CURRENT LAW STATUTES ANNOTATED
1986

VOLUME FOUR

AUSTRALIA AND NEW ZEALAND
The Law Book Company Ltd.
Sydney : Melbourne : Perth

CANADA AND U.S.A.
The Carswell Company Ltd.
Agincourt, Ontario

INDIA
N. M. Tripathi Private Ltd.
Bombay
and
Eastern Law House Private Ltd.
Calcutta and Delhi

M.P.P. House
Bangalore

ISRAEL
Steimatzky's Agency Ltd.
Jerusalem : Tel Aviv : Haifa

MALAYSIA : SINGAPORE : BRUNEI
Malayan Law Journal (Pte.) Ltd.
Singapore

PAKISTAN
Pakistan Law House
Karachi

CURRENT LAW
STATUTES
ANNOTATED
1986

VOLUME FOUR

EDITOR IN CHIEF

PETER ALLSOP, C.B.E., M.A.
Barrister

GENERAL EDITOR

KEVAN NORRIS, LL.B.
Solicitor

ASSISTANT GENERAL EDITOR

JULIE HARRIS, LL.B.

ADMINISTRATION

GILLIAN BRONZE, LL.B.

LONDON

SWEET & MAXWELL   STEVENS & SONS

EDINBURGH

W. GREEN & SON

1987

Published by
SWEET & MAXWELL LIMITED
and STEVENS & SONS LIMITED
of 11 New Fetter Lane, London,
and W. GREEN & SON LIMITED
of St. Giles Street, Edinburgh,
and Printed in Great Britain
by The Eastern Press Ltd.,
London and Reading

ISBN This Volume only : 0 421 38050 0
As a set : 0 421 38060 8

CONTENTS

CHRONOLOGICAL TABLE

STATUTES 1986

VOLUME ONE

c. 1. Education (Amendment) Act 1986
   2. Australia Act 1986
   3. Atomic Energy Authority Act 1986
   4. Consolidated Fund Act 1986
   5. Agricultural Holdings Act 1986
   6. Prevention of Oil Pollution Act 1986
   7. Marriage (Wales) Act 1986
   8. Museum of London Act 1986
   9. Law Reform (Parent and Child) (Scotland) Act 1986
  10. Local Government Act 1986
  11. Gaming (Amendment) Act 1986
  12. Statute Law (Repeals) Act 1986
  13. Highways (Amendment) Act 1986
  14. Animals (Scientific Procedures) Act 1986
  15. Industrial Training Act 1986
  16. Marriage (Prohibited Degrees of Relationship) Act 1986
  17. Drainage Rates (Disabled Persons) Act 1986
  18. Corneal Tissue Act 1986
  19. British Shipbuilders (Borrowing Powers) Act 1986
  20. Horticultural Produce Act 1986
  21. Armed Forces Act 1986
  22. Civil Protection in Peacetime Act 1986
  23. Safety at Sea Act 1986
  24. Health Service Joint Consultative Committees (Access to Information) Act 1986
  25. Commonwealth Development Corporation Act 1986
  26. Land Registration Act 1986
  27. Road Traffic Regulation (Parking) Act 1986
  28. Children and Young Persons (Amendment) Act 1986
  29. Consumer Safety (Amendment) Act 1986
  30. Forestry Act 1986
  31. Airports Act 1986
  32. Drug Trafficking Offences Act 1986
  33. Disabled Persons (Services, Consultation and Representation) Act 1986

INDEX OF SHORT TITLES

STATUTES 1986

References are to chapter numbers of 1986

Index of Short Titles

FINANCIAL SERVICES ACT 1986*

(1986 c. 60)

ARRANGEMENT OF SECTIONS

PART I

REGULATION OF INVESTMENT BUSINESS

CHAPTER I

PRELIMINARY

CHAPTER II

RESTRICTION ON CARRYING ON BUSINESS

CHAPTER III

AUTHORISED PERSONS

Members of recognised self-regulating organisations

Persons authorised by recognised professional bodies

Insurance companies

Friendly societies

---

* Annotations by Robert Ferguson, LL.B., Ph.D. and Alan Page, LL.B., Ph.D.

PART II

INSURANCE BUSINESS

PART III

FRIENDLY SOCIETIES

PART IV

OFFICIAL LISTING OF SECURITIES

An Act to regulate the carrying on of investment business; to make related provision with respect to insurance business and business carried on by friendly societies; to make new provision with respect to the official listing of securities, offers of unlisted securities, takeover offers and insider dealing; to make provision as to the disclosure of information obtained under enactments relating to fair trading, banking, companies and insurance; to make provision for securing reciprocity with other countries in respect of facilities for the provision of financial services; and for connected purposes.   [7th November 1986]

INTRODUCTION AND GENERAL NOTE

The Financial Services Act 1986 effects a complete overhaul of the existing statutory framework for the regulation of investment business. It is the first such overhaul to have been undertaken since the framework was established almost half a century ago by the Prevention of Fraud (Investments) Act 1939 in response to the share dealing scandals of the early 1930s (*Report of the Departmental Committee on Sharepushing*, Cmd. 5539 (1937)) and the growth of unit trusts (*Fixed Trusts: Report of a Departmental Committee Appointed by the Board of Trade*, Cmd. 5259 (1936)). That Act, the implementation of which was delayed by the war until 1944, made it an offence for non-exempted persons to carry on the business of dealing in securities without a licence. Its provisions, as amended in various minor respects, were subsequently re-enacted by the consolidating enactment, the Prevention of Fraud (Investments) Act 1958. This Act will continue to provide the principal source of statutory control over investment business until the Financial Services Act is brought into force in the course of 1987.

The enactment of the Financial Services Act comes some ten years after there was first proposed the revision of the Prevention of Fraud (Investments) Act to bring it into line with modern conditions. Following an internal review of the arrangements for the supervision of the securities market conducted between 1974 and 1976, the Government announced its intention to amend the Act; and in a consultative document published in 1977 (Cmnd. 6893) proposals were outlined for the revision of the Act itself and the then Licensed Dealers (Conduct of Business) Rules (S.I. 1960 No. 1216). Among the main proposals was that the scope of the Act should be widened to include investment advisers and consultants, that the number of exemptions should be reduced, that fuller information should be required from applicants for licences, that power should be taken to suspend, as well as to revoke, licences and that the enforcement provisions of the Act should be strengthened.

With the change of Government in 1979 preliminary work on the amending legislation was shelved, but it was resumed in 1981 in the wake of the collapse of four licensed dealers in securities including Norton Warburg. Shortly afterwards, Professor L. C. B. Gower was appointed by the Secretary of State to undertake a review of the protection required by investors and to advise on the need for new legislation. A Discussion Document was published in 1982; and in 1983 new Dealers in Securities (Licensing) Regulations (S.I. 1983 No. 587) and Licensed Dealers (Conduct of Business) Rules (S.I. 1983 No. 585) were introduced.

At the time Professor Gower's appointment was widely regarded as a political sop. The Government had to do something, but it was not clear that the political will existed to do anything beyond tightening the licensed dealers rules. By the time Part I of Professor Gower's Report (*Review of Investor Protection*, Cmnd. 9125 (1984)) was published, however, a marked shift in political attitudes had occurred. Partly this was the result of the steady succession of further scandals in the insurance and commodities markets. But, more importantly, it stemmed from the wave of change which engulfed The Stock Exchange in the wake of the agreement reached between the Secretary of State for Trade and Industry and the Chairman of The Stock Exchange in July 1983 which led to the abatement of the proceedings then pending before the Restrictive Practices Court and the removal of The Stock Exchange's rule book from the scope of the restrictive trade practices legislation (Restrictive Trade Practices (Stock Exchange) Act 1984). The projected abandonment of The Stock Exchange's system of fixed minimum commissions and its single capacity dealing system, together with the emergence of financial services conglomerates as a result of the removal of the restrictions on the outside ownership of member firms, all combined to give the issue of investor protection a much greater prominence and to highlight the link between it and the maintenance of London's position as a leading international financial centre.

Professor Gower's principal recommendation was that the Prevention of Fraud (Investments) Act should be replaced by a new Investor Protection Act. This would provide the framework for a comprehensive system for the regulation of investment business "based so far as possible on self-regulation subject to governmental surveillance". Following the publication of Professor Gower's report, two groups of practitioners were appointed, one by the Governor of the Bank of England to advise on the structure and operation of self-regulatory groupings that would most appropriately cover all types of securities activity (including investment management) together with commodity and financial futures, the other by the Parliamentary Under Secretary of State for Corporate and Consumer Affairs to advise on the prospects for practitioner-based regulation of the marketing of life insurance and unit trusts. In October 1984, the Government announced its intention to proceed.

In much of its content the White Paper published in January 1985 (*Financial Services in the United Kingdom: A New Framework for Investor Protection*, Cmnd. 9432) followed Professor Gower's recommendations. New legislation would be introduced which would make it an offence to carry on investment business without authorisation or exemption. The power of authorisation would be assumed by the Secretary of State, but he would be empowered to delegate this and other functions to a practitioner-based body designated by him which matched a number of criteria laid down in the legislation. This body would operate in turn through a number of self-regulating organisations recognised by it. The White Paper envisaged the establishment of two practitioner-based bodies, a Securities and Investments Board (SIB), covering the regulation of securities and investments, and a Marketing of Investments Board (MIB), covering the marketing of investments such as life insurance and unit trusts. After the White Paper was published these two bodies were established, the latter in the form of an organising committee (MIBOC), but it was subsequently decided that they should be merged to form a single body, the SIB.

Outline of the Act

Part I of the Act establishes a new regime for the regulation of investment business which replaces the old regime based on the Prevention of Fraud (Investments) Act 1958. The new regime differs from the old in several important respects. First, a new regulatory authority, the Securities and Investments Board Ltd., assumes general responsibility for a system of regulation—"practitioner-based, statute-backed" regulation—which is designed to combine the strengths of self-regulation and statutory regulation. Secondly, the coverage of the new regime is wider in that it applies to "investments" (not just securities) and to the carrying on of investment business (not just the business of dealing in securities). Moreover, while a large number of investment firms enjoyed exemptions of one form or another under the old regime, the opportunities for exemption are more limited under the new regime. Thirdly, the new legislation, as well as providing for the standard criminal and administrative sanctions, affords civil remedies to investors who suffer loss as a result of contraventions of its provisions, or those of subordinate rules and regulations or the corresponding provisions of recognised self-regulation organisations.

Chapter I of Part I (in conjunction with Sched. 1) defines the scope of the legislation by enumerating the investments covered and the activities constituting investment business. Flexibility is retained by means of a power to amend the lists by means of subordinate legislation.

Chapter II of Part I prohibits the carrying on of investment business without authorisation or exemption. An investment firm which contravenes this prohibition commits a criminal offence. Agreements entered into in contravention of the prohibition will normally be unenforceable by the firm entering into them, although they will be enforceable by the person with whom they are entered into. And the Board is empowered to apply to the court for injunctions against investment firms which contravene the prohibition, and also for restitution orders, to compensate investors adversely affected by a contravention.

Chapter III of Part I deals with the authorisation of investment firms. There are two main alternatives: direct authorisation by the Board and indirect authorisation through membership of a recognised self-regulating organisation. Direct authorisation is confined to "fit and proper" persons and the Board is empowered to suspend or withdraw the authorisation of firms which cease to satisfy this requirement or which fail to comply with their obligations. A firm which is refused authorisation by the Board, or whose direct authorisation is suspended or withdrawn, may appeal to the Financial Services Tribunal established under Chapter IX of Part I. As regards indirect authorisation, provision is made (in conjunction with Sched. 2) for the recognition of self-regulating organisations where the conditions and requirements laid down are satisfied. Should these conditions and requirements cease to be met, the Board is empowered to revoke their recognition. Less drastically, it is also empowered to seek compliance orders from the court against them and to alter their rules in order to protect investors. A firm may also be authorised indirectly by certification by a recognised professional body, but this method is confined to firms whose main business is the practice of their profession. Provision is made (in conjunction with Sched. 3) for the recognition of professional bodies at the discretion of the Board, and the Board is empowered to revoke their recognition and to seek compliance against them, but not to alter their rules. Chapter III also makes provision for the automatic authorisation of certain insurance companies, registered friendly societies and operators or trustees of recognised collective investment schemes. Unlike directly authorised firms, members of recognised self-regulating organisations and firms certificated by recognised professional bodies, the authorisation conferred upon them is limited. Finally, provision is made for the authorisation of firms authorised in other Member States of the European Community. Their authorisation may be suspended or withdrawn in the same way and subject to the same safeguards as that of directly authorised firms.

Chapter IV of Part I deals with exemptions from the requirement of authorisation. Provision is made for the recognition and exemption of investment exchanges (in conjunction with Sched. 4) and clearing houses; and for the exemption of the Bank of England, Lloyd's, listed money market institutions (in conjunction with Sched. 5), appointed representatives and miscellaneous other persons performing functions regulated under other enactments. Flexibility is retained by the conferral of a power on the Secretary of State, exercisable by statutory instrument, to create additional exemptions and to remove or restrict certain of the exemptions conferred by this Chapter.

Chapter V of Part I deals with the conduct of investment business. The making of misleading statements, market manipulation, and investment advertising by unauthorised persons are defined as criminal offences. "Cold-calling" is, in general, prohibited, but not subjected to criminal sanctions. The Board is empowered to make various kinds of rules and regulations by means of which it will be able to regulate the conduct of investment business by authorised persons, impose capital adequacy requirements, lay down a "cooling-off" period in connection with the purchase of specified investments, provide for the safe-keeping of client's money and establish a compensation fund. The Board is also empowered to give "disqualification directions" banning individuals from employment in connection with investment business, to make a public statement as to a person's misconduct, and to apply to the court for injunctions against investment firms which break the rules, and also for restitution orders to compensate investors adversely affected by a breach. Investors who suffer loss as a result of a breach of the rules are themselves given the remedy of an action for damages.

Chapter VI of Part I confers a number of powers of intervention on the Board. In the exercise of these powers the Board will be able to restrict the kinds of business authorised persons may undertake, to prohibit them from disposing of assets, to require them to vest assets in an approved trustee and to require them to maintain assets in the United Kingdom. A firm upon which a prohibition or requirement is imposed in the exercise of these powers will be able to appeal to the Financial Services Tribunal established under Chaper IX of Part I. Should a firm breach a prohibition or requirement imposed upon it, the Board may make a public statement, apply it to the court for an injunction, and also a restitution order to compensate investors adversely affected. Investors who suffer loss as a result of any breach are themselves given the remedy of an action for damages.

Chapter VII of Part I empowers the Securities and Investments Board to petition for the winding-up of an authorised company or partnership which defaults in an obligation to pay what it owes to an investor. Various regulatory authorities are empowered to petition for the appointment of an administrator under the Insolvency Act 1986.

Chapter VIII of Part I introduces the concept of a collective investment scheme. This embraces unit trusts, open-ended investment companies and various other collective investment arrangements. By and large, only an authorised unit trust scheme and recognised overseas schemes may be promoted to the general public. A procedure for the authorisation and de-authorisation of unit trust schemes is set out, and the Securities and Investments Board is empowered to make rules governing the constitution and management of such schemes and to require the publication of "scheme particulars" covering stipulated matters. The management companies of authorised unit trust schemes are required to confine their activities to the management of pooled investment vehicles, and any clause in a trust deed purporting to exempt the manager or trustee from liability for negligence is nullified. The Board is given certain powers of intervention in relation to authorised schemes. Criteria for the recognition of overseas schemes are also set out. In conformity to the UCITS directive, the recognition of UCITS (undertakings for collective investment in transferable securities) certified in another member State is more or less automatic if appropriate notice is given. The Secretary of State is empowered to order investigations into the affairs of collective investment schemes. Contraventions of Chapter VIII and of regulations made under it are under certain circumstances assimilated to contraventions of Chapter V.

Chaper IX of Part I makes provision for the establishment of a Financial Services Tribunal, consisting in individual cases of a legally qualified chairman and two other members of an appointed Panel. The Chapter identifies the applications and other matters which must be referred to the Tribunal and the options open to the Tribunal in reporting on them. Schedule 6 makes additional provisions in relation to the Tribunal.

Chapter X of Part I makes provision for the maintenance of a register of information by the Board and for it to be open for public inspection. The register will contain information about authorised persons, recognised organisations, authorised unit trust schemes, recognised schemes and individuals who are the subject of disqualification directions. Provision is also made for information to be obtained by the Board and for investigations to be undertaken by the Board and the Secretary of State.

Chapter XI of Part I is concerned with the role of the auditor in the supervision of investment firms. Auditors are free from any legal constraint which might prevent them from communicating to the appropriate supervisory authorities matters of regulatory concern. All firms directly regulated by the Board must have an auditor, and where it has good reason the Board may require such firms to submit to a second audit.

Chapter XII of Part I makes provision for the payment of fees both on applications to the Board and periodically thereafter.

Chapter XIII of Part I makes provision for the transfer by the Secretary of State, by draft order subject to affirmative resolution procedure, of all or any of a range of identified functions to a designated agency, which agency is initially to be the Securities and

Investments Board. Before transferring any functions, it must appear to the Secretary of State that the agency is able and willing to discharge the transferred functions; that the requirements of Schedule 7 are satisfied; that its rules and regulations afford investors an adequate level of protection and comply with the principles set out in Schedule 8; and that the likely effects on competition of its rules, regulations and guidance do not exceed those necessary for the protection of investors. Should these requirements cease to be met, provision is made for the resumption of transferred functions either in their entirety or selectively as regards both the functions and the classes of investments or investment business in respect of which they are to be resumed. Schedule 9 make additional provision in relation to the status of designated agencies and the exercise of transferred functions.

Chapter XIV of Part I establishes a special regime for the application of competition policy to recognised bodies and designated agencies. Its general import is to reserve the power of decision to the Secretary of State rather than the Restrictive Practices Court. Before a body, other than a professional body, can be recognised, or functions transferred to a designated agency, the Secretary of State must be satisfied that the anti-competitive effects of their rules, regulations, guidance and clearing arrangements do not exceed those necessary for the protection of investors. Before deciding this question, the Secretary of State must obtain and have regard to a report from the Director General of Fair Trading, The DGFT will also be responsible for the subsequent monitoring of recognised bodies' and designated agencies' compliance with this requirement. Should they breach it, the Secretary of State may impose various sanctions including the revocation of recognition or the resumption of transferred functions. Consequential exemptions are provided from the monopoly provisions of the Fair Trading Act 1973, the Restrictive Trade Practices Act 1976, which is also modified in its application to recognised professional bodies, and the Competition Act 1980.

Part II of the Act (coupled with Sched. 10) adapts the investment business regime to life assurance (where used as an investment medium) in a way that takes account of the regulation of insurers under the Insurance Companies Act 1982. The broad effect is that only the life assurance marketing and pension fund management activities of insurance companies fall within the scope of the investment business regime. Promotion of the life policies of unauthorised insurers is restricted. Insurance companies must have arrangements to secure that they do not act unfairly as between their different funds. It becomes possible to extend the range of permitted links for linked life assurance policies. At the same time, the opportunity has been taken to effect various reforms of the law relating to the regulation of insurance in general. The legal status of contracts entered into with unauthorised insurers is elaborated. A revised offence of making misleading statements as to insurance contracts is enacted. The definition of an insurance company "controller" is altered. And there is a provision designed to facilitate communications between insurance company auditors and supervisors.

Part III of the Act (coupled with Sched. 11) establishes a framework for friendly societies parallel to the main investment business regime.

Part IV of the Act creates a new framework from the official listing of securities on The Stock Exchange. The Stock Exchange (Listing) Regulations 1984 (S.I. 1984 No. 716) made under the European Communities Act 1972 to implement various company law directives are wholly revoked. The new legislation puts beyond question the power of The Stock Exchange not only to make rules implementing the requirements of the directives but also to impose additional requirements. The general duty of disclosure in listing particulars is now enshrined in primary legislation, and the opportunity has been taken to revise and clarify the law governing compensation for false or misleading particulars.

Part V of the Act deals with offers of unlisted securities. It empowers the Secretary of State to lay down modern prospectus requirements in subordinate legislation; Sched. 3 of the Companies Act 1985 (mandatory contents of prospectus) is repealed. The concept of an "approved" recognised investment exchange is introduced; in certain circumstances the continuing disclosure requirements of an approved exchange will displace the statutory prospectus requirements. A general duty of disclosure in prospectuses is also introduced, and provision (parallel to that in respect of listing particulars) is made for compensation for false or misleading prospectuses.

Part VI of the Act (coupled with Sched. 12) substitutes fresh provisions for ss. 428–30 of the Companies Act 1985. These up-date and rationalise the rules governing the compulsory acquisition of the shares of a dissentient minority after a takeover.

Part VII extends the coverage of the insider dealing legislation to include the abuse of information held by public servants in general. The Secretary of State is empowered to appoint inspectors to investigate cases of suspected insider dealing, and penalties are stipulated for failure to co-operate. At the same time market makers are exempted from the legislation, and special provision is made for price stabilisation.

Part VIII deals with the disclosure of information. Restrictions are imposed on the disclosure of information obtained under the Act and their contravention is made a criminal offence. A series of exceptions are created, however, the purpose of which is to ensure that the disclosure of information to other authorities is not unduly inhibited, and parallel provision is made (in conjunction with Sched. 13) for the disclosure of information obtained under the fair trading, banking, insurance and companies legislation to other authorities including the authorities responsible for the administration of this Act. Information may also be disclosed to overseas authorities, but provision is made for the prohibition or restriction of the disclosure of information to them.

Part IX of the Act is designed to provide the United Kingdom with leverage in negotiating reciprocity of access for financial services firms to foreign markets. The Secretary of State and the Treasury are empowered to serve notices on firms from foreign countries disqualifying them from, or restricting them in, carrying on investment, insurance or banking business in the United Kingdom where it appears that the country from which they come prevents by law or governmental action United Kingdom investment, insurance or banking firms from carrying on business in that country on terms as favourable as those afforded to firms from that country in the United Kingdom, and if it is considered in the national interest to do so. The different types of notices and their effects are defined, and provision is made for their variation and revocation.

Part X contains miscellaneous and supplementary provisions. These include the exemption of regulatory authorities, other than recognised professional bodies, from liability for damages in certain circumstances, and the extension of the coverage of the investment business regime to occupational pension fund managers who would not otherwise be required to seek authorisation under Part I. The Secretary of State is empowered to direct certain regulatory authorities to take action to comply with the United Kingdom's international obligations. An offence of making false and misleading statements in connection with the administration of the Act is created. Various minor changes in company law are effected.

SPECIAL NOTE

In Part I of the Act (regulation of investment business) many powers are conferred upon the Secretary of State which he is authorised (by s.114) to transfer to a designated agency. The Securities and Investment Board Ltd. is to be the designated agency, and it is anticipated that the Secretary of State will transfer his transferable powers to it. Accordingly the annotation to Part I proceeds on the assumption that transferable powers will be transferred, and references in the annotation to Part I to the Secretary of State's powers are references to those powers of the Secretary of State which cannot be transferred. Where a power is transferable subject to a reservation that it is to be exercisable by the Secretary of State concurrently with the designated agency the annotation makes this clear.

COMMENCEMENT

See Note to s.211.

ABBREVIATIONS

In the annotations the following abbreviations are used:

Admission directive: Council directive of March 5, 1979 co-ordinating the conditions for the admission of securities to official stock exchange listing (79/279/EEC).

DTI: Department of Trade and Industry.

Financial Services in the UK: Financial Services in the United Kingdom: A New Framework for Investor Protection, January 1985 (Cmnd. 9432).

Listing Particulars directive: Council directive of March 17, 1980 coordinating the requirements for the drawing up, scrutiny and distribution of the listing particulars to be published for the admission of securities to official stock exchange listing (80/390/EEC).

PFI Act: Prevention of Fraud (Investments) Act 1958.

RCH: Recognised clearing house.

RIE: Recognised investment exchange.

RPB: Recognised professional body.

The Regulation of Authorised Unit Trust Schemes: The Regulation of Authorised Unit Trust Schemes: A consultative document on the proposed regulations for unit trust schemes authorised under the Financial Services Bill, August 1986 (DTI).

SIB: Securities and Investments Board.

SRO: Self-regulating organisation.

UCITS: Undertakings for collective investment in transferable securities.

UCITS directive: Council directive of December 20, 1985 on the coordination of laws, regulations and administrative provisions relating to undertakings for collective investment in transferable securities (85/611/EEC).

PARLIAMENTARY DEBATES
   Hansard: H.C. Vol. 89, cols. 344, 940; Vol. 99, cols. 386, 520, 613; Vol. 103, cols. 489, 594; H.L. Vol. 477, col. 74; Vol. 478, col. 584; Vol. 479, cols. 37, 216, 564, 720; Vol. 480, cols. 684, 913; Vol. 481, cols. 97, 509.
   This Bill was considered in Standing Committee E, January 28 to March 25, 1986.

PART I

REGULATION OF INVESTMENT BUSINESS

CHAPTER I

PRELIMINARY

Investments and investment business

1.—(1) In this Act, unless the context otherwise requires, "investment" means any asset, right or interest falling within any paragraph in Part I of Schedule 1 to this Act.
   (2) In this Act "investment business" means the business of engaging in one or more of the activities which fall within the paragraphs in Part II of that Schedule and are not excluded by Part III of that Schedule.
   (3) For the purposes of this Act a person carries on investment business in the United Kingdom if he—
   (*a*) carries on investment business from a permanent place of business maintained by him in the United Kingdom; or
   (*b*) engages in the United Kingdom in one or more of the activities which fall within the paragraphs in Part II of that Schedule and are not excluded by Part III or IV of that Schedule and his doing so constitutes the carrying on by him of a business in the United Kingdom.
   (4) Parts I to IV of that Schedule shall be construed in accordance with Part V.

GENERAL NOTE
   This section lays down the definitions which delimit the scope of the regulatory scheme for investment business. See also the general note to Sched. 1.

Subs. (2)
   "Investment business" means the *business* of engaging in one or more of the activities listed in the Schedule. Entering into a transaction falling within a paragraph of the Schedule does not *per se* constitute investment business.

Subs. (3)
   Carries on investment business: The notion of "carrying on" business has connotations of continuity: "it imports a series or repetition of acts": *Kirkwood* v. *Gadd* [1910] A.C. 422, *per* Lord Loreburn L.C. at p.423.
   The Act makes no provision for the authorisation of employees (employed under a contract of service). This presupposes that where an employee enters into investment transactions on behalf of his employer, the employee is not carrying on investment business. On the other hand, appointed representatives (employed under a contract for services) do carry on investment business, and would require authorisation were they are not exempted persons under s.44.
   Certain occupational pension fund managers who do not fall within this section's definition of carrying on investment business are to be treated as doing so by virtue of s.191.

Power to extend or restrict scope of Act

2.—(1) The Secretary of State may by order amend Schedule 1 to this Act so as—
  (a) to extend or restrict the meaning of investment for the purposes of all or any provisions of this Act; or
  (b) to extend or restrict for the purposes of all or any of those provisions the activities that are to constitute the carrying on of investment business or the carrying on of such business in the United Kingdom.

(2) The amendments that may be made for the purposes of subsection (1)(b) above include amendments conferring powers on the Secretary of State, whether by extending or modifying any provision of that Schedule which confers such powers or by adding further such provisions.

(3) An order under this section which extends the meaning of investment or extends the activities that are to constitute the carrying on of investment business or the carrying on of such business in the United Kingdom shall be laid before Parliament after being made and shall cease to have effect at the end of the period of twenty-eight days beginning with the day on which it is made (but without prejudice to anything done under the order or to the making of a new order) unless before the end of that period the order is approved by a resolution of each House of Parliament.

(4) In reckoning the period mentioned in subsection (3) above no account shall be taken of any time during which Parliament is dissolved or prorogued or during which both Houses are adjourned for more than four days.

(5) Any order under this section to which subsection (3) above does not apply shall be subject to annulment in pursuance of a resolution of either House of Parliament.

(6) An order under this section may contain such transitional provisions as the Secretary of State thinks necessary or expedient.

DEFINITIONS
  "carrying on of investment business": s.1(3).
  "investment": s.1(1).
  "investment business": s.1(2).

GENERAL NOTE
  This section enables the scope of the regulatory system to be altered by orders of the Secretary of State redefining the meaning of "investment," or the activities that are to constitute the carrying on of investment business.
  As to the making of such orders, see s.205(2) and subss. (3) and (5) of this section.

Subs. (2)
  Para. 23 of Sched. 1 empowers the Secretary of State to exclude certain dealings done in the course of non-investment business from the activities constituting investment business by granting a "permission" to particular applicants.
  The significance of this subsection is that it enables the Secretary of State to modify the criteria governing the grant of permissions, and to assume the power to grant permissions in respect of other activities.

Subs. (3)
  Orders whose effect is to extend the scope of the regulatory system are subject to an affirmative resolution procedure.

Subs. (5)
  Other orders are merely subject to annulment.

CHAPTER II

RESTRICTION ON CARRYING ON BUSINESS

Persons entitled to carry on investment business

3. No person shall carry on, or purport to carry on, investment business in the United Kingdom unless he is an authorised person under Chapter III or an exempted person under Chapter IV of this Part of this Act.

DEFINITIONS
"authorised person": s.207(1).
"carry on investment business": s.1(3).
"exempted person": s.207(1).

GENERAL NOTE
This section prohibits the carrying on, or purported carrying on, of investment business without authorisation or exemption. This prohibition does not apply to persons acting as agents or otherwise on behalf of the Crown. (s.207(11)). As to penalties for breach of this prohibition, see sections 4–6.
Authorised person: A person may be authorised directly by the SIB (s.25), or indirectly through membership of a recognised SRO (s.7) or certification by a recognised body (s.15). Chapter III also makes provision for the automatic authorisation of insurers (s.22), registered friendly societies (s.23), operators of trustees of recognised collective investment schemes (s.24) and persons authorised in other Member States of the European Community (s.31).
Exempted person: Chapter IV exempts the following from the requirement of authorisation: the Bank of England (s.35), recognised investment exchanges (s.36), recognised clearing houses (s.38), Lloyd's (s.42), listed money market institutions (s.43), appointed representatives (s.44) together with a miscellaneous group of persons which includes official receivers (s.45).

Offences

4.—(1) Any person who carries on, or purports to carry on, investment business in contravention of section 3 above shall be guilty of an offence and liable—

(*a*) on conviction on indictment, to imprisonment for a term not exceeding two years or to a fine or to both;

(*b*) on summary conviction, to imprisonment for a term not exceeding six months or to a fine not exceeding the statutory maximum or to both.

(2) In proceedings brought against any person for an offence under this section it shall be a defence for him to prove that he took all reasonable precautions and exercised all due diligence to avoid the commission of the offence.

DEFINITION
"carries on investment business": s.1(3).

GENERAL NOTE
Subs. (1)
This subsection makes contravention of the prohibition in section 3 an offence.

Subs. (2)
All reasonable precautions . . . all due diligence: An investment business may succeed in the defence if it can prove that it set up an adequate administrative system for the avoidance of the offence and took the necessary measures to see that it was properly implemented. (*Tesco Supermarkets Ltd.* v. *Nattrass* [1972] A.C. 153.)

Agreements made by or through unauthorised persons

5.—(1) Subject to subsection (3) below, any agreement to which this subsection applies—

(*a*) which is entered into by a person in the course of carrying on investment business in contravention of section 3 above; or

(*b*) which is entered into—

(i) by a person who is an authorised person or an exempted person in respect of the investment business in the course of which he enters into the agreement; but

(ii) in consequence of anything said or done by a person in the course of carrying on investment business in contravention of that section,

shall be unenforceable against the other party; and that party shall be entitled to recover any money or other property paid or transferred by him under the agreement, together with compensation for any loss sustained by him as a result of having parted with it.

(2) The compensation recoverable under subsection (1) above shall be such as the parties may agree or as the court may, on the application of either party, determine.

(3) A court may allow an agreement to which subsection (1) above applies to be enforced or money and property paid or transferred under it to be retained if it is satisfied—

(*a*) in a case within paragraph (*a*) of that subsection, that the person mentioned in that paragraph reasonably believed that his entering into the agreement did not constitute a contravention of section 3 above;

(*b*) in a case within paragraph (*b*) of that subsection, that the person mentioned in sub-paragraph (i) of that paragraph did not know that the agreement was entered into as mentioned in sub-paragraph (ii) of that paragraph; and

(*c*) in either case, that it is just and equitable for the agreement to be enforced or, as the case may be, for the money or property paid or transferred under it to be retained.

(4) Where a person elects not to perform an agreement which by virtue of this section is unenforceable against him or by virtue of this section recovers money paid or other property transferred by him under an agreement he shall repay any money and return any other property received by him under the agreement.

(5) Where any property transferred under an agreement to which this section applies has passed to a third party the references to that property in subsections (1), (3) and (4) above shall be construed as references to its value at the time of its transfer under the agreement.

(6) A contravention of section 3 above shall not make an agreement illegal or invalid to any greater extent than is provided in this section.

(7) Subsection (1) above applies to any agreement the making or performance of which by the person seeking to enforce it or from whom money or other property is recoverable under this section constitutes an activity which falls within any paragraph of Part II of Schedule 1 to this Act and is not excluded by Part III or IV of that Schedule.

DEFINITIONS

"agreement": s.5(7).
"authorised person": s.207(1).
"carrying on investment business": s.1(3).
"exempted person": s.207(1).

GENERAL NOTE

This section governs the enforceability of agreements, as defined in subsection (7), when section 3 has been contravened either by an investment business or by a third party, *e.g.* an introducer.

Subs. (1)
The basic position is as stated in this subsection: such agreements are unenforceable.

Compensation for any loss sustained: This is broader than the original proposal which restricted compensation to the payment of interest on money transferred. Now compensation is also payable in respect of opportunities missed, *e.g.* to participate in a bonus or rights issue.

Subs. (3)
However, such an agreement may be enforceable when the conditions stipulated are satisfied.

May: Even if the court is satisfied, it is not obliged to allow the agreement to be enforced.

Para. (a)
Reasonably believed: Covers, *e.g.* the person "who concludes on reasonable grounds that he is not carrying on an authorisable business", or "who did not know that he had to be authorised and whose ignorance was reasonable". It does not cover "the careless and the criminal". (H.L. Vol. 480, cols. 775–776).

Para. (b)
Did not know: Difficult though it is to prove a negative, this is less onerous than the original proposal which required the investment business to satisfy the court that it "neither knew nor ought to have known". Constructive knowledge is therefore no longer directly relevant, although the onus is still probably on the investment business "to take care that none of its investment agreements arise because of the involvement of an unauthorised person". (H.L. Vol. 479, col. 230).

Subs. (6)
This subsection makes it plain that the party with whom the agreement is made may, if he so chooses, treat the agreement as valid and enforce it accordingly.

Subs. (7)
And is not excluded by Part III or IV: Agreements falling within the scope of these exclusions are enforceable regardless of any contravention of section 3.

Injunctions and restitution orders

6.—(1) If, on the application of the Secretary of State, the court is satisfied—
  (*a*) that there is a reasonable likelihood that a person will contravene section 3 above; or
  (*b*) that any person has contravened that section and that there is a reasonable likelihood that the contravention will continue or be repeated.
the court may grant an injunction restraining the contravention or, in Scotland, an interdict prohibiting the contravention.

  (2) If, on the application of the Secretary of State, the court is satisfied that a person has entered into any transaction in contravention of section 3 above the court may order that person and any other person who appears to the court to have been knowingly concerned in the contravention to take such steps as the court may direct for restoring the parties to the position in which they were before the transaction was entered into.

  (3) The court may, on the application of the Secretary of State, make an order under subsection (4) below or, in relation to Scotland, under subsection (5) below if satisfied that a person has been carrying on investment business in contravention of section 3 above and—
  (*a*) that profits have accrued to that person as a result of carrying on that business; or
  (*b*) that one or more investors have suffered loss or been otherwise adversely affected as a result of his contravention of section 47 or 56 below or failure to act substantially in accordance with any of the rules or regulations made under Chapter V of this Part of this Act.

(4) The court may under this subsection order the person concerned to pay into court, or appoint a receiver to recover from him, such sum as appears to the court to be just having regard—

    (a) in a case within paragraph (a) of subsection (3) above, to the profits appearing to the court to have accrued;

    (b) in a case within paragraph (b) of that subsection, to the extent of the loss or other adverse effect; or

    (c) in a case within both paragraphs (a) and (b) of that subsection, to the profits and to the extent of the loss or other adverse effect.

(5) The court may under this subsection order the person concerned to pay to the applicant such sum as appears to the court to be just having regard to the considerations mentioned in paragraphs (a) to (c) of subsection (4) above.

(6) Any amount paid into court by or recovered from a person in pursuance of an order under subsection (4) or (5) above shall be paid out to such person or distributed among such persons as the court may direct, being a person or persons appearing to the court to have entered into transactions with that person as a result of which the profits mentioned in paragraph (a) of subsection (3) above have accrued to him or the loss or other adverse effect mentioned in paragraph (b) of that subsection has been suffered.

(7) On an application under subsection (3) above the court may require the person concerned to furnish it with such accounts or other information as it may require for establishing whether any and, if so, what profits have accrued to him as mentioned in paragraph (a) of that subsection and for determining how any amounts are to be paid or distributed under subsection (6) above; and the court may require any such accounts or other information to be verified in such manner as it may direct.

(8) The jurisdiction conferred by this section shall be exercisable by the High Court and the Court of Session.

(9) Nothing in this section affects the right of any person other than the Secretary of State to bring proceedings in respect of any of the matters to which this section applies.

DEFINITION

"carrying on investment business": s.1(3).

GENERAL NOTE

This section empowers the SIB to seek injunctions and restitution orders. Depending on the terms of the delegation order, as to which see section 114, these powers may also be exercisable by the Secretary of State.

Subs. (2)

An aggrieved investor cannot compel the Board to seek a restitution order, but the Board's power to do so provides a potentially important additional (subs. (9)) avenue of redress for the aggrieved investor which the SIB has said it will be prepared to use "particularly as many investors are likely to be hesitant about incurring costs themselves in an action for damages". (*Regulation of Investment Business: The New Framework* (1985), para. 1.40).

Transaction: Presumably the term is used to make it clear that not just agreements as defined in section 5(7) are covered, but also other arrangements not falling within the scope of their definition.

Knowingly: Note this requirement.

CHAPTER III

AUTHORISED PERSONS

Members of recognised self-regulating organisations

Authorisation by membership of recognised self-regulating organisation

7.—(1) Subject to subsection (2) below, a member of a recognised self-regulating organisation is an authorised person by virtue of his membership of that organisation.

(2) This section does not apply to a member who is an authorised person by virtue of section 22 or 23 below or an insurance company which is an authorised person by virtue of section 31 below.

DEFINITIONS
    "authorised person": s.207(1).
    "recognised self-regulating organisation": s.207(1).

GENERAL NOTE
Subs. (1)
    Sections 7–14 establish the basic framework for the regulation of investment business carried on by members of recognised SROs. In terms of this subsection a member of a recognised SRO is an authorised person and hence does not fall foul of the basic prohibition in section 3. The expectation, indeed hope, is that the vast majority of investment businesses will become authorised through membership of SROs.

Subs. (2)
    The bodies referred to are supervised under other regimes. The purpose of this subsection is to ensure that they cannot, by means of membership of an SRO, evade the restrictions imposed under those regimes on the kinds of investment business they may undertake.

Self-regulating organisations

8.—(1) In this Act a "self-regulating organisation" means a body (whether a body corporate or an unincorporated association) which regulates the carrying on of investment business of any kind by enforcing rules which are binding on persons carrying on business of that kind either because they are members of that body or because they are otherwise subject to its control.

(2) In this Act references to the members of a self-regulating organisation are references to the persons who, whether or not members of the organisation, are subject to its rules in carrying on the business in question.

(3) In this Act references to the rules of a self-regulating organisation are references to the rules (whether or not laid down by the organisation itself) which the organisation has power to enforce in relation to the carrying on of the business in question or which relate to the admission and expulsion of members of the organisation or otherwise to its constitution.

(4) In this Act references to guidance issued by a self-regulating organisation are references to guidance issued or any recommendation made by it to all or any class of its members or persons seeking to become members which would, if it were a rule, fall within subsection (3) above.

DEFINITION
    "carrying on of investment business": s.1(3).

GENERAL NOTE
    This section defines self-regulation organisations, their members, rules and guidance.

Subs. (3)

Not laid down by the organisation itself: *e.g.* rules laid down by the SIB in respect of clients' money (s.55) and cold calling (s.56).

Subs. (4)

The essential difference between rules and guidance is that the former are binding whereas the latter is not.

Applications for recognition

9.—(1) A self-regulating organisation may apply to the Secretary of State for an order declaring it to be a recognised self-regulating organisation for the purposes of this Act.

(2) Any such application—

(*a*) shall be made in such manner as the Secretary of State may direct; and

(*b*) shall be accompanied by such information as the Secretary of State may reasonably require for the purpose of determining the application.

(3) At any time after receiving an application and before determining it the Secretary of State may require the applicant to furnish additional information.

(4) The directions and requirements given or imposed under subsections (2) and (3) above may differ as between different applications.

(5) Any information to be furnished to the Secretary of State under this section shall, if he so requires, be in such form or verified in such manner as he may specify.

(6) Every application shall be accompanied by a copy of the applicant's rules and of any guidance issued by the applicant which is intended to have continuing effect and is issued in writing or other legible form.

DEFINITIONS

"guidance": s.8(4).

"recognised self-regulating organisation": s.207(1).

"rules": s.8(3).

"self-regulating organisation": s.8(1).

GENERAL NOTE

This section governs the making of applications for recognition as a self-regulating organisation. As to fees payable, see section 112(1).

Subs. (1), para. (b)

Reasonably: Note this additional qualification of the accompanying information which may be required.

Subs. (6)

Continuing effect: Purely temporary guidance need not be submitted.

Or other legible form: *e.g.* guidance which may be retrieved from a computer (H.L. Vol. 479, cols. 235–237).

Grant and refusal of recognition

10.—(1) The Secretary of State may, on an application duly made in accordance with section 9 above and after being furnished with all such information as he may require under that section, make or refuse to make an order ("a recognition order") declaring the applicant to be a recognised self-regulating organisation.

(2) Subject to subsection (4) below and to Chapter XIV of this Part of this Act, the Secretary of State shall make a recognition order if it appears to him from the information furnished by the organisation making the application and having regard to any other information in his possession

that the requirements of subsection (3) below and of Schedule 2 to this Act are satisfied as respects that organisation.

(3) Where there is a kind of investment business with which the organisation is not concerned, its rules must preclude a member from carrying on investment business of that kind unless he is an authorised person otherwise than by virtue of his membership of the organisation or an exempted person in respect of that business.

(4) The Secretary of State may refuse to make a recognition order in respect of an organisation if he considers that its recognition is unnecessary having regard to the existence of one or more other organisations which are concerned with investment business of a kind with which the applicant is concerned and which have been or are likely to be recognised under this section.

(5) Where the Secretary of State refuses an application for a recognition order he shall give the applicant a written notice to that effect specifying a requirement which in the opinion of the Secretary of State is not satisfied, stating that the application is refused on the ground mentioned in subsection (4) above or stating that it is refused by virtue of Chapter XIV.

(6) A recognition order shall state the date on which it takes effect.

DEFINITIONS
"authorised persons": s.207(1).
"exempted persons": s.207(1).
"investment business": s.1(2).
"members": s.8(2).
"recognised self-regulating organisation": s.207(1).
"recognition order": s.207(1).
"rules": s.8(3).

GENERAL NOTE
This section identifies the factors to be taken into account by the SIB when making, or refusing to make, an order declaring an organisation to be a recognised SRO.

Subs. (2)
Chapter XIV: The likely effects on competition of an SRO's rules and guidance must not exceed those necessary for the protection of investors. Whether or not this condition is satisfied is a matter for the Secretary of State (s.120(2)).
Shall: Although a recognition order must be made where the requirements and conditions stipulated are satisfied, whether or not they are is a matter for the discretion of the SIB and, in the case of the competitive effects of an organisation's rules and guidance, the Secretary of State.
Schedule 2: This schedule sets out a number of requirements which an organisation must satisfy.

Subs. (3)
No single recognised SRO is expected to cover all kinds of investment business. Organisations must therefore include in their rules a "scope" rule preventing their members from carrying on, without separate authorisation or exemption, the kinds of investment business not covered by the organisation. Such authorisation may therefore have to be sought from another organisation (or organisations) or from the SIB.

Subs. (4)
This subsection imports a "need" test designed to prevent a proliferation of recognised SROs. As is clear from the section overall, need is only one of the factors to be taken into account in the grant or refusal of recognition. Keeping the numbers down is therefore not to be pursued regardless of the likely effectiveness of the arrangements proposed.

Revocation of recognition

11.—(1) A recognition order may be revoked by a further order made by the Secretary of State if at any time it appears to him—

   (*a*) that section 10(3) above or any requirement of Schedule 2 to this Act is not satisfied in the case of the organisation to which the recognition order relates ("the recognised organisation");

   (*b*) that the recognised organisation has failed to comply with any obligation to which it is subject by virtue of this Act; or

   (*c*) that the continued recognition of the organisation is undesirable having regard to the existence of one or more other organisations which have been or are to be recognised under section 10 above.

(2) An order revoking a recognition order shall state the date on which it takes effect and that date shall not be earlier than three months after the day on which the revocation order is made.

(3) Before revoking a recognition order the Secretary of State shall give written notice of his intention to do so to the recognised organisation, take such steps as he considers reasonably practicable for bringing the notice to the attention of members of the organisation and publish it in such manner as he thinks appropriate for bringing it to the attention of any other persons who are in his opinion likely to be affected.

(4) A notice under subsection (3) above shall state the reasons for which the Secretary of State proposes to act and give particulars of the rights conferred by subsection (5) below.

(5) An organisation on which a notice is served under subsection (3) above, any member of the organisation and any other person who appears to the Secretary of State to be affected may within three months after the date of service or publication, or within such longer time as the Secretary of State may allow, make written representations to the Secretary of State and, if desired, oral representations to a person appointed for that purpose by the Secretary of State; and the Secretary of State shall have regard to any representations made in accordance with this subsection in determining whether to revoke the recognition order.

(6) If in any case the Secretary of State considers it essential to do so in the interests of investors he may revoke a recognition order without regard to the restriction imposed by subsection (2) above and notwithstanding that no notice has been given or published under subsection (3) above or that the time for making representations in pursuance of such a notice has not expired.

(7) An order revoking a recognition order may contain such transitional provisions as the Secretary of State thinks necessary or expedient.

(8) A recognition order may be revoked at the request or with the consent of the recognised organisation and any such revocation shall not be subject to the restrictions imposed by subsections (1) and (2) or the requirements of subsections (3) to (5) above.

(9) On making an order revoking a recognition order the Secretary of State shall give the organisation written notice of the making of the order, take such steps as he considers reasonably practicable for bringing the making of the order to the attention of members of the organisation and publish a notice of the making of the order in such manner as he thinks appropriate for bringing it to the attention of any other persons who are in his opinion likely to be affected.

DEFINITIONS
  "members": s.8(2).
  "recognised organisation": s.11(1)(*a*).
  "recognition order": s.107(1).

GENERAL NOTE
  This section empowers the SIB to revoke a recognition order. Revocation is the most drastic weapon in the SIB armoury. It deprives the SRO's members of their authorisation to carry on investment business unless they are separately authorised or exempted. Less

drastically, the SIB is also empowered to seek compliance orders (s.12) and to alter an SRO's rules (s.13). Revocation may also take place at the request or with the consent of the SRO (subs. (8)).

Subs. (1)
    Any obligation . . . this Act: Covers obligations imposed both by the Act as well as under it.
    An order may also be revoked by the Secretary of State where the anti-competitive effects of an SRO's rules, guidance or practices, or the practice of its members, exceed those necessary for the protection of investors (s.120(4)).

Subs. (2)
    A revocation order may take effect earlier (subs. (6)).

Subs. (3)
    The requirement of notice may be dispensed with (subs. (6)). As to the service of notices, see section 204.

Subss. (4), (5)
    These requirements may also be dispensed with (subs. (6)).

Subs. (9)
    As to the service of notices, see section 204.

Compliance orders

12.—(1) If at any time it appears to the Secretary of State—
    (*a*) that subsection (3) of section 10 above or any requirement of Schedule 2 to this Act is not satisfied in the case of a recognised organisation; or
    (*b*) that a recognised organisation has failed to comply with any obligation to which it is subject by virtue of this Act,
he may, instead of revoking the recognition order under section 11 above, make an application to the court under this section.
    (2) If on any such application the court decides that subsection (3) of section 10 or the requirement in question is not satisfied or, as the case may be, that the organisation has failed to comply with the obligation in question it may order the organisation to take such steps as the court directs for securing that that subsection or requirement is satisfied or that that obligation is complied with.
    (3) The jurisdiction conferred by this section shall be exercisable by the High Court and the Court of Session.

DEFINITIONS
    "recognised organisation": s.11(1)(*a*).
    "recognition order": s.207(1).

GENERAL NOTE
    This section empowers the SIB to seek compliance orders in respect of SROs. In addition, the Secretary of State has the power, exercisable through the SIB, to cause an SRO to take remedial action where the anti-competitive effects of its rules, guidance or practices, or the practices of its members, exceed those necessary for the protection of investors (s.120(4)).

Subs. (1)
    Any obligation . . . this Act: see annotation to section 11(1).

Alteration of rules for protection of investors

13.—(1) If at any time it appears to the Secretary of State that the rules of a recognised organisation do not satisfy the requirements of paragraph 3(1) of Schedule 2 to this Act he may, instead of revoking the recognition order or making an application under section 12 above, direct the organisation to alter, or himself alter, its rules in such manner as he considers necessary for securing that the rules satisfy those requirements.

(2) If at any time it appears to the Secretary of State that the rules or practices of a recognised organisation which is concerned with two or more kinds of investment business do not satisfy any requirement of Schedule 2 to this Act in respect of investment business of any of those kinds he may, instead of revoking the recognition order or making an application under section 12 above, direct the organisation to alter, or himself alter, its rules so that they preclude a member from carrying on investment business of that kind unless he is an authorised person otherwise than by virtue of membership of the organisation or an exempted person in respect of that business.

(3) Any direction given under this section shall, on the application of the Secretary of State, be enforceable by mandamus or, in Scotland, by an order for specific performance under section 91 of the Court of Session Act 1868.

(4) Before giving a direction or making any alteration under subsection (1) above the Secretary of State shall consult the organisation concerned.

(5) A recognised organisation whose rules have been altered by or pursuant to a direction given by the Secretary of State under subsection (1) above may apply to the court and if the court is satisfied—

    (*a*) that the rules without the alteration satisfied the requirements mentioned in that subsection; or

    (*b*) that other alterations proposed by the organisation would result in the rules satisfying those requirements,

the court may set aside the alterations made by or pursuant to the direction given by the Secretary of State and, in a case within paragraph (*b*) above, order the organisation to make the alterations proposed by it; but the setting aside of an alteration under this subsection shall not affect its previous operation.

(6) The jurisdiction conferred by subsection (5) above shall be exercisable by the High Court and the Court of Session.

(7) Section 11(2) to (7) and (9) above shall, with the necessary modifications, have effect in relation to any direction given or alteration made by the Secretary of State under subsection (2) above as they have effect in relation to an order revoking a recognition order.

(8) The fact that the rules of a recognised organisation have been altered by or pursuant to a direction given by the Secretary of State or pursuant to an order made by the court under this section shall not preclude their subsequent alteration or revocation by that organisation.

DEFINITIONS
    "investment business": s.1(2).
    "member": s.8(2).
    "recognised organisation": s.11(1)(*a*).
    "recognition order": s.207(1).
    "rules": s.8(3).

GENERAL NOTE
    This section empowers the SIB to alter an SRO's rules for the protection of investors.

Subs. (1)
    This subsection stems from an undertaking given during the Commons' Committee Stage that the Bill would be amended to empower the SIB to direct an SRO to alter, or itself to alter, its rules should they not comply with the principle of equivalence laid down in Sched. 2, para. 3 (H.C. Standing Committee E, col. 237). As to safeguards, see subsections (4), (5). Rule changes may also be imposed under sections 120(4) and 192.

Subs. (2)

This subsection empowers the SIB to restrict the kinds of investment business an SRO's members are authorised to undertake by virtue of their membership of the organisation. As to safeguards, see subsection (7).

Practices: The practices referred to are to those of the organisation itself and by implication not those of its members; *cf.* Sched. 2 and s.119.

Subs. (5)

In return for conceding the power to impose rule changes, this subsection gives SROs the right to make a judicial application to have any rule change imposed under subsection (1) set aside. Absent this right, an SRO would have to seek judicial review of the exercise of the power or await the attempted enforcement of any direction under subsection (3).

Subs. (8)

The purpose of this subsection is to ensure that a rule which has been changed does not become "set in stone despite later changes in circumstances in which a change would be not only acceptable but positively desirable" (H.L. Vol. 479, col. 261). The possibility of its abuse to overturn imposed rule changes can be countered by recourse to sections 11 or 12.

Notification requirements

14.—(1) The Secretary of State may make regulations requiring a recognised organisation to give him forthwith notice of the occurrence of such events relating to the organisation or its members as are specified in the regulations and such information in respect of those events as is so specified.

(2) The Secretary of State may make regulations requiring a recognised organisation to furnish him at such times or in respect of such periods as are specified in the regulations with such information relating to the organisation or its members as is so specified.

(3) The notices and information required to be given or furnished under the foregoing provisions of this section shall be such as the Secretary of State may reasonably require for the exercise of his functions under this Act.

(4) Regulations under the foregoing provisions of this section may require information to be given in a specified form and to be verified in a specified manner.

(5) Any notice or information required to be given or furnished under the foregoing provisions of this section shall be given in writing or in such other manner as the Secretary of State may approve.

(6) Where a recognised organisation amends, revokes or adds to its rules or guidance it shall within seven days give the Secretary of State written notice of the amendment, revocation or addition; but notice need not be given of the revocation of guidance other than such as is mentioned in section 9(6) above or of any amendment of or addition to guidance which does not result in or consist of such guidance as is there mentioned.

(7) Contravention of, or of regulations under, this section shall not be an offence.

DEFINITIONS
"guidance": s.8(4).
"members": s.8(2).
"recognised organisations": s.11(1)(*a*).
"rules": s.8(3).

GENERAL NOTE
This section makes provision for the notification of information by SROs to the SIB.

Subss. (1), (2)

These subsections empower the SIB to make regulations (notification regulations) specifying the information with which it is to be supplied by SROs. As to their likely content, and accompanying memoranda of understanding, see *Regulation of Investment Business: The New Framework* (1985), para. 2.16. As to the making of regulations by the Board, see section 114(9) and Schedule 9, paras. 4–9. Breach of these regulations is not an offence (subs. (7)), nor does it give rise to liability in damages (s.187).

Subs. (3)
    Reasonably . . . functions under this Act: Note the twin qualifications.

Subs. (6)
    This subsection requires SROs to give the SIB notice of alterations in their rules and guidance. The SIB must in turn notify them to the Secretary of State (s.120(3)). Breach of this requirement is not an offence (subs. (7)), nor does it give rise to liability in damages (s.187).
    Other than such . . . mentioned: Guidance which is intended to have continuing effect and is issued in writing or other legible form.

Persons authorised by recognised professional bodies

Authorisation by certification by recognised professional body

15.—(1) A person holding a certificate issued for the purposes of this Part of this Act by a recognised professional body is an authorised person.
    (2) Such a certificate may be issued by a recognised professional body to an individual, a body corporate, a partnership or an unincorporated association.
    (3) A certificate issued to a partnership—
    (*a*) shall be issued in the partnership name; and
    (*b*) shall authorise the carrying on of investment business in that name by the partnership to which the certificate is issued, by any partnership which succeeds to that business or by any person who succeeds to that business having previously carried it on in partnership;
and, in relation to a certificate issued to a partnership constituted under the law of England and Wales or Northern Ireland or the law of any other country or territory under which a partnership is not a legal person, references in this Act to the person who holds the certificate or is certified shall be construed as references to the persons or person for the time being authorised by the certificate to carry on investment business as mentioned in paragraph (*b*) above.

DEFINITIONS
    "authorised person": s.207(1).
    "body corporate": s.207(1).
    "partnership": s.207(1).
    "recognised professional body": s.207(1).

GENERAL NOTE
    Sections 15–21 establish a separate framework for the regulation of investment business carried on by professional people such as solicitors, accountants and surveyors incidentally to the practice of their profession. In terms of this subsection a person certificated by a recognised professional body is an authorised person and hence does not fall foul of the basic prohibition in section 3. As to certification, see Schedule 3, para. 2.

Subs. (2)
    Body corporate: The inclusion of bodies corporate is intended to allow for changing patterns of professional organisation. A body corporate may thus be certificated although it may not be a member of the RPB.

Subs. (3)
    Absent this provision a certificate issued to a partnership constituted under English law would cease to authorise the carrying on of investment business whenever the partnership's

membership changed because the partnership itself would cease to exist. By virtue of this subsection the authorisation granted to a partnership continues in force "notwithstanding any subsequent change in the partners so long as . . . the business continues to be carried on in the original name" (H.L. Vol. 480, col. 926).

Professional bodies

16.—(1) In this Act a "professional body" means a body which regulates the practice of a profession and references to the practice of a profession do not include references to carrying on a business consisting wholly or mainly of investment business.

(2) In this Act references to the members of a professional body are references to individuals who, whether or not members of the body, are entitled to practise the profession in question and, in practising it, are subject to the rules of that body.

(3) In this Act references to the rules of a professional body are references to the rules (whether or not laid down by the body itself) which the body has power to enforce in relation to the practice of the profession in question and the carrying on of investment business by persons practising that profession or which relate to the grant, suspension or withdrawal of certificates under section 15 above, the admission and expulsion of members or otherwise to the constitution of the body.

(4) In this Act references to guidance issued by a professional body are references to guidance issued or any recommendation made by it to all or any class of its members or persons seeking to become members, or to persons or any class of persons who are or are seeking to be certified by the body, and which would, if it were a rule, fall within subsection (3) above.

DEFINITION
  "carrying on of investment business": s.1(3).

GENERAL NOTE
  This section defines professional bodies, their members, rules and guidance. It is modelled on section 8 in respect of SROs.

Subs. (1)
  Note that by definition the carrying on of business consisting wholly or mainly of investment business is not the practice of a profession.

Subs. (3)
  Not laid down by the body itself: *e.g.* rules laid down by the SIB in respect of clients' money (s.55) and cold-calling (s.56).

Subs. (4)
  Whereas rules are binding, guidance is not.

Applications for recognition

17.—(1) A professional body may apply to the Secretary of State for an order declaring it to be a recognised professional body for the purposes of this Act.

(2) Subsections (2) to (6) of section 9 above shall have effect in relation to an application under subsection (1) above as they have effect in relation to an application under subsection (1) of that section.

DEFINITIONS
  "professional body": s.16(1).
  "recognised professional body": s.207(1).

GENERAL NOTE
This section governs the making of applications for recognition. The same arrangements apply as apply in respect of applications for recognition by SROs; as to fees, see section 112(1). The Act also makes provision for the interim recognition of professional bodies; as to the making of applications for interim recognition orders, see Sched. 15, para. 4.

Grant and refusal of recognition

18.—(1) The Secretary of State may, on an application duly made in accordance with section 17 above and after being furnished with all such information as he may require under that section, make or refuse to make an order ("a recognition order") declaring the applicant to be a recognised professional body.

(2) The Secretary of State may make a recognition order if it appears to him from the information furnished by the body making the application and having regard to any other information in his possession that the requirements of subsection (3) below and of Schedule 3 to this Act are satisfied as respects that body.

(3) The body must have rules which impose acceptable limits on the kinds of investment business which may be carried on by persons certified by it and the circumstances in which they may carry on such business and which preclude a person certified by that body from carrying on any investment business outside those limits unless he is an authorised person otherwise than by virtue of the certification or an exempted person in respect of that business.

(4) Where the Secretary of State refuses an application for a recognition order he shall give the applicant a written notice to that effect, stating the reasons for the refusal.

(5) A recognition order shall state the date on which it takes effect.

DEFINITIONS
"authorised person": s.207(1).
"exempted person": s.207(1).
"investment business": s.1(2).
"recognised professional body": s.207(1).
"recognition order": s.207(1).
"rules": s.16(3).

GENERAL NOTE
This section identifies some of the factors to be taken into account by the SIB when making, or refusing to make, an order declaring a professional body to be a recognised professional body.

Subs. (1)
As to the making of interim recognition orders, see Sched. 15, para. 4.

Subs. (2)
May: the SIB is not obliged to recognise a professional body; contrast section 10(2). One important consequence of this is that the criteria referred to in this section are not the only criteria to be taken into account in deciding whether to grant or refuse recognition. As to possible additional criteria, see H.L. Vol. 480, col. 935. Compare also in this respect subsection (4) with section 10(5).
Schedule 3: This Schedule sets out a number of requirements which a body must satisfy.

Subs. (3)
Acceptable limits: These are not quantitative limits, but limits on the *kinds* of, and *circumstances* in which, investment business may be undertaken by certified persons. The requirement of *limits* on the kind of investment business which may be undertaken means the professional bodies must have their equivalent of the "scope" rule required of SROs (s.10(3)); the requirement of limits on the *circumstances* in which investment business may be undertaken is intended to reinforce the restriction of certification to persons whose main

business is the practice of their profession (s.16(1); Sched. 3, para. 2). Investment business carried on under the supervision of an RPB is thus to be confined to that carried on incidentally to the practice of the profession (H.C. Vol. 103, col. 518).

Revocation of recognition

19.—(1) A recognition order under section 18 above may be revoked by a further order made by the Secretary of State if at any time it appears to him—

(a) that section 18(3) above or any requirement of Schedule 3 to this Act is not satisfied in the case of the body to which the recognition order relates; or

(b) that the body has failed to comply with any obligation to which it is subject by virtue of this Act.

(2) Subsections (2) to (9) of section 11 above shall have effect in relation to the revocation of a recognition order under this section as they have effect in relation to the revocation of a recognition order under subsection (1) of that section.

DEFINITION
"recognition order": s.207(1).

GENERAL NOTE
This section empowers the SIB to revoke a recognition order. Again, revocation is the most drastic weapon in the SIB's armoury; it deprives certificated persons of their authorisation to carry on investment business without separate authorisation or exemption. As a less drastic alternative the SIB may seek a compliance order (s.20), but neither it, nor the Secretary of State, has power to alter an RPB's rules. The same procedural safeguards apply to the revocation of an RPB's recognition as apply to the revocation of the recognition of an SRO.

Subs. (1)
Any obligation . . . this Act: See annotation to section 11(1).

Compliance orders

20.—(1) If at any time it appears to the Secretary of State—

(a) that subsection (3) of section 18 above or any requirement of Schedule 3 to this Act is not satisfied in the case of a recognised professional body; or

(b) that such a body has failed to comply with any obligation to which it is subject by virtue of this Act,

he may, instead of revoking the recognition order under section 19 above, make an application to the court under this section.

(2) If on any such application the court decides that subsection (3) of section 18 above or the requirement in question is not satisfied or, as the case may be, that the body has failed to comply with the obligation in question it may order the body to take such steps as the court directs for securing that that subsection or requirement is satisfied or that that obligation is complied with.

(3) The jurisdiction conferred by this section shall be exercisable by the High Court and the Court of Session.

DEFINITIONS
"recognised professional body": s.207(1).
"recognition order": s.207(1).

GENERAL NOTE
This section empowers the SIB to seek compliance orders in respect of RPBs.

Subs. (1)
    Any obligation . . . this Act: See annotation to section 11(1).

Notification requirements
    21.—(1) The Secretary of State may make regulations requiring a recognised professional body to give him forthwith notice of the occurrence of such events relating to the body, its members or persons certified by it as are specified in the regulations and such information in respect of those events as is so specified.
    (2) The Secretary of State may make regulations requiring a recognised professional body to furnish him at such times or in respect of such periods as are specified in the regulations with such information relating to the body, its members and persons certified by it as is so specified.
    (3) The notices and information required to be given or furnished under the foregoing provisions of this section shall be such as the Secretary of State may reasonably require for the exercise of his functions under this Act.
    (4) Regulations under the foregoing provisions of this section may require information to be given in a specified form and to be verified in a specified manner.
    (5) Any notice or information required to be given or furnished under the foregoing provisions of this section shall be given in writing or in such other manner as the Secretary of State may approve.
    (6) Where a recognised professional body amends, revokes or adds to its rules or guidance it shall within seven days give the Secretary of State written notice of the amendment, revocation or addition; but—
      (*a*) notice need not be given of the revocation of guidance other than such as is mentioned in section 9(6) above or of any amendment of or addition to guidance which does not result in or consist of such guidance as is there mentioned; and
      (*b*) notice need not be given in respect of any rule or guidance, or rules or guidance of any description, in the case of which the Secretary of State has waived compliance with this subsection by notice in writing to the body concerned;
and any such waiver may be varied or revoked by a further notice in writing.
    (7) Contravention of, or of regulations under, this section shall not be an offence.

Definitions
    "guidance": s.16(4).
    "members": s.16(2).
    "recognised professional body": s.207(1).
    "rules": s.16(3).

General Note
    This section makes provision for the notification of information by RPBs to the SIB. It replicates substantially the equivalent provision in respect of SROs, section 14, to the annotations to which reference should be made.

Subs. (6)
    Note the power to waive this requirement. Presumably it will be exercised in respect of rules and guidance which do not relate to the carrying on of investment business by persons certified by the RPB. As to the service of notices, see section 204.

Subs. (7)
    The immunity from civil action conferred on SROs by section 187 does not extend to RPBs. Consequently, a failure to comply with the regulations or subsection (6) may give rise to civil remedies. See in this respect, H.L. Vol. 479, col. 266.

Insurance companies

Authorised insurers

22. A body which is authorised under section 3 or 4 of the Insurance Companies Act 1982 to carry on insurance business which is investment business and carries on such insurance business in the United Kingdom is an authorised person as respects—

(*a*) any insurance business which is investment business; and

(*b*) any other investment business which that body may carry on without contravening section 16 of that Act.

DEFINITIONS
"authorised persons": s.207(1).
"insurance business": s.207(7).
"investment business": s.1(2).

GENERAL NOTE
This section applies only to insurance companies authorised under section 3 or 4 of the Insurance Companies Act. It automatically authorises them to carry on investment business. They do not therefore require, nor indeed are they permitted to obtain, any further authorisation to carry on investment business (Sched. 10, para. 2(1)). Note that, in contrast to sections 7 and 15, their authorisation is confined to (a) and (b). As to the position of insurance companies to which Part II of the Insurance Companies Act applies, but to which this section does not apply, see Schedule 10, para. 2(2). As to the regulation of investment business carried on by insurance companies, see Part II of the Act.

Friendly societies

Registered friendly societies

23.—(1) A society which—

(*a*) is a friendly society within the meaning of section 7(1)(*a*) of the Friendly Societies Act 1974;

(*b*) is registered within the meaning of that Act as a society but not as a branch of a society;

(*c*) under its rules has its registered office at a place situated in Great Britain; and

(*d*) carries on investment business in the United Kingdom,

is an authorised person as respects any investment business which it carries on for or in connection with any of the purposes mentioned in Schedule 1 to that Act.

(2) A society which—

(*a*) is a friendly society within the meaning of section 1(1)(*a*) of the Friendly Societies Act (Northern Ireland) 1970;

(*b*) is registered or deemed to be registered as a society but not as a branch of a society under that Act;

(*c*) under its rules has its registered office at a place situated in Northern Ireland; and

(*d*) carries on investment business in the United Kingdom,

is an authorised person as respects any investment business which it carries on for or in connection with any of the purposes mentioned in Schedule 1 to that Act.

DEFINITIONS
"authorised person": s.207(1).
"investment business": s.1(2).

GENERAL NOTE
Friendly societies which carry on investment business do not require separate authorisation to do so: they are automatically authorised by virtue of this section. Note, however, that in

common with insurance companies, the authorisation conferred by this section is limited. As to the regulation of investment business carried on by friendly societies, see Schedule 11.

Subss. (1)(b), (2)(b)
Branch of a society: Branches of a society are also automatically authorised (H.L. Vol. 479, cols. 270–271).

Collective investment schemes

Operators and trustees of recognised schemes

24. The operator or trustee of a scheme recognised under section 86 below is an authorised person as respects—
(*a*) investment business which consists in operating or acting as trustee in relation to that scheme; and
(*b*) any investment business which is carried on by him in connection with or for the purposes of that scheme.

DEFINITIONS
"authorised person": s.207(1).
"investment business": s.1(2).
"operator": s.207(1).
"trustee": s.207(1).

GENERAL NOTE
This section, which gives effect to the United Kingdom's obligations under the UCITS Directive, confers automatic authorisation on the operator or trustee of a collective investment scheme which is authorised in another Member State in accordance with the provisions of the Directive and which is recognised under section 86. Note that, in common with insurance companies and friendly societies, the authorisation conferred by this section is limited.

Persons authorised by the Secretary of State

Authorisation by Secretary of State

25. A person holding an authorisation granted by the Secretary of State under the following provisions of this Chapter is an authorised person.

DEFINITION
"authorised person": s.207(1).

GENERAL NOTE
Sections 25–30 establish the basic framework for the regulation of directly authorised investment businesses. For the majority of investment businesses, direct authorisation by the SIB will constitute the only real alternative to obtaining authorisation through membership of an SRO. Although, by virtue of this section, a directly authorised person does not contravene the basic prohibition in section 3, such a person will be required to confine himself to the kinds of investment business for which he is approved by the SIB.

Applications for authorisation

26.—(1) An application for authorisation by the Secretary of State may be made by—
(*a*) an individual;
(*b*) a body corporate;
(*c*) a partnership; or
(*d*) an unincorporated association.
(2) Any such application—
(*a*) shall be made in such manner as the Secretary of State may direct;
(*b*) shall contain or be accompanied by—

(i) information as to the investment business which the applicant proposes to carry on and the services which he will hold himself out as able to provide in the carrying on of that business; and

(ii) such other information as the Secretary of State may reasonably require for the purpose of determining the application; and

(c) shall contain the address of a place in the United Kingdom for the service on the applicant of any notice or other document required or authorised to be served on him under this Act.

(3) At any time after receiving an application and before determining it the Secretary of State may require the applicant to furnish additional information.

(4) The directions and requirements given or imposed under subsections (2) and (3) above may differ as between different applications.

(5) Any information to be furnished to the Secretary of State under this section shall, if he so requires, be in such form or verified in such manner as he may specify.

DEFINITIONS
"appointed representative": s.44(2).
"body corporate" s.207(1).
"investment business": s.1(2).
"partnership": s.207(1).

GENERAL NOTE
This section governs the making of applications for authorisation. For the information which the SIB will require, in the form of a completed general application form and business plan questionnaire, see *Regulation of Investment Business* (the SIB's rule book), chapter 1. As to fees, see section 112(5). As to the withdrawal of applications, see section 30.

Grant and refusal of authorisation

27.—(1) The Secretary of State may, on an application duly made in accordance with section 26 above and after being furnished with all such information as he may require under that section, grant or refuse the application.

(2) The Secretary of State shall grant the application if it appears to him from the information furnished by the applicant and having regard to any other information in his possession that the applicant is a fit and proper person to carry on the investment business and provide the services described in the application.

(3) In determining whether to grant or refuse an application the Secretary of State may take into account any matter relating to any person who is or will be employed by or associated with the applicant for the purposes of the business in question, to any person who is or will be acting as an appointed representative in relation to that business and—

(a) if the applicant is a body corporate, to any director or controller of that body, to any other body corporate in the same group or to any director or controller of any such other body corporate;

(b) if the applicant is a partnership, to any of the partners;

(c) if the applicant is an unincorporated association, to any member of the governing body of the association or any officer or controller of the association.

(4) In determining whether to grant or refuse an application the Secretary of State may also have regard to any business which the applicant proposes to carry on in connection with his investment business.

(5) In the case of an applicant who is authorised to carry on investment business in a member State other than the United Kingdom the Secretary of State shall have regard to that authorisation.

(6) An authorisation granted to a partnership—
(a) shall be granted in the partnership name; and
(b) shall authorise the carrying on of investment business in that name (or with the Secretary of State's consent in any other name) by the partnership to which the authorisation is granted, by any partnership which succeeds to that business or by any person who succeeds to that business having previously carried it on in partnership;

and, in relation to an authorisation granted to a partnership constituted under the law of England and Wales or Northern Ireland or the law of any other country or territory under which a partnership is not a legal person, references in this Act to the holder of the authorisation or the authorised person shall be construed as references to the persons or person for the time being authorised by the authorisation to carry on investment business as mentioned in paragraph (b) above.

(7) An authorisation granted to an unincorporated association shall apply to the carrying on of investment business in the name of the association and in such manner as may be specified in the authorisation.

(8) The Secretary of State shall give an applicant for authorisation written notice of the grant of authorisation specifying the date on which it takes effect.

DEFINITIONS
  "appointed representative": s.44(2).
  "controller": s.207(1).
  "director": s.207(1).
  "group": s.207(1).
  "investment business": s.1(2).
  "partnership": s.207(1).

GENERAL NOTE
  This section specifies the circumstances in which the SIB may grant or refuse an application for authorisation.

Subs. (1)
  Grant or refuse: As to the refusal of an application, see section 29. As to interim authorisation, see Schedule 15, para. 1.

Subs. (2)
  Shall: If the applicant is adjudged a fit and proper person his application must be granted.
  Fit and proper person: Although this term is widely used, there is little judicial authority on its meaning (*R.* v. *Hyde Justices* [1912] 1 K.B. 645; *R.* v. *Holborn Licensing Justices* (1926) 136 L.T. 278). Given the wide variety of different contexts in which it is used, its meaning arguably falls to be determined in the light of its particular context. In this context, the carrying on of investment business and the provision of the services described, it clearly embraces the honesty and competence of the applicant. Whether it also embraces the financial standing of the applicant, as arguably it does, is apparently regarded as less clear; hence the inclusion of section 49.

Subs. (6)
  See the annotation to section 15(3).

Subs. (8)
  As to the giving of notices, see section 204.

Withdrawal and suspension of authorisation

28.—(1) The Secretary of State may at any time withdraw or suspend any authorisation granted by him if it appears to him—
(a) that the holder of the authorisation is not a fit and proper person to carry on the investment business which he is carrying on or proposing to carry on; or

(b) without prejudice to paragraph (a) above, that the holder of the authorisation has contravened any provision of this Act or any rules or regulations made under it or, in purported compliance with any such provision, has furnished the Secretary of State with false, inaccurate or misleading information or has contravened any prohibition or requirement imposed under this Act.

(2) For the purposes of subsection (1)(a) above the Secretary of State may take into account any such matters as are mentioned in section 27(3) and (4) above.

(3) Where the holder of the authorisation is a member of a recognised self-regulating organisation the rules, prohibitions and requirements referred to in paragraph (b) of subsection (1) above include the rules of that organisation and any prohibition or requirement imposed by virtue of those rules; and where he is a person certified by a recognised professional body the rules, prohibitions and requirements referred to in that paragraph include the rules of that body which regulate the carrying on by him of investment business and any prohibition or requirement imposed by virtue of those rules.

(4) The suspension of an authorisation shall be for a specified period or until the occurrence of a specified event or until specified conditions are complied with; and while an authorisation is suspended the holder shall not be an authorised person.

(5) Any period, event or conditions specified under subsection (4) above in the case of an authorisation may be varied by the Secretary of State on the application of the holder.

DEFINITIONS
"carry on investment business": s.1(3).
"investment business": s.1(2).
"member": s.8(2).
"recognised professional body": s.207(1).
"recognised self-regulating organisation": s.207(1).
"rules": ss.8(3), 16(3).

GENERAL NOTE
This section empowers the SIB to withdraw or suspend authorisation. As to safeguards, see section 29.

Subs. (1)
Fit and proper person: see the annotation to section 27(2).

Subs. (3)
This subsection takes account of the fact that a directly authorised person may also be authorised by virtue of membership of an SRO or certification by an RPB. In terms of it, contravention of the SRO's or RPB's rules, etc., may also lead to the suspension or withdrawal of direct authorisation.

Subs. (5)
As to the refusal of an application, see section 29.

Notice of proposed refusal, withdrawal or suspension

29.—(1) Where the Secretary of State proposes—
  (a) to refuse an application under section 26 or 28(5) above; or
  (b) to withdraw or suspend an authorisation,
he shall give the applicant or the authorised person written notice of his intention to do so, stating the reasons for which he proposes to act.

(2) In the case of a proposed withdrawal or suspension the notice shall state the date on which it is proposed that the withdrawal or suspension

should take effect and, in the case of a proposed suspension, its proposed duration.

(3) Where the reasons stated in a notice under this section relate specifically to matters which—

    (*a*) refer to a person identified in the notice other than the applicant or the holder of the authorisation; and

    (*b*) are in the opinion of the Secretary of State prejudicial to that person in any office or employment,

the Secretary of State shall, unless he considers it impracticable to do so, serve a copy of the notice on that person.

(4) A notice under this section shall give particulars of the right to require the case to be referred to the Tribunal under Chapter IX of this Part of this Act.

(5) Where a case is not required to be referred to the Tribunal by a person on whom a notice is served under this section the Secretary of State shall, at the expiration of the period within which such a requirement can be made—

    (*a*) give that person written notice of the refusal, withdrawal or suspension; or

    (*b*) give that person written notice of the grant of the application or, as the case may be, written notice that the authorisation is not to be withdrawn or suspended;

and the Secretary of State may give public notice of any decision notified by him under paragraph (*a*) or (*b*) above and the reasons for the decision except that he shall not do so in the case of a decision notified under paragraph (*b*) unless the person concerned consents to his doing so.

DEFINITIONS
    "authorised person": s.207(1).
    "the Tribunal": s.207(1).

GENERAL NOTE
    This section imposes a duty upon the SIB to give notice of its intention to refuse an application for direct authorisation or for the variation of the suspension of direct authorisation, or to suspend or withdraw direct authorisation. As to the service of notices, see section 204.

Subs. (3)
    Note that identified third parties must in the circumstances specified be served with a copy of the notice.

Subs. (4)
    The notice must include details of the person's right to require the SIB to refer the case to the Financial Services Tribunal. As to references to the Tribunal, see section 97.

Subs. (5)
    Note that SIB is not bound by its notice of intention.
    Expiration of the period: Normally within 28 days, excluding public holidays (ss.97(1), (4), (5), 207(10)).

Withdrawal of applications and authorisations by consent

30.—(1) An application under section 26 above may be withdrawn before it is granted or refused; and, subject to subsections (2) and (3) below, an authorisation granted under section 27 above may be withdrawn by the Secretary of State at the request or with the consent of the authorised person.

(2) The Secretary of State may refuse to withdraw any such authorisation if he considers that the public interest requires any matter affecting the authorised person to be investigated as a preliminary to a decision on the

question whether the Secretary of State should in respect of that person exercise his powers under section 28 above or under any other provision of this Part of this Act.

(3) The Secretary of State may also refuse to withdraw an authorisation where in his opinion it is desirable that a prohibition or restriction should be imposed on the authorised person under Chapter VI of this Part of this Act or that a prohibition or restriction imposed on that person under that Chapter should continue in force.

(4) The Secretary of State may give public notice of any withdrawal of authorisation under subsection (1) above.

DEFINITION
"authorised person": s.207(1).

GENERAL NOTE
This section makes provision for the withdrawal of applications and authorisations by consent.

Subss. (2), (3)
The purpose of these provisions is to ensure that an investment business cannot prevent the SIB from exercising its powers in relation to it by simply requesting that its authorisation be withdrawn.

Persons authorised in other member States

Authorisation in other member State

31.—(1) A person carrying on investment business in the United Kingdom is an authorised person if—
   (a) he is established in a member State other than the United Kingdom;
   (b) the law of that State recognises him as a national of that or another member State; and
   (c) he is for the time being authorised under that law to carry on investment business or investment business of any particular kind.

(2) For the purposes of this Act a person is established in a member State other than the United Kingdom if his head office is situated in that State and he does not transact investment business from a permanent place of business maintained by him in the United Kingdom.

(3) This section applies to a person only if the provisions of the law under which he is authorised to carry on the investment business in question—
   (a) afford to investors in the United Kingdom protection, in relation to his carrying on of that business, which is at least equivalent to that provided for them by the provisions of this Chapter relating to members of recognised self-regulating organisations or to persons authorised by the Secretary of State; or
   (b) satisfy the conditions laid down by a Community instrument for the co-ordination or approximation of the laws, regulations or administrative provisions of member States relating to the carrying on of investment business or investment business of the relevant kind.

(4) A certificate issued by the Secretary of State and for the time being in force to the effect that the provisions of the law of a member State comply with the requirements of subsection (3)(a) above, either as respects all investment business or as respects investment business of a particular kind, shall be conclusive evidence of that matter but the absence or revocation of such a certificate shall not be regarded as indicating that those requirements are not complied with.

(5) This section shall not apply to a person by virtue of paragraph (*b*) of subsection (3) above unless the authority by which he is authorised to carry on the investment business in question certifies that he is authorised to do so under a law which complies with the requirements of that paragraph.

DEFINITIONS
"authorised person": s.207(1).
"carrying on investment business": s.1(3).
"investment business": s.1(2).

GENERAL NOTE
This section makes provision for the authorisation of nationals of other Member States of the European Community who are not established in the United Kingdom. It gives effect to the United Kingdom's obligation under the EEC Treaty to refrain from imposing discriminatory restrictions on the free movement of services. For the purposes of this section Gibraltar is treated as if it were a Member State (s.208). Insurance companies which are authorised by virtue of this section may not obtain authorisation under any other provision (Sched. 10, para. 2(3)).

Subs. (1)
To be authorised by virtue of this provision, the three conditions listed must be satisfied. Before carrying on investment business in the United Kingdom, an authorised person must also give notice of his intention to do so (s.32.).

Para. (a)
Establishment is defined in subsection (2).

Para. (b)
The person must be a national of *a* Member State, not necessarily of the State in which he is established.

Para. (c)
The law under which the person is authorised must comply with either of the two requirements laid down in subsection (3).

Subs. (3)
Para. (a)
Note the Secretary of State's power to issue a certificate under subsection (4).

Para. (b)
Note the additional requirement in subsection (5).

Subs. (4)
The reason why a certificate, or its lack, cannot be conclusive of the absence of equivalence is that the right to provide services derives from Community law independently of national law. Whether or not the equivalence test is satisfied falls, therefore, to be decided by the courts with the assistance of the European Court.
The power to issue certificates is reserved to the Secretary of State and cannot be transferred to the SIB (s.114(5)).

Notice of commencement of business

32.—(1) A person who is an authorised person by virtue of section 31 above shall be guilty of an offence unless, not less than seven days before beginning to carry on investment business in the United Kingdom, he has given notice of his intention to do so to the Secretary of State either in writing or in such other manner as the Secretary of State may approve.
(2) The notice shall contain—
(*a*) information as to the investment business which that person proposes to carry on in the United Kingdom and the services which he

will hold himself out as able to provide in the carrying on of that
business;

(*b*) information as to the authorisation of that person in the member
State in question;

(*c*) the address of a place (whether in the United Kingdom or elsewhere) for the service on that person of any notice or other
document required or authorised to be served on him under this
Act;

(*d*) such other information as may be prescribed;

and the notice shall comply with such requirements as to the form in
which any information is to be given and as to its verification as may be
prescribed.

(3) A notice by a person claiming to be authorised by virtue of
subsection (3)(*b*) of section 31 above shall be accompanied by a copy of
the certificate required by subsection (5) of that section.

(4) A person guilty of an offence under subsection (1) above shall be
liable—

(*a*) on conviction or indictment, to a fine;

(*b*) on summary conviction, to a fine not exceeding the statutory
maximum.

(5) In proceedings brought against any person for an offence under
subsection (1) above it shall be a defence for him to prove that he took
all reasonable precautions and exercised all due diligence to avoid the
commission of the offence.

DEFINITIONS
"authorised person": s.207(1).
"carry on investment business": s.1(3).
"investment business": s.1(2).
"prescribed": s.207(1).

GENERAL NOTE
This section requires a person authorised by virtue of section 31 to give the SIB notice of
his intention to carry on investment business in the United Kingdom. Where a person is
carrying on investment business in the United Kingdom on the day on which section 31
comes into force, notice must be given "forthwith" (Sched. 15, para. 8). Contravention of
this requirement is an offence. As to fees, see section 112(5).

Subs. (5)
All reasonable precautions . . . all due diligence: See annotation to section 4(2).

Termination and suspension of authorisation

33.—(1) If it appears to the Secretary of State that a person who is an
authorised person by virtue of section 31 above has contravened any
provision of this Act or of any rules or regulations made under it or, in
purported compliance with any such provision, has furnished the Secretary
of State with false, inaccurate or misleading information or has contravened any prohibition or requirement imposed under this Act the Secretary of State may direct—

(*a*) that he shall cease to be an authorised person by virtue of that
section; or

(*b*) that he shall not be an authorised person by virtue of that section
for a specified period or until the occurrence of a specified event or
until specified conditions are complied with.

(2) In the case of a person who is a member of a recognised self-
regulating organisation the rules, prohibitions and requirements referred
to in subsection (1) above include the rules of that organisation and any
prohibition or requirement imposed by virtue of those rules; and in the

case of a person who is certified by a recognised professional body the rules, prohibitions and requirements referred to in that subsection include the rules of that body which regulate the carrying on by him of investment business and any prohibition or requirement imposed by virtue of those rules.

(3) Any period, event or condition specified in a direction under subsection (1)(*b*) above may be varied by the Secretary of State on the application of the person to whom the direction relates.

(4) The Secretary of State shall consult the relevant supervisory authority before giving a direction under this section unless he considers it essential in the interests of investors that the direction should be given forthwith but in that case he shall consult the authority immediately after giving the direction and may then revoke or vary it if he considers it appropriate to do so.

(5) The Secretary of State shall revoke a direction under this section if he is satisfied, after consulting the relevant supervisory authority, that it will secure that the person concerned will comply with the provisions mentioned in subsection (1) above.

(6) In this section "the relevant supervisory authority" means the authority of the member State where the person concerned is established which is responsible for supervising the carrying on of investment business of the kind which that person is or was carrying on.

DEFINITIONS
"authorised person": s.207(1).
"investment business": s.1(2).
"recognised professional body": s.207(1).
"recognised self-regulating organisation": s.207(1).
"relevant supervisory authority": subs. (6).
"rules": ss.8(3), 16(3).

GENERAL NOTE
This section empowers the SIB to suspend or terminate the authorisation of a person authorised by virtue of section 31. As to safeguards, see section 34.

Subs. (2)
See the annotation to section 28(3).

Notice of proposed termination or suspension

34.—(1) Where the Secretary of State proposes—
   (*a*) to give a direction under section 33 above; or
   (*b*) to refuse an application under subsection (3) of that section,
he shall give the authorised person written notice of his intention to do so, stating the reasons for which he proposes to act.

(2) In the case of a proposed direction under section 33 above the notice shall state the date on which it is proposed that the direction should take effect and, in the case of a proposed direction under subsection (1)(*b*) of that section, its proposed duration.

(3) Where the reasons stated in a notice under this section relate specifically to matters which—
   (*a*) refer to a person identified in the notice other than the authorised person; and
   (*b*) are in the opinion of the Secretary of State prejudicial to that person in any office or employment,
the Secretary of State shall, unless he considers it impracticable to do so, serve a copy of the notice on that other person.

(4) A notice under this section shall give particulars of the right to require the case to be referred to the Tribunal under Chapter IX of this Part of this Act.

(5) Where a case is not required to be referred to the Tribunal by a person on whom a notice is served under this section the Secretary of State shall, at the expiration of the period within which such a requirement can be made—

(*a*) give that person written notice of the direction or refusal; or

(*b*) give that person written notice that the direction is not to be given or, as the case may be, of the grant of the application;

and the Secretary of State may give public notice of any decision notified by him under paragraph (*a*) or (*b*) above and the reasons for the decision except that he shall not do so in the case of a decision within paragraph (*b*) unless the person concerned consents to his doing so.

DEFINITIONS
  "authorised person": s.207(1).
  "the Tribunal": s.207(1).

GENERAL NOTE
This section imposes a duty upon the SIB to give notice of its intention to terminate or suspend authorisation by virtue of section 31, or to refuse an application for the variation of the suspension of authorisation under that section. It replicates substantially the equivalent provision in respect of directly authorised persons, section 29, to the annotations to which reference should be made.

CHAPTER IV

EXEMPTED PERSONS

The Bank of England

The Bank of England

35. The Bank of England is an exempted person.

DEFINITION
  "exempted person": s.207(1).

GENERAL NOTE
This section exempts the Bank of England from the requirement of authorisation.

Recognised investment exchanges and clearing houses

Investment exchanges

36.—(1) A recognised investment exchange is an exempted person as respects anything done in its capacity as such which constitutes investment business.

(2) In this Act references to the rules of an investment exchange are references to the rules made or conditions imposed by it with respect to the matters dealt with in Schedule 4 to this Act, with respect to the admission of persons to or their exclusion from the use of its facilities or otherwise relating to its constitution.

(3) In this Act references to guidance issued by an investment exchange are references to guidance issued or any recommendation made by it to all or any class of its members or users or persons seeking to become members of the exchange or to use its facilities and which would, if it were a rule, fall within subsection (2) above.

DEFINITIONS
"exempted person": s.207(1).
"investment business": s.207(1).
"recognised investment exchange": s.207(1).

GENERAL NOTE
This section exempts recognised investment exchanges (RIEs) from the requirement of authorisation. It also defines investment exchanges' rules and guidance. Investment exchanges do not have to be recognised: authorisation constitutes a sufficient alternative. Recognition thus operates as "a seal of good practice", indicating that the exchange meets the requirements laid down for recognition (H.C. Standing Committee E, col. 335). See also *Regulation of Investment Business: The New Framework* (1985) paras. 1.24–1.29.

Subs. (1)
Note that the exemption is confined to investment business undertaken in the RIE's capacity as an investment exchange.

Subs. (3)
Whereas rules are binding, guidance is not.

Grant and revocation of recognition

37.—(1) Any body corporate or unincorporated association may apply to the Secretary of State for an order declaring it to be a recognised investment exchange for the purposes of this Act.

(2) Subsections (2) to (5) of section 9 above shall have effect in relation to an application under subsection (1) above as they have effect in relation to an application under subsection (1) of that section; and every application under subsection (1) above shall be accompanied by—

(a) a copy of the applicant's rules;

(b) a copy of any guidance issued by the applicant which is intended to have continuing effect and is issued in writing or other legible form; and

(c) particulars of any arrangements which the applicant has made or proposes to make for the provision of clearing services.

(3) The Secretary of State may, on an application duly made in accordance with subsection (1) above and after being furnished with all such information as he may require in connection with the application, make or refuse to make an order ("a recognition order") declaring the applicant to be a recognised investment exchange for the purposes of this Act.

(4) Subject to Chapter XIV of this Part of this Act, the Secretary of State may make a recognition order if it appears to him from the information furnished by the exchange making the application and having regard to any other information in his possession that the requirements of Schedule 4 to this Act are satisfied as respects that exchange.

(5) Where the Secretary of State refuses an application for a recognition order he shall give the applicant a written notice to that effect stating the reasons for the refusal.

(6) A recognition order shall state the date on which it takes effect.

(7) A recognition order may be revoked by a further order made by the Secretary of State if at any time it appears to him—

(a) that any requirement of Schedule 4 to this Act is not satisfied in the case of the exchange to which the recognition order relates; or

(b) that the exchange has failed to comply with any obligation to which it is subject by virtue of this Act;

and subsections (2) to (9) of section 11 above shall have effect in relation to the revocation of a recognition order under this subsection as they have effect in relation to the revocation of such an order under subsection (1) of that section.

(8) Section 12 above shall have effect in relation to a recognised investment exchange and the requirements and obligations referred to in subsection (7) above as it has effect in relation to the requirements and obligations there mentioned.

DEFINITIONS
"body corporate": s.207(1).
"clearing arrangements": s.38(2).
"guidance": s.36(3).
"recognised investment exchange": s.207(1).
"recognition order": s.207(1).
"rules": s. 36(2).

GENERAL NOTE
This section governs the grant and revocation of orders declaring a body to be a recognised investment exchange. As to fees, see section 112(1). As to overseas investment exchanges, see section 40.

Subs. (2)
This subsection governs the making of applications for recognition.

Para. (b)
Continuing effect: Purely temporary guidance need not be submitted.
Or other legible form: *e.g.* guidance which may be retrieved from a computer (H.L. Vol. 479, cols. 235–237).

Subs. (4)
This subsection identifies the criteria which must be satisfied before the SIB is empowered to make a recognition order.
Chapter XIV: The likely effects on competition of an investment exchange's rules, guidance and clearing arrangements must not exceed those necessary for the protection of investors. Whether or not this condition is satisfied is a matter for the Secretary of State (s.120(2)).
May: The Board is not obliged to recognise an investment exchange. See also in this regard the annotation to section 18(2).
Schedule 4: This schedule sets out a number of requirements which an exchange must satisfy.

Subs. (5)
As to the service of notices, see section 204.

Subs. (7)
This subsection empowers the SIB to revoke a recognition order.
Any obligation . . . this Act: Covers obligations imposed both by the Act as well as under it.
An order may also be revoked by the Secretary of State when the anti-competitive effects of an RIE's rules, guidance or practices, or the practices off its members, exceed those necessary for the protection of investors (s.120(4)).

Subs. (8)
This subsection empowers the SIB to seek compliance orders in respect of RIEs.
Note also that where the anti-competitive effects of an RIE's rules, guidance or practices, or the practices of its members, exceed those necessary for the protection of investors, the Secretary of State also has the power, exercisable through the SIB, to alter its rules and to direct it to take remedial action (s.120(4)).

Clearing houses

38.—(1) A recognised clearing house is an exempted person as respects anything done by it in its capacity as a person providing clearing services for the transaction of investment business.

(2) In this Act references to the rules of a clearing house are references to the rules made or conditions imposed by it with respect to the provision by it or its members of clearing services under clearing arrangements, that is to say, arrangements with a recognised investment exchange for the

provision of clearing services in respect of transactions effected on the exchange.

(3) In this Act references to guidance issued by a clearing house are references to guidance issued or any recommendation made by it to all or any class of its members or persons using or seeking to use its services and which would, if it were a rule, fall within subsection (2) above.

DEFINITIONS
    "exempted person": s.207(1).
    "investment business": s.1(2).
    "recognised clearing house": s.207(1).

GENERAL NOTE
    An RIE is required to provide facilities for the completion of transactions. These facilities may be provided by a recognised clearing house (RCH) (Sched. 4, para. 4). This section exempts RCHs from the requirement of authorisation. It also defines clearing houses' rules and guidance.

Subs. (1)
    Note that the exemption is confined to investment business undertaken in the RCH's capacity as a provider of clearing services.

Subs. (2)
    On the exchange: Bargains struck "off the exchange" are covered if subject to the exchange's rules on reporting, clearing and so on. (H.L. Vol. 479, col. 297).

Subs. (3)
    Whereas rules are binding, guidance is not.

Grant and revocation of recognition

39.—(1) Any body corporate or unincorporated association may apply to the Secretary of State for an order declaring it to be a recognised clearing house for the purposes of this Act.

(2) Subsections (2) to (5) of section 9 above shall have effect in relation to an application under subsection (1) above as they have effect in relation to an application under subsection (1) of that section; and any application under subsection (1) above shall be accompanied by—

    (*a*) a copy of the applicant's rules;
    (*b*) a copy of any guidance issued by the applicant which is intended to have continuing effect and is issued in writing or other legible form; and
    (*c*) particulars of any recognised investment exchange with which the applicant proposes to make clearing arrangements and of any other person (whether or not such an exchange) for whom the applicant provides clearing services.

(3) The Secretary of State may, on an application duly made in accordance with subsection (1) above and after being furnished with all such information as he may require in connection with the application, make or refuse to make an order ("a recognition order") declaring the applicant to be a recognised clearing house for the purposes of this Act.

(4) Subject to Chapter XIV of this Part of this Act, the Secretary of State may make a recognition order if it appears to him from the information furnished by the clearing house making the application and having regard to any other information in his possession that the clearing house—

    (*a*) has financial resources sufficient for the proper performance of its functions;
    (*b*) has adequate arrangements and resources for the effective monitoring and enforcement of compliance with its rules or, as respects monitoring, arrangements providing for that function to be performed on behalf of the clearing house (and without affecting its

responsibility) by another body or person who is able and willing to perform it;

(c) provides or is able to provide clearing services which would enable a recognised investment exchange to make arrangements with it that satisfy the requirements of Schedule 4 to this Act; and

(d) is able and willing to comply with duties corresponding to those imposed in the case of a recognised investment exchange by paragraph 5 of that Schedule.

(5) Where the Secretary of State refuses an application for a recognition order he shall give the applicant a written notice to that effect stating the reasons for the refusal.

(6) A recognition order shall state the date on which it takes effect.

(7) A recognition order may be revoked by a further order made by the Secretary of State if at any time it appears to him—

(a) that any requirement of subsection (4) above is not satisfied in the case of the clearing house; or

(b) that the clearing house has failed to comply with any obligation to which it is subject by virtue of this Act;

and subsections (2) to (9) of section 11 above shall have effect in relation to the revocation of a recognition order under this subsection as they have effect in relation to the revocation of such an order under subsection (1) of that section.

(8) Section 12 above shall have effect in relation to a recognised clearing house and the requirements and obligations referred to in subsection (7) above as it has effect in relation to the requirements and obligations there mentioned.

DEFINITIONS
"body corporate": s.207(1).
"clearing arrangements": s.38(2).
"guidance": s.38(3).
"recognised clearing house": s.207(1).
"recognised investment exchange": s.207(1).
"recognition order": s.207(1).
"rules": s.38(2).

GENERAL NOTE
This section governs the grant and revocation of orders declaring a body to be a recognised clearing house. As to fees, see section 112(1). As to overseas clearing houses, see section 40.

Subs. (2)
This subsection governs the making of applications for recognition.

Para. (b)
Continuing effect: Purely temporary guidance need not be submitted.
Or other legible form: *e.g.* guidance which may be retrieved from a computer. (H.L. Vol. 479, cols. 235–237).

Subs. (4)
This section identifies the criteria which must be satisfied before the SIB is empowered to make a recognition order.
Chapter XIV: The likely effects on competition of a clearing house's rules and guidance must not exceed those necessary for the protection of investors. Whether or not this condition is satisfied is a matter for the Secretary of State (s.120(2)).
May: The SIB is not obliged to recognise a clearing house. See also in this regard the annotation to section 18(2).

Subs. (5)
As to the service of notices, see section 204.

Subs. (7)
This subsection empowers the SIB to revoke a recognition order.
Any obligation . . . this Act: Covers obligations imposed both by the Act as well as under it. An order may also be revoked by the Secretary of State where the anti-competitive

effects of an RCH's rules, guidance, clearing arrangements or practices, or the practices of its members, exceed those necessary for the protection of investors. (s.120(4)).

Subs. (8)

This subsection empowers the SIB to seek compliance orders in respect of RCHs.

Note also that where anti-competitive effects of an RCH's rules, guidance, clearing arrangements or practices, or the practices of its members, exceed those necessary for the protection of investors, the Secretary of State also has power exercisable through the SIB to alter its rules and to direct it to take remedial action. (s.120(4)).

Overseas investment exchanges and clearing houses

40.—(1) Any application under section 37(1) or 39(1) above by a body or association whose head office is situated in a country outside the United Kingdom shall contain the address of a place in the United Kingdom for the service on that body or association of notices or other documents required or authorised to be served on it under this Act.

(2) In relation to any such body or association sections 37(4) and 39(4) above shall have effect with the substitution for the requirements there mentioned of the following requirements, that is to say—

(*a*) that the body or association is, in the country in which its head office is situated, subject to supervision which, together with the rules and practices of that body or association, is such that investors in the United Kingdom are afforded protection in relation to that body or association at least equivalent to that provided by the provisions of this Act in relation to investment exchanges and clearing houses in respect of which recognition orders are made otherwise than by virtue of this subsection; and

(*b*) that the body or association is able and willing to co-operate, by the sharing of information and otherwise, with the authorities, bodies and persons responsible in the United Kingdom for the supervision and regulation of investment business or other financial services; and

(*c*) that adequate arrangements exist for such co-operation between those responsible for the supervision of the body or association in the country mentioned in paragraph (*a*) above and the authorities, bodies and persons mentioned in paragraph (*b*) above.

(3) In determining whether to make a recognition order by virtue of subsection (2) above the Secretary of State may have regard to the extent to which persons in the United Kingdom and persons in the country mentioned in that subsection have access to the financial markets in each others' countries.

(4) In relation to a body or association declared to be a recognised investment exchange or recognised clearing house by a recognition order made by virtue of subsection (2) above—

(*a*) the reference in section 36(2) above to the matters dealt with in Schedule 4 to this Act shall be construed as a reference to corresponding matters;

(*b*) sections 37(7) and (8) and 39(7) and (8) above shall have effect as if the requirements mentioned in section 37(7)(*a*) and in section 39(7)(*a*) were those of subsection (2)(*a*) and (*b*) above; and

(*c*) the grounds on which the order may be revoked under section 37(7) or 39(7) above shall include the ground that it appears to the Secretary of State that revocation is desirable in the interests of investors and potential investors in the United Kingdom.

(5) In this section "country" includes any territory or any part of a country or territory.

(6) A body or association declared to be a recognised investment exchange or recognised clearing house by a recognition order made by

virtue of subsection (2) above is in this Act referred to as an "overseas investment exchange" or an "overseas clearing house".

DEFINITIONS
"country": subs. (5).
"recognised clearing house": s.207(1).
"recognised investment exchange": s.207(1).
"recognition order": s.207(1).

GENERAL NOTE
This section makes separate provision regarding overseas investment exchanges and clearing houses. Note that the powers which it confers are reserved to the Secretary of State and cannot be transferred to the SIB (s.114(6)).

Subs. (2)
This subsection empowers the Secretary of State to recognise, and thus exempt, overseas investment exchanges and clearing houses. To this end it identifies the criteria which they must satisfy before a recognition order can be made. Note that they must also satisfy the requirements of Chapter XIV, as to which see the annotations to sections 37(4) and 39(4), and that the Secretary of State may also have regard to the extent to which access to financial markets is reciprocated (subs. (3)).

Para. (a)
Otherwise than by virtue . . . subsection: *i.e.* by virtue of sections 37(3) or 39(3).

Para. (c)
In the country: *i.e.* in the country in which the head office is situated.

Subs. (4)
Para. (a)
This paragraph adjusts the definition of an overseas investment exchange's rules. Their definition is relevant to the revocation of recognition.

Paras. (b), (c)
These paragraphs empower the Secretary of State to revoke an overseas investment exchange's or clearing house's recognition and to seek compliance orders in respect of them. Recognition may be revoked on the following grounds: (i) that the requirements of subsection 2(*a*) and (*b*) are not satisfied; (ii) that the exchange or clearing house has failed to comply with any obligation to which it is subject (ss.37(7)(*b*), 39(7)(*b*)); or (iii) that the anti-competitive effects of their rules, etc., are adjudged excessive (s.119(3)). As regards compliance orders, note that where the anti-competitive effects of an exchange or clearing house's rules etc. are adjudged excessive, the Secretary of State also has power to direct it to take remedial action, but not to alter its rules (s.119(3), (4)).

Notification requirements

41.—(1) The Secretary of State may make regulations requiring a recognised investment exchange or recognised clearing house to give him forthwith notice of the occurrence of such events relating to the exchange or clearing house as are specified in the regulations and such information in respect of those events as is so specified.

(2) The Secretary of State may make regulations requiring a recognised investment exchange or recognised clearing house to furnish him at such times or in respect of such periods as are specified in the regulations with such information relating to the exchange or clearing house as is so specified.

(3) The notices and information required to be given or furnished under the foregoing provisions of this section shall be such as the Secretary of State may reasonably require for the exercise of his functions under this Act.

(4) Regulations under the foregoing provisions of this section may require information to be given in a specified form and to be verified in a specified manner.

(5) Where a recognised investment exchange—
(*a*) amends, revokes or adds to its rules or guidance; or

(*b*) makes, terminates or varies any clearing arrangements,
it shall within seven days give written notice to the Secretary of State of the amendment, revocation or addition or, as the case may be, of the matters mentioned in paragraph (*b*) above.

(6) Where a recognised clearing house—
    (*a*) amends, revokes or adds to its rules or guidance; or
    (*b*) makes a change in the persons for whom it provides clearing services,
it shall within seven days give written notice to the Secretary of State of the amendment, revocation or addition or, as the case may be, of the change.

(7) Notice need not be given under subsection (5) or (6) above of the revocation of guidance other than such as is mentioned in section 37(2)(*b*) or 39(2)(*b*) above or of any amendment of or addition to guidance which does not result in or consist of such guidance as is there mentioned.

DEFINITIONS
    "clearing arrangements": s.38(2).
    "guidance": ss.36(5), 38(3).
    "recognised clearing house": s.207(1).
    "recognised investment exchange": s.207(1)
    "rules": ss.36(2), 38(2).

GENERAL NOTE
Subss. (1), (2)
    These subsections empower the SIB to make regulations (notification regulations) specifying the information with which it is to be supplied by RIEs and RCHs. As to the making of regulations by the SIB, see section 114(9) and Schedule 9, paras. 4–9.

Subss. (5), (6)
    These subsections require RIEs and RCHs to give the SIB notice of alterations in their rules, guidance and clearing arrangements. The SIB must in turn notify them to the Secretary of State (s.120(3)).

Subs. (7)
    Other than such mentioned: Guidance which is intended to have continuing effect and is issued in writing or other legible form.

Other exemptions
Lloyd's

42. The Society of Lloyd's and persons permitted by the Council of Lloyd's to act as underwriting agents at Lloyd's are exempted persons as respects investment business carried on in connection with or for the purpose of insurance business at Lloyd's.

DEFINITIONS
    "exempted person": s.207(1).
    "insurance business": s.207(7).
    "investment business": s.1(2).

GENERAL NOTE
    This section, one of the Act's most contentious provisions, exempts the Society of Lloyd's and its underwriting agents from the requirement of authorisation. Note that the exemption itself is restricted and that it may be further restricted or removed by an order made under section 46. The three main activities which it covers, which it was conceded would otherwise require authorisation, are: the collective management by managing agents of the affairs of Lloyd's syndicates; the provision of advice and assistance to members and potential members by members' agents; and the investment management of members' insurance funds by underwriting agents (H.C. Standing Committee E, col. 121).

Listed money market institutions

43.—(1) A person for the time being included in a list maintained by the Bank of England for the purposes of this section ("a listed institution") is an exempted person in respect of, and of anything done for the purposes of, any transaction to which Part I or Part II of Schedule 5 to this Act applies and in respect of any arrangements made by him with a view to other persons entering into a transaction to which Part III of that Schedule applies.

(2) The conditions imposed by the Bank of England for admission to the list referred to in this section and the arrangements made by it for a person's admission to and removal from the list shall require the approval of the Treasury; and this section shall cease to have effect if that approval is withdrawn but without prejudice to its again having effect if approval is given for fresh conditions or arrangements.

(3) The Bank of England shall publish the list as for the time being in force and provide a certified copy of it at the request of any person wishing to refer to it in legal proceedings.

(4) Such a certified copy shall be evidence or, in Scotland, sufficient evidence of the contents of the list; and a copy purporting to be certified by or on behalf of the Bank shall be deemed to have been duly certified unless the contrary is shown.

DEFINITION
    "exempted person": s.207(1).

GENERAL NOTE
    This section exempts listed institutions, as defined in subsection (1), from the requirement of authorisation in respect of transactions in money market instruments. It gives effect to a decision that the wholesale has been money, bullion and foreign currency markets should be regulated by the Bank of England. A consultative document on their regulation published: *The future regulation of the wholesale markets in sterling, foreign exchange and bullion* (Bank of England, December 1986). Note that the exemption which this section confers may be restricted or removed by an order made under section 46.

Appointed representatives

44.—(1) An appointed representative is an exempted person as respects investment business carried on by him as such a representative.

(2) For the purposes of this Act an appointed representative is a person—
    (a) who is employed by an authorised person (his "principal") under a contract for services which—
        (i) requires or permits him to carry on investment business to which this section applies; and
        (ii) complies with subsections (4) and (5) below; and
    (b) for whose activities in carrying on the whole or part of that investment business his principal has accepted responsibility in writing;
and the investment business carried on by an appointed representative as such is the investment business for which his principal has accepted responsibility.

(3) This section applies to investment business carried on by an appointed representative which consists of—
    (a) procuring or endeavouring to procure the persons with whom he deals to enter into investment agreements with his principal or (if not prohibited by his contract) with other persons;
    (b) giving advice to the persons with whom he deals about entering into investment agreements with his principal or (if not prohibited by his contract) with other persons; or

(*c*) giving advice as to the sale of investments issued by his principal or as to the exercise of rights conferred by an investment whether or not issued as aforesaid.

(4) If the contract between an appointed representative and his principal does not prohibit the representative from procuring or endeavouring to procure persons to enter into investment agreements with persons other than his principal it must make provision for enabling the principal either to impose such a prohibition or to restrict the kinds of investment to which those agreements may relate or the other persons with whom they may be entered into.

(5) If the contract between an appointed representative and his principal does not prohibit the representative from giving advice about entering into investment agreements with persons other than his principal it must make provision for enabling the principal either to impose such a prohibition or to restrict the kinds of advice which the representative may give by reference to the kinds of investment in relation to which or the persons with whom the representative may advise that investment agreements should be made.

(6) The principal of an appointed representative shall be responsible, to the same extent as if he had expressly authorised it, for anything said or done or omitted by the representative in carrying on the investment business for which he has accepted responsibility.

(7) In determining whether an authorised person has complied with—

(*a*) any provision contained in or made under this Act; or

(*b*) any rules of a recognised self-regulating organisation or recognised professional body,

anything which a person who at the material time is or was an appointed representative of the authorised person has said, done or omitted as respects investment business for which the authorised person has accepted responsibility shall be treated as having been said, done or omitted by the authorised person.

(8) Nothing in subsection (7) above shall cause the knowledge or intentions of an appointed representative to be attributed to his principal for the purpose of determining whether the principal has committed a criminal offence unless in all the circumstances it is reasonable for them to be attributed to him.

(9) In this Act "investment agreement" means any agreement the making or performance of which by either party constitutes an activity which falls within any paragraph of Part II of Schedule 1 to this Act or would do so apart from Parts III and IV of that Schedule.

DEFINITIONS

"appointed representative": subs. (2),
"authorised person": s.207(1).
"exempted person": s.207(1).
"investment agreement": subs. (9).
"investment business": s.1(2).
"rules": ss. 8(3), 16(3).

GENERAL NOTE

This section exempts appointed representatives, as defined in subsection (2), from the requirement of authorisation. In the insurance industry in particular it is common for company representatives to be self-employed rather than directly employed by a company. Without exemption these representatives would have to become employees of authorised persons or themselves authorised. In return for exemption their authorised principals are made responsible for their actions. The intention is therefore that appointed representatives should be treated as if they were employees of their authorised principal and not as independent businesses. (H.L. Vol. 480, cols. 991–992).

Subs. (1)
Note that the exemption is limited.

Subs. (2)
This subsection defines an appointed representative. Note that an appointed representative may have more than one principal, but that the Board will make rules restricting the kinds of principal an appointed representative may have, presumably under section 48(2)(*f*).

Para. (c)
Contract for services: Not contract of service which would make him an employee.
Investment business . . . applies: Defined in subsection (3).

Subss. (6), (7)
These subsections place principals in the same position in relation to their appointed representatives as they are in relation to their employees.

Subs. (8)
This subsection is designed to ensure that principals are only made criminally liable for the activities of their appointed representatives in circumstances broadly comparable to those in which a corporate employer would be made criminally liable for the criminal actions of their employees. (H.L. Vol. 479, col. 137).

Subs. (9)
Note that the definition of investment agreement is broader than the definition of carrying on investment business in the United Kingdom in section 1(3).

Miscellaneous exemptions

45.—(1) Each of the following persons is an exempted person to the extent specified in relation to that person—
   (*a*) the President of the Family Division of the High Court when acting in the exercise of his functions under section 9 of the Administration of Estates Act 1925;
   (*b*) the Probate Judge of the High Court of Northern Ireland when acting in the exercise of his functions under section 3 of the Administration of Estates Act (Northern Ireland) 1955;
   (*c*) the Accountant General of the Supreme Court when acting in the exercise of his functions under Part VI of the Administration of Justice Act 1982;
   (*d*) the Accountant of Court when acting in the exercise of his functions in connection with the consignment or deposit of sums of money;
   (*e*) the Public Trustee when acting in the exercise of his functions under the Public Trustee Act 1906;
   (*f*) the Master of the Court of Protection when acting in the exercise of his functions under Part VII of the Mental Health Act 1983;
   (*g*) the Official Solicitor to the Supreme Court when acting as judicial trustee under the Judicial Trustees Act 1896;
   (*h*) a registrar of a county court when managing funds paid into court;
   (*i*) a sheriff clerk when acting in the exercise of his functions in connection with the consignation or deposit of sums of money;
   (*j*) a person acting in his capacity as manager of a fund established under section 22 of the Charities Act 1960, section 25 of the Charities Act (Northern Ireland) 1964, section 11 of the Trustee Investments Act 1961 or section 42 of the Administration of Justice Act 1982;
   (*k*) the Central Board of Finance of the Church of England or a Diocesan Authority within the meaning of the Church Funds Investment Measure 1958 when acting in the exercise of its functions under that Measure;
   (*l*) a person acting in his capacity as an official receiver within the meaning of section 399 of the Insolvency Act 1986 or in that capacity within the meaning of any corresponding provision in force in Northern Ireland.

(2) Where a bankruptcy order is made in respect of an authorised person or of a person whose authorisation is suspended under section 28 above or who is the subject of a direction under section 33(1)(*b*) above or a winding-up order is made in respect of a partnership which is such a person, the trustee in bankruptcy or liquidator acting in his capacity as such is an exempted person but—

(*a*) sections 48 to 71 below and, so far as relevant to any of those provisions, Chapter IX of this Part of this Act; and

(*b*) sections 104, 105 and 106 below,

shall apply to him to the same extent as they applied to the bankrupt or partnership and, if the bankrupt or partnership was subject to the rules of a recognised self-regulating organisation or recognised professional body, he shall himself also be subject to those rules.

(3) In the application of subsection (2) above to Scotland—

(*a*) for the reference to a bankruptcy order being made in respect of a person there shall be substituted a reference to the estate of that person being sequestrated;

(*b*) the reference to a winding-up order in respect of a partnership is a reference to such an order made under section 72 below;

(*c*) for the reference to the trustee in bankruptcy there shall be substituted a reference to the interim trustee or permanent trustee within the meaning of the Bankruptcy (Scotland) Act 1985; and

(*d*) for the references to the bankrupt there shall be substituted references to the debtor.

(4) In the application of subsection (2) above to Northern Ireland for the reference to a bankruptcy order there shall be substituted a reference to an order of adjudication of bankruptcy and the reference to a trustee in bankruptcy shall include a reference to an assignee in bankruptcy.

DEFINITIONS
"authorised person": s.207(1).
"exempted person": s.207(1).
"partnership": s.207(1).

GENERAL NOTE
This section exempts the persons listed from the requirement of authorisation. Note that the exemptions are restricted and that they may be further restricted or removed by an order made under section 46.

Subs. (2)
This subsection, as amended in its application to Scotland and Northern Ireland by subsections (3) and (4), exempts trustees in bankruptcy of sole traders and liquidators of partnerships from the requirement of authorisation. Note that they are subject to the provisions mentioned as well as to the rules of any SRO or RPB to which the sole trader or partnership was subject.

Supplemental

Power to extend or restrict exemptions

46.—(1) The Secretary of State may by order provide—

(*a*) for exemptions additional to those specified in the foregoing provisions of this Chapter; or

(*b*) for removing or restricting any exemption conferred by section 42, 43 or 45 above;

and any such order may contain such transitional provisions as the Secretary of State thinks necessary or expedient.

(2) An order making such provision as is mentioned in paragraph (*a*) of subsection (1) above shall be subject to annulment in pursuance of a resolution of either House of Parliament; and no order making such

provision as is mentioned in paragraph (*b*) of that subsection shall be made unless a draft of it has been laid before and approved by a resolution of each House of Parliament.

GENERAL NOTE

This section confers a power on the Secretary of State, exercisable by statutory instrument (s.205(2)), to create additional exemptions, or to remove or restrict the exemptions conferred by sections 42 (Lloyd's), 43 (listed money market institutions) or 45 (miscellaneous).

CHAPTER V

CONDUCT OF INVESTMENT BUSINESS

Misleading statements and practices

47.—(1) Any person who—
(*a*) makes a statement, promise or forecast which he knows to be misleading, false or deceptive or dishonestly conceals any material facts; or
(*b*) recklessly makes (dishonestly or otherwise) a statement, promise or forecast which is misleading, false or deceptive,
is guilty of an offence if he makes the statement, promise or forecast or conceals the facts for the purpose of inducing, or is reckless as to whether it may induce, another person (whether or not the person to whom the statement, promise or forecast is made or from whom the facts are concealed) to enter or offer to enter into, or to refrain from entering or offering to enter into, an investment agreement or to exercise, or refrain from exercising, any rights conferred by an investment.

(2) Any person who does any act or engages in any course of conduct which creates a false or misleading impression as to the market in or the price or value of any investments is guilty of an offence if he does so for the purpose of creating that impression and of thereby inducing another person to acquire, dispose of, subscribe for or underwrite those investments or to refrain from doing so or to exercise, or refrain from exercising, any rights conferred by those investments.

(3) In proceedings brought against any person for an offence under subsection (2) above it shall be a defence for him to prove that he reasonably believed that his act or conduct would not create an impression that was false or misleading as to the matters mentioned in that subsection.

(4) Subsection (1) above does not apply unless—
(*a*) the statement, promise or forecast is made in or from, or the facts are concealed in or from, the United Kingdom;
(*b*) the person on whom the inducement is intended to or may have effect is in the United Kingdom; or
(*c*) the agreement is or would be entered into or the rights are or would be exercised in the United Kingdom.

(5) Subsection (2) above does not apply unless—
(*a*) the act is done or the course of conduct is engaged in in the United Kingdom; or
(*b*) the false or misleading impression is created there.

(6) A person guilty of an offence under this section shall be liable—
(*a*) on conviction on indictment, to imprisonment for a term not exceeding seven years or to a fine or to both;
(*b*) on summary conviction, to imprisonment for a term not exceeding six months or to a fine not exceeding the statutory maximum or to both.

DEFINITIONS

"investment": s.1(1).

"investment agreement": s.44(9).

GENERAL NOTE

This section replaces s.13 of the PFI Act 1958 and also introduces the offence of market manipulation.

Subs. (1)

Cognate provisions are to be found in the Banking Act 1979, s.39 and in s.133 of this Act. Note the qualification of this subsection by s.48(6).

Dishonestly: The meaning of "dishonesty" has been discussed in *Feely* [1973] Q.B. 530 and *Ghosh* [1982] Q.B. 1053.

Conceals any material facts: A prosecution of dishonest concealment might be considered in relation to insider dealings falling beyond the scope of the Company Securities (Insider Dealing) Act 1985, since any insider dealer who failed to disclose to his counterparty that he was in possession of unpublished price-sensitive information might be regarded as having dishonestly concealed a material fact.

Recklessly/reckless: Decisions on the meaning of "recklessness"in the context of earlier versions of this subsection (*Bates* [1952] 2 All E.R. 842, affirmed *sub. nom. Russell* [1953] 1 W.L.R. 77; *Grunwald* [1961] 2 W.L.R. 606) must now be read in the light of the House of Lords decisions in *Caldwell* [1982] A.C. 341 and *Lawrence* [1982] A.C. 510.

Dishonestly or otherwise: These words were introduced into s.13 of the PFI Act by s.21(*a*) of the Protection of Depositors Act 1963 to effect a statutory reversal of the decision in *Mackinnon* [1959] 1 Q.B. 150 in which it was held that recklessness entailed a fraudulent (*i.e.* dishonest) state of mind.

Subs. (2)

This subsection makes it a criminal offence to engage in market manipulation (*e.g.* by entering into spurious transactions at inflated prices). The prosecution must show that the accused did something which created a false or misleading impression as to the market in or the price or value of any investments, and that the accused created the impression in question on purpose. But the prosecution need not show that the accused intended the impression to be false or misleading. However by virtue of subs. (3) it is a defence for the accused to prove that he reasonably believed that what he did would not create a false or misleading impression.

Subs. (2) is qualified by s.48(6) and (7) which, *inter alia*, deal with the circumstances in which price stabilisation activities cannot be regarded as market manipulation.

Subss. (4), (5)

These subsections build on the decision of the House of Lords in *Secretary of State* v. *Markus* [1976] A.C. 35. Someone engaging in a "boilerhouse" operation from (say) Amsterdam falls within the scope of subs. (2) if a false or misleading impression is created in the U.K. and the other elements of the offence are present.

Conduct of business rules

48.—(1) The Secretary of State may make rules regulating the conduct of investment business by authorised persons but those rules shall not apply to members of a recognised self-regulating organisation or persons certified by a recognised professional body in respect of investment business in the carrying on of which they are subject to the rules of the organisation or body.

(2) Rules under this section may in particular make provision—

(*a*) prohibiting a person from carrying on, or holding himself out as carrying on—

(i) investment business of any kind specified in the rules; or

(ii) investment business of a kind or on a scale other than that notified by him to the Secretary of State in connection with an application for authorisation under Chapter III of this Part of this Act, in a notice under section 32 above or in accordance with any provision of the rules or regulations in that behalf;

(*b*) prohibiting a person from carrying on investment business in relation to persons other than those of a specified class or description;

(c) regulating the manner in which a person may hold himself out as carrying on investment business;

(d) regulating the manner in which a person makes a market in any investments;

(e) as to the form and content of advertisements in respect of investment business;

(f) requiring the principals of appointed representatives to impose restrictions on the investment business carried on by them;

(g) requiring the disclosure of the amount or value, or of arrangements for the payment or provision, of commissions or other inducements in connection with investment business and restricting the matters by reference to which or the manner in which their amount or value may be determined;

(h) enabling or requiring information obtained by an authorised person in the course of carrying on one part of his business to be withheld by him from persons with whom he deals in the course of carrying on another part and for that purpose enabling or requiring persons employed in one part of that business to withhold information from those employed in another part;

(i) as to the circumstances and manner in which and the time when or the period during which action may be taken for the purpose of stabilising the price of investments of any specified description;

(j) for arrangements for the settlement of disputes;

(k) requiring the keeping of accounts and other records, as to their form and content and for their inspection;

(l) requiring a person to whom the rules apply to make provision for the protection of investors in the event of the cessation of his investment business in consequence of his death, incapacity or otherwise.

(3) Subsection (2) above is without prejudice to the generality of subsection (1) above and accordingly rules under this section may make provision for matters other than those mentioned in subsection (2) or further provision as to any of the matters there mentioned except that they shall not impose limits on the amount or value of commissions or other inducements paid or provided in connection with investment business.

(4) Rules under this section may also regulate or prohibit the carrying on in connection with investment business of any other business or the carrying on of any other business which is held out as being for the purposes of investment.

(5) In paragraph (e) of subsection (2) above "advertisement" does not include any advertisement which is subject to section 154 below or which is required or permitted to be published by listing rules under Part IV of this Act and relates to securities which have been admitted to listing under that Part; and rules under that paragraph shall have effect subject to the provisions of Part V of this Act.

(6) Nothing done in conformity with rules made under paragraph (h) of subsection (2) above shall be regarded as a contravention of section 47 above.

(7) Section 47(2) above shall not be regarded as contravened by anything done for the purpose of stabilising the price of investments if it is done in conformity with rules made under this section and—

(a) in respect of investments which fall within any of paragraphs 1 to 5 of Schedule 1 to this Act and are specified by the rules; and

(b) during such period before or after the issue of those investments as is specified by the rules.

(8) The Secretary of State may by order amend subsection (7) above—

(a) by restricting or extending the kinds of investment to which it applies;

(b) by restricting it so as to apply only in relation to the issue of investments in specified circumstances or by extending it, in respect of investments of any kind specified in the order, so as to apply to things done during a specified period before or after events other than the issue of those investments.

(9) No order shall be made under subsection (8) above unless a draft of it has been laid before and approved by a resolution of each House of Parliament.

(10) Rules under this section may contain such incidental and transitional provisions as the Secretary of State thinks necessary or expedient.

DEFINITIONS
"advertisement": s.207(2), (3).
"appointed representative": s.44(2).
"authorised person": s.207(1).
"carrying on investment business": s.1(3).
"certified": s.207(1).
"investment": s.1(1).
"investment business": s.1(2).
"listing": s.142(7).
"listing rules": s.142(6).
"member": s.207(1).
"recognised professional body": s.207(1).
"securities": s.142(7).

GENERAL NOTE
This section empowers the SIB to make Conduct of Business Rules. These rules must satisfy the requirements set out in Schedule 8.

As to the consequences of contravening these rules, see ss.28, 60–62, and Chap. VI. As to the manner of making these rules, see Sched. 9, paras. 4–9.

Subs. (1)
The Conduct of Business Rules made under this section will apply to persons directly authorised under ss. 25–30 and to persons authorised in other member States (ss. 31–34).

They will not apply to members of an SRO or persons certified by an RPB in respect of investment business regulated by the organisation or body in question. They will, however, apply to SRO members and persons authorised by virtue of certification by an RPB in respect of investment business in the carrying on of which they are *not* subject to the rules of the organisation or body. In this case the Conduct of Business Rules will apply whether or not the person in question has actually obtained direct authorisation.

Nor will the Conduct of Business Rules apply:
to the operator or trustee of a collective investment scheme recognised under s.86 (*i.e.* a UCITS), except so far as the rules make provision in respect of marketing such schemes and giving advice on them (s.86(7));
to regulated insurance companies, except so far as the rules make provision in respect of their marketing, advisory and pension fund management activities (Sched. 10, para. 4(1), (2));
to regulated friendly societies, subject to the proviso that the Chief Registrar of Friendly Societies (or the transferee body, *i.e.* the SIB) may make rules (parallel to those which may be made in respect of regulated insurance companies) applicable to societies which are not members of an appropriate SRO (Sched. 11, para. 14(1), (2)).

Subs. (2)
The purpose of this subsection is to make it clear that the Conduct of Business Rules may properly make provision in respect of the matters enumerated which, it was feared, might conceivably otherwise have been regarded as falling beyond the scope of the rule-making power conferred by subs. (1). This subsection is without prejudice to the generality of subs. (1): subs. (3).

Para. (a)(ii): This enables the SIB to restrict the kind or scale of investment business that a directly authorised person may do to what is set out in its "business plan."

Para. (e): "Advertisements" in this context does not include advertisements published in connection with the admission of securities to listing (under Part IV of the Act); and rules made under this paragraph cannot derogate from the provisions of Part V (prospectuses in connection with unlisted securities): subs. (5).

Para. (h): This paragraph contemplates the making of rules recognising Chinese walls, *e.g.* as an alternative to the disclosure of conflicts of interest.

Para. (i): This paragraph contemplates the making of rules regulating price stabilisation practices. The rules made under this paragraph must make proper provision for price stabilisation actions to be accompanied by adequate disclosure of their possible effect on the price of the investments concerned: see Sched. 8, para. 8.

As to the circumstances under which conformity with the rules regulating price stabilisation puts one beyond the scope of the market manipulation offence defined in s.47(2), see subs. (7).

Subs. (3)

Shall not impose limits on the amount or value of commissions: There is no power to control the level of commissions "since this would amount to statutory price control and be incompatible with the Government's policy: *Financial Services in the United Kingdom*, para. 10.1.

Subs. (4)

The Conduct of Business Rules may also regulate business other than investment business either if it is carried on in connection with investment business or if it is held out as being for the purposes of investment.

For the purposes of investment: By implication, investment in this particular context is to be distinguished from the specific "investments" enumerated in Sched. 1, Part I. For example, real property or collectibles may be acquired "for the purposes of investment."

Subs. (6)

The effect of this subsection is that things done in conformity with rules made under subs. (2)(*h*) (allowing for the construction of Chinese walls) cannot be regarded as the dishonest concealment of material facts or as market manipulation.

In conformity with rules made: see subs. (7).

Subs. (7)

Things done for price stabilisation purposes cannot be regarded as market manipulation if three conditions are satisfied. First, they must be done in conformity with "rules made under this section." (This, in contrast to the preceding subsection, appears to require conformity with all of the Conduct of Business Rules, not just those made under subs. (2)(*i*).) Secondly, they must relate to specified investments. (At the moment only investments falling within paras. 1 to 5 of Sched. 1—*i.e.* broadly speaking, securities—can be specified by the rules.) Thirdly, they must be done during the specified period before or after the *issue* of the investments. (At the moment this subsection does not extend to stabilisation in circumstances unconnected with new issues.) As to the possible amendment of this subsection, see subs. (8).

This subsection merely specifies circumstances in which price stabilisation cannot amount to the offence of market manipulation. It by no means follows that price stabilisation practices falling beyond this subsection necessarily do amount to the offence of market manipulation.

In conformity with rules made: The rules made under this section do not apply, for example, to persons authorised by virtue of membership of an SRO. Nevertheless, such persons may avail themselves of the "defence" afforded by this subsection provided they have acted in accordance with those rules.

Subs. (8)

This subsection empowers the Secretary of State to restrict or extend the kinds of investment to which the preceding subsection applies, and to restrict it to specified issues or to extend it beyond issues (*i.e.* to certain offers of existing investments). This is a non-transferable function of the Secretary of State. s.114(5)(*c*).

As to the manner of its exercise, see s.205(2) and subs. (9) of this section.

Financial resources rules

49.—(1) The Secretary of State may make rules requiring persons authorised to carry on investment business by virtue of section 25 or 31 above to have and maintain in respect of that business such financial resources as are required by the rules.

(2) Without prejudice to the generality of subsection (1) above, rules under this section may—

   (*a*) impose requirements which are absolute or which are to vary from time to time by reference to such factors as are specified in or determined in accordance with the rules;

   (*b*) impose requirements which take account of any business (whether or not investment business) carried on by the person concerned in conjunction with or in addition to the business mentioned in subsection (1) above;

   (*c*) make provision as to the assets, liabilities and other matters to be taken into account in determining a person's financial resources for the purposes of the rules and the extent to which and the manner in which they are to be taken into account for that purpose.

DEFINITIONS
"carry on investment business": s.1(3).
"investment business": s.1(2).

GENERAL NOTE
This section empowers the SIB to make financial resources or capital adequacy rules. Under the legislation as originally conceived capital adequacy requirements were to have been imposed under the Conduct of Business Rules or by means of the "fit and proper" test. The present section was introduced to put the SIB's power to impose capital adequacy requirements beyond doubt.

The rules made under this section will apply to directly authorised persons and to persons authorised in other Member States.

As to the manner of making these rules, see Sched. 9, paras. 4–9.

As to the consequences of contravening them, see ss.28, 60, 61, 62(3), (4), and Chap. VI.

Modification of conduct of business and financial resources rules for particular cases

50.—(1) The Secretary of State may, on the application of any person to whom any rules made under section 48 or 49 above apply, alter the requirements of the rules so as to adapt them to the circumstances of that person or to any particular kind of business carried on or to be carried on by him.

(2) The Secretary of State shall not exercise the powers conferred by subsection (1) above in any case unless it appears to him that—

   (*a*) compliance with the requirements in question would be unduly burdensome for the applicant having regard to the benefit which compliance would confer on investors; and

   (*b*) the exercise of those powers will not result in any undue risk to investors.

(3) The powers conferred by subsection (1) above may be exercised unconditionally or subject to conditions.

GENERAL NOTE
This section enables the SIB to tailor the Conduct of Business Rules and the Financial Resources Rules to fit the particular circumstances or activities of individual authorised persons. This power is not to be exercised unless its exercise is warranted by a cost-benefit analysis (subs. (2)(*a*)) and will not occasion any undue risk to investors (subs. (2)(*b*)).

Cancellation rules

51.—(1) The Secretary of State may make rules for enabling a person who has entered or offered to enter into an investment agreement with an authorised person to rescind the agreement or withdraw the offer within such period and in such manner as may be prescribed.

(2) Without prejudice to the generality of subsection (1) above, rules under this section may make provision—

(a) for requiring the service of notices with respect to the rights exercisable under the rules;

(b) for the restitution of property and the making or recovery of payments where those rights are exercised; and

(c) for such other incidental matters as the Secretary of State thinks necessary or expedient.

DEFINITIONS
"authorised person": s.207(1).
"investment agreement": s.44(9).

GENERAL NOTE
This section empowers the SIB to prescribe a cooling-off period in respect of investment agreements, during which the investor may resile from the transaction. Broadly speaking, the investments in respect of which a cooling-off period will be prescribed will be those in respect of which cold-calling will be permitted by the Unsolicited Calls Regulations to be made under s.56 (*i.e.* in the main, life assurance and unit trust products).

Persons authorised by virtue of SRO membership or certification by an RPB are not excluded from the application of the Cancellation Rules.

As to the manner of making the rules, see Sched. 9, paras. 4–9.

As to the consequences of contravening them, see ss.28, 60–62, and Chap. VI.

Notification regulations

52.—(1) The Secretary of State may make regulations requiring authorised persons to give him forthwith notice of the occurrence of such events as are specified in the regulations and such information in respect of those events as is so specified.

(2) The Secretary of State may make regulations requiring authorised persons to furnish him at such times or in respect of such periods as are specified in the regulations with such information as is so specified.

(3) Regulations under this section shall not apply to a member of a recognised self-regulating organisation or a person certified by a recognised professional body unless he carries on investment business in the carrying on of which he is subject to any of the rules made under section 48 above.

(4) Without prejudice to the generality of subsections (1) and (2) above, regulations under this section may relate to—

(a) the nature of the investment business being carried on;

(b) the nature of any other business carried on with or for the purposes of the investment business;

(c) any proposal of an authorised person to alter the nature or extent of any business carried on by him;

(d) any person becoming or ceasing to be a person of the kind to whom regard could be had by the Secretary of State under subsection (3) of section 27 above in deciding an application for authorisation under that section;

(e) the financial position of an authorised person as respects his investment business or any other business carried on by him;

(f) any property managed, and any property or money held, by an authorised person on behalf of other persons.

(5) Regulations under this section may require information to be given in a specified form and to be verified in a specified manner.

(6) Any notice or information required to be given or furnished under this section shall be given in writing or in such other manner as the Secretary of State may approve.

"authorised person": s.207(1).
"certified": s.207(1).
"investment business": s.1(2).
"member": s.207(1).
"recognised professional body": s.207(1).
"recognised self-regulating organisation": s.207(1).

GENERAL NOTE
This section empowers the SIB to make Notification Regulations requiring authorised persons to give notice of the occurrence of specified events and to furnish the SIB with specified information.
As to the manner of making the regulations, see Sched. 9, paras. 4–9.
As to the consequences of contravening them, see ss.28, 60–62, and Chap. VI.

Subs. (3)
The regulations will not apply to persons authorised by virtue of SRO membership or certification by an RPB unless they are carrying on a kind of investment business with which the organisation or body is not concerned.

Indemnity rules

53.—(1) The Secretary of State may make rules concerning indemnity against any claim in respect of any description of civil liability incurred by an authorised person in connection with his investment business.

(2) Rules under this section shall not apply to a member of a recognised self-regulating organisation or a person certified by a recognised professional body in respect of investment business in the carrying on of which he is subject to the rules of the organisation or body unless that organisation or body has requested that rules under this section should apply to him; and any such request shall not be capable of being withdrawn after rules giving effect to it have been made but without prejudice to the power of the Secretary of State to revoke the rules if he thinks fit.

(3) For the purpose of providing indemnity the rules—
(a) may authorise the Secretary of State to establish and maintain a fund or funds;
(b) may authorise the Secretary of State to take out and maintain insurance with insurers authorised to carry on insurance business under the law of the United Kingdom or any other member State;
(c) may require any person to whom the rules apply to take out and maintain insurance with any such insurer.

(4) Without prejudice to the generality of the foregoing provisions, the rules may—
(a) specify the terms and conditions on which, and the extent to which, indemnity is to be available and any circumstances in which the right to it is to be excluded or modified;
(b) provide for the management, administration and protection of any fund maintained by virtue of subsection (3)(a) above and require persons to whom the rules apply to make payments to any such fund;
(c) require persons to whom the rules apply to make payments by way of premium on any insurance policy maintained by the Secretary of State by virtue of subsection 3(b) above;
(d) prescribe the conditions which an insurance policy must satisfy for the purposes of subsection (3)(c) above;
(e) authorise the Secretary of State to determine the amount which the rules require to be paid to him or an insurer, subject to such limits or in accordance with such provisions as may be prescribed by the rules;
(f) specify circumstances in which, where sums are paid by the Secre-

tary of State or an insurer in satisfaction of claims against a person subject to the rules, proceedings may be taken against that person by the Secretary of State or the insurer;

(*g*) specify circumstances in which persons are exempt from the rules;

(*h*) empower the Secretary of State to take such steps as he considers necessary or expedient to ascertain whether or not the rules are being complied with; and

(*i*) contain incidental or supplementary provisions.

DEFINITIONS

"authorised person": s.207(1).
"carrying on investment business": s.1(3).
"certified": s.207(1).
"investment business": s.1(2).
"member": s.207(1).
"recognised professional body": s.207(1).
"recognised self-regulating organisation": s.207(1).
"rules": s.207(1).

GENERAL NOTE

This section empowers the SIB to make Indemnity Rules for the purpose of providing indemnity against claims by investors in respect of any kind of civil liability incurred by an authorised person in connection with his investment business. Rules covering claims based on negligence as well as default are thus contemplated: subs. (1). The rules might provide indemnity by means of a fund based on levies, or a master policy based on compulsory premiums, or compulsory individual insurance: subs. (3).

The effect of subs. (2) is that the Indemnity Rules would not apply to SROs or RPBs unless the organisation or body in question opted in favour of participation. (Having done so, it could not withdraw at will.) The "voluntary" character of the indemnity scheme gave rise to doubts as to whether a scheme based largely on the participation of directly authorised persons would be sufficiently broadly based to offer adequate cover and, in view of these doubts, s.54 (providing for a compulsory compensation fund) was introduced: H.L. Vol. 480, cols. 784–95 (October 14, 1986). This section has, nevertheless, been retained on the footing that "there may still be scope for compulsory insurance arrangements to play a part in this area": H.C. Vol. 103, col. 554 (October 30, 1986)—presumably in relation to directly authorised persons.

Rules under this section must make "the best provision that can reasonably be made" under this section: Sched. 8, para. 10.

As to the manner of making any rules under this section, see Sched. 9, paras. 4–9.

As to the consequences of contravening any rules made under this section, see ss.28, 60–62 and Chap. VI.

Compensation fund

54.—(1) The Secretary of State may by rules establish a scheme for compensating investors in cases where persons who are or have been authorised persons are unable, or likely to be unable, to satisfy claims in respect of any description of civil liability incurred by them in connection with their investment businesses.

(2) Without prejudice to the generality of subsection (1) above, rules under this section may—

(*a*) provide for the administration of the scheme and, subject to the rules, the determination and regulation of any matter relating to its operation by a body appearing to the Secretary of State to be representative of, or of any class of, authorised persons;

(*b*) establish a fund out of which compensation is to be paid;

(*c*) provide for the levying of contributions from, or from any class of, authorised persons and otherwise for financing the scheme and for the payment of contributions and other money into the fund;

(*d*) specify the terms and conditions on which, and the extent to which, compensation is to be payable and any circumstances in which the right to compensation is to be excluded or modified;

(*e*) provide for treating compensation payable under the scheme in respect of a claim against any person as extinguishing or reducing the liability of that person in respect of the claim and for conferring on the body administering the scheme a right of recovery against that person, being, in the event of his insolvency, a right not exceeding such right, if any, as the claimant would have had in that event; and

(*f*) contain incidental and supplementary provisions.

(3) A scheme under this section shall not be made so as to apply to persons who are members of a recognised self-regulating organisation except after consultation with that organisation or, except at the request of a recognised professional body, to persons who are certified by it and subject to its rules in carrying on all the investment business carried on by them; and no scheme applying to such persons shall be made unless the Secretary of State is satisfied that the rules establishing it make sufficient provision—

(*a*) for the administration of the scheme by a body on which the interests of those persons are adequately represented; and

(*b*) for securing that the amounts which they are liable to contribute reflect, so far as practicable, the amount of the claims made or likely to be made in respect of those persons.

(4) Where a scheme applies to such persons as are mentioned in subsection (3) above the rules under this section may—

(*a*) constitute the recognised self-regulating organisation or recognised professional body in question as the body administering the scheme in relation to those persons;

(*b*) provide for the levying of contributions from that organisation or body instead of from those persons; and

(*c*) establish a separate fund for the contributions and compensation payable in respect of those persons, with or without provision for payments and repayments in specified circumstances between that and any other fund established by the scheme.

(5) A request by a recognised professional body under subsection (3) above shall not be capable of being withdrawn after rules giving effect to it have been made but without prejudice to the power of the Secretary of State to revoke the rules if he thinks fit.

(6) Rules may be made—

(*a*) for England and Wales, under sections 411 and 412 of the Insolvency Act 1986;

(*b*) for Scotland—

(i) under the said section 411; and

(ii) in relation to the application of this section where the persons who are or have been authorised persons are persons whose estates may be sequestrated under the Bankruptcy (Scotland) Act 1985, by the Secretary of State under this section; and

(*c*) for Northern Ireland, under Article 613 of the Companies (Northern Ireland) Order 1986 and section 65 of the Judicature (Northern Ireland) Act 1978,

for the purpose of integrating any procedure for which provision is made by virtue of subsection (2)(*e*) above into the general procedure on a winding-up, bankruptcy or sequestration.

DEFINITIONS
"authorised person": s.207(1).
"carrying on investment business": s.1(3).
"certified": s.207(1).

"investment business": s.1(2).
"member": s.207(1).
"recognised professional body": s.207(1).
"recognised self-regulating organisation": s.207(1).
"rules": s.207(1).

GENERAL NOTE
This section empowers the SIB to set up a funded central compensation scheme.
As to the manner of making rules under this section, see Sched. 9, paras. 4–9.
As to the consequences of contravening them, see ss.28, 60–62, and Chap. VI.

Subs. (1)
The scheme is to be for the compensation of investors in cases where authorised persons
arc unable, or likely to be unable, to satisfy claims in respect of any description of civil
liability in connection with their investment businesses. Compensation for fraud, negligence
and failure to comply with the rules as well as for default is thus contemplated. The
compensation scheme is to extend to claims against persons whose authorisation has been
revoked.

Subs. (2)
This subsection enumerates various matters which may be covered in the scheme rules.
The rules may provide for the establishment of a body to administer the scheme and of a
compensation fund based on levies of authorised persons. They may also specify the
circumstances under which compensation is to be payable. Under para. (*e*) provision may be
made for subrogation, and in this connection insolvency rules may be made under the
insolvency legislation to integrate the subrogation procedure into the general insolvency
procedures: subs. (6).

Subs. (3)
SRO members can be compulsorily incorporated in the compensation scheme after
consultation with the SRO in question. Certified RPB members *all* of whose investment
business is regulated by the RPB cannot be incorporated, save at the request of the RPB in
question. (But if an RPB does ask to join in, it cannot unilaterally withdraw once the rules
giving effect to its request have been made: subs. (5).) Neither SRO nor RPB members are
to be incorporated unless the rules make sufficient provision for the representation of the
interests of those affected on the body administering the scheme (para. (*a*)) and for securing
that their contributions broadly reflect the risk that they present (para. (*b*)). (This latter
provision is designed to reduce the scope for cross-subsidisation of one SRO by another—a
concern expressed by The Stock Exchange.)

Subs. (4)
This subsection makes it possible for the scheme to have a "federal" structure. Where the
scheme applies to SRO (or RPB) members the SRO (or RPB) can be constituted as the
body administering the scheme in relation to its own members: para. (*a*). A block
contribution may be levied from the SRO (or RPB) in lieu of individual contributions from
its members: para. (*b*). And a separate fund may be established for the contributions and
compensation payable in respect of those members (with or without provision for cross-
subsidisation): para. (*c*).

Clients' money

55.—(1) The Secretary of State may make regulations with respect to
money (in this section referred to as "clients' money") which authorised
persons, or authorised persons of any description, hold in such circumstances as are specified in the regulations.

(2) Without prejudice to the generality of subsection (1) above, regulations under this section may—

(*a*) provide that clients' money held by an authorised person is held on
trust;

(*b*) require clients' money to be paid into an account the title of which
contains the word "client" and which is with an institution of a
kind specified in the regulations or, in the case of a member of

a recognised self-regulating organisation or a person certified by a recognised professional body, by the rules of that organisation or body;

(*c*) make provision with respect to the opening and keeping of clients' accounts, including provision as to the circumstances in which money other than clients' money may be paid into such accounts and the circumstances in which and the persons to whom money held in such accounts may be paid out;

(*d*) require the keeping of accounts and records in respect of clients' money;

(*e*) require any such accounts to be examined by an accountant having such qualifications as are specified in the regulations and require the accountant to report to the Secretary of State, or in the case of a member of a recognised self-regulating organisation or a person certified by a recognised professional body, to that organisation or body, whether in his opinion the provisions of the regulations have been complied with and on such other matters as may be specified in the regulations;

(*f*) authorise the retention, to such extent and in such cases as may be specified in regulations, of so much of clients' money as represents interest.

(3) Where an authorised person is required to have an auditor, whether by virtue of any provision contained in or made under any enactment (including this Act) or of the rules of any such organisation or body as is mentioned in paragraph (*b*) of subsection (2) above, the regulations may require the examination and report referred to in paragraph (*e*) of that subsection to be carried out and made by that auditor.

(4) An institution with which an account is kept in pursuance of regulations made under this section does not incur any liability as constructive trustee where money is wrongfully paid from the account unless the institution permits the payment with knowledge that it is wrongful or having deliberately failed to make enquiries in circumstances in which a reasonable and honest person would have done so.

(5) In the application of this section to Scotland for the reference to money being held on trust there shall be substituted a reference to its being held as agent for the person who is entitled to call for it to be paid over to him or to be paid on his direction or to have it otherwise credited to him.

DEFINITIONS
"authorised persons": s.207(1).
"certified": s.207(1).
"member": s.207(1).
"recognised professional body": s.207(1).
"recognised self-regulating organisation": s.207(1).
"rules": s.207(1).

GENERAL NOTE
This section empowers the SIB to make Clients' Money Regulations. The aim is to safeguard clients' money held by authorised persons by ensuring that it is held on trust, so that upon the insolvency of the authorised person the client does not fall to be treated as an ordinary creditor and the client's money cannot be used to meet the claims of the creditors.

As to the manner of making the regulations, see Sched. 9, paras. 4–9.

As to the consequences of contravening them, see ss.28, 60–62, and Chap. VI.

Subs. (2)
Para. (a): held on trust: For the Scottish equivalent, see subs. (5). For a discussion of special characteristics of Scots law in this connection, see SIB, Draft Clients' Money Regulations (May 1986), Explanatory Memorandum, paras. 8–13.

Para. (b): This paragraph envisages that SROs and RPBs may be allowed to specify for their own members the kinds of institution with which clients' accounts may be opened.

Para. (c): The regulations may regulate the payment of money out of clients' accounts. Where money is wrongfully paid out of such an account, the institution with which it is kept does not incur any liability as constructive trustee unless it knew the payment to be wrongful or deliberately failed to make enquiries when a reasonable and honest person would have done so: subs. (4).

Para. (e): The regulations may require clients' accounts to be examined by an accountant. Where an authorised person is required to have an auditor, the regulations may require the examination to be carried out by that auditor: subs. (3).

Para. (f): The implication is that interest is indeed clients' money although its retention may be authorised in specified circumstances.

Unsolicited calls

56.—(1) Except so far as permitted by regulations made by the Secretary of State, no person shall in the course of or in consequence of an unsolicited call—

(a) made on a person in the United Kingdom; or

(b) made from the United Kingdom on a person elsewhere,

by way of business enter into an investment agreement with the person on whom the call is made or procure or endeavour to procure that person to enter into such an agreement.

(2) A person shall not be guilty of an offence by reason only of contravening subsection (1) above, but subject to subsection (4) below—

(a) any investment agreement which is entered into in the course of or in consequence of the unsolicited call shall not be enforceable against the person on whom the call was made; and

(b) that person shall be entitled to recover any money or other property paid or transferred by him under the agreement, together with compensation for any loss sustained by him as a result of having parted with it.

(3) The compensation recoverable under subsection (2) above shall be such as the parties may agree or as a court may, on the application of either party, determine.

(4) A court may allow an agreement to which subsection (2) above applies to be enforced or money and property paid or transferred under it to be retained if it is satisfied—

(a) that the person on whom the call was made was not influenced, or not influenced to any material extent, by anything said or done in the course of or in consequence of the call;

(b) without prejudice to paragraph (a) above, that the person on whom the call was made entered into the agreement—

(i) following discussions between the parties of such a nature and over such a period that his entering into the agreement can fairly be regarded as a consequence of those discussions rather than the call; and

(ii) was aware of the nature of the agreement and any risks involved in entering into it; or

(c) that the call was not made by—

(i) the person seeking to enforce the agreement or to retain the money or property or a person acting on his behalf or an appointed representative whose principal he was; or

(ii) a person who has received or is to receive, or in the case of an appointed representative whose principal has received or is to receive, any commission or other inducement in respect of the agreement from a person mentioned in sub-paragraph (i) above.

(5) Where a person elects not to perform an agreement which by virtue of this section is unenforceable against him or by virtue of this section recovers money paid or other property transferred by him under an

agreement he shall repay any money and return any other property received by him under the agreement.

(6) Where any property transferred under an agreement to which this section applies has passed to a third party the references to that property in this section shall be construed as references to its value at the time of its transfer under the agreement.

(7) In the application of this section to anything done by a member of a recognised self-regulating organisation or a person certified by a recognised professional body in carrying on investment business in the carrying on of which he is subject to the rules of the organisation or body the reference in subsection (1) above to regulations made by the Secretary of State shall be construed as references to the rules of the organisation or body.

(8) In this section "unsolicited call" means a personal visit or oral communication made without express invitation.

DEFINITIONS
"appointed representative": s.44(2).
"carrying on investment business": s.1(3).
"certified": s.207(1).
"investment agreement": s.44(9).
"investment business": s.1(2).
"member": s.207(1).
"recognised professional body": s.207(1).
"recognised self-regulating organisation": s.207(1).
"rules": s.207(1).
"unsolicited call": s.56(8).

GENERAL NOTE
This section deals with "cold-calling" by prohibiting the pushing of investments through unsolicited calls. That prohibition may, however, be relaxed in certain circumstances.

Subs. (1)
It is prohibited during or in consequence of an unsolicited call by way of business to enter into an investment agreement with the person called or to try and persuade him to enter into an investment agreement.
No person: The prohibition applies to persons generally, not just to authorised persons.
Unsolicited call: See the definition in subs. (8). A bank manager who raises the subject of investments in the course of a conversation initiated by a bank customer is not making an oral communication without express invitation: the notion of "oral communication" refers to the conversation as a whole: H.L. Vol. 479, col. 350 (July 23, 1986).
By way of business: A person who suggests an investment to a friend in the course of an unsolicited call, and who stands to gain nothing from the agreement, presumably acts otherwise than by way of business.
Except so far as permitted by regulations: Regulations made by the SIB may exclude cold-calling in certain circumstances, or the cold-calling of certain investments (*e.g.* those for which there is a cooling-off period), from the general prohibition. As to the manner of making these regulations, see Sched. 9, paras. 4–9. In relation to SRO and RPB members carrying on investment business regulated by the SRO or RPB the power to make exceptions to the general prohibition is exercisable by the SRO or RPB: subs. (7).
As to the consequences of contravening this subsection, see subs. (2) of this section, ss.28, 60, 61 and Chap. VI.

Subs. (2)
This subsection establishes a general presumption that an investment agreement tainted by cold-calling is unenforceable against the person on whom the call was made, and that anything parted with is recoverable by him along with compensation for any loss sustained. A person taking advantage of this subsection must return anything received by him under the agreement: subss. (5), (6).
This subsection is subject to subs. (4).

Subs. (4)

This subsection enumerates the circumstances in which a court may allow an agreement tainted by cold-calling to be enforced notwithstanding subs. (2). The broad effect is that the agreement may be enforceable if the investor was not materially influenced by the call, or if he went into it with his eyes open following discussions overshadowing the initial call, or if the caller was a disinterested third party.

Restrictions on advertising

57.—(1) Subject to section 58 below, no person other than an authorised person shall issue or cause to be issued an investment advertisement in the United Kingdom unless its contents have been approved by an authorised person.

(2) In this Act "an investment advertisement" means any advertisement inviting persons to enter or offer to enter into an investment agreement or to exercise any rights conferred by an investment to acquire, dispose of, underwrite or convert an investment or containing information calculated to lead directly or indirectly to persons doing so.

(3) Subject to subsection (4) below, any person who contravenes this section shall be guilty of an offence and liable—

(*a*) on conviction on indictment, to imprisonment for a term not exceeding two years or to a fine or to both;

(*b*) on summary conviction, to imprisonment for a term not exceeding six months or to a fine not exceeding the statutory maximum or to both.

(4) A person who in the ordinary course of a business other than investment business issues an advertisement to the order of another person shall not be guilty of an offence under this section if he proves that he believed on reasonable grounds that the person to whose order the advertisement was issued was an authorised person, that the contents of the advertisement were approved by an authorised person or that the advertisement was permitted by or under section 58 below.

(5) If in contravention of this section a person issues or causes to be issued an advertisement inviting persons to enter or offer to enter into an investment agreement or containing information calculated to lead directly or indirectly to persons doing so, then, subject to subsection (8) below—

(*a*) he shall not be entitled to enforce any agreement to which the advertisement related and which was entered into after the issue of the advertisement; and

(*b*) the other party shall be entitled to recover any money or other property paid or transferred by him under the agreement, together with compensation for any loss sustained by him as a result of having parted with it.

(6) If in contravention of this section a person issues or causes to be issued an advertisement inviting persons to exercise any rights conferred by an investment or containing information calculated to lead directly or indirectly to persons doing so, then, subject to subsection (8) below—

(*a*) he shall not be entitled to enforce any obligation to which a person is subject as a result of any exercise by him after the issue of the advertisement of any rights to which the advertisement related; and

(*b*) that person shall be entitled to recover any money or other property paid or transferred by him under any such obligation, together with compensation for any loss sustained by him as a result of having parted with it.

(7) The compensation recoverable under subsection (5) or (6) above shall be such as the parties may agree or as a court may, on the application of either party, determine.

(8) The court may allow any such agreement or obligation as is mentioned in subsection (5) or (6) above to be enforced or money or property paid or transferred under it to be retained if it is satisfied—

(*a*) that the person against whom enforcement is sought or who is seeking to recover the money or property was not influenced, or not influenced to any material extent, by the advertisement in making his decision to enter into the agreement or as to the exercise of the rights in question; or

(*b*) that the advertisement was not misleading as to the nature of the investment, the terms of the agreement or, as the case may be, the consequences of exercising the rights in question and fairly stated any risks involved in those matters.

(9) Where a person elects not to perform an agreement or an obligation which by virtue of subsection (5) or (6) above is unenforceable against him or by virtue of either of those subsections recovers money paid or other property transferred by him under an agreement or obligation he shall repay any money and return any other property received by him under the agreement or, as the case may be, as a result of exercising the rights in question.

(10) Where any property transferred under an agreement or obligation to which subsection (5) or (6) above applies has passed to a third party the references to that property in this section shall be construed as references to its value at the time of its transfer under the agreement or obligation.

DEFINITIONS

"advertisement": s.207(2), (3).
"authorised person": s.207(1).
"investment": s.1(1).
"investment advertisement": s.57(2).
"investment agreement": s.44(9).

GENERAL NOTE

This section prohibits the issue by an unauthorised person of an investment advertisement unless its contents have been approved by an authorised person. The purpose of this provision is "to ensure that all investment advertisements are subject to rules concerning form and content [s.48(2)(*e*)] and that an authorised person who could be called to account by an appropriate regulator is responsible for ensuring that those rules are met": H.L. Vol. 481, col. 37 (October 20, 1986).

Various exceptions to this prohibition are set out in section 58. Section 57 does not apply to investment advertisements issued by the National Enterprise Board (now the British Technology Group), the Scottish Development Agency or the Welsh Development Agency in the discharge of their functions: Sched. 16, paras. 10–12. As to advertisements broadcast by the Independent Broadcasting Authority, see s.207(4).

Contravention of this section is a criminal offence (subs. (3)) and may entail various civil consequences (subss. (5) and (6), and ss.60 and 61).

Subs. (4)

This subsection sets out a defence to the criminal charge under subs. (3). The burden of proof is on the accused.

Subs. (5)

This subsection establishes a general presumption that an investment agreement entered into after the issue of an advertisement in breach of this section is unenforceable by the issuer. The advertisement must relate to the agreement in question, but there is no need to show that the agreement was entered into in consequence of the advertisement. By the same token the investor can recover anything he has parted with along with compensation for any loss sustained. A person taking advantage of this subsection must return anything received by him under the agreement: subss. (9), (10).

This subsection is subject to subs. (8).

Subs. (6)

This subsection applies to an advertisement inviting persons to exercise any rights conferred by an investment. Again, the general presumption is that the issuer cannot enforce any obligation incurred by an investor exercising those rights after the issue of a related advertisement in breach of this section.

This subsection is also subject to subs. (8).

Subs. (8)

This specifies the circumstances under which an agreement or obligation may be upheld notwithstanding its prima facie unenforceability. These are where the investor was not materially influenced by the advertisement, or where the advertisement was not misleading and fairly stated the risks involved.

Exceptions from restrictions on advertising

58.—(1) Section 57 above does not apply to—
(*a*) any advertisement issued or caused to be issued by, and relating only to investments issued by—
 (i) the government of the United Kingdom, of Northern Ireland or of any country or territory outside the United Kingdom;
 (ii) a local authority in the United Kingdom or elsewhere;
 (iii) the Bank of England or the central bank of any country or territory outside the United Kingdom; or
 (iv) any international organisation the members of which include the United Kingdom or another member State;
(*b*) any advertisement issued or caused to be issued by a person who is exempt under section 36, 38, 42, 43, 44 or 45 above, or by virtue of an order under section 46 above, if the advertisement relates to a matter in respect of which he is exempt.
(*c*) any advertisement which is issued or caused to be issued by a national of a member State other than the United Kingdom in the course of investment business lawfully carried on by him in such a State and which conforms with any rules made under section 48(2)(*e*) above;
(*d*) any advertisement which—
 (i) is subject to section 154 below; or
 (ii) consists of or any part of listing particulars, supplementary listing particulars or any other document required or permitted to be published by listing rules under Part IV of this Act or by an approved exchange under Part V of this Act.

(2) Section 57 above does not apply to an advertisement inviting persons to subscribe in cash for any investments to which Part V of this Act applies if the advertisement is issued or caused to be issued by the person by whom the investments are to be issued and either the advertisement consists of a prospectus registered in accordance with that Part or the following matters (and no others that would make it an investment advertisement) are contained in the advertisement—
(*a*) the name of that person and his address or particulars of other means of communicating with him;
(*b*) the nature of the investments, the number offered for subscription and their nominal value and price;
(*c*) a statement that a prospectus for the purposes of that Part of this Act is or will be available and, if it is not yet available, when it will be; and
(*d*) instructions for obtaining a copy of the prospectus.

(3) Section 57 above does not apply to an advertisement issued in such circumstances as may be specified in an order made by the Secretary of State for the purpose of exempting from that section—
(*a*) advertisements appearing to him to have a private character,

whether by reason of a connection between the person issuing them and those to whom they are issued or otherwise;

(*b*) advertisements appearing to him to deal with investment only incidentally;

(*c*) advertisements issued to persons appearing to him to be sufficiently expert to understand any risks involved; or

(*d*) such other classes of advertisement as he thinks fit.

(4) An order under subsection (3) above may require any person who by virtue of the order is authorised to issue an advertisement to comply with such requirements as are specified in the order.

(5) An order made by virtue of paragraph (*a*), (*b*) or (*c*) of subsection (3) above shall be subject to annulment in pursuance of a resolution of either House of Parliament; and no order shall be made by virtue of paragraph (*d*) of that subsection unless a draft of it has been laid before and approved by a resolution of each House of Parliament.

(6) Subsections 1(*c*) and (2) above do not apply to any advertisement relating to an investment falling within paragraph 5 of Schedule 1 to this Act.

DEFINITIONS

"advertisement": s.207(2), (3).
"approved exchange": s.158(6).
"investment": s.1(1).
"investment advertisement": s.57(2).
"listing particulars": s.144(2).
"listing rules": s.142(6).
"prospectus": s.159(1)(*a*).

GENERAL NOTE

This section enumerates advertisements to which s.57 does not apply.

Subs. (1)

This subsection exempts advertisements issued or caused to be issued by (*a*) various issuers of public sector securities, (*b*) a recognised investment exchange, a recognised clearing house, Lloyd's, listed money market institutions, appointed representatives or miscellaneous others, if the advertisement relates to a matter in respect of which there is exemption, and (*c*) nationals of member States other than the U.K. (in this context Gibraltar is deemed to be a member State: s.208(1)) in the course of investment business lawfully carried on in such a State—provided the advertisement conforms to the Conduct of Business Rules on the form and content of investment advertisements and does not relate to certificates representing securities: subs. (6). This subsection also exempts (*d*) advertisements in connection with listing applications, or consisting of listing particulars or any other documents whose publication is countenanced by The Stock Exchange's listing rules or by an approved recognised investment exchange.

Subs. (2)

This subsection exempts advertisements inviting subscription in cash for unlisted securities (other than certificates representing securities: subs. (6)) if the advertisement is issued by the issuer of the securities and either consists of a prospectus or confines itself to the matters enumerated.

Subs. (3)

This subsection exempts such classes of investment advertisements as may be specified in orders made by the Secretary of State. Making such an order is a non-transferable function of the Secretary of State: s.114(5)(*d*). As to the manner of making an order, see s.205(2) and subs. (5) of this section.

Para. (a): private character: Under this heading it is proposed to exempt directors' communications to shareholders about company results and prospects: H.L. Vol. 481, col. 43 (October 20, 1986).

Employment of prohibited persons

59.—(1) If it appears to the Secretary of State that any individual is not a fit and proper person to be employed in connection with investment business or investment business of a particular kind he may direct that he shall not, without the written consent of the Secretary of State, be employed in connection with investment business or, as the case may be, investment business of that kind—

  (*a*) by authorised persons or exempted persons; or

  (*b*) by any specified person or persons, or by persons of any specified description, falling within paragraph (*a*) above.

(2) A direction under this section ("a disqualification direction") shall specify the date on which it is to take effect and a copy of it shall be served on the person to whom it relates.

(3) Any consent by the Secretary of State to the employment of a person who is the subject of a disqualification direction may relate to employment generally or to employment of a particular kind, may be given subject to conditions and restrictions and may be varied by him from time to time.

(4) Where the Secretary of State proposes—

  (*a*) to give a disqualification direction in respect of any person; or

  (*b*) to refuse an application for his consent under this section or for the variation of such consent,

he shall give that person or the applicant written notice of his intention to do so, stating the reasons for which he proposes to act and giving particulars of the right to require the case to be referred to the Tribunal under Chapter IX of this Part of this Act.

(5) Any person who accepts or continues in any employment in contravention of a disqualification direction shall be guilty of an offence and liable on summary conviction to a fine not exceeding the fifth level on the standard scale.

(6) It shall be the duty of an authorised person and an appointed representative to take reasonable care not to employ or continue to employ a person in contravention of a disqualification direction.

(7) The Secretary of State may revoke a disqualification direction.

(8) In this section references to employment include references to employment otherwise than under a contract of service.

DEFINITIONS

  "authorised person": s.207(1).
  "disqualification direction": s.59(2).
  "employment": s.59(8).
  "exempted person": s.207(1).
  "investment business": s.1(2).
  "Tribunal": s.207(1).

GENERAL NOTE

  This section enables the SIB to give a disqualification direction in respect of any individual who is not fit and proper to be employed in connection with investment business. An individual who is the subject of such a direction is not to be employed in connection with investment business, without the SIB's written consent, either by authorised persons or by exempted persons.

Subs. (1)

  Fit and proper person: See s.27(2).

  Employed: This includes being employed otherwise than under a contract of service: subs. (8). It thus includes employment under a contract for services.

Subs. (4)

The right to require the case to be referred to the Financial Services Tribunal arises not only when it is proposed to give a disqualification direction but also when it is proposed to refuse consent to employment or to vary such consent.

As to the service of notices, see s.204.

Subs. (5)

It is a criminal offence for a disqualified individual to accept or continue in any employment ruled out by the disqualification order. As to the civil consequences of doing so, see ss.60 and 61.

Subs. (6)

This puts authorised persons under a duty to take reasonable care not to employ anyone in contravention of a disqualification direction. The same duty is imposed on appointed representatives, but not on other exempted persons. As to the consequences of contravening this duty, see ss.60–62.

Taking reasonable care is likely to entail checking the register of individuals subject to a disqualification direction, established under s.102(1)(*e*).

Public statement as to person's misconduct

60.—(1) If it appears to the Secretary of State that a person who is or was an authorised person by virtue of section 22, 24, 25 or 31 above has contravened—

(*a*) any provision of rules or regulations made under this Chapter or of section 56 or 59 above; or

(*b*) any condition imposed under section 50 above,

he may publish a statement to that effect.

(2) Before publishing a statement under subsection (1) above the Secretary of State shall give the person concerned written notice of the proposed statement and of the reasons for which he proposes to act.

(3) Where the reasons stated in the notice relate specifically to matters which—

(*a*) refer to a person identified in the notice other than the person who is or was the authorised person; and

(*b*) are in the opinion of the Secretary of State prejudicial to that person in any office or employment,

the Secretary of State shall, unless he considers it impracticable to do so, serve a copy of the notice on that other person.

(4) A notice under this section shall give particulars of the right to have the case referred to the Tribunal under Chapter IX of this Part of this Act.

(5) Where a case is not required to be referred to the Tribunal by a person on whom a notice is served under this section the Secretary of State shall, at the expiration of the period within which such a requirement can be made, give that person written notice that the statement is or is not to be published; and if it is to be published the Secretary of State shall after publication send a copy of it to that person and to any person on whom a copy of the notice under subsection (2) above was served.

DEFINITIONS

"authorised person": s.207(1).

"Tribunal": s.207(1).

GENERAL NOTE

This section specifies the circumstances under which the SIB may make a public statement as to a person's misconduct, and lays down the procedure to be followed.

Subs. (1)

A statement may be published regarding a person who is or was authorised under s.22 (insurance companies), s.24 (operators and trustees of UCITS), s.25 (directly authorised persons) and s.31 (persons authorised in other member States). The statement may relate to a contravention of any provision of rules and regulations made under Chapter V (or any condition attached to the modification of rules under s.50) or any provision of ss.56 or 59 (cold-calling, disqualified individuals).

Subs. (2)
As to the service of notices, see s.204.

Subs. (4)
The right to require the case to be referred to the Financial Services Tribunal belongs not only to the authorised person as to whose conduct a public statement is proposed but also to any third party upon whom a copy is served by virtue of subs. (3): s.97(1)(*b*).

Injunctions and restitution orders

61.—(1) If on the application of the Secretary of State the court is satisfied—
   (*a*) that there is a reasonable likelihood that any person will contravene any provision of—
      (i) rules or regulations made under this Chapter;
      (ii) sections 47, 56, 57, or 59 above;
      (iii) any requirements imposed by an order under section 58(3) above; or
      (iv) the rules of a recognised self-regulating organisation, recognised professional body, recognised investment exchange or recognised clearing house to which that person is subject and which regulate the carrying on by him of investment business,
      or any condition imposed under section 50 above;
   (*b*) that any person has contravened any such provision or condition and that there is a reasonable likelihood that the contravention will continue or be repeated; or
   (*c*) that any person has contravened any such provision or condition and that there are steps that could be taken for remedying the contravention,
the court may grant an injunction restraining the contravention or, in Scotland, an interdict prohibiting the contravention or, as the case may be, make an order requiring that person and any other person who appears to the court to have been knowingly concerned in the contravention to take such steps as the court may direct to remedy it.
   (2) No application shall be made by the Secretary of State under subsection (1) above in respect of any such rules as are mentioned in subsection (1)(*a*)(iv) above unless it appears to him that the organisation, body, exchange or clearing house is unable or unwilling to take appropriate steps to restrain the contravention or to require the person concerned to take such steps as are mentioned in subsection (1) above.
   (3) The court may, on the application of the Secretary of State, make an order under subsection (4) below or, in relation to Scotland, under subsection (5) below if satisfied—
   (*a*) that profits have accrued to any person as a result of his contravention of any provision or condition mentioned in subsection (1)(*a*) above; or
   (*b*) that one or more investors have suffered loss or been otherwise adversely affected as a result of that contravention.
   (4) The court may under this subsection order the person concerned to pay into court, or appoint a receiver to recover from him, such sum as appears to the court to be just having regard—
   (*a*) in a case within paragraph (*a*) of subsection (3) above, to the profits appearing to the court to have accrued;

(b) in a case within paragraph (b) of that subsection, to the extent of the loss or other adverse effect; or

(c) in a case within both paragraphs (a) and (b) of that subsection, to the profits and to the extent of the loss or other adverse effect.

(5) The court may under this subsection order the person concerned to pay to the applicant such sum as appears to the court to be just having regard to the considerations mentioned in paragraphs (a) to (c) of subsection (4) above.

(6) Any amount paid into court by or recovered from a person in pursuance of an order under subsection (4) or (5) above shall be paid out to such person or distributed among such persons as the court may direct, being a person or persons appearing to the court to have entered into transactions with that person as a result of which the profits mentioned in paragraph (a) of subsection (3) above have accrued to him or the loss or adverse effect mentioned in paragraph (b) of that subsection has been suffered.

(7) On an application under subsection (3) above the court may require the person concerned to furnish it with such accounts or other information as it may require for establishing whether any and, if so, what profits have accrued to him as mentioned in paragraph (a) of that subsection and for determining how any amounts are to be paid or distributed under subsection (6) above; and the court may require any such accounts or other information to be verified in such manner as it may direct.

(8) The jurisdiction conferred by this section shall be exercisable by the High Court and the Court of Session.

(9) Nothing in this section affects the right of any person other than the Secretary of State to bring proceedings in respect of the matters to which this section applies.

DEFINITIONS
"carrying on investment business": s.1(3).
"investment business": s.1(2).
"recognised clearing house": s.207(1).
"recognised investment exchange": s.207(1).
"recognised professional body": s.207(1).
"recognised self-regulating organisation": s.207(1).
"rules": s.207(1).

GENERAL NOTE
This section empowers the SIB to seek injunctions (in Scotland, interdicts), as a means of enforcement (subss. (1) and (2)), and to apply for restitution orders (also known as disgorgement orders) on behalf of investors (subss. (3)–(7)).

The transfer of a function exercisable by virtue of subs. (1)(a)(ii) or (iii) may be subject to a reservation that it is to be exercisable by the Secretary of State concurrently with the SIB: s.114(8).

Subs. (1)
If there is a reasonable likelihood that a person will contravene any of the enumerated provisions, or if one of these provisions has already been contravened and there is a reasonable likelihood that the contravention will continue or be repeated, then the court may grant an injunction restraining the contravention.

If a person has contravened one of the enumerated provisions and there are steps that could be taken for remedying the contravention, then the court may make an order requiring steps to be taken to remedy it.

The enumerated provisions are any provision of (i) the rules or regulations made under Chapter V, (ii) s.47 (misleading statements and market manipulation), s.56 (cold-calling), s.57 (advertising) or s.59 (disqualified individuals), or (iii) any requirements imposed by an order under s.58(3) (exempted advertisements). An injunction may also be sought in connection with a contravention of a condition attached to the modification of rules under s.50.

This subsection also allows the SIB to apply for an injunction in connection with a contravention of the investment business rules of an SRO, RPB, RIE or RCH: para. (*a*)(iv)—but no such application is to be made unless the regulatory authority concerned appears unable or unwilling to deal with the contravention itself: subs. (2).

Subs. (3)
This subsection sets out the grounds upon which a disgorgement order may be made by the court upon the application of the SIB.
Para. (a): profits accrued: As to the assessment of these, see subs. (7).
Para. (b): adversely affected: This phrase makes it clear that an investor's failure to realise a profit to which he is entitled is a relevant ground.

Subs. (4)
This subsection empowers the court to make a restitution order, requiring the person in question to pay over such sum "as appears to the court to be just" having regard to the criteria enumerated.
This subsection applies to applications to the High Court.

Subs. (5)
This subsection applies to applications to the Court of Session.
The principles applicable to the making of the restitution order are those laid down in subs. (4), but the sum to be disgorged must be paid to the SIB.

Subs. (6)
This subsection identifies the persons who may benefit from the distribution of the sum disgorged. They are the investors whose transactions with the person concerned have generated his profits or occasioned the losses or adverse effects suffered by them.

Actions for damages

62.—(1) Without prejudice to section 61 above, a contravention of—
 (*a*) any rules or regulations made under this Chapter;
 (*b*) any conditions imposed under section 50 above;
 (*c*) any requirements imposed by an order under section 58(3) above;
 (*d*) the duty imposed by section 59(6) above,
shall be actionable at the suit of a person who suffers loss as a result of the contravention subject to the defences and other incidents applying to actions for breach of statutory duty.

(2) Subsection (1) applies also to a contravention by a member of a recognised self-regulating organisation or a person certified by a recognised professional body of any rules of the organisation or body relating to a matter in respect of which rules or regulations have been or could be made under this Chapter in relation to an authorised person who is not such a member or so certified.

(3) Subsection (1) above does not apply—
 (*a*) to a contravention of rules made under section 49 or conditions imposed under section 50 in connection with an alteration of the requirements of those rules; or
 (*b*) by virtue of subsection (2) above to a contravention of rules relating to a matter in respect of which rules have been or could be made under section 49.

(4) A person shall not be guilty of an offence by reason of any contravention to which subsection (1) above applies or of a contravention of rules made under section 49 above or such conditions as are mentioned in subsection (3)(*a*) above and no such contravention shall invalidate any transaction.

DEFINITIONS
 "at the suit": s.207(9).
 "certified": s.207(1).
 "member": s.207(1).

"recognised professional body": s.207(1).
"recognised self-regulating organisation": s.207(1).
"rules": s.207(1).

GENERAL NOTE

This section confers a right of action upon an investor who suffers loss as a result of a contravention of any of the provisions enumerated in subs. (1). The action is for breach of statutory duty.

Subs. (1)

Contravention of any of the following is actionable—(*a*) any rules or regulations made under Chapter V (except the Financial Resources Rules made under s.49: subs. (3)(*a*)); (*b*) any condition imposed in connection with a modification of the Conduct of Business Rules under s.50 (but not in connection with a modification of the Financial Resources Rules: subs. (3)(*e*)); (*c*) any requirements imposed by an order under s.58(3) (exempted advertisements); (*d*) the duty to take reasonable care not to employ a person in contravention of a disqualification direction.

Subs. (2)

Contraventions by SRO members or by persons certified by an RPB of relevant SRO or RPB rules are also actionable. The relevant SRO or RPB rules are those relating to a matter in respect of which rules or regulations *have been made* or *could be made* under Chapter V in relation to a directly authorised person. Thus the SRO or RPB rules upon which an action may be founded are not only those which correspond to the SIB's actual rules and regulations, but also those which correspond to rules and regulations which the SIB might hypothetically make.

Even if the SRO or RPB rules are contractual rather than statutory in character, the action remains "subject to the defences and other incidents applying to actions for breach of statutory duty."

Contravention of an SRO or RPB's capital adequacy requirements is not actionable: subs. (3)(*b*).

Subs. (4)

A person is not guilty of a criminal offence by reason of any of the contraventions mentioned in this section.

No contravention mentioned in this section invalidates any transaction.

Gaming contracts

63.—(1) No contract to which this section applies shall be void or unenforceable by reason of—

(*a*) section 18 of the Gaming Act 1845, section 1 of the Gaming Act 1892 or any corresponding provisions in force in Northern Ireland; or

(*b*) any rule of the law of Scotland whereby a contract by way of gaming or wagering is not legally enforceable.

(2) This section applies to any contract entered into by either or each party by way of business and the making or performance of which by either party constitutes an activity which falls within paragraph 12 of Schedule 1 to this Act or would do so apart from Parts III and IV of that Schedule.

GENERAL NOTE

This section ensures that no contract the making or performance of which by either party constitutes dealing in investments is unenforceable by reason of the English gaming legislation or the common law of Scotland. It is thus designed to remove doubts as to the enforceability, for example, of futures contracts.

Subs. (2)

By way of business: This section applies provided at least one party to the contract has entered into it "by way of business." It does not therefore render enforceable a friendly wager.

CHAPTER VI

POWERS OF INTERVENTION
Scope of powers

64.—(1) The powers conferred on the Secretary of State by this Chapter shall be exercisable in relation to any authorised person or, except in the case of the power conferred by section 65 below, any appointed representative of his if it appears to the Secretary of State—

(*a*) that the exercise of the powers is desirable for the protection of investors;

(*b*) that the authorised person is not fit to carry on investment business of a particular kind or to the extent to which he is carrying it on or proposing to carry it on; or

(*c*) that the authorised person has contravened any provision of this Act or of any rules or regulations made under it or, in purported compliance with any such provision, has furnished the Secretary of State with false, inaccurate or misleading information or has contravened any prohibition or requirement imposed under this Act.

(2) For the purposes of subsection (1)(*b*) above the Secretary of State may take into account any matters that could be taken into account in deciding whether to withdraw or suspend an authorisation under Chapter III of this Part of this Act.

(3) The powers conferred by this Chapter may be exercised in relation to a person whose authorisation is suspended under section 28 above or who is the subject of a direction under section 33(1)(*b*) above and references in this Chapter to an authorised person shall be construed accordingly.

(4) The powers conferred by this Chapter shall not be exercisable in relation to—

(*a*) an authorised person who is a member of a recognised self-regulating organisation or a person certified by a recognised professional body and is subject to the rules of such an organisation or body in carrying on all the investment business carried on by him; or

(*b*) an appointed representative whose principal or, in the case of such a representative with more than one principal, each of whose principals is a member of such an organisation or body and is subject to the rules of such an organisation or body in carrying on the investment business in respect of which his principal or each of his principals has accepted responsibility for his activities;

except that the powers conferred by virtue of section 67(1)(*b*) below may on any of the grounds specified in subsection (1) above be exercised in relation to such a person at the request of any such organisation of which he or, in the case of an appointed representative, any of his principals is a member or any such body by which he or, as the case may be, any of his principals is certified.

DEFINITIONS
  "appointed representative": s.44(2).
  "authorised person": s.207(1).
  "certified": s.207(1).
  "investment business": s.1(2).
  "member": s.8(2).
  "principal": s.44.
  "recognised professional body": s.207(1).
  "recognised self-regulating organisation": s.207(1).

GENERAL NOTE

This section specifies the persons in respect of which the powers of intervention conferred by this Chapter are exercisable and the grounds upon which they are exercisable.

(a) *Persons in respect of whom exercisable*:

(i) persons directly authorised by virtue of section 25, including persons whose authorisation is suspended under section 28;

(ii) insurers authorised by virtue of section 22, but see Schedule 10, para. 6;

(iii) registered friendly societies authorised by virtue of section 23, but see Schedule 11, para. 23;

(iv) operators or trustees of recognised collective investment schemes authorised by virtue of section 24;

(v) persons authorised in other Member States of the European Community by virtue of section 31, including persons whose authorisation is suspended under section 33(1)(*b*); and

(vi) appointed representatives, other than appointed representatives whose principal or principals are members of an SRO or certificated by an RPB.

(b) *Persons in respect of whom not exercisable*, save to the extent and in the circumstances stipulated in subsection (4):

(i) members of SROs (note that SROs must have corresponding powers (Sched. 2, para. 3), and note also section 71(2));

(ii) persons certificated by RPBs (but note section 71(2)); and

(iii) appointed representatives whose principal or principals are members of an SRO or certificated by an RPB.

(c) *Grounds upon which exercisable*:

These are set out in subsection (1). Note, in relation to paragraph (*b*), subsection (2). Account may thus be taken of matters relating to employees, associates and appointed representatives, etc. (s.27(3)), business carried on in connection with the investment business (s.27(4)) and any breaches of the rules etc. of SROs and RPBs (ss.27(3), 33(3)).

Restriction of business

65.—(1) The Secretary of State may prohibit an authorised person from—

    (*a*) entering into transactions of any specified kind or entering into them except in specified circumstances or to a specified extent;

    (*b*) soliciting business from persons of a specified kind or otherwise than from such persons or in a specified country or territory outside the United Kingdom;

    (*c*) carrying on business in a specified manner or otherwise than in a specified manner.

(2) A prohibition under this section may relate to transactions entered into in connection with or for the purposes of investment business or to other business which is carried on in connection with or for the purposes of investment business.

DEFINITIONS

"authorised person": s.207(1).

"investment business": s.1(2).

GENERAL NOTE

Where the SIB has grounds for doing so, as to which see section 64(1), this section empowers it to restrict the business, including non-investment business, undertaken by an authorised person. This power is not exercisable in respect of appointed representatives (s.64(1)). As to the imposition of prohibitions, see section 70; as to breach of a prohibition, see section 71.

Restriction on dealing with assets

66.—(1) The Secretary of State may prohibit an authorised person or appointed representative from disposing of or otherwise dealing with any assets, or any specified assets, of that person or, as the case may be, representative in any specified manner or otherwise than in a specified manner.

(2) A prohibition under this section may relate to assets outside the United Kingdom.

DEFINITIONS
"appointed representative": s.44(2).
"authorised person": s.207(1).

GENERAL NOTE
Where the SIB has grounds for doing so, as to which see section 64(1), this section empowers it to prohibit an authorised person or appointed representative from disposing of or otherwise in dealing with any of his assets. As to the imposition of prohibitions, see section 70; as to breach of a prohibition, see section 71.

Vesting of assets in trustee

67.—(1) The Secretary of State may impose a requirement that all assets, or all assets of any specified class or description, which at any time while the requirement is in force—

(a) belong to an authorised person or appointed representative; or

(b) belong to investors and are held by or to the order of an authorised person or appointed representative,

shall be transferred to and held by a trustee approved by the Secretary of State.

(2) Where a requirement is imposed under this section it shall be the duty of the authorised person or, as the case may be, appointed representative to transfer the assets to the trustee and to give him all such other assistance as may be required to enable him to discharge his functions in accordance with the requirement.

(3) Assets held by a trustee in accordance with a requirement under this section shall not be released or dealt with except in accordance with directions given by the Secretary of State or in such circumstances as may be specified by him.

(4) A requirement under this section may relate to assets outside the United Kingdom.

DEFINITIONS
"appointed representative": s.44(2).
"authorised person": s.207(1).

GENERAL NOTE
Where the SIB has grounds for doing so, as to which see section 64(1), this section empowers it to require the vesting in an approved trustee of assets belonging to an authorised person or appointed representative or held by them for investors. This power is also exercisable at the request of an SRO or RPB in respect of its members or persons certificated by it as well as in respect of appointed representatives whose principal or principals are members of the SRO or certificated by the RPB (s.64(4)). As to the imposition of requirements, see section 70; as to breach of a requirement, see section 71.

Maintenance of assets in United Kingdom

68.—(1) The Secretary of State may require an authorised person or appointed representative to maintain in the United Kingdom assets of such value as appears to the Secretary of State to be desirable with a view to ensuring that the authorised person or, as the case may be, appointed representative will be able to meet his liabilities in respect of investment business carried on by him in the United Kingdom.

(2) The Secretary of State may direct that for the purposes of any requirement under this section assets of any specified class or description shall or shall not be taken into account.

DEFINITIONS
"appointed representative": s.44(2).
"authorised person": s.207(1).
"investment business": s.1(2).

GENERAL NOTE
Where the SIB has grounds for doing so, as to which see section 64(1), this section empowers it to require an authorised person or appointed representative to maintain assets in the United Kingdom. As to the imposition of requirements, see section 70; as to breach of a requirement, see section 71.

Rescission and variation

69. The Secretary of State may, either of his own motion or on the application of a person on whom a prohibition or requirement has been imposed under this Chapter, rescind or vary the prohibition or requirement if it appears to the Secretary of State that it is no longer necessary for the prohibition or requirement to take effect or continue in force or, as the case may be, that it should take effect or continue in force in a different form.

GENERAL NOTE
This section empowers the Secretary of State to rescind or vary prohibitions and requirements imposed under sections 65 to 68. As to the refusal of an application for the rescission or variation of a prohibition or requirement, see section 70(2).

Notices

70.—(1) The power to impose, rescind or vary a prohibition or requirement under this Chapter shall be exercisable by written notice served by the Secretary of State on the person concerned; and any such notice shall take effect on such date as is specified in the notice.

(2) If the Secretary of State refuses to rescind or vary a prohibition or requirement on the application of the person to whom it applies he shall serve that person with a written notice of the refusal.

(3) A notice imposing a prohibition or requirement, or varying a prohibition or requirement otherwise than on the application of the person to whom it applies, and a notice under subsection (2) above shall state the reasons for which the prohibition or requirement was imposed or varied or, as the case may be, why the application was refused.

(4) Where the reasons stated in a notice to which subsection (3) above applies relate specifically to matters which—

(a) refer to a person identified in the notice other than the person to whom the prohibition or requirement applies; and

(b) are in the opinion of the Secretary of State prejudicial to that person in any office or employment,

the Secretary of State shall, unless he considers it impracticable to do so, serve a copy of the notice on that person.

(5) A notice to which subsection (3) above applies shall give particulars of the right to have the case referred to the Tribunal under Chapter IX of this Part of this Act.

(6) The Secretary of State may give public notice of any prohibition or requirement imposed by him under this Chapter and of the rescission and variation of any such prohibition or requirement; and any such notice may, if the Secretary of State thinks fit, include a statement of the reasons for which the prohibition or requirement was imposed, rescinded or varied.

DEFINITION
"Tribunal": s.207(1).

GENERAL NOTE
This section governs the imposition, rescission or variation of prohibitions and requirements. It provides that these powers are exercisable by notice. As to the service of notices, see section 204.

A notice imposing or varying prohibitions or requirements, except where they are varied on the application of the person to whom they apply, or refusing an application for their variation or rescission must include a statement of the reasons for doing so, and details of the person's right to require the SIB to refer his case to the Financial Services Tribunal. As to references to the Tribunal, see section 97.

Breach of prohibition or requirement

71.—(1) Sections 60, 61, and 62 above shall have effect in relation to a contravention of a prohibition or requirement imposed under this Chapter as they have effect in relation to any such contravention as is mentioned in those sections.

(2) In its application by virtue of this section, section 62(2) shall have effect with the substitution—

(*a*) for the reference to the rules of a recognised self-regulating organisation of a reference to any prohibition or requirement imposed by it in the exercise of powers for purposes corresponding to those of this Chapter; and

(*b*) for the reference to the rules of a recognised professional body of a reference to any prohibition or requirement imposed in the exercise of powers for such purposes by that body or by any other body or person having functions in respect of the enforcement of the recognised professional body's rules relating to the carrying on of investment business.

(3) This section is without prejudice to any equitable remedy available in respect of property which by virtue of a requirement under section 67 above is subject to a trust.

DEFINITIONS
"investment business": s.1(2).
"recognised professional body": s.207(1).
"rules": s.16(3).

GENERAL NOTE
This section provides sanctions for breaches of prohibitions and requirements imposed either by the SIB in the exercise of its powers under this Chapter or by SROs and RPBs in the exercise of their corresponding powers.

Subs. (1)
Where breaches occur, the SIB may make public statements and seek injuctions and restitution orders (ss.60, 61). Breaches are also actionable at the suit of any person suffering loss as a result. This is without prejudice to the SIB's power to suspend or withdraw authorisation.

Subs. (2)
A breach by a member of an SRO of any prohibition or requirement imposed in the exercise of its corresponding powers is also actionable, as is a breach by a person certified by an RPB of any prohibition or requirement similarly imposed upon him.

Para. (b)
Any other body or person: See Schedule 3, para. 4(4).

CHAPTER VII

WINDING UP AND ADMINISTRATION ORDERS

Winding up orders

72.—(1) On a petition presented by the Secretary of State by virtue of this section, the court having jurisdiction under the Insolvency Act 1986 may wind up an authorised person or appointed representative to whom this subsection applies if—

(a) the person is unable to pay his debts within the meaning of section 123 or, as the case may be, section 221 of that Act; or

(b) the court is of the opinion that it is just and equitable that the person should be wound up.

(2) Subsection (1) above applies to any authorised person, any person whose authorisation is suspended under section 28 above or who is the subject of a direction under section 33(1)(b) above or any appointed representative who is—

(a) a company within the meaning of section 735 of the Companies Act 1985;

(b) an unregistered company within the meaning of section 220 of the Insolvency Act 1986;

(c) an oversea company within the meaning of section 744 of the Companies Act 1985; or

(d) a partnership.

(3) For the purposes of a petition under subsection (1) above a person who defaults in an obligation to pay any sum due and payable under any investment agreement shall be deemed to be unable to pay his debts.

(4) Where a petition is presented under subsection (1) above for the winding up of a partnership on the ground mentioned in paragraph (b) of subsection (1) above or, in Scotland, on a ground mentioned in paragraph (a) or (b) of that subsection, the court shall have jurisdiction and the Insolvency Act 1986 shall have effect as if the partnership were an unregistered company within the meaning of section 220 of that Act.

(5) The Secretary of State shall not present a petition under subsection (1) above for the winding up of any person who is an authorised person by virtue of membership of a recognised self-regulating organisation or certification by a recognised professional body and is subject to the rules of the organisation or body in the carrying on of all investment business carried on by him, unless that organisation or body has consented to his doing so.

DEFINITIONS

"appointed representative": s.44.
"authorised person": s.207(1).
"carrying on investment business": s.1(3).
"certification": s.207(1).
"investment agreement": s.44(9).
"investment business": s.1(2).
"membership": s.207(1).
"recognised professional body": s.207(1).
"recognised self-regulating organisation": s.207(1).
"rules": s.207(1).

GENERAL NOTE

This section empowers the SIB to petition the court for the winding up of an authorised person or appointed representative which is a company or partnership. A comparable provision is to be found in the Banking Act 1979, s.18.

Subs. (1)

A winding-up order may be granted on the grounds that it is just and equitable that the authorised person or appointed representative should be wound up, or that it is unable to pay its debts within the meaning of the Insolvency Act 1986. Note, however, that in the present context defaulting on an obligation to pay any sum due and payable under an investment agreement is deemed to be inability to pay one's debts: subs. (3).

Subs. (2)

This subsection specifies precisely the authorised persons and appointed representatives to which the section applies.

Subs. (5)

The SIB is not to petition for the winding up of a company or partnership *all* of whose investment business is covered by its membership of an SRO or certification by an RPB, except with the consent of the organisation or body in question.

Winding up orders: Northern Ireland

73.—(1) On a petition presented by the Secretary of State by virtue of this section, the High Court in Northern Ireland may wind up an authorised person or appointed representative to whom this subsection applies if—

(*a*) the person is unable to pay his debts within the meaning of Article 480 or, as the case may be, Article 616 of the Companies (Northern Ireland) Order 1986; or

(*b*) the court is of the opinion that it is just and equitable that the person should be wound up.

(2) Subsection (1) above applies to any authorised person, any person whose authorisation is suspended under section 28 above or who is the subject of a direction under section 33(1)(*b*) above or any appointed representative who is—

(*a*) a company within the meaning of Article 3 of the Companies (Northern Ireland) Order 1986;

(*b*) an unregistered company within the meaning of Article 615 of that Order; or

(*c*) a Part XXIII company within the meaning of Article 2 of that Order; or

(*d*) a partnership.

(3) For the purposes of a petition under subsection (1) above a person who defaults in an obligation to pay any sum due and payable under any investment agreement shall be deemed to be unable to pay his debts.

(4) Where a petition is presented under subsection (1) above for the winding up of a partnership on the ground mentioned in paragraph (*b*) of subsection (1) above, the High Court in Northern Ireland shall have jurisdiction and the Companies (Northern Ireland) Order 1986 shall have effect as if the partnership were an unregistered company within the meaning of Article 615 of that Order.

(5) The Secretary of State shall not present a petition under subsection (1) above for the winding up of any person who is an authorised person by virtue of membership of a recognised self-regulating organisation or certification by a recognised professional body and is subject to the rules of the organisation or body in the carrying on of all investment business carried on by him, unless that organisation or body has consented to his doing so.

DEFINITIONS

"appointed representative": s.44.
"authorised person": s.207(1).
"carrying on investment business": s.1(3).
"certification": s.207(1).
"investment agreement": s.44(9).
"investment business": s.207(1).
"membership": s.207(1).
"recognised professional body": s.207(1).
"recognised self-regulating organisation": s.207(1).
"rules": s.207(1).

GENERAL NOTE

This section has the same effect in relation to Northern Ireland as the preceding section has in relation to the rest of the United Kingdom.

Administration orders

74. A petition may be presented under section 9 of the Insolvency Act 1986 (applications for administration orders) in relation to a company to which section 8 of that Act applies which is an authorised person, a person whose authorisation is suspended under section 28 above or who is the subject of a direction under section 33(1)(*b*) above or an appointed representative—

(*a*) in the case of an authorised person who is an authorised person by virtue of membership of a recognised self-regulating organisation or certification by a recognised professional body, by that organisation or body; and

(*b*) in the case of an appointed representative or an authorised person who is not authorised as mentioned in paragraph (*a*) above or is so authorised but is not subject to the rules of the organisation or body in question in the carrying on of all investment business carried on by him, by the Secretary of State.

DEFINITIONS
"appointed representative": s.44.
"authorised person": s.207(1).
"carrying on investment business": s.1(3).
"certification": s.207(1).
"investment business": s.1(2).
"membership": s.207(1).
"recognised professional body": s.207(1).
"recognised self-regulating organisation": s.207(1).
"rules": s.207(1).

GENERAL NOTE
This section empowers certain regulatory authorities to petition the court for the appointment of an administrator under the insolvency legislation for a company which is an authorised person or an appointed representative.

Para. (a): SROs are empowered to present a petition in relation to their own members, and RPBs in relation to their certified members, where *all* the investment business of the company in question is regulated by the petitioning SRO or SROs, or RPB or RPBs.

Para. (b): The SIB is empowered to present a petition in relation to an appointed representative, or in relation to an authorised company whose authorisation does not derive from membership of an SRO or RPB or which is not SRO-regulated or RPB-regulated in respect of *all* its investment business.

CHAPTER VIII

COLLECTIVE INVESTMENT SCHEMES

Preliminary

Interpretation

75.—(1) In this Act "a collective investment scheme" means, subject to the provisions of this section, any arrangements with respect to property of any description, including money, the purpose or effect of which is to enable persons taking part in the arrangements (whether by becoming owners of the property or any part of it or otherwise) to participate in or receive profits or income arising from the acquisition, holding, management or disposal of the property or sums paid out of such profits or income.

(2) The arrangements must be such that the persons who are to participate as mentioned in subsection (1) above (in this Act referred to as "participants") do not have day to day control over the management

of the property in question, whether or not they have the right to be consulted or to give directions; and the arrangements must also have either or both of the characteristics mentioned in subsection (3) below.

(3) Those characteristics are—

(a) that the contributions of the participants and the profits or income out of which payments are to be made to them are pooled;

(b) that the property in question is managed as a whole by or on behalf of the operator of the scheme.

(4) Where any arrangements provide for such pooling as is mentioned in paragraph (a) of subsection (3) above in relation to separate parts of the property in question, the arrangements shall not be regarded as constituting a single collective investment scheme unless the participants are entitled to exchange rights in one part for rights in another.

(5) Arrangements are not a collective investment scheme if—

(a) the property to which the arrangements relate (other than cash awaiting investment) consists of investments falling within any of paragraphs 1 to 5, 6 (so far as relating to units in authorised unit trust schemes and recognised schemes) and 10 of Schedule 1 to this Act;

(b) each participant is the owner of a part of that property and entitled to withdraw it at any time; and

(c) the arrangements do not have the characteristics mentioned in paragraph (a) of subsection (3) above and have those mentioned in paragraph (b) of that subsection only because the parts of the property belonging to different participants are not bought and sold separately except where a person becomes or ceases to be a participant.

(6) The following are not collective investment schemes—

(a) arrangements operated by a person otherwise than by way of business;

(b) arrangements where each of the participants carries on a business other than investment business and enters into the arrangements for commercial purposes related to that business;

(c) arrangements where each of the participants is a body corporate in the same group as the operator;

(d) arrangements where—

    (i) each of the participants is a bona fide employee or former employee (or the wife, husband, widow, widower, child or step-child under the age of eighteen of such an employee or former employee) of a body corporate in the same group as the operator; and

    (ii) the property to which the arrangements relate consists of shares or debentures (as defined in paragraph 20(4) of Schedule 1 to this Act) in or of a member of that group;

(e) arrangements where the receipt of the participants' contributions constitutes the acceptance of deposits in the course of a business which is a deposit-taking business for the purposes of the Banking Act 1979 and does not constitute a transaction prescribed for the purposes of section 2 of that Act by regulations made by the Treasury;

(f) franchise arrangements, that is to say, arrangements under which a person earns profits or income by exploiting a right conferred by the arrangements to use a trade name or design or other intellectual property or the good-will attached to it;

(g) arrangements the predominant purpose of which is to enable persons participating in them to share in the use or enjoyment of a particular property or to make its use or enjoyment available gratuitously to other persons;

(*h*) arrangements under which the rights or interests of the participants are investments falling within paragraph 5 of Schedule 1 to this Act;

(*i*) arrangements the purpose of which is the provision of clearing services and which are operated by an authorised person, a recognised clearing house or a recognised investment exchange;

(*j*) contracts of insurance;

(*k*) occupational pension schemes.

(7) No body incorporated under the law of, or of any part of, the United Kingdom relating to building societies or industrial and provident societies or registered under any such law relating to friendly societies, and no other body corporate other than an open-ended investment company, shall be regarded as constituting a collective investment scheme.

(8) In this Act—

"a unit trust scheme" means a collective investment scheme under which the property in question is held on trust for the participants;

"an open-ended investment company" means a collective investment scheme under which—

(*a*) the property in question belongs beneficially to, and is managed by or on behalf of, a body corporate having as its purpose the investment of its funds with the aim of spreading investment risk and giving its members the benefit of the results of the management of those funds by or on behalf of that body; and

(*b*) the rights of the participants are represented by shares in or securities of that body which—

(i) the participants are entitled to have redeemed or repurchased, or which (otherwise than under Chapter VII of Part V of the Companies Act 1985 or the corresponding Northern Ireland provision) are redeemed or repurchased from them by, or out of funds provided by, that body; or

(ii) the body ensures can be sold by the participants on an investment exchange at a price related to the value of the property to which they relate;

"trustee", in relation to a unit trust scheme, means the person holding the property in question on trust for the participants and, in relation to a collective investment scheme constituted under the law of a country or territory outside the United Kingdom, means any person who (whether or not under a trust) is entrusted with the custody of the property in question;

"units" means the rights or interests (however described) of the participants in a collective investment scheme;

"the operator", in relation to a unit trust scheme with a separate trustee, means the manager and, in relation to an open-ended investment company, means that company.

(9) If an order under section 2 above amends the references to a collective investment scheme in Schedule 1 to this Act it may also amend the provisions of this section.

DEFINITIONS

"body corporate": s.207(1).

"occupational pension scheme": s.207(1).

GENERAL NOTE

This section defines "collective investment scheme" and associated concepts. The definition has three basic components: (i) there must be participation in profits or income (subs. (1)); (ii) participants must not have day to day control over the management of scheme property (subs. (2)); and (iii) either there must be pooling, or the scheme operator must manage the scheme property as a whole (subs. (3)). Various arrangements are, however, specifically excluded from this definition (subss. (5), (6), (7)). Moreover the definitions in this section are susceptible to amendment by the Secretary of State (subs. (9)).

Subs. (1)

Property of any description: A collective investment scheme is an arrangement with respect to "property of any description." Hence the definition is not confined to arrangements respecting "investments" as enumerated in Sched. 1, Part I, but extends to arrangements respecting any kind of property.

Subs. (4)

Pooling arrangements in respect of property divided into a number of separate parts constitute a corresponding number of collective investment schemes, unless participants are entitled to "switch" from one part to another.

Subs. (5)

This subsection is designed to allow the marketing of mass-produced (as opposed to individualised) Personal Equity Plans, which would otherwise be caught by subs. (3)(*b*). Provided the stipulated conditions are satisfied, subs. (5) has the effect of excluding from the definition of collective investment schemes common management arrangements whereby an investment manager buys and sells investments for more than one portfolio at the same time on the basis of a series of discretionary investment management contracts on standard terms (see H.L. Vol. 479, col. 564, July 28, 1986). As a result such arrangements are not subject to the restrictions of s.76.

Subs. (6)

Para. (a): by way of business: That which is done by way of business may be contrasted with that which is done (for example) out of friendship, or for fun, or from charitable motives. So an investment club that is run by an unpaid volunteer is not a collective investment scheme.

Para. (b): Excludes joint ventures from the definition of collective investment schemes.

Para. (d): Excludes employee share schemes.

Para. (e): Excludes certain deposit-taking activities.

Para. (g): Excludes time-sharing arrangements which pass the "predominant purpose" test stipulated in the paragraph. Time-shares sold primarily as investments are not excluded.

Para. (h): Excludes arrangements under which are issued certificates representing securities (such as depositary receipts).

Subs. (7)

This subsection excludes bodies corporate, other than open-ended investment companies as defined in subs. (8), from the definition of collective investment schemes. Thus investment trust companies are not collective investment schemes.

Subs. (8)

Open-ended investment company: Para. (*b*) of the definition is satisfied either if participants are entitled *de jure* to redemption, *or* if participants' shares are as a matter of practice redeemed (otherwise than under the special Companies Act procedure designed to secure maintenance of capital), *or* if the company *ensures* (*i.e.* by intervening in the market) that they can be sold on an investment exchange at a price related to the value of the underlying assets. The necessary relationship between price and net asset value is a matter for stipulation under s.81. See *The Regulation of Authorised Unit Trust Schemes*, para. 9.11.

Subs. (9)

This subsection enables the Secretary of State to amend s.75, but only if he amends the references to a collective investment scheme in Sched. 1.

Promotion of schemes

Restrictions on promotion

76.—(1) Subject to subsections (2), (3) and (4) below, an authorised person shall not—

(*a*) issue or cause to be issued in the United Kingdom any advertisement inviting persons to become or offer to become participants in a collective investment scheme or containing information calculated to lead directly or indirectly to persons becoming or offering to become participants in such a scheme; or (*b*) advise or procure any person in the United Kingdom to become or offer to become a participant in such a scheme,

unless the scheme is an authorised unit trust scheme or a recognised scheme under the following provisions of this Chapter.

(2) Subsection (1) above shall not apply if the advertisement is issued to or the person mentioned in paragraph (*b*) of that subsection is—

(*a*) an authorised person; or

(*b*) a person whose ordinary business involves the acquisition and disposal of property of the same kind as the property, or a substantial part of the property, to which the scheme relates.

(3) Subsection (1) above shall not apply to anything done in accordance with regulations made by the Secretary of State for the purpose of exempting from that subsection the promotion otherwise than to the general public of schemes of such descriptions as are specified in the regulations.

(4) The Secretary of State may by regulations make provision for exempting single property schemes from subsection (1) above.

(5) For the purposes of subsection (4) above a single property scheme is a scheme which has the characteristics mentioned in subsection (6) below and satisfies such other requirements as are specified in the regulations conferring the exemption.

(6) The characteristics referred to above are—

(*a*) that the property subject to the scheme (apart from cash or other assets held for management purposes) consists of—

(i) a single building (or a single building with ancillary buildings) managed by or on behalf of the operator of the scheme; or

(ii) a group of adjacent or contiguous buildings managed by him or on his behalf as a single enterprise,

with or without ancillary land and with or without furniture, fittings or other contents of the building or buildings in question; and

(*b*) that the units of the participants in the scheme are either dealt in on a recognised investment exchange or offered on terms such that any agreement for their acquisition is conditional on their admission to dealings on such an exchange.

(7) Regulations under subsection (4) above may contain such supplementary and transitional provisions as the Secretary of State thinks necessary and may also contain provisions imposing obligations or liabilities on the operator and trustee (if any) of an exempted scheme, including, to such extent as he thinks appropriate, provisions for purposes corresponding to those for which provision can be made under section 85 below in relation to authorised unit trust schemes.

DEFINITIONS

"advertisement": s.207(2), (3).

"authorised person": s.207(1).

"authorised unit trust scheme": s.207(1).

"collective investment scheme": s.75.

"participant": s.75(2).

"recognised investment exchange": s.207(1).

"recognised scheme": s.207(1).

GENERAL NOTE

Subject to certain exceptions, this key section confines the promotion of collective investment schemes by *authorised* persons to authorised unit trust schemes and recognised schemes (*i.e.* to those rendered suitable for promotion by virtue of regulation). (The promotion of collective investment schemes by *unauthorised* persons is a criminal offence: s.57.)

As to the consequences for an authorised person of contravening this section, see s.95.

Subs. (2)

This is a variant of the familiar "professionals only" exemption. It allows an authorised person to promote to another authorised person any collective investment scheme, and to a business investor an unauthorised, unrecognised scheme whose underlying assets are of the same kind as those ordinarily traded by the business investor.

Subs. (3)

This subsection empowers the SIB to make regulations exempting the selective promotion of specified unauthorised, unrecognised schemes from the prohibition in subs. (1). Any exemption given will presumably relate to "sophisticated" investors.

As to the manner of making regulations under this subsection, see s.205(2) as qualified by Sched. 9, paras. 4–9.

Subss. (4), (5), (6), (7)

These subsections empower the SIB to make regulations exempting the promotion of single property schemes from the prohibition in subs. (1). The underlying assets of a single property scheme must be a single building or a group of adjacent or contiguous buildings, and the units must be traded on a recognised investment exchange. The purpose of the provision is to facilitate the formation of "co-ownership trusts" as a vehicle for investment in single properties as advocated by the Royal Institution of Chartered Surveyors. The need for such trusts has, however, been diminished by the The Stock Exchange's willingness to list property income certificates (PINCs), which perform a similar economic function.

As to the manner of making regulation under subs. (4), see s.205(2) as qualified by Sched. 9, paras. 4–9.

Authorised unit trust schemes

Applications for authorisation

77.—(1) Any application for an order declaring a unit trust scheme to be an authorised unit trust scheme shall be made by the manager and trustee, or proposed manager and trustee, of the scheme and the manager and trustee shall be different persons.

(2) Any such application—

(*a*) shall be made in such manner as the Secretary of State may direct; and

(*b*) shall contain or be accompanied by such information as he may reasonably require for the purpose of determining the application.

(3) At any time after receiving an application and before determining it the Secretary of State may require the applicant to furnish additional information.

(4) The directions and requirements given or imposed under subsections (2) and (3) above may differ as between different applications.

(5) Any information to be furnished to the Secretary of State under this section shall, if he so requires, be in such form or verified in such manner as he may specify.

DEFINITIONS

"authorised unit trust scheme": s.207(1).
"trustee": s.75(8).
"unit trust scheme": s.75(8).

GENERAL NOTE

This section requires applications for the authorisation of a unit trust scheme to be made in such a manner as the SIB may direct, with such information as it may reasonably require.

Subs. (1)

Manager and trustee shall be different persons: see further, s.78(2).

Authorisation orders

78.—(1) The Secretary of State may, on an application duly made in accordance with section 77 above and after being furnished with all such information as he may require under that section, make an order declaring a unit trust scheme to be an authorised unit trust scheme for the purposes of this Act if—

(*a*) it appears to him that the scheme complies with the requirements of the regulations made under section 81 below and that the following provisions of this section are satisfied; and

(*b*) he has been furnished with a copy of the trust deed and a certificate signed by a solicitor to the effect that it complies with such of those requirements as relate to its contents.

(2) The manager and the trustee must be persons who are independent of each other.

(3) The manager and the trustee must each be a body corporate incorporated in the United Kingdom or another member State, the affairs of each must be administered in the country in which it is incorporated, each must have a place of business in the United Kingdom and, if the manager is incorporated in another member State, the scheme must not be one which satisfies the requirements prescribed for the purposes of section 86 below.

(4) The manager and the trustee must each be an authorised person and neither must be prohibited from acting as manager or trustee, as the case may be, by or under rules under section 48 above, by or under the rules of any recognised self-regulating organisation of which the manager or trustee is a member or by a prohibition imposed under section 65 above.

(5) The name of the scheme must not be undesirable or misleading; and the purposes of the scheme must be reasonably capable of being successfully carried into effect.

(6) The participants must be entitled to have their units redeemed in accordance with the scheme at a price related to the net value of the property to which the units relate and determined in accordance with the scheme; but a scheme shall be treated as complying with this subsection if it requires the manager to ensure that a participant is able to sell his units on an investment exchange at a price not significantly different from that mentioned in this subsection.

(7) The Secretary of State shall inform the applicants of his decision on the application not later than six months after the date on which the application was received.

(8) On making an order under this section the Secretary of State may issue a certificate to the effect that the scheme complies with the conditions necessary for it to enjoy the rights conferred by any relevant Community instrument.

DEFINITIONS
"authorised unit trust scheme": s.207(1).
"body corporate": s.207(1).
"member": s.207(1).
"recognised self-regulating organisation": s.207(1).
"rules": s.207(1).
"trustee": s.75(8).
"unit trust scheme": s.75(8).

GENERAL NOTE
This section lays down conditions which must be satisfied before a unit trust scheme can be authorised. For reasons of Community law no power of authorisation of unit trust schemes is conferred upon SROs: *The Regulation of Authorised Unit Trust Schemes*, para. 3.5. The ban on promotion in s.76(1) does not apply to authorised unit trust schemes.

Subs. (1)
May: The SIB "may" authorise a unit trust scheme which satisfies the statutory conditions. Contrast the use of "shall" in the context of the provisions governing the recognition of the self-regulating organisations (s.10(2)) and the authorisation of direct

applicants (s.27(2)). Section 16(1)(c) of the repealed Prevention of Fraud (Investments) Act 1939 (corresponding to PFI Act 1958, s.17(1)(c) (also repealed)) provided that the Board of Trade "may by order declare to be an authorised unit trust scheme . . . any unit trust scheme in relation to which the Board are satisfied that the [Act's] conditions are fulfilled . . ." In *Allied Investors' Trusts Ltd.* v. *Board of Trade* [1956] Ch. 232, [1956] 2 W.L.R. 224, the court took the view that this provision conferred a general discretion to give or withhold authorisation, and accordingly the Board might impose conditions ("discretionary requirements") over and above those stipulated in the legislation. A similar view must be taken of the significance of "may" in the present context.

As to the manner of making an authorisation order, see s.205(5).

Subs. (2)

"Because the trustee is independent he can be given the main supervisory role, thereby reducing the need for external supervision by the central regulatory body . . .": *The Regulation of Authorised Unit Trust Schemes*, para. 1.11. This provision is thus the keystone of a system of "devolved self-regulation" under which it will be the trustee's responsibility "to see that the manager acts in accordance with the regulations and the provisions of the trust deed": *ibid.*, para. 6.5.

Subs. (3)

Where the manager is incorporated in a member State other than the United Kingdom, and the scheme qualifies for recognition under s.86 (schemes constituted in other member States), it is not eligible for authorisation under s.78.

Subs. (4)

Not only must the manager and trustee be authorised persons, but the *scope* of their authorisation (whether conferred by the SIB or by an SRO) must extend to their acting as manager or trustee.

Subs. (6)

Regulations to be made under s.81 will lay down the minimum redemption requirements: *The Regulation of Authorised Unit Trust Schemes*, para. 9.8. The second limb of this subsection, reflecting the UCITS directive, contemplates as an alternative to the standard method of redemption the listing of the units on an investment exchange, coupled with intervention in the market by the manager to ensure that the market price is a fair reflection of the net asset value. It remains to be seen whether the regulations will allow this alternative to the standard method of redemption: *ibid.*, para. 9. 11.

Subs. (8)

Any relevant community instrument: The UCITS directive is such.

Revocation of authorisation

79.—(1) The Secretary of State may revoke an order declaring a unit trust scheme to be an authorised unit trust scheme if it appears to him—

   (*a*) that any of the requirements for the making of the order are no longer satisfied;

   (*b*) that it is undesirable in the interests of the participants or potential participants that the scheme should continue to be authorised; or

   (*c*) without prejudice to paragraph (*b*) above, that the manager or trustee of the scheme has contravened any provision of this Act or any rules or regulations made under it or, in purported compliance with any such provision, has furnished the Secretary of State with false, inaccurate or misleading information or has contravened any prohibition or requirement imposed under this Act.

(2) For the purposes of subsection (1)(*b*) above the Secretary of State may take into account any matter relating to the scheme, the manager or trustee, a director or controller of the manager or trustee or any person employed by or associated with the manager or trustee in connection with the scheme.

(3) In the case of a manager or trustee who is a member of a recognised self-regulating organisation the rules, prohibitions and requirements referred to in subsection (1)(*c*) above include the rules of that organisation and any prohibition or requirement imposed by virtue of those rules.

(4) The Secretary of State may revoke an order declaring a unit trust scheme to be an authorised unit trust scheme at the request of the manager or trustee of the scheme; but he may refuse to do so if he considers that any matter concerning the scheme should be investigated as a preliminary to a decision on the question whether the order should be revoked or that revocation would not be in the interests of the participants or would be incompatible with a Community obligation.

DEFINITIONS
"authorised unit trust scheme": s.207(1).
"controller": s.207(5).
"director": s.207(1).
"member": s.207(1).
"participants": s.75(2).
"recognised self-regulating organisation": s.207(1).
"rules": s.207(1).
"trustee": s.75(8).
"unit trust scheme": s.75(8).

GENERAL NOTE
This section sets out the grounds upon which the authorisation of a unit trust scheme may be revoked by the SIB.

Subs. (1)
In para. (*a*) the "requirements" in question are those laid down in s.78(1). Para. (*b*) must be read in conjunction with subs. (2). Para. (*c*) must be read in conjunction with subs. (3).
As to the manner of revocation, see s.205(5).

Subs. (4)
This subsection empowers the SIB to revoke an authorisation at the request of the manager or trustee. It sets out three grounds upon which a request for revocation may be refused. It does not follow that the SIB is otherwise obliged to revoke authorisation on request.

Representations against refusal or revocation

80.—(1) Where the Secretary of State proposes—
   (*a*) to refuse an application for an order under section 78 above; or
   (*b*) to revoke such an order otherwise than at the request of the manager or trustee of the scheme,
he shall give the applicants or, as the case may be, the manager and trustee of the scheme written notice of his intention to do so, stating the reasons for which he proposes to act and giving particulars of the rights conferred by subsection (2) below.

(2) A person on whom a notice is served under subsection (1) above may, within twenty-one days of the date of service, make written representations to the Secretary of State and, if desired, oral representations to a person appointed for that purpose by the Secretary of State.

(3) The Secretary of State shall have regard to any representations made in accordance with subsection (2) above in determining whether to refuse the application or revoke the order, as the case may be.

DEFINITIONS
"trustee": s.75(8).

GENERAL NOTE
This section requires an opportunity to make representations to be afforded to the actual or proposed manager and trustee of a unit trust scheme in respect of which the SIB proposes to refuse an application for authorisation or to revoke authorisation.

There is, in connection with the refusal or revocation of authorisation for a unit trust scheme, no right to require the case to be referred to the Financial Services Tribunal.

Constitution and management

81.—(1) The Secretary of State may make regulations as to the constitution and management of authorised unit trust schemes, the powers and duties of the manager and trustee of any such scheme and the rights and obligations of the participants in any such scheme.

(2) Without prejudice to the generality of subsection (1) above, regulations under this section may make provision—

(*a*) as to the issue and redemption of the units under the scheme;

(*b*) as to the expenses of the scheme and the means of meeting them;

(*c*) for the appointment, removal, powers and duties of an auditor for the scheme;

(*d*) for restricting or regulating the investment and borrowing powers exercisable in relation to the scheme;

(*e*) requiring the keeping of records with respect to the transactions and financial position of the scheme and for the inspection of those records;

(*f*) requiring the preparation of periodical reports with respect to the scheme and the furnishing of those reports to the participants and to the Secretary of State; and

(*g*) with respect to the amendment of the scheme.

(3) Regulations under this section may make provision as to the contents of the trust deed, including provision requiring any of the matters mentioned in subsection (2) above to be dealt with in the deed; but regulations under this section shall be binding on the manager, trustee and participants independently of the contents of the deed and, in the case of the participants, shall have effect as if contained in it.

(4) Regulations under this section shall not impose limits on the remuneration payable to the manager of a scheme.

(5) Regulations under this section may contain such incidental and transitional provisions as the Secretary of State thinks necessary or expedient.

DEFINITIONS
"authorised unit trust scheme": s.207(1).
"participants": s.75(2).
"trustee": s.75(8).

GENERAL NOTE
This section gives power to make regulations as to the constitution and management, etc., of authorised unit trust schemes. For an account of the proposed regulations, see *The Regulation of Authorised Unit Trust Schemes*, chaps. 4–14. The powers given, save that conferred by subs. (2)(*d*), are to be transferred to the SIB. The regulations made under this section will apply to all managers and trustees—whether or not they are members of SROs—of authorised schemes. Managers and trustees must, of course, be authorised persons (s.78(4)), and as such they will, in addition, be bound by the conduct of business and other rules made by the SIB under Chapter V, or by the equivalent rules of an SRO.

As to the manner of making regulations under this section, see s.205(2) as qualified by Sched. 9, paras. 4–9.

As to the consequences of contravening the regulations made, see subs. (3), s.79(1)(*c*) and s.95(1).

Subs. (2)
Para. (d): "The power to control the investments of authorised schemes, which could be used to allow the creation of new investment products thus altering the characteristics of authorised schemes, will be retained by the Secretary of State": *The Regulation of Authorised Unit Trust Schemes*, para. 1.13.

Subs. (3)
Regulations made under this section are binding independently of the contents of the trust deed. Thus they are binding whether or not incorporated in the deed, and override contrary

provisions in it. Regulations binding on the participants have effect as if contained in the trust deed, so that a contravention by a participant is tantamount to a breach of a provision of the trust deed. A contravention of the regulations by a manager or trustee engenders the legal consequences stipulated in s.95.

Subs. (4)
This subsection embodies the same policy of hostility to statutory price controls as s.48(3).

Alteration of schemes and changes of manager or trustee

82.—(1) The manager of an authorised unit trust scheme shall give written notice to the Secretary of State of—
    (*a*) any proposed alteration to the scheme; and
    (*b*) any proposal to replace the trustee of the scheme;
and any notice given in respect of a proposed alteration involving a change in the trust deed shall be accompanied by a certificate signed by a solicitor to the effect that the change will not affect the compliance of the deed with the regulations made under section 81 above.

(2) The trustee of an authorised unit trust scheme shall give written notice to the Secretary of State of any proposal to replace the manager of the scheme.

(3) Effect shall not be given to any such proposal unless—
    (*a*) the Secretary of State has given his approval to the proposal; or
    (*b*) one month has elapsed since the date on which the notice was given under subsection (1) or (2) above without the Secretary of State having notified the manager or trustee that the proposal is not approved.

(4) Neither the manager nor the trustee of an authorised unit trust scheme shall be replaced except by persons who satisfy the requirements of section 78(2) to (4) above.

DEFINITIONS
"authorised unit trust scheme": s.207(1).
"trustee": s.75(8).

GENERAL NOTE
This section requires notification to the SIB of any proposal to alter an authorised unit trust scheme or to replace the trustee or manager. Such proposals are not to be effectuated without the approval of the SIB.

Restrictions on activities of manager

83.—(1) The manager of an authorised unit trust scheme shall not engage in any activities other than those mentioned in subsection (2) below.

(2) Those activities are—
    (*a*) acting as manager of—
        (i) a unit trust scheme;
        (ii) an open-ended investment company or any other body corporate whose business consists of investing its funds with the aim of spreading investment risk and giving its members the benefit of the results of the management of its funds by or on behalf of that body; or
        (iii) any other collective investment scheme under which the contributions of the participants and the profits or income out of which payments are to be made to them are pooled;
    (*b*) activities for the purposes of or in connection with those mentioned in paragraph (*a*) above.

(3) A prohibition under section 65 above may prohibit the manager of an authorised unit trust scheme from inviting persons in any specified

country or territory outside the United Kingdom to become participants in the scheme.

GENERAL NOTE
    This section gives effect to a provision of the UCITS directive by restricting the manager of an authorised unit trust scheme to the activities listed in subs. (2). In essence the manager is confined to the management of pooled investment vehicles. One consequence of this is that persons authorised by RPBs cannot act as managers of authorised unit trust schemes.
    This section does not apply to a manager appointed by an order made on an application to the court under s.93(1)(*b*): s.93(5).

Subs. (2)
    Para. (a)(ii): This allows the managing of authorised unit trust schemes to be combined with the managing of investment trust companies as well as open-ended investment companies. The definition of a "manager" in s.207(6) cannot sensibly be applied to "acting as a manager" of such companies, notwithstanding the apparent requirement of s.207(6) that it should be applied.
    Para. (a)(iii): this allows the managing of authorised unit trust schemes to be combined with the managing of such collective investment schemes as are characterised by pooling arrangements, *i.e.* as fall within s.75(3)(*a*) rather than s.75(3)(*b*). So a unit trust management company cannot itself manage Personal Equity Plans.

Avoidance of exclusion clauses

84. Any provision of the trust deed of an authorised unit trust scheme shall be void in so far as it would have the effect of exempting the manager or trustee from liability for any failure to exercise due care and diligence in the discharge of his functions in respect of the scheme.

Publication of scheme particulars

85.—(1) The Secretary of State may make regulations requiring the manager of an authorised unit trust scheme to submit to him and publish or make available to the public on request a document ("scheme particulars") containing information about the scheme and complying with such requirements as are specified in the regulations.

(2) Regulations under this section may require the manager of an authorised unit trust scheme to submit and publish or make available revised or further scheme particulars if—

   (*a*) there is a significant change affecting any matter contained in such particulars previously published or made available whose inclusion was required by the regulations; or

   (*b*) a significant new matter arises the inclusion of information in respect of which would have been required in previous particulars if it had arisen when those particulars were prepared.

(3) Regulations under this section may provide for the payment, by the person or persons who in accordance with the regulations are treated as responsible for any scheme particulars, of compensation to any person who has become or agreed to become a participant in the scheme and suffered loss as a result of any untrue or misleading statement in the

particulars or the omission from them of any matter required by the regulations to be included.

(4) Regulations under this section shall not affect any liability which any person may incur apart from the regulations.

DEFINITIONS
"authorised unit trust scheme": s.207(1).
"participant": s.75(2).

GENERAL NOTE
This section requires the manager of an authorised unit trust scheme to publish scheme particulars (*i.e.* a document giving information about the scheme) in accordance with regulations to be made by the SIB. In addition to requiring specific disclosures, the regulations will put the manager under a general duty to disclose any other information about the scheme which an investor would reasonably require for the purpose of deciding whether to invest in the scheme: *The Regulation of Authorised Unit Trust Schemes*, para. 15.2. This reflects the UCITS directive, art. 28.

As to the manner of making regulations under this section, see s.205(2) as qualfied by Sched. 9, paras. 4–9.

As to the consequences of contravening regulations made under this section, see subss. (3) and (4), s.79(1)(*c*) and s.95(1).

Subs. (2)
The obligation to publish scheme particulars is a continuing obligation and the manager must keep the scheme particulars up-to-date.

Subs. (3)
This subsection enables regulations to be made providing for compensation for scheme participants who suffer loss as a result of an untrue or misleading statement in the particulars on a significant omission from them. The compensation is payable by the person(s) designated responsible for the scheme particulars by the regulations. The regulations will certainly fix responsibility for the scheme particulars upon the manager, and it is unlikely that responsibility will also be ascribed to the trustee: *The Regulation of Authorised Unit Trust Schemes*, paras. 15.3–15.5.

Subs. (4)
Any liability incurred under the common law of negligence or under the Misrepresentation Act 1967 is unaffected by the incurrence of liability under the subs. (3) regulations. Liability under s.95 (contraventions) is presumably also unaffected.

Recognition of overseas schemes

Schemes constituted in other member States

86.—(1) Subject to subsection (2) below, a collective investment scheme constituted in a member State other than the United Kingdom is a recognised scheme if it satisfies such requirements as are prescribed for the purposes of this section.

(2) Not less than two months before inviting persons in the United Kingdom to become participants in the scheme the operator of the scheme shall give written notice to the Secretary of State of his intention to do so, specifying the manner in which the invitation is to be made; and the scheme shall not be a recognised scheme by virtue of this section if within two months of receiving the notice the Secretary of State notifies—

(*a*) the operator of the scheme; and
(*b*) the authorities of the State in question who are responsible for the authorisation of collective investment schemes,

that the manner in which the invitation is to be made does not comply with the law in force in the United Kingdom.

(3) The notice to be given to the Secretary of State under subsection (2) above—

(*a*) shall be accompanied by a certificate from the authorities mentioned in subsection (2)(*b*) above to the effect that the scheme complies with the conditions necessary for it to enjoy the rights conferred by any relevant Community instrument;

(*b*) shall contain the address of a place in the United Kingdom for the service on the operator of notices or other documents required or authorised to be served on him under this Act; and

(*c*) shall contain or be accompanied by such other information and documents as may be prescribed.

(4) A notice given by the Secretary of State under subsection (2) above shall give the reasons for which he considers that the law in force in the United Kingdom will not be complied with and give particulars of the rights conferred by subsection (5) below.

(5) A person on whom a notice is served by the Secretary of State under subsection (2) above may, within twenty-one days of the date of service, make written representations to the Secretary of State and, if desired, oral representations to a person appointed for that purpose by the Secretary of State.

(6) The Secretary of State may in the light of any representations made in accordance with subsection (5) above withdraw his notice and in that event the scheme shall be a recognised scheme from the date on which the notice is withdrawn.

(7) Rules under section 48 above shall not apply to investment business in respect of which the operator or trustee of a scheme recognised under this section is an authorised person by virtue of section 24 above except so far as they make provision as respects—

(*a*) procuring persons to become participants in the scheme and advising persons on the scheme and the exercise of the rights conferred by it;

(*b*) matters incidental to those mentioned in paragraph (*a*) above.

(8) For the purposes of this section a collective investment scheme is constituted in a member State if—

(*a*) it is constituted under the law of that State by a contract or under a trust and is managed by a body corporate incorporated under that law; or

(*b*) it takes the form of an open-ended investment company incorporated under that law.

(9) If the operator of a scheme recognised under this section gives written notice to the Secretary of State stating that he desires the scheme no longer to be recognised under this section it shall cease to be so recognised when the notice is given.

DEFINITIONS

"body corporate": s.207(1).
"collective investment scheme": s.75.
"open-ended investment company": s.75(8).
"operation": s.75(8).
"participants": s.75(2).
"recognised scheme": s.207(1).

GENERAL NOTE

This section (coupled with requirements prescribed under it) implements the obligation arising from the UCITS directive to recognise UCITS (undertakings for collective investment in transferable securities) constituted in the Member States of the EEC when those collective investment undertakings comply with the conditions stipulated in the directive. As to the position of schemes constituted in Gibraltar, see s.208.

The ban on promotion in s.76(1) does not apply to a recognised scheme, and the operator or trustee of such a scheme enjoys the privileges conferred by s.24 (authorised person status) and subs. (7) below.

Subs. (1)

The prescription of requirements under this subsection is a non-transferable function of the Secretary of State: s.114(5)(*e*).

Constituted: see subs. (8).

As to the prescription of requirements, see s.205(1).

Subs. (2)

If the requisite notice is given, recognition is automatic, unless the SIB gives notice that the proposed marketing arrangements do not comply with U.K. law. Such notice must be reasoned (subs. (4)).

Subs. (3)

Para. (a): The UCITS seeking recognition must submit a certificate of compliance with the conditions stipulated in the directive, issued by the responsible authorities in its home State.

Para. (b): As to the service of notices, see s.204.

Subss. (5), (6)

There is, in connection with the service or confirmation of notices by the Secretary of State, no right to require the case to be referred to the Financial Services Tribunal.

Subs. (7)

The only Conduct of Business Rules which apply to operating or acting as trustee of a recognised scheme, or to other investment business carried on in connection with or for the purposes of such a scheme, are those which address the matters mentioned in paras. (*a*) and (*b*).

Schemes authorised in designated countries or territories

87.—(1) Subject to subsection (3) below, a collective investment scheme which is not a recognised scheme by virtue of section 86 above but is managed in and authorised under the law of a country or territory outside the United Kingdom is a recognised scheme if—

(*a*) that country or territory is designated for the purposes of this section by an order made by the Secretary of State; and

(*b*) the scheme is of a class specified by the order.

(2) The Secretary of State shall not make an order designating any country or territory for the purposes of this section unless he is satisfied that the law under which collective investment schemes of the class to be specified by the order are authorised and supervised in that country or territory affords to investors in the United Kingdom protection at least equivalent to that provided for them by this Chapter in the case of an authorised unit trust scheme.

(3) A scheme shall not be recognised by virtue of this section unless the operator of the scheme gives written notice to the Secretary of State that he wishes it to be recognised; and the scheme shall not be recognised if within such period from receiving the notice as may be prescribed the Secretary of State notifies the operator that the scheme is not to be recognised.

(4) The notice given by the operator under subsection (3) above—

(*a*) shall contain the address of a place in the United Kingdom for the service on the operator of notices or other documents required or authorised to be served on him under this Act; and

(*b*) shall contain or be accompanied by such information and documents as may be prescribed.

(5) Section 85 above shall have effect in relation to a scheme recognised under this section as it has effect in relation to an authorised unit trust scheme, taking references to the manager as references to the operator and, in the case of an operator who is not an authorised person, references to publishing particulars as references to causing them to be published;

and regulations made by virtue of this subsection may make provision whereby compliance with any requirements imposed by or under the law of a country or territory designated under this section is treated as compliance with any requirement of the regulations.

(6) An order under subsection (1) above may contain such transitional provisions as the Secretary of State thinks necessary or expedient and shall be subject to annulment in pursuance of a resolution of either House of Parliament.

DEFINITIONS
"authorised person": s.207(1).
"collective investment scheme": s.75.
"operators": s.75(8).
"recognised scheme": s.207(1).

GENERAL NOTE
This section provides for the discretionary recognition of collective investment schemes (other than UCITS) managed in and authorised under the law of a *designated* country or territory outside the U.K. A precondition of designation is that the law of the country or territory in question affords scheme investors in the U.K. protection at least equivalent to that given by the legislation in the case of an authorised unit trust scheme.

The prohibition of promotion in s.76(1) does not apply to a scheme recognised by virtue of this section, but the operator does not enjoy the other privileges associated with UCITS (see ss.24 and 86(7)).

Subs. (1)
The making of a designation order under this subsection is a non-transferable function of the Secretary of State: s.114(5)(*e*).

As to the manner of making a designation order, see s.205(2) and subs. (6) of this section.

Subs. (2)
The Secretary of State must not make a designation order unless the criterion of equivalent protection is satisfied. The satisfaction of this condition does not, however, oblige him to make an order, and the imposition of further non-statutory conditions is contemplated by the government. These are: (i) "the scheme would have to be limited to investment in the same kind of assets within similar limits as United Kingdom authorised schemes"; (ii) "equivalent United Kingdom authorised schemes would have to be able to market freely in the country concerned"; and (iii) "there would have to be . . . satisfactory arrangements for collaboration between regulators": H.C. Standing Committee E, col. 471 (March 6, 1986).

Subs. (3)
If the requisite notice is given recognition is automatic, unless the SIB gives notice within a period to be prescribed that the scheme is not to be recognised. No particular ground upon which a decision not to recognise must be based is specified: contrast s.86(2).

As to the prescription of the relevant period, see s.205(1).

As to the procedure to be followed upon notification of non-recognition, see s.89(5)–(7).

Subs. (4)
As to the service of notices on the operator, see s.204.

Subs. (5).
This subsection applies the requirement to publish scheme particulars (s.85) to schemes recognised under this section, *mutatis mutandis.*

Where the operator of a scheme recognised under this section is not an authorised person, the scheme particulars must (by virtue of s.57) be published by some other person who is an authorised person. There is likely to be a requirement that the scheme particulars disclose that the scheme is a foreign one: H.L. Vol. 479, col. 586 (July 28, 1986).

As to the manner of making of regulations under this subsection, see s.205(2) as qualified by Sched. 9, paras. 4–9.

Other overseas schemes

88.—(1) The Secretary of State may, on the application of the operator of a scheme which—

(*a*) is managed in a country or territory outside the United Kingdom; but

(*b*) does not satisfy the requirements mentioned in section 86(1) above and in relation to which there is no relevant order under section 87(1) above,

make an order declaring the scheme to be a recognised scheme if it appears to him that it affords adequate protection to the participants, makes adequate provision for the matters dealt with by regulations under section 81 above and satisfies the following provisions of this section.

(2) The operator must be a body corporate or the scheme must take the form of an open-ended investment company.

(3) Subject to subsection (4) below, the operator and the trustee, if any, must be fit and proper persons to act as operator or, as the case may be, as trustee; and for that purpose the Secretary of State may take into account any matter relating to—

(*a*) any person who is or will be employed by or associated with the operator or trustee for the purposes of the scheme;

(*b*) any director or controller of the operator or trustee;

(*c*) any other body corporate in the same group as the operator or trustee and any director or controller of any such other body.

(4) Subsection (3) above does not apply to an operator or trustee who is an authorised person and not prohibited from acting as operator or trustee, as the case may be, by or under rules under section 48 above, by or under the rules of any recognised self-regulating organisation of which he is a member or by any prohibition imposed under section 65 above.

(5) If the operator is not an authorised person he must have a representative in the United Kingdom who is an authorised person and has power to act generally for the operator and to accept service of notices and other documents on his behalf.

(6) The name of the scheme must not be undesirable or misleading; and the purposes of the scheme must be reasonably capable of being successfully carried into effect.

(7) The participants must be entitled to have their units redeemed in accordance with the scheme at a price related to the net value of the property to which the units relate and determined in accordance with the scheme; but a scheme shall be treated as complying with this subsection if it requires the operator to ensure that a participant is able to sell his units on an investment exchange at a price not significantly different from that mentioned in this subsection.

(8) Subsections (2) to (5) of section 77 above shall apply also to an application under this section.

(9) So much of section 82 above as applies to an alteration of the scheme shall apply also to a scheme recognised under this section, taking references to the manager as references to the operator and with the omission of the requirement relating to the solicitor's certificate; and if the operator or trustee of any such scheme is to be replaced the operator or, as the case may be, the trustee, or in either case the person who is to replace him, shall give at least one month's notice to the Secretary of State.

(10) Section 85 above shall have effect in relation to a scheme recognised under this section as it has effect in relation to an authorised unit trust scheme, taking references to the manager as references to the operator and, in the case of an operator who is not an authorised person, references to publishing particulars as references to causing them to be published.

DEFINITIONS
"authorised person": s.207(1).
"authorised unit trust scheme": s.207(1).
"body corporate": s.207(1).
"controller": s.207(5).
"director": s.207(1).
"member": s.207(1).
"open-ended investment company": s.75(8).
"operator": s.75(8).
"participants": s.75(2).
"recognised scheme": s.207(1).
"recognised self-regulating organisation": s.207(1).
"rules": s.207(1).
"trustee": s.75(8).

GENERAL NOTE
This section provides for the discretionary recognition of collective investment schemes (other than UCITS and schemes in relation to which there is a designation order under the preceding section) managed in a country or territory outside the U.K. An order declaring a scheme to be recognised *may* be made if it affords adequate protection to the participants, if there is adequate provision regarding the constitution and management of the scheme, etc., and if the scheme satisfies the other requirements of this section.

The ban on promotion in s.76(1) does not apply to a scheme recognised by virtue of this section, but the operator deos not enjoy the other privileges associated with UCITS (see ss.24 and 86(7)).

Subs. (1)
The making of an order declaring the scheme to be a recognised scheme is a transferable function of the Secretary of State: contrast s.87(1).
As to the manner of making of such an order, see s.205(5).

Subs. (3)
Fit and proper persons: As to the meaning of this, see s.27(2).

Subs. (4)
The special fit and proper persons requirement under subs. (3) does not apply to an operator or trustee who is an authorised person (and hence, *ex hypothesi*, fit and proper) with an authorisation of appropriate scope. *Cf.* s.78(4).

Subs. (5)
As to the service of notices on the United Kingdom representative, see s.204.

Subss. (6), (7)
Virtually identical requirements apply to unit trust schemes for which authorisation is sought: s.78(5), (6).

Subs. (8)
The same application procedure applies as for unit trust schemes for which authorisation is sought.

Subs. (9)
So much of s.82 as applies to the replacement of a trustee does not apply to a scheme recognised under this section.

Subs. (10)
This subsection is identical to the first limb of s.87(5), *q.v.*

Refusal and revocation of recognition

89.—(1) The Secretary of State may at any time direct that a scheme shall cease to be recognised by virtue of section 87 above or revoke an order under section 88 above if it appears to him—

 (*a*) that it is undesirable in the interests of the participants or potential participants in the United Kingdom that the scheme should continue to be recognised;

(b) without prejudice to paragraph (a) above, that the operator or trustee of the scheme has contravened any provision of this Act or any rules or regulations made under it or, in purported compliance with any such provision, has furnished the Secretary of State with false, inaccurate or misleading information or has contravened any prohibition or requirement imposed under this Act; or

(c) in the case of an order under section 88 that any of the requirements for the making of the order are no longer satisfied.

(2) For the purposes of subsection (1)(a) above the Secretary of State may take into account any matter relating to the scheme the operator or trustee, a director or controller of the operator or trustee or any person employed by or associated with the operator or trustee in connection with the scheme.

(3) In the case of an operator or trustee who is a member of a recognised self-regulating organisation the rules, prohibitions and requirements referred to in subsection (1)(b) above include the rules of that organisation and any prohibition or requirement imposed by virtue of those rules.

(4) The Secretary of State may give such a direction or revoke such an order as is mentioned in subsection (1) above at the request of the operator or trustee of the scheme; but he may refuse to do so if he considers that any matter concerning the scheme should be investigated as a preliminary to a decision on the question whether the direction should be given or the order revoked or that the direction or revocation would not be in the interests of the participants.

(5) Where the Secretary of State proposes—

(a) to notify the operator of a scheme under section 87(3) above; or

(b) to give such a direction or to refuse to make or to revoke such an order as is mentioned in subsection (1) above,

he shall give the operator written notice of his intention to do so, stating the reasons for which he proposes to act and giving particulars of the rights conferred by subsection (6) below.

(6) A person on whom a notice is served under subsection (5) above may, within twenty-one days of the date of service, make written representations to the Secretary of State and, if desired, oral representations to a person appointed for that purpose by the Secretary of State.

(7) The Secretary of State shall have regard to any representations made in accordance with subsection (6) above in determining whether to notify the operator, give the direction or refuse to make or revoke the order, as the case may be.

DEFINITIONS
   "controller": s.207(5).
   "director": s.207(1).
   "member": s.207(1).
   "operator": s.75(8).
   "participants": s.75(2).
   "recognised self-regulating organisation": s.207(1).
   "rules": s.207(1).

GENERAL NOTE
   This section, which contains provisions broadly parallel to those of ss.79 and 80, sets out the grounds upon which the recognition of a recognised scheme (other than a UCITS) may be withdrawn by the SIB.
   Also by virtue of this section, where the SIB proposes to *withdraw* recognition of a scheme (other than a UCITS) it must afford an opportunity to make representations to the scheme operator. Where the SIB proposes to *refuse* recognition of a scheme in relation to which

there is a designation order under s.87 the same opportunity must be afforded. Where, however, the SIB proposes to *refuse* recognition of a scheme for which recognition is sought under s.88 (other overseas schemes) no such opportunity need be afforded. No right to require a case to be referred to the Financial Services Tribunal is conferred by this section.

Subs. (1)
Para. (*a*) must be read in conjunction with subs. (2). Para. (*b*) must be read in conjunction with subs. (3).
As to the manner of revoking an order under s.88, see s.205(5).

Subs. (4)
This subsection empowers the SIB to withdraw recognition at the request of the operator or trustee. It sets out two grounds upon which a request for withdrawal might be refused. It does not follow that the SIB is otherwise obliged to withdraw recognition on request.

Subs. (5)
Where the SIB proposes to withdraw the recognition of a scheme recognised under ss.87 or 88 it must give the operator written notice of its intention to do so. Where the SIB proposes to refuse to recognise a scheme in respect of which there is an application under s.87, again it must give notice. But where the refusal of an application under s.88 is contemplated, no notice need be given.

Subs. (6)
As to the service of a notice on an operator, see s.204.

Facilities and information in the United Kingdom

90.—(1) The Secretary of State may make regulations requiring operators of recognised schemes to maintain in the United Kingdom, or in such part or parts of it as may be specified in the regulations, such facilities as he thinks desirable in the interests of participants and as are specified in the regulations.

(2) The Secretary of State may by notice in writing require the operator of any recognised scheme to include such explanatory information as is specified in the notice in any investment advertisement issued or caused to be issued by him in the United Kingdom in which the scheme is named.

DEFINITIONS
"investment advertisement": s.57(2).
"operator": s.75(8).
"recognised scheme": s.207(1).

GENERAL NOTE
The powers conferred by this section are, of course, exercisable only in relation to overseas schemes.

Subs. (1)
Recognised schemes might, for example, be required to maintain in the U.K. facilities enabling participants to redeem their units in this country: H.L. Vol. 479, col. 589 (July 28, 1986).
As to the manner of making regulations under this subsection, see s.205(2) as qualified by Sched. 9, paras. 4–9.
As to the consequences of contravening such regulations, see ss.89(1)(*b*) and 95(1).

Subs. (2)
As to the consequences of contravening such a requirement, see ss.89(1)(*b*) and 95(2).

Powers of intervention

Directions

91.—(1) If it appears to the Secretary of State—
(*a*) that any of the requirements for the making of an order declaring

a scheme to be an authorised unit trust scheme are no longer satisfied;

(b) that the exercise of the power conferred by this subsection is desirable in the interests of participants or potential participants in the scheme; or

(c) without prejudice to paragraph (b) above, that the manager or trustee of such a scheme has contravened any provision of this Act or any rules or regulations made under it or, in purported compliance with any such provision, has furnished the Secretary of State with false, inaccurate or misleading information or has contravened any prohibition or requirement imposed under this Act,

he may give a direction under subsection (2) below.

(2) A direction under this subsection may—

(a) require the manager of the scheme to cease the issue or redemption, or both the issue and redemption, of units under the scheme on a date specified in the direction until such further date as is specified in that or another direction;

(b) require the manager and trustee of the scheme to wind it up by such date as is specified in the direction or, if no date is specified, as soon as practicable.

(3) The revocation of the order declaring an authorised unit trust scheme to be such a scheme shall not affect the operation of any direction under subsection (2) above which is then in force; and a direction may be given under that subsection in relation to a scheme in the case of which the order declaring it to be an authorised unit trust scheme has been revoked if a direction under that subsection was already in force at the time of revocation.

(4) Sections 60, 61 and 62 above shall have effect in relation to a contravention of a direction under subsection (2) above as they have effect in relation to any such contravention as is mentioned in those sections.

(5) It it appears to the Secretary of State—

(a) that the exercise of the power conferred by this subsection is desirable in the interests of participants or potential participants in a scheme recognised under section 87 or 88 above who are in the United Kingdom;

(b) without prejudice to paragraph (a) above, that the operator of such a scheme has contravened any provision of this Act or any rules or regulations made under it or, in purported compliance with any such provision, has furnished the Secretary of State with false, inaccurate or misleading information or has contravened any prohibition or requirement imposed under this Act; or

(c) that any of the requirements for the recognition of a scheme under section 88 above are no longer satisfied.

he may direct that the scheme shall not be a recognised scheme for a specified period or until the occurrence of a specified event or until specified conditions are complied with.

(6) For the purposes of subsections (1)(b) and (5)(a) above the Secretary of State may take into account any matter relating to the scheme, the manager, operator or trustee, a director or controller of the manager, operator or trustee or any person employed by or associated with the manager, operator or trustee in connection with the scheme.

(7) In the case of a manager, operator or trustee who is a member of a recognised self-regulating organisation the rules, prohibitions and requirements referred to in subsections (1)(c) and 5(b) above include the rules of that organisation and any prohibition or requirement imposed by virtue of those rules.

(8) The Secretary of State may, either of his own motion or on the application of the manager, trustee or operator of the scheme concerned, withdraw or vary a direction given under this section if it appears to the Secretary of State that it is no longer necessary for the direction to take effect or continue in force or, as the case may be, that it should take effect or continue in force in a different form.

DEFINITIONS
"authorised unit trust scheme": s.207(1).
"controller": s.207(5).
"director": s.207(1).
"member": s.207(1).
"operator": s.75(8).
"participant": s.75(2).
"recognised scheme": s.207(1).
"recognised self-regulating organisation": s.207(1).
"rules": s.207(1).
"trustee": s.75(8).

GENERAL NOTE
This section confers power to give certain directions upon the SIB—first, in relation to authorised unit trust schemes, and secondly in relation to recognised schemes (other than UCITS)—and sets out the grounds upon which directions may be given.

Subs. (1)
This subsection sets out the grounds upon which a direction may be given in relation to an authorised unit trust scheme. Para. (*b*) must be read in conjunction with subs. (6). Para. (*c*) must be read in conjunction with subs. (7).

Subs. (2)
A direction may require the suspension of the issue and/or redemption of units, or the winding-up of an authorised unit trust scheme.
As to the consequences of contravening such a direction, see subs. (4) below.

Subs. (3)
This subsection provides that a direction is unaffected by the revocation of a unit trust scheme's authorisation, and that revocation is no bar to subsequent directions where the first direction preceded revocation.

Subs. (5)
This subsection sets out the grounds upon which a direction may be given in relation to a recognised collective investment scheme (other than a UCITS). The effect of a direction is to suspend recognition. Para. (*b*) must be read in conjunction with subs. (7).

Notice of directions

92.—(1) The power to give a direction under section 91 above in relation to a scheme shall be exercisable by written notice served by the Secretary of State on the manager and trustee or, as the case may be, on the operator of the scheme and any such notice shall take effect on such date as is specified in the notice.

(2) If the Secretary of State refuses to withdraw or vary a direction on the application of the manager, trustee or operator of the scheme concerned he shall serve that person with a written notice of refusal.

(3) A notice giving a direction, or varying it otherwise than on the application of the manager, trustee or operator concerned, or refusing to withdraw or vary a direction on the application of such a person shall state the reasons for which the direction was given or varied or, as the case may be, why the application was refused.

(4) The Secretary of State may give public notice of a direction given by him under section 91 above and of any withdrawal or variation of such

a direction; and any such notice may, if the Secretary of State thinks fit, include a statement of the reasons for which the direction was given, withdrawn or varied.

DEFINITIONS
"operator": s.75(8).
"trustee": s.75(8).

GENERAL NOTE
This section requires the power to give directions under the preceding section to be exercised by written notice, and decisions made in connection with directions to be reasoned. As to the service of notices, see s.204.

Subs. (1)
A notice takes effect on the date specified in it and, accordingly, may be expressed so as to take immediate effect.

Applications to the court

93.—(1) In any case in which the Secretary of State has power to give a direction under section 91(2) above in relation to an authorised unit trust scheme or, by virtue of subsection (3) of that section, in relation to a scheme which has been such a scheme, he may apply to the court—
  (*a*) for an order removing the manager or trustee, or both the manager and trustee, of the scheme and replacing either or both of them with a person or persons nominated by him and appearing to him to satisfy the requirements of section 78 above; or
  (*b*) if it appears to the Secretary of State that no, or no suitable, person satisfying those requirements is available, for an order removing the manager or trustee, or both the manager and trustee, and appointing an authorised person to wind the scheme up.
(2) On an application under this section the court may make such order as it thinks fit; and the court may, on the application of the Secretary of State, rescind any such order as is mentioned in paragraph (*b*) of subsection (1) above and substitute such an order as is mentioned in paragraph (*a*) of that subsection.
(3) The Secretary of State shall give written notice of the making of an application under this section to the manager and trustee of the scheme concerned and take such steps as he considers appropriate for bringing the making of the application to the attention of the participants.
(4) The jurisdiction conferred by this section shall be exercisable by the High Court and the Court of Session.
(5) Section 83 above shall not apply to a manager appointed by an order made on an application under subsection (1)(*b*) above.

DEFINITIONS
"authorised person": s.207(1).
"authorised unit trust scheme": s.207(1).
"trustee": s.75(8).

GENERAL NOTE
This section empowers the SIB to apply to the court for an order removing the manager and/or trustee of an authorised unit trust scheme. Such an application may be made only on the basis of the grounds specified in s.91(1).

Subs. (1)
Requirements of s.78: The allusion is presumably to s.78(2)–(4).

Supplemental

Investigations

94.—(1) The Secretary of State may appoint one or more competent inspectors to investigate and report on—

(*a*) the affairs of, or of the manager or trustee of, any authorised unit trust scheme;

(*b*) the affairs of, or of the operator or trustee of, any recognised scheme so far as relating to activities carried on in the United Kingdom; or

(*c*) the affairs of, or of the operator or trustee of, any other collective investment scheme,

if it appears to the Secretary of State that it is in the interests of the participants to do so or that the matter is of public concern.

(2) An inspector appointed under subsection (1) above to investigate the affairs of, or of the manager, trustee or operator of, any scheme may also, if he thinks it necessary for the purposes of that investigation, investigate the affairs of, or of the manager, trustee or operator of, any other such scheme as is mentioned in that subsection whose manager, trustee or operator is the same person as the manager, trustee or operator of the first-mentioned scheme.

(3) Sections 434 to 436 of the Companies Act 1985 (production of documents and evidence to inspectors), except section 435(1)(*a*) and (*b*) and (2), shall apply in relation to an inspector appointed under this section as they apply to an inspector appointed under section 431 of that Act but with the modifications specified in subsection (4) below.

(4) In the provisions applied by subsection (3) above for any reference to a company or its affairs there shall be substituted a reference to the scheme under investigation by virtue of this section and the affairs mentioned in subsection (1) or (2) above and any reference to an officer or director of the company shall include a reference to any director of the manager, trustee or operator of the scheme.

(5) A person shall not under this section be required to disclose any information or produce any document which he would be entitled to refuse to disclose or produce on grounds of legal professional privilege in proceedings in the High Court or on grounds of confidentiality as between client and professional legal adviser in proceedings in the Court of Session except that a lawyer may be required to furnish the name and address of his client.

(6) Where a person claims a lien on a document its production under this section shall be without prejudice to the lien.

(7) Nothing in this section shall require a person carrying on the business of banking to disclose any information or produce any document relating to the affairs of a customer unless—

(*a*) the customer is a person who the inspector has reason to believe may be able to give information relevant to the investigation; and

(*b*) the Secretary of State is satisfied that the disclosure or production is necessary for the purposes of the investigation.

(8) An inspector appointed under this section may, and if so directed by the Secretary of State shall, make interim reports to the Secretary of State and on the conclusion of his investigation shall make a final report to him.

(9) Any such report shall be written or printed as the Secretary of State may direct and the Secretary of State may, if he thinks fit—

(*a*) furnish a copy, on request and on payment of the prescribed fee, to the manager, trustee or operators or any participant in a scheme under investigation or any other person whose conduct is referred to in the report; and

(b) cause the report to be published.

DEFINITIONS
"authorised unit trust scheme": s.207(1).
"collective investment scheme": s.75.
"director": s.207(1).
"operator": s.75(8).
"participant": s.75(2).
"trustee": s.75(8).

GENERAL NOTE
This section empowers the Secretary of State to appoint inspectors to investigate and report on the affairs of collective investment schemes or on the affairs of their trustees, managers or operators. The power to appoint inspectors is transferable to the SIB, but any transfer must be subject to the reservation that the power is to be exercisable by the Secretary of State concurrently with the Board: s.114(8).

Subss. (3), (4)
These subsections apply ss.434–36 of the Companies Act, with appropriate modifications, to investigations of collective investment schemes. Accordingly the inspectors can compel the production of documents and examine on oath company officers and directors and other persons possessed of relevant information. An answer given by a person to a question put to him in exercise of these powers may be used in evidence against him. See also s.199(2) (search warrants).

Subs. (7)
The business of banking: This phrase is not defined.

Contraventions

95.—(1) A person who contravenes any provision of this Chapter, a manager or trustee of an authorised unit trust scheme who contravenes any regulations made under section 81 above and a person who contravenes any other regulations made under this Chapter shall be treated as having contravened rules made under Chapter V of this Part of this Act or, in the case of a person who is an authorised person by virtue of his membership of a recognised self-regulating organisation or certification by a recognised professional body, the rules of that organisation or body.

(2) Subsection (1) above applies also to any contravention by the operator of a recognised scheme of a requirement imposed under section 90(2) above.

DEFINITIONS
"authorised person": s.207(1).
"authorised unit trust scheme": s.207(1).
"certification": s.207(1).
"member": s.207(1).
"recognised scheme": s.207(1).
"recognised professional body": s.207(1).
"recognised self-regulating organisation": s.207(1).
"rules": s.207(1).

GENERAL NOTE

Subs. (1)
In general, a person who contravenes any provision of Chapter VIII (collective investment schemes) or any regulations made under it is to be treated as having contravened rules made under Chapter V (conduct of investment business). Hence contraventions under Chapter VIII may bring into play s.60 (public statement as to person's misconduct), s.61 (injunctions and restitution orders) and s.62 (actions for damages). (There is an exception in favour of *participants* in an authorised unit trust scheme who contravene regulations made under s.81.)

In the case of a person authorised by virtue of membership of an SRO or certification by a recognised professional body, however, a contravention under Chapter VIII is to be treated as a contravention of the rules of the relevant SRO or professional body. It is only a contravention of particular rules of an SRO or a recognised professional body (*viz.* those rules specified in s.61(1)(*a*)(iv) and s.62(2)) that makes it possible to apply for an injunction or restitution order under s.61 and to sue for damages under s.62. Section 95(1) does not provide that a contravention of the Chapter VIII regulations is to be treated as a contravention of these particular rules. It seems therefore that these civil remedies are not available. The effect of s.95(1) in relation to members of SROs and RPBs is merely to make a contravention of the Chapter VIII regulations a disciplinary matter for the relevant SRO or RPB.

CHAPTER IX

THE TRIBUNAL

The Financial Services Tribunal

96.—(1) For the purposes of this Act there shall be a Tribunal known as the Financial Services Tribunal (in this Act referred to as "the Tribunal").

(2) There shall be a panel of not less than ten persons to serve as members of the Tribunal when nominated to do so in accordance with subsection (3) below; and that panel shall consist of—

(*a*) persons with legal qualifications appointed by the Lord Chancellor after consultation with the Lord Advocate, including at least one person qualified in Scots law; and

(*b*) persons appointed by the Secretary of State who appear to him to be qualified by experience or otherwise to deal with the cases that may be referred to the Tribunal.

(3) Where a case is referred to the Tribunal the Secretary of State shall nominate three persons from the panel to serve as members of the Tribunal in respect of that case and nominate one of them to be chairman.

(4) The person nominated to be chairman of the Tribunal in respect of any case shall be a person with legal qualifications and, so far as practicable, at least one of the other members shall be a person with recent practical experience in business relevant to the case.

(5) If while a case is being dealt with by the Tribunal one of the three persons serving as members in respect of that case becomes unable to act the case may, with the consent of the Secretary of State and of the person or persons at whose request the case was referred to the Tribunal, be dealt with by the other two members.

(6) Schedule 6 to this Act shall have effect as respects the Tribunal and its proceedings.

GENERAL NOTE

This section makes provision for the establishment of a Financial Services Tribunal and for the appointment of a panel of members. In individual cases the Tribunal will consist of a legally qualified chairman and two other members of the panel. Schedule 6 makes further provision in relation to the Tribunal.

References to the Tribunal

97.—(1) Any person—

(*a*) on whom a notice is served under section 29, 34, 59(4), 60(2) or 70 above; or

(*b*) on whom a copy of a notice under section 29, 34, 60(2) or 70 above is served or on whom the Secretary of State considers that a copy of such a notice would have been served if it had been practicable to do so,

may within twenty-eight days of the date of service of the notice require the Secretary of State to refer the matter to which the notice relates to the Tribunal and, subject to the provisions of this section, the Secretary of State shall refer that matter accordingly.

(2) The Secretary of State need not refer a matter to the Tribunal at the request of the person on whom a notice was served under section 29, 34, 59(4) or 60(2) above if within the period mentioned in subsection (1) above he—

    (*a*) decides to grant the application or, as the case may be, decides not to withdraw or suspend the authorisation, give the direction or publish the statement to which the notice relates; and

    (*b*) gives written notice of his decision to that person.

(3) The Secretary of State need not refer a matter to the Tribunal at the request of the person on whom a notice is served under section 70 above if—

    (*a*) that matter is the refusal of an application for the rescission or variation of a prohibition or requirement and within the period mentioned in subsection (1) above he—

        (i) decides to grant the application; and

        (ii) gives written notice of his decision to that person; or

    (*b*) that matter is the imposition or variation of a prohibition or requirement, being a prohibition, requirement or variation which has not yet taken effect, and within the period mentioned in subsection (1) above and before the prohibition, requirement or variation takes effect he—

        (i) decides to rescind the prohibition or requirement or decides not to make the variation; and

        (ii) gives written notice of his decision to that person.

(4) Where the notice served on a person under section 29 or 34 above—

    (*a*) proposed the withdrawal of an authorisation or the giving of a direction under section 33(1)(*a*) above; or

    (*b*) proposed the suspension of an authorisation or the giving of a direction under section 33(1)(*b*) above,

and at any time within the period mentioned in subsection (1) above the Secretary of State serves a new notice on that person in substitution for that previously served, then, if the substituted notice complies with subsection (5) below, subsection (1) above shall have effect in relation to the substituted notice instead of the original notice as if the period there mentioned were twenty-eight days after the date of service of the original notice or fourteen days after the date of service of the substituted notice, whichever ends later.

(5) A notice served in substitution for a notice within subsection (4)(*a*) above complies with this subsection if it proposes—

    (*a*) the suspension of an authorisation or the giving of a direction under section 33(1)(*b*) above; or

    (*b*) the exercise of the power conferred by section 60 above;

and a notice served in substitution for a notice within subsection (4)(*b*) above complies with this subsection if it proposes a less severe suspension or direction under section 33(1)(*b*) or the exercise of the power conferred by section 60 above.

(6) The reference of the imposition or variation of a prohibition or requirement under Chapter VI of this Part of this Act to the Tribunal shall not affect the date on which it comes into effect.

DEFINITION
"the Tribunal": s.207(1).

GENERAL NOTE
This section governs references to the Tribunal.

Subs. (1)
The following may require the SIB to refer their case to the Tribunal.
(a) *applicants* whose applications the SIB propose to refuse, namely:
    (i) applicants for direct authorisation (s.28);
    (ii) applicants for the variation of the suspension of direct authorisation (s.29);
    (iii) applicants for the variation of the suspension of authorisation under section 31 (s.34);
    (iv) applicants for consent to employment (s.59(4));
    (v) applicants for variation of consent to employment s.59(4));
    (vi) applicants for rescission or variation of prohibitions or requirements imposed under Chapter VI (s.70);
(b) *persons*
    (i) whose direct authorisation the SIB proposes to suspend or withdraw (s.29);
    (ii) whose authorisation under section 31 the SIB proposes to terminate or suspend (s.34);
    (iii) whom the SIB proposes to disqualify from employment (s.59(4));
    (iv) in respect of whom the SIB proposes to make a public statement (s.60(2));
    (v) upon whom the SIB has imposed a prohibition or requirement under Chapter VI (s.70);
    (vi) in respect of whom the SIB varies a prohibition or requirement imposed under Chapter VI (s.70); and
(c) *third parties* named in notices under sections 29, 34, 60(2) or 70.
The right to require the SIB to refer a case to the Tribunal is exercisable within 28 days. If within the period, the SIB reverses its decision, it need not refer the case to the Tribunal (subss. (2), (3)). Otherwise it must. In cases (b)(i) and (ii) above, if the SIB decides within the 28 day period to adopt a less severe course of action the period may be extended (subss. (4), (5)). In calculating the relevant period no account is taken of public holidays (s.207(10)). As to the service of notices, see section 204.

Decisions on references by applicant or authorised person etc.

98.—(1) Where a case is referred to the Tribunal at the request of a person within section 97(1)(*a*) above the Tribunal shall—
    (*a*) investigate the case; and
    (*b*) make a report to the Secretary of State stating what would in its opinion be the appropriate decision in the matter and the reasons for that opinion;
and it shall be the duty of the Secretary of State to decide the matter forthwith in accordance with the Tribunal's report.
    (2) Where the matter referred to the Tribunal is the refusal of an application the Tribunal may under this section report that the appropriate decision would be to grant or refuse the application or—
    (*a*) in the case of an application for the variation of a suspension, direction, consent, prohibition or requirement, to vary it in a specified manner;
    (*b*) in the case of an application for the rescission of a prohibition or requirement, to vary the prohibition or requirement in a specified manner.
    (3) Where the matter referred to the Tribunal is any action of the Secretary of State other than the refusal of an application the Tribunal may report that the appropriate decision would be—
    (*a*) to take or not to take the action taken or proposed to be taken by the Secretary of State or to take any other action that he could take under the provision in question; or
    (*b*) to take instead or in addition any action that he could take in the

case of the person concerned under any one or more of the provisions mentioned in subsection (4) below other than that under which he was acting or proposing to act.

(4) Those provisions are sections 28, 33 and 60 above and Chapter VI of this Part of this Act; and sections 29, 34, 60(2) and (3) and 70(2) and (4) above shall not apply to any action taken by the Secretary of State in accordance with the Tribunal's report.

(5) The Tribunal shall send a copy of its report under this section to the person at whose request the case was referred to it; and the Secretary of State shall serve him with a written notice of the decision made by him in accordance with the report.

DEFINITION
"the Tribunal": s.207(1).

GENERAL NOTE
This section governs the disposal of references other than those made at the instance of third parties. The disposal of third parties' references is governed by section 99.

Subs. (1)
This subsection imposes a duty on the Tribunal to investigate and report, and on the SIB to implement the Tribunal's report. Note that the Tribunal's report is to be implemented forthwith.

Subs. (2)
This subsection sets out the options open to the Tribunal in reporting on applications. For a list of the relevant applications, see the annotations to section 97(1).

Subs. (3)
This subsection sets out the options open to the Tribunal in reporting on matters other than applications. For a list of the relevant matters, see the annotation to section 97(1).

Subs. (4)
Section 28: Power to suspend or withdraw direct authorisation.
Section 33: Power to suspend or terminate authorisation under section 31.
Section 60: Power to issue a public statement.
Chapter VI: Powers of intervention.
And sections 29 . . . shall not apply: In implementing the Tribunal's report, the SIB is not obliged to give notice in accordance with those provisions.

Subs. (5)
As to the service of notices, see section 204.

Decisions on references by third parties

99. Where a case is referred to the Tribunal at the request of a person within section 97(1)(*b*) above the Tribunal shall report to the Secretary of State whether the reasons stated in the notice in question which relate to that person are substantiated; and the Tribunal shall send a copy of the report to that person and to the person on whom the notice was served.

DEFINITION
"the Tribunal": s.207(1).

GENERAL NOTE
This section governs the disposal of references made at the instance of third parties.

Withdrawal of references

100.—(1) A person who has required a case to be referred to the Tribunal may at any time before the conclusion of the proceedings before the Tribunal withdraw the reference.

(2) The Secretary of State may at any such time withdraw any reference made at the request of a person on whom a notice was served under any of the provisions mentioned in subsection (1)(a) of section 97 above if he—

(a) decides as mentioned in subsection (2)(a) or (3)(a)(i) or (b)(i) of that section; and

(b) gives such a notice as is mentioned in subsection (2)(b) or (3)(a)(ii) or (b)(ii) of that section;

but a reference shall not be withdrawn by virtue of such a decision and notice as are mentioned in paragraph (b) of subsection (3) unless the decision is made and the notice is given before the prohibition, requirement or variation has taken effect.

(3) Where a case is withdrawn from the Tribunal under this section the Tribunal shall not further investigate the case or make a report under section 98 or 99 above; but where the reference is withdrawn otherwise than by the Secretary of State he may require the Tribunal to make a report to him on the results of its investigation up to the time when the reference was withdrawn.

(4) Where two or more persons have required a case to be referred to the Tribunal the withdrawal of the reference by one or more of them shall not affect the functions of the Tribunal as respects the case so far as relating to a person who has not withdrawn the reference.

(5) Where a person on whom a notice was served under section 29, 34 or 60 above withdraws a case from the Tribunal subsection (5) of each of those sections shall apply to him as if he had not required the case to be referred.

DEFINITION
"the Tribunal": s.207(1).

GENERAL NOTE
This section makes provision for the withdrawal of references.

Subs. (1)
Note subss. (3)–(5).

Subs. (2)
The Board may withdraw the reference if it reverses its decision.
But a reference shall not be withdrawn: This proviso preserves the jurisdiction of the Tribunal where a prohibition or requirement imposed or varied under Chapter VI has taken effect.

Subs. (3)
Note that the first part of this subsection does not make sense. Presumably the intention is that where a reference is withdrawn by the Secretary of State the Tribunal should not consider it further.

Reports

101.—(1) In preparing its report on any case the Tribunal shall have regard to the need to exclude, so far as practicable, any matter which relates to the affairs of a particular person (not being a person who required or could have required the case to be referred to the Tribunal) where the publication of that matter would or might, in the opinion of the Tribunal, seriously and prejudicially affect the interests of that person.

(2) The Secretary of State may, in such cases as he thinks fit, publish the report of the Tribunal and offer copies of any such report for sale.

(3) The Secretary of State may, on request and on payment of the prescribed fee, supply a copy of a report of the Tribunal to any person whose conduct is referred to in the report or whose interests as a client or

creditor are affected by the conduct of a person to whom the proceedings before the Tribunal related.

(4) If the Secretary of State is of opinion that there is good reason for not disclosing any part of a report he may cause that part to be omitted from the report as published under subsection (2) or from the copy of it supplied under subsection (3) above.

(5) A copy of a report of the Tribunal endorsed with a certificate signed by or on behalf of the Secretary of State stating that it is a true copy shall be admissible as evidence of the opinion of the Tribunal as to any matter referred to in the report; and a certificate purporting to be signed as aforesaid shall be deemed to have been duly signed unless the contrary is shown.

DEFINITIONS
"prescribed": s.207(1).
"the Tribunal": s.207(1).

CHAPTER X

INFORMATION

Register of authorised persons and recognised organisations etc.

102.—(1) The Secretary of State shall keep a register containing an entry in respect of—

(a) each person who is an authorised person by virtue of an authorisation granted by the Secretary of State;

(b) each other person who appears to him to be an authorised person by virtue of any provision of this Part of this Act;

(c) each recognised self-regulating organisation, recognised professional body, recognised investment exchange and recognised clearing house;

(d) each authorised unit trust scheme and recognised scheme;

(e) each person in respect of whom a direction under section 59 above is in force.

(2) The entry in respect of each authorised person shall consist of—

(a) a statement of the provision by virtue of which he is an authorised person;

(b) in the case of a person who is an authorised person by virtue of membership of a recognised self-regulating organisation or certification by a recognised professional body, the name and address of the organisation or body;

(c) in the case of a person who is an authorised person by virtue of section 25 or 31 above, information as to the services which that person holds himself out as able to provide;

(d) in the case of a person who is an authorised person by virtue of section 31 above, the address notified to the Secretary of State under section 32 above;

(e) in the case of a person who is an authorised person by virtue of any provision other than section 31 above, the date on which he became an authorised person by virtue of that provision; and

(f) such other information as the Secretary of State may determine.

(3) The entry in respect of each such organisation, body, exchange or clearing house as is mentioned in subsection (1)(c) above shall consist of its name and address and such other information as the Secretary of State may determine.

(4) The entry in respect of each such scheme as is mentioned in subsection (1)(*d*) above shall consist of its name and, in the case of an authorised unit trust scheme, the name and address of the manager and trustee and, in the case of a recognised scheme, the name and address of the operator and of any representative of the operator in the United Kingdom and, in either case, such other information as the Secretary of State may determine.

(5) The entry in respect of each such person as is mentioned in subsection (1)(*e*) above shall include particulars of any consent for that person's employment given by the Secretary of State.

(6) Where it appears to the Secretary of State that any person in respect of whom there is an entry in the register by virtue of subsection (1)(*a*) or (*b*) above has ceased to be an authorised person (whether by death, by withdrawal or other cessation of his authorisation, as a result of his ceasing to be a member of a recognised self-regulating organisation or otherwise) the Secretary of State shall make a note to that effect in the entry together with the reason why the person in question is no longer an authorised person.

(7) Where—

(*a*) an organisation, body, exchange or clearing house in respect of which there is an entry in the register by virtue of paragraph (*c*) of subsection (1) above has ceased to be recognised or ceased to exist;

(*b*) an authorised unit trust scheme or recognised scheme in respect of which there is an entry in the register by virtue of paragraph (*d*) of that subsection has ceased to be authorised or recognised; or

(*c*) the direction applying to a person in respect of whom there is an entry in the register by virtue of paragraph (*e*) of that subsection has ceased to have effect,

the Secretary of State shall make a note to that effect in the entry.

(8) An entry in respect of which a note is made under subsection (6) or (7) above may be removed from the register at the end of such period as the Secretary of State thinks appropriate.

Definitions
    "authorised person": s.207(1).
    "authorised unit trust scheme": s.207(1).
    "operator": s.207(1).
    "recognised clearing house": s.207(1).
    "recognised investment exchange": s.207(1).
    "recognised professional body": s.207(1).
    "recognised self-regulating organisation": s.207(1).
    "recognised scheme": s.207(1).
    "trustee": s.207(1).

General Note
    This section requires the SIB to maintain a register of information about authorised persons, recognised organisations, authorised unit trust schemes, recognised schemes and individuals who are the subject of a disqualification direction. As to inspection of the register see section 103.

Inspection of register

103.—(1) The information contained in the entries included in the register otherwise than by virtue of section 102(1)(*e*) above shall be open to inspection; and the Secretary of State may publish the information contained in those entries in any form he thinks appropriate and may offer copies of any such information for sale.

(2) A person shall be entitled to ascertain whether there is an entry in the register by virtue of subsection (1)(*e*) of section 102 above (not being an entry in respect of which there is a note under subsection (7) of that

section) in respect of a particular person specified by him and, if there is such an entry, to inspect it.

(3) Except as provided by subsection (2) above the information contained in the register by virtue of section 102(1)(*e*) above shall not be open to inspection by any person unless he satisfies the Secretary of State that he has a good reason for seeking the information.

(4) A person to whom information is made available by the Secretary of State under subsection (3) above shall not, without the consent of the Secretary of State or of the person to whom the information relates, make use of it except for the purpose for which it was made available.

(5) Information which by virtue of this section is open to inspection shall be open to inspection free of charge but only at such times and places as the Secretary of State may appoint; and a person entitled to inspect any information may obtain a certified copy of it from the Secretary of State on payment of the prescribed fee.

(6) The register may be kept by the Secretary of State in such form as he thinks appropriate with a view to facilitating inspection of the information which it contains.

GENERAL NOTE
This section makes provision regarding inspection of the register. Except in the case of disqualification directions, there is no restriction on access to the register.

Subs. (2)
Note that the right is confined to the inspection of entries in respect of specified persons.

Subs. (3)
To exercise the general right of inspection conferred by this subsection, the person must have "good reason" for doing so. A person who was uncertain about the disqualified person's name would have good reason, as would a *bona fide* investigative journalist. (H.C. Standing Committee E, col. 484.)

Power to call for information

104.—(1) The Secretary of State may by notice in writing require a person who is authorised to carry on investment business by virtue of section 22, 24, 25 or 31 above to furnish him with such information as he may reasonably require for the exercise of his functions under this Act.

(2) The Secretary of State may by notice in writing require a recognised self-regulating organisation, recognised professional body, recognised investment exchange or recognised clearing house to furnish him with such information as he may reasonably require for the exercise of his functions under this Act.

(3) The Secretary of State may require any information which he requires under this section to be furnished within such reasonable time and verified in such manner as he may specify.

(4) Sections 60, 61 and 62 above shall have effect in relation to a contravention of a requirement imposed under subsection (1) above as they have effect in relation to a contravention of the provisions to which those sections apply.

DEFINITIONS
"recognised clearing house": s.207(1).
"recognised investment exchange": s.207(1).
"recognised professional body": s.207(1).
"recognised self-regulating organisation": s.207(1).

GENERAL NOTE
This section confers a power on the SIB, exercisable by notice, to call for information. As to the service of notices, see section 204.

Subs. (1)

By virtue of . . . 31: i.e. authorised insurers, operators or trustees of recognised collective investment schemes, directly authorised persons and persons authorised in other Member States.

Reasonably: Note the qualification.

As to contraventions of requirements imposed under this subsection, see subs. (4).

Subs. (2)

Reasonably: Note the qualification.

Investigation powers

105.—(1) The powers of the Secretary of State under this section shall be exercisable in any case in which it appears to him that there is good reason to do so for the purpose of investigating the affairs, or any aspect of the affairs, of any person so far as relevant to any investment business which he is or was carrying on or appears to the Secretary of State to be or to have been carrying on.

(2) Those powers shall not be exercisable for the purpose of investigating the affairs of any exempted person unless he is an appointed representative or the investigation is in respect of investment business in respect of which he is not an exempted person and shall not be exercisable for the purpose of investigating the affairs of a member of a recognised self-regulating organisation or a person certified by a recognised professional body in respect of investment business in the carrying on of which he is subject to its rules unless—

(a) that organisation or body has requested the Secretary of State to investigate those affairs; or

(b) it appears to him that the organisation or body is unable or unwilling to investigate them in a satisfactory manner.

(3) The Secretary of State may require the person whose affairs are to be investigated ("the person under investigation") or any connected person to attend before the Secretary of State at a specified time and place and answer questions or otherwise furnish information with respect to any matter relevant to the investigation.

(4) The Secretary of State may require the person under investigation or any other person to produce at a specified time and place any specified documents which appear to the Secretary of State to relate to any matter relevant to the investigation; and—

(a) if any such documents are produced, the Secretary of State may take copies or extracts from them or require the person producing them or any connected person to provide an explanation of any of them;

(b) if any such documents are not produced, the Secretary of State may require the person who was required to produce them to state, to the best of his knowledge and belief, where they are.

(5) A statement by a person in compliance with the requirement imposed by virtue of this section may be used in evidence against him.

(6) A person shall not under this section be required to disclose any information or produce any document which he would be entitled to refuse to disclose or produce on grounds of legal professional privilege in proceedings in the High Court or on grounds of confidentiality as between client and professional legal adviser in proceedings in the Court of Session except that a lawyer may be required to furnish the name and address of his client.

(7) The Secretary of State shall not require a recognised bank or licensed institution within the meaning of the Banking Act 1979 to disclose any information or produce any document relating to the affairs of a customer unless the Secretary of State considers it necessary to do so for

the purpose of investigating any investment business carried on, or appearing to the Secretary of State to be carried on or to have been carried on, by the bank, institution or customer or, if the customer is a related company of the person under investigation, by that person.

(8) Where a person claims a lien on a document its production under this section shall be without prejudice to the lien.

(9) In this section—

"connected person", in relation to any other person means—

    (a) any person who is or was that other person's partner, employee, agent, appointed representative, banker, auditor or solicitor; and

    (b) where the other person is a body corporate, any person who is or was a director, secretary or controller of that body corporate or of another body corporate of which it is or was a subsidiary; and

    (c) where the other person is an unincorporated association, any person who is or was a member of the governing body or an officer or controller of the association; and

    (d) where the other person is an appointed representative, any person who is or was his principal; and

    (e) where the other person is the person under investigation (being a body corporate), any related company of that body corporate and any person who is a connected person in relation to that company;

"documents" includes information recorded in any form and, in relation to information recorded otherwise than in legible form, references to its production include references to producing a copy of the information in legible form;

"related company", in relation to a person under investigation (being a body corporate), means any other body corporate which is or at any material time was—

    (a) a holding company or subsidiary of the person under investigation;

    (b) a subsidiary of a holding company of that person; or

    (c) a holding company of a subsidiary of that person,

and whose affairs it is in the Secretary of State's opinion necessary to investigate for the purpose of investigating the affairs of that person.

(10) Any person who without reasonable excuse fails to comply with a requirement imposed on him under this section shall be guilty of an offence and liable on summary conviction to imprisonment for a term not exceeding six months or to a fine not exceeding the fifth level on the standard scale or to both.

DEFINITIONS

"appointed representative": s.44(2).
"body corporate": s.207(1).
"carrying on investment business": s.1(3).
"certified": s.207(1).
"connected person": subs. (9).
"controller": s.207(5).
"documents": subs. (9).
"exempted person": s.207(1).
"holding company": s.207(8).
"member": s.8(2).
"principal": s.44(2).
"recognised professional body": s.207(1).
"recognised self-regulating organisation": s.207(1).
"related company": subs. (9).
"subsidiary": s.207(8).

General Note
This section empowers the SIB to investigate the affairs of a person who is, or was, or appears to be carrying on investment business, and to impose requirements on persons for the purpose of the investigation. Failure to comply with a requirement is an offence (subs. 10). It may also provide grounds for the withdrawal of authorisation. These powers are also exercisable by the Secretary of State (s.114(8)).

Subs. (2)
Note that the SIB has no general power to investigate the affairs of exempted persons (other than appointed representatives), members of SROs or persons certified by RPBs.

Subss. (3), (4)
These subsections set out the SIB's powers. Note that the power to compel attendance, answers to questions and the provision of information is exercisable in respect of persons under investigation and connected persons only, whereas the power to require the production of documents is exercisable in respect of anyone. Where documents are not produced, a search warrant may be obtained (s.199(1)(*b*)).

Subss. (6), (7)
These subsections impose restrictions on the Board's power to require the disclosure of information and the production of documents. Note that the confidentiality of a bank's customer's affairs may be overridden where the SIB considers it "necessary".

Exercise of investigation powers by officer etc.

106.—(1) The Secretary of State may authorise any officer of his or any other competent person to exercise on his behalf all or any of the powers conferred by section 105 above but no such authority shall be granted except for the purpose of investigating the affairs, or any aspects of the affairs, of a person specified in the authority.

(2) No person shall be bound to comply with any requirement imposed by a person exercising powers by virtue of an authority granted under this section unless he has, if required to do so, produced evidence of his authority.

(3) Where the Secretary of State authorises a person other than one of his officers to exercise any powers by virtue of this section that person shall make a report to the Secretary of State in such manner as he may require on the exercise of those powers and the results of exercising them.

General Note
This section authorises the SIB to appoint competent persons to exercise its powers under section 105. This power is also exercisable by the Secretary of State (s.114(8)).

Chapter XI

Auditors

Appointment of auditors

107.—(1) The Secretary of State may make rules requiring a person who is authorised to carry on investment business by virtue of section 25 or 31 above and who, apart from the rules, is not required by or under any enactment to appoint an auditor to appoint as an auditor a person satisfying such conditions as to qualifications and otherwise as may be specified in or imposed under the rules.

(2) Rules under this section may make provision—
(*a*) specifying the manner in which and the time within which an auditor is to be appointed;

(*b*) requiring the Secretary of State to be notified of any such appointment and enabling the Secretary of State to make an appointment if no appointment is made or notified as required by the rules;

(*c*) with respect to the remuneration of an auditor appointed under the rules;

(*d*) with respect to the term of office, removal and resignation of any such auditor;

(*e*) requiring any such auditor who is removed, resigns or is not reappointed to notify the Secretary of State whether there are any circumstances connected with his ceasing to hold office which he considers should be brought to the Secretary of State's attention.

(3) An auditor appointed under the rules shall in accordance with the rules examine and report on the accounts of the authorised person in question and shall for that purpose have such duties and powers as are specified in the rules.

DEFINITIONS
"authorised person": s.207(1).
"carry on investment business": s.1(3).

GENERAL NOTE
This section empowers the SIB to make rules requiring directly authorised persons and persons authorised in other Member States to appoint an auditor.

Subs. (1)
The rules will not apply to persons already required by or under any enactment to appoint an auditor. (So, for example, they will not apply to United Kingdom registered companies.) A person incorporated or having his head office outside the United Kingdom is, however, subject to s.110 whether or not he is already required to appoint an auditor.
The rules will not apply to persons authorised exclusively by virtue of their membership of an SRO or RPB.
As to the manner of making the rules, see s.205(2) as qualified by Sched. 9, paras. 4–9.

Subs. (2)
It is to be anticipated that the rules made will be comparable with the provisions of the Companies Act 1985 (ss.384–91) respecting the appointment, removal and resignation of auditors.

Power to require second audit

108.—(1) If in any case it appears to the Secretary of State that there is good reason to do so he may direct any person who is authorised to carry on investment business by virtue of section 25 or 31 above to submit for further examination by a person approved by the Secretary of State—

(*a*) any accounts on which that person's auditor has reported or any information given under section 52 or 104 above which has been verified by that auditor; or

(*b*) such matters contained in any such accounts or information as are specified in the direction;

and the person making the further examination shall report his conclusions to the Secretary of State.

(2) Any further examination and report required by a direction under this section shall be at the expense of the authorised person concerned and shall be carried out and made within such time as is specified in the direction or within such further time as the Secretary of State may allow.

(3) The person carrying out an examination under this section shall have all the powers that were available to the auditor; and it shall be the duty of the auditor to afford him all such assistance as he may require.

(4) Where a report made under this section relates to accounts which under any enactment are required to be sent to or made available for inspection by any person or to be delivered for registration, the report, or any part of it (or a note that such a report has been made) may be similarly sent, made available or delivered by the Secretary of State.

DEFINITIONS
"authorised person": s.207(1).
"carry on investment business": s.1(3).

GENERAL NOTE
This section empowers the SIB to direct directly authorised persons and persons authorised in other Member States to submit (at their own expense) to a second audit, the conclusions of which are to be reported to the SIB.

Subs. (1)
Good reason: A second audit might be required, for example, if the work of the original auditor appears to be substandard: H.L. Vol. 479, col. 605 (July 28, 1986).

Subs. (3)
The original auditor's duty to co-operate is enforceable in the manner specified in s.111(2).

Communication by auditor with supervisory authorities

109.—(1) No duty to which an auditor of an authorised person may be subject shall be regarded as contravened by reason of his communicating in good faith to the Secretary of State, whether or not in response to a request from him, any information or opinion on a matter of which the auditor has become aware in his capacity as auditor of that person and which is relevant to any functions of the Secretary of State under this Act.

(2) If it appears to the Secretary of State that any auditor or class of auditor to whom subsection (1) above applies is not subject to satisfactory rules made or guidance issued by a professional body specifying circumstances in which matters are to be communicated to the Secretary of State as mentioned in that subsection the Secretary of State may himself make rules applying to that auditor or that class of auditor and specifying such circumstances; and it shall be the duty of an auditor to whom the rules made by the Secretary of State apply to communicate a matter to the Secretary of State in the circumstances specified by the rules.

(3) The matters to be communicated to the Secretary of State in accordance with any such rules or guidance may include matters relating to persons other than the authorised person.

(4) No such rules as are mentioned in subsection (2) above shall be made by the Secretary of State unless a draft of them has been laid before and approved by a resolution of each House of Parliament.

(5) This section applies to—
 (*a*) the communication by an auditor to a recognised self-regulating organisation or recognised professional body of matters relevant to its function of determining whether a person is a fit and proper person to carry on investment business; and
 (*b*) the communication to such an organisation or body or any other authority or person of matters relevant to its or his function of determining whether a person is complying with the rules applicable to his conduct of investment business,

as it applies to the communication to the Secretary of State of matters relevant to his functions under this Act.

DEFINITIONS
"authorised person": s.207(1).
"recognised professional body": s.207(1).
"recognised self-regulating organisation": s.207(1).

GENERAL NOTE

The aim of this section is to facilitate communication between solicitors and supervisory authorities. Accordingly, relevant communications made by an auditor in good faith to the appropriate supervisory authority are not to be regarded as a breach of any duty (*e.g.* of confidentiality) to which the auditor may be subject.

Subs. (1)

This subsection covers communications to the Secretary of State (and by implication, to the SIB). The test of relevance is satisfied if the information or opinion communicated is relevant to any of the Secretary of State's functions under the Act. Note that no *statutory duty* to communicate is imposed upon the auditor.

Subs. (2)

The government expects the various accountancy bodies to make rules or issue guidance specifying circumstances (not "the" circumstances) in which matters are to be communicated to the Secretary of State. Under the specified circumstances the auditor may be under a professional duty to communicate to the Secretary of State. Communications unprompted by the professional body's rules on guidance are not, however, excluded from the benefit conferred by subs. (1).

If some auditors are left uncovered by satisfactory rules or guidance, the Secretary of State may himself make rules applicable to them. Auditors subject to these rules will be under a statutory duty to communicate to the Secretary of State in the circumstances the rules specify. As to the consequences of failing to comply with this duty, see s.111(3), (4).

The making of rules under this subsection is a non-transferable function of the Secretary of State: s.114(5)(*g*). As to the manner of its exercise, see s.205(2) and subs. (4) of this section.

Subs. (5)

This subsection extends the coverage of the section to a communication by an auditor (*a*) to an SRO or RBP relevant to its function of determining whether a person is "fit and proper," and (*b*) to an SRO or RBP "or any other authority or person" relevant to its function of monitoring compliance with the applicable rules for the conduct of investment business.

Any other authority or person: This covers communications to a "lead regulator" where an authorised person is subject to the supervision of several regulatory authorities. See Securities and Investments Board/Marketing of Investments Board Organising Committee, *Regulation of Investment Business: The New Framework* (December 1985), paras. 1.18–1.23. See also Sched. 2, para. 4(2) and Sched. 3, para. 4(4).

Fit and proper person: see s.27(2).

Overseas business

110.—(1) A person incorporated or having his head office outside the United Kingdom who is authorised as mentioned in subsection (1) of section 107 above may, whether or not he is required to appoint an auditor apart from the rules made under that subsection, appoint an auditor in accordance with those rules in respect of the investment business carried on by him in the United Kingdom and in that event that person shall be treated for the purposes of this Chapter as the auditor of that person.

(2) In the case of a person to be appointed as auditor of a person incorporated or having his head office outside the United Kingdom the conditions as to qualifications imposed by or under the rules made under that section may be regarded as satisfied by qualifications obtained outside the United Kingdom which appear to the Secretary of State to be equivalent.

(3) A person incorporated or having his head office outside the United Kingdom shall not be regarded for the purposes of section 25 above as a fit and proper person to carry on investment business unless—

    (*a*) he has appointed an auditor in accordance with rules made under section 107 above in respect of the investment business carried on by him in the United Kingdom; or (*b*) he has an auditor having qualifications, powers and duties appearing to the Secretary of State to be equivalent to those applying to an auditor appointed in accordance with those rules,

and, in either case, the auditor is able and willing to communicate with the Secretary of State and other bodies and persons as mentioned in section 109 above.

GENERAL NOTE
The effect of this section is that a person incorporated or having his head office outside the United Kingdom must have, in respect of his United Kingdom investment business, an auditor who is able and willing to communicate with the supervisory authorites as mentioned in the preceding section. That auditor must either have been appointed in accordance with the rules made under s.107 or have qualifications, powers and duties equivalent to those stipulated under the rules. Without such an auditor, a person incorporated or having his head office outside the United Kingdom is not to be regarded as a fit and proper person for the purposes of s.25 (direct authorisation).

Offences and enforcement

111.—(1) Any authorised person and any officer, controller or manager of an authorised person, who knowingly or recklessly furnishes an auditor appointed under the rules made under section 107 or a person carrying out an examination under section 108 above with information which the auditor or that person requires or is entitled to require and which is false or misleading in a material particular shall be guilty of an offence and liable—

(*a*) on conviction on indictment, to imprisonment for a term not exceeding two years or to a fine or to both;

(*b*) on summary conviction, to imprisonment for a term not exceeding six months or to a fine not exceeding the statutory maximum or to both.

(2) The duty of an auditor under section 108(3) above shall be enforceable by mandamus or, in Scotland, by an order for specific performance under section 91 of the Court of Session Act 1868.

(3) If it appears to the Secretary of State that an auditor has failed to comply with the duty mentioned in section 109(2) above, the Secretary of State may disqualify him from being the auditor of an authorised person or any class of authorised person; but the Secretary of State may remove any disqualification imposed under this subsection if satisfied that the person in question will in future comply with that duty.

(4) An authorised person shall not appoint as auditor a person disqualified under subsection (3) above; and a person who is an authorised person by virtue of membership of a recognised self-regulating organisation or certification by a recognised professional body who contravenes this subsection shall be treated as having contravened the rules of the organisation or body.

GENERAL NOTE
Subs. (1)
   This subsection makes it a criminal offence to furnish (knowingly or recklessly) false or misleading information to a second auditor or to an auditor appointed *under* the rules made under s.107. (Note that an auditor appointed under s.110 is appointed not "under" but "in accordance with" the rules made under s.107.)

Subs. (4)
   For a person authorised by virtue of membership of an SRO or RPB contravention of this subsection is a domestic disciplinary matter. As to the consequences of contravention for a directly authorised person, see s.28(1)(*b*) and s.64(1)(*c*). A contravention of this subsection is not tantamount to a contravention of a provision of Chapter V: contrast s.95.

CHAPTER XII

FEES

Application fees

   112.—(1) An applicant for a recognition order under Chapter III or IV of this Part of this Act shall pay such fees in respect of his application as may be required by a scheme made and published by the Secretary of State; and no application for such an order shall be regarded as duly made unless this subsection is complied with.
   (2) A scheme made for the purposes of subsection (1) above shall specify the time when the fees are to be paid and may—
   (*a*) provide for the determination of the fees in accordance with a specified scale or other specified factors;
   (*b*) provide for the return or abatement of any fees where an application is refused or withdrawn; and
   (*c*) make different provision for different cases.
   (3) Any scheme made for the purposes of subsection (1) above shall come into operation on such date as is specified in the scheme (not being earlier than the day on which it is first published) and shall apply to applications made on or after the date on which it comes into operation.
   (4) The power to make a scheme for the purposes of subsection (1) above includes power to vary or revoke a previous scheme made under those provisions.
   (5) Every application under section 26, 77 or 88 above shall be accompanied by the prescribed fee and every notice given to the Secretary of State under section 32, 86(2) or 87(3) above shall be accompanied by such fee as may be prescribed; and no such application or notice shall be regarded as duly made or given unless this subsection is complied with.

DEFINITIONS
   "prescribed": s.107(1).
   "recognition order": s.207(1).

GENERAL NOTE
   This section makes provision for the payment of fees by applicants for recognition or authorisation and by persons giving notice under sections 32, 86(2) or 87(3). Note that in setting fees, the SIB may take into account its initial costs. (Sched. 9, para. 11). As to fees payable, see *Regulation of Investment Business* (the SIB's rule book), Ch. 10.

Periodical fees

   113.—(1) Every recognised self-regulating organisation, recognised professional body, recognised investment exchange and recognised clearing house shall pay such periodical fees to the Secretary of State as may be prescribed.

(2) So long as a body is authorised under section 22 above to carry on insurance business which is investment business it shall pay to the Secretary of State such periodical fees as may be prescribed.

(3) So long as a society is authorised under section 23 above to carry on investment business it shall—

(*a*) if it is authorised by virtue of subsection (1) of that section, pay to the Chief Registrar of friendly societies such periodical fees as he may be by regulations specify; and

(*b*) if it is authorised by virtue of subsection (2) of that section, pay to the Registrar of Friendly Societies for Northern Ireland such periodical fees as he may by regulations specify.

(4) A person who is an authorised person by virtue of section 25 or 31 above shall pay such periodical fees to the Secretary of State as may be prescribed.

(5) If a person fails to pay any fee which is payable by him under subsection (4) above the Secretary of State may serve on him a written notice requiring him to pay the fee within twenty-eight days of service of the notice; and if the fee is not paid within that period that person's authorisation shall cease to have effect unless the Secretary of State otherwise directs.

(6) A direction under subsection (5) above may be given so as to have retrospective effect; and the Secretary of State may under that subsection direct that the person in question shall continue to be an authorised person only for such period as is specified in the direction.

(7) Subsection (5) above is without prejudice to the recovery of any fee as a debt due to the Crown.

(8) The manager of each authorised unit trust scheme and the operator of each recognised scheme shall pay such periodical fees to the Secretary of State as may be prescribed.

DEFINITIONS
"authorised unit trust scheme": s.207(1).
"insurance business": s.207(7).
"investment business": s.1(2).
"operator": s.207(1).
"prescribed": s.207(1).
"recognised clearing house": s.207(1).
"recognised investment exchange": s.207(1).
"recognised professional body": s.207(1).
"recognised scheme": s.207(1).
"recognised self-regulating organisation": s.207(1).

GENERAL NOTE
This section makes provisions for the payment of periodic fees. Note that in setting fees, the SIB may take into account its initial costs (Sched. 9, para. 11). As to fees payable, see *Regulation of Investment Business* (the SIB's rule book), Ch. 10.

Subs. (5)
As to service of notices, see section 204.

CHAPTER XIII

TRANSFER OF FUNCTIONS TO DESIGNATED AGENCY

Power to transfer functions to designated agency

114.—(1) If it appears to the Secretary of State—
(*a*) that a body corporate has been established which is able and willing

to discharge all or any of the functions to which this section applies; and

(*b*) that the requirements of Schedule 7 to this Act are satisfied in the case of that body,

he may, subject to the provisions of this section and Chapter XIV of this Part of this Act, make an order transferring all or any of those functions to that body.

(2) The body to which functions are transferred by the first order made under subsection (1) above shall be the body known as The Securities and Investments Board Limited if it appears to the Secretary of State that it is able and willing to discharge them, that the requirements mentioned in paragraph (*b*) of that subsection are satisfied in the case of that body and that he is not precluded from making the order by the subsequent provisions of this section or Chapter XIV of this Part of this Act.

(3) An order under subsection (1) above is in this Act referred to as "a delegation order" and a body to which functions are transferred by a delegation order is in this Act referred to as "a designated agency".

(4) Subject to subsections (5) and (6) below, this section applies to any functions of the Secretary of State under Chapters II to XII of this Part of this Act and to his functions under paragraphs 23 and 25(2) of Schedule 1 and paragraphs 4, 5 and 15 of Schedule 15 to this Act.

(5) This section does not apply to any functions under—

(*a*) section 31(4);
(*b*) section 46;
(*c*) section 48(8);
(*d*) section 58(3);
(*e*) section 86(1) or 87(1);
(*f*) section 96;
(*g*) section 109(2) above.

(6) This section does not apply to the making or revocation of a recognition order in respect of an overseas investment exchange or overseas clearing house or the making of an application to the court under section 12 above in respect of any such exchange or clearing house.

(7) Any function may be transferred by a delegation order either wholly or in part.

(8) In the case of a function under section 6 or 72 or a function under section 61 which is exercisable by virtue of subsection (1)(*a*)(ii) or (iii) of that section, the transfer may be subject to a reservation that it is to be exercisable by the Secretary of State concurrently with the designated agency and any transfer of a function under section 94, 105 or 106 shall be subject to such reservation.

(9) The Secretary of State shall not make a delegation order transferring any function of making rules or regulations to a designated agency unless—

(*a*) the agency has furnished him with a copy of the rules and regulations which it proposes to make in the exercise of those functions; and

(*b*) he is satisfied that those rules and regulations will afford investors an adequate level of protection and, in the case of such rules and regulations as are mentioned in Schedule 8 to this Act, comply with the principles set out in that Schedule.

(10) The Secretary of State shall also before making a delegation order transferring any functions to a designated agency require it to furnish him with a copy of any guidance intended to have continuing effect which it proposes to issue in writing or other legible form and the Secretary of State may take any such guidance into account in determining whether he is satisfied as mentioned in subsection (9)(*b*) above.

(11) No delegation order shall be made unless a draft of it has been laid before and approved by a resolution of each House of Parliament.

(12) In this Act references to guidance issued by a designated agency are references to guidance issued or any recommendation made by it which is issued or made to persons generally or to any class of persons, being, in either case, persons who are or may be subject to rules or regulations made by it, or who are or may be recognised or authorised by it, in the exercise of its functions under a delegation order.

DEFINITIONS
"body corporate": s.207(1).
"delegation order": subs. (3).
"designated agency": subs. (3).
"guidance": subs. (12).
"recognition order": s.207(1).

GENERAL NOTE
This section makes provision for the transfer by the Secretary of State, by draft order subject to affirmative resolution procedure, of all or any of the functions identified to a designated agency, which agency initially is to be the SIB. As to the status of the SIB and the exercise of transferred functions, see Schedule 9.

Subss. (1), (2)
Before transferring any functions, whether to the SIB or subsequently to another designated agency, it must appear to the Secretary of State:
(a) that it is able and willing to discharge the transferred functions;
(b) that the requirements of Schedule 7 are satisfied;
(c) that its rules and regulations afford investors an adequate level of protection and comply with the principles set out in Schedule 8 (subs. 9(*b*)). In determining whether they do, the Secretary of State may take into account any guidance which it proposes to issue (subs. (10)); and
(d) that the likely effects on competition of its rules, regulations and guidance do not exceed those necessary for the protection of investors (s.121(1)).
As to the making of orders, see subsection (11); as to transitional and supplementary provisions, see section 118.

Subss. (4)–(6)
These subsections identify, with exclusions, the functions which may be transferred for the purposes of subsections (1) and (2).

Subs. (8)
This subsection makes provision for the continued exercise of transferred functions by the Secretary of State. Depending on the terms of the delegation order, the first group of functions *may* continue to be exercised by the Secretary of State; the second group *are* so exercisable.

Subs. (10)
Continuing effect: Purely temporary guidance need not be submitted.
Or other legible form: *e.g.* guidance which may be retrieved from a computer. (H.L. Vol. 479, cols. 235–237).

Subs. (12)
Whereas rules and regulations are binding, guidance is not.

Resumption of transferred functions

115.—(1) The Secretary of State may at the request or with the consent of a designated agency make an order resuming all or any of the functions transferred to the agency by a delegation order.

(2) The Secretary of State may, in the circumstances mentioned in subsection (3), (4) or (5) below, make an order resuming—
(*a*) all the functions transferred to a designated agency by a delegation order; or
(*b*) all, all legislative or all administrative functions transferred to a

designated agency by a delegation order so far as relating to investments or investment business of any class.

(3) An order may be made under subsection (2) above if at any time it appears to the Secretary of State that any of the requirements of Schedule 7 to this Act are not satisfied in the case of the agency.

(4) An order may be made under subsection (2) above as respects functions relating to any class of investment or investment business if at any time it appears to the Secretary of State that the agency is unable or unwilling to discharge all or any of the transferred functions in respect of all or any investments or investment business falling within that class.

(5) Where the transferred functions consist of or include any functions of making rules or regulations an order may be made under subsection (2) above if at any time it appears to the Secretary of State that the rules or regulations made by the agency do not satisfy the requirements of section 114(9)(*b*) above.

(6) An order under subsection (1) above shall be subject to annulment in pursuance of a resolution of either House of Parliament; and no other order shall be made under this section unless a draft of it has been laid before and approved by a resolution of each House of Parliament.

(7) In subsection (2)(*b*) above—

(*a*) "legislative functions" means functions of making rules or regulations;

(*b*) "administrative functions" means functions other than legislative functions;

but the resumption of legislative functions shall not deprive a designated agency of any function of prescribing fees to be paid or information to be furnished in connection with administrative functions retained by the agency; and the resumption of administrative functions shall extend to the function of prescribing fees to be paid and information to be furnished in connection with those administrative functions.

DEFINITIONS

"administrative functions": subs. 7(1)(*b*).
"delegation order": s.114(3).
"designated agency": s.114(3).
"investment business": s.1(2).
"investments": s.1(1).
"legislative functions": subs. 7(1)(*a*).

GENERAL NOTE

This section makes provision for the resumption of functions transferred under section 114.

Subs. (1)

Under this subsection all or any of the transferred powers may be resumed at the request or with the consent of the designated agency. The power of resumption is exercisable by order subject to negative resolution procedure (subs. (6)). As to transitional and supplementary provisions, see section 118.

Subs. (2)

This subsection makes provision for the resumption of transferred functions either in their entirety or selectively as regards both the functions and the classes of investments or investment business in respect of which they are to be resumed. In relation to the resumption of legislative and administrative functions, note the provisos to subsection (7). The power of resumption under this subsection is exercisable by draft order subject to affirmative resolution procedure (subs. (6)). As to transitional and supplementary provisions, see section 118.

Subss. (3)–(6)

These subsections identify the circumstances in which an order may be made under subs. (2). An order may also be made where the anti-competitive effects of a designated agency's regulations etc., exceed those necessary for the protection of investors. Alternatively the agency may be directed to take remedial action. (s.121(3)).

Status and exercise of transferred functions

116. Schedule 9 to this Act shall have effect as respects the status of a designated agency and the exercise of the functions transferred to it by a delegation order.

DEFINITIONS
 "delegation order": s.114(3).
 "designated agency": s.114(3).

GENERAL NOTE
 As to exemption from liability in damages, see section 187(3).

Reports and accounts

117.—(1) A designated agency shall at least once in each year for which the delegation order is in force make a report to the Secretary of State on the discharge of the functions transferred to it by the order and on such other matters as the order may require.

(2) The Secretary of State shall lay before Parliament copies of each report received by him under this section.

(3) The Secretary of State may give directions to a designated agency with respect to its accounts and the audit of its accounts; and it shall be the duty of the agency to comply with the directions.

(4) Subsection (3) above shall not apply to a designated agency which is a company to which section 227 of the Companies Act 1985 applies; but the Secretary of State may require any designated agency (whether or not such a company) to comply with any provisions of that Act which would not otherwise apply to it or direct that any provision of that Act shall apply to the agency with such modifications as are specified in the direction; and it shall be the duty of the agency to comply with any such requirement or direction.

(5) In subsection (4) above the references to the Companies Act 1985 and section 227 of that Act include references to the corresponding Northern Ireland provisions.

DEFINITIONS
 "delegation order": s.114(3).
 "designated agency": s.114(3).

GENERAL NOTE
 This section imposes a duty on a designated agency to prepare an annual report on the discharge of its functions, and on the Secretary of State to lay copies of its report before Parliament. The Secretary of State is also empowered to give an agency directions about its accounts and their audit.

Transitional and supplementary provisions

118.—(1) A delegation order shall not affect anything previously done in the exercise of a function which is transferred by the order; and any order resuming a function shall not affect anything previously done by the designated agency in the exercise of a function which is resumed.

(2) A delegation order and an order resuming any functions transferred by a delegation order may contain, or the Secretary of State may by a separate order under this section make, such transitional and other supplementary provisions as he thinks necessary or expedient in connection with the delegation order or the order resuming the functions in question.

(3) The provisions that may be made under subsection (2) above in connection with a delegation order include, in particular, provisions—

(*a*) for modifying or excluding any provision of this Act in its application to any function transferred by the order;

(*b*) for applying to a designated agency, in connection with any such function, any provision applying to the Secretary of State which is contained in or made under any other enactment;

(*c*) for the transfer of any property, rights or liabilities from the Secretary of State to a designated agency;

(*d*) for the carrying on and completion by a designated agency of anything in process of being done by the Secretary of State when the order takes effect; and

(*e*) for the substitution of a designated agency for the Secretary of State in any instrument, contract or legal proceedings.

(4) The provisions that may be made under subsection (2) above in connection with an order resuming any functions include, in particular, provisions—

(*a*) for the transfer of any property, rights or liabilities from the agency to the Secretary of State;

(*b*) for the carrying on and completion by the Secretary of State of anything in process of being done by the agency when the order takes effect;

(*c*) for the substitution of the Secretary of State for the agency in any instrument, contract or legal proceedings; and

(*d*) in a case where some functions remain with the agency, for modifying or excluding any provision of this Act in its application to any such functions.

(5) In a case where any function of a designated agency is resumed and is to be immediately transferred by a delegation order to another designated agency, the provisions that may be made under subsection (2) above may include provisions for any of the matters mentioned in paragraphs (*a*) to (*c*) of subsection (4) above, taking references to the Secretary of State as references to that other agency.

(6) Any order under this section shall be subject to annulment in pursuance of a resolution of either House of Parliament.

DEFINITIONS
"delegation order": s.114(3).
"designated agency": s.114(3).

GENERAL NOTE

Subs. (1)
This subsection preserves the validity of things done prior to the transfer or resumption of functions under sections 114 and 115.

Subs. (2)
This subsection empowers the Secretary of State to make transitional and other supplementary provisions when transferring or resuming functions, either in the order itself or by separate order subject to negative resolution procedure (subs. (6)).

Subs. (3)
This subsection is illustrative and not definitive of the provisions that can be made.

Para. (a): Note the width of this power.

Subs. (4)
Again, this subsection is illustrative and not definitive. See also subsection (5).

CHAPTER XIV

PREVENTION OF RESTRICTIVE PRACTICES

Examination of rules and practices

Recognised self-regulating organisations, investment exchanges and clearing houses

119.—(1) The Secretary of State shall not make a recognition order in respect of a self-regulating organisation, investment exchange or clearing house unless he is satisfied that—

(a) the rules and any guidance of which copies are furnished with the application for the order; and

(b) in the case of an investment exchange, any arrangements of which particulars are furnished with the application,

do not have, and are not intended or likely to have, to any significant extent the effect of restricting, distorting or preventing competition or, if they have or are intended or likely to have that effect to any significant extent, that the effect is not greater than is necessary for the protection of investors.

(2) The powers conferred by subsection (3) below shall be exercisable by the Secretary of State if at any time it appears to him that—

(a) any rules made or guidance issued by a recognised self-regulating organisation, investment exchange or clearing house or any clearing arrangements made by a recognised clearing house;

(b) any practices of any such organisation, exchange or clearing house; or

(c) any practices of persons who are members of, or otherwise subject to the rules made by, any such organisation, exchange or clearing house,

have, or are intended or likely to have, to a significant extent the effect of restricting, distorting or preventing competition and that that effect is greater than is necessary for the protection of investors.

(3) The powers exercisable under this subsection are—

(a) to revoke the recognition order of the organisation, exchange or clearing house;

(b) to direct it to take specified steps for the purpose of securing that the rules, guidance, arrangements or practices in question do not have the effect mentioned in subsection (2) above;

(c) to make alterations in the rules for that purpose;

and subsections (2) to (5), (7) and (9) of section 11 above shall have effect in relation to the revocation of a recognition order under this subsection as they have effect in relation to the revocation of such an order under subsection (1) of that section.

(4) Subsection (3)(c) above does not apply to an overseas investment exchange or overseas clearing house.

(5) The practices referred to in paragraph (b) of subsection (2) above are practices of the organisation, exchange or clearing house in its capacity as such, being, in the case of a clearing house, practices in respect of its clearing arrangements; and the practices referred to in paragraph (c) of that subsection are practices in relation to business in respect of which the persons in question are subject to the rules of the organisation, exchange or clearing house and which are required or contemplated by its rules or guidance or otherwise attributable to its conduct in its capacity as such.

DEFINITIONS
"clearing arrangements": s.38(2).
"guidance": s.207(1).

"members": s.8(2).
"practices": subs. (5).
"recognised clearing house": s.207(1).
"recognised investment exchange": s.207(1).
"recognised self-regulating organisation": s.207(1).
"recognition order": s.207(1).
"rules": s.207(1).
"self-regulatory organisation": s.8(1).

GENERAL NOTE

Chapter XIV establishes a special regime for the application of competition policy to recognised bodies and designated agencies. Its general import is to reserve the power of decision to the Secretary of State rather than the Restrictive Practices Court. The Secretary of State's functions under this Chapter are not transferable to the Board.

This section makes provision for the application of competition policy to recognised bodies other than professional bodies. It applies where they are recognised by the Secretary of State; where they are recognised by the Board, section 120 applies. As to recognised professional bodies, see section 127.

Subs. (1)

This subsection prohibits the Secretary of State from making a recognition order except in the circumstances stipulated. As regards those circumstances, it should be noted that two questions have to be asked. The first is whether the rules, guidance or clearing arrangements affect competition "to any significant extent". Before answering this question, the Secretary of State must obtain, and have regard to, a report from the Director General of Fair Trading (s.122(2)). Although the Secretary of State is not bound by the DGFT's report, a negative answer by the DGFT to this question will effectively dispose of the matter. If as is more likely, however, the answer to the first question is that they do affect competition to a significant extent, the second question must then be asked; namely does that effect exceed that necessary for the protection of investors? As with the first question the Secretary of State is the sole judge of the answer to this question with the difference that he does not have to obtain and have regard to the opinion of the DGFT in answering it.

Subs. (2)

This subsection defines the circumstances in which the sanctions provided by subsection (3) may be invoked. Note that although the essence of guidance is that it is not binding, the Secretary of State is entitled to assume that it will be observed (s.128(5)). As to practices, see subsection (5).

Subs. (3)

Note that the initiative in the application of these sanctions rests with the DGFT (s.122(7)). It is for the Secretary of State, however, to decide whether they should be applied.

Para. (a): As to safeguards, see the proviso to this subsection, and note that by virtue of the exclusion of subsection (6) from the list of subsections applicable, these safeguards cannot be dispensed with.

Para. (b): As to safeguards and the enforcement of directives, see section 128.

Para. (c): This power is not exercisable in respect of overseas investment exchanges and clearing houses (subs. (4)). As to safeguards, see section 128; and note that the fact that rule changes have been imposed does not preclude their subsequent alteration or revocation (s.128(4)).

Modification of s.119 where recognition function is transferred

120.—(1) This section applies instead of section 119 above where the function of making or revoking a recognition order in respect of a self-regulating organisation, investment exchange or clearing house is exercisable by a designated agency.

(2) The designated agency—

(*a*) shall send to the Secretary of State a copy of the rules and of any guidance or arrangements of which copies or particulars are furnished with any application made to the agency for a recognition order together with any other information supplied with or in connection with the application; and

(*b*) shall not make the recognition order without the leave of the Secretary of State;

and he shall not give leave in any case in which he would (apart from the delegation order) have been precluded by section 119(1) above from making the recognition order.

(3) A designated agency shall send the Secretary of State a copy of any notice received by it under section 14(6) or 41(5) or (6) above.

(4) If at any time it appears to the Secretary of State in the case of a recognised self-regulating organisation, recognised investment exchange or recognised clearing house that there are circumstances such that (apart from the delegation order) he would have been able to exercise any of the powers conferred by subsection (3) of section 119 above he may, notwithstanding the delegation order, himself exercise the power conferred by paragraph (*a*) of that subsection or direct the designated agency to exercise the power conferred by paragraph (*b*) or (*c*) of that subsection in such manner as he may specify.

DEFINITIONS
"clearing arrangements": s.38(2).
"delegation order": s.114(3).
"designated agency": s.114(3).
"guidance": s.207(1).
"recognition order": s.207(1).
"rules": s.207(1).
"self-regulatory organisation": s.8(1).

GENERAL NOTE
This section applies instead of section 119 where the function of granting or revoking recognition has been transferred.

Subs. (2)
This subsection prevents a recognition order being made without leave of the Secretary of State. Leave is to be withheld where section 119(1) would preclude him from making a recognition order. See generally the annotation to that subsection, noting that the DGFT plays the same role in relation to this subsection as he plays in relation to that (s.122(2)). As to safeguards where the Secretary of State proposes to withhold leave, see section 128.

Subs. (3)
Section 120(3) in turn obliges the Secretary of State to supply the DGFT with any details of alterations in rules, guidance and clearing arrangements with which he is supplied by virtue of this provision.

Subs. (4)
This subsection makes provision for the exercise of the powers conferred by section 119(3), either by the Secretary of State himself in the case of the revocation of a recognition order, or in other cases by the SIB acting at his direction. Again, the initiative in the exercise of those powers rests with the DGFT (s.122(7)). As to safeguards in respect of directions and their enforcement, see section 128.

Designated agencies

121.—(1) The Secretary of State shall not make a delegation order transferring any function to a designated agency unless he is satisfied that any rules, regulations and guidance of which copies are furnished to him under section 114(9) or (10) above do not have, and are not intended or likely to have, to any significant extent the effect of restricting, distorting or preventing competition or, if they have or are intended or likely to have that effect to any significant extent, that the effect is not greater than is necessary for the protection of investors.

(2) The powers conferred by subsection (3) below shall be exercisable by the Secretary of State if at any time it appears to him that—

    (*a*) any rules or regulations made by a designated agency in the exercise of functions transferred to it by a delegation order or any guidance issued by a designated agency;

    (*b*) any practices of a designated agency; or

    (*c*) any practices of persons who are subject to rules or regulations made by it in the exercise of those functions,

have, or are intended or are likely to have, to any significant extent the effect of restricting, distorting or preventing competition and that that effect is greater than is necessary for the protection of investors.

(3) The powers exercisable under this subsection are—

    (*a*) to make an order in respect of the agency under section 115(2) above as if the circumstances were such as are there mentioned; or

    (*b*) to direct the agency to take specified steps for the purpose of securing that the rules, regulations, guidance or practices in question do not have the effect mentioned in subsection (2) above.

(4) The practices referred to in paragraph (*b*) of subsection (2) above are practices of the designated agency in its capacity as such; and the practices referred to in paragraph (*c*) of that subsection are practices in relation to business in respect of which the persons in question are subject to any such rules or regulations as are mentioned in paragraph (*a*) of that subsection and which are required or contemplated by those rules or regulations or by any such guidance as is there mentioned or are otherwise attributable to the conduct of the agency in its capacity as such.

DEFINITIONS
    "delegation order": s.114(3).
    "designated agency": s.114(3).
    "guidance": s.114(12).

GENERAL NOTE
This section applies the same regime to designated agencies as applies to recognised bodies under sections 119 and 120.

Subs. (1)
See the annotation to section 119(1). Again the Secretary of State must obtain and have regard to a report from the DGFT (s.122(2)).

Subs. (2)
This subsection defines the circumstances in which the sanctions provided by subsection (3) may be invoked. Note that the Secretary of State is entitled to assume that guidance will be observed (s.128(5)). As to practices, see subsection (4).

Subs. (3)
Note that the initiative in the application of these sanctions rests with the DGFT (s.122(7)). It is for the Secretary of State, however, to decide whether they should be applied.

Para. (b)
As to safeguards and the enforcement of directions, see section 128. The fact that rules and regulations have been altered pursuant to a direction given by the Secretary of State does not preclude their subsequent alteration or revocation (s.128(4)).

Consultation with Director General of Fair Trading

Reports by Director General of Fair Trading

122.—(1) The Secretary of State shall before deciding—

    (*a*) whether to refuse to make, or to refuse to leave for the making of,

a recognition order in pursuance of section 119(1) or 120(2) above;
or

(*b*) whether he is precluded by section 121(1) above from making a
delegation order,

send to the Director General of Fair Trading (in this Chapter referred to
as "the Director") a copy of the rules and regulations and of any guidance
or arrangements which the Secretary of State is required to consider in
making that decision together with such other information as the Secretary
of State considers will assist the Director in discharging his functions
under subsection (2) below.

(2) The Director shall report to the Secretary of State whether, in his
opinion, the rules, regulations, guidance or arrangements of which copies
are sent to him under subsection (1) above have, or are intended or likely
to have, to any significant extent the effect of restricting, distorting, or
preventing competition and, if so, what that effect is likely to be; and in
making any such decision as is mentioned in that subsection the Secretary
of State shall have regard to the Director's report.

(3) The Secretary of State shall send the Director copies of any notice
received by him under section 14(6), 41(5) or (6) or 120(3) above or under
paragraph 4 of Schedule 9 to this Act together with such information as
the Secretary of State considers will assist the Director in discharging his
functions under subsections (4) and (5) below.

(4) The Director shall keep under review—

(*a*) the rules, guidance, arrangements and regulations mentioned in
section 119(2) and 121(2) above; and

(*b*) the matters specified in the notices of which copies are sent to him
under subsection (3) above;

and if at any time he is of the opinion that any such rules, guidance,
arrangements, regulations or matters, or any such rules, guidance,
arrangements or regulations taken together with any such matters, have,
or are intended or likely to have, to any significant extent the effect
mentioned in subsection (2) above, he shall make a report to the Secretary
of State stating his opinion and what that effect is or is likely to be.

(5) The Director may report to the Secretary of State his opinion that
any such matter as is mentioned in subsection (4)(*b*) above does not in his
opinion have, and is not intended or likely to have, to any significant
extent the effect mentioned in subsection (2) above.

(6) The Director may from time to time consider whether any such
practices as are mentioned in section 119(2) or 121(2) above have, or are
intended or likely to have, to any significant extent the effect mentioned
in subsection (2) above and, if so, what that effect is or is likely to be; and
if he is of that opinion he shall make a report to the Secretary of State
stating his opinion and what the effect is or is likely to be.

(7) The Secretary of State shall not exercise his powers under section
119(3), 120(4) or 121(3) above except after receiving and considering a
report from the Director under subsection (4) or (6) above.

(8) The Director may, if he thinks fit, publish any report made by him
under this section but shall exclude from a published report, so far as
practicable, any matter which relates to the affairs of a particular person
(other than the self-regulating organisation, investment exchange, clearing
house or designated agency concerned) the publication of which would or
might in his opinion seriously and prejudicially affect the interests of that
person.

DEFINITIONS
  "arrangements": s.38(2).
  "delegation order": s.114(3).
  "guidance": s.207(1).

"recognition order": s.207(1).
"rules": s.207(1).

GENERAL NOTE

This section defines the role of the Director General of Fair Trading.

Subs. (2)

The DGFT is only required to report whether the rules, regulations, guidance or arrangements affect competition to any significant extent. He is not required to report whether their effect is greater than is necessary for the protection of investors.

Subs. (3)

These are notices of alterations in the rules, guidance and clearing arrangements of recognised bodies and of alterations in the rules, regulations and guidance of designated agencies.

Subs. (4)

This subsection imposes two duties on the DGFT. First, he is to keep under review the competitive effects of rules, regulations, guidance and clearing arrangements together with alterations in them. Secondly, he is to make a report to the Secretary of State where they affect or are likely to affect competition to any significant extent. Note that the DGFT is entitled to assume that guidance will be observed (s.128(5)). As to practices, see subsection (6).

Subs. (5)

This subsection allows the DGFT to clear alterations in rules, regulations, guidance and clearing arrangements. It is a negative clearance procedure: clearance does not relieve the DGFT of his duties under subsection (4).

Subs. (6)

This subsection allows the DGFT to examine the competitive effects of practices and to report. Note that in contrast to subsection (4) he is not under an obligation to do so.

Subs. (7)

By virtue of this subsection the initiative in the application of sanctions rests with the DGFT.

Investigations by Director General of Fair Trading

123.—(1) For the purpose of investigating any matter with a view to its consideration under section 122 above the Director may by a notice in writing—

(*a*) require any person to produce, at a time and place specified in the notice, to the Director or to any person appointed by him for the purpose, any documents which are specified or described in the notice and which are documents in his custody or under his control and relating to any matter relevant to the investigation; or

(*b*) require any person carrying on any business to furnish to the Director such information as may be specified or described in the notice, and specify the time within which, and the manner and form in which, any such information is to be furnished.

(2) A person shall not under this section be required to produce any document or disclose any information which he would be entitled to refuse to produce or disclose on grounds of legal professional privilege in proceedings in the High Court or on grounds of confidentiality as between client and professional legal adviser in proceedings in the Court of Session.

(3) Subsections (5) to (8) of section 85 of the Fair Trading Act 1973 (enforcement provisions) shall apply in relation to a notice under this section as they apply in relation to a notice under subsection (1) of that section.

GENERAL NOTE

This section empowers the DGFT to obtain documents and information for the purpose of the discharge of his functions under section 122. As to the service of notices, see section 204.

Subs. (3)

A refusal, or a failure without reasonable excuse, to do anything required is an offence punishable on summary conviction by a fine not exceeding level 5 on the standard scale. (Fair Trading Act 1973, s.85(5)). It is also an offence to wilfully alter, suppress or destroy any document, or to knowingly or recklessly make any statement which is false in a material particular. This offence is punishable on summary conviction by a fine not exceeding the prescribed sum under the Magistrates' Courts Act 1980, s.32(2) or on conviction on indictment by imprisonment for a term not exceeding two years or a fine or both. (Fair Trading Act 1973, s.85(6)). The Secretary of State is also empowered to apply to court for an order to have made good any default in complying with a notice under subsection (1). (Fair Trading Act 1973, s.85(7)).

Consequential exemptions from competition law

The Fair Trading Act 1973

124.—(1) For the purpose of determining whether a monopoly situation within the meaning of the Fair Trading Act 1973 exists by reason of the circumstances mentioned in section 7(1)(*c*) of that Act, no account shall be taken of—

  (*a*) the rules made or guidance issued by a recognised self-regulating organisation, recognised investment exchange or recognised clearing house or any conduct constituting such a practice as is mentioned in section 119(2) above;

  (*b*) any clearing arrangements or any conduct required or contemplated by any such arrangements; or

  (*c*) the rules or regulations made or guidance issued by a designated agency in the exercise of functions transferred to it by a delegation order or any conduct constituting such a practice as is mentioned in section 121(2) above.

(2) Where a recognition order is revoked there shall be disregarded for the purpose mentioned in subsection (1) above any such conduct as is mentioned in that subsection which occurred while the order was in force.

(3) Where on a monopoly reference under section 50 or 51 of the said Act of 1973 falling within section 49 of that Act the Monopolies and Mergers Commission find that a monopoly situation within the meaning of that Act exists and—

  (*a*) that the person (or, if more than one, any of the persons) in whose favour it exists is subject to the rules of a recognised self-regulating organisation, recognised investment exchange or recognised clearing house or to the rules or regulations made by a designated agency in the exercise of functions transferred to it by a delegation order; or

  (*b*) that any such person's conduct in carrying on any business to which those rules or regulations relate is the subject of guidance issued by such an organisation, exchange, clearing house or agency; or

  (*c*) that any such person is a party to any clearing arrangements; or

  (*d*) that the person (or, if more than one, any of the persons) in whose favour the monopoly situation exists is such an organisation, exchange or clearing house as is mentioned in paragraph (*a*) above or a designated agency,

the Commission, in making their report on that reference, shall exclude from their consideration the question whether the rules, regulations, guidance or clearing arrangements or any acts or omissions of such an organisation, exchange, clearing house or agency as is mentioned in paragraph (*d*) above in its capacity as such operate, or may be expected to operate, against the public interest; and section 54(3) of that Act shall have effect subject to the provisions of this subsection.

DEFINITIONS
"clearing arrangements": s.38(2).
"delegation order": s.114(3).
"designated agency": s.114(3).
"guidance": s.207(1).
"recognised clearing house": s.207(1).
"recognised investment exchange": s.207(1).
"recognised self-regulating organisation": s.207(1).
"rules": s.207(1).

GENERAL NOTE
This section provides for consequential exemptions from the provisions mentioned of the Fair Trading Act 1973 relating to monopolies. The merger provisions of that Act continue to apply.

Subs. (1)
This subsection provides that in determining whether a monopoly situation exists in relation to the supply of services, no account is to be taken of the rules, regulations, guidance, clearing arrangements or conduct stemming from them of recognised bodies and designated agencies.

Subs. (3)
Where on a monopoly reference not limited to the facts the Monopolies and Mergers Commission find that a monopoly situation exists, this subsection prevents the Commission from considering and reporting on the compatibility of the matters specified with the public interest.

The Restrictive Trade Practices Act 1976

125.—(1) The Restrictive Trade Practices Act 1976 shall not apply to any agreement for the constitution of a recognised self-regulating organisation, recognised investment exchange or recognised clearing house, including any term deemed to be contained in it by virtue of section 8(2) or 16(3) of that Act.

(2) The said Act of 1976 shall not apply to any agreement the parties to which consist of or include—

(*a*) any such organisation, exchange or clearing house as is mentioned in subsection (1) above; or

(*b*) a person who is subject to the rules of any such organisation, exchange or clearing house or to the rules or regulations made by a designated agency in the exercise of functions transferred to it by a delegation order,

by reason of any term the inclusion of which in the agreement is required or contemplated by the rules, regulations or guidance of that organisation, exchange, clearing house or agency.

(3) The said Act of 1976 shall not apply to any clearing arrangements or to any agreement between a recognised investment exchange and a recognised clearing house by reason of any term the inclusion of which in the agreement is required or contemplated by any clearing arrangements.

(4) Where the recognition order in respect of a self-regulating organisation, investment exchange or clearing house is revoked the foregoing provisions shall have effect as if the organisation, exchange or clearing house had continued to be recognised until the end of the period of six months beginning with the day on which the revocation takes effect.

(5) Where an agreement ceases by virtue of this section to be subject to registration—

(*a*) the Director shall remove from the register maintained by him under the said Act of 1976 any particulars which are entered or filed in that register in respect of the agreement; and

(b) any proceedings in respect of the agreement which are pending before the Restrictive Practices Court shall be discontinued.

(6) Where an agreement which has been exempt from registration by virtue of this section ceases to be exempt in consequence of the revocation of a recognition order, the time within which particulars of the agreement are to be furnished in accordance with section 24 of and Schedule 2 to the said Act of 1976 shall be the period of one month beginning with the day on which the agreement ceased to be exempt from registration.

(7) Where in the case of an agreement registered under the said Act of 1976 a term ceases to fall within subsection (2) or (3) above in consequence of the revocation of a recognition order and particulars of that term have not previously been furnished to the Director under section 24 of that Act, those particulars shall be furnished to him within the period of one month beginning with the day on which the term ceased to fall within that subsection.

(8) The Restrictive Trade Practices (Stock Exchange) Act 1984 shall cease to have effect.

DEFINITIONS
    "delegation order": s.114(3).
    "designated agency": s114(3).
    "recognised clearing house": s.207(1).
    "recognised investment exchange": s207(1).
    "recognised self-regulating organisation": s.207(1).
    "rules": s.207(1).

GENERAL NOTE
    This section makes provision for consequential exemptions from the Restrictive Trade Practices Act 1976. Agreements, and terms of agreements not specifically exempted, all fall within the scope of that Act.

Subs. (1)
    This subsection exempts agreements for the constitution of SROs, RIEs and RCHs from the scope of the Restrictive Trade Practices Act.

Subs. (2)
    This subsection exempts the terms of agreement which are required or contemplated by the rules, regulations and guidance mentioned from the scope of the Restrictive Trade Practices Act. Insofar as they include other terms, which are not so required or contemplated, they do fall within the scope of the Act.

Subs. (4)
    This subsection exempts clearing arrangements and the terms of agreements between RIEs and RCHs which are required or contemplated by clearing arrangements, from the scope of the Restrictive Trade Practices Act.
    As to the consequences of the revocation of recognition, see subsections (4), (6) and (7).

The Competition Act 1980

126.—(1) No course of conduct constituting any such practice as is mentioned in section 119(2) or 121(2) above shall constitute an anti-competitive practice for the purposes of the Competition Act 1980.

(2) Where a recognition order or delegation order is revoked, there shall not be treated as an anti-competitive practice for the purposes of that Act any such course of conduct as is mentioned in subsection (1) above which occurred while the order was in force.

DEFINITIONS
    "delegation order": s.114(3).
    "recognition order": s.207(1).

This section makes provision for consequential exemptions from the Competition Act 1980.

Recognised professional bodies

Modification of Restrictive Trade Practices Act 1976 in relation to recognised professional bodies

127.—(1) This section applies to—

(a) any agreement for the constitution of a recognised professional body, including any term deemed to be contained in it by virtue of section 16(3) of the Restrictive Trade Practices Act 1976; and

(b) any other agreement—

(i) the parties to which consist of or include such a body, or person certified by such a body or a member of such a body; and

(ii) to which that Act applies by virtue of any term the inclusion of which in the agreement is required or contemplated by rules or guidance of that body relating to the carrying on of investment business by persons certified by it.

(2) If it appears to the Secretary of State that the restrictions in an agreement to which this section applies—

(a) do not have, and are not intended or likely to have, to any significant extent the effect of restricting, distorting or preventing competition; or

(b) if all or any of them have, or are intended or likely to have, that effect to any significant extent, that the effect is not greater than is necessary for the protection of investors,

he may give a direction to the Director requiring him not to make an application to the Restrictive Practices Court under Part I of the said Act of 1976 in respect of the agreement.

(3) If it appears to the Secretary of State that one or more (but not all) of the restrictions in an agreement to which this section applies—

(a) do not have, and are not intended or likely to have, to any significant extent the effect mentioned in subsection (2) above; or

(b) if they have, or are intended or likely to have, that effect to any significant extent that the effect is not greater than is necessary for the protection of investors,

he may make a declaration to that effect and give notice of it to the Director and the Restrictive Practices Court.

(4) The Restrictive Practices Court shall not in any proceedings begun by an application made after notice has been given to it of a declaration under this section make any finding or exercise any power under Part I of the said Act of 1976 in relation to a restriction in respect of which the declaration has effect.

(5) The Director shall not make any application to the Restrictive Practices Court under Part I of the said Act of 1976 in respect of any agreement to which this section applies unless—

(a) he has notified the Secretary of State of his intention to do so; and

(b) the Secretary of State has either notified him that he does not intend to give a direction or make a declaration under this section or has given him notice of a declaration in respect of it;

and where the Director proposes to make any such application he shall furnish the Secretary of State with particulars of the agreement and the restrictions by virtue of which the said Act of 1976 applies to it and such other information as he considers will assist the Secretary of State in deciding whether to exercise his powers under this section or as the Secretary of State may request.

(6) The Secretary of State may—

(*a*) revoke a direction or declaration under this section;

(*b*) vary any such declaration; or

(*c*) give a direction to make a declaration notwithstanding a previous notification to the Director that he did not intend to give a direction or make a declaration,

if he is satisfied that there has been a material change of circumstances such that the grounds for the direction or declaration have ceased to exist, that there are grounds for a different declaration or that there are grounds for giving a direction or making a declaration, as the case may be.

(7) The Secretary of State shall give notice to the Director of the revocation of a direction and to the Director and the Restrictive Practices Court of the revocation or variation of a declaration; and no such variation shall have effect so as to restrict the powers of the Court in any proceedings begun by an application already made by the Director.

(8) A direction or declaration under this section shall cease to have effect if the agreement in question ceases to be one to which this section applies.

(9) This section applies to information provisions as it applies to restrictions.

DEFINITIONS
  "certified": s.207(1).
  "guidance": s.16(4).
  "investment business": s.1(2).
  "member": s.16(2).
  "recognised professional body": s.207(1).
  "rules": s.16(3).

GENERAL NOTE

This section modifies the Restrictive Trade Practices Act 1976 in its application to recognised professional bodies. Its effect is "to put the rules and practices of a recognised professional body on broadly the same footing as those of recognised self-regulating organisations to the extent that they are concerned with investment business, while leaving unchanged the existing provisions of competition law as they apply to the great bulk of the body's activities". (H.L. Vol. 479, col. 658).

Subs. (1)

This subsection defines the agreements to which this section applies.

Para. (b)

Note that agreements to which the Act applies, by virtue of terms other than those required or contemplated by the RPB's rules or guidance relating to the carrying on of investment business, do not fall within the scope of this section.

Subs. (2)

This subsection applies the same test as applies to other recognised bodies and designated agencies under sections 119(1) and 121(1), with the difference that the Secretary of State is not obliged to obtain and have regard to a report from the DGFT before deciding whether the restrictions affect competition to any significant extent. As to the enforcement of directions, see section 128(3). The Secretary of State also has power to give directions in respect of information provisions in agreements.

Subs. (3)

In contrast to subsection (2), which applies to all of the restrictions or information provisions in an agreement, this subsection empowers the Secretary of State to make a declaration that, where they exist, the anti-competitive effects of some restrictions or information provisions are no greater than is necessary for the protection of investors. As to the service of notices, see section 204.

Supplemental

Supplementary provisions

128.—(1) Before the Secretary of State exercises a power under section 119(3)(*b*) or (*c*) above, his power to refuse leave under section 120(2) above or his power to give a direction under section 120(4) above in respect of a self-regulating organisation, investment exchange or clearing house, or his power under section 121(3)(*b*) above in respect of a designated agency, he shall—

(*a*) give written notice of his intention to do so to the organisation, exchange, clearing house or agency and take such steps (whether by publication or otherwise) as he thinks appropriate for bringing the notice to the attention of any other person who in his opinion is likely to be affected by the exercise of the power; and

(*b*) have regard to any representation made within such time as he considers reasonable by the organisation, exchange, clearing house or agency or by any such other person.

(2) A notice under subsection (1) above shall give particulars of the manner in which the Secretary of State proposes to exercise the power in question and state the reasons for which he proposes to act; and the statement of reasons may include matters contained in any report received by him under section 122 above.

(3) Any direction given under this Chapter shall, on the application of the person by whom it was given, be enforceable by mandamus or, in Scotland, by an order for specific performance under section 91 of the Court of Session Act 1868.

(4) The fact that any rules or regulations made by a recognised self-regulating organisation, investment exchange or clearing house or by a designated agency have been altered by or pursuant to a direction given by the Secretary of State under this Chapter shall not preclude their subsequent alteration or revocation by that organisation, exchange, clearing house or agency.

(5) In determining under this Chapter whether any guidance has, or is likely to have, any particular effect the Secretary of State and the Director may assume that the persons to whom it is addressed will act in conformity with it.

DEFINITIONS
    "designated agency": s.114(3).
    "guidance": s.207(1).
    "recognised clearing house": s.207(1).
    "recognised investment exchange": s.207(1).
    "recognised self-regulating organisation": s.207(1).
    "rules": s.207(1).

GENERAL NOTE
    This section makes supplementary provisions which are referred to in the annotations to the relevant sections.

Subs. (1)
    As to the service of notices, see section 204.

Subs. (4)
    As to the purpose of this provision, see the annotation to section 13(8).

PART II

INSURANCE BUSINESS

Application of investment business provisions to regulated insurance companies

129. Schedule 10 to this Act shall have effect with respect to the application of the foregoing provisions of this Act to regulated insurance companies, that is to say—

 (*a*) insurance companies to which Part II of the Insurance Companies Act 1982 applies; and

 (*b*) insurance companies which are authorised persons by virtue of section 31 above.

DEFINITIONS
 "authorised person": s.207(1).
 "insurance company": s.207(7).

GENERAL NOTE
 This section applies Sched. 10 to "regulated insurance companies," *i.e.* companies subject to Part II of the Insurance Companies Act 1982 and companies authorised in other member States.
 As to the effect of Sched. 10, see General Note thereto.

Restriction on promotion of contracts of insurance

130.—(1) Subject to subsections (2) and (3) below, no person shall—

 (*a*) issue or cause to be issued in the United Kingdom an advertisement—

   (i) inviting any person to enter or offer to enter into a contract of insurance rights under which constitute an investment for the purposes of this Act, or

   (ii) containing information calculated to lead directly or indirectly to any person doing so; or

 (*b*) in the course of a business, advise or procure any person in the United Kingdom to enter into such a contract.

(2) Subsection (1) above does not apply where the contract of insurance referred to in that subsection is to be with—

 (*a*) a body authorised under section 3 or 4 of the Insurance Companies Act 1982 to effect and carry out such contracts of insurance;

 (*b*) a body registered under the enactments relating to friendly societies;

 (*c*) an insurance company the head office of which is in a member State other than the United Kingdom and which is entitled to carry on there insurance business of the relevant class;

 (*d*) an insurance company which has a branch or agency in such a member State and is entitled under the law of that State to carry on there insurance business of the relevant class;

and in this subsection "the relevant class" means the class of insurance business specified in Schedule 1 or 2 to the Insurance Companies Act 1982 into which the effecting and carrying out of the contract in question falls.

(3) Subsection (1) above also does not apply where—

 (*a*) the contract of insurance referred to in that subsection is to be with an insurance company authorised to effect or carry out such contracts of insurance in any country or territory which is for the time being designated for the purposes of this section by an order made by the Secretary of State; and (*b*) any conditions imposed by the order designating the country or territory have been satisfied.

(4) The Secretary of State shall not make an order designating any country or territory for the purposes of this section unless he is satisfied that the law under which insurance companies are authorised and supervised in that country or territory affords adequate protection to policy holders and potential policy holders against the risk that the companies may be unable to meet their liabilities; and, if at any time it appears to him that the law of a country or territory which has been designated under this section does not satisfy that requirement, he may by a further order revoke the order designating that country or territory.

(5) An order under this section shall be subject to annulment in pursuance of a resolution of either House of Parliament.

(6) Subject to subsections (7) and (8) below, any person who contravenes this section shall be guilty of an offence and liable—

    (*a*) on conviction on indictment, to imprisonment for a term not exceeding two years or to a fine or to both;

    (*b*) on summary conviction, to imprisonment for a term not exceeding six months or to a fine not exceeding the statutory maximum or to both.

(7) A person who in the ordinary course of a business other than investment business issues an advertisement to the order of another person shall not be guilty of an offence under this section if he proves that the matters contained in the advertisement were not (wholly or in part) devised or selected by him or by any person under his direction or control and that he believed on reasonable grounds after due enquiry that the person to whose order the advertisement was issued was an authorised person.

(8) A person other than the insurance company with which the contract of insurance is to be made shall not be guilty of an offence under this section if he proves that he believed on reasonable grounds after due enquiry that subsection (2) or (3) above applied in the case of the contravention in question.

DEFINITIONS

"advertisement": s.207(2), (3).
"authorised person": s.207(1).
"contract of insurance": s.207(7).
"insurance company": s.207(7).
"investment": s.1(1).
"investment business": s.1(2).

GENERAL NOTE

This section prohibits, subject to specified exceptions, the promotion of life assurance as an investment medium.

Subs. (1)

Contract of insurance rights under which constitute an investment for the purposes of this Act: see Sched. 1, para. 10, which, *inter alia*, excludes pure protection policies.

The ban on promotion covers both life assurance advertisements and advice given in the course of a business (*e.g.* by an intermediary).

Contravention of the ban is a criminal offence: subs. (6). As to the civil consequences of a contravention, see s.131.

Subs. (2)

Regardless of who issues the advertisement or gives the advice, the ban does not apply if the contract is to be *with* one of the bodies enumerated (*i.e.* broadly speaking, authorised insurance companies, friendly societies and EEC-based (or Gibraltar-based: s.208(1)) insurance companies.

Subs. (3)

The promotion of contracts with non-EEC insurers is banned unless the contract is to be with an insurance company authorised in a country or territory designated by an order of the Secretary of State.

As to the manner of making a designation order, see s.205(2) and subs. (5) of this section.

Subs. (4)

The Secretary of State must not make a designation order unless satisfied that the law of the country/territory to be designated affords adequate protection to policyholders against the risk that insurers may be unable to meet their liabilities—another application of the principle of equivalence.

Subs. (7)

This subsection makes it a defence for the person who in the ordinary course of a non-investment business has issued an advertisement to the order of another person to *prove* that he had no say in the contents to the advertisement *and* that he reasonably believed the other person to be an authorised person.

Authorised person: That is, authorised under this Act, not the Insurance Companies Act 1982.

Subs. (8)

This subsection affords a defence to the promoter of a policy who reasonably believed that the insurer fell within subss. (2) or (3). Again, the burden of proof is on the accused.

Contracts made after contravention of s.130

131.—(1) Where there has been a contravention of section 130 above, then, subject to subsections (3) and (4) below—

(a) the insurance company shall not be entitled to enforce any contract of insurance with which the advertisement, advice or procurement was concerned and which was entered into after the contravention occurred; and

(b) the other party shall be entitled to recover any money or other property paid or transferred by him under the contract, together with compensation for any loss sustained by him as a result of having parted with it.

(2) The compensation recoverable under subsection (1) above shall be such as the parties may agree or as a court may, on the application of either party, determine.

(3) In a case where the contravention referred to in subsection (1) above was a contravention by the insurance company with which the contract was made, the court may allow the contract to be enforced or money or property paid or transferred under it to be retained if it is satisfied—

(a) that the person against whom enforcement is sought or who is seeking to recover the money or property was not influenced, or not influenced to any material extent, by the advertisement or, as the case may be, the advice in making his decision to enter into the contract; or

(b) that the advertisement or, as the case may be, the advice was not misleading as to the nature of the company with which the contract was to be made or the terms of the contract and fairly stated any risks involved in entering into it.

(4) In a case where the contravention of section 130 above referred to in subsection (1) above was a contravention by a person other than the insurance company with which the contract was made the court may allow the contract to be enforced or money or property paid or transferred under it to be retained if it is satisfied that at the time the contract was made the company had no reason to believe that any contravention of section 130 above had taken place in relation to the contract.

(5) Where a person elects not to perform a contract which by virtue of subsection (1) above is unenforceable against him or by virtue of that

subsection recovers money paid or other property transferred to him under a contract he shall not be entitled to any benefits under the contract and shall repay any money and return any other property received by him under the contract.

(6) Where any property transferred under a contract to which this section applies has passed to a third party the references to that property in this section shall be construed as references to its value at the time of its transfer under the contract.

(7) A contravention of section 130 above by an authorised person shall be actionable at the suit of any person who suffers loss as a result of the contravention.

(8) Section 61 above shall have effect in relation to a contravention or proposed contravention of section 130 above as it has effect in relation to a contravention or proposed contravention of section 57 above.

DEFINITIONS
"advertisement": s.207(2), (3).
"at the suit": s.207(9).
"authorised person": s.207(1).
"contract of insurance": s.207(7).
"insurance company": s.207(7).

GENERAL NOTE
This section (comparable to s.57(5)–(10)) lays down the civil consequences of a contravention of the preceding section.

Subs. (1)
This subsection renders prima facie unenforceable by the insurance company any contract with which the advertisement or advice was concerned and which was entered into after the contravention. It need not be shown that the contravention brought about the making of the contract. In addition the insured is prima facie entitled to unravel the transaction, recovering anything parted with by him under it, along with compensation for any loss sustained as a result of having parted with it. But if the insured opts not to perform the contract or opts to unravel it, he is not entitled to any benefits under it and must return anything received under it: subss. (5), (6).

This presumption of unenforceability may be overturned in the circumstances specified in subss. (3) and (4).

Subs. (3)
This subsection applies where the contravention of s.130 was by the contracting *insurance company itself*. Here the court may uphold the contract if the insured was not materially influenced by the advertisement or advice in deciding to buy the policy, or if the advertisement or advice was not misleading and fairly stated the risks involved.

Subs. (4)
This subsection applies where the contravention of s.130 was by *someone other than* the contracting insurance company (*e.g.* an intermediary). Here the court may uphold the contract if, when it was made, the company had no reason to believe that s.130 had been contravened in relation to it.

As to the position of the intermediary in such circumstances, see subss. (7) and (8).

Subs. (7)
An authorised person who contravenes s.130 is exposed to actions for damages by anyone who has suffered loss as a result. Note the failure to amend this provision along the lines of ss.62(1) and 171(6) (which allow an action "subject to the defences and other incidents applying to actions for breach of statutory duty").

Subs. (8)
The effect is that the SIB may seek injunctions and restitution orders in connection with an actual or proposed contravention of s.130.

Insurance contracts effected in contravention of s.2 of Insurance Companies Act 1982

132.—(1) Subject to subsection (3) below, a contract of insurance (not being an agreement to which section 5(1) above applies) which is entered into by a person in the course of carrying on insurance business in contravention of section 2 of the Insurance Companies Act 1982 shall be unenforceable against the other party; and that party shall be entitled to recover any money or other property paid or transferred by him under the contract, together with compensation for any loss sustained by him as a result of having parted with it.

(2) The compensation recoverable under subsection (1) above shall be such as the parties may agree or as a court may, on the application of either party, determine.

(3) A court may allow a contract to which subsection (1) above applies to be enforced or money or property paid or transferred under it to be retained if it is satisfied—

(*a*) that the person carrying on insurance business reasonably believed that his entering into the contract did not constitute a contravention of section 2 of the said Act of 1982; and

(*b*) that it is just and equitable for the contract to be enforced or, as the case may be, for the money or property paid or transferred under it to be retained.

(4) Where a person elects not to perform a contract which by virtue of this section is unenforceable against him or by virtue of this section recovers money or property paid or transferred under a contract he shall not be entitled to any benefits under the contract and shall repay any money and return any other property received by him under the contract.

(5) Where any property transferred under a contract to which this section applies has passed to a third party the references to that property in this section shall be construed as references to its value at the time of its transfer under the contract.

(6) A contravention of section 2 of the said Act of 1982 shall not make a contract of insurance illegal or invalid to any greater extent than is provided in this section; and a contravention of that section in respect of a contract of insurance shall not affect the validity of any re-insurance contract entered into in respect of that contract.

DEFINITION
    "contract of insurance": s.207(7).

GENERAL NOTE
    This section (comparable to s.5) lays down the civil consequences of a contravention of s.2 of the Insurance Companies Act 1982 (carrying on insurance business without authorisation) in relation to a contract of insurance not covered by s.5(7) of the Financial Services Act.
    This section is designed to supersede the common law position, with its uncertainties, complications and practical inconvenience, as expressed in *Bedford Insurance Co. Ltd.* v. *I.R.B.* [1985] Q.B. 966, *Stewart* v. *Oriental Fire and Marine Insurance Co. Ltd.* [1985] Q.B. 988, and *Phoenix Central Insurance Co. Greece S.A.* v. *Administratia Asiguraliror de Stat.*, *Financial Times*, October 15, 1986.

Subs. (1)
    This section applies to contracts of insurance which are not agreements to which s.5(1) applies. It thus applies to insurance contracts the making or performance of which does not constitute an activity falling within Sched. 1, Part II (activities constituting investment business) and also to insurance contracts the making or performance of which would fall within Sched. 1, Part II were it not for Parts III and IV. Broadly speaking, therefore, this section applies to general insurance contracts and to life assurance contracts when not used as an investment medium; it is intended to be complementary to s.5.
    Subs. (1) creates a presumption that an insurance contract, to which this section applies, which is entered into in contravention of s.2 of the 1982 Act is unenforceable against the insured. There is also a presumption that the insured may unravel the transaction, recovering anything he has parted with under the contract, along with compensation for any loss sustained by him as a result of having parted with it. But if the insured opts not to perform

the contract or opts to unravel it, he is not entitled to any benefits under it and must return anything received under it: subss. (4), (5).

The presumption of unenforceability may be overturned in the circumstances specified in subs. (3).

Subs. (3)

The court may uphold the contract if the insurer reasonably believed that in entering into it he was not contravening s.2 of the 1982 Act, *and* it would be just and equitable for it to be upheld.

Subs. (6)

This subsection is designed to neutralise the judicial decisions cited above.

Misleading statements as to insurance contracts

133.—(1) Any person who—

(a) makes a statement, promise or forecast which he knows to be misleading, false or deceptive or dishonestly conceals any material facts; or

(b) recklessly makes (dishonestly or otherwise) a statement, promise or forecast which is misleading, false or deceptive,

is guilty of an offence if he makes the statement, promise or forecast or conceals the facts for the purpose of inducing, or is reckless as to whether it may induce, another person (whether or not the person to whom the statement, promise or forecast is made or from whom the facts are concealed) to enter into or offer to enter into, or to refrain from entering or offering to enter into, a contract of insurance with an insurance company (not being an investment agreement) or to exercise or refrain from exercising, any rights conferred by such a contract.

(2) Subsection (1) above does not apply unless—

(a) the statement, promise or forecast is made in or from, or the facts are concealed in or from, the United Kingdom;

(b) the person on whom the inducement is intended to or may have effect is in the United Kingdom; or

(c) the contract is or would be entered into or the rights are or would be exercisable in the United Kingdom.

(3) A person guilty of an offence under this section shall be liable—

(a) on conviction on indictment, to imprisonment for a term not exceeding seven years or to a fine or to both;

(b) on summary conviction, to imprisonment for a term not exceeding six months or to a fine not exceeding the statutory maximum or to both.

DEFINITIONS

"contract of insurance": s.207(7).

"insurance company": s.207(7).

"investment agreement": s.44(9).

GENERAL NOTE

Section 47 penalises misleading statements, etc., as to investment agreements. This precisely parallel provision penalises misleading statements, etc., as to insurance contracts which are not investment agreements.

Subs. (1)

Cf. s.47(1).

Subs. (2)

Cf. s.47(4).

Para. (c): exercisable: Contrast "exercised" in s.47(4)(c).

Controllers of insurance companies

134. In section 7(4)(*c*)(ii) of the Insurance Companies Act 1982 (definition of controller by reference to exercise of not less than one-third of voting power) for the words "one-third" there shall be substituted the words "15 per cent.".

GENERAL NOTE
This section changes, for the purposes of the Insurance Companies Act 1982, the proportion of voting power a person must have in order to be a "controller." It is thereby brought into line with the proportion laid down for the purpose of the present legislation: s.207(5).

Communication by auditor with Secretary of State

135.—(1) After section 21 of the Insurance Companies Act 1982 there shall be inserted—

"Communication by auditor with Secretary of State

21A.—(1) No duty to which an auditor of an insurance company to which this Part of this Act applies may be subject shall be regarded as contravened by reason of his communicating in good faith to the Secretary of State, whether or not in response to a request from him, any information or opinion on a matter of which the auditor has become aware in his capacity as auditor of that company and which is relevant to any functions of the Secretary of State under this Act.

(2) If it appears to the Secretary of State that any auditor or class of auditor to whom subsection (1) above applies is not subject to satisfactory rules made or guidance issued by a professional body specifying circumstances in which matters are to be communicated to the Secretary of State as mentioned in that subsection the Secretary of State may make regulations applying to that auditor or class of auditor and specifying such circumstances; and it shall be the duty of an auditor to whom the regulations made by the Secretary of State apply to communicate a matter to the Secretary of State in the circumstances specified by the regulations.

(3) The matters to be communicated to the Secretary of State in accordance with any such rules or guidance or regulations may include matters relating to persons other than the company.

(4) No regulations shall be made under subsection (2) above unless a draft of them has been laid before and approved by a resolution of each House of Parliament.

(5) If it appears to the Secretary of State that an auditor has failed to comply with the duty mentioned in subsection (2) above, the Secretary of State may disqualify him from being the auditor of an insurance company or any class of insurance company to which Part II of this Act applies; but the Secretary of State may remove any disqualification imposed under this subsection if satisfied that the person in question will in future comply with that duty.

(6) An insurance company to which this Part of this Act applies shall not appoint as auditor a person disqualified under subsection (5) above.".

(2) In section 71(7) of that Act (which lists the provisions of that Act default in complying with which is not an offence) after the words "section 16" there shall be inserted the words "21A", and in section 97(4) of that Act (which provides that regulations under that Act are to be subject to annulment) after the word "Act" there shall be inserted the words ", except regulations under section 21A(3),".

DEFINITION
"insurance company": Insurance Companies Act 1982, s.96(1).

This section makes provision for the auditors of insurance companies to report to the Secretary of State matters relevant to the DTI's functions under the insurance companies legislation. It is envisaged that the role of auditors in the regulation of insurance companies will be parallel to their role in the regulation of investment businesses (*cf.* also Building Societies Act 1986, s.82).

Subs. (1)
A new section is inserted in the Insurance Companies Act 1982.
Section 21A(1)–(3): This corresponds to Financial Services Act, s.109(1)–(3), *q.v.*
Section 21A(4), (5): This corresponds to Financial Services Act, s.111(3) and the first limb of s.111(4), *q.v.*

Arrangements to avoid unfairness between separate insurance funds etc.

136.—(1) After section 31 of the Insurance Companies Act 1982 there shall be inserted—

> **"Arrangements to avoid unfairness between separate insurance funds etc.**
>
> 31A.—(1) An insurance company to which this Part of this Act applies which carries on long term business in the United Kingdom shall secure that adequate arrangements are in force for securing that transactions affecting assets of the company (other than transactions outside its control) do not operate unfairly between the section 28 fund or funds and the other assets of the company or, in a case where the company has more than one identified fund, between those funds.
>
> (2) In this section—
>> "the section 28 fund or funds" means the assets representing the fund or funds maintained by the company under section 28(1)(*b*) above; and
>>
>> "identified fund", in relation to a company, means assets representing the company's receipts from a particular part of its long term business which can be identified as such by virtue of accounting or other records maintained by the company."

(2) In section 71(7) of that Act (which lists the provisions of that Act default in complying with which is not an offence) before the word "or" there shall be inserted the word "31A".

"insurance company": Insurance Companies Act 1981, s.96(1).
"long term business": Insurance Companies Act 1982, s.1(1).

Because of the special characteristics of insurance company funds and the pre-existing DTI system of regulating solvency, the investment management activities of insurance companies are not (leaving aside pension fund management) to be regulated by the Conduct of Business Rules made under s.48. However, this section provides that insurance companies must have arrangements to secure that they do not act unfairly as between their different funds. It thus enshrines in the insurance companies legislation "the single most important principle of investment management: that of dealing fairly as between different clients": H.L. Vol. 479, col. 663 (July 28, 1986).

Subs. (1)
The new provision is inserted in the Insurance Companies Act 1982. Accordingly compliance with it will be monitored, and its breach will trigger the powers of intervention conferred by that Act.
Section 28 fund: The 1982 Act requires insurance companies to separate the assets and liabilities attributable to long term business into a distinct fund.

Regulations in respect of linked long term policies

137. In section 78(2) of the Insurance Companies Act 1982 (regulations in respect of linked long term policies) after paragraph (a) there shall be inserted—

"(aa) restricting the proportion of those benefits which may be determined by reference to property of a specified description or a specified index;".

GENERAL NOTE

The Insurance Companies Act 1982, s.78(2)(a), empowers the DTI to make regulations restricting the descriptions of property, or the indices of the value of property, by reference to which benefits under linked long term policies (usually unit-linked policies) may be determined. But the 1982 Act made no provision for permitted links to be subject to quantitative limits. The new provision, hereby inserted into s.78(2) of the 1982 Act, allows regulations to be made stipulating that only a specified proportion of funds is to be linked to a particular description of property, or a particular index.

This will enable the range of permitted links for life assurance policies to be extended. This reflects the policy that, as far as possible, "there should be parity between the permitted investments of unit trusts and the permitted links for life assurance policies": *Financial Services in the United Kingdom*, para. 9.10.

Insurance brokers

138.—(1) Rules made under section 8 of the Insurance Brokers (Registration) Act 1977 may require an applicant for registration or enrolment to state whether he is an authorised person or exempted person under Part I of this Act and, if so, to give particulars of the authorisation or exemption; and an individual shall be treated as satisfying the requirements of section 3(2)(a) of that Act (applicant for registration to satisfy Council as to his character and suitability) if he is an authorised person or a member of a partnership or unincorporated association which is an authorised person.

(2) In drawing up any statement under section 10 of that Act or making any rules under section 11 or 12 of that Act after the coming into force of this section the Insurance Brokers Registration Council shall take proper account of any provisions applicable to, and powers exercisable in relation to, registered insurance brokers or enrolled bodies corporate under this Act.

(3) In section 12(1) and (2) of that Act (which requires the Council to make professional indemnity rules) for the words "The Council shall" there shall be substituted the words "The Council may".

(4) In section 15 of that Act (erasure from register and list for unprofessional conduct etc.) after subsection (2) there shall be inserted—

"(2A) The Disciplinary Committee may, if they think fit, direct that the name of a registered insurance broker or enrolled body corporate shall be erased from the register or list if it appears to the Committee that any responsible person has concluded that the broker (or a related person) or the body corporate has contravened or failed to comply with—

(a) any provision of the Financial Services Act 1986 or any rule or regulation made under it to which he or it is or was subject at the time of the contravention or failure; or

(b) any rule of any recognised self-regulating organisation or recognised professional body (within the meaning of that Act), to which he is or was subject at that time.

(2B) In subsection (2A) above—

(a) "responsible person" means a person responsible under the Financial Services Act 1986 or under the rules of any recognised self-regulating organisation or recognised professional body (within the meaning of that Act) for determining whether any contravention of any provision of that Act or rules or regulations made under it or any rules of that organisation or body has occurred; and

(b) "related person" means a partnership or unincorporated association of which the broker in question is (or was at the time of the failure or contravention in question) a member or a body corporate of which he is (or was at that time) a director."

(5) The Insurance Brokers Registration Council shall co-operate, by the sharing of information and otherwise, with the Secretary of State and any other authority, body or person having responsibility for the supervision or regulation of investment business or other financial services.

(6) For the purposes of the said Act of 1977 "authorised insurers" shall include—

(a) an insurance company the head office of which is in a member State other than the United Kingdom and which is entitled to carry on there insurance business corresponding to that mentioned in the definition of "authorised insurers" in that Act; and

(b) an insurance company which has a branch or agency in such a member State and is entitled under the law of that State to carry on there insurance business corresponding to that mentioned in that definition.

DEFINITIONS
"authorised person": s.207(1).
"enrolled": Insurance Brokers (Registration) Act 1977, s.29(1).
"exempted person": s.207(1).
"recognised professional body": s.207(1).
"recognised self-regulating organisation": s.207(1).
"register": Insurance Brokers (Registration) Act 1977, s.29(1).
"registered insurance broker": Insurance Brokers (Registration) Act 1977, s.29(1).
"rules": s.207(1).

GENERAL NOTE
This section addresses the relationship between the present legislation and the Insurance Brokers (Registration) Act 1977. The intention behind it is "to reduce to a minimum the supervision by the Insurance Brokers Registration Council of a person who is subject to the financial services legislation and the insurance brokers legislation": H.L. Vol. 481, col. 110 (October 20, 1986).

Subs. (1)
The effect of this subsection is that authorised persons are entitled to be registered as insurance brokers if they are qualified by the requisite experience of insurance business.

Subs. (2)
This requires the Insurance Brokers Registration Council to take proper account of the subjection of life assurance brokers to the investment business regime in drawing up its Code of Conduct and in making its rules for financial regulation and professional indemnity.

Subs. (3)
The Insurance Brokers Registration Council is thus no longer legally required to make professional indemnity rules.

Subs. (4)
This inserts new provisions in the 1977 Act which enable the Insurance Brokers Registration Council to act on disciplinary decisions made by the regulatory authorities of the investment business regime, by striking off the broker concerned.

Subs. (5)

Subs. (5)

This subsection imposes the standard co-operation obligation on the Insurance Brokers
Registration Council.

Industrial assurance

139.—(1) In section 5 of the Industrial Assurance Act 1923 (prohibition
on issue of illegal policies) the references to policies which are illegal or
not within the legal powers of a society or company shall not be construed
as applying to any policy issued—

    (*a*) in the course of carrying on investment business in contravention
        of section 3 above; or

    (*b*) in the course of carrying on insurance business in contravention of
        section 2 of the Insurance Companies Act 1982.

(2) In section 20(4) of the said Act of 1923 the reference to a person
employed by a collecting society or industrial assurance company and in
section 34 of that Act the references to a person in the regular employment
of such a society or company shall include references to an appointed
representative of such a society or company but as respects section 34
only if the contract in question is an investment agreement.

(3) Where it appears to the Industrial Assurance Commissioner that
rules made by virtue of section 48(2)(*j*) (or corresponding rules made by
a recognised self-regulating organisation) make arrangements for the
settlement of a dispute referred to him under section 32 of the said Act
of 1923 or that such rules relate to some of the matters in dispute he may,
if he thinks fit, delegate his functions in respect of the dispute so as to
enable it to be settled in accordance with the rules.

(4) If such rules provide that any dispute may be referred to the
Industrial Assurance Commissioner he may deal with any dispute referred
to him in pursuance of those rules as if it were a dispute referred under
section 77 of the Friendly Societies Act 1974 and may delegate his
functions in respect of any such dispute to any other person.

(5) The foregoing provisions of this section shall apply to Northern
Ireland with the substitution for the references to sections 5, 20(4), 32
and 34 of the said Act of 1923 and section 77 of the said Act of 1974 of
references to Articles 20, 27(2), 36 and 38 of the Industrial Assurance
(Northern Ireland) Order 1979 and section 65 of the Friendly Societies
Act (Northern Ireland) 1970 and for the references to the Industrial
Assurance Commissioner of references to the Industrial Assurance Com-
missioner for Northern Ireland.

D<small>EFINITIONS</small>
    "appointed representative": s.44.
    "carrying on investment business": s.1(3).
    "investment agreement": s.44(9).
    "investment business": s.1(2).
    "recognised self-regulating organisation": s.207(1).
    "rules": s.207(1).

G<small>ENERAL</small> N<small>OTE</small>
    This section co-ordinates the present legislation with the industrial assurance legislation.

Subs. (1)
    This subsection disapplies s.5 of the Industrial Assurance Act 1923 (which provides for a
refund of premiums paid on an illegal industrial assurance policy) to policies issued in the
course of carrying on investment business or insurance business without the appropriate
authorisation. The civil consequences of issuing such policies are thus those laid down in ss.5
and 132 of the Financial Services Act.

Subs. (2)

Section 20(4) of the 1923 Act provides that if a proposal form for an industrial assurance policy is filled in by a person employed by a collecting society or industrial assurance company then, in the absence of fraud, the validity of the policy cannot be questioned on the ground of misstatement in the proposal. For the purposes of this provision an appointed representative is a "person employed."

Section 34 of the 1923 Act provides that only persons in the regular employment of the society or company are to procure anyone to enter into a contract of industrial assurance. For the purposes of this provision an appointed representative is a person in the regular employment of the society or company if the contract in question is an investment agreement.

Subs. (3)

Under s.48(2)(*j*) the Conduct of Business Rules may make provision for arrangements for the settlement of disputes, *e.g.* by establishing an Investment Ombudsman. The Industrial Assurance Commissioner may, where appropriate, delegate his dispute-settlement functions to such an ombudsman or the SRO equivalent.

Subs. (4)

Such rules: *i.e.*, the SIB's Conduct of Business Rules on dispute-settlement, or the corresponding rules of an SRO.

Section 77 of the Friendly Societies Act 1974 empowers the Industrial Assurance Commissioner to order the attendance of concerned parties and witnesses, to require the production of books and documents, to determine the dispute, and to order the payment of expenses.

PART III

FRIENDLY SOCIETIES

Friendly societies

140. Schedule 11 to this Act shall have effect as respects the regulation of friendly societies.

GENERAL NOTE

As to the effect of Sched. 11, see the general note thereto.

Indemnity schemes

141.—(1) Any two or more registered friendly societies may, notwithstanding any provision to the contrary in their rules, enter into arrangements for the purpose of making funds available to meet losses incurred by any society which is a party to the arrangements or by the members of any such society by virtue of their membership of it.

(2) No such arrangements shall come into force unless they have been approved by the Chief Registrar of friendly societies or, as the case may be, the Registrar of Friendly Societies for Northern Ireland.

DEFINITION

"registered friendly society": s.207(1).

GENERAL NOTE

This section, which overrides any contrary provision in a friendly society's rules, allows friendly societies to enter into mutual indemnity arrangements, subject to the approval of the Chief Registrar of Friendly Societies.

PART IV

OFFICIAL LISTING OF SECURITIES

Official listing

142.—(1) No investment to which this section applies shall be admitted to the Official List of The Stock Exchange except in accordance with the provisions of this Part of this Act.

(2) Subject to subsections (3) and (4) below, this section applies to any investment falling within paragraph 1, 2, 4 or 5 of Schedule 1 to this Act.

(3) In the application of those paragraphs for the purposes of subsection (2) above—

(*a*) paragraphs 1, 4 and 5 shall have effect as if paragraph 1 did not contain the exclusion relating to building societies, industrial and provident societies or credit unions;

(*b*) paragraph 2 shall have effect as if it included any instrument falling within paragraph 3 issued otherwise than by the government of a member State or a local authority in a member State; and

(*c*) paragraphs 4 and 5 shall have effect as if they referred only to investments falling within paragraph 1.

(4) The Secretary of State may by order direct that this section shall apply also to investments falling within paragraph 6 of Schedule 1 to this Act or to such investments of any class or description.

(5) An order under subsection (4) above shall be subject to annulment in pursuance of a resolution of either House of Parliament.

(6) In this Part of this Act "the competent authority" means, subject to section 157 below, the Council of The Stock Exchange; and that authority may make rules (in this Act referred to as "listing rules") for the purposes of any of the following provisions.

(7) In this Part of this Act—

"issuer", in relation to any securities, means the person by whom they have been or are to be issued except that in relation to a certificate or other instrument falling within paragraph 5 of Schedule 1 to this Act it means the person who issued or is to issue the securities to which the certificate or instrument relates;

"the Official List" means the Official List of The Stock Exchange;

"securities" means investments to which this section applies;

and references to listing are references to inclusion in the Official List in pursuance of this Part of this Act.

(8) Any functions of the competent authority under this Part of this Act may be exercised by any committee, sub-committee, officer or servant of the authority except that listing rules—

(*a*) shall be made only by the authority itself or by a committee or sub-committee of the authority; and

(*b*) if made by a committee or sub-committee, shall cease to have effect at the end of the period of twenty-eight days beginning with the day on which they are made (but without prejudice to anything done under them) unless before the end of that period they are confirmed by the authority.

(9) Nothing in this Part of this Act affects the powers of the Council of The Stock Exchange in respect of investments to which this section does not apply and such investments may be admitted to the Official List otherwise than in accordance with this Part of this Act.

DEFINITIONS

"instrument": Sched. 1, para. 28(1)(*b*).

"investment": s.1(1).

GENERAL NOTE

This section provides that no investment to which it applies is to be listed on The Stock Exchange save in accordance with the provisions of Part IV. It applies to the investments enumerated in subss. (2) and (3) for the purposes of Part IV which it defines as "securities."

This section also defines various other terms, including "the competent authority," and specifies how the competent authority may exercise its functions.

Subss. (2), (3)

This section applies to shares, debentures, government and public securities (other than those issued by a member State or its local authorities), instruments entitling to shares and certificates representing shares.

Subs. (4)

This subsection enables the Secretary of State to bring the units of collective investment schemes within the scope of the official listing provisions, as would be permitted by art. 1(2) of the Admission directive.

As to the manner of making an order under this subsection, see s.205(2) and subs. (5) of this section.

Subs. (6)

This subsection identifies the Council of The Stock Exchange as the competent authority in the first instance and empowers it to make rules ("listing rules") for the purposes of the official listing provisions.

As to the manner of making of listing rules, see s.156 and subs. (8) of this section.

Subs. (8)

The special procedure for the making of listing rules is designed to enable The Stock Exchange to make rules for urgent cases without having to convene a Council meeting forthwith: H.C. St. Ctte. E, col. 807 (March 13, 1986).

Applications for listing

143.—(1) An application for listing shall be made to the competent authority in such manner as the listing rules may require.

(2) No application for the listing of any securities shall be made except by or with the consent of the issuer of the securities.

(3) No application for listing shall be made in respect of securities to be issued by a private company or by an old public company within the meaning of section 1 of the Companies Consolidation (Consequential Provisions) Act 1985 or the corresponding Northern Ireland provision.

DEFINITIONS

"competent authority": s.142(6).
"issuer": s.142(7).
"listing": s.142(7).
"listing rules": s.142(6).
"securities": s.142(7).

GENERAL NOTE

Subs. (2)

In the case of an application for the listing of certificates representing securities (Sched. 1, para. 5) the effect of s.142(7) is that the consent necessary is that of the issuer of the underlying securities.

Admission to list

144.—(1) The competent authority shall not admit any securities to the Official List except on an application duly made in accordance with section 143 above and unless satisfied that—

　(*a*)　the requirements of the listing rules made by the authority for the purposes of this section and in force when the application is made; and (*b*) any other requirements imposed by the authority in relation to that application,

are complied with.

(2) Without prejudice to the generality of the power of the competent authority to make listing rules for the purposes of this section, such rules may, in particular, require as a condition of the admission of any securities to the Official List—

(*a*) the submission to, and approval of, the authority of a document (in this Act referred to as "listing particulars") in such form and containing such information as may be specified in the rules; and

(*b*) the publication of that document;

or, in such cases as may be specified by the rules, the publication of a document other than listing particulars.

(3) The competent authority may refuse an application—

(*a*) if it considers that by reason of any matter relating to the issuer the admission of the securities would be detrimental to the interests of investors; or

(*b*) in the case of securities already officially listed in another member State, if the issuer has failed to comply with any obligations to which he is subject by virtue of that listing.

(4) The competent authority shall notify the applicant of its decision on the application within six months from the date on which the application is received or, if within that period the authority has required the applicant to furnish further information in connection with the application, from the date on which that information is furnished.

(5) If the competent authority does not notify the applicant of its decision within the time required by subsection (4) above it shall be taken to have refused the application.

(6) When any securities have been admitted to the Official List their admission shall not be called in question on the ground that any requirement or condition for their admission has not been complied with.

DEFINITIONS
  "competent authority": s.142(6).
  "issuer": s.142(7).
  "listing rules": s.142(6).
  "official list": s.142(7).
  "securities": s.142(7).

GENERAL NOTE
  This section specifies conditions which must be satisfied before securities can be admitted to the Official List, and empowers The Stock Exchange to lay down conditions regarding listing particulars. It also specifies circumstances under which The Stock Exchange may refuse an application, and deals with notification of refusal.

Subs. (1)
  The Stock Exchange *must not* admit any securities to listing unless satisfied that the requirements of the listing rules and any other requirements imposed by the exchange are complied with. Thus, when the Stock Exchange chooses to impose conditions on admission to listing additional to, or more stringent than, those required by the Admissions directive, it cannot waive those conditions on an individualised basis. On the other hand, the listing rules themselves may authorise The Stock Exchange to dispense with or modify the application of the rules in particular cases and by reference to any circumstances: s.156(2). This reflects arts. 5(3) and 7 of the directive, which provide that any derogations "must apply generally for all issuers where the circumstances justifying them are similar."

Subs. (6)
  This subsection is designed to ensure that a transaction involving a listed security is not void or voidable if it emerges that, notwithstanding the admission of the security to listing, some listing requirement has not been complied with.

Discontinuance and suspension of listing

145.—(1) The competent authority may, in accordance with the listing rules, discontinue the listing of any securities if satisfied that there are special circumstances which preclude normal regular dealings in the securities.

(2) The competent authority may in accordance with the listing rules suspend the listing of any securities.

(3) Securities the listing of which is suspended under subsection (2) above shall nevertheless be regarded as listed for the purposes of sections 153 and 155 below.

(4) This section applies to securities included in the Official List at the coming into force of this Part of this Act as it applies to securities included by virtue of this Part.

DEFINITIONS
  "competent authority": s.142(6).
  "listing": s.142(7).
  "listing rules": s.142(6).
  "securities": s.142(7).

GENERAL NOTE
  This section empowers The Stock Exchange to discontinue or suspend the listing of any securities in accordance with the listing rules.

General duty of disclosure in listing particulars

146.—(1) In addition to the information specified by listing rules or required by the competent authority as a condition of the admission of any securities to the Official List any listing particulars submitted to the competent authority under section 144 above shall contain all such information as investors and their professional advisers would reasonably require, and reasonably expect to find there, for the purpose of making an informed assessment of—

   (*a*) the assets and liabilities, financial position, profits and losses, and prospects of the issuer of the securities; and

   (*b*) the rights attaching to those securities.

(2) The information to be included by virtue of this section shall be such information as is mentioned in subsection (1) above which is within the knowledge of any person responsible for the listing particulars or which it would be reasonable for him to obtain by making enquiries.

(3) In determining what information is required to be included in listing particulars by virtue of this section regard shall be had—

   (*a*) to the nature of the securities and of the issuer of the securities;

   (*b*) to the nature of the persons likely to consider their acquisition;

   (*c*) to the fact that certain matters may reasonably be expected to be within the knowledge of professional advisers of any kind which those persons may reasonably be expected to consult; and

   (*d*) to any information available to investors or their professional advisers by virtue of requirements imposed under section 153 below or by or under any other enactment or by virtue of requirements imposed by a recognised investment exchange for the purpose of complying with paragraph 2(2)(*b*) of Schedule 4 to this Act.

DEFINITIONS
  "competent authority": s.142(6).
  "issuer": s.142(7).
  "listing": s.142(7).
  "listing particulars": s.144(2).
  "official list": s.142(7).

"persons responsible for listing particulars": s.152.
"recognised investment exchange": s.207(1).
"securities": s.142(7).

General Note
This section, reflecting art. 4 of the Listing Particulars directive, imposes a general duty of disclosure on persons responsible for listing particulars.

Subs. (1)
The general duty of disclosure supplements the specific disclosure requirements of the listing rules. The listing particulars must contain all such information as investors and their professional advisers would reasonably require, and reasonably expect to find there, for the purpose of making an informed assessment of the matters mentioned. There is, however, no obligation to disclose information covered by s.148.

Subs. (2)
Any person responsible for the listing particulars: See s.152.

Subs. (3)
In determining the reasonable requirements and expectations of investors and their professional advisers, regard is to be had to the factors enumerated.
Para. (b): Information needed by unsophisticated investors might be redundant if the issue is aimed at sophisticated investors.
Para. (d): It is reasonable to take into account what information is already available by virtue of statutory disclosure requirements or the continuing disclosure requirements of a recognised investment exchange.

Supplementary listing particulars

147.—(1) If at any time after the preparation of listing particulars for submission to the competent authority under section 144 above and before the commencement of dealings in the securities following their admission to the Official List—

(*a*) there is a significant change affecting any matter contained in those particulars whose inclusion was required by section 146 above or by listing rules or by the competent authority; or

(*b*) a significant new matter arises the inclusion of information in respect of which would have been so required if it had arisen when the particulars were prepared,

the issuer of the securities shall, in accordance with listing rules made for the purposes of this section, submit to the competent authority for its approval and, if approved, publish supplementary listing particulars of the change or new matter.

(2) In subsection (1) above "significant" means significant for the purpose of making an informed assessment of the matters mentioned in section 146(1) above.

(3) Where the issuer of the securities is not aware of the change or new matter in question he shall not be under any duty to comply with subsection (1) above unless he is notified of it by a person responsible for the listing particulars; but it shall be the duty of any person responsible for those particulars who is aware of such a matter to give notice of it to the issuer.

(4) Subsection (1) above applies also as respects matters contained in any supplementary listing particulars previously published under this section in respect of the securities in question.

Definitions
"competent authority": s.142(6).
"issuer": s.142(7).
"listing particulars": s.144(2).
"listing rules": s.142(6).

"official list": s.142(7).
"persons responsible for listing particulars": s.152.

GENERAL NOTE
This section specifies the circumstances under which supplementary listing particulars must be prepared.

Subs. (1)
If there is a significant development during the time between the preparation of listing particulars and the commencement of dealings, the listing particulars must be kept up-to-date by means of one or more supplements.
As to the meaning of "significant," see subs. (2).

Subs. (3)
Person responsible for the listing particulars: See s.152.

Exemptions from disclosure

148.—(1) The competent authority may authorise the omission from listing particulars or supplementary listing particulars of any information the inclusion of which would otherwise be required by section 146 above—

(*a*) on the ground that its disclosure would be contrary to the public interest;

(*b*) subject to subsection (2) below, on the ground that its disclosure would be seriously detrimental to the issuer of the securities; or

(*c*) in the case of securities which fall within paragraph 2 of Schedule 1 to this Act as modified by section 142(3)(*b*) above and are of any class specified by listing rules, on the ground that its disclosure is unnecessary for persons of the kind who may be expected normally to buy or deal in the securities.

(2) No authority shall be granted under subsection (1)(*b*) above in respect of, and no such authority shall be regarded as extending to, information the non-disclosure of which would be likely to mislead a person considering the acquisition of the securities as to any facts the knowledge of which it is essential for him to have in order to make an informed assessment.

(3) The Secretary of State or the Treasury may issue a certificate to the effect that the disclosure of any information (including information that would otherwise have to be included in particulars for which they are themselves responsible) would be contrary to the public interest and the competent authority shall be entitled to act on any such certificate in exercising its powers under subsection (1)(*a*) above.

(4) This section is without prejudice to any powers of the competent authority under rules made by virtue of section 156(2) below.

DEFINITIONS
"competent authority": s.142(6).
"listing particulars": s.144(2).
"listing rules": s.142(6).
"securities": s.142(7).

GENERAL NOTE
This section specifies circumstances under which The Stock Exchange is empowered to authorise the omission from listing particulars of information whose inclusion would otherwise be required by s.146.
The omission of information may be authorised on the ground that its disclosure would be contrary to the public interest: subs. (1)(*a*). The Secretary of State and the Treasury are empowered to issue certificates to this effect, and The Stock Exchange is entitled to act on them: subs. (3). Even in the absence of a certificate, however, The Stock Exchange may act on public interest grounds.

The omission of information may also be authorised on the ground that its disclosure would be seriously detrimental to the issuer of the securities: subs. (1)(b). But information may not be suppressed on this ground if its non-disclosure would be likely to mislead a potential acquirer as to any facts he must know in order to make an informed assessment: subs. (2).

The omission of information may be authorised, thirdly, in the case of debt instruments covered by Part IV (see s.142) of any class specified by listing rules, on the ground that its disclosure is unnecessary for the kind of investors at whom the issue is aimed (i.e. presumably, sophisticated investors): subs. (1)(c).

Registration of listing particulars

149.—(1) On or before the date on which listing particulars or supplementary listing particulars are published as required by listing rules a copy of the particulars shall be delivered for registration to the registrar of companies and a statement that a copy has been delivered to him shall be included in the particulars.

(2) In subsection (1) above "the registrar of companies" means—

(a) if the securities in question are or are to be issued by a company incorporated in Great Britain, the registrar of companies in England and Wales or the registrar of companies in Scotland according to whether the company's registered office is in England and Wales or in Scotland;

(b) if the securities in question are or are to be issued by a company incorporated in Northern Ireland, the registrar of companies for Northern Ireland;

(c) in any other case, any of those registrars.

(3) If any particulars are published without a copy of them having been delivered as required by this section the issuer of the securities in question and any person who is knowingly a party to the publication shall be guilty of an offence and liable—

(a) on conviction on indictment, to a fine;

(b) on summary conviction, to a fine not exceeding the statutory maximum.

DEFINITIONS
"insurer": s.142(7).
"listing particulars": s.144(2).
"listing rules": s.142(6).
"securities": s.142(7).

GENERAL NOTE
This section requires the registration of listing particulars with one of the registrars of companies. In the case of a company incorporated outside Great Britain and Northern Ireland, any of the registrars may be selected.

Compensation for false or misleading particulars

150.—(1) Subject to section 151 below, the person or persons responsible for any listing particulars or supplementary listing particulars shall be liable to pay compensation to any person who has acquired any of the securities in question and suffered loss in respect of them as a result of any untrue or misleading statement in the particulars or the omission from them of any matter required to be included by section 146 or 147 above.

(2) Where listing rules require listing particulars to include information as to any particular matter on the basis that the particulars must include a statement either as to that matter or, if such is the case, that there is no such matter, the omission from the particulars of the information shall be treated for the purposes of subsection (1) above as a statement that there is no such matter.

(3) Subject to section 151 below, a person who fails to comply with section 147 above shall be liable to pay compensation to any person who has acquired any of the securities in question and suffered loss in respect of them as a result of the failure.

(4) This section does not affect any liability which any person may incur apart from this section.

(5) References in this section to the acquisition by any person of securities include references to his contracting to acquire them or an interest in them.

(6) No person shall by reason of being a promoter of a company or otherwise incur any liability for failing to disclose any information which he would not be required to disclose in listing particulars in respect of a company's securities if he were responsible for those particulars or, if he is responsible for them, which he is entitled to omit by virtue of section 148 above.

DEFINITIONS
"listing particulars": s.144(2).
"listing rules": s.142(6).
"persons responsible for listing particulars": s.152.
"securities": s.142(7).

GENERAL NOTE
Subject to the next section, this section specifies the circumstances in which compensation is payable for false or misleading listing particulars by the persons responsible for them.

Subs. (1)
Person who has acquired: see subs. (5) below.
This subsection provides that compensation is payable by the persons responsible for listing particulars for a loss occasioned by an untrue or misleading statement, by an omission in breach of the general duty of disclosure, or by an omission in breach of the supplementary disclosure requirements imposed by s.147. Subs. (1) does *not* state that compensation is payable for a loss occasioned by an omission in breach of listing rules, but such omissions are addressed in subs. (2).

Subs. (2)
Where listing rules require something to be disclosed or a positive statement to be made that there is nothing to be disclosed (a positive negative), a failure to make any disclosure or statement is to be treated as a statement that there is nothing to be disclosed. The truth or untruth of this notional statement can then be determined for the purposes of subs. (1).

Subs. (3)
Compensation is also payable for a loss occasioned by a failure to comply with subss. (1) or (3) of s.147.

Subs. (4)
Any liability incurred under the common law of negligence or under the Misrepresentation Act 1967 is unaffected by the incurrence of liability under this section.

Exemption from liability to pay compensation

151.—(1) A person shall not incur[r]* any liability under section 150(1) above for any loss in respect of securities caused by any such statement or omission as is there mentioned if he satisfies the court that at the time when the particulars were submitted to the competent authority he reasonably believed, having made such enquiries (if any) as were reasonable, that the statement was true and not misleading or that the matter whose omission caused the loss was properly omitted and—

---

* [ ] denotes typographical error in Queen's Printer's copy of Act.

(*a*) that he continued in that belief until the time when the securities were acquired; or

(*b*) that they were acquired before it was reasonably practicable to bring a correction to the attention of persons likely to acquire the securities in question; or

(*c*) that before the securities were acquired he had taken all such steps as it was reasonable for him to have taken to secure that a correction was brought to the attention of those persons; or

(*d*) that he continued in that belief until after the commencement of dealings in the securities following their admission to the Official List and that the securities were acquired after such a lapse of time that he ought in the circumstances to be reasonably excused.

(2) A person shall not incur any liability under section 150(1) above for any loss in respect of securities caused by a statement purporting to be made by or on the authority of another person as an expert which is, and is stated to be, included in the particulars with that other person's consent if he satisfies the court that at the time when the particulars were submitted to the competent authority he believed on reasonable grounds that the other person was competent to make or authorise the statement and had consented to its inclusion in the form and context in which it was included and—

(*a*) that he continued in that belief until the time when the securities were acquired; or

(*b*) that they were acquired before it was reasonably practicable to bring the fact that the expert was not competent or had not consented to the attention of persons likely to acquire the securities in question; or

(*c*) that before the securities were acquired he had taken all such steps as it was reasonable for him to have taken to secure that that fact was brought to the attention of those persons; or

(*d*) that he continued in that belief until after the commencement of dealings in the securities following their admission to the Official List and that the securities were acquired after such a lapse of time that he ought in the circumstances to be reasonably excused.

(3) Without prejudice to subsections (1) and (2) above, a person shall not incur any liability under section 150(1) above for any loss in respect of any securities caused by any such statement or omissions as is there mentioned if he satisfies the court—

(*a*) that before the securities were acquired a correction, or where the statement was such as is mentioned in subsection (2), the fact that the expert was not competent or had not consented had been published in a manner calculated to bring it to the attention of persons likely to acquire the securities in question; or

(*b*) that he took all such steps as it was reasonable for him to take to secure such publication and reasonably believed that it had taken place before the securities were acquired.

(4) A person shall not incur any liability under section 150(1) above for any loss resulting from a statement made by an official person or contained in a public official document which is included in the particulars if he satisfies the court that the statement is accurately and fairly reproduced.

(5) A person shall not incur any liability under section 150(1) or (3) above if he satisfies the court that the person suffering the loss acquired the securities in question with knowledge that the statement was false or misleading, of the omitted matter or of the change or new matter, as the case may be.

(6) A person shall not incur any liability under section 150(3) above if he satisfies the court that he reasonably believed that the change or new

matter in question was not such as to call for supplementary listing particulars.

(7) In this section "expert" includes any engineer, valuer, accountant or other person whose profession, qualifications or experience give authority to a statement made by him; and references to the acquisition of securities include references to contracting to acquire them or an interest in them.

DEFINITIONS
    "acquisition of securities": s.151(7).
    "competent authority": s.142(6).
    "expert": s.151(7).
    "official list": s.142(7).
    "securities": s.142(7).

GENERAL NOTE
This section provides various defences to claims for compensation under s.150(1) (in the case of subss. (1) to (5)) and s.150(3) (in the case of subs. (6)). In each case the onus is on the person from whom compensation is sought to satisfy the court of the existence of the circumstances which found the exemption.

Subs. (1)
This subsection provides a defence of reasonable belief in the truth of the relevant statement or in the propriety of the relevant omission. This reasonable belief, to afford a defence, must be coupled with one of the eventualities enumerated in paras. (*a*) to (*d*).
    Para. (d): This paragraph appears to contemplate that lapse of time can cure a failure to take such steps as are reasonable to secure that a correction is brought to the attention of potential acquirers.

Subs. (2)
This subsection provides a defence of reasonable belief in the competence of an expert and in that expert's consent to the relevant statement's inclusion. Again this reasonable belief, to afford a defence, must be coupled with one of the eventualities enumerated in paras. (*a*) to (*d*).

Subs. (3)
This subsection contemplates a situation where a person responsible for defective listing particulars cannot satisfy the court of his reasonable belief in their accuracy, or in the competence and consent of the expert. In such a situation he incurs no liability if, before the acquisition of securities, an appropriate correction is published, or he takes reasonable steps to secure its publication and reasonably believes it to have been published.

Subs. (4)
This subsection exempts from liability if the loss was occasioned by an official statement reproduced in the listing particulars.

Subs. (5)
No liability is incurred if the person acquiring the securities knew of the defect in the listing particulars.

Persons responsible for particulars

152.—(1) For the purposes of this Part of this Act the persons responsible for listing particulars or supplementary listing particulars are—
    (*a*) the issuer of the securities to which the particulars relate;
    (*b*) where the issuer is a body corporate, each person who is a director of that body at the time when the particulars are submitted to the competent authority;
    (*c*) where the issuer is a body corporate, each person who has authorised himself to be named, and is named, in the particulars as a director or as having agreed to become a director of that body either immediately or at a future time;

    (*d*) each person who accepts, and is stated in the particulars as accepting, responsibility for, or for any part of, the particulars;

    (*e*) each person not falling within any of the foregoing paragraphs who has authorised the contents of, or any part of, the particulars.

(2) A person is not responsible for any particulars by virtue of subsection (1)(*b*) above if they are published without his knowledge or consent and on becoming aware of their publication he forthwith gives reasonable public notice that they were published without his knowledge or consent.

(3) Where a person has accepted responsibility for, or authorised, only part of the contents of any particulars, he is responsible under subsection (1)(*d*) or (*e*) above for only that part and only if it is included in (or substantially in) the form and context to which he has agreed.

(4) Where the particulars relate to securities which are to be issued in connection with an offer by (or by a wholly-owned subsidiary of), the issuer for, or an agreement for the acquisition by (or by a wholly-owned subsidiary of) the issuer of, securities issued by another person or in connection with any arrangement whereby the whole of the undertaking of another person is to become the undertaking of the issuer (of a wholly-owned subsidiary of the issuer or of a body corporate which will become such a subsidiary by virtue of the arrangement) then if—

    (*a*) that other person; and

    (*b*) where that other person is a body corporate, each person who is a director of that body at the time when the particulars are submitted to the competent authority and each other person who has authorised himself to be named, and is named, in the particulars as a director of that body,

is responsible by virtue of paragraph (*d*) of subsection (1) above for any part of the particulars relating to that other person or to the securities or undertaking to which the offer, agreement or arrangement relates, no person shall be responsible for that part under paragraph (*a*), (*b*) or (*c*) of that subsection but without prejudice to his being responsible under paragraph (*d*).

(5) Neither paragraph (*b*) nor paragraph (*c*) of subsection (1) above applies in the case of an issuer of international securities of a class specified by listing rules for the purposes of section 148(1)(*c*) above; and neither of those paragraphs nor paragraph (*b*) of subsection (4) above applies in the case of any director certified by the competent authority as a person to whom that paragraph should not apply by reason of his having an interest, or of any other circumstances, making it inappropriate for him to be responsible by virtue of that paragraph.

(6) In subsection (5) above "international securities" means any investment falling within paragraph 2 of Schedule 1 to this Act as modified by section 142(3)(*b*) above which is of a kind likely to be dealt in by bodies incorporated in or persons resident in a country or territory outside the United Kingdom, is denominated in a currency other than sterling or is otherwise connected with such a country or territory.

(7) In this section "wholly-owned subsidiary", in relation to a person other than a body corporate, means any body corporate that would be his wholly-owned subsidiary if he were a body corporate.

(8) Nothing in this section shall be construed as making a person responsible for any particulars by reason of giving advice as to their contents in a professional capacity.

(9) Where by virtue of this section the issuer of any shares pays or is liable to pay compensation under section 150 above for loss suffered in respect of shares for which a person has subscribed no account shall be taken of that liability or payment in determining any question as to the amount paid on subscription for those shares or as to the amount paid up or deemed to be paid up on them.

DEFINITIONS
"body corporate": s.207(1).
"competent authority": s.142(6).
"director": s.207(1).
"issuer": s.142(7).
"listing rules": s.142(6).
"securities": s.142(7).
"subsidiary": s.207(8).

GENERAL NOTE
This section is concerned with the attribution of responsibility for listing particulars and supplementary listing particulars.

Subs. (1)
This subsection enumerates the persons responsible for listing particulars.
Para. (a): This paragraph is qualified by subs. (4).
Para. (b): This paragraph is qualified by subss. (2), (4) and (5).
Para. (c): This paragraph is qualified by subss. (4) and (5).
Para. (d): This paragraph is qualified by subs. (3).
Para. (e): Other persons who authorise particulars (or parts thereof) include the sponsoring issuing house and experts (*e.g.* accountants).
This paragraph is qualified by subs. (3).

Subs. (2)
This subsection provides that a person is not responsible *qua* director for particulars published without his knowledge or consent, etc. That person might still be responsible by virtue of having avowed responsibility for them (subs. (1)(*d*)).

Subs. (4)
This subsection is concerned with responsibility for listing particulars relating to securities issued in connection with an agreed takeover. Its main application is to the issuer's acquisition of another company's shares. In such a case, if the other company *and* its directors avow responsibility for any part of the particulars relating to that company, then no person incurs responsibility for that part by virtue of being the issuer of the new securities or a director of the issuer. Responsibility may still be incurred, however, by an avowal of responsibility.
This subsection also applies to the acquisition of the whole of an undertaking owned by another person (whether that person is a body corporate or not).
This subsection is qualified by subs. (5).
As to the meaning of "wholly-owned subsidiary" in this context, see subs. (7).

Subs. (5)
The first limb of this subsection absolves from responsibility for listing particulars the directors (and ostensible directors and directors-to-be) of an issue of international securities of a class specified by listing rules unless they avow responsibility for the particulars or authorise their contents.
As to the meaning "international securities" in this context, see subs. (6) below.
The second limb of this subsection aims to absolve from responsibility for listing particulars directors (and ostensible directors and directors-to-be) certified by The Stock Exchange. In addition, an avowal of responsibility by a certified director is not necessary for the benefit of subs. (4) to be gained. The import of the certificate is that the director in question is a person to whom "that paragraph" should not apply by reason of his having an interest, or of any other circumstances, making it inappropriate (*e.g.* because of a conflict of interest) for him to be responsible by virtue of "that paragraph."
But what is "that paragraph"? In the Financial Services Bill as amended in Committee in the House of Lords (Bill 238) "that paragraph" was para. (*b*) of subs. (1), so that the effect of a certificate would be to relieve the director of responsibility *qua* director. In the subsection as amended and enacted, however, "that paragraph" appears to have become para. (*b*) of subs. (4), which may cause difficulties.

Subs. (6)
"International securities" are thus debt instruments covered by Part IV (see s.142) which satisfy one of the criteria specified.

Subs. (8)
This is modelled on part of s.741(2) of the Companies Act 1985.

Subs. (9)
The effect of this subsection is that the liability of a shareholder in respect of shares not fully paid up cannot be offset against the liability of the company to pay that shareholder compensation in respect of false or misleading particulars.

Obligations of issuers of listed securities

153.—(1) Listing rules may specify requirements to be complied with by issuers of listed securities and make provision with respect to the action that may be taken by the competent authority in the event of non-compliance, including provision—
  (*a*) authorising the authority to publish the fact that an issuer has contravened any provision of the rules; and
  (*b*) if the rules require an issuer to publish any information, authorising the authority to publish it in the event of his failure to do so.
  (2) This section applies to the issuer of securities included in the Official List at the coming into force of this Part of this Act as it applies to the issuer of securities included by virtue of this Part.

DEFINITIONS
  "competent authority": s.142(6).
  "issuer": s.142(7).
  "listing rules": s.142(6).

GENERAL NOTE
  This section enables The Stock Exchange in the listing rules to specify requirements to be complied with by issuers, and to make provision for the publicising of contraventions and for the publication by The Stock Exchange of information which the issuer ought under the rules to have published.

Subs. (1)
  Listed securities: This includes securities the listing of which is suspended: s.145(3).

Advertisements etc. in connection with listing applications

154.—(1) Where listing particulars are or are to be published in connection with an application for the listing of any securities no advertisement or other information of a kind specified by listing rules shall be issued in the United Kingdom unless the contents of the advertisement or other information have been submitted to the competent authority and that authority has either—
  (*a*) approved those contents; or
  (*b*) authorised the issue of the advertisement or information without such approval.
  (2) An authorised person who contravenes this section shall be treated as having contravened rules made under Chapter V of Part I of this Act or, in the case of a person who is an authorised person by virtue of his membership of a recognised self-regulating organisation or certification by a recognised professional body, the rules of that organisation or body.
  (3) Subject to subsection (4) below, a person other than an authorised person, who contravenes this section shall be guilty of an offence and liable—
  (*a*) on conviction on indictment, to imprisonment for a term not exceeding two years or to a fine or to both;
  (*b*) on summary conviction, to a fine not exceeding the statutory maximum.

(4) A person who in the ordinary course of a business other than investment business issues an advertisement or other information to the order of another person shall not be guilty of an offence under this section if he proves that he believed on reasonable grounds that the advertisement or information had been approved or its issue authorised by the competent authority.

(5) Where information has been approved, or its issue has been authorised, under this section neither the person issuing it nor any person responsible for, or for any part of, the listing particulars shall incur any civil liability by reason of any statement in or omission from the information if that information and the listing particulars, taken together, would not be likely to mislead persons of the kind likely to consider the acquisition of the securities in question.

DEFINITIONS
"advertisement": s.207(2), (3).
"authorised person": s.207(1).
"certification": s.270(1).
"competent authority": s.142(6).
"investment business": s.1(2).
"listing": s.142(7).
"listing rules": s.142(6).
"recognised professional body": s.207(1).
"recognised self-regulating organisation": s.207(1).
"securities": s.147(7).

GENERAL NOTE
This section lays down the procedure to be followed where it is proposed to publish an advertisement in connection with the listing of securities. It also specifies the consequences of contravening this procedure, creates a special defence, and limits the scope of civil liability in connection with such advertisements.

Subs. (1)
It is up to The Stock Exchange to specify in the listing rules what documents are to be submitted to it. It is also up to The Stock Exchange to decide whether to vet the advertisement or information, or to authorise its issue without vetting it.

Subs. (2)
This subsection specifies the consequences for authorised persons of issuing advertisements or information caught by the listing rules without the approval or authorisation of The Stock Exchange. The provision is parallel to that made in s.95, and raises parallel difficulties. A directly authorised person who contravenes this section is to be treated as having contravened rules made under Chapter V and, accordingly, is exposed to civil actions. A person authorised by virtue of membership of an SRO or RPB, on the other hand, is to be treated as having contravened the rules of the SRO or RPB in question. This formulation seems apt to make contravention a disciplinary matter for the SRO or RPB but not to expose the violator to civil actions. Contrast the formulations in s.61(1)(a)(iv) and s.62(2).

Subs. (3)
This subsection makes it a criminal offence, subject to subs. (4), for an unauthorised person to contravene subs. (1).

Subs. (4)
This subsection provides a defence for an unauthorised person who, in the ordinary course of a business other than investment business, issues an advertisement to the order of another person. However, the onus is on the issuer of the advertisement to prove that he believed on reasonable grounds that subs. (1) had been complied with.

Subs. (5)
The effect of this subsection is that a misleading statement in or omission from an approved or authorised advertisement does not expose the issuer of the advertisement to civil liability if the advertisement read in conjunction with the listing particulars would not be likely to mislead persons of the kind likely to consider the acquisition of the securities in question.

Fees

155. Listing rules may require the payment of fees to the competent authority in respect of applications for listing and the retention of securities in the Official List.

DEFINITIONS
    "competent authority": s.142(6).
    "listing": s.142(7).
    "listing rules": s.142(6).
    "official list": s.142(7).
    "securities": s.142(7).

GENERAL NOTE
Securities whose listing is suspended are to be regarded as listed for the purposes of this section: s.145(3).

Listing rules: general provisions

156.—(1) Listing rules may make different provision for different cases.

(2) Listing rules may authorise the competent authority to dispense with or modify the application of the rules in particular cases and by reference to any circumstances.

(3) Listing rules shall be made by an instrument in writing.

(4) Immediately after an instrument containing listing rules is made it shall be printed and made available to the public with or without payment.

(5) A person shall not be taken to have contravened any listing rule if he shows that at the time of the alleged contravention the instrument containing the rule had not been made available as required by subsection (4) above.

(6) The production of a printed copy of an instrument purporting to be made by the competent authority on which is endorsed a certificate signed by an officer of the authority authorised by it for that purpose and stating—

(*a*) that the instrument was made by the authority;

(*b*) that the copy is a true copy of the instrument; and

(*c*) that on a specified date the instrument was made available to the public as required by subsection (4) above,

shall be prima facie evidence or, in Scotland, sufficient evidence of the facts stated in the certificate.

(7) Any certificate purporting to be signed as mentioned in subsection (6) above shall be deemed to have been duly signed unless the contrary is shown.

(8) Any person wishing in any legal proceedings to cite an instrument made by the competent authority may require the authority to cause a copy of it to be endorsed with such a certificate as is mentioned in subsection (6) above.

DEFINITIONS
    "competent authorities": s.142(6).
    "listing rules": s.142(6).

GENERAL NOTE
Subss. (3)–(8)
These subsections contain provisions governing the promulgation and citation of listing rules. The provisions are those usually associated with subordinate legislation other than statutory instruments.

Alteration of competent authority

157.—(1) The Secretary of State may by order transfer the functions as competent authority of the Council of The Stock Exchange to another body or other bodies either at the request of the Council or if it appears to him—

(a) that the Council is exercising those functions in a manner which is unnecessary for the protection of investors and fails to take into account the proper interests of issuers and proposed issuers of securities; or

(b) that it is necessary to do so for the protection of investors.

(2) The Secretary of State may by order transfer all or any of the functions as competent authority from any body or bodies to which they have been previously transferred under this section to another body or bodies.

(3) Any order made under subsection (1) above at the request of the Council shall be subject to annulment in pursuance of a resolution of either House of Parliament; and no other order shall be made under this section unless a draft of it has been laid before and approved by a resolution of each House of Parliament.

(4) An order under this section shall not affect anything previously done by any body ("the previous authority") in the exercise of functions which are transferred by the order to another body ("the new authority") and may contain such supplementary provisions as the Secretary of State thinks necessary or expedient, including provisions—

(a) for modifying or excluding any provision of this Part of this Act in its application to any such functions;

(b) for the transfer of any property, rights or liabilities relating to any such functions from the previous authority to the new authority;

(c) for the carrying on and completion by the new authority of anything in process of being done by the previous authority when the order takes effect; and

(d) for the substitution of the new authority for the previous authority in any instrument, contract or legal proceedings.

(5) If by virtue of this section the function of admission to or discontinuance or suspension of listing is exercisable otherwise than by the Council of The Stock Exchange, references in this Part of this Act to the competent authority admitting securities to the Official List or to discontinuing or suspending the listing of any securities shall be construed as references to the giving of directions to the Council of The Stock Exchange to admit the securities or to discontinue or suspend their listing; and it shall be the duty of the Council to comply with any such direction.

DEFINITIONS
    "issuer": s.142(7).
    "listing": s.142(7).
    "official list": s.142(7).
    "securities": s.142(7).

GENERAL NOTE
    This section empowers the Secretary of State to substitute some other body for the Council of The Stock Exchange as the "competent authority." It also empowers him to make subsequent alterations of the competent authority.

Subs. (1)
    This subsection sets out the three grounds upon which a transfer of the functions of the Council of The Stock Exchange as competent authority might be ordered.
    As to the manner of making such an order, see s.205(2) and subs. (3) of this section.

Subs. (2)
    This subsection empowers the Secretary of State to order the transfer of *all or any* of the functions as competent authority from any body to which they have previously been transferred to another body. The grounds upon which such an order might be made are not limited by enumeration.

As to the manner of making an order under this subsection, see s.205(2) and subs. (3) of this section.

Subs. (4)

A transfer order under this section does not affect anything done by a previous competent authority in the exercise of its functions. The order may contain various transitional provisions, including ones that modify or exclude provisions of Part IV of the Act in its application to the functions transferred.

Subs. (5)

In the unlikely event of The Stock Exchange being stripped of the function of admitting securities to listing, or discontinuing or suspending their listing, the Council could be directed to carry out the requisite formal acts.

Part V

Offers of Unlisted Securities

Preliminary

158.—(1) This Part of this Act applies to any investment—
  (a) which is not listed, or the subject of an application for listing, in accordance with Part IV of this Act; and
  (b) falls within paragraph 1, 2, 4 or 5 of Schedule 1 to this Act.
  (2) In the application of those paragraphs for the purposes of subsection (1) above—
  (a) paragraphs 4 and 5 shall have effect with the omission of references to investments falling within paragraph 3; and
  (b) paragraph 4 shall have effect as if it referred only to instruments issued by the person issuing the investment to be subscribed for.
  (3) In this Part of this Act—
    "issuer", in relation to any securities, means the person by whom they have been or are to be issued except that in relation to a certificate or other instrument falling within paragraph 5 of Schedule 1 to this Act it means the person who issued or is to issue the securities to which the certificate or instrument relates;
    "securities" means investments to which this section applies.
  (4) For the purposes of this Part of this Act an advertisement offers securities if—
  (a) it invites a person to enter into an agreement for or with a view to subscribing for or otherwise acquiring or underwriting any securities; or
  (b) it contains information calculated to lead directly or indirectly to a person entering into such an agreement.
  (5) In this Part of this Act "the registrar of companies", in relation to any securities, means—
  (a) if the securities are or are to be issued by a company incorporated in Great Britain, the registrar of companies in England and Wales or the registrar of companies in Scotland according to whether the company's registered office is in England and Wales or in Scotland;
  (b) if the securities are or are to be issued by a company incorporated in Northern Ireland, the registrar of companies for Northern Ireland;
  (c) in any other case, any of those registrars.
  (6) In this Part of this Act "approved exchange", in relation to dealings in any securities, means a recognised investment exchange approved by the Secretary of State for the purposes of this Part of this Act either generally or in relation to such dealings, and the Secretary of State shall

give notice in such manner as he thinks appropriate of the exchanges which are for the time being approved.

DEFINITIONS
"advertisement": s.207(2), (3).
"investment": s.1(1).
"listing": s.142(7).
"recognised investment exchange": s.207(1).

GENERAL NOTE
This section specifies the investments to which Part V of the Act applies and defines them, *for the purposes of Part V*, as "securities."
This section also defines various other terms for the purposes of this Part.

Subss. (1), (2)
This part of the Act applies to shares, debentures, certificates representing shares or debentures, and instruments entitling to shares or debentures if issued by the person issuing the underlying shares or debentures—all if unlisted.

Subs. (3)
Note that "securities" for the purposes of Part V (offers of unlisted securities) are not the same thing as "securities" for the purposes of Part IV (official listing of securities).

Subs. (6)
This subsection introduces the concept of an approved recognised investment exchange. In certain circumstances the continuous disclosure requirements of such an exchange allow offerors to be relieved of the need to produce a prospectus.

Offers of securities on admission to approved exchange

159.—(1) Subject to subsection (2) and section 161 below, no person shall issue or cause to be issued in the United Kingdom an advertisement offering any securities on the occasion of their admission to dealings on an approved exchange or on terms that they will be issued if admitted to such dealings unless—

    (*a*) a document (in this Part of this Act referred to as a "prospectus") containing information about the securities has been submitted to and approved by the exchange and delivered for registration to the registrar of companies; or

    (*b*) the advertisement is such that no agreement can be entered into in pursuance of it until such a prospectus has been submitted, approved and delivered as aforesaid.

(2) Subsection (1) above does not apply if a prospectus relating to the securities has been delivered for registration under this Part of this Act in the previous twelve months and the approved exchange certifies that it is satisfied that persons likely to consider acquiring the securities will have sufficient information to enable them to decide whether to do so from that prospectus and any information published in connection with the admission of the securities.

DEFINITIONS
"advertisement": s.207(2), (3).
"advertisement offering securities": s.158(4).
"approved exchange": s.158(6).
"registrar of companies": s.158(5).
"securities": s.158(3).

GENERAL NOTE
This section prohibits the issue of an advertisement offering securities on the occasion of their admission to dealings on an approved exchange (or to be admitted) unless a prospectus has been approved by the exchange and delivered to the registrar of companies, or unless a prospectus is to be approved and delivered before the offer can be accepted. (This latter alternative allows a takeover bid to be made before a prospectus is produced.)

The prohibition does not apply, however, if there is already a registered prospectus less than a year old, and the exchange certifies that it (coupled with any information published in connection with the admission of the securities) will give potential acquirers enough information to go on.

As to circumstances in which this section does not apply, see s.161 and especially s.161(3) (compliance with continuing disclosure obligations as an alternative to a prospectus).

As to the consequence of contravening this section, see s.171.

Other offers of securities

160.—(1) Subject to subsections (5) and (6) and section 161 below, no person shall issue or cause to be issued in the United Kingdom an advertisement offering any securities which is a primary or secondary offer within the meaning of this section unless—

(a) he has delivered for registration to the registrar of companies a prospectus relating to the securities and expressed to be in respect of the offer; or

(b) the advertisement is such that no agreement can be entered into in pursuance of it until such a prospectus has been delivered by him as aforesaid.

(2) For the purposes of this section a primary offer is an advertisement issued otherwise than as mentioned in section 159(1) above inviting persons to enter into an agreement for or with a view to subscribing (whether or not in cash) for or underwriting the securities to which it relates or containing information calculated to lead directly or indirectly to their doing so.

(3) For the purposes of this section a secondary offer is any other advertisement issued otherwise than as mentioned in section 159(1) above inviting persons to enter into an agreement for or with a view to acquiring the securities to which it relates or containing information calculated to lead directly or indirectly to their doing so, being an advertisement issued or caused to be issued by—

(a) a person who has acquired the securities from the issuer with a view to issuing such an advertisement in respect of them;

(b) a person who, with a view to issuing such an advertisement in respect of them, has acquired the securities otherwise than from the issuer but without their having been admitted to dealings on an approved exchange or held by a person who acquired them as an investment and without any intention that such an advertisement should be issued in respect of them; or

(c) a person who is a controller of the issuer or has been such a controller in the previous twelve months and who is acting with the consent or participation of the issuer in issuing the advertisement.

(4) For the purposes of subsection (3)(a) above it shall be presumed in the absence of evidence to the contrary that a person has acquired securities with a view to issuing an advertisement offering the securities if he issues it or causes it to be issued—

(a) within six months after the issue of the securities; or

(b) before the consideration due from him for their acquisition is received by the person from whom he acquired them.

(5) Subsection (1) above does not apply to a secondary offer if such a prospectus as is mentioned in that subsection has been delivered in accordance with that subsection in respect of an offer of the same securities made in the previous six months by a person making a primary offer or a previous secondary offer.

(6) Subsection (1) above does not apply to an advertisement issued in such circumstances as may be specified by an order made by the Secretary of State for the purpose of exempting from that subsection—

(a) advertisements appearing to him to have a private character, whether by reason of a connection between the person issuing them and those to whom they are addressed or otherwise;

(b) advertisements appearing to him to deal with investments only incidentally;

(c) advertisements issued to persons appearing to him to be sufficiently expert to understand any risks involved; or

(d) such other classes of advertisement as he thinks fit.

(7) Without prejudice to subsection (6)(c) above an order made by the Secretary of State may exempt from subsection (1) above an advertisement issued in whatever circumstances if it relates to securities appearing to him to be of a kind that can be expected normally to be bought or dealt in only by persons sufficiently expert to understand any risks involved.

(8) An order under subsection (6) or (7) above may require any person who by virtue of the order is authorised to issue an advertisement to comply with such requirements as are specified in the order.

(9) An order made by virtue of subsection (6)(a), (b) or (c) or by virtue of subsection (7) above shall be subject to annulment in pursuance of a resolution of either House of Parliament; and no order shall be made by virtue of subsection (6)(d) above unless a draft of it has been laid before and approved by a resolution of each House of Parliament.

DEFINITIONS

"advertisement": s.207(2), (3).
"advertisement offering securities": s.158(4).
"controller": s.207(5).
"issuer": s.158(3).
"registrar of companies": s.158(5).
"securities": s.158(3).

GENERAL NOTE

This section applies to advertisements making a primary or secondary offer of securities not covered by the preceding section. The underlying policy is that a prospectus should be required when securities not admitted to an approved exchange are offered *for the first time* by the issuer or by someone else who has acquired them with a view to offering them: H.L. Vol. 479, col. 702 (July 28, 1986).

Subs. (1)

This subsection lays down the general rule that a primary or secondary offer of such securities is prohibited unless a prospectus, expressed to be in respect of the offer, has been delivered to the registrar of companies, or unless a prospectus is to be delivered before the offer can be accepted. (As in the previous section, this latter alternative allows a takeover bid to be made before a prospectus is produced.)

This general rule does not apply, however, in the circumstances set out in subss. (5) and (6).

As to the consequences of contravening subs. (1), see s.171.

"Primary offer" is defined in subs. (2), and "secondary offer" in subs. (3).

Subs. (2)

This defines "primary offer."

A prospectus is required if the advertisement may lead people to *subscribe for* or *underwrite* the securities in question.

Subs. (3)

This defines "secondary offer."

A prospectus is required if the advertisement may lead people to *acquire* the securities in question and the advertiser has acquired the securities from their actual issuer with a view to advertising them: para. (a). Subs. (4) creates a rebuttable presumption that a person has acquired securities with a view to advertising them if he advertises them within six months of their issue or before he has paid for them.

A prospectus is also required if the advertisement may lead people to acquire the securities in question and the advertiser has acquired the securities from someone *other than* their issuer. But a prospectus is not required if the securities in question have been held by someone who acquired them "as an investment" and without any intention that they should be offered by advertisement. And a prospectus is not required if the securities in question have been admitted to dealings on an approved exchange: para. (*b*). (This latter exception appears here because s.159 does not cover advertisements issued *after* the occasion of securities' admission to dealings on an approved exchange.)

A prospectus is required if the advertisement may lead people to acquire the securities in question and the advertiser is a controller of the issuer of the securities acting with the consent or participation of the issuer: para. (*c*).

A prospectus is not required in the circumstances set out in subs. (5).

Subs. (5)

A prospectus is not required in connection with a secondary offer if the securities in question are already covered by a prospectus, less than six months old, registered in connection with a primary offer or a previous secondary offer.

Subs. (6)

A prospectus is not required in connection with advertisements exempted by the Secretary of State, who may exempt the classes of advertisements enumerated in paras. (*a*), (*b*) and (*c*), and such other classes of advertisement as he thinks fit.

Para. (a): The notion of advertisements having a "private character" replaces that of "domestic concern" under the Companies Act 1986, s.60 with the difference that its precise scope will be delineated in the Secretary of State's order.

Para. (b): Advertisements dealing with investments only incidentally might include, for example, an offer to residents of shares in a management company to run a block of flats.

Para. (c): This subsection permits the Secretary of State to fashion a "professionals-only" exemption. See also subs. (7).

As to the manner of making an order under this subsection, see s.205(2) and subs. (9).

Subs. (7)

Whereas subs. 6(*c*) applies to advertisements issued to certain *persons*, this subsection applies to advertisements relating to certain *securities*. It empowers the Secretary of State to exempt advertisements of securities normally dealt in by experts who do not need a prospectus to enable them to assess the risks. For example, offers of short-dated debentures traded in very high denominations (sterling commercial paper). See also s.195. As to the manner of making an order under this subsection, see s.205(2) and subs. (9).

Exceptions

161.—(1) Sections 159 and 160 above do not apply to any advertisement offering securities if the offer is conditional on their admission to listing in accordance with Part IV of this Act and section 159 above does not apply to any advertisement offering securities if they have been listed in accordance with that Part in the previous twelve months and the approved exchange in question certifies that persons likely to consider acquiring them will have sufficient information to enable them to decide whether to do so.

(2) Neither of those sections applies to any such advertisement as is mentioned in section 58(2) above.

(3) Neither of those sections applies if other securities issued by the same person (whether or not securities of the same class as those to which the offer relates) are already dealt in on an approved exchange and the exchange certifies that persons likely to consider acquiring the securities to which the offer relates will have sufficient information to enable them to decide whether to do so having regard to the steps that have been taken to comply in respect of those other securities with the requirements imposed by the exchange for the purpose of complying with paragraph 2(2)(*b*) of Schedule 4 to this Act, to the nature of the securities to which the offer relates, to the circumstances of their issue and to the information about the issuer which is available to investors by virtue of any enactment.

(4) If it appears to the Secretary of State that the law of a country or territory outside the United Kingdom provides investors in the United Kingdom with protection at least equivalent to that provided by Part IV of this Act or this Part of this Act in respect of securities dealt in on an

exchange or exchanges in that country or territory he may by order specify circumstances in which those sections are not to apply to advertisements offering those securities.

(5) An order under subsection (4) above shall be subject to annulment in pursuance of a resolution of either House of Parliament.

DEFINITIONS
"advertisement": s.207(2), (3).
"advertisement offering securities": s.158(4).
"approved exchange": s.158(6).
"listing": s.142(7).
"securities": s.158(3).

GENERAL NOTE
This section specifies circumstances under which a prospectus is not required in connection with an advertisement offering securities.

Subs. (1)
No prospectus is required if the offer is conditional on the admission of the advertised securities to listing. (Normally, however, listing particulars will be necessary.)
No prospectus is required under s.159 if the securities advertised have been listed in the previous 12 months and the approved exchange certifies that potential acquirers will have enough information to go on.

Subs. (2)
The effect of this subsection is that an issuer of securities may advertise the forthcoming availability of a prospectus provided the contents of the advertisement are limited to those enumerated in s.58(2).

Subs. (3)
Paragraph 2(2)(*b*) of Schedule 4 requires recognised investment exchanges to impose continuing disclosure obligations ("such obligations as will . . . afford to persons dealing in the investments proper information for determining their current value").
The effect of subs. (3) is that no prospectus is required if other securities issued by the same person are already dealt in on the approved recognised investment exchange, and the exchange certifies that potential acquirers of the securities to be advertised will have enough information to go on (without a prospectus) having regard to the issuer's compliance (in respect of securities already dealt in) with the continuing disclosure requirements, to the nature of the securities to be advertised, to the circumstances of their issue, and to the information about the issuer statutorily available to investors. (Note that the securities already dealt in need not be securities of the same class as those to be advertised.)

Subs. (4)
This subsection empowers the Secretary of State to make an order exempting overseas issuers whose securities are dealt in on an overseas exchange from the requirement to register a prospectus if their domestic law affords United Kingdom investors protection at least equivalent to Part IV (official listing) or Part V (offers of unlisted securities) of the Act.
As to the manner of making an order under this subsection, see s.205(2) and subs. (5) of this section.

Form and content of prospectus

162.—(1) A prospectus shall contain such information and comply with such other requirements as may be prescribed by rules made by the Secretary of State for the purposes of this section.

(2) Rules under this section may make provision whereby compliance with any requirements imposed by or under the law of a country or territory outside the United Kingdom is treated as compliance with any requirements of the rules.

(3) If it appears to the Secretary of State that an approved exchange has rules in respect of prospectuses relating to securities dealt in on the

exchange, and practices in exercising any powers conferred by the rules, which provide investors with protection at least equivalent to that provided by rules under this section he may direct that any such prospectus shall be subject to the rules of the exchange instead of the rules made under this section.

DEFINITIONS
"approved exchange": s.158(6).
"prospectus": s.159(1)(*a*).
"securities": s.158(3).

GENERAL NOTE
This section empowers the Secretary of State to makes rules prescribing the form and content of prospectuses and provides for the displacement of those rules. The rules made will replace Schedule 3 of the Companies Act 1985.

Subs. (1)
As to the manner of making rules under this subsection, see s.205(2).

Subs. (3)
This subsection allows the Secretary of State to direct that prospectuses relating to securities dealt in on an approved exchange are to be subject to the rules of the exchange (instead of the Secretary of State's rules). Such a direction may be made if the exchange's rules and practices afford investors protection at least equivalent to that provided by the Secretary of State's rules.

General duty of disclosure in prospectus

163.—(1) In addition to the information required to be included in a prospectus by virtue of rules applying to it by virtue of section 162 above a prospectus shall contain all such information as investors and their professional advisers would reasonably require, and reasonably expect to find there, for the purpose of making an informed assessment of—
  (*a*) the assets and liabilities, financial position, profits and losses, and prospects of the issuer of the securities; and
  (*b*) the rights attaching to those securities.
  (2) The information to be included by virtue of this section shall be such information as is mentioned in subsection (1) above which is within the knowledge of any person responsible for the prospectus or which it would be reasonable for him to obtain by making enquiries.
  (3) In determining what information is required to be included in a prospectus by virtue of this section regard shall be had—
  (*a*) to the nature of the securities and of the issuer of the securities;
  (*b*) to the nature of the persons likely to consider their acquisition;
  (*c*) to the fact that certain matters may reasonably be expected to be within the knowledge of professional advisers of any kind which those persons may reasonably be expected to consult; and
  (*d*) to any information available to investors or their professional advisers by virtue of any enactment or by virtue of requirements imposed by a recognised investment exchange for the purpose of complying with paragraph 2(2)(*b*) of Schedule 4 to this Act.

DEFINITIONS
"issuer": s.158(3).
"persons responsible for prospectus": s.168.
"prospectus": s.159(1)(*a*).
"recognised investment exchange": s.207(1).
"securities": s.158(3).

GENERAL NOTE
This section is the Part V analogue of s.146. It imposes a general duty of disclosure on persons responsible for listing particulars.

Subs. (1)
The general duty of disclosure supplements the specific disclosure requirements of the prospectus rules made under the previous section. The prospectus must contain all such information as investors and their professional advisers would reasonably require, and reasonably expect to find there, for the purpose of making an informed assessment of the matters mentioned. There is, however, no obligation to disclose information covered by s.165.

Subs. (2)
Any person responsible for the prospectus: see s.168.

Subs. (3)
In determining the reasonable requirements and expectations of investors and their professional advisers regard is to be had to the factors enumerated.

Para. (b): Information needed by unsophisticated investors might be redundant if the issue is aimed at sophisticated investors.

Para. (d): It is reasonable to take into account what information is already available by virtue of statutory disclosure requirements or the continuing disclosure requirements of a recognised investment exchange.

Supplementary prospectus

164.—(1) Where a prospectus has been registered under this Part of this Act in respect of an offer of securities and at any time while an agreement in respect of those securities can be entered into in pursuance of that offer—
  (a) there is a significant change affecting any matter contained in the prospectus whose inclusion was required by rules applying to it by virtue of section 162 above or by section 163 above; or
  (b) a significant new matter arises the inclusion of information in respect of which would have been so required if it had arisen when the prospectus was prepared,
the person who delivered the prospectus for registration to the registrar of companies shall deliver to him for registration a supplementary prospectus containing particulars of the change or new matter.

(2) In subsection (1) above "significant" means significant for the purpose of making an informed assessment of the matters mentioned in section 163(1) above.

(3) Where the person who delivered the prospectus for registration is not aware of the change or new matter in question he shall not be under any duty to comply with subsection (1) above unless he is notified of it by a person responsible for the prospectus; but any person responsible for the prospectus who is aware of such a matter shall be under a duty to give him notice of it.

(4) Subsection (1) above applies also as respects matters contained in a supplementary prospectus previously registered under this section in respect of the securities in question.

DEFINITIONS
  "persons responsible for prospectus": s.168.
  "prospectus": s.159(1)(a).
  "registrar of companies": s.158(5).
  "securities": s.158(3).

This section is the Part V parallel to s.147. It specifies the circumstances under which a supplementary prospectus must be prepared.

Subs. (1)
A prospectus must be kept up-to-date by means of one or more supplements if there is a significant development during the period in which an agreement can be entered into in pursuance of the offer in respect of which the prospectus has been registered.
As to the meaning of "significant," see subs. (2).

Subs. (3)
Persons responsible for the prospectus: See s.168.

Exemptions from disclosure

165.—(1) If in the case of any approved exchange the Secretary of State so directs, the exchange shall have power to authorise the omission from a prospectus or supplementary prospectus of any information the inclusion of which would otherwise be required by section 163 above—

(*a*) on the ground that its disclosure would be contrary to the public interest;

(*b*) subject to subsection (2) below, on the ground that its disclosure would be seriously detrimental to the issuer of the securities; or

(*c*) in the case of securities which fall within paragraph 2 of Schedule 1 to this Act and are of any class specified by the rules of the exchange, on the ground that its disclosure is unnecessary for persons of the kind who may be expected normally to buy or deal in the securities.

(2) No authority shall be granted under subsection (1)(*b*) above in respect of, and no such authority shall be regarded as extending to, information the non-disclosure of which would be likely to mislead a person considering the acquisition of the securities as to any facts the knowledge of which it is essential for him to have in order to make an informed assessment.

(3) The Secretary of State or the Treasury may issue a certificate to the effect that the disclosure of any information (including information that would otherwise have to be included in a prospectus or supplementary prospectus for which they are themselves responsible) would be contrary to the public interest and the exchange shall be entitled to act on any such certificate in exercising its powers under subsection (1)(*a*) above.

DEFINITIONS
  "approved exchange": s.158(6).
  "prospectus": s.159(1)(*a*).
  "securities": s.158(3).

GENERAL NOTE
This section is the Part V parallel to s.148. It enables the Secretary of State to direct that an approved exchange is to have the power to authorise, in the circumstances specified in this section, the omission from a prospectus of information whose inclusion would otherwise be required by s.163.
The omission of information may be authorised on the ground that its disclosure would be contrary to the public interest: subs. (1)(*a*). The Secretary of State and the Treasury are empowered to issue certificates to this effect, and the exchange is entitled to act on them: subs. (3). Even in the absence of a certificate, however, the exchange may act on public interest grounds.
The omission of information may also be authorised on the ground that its disclosure would be seriously detrimental to the issuer of the securities: subs. (1)(*b*). But information may not be suppressed on this ground if its non-disclosure would be likely to mislead a potential acquirer as to any facts he must know in order to make an informed assessment: subs. (2).

The omission of information may be authorised, thirdly, in the case of debentures of any class specified by the rules of the exchange, on the ground that its disclosure is unnecessary for the kind of investors at whom the issue is aimed (*i.e.*, presumably, sophisticated investors): subs. (1)(*c*).

Compensation for false or misleading prospectus

166.—(1) Subject to section 167 below, the person or persons responsible for a prospectus or supplementary prospectus shall be liable to pay compensation to any person who has acquired the securities to which the prospectus relates and suffered loss in respect of them as a result of any untrue or misleading statement in the prospectus or the omission from it of any matter required to be included by section 163 or 164 above.

(2) Where rules applicable to a prospectus by virtue of section 162 above require it to include information as to any particular matter on the basis that the prospectus must include a statement either as to that matter or, if such is the case, that there is no such matter, the omission from the prospectus of the information shall be treated for the purpose of subsection (1) above as a statement that there is no such matter.

(3) Subject to section 167 below, a person who fails to comply with section 164 above shall be liable to pay compensation to any person who has acquired any of the securities in question and suffered loss in respect of them as a result of the failure.

(4) This section does not affect any liability which any person may incur apart from this section.

(5) References in this section to the acquisition by any person of securities include references to his contracting to acquire them or an interest in them.

DEFINITIONS
"persons responsible for prospectus": s.168.
"prospectus": s.159(1)(*a*).
"securities": s.158(3).

GENERAL NOTE
This section is the Part V parallel to s.150. Subject to the next section, it specifies the circumstances in which compensation is payable for false or misleading prospectuses by the persons responsible for them.

Subs. (1)
Person who has acquired: see subs. (5) below.
This subsection provides that compensation is payable by the persons responsible for a prospectus for a loss occasioned by an untrue or misleading statement, by an omission in breach of the general duty of disclosure, or by an omission in breach of the supplementary disclosure requirements imposed by s.164. Subs. (1) does not state that compensation is payable for a loss occasioned by an omission in breach of the prospectus rules made under s.162, but such omissions are addressed in subs. (2).

Subs. (2)
Where prospectus rules require something to be disclosed or a positive statement to be made that there is nothing to be disclosed (a positive negative), a failure to make any disclosure or statement is to be treated as a statement that there is nothing to be disclosed. The truth or untruth of this notional statement can then be determined for the purposes of subs. (1).

Subs. (3)
Compensation is also payable for a loss occasioned by a failure to comply with subss. (1) or (3) of s.164.

Subs. (4)
Any liability incurred under the common law of negligence or under the Misrepresentation Act 1967 is unaffected by the incurrence of liability under this section.

Exemption from liability to pay compensation

167.—(1) A person shall not incur any liability under section 166(1) above for any loss in respect of securities caused by any such statement or omission as is there mentioned if he satisfies the court that at the time when the prospectus or supplementary prospectus was delivered for registration he reasonably believed, having made such enquiries (if any) as were reasonable, that the statement was true and not misleading or that the matter whose omission caused the loss was properly omitted and—

    (*a*) that he continued in that belief until the time when the securities were acquired; or

    (*b*) that they were acquired before it was reasonably practicable to bring a correction to the attention of persons likely to acquire the securities in question; or

    (*c*) that before the securities were acquired he had taken all such steps as it was reasonable for him to have taken to secure that a correction was brought to the attention of those persons; or

    (*d*) that the securities were acquired after such a lapse of time that he ought in the circumstances to be reasonably excused;

but paragraph (*d*) above does not apply where the securities are dealt in on an approved exchange unless he satisfies the court that he continued in that belief until after the commencement of dealings in the securities on that exchange.

(2) A person shall not incur any liability under section 166(1) above for any loss in respect of securities caused by a statement purporting to be made by or on the authority of another person as an expert which is, and is stated to be, included in the prospectus or supplementary prospectus with that other person's consent if he satisfies the court that at the time when the prospectus or supplementary prospectus was delivered for registration he believed on reasonable grounds that the other person was competent to make or authorise the statement and had consented to its inclusion in the form and context in which it was included and—

    (*a*) that he continued in that belief until the time when the securities were acquired; or

    (*b*) that they were acquired before it was reasonably practicable to bring the fact that the expert was not competent or had not consented to the attention of persons likely to acquire the securities in question; or

    (*c*) that before the securities were acquired he had taken all such steps as it was reasonable for him to have taken to secure that that fact was brought to the attention of those persons; or

    (*d*) that the securities were acquired after such a lapse of time that he ought in the circumstances to be reasonably excused;

but paragraph (*d*) above does not apply where the securities are dealt in on an approved exchange unless he satisfies the court that he continued in that belief until after the commencement of dealings in the securities on that exchange.

(3) Without prejudice to subsections (1) and (2) above, a person shall not incur any liability under section 166(1) above for any loss in respect of any securities caused by any such statement or omission as is there mentioned if he satisfies the court—

    (*a*) that before the securities were acquired a correction or, where the statement was such as is mentioned in subsection (2) above, the fact that the expert was not competent or had not consented had been published in a manner calculated to bring it to the attention of persons likely to acquire the securities in question; or (*b*) that he took all such steps as it was reasonable for him to take to secure such publication and reasonably believed that it had taken place before the securities were acquired.

(4) A person shall not incur any liability under section 166(1) above for any loss resulting from a statement made by an official person or contained in a public official document which is included in the prospectus or supplementary prospectus if he satisfies the court that the statement is accurately and fairly reproduced.

(5) A person shall not incur any liability under section 166(1) or (3) above if he satisfies the court that the person suffering the loss acquired the securities in question with knowledge that the statement was false or misleading, of the omitted matter or of the change or new matter, as the case may be.

(6) A person shall not incur any liability under section 166(3) above if he satisfies the court that he reasonably believed that the change or new matter in question was not such as to call for a supplementary prospectus.

(7) In this section "expert" includes any engineer, valuer, accountant or other person whose profession, qualifications or experience give authority to a statement made by him; and references to the acquisition of securities include references to contracting to acquire them or an interest in them.

DEFINITIONS
"acquisition of securities": s.167(7).
"approved exchange": s.158(6).
"expert": s.151(7).
"prospectus": s.159(1)(*a*).
"securities": s.158(3).

GENERAL NOTE
This section is the Part V analogue of s.151. It provides various defences to claims for compensation under s.166(1) (in the case of subss. (1) to (5)) and s.166(3) (in the case of subs. (6)). In each case the onus is on the person from whom compensation is sought to satisfy the court of the existence of the circumstances which found the exemption.

Subs. (1)
This subsection (replacing s.68(2)(*a*) of the Companies Act 1985) provides a defence of reasonable belief in the truth of the relevant statement or in the propriety of the relevant omission. This reasonable belief, to afford a defence, must be coupled with one of the eventualities enumerated in paras. (*a*) to (*d*).

Para. (d): This paragraph appears to contemplate that lapse of time can cure a failure to take such steps as are reasonable to secure that a correction is brought to the attention of potential acquirers.

Subs. (2)
This subsection (replacing s.68(2)(*b*) of the Companies Act 1985) provides a defence of reasonable belief in the competence of an expert and in that expert's consent to the relevant statement's inclusion. Again this reasonable belief, to afford a defence, must be coupled with one of the eventualities enumerated in paras. (*a*) to (*d*).

Subs. (3)
This subsection contemplates a situation where a person responsible for a defective prospectus cannot satisfy the court of his reasonable belief in its accuracy, or in the competence and consent of the expert. In such a situation he incurs no liability if, before the acquisition of the securities, an appropriate correction is published, or he takes reasonable steps to secure its publication and reasonably believes it to have been published.

Subs. (4)
This subsection (replacing s.68(2)(*c*) of the Companies Act 1985) exempts from liability if the loss was occasioned by an official statement reproduced in the prospectus.

No liability is incurred if the person acquiring the securities knew of the defect in the prospectus.

Persons responsible for prospectus

168.—(1) For the purposes of this Part of this Act the persons responsible for a prospectus or supplementary prospectus are—

(a) the issuer of the securities to which the prospectus or supplementary prospectus relates;

(b) where the issuer is a body corporate, each person who is a director of that body at the time when the prospectus or supplementary prospectus is delivered for registration;

(c) where the issuer is a body corporate, each person who has authorised himself to be named, and is named, in the prospectus or supplementary prospectus as a director or as having agreed to become a director of that body either immediately or at a future time;

(d) each person who accepts, and is stated in the prospectus or supplementary prospectus as accepting, responsibility for, or for any part of, the prospectus or supplementary prospectus;

(e) each person not falling within any of the foregoing paragraphs who has authorised the contents of, or of any part of, the prospectus or supplementary prospectus.

(2) A person is not responsible under subsection (1)(a), (b) or (c) above unless the issuer has made or authorised the offer in relation to which the prospectus or supplementary prospectus was delivered for registration; and a person is not responsible for a prospectus or supplementary prospectus by virtue of subsection (1)(b) above if it is delivered for registration without his knowledge or consent and on becoming aware of its delivery he forthwith gives reasonable public notice that it was delivered without his knowledge or consent.

(3) Where a person has accepted responsibility for, or authorised, only part of the contents of any prospectus or supplementary prospectus he is responsible under subsection (1)(d) or (e) above for only that part and only if it is included in (or substantially in) the form and context to which he has agreed.

(4) Where a prospectus or supplementary prospectus relates to securities which are to be issued in connection with an offer by (or by a wholly-owned subsidiary of) the issuer for, or an agreement for the acquisition by (or by a wholly-owned subsidiary of) the issuer of, securities issued by another person or in connection with any arrangement whereby the whole of the undertaking of another person is to become the undertaking of the issuer (of a wholly-owned subsidiary of the issuer or of a body corporate which will become such a subsidiary by virtue of the arrangement) then if—

(a) that other person; and

(b) where that other person is a body corporate, each person who is a director of that body at the time when the prospectus or supplementary prospectus is delivered for registration and each other person who has authorised himself to be named, and is named, in the prospectus or supplementary prospectus as a director of that body,

is responsible by virtue of paragraph (d) of subsection (1) above for any part of the prospectus or supplementary prospectus relating to that other person or to the securities or undertaking to which the offer, agreement or arrangement relates, no person shall be responsible for that part under paragraph (a), (b) or (c) of that subsection but without prejudice to his being responsible under paragraph (d).

(5) Neither paragraph (*b*) nor paragraph (*c*) of subsection (1) above nor paragraph (*b*) of subsection (4) above applies in the case of any director if the prospectus or supplementary prospectus is subject to the rules of an approved exchange by virtue of section 162(3) above and he is certified by the exchange as a person to whom that paragraph should not apply by reason of his having an interest, or of any other circumstances, making it inappropriate for him to be responsible by virtue of that paragraph.

(6) In this section "wholly-owned subsidiary", in relation to a person other than a body corporate, means any body corporate that would be his wholly-owned subsidiary if he were a body corporate.

(7) Nothing in this section shall be construed as making a person responsible for any prospectus or supplementary prospectus by reason only of giving advice as to its contents in a professional capacity.

(8) Where by virtue of this section the issuer of any shares pays or is liable to pay compensation under section 166 above for loss suffered in respect of shares for which a person has subscribed no account shall be taken of that liability or payment in determining any question as to the amount paid on subscription for those shares or as to the amount paid up or deemed to be paid up on them.

DEFINITIONS
"approved exchange": s.158(6).
"body corporate": s.207(1).
"director": s.207(1).
"issuer": s.158(3).
"prospectus": s.159(1)(*a*).
"securities": s.158(3).
"subsidiary": s.207(8).

GENERAL NOTE
This section is the Part V parallel to s.152. It is concerned with the attribution of responsibility for prospectuses and supplementary prospectuses.

Subs. (1)
This subsection enumerates the persons responsible for prospectuses.

Para. (a): This paragraph is qualified by subss. (2) and (4).

Para. (b): This paragraph is qualified by subss. (2), (4) and (5).

Para. (c): This paragraph is qualified by subss. (2), (4) and (5).

Para. (d): This paragraph is qualified by subs. (3).

Para. (e): Other persons who authorise prospectuses (or parts thereof) include the sponsoring issuing house and experts (*e.g.* accountants).
This paragraph is qualified by subs. (3).

Subs. (2)
The first limb of this subsection absolves the issuer and its directors of responsibility for the prospectus if the issuer has not made or authorised the offer to which the prospectus relates. No corresponding provision appears in connection with responsibility for listing particulars (s.152(2)), since no application for listing can be made without the consent of the issuer (s.143(2)).
The second limb of this subsection (replacing s.68(1)(*b*) of the Companies Act 1985) provides that a person is not responsible *qua* director for a prospectus published without his knowledge or consent, *etc.* That person might still be responsible by virtue of having avowed responsibility for the prospectus (subs. (1)(*d*)).

Subs. (4)

This subsection is concerned with responsibility for a prospectus relating to securities issued in connection with an agreed takeover. Its main application is to the issuer's acquisition of another company's shares. In such a case, if the other company *and* its directors avow responsibility for any part of the prospectus relating to that company, then no person incurs responsibility for that part by virtue of being the issuer of the new securities or a director of the issuer. Responsibility may still be incurred, however, by an avowal of responsibility.

This subsection also applies to the acquisition of the whole of an undertaking owned by another person (whether that person is a body corporate or not).

This subsection is qualified by subs. (5).

As to the meaning of "wholly-owned subsidiary" in this context, see subs. (6).

Subs. (5)

This subsection aims to absolve from responsibility for a prospectus issued under the rules of an approved exchange directors (and ostensible directors and directors-to-be) certified by the exchange. In addition, an avowal of responsibility by a certified director is not necessary for the benefit of subs. (4) to be gained. The import of the certificate is that the director in question is a person to whom "that paragraph" (presumably para. (*b*) of subs. (1)) should not apply by reason of his having an interest, or of any other circumstances, making it inappropriate (*e.g.* because of a conflict of interest) for him to be responsible by virtue of "that paragraph."

Subs. (7)

This is modelled on part of s.741(2) of the Companies Act 1985.

Subs. (8)

The effect of this subsection is that the liability of a shareholder in respect of shares not fully paid up cannot be offset against the liability of the company to pay that shareholder compensation in respect of a false or misleading prospectus.

Terms and implementation of offer

169.—(1) The Secretary of State may make rules—

(*a*) regulating the terms on which a person may offer securities by an advertisement to which this Part of this Act applies; and

(*b*) otherwise regulating his conduct with a view to ensuring that the persons to whom the offer is addressed are treated equally and fairly.

(2) Rules under this section may, in particular, make provision with respect to the giving of priority as between persons to whom an offer is made and with respect to the payment of commissions.

(3) Section 162(2) above shall apply also to rules made under this section.

DEFINITIONS
"advertisement": s.207(2), (3).
"securities": s.158(3).

GENERAL NOTE

This section empowers the Secretary of State to make rules regulating the terms of offers and the conduct of offerors. The rules may provide that compliance with overseas requirements is to be treated as compliance with requirements of the rules.

As to the manner of making rules under this section, see s.205(2).

As to the consequences of contravening rules made under this section, see s.171.

Advertisements by private companies and old public companies

170.—(1) No private company and no old public company shall issue or cause to be issued in the United Kingdom any advertisement offering securities to be issued by that company.

(2) Subsection (1) above shall not apply to an advertisement issued in such circumstances as may be specified by an order made by the Secretary of State for the purpose of exempting from that subsection such advertisements as are mentioned in section 160(6)(*a*), (*b*) or (*c*) above.

(3) An order under subsection (2) above may require any person who by virtue of the order is authorised to issue an advertisement to comply with such requirements as are specified in the order.

(4) An order under subsection (2) above shall be subject to annulment in pursuance of a resolution of either House of Parliament.

(5) In this section "old public company" has the meaning given in section 1 of the Companies Consolidation (Consequential Provisions) Act 1985 or the corresponding Northern Ireland provision.

DEFINITIONS
"advertisement": s.207(2), (3).
"advertisement offering securities": s.158(4).
"private company": s.207(1).
"securities": s.158(3).

GENERAL NOTE
This section (replacing s.81 of the Companies Act 1985) generally prohibits the issue of advertisements offering securities by private companies and old public companies.

Subs. (1)
As to the meaning of "old public company," see subs. (5).
As to the consequences of contravening this prohibition, see s.171.
An authorised person who issues on behalf of a company an advertisement, which that company itself is prohibited from issuing by this subsection, is caught by s.171(1)(*c*). An unauthorised person who does this is caught by s.57.

Subs. (2)
This subsection empowers the Secretary of State to exempt from the general prohibition advertisements mentioned in s.160(6)(*a*), (*b*) or (*c*), *q.v.*
As to the manner of making an order under this subsection, see s.205(2) and subs. (4) of this section.

Contraventions

171.—(1) An authorised person who—
   (*a*) contravenes section 159 or 160 above or rules made under section 169 above;
   (*b*) contravenes any requirement imposed by an order under section 160(6) or (7) or 170 above; or
   (*c*) on behalf of a company issues or causes to be issued an advertisement which that company is prohibited from issuing by section 170 above,
shall be treated as having contravened rules made under Chapter V of Part I of this Act or, in the case of a person who is an authorised person by virtue of his membership of a recognised self-regulating organisation or certification by a recognised professional body, the rules of that organisation or body.

(2) Section 57 above shall apply to a company which issues or causes to be issued an advertisement in contravention of section 170 above as it applies to a person who issues an advertisement in contravention of that section.

(3) A person, other than an authorised person, who contravenes section 159 or 160, the rules made under section 169 or any requirement imposed by an order under section 160(6) or (7) or 170 above shall be guilty of an offence and liable—

(*a*) on conviction on indictment, to imprisonment for a term not exceeding two years or to a fine or to both;

(*b*) on summary conviction, to imprisonment for a term not exceeding six months or to a fine not exceeding the statutory maximum or to both.

(4) A person who in the ordinary course of a business other than investment business issues an advertisement to the order of another person shall not be guilty of an offence under subsection (3) above in respect of a contravention of section 159 or 160 above if he proves that he believed on reasonable grounds that neither section 159 nor section 160 above applied to the advertisement or that one of those sections had been complied with in respect of the advertisement.

(5) Without prejudice to any liability under section 166 above, a person shall not be regarded as having contravened section 159 or 160 above by reason only of a prospectus not having fully complied with the requirements of this Part of this Act as to its form and content.

(6) Any contravention to which this section applies shall be actionable at the suit of a person who suffers loss as a result of the contravention subject to the defences and other incidents applying to actions for breach of statutory duty.

DEFINITIONS
"advertisement": s.207(2), (3).
"at the suit": s.207(9).
"authorised person": s.207(1).
"certification": s.207(1).
"recognised professional body": s.207(1).
"recognised self-regulating organisation": s.207(1).
"rules": s.207(1).

GENERAL NOTE
This section specifies the consequences of contravening certain provisions of Part V and various subordinate instruments.

Subs. (1)
Directly authorised persons who contravene any of the provisions, rules and requirements enumerated, or issue a private company's advertisement, are to be treated as having contravened rules made under Chapter V of Part I, with all the consequences which that entails (see ss.60–62). Persons authorised by virtue of membership of an SRO or RPB are to be treated as having contravened the rules of the SRO or RPB in question. Contravention is thus a disciplinary matter for the SRO or RPB. Note, however, the effect of subs. (6).

Subs. (2)
The effect of this subsection is that a company advertising its securities in contravention of s.170 commits a criminal offence (s.57(3)) and cannot as a rule enforce any subsequent agreement to which the advertisement related (s.57(5)).

Subs. (3)
Unauthorised persons who contravene any of the provisions, rules or requirements enumerated commit a criminal offence.

Subs. (4)
This subsection provides a defence to a charge of issuing an advertisement offering securities, no prospectus having been approved or registered, for an unauthorised person who in the ordinary course of a business other than investment business issues an advertisement to the order of another person. However, the onus is on the issuer of the advertisement to prove that he believed on reasonable grounds either that ss.159 and 160 did not apply or that one of them had been complied with.

Subs. (5)
The effect of this subsection is that a person is not to be regarded as having failed to register a prospectus, or secure its approval if need be, by reason only of a technical defect in its form or content.

Subs. (6)
Any person who suffers loss as a result of any contravention to which this section applies may sue for damages. Thus, a person who suffers loss as a result of a contravention of s.170 has the choice of taking action under this subsection or s.57(5).

PART VI

TAKEOVER OFFERS

Takeover offers

172.—(1) The provisions set out in Schedule 12 to this Act shall be substituted for sections 428, 429 and 430 of the Companies Act 1985.

(2) Subsection (1) above does not affect any case in which the offer in respect of the scheme or contract mentioned in section 428(1) was made before the coming into force of this section.

GENERAL NOTE
See general note to Sched. 12.

PART VII

INSIDER DEALING

Information obtained in official capacity: public bodies etc.

173.—(1) In section 2 of the Company Securities (Insider Dealing) Act 1985 (abuse of information obtained by Crown servants in official capacity) for the word "Crown" wherever it occurs there shall be substituted the word "public".

(2) At the end of that section there shall be added—
"(4) 'Public servant' means—
   (*a*) a Crown servant;
   (*b*) a member, officer or servant of a designated agency, competent authority or transferee body (within the meaning of the Financial Services Act 1986);
   (*c*) an officer or servant of a recognised self-regulating organisation, recognised investment exchange or recognised clearing house (within the meaning of that Act);
   (*d*) any person declared by an order for the time being in force under subsection (5) to be a public servant for the purposes of this section.

(5) If it appears to the Secretary of State that the members, officers or employees of or persons otherwise connected with any body appearing to him to exercise public functions may have access to unpublished price sensitive information relating to securities, he may by order declare that those persons are to be public servants for the purposes of this section.

(6) The power to make an order under subsection (5) shall be exercisable by statutory instrument and an instrument containing such an order shall be subject to annulment in pursuance of a resolution of either House of Parliament."

DEFINITIONS
"competent authority": s.142(6).
"Crown servant": Company Securities (Insider Dealing) Act 1985, s.16(1).
"designated agency": s.114(3).
"recognised clearing house": s.207(1).
"recognised investment exchange": s.207(1).
"recognised self-regulating organisation": s.207(1).
"securities": Company Securities (Insider Dealing) Act 1985, s.12.
"transferee body": Sched. 11, para. 28.
"unpublished price sensitive information": Company Securities (Insider Dealing) Act 1985, s.10.

GENERAL NOTE
This section extends the scope of s.2 of the Company Securities (Insider Dealing) Act 1985. As amended s.2 will cover not only the abuse of information held by Crown servants, by virtue of their position, but also the abuse of information by other public servants. The persons enumerated in new subs. (4) of s.2 of the 1985 Act are public servants, as are the persons declared to be public servants by order of the Secretary of State under new subs. (5). As to the manner of making an order under this subsection, see new subs. (6).

Market makers, off-market dealers etc.

174.—(1) In subsection (1) of section 3 of the Company Securities (Insider Dealing) Act 1985 (actions not prohibited by sections 1 and 2 of that Act) at the end of paragraph (*c*) there shall be inserted the words "; or
   (*d*) doing any particular thing in relation to any particular securities if the information—
      (i) was obtained by him in the course of a business of a market maker in those securities in which he was engaged or employed, and
      (ii) was of a description which it would be reasonable to expect him to obtain in the ordinary course of that business,
   and he does that thing in good faith in the course of that business.".
(2) At the end of that subsection there shall be inserted—
   " 'Market maker' means a person (whether an individual, partnership or company) who—
      (*a*) holds himself out at all normal times in compliance with the rules of a recognised stock exchange as willing to buy and sell securities at prices specified by him; and
      (*b*) is recognised as doing so by that recognised stock exchange.".
(3) The existing provisions of section 4 of that Act (off-market deals in advertised securities) shall become subsection (1) of that section and after that subsection there shall be inserted—
   "(2) In its application by virtue of this section the definition of "market maker" in section 3(1) shall have effect as if the references to a recognised stock exchange were references to a recognised investment exchange (other than an overseas investment exchange) within the meaning of the Financial Services Act 1986.".
(4) In section 13 of that Act—
   (*a*) in subsection (1) (which defines dealing in securities and provides that references to dealing on a recognised stock exchange include dealing through an investment exchange) the words from "and references" onwards shall be omitted; and
   (*b*) for subsection (3) (definition of off-market dealer) there shall be substituted—
      "(3) 'Off-market dealer' means a person who is an authorised person within the meaning of the Financial Services Act 1986.".

"authorised person": s.207(1).
"company": Company Securities (Insider Dealing) Act 1985, s.11(*a*).
"overseas investment exchange": s.207(1).
"recognised investment exchange": s.207(1).
"recognised stock exchange": Sched. 16, para. 28(*a*).
"securities": Company Securities (Insider Dealing) Act 1985, s.12.

GENERAL NOTE

Subss. (1), (2)
These subsections add a market-maker's exemption to the existing jobber's exemption in the insider dealing legislation. The role of market-maker became recognised on The Stock Exchange on October 27, 1986. Note, however, that the definition of "market-maker" in subs. (2) extends to market-makers on other stock exchanges recognised under the 1985 Act.

Subs. (3)
The effect of this subsection is that the market-maker's exemption applies to an authorised person making a market in advertised securities, not on a recognised stock exchange, but on a recognised investment exchange other than an overseas investment exchange.

Price stabilisation

175. For section 6 of the Company Securities (Insider Dealing) Act 1985 (international bonds) there shall be substituted—

> **"Price stabilisation**
>   **6.**—(1) No provision of section 1, 2, 4 or 5 prohibits an individual from doing anything for the purpose of stabilising the price of securities if it is done in conformity with rules made under section 48 of the Financial Services Act 1986 and—
>   (*a*) in respect of securities which fall within any of paragraphs 1 to 5 of Schedule 1 to that Act and are specified by the rules; and
>   (*b*) during such period before or after the issue of those securities as is specified by the rules.
>   (2) Any order under subsection (8) of section 48 of that Act shall apply also in relation to subsection (1) of this section.".

DEFINITION
"securities": Company Securities (Insider Dealing) Act 1985, s.12.

GENERAL NOTE
S.6 of the Company Securities (Insider Dealing) Act 1985 creates an exemption from the prohibition of insider dealing. The old exemption covered things done in connection with an international bond issue. The new exemption covers things done for the purpose of price stabilisation in conformity with the rules made under s.48(2)(*i*) of the Financial Services Act. The rules may legitimate price stabilisation in respect of securities falling within any of paras. 1 to 5 of Sched. 1 (not just international securities). The rules will specify the period before or after issue during which price stabilisation is legitimate and may indeed allow stabilisation to be undertaken in relation to certain offers of existing securities. The price stabilisation "defence" to a charge of insider dealing thus parallels the price stabilisation "defence" (s.48(7)) to a charge of market manipulation under s.47(2).

Contracts for differences by reference to securities

176. After subsection (1) of section 13 of the Company Securities (Insider Dealing) Act 1985 (definition of dealing in securities), there shall be inserted—

> "(1A) For the purposes of this Act a person who (whether as principal or agent) buys or sells or agrees to buy or sell investments within paragraph 9 of Schedule 1 to the Financial Services Act 1986 (contracts for differences etc.) where the purpose or pretended purpose

mentioned in that paragraph is to secure a profit or avoid a loss wholly or partly by reference to fluctuations in the value or price of securities shall be treated as if he were dealing in those securities.".

DEFINITION

"securities": Company Securities (Insider Dealing) Act 1985, s.12.

GENERAL NOTE

The effect of this section is to bring dealings in contracts for differences within the scope of the insider dealing legislation if the underlying investments are "securities" within the meaning of that legislation.

Investigations into insider dealing

177.—(1) If it appears to the Secretary of State that there are circumstances suggesting that there may have been a contravention of section 1, 2, 4 or 5 of the Company Securities (Insider Dealing) Act 1985, he may appoint one or more competent inspectors to carry out such investigations as are requisite to establish whether or not any such contravention has occurred and to report the results of their investigations to him.

(2) The appointment under this section of an inspector may limit the period during which he is to continue his investigation or confine it to particular matters.

(3) If the inspectors consider that any person is or may be able to give information concerning any such contravention they may require that person—

(a) to produce to them any documents in his possession or under his control relating to the company in relation to whose securities the contravention is suspected to have occurred or to its securities;

(b) to attend before them; and

(c) otherwise to give them all assistance in connection with the investigation which he is reasonably able to give;

and it shall be the duty of that person to comply with that requirement.

(4) An inspector may examine on oath any person who he considers is or may be able to give information concerning any such contravention, and may administer an oath accordingly.

(5) The inspectors shall make such interim reports to the Secretary of State as they think fit or he may direct and on the conclusion of the investigation they shall make a final report to him.

(6) A statement made by a person in compliance with a requirement imposed by virtue of this section may be used in evidence against him.

(7) A person shall not under this section be required to disclose any information or produce any document which he would be entitled to refuse to disclose or produce on grounds of legal professional privilege in proceedings in the High Court or on grounds of confidentiality as between client and professional legal adviser in proceedings in the Court of Session.

(8) Nothing in this section shall require a person carrying on the business of banking to disclose any information or produce any document relating to the affairs of a customer unless—

(a) the customer is a person who the inspectors have reason to believe may be able to give information concerning a suspected contravention; and

(b) the Secretary of State is satisfied that the disclosure or production is necessary for the purposes of the investigation.

(9) Where a person claims a lien on a document its production under this section shall be without prejudice to his lien.

(10) In this section "document" includes information recorded in any form; and in relation to information recorded otherwise than in legible

form references to its production include references to producing a copy of the information in legible form.

GENERAL NOTE
This section empowers the Secretary of State to appoint inspectors to investigate and report on suspected contraventions of the insider dealing legislation. The inspectors can compel the production of documents and examine on oath persons possessed of relevant information. Respondents' statements may be used in evidence against them. There are savings in respect of legal professional privilege and banking confidentiality, though the latter is heavily qualified.

Subs. (3)
Documents: see subs. (10).
Securities: This section is not inserted into the Company Securities (Insider Dealing) Act 1985, but since investigations will relate to contraventions of that Act "securities" here presumably bears the meaning given by s.12 of that Act.
As to the consequences of refusing to comply with a request made under this subsection, see s.178.

Subs. (4)
As to the consequences of refusing to answer any question, see s.178.

Subs. (8)
The business of banking: This phrase is not defined.

Penalties for failure to co-operate with s.177 investigations

178.—(1) If any person—
  (a) refuses to comply with any request under subsection (3) of section 177 above; or
  (b) refuses to answer any question put to him by the inspectors appointed under that section with respect to any matter relevant for establishing whether or not any suspected contravention has occurred,
the inspectors may certify that fact in writing to the court and the court may inquire into the case.
  (2) If, after hearing any witness who may be produced against or on behalf of the alleged offender and any statement which may be offered in defence, the court is satisfied that he did without reasonable excuse refuse to comply with such a request or answer any such question, the court may—
  (a) punish him in like manner as if he had been guilty of contempt of the court; or
  (b) direct that the Secretary of State may exercise his powers under this section in respect of him;
and the court may give a direction under paragraph (b) above notwithstanding that the offender is not within the jurisdiction of the court if the court is satisfied that he was notified of his right to appear before the court and of the powers available under this section.
  (3) Where the court gives a direction under subsection (2)(b) above in respect of an authorised person the Secretary of State may serve a notice on him—
  (a) cancelling any authorisation of his to carry on investment business after the expiry of a specified period after the service of the notice;
  (b) disqualifying him from becoming authorised to carry on investment business after the expiry of a specified period;
  (c) restricting any authorisation of his in respect of investment business during a specified period to the performance of contracts entered into before the notice comes into force;
  (d) prohibiting him from entering into transactions of a specified kind

or entering into them except in specified circumstances or to a specified extent;

(*e*) prohibiting him from soliciting business from persons of a specified kind or otherwise than from such persons; or

(*f*) prohibiting him from carrying on business in a specified manner or otherwise than in a specified manner.

(4) The period mentioned in paragraphs (*a*) and (*c*) of subsection (3) above shall be such period as appears to the Secretary of State reasonable to enable the person on whom the notice is served to complete the performance of any contracts entered into before the notice comes into force and to terminate such of them as are of a continuing nature.

(5) Where the court gives a direction under subsection (2)(*b*) above in the case of an unauthorised person the Secretary of State may direct that any authorised person who knowingly transacts investment business of a specified kind, or in specified circumstances or to a specified extent, with or on behalf of that unauthorised person shall be treated as having contravened rules made under Chapter V of Part I of this Act or, in the case of a person who is an authorised person by virtue of his membership of a recognised self-regulating organisation or certification by a recognised professional body, the rules of that organisation or body.

(6) A person shall not be treated for the purposes of subsection (2) above as having a reasonable excuse for refusing to comply with a request or answer a question in a case where the contravention or suspected contravention being investigated relates to dealing by him on the instructions or for the account of another person, by reason that at the time of the refusal—

(*a*) he did not know the identity of that other person; or

(*b*) he was subject to the law of a country or territory outside the United Kingdom which prohibited him from disclosing information relating to the dealing without the consent of that other person, if he might have obtained that consent or obtained exemption from that law.

(7) A notice served on a person under subsection (3) above may be revoked at any time by the Secretary of State by serving a revocation notice on him; and the Secretary of State shall revoke such a notice if it appears to him that he has agreed to comply with the relevant request or answer the relevant question.

(8) The revocation of such notice as is mentioned in subsection (3)(*a*) shall not have the effect of reviving the authorisation cancelled by the notice except where the person would (apart from the notice) at the time of the revocation be an authorised person by virtue of his membership of a recognised self-regulating organisation or certification by a recognised professional body; but nothing in this subsection shall be construed as preventing any person who has been subject to such a notice from again becoming authorised after the revocation of the notice.

(9) If it appears to the Secretary of State—

(*a*) that a person on whom he serves a notice under subsection (3) above is an authorised person by virtue of an authorisation granted by a designated agency or by virtue of membership of a recognised self-regulating organisation or certification by a recognised professional body; or

(*b*) that a person on whom he serves a revocation notice under subsection (7) above was such an authorised person at the time that the notice which is being revoked was served,

he shall serve a copy of the notice on that agency, organisation or body.

(10) The functions to which section 114 above applies shall include the functions of the Secretary of State under this section but any transfer of those functions shall be subject to a reservation that they are to be

exercisable by him concurrently with the designated agency and so as to be exercisable by the agency subject to such conditions or restrictions as the Secretary of State may from time to time impose.

DEFINITIONS
"authorised person": s.207(1).
"carry on investment business": s.1(3).
"certification": s.207(1).
"designated agency": s.114(3).
"investment business": s.1(2).
"member": s.207(1).
"recognised professional body": s.207(1).
"recognised self-regulating organisation": s.207(1).
"rules": s.207(1).

GENERAL NOTE
This section sets out the possible consequences of a failure to co-operate (subs. (1)) with inspectors appointed under s.177. Cases of non co-operation may be referred by the inspectors to the court which, if satisfied that the failure to co-operate lacked reasonable excuse, may punish the offender as though he were guilty of contempt of court or direct that the Secretary of State may exercise the powers conferred by this section: subs. (2). (These powers are transferable to the SIB subject to the reservation that they are to be exercisable by the Secretary of State concurrently with the SIB: subs. (10).) The powers available depend on whether the person in respect of whom they are to be exercised is authorised in this country (subs. (3)) or not (subs. (5)):
In relation to the latter, the aim of the section "to enable pressure to be applied, within the proper limits of United Kingdom jurisdiction, to dispose offshore intermediaries to co-operate with investigations into suspected insider dealing on United Kingdom markets": H.C., Vol. 99, col. 524 (June 12, 1986). The government has undertaken that "where arrangements are in place to ensure that the information we need can be obtained by other means through the co-operation of the relevant foreign authorities, we shall always resort to those means: *ibid.*, col. 525. (On September 23, 1986, the United Kingdom and the USA published details of a Memorandum of Understanding providing for the exchange between United Kingdom and USA regulatory authorities of information relevant to investigations of fraud and malpractice in financial markets including insider dealing.)

Subs. (2)
Offender: *i.e.* the person guilty of not co-operating with the inspectors.
Reasonable excuse: see subs. (6).

Subs. (3)
This subsection enumerates the options open to the Secretary of State where the offender is an *authorised* person.
As to the manner of serving a notice, see s.204. As to the revocation of a notice, see subs. (7).
Para. (a): As to the effect of revoking a notice cancelling authorisation, see subs. (8).
Paras. (a), (c): specified period: see subs. (4).

Subs. (5)
This subsection states the options open to the Secretary of State where the offender is an *unauthorised* person. Here the Secretary of State may prohibit any authorised person from transacting investment business of a specified kind, or in specified circumstances or to a specified extent, with or on behalf of the offender. The aim is thus to bring pressure to bear on him indirectly by means of an orchestrated boycott.
A directly authorised person who knowingly contravenes such a prohibition is to be treated as having contravened rules made under Chapter V of Part I, with all the consequences which that entails (see ss.60–62). A person authorised by virtue of membership of an SRO or RPB is to be treated as having contravened the rules of the SRO or RPB in question. Contravention is thus a disciplinary matter for the SRO or RPB.

Subs. (6)
This subsection applies where the alleged offender has been dealing on the instructions or for the account of another person. In such a case, not knowing the identity of one's principal

is not to be regarded as a reasonable cause for refusing to comply with a request or answer a question. Nor is being subject to an overseas banking secrecy law if one might have obtained a waiver. This provision is thus based on the premise that "if an overseas bank could know the identity of the principal behind a transaction on a United Kingdom market, who may have committed a criminal offence, but chooses not to find out, then it is reasonable for that bank to have restrictions imposed on its United Kingdom activities": H.C., Vol. 99, col. 525 (June 12, 1986).

PART VIII

RESTRICTIONS ON DISCLOSURE OF INFORMATION

Restrictions on disclosure of information

179.—(1) Subject to section 180 below, information which is restricted information for the purposes of this section and relates to the business or other affairs of any person shall not be disclosed by a person mentioned in subsection (3) below ("the primary recipient") or any person obtaining the information directly or indirectly from him without the consent of the person from whom the primary recipient obtained the information and if different, the person to whom it relates.

(2) Subject to subsection (4) below, information is restricted information for the purposes of this section if it was obtained by the primary recipient for the purposes of, or in the discharge of his functions under, this Act or any rules or regulations made under this Act (whether or not by virtue of any requirement to supply it made under those provisions).

(3) The persons mentioned in subsection (1) above are—

(*a*) the Secretary of State;

(*b*) any designated agency, transferee body or body administering a scheme under section 54 above;

(*c*) the Director General of Fair Trading;

(*d*) the Chief Registrar of friendly societies;

(*e*) the Registrar of Friendly Societies for Northern Ireland;

(*f*) the Bank of England;

(*g*) any member of the Tribunal;

(*h*) any person appointed or authorised to exercise any powers under section 94, 106 or 177 above; and

(*i*) any officer or servant of any such person.

(4) Information shall not be treated as restricted information for the purposes of this section if it has been made available to the public by virtue of being disclosed in any circumstances in which or for any purpose for which disclosure is not precluded by this section.

(5) Subject to section 180 below, information obtained by the competent authority in the exercise of its functions under Part IV of this Act or received by it pursuant to a Community obligation from any authority exercising corresponding functions in another member State shall not be disclosed without the consent of the person from whom the competent authority obtained the information and, if different, the person to whom it relates.

(6) Any person who contravenes this section shall be guilty of an offence and liable—

(*a*) on conviction on indictment, to imprisonment for a term not exceeding two years or to a fine or to both;

(*b*) on summary conviction, to imprisonment for a term not exceeding three months or to a fine not exceeding the statutory maximum or to both.

DEFINITIONS
  "competent authority": s.207(1).
  "designated agency": s.114(3).
  "primary recipient": subs. (3).
  "restricted information": subss. (2), (4).
  "the Tribunal": s.207(1).
  "transferee body": Sched. 11, para. 28(4).

GENERAL NOTE
  This section imposes restrictions on the disclosure of information obtained under the Act and provides that their contravention is an offence. As to exceptions, see section 180.

Exceptions from restrictions on disclosure

180.—(1) Section 179 above shall not preclude the disclosure of information—
  (*a*) with a view to the institution of or otherwise for the purposes of criminal proceedings;
  (*b*) with a view to the institution of or otherwise for the purposes of any civil proceedings arising under or by virtue of this Act or proceedings before the Tribunal;
  (*c*) for the purpose of enabling or assisting the Secretary of State to exercise any powers conferred on him by this Act or by the enactments relating to companies insurance companies or insolvency or for the purpose of enabling or assisting any inspector appointed by him under the enactments relating to companies to discharge his functions;
  (*d*) for the purpose of enabling or assisting the Department of Economic Development for Northern Ireland to exercise any powers conferred on it by the enactments relating to companies or insolvency or for the purpose of enabling or assisting any inspector appointed by it under the enactments relating to companies to discharge his functions;
  (*e*) for the purpose of enabling or assisting a designated agency or transferee body or the competent authority to discharge its functions under this Act or of enabling or assisting the body administering a scheme under section 54 above to discharge its functions under the scheme;
  (*f*) for the purpose of enabling or assisting the Bank of England to discharge its functions under the Banking Act 1979 or any other functions;
  (*g*) for the purpose of enabling or assisting the Deposit Protection Board to discharge its functions under that Act;
  (*h*) for the purpose of enabling or assisting the Chief Registrar of friendly societies or the Registrar of Friendly Societies for Northern Ireland to discharge his functions under this Act or under the enactments relating to friendly societies or building societies;
  (*i*) for the purpose of enabling or assisting the Industrial Assurance Commissioner or the Industrial Assurance Commissioner for Northern Ireland to discharge his functions under the enactments relating to industrial assurance;
  (*j*) for the purpose of enabling or assisting the Insurance Brokers Registration Council to discharge its functions under the Insurance Brokers (Registration) Act 1977;
  (*k*) for the purpose of enabling or assisting an official receiver to discharge his functions under the enactments relating to insolvency or for the purpose of enabling or assisting a body which is for the time being a recognised professional body for the purposes of section 391 of the Insolvency Act 1986 to discharge its functions as such;

(*l*) for the purpose of enabling or assisting the Building Societies Commission to discharge its functions under the Building Societies Act 1986;

(*m*) for the purpose of enabling or assisting the Director General of Fair Trading to discharge his functions under this Act;

(*n*) for the purpose of enabling or assisting a recognised self-regulating organisation, recognised investment exchange, recognised professional body, or recognised clearing house to discharge its functions as such;

(*o*) with a view to the institution of, or otherwise for the purposes of, any disciplinary proceedings relating to the exercise by a solicitor, auditor, accountant, valuer or actuary of his professional duties;

(*p*) for the purpose of enabling or assisting any person appointed or authorised to exercise any powers under section 94, 106 or 177 above to discharge his functions;

(*q*) for the purpose of enabling or assisting an auditor of an authorised person or a person approved under section 108 above to discharge his functions;

(*r*) if the information is or has been available to the public from other sources;

(*s*) in a summary or collection of information framed in such a way as not to enable the identity of any person to whom the information relates to be ascertained; or

(*t*) in pursuance of any Community obligation.

(2) Section 179 above shall not preclude the disclosure of information to the Secretary of State or to the Treasury if the disclosure is made in the interests of investors or in the public interest.

(3) Subject to subsection (4) below, section 179 above shall not preclude the disclosure of information for the purpose of enabling or assisting any public or other authority for the time being designated for the purposes of this section by an order made by the Secretary of State to discharge any functions which are specified in the order.

(4) An order under subsection (3) above designating an authority for the purposes of that subsection may—

(*a*) impose conditions subject to which the disclosure of information is permitted by that subsection; and

(*b*) otherwise restrict the circumstances in which that subsection permits disclosure.

(5) Section 179 above shall not preclude the disclosure—

(*a*) of any information contained in an unpublished report of the Tribunal which has been made available to any person under this Act, by the person to whom it was made available or by any person obtaining the information directly or indirectly from him;

(*b*) of any information contained in any notice or copy of a notice served under this Act, notice of the contents of which has not been given to the public, by the person on whom it was served or any person obtaining the information directly or indirectly from him;

(*c*) of any information contained in the register kept under section 102 above by virtue of subsection (1)(*e*) of that section, by a person who has inspected the register under section 103(2) or (3) above or any person obtaining the information directly or indirectly from him.

(6) Section 179 above shall not preclude the disclosure of information for the purpose of enabling or assisting an authority in a country or territory outside the United Kingdom to exercise functions corresponding to those of the Secretary of State under this Act or the Insurance

Companies Act 1982 or to those of the Bank of England under the Banking Act 1979 or to those of the competent authority under this Act or any other functions in connection with rules of law corresponding to the provisions of the Companies Securities (Insider Dealing) Act 1985 or Part VII of this Act.

(7) Section 179 above shall not preclude the disclosure of information by the Director General of Fair Trading or any officer or servant of his or any person obtaining the information directly or indirectly from the Director or any such officer or servant if the information was obtained by the Director or any such officer or servant for the purposes of or in the discharge of his functions under this Act (whether or not he was the primary recipient of the information within the meaning of section 179 above) and the disclosure is made—

> (*a*) for the purpose of enabling or assisting the Director, the Secretary of State or any other Minister, the Monopolies and Mergers Commission or any Northern Ireland department to discharge any function conferred on him or them by the Fair Trading Act 1973 (other than Part II or III of that Act), the Restrictive Trade Practices Act 1976 or the Competition Act 1980; or
>
> (*b*) for the purposes of any civil proceedings under any of those provisions;

and information shall not be treated as restricted information for the purposes of section 179 above if it has been made available to the public by virtue of this subsection.

(8) The Secretary of State may by order modify the application of any provision of this section so as—

> (*a*) to prevent the disclosure by virtue of that provision; or
>
> (*b*) to restrict the extent to which disclosure is permitted by virtue of that provision,

of information received by a person specified in the order pursuant to a Community obligation from a person exercising functions in relation to a collective investment scheme who is also so specified.

(9) An order under subsection (3) or (8) above shall be subject to annulment in pursuance of a resolution of either House of Parliament.

DEFINITIONS
"authorised person": s.207(1).
"collective investment scheme": s.75.
"competent authority": s.207(1).
"designated agency": s.114(3).
"recognised clearing house": s.207(1).
"recognised investment exchange": s.207(1).
"recognised professional body": s.207(1).
"recognised self-regulating organisation": s.207(1).
"the Tribunal": s.207(1).
"transferee body": Sched. 11, para. 28(4).

GENERAL NOTE
This section creates a series of exceptions from the restrictions on the disclosure of information contained in section 179. Their purpose is to ensure that the restrictions do not "unduly inhibit" the disclosure of information obtained under the Act to other authorities. (H.C. Standing Committee E, cols. 905–906).

Subs. (3)
This subsection empowers the Secretary of State to designate, by order subject to negative procedure, public and other authorities as ones to whom information may be disclosed for the purpose of enabling or assisting them to discharge specified functions.

Subs. (6)
By virtue of this subsection, information may also be disclosed to overseas authorities. In determining whether functions correspond, regard may be had to provisions of this Act which have not yet come into force (Sched. 15, para. 13). As to restrictions on the disclosure of information overseas, see section 181.

Directions restricting disclosure of information overseas

181.—(1) If it appears to the Secretary of State to be in the public interest to do so, he may give a direction prohibiting the disclosure to any person in a country or territory outside the United Kingdom which is specified in the direction, or to such persons in such a country or territory as may be so specified, of such information to which this section applies as may be so specified.

(2) A direction under subsection (1) above—

(*a*) may prohibit disclosure of the information to which it applies by all persons or only by such persons or classes of person as may be specified in it; and

(*b*) may prohibit such disclosure absolutely or in such cases or subject to such conditions as to consent or otherwise as may be specified in it;

and a direction prohibiting disclosure by all persons shall be published by the Secretary of State in such manner as appears to him to be appropriate.

(3) This section applies to any information relating to the business or other affairs of any person which was obtained (whether or not by virtue of any requirement to supply it) directly or indirectly—

(*a*) by a designated agency, a transferee body, the competent authority or any person appointed or authorised to exercise any powers under section 94, 106 or 177 above (or any officer or servant of any such body or person) for the purposes or in the discharge of any functions of that body or person under this Act or any rules or regulations made under this Act or of any monitoring agency functions; or

(*b*) by a recognised self-regulating organisation, a recognised professional body, a recognised investment exchange or a recognised clearing house other than an overseas investment exchange or clearing house (or any officer or servant of such an organisation, body, investment exchange or clearing house) for the purposes or in the discharge of any of its functions as such or of any monitoring agency functions.

(4) In subsection (3) above "monitoring agency functions" means any functions exercisable on behalf of another body by virtue of arrangements made pursuant to paragraph 4(2) of Schedule 2, paragraph 4(6) of Schedule 3, paragraph 3(2) of Schedule 4 or paragraph 3(2) of Schedule 7 to this Act or of such arrangements as are mentioned in section 39(4)(*b*) above.

(5) A direction under this section shall not prohibit the disclosure by any person other than a person mentioned in subsection (3) above of—

(*a*) information relating only to the affairs of that person; or

(*b*) information obtained by that person otherwise than directly or indirectly from a person mentioned in subsection (3) above.

(6) A direction under this section shall not prohibit the disclosure of information in pursuance of any Community obligation.

(7) A person who knowingly discloses information in contravention of a direction under this section shall be guilty of an offence and liable—

(*a*) on conviction on indictment, to imprisonment for a term not exceeding two years or to a fine or to both;

(*b*) on summary conviction, to imprisonment for a term not exceeding three months or to a fine not exceeding the statutory maximum or to both.

(8) A person shall not be guilty of an offence under this section by virtue of anything done or omitted to be done by him outside the United Kingdom unless he is a British citizen, a British Dependent Territories

citizen, a British Overseas citizen or a body corporate incorporated in the United Kingdom.

DEFINITIONS
"competent authority": s.207(1).
"designated agency": s.114(3).
"monitoring agency functions": subs. (4).
"overseas clearing house": s.207(1).
"overseas investment exchange": s.207(1).
"recognised investment exchange": s.207(1).
"recognised professional body": s.207(1).
"recognised self-regulating organisation": s.207(1).
"transferee body": Sched. 11, para. 28(4).

GENERAL NOTE
This section empowers the Secretary of State to give directions prohibiting or otherwise restricting the disclosure of information overseas. As to the circumstances in which this power might be used, see H.L. Vol. 479, col. 749. Contravention of a direction is an offence (subss. (7), (8)).

Subs. (8)
Note that the offence may be committed outside the United Kingdom by the persons listed.

Disclosure of information under enactments relating to fair trading, banking, insurance and companies

182. The enactments mentioned in Schedule 13 to this Act shall have effect with the amendments there specified (which relate to the circumstances in which information obtained under those enactments may be disclosed).

GENERAL NOTE
Schedule 13 makes provision for the disclosure of information obtained under the fair trading, banking, insurance and companies legislation to other authorities, including overseas authorities. As to restrictions on the disclosure of information overseas, see section 181.

PART IX

RECIPROCITY

Reciprocal facilities for financial business

183.—(1) If it appears to the Secretary of State or the Treasury that by reason of—
(a) the law of any country outside the United Kingdom; or
(b) any action taken by or the practices of the government or any other authority or body in that country,
persons connected with the United Kingdom are unable to carry on investment, insurance or banking business in, or in relation to, that country on terms as favourable as those on which persons connected with that country are able to carry on any such business in, or in relation to, the United Kingdom, the Secretary of State or, as the case may be, the Treasury may serve a notice under this subsection on any person connected with that country who is carrying on or appears to them to intend to carry on any such business in, or in relation to, the United Kingdom.

(2) No notice shall be served under subsection (1) above unless the Secretary of State, or as the case may be, the Treasury consider it in the national interest to serve it; and before doing so the Secretary of State or, as the case may be, the Treasury shall so far as they consider expedient

consult such body or bodies as appear to them to represent the interests of persons likely to be affected.

(3) A notice under subsection (1) above shall state the grounds on which it is given (identifying the country in relation to which those grounds are considered to exist); and any such notice shall come into force on such date as may be specified in it.

(4) For the purposes of this section a person is connected with a country if it appears to the Secretary of State or, as the case may be, the Treasury—

    (*a*) in the case of an individual, that he is a national of or resident in that country or carries on investment, insurance or banking business from a principal place of business there;

    (*b*) in the case of a body corporate, that it is incorporated or has a principal place of business in that country or is controlled by a person or persons connected with that country;

    (*c*) in the case of a partnership, that it has a principal place of business in that country or that any partner is connected with that country;

    (*d*) in the case of an unincorporated association which is not a partnership, that it is formed under the law of that country, has a principal place of business there or is controlled by a person or persons connected with that country.

(5) In this section "country" includes any territory or part of a country or territory; and where it appears to the Secretary of State or, as the case may be, the Treasury that there are such grounds as are mentioned in subsection (1) above in the case of any part of a country or territory their powers under that subsection shall also be exercisable in respect of any person who is connected with that country or territory or any other part of it.

DEFINITIONS

  "body corporate": s.207(1).
  "carry on investment business": s.1(3).
  "controller": s.207(5).
  "country": subs. (5).
  "insurance business": s.207(7).
  "partnership": s.207(1).
  "person connected": subs. (4).

GENERAL NOTE

The purpose of this Part of the Act is to provide the United Kingdom with leverage in negotiating reciprocity of access for financial services firms to foreign markets. To that end this section empowers the Secretary of State or the Treasury to serve notices on persons from foreign countries disqualifying them from, or restricting them in, carrying on investment, insurance or banking business in the United Kingdom. Notices may only be served if it appears that the country from which they come prevents by law or governmental action United Kingdom investment, insurance or banking firms from carrying on business in that country on terms as favourable as those afforded to firms from that country in the United Kingdom and if it is considered in the national interest to do so (subss. (1), (2)).

Subs. (1)

Banking business: This term is not defined.

As to types of notices and their effects, see sections 184 and 185. As to the variation and revocation of notices, see section 186. As to the service of notices, see section 204.

Investment and insurance business

184.—(1) A notice under section 183 above relating to the carrying on of investment business or insurance business shall be served by the Secretary of State and such a notice may be a disqualification notice, a restriction notice or a partial restriction notice and may relate to the carrying on of business of both kinds.

(2) A disqualification notice as respects investment business or insurance business shall have the effect of—

(a) cancelling any authorisation of the person concerned to carry on that business after the expiry of such period after the service of the notice as may be specified in it;

(b) disqualifying him from becoming authorised to carry on that business after the expiry of that period; and

(c) restricting any authorisation of the person concerned in respect of that business during that period to the performance of contracts entered into before the notice comes into force;

and the period specified in such a notice shall be such period as appears to the Secretary of State to be reasonable to enable the person on whom it is served to complete the performance of those contracts and to terminate such of them as are of a continuing nature.

(3) A restriction notice as respects investment business or insurance business shall have the effect of restricting any authorisation of the person concerned in respect of that business to the performance of contracts entered into before the notice comes into force.

(4) A partial restriction notice as respects investment business may prohibit the person concerned from—

(a) entering into transactions of any specified kind or entering into them except in specified circumstances or to a specified extent;

(b) soliciting business from persons of a specified kind or otherwise than from such persons;

(c) carrying on business in a specified manner or otherwise than in a specified manner.

(5) A partial restriction notice as respects insurance business may direct that the person concerned shall cease to be authorised under section 3 or 4 of the Insurance Companies Act 1982 to effect contracts of insurance of any description specified in the notice.

(6) If it appears to the Secretary of State that a person on whom he serves a notice under section 183 above as respects investment business is an authorised person by virtue of an authorisation granted by a designated agency or by virtue of membership of a recognised self-regulating organisation or certification by a recognised professional body he shall serve a copy of the notice on that agency, organisation or body.

(7) If it appears to the Secretary of State—

(a) that any person on whom a partial restriction notice has been served by him has contravened any provision of that notice or, in the case of a notice under subsection (5) above, effected a contract of insurance of a description specified in the notice; and

(b) that any such grounds as are mentioned in subsection (1) of section 183 above still exist in the case of the country concerned,

he may serve a disqualification notice or a restriction notice on him under that section.

(8) Sections 28, 33, 60, 61 and 62 above shall have effect in relation to a contravention of such a notice as is mentioned in subsection (4) above as they have effect in relation to any such contravention as is mentioned in those sections.

DEFINITIONS
"authorised person": s.207(1).
"carrying on of investment business": s.1(3).
"certification": s.207(1).
"contracts of insurance": s.207(7).
"designated agency": s.114(3).

"insurance business": s.207(7).
"membership": s.8(2).
"recognised professional body": s.207(1).
"recognised self-regulating organisation": s.207(1).

GENERAL NOTE
This section sets out the different types of notices, and their effects, which may be served by the Secretary of State under section 183(1) on persons carrying on investment or insurance business. The three types of notices which may be served are disqualification notices, restriction notices and partial restriction notices.

Subs. (2)
A disqualification notice cancels, disqualifies and restricts.

Subs. (3)
Unlike a disqualification notice, a restriction notice does not have the effect of cancelling the person's authorisation. Instead it is effectively suspended pending the possible serving of a revocation notice under section 186(2).

Subs. (4)
This subsection deals with partial restriction notices in respect of investment business. It follows closely the equivalent provisions of section 65. Contravention of any provision of a partial restriction notice may be penalised in the following ways: by the serving of a restriction notice or disqualification notice (subs. (7)); by the suspension or withdrawal of authorisation under sections 28 or 33; by the issue of a public reprimand under section 60; by injunctions or restitution obtained under section 61; and by actions for damages brought under section 62 (subs. 8).

Subs. (5)
This subsection deals with partial restriction notices in respect of insurance business. If contracts of insurance of a description specified in the notice are effected, a restriction notice or disqualification notice may be served (subs. (7)).

Banking business

185.—(1) A notice under section 183 above relating to the carrying on of a deposit-taking business as a recognised bank or licensed institution within the meaning of the Banking Act 1979 shall be served by the Treasury and may be either a disqualification notice or a partial restriction notice.

(2) A disqualification notice relating to such business shall have the effect of—

(*a*) cancelling any recognition or licence granted to the person concerned under the Banking Act 1979; and

(*b*) disqualifying him from becoming a recognised bank or licensed institution within the meaning of that Act.

(3) A partial restriction notice relating to such business may—

(*a*) prohibit the person concerned from dealing with or disposing of his assets in any manner specified in the direction;

(*b*) impose limitations on the acceptance by him of deposits;

(*c*) prohibit him from soliciting deposits either generally or from persons who are not already depositors;

(*d*) prohibit him from entering into any other transaction or class of transactions;

(*e*) require him to take certain steps, to pursue or refrain from pursuing a particular course of activities or to restrict the scope of his business in a particular way.

(4) The Treasury shall serve on the Bank of England a copy of any notice served by them under section 183 above.

(5) Any person who contravenes any provision of a partial restriction notice served on him by the Treasury under this section shall be guilty of an offence and liable—

(*a*) on conviction on indictment, to a fine;

(*b*) on summary conviction, to a fine not exceeding the statutory maximum.

(6) Any such contravention shall be actionable at the suit of a person who suffers loss as a result of the contravention subject to the defences and other incidents applying to actions for breach of statutory duty, but no such contravention shall invalidate any transaction.

(7) At the end of subsection (1) of section 8 of the Banking Act 1979 (power to give directions in connection with termination of deposit-taking authority) there shall be inserted—

"(*d*) at any time after a disqualification notice has been served on the institution by the Treasury under section 183 of the Financial Services Act 1986.".

GENERAL NOTE

This section sets out the different types of notices, and their effects, which may be served by the Treasury under section 183(1) on persons carrying on banking business. The two types of notices which may be served are disqualification notices and partial restriction notices (subss. (2), (3)). Contravention of any provision of a partial restriction notice exposes the person to criminal and civil penalties (subss. (5), (6)). Note, in relation to civil remedies, that the validity of transactions entered into in contravention of the provisions of a partial restriction notice is expressly preserved (subs. (6)).

Variation and revocation of notices

186.—(1) The Secretary of State or the Treasury may vary a partial restriction notice served under section 183 above by a notice in writing served on the person concerned; and any such notice shall come into force on such date as is specified in the notice.

(2) A notice under section 183 above may be revoked at any time by the Secretary of State or, as the case may be, the Treasury by serving a revocation notice on the person concerned; and the Secretary of State or, as the case may be, the Treasury shall revoke a notice if it appears to them that there are no longer any such grounds as are mentioned in subsection (1) of that section in the case of the country concerned.

(3) The revocation of a disqualification notice as respects investment business or insurance business shall not have the effect of reviving the authorisation which was cancelled by the notice except where the notice relates to investment business and the person concerned would (apart from the disqualification notice) at the time of the revocation be an authorised person as respects the investment business in question by virtue of his membership of a recognised self-regulating organisation or certification by a recognised professional body.

(4) The revocation of a disqualification notice as respects banking business shall not have the effect of reviving the recognition or licence which was cancelled by the notice.

(5) Nothing in subsection (3) or (4) above shall be construed as preventing any person who has been subject to a disqualification notice as respects any business from again becoming authorised or, as the case may be, becoming a recognised bank or licensed institution within the meaning of the Banking Act 1979 after the revocation of the notice.

(6) If it appears to the Secretary of State that a person on whom he serves a notice under this section as respects investment business was an authorised person by virtue of an authorisation granted by a designated agency or by virtue of membership of a recognised self-regulating organisation or certification by a recognised professional body at the time that

the notice which is being varied or revoked was served, he shall serve a copy of the notice on that agency, organisation or body.

(7) The Treasury shall serve on the Bank of England a copy of any notice served by them under this section.

DEFINITIONS
"authorised person": s.207(1).
"certification": s.207(1).
"designated agency": s.114(3).
"insurance business": s.207(7).
"investment business": s.1(2).
"membership": s.8(2).
"recognised professional body": s.207(1).
"recognised self-regulating organisation": s.207(1).

GENERAL NOTE
This section makes provision for the variation and revocation of notices served under section 183(1). As to the service of notices, see section 204.

Subs. (2)
Note that a notice must be revoked where the grounds mentioned in section 183(1) no longer obtain.

Subs. (3)
Save in the circumstances specified, a person in respect of whom a disqualification notice has been revoked will have to seek authorisation afresh.

PART X

MISCELLANEOUS AND SUPPLEMENTARY

Exemption from liability for damages

187.—(1) Neither a recognised self-regulating organisation nor any of its officers or servants or members of its governing body shall be liable in damages for anything done or omitted in the discharge or purported discharge of any functions to which this subsection applies unless the act or omission is shown to have been in bad faith.

(2) The functions to which subsection (1) above applies are the functions of the organisation so far as relating to, or to matters arising out of—

(a) the rules, practices, powers and arrangements of the organisation to which the requirements in paragraphs 1 to 6 of Schedule 2 to this Act apply;

(b) the obligations with which paragraph 7 of that Schedule requires the organisation to comply;

(c) any guidance issued by the organisation;

(d) the powers of the organisation under section 53(2), 64(4), 72(5), 73(5) or 105(2)(a) above; or

(e) the obligations to which the organisation is subject by virtue of this Act.

(3) No designated agency or transferee body nor any member, officer or servant of a designated agency or transferee body shall be liable in damages for anything done or omitted in the discharge or purported discharge of the functions exercisable by the agency by virtue of a delegation order or, as the case may be, the functions exercisable by the body by virtue of a transfer order unless the act or omission is shown to have been in bad faith.

(4) Neither the competent authority nor any member, officer, or servant of that authority shall be liable in damages for anything done or omitted

in the discharge or purported discharge of any functions of the authority under Part IV of this Act unless the act or omission is shown to have been in bad faith.

(5) The functions to which subsections (1) and (3) above apply also include any functions exercisable by a recognised self-regulating organisation, designated agency or transferee body on behalf of another body by virtue of arrangements made pursuant to paragraph 4(2) of Schedule 2, paragraph 4(6) of Schedule 3, paragraph 3(2) of Schedule 4 or paragraph 3(2) of Schedule 7 to this Act or of such arrangements as are mentioned in section 39(4)(*b*) above.

(6) A recognised professional body may make it a condition of any certificate issued by it for the purposes of Part I of this Act that neither the body nor any of its officers or servants or members of its governing body is to be liable in damages for anything done or omitted in the discharge or purported discharge of any functions to which this subsection applies unless the act or omission is shown to have been in bad faith.

(7) The functions to which subsection (6) above applies are the functions of the body so far as relating to, or to matters arising out of—

(*a*) the rules, practices and arrangements of the body to which the requirements in paragraphs 2 to 5 of Schedule 3 to this Act apply;

(*b*) the obligations with which paragraph 6 of that Schedule requires the body to comply;

(*c*) any guidance issued by the body in respect of any matters dealt with by such rules as are mentioned in paragraph (*a*) above;

(*d*) the powers of the body under the provisions mentioned in subsection (2)(*d*) above or under section 54(3) above; or

(*e*) the obligations to which the body is subject by virtue of this Act.

DEFINITIONS
"competent authority": s.207(1).
"delegation order": s.114(3).
"designated agency": s.114(3).
"guidance": s.207(1).
"recognised professional body": s.207(1).
"recognised self-regulating organisation": s.207(1).
"rules": s.207(1).
"transferee body": Sched. 11, para. 28(4).
"transfer order": Sched. 11, para. 28(4).

GENERAL NOTE
This section grants immunity from liability in damages to SROs, designated agencies, transferee bodies and competent authorities for acts or omissions in the discharge or purported discharge of the functions identified (subss. (1), (3), (4)). The immunity thus granted extends to investors as well as to persons supervised by those bodies. However, the immunity is confined to immunity from liability in damages: judicial review is therefore not excluded. And it does not extend to acts or omissions shown to have been in bad faith.

Subs. (1)
As to the functions to which this subsection applies, see subsections (2) and (5).

Subs. (3)
As to the functions in respect of which immunity is granted, see also subs. (5).

Subs. (6)
Despite strenuous efforts to achieve it, the immunity granted by this section does not extend to RPBs. Instead this subsection empowers them to make it a condition of certification that they are not to be liable for anything done or omitted in good faith in the discharge of the functions identified in subsection (7). Such a condition would bind a person certified by an RPB but would not prevent an aggrieved investor from suing the RPB.

Jurisdiction as respects actions concerning designated agency etc.

188.—(1) Proceedings arising out of any act or omission (or proposed act or omission) of a designated agency, transferee body or the competent authority in the discharge or purported discharge of any of its functions under this Act may be brought in the High Court or the Court of Session.

(2) At the end of Schedule 5 to the Civil Jurisdiction and Judgments Act 1982 (exclusion of certain proceedings from the provisions of Schedule 4 to that Act which determine whether the courts in each part of the United Kingdom have jurisdiction in proceedings) there shall be inserted—

"*Proceedings concerning financial services agencies*
10. Such proceedings as are mentioned in section 188 of the Financial Services Act 1986.".

DEFINITIONS
"competent authority": s.207(1).
"designated agency": s.114(3).
"transferee body": Sched. 11, para. 28(4).

GENERAL NOTE
This section makes it plain, in response to doubts which were expressed when the Bill was first published, that proceedings may be brought against a designated agency, transferee body or competent authority in the courts in any part of the United Kingdom.

Restriction of Rehabilitation of Offenders Act 1974

189.—(1) The Rehabilitation of Offenders Act 1974 shall have effect subject to the provisions of this section in cases where the spent conviction is for—
  (*a*) an offence involving fraud or other dishonesty; or
  (*b*) an offence under legislation (whether or not of the United Kingdom) relating to companies (including insider dealing), building societies, industrial and provident societies, credit unions, friendly societies, insurance, banking or other financial services, insolvency, consumer credit or consumer protection.

(2) Nothing in section 4(1) (restriction on evidence as to spent convictions in proceedings) shall prevent the determination in any proceedings specified in Part I of Schedule 14 to this Act of any issue, or prevent the admission or requirement in any such proceedings of any evidence, relating to a person's previous convictions for any such offence as is mentioned in subsection (1) above or to circumstances ancillary thereto.

(3) A conviction for any such offence as is mentioned in subsection (1) above shall not be regarded as spent for the purposes of section 4(2) (questions relating to an individual's previous convictions) if—
  (*a*) the question is put by or on behalf of a person specified in the first column of Part II of that Schedule and relates to an individual (whether or not the person questioned) specified in relation to the person putting the question in the second column of that Part; and
  (*b*) the person questioned is informed when the question is put that by virtue of this section convictions for any such offence are to be disclosed.

(4) Section 4(3)(*b*) (spent conviction not to be ground for excluding person from office, occupation etc.) shall not prevent a person specified in the first column of Part III of that Schedule from taking such action as is specified in relation to that person in the second column of that Part by reason, or partly by reason, of a spent conviction for any such offence as is mentioned in subsection (1) above of an individual who is—
  (*a*) the person in respect of whom the action is taken;

(b) as respects action within paragraph 1 or 4 of that Part, an associate of that person; or

(c) as respects action within paragraph 1 of that Part consisting of a decision to refuse or revoke an order declaring a collective investment scheme to be an authorised unit trust scheme or a recognised scheme, the operator or trustee of the scheme or an associate of his,

or of any circumstances ancillary to such a conviction or of a failure (whether or not by that individual) to disclose such a conviction or any such circumstances.

(5) Parts I, II and III of that Schedule shall have effect subject to Part IV.

(6) In this section and that Schedule "associate" means—

(a) in relation to a body corporate, a director, manager or controller;

(b) in relation to a partnership, a partner or manager;

(c) in relation to a registered friendly society, a trustee, manager or member of the committee of the society;

(d) in relation to an unincorporated association, a member of its governing body or an officer, manager or controller;

(e) in relation to an individual, a manager.

(7) This section and that Schedule shall apply to Northern Ireland with the substitution for the references to the said Act of 1974 and section 4(1), (2) and (3)(b) of that Act of references to the Rehabilitation of Offenders (Northern Ireland) Order 1978 and Article 5(1), (2) and (3)(b) of that Order.

DEFINITIONS

"associate": subs. (6).
"authorised unit trust scheme": s.207(1).
"body corporate": s.207(1).
"collective investment scheme": s.75.
"controller": s.207(5).
"manager": s.207(6).
"operator": s.207(1).
"partnership": s.207(1).
"recognised scheme": s.207(1).
"trustee": s.207(1).

GENERAL NOTE

This section and Schedule 14 make provision for the disclosure of convictions which would otherwise be treated as spent by virtue of the Rehabilitation of Offenders Act 1974 and for those convictions to be taken into account in the discharge of functions under this Act.

Subs. (1)

This subsection identifies the convictions which are to be disclosed and which may be taken into account.

Subs. (2)

This subsection, in conjunction with Schedule 14, Part I, permits the determination of issues, or the admission or requirement of evidence relating to previous convictions in exempted proceedings.

Subs. (3)

This subsection, in conjunction with Schedule 14, Part II, makes provision for questions to be put regarding previous convictions.

Subs. (4)

This subsection permits spent convictions to be taken into account for the purposes listed in Schedule 14, Part III.

Data protection

190. An order under section 30 of the Data Protection Act 1984 (exemption from subject access provisions of data held for the purpose of discharging designated functions conferred by or under enactments relating to the regulation of financial services etc.) may designate for the purposes of that section as if they were functions conferred by or under such an enactment as is there mentioned—

(a) any functions of a recognised self-regulating organisation in connection with the admission or expulsion of members, the suspension of a person's membership or the supervision or regulation of persons carrying on investment business by virtue of membership of the organisation;

(b) any functions of a recognised professional body in connection with the issue of certificates for the purposes of Part I of this Act, the withdrawal or suspension of such certificates or the supervision or regulation of persons carrying on investment business by virtue of certification by that body;

(c) any functions of a recognised self-regulating organisation for friendly societies in connection with the supervision or regulation of its member societies.

DEFINITIONS
"carrying on investment business": s.1(3).
"certification": s.207(1).
"members": s.8(2).
"recognised professional body": s.207(1).
"recognised self-regulating orgnisation for friendly societies": Sched. 11, para. 1.
"recognised self-regulating organisation": s.207(1).

GENERAL NOTE
Section 30 of the Data Protection Act makes provision for the exemption from the subject access provisions of the Act of data held for the purpose of discharging functions conferred by or under statute. Given that it could be argued that SROs' and RPBs' supervisory functions are not so conferred, this section puts the matter beyond doubt by making provision for the exemption by order of data held by them for the purpose of their supervisory functions.

Occupational pension schemes

191.—(1) Subject to the provisions of this section, a person who apart from this section would not be regarded as carrying on investment business shall be treated as doing so if he engages in the activity of management falling within paragraph 14 of Schedule 1 to this Act in a case where the assets referred to in that paragraph are held for the purposes of an occupational pension scheme.

(2) Subsection (1) above does not apply where all decisions, or all day to day decisions, in the carrying on of that activity so far as relating to assets which are investments are taken on behalf of the person concerned by—

(a) an authorised person;

(b) an exempted person who in doing so is acting in the course of the business in respect of which he is exempt; or

(c) a person who does not require authorisation to manage the assets by virtue of Part IV of Schedule 1 to this Act.

(3) The Secretary of State may by order direct that a person of such description as is specified in the order shall not by virtue of this section be treated as carrying on investment business where the assets are held for the purposes of an occupational pension scheme of such description as is so specified, being a scheme in the case of which it appears to the

Secretary of State that management by an authorised or exempted person is unnecessary having regard to the size of the scheme and the control exercisable over its affairs by the members.

(4) An order under subsection (3) above shall be subject to annulment in pursuance of a resolution of either House of Parliament.

(5) For the purposes of subsection (1) above paragraph 14 of Schedule 1 to this Act shall be construed without reference to paragraph 22 of that Schedule.

DEFINITIONS
"authorised person": s.207(1).
"carrying on investment business": s.1(3).
"exempted person": s.207(1).
"investment business": s.1(2).
"occupational pension scheme": s.207(1).

GENERAL NOTE
This section is designed to ensure that persons who engage in day-to-day management of an occupational pension scheme's investments must be authorised (or exempted) persons whether or not they would otherwise be regarded as carrying on investment business. It thus affects company employees who manage the assets of their company pension scheme in-house, and also trustees who actively manage the assets of an occupational pension scheme.

Subs. (1)
Persons who engage in investment management for an occupational pension scheme are to be regarded as carrying on investment business. The exemption in favour of trustees engaged in investment management is not applicable in the present context: subs. (5).

Subs. (2)
This subsection qualifies the preceding one: "A person such as a trustee who is responsible for the management of the assets of an occupational pension scheme will not be required to be authorised if he delegates day-to-day management of those assets to an authorised or exempted person. This does not mean that he would have to distance himself entirely from the management of the assets. He would still be able to take what might be called strategic decisions, for example, about the proportion of the assets that should constitute investments of particular kinds or the desired balance between growth and income . . .": H.L. Vol. 479, col. 781 (July 29, 1986).

Part IV of Schedule 1: *i.e.,* exclusions for persons without a permanent place of business in the United Kingdom.

Subs. (3)
This empowers the Secretary of State to exempt from the need to seek authorisation persons managing the investments of a scheme where management by an authorised/exempted person is unnecessary in view of the size of the scheme and the control that its members have over it. This subsection thus makes it possible to exempt the managers of small self-administered schemes.

As to the making of an order under this subsection, see s.205(2) and subs. (4) of this section.

International obligations

192.—(1) If it appears to the Secretary of State—

    (*a*) that any action proposed to be taken by a recognised self-regulating organisation, designated agency, transferee body or competent authority would be incompatible with Community obligations or any other international obligations of the United Kingdom; or

    (*b*) that any action which that organisation, agency, body or authority has power to take is required for the purpose of implementing any such obligations,

he may direct the organisation, agency, body or authority not to take or, as the case may be, to take the action in question.

(2) Subsection (1) above applies also to an approved exchange within the meaning of Part V of this Act in respect of any action which it proposes to take or has power to take in respect of rules applying to a prospectus by virtue of a direction under section 162(3) above.

(3) A direction under this section may include such supplementary or incidental requirements as the Secretary of State thinks necessary or expedient.

(4) Where the function of making or revoking a recognition order in respect of a self-regulating organisation is exercisable by a designated agency any direction under subsection (1) above in respect of that organisation shall be a direction requiring the agency to give the organisation such a direction as is specified in the direction given by the Secretary of State.

(5) Any direction under this section shall, on the application of the person by whom it was given, be enforceable by mandamus or, in Scotland, by an order for specific performance under section 91 of the Court of Session Act 1868.

DEFINITIONS
"approved exchange": s.158(6).
"competent authority": s.207(1).
"designated agency": s.114(3).
"recognised self-regulating organisation": s.207(1).
"transferee body": Sched. 11, para. 28(4).

GENERAL NOTE
This section empowers the Secretary of State to prevent the bodies listed from taking action incompatible with the United Kingdom's Community or other international obligations. He may also require them to take such action as is required for their implementation. The action which they may be prevented from taking or required to take includes altering their rules. In the case of SROs the Secretary of State's powers are exercisable through the SIB (subs. (4)).

Exemption from Banking Act 1979

193.—(1) Section 1(1) of the Banking Act 1979 (control of deposit-taking) shall not apply to the acceptance of a deposit by an authorised or exempted person in the course or for the purpose of engaging in any activity falling within paragraph 12 of Schedule 1 to this Act with or on behalf of the person by whom or on whose behalf the deposit is made or any activity falling within paragraph 13, 14 or 16 of that Schedule on behalf of that person.

(2) Subsection (1) above applies to an exempted person only if the activity is one in respect of which he is exempt; and for the purposes of that subsection the paragraphs of Schedule 1 there mentioned shall be construed without reference to Parts III and IV of that Schedule.

(3) This section is without prejudice to any exemption from the said Act of 1979 which applies to an authorised or exempted person apart from this section.

DEFINITIONS
"authorised person": s.207(1).
"exempted person": s.207(1).

GENERAL NOTE
Section 1(1) of the Banking Act 1979 prohibits the acceptance of deposits unless the person is exempted by virtue of section 2 of that Act. Since most investment businesses accept deposits they require exemption if they are to avoid contravening this prohibition. This section duly exempts persons who are authorised or exempted under this Act in respect of the activities listed. Note that the exemptions created in favour of exempted persons

under this Act are confined to the activities in respect of which they are exempted, and that persons may be exempted independently of this provision by the Banking Act itself. As to the exemptions which exist under the Banking Act, see section 2 of that Act and the statutory instruments made thereunder.

Transfers to or from recognised clearing houses

194.—(1) In section 5 of the Stock Exchange (Completion of Bargains) Act 1976 (protection of trustees etc. in case of transfer of shares etc. to or from a stock exchange nominee)—

    (*a*) for the words "a stock exchange nominee", in the first place where they occur, there shall be substituted the words "a recognised clearing house or a nominee of a recognised clearing house or of a recognised investment exchange";

    (*b*) for those words in the second place where they occur there shall be substituted the words "such a clearing house or nominee";

    (*c*) at the end there shall be added the words "; but no person shall be a nominee for the purposes of this section unless he is a person designated for the purposes of this section in the rules of the recognised investment exchange in question".

(2) The provisions of that section as amended by subsection (1) above shall become subsection (1) of that section and after that subsection there shall be inserted—

    "(2) In this section "a recognised clearing house" means a recognised clearing house within the meaning of the Financial Services Act 1986 acting in relation to a recognised investment exchange within the meaning of that Act and "a recognised investment exchange" has the same meaning as in that Act."

(3) In Article 7 of the Stock Exchange (Completion of Bargains) (Northern Ireland) Order 1977 (protection of trustees etc. in case of transfer of shares etc. to or from a stock exchange nominee)—

    (*a*) for the words "a stock exchange nominee", in the first place where they occur, there shall be substituted the words "a recognised clearing house or a nominee of a recognised clearing house or of a recognised investment exchange";

    (*b*) for those words in the second place where they occur there shall be substituted the words "such a clearing house or nominee";

    (*c*) at the end there shall be added the words "; but no person shall be a nominee for the purposes of this Article unless he is a person designated for the purposes of this Article in the rules of the recognised investment exchange in question".

(4) The provisions of that Article as amended by subsection (3) above shall become paragraph (1) of that Article and after that paragraph there shall be inserted—

    "(2) In this Article "a recognised clearing house" means a recognised clearing house within the meaning of the Financial Services Act 1986 acting in relation to a recognised investment exchange within the meaning of that Act and "a recognised investment exchange" has the same meaning as in that Act."

(5) In subsection (4) of section 185 of the Companies Act 1985 (exemption from duty to issue certificates in respect of shares etc. in cases of allotment or transfer to a stock exchange nominee)—

    (*a*) for the words "a stock exchange nominee" in the first place where they occur there shall be substituted the words "a recognised clearing house or a nominee of a recognised clearing house or of a recognised investment exchange";

    (*b*) for those words in the second place where they occur there shall be substituted the words "such a clearing house or nominee";

    (*c*) at the end of the first paragraph in that subsection there shall be inserted the words "; but no person shall be a nominee for the purposes of this section unless he is a person designated for the purposes of this section in the rules of the recognised investment exchange in question"; and

(*d*) for the second paragraph in that subsection there shall be substituted—

" 'Recognised clearing house' means a recognised clearing house within the meaning of the Financial Services Act 1986 acting in relation to a recognised investment exchange and 'recognised investment exchange' has the same meaning as in that Act.".

(6) In paragraph (4) of Article 195 of the Companies (Northern Ireland) Order 1986 (duty to issue certificates in respect of shares etc. in cases of allotment or transfer unless it is to a stock exchange nominee)—

(*a*) for the words "a stock exchange nominee" in the first place where they occur there shall be substituted the words "a recognised clearing house or a nominee of a recognised clearing house or of a recognised investment exchange";

(*b*) for those words in the second place where they occur there shall be substituted the words "such a clearing house or nominee";

(*c*) at the end of the first sub-paragraph in that paragraph there shall be inserted the words "; but no person shall be a nominee for the purposes of this Article unless he is a person designated for the purposes of this Article in the rules of the recognised investment exchange in question"; and

(*d*) for the second sub-paragraph in that paragraph there shall be substituted " 'recognised clearing house' means a recognised clearing house within the meaning of the Financial Services Act 1986 acting in relation to a recognised investment exchange and 'recognised investment exchange' has the same meaning as in that Act.".

DEFINITIONS
"recognised clearing house": s.207(1).
"recognised investment exchange": s.207(1).

GENERAL NOTE

Subs. (1)

Section 5 of the Stock Exchange (Completion of Bargains) Act 1976 provides that it is not breach of trust for a trustee to pay for securities held by the Stock Exchange nominee (SEPON Ltd.) before their transfer to him. Conversely it is not breach of trust to transfer securities to SEPON before receiving payment for them.

This subsection assimilates the legal position of trustees *vis-à-vis* other recognised clearing houses or their nominees or the nominees of recognised investment exchanges to their position *vis-à-vis* SEPON Ltd.

Subs. (5)

Section 185(4) of the Companies Act 1985 exempts company registrars, in the case of a transfer to SEPON Ltd., from the obligation to issue a share certificate within two months of the transfer.

This subsection extends that exemption to transfers to recognised clearing houses or their nominees or the nominees of recognised investment exchanges.

Offers of short-dated debentures

195. As respects debentures which, under the terms of issue, must be repaid within less than one year of the date of issue—

(*a*) section 79(2) of the Companies Act 1985 (offer of debentures of oversea company deemed not to be an offer to the public if made to professional investor) shall apply for the purposes of Chapter I of Part III of that Act as well as for those of Chapter II of that Part; and

(b) Article 89(2) of the Companies (Northern Ireland) Order 1986 (corresponding provisions for Northern Ireland) shall apply for the purposes of Chapter I of Part IV of that Order as well as for those of Chapter II of that Part.

DEFINITIONS

"offer to the public": Companies Act 1985, s.50.
"oversea company": Companies Act 1985, s.744.

GENERAL NOTE

By virtue of s.79(2) of the Companies Act 1985, an offer of the debentures of an oversea company to persons whose ordinary business is to buy or sell shares or debentures is not to be regarded as an offer to the public. Hence no prospectus is required. Section 195 of the present Act extends this privilege to offers of the debentures of companies to professional investors. This provision thus gives United Kingdom companies the same freedom to issue sterling commercial paper as foreign companies already enjoy.

This section came into force when the Act was passed: s.211(2). But it will be repealed when Sched. 17, Part I is brought into force. This is because s.195 is an interim provision which will be superseded by an order made under s.160(7).

Financial assistance for employees' share schemes

196.—(1) Section 153 of the Companies Act 1985 (transactions not prohibited by section 151) shall be amended as follows.

(2) After subsection (4)(b) there shall be inserted—

"(bb) without prejudice to paragraph (b), the provision of financial assistance by a company or any of its subsidiaries for the purposes of or in connection with anything done by the company (or a company connected with it) for the purpose of enabling or facilitating transactions in shares in the first-mentioned company between, and involving the acquisition of beneficial ownership of those shares by, any of the following persons—

(i) the bona fide employees or former employees of that company or of another company in the same group; or

(ii) the wives, husbands, widows, widowers, children or step-children under the age of eighteen of any such employees or former employees.".

(3) After subsection (4) there shall be inserted—

"(5) For the purposes of subsection (4)(bb) a company is connected with another company if—

(a) they are in the same group; or

(b) one is entitled, either alone or with any other company in the same group, to exercise or control the exercise of a majority of the voting rights attributable to the share capital which are exercisable in all circumstances at any general meeting of the other company or of its holding company;

and in this section "group", in relation to a company, means that company, any other company which is its holding company or subsidiary and any other company which is a subsidiary of that holding company.".

(4) Article 163 of the Companies (Northern Ireland) Order 1986 (transactions not prohibited by Article 161) shall be amended as follows.

(5) After paragraph (4)(b) there shall be inserted—

"(bb) without prejudice to sub-paragraph (b), the provision of financial assistance by a company or any of its subsidiaries for the purposes of or in connection with anything done by the company (or a company connected with it) for the purpose of enabling or facilitating transactions in shares in the first-mentioned company between, and involving the acquisition of beneficial ownership of those shares by, any of the following persons—

(i) the bona fide employees or former employees of that company or of another company in the same group; or

(ii) the wives, husbands, widows, widowers, children, step-children or adopted children under the age of eighteen of such employees or former employees.".

(6) After paragraph (4) there shall be inserted—

"(5) For the purposes of paragraph (4)(*bb*) a company is connected with another company if—

(*a*) they are in the same group; or

(*b*) one is entitled, either alone or with any other company in the same group, to exercise or control the exercise of a majority of the voting rights attributable to the share capital which are exercisable in all circumstances at any general meeting of the other company or of its holding company;

and in this Article "group", in relation to a company, means that company, any other company which is its holding company or subsidiary and any other company which is a subsidiary of that holding company.".

DEFINITIONS

"company": Companies Act 1985, s.735.
"holding company": Companies Act 1985, s.736.
"subsidiary": Companies Act 1985, s.736.

GENERAL NOTE

In general, of course, a company must not give financial assistance towards the purchase of its own shares: Companies Act 1985, s.151. But s.153(4)(*b*) of the 1985 Act allows a company to provide money in accordance with an employees' share scheme for the acquisition of its own fully paid shares. The new provision inserted by the present legislation makes it clear that a company may provide financial assistance for facilities helping beneficiaries of the scheme and their dependants to trade company shares among themselves.

Disclosure of interests in shares: interest held by market maker

197.—(1) In section 209 of the Companies Act 1985 (interests to be disregarded for purposes of sections 198 to 202)—

(*a*) in subsection (1)(*f*) after the word "jobber" there shall be inserted the words "or market maker";

(*b*) after subsection (4) there shall be inserted—

"(4A) A person is a market maker for the purposes of subsection (1)(*f*) if—

(*a*) he holds himself out at all normal times in compliance with the rules of a recognised investment exchange other than an overseas investment exchange (within the meaning of the Financial Services Act 1986) as willing to buy and sell securities at prices specified by him; and

(*b*) is recognised as doing so by that investment exchange;

and an interest of such a person in shares is an exempt interest if he carries on business as a market maker in the United Kingdom, is subject to such rules in the carrying on of that business and holds the interest for the purposes of that business.".

(2) In Article 217 of the Companies (Northern Ireland) Order 1986 (interests to be disregarded for purposes of Articles 206 to 210 (disclosure of interests in shares))—

(*a*) in paragraph (1)(*d*) after the word "jobber" there shall be inserted the words "or market maker";

(*b*) after paragraph (4) there shall be inserted—

"(4A) A person is a market maker for the purposes of paragraph (1)(*d*) if—

(*a*) he holds himself out at all normal times in compliance with the rules of a recognised investment exchange other than an overseas investment exchange (within the meaning of the Financial Services Act 1986) as willing to buy and sell securities at prices specified by him; and

(*b*) is recognised as doing so by that investment exchange,

and an interest of such a person in shares is an exempt interest if he carries on business as a market maker in the United Kingdom, is subject to such rules in the carrying on of that business and holds the interest for the purposes of that business.".

DEFINITIONS
"overseas investment exchange": s.207(1).
"recognised investment exchange": s.207(1).
"rules": s.207(1).

GENERAL NOTE
Under Part VI of the Companies Act 1985 jobbers are exempt from the obligation to give notice of acquisition of interests in shares in excess of five per cent. of the share capital. This provision extends that exemption to market makers as defined.

Power to petition for winding up etc. on information obtained under Act

198.—(1) In section 440 of the Companies Act 1985—

(*a*) after the words "section 437" there shall be inserted the words "above or section 94 of the Financial Services Act 1986"; and

(*b*) after the words "448 below" there shall be inserted the words "or section 105 of that Act".

(2) In section 8 of the Company Directors Disqualification Act 1986—

(*a*) after the words "the Companies Act" there shall be inserted the words "or section 94 or 177 of the Financial Services Act 1986"; and

(*b*) for the words "that Act" there shall be substituted the words "the Companies Act or section 105 of the Financial Services Act 1986".

(3) In Article 433 of the Companies (Northern Ireland) Order 1986—

(*a*) after the words "Article 430" there shall be inserted the words "or section 94 of the Financial Services Act 1986"; and

(*b*) after the word "441" there shall be inserted the words "or section 105 of that Act".

GENERAL NOTE

Subs. (1)

Section 440 of the Companies Act 1985 empowers the Secretary of State to petition for the winding up of a company in the public interest. But he may present a petition only on the basis of a report obtained by inspectors appointed, or of information or documents obtained, under the companies legislation. This new provision enables the Secretary of State to petition for a winding up under the companies legislation on the basis of the report of an investigation into a collective investment scheme or an investment business under the financial services legislation.

Subs. (2)

Likewise s.8 of the Company Directors Disqualification Act 1986 only allows the Secretary of State to apply to the court for the disqualification of a director in the public interest on the basis of information obtained under the Companies Act 1985. The new provision enables the Secretary of State to base his application on the report of an investigation under the financial services legislation into a collective investment scheme, an investment business, or a case of suspected insider dealing.

Powers of entry

199.—(1) A justice of the peace may issue a warrant under this section if satisfied on information on oath laid by or on behalf of the Secretary of State that there are reasonable grounds for believing—

(*a*) that an offence has been committed under section 4, 47, 57, 130, 133 or 171(2) or (3) above or section 1, 2, 4 or 5 of the Company Securities (Insider Dealing) Act 1985 and that there are on any premises documents relevant to the question whether that offence has been committed; or

(*b*) that there are on any premises owned or occupied by a person whose affairs, or any aspect of whose affairs, are being investigated under section 105 above documents whose production has been required under that section and which have not been produced in compliance with that requirement;

but paragraph (*b*) above applies only if the person there mentioned is an authorised person, a person whose authorisation has been suspended or who is the subject of a direction under section 33(1)(*b*) above or an appointed representative of an authorised person.

(2) A justice of the peace may issue a warrant under this section if satisfied on information on oath laid by an inspector appointed under section 94 above that there are reasonable grounds for believing that there are on any premises owned or occupied by—

(*a*) the manager, trustee or operator of any scheme the affairs of which are being investigated under subsection (1) of that section; or

(*b*) a manager, trustee or operator whose affairs are being investigated under that subsection,

any documents whose production has been required under that section and which have not been produced in compliance with that requirement.

(3) A warrant under this section shall authorise a constable, together with any other person named in it and any other constables—

(*a*) to enter the premises specified in the information, using such force as is reasonably necessary for the purpose;

(*b*) to search the premises and take possession of any documents appearing to be such documents as are mentioned in subsection (1)(*a*) or (*b*) or, as the case may be, in subsection (2) above or to take, in relation to any such documents, any other steps which may appear to be necessary for preserving them or preventing interference with them;

(*c*) to take copies of any such documents; and

(*d*) to require any person named in the warrant to provide an explanation of them or to state where they may be found.

(4) A warrant under this section shall continue in force until the end of the period of one month beginning with the day on which it is issued.

(5) Any documents of which possession is taken under this section may be retained—

(*a*) for a period of three months; or

(*b*) if within that period proceedings to which the documents are relevant are commenced against any person for an offence under this Act or section 1, 2, 4 or 5 of the said Act of 1985, until the conclusion of those proceedings.

(6) Any person who obstructs the exercise of any rights conferred by a warrant issued under this section or fails without reasonable excuse to comply with any requirement imposed in accordance with subsection (3)(*d*) above shall be guilty of an offence and liable—

(*a*) on conviction on indictment, to a fine;

(b) on summary conviction, to a fine not exceeding the statutory maximum.

(7) The functions to which section 114 above applies shall include the functions of the Secretary of State under this section; but if any of those functions are transferred under that section the transfer may be subject to a reservation that they are to be exercisable by the Secretary of State concurrently with the designated agency and, in the case of functions exercisable by virtue of subsection (1)(a) above, so as to be exercisable by the agency subject to such conditions or restrictions as the Secretary of State may from time to time impose.

(8) In the application of this section to Scotland the references to a justice of the peace shall include references to a sheriff and for references to the laying of information on oath there shall be substituted references to furnishing evidence on oath; and in the application of this section to Northern Ireland for references to the laying of information on oath there shall be substituted references to making a complaint on oath.

(9) In this section "documents" includes information recorded in any form and, in relation to information recorded otherwise than in legible form, references to its production include references to producing a copy of the information in legible form.

DEFINITIONS
"appointed representative": s.44(2).
"authorised person": s.207(1).
"designated agency": s.114(3).
"documents": subs. (9).
"operator": s.75(8).
"trustee": s.75(8).

GENERAL NOTE
This section makes provision for the issue of search warrants. Warrants may be issued in three types of case:

(a) Where the commission of an offence is suspected (subs. 1(a)). Warrants may be obtained on the application of the Secretary of State or the SIB. The SIB's power to obtain warrants may be subject to restrictions or conditions imposed by the Secretary of State (subs. (7)). Note that warrants may be obtained in respect of "any premises".

(b) Where documents have not been produced in compliance with a requirement imposed under section 105 (subs. (1)(b)). Again, warrants may be obtained on the application of the Secretary of State or the SIB. Note that warrants may only be obtained in respect of premises "owned or occupied" by the person under investigation, and only in respect of the persons mentioned; and

(c) Where documents have not been produced in compliance with a requirement imposed under section 94 (subs. (2)). Again warrants may only be obtained in respect of premises "owned or occupied".

As to offences in connection with warrants, see subsection (6).

False and misleading statements

200.—(1) A person commits an offence if—
   (a) for the purposes of or in connection with any application under this Act; or
   (b) in purported compliance with any requirement imposed on him by or under this Act,
he furnishes information which he knows to be false or misleading in a material particular or recklessly furnishes information which is false or misleading in a material particular.

(2) A person commits an offence if, not being an authorised person or exempted person, he—
   (a) describes himself as such a person; or
   (b) so holds himself out as to indicate or be reasonably understood to indicate that he is such a person.

(3) A person commits an offence if, not having a status to which this subsection applies, he—

(*a*) describes himself as having that status, or

(*b*) so holds himself out as to indicate or be reasonably understood to indicate that he has that status.

(4) Subsection (3) above applies to the status of recognised self-regulating organisation, recognised professional body, recognised investment exchange or recognised clearing house.

(5) A person guilty of an offence under subsection (1) above shall be liable—

(*a*) on conviction on indictment, to imprisonment for a term not exceeding two years or to a fine or to both;

(*b*) on summary conviction, to imprisonment for a term not exceeding six months or to a fine not exceeding the statutory maximum or to both.

(6) A person guilty of an offence under subsection (2) or (3) above shall be liable on summary conviction to imprisonment for a term not exceeding six months or to a fine not exceeding the fifth level on the standard scale or to both.

(7) Where a contravention of subsection (2) or (3) above involves a public display of the offending description or other matter the maximum fine that may be imposed under subsection (6) above shall be an amount equal to the fifth level on the standard scale multiplied by the number of days for which the display has continued.

(8) In proceedings brought against any person for an offence under subsection (2) or (3) above it shall be a defence for him to prove that he took all reasonable precautions and exercised all due diligence to avoid the commission of the offence.

DEFINITIONS

"authorised person": s.207(1).

"exempted person": s.207(1).

"recognised clearing house": s.207(1).

"recognised investment exchange": s.207(1).

"recognised professional body": s.207(1).

"recognised self-regulating organisation": s.207(1).

GENERAL NOTE

This section creates three separate offences.

Subs. (1)

This subsection makes it an offence to knowingly or recklessly furnish information which is false or misleading in a material particular.

Recklessly: See the annotation to section 47(1).

As to penalties see subsection (5); as to offences by bodies corporate, *etc.*, see section 204.

Subs. (2)

This subsection makes it an offence for a person to falsely describe himself or to hold himself out as being authorised or exempted. It is a defence to prove that all reasonable steps were taken and all due diligence exercised to avoid the commission of the offence (subs. (8)). As to penalties, see subsections (6) and (7); as to offences by bodies corporate, *etc.*, see section 204.

Subs. (3)

This subsection makes it an offence for a body to falsely describe itself or to hold itself out as being recognised. It is a defence to prove that all reasonable steps were taken and all due diligence exercised to avoid the commission of the offence (subs. (8)). As to penalties, see subsections (6) and (7); as to offences by bodies corporate, *etc.*, see section 204.

Subs. (8)

All reasonable precautions . . . all due diligence: See the annotation to section 4(2).

Prosecutions

201.—(1) Proceedings in respect of an offence under any provision of this Act other than section 133 or 185 shall not be instituted—

(a) in England and Wales, except by or with the consent of the Secretary of State or the Director of Public Prosecutions; or

(b) in Northern Ireland, except by or with the consent of the Secretary of State or the Director of Public Prosecutions for Northern Ireland.

(2) Proceedings in respect of an offence under section 133 above shall not be instituted—

(a) in England and Wales, except by or with the consent of the Secretary of State, the Industrial Assurance Commissioner or the Director of Public Prosecutions; or

(b) in Northern Ireland, except by or with the consent of the Secretary of State or the Director of Public Prosecutions for Northern Ireland.

(3) Proceedings in respect of an offence under section 185 above shall not be instituted—

(a) in England and Wales, except by or with the consent of the Treasury or the Director of Public Prosecutions; or

(b) in Northern Ireland, except by or with the consent of the Treasury or the Director of Public Prosecutions for Northern Ireland.

(4) The functions to which section 114 above applies shall include the function of the Secretary of State under subsection (1) above to institute proceedings but any transfer of that function shall be subject to a reservation that it is to be exercisable by him concurrently with the designated agency and so as to be exercisable by the agency subject to such conditions or restrictions as the Secretary of State may from time to time impose.

DEFINITION
"designated agency": s.114(3).

GENERAL NOTE
This section deals with prosecutions in respect of offences under the Act. Note that save in respect of offences under sections 133 and 185, the power to bring prosecutions may be conferred upon the SIB, subject however to a reservation that it is to be exercisable concurrently with the Secretary of State as well as to such conditions or restrictions as may be imposed by the Secretary of State (subs. (4)). The SIB will certainly be given the power to prosecute in repect of offences under s. 4. In Scotland, where prosecutions are initiated by or with the consent of the Lord Advocate, the Secretary of State has no power to initiate prosecutions and hence there would appear to be no scope for the SIB to initiate prosecutions either.

Offences by bodies corporate, partnerships and unincorporated associations

202.—(1) Where an offence under this Act committed by a body corporate is proved to have been committed with the consent or connivance of, or to be attributable to any neglect on the part of—

(a) any director, manager, secretary or other similar officer of the body corporate, or any person who was purporting to act in any such capacity; or

(b) a controller of the body corporate,

he, as well as the body corporate, shall be guilty of that offence and liable to be proceeded against and punished accordingly.

(2) Where the affairs of a body corporate are managed by the members subsection (1) above shall apply in relation to the acts and defaults of a member in connection with his functions of management as if he were a director of the body corporate.

(3) Where a partnership is guilty of an offence under this Act every partner, other than a partner who is proved to have been ignorant of or to have attempted to prevent the commission of the offence, shall also be guilty of that offence and be liable to be proceeded against and punished accordingly.

(4) Where an unincorporated association (other than a partnership) is guilty of an offence under this Act—

(a) every officer of the association who is bound to fulfil any duty of which the breach is the offence; or

(b) if there is no such officer, every member of the governing body other than a member who is proved to have been ignorant of or to have attempted to prevent the commission of the offence,

shall also be guilty of the offence and be liable to be proceeded against and punished accordingly.

DEFINITIONS

"body corporate": s.207(1).
"controller": s.207(5).
"director": s.207(1).
"manager": s.207(6).
"partnership": s.207(1).

GENERAL NOTE

This section enables proceedings to be brought against the individuals identified in respect of offences committed by bodies corporate, partnerships and unincorporated associations. Identical provisions are contained in the Banking Act 1979 (ss.41, 42).

Subs. (1)

Consent: Knowledge is implied, but constructive rather than actual knowledge may be sufficient. (*Ex parte Todd; Re Caughey* (1876) 1 Ch.D. 521 at 528; *Mallon* v. *Allon* [1964] 1 Q.B. 385 at 394).

Connivance: Save in the context of matrimonial law, there is little authority on the meaning of connivance, but encouragement would seem to be essential. (*Godfrey* v. *Godfrey* [1965] A.C. 444.)

Neglect: Implies failure to perform a duty of which the person charged knows or ought to have known (*Re Hughes; Rea* v. *Black* [1943] Ch. 296 at 298.

Subss. (3), (4)

Other than . . . commission of the offence "the onus of proof will lie on the person seeking to avoid liability for the offence . . ." (H.L. Vol. 481, col. 576.)

Jurisdiction and procedure in respect of offences

203.—(1) Summary proceedings for an offence under this Act may, without prejudice to any jurisdiction exercisable apart from this section, be taken against any body corporate or unincorporated association at any place at which it has a place of business and against an individual at any place where he is for the time being.

(2) Proceedings for an offence alleged to have been committed under this Act by an unincorporated association shall be brought in the name of the association (and not in that of any of its members) and for the purposes of any such proceedings any rules of court relating to the service of documents shall have effect as if the association were a corporation.

(3) Section 33 of the Criminal Justice Act 1925 and Schedule 3 to the Magistrates' Courts Act 1980 (procedure on charge of offence against a corporation) shall have effect in a case in which an unincorporated association is charged in England and Wales with an offence under this Act in like manner as they have effect in the case of a corporation.

(4) In relation to any proceedings on indictment in Scotland for an offence alleged to have been committed under this Act by an unincorporated association, section 74 of the Criminal Procedure (Scotland) Act

1975 (proceedings on indictment against bodies corporate) shall have effect as if the association were a body corporate.

(5) Section 18 of the Criminal Justice Act (Northern Ireland) 1945 and Schedule 4 to the Magistrates' Courts (Northern Ireland) Order 1981 (procedure on charge of offence against a corporation) shall have effect in a case in which an unincorporated association is charged in Northern Ireland with an offence under this Act in like manner as they have effect in the case of a corporation.

(6) A fine imposed on an unincorporated association on its conviction of an offence under this Act shall be paid out of the funds of the association.

DEFINITION
"body corporate": s.207(1).

GENERAL NOTE
This section deals with the jurisdiction of the courts and procedures to be adopted in respect of offences.

Service of notices

204.—(1) This section has effect in relation to any notice, direction or other document required or authorised by or under this Act to be given to or served on any person other than the Secretary of State, the Chief Registrar of friendly societies or the Registrar of Friendly Societies for Northern Ireland.

(2) Any such document may be given to or served on the person in question—
  (a) by delivering it to him;
  (b) by leaving it at his proper address; or
  (c) by sending it by post to him at that address.

(3) Any such document may—
  (a) in the case of a body corporate, be given to or served on the secretary or clerk of that body;
  (b) in the case of a partnership, be given to or served on any partner;
  (c) in the case of an unincorporated association other than a partnership, be given to or served on any member of the governing body of the association;
  (d) in the case of an appointed representative, be given to or served on his principal.

(4) For the purposes of this section and section 7 of the Interpretation Act 1978 (service of documents by post) in its application to this section, the proper address of any person is his last known address (whether of his residence or of a place where he carries on business or is employed) and also any address applicable in his case under the following provisions—
  (a) in the case of a member of a recognised self-regulating organisation or a person certified by a recognised professional body who does not have a place of business in the United Kingdom, the address of that organisation or body;
  (b) in the case of a body corporate, its secretary or its clerk, the address of its registered or principal office in the United Kingdom;
  (c) in the case of an unincorporated association (other than a partnership) or a member of its governing body, its principal office in the United Kingdom.

(5) Where a person has notified the Secretary of State of an address or a new address at which documents may be given to or served on him under this Act that address shall also be his proper address for the purposes mentioned in subsection (4) above or, as the case may be, his

proper address for those purposes in substitution for that previously notified.

DEFINITIONS
"appointed representative": s.44(2).
"body corporate": s.207(1).
"certified": s.207(1).
"member": s.8(2).
"partnership": s.207(1).
"principal": s.207(1).
"proper address": subss. (4), (5).
"recognised professional body": s.207(1).
"recognised self-regulating organisation": s.207(1).

GENERAL NOTE
This section sets out the manner in which a notice, direction or other document can be given or served. As to the service of documents by post, see the Interpretation Act 1978, section 7.

Regulations, rules and orders

205.—(1) The Secretary of State may make regulations prescribing anything which by this Act is authorised or required to be prescribed.

(2) Subject to subsection (5) below, any power of the Secretary of State to make regulations, rules or orders under this Act shall be exercisable by statutory instrument.

(3) Subject to subsection (5) below, any regulations, rules or orders made under this Act by the Secretary of State may make different provision for different cases.

(4) Except as otherwise provided, a statutory instrument containing regulations or rules under this Act shall be subject to annulment in pursuance of a resolution of either House of Parliament.

(5) Subsections (2) and (3) above do not apply to a recognition order, an order declaring a collective investment scheme to be an authorised unit trust scheme or a recognised scheme or to an order revoking any such order.

DEFINITIONS
"authorised unit trust scheme": s.207(1).
"collective investment scheme": s.75.
"recognised scheme": s.207(1).
"recognition order": s.207(1).

GENERAL NOTE
This section contains provisions concerning the making of regulations, rules and orders under the Act. As to rules and regulations made by the SIB in the exercise of functions transferred to it by a delegation order, see Schedule 9, paragraphs 4 to 9.

Publication of information and advice

206.—(1) The Secretary of State may publish information or give advice, or arrange for the publication of information or the giving of advice, in such form and manner as he considers appropriate with respect to—

(a) the operation of this Act and the rules and regulations made under it, including in particular the rights of investors, the duties of authorised persons and the steps to be taken for enforcing those rights or complying with those duties;

(b) any matters relating to the functions of the Secretary of State under this Act or any such rules or regulations;

(c) any other matters about which it appears to him to be desirable to publish information or give advice for the protection of investors or any class of investors.

(2) The Secretary of State may offer for sale copies of information published under this section and may, if he thinks fit, make a reasonable charge for advice given under this section at any person's request.

(3) This section shall not be construed as authorising the disclosure of restricted information within the meaning of section 179 above in any case in which it could not be disclosed apart from the provisions of this section.

(4) The functions to which section 114 above applies shall include the functions of the Secretary of State under this section.

DEFINITIONS
"authorised persons": s.207(1).
"restricted information": s.179(2).

GENERAL NOTE
This section empowers the SIB to publish information and to give advice about the matters specified.

Interpretation

207.—(1) In this Act, except where the context otherwise requires—

"appointed representative" has the meaning given in section 44 above;

"authorised person" means a person authorised under Chapter III of Part I of this Act;

"authorised unit trust scheme" means a unit trust scheme declared by an order of the Secretary of State for the time being in force to be an authorised unit trust scheme for the purposes of this Act;

"body corporate" includes a body corporate constituted under the law of a country or territory outside the United Kingdom;

"certified" and "certification" mean certified or certification by a recognised professional body for the purposes of Part I of this Act;

"clearing arrangements" has the meaning given in section 38(2) above;

"competent authority" means the competent authority for the purposes of Part IV of this Act;

"collective investment scheme" has the meaning given in section 75 above;

"delegation order" and "designated agency" have the meaning given in section 114(3) above;

"director", in relation to a body corporate, includes a person occupying in relation to it the position of a director (by whatever name called) and any person in accordance with whose directions or instructions (not being advice given in a professional capacity) the directors of that body are accustomed to act;

"exempted person" means a person exempted under Chapter IV of Part I of this Act;

"group", in relation to a body corporate, means that body corporate, any other body corporate which is its holding company or subsidiary and any other body corporate which is a subsidiary of that holding company;

"guidance", in relation to a self-regulating organisation, professional body, investment exchange, clearing house or designated agency, has the meaning given in section 8(4), 16(4), 36(3), 38(3) or 114(12) above;

"investment advertisement" has the meaning given in section 57(2) above;

"investment agreement" has the meaning given in section 44(9) above;

"listing particulars" has the meaning given in section 144(2) above;

"member", in relation to a self-regulating organisation or professional body, has the meaning given in section 8(2) or 16(2) above;

"occupational pension scheme" means any scheme or arrangement which is comprised in one or more instruments or agreements and which has, or is capable of having, effect in relation to one or more descriptions or categories of employment so as to provide benefits, in the form of pensions or otherwise, payable on termination of service, or on death or retirement, to or in respect of earners with qualifying service in an employment of any such description or category;

"operator", in relation to a collective investment scheme, shall be construed in accordance with section 75(8) above;

"open-ended investment company" has the meaning given in section 75(8) above;

"overseas investment exchange" and "overseas clearing house" mean a recognised investment exchange or recognised clearing house in the case of which the recognition order was made by virtue of section 40 above;

"participant" has the meaning given in section 75(2) above;

"partnership" includes a partnership constituted under the law of a country or territory outside the United Kingdom;

"prescribed" means prescribed by regulations made by the Secretary of State;

"principal", in relation to an appointed representative, has the meaning given in section 44 above;

"private company" has the meaning given in section 1(3) of the Companies Act 1985 or the corresponding Northern Ireland provision;

"recognised clearing house" means a body declared by an order of the Secretary of State for the time being in force to be a recognised clearing house for the purposes of this Act;

"recognised investment exchange" means a body declared by an order of the Secretary of State for the time being in force to be a recognised investment exchange for the purposes of this Act;

"recognised professional body" means a body declared by an order of the Secretary of State for the time being in force to be a recognised professional body for the purposes of this Act;

"recognised scheme" means a scheme recognised under section 86, 87 or 88 above;

"recognised self-regulating organisation" means a body declared by an order of the Secretary of State for the time being in force to be a recognised self-regulating organisation for the purposes of this Act;

"recognised self-regulating organisation for friendly societies" has the meaning given in paragraph 1 of Schedule 11 to this Act;

"recognition order" means an order declaring a body to be a recognised self-regulating organisation, self-regulating organisation for friendly societies, professional body, investment exchange or clearing house;

"registered friendly society" means—

(*a*) a society which is a friendly society within the meaning of section 7(1)(*a*) of the Friendly Societies Act 1974 and is registered within the meaning of that Act; or

(*b*) a society which is a friendly society within the meaning of section 1(1)(*a*) of the Friendly Societies Act (Northern Ireland) 1970 and is registered or deemed to be registered under that Act;

"rules", in relation to a self-regulating organisation, professional body, investment exchange or clearing house, has the meaning given in section 8(3), 16(3), 36(2) or 38(2) above;

"transfer order" and "transferee body" have the meaning given in paragraph 28(4) of Schedule 11 to this Act;

"the Tribunal" means the Financial Services Tribunal;

"trustee", in relation to a collective investment scheme, has the meaning given in section 75(8) above;

"unit trust scheme" and "units" have the meaning given in section 75(8) above.

(2) In this Act "advertisement" includes every form of advertising, whether in a publication, by the display of notices, signs, labels or showcards, by means of circulars, catalogues, price lists or other documents, by an exhibition of pictures or photographic or cinematographic films, by way of sound broadcasting or television, by the distribution of recordings, or in any other manner; and references to the issue of an advertisement shall be construed accordingly.

(3) For the purposes of this Act an advertisement or other information issued outside the United Kingdom shall be treated as issued in the United Kingdom if it is directed to persons in the United Kingdom or is made available to them otherwise than in a newspaper, journal, magazine or other periodical publication published and circulating principally outside the United Kingdom or in a sound or television broadcast transmitted principally for reception outside the United Kingdom.

(4) The Independent Broadcasting Authority shall not be regarded as contravening any provision of this Act by reason of broadcasting an advertisement in accordance with the provisions of the Broadcasting Act 1981.

(5) In this Act "controller" means—

(*a*) in relation to a body corporate, a person who, either alone or with any associate or associates, is entitled to exercise, or control the exercise of, 15 per cent. or more of the voting power at any general meeting of the body corporate or another body corporate of which it is a subsidiary; and

(*b*) in relation to an unincorporated association—

(i) any person in accordance with whose directions or instructions, either alone or with those of any associate or associates, the officers or members of the governing body of the association are accustomed to act (but disregarding advice given in a professional capacity); and

(ii) any person who, either alone or with any associate or associates, is entitled to exercise, or control the exercise of, 15 per cent. or more of the voting power at any general meeting of the association;

and for the purposes of this subsection "associate", in relation to any person, means that person's wife, husband or minor child or step-child, any body corporate of which that person is a director, any person who is an employee or partner of that person and, if that person is a body corporate, any subsidiary of that body corporate and any employee of any such subsidiary.

(6) In this Act, except in relation to a unit trust scheme or a registered friendly society, "manager" means an employee who—

(*a*) under the immediate authority of his employer is responsible, either alone or jointly with one or more other persons, for the conduct of his employer's business; or

(*b*) under the immediate authority of his employer or of a person who is a manager by virtue of paragraph (*a*) above exercises managerial functions or is responsible for maintaining accounts or other records of his employer;

and, where the employer is not an individual, references in this subsection to the authority of the employer are references to the authority, in the case of a body corporate, of the directors, in the case of a partnership, of the partners and, in the case of an unincorporated association, of its officers or the members of its governing body.

(7) In this Act "insurance business", "insurance company" and "contract of insurance" have the same meanings as in the Insurance Companies Act 1982.

(8) Section 736 of the Companies Act 1985 (meaning of subsidiary and holding company) shall apply for the purposes of this Act.

(9) In the application of this Act to Scotland, references to a matter being actionable at the suit of a person shall be construed as references to the matter being actionable at the instance of that person.

(10) For the purposes of any provision of this Act authorising or requiring a person to do anything within a specified number of days no account shall be taken of any day which is a public holiday in any part of the United Kingdom.

(11) Nothing in Part I of this Act shall be construed as applying to investment business carried on by any person when acting as agent or otherwise on behalf of the Crown.

Gibraltar

208.—(1) Subject to the provisions of this section, section 31, 58(1)(*c*), 86 and 130(2)(*c*) and (*d*) above shall apply as if Gibraltar were a member State.

(2) References in those provisions to a national of a member State shall, in relation to Gibraltar, be construed as references to a British Dependent Territories citizen or a body incorporated in Gibraltar.

(3) In the case of a collective investment scheme constituted in Gibraltar the reference in subsection (3)(*a*) of section 86 above to a relevant Community instrument shall be taken as a reference to any Community instrument the object of which is the co-ordination or approximation of the laws, regulations or administrative provisions of member States relating to collective investment schemes of a kind which satisfy the requirements prescribed for the purposes of that section.

(4) The Secretary of State may by regulations make such provision as appears to him to be necessary or expedient to secure—

(*a*) that he may give notice under subsection (2) of section 86 above on grounds relating to the law of Gibraltar; and

(*b*) that this Act applies as if a scheme which is constituted in a member State other than the United Kingdom and recognised in Gibraltar under provisions which appear to the Secretary of State to give effect to the provisions of a relevant Community instrument were a scheme recognised under that section.

DEFINITION
"collective investment scheme": s.75.

GENERAL NOTE
The effect of this section is to treat Gibraltar as if it were a Member State in its own right. It will not be brought into operaton until Gibraltar has enacted the necessary implementing legislation (H.L. Vol. 479, cols. 813–816).

Northern Ireland

209.—(1) This Act extends to Northern Ireland.

(2) Subject to any Order made after the passing of this Act by virtue of subsection (1)(*a*) of section 3 of the Northern Ireland Constitution Act 1973 the regulation of investment business, the official listing of securities and offers of unlisted securities shall not be transferred matters for the purposes of that Act but shall for the purposes of subsection (2) of that section be treated as specified in Schedule 3 to that Act.

Expenses and receipts

210.—(1) Any expenses incurred by the Secretary of State under this Act shall be defrayed out of moneys provided by Parliament.

(2) Any fees or other sums received by the Secretary of State under this Act shall be paid into the Consolidated Fund.

(3) Subsections (1) and (2) above apply also to expenses incurred and fees received under this Act by the Chief Registrar of friendly societies; and any fees received under this Act by the Registrar of Friendly Societies for Northern Ireland shall be paid into the Consolidated Fund of Northern Ireland.

Commencement and transitional provisions

211.—(1) This Act shall come into force on such day as the Secretary of State may by order appoint and different days may be appointed for different provisions or different purposes.

(2) Subsection (1) above does not apply to section 195 which shall come into force when this Act is passed.

(3) Schedule 15 to this Act shall have effect with respect to the transitional matters there mentioned.

GENERAL NOTE

The DTI's provisional timetable for the implementation of Part I of the Act (regulation of investment business) is as follows:

Spring 1987 Delegation order laid before Parliament proposing transfer of functions to the SIB.

First half of 1987 The SIB undertakes recognition procedure of SROs, professional bodies, investment exchanges and clearing houses.

Summer/Autumn 1987 Investment businesses wishing to obtain authorisation from the SIB may apply; applications considered.

Late 1987 Appointed day for s.3 to come into effect.

The following orders had already been made by the end of 1986:

The Financial Services Act 1986 (Commencement No. 1) Order 1986, S.I. 1986 No. 1940.

The Financial Services Act 1986 (Commencement No. 2) Order 1986, S.I. 1986 No. 2031.

The Financial Services (Disclosure of Information) (Designated Authorities) Order 1986, S.I. 1986 No. 2046.

The Financial Services Act (Commencement No. 3) Order 1986, S.I. 1986 No. 2246.

Short title, consequential amendments and repeals

212.—(1) This Act may be cited as the Financial Services Act 1986.

(2) The enactments and instruments mentioned in Schedule 16 to this Act shall have effect with the amendments there specified, being amendments consequential on the provisions of this Act.

(3) The enactments mentioned in Part I of Schedule 17 to this Act and the instruments mentioned in Part II of that Schedule are hereby repealed or revoked to the extent specified in the third column of those Parts.

SCHEDULES

SCHEDULE 1

INVESTMENTS AND INVESTMENT BUSINESS

PART I

INVESTMENTS

Shares etc.

1. Shares and stock in the share capital of a company.
   Note. In this paragraph "company" includes any body corporate and also any unincorporated body constituted under the law of a country or territory outside the United Kingdom but does not include an open-ended investment company or any body incorporated under the law of, or of any part of, the United Kingdom relating to building societies, industrial and provident societies or credit unions.

Debentures

2. Debentures, including debenture stock, loan stock, bonds, certificates of deposit and other instruments creating or acknowledging indebtedness, not being instruments falling within paragraph 3 below.
   Note. This paragraph shall not be construed as applying—
   (a) to any instrument acknowledging or creating indebtedness for, or for money borrowed to defray, the consideration payable under a contract for the supply of goods or services;
   (b) to a cheque or other bill of exchange, a banker's draft or a letter of credit; or
   (c) to a banknote, a statement showing a balance in a current, deposit or savings account or (by reason of any financial obligation contained in it) to a lease or other disposition of property, a heritable security or an insurance policy.

Government and public securities

3. Loan stock, bonds and other instruments creating or acknowledging indebtedness issued by or on behalf of a government, local authority or public authority.
   Notes
   (1) In this paragraph "government, local authority or public authority" means—
   (a) the government of the United Kingdom, of Northern Ireland, or of any country or territory outside the United Kingdom;
   (b) a local authority in the United Kingdom or elsewhere;
   (c) any international organisation the members of which include the United Kingdom or another member State.
   (2) The Note to paragraph 2 above shall, so far as applicable, apply also to this paragraph.

Instruments entitling to shares or securities

4. Warrants or other instruments entitling the holder to subscribe for investments falling within paragraph 1, 2 or 3 above.
   Notes
   (1) It is immaterial whether the investments are for the time being in existence or identifiable.
   (2) An investment falling within this paragraph shall not be regarded as falling within paragraph 7, 8 or 9 below.

Certificates representing securities

5. Certificates or other instruments which confer—

(a) property rights in respect of any investment falling within paragraph 1, 2, 3 or 4 above;

(b) any right to acquire, dispose of, underwrite or convert an investment, being a right to which the holder would be entitled if he held any such investment to which the certificate or instrument relates; or

(c) a contractual right (other than an option) to acquire any such investment otherwise than by subscription.

Note. This paragraph does not apply to any instrument which confers rights in respect of two or more investments issued by different persons or in respect of two or more different investments falling within paragraph 3 above and issued by the same person.

Units in collective investment scheme

6. Units in a collective investment scheme, including shares in or securities of an open-ended investment company.

Options

7. Options to acquire or dispose of—

(a) an investment falling within any other paragraph of this Part of this Schedule;

(b) currency of the United Kingdom or of any other country or territory;

(c) gold or silver; or

(d) an option to acquire or dispose of an investment falling within this paragraph by virtue of (a), (b) or (c) above.

Futures

8. Rights under a contract for the sale of a commodity or property of any other description under which delivery is to be made at a future date and at a price agreed upon when the contract is made.

Notes

(1) This paragraph does not apply if the contract is made for commercial and not investment purposes.

(2) A contract shall be regarded as made for investment purposes if it is made or traded on a recognised investment exchange or made otherwise than on a recognised investment exchange but expressed to be as traded on such an exchange or on the same terms as those on which an equivalent contract would be made on such an exchange.

(3) A contract not falling within Note (2) above shall be regarded as made for commercial purposes if under the terms of the contract delivery is to be made within seven days.

(4) The following are indications that any other contract is made for a commercial purpose and the absence of any of them is an indication that it is made for investment purposes—

(a) either or each of the parties is a producer of the commodity or other property or uses it in his business;

(b) the seller delivers or intends to deliver the property or the purchaser takes or intends to take delivery of it.

(5) It is an indication that a contract is made for commercial purposes that the price, the lot, the delivery date or the other terms are determined by the parties for the purposes of the particular contract and not by reference to regularly published prices, to standard lots or delivery dates or to standard terms.

(6) The following are also indications that a contract is made for investment purposes—

(a) it is expressed to be as traded on a market or on an exchange;

(b) performance of the contract is ensured by an investment exchange or a clearing house;

(c) there are arrangements for the payment or provision of margin.

(7) A price shall be taken to have been agreed upon when a contract is made—

(a) notwithstanding that it is left to be determined by reference to the price at which a contract is to be entered into on a market or exchange or could be entered into at a time and place specified in the contract; or

(*b*) in a case where the contract is expressed to be by reference to a standard lot and quality, notwithstanding that provision is made for a variation in the price to take account of any variation in quantity or quality on delivery.

Contracts for differences etc.

9. Rights under a contract for differences or under any other contract the purpose or pretended purpose of which is to secure a profit or avoid a loss by reference to fluctuations in the value or price of property of any description or in an index or other factor designated for that purpose in the contract.

Note. This paragraph does not apply where the parties intend that the profit is to be obtained or the loss avoided by taking delivery of any property to which the contract relates.

Long term insurance contracts

10. Rights under a contract the effecting and carrying out of which constitutes long term business within the meaning of the Insurance Companies Act 1982.

Notes

(1) This paragraph does not apply to rights under a contract of insurance if—

(*a*) the benefits under the contract are payable only on death or in respect of incapacity due to injury, sickness or infirmity;

(*b*) no benefits are payable under the contract on a death (other than a death due to accident) unless it occurs within ten years of the date on which the life of the person in question was first insured under the contract or before that person attains a specified age not exceeding seventy years;

(*c*) the contract has no surrender value or the consideration consists of a single premium and the surrender value does not exceed that premium; and

(*d*) the contract does not make provision for its conversion or extension in a manner that would result in its ceasing to comply with paragraphs (*a*), (*b*) and (*c*) above.

(2) Where the provisions of a contract of insurance are such that the effecting and carrying out of the contract—

(*a*) constitutes both long term business within the meaning of the Insurance Companies Act 1982 and general business within the meaning of that Act; or

(*b*) by virtue of section 1(3) of that Act constitutes long term business notwithstanding the inclusion of subsidiary general business provisions,

references in this paragraph to rights and benefits under the contract are references only to such rights and benefits as are attributable to the provisions of the contract relating to long term business.

(3) This paragraph does not apply to rights under a re-insurance contract.

(4) Rights falling within this paragraph shall not be regarded as falling within paragraph 9 above.

Rights and interests in investments

11. Rights to and interests in anything which is an investment falling within any other paragraph of this Part of this Schedule.

Notes

(1) This paragraph does not apply to interests under the trusts of an occupational pension scheme.

(2) This paragraph does not apply to rights or interests which are investments by virtue of any other paragraph of this Part of this Schedule.

Part II

Activities Constituting Investment Business

Dealing in investments

12. Buying, selling, subscribing for or underwriting investments or offering or agreeing to do so, either as principal or as an agent.

Arranging deals in investments

13. Making or offering or agreeing to make—
(a) arrangements with a view to another person buying, selling, subscribing for or underwriting a particular investment; or
(b) arrangements with a view to a person who participates in the arrangements buying, selling, subscribing for or underwriting investments.
   Notes
   (1) This paragraph does not apply to a person by reason of his making, or offering or agreeing to make, arrangements with a view to a transaction to which he will himself be a party as principal or which will be entered into by him as agent for one of the parties.
   (2) The arrangements in (a) above are arrangements which bring about or would bring about the transaction in question.

Managing investments

14. Managing, or offering or agreeing to manage, assets belonging to another person if—
(a) those assets consist of or include investments; or
(b) the arrangements for their management are such that those assets may consist of or include investments at the discretion of the person managing or offering or agreeing to manage them and either they have at any time since the date of the coming into force of section 3 of this Act done so or the arrangements have at any time (whether before or after that date) been held out as arrangements under which they would do so.

Investment advice

15. Giving, or offering or agreeing to give, to persons in their capacity as investors or potential investors advice on the merits of their purchasing, selling, subscribing for or underwriting an investment, or exercising any right conferred by an investment to acquire, dispose of, underwrite or convert an investment.

Establishing etc. collective investment schemes

16. Establishing, operating or winding up a collective investment scheme, including acting as trustee of an authorised unit trust scheme.

Part III

Excluded Activities

Dealings as principal

17.—(1) Paragraph 12 above applies to a transaction which is or is to be entered into by a person as principal only if—
(a) he holds himself out as willing to enter into transactions of that kind at prices determined by him generally and continuously rather than in respect of each particular transaction; or
(b) he holds himself out as engaging in the business of buying investments with a view to selling them and those investments are or include investments of the kind to which the transaction relates; or
(c) he regularly solicits members of the public for the purpose of inducing them to enter

as principals or agents into transactions to which that paragraph applies and the transaction is or is to be entered into as a result of his having solicited members of the public in that manner.

(2) In sub-paragraph (1) above "buying" and "selling" means buying and selling by transactions to which paragraph 12 above applies and "members of the public", in relation to the person soliciting them ("the relevant person"), means any other persons except—

(*a*) authorised persons, exempted persons, or persons holding a permission under paragraph 23 below;

(*b*) members of the same group as the relevant person;

(*c*) persons who are, or propose to become, participators with the relevant person in a joint enterprise;

(*d*) any person who is solicited by the relevant person with a view to—

　(i) the acquisition by the relevant person of 20 per cent. or more of the voting shares in a body corporate (that is to say, shares carrying not less than that percentage of the voting rights attributable to share capital which are exercisable in all circumstances at any general meeting of the body); or

　(ii) if the relevant person (either alone or with other members of the same group as himself) holds 20 per cent. or more of the voting shares in a body corporate, the acquisition by him of further shares in the body or the disposal by him of shares in that body to the person solicited or to a member of the same group as that person; or

　(iii) if the person solicited (either alone or with other members of the same group as himself) hold 20 per cent. or more of the voting shares in a body corporate, the disposal by the relevant person of further shares in that body to the person solicited or to a member of the same group as that person;

(*e*) any person whose head office is outside the United Kingdom, who is solicited by an approach made or directed to him at a place outside the United Kingdom and whose ordinary business involves him in engaging in activities which fall within Part II of this Schedule or would do so apart from this Part or Part IV.

(3) Sub-paragraph (1) above applies only if the investment to which the transaction relates or will relate falls within any of paragraphs 1 to 6 above or, so far as relevant to any of those paragraphs, paragraph 11 above.

(4) Paragraph 12 above does not apply to a transaction which relates or is to relate to any other investment and which is or is to be entered into by a person as principal if he is not an authorised person and the transaction is or is to be entered into by him—

(*a*) with or through an authorised person, an exempted person or a person holding a permission under paragraph 23 below; or

(*b*) through an office outside the United Kingdom, maintained by a party to the transaction, and with or through a person whose head office is situated outside the United Kingdom and whose ordinary business is such as is mentioned in sub-paragraph (2)(*e*) above.

Groups and joint enterprises

18.—(1) Paragraph 12 above does not apply to any transaction which is or is to be entered into by a person as principal with another person if—

(*a*) they are bodies corporate in the same group; or

(*b*) they are, or propose to become, participators in a joint enterprise and the transaction is or is to be entered into for the purposes of, or in connection with, that enterprise.

(2) Paragraph 12 above does not apply to any transaction which is or is to be entered into by any person as agent for another person in the circumstances mentioned in sub-paragraph (1)(*a*) or (*b*) above if—

(*a*) where the investment falls within any of paragraphs 1 to 6 above or, so far as relevant to any of those paragraphs, paragraph 11 above, the agent does not—

　(i) hold himself out (otherwise than to other bodies corporate in the same group or persons who are or propose to become participators with him in a joint enterprise) as engaging in the business of buying investments with a view to selling them and those investments are or include investments of the kind to which the transaction relates; or

　(ii) regularly solicit members of the public for the purpose of inducing them to enter as principals or agents into transactions to which paragraph 12 above applies; and the transaction is not or is not to be entered into as a result of his having solicited members of the public in that manner;

(*b*) where the investment is not as mentioned in paragraph (*a*) above—

(i) the agent enters into the transaction with or through an authorised person, an exempted person or a person holding a permission under paragraph 23 below; or

(ii) the transaction is effected through an office outside the United Kingdom, maintained by a party to the transaction, and with or through a person whose head office is situated outside the United Kingdom and whose ordinary business involves him in engaging in activities which fall within Part II of this Schedule or would do so apart from this Part or Part IV.

(3) Paragraph 13 above does not apply to arrangements which a person makes or offers or agrees to make if—

(*a*) that person is a body corporate and the arrangements are with a view to another body corporate in the same group entering into a transaction of the kind mentioned in that paragraph; or

(*b*) that person is or proposes to become a participator in a joint enterprise and the arrangements are with a view to another person who is or proposes to become a participator in the enterprise entering into such a transaction for the purposes of or in connection with that enterprise.

(4) Paragraph 14 above does not apply to a person by reason of his managing or offering or agreeing to manage the investments of another person if—

(*a*) they are bodies corporate in the same group; or

(*b*) they are, or propose to become, participators in a joint enterprise and the investments are or are to be managed for the purposes of, or in connection with, that enterprise.

(5) Paragraph 15 above does not apply to advice given by a person to another person if—

(*a*) they are bodies corporate in the same group; or

(*b*) they are, or propose to become, participators in a joint enterprise and the advice is given for the purposes of, or in connection with, that enterprise.

(6) The definitions in paragraph 17(2) above shall apply also for the purposes of sub-paragraph (2)(*a*) above except that the relevant person referred to in paragraph 17(2)(*d*) shall be the person for whom the agent is acting.

Sale of goods and supply of services

19.—(1) This paragraph has effect where a person ("the supplier") sells or offers or agrees to sell goods to another person ("the customer") or supplies or offers or agrees to supply him with services and the supplier's main business is to supply goods or services and not to engage in activities falling within Part II of this Schedule.

(2) Paragraph 12 above does not apply to any transaction which is or is to be entered into by the supplier as principal if it is or is to be entered into by him with the customer for the purposes of or in connection with the sale or supply or a related sale or supply (that is to say, a sale or supply to the customer otherwise than by the supplier but for or in connection with the same purpose as the first-mentioned sale or supply).

(3) Paragraph 12 above does not apply to any transaction which is or is to be entered into by the supplier as agent for the customer if it is or is to be entered into for the purposes of or in connection with the sale or supply or a related sale or supply and—

(*a*) where the investment falls within any of paragraphs 1 to 6 above or, so far as relevant to any of those paragraphs, paragraph 11 above, the supplier does not—

(i) hold himself out (otherwise than to the customer) as engaging in the business of buying investments with a view to selling them and those investments are or include investments of the kind to which the transaction relates; or

(ii) regularly solicit members of the public for the purpose of inducing them to enter as principals or agents into transactions to which paragraph 12 above applies; and the transaction is not or is not to be entered into as a result of his having solicited members of the public in that manner;

(*b*) where the investment is not as mentioned in paragraph (*a*) above, the supplier enters into the transaction—

(i) with or through an authorised person, an exempted person or a person holding a permission under paragraph 23 below; or

(ii) through an office outside the United Kingdom, maintained by a party to the transaction, and with or through a person whose head office is situated outside the United Kingdom and whose ordinary business involves him in engaging in activities which fall within Part II of this Schedule or would do so apart from this Part or Part IV.

(4) Paragraph 13 above does not apply to arrangements which the supplier makes or offers or agrees to make with a view to the customer entering into a transaction for the purposes of or in connection with the sale or supply or a related sale or supply.

(5) Paragraph 14 above does not apply to the supplier by reason of his managing or offering or agreeing to manage the investments of the customer if they are or are to be managed for the purposes of or in connection with the sale or supply or a related sale or supply.

(6) Paragraph 15 above does not apply to advice given by the supplier to the customer for the purposes of or in connection with the sale or supply or a related sale or supply or to a person with whom the customer proposes to enter into a transaction for the purposes of or in connection with the sale or supply or a related sale or supply.

(7) Where the supplier is a body corporate and a member of a group sub-paragraphs (2) to (6) above shall apply to any other member of the group as they apply to the supplier; and where the customer is a body corporate and a member of a group references in those sub-paragraphs to the customer include references to any other member of the group.

(8) The definitions in paragraph 17(2) above shall apply also for the purposes of sub-paragraph (3)(a) above.

Employees' share schemes

20.—(1) Paragraphs 12 and 13 above do not apply to anything done by a body corporate, a body corporate connected with it or a relevant trustee for the purpose of enabling or facilitating transactions in shares in or debentures of the first-mentioned body between or for the benefit of any of the persons mentioned in sub-paragraph (2) below or the holding of such shares or debentures by or for the benefit of any such persons.

(2) The persons referred to in sub-paragraph (1) above are—

(a) the bona fide employees or former employees of the body corporate or of another body corporate in the same group; or

(b) the wives, husbands, widows, widowers, or children or step-children under the age of eighteen of such employees or former employees.

(3) In this paragraph "a relevant trustee" means a person holding shares in or debentures of a body corporate as trustee in pursuance of arrangements made for the purpose mentioned in sub-paragraph (1) above by, or by a body corporate connected with, that body corporate.

(4) In this paragraph "shares" and "debentures" include any investment falling within paragraph 1 or 2 above and also include any investment falling within paragraph 4 or 5 above so far as relating to those paragraphs or any investment falling within paragraph 11 above so far as relating to paragraph 1, 2, 4 or 5.

(5) For the purposes of this paragraph a body corporate is connected with another body corporate if—

(a) they are in the same group; or

(b) one is entitled, either alone or with any other body corporate in the same group, to exercise or control the exercise of a majority of the voting rights attributable to the share capital which are exercisable in all circumstances at any general meeting of the other body corporate or of its holding company.

Sale of private company

21.—(1) Paragraphs 12 and 13 above do not apply to the acquisition or disposal of, or to anything done for the purposes of the acquisition or disposal of, shares in a private company, and paragraph 15 above does not apply to advice given in connection with the acquisition or disposal of such shares, if—

(a) the shares consist of or include shares carrying 75 per cent. or more of the voting rights attributable to share capital which are exercisable in all circumstances at any general meeting of the company; or

(b) the shares, together with any already held by the person acquiring them, carry not less than that percentage of those voting rights; and

(c) in either case, the acquisition and disposal is, or is to be, between parties each of whom is a body corporate, a partnership, a single individual or a group of connected individuals.

(2) For the purposes of subsection (1)(c) above "a group of connected individuals", in relation to the party disposing of the shares, means persons each of whom is, or is a close relative of, a director or manager of the company and, in relation to the party acquiring the shares, means persons each of whom is, or is a close relative of, a person who is to be a director or manager of the company.

(3) In this paragraph "private company" means a private company within the meaning of section 1(3) of the Companies Act 1985 or the corresponding Northern Ireland Provision and "close relative" means a person's spouse, his children and step-children, his parents and step-parents, his brothers and sisters and his step-brothers and step-sisters.

Trustees and personal representatives

22.—(1) Paragraph 12 above does not apply to a person by reason of his buying, selling or subscribing for an investment or offering or agreeing to do so if—
 (a) the investment is or, as the case may be, is to be held by him as bare trustee or, in Scotland, as nominee for another person;
 (b) he is acting on that person's instructions; and
 (c) he does not hold himself out as providing a service of buying and selling investments.
 (2) Paragraph 13 above does not apply to anything done by a person as trustee or personal representative with a view to—
 (a) a fellow trustee or personal representative and himself engaging in their capacity as such in an activity falling within paragraph 12 above; or
 (b) a beneficiary under the trust, will or intestacy engaging in any such activity,
unless that person is remunerated for what he does in addition to any remuneration he receives for discharging his duties as trustee or personal representative.
 (3) Paragraph 14 above does not apply to anything done by a person as trustee or personal representative unless he holds himself out as offering investment management services or is remunerated for providing such services in addition to any remuneration he receives for discharging his duties as trustee or personal representative.
 (4) Paragraph 15 above does not apply to advice given by a person as trustee or personal representative to—
 (a) a fellow trustee or personal representative for the purposes of the trust or estate; or
 (b) a beneficiary under the trust, will or intestacy concerning his interest in the trust fund or estate,
unless that person is remunerated for doing so in addition to any remuneration he receives for discharging his duties as trustee or personal representative.
 (5) Sub-paragraph (1) above has effect to the exclusion of paragraph 17 above as respects any transaction in respect of which the conditions in sub-paragraph (1)(a) and (b) are satisfied.

Dealings in course of non-investment business

23.—(1) Paragraph 12 above does not apply to anything done by a person—
 (a) as principal;
 (b) if that person is a body corporate in a group, as agent for another member of the group; or
 (c) as agent for a person who is or proposes to become a participator with him in a joint enterprise and for the purposes of or in connection with that enterprise,
if it is done in accordance with the terms and conditions of a permission granted to him by the Secretary of State under this paragraph.
 (2) Any application for permission under this paragraph shall be accompanied or supported by such information as the Secretary of State may require and shall not be regarded as duly made unless accompanied by the prescribed fee.
 (3) The Secretary of State may grant a permission under this paragraph if it appears to him—
 (a) that the applicant's main business, or if he is a member of a group the main business of the group, does not consist of activities for which a person is required to be authorised under this Act;
 (b) that the applicant's business is likely to involve such activities which fall within paragraph 12 above; and
 (c) that, having regard to the nature of the applicant's main business and, if he is a member of a group, the main business of the group taken as a whole, the manner in which, the persons with whom and the purposes for which the applicant proposes to engage in activities that would require him to be an authorised person and to any other relevant matters, it is inappropriate to require him to be subject to regulation as an authorised person.
 (4) Any permission under this paragraph shall be granted by a notice in writing; and the Secretary of State may by a further notice in writing withdraw any such permission if for any reason it appears to him that is not appropriate for it to continue in force.

(5) The Secretary of State may make regulations requiring persons holding permissions under this paragraph to furnish him with information for the purpose of enabling him to determine whether those permissions should continue in force; and such regulations may, in particular, require such persons—

(a) to give him notice forthwith of the occurrence of such events as are specified in the regulations and such information in respect of those events as is so specified;

(b) to furnish him at such times or in respect of such periods as are specified in the regulations with such information as is so specified.

(6) Section 61 of this Act shall have effect in relation to a contravention of any condition imposed by a permission under this paragraph as it has effect in relation to any such contravention as is mentioned in subsection (1)(a) of that section.

(7) Section 104 of this Act shall apply to a person holding a permission under this paragraph as if he were authorised to carry on investment business as there mentioned; and sections 105 and 106 of this Act shall have effect as if anything done by him in accordance with such permission constituted the carrying on of investment business.

Advice given in course of profession or non-investment business

24.—(1) Paragraph 15 above does not apply to advice—

(a) which is given in the course of the carrying on of any profession or of a business not otherwise constituting investment business; and

(b) the giving of which is a necessary part of other advice or services given in the course of carrying on that profession or business.

(2) Advice shall not be regarded as falling within sub-paragraph (1)(b) above if it is remunerated separately from the other advice or services.

Newspapers

25.—(1) Paragraph 15 above does not apply to advice given in a newspaper, journal, magazine or other periodical publication if the principal purpose of the publication, taken as a whole and including any advertisements contained in it, is not to lead persons to invest in any particular investment.

(2) The Secretary of State may, on the application of the proprietor of any periodical publication, certify that it is of the nature described in sub-paragraph (1) above and revoke any such certificate if he considers that it is no longer justified.

(3) A certificate given under sub-paragraph (2) above and not revoked shall be conclusive evidence of the matters certified.

Part IV

Additional Exclusions for Persons without Permanent Place of Business in United Kingdom

Transactions with or through authorised or exempted persons

26.—(1) Paragraph 12 above does not apply to any transaction by a person not falling within section 1(3)(a) of this Act ("an overseas person") with or through—

(a) an authorised person; or

(b) an exempted person acting in the course of business in respect of which he is exempt.

(2) Paragraph 13 above does not apply if—

(a) the arrangements are made by an overseas person with, or the offer or agreement to make them is made by him to or with, an authorised person or an exempted person and, in the case of an exempted person, the arrangements are with a view to his entering into a transaction in respect of which he is exempt; or

(b) the transactions with a view to which the arrangements are made are, as respects transactions in the United Kingdom, confined to transactions by authorised persons and transactions by exempted persons in respect of which they are exempt.

Unsolicited or legitimately solicited transactions etc. with or for other persons

27.—(1) Paragraph 12 above does not apply to any transaction entered into by an overseas person as principal with, or as agent for, a person in the United Kingdom, paragraphs 13, 14 and 15 above do not apply to any offer made by an overseas person to or agreement made by him with a person in the United Kingdom and paragraph 15 above does not apply to any advice given by an overseas person to a person in the United Kingdom if the transaction, offer, agreement or advice is the result of—

(*a*) an approach made to the overseas person by or on behalf of the person in the United Kingdom which either has not been in any way solicited by the overseas person or has been solicited by him in a way which has not contravened section 56 or 57 of this Act; or

(*b*) an approach made by the overseas person which has not contravened either of those sections.

(2) Where the transaction is entered into by the overseas person as agent for a person in the United Kingdom, sub-paragraph (1) above applies only if—

(*a*) the other party is outside the United Kingdom; or

(*b*) the other party is in the United Kingdom and the transaction is the result of such an approach by the other party as is mentioned in sub-paragraph (1)(*a*) above or of such an approach as is mentioned in sub-paragraph (1)(*b*) above.

PART V

INTERPRETATION

28.—(1) In this Schedule—

(*a*) "property" includes currency of the United Kingdom or any other country or territory;

(*b*) references to an instrument include references to any record whether or not in the form of a document;

(*c*) references to an offer include references to an invitation to treat;

(*d*) references to buying and selling include references to any acquisition or disposal for valuable consideration.

(2) In sub-paragraph (1)(*d*) above "disposal" includes—

(*a*) in the case of an investment consisting of rights under a contract or other arrangements, assuming the corresponding liabilities under the contract or arrangements;

(*b*) in the case of any other investment, issuing or creating the investment or granting the rights or interests of which it consists;

(*c*) in the case of an investment consisting of rights under a contract, surrendering, assigning or converting those rights.

(3) A company shall not by reason of issuing its own shares or share warrants, and a person shall not by reason of issuing his own debentures or debenture warrants, be regarded for the purposes of this Schedule as disposing of them or, by reason of anything done for the purpose of issuing them, be regarded as making arrangements with a view to a person subscribing for or otherwise acquiring them or underwriting them.

(4) In sub-paragraph (3) above "company" has the same meaning as in paragraph 1 above, "shares" and "debentures" include any investments falling within paragraph 1 or 2 above and "share warrants" and "debenture warrants" means any investment which falls within paragraph 4 above and relates to shares in the company concerned or, as the case may be, to debentures issued by the person concerned.

29. For the purposes of this Schedule a transaction is entered into through a person if he enters into it as agent or arranges for it to be entered into by another person as principal or agent.

30. For the purposes of this Schedule a group shall be treated as including any body corporate which is a related company within the meaning of paragraph 92 of Schedule 4 to the Companies Act 1985 of any member of the group or would be such a related company if the member of the group were a company within the meaning of that Act.

31. In this Schedule "a joint enterprise" means an enterprise into which two or more persons ("the participators") enter for commercial reasons related to a business or businesses (other than investment business) carried on by them; and where a participator is a body corporate and a member of a group each other member of the group shall also be regarded as a participator in the enterprise.

32. Where a person is an exempted person as respects only part of the investment business carried on by him anything done by him in carrying on that part shall be disregarded in determining whether any paragraph of Part III or IV of this Schedule applies to anything done by him in the course of business in respect of which he is not exempt.

33. In determining for the purposes of this Schedule whether anything constitutes an investment or the carrying on of investment business section 18 of the Gaming Act 1845, section 1 of the Gaming Act 1892, any corresponding provision in force in Northern Ireland and any rule of the law of Scotland whereby a contract by way of gaming or wagering is not legally enforceable shall be disregarded.

60–238

GENERAL NOTE

"The general principle underlying the definition of 'investments' . . . is that it excludes physical property which a potential purchaser can inspect and which passes under his direct control on purchase": H.L. Vol. 479, col. 64 (July 21, 1986).

Para. 2

Note (*a*) serves to exclude from the definition of investments instruments such as promissory notes when used in connection with the financing of trade. The exclusion only applies, however, when the instrument relates to the consideration payable under a particular contract for the supply of goods or services.

Para. 4

This paragraph applies to instruments entitling the holder to *subscribe* for investments within paras. 1, 2 or 3 (*e.g.* share warrants).

Para. 5

This paragraph applies, for example, to depositary receipts.

Para. 6

See the definitions in s.75.

Para. 7

This paragraph covers options over investments listed in Part I of the schedule, currency options, gold and silver options, and options over options.

Para. 8

This paragraph covers futures contracts and attempts to supply criteria whereby futures contracts (designed to allocate the risk of price fluctuations) can be distinguished from forward delivery contracts where delivery is actually contemplated.

Price agreed upon when the contract is made: see Note (7).

Note (1) provides that rights under a contract made for commercial purposes are not investments. Note (2) provides that contracts made or traded on an RIE are to be regarded as made for investment purposes, as are off-exchange contracts which simulate such contracts. On the other hand, a contract is made for commercial purposes if delivery is to be made within seven days (Note (3))—this is intended to cover "spot" or "cash" contracts. Notes (4) to (6) supply pointers as to the purposes (commercial/investment) underlying a contract. Observe that Note (4) expressly provides that the absence of the indications in question points to a contrary inference, whereas Notes (5) and (6) do not provide for any inference to be drawn from the absence of the indications they mention.

Para. 9

This applies, for example, to bets on the movements of a stock market index. See also para. 33.

Para. 10

Rights under a *long term* insurance contract are investments unless the contract is excluded by the cumulative criteria laid down in Note (1). The aim is to exclude policies taken out purely for "protection" purposes.

Para. 11

Note (1) makes it clear that the interests of the members and beneficiaries of an occupational pension scheme are not "investments."

Para. 12

Various activities otherwise falling within this paragraph are excluded by paras. 17(1), 17(4), 18(1), 18(2), 19(2), 19(3), 20(1), 21(1), 22(1), 23(1), 26(1), and 27(1).

Para. 13

Various activities otherwise falling within this paragraph are excluded by paras. 18(3), 19(4), 20(1), 21(1), 22(2), 26(2) and 27(1).

The effect of Note (1) is that a person who makes arrangements with a view to contracting as principal or as agent for one of the parties is "dealing" rather than "arranging deals." The effect of (*b*) is that the activities of an investment exchange constitute investment business; accordingly unrecognised exchanges must seek authorisation.

Para. 14

Various activities otherwise falling within this paragraph are excluded by paras. 18(4), 19(5), 22(3) and 27(1).

The effect of (*b*) is to exclude from the scope of the legislation asset management arrangements where the manager has discretion to invest some of the assets in investments, but in practice he never does so and there is no expectation that he will do so.

Para. 15

Various activities otherwise falling within this paragraph are excluded by paras. 18(5), 19(6), 22(4), 24, 25 and 27(1).

This paragraph covers the giving of advice to persons in their capacity as investors or potential investors on the merits of making or disposing of a particular investment. Abstract, general advice does not fall within the scope of the provision.

Para. 17

This paragraph in general exempts dealings on one's own account from para. 12 (dealing in investments as constituting investment business).

As regards paras. 1 to 6 investments, para. 12 applies to a transaction to be entered by a person as principal only if he is in effect a continuous or occasional market maker, or if he regularly solicits "members of the public" to transact. "Members of the public" is defined in sub-para. (2). Note that the effect of (*d*) is that a person need not be authorised in order to solicit shareholders for the purpose of acquiring a strategic stake in a company. (The restrictions on cold-calling (s.56) and investment advertisements (s.57) remain applicable.)

As regards paras. 7 to 10 investments, the effect of sub-para. (4) is that para. 12 does not apply to transactions entered into as principal by a person dealing with authorised persons and the like.

Para. 18

The principle underlying this paragraph is "that nothing which is done between companies in the same group or between participators in a joint enterprise is to be regarded as constituting investment business, and that in considering transactions between any member of the group or participator in the enterprise and a third party, any transaction into which a member or participator enters on behalf of another member or participator is treated as if it were entered into by him as principal": H.L. Vol. 480, col. 740 (October 14, 1986).

Para. 19

This paragraph is intended to allow exporters and other sellers to offer their customers financial packages incorporating investments for the purposes of or in connection with the sale. Where (sub-para.(3)) the seller acts as the customer's agent he gains the exemption only if he confines himself to activities which would be exempted were he dealing on his own account.

Para. 20

This paragraph ensures that neither a company operating an employees' share scheme nor the scheme trustees need seek authorisation in order to facilitate transactions in company shares between beneficiaries of the scheme (*e.g.* by running a company "share shop").

Para. 21

This paragraph excludes from the definition of investment business the acquisition or disposal of control of a private company (the criterion being command of at least 75 per cent. of the voting rights). The effect is that transfer agents need not become authorised persons.

Para. 22

This paragraph creates an exemption for trustees and personal representatives. The exemption is not available (save in relation to para. 12) if the trustee is remunerated for what he does in addition to his remuneration as a trustee. Moreover the exemption in relation to investment management is unavailable if the trustee holds himself out as offering investment management services. Similarly the exemption in relation to para. 12 (dealing) is unavailable if the bare trustee/nominee holds himself out as providing a dealing service.

Para. 23

Paras. 18 (groups and joint enterprises) and 19 (sale of goods and supply of services) are designed to exempt from the need to be authorised industrial and commercial companies whose business leads them to engage in investment-related activities. This paragraph is designed to afford an additional escape route, if necessary, for such companies.

A company which would otherwise require to be authorised by virtue of para. 12 (dealing in investments) because of dealings as principal, or as agent for another company in the same group, or as agent for a participator in a joint enterprise, need not seek authorisation if it obtains and complies with a permission which may be granted at the discretion of the Secretary of State. (The Secretary of State's power to grant permissions is a function transferable to the SIB: s.114(4).)

The Secretary of State/SIB *may* (but is not obliged to) grant a permission if the applicant company's main business is non-investment business and if, having regard to the company's main business, and to the character of its proposed investment-related activities, it would be inappropriate for the company to be subject to the investment business régime.

No particular procedure for the grant or withdrawal of permissions is laid down, but it is anticipated that the Secretary of State/SIB will publish guidelines setting out the criteria on which the exercise of discretion will be based. In practice permissions will only be available to companies who do not deal (in investments) with members of the public: H.L. Vol. 480, cols. 756–57 (October 14, 1968).

A contravention of a condition imposed by a permission may enable the SIB to seek an injunction or restitution order under s.61: sub-para. (6). The power to call for information under s.104 is also extended to companies with para. 23 permissions, as is the power to investigate under s.105: sub-para. (7).

Para. 24

Advice given in the course of carrying on a profession or a non-investment business is excluded from para. 15 (investment advice) if it is a necessary part of the professional or non-investment advice given. " 'Necessary' means that without giving the investment advice in question, the function of giving other advice or providing other services could not properly be performed": H.C. St. Cttee. E, col. 104 (February 4, 1986). "Necessary" advice, therefore, would almost certainly have to be confined to advice about *types* of investments rather than (say) the insurance policy of a particular life office. In any event, advice which attracts commission is not "necessary."

Para. 25

The effect of this paragraph is that the publication of a tip-sheet or a broker's circular is investment business, while the publication of the *Financial Times* is not. Note, however, that financial journalists are subject to (though not, of course, legally bound by) a code of practice, *viz. The Press Council Declaration of Principle on Financial Journalism* (June 6, 1985).

The power to certify a publication under sub-para. (2) is a function transferable to the SIB: s.114(4). A certificate is conclusive evidence of exemption from the need to obtain authorisation by virtue of para. 15 (investment advice), but exemption is not dependent on the possession of a certificate.

Para. 26

This paragraph creates an exemption in favour of persons who would otherwise be regarded as carrying on investment business in the United Kingdom without maintaining a permanent place of business here. Such "overseas persons" need not seek authorisation if they confine themselves to dealing and arranging deals involving authorised and exempted persons (in short, "professionals") exclusively.

Para. 27

This paragraph exempts overseas persons in respect of transactions entered into with or on behalf of a United Kingdom person provided the initiative was taken by the United Kingdom person; or if taken by the overseas person, he did not engage in illegal advertising or cold-calling.

Section 10   SCHEDULE 2

REQUIREMENTS FOR RECOGNITION OF SELF-REGULATING ORGANISATION

Members to be fit and proper persons

1.—(1) The rules and practices of the organisation must be such as to secure that its members are fit and proper persons to carry on investment business of the kind with which the organisation is concerned.

(2) Where the organisation is concerned with investment business of different kinds its rules and practices must be such as to secure that a member carrying on investment business of any of those kinds is a fit and proper person to carry on investment business of that kind.

(3) The matters which may be taken into account under the rules in determining whether a person is a fit and proper person must include those that the Secretary of State may take into account under section 27 above.

(4) This paragraph does not apply to a person who is not an authorised person by virtue of being a member of the organisation.

Admission, expulsion and discipline

2. The rules and practices of the organisation relating to—
(*a*) the admission and expulsion of members; and
(*b*) the discipline it exercises over its members,
must be fair and reasonable and include adequate provision for appeals.

Safeguards for investors

3.—(1) The rules of the organisation governing the carrying on of investment business of any kind by its members must afford investors protection at least equivalent to that afforded in respect of investment business of that kind by the rules and regulations for the time being in force under Chapter V of Part I of this Act.

(2) The rules under that Chapter to be taken into account for the purposes of sub-paragraph (1) above include the rules made under section 49 and under sections 53 and 54 so far as not themselves applying to the members of the organisation.

(3) The organisation must, so far as practicable, have powers for purposes corresponding to those of Chapter VI of Part I of this Act.

(4) The rules of the organisation must enable it to prevent a member resigning from the organisation if the organisation considers that any matter affecting him should be investigated as a preliminary to a decision on the question whether he should be expelled or otherwise disciplined or if it considers that it is desirable that a prohibition or requirement should be imposed on him under the powers mentioned in sub-paragraph (3) above or that any prohibition or requirement imposed on him under those powers should continue in force.

Monitoring and enforcement

4.—(1) The organisation must have adequate arrangements and resources for the effective monitoring and enforcement of compliance with its rules and with any rules or regulations to which its members are subject under Chapter V of Part I of this Act in respect of investment business of a kind regulated by the organisation.

(2) The arrangements for monitoring may make provision for that function to be performed on behalf of the organisation (and without affecting its responsibility) by any other body or person who is able and willing to perform it.

The governing body

5.—(1) The arrangements of the organisation with respect to the appointment, removal from office and functions of the persons responsible for making or enforcing the rules of the organisation must be such as to secure a proper balance—
(*a*) between the interests of the different members of the organisation; and
(*b*) between the interests of the organisation or its members and the interests of the public.

(2) The arrangements shall not be regarded as satisfying the requirements of this paragraph unless the persons responsible for those matters include a number of persons independent of the organisation and its members sufficient to secure the balance referred to in sub-paragraph (1)(*b*) above.

Investigation of complaints

6.—(1) The organisation must have effective arrangements for the investigation of complaints against the organisation or its members.

(2) The arrangements may make provision for the whole or part of that function to be performed by and to be the responsibility of a body or person independent of the organisation.

Promotion and maintenance of standards

7. The organisation must be able and willing to promote and maintain high standards of integrity and fair dealing in the carrying on of investment business and to co-operate, by the sharing of information and otherwise, with the Secretary of State and any other authority, body or person having responsibility for the supervision or regulation of investment business or other financial services.

GENERAL NOTE

Para. 1

Fit and Proper: See the annotation to section 27. During the Commons' Committee Stage it was stated that an SRO would not be eligible for recognition "unless in applying the test, it has regard to the capital that the applicant proposes to devote to the business; the competence, qualifications, experience and honesty of people who will be running the business or occupying key positions; and the applicant's ability to comply with the SRO's rules". (H.C. St. Cttee. E., col. 168). In view of the Bill's later amendment (as to which, see s.49) it is questionable whether the adequacy of the applicant's financial resources falls to be treated under this paragraph or paragraph 3 below.

As to interim authorisation, see Sched. 15, para. 1.

Para. 3

Equivalent: Does not mean identical.

Para. 4

In respect of investment business . . . by the organisation: The only rules which an SRO has to monitor and enforce are those in respect of the kinds of investment business which it regulates. It does not have to monitor or enforce any other rules to which its members may be subject, *e.g.* because they are also directly authorised.

Para. 5

The issue of how many of the governing body's members should be independent of the organisation and its members was debated at some length. Sub-paragraph (2) was added on Commons' Report and then amended on Lords' Report and again on Third Reading. Earlier the figure of between one-quarter and one-third was quoted with approval. (See, *e.g.* H.L. Vol. 479, col. 248).

Para. 6

Body or person independent . . . organisation: This allows the possibility of complaints being investigated by an ombudsman or arbitrator. The SIB will establish its own ombudsman scheme to which SRO's will be able to subscribe. Note that, in contrast to paragraph 4(2), the SRO may divest itself of the responsibility also. The purpose of allowing it to do so is to underline the ombudsman or arbitrator's independence.

Section 18   SCHEDULE 3

REQUIREMENTS FOR RECOGNITION OF PROFESSIONAL BODY

Statutory status

1. The body must—
(*a*) regulate the practice of a profession in the exercise of statutory powers; or
(*b*) be recognised (otherwise than under this Act) for a statutory purpose by a Minister of the Crown or by, or by the head of, a Northern Ireland department; or
(*c*) be specified in a provision contained in or made under an enactment as a body whose members are qualified to exercise functions or hold offices specified in that provision.

Certification

2.—(1) The body must have rules, practices and arrangements for securing that no person can be certified by the body for the purposes of Part I of this Act unless the following conditions are satisfied.

(2) The certified person must be either—
(*a*) an individual who is a member of the body; or
(*b*) a person managed and controlled by one or more individuals each of whom is a member of a recognised professional body and at least one of whom is a member of the certifying body.

(3) Where the certified person is an individual his main business must be the practice of the profession regulated by the certifying body and he must be practising that profession otherwise than in partnership; and where the certified person is not an individual that person's main business must be the practice of the profession or professions regulated by the recognised professional body or bodies of which the individual or individuals mentioned in sub-paragraph (2)(*b*) above are members.

(4) In the application of sub-paragraphs (2) and (3) above to a certificate which is to be or has been issued to a partnership constituted under the law of England and Wales or Northern Ireland or the law of any other country or territory under which a partnership is not a legal person, references to the certified person shall be construed as references to the partnership.

Safeguards for investors

3.—(1) The body must have rules regulating the carrying on of investment business by persons certified by it; and those rules must in respect of investment business of any kind regulated by them afford to investors protection at least equivalent to that afforded in respect of investment business of that kind by the rules and regulations for the time being in force under Chapter V of Part I of this Act.

(2) The rules under that Chapter to be taken into account for the purposes of this paragraph include the rules made under section 49 and under sections 53 and 54 so far as not themselves applying to persons certified by the body.

Monitoring and enforcement

4.—(1) The body must have adequate arrangements and resources for the effective monitoring of the continued compliance by persons certified by it with the conditions mentioned in paragraph 2 above and rules, practices and arrangements for the withdrawal or suspension of certification (subject to appropriate transitional provisions) in the event of any of those conditions ceasing to be satisfied.

(2) The body must have adequate arrangements and resources for the effective monitoring and enforcement of compliance by persons certified by it with the rules of the body relating to the carrying on of investment business and with any rules or regulations to which those persons are subject under Chapter V of Part I of this Act in respect of business of a kind regulated by the body.

(3) The arrangements for enforcement must include provision for the withdrawal or suspension of certification and may include provision for disciplining members of the body who manage or control a certified person.

(4) The arrangements for enforcement may make provision for the whole or part of that function to be performed by and to be the responsibility of a body or person independent of the professional body.

(5) The arrangements for enforcement must be such as to secure a proper balance between the interests of persons certified by the body and the interests of the public; and the arrangements shall not be regarded as satisfying that requirement unless the persons responsible for enforcement include a sufficient number of persons who are independent of the body and its members and of persons certified by it.

(6) The arrangements for monitoring may make provision for that function to be performed on behalf of the body (and without affecting its responsibility) by any other body or person who is able and willing to perform it.

Investigation of complaints

5.—(1) The body must have effective arrangements for the investigation of complaints relating to—
   (a) the carrying on by persons certified by it of investment business in respect of which they are subject to its rules; and
   (b) its regulation of investment business.

(2) Paragraph 4(4) above applies also to arrangements made pursuant to this paragraph.

Promotion and maintenance of standards

6. The body must be able and willing to promote and maintain high standards of integrity and fair dealing in the carrying on of investment business and to co-operate, by the sharing of information and otherwise, with the Secretary of State and any other authority, body or person having responsibility for the supervision or regulation of investment business or other financial services.

GENERAL NOTE

These requirements follow closely the requirements in respect of SROs set out in Sched. 2, the annotations to which should also be referred to.

Para. 2

As to interim certification, see Sched. 15, para. 5.

Para. 4

Sub-para. (3)

May: Not must. Note the absence of any provision equivalent to Sched. 2, para. 2.

Sub-para. (4)

This provision takes account of the fact that some professional bodies have independent disciplinary arrangements.

Sub-para. (5)

Contrast Sched. 5, para. 5. Does "sufficient" mean between one-quarter and one-third as has been suggested in relation to SROs?

Sections 36 and 37   SCHEDULE 4

REQUIREMENTS FOR RECOGNITION OF INVESTMENT EXCHANGE

Financial resources

1. The exchange must have financial resources sufficient for the proper performance of its functions.

Safeguards for investors

2.—(1) The rules and practices of the exchange must ensure that business conducted by means of its facilities is conducted in an orderly manner and so as to afford proper protection to investors.

(2) The exchange must—

(*a*) limit dealings on the exchange to investments in which there is a proper market; and

(*b*) where relevant, require issuers of investments dealt in on the exchange to comply with such obligations as will, so far as possible, afford to persons dealing in the investments proper information for determining their current value.

(3) In the case of securities to which Part IV of this Act applies compliance by The Stock Exchange with the provisions of that Part shall be treated as compliance by it with sub-paragraph (2) above.

(4) The exchange must either have its own arrangements for ensuring the performance of transactions effected on the exchange or ensure their performance by means of services provided under clearing arrangements made by it with a recognised clearing house.

(5) The exchange must either itself have or secure the provision on its behalf of satisfactory arrangements for recording the transactions effected on the exchange.

(6) Sub-paragraphs (2), (4) and (5) above are without prejudice to the generality of sub-paragraph (1) above.

Monitoring and enforcement

3.—(1) The exchange must have adequate arrangements and resources for the effective monitoring and enforcement of compliance with its rules and any clearing arrangements made by it.

(2) The arrangements for monitoring may make provision for that function to be performed on behalf of the exchange (and without affecting its responsibility) by any other body or person who is able and willing to perform it.

Investigation of complaints

4. The exchange must have effective arrangements for the investigation of complaints in respect of business transacted by means of its facilities.

Promotion and maintenance of standards

5. The exchange must be able and willing to promote and maintain high standards of integrity and fair dealing in the carrying on of investment business and to co-operate, by the sharing of information and otherwise, with the Secretary of State and any other authority, body or person having responsibility for the supervision or regulation of investment business or other financial services.

GENERAL NOTE

These requirements are expressed in more general terms than the corresponding requirements of Scheds. 2 and 3 in order to cover the variety of forms which investment exchanges may take.

Para. 2

Sub-para. (1)

This general requirement entails, among other things, that an investment exchange should vet users of its facilities, make conduct of business rules and have "the power to refuse access, or expel or exclude anyone who is not prepared to observe those rules". (H.C. St. Cttee. E., cols. 342–343.) Although there are no requirements governing access, restrictions on access will be within the purview of the DGFT in the discharge of his functions under section 122.

Sub-para. (2)

Proper market: This requirement "does not mean that there must be frequent or day-to-day dealings. It means only that there must be a properly registered two-way market in which the investment can be bought and sold at a fair price, subject to proper safeguards, even if dealings take place only at intervals". (H.C. St. Cttee. E., cols. 341–342.)

Section 43   SCHEDULE 5

LISTED MONEY MARKET INSTITUTIONS

PART I

TRANSACTIONS NOT SUBJECT TO MONETARY LIMIT

1. This Part of this Schedule applies to any transaction entered into by the listed institution as principal (or as agent for another listed institution) with another listed institution or the Bank of England (whether acting as principal or agent) if the transaction falls within paragraph 2 or 3 below.

2.—(1) A transaction falls within this paragraph if it is in respect of an investment specified in sub-paragraph (2) below and—

(a) in the case of an investment within any of paragraphs (a) to (d) of that sub-paragraph, the transaction is not regulated by the rules of a recognised investment exchange; and

(b) in the case of any other investment specified in that sub-paragraph, the transaction is not made on such an exchange or expressed to be as so made.

(2) The investments referred to above are—

(a) a debenture or other instrument falling within paragraph 2 of Schedule 1 to this Act which is issued—

(i) by a recognised bank or licensed institution within the meaning of the Banking Act 1979 or a building society incorporated in, or in any part of, the United Kingdom; and

(ii) on terms requiring repayment not later than five years from the date of issue;

(b) any other debenture or instrument falling within paragraph 2 of Schedule 1 to this Act which is issued on terms requiring repayment not later than one year from the date of issue;

(c) loan stock, or any other instrument, falling within paragraph 3 of Schedule 1 to this Act which is issued on terms requiring repayment not later than one year or, if issued by a local authority in the United Kingdom, five years from the date of issue;

(d) a warrant or other instrument falling within paragraph 4 of Schedule 1 to this Act which entitles the holder to subscribe for an investment within paragraph (*a*), (*b*) or (*c*) above;

(*e*) any certificate or other instrument falling within paragraph 5 or 11 of Schedule 1 to this Act and relating to an investment within paragraph (*a*), (*b*) or (*c*) above;

(*f*) an option falling within paragraph 7 of Schedule 1 to this Act and relating to—
    (i) an investment within paragraph (*a*), (*b*) or (*c*) above;
    (ii) currency of the United Kingdom or of any other country or territory; or
    (iii) gold or silver;

(*g*) rights under a contract falling within paragraph 8 of Schedule 1 to this Act for the sale of—
    (i) an investment within paragraph (*a*), (*b*) or (*c*) above;
    (ii) currency of the United Kingdom or of any other country or territory; or
    (iii) gold or silver;

(*h*) rights under a contract falling within paragraph 9 of Schedule 1 to this Act by reference to fluctuations in—
    (i) the value or price of any investment falling within any of the foregoing paragraphs; or
    (ii) currency of the United Kingdom or of any other country or territory; or
    (iii) the rate of interest on loans in any such currency or any index of such rates;

(*i*) an option to acquire or dispose of an investment within paragraph (*f*), (*g*) or (*h*) above.

3.—(1) A transaction falls within this paragraph if it is a transaction by which one of the parties agrees to sell or transfer an investment falling within paragraph 2 or 3 of Schedule 1 to this Act and by the same or a collateral agreement that party agrees, or acquires an option, to buy back or re-acquire that investment or an equivalent amount of a similar investment within twelve months of the sale or transfer.

(2) For the purposes of this paragraph investments shall be regarded as similar if they entitle their holders to the same rights against the same persons as to capital and interest and the same remedies for the enforcement of those rights.

PART II

TRANSACTIONS SUBJECT TO MONETARY LIMIT

4.—(1) This Part of this Schedule applies to any transaction entered into by the listed institution—

(*a*) as principal (or as agent for another listed institution) with an unlisted person (whether acting as principal or agent);

(*b*) as agent for an unlisted person with a listed institution or the Bank of England (whether acting as principal or agent); or

(*c*) as agent for an unlisted person with another unlisted person (whether acting as principal or agent),

if the transaction falls within paragraph 2 or 3 above and the conditions in paragraph 5 or, as the case may be, paragraph 7 below are satisfied.

(2) In this Part of this Schedule and in Part III below "unlisted person" means a person who is neither a listed institution nor the Bank of England.

5.—(1) In the case of a transaction falling within paragraph 2 above the conditions referred to above are as follows but subject to paragraph 6 below.

(2) The consideration for a transaction in respect of an investment falling within paragraph 2(2)(*a*), (*b*), (*c*) or (*e*) above must be not less than £100,000.

(3) The consideration payable on subscription in the case of an investment falling within paragraph 2(2)(*d*) must not be less than £500,000.

(4) The value or price of the property in respect of which an option within paragraph 2(2)(*f*) above is granted must not be less than £500,000.

(5) The price payable under a contract within paragraph 2(2)(*g*) above must be not less than £500,000.

(6) The value or price the fluctuation in which, or the amount the fluctuation in the interest on which, is relevant for the purposes of a contract within paragraph 2(2)(*h*) above must not be less than £500,000.

(7) In the case of an option falling within paragraph 2(2)(*i*) above the condition in sub-paragraph (4), (5) or (6) above, as the case may be, must be satisfied in respect of the investment to which the option relates.

6. The conditions in paragraph 5 above do not apply to a transaction entered into by the listed institution as mentioned in paragraph (*a*), (*b*) or (*c*) of paragraph 4(1) above if—

(a) the unlisted person mentioned in paragraph (a) or (b) or, as the case may be, each of the unlisted persons mentioned in paragraph (c) has in the previous eighteen months entered into another transaction in respect of an investment specified in paragraph 2(2) above;

(b) those conditions were satisfied in the case of that other transaction; and

(c) that other transaction was entered into by that person (whether acting as principal or agent) with the listed institution (whether acting as principal or agent) or was entered into by that person through the agency of that institution or was entered into by him (whether acting as principal or agent) as a result of arrangements made by that institution.

7. In the case of a transaction falling within paragraph 3 above the condition referred to in paragraph 4 above is that the consideration for the sale or transfer must be not less than £100,000.

8. The monetary limits mentioned in this Part of this Schedule refer to the time when the transaction is entered into; and where the consideration, value, price or amount referred to above is not in sterling it shall be converted at the rate of exchange prevailing at that time.

PART III

TRANSACTIONS ARRANGED BY LISTED INSTITUTIONS

9. Subject to paragraphs 10 and 11 below, this Part of this Schedule applies to any transaction arranged by the listed institution which—

(a) is entered into by another listed institution as principal (or as agent for another listed institution) with another listed institution or the Bank of England (whether acting as principal or agent);

(b) is entered into by another listed institution (whether acting as principal or agent) with an unlisted person (whether acting as principal or agent); or

(c) is entered into between unlisted persons (whether acting as principal or agent), if the transaction falls within paragraph 2 or 3 above.

10. In the case of a transaction falling within paragraph 2 above paragraph 9(b) and (c) above do not apply unless either the conditions in paragraph 5 above are satisfied or—

(a) the unlisted person mentioned in paragraph (b) or, as the case may be, each of the unlisted persons mentioned in paragraph (c) has in the previous eighteen months entered into another transaction in respect of an investment specified in paragraph 2(2) above;

(b) those conditions were satisfied in the case of that other transaction; and

(c) that other transaction was entered into by that person (whether acting as principal or agent) with the listed institution making the arrangements (whether acting as principal or agent) or through the agency of that institution or was entered into by that person (whether acting as principal or agent) as a result of arrangements made by that institution.

11. In the case of a transaction falling within paragraph 3 above paragraph 9(b) and (c) above do not apply unless the condition in paragraph 7 above is satisfied.

GENERAL NOTE

Part I of this Schedule covers transactions between listed institutions. These transactions are exempt. Part II covers transactions between listed institutions and others. These transactions are exempt if they exceed the limits set or if the person with whom they are entered into can be treated as a wholesale counterparty. Part III extends the exemption to wholesale market transactions arranged by a listed institution.

Section 96(6)   SCHEDULE 6

THE FINANCIAL SERVICES TRIBUNAL

Term of office of members

1.—(1) A person appointed to the panel mentioned in section 96(2) of this Act shall hold and vacate his office in accordance with the terms of his appointment and on ceasing to hold office shall be eligible for re-appointment.

(2) A member of the panel appointed by the Lord Chancellor may resign his office by notice in writing to the Lord Chancellor; and a member of the panel appointed by the Secretary of State may resign his office by notice in writing to the Secretary of State.

Expenses

2. The Secretary of State shall pay to the persons serving as members of the Tribunal such remuneration and allowances as he may determine and shall defray such other expenses of the Tribunal as he may approve.

Staff

3. The Secretary of State may provide the Tribunal with such officers and servants as he thinks necessary for the proper discharge of its functions.

Procedure

4.—(1) The Secretary of State may make rules for regulating the procedure of the Tribunal, including provision for the holding of any proceedings in private, for the awarding of costs (or, in Scotland, expenses) and for the payment of expenses to persons required to attend before the Tribunal.

(2) The Tribunal may appoint counsel or a solicitor to assist it in proceedings before the Tribunal.

Evidence

5.—(1) The Tribunal may by summons require any person to attend, at such time and place as is specified in the summons, to give evidence or to produce any document in his custody or under his control which the Tribunal considers it necessary to examine.

(2) The Tribunal may take evidence on oath and for that purpose administer oaths or may, instead of administering an oath, require the person examined to make and subscribe a declaration of the truth of the matters in respect of which he is examined.

(3) Any person who without reasonable excuse—

(a) refuses or fails to attend in obedience to a summons issued by the Tribunal or to give evidence; or

(b) alters, suppresses, conceals or destroys or refuses to produce a document which he may be required to produce for the purposes of proceedings before the Tribunal,

shall be guilty of an offence.

(4) A person guilty of an offence under paragraph (a) of sub-paragraph (3) above shall be liable on summary conviction to a fine not exceeding the fifth level on the standard scale; and a person guilty of an offence under paragraph (b) of that sub-paragraph shall be liable—

(a) on conviction on indictment, to imprisonment for a term not exceeding two years or to a fine or to both;

(b) on summary conviction, to a fine not exceeding the statutory maximum.

(5) A person shall not under this paragraph be required to disclose any information or produce any document which he would be entitled to refuse to disclose or produce on grounds of legal professional privilege in proceedings in the High Court or on grounds of confidentiality as between client and professional legal adviser in proceedings in the Court of Session except that a lawyer may be required to furnish the name and address of his client.

(6) Any reference in this paragraph to the production of a document includes a reference to the production of a legible copy of information recorded otherwise than in legible form; and the reference to suppressing a document includes a reference to destroying the means of reproducing information recorded otherwise than in legible form.

Appeals and supervision by Council on Tribunals

6. The Tribunals and Inquiries Act 1971 shall be amended as follows—

(a) in section 8(2) after "6A" there shall be inserted "6B";

(b) in section 13(1) after "6" there shall be inserted "6B";

(c) in Schedule 1, after paragraph 6A there shall be inserted—

"Financial services.   6B. The Financial Services Tribunal established by section 96 of the Financial Services Act 1986."

B.V.S. (4)—9

Parliamentary disqualification

7.—(1) In Part III of Schedule 1 to the House of Commons Disqualification Act 1975 (disqualifying offices) there shall be inserted at the appropriate place "Any member of the Financial Services Tribunal in receipt of remuneration".

(2) A corresponding amendment shall be made in Part III of Schedule 1 to the Northern Ireland Assembly Disqualification Act 1975.

Section 114   SCHEDULE 7

QUALIFICATIONS OF DESIGNATED AGENCY

Constitution

1.—(1) The constitution of the agency must provide for it to have—
(a) a chairman; and
(b) a governing body consisting of the chairman and other members;
and the provisions of the constitution relating to the chairman and the other members of the governing body must comply with the following provisions of this paragraph.

(2) The chairman and other members of the governing body must be persons appointed and liable to removal from office by the Secretary of State and the Governor of the Bank of England acting jointly.

(3) The members of the governing body must include—
(a) persons with experience of investment business of a kind relevant to the functions or proposed functions of the agency; and
(b) other persons, including regular users on their own account or on behalf of others of services provided by persons carrying on investment business of any such kind;
and the composition of that body must be such as to secure a proper balance between the interests of persons carrying on investment business and the interests of the public.

Arrangements for discharge of functions

2.—(1) The agency's arrangements for the discharge of its functions must comply with the following provisions of this paragraph.

(2) Any rules or regulations must be made by the governing body of the agency.

(3) Any decision taken in the exercise of other functions must be taken at a level appropriate to the importance of the decision.

(4) In the case of functions to be discharged by the governing body, the members falling respectively within paragraphs (a) and (b) of paragraph 1(3) above must, so far as practicable, have an opportunity to express their opinions.

(5) Subject to sub-paragraphs (2) to (4) above, the arrangements may enable any functions to be discharged by a committee, sub-committee, officer or servant of the agency.

Monitoring and enforcement

3.—(1) The agency must have a satisfactory system—
(a) for enabling it to determine whether persons regulated by it are complying with the obligations which it is the responsibility of the agency to enforce; and
(b) for the discharge of the agency's responsibility for the enforcement of those obligations.

(2) The system may provide for the functions mentioned in sub-paragraph (1)(a) to be performed on its behalf (and without affecting its responsibility) by any other body or person who is able and willing to perform them.

Investigation of complaints

4.—(1) The agency must have effective arrangements for the investigation of complaints arising out of the conduct of investment business by authorised persons or against any recognised self-regulating organisation, professional body, investment exchange or clearing house.

(2) The arrangements must make provision for the investigation of complaints in respect of authorised persons to be carried out in appropriate cases independently of the agency and those persons.

Promotion and maintenance of standards

5. The agency must be able and willing to promote and maintain high standards of integrity and fair dealing in the carry on of investment business and to co-operate, by the sharing of information and otherwise, with the Secretary of State and any other authority, body or person having responsibility for the supervision or regulation of investment business or other financial services.

Records

6. The agency must have satisfactory arrangements for recording decisions made in the exercise of its functions and for the safekeeping of those records which ought to be preserved.

Section 114   SCHEDULE 8

Principles applicable to Designated Agency's Rules and Regulations

Standards

1. The rules made under section 48 of this Act (in this Schedule referred to as "conduct of business rules") and the other rules and regulations made under Part I of this Act must promote high standards of integrity and fair dealing in the conduct of investment business.

2. The conduct of business rules must make proper provision for requiring an authorised person to act with due skill, care and diligence in providing any service which he provides or holds himself out as willing to provide.

3. The conduct of business rules must make proper provision for requiring an authorised person to subordinate his own interests to those of his clients and to act fairly between his clients.

4. The conduct of business rules must make proper provision for requiring an authorised person to ensure that, in anything done by him for the persons with whom he deals, due regard is had to their circumstances.

Disclosure

5. The conduct of business rules must make proper provision for the disclosure by an authorised person of interests in, and facts material to, transactions which are entered into by him in the course of carrying on investment business or in respect of which he gives advice in the course of carrying on such business, including information as to any commissions or other inducements received or receivable from a third party in connection with any such transaction.

6. The conduct of business rules must make proper provision for the disclosure by an authorised person of the capacity in which and the terms on which he enters into any such transaction.

7. The conduct of business rules, or those rules and rules under section 51 of this Act, must make proper provision for requiring an authorised person who in the course of carrying on investment business enters or offers to enter into a transaction in respect of an investment with any person, or gives any person advice about such a transaction, to give that person such information as to the nature of the investment and the financial implications of the transaction as will enable him to make an informed decision.

8. Rules made under section 48 of this Act regulating action for the purpose of stabilising the price of investments must make proper provision for ensuring that where action is or is to be taken in conformity with the rules adequate arrangements exist for making known that the price of the investments in respect of which the action is or is to be taken (and, where relevant, of any other investments) may be affected by that action and the period during which it may be affected; and where a transaction is or is to be entered into during a period when it is known that the price of the investment to which it relates may be affected by any

such action the information referred to in paragraph 7 above includes information to that effect.

Protection

9. The conduct of business rules and any regulations made under section 55 of this Act must make proper provision for the protection of property for which an authorised person is liable to account to another person.

10. Rules made under sections 53 and 54 of this Act must make the best provision that can reasonably be made under those sections.

Records

11. The conduct of business rules must require the keeping of proper records and make provision for their inspection in appropriate cases.

Classes of investors

12. The conduct of business rules and the other rules and regulations made under Chapter V of Part I of this Act must take proper account of the fact that provisions that are appropriate for regulating the conduct of business in relation to some classes of investors may not (by reason of their knowledge, experience or otherwise) be appropriate in relation to others.

GENERAL NOTE
This schedule sets out the principles applicable to the SIB's rules and regulations. Authorised persons are not bound by these principles, nor may the validity of the SIB's rules and regulations be impugned on the grounds that they fall short of the schedule's requirements or go beyond them. However the Secretary of State must not transfer his legislative functions to the SIB unless he is satisfied that its rules and regulations comply with the scheduled principles where relevant: s.114(9)(*b*). And he may resume those functions if at any time it appears to him that the SIB's rules and regulations no longer comply with the principles set out: s.115(5).

Section 116 SCHEDULE 9

DESIGNATED AGENCIES: STATUS AND EXERCISE OF TRANSFERRED FUNCTIONS

Status

1.—(1) A designated agency shall not be regarded as acting on behalf of the Crown and its members, officers and servants shall not be regarded as Crown servants.

(2) In Part III of Schedule 1 to the House of Commons Disqualification Act 1975 (disqualifying offices) there shall be inserted at the appropriate place—
    "Chairman of a designated agency within the meaning of the Financial Services Act 1986 if he is in receipt of remuneration".

(3) An amendment corresponding to that in sub-paragraph (2) above shall be made in Part III of Schedule 1 to the Northern Ireland Assembly Disqualification Act 1975.

Exemption from requirement of "limited" in name of designated agency

2.—(1) A company is exempt from the requirements of the Companies Act 1985 relating to the use of "limited" as part of the company name if—
    (*a*) it is a designated agency; and
    (*b*) its memorandum or articles comply with the requirements specified in paragraph (*b*) of subsection (3) of section 30 of that Act.

(2) In subsection (4) of that section (statutory declaration of compliance with requirements entitling company to exemption) the reference to the requirements of subsection (3) of that section shall include a reference to the requirements of sub-paragraph (1) above.

(3) In section 31 of that Act (provisions applicable to exempted companies) the reference to a company which is exempt under section 30 of that Act shall include a reference to a company that is exempt under this paragraph and, in relation to such a company, the power conferred by subsection (2) of that section (direction to include "limited" in company name)

shall be exercisable on the ground that the company has ceased to be a designated agency instead of the ground mentioned in paragraph (*a*) of that subsection.

(4) In this paragraph references to the said Act of 1985 and sections 30 and 31 of that Act include references to the corresponding provisions in force in Northern Ireland.

The Tribunal

3.—(1) Where a case is referred to the Tribunal by a designated agency the Tribunal shall send the Secretary of State a copy of any report made by it to the agency in respect of that case.

(2) Where the powers which the Tribunal could, apart from any delegation order, require the Secretary of State to exercise are, by virtue of such an order or of an order resuming any function transferred by it, exercisable partly by the Secretary of State and partly by a designated agency or designated agencies the Tribunal may require any of them to exercise such of those powers as are exercisable by them respectively.

Legislative functions

4.—(1) A designated agency shall send the Secretary of State a copy of any rules or regulations made by it by virtue of functions transferred to it by a delegation order and give him written notice of any amendment or revocation of or addition to any such rules or regulations.

(2) A designated agency shall—

(*a*) send the Secretary of State a copy of any guidance issued by the agency which is intended to have continuing effect and is issued in writing or other legible form; and

(*b*) give him written notice of any amendment, revocation of or addition to guidance issued by it;

but notice need not be given of the revocation of guidance other than such as is mentioned in paragraph (*a*) above or of any amendment or addition which does not result in or consist of such guidance as is there mentioned.

5. Paragraphs 6 to 9 below shall have effect instead of section 205(2) and (4) of this Act in relation to rules and regulations made by a designated agency in the exercise of functions transferred to it by a delegation order.

6. The rules and regulations shall be made by an instrument in writing.

7. The instrument shall specify the provision of this Act under which it is made.

8.—(1) Immediately after an instrument is made it shall be printed and made available to the public with or without payment.

(2) A person shall not be taken to have contravened any rule or regulation if he shows that at the time of the alleged contravention the instrument containing the rule or regulation had not been made available as required by this paragraph.

9.—(1) The production of a printed copy of an instrument purporting to be made by the agency on which is endorsed a certificate signed by an officer of the agency authorised by it for that purpose and stating—

(*a*) that the instrument was made by the agency;

(*b*) that the copy is a true copy of the instrument; and

(*c*) that on a specified date the instrument was made available to the public as required by paragraph 8 above,

shall be prima facie evidence or, in Scotland, sufficient evidence of the facts stated in the certificate.

(2) Any certificate purporting to be signed as mentioned in sub-paragraph (1) above shall be deemed to have been duly signed unless the contrary is shown.

(3) Any person wishing in any legal proceedings to cite an instrument made by the agency may require the agency to cause a copy of it to be endorsed with such a certificate as is mentioned in this paragraph.

Fees

10.—(1) A designated agency may retain any fees payable to it by virtue of the delegation order.

(2) Any such fees shall be applicable for meeting the expenses of the agency in discharging its functions under the order and for any purposes incidental thereto.

(3) Any fees payable to a designated agency by virtue of a delegation order made before the coming into force of section 3 of this Act may also be applied for repaying the principal of, and paying interest on, any money borrowed by the agency (or by any other person

whose liabilities in respect of the money are assumed by the agency) which has been used for the purpose of defraying expenses incurred before the making of the order (whether before or after the passing of this Act) in making preparations for the agency becoming a designated agency.

11. If the function of prescribing the amount of any fee, or of making a scheme under section 112 above, is exercisable by a designated agency it may prescribe or make provision for such fees as will enable it to defray any such expenses as are mentioned in paragraph 10 above.

Consultation

12.—(1) Before making any rules or regulations by virtue of functions transferred to it by a delegation order a designated agency shall, subject to sub-paragraphs (2) and (3) below, publish the proposed rules and regulations in such manner as appears to the agency to be best calculated to bring them to the attention of the public, together with a statement that representations in respect of the proposals can be made to the agency within a specified period; and before making the rules or regulations the agency shall have regard to any representations duly made in accordance with that statement.

(2) Sub-paragraph (1) above does not apply in any case in which the agency considers that the delay involved in complying with that sub-paragraph would be prejudicial to the interests of investors.

(3) Sub-paragraph (1) above does not apply to the making of any rule or regulation if it is in the same terms (or substantially the same terms) as a proposed rule or regulation which was furnished by the agency to the Secretary of State for the purposes of section 114(9) of this Act.

Exchange of information

13.—(1) The Secretary of State may communicate to a designated agency any information in his possession of which he could have availed himself for the purpose of exercising any function which by virtue of a delegation order is for the time being exercisable by the agency.

(2) A designated agency may in the exercise of any function which by virtue of a delegation order is for the time being exercisable by it communicate to any other person any information which has been communicated to the agency by the Secretary of State and which the Secretary of State could have communicated to that person in the exercise of that function.

(3) No communication of information under sub-paragraph (1) above shall constitute publication for the purposes of the law of defamation.

GENERAL NOTE

The most important of these provisions are those concerning the SIB's legislative functions (paras. 4–9). Note also the requirement of consultation (para. 12), and the special defence provided by para. 8(2) which is modelled on s.3(2) of the Statutory Instruments Act 1946.

Section 129   SCHEDULE 10

REGULATED INSURANCE COMPANIES

Preliminary

1. In this Part of this Schedule "a regulated insurance company" means any such company as is mentioned in section 129 of this Act.

Authorisations for investment business and insurance business

2.—(1) An insurance company to which section 22 of this Act applies shall not be an authorised person except by virtue of that section.

(2) If an insurance company to which Part II of the Insurance Companies Act 1982 applies but to which section 22 of this Act does not apply becomes an authorised person by virtue of any other provision of this Act it shall be an authorised person only as respects the management of the investments of any pension fund which is established solely for the

benefit of the officers or employees and their dependants of that company or of any other body corporate in the same group as that company.

(3) An insurance company to which section 31 of this Act applies shall not, so long as it is an authorised person by virtue of that section, be an authorised person by virtue of any other provision of this Act.

(4) None of the provisions of Part I of this Act shall be construed as authorising any person to carry on insurance business in any case in which he could not lawfully do so apart from those provisions.

Recognition of self-regulating organisation with insurance company members

3.—(1) In the case of a self-regulating organisation whose members include or may include regulated insurance companies the requirements of Schedule 2 to this Act shall include a requirement that the rules of the organisation must take proper account of Part II of the Insurance Companies Act 1982 or, as the case may be, of the provisions for corresponding purposes in the law of any member State in which such companies are established.

(2) Where the function of making or revoking a recognition order in respect of such a self-regulating organisation is exercisable by a designated agency it shall not regard that requirement as satisfied unless the Secretary of State has certified that he also regards it as satisfied.

(3) A delegation order—

(a) may reserve to the Secretary of State the function of revoking a recognition order in respect of such a self-regulating organisation as is mentioned in sub-paragraph (1) above on the ground that the requirement there mentioned is not satisfied; and

(b) shall not transfer to a designated agency the function of revoking any such recognition order on the ground that the organisation has contravened sub-paragraphs (3) or (4) of paragraph 6 below as applied by sub-paragraph (5) of that paragraph.

(4) In the case of such a self-regulating organisation as is mentioned in sub-paragraph (1) above the requirements of Schedule 2 to this Act referred to in section 187(2)(a) of this Act shall include the requirement mentioned in that sub-paragraph.

Modification of provisions as to conduct of investment business

4.—(1) The rules under section 48 of this Act shall not apply to a regulated insurance company except so far as they make provision as respects the matters mentioned in sub-paragraph (2) below.

(2) The matters referred to in sub-paragraph (1) above are—

(a) procuring proposals for policies the rights under which constitute an investment for the purposes of this Act and advising persons on such policies and the exercise of the rights conferred by them;

(b) managing the investments of pension funds, procuring persons to enter into contracts for the management of such investments and advising persons on such contracts and the exercise of the rights conferred by them;

(c) matters incidental to those mentioned in paragraph (a) and (b) above.

(3) The rules under section 49 of this Act shall not apply to an insurance company which is an authorised person by virtue of section 31 of this Act.

(4) The rules under sections 53 and 54 of this Act shall not apply to loss arising as a result of a regulated insurance company being unable to meet its liabilities under a contract of insurance.

(5) A direction under section 59 of this Act shall not prohibit the employment of a person by a regulated insurance company except in connection with—

(a) the matters mentioned in sub-paragraph (2) above; or

(b) investment business carried on in connection with or for the purposes of those matters.

(6) The Secretary of State shall not make a delegation order transferring any functions of making rules or regulations under Chapter V of Part I of this Act in relation to a regulated insurance company unless he is satisfied that those rules and regulations will take proper account of Part II of the Insurance Companies Act 1982 or, as the case may be, of the provisions for corresponding purposes in the law of the member State in which the company is established; and in section 115(5) of this Act the reference to the requirements of section 114(9)(b) shall include a reference to the requirements of this sub-paragraph.

Restriction of provisions as to conduct of insurance business

5.—(1) Regulations under section 72 of the Insurance Companies Act 1982 (insurance advertisements) shall not apply to so much of any advertisement issued by an authorised person as relates to a contract of insurance the rights under which constitute an investment for the purposes of this Act.

(2) No requirement imposed under section 74 of that Act (intermediaries in insurance transactions) shall apply in respect of an invitation issued by, or by an appointed representative of, an authorised person in relation to a contract of insurance the rights under which constitute an investment for the purposes of this Act.

(3) Subject to sub-paragraph (4) below, sections 75 to 77 of that Act (right to withdraw from long-term policies) shall not apply to a regulated insurance company in respect of a contract of insurance the rights under which constitute an investment for the purposes of this Act.

(4) Sub-paragraph (3) above does not affect the operation of the said sections 75 to 77 in a case in which the statutory notice required by those sections has been or ought to have been served before the coming into force of that sub-paragraph.

Exercise of powers of intervention etc.

6.—(1) The powers conferred by Chapter VI of Part I of this Act shall not be exercisable in relation to a regulated insurance company on the ground specified in section 64(1)(*a*) of this Act for reasons relating to the ability of the company to meet its liabilities to policy holders or potential policy holders.

(2) The powers conferred by sections 66 and 68 of this Act, and those conferred by section 67 of this Act so far as applicable to assets belonging to the authorised person, shall not be exercisable in relation to a regulated insurance company.

(3) A designated agency shall not in the case of a regulated insurance company impose any prohibition or requirement under section 65 or 67 of this Act, or vary any such prohibition or requirement, unless it has given reasonable notice of its intention to do so to the Secretary of State and informed him—

(*a*) of the manner in which and the date on or after which it intends to exercise that power; and

(*b*) in the case of a proposal to impose a prohibition or requirement, on which of the grounds specified in section 64(1) of this Act it proposes to act and its reasons for considering that the ground in question exists and that it is necessary to impose the prohibition or requirement.

(4) A designated agency shall not exercise any power to which sub-paragraph (3) above applies if the Secretary of State has before the date specified in accordance with sub-paragraph (3), above served on it a notice in writing directing it not to do so; and the Secretary of State may serve such a notice if he considers it desirable for protecting policy holders or potential policy holders of the company against the risk that it may be unable to meet its liabilities or to fulfil the reasonable expectations of its policy holders or potential policy holders.

(5) Sub-paragraphs (3) and (4) above shall, with the necessary modifications, apply also where a recognised self-regulating organisation proposes to exercise, in the case of a member who is a regulated insurance company, any powers of the organisation for purposes corresponding to those of Chapter VI of Part I of this Act.

(6) The powers conferred by sections 72 and 73 of this Act shall not be exercisable in relation to a regulated insurance company.

Withdrawal of insurance business authorisation

7.—(1) At the end of section 11(2)(*a*) of the Insurance Companies Act 1982 (withdrawal of authorisation in respect of new business where insurance company has failed to satisfy an obligation to which it is subject by virtue of that Act) there shall be inserted the words "or the Financial Services Act 1986 or, if it is a member of a recognised self-regulating organisation within the meaning of that Act, an obligation to which it is subject by virtue of the rules of that organisation".

(2) After subsection (2) of section 13 of that Act (final withdrawal of authorisation) there shall be inserted—

"(2A) The Secretary of State may direct that an insurance company shall cease to be authorised to carry on business which is insurance business by virtue of section 95(*c*)(ii) of this Act if it appears to him that the company has failed to satisfy an obligation to which it is subject by virtue of the Financial Services Act 1986 or, if it is a member of a recognised self-regulating organisation within the meaning of that Act, an obligation to which it is subject by virtue of the rules of that organisation.

(2B) Subsections (3), (5) and (6) of section 11 and subsections (1) and (5) to (8) of section 12 above shall apply to a direction under subsection (2A) above as they apply to a direction under section 11."

Termination of investment business authorisation of insurer established in other member State

8.—(1) Sections 33(1)(*b*) and 34 of this Act shall not apply to a regulated insurance company.

(2) A direction under section 33(1)(*a*) of this Act in respect of such an insurance company may provide that the company shall cease to be an authorised person except as respects investment business of a kind specified in the direction and shall not make it unlawful for the company to effect a contract of insurance in pursuance of a subsisting contract of insurance.

(3) Where the Secretary of State proposes to give a direction under section 33(1)(*a*) of this Act in respect of such an insurance company he shall give it written notice of his intention to do so, giving particulars of the grounds on which he proposes to act and of the rights exercisable under sub-paragraph (4) below.

(4) An insurance company on which a notice is served under sub-paragraph (3) above may within fourteen days after the date of service make written representations to the Secretary of State and, if desired, oral representations to a person appointed for that purpose by the Secretary of State; and the Secretary of State shall have regard to any representations made in accordance with this sub-paragraph in determining whether to give the direction.

(5) After giving a direction under section 33(1)(*a*) of this Act in respect of a regulated insurance company the Secretary of State shall inform the company in writing of the reasons for giving the direction.

(6) A delegation order shall not transfer to a designated agency the function of giving a direction under section 33(1)(*a*) of this Act in respect of a regulated insurance company.

Powers of Tribunal

9. In the case of a regulated insurance company the provisions mentioned in section 98(4) of this Act shall include sections 11 and 13(2A) of the Insurance Companies Act 1982 but where the Tribunal reports that the appropriate decision would be to take action under either of those sections or under section 33(1)(*a*) of this Act the Secretary of State shall take the report into consideration but shall not be bound to act upon it.

Consultation with designated agencies

10.—(1) Where any functions under this Act are for the time being exercisable by a designated agency in relation to regulated insurance companies the Secretary of State shall, before issuing an authorisation under section 3 of the Insurance Companies Act 1982 to an applicant who proposes to carry on in the United Kingdom insurance business which is investment business—

(*a*) seek the advice of the designated agency with respect to any matters which are relevant to those functions of the agency and relate to the applicant, his proposed business or persons who will be associated with him in, or in connection with, that business; and

(*b*) take into account any advice on those matters given to him by the agency before the end of the period within which the application is required to be decided.

(2) The Secretary of State may for the purpose of obtaining the advice of a designated agency under sub-paragraph (1) above furnish it with any information obtained by him in connection with the application.

(3) If a designated agency by which any functions under this Act are for the time being exercisable in relation to regulated insurance companies has reasonable grounds for believing that any such insurance company has failed to comply with an obligation to which it is subject by virtue of this Act it shall forthwith give notice of that fact to the Secretary of State so that he can take it into consideration in deciding whether to give a direction in respect of the company under section 11 or 13(2A) of the said Act of 1982 or section 33 of this Act.

(4) A notice under sub-paragraph (3) above shall contain particulars of the obligation in question and of the agency's reasons for considering that the company has failed to satisfy that obligation.

(5) A designated agency need not give a notice under sub-paragraph (3) above in respect of any matter unless it considers that that matter (either alone or in conjunction with other matters) would justify the withdrawal of authorisation under section 28 of this Act in the case of a person to whom that section applies.

GENERAL NOTE

This schedule modifies Part I of the Act in its application to regulated insurance companies. This modification reflects the fact that insurance companies are already subject to a regime of prudential supervision by the Department of Trade and Industry. This regime focuses in particular on the solvency of insurance companies and their ability to fulfil the reasonable expectations of policy holders.

Accordingly this schedule makes the provisions and regulations of insurance companies legislation paramount in relation to solvency matters (so that, for example, indemnity and compensation fund rules under the Act are not to apply to regulated insurance companies: para. 4(4)). At the same time, the provisions and rules and regulations of the financial services legislation in relation to the life assurance marketing and pension fund management activities of regulated insurance companies are to be paramount, and various insurance companies legislation provisions are therefore disapplied: paras. 4(1), (2), 5.

Sched. 10 also co-ordinates the regulatory jurisdictions of the DTI and the SIB in relation to the recognition of any SRO with insurance company members (para. 3), and the exercise of powers of intervention (para. 6). In relation to questions of authorisation and de-authorisation of insurance companies, the DTI continues to have the last word: paras. 7–10.

Section 140   SCHEDULE 11

FRIENDLY SOCIETIES

PART I

PRELIMINARY

1. In this Schedule—
    "a regulated friendly society" means a society which is an authorised person by virtue of section 23 of this Act as respects such investment business as is mentioned in that section;
    "regulated business", in relation to a regulated friendly society, means investment business as respects which the society is authorised by virtue of that section;
    "a self-regulating organisation for friendly societies" means a self-regulating organisation which is permitted under its rules to admit regulated friendly societies as members and to regulate the carrying on by such societies of regulated business;
    "a recognised self-regulating organisation for friendly societies" means a body declared by an order of the Registrar for the time being in force to be a recognised self-regulating organisation for friendly societies for the purposes of this Schedule;
    "a member society" means a regulated friendly society which is a member of an appropriate recognised self-regulating organisation for friendly societies and is subject to its rules in carrying on all its regulated business and, for the purposes of this definition, "an appropriate recognised self-regulating organisation for friendly societies" means—
        (a) in the case of any such society as is mentioned in section 23(1) of this Act, an organisation declared by an order of the Chief Registrar of friendly societies for the time being in force to be a recognised self-regulating organisation for friendly societies for the purposes of this Schedule; and
        (b) in the case of any such society as is mentioned in section 23(2) of this Act, an organisation declared by an order of the Registrar of Friendly Societies for Northern Ireland for the time being in force to be such an organisation;
    "the Registrar" means—
        (a) in relation to any such society as is mentioned in section 23(1) of this Act, or to any self-regulating organisation for friendly societies which has

applied for or been granted a recognition order made by him, the Chief Registrar of friendly societies; and

(*b*) in relation to any such society as is mentioned in section 23(2) of this Act, or to any self-regulating organisation for friendly societies which has applied for or been granted a recognition order made by him, the Registrar of Friendly Societies for Northern Ireland.

PART II

SELF-REGULATING ORGANISATIONS FOR FRIENDLY SOCIETIES

Recognition

2.—(1) A self-regulating organisation for friendly societies may apply to the Chief Registrar of friendly societies or the Registrar of Friendly Societies for Northern Ireland for an order declaring it to be a recognised self-regulating organisation for friendly societies for the purposes of this Schedule.

(2) An application under sub-paragraph (1) above—

(*a*) shall be made in such manner as the Registrar may direct; and

(*b*) shall be accompanied by such information as the Registrar may reasonably require for the purpose of determining the application.

(3) At any time after receiving an application and before determining it the Registrar may require the applicant to furnish additional information.

(4) The directions and requirements given or imposed under sub-paragraphs (2) and (3) above may differ as between different applications.

(5) Any information to be furnished to the Registrar under this paragraph shall, if he so requires, be in such form or verified in such manner as he may specify.

(6) Every application shall be accompanied by a copy of the applicant's rules and of any guidance issued by the applicant which is intended to have continuing effect and is issued in writing or other legible form.

3.—(1) If, on an application duly made in accordance with paragraph 2 above and after being furnished with all such information as he may require under that paragraph, it appears to the Registrar from that information and having regard to any other information in his possession that the requirements mentioned in paragraph 4 below are satisfied as respects that organisation, he may, with the consent of the Secretary of State and subject to sub-paragraph (2) below, make an order ("a recognition order") declaring the applicant to be a recognised self-regulating organisation for friendly societies.

(2) Where the Registrar proposes to grant an application for a recognition order he shall send to the Secretary of State a copy of the application together with a copy of the rules and any guidance accompanying the application and the Secretary of State shall not consent to the making of the recognition order unless he is satisfied that the rules and guidance of which copies have been sent to him under this sub-paragraph do not have, and are not intended or likely to have, to any significant extent the effect of restricting, distorting or preventing competition or, if they have or are intended or likely to have that effect to any significant extent, that the effect is not greater than is necessary for the protection of investors.

(3) Section 122 of this Act shall apply in relation to the decision whether to consent to the making of a recognition order under this paragraph as it applies to the decisions mentioned in subsection (1) of that section.

(4) Subsections (1) and (2) of section 128 of this Act shall apply for the purposes of this paragraph as if the powers there mentioned included the power of refusing consent to the making of a recognition order under this paragraph and subsection (5) of that section shall apply for that purpose as if the reference to Chapter XIV of Part I included a reference to this paragraph.

(5) The Registrar may refuse to make a recognition order in respect of an organisation if he considers that its recognition is unnecessary having regard to the existence of one or more other organisations which are concerned with such investment business as is mentioned in section 23 of this Act and which have been or are likely to be recognised under this paragraph.

(6) Where the Registrar refuses an application for a recognition order he shall give the applicant a written notice to that effect specifying a requirement which in the opinion of the Registrar is not satisfied, stating that the application is refused on the ground mentioned in sub-paragraph (5) above or stating that the Secretary of State has refused to consent to the making of the order.

(7) A recognition order shall state the date on which it takes effect.

4.—(1) The requirements referred to in paragraph 3 above are that mentioned in sub-paragraph (2) below and those set out in paragraphs 2 to 7 of Schedule 2 to this Act as modified in sub-paragraphs (3) to (5) below.

(2) The rules of the organisation must take proper account of the Friendly Societies Act 1974, or as the case may be, the Friendly Societies Act (Northern Ireland) 1970.

(3) References in paragraphs 2, 3, 4 and 6 of Schedule 2 to members are to members who are regulated friendly societies.

(4) In paragraph 3 of that Schedule—

(a) in sub-paragraph (1) for the reference to Chapter V of Part I of this Act there shall be substituted a reference to paragraphs 14 to 22 below; and

(b) in sub-paragraph (2) the reference to section 49 of this Act shall be omitted and for the reference to sections 53 and 54 there shall be substituted a reference to paragraphs 17 and 18 below; and

(c) in sub-paragraph (3) for the reference to Chapter VI of that Part there shall be substituted a reference to the powers exercisable by the Registrar by virtue of paragraph 23 below.

(5) In paragraph 4 of that Schedule for the reference to Chapter V of Part I of this Act there shall be substituted references to paragraphs 14 to 22 below.

Revocation of recognition

5.—(1) A recognition order may be revoked by a further order made by the Registrar if at any time it appears to him—

(a) that any requirement mentioned in paragraph 4(1) above is not satisfied in the case of the organisation to which the recognition order relates ("the recognised organisation");

(b) that the recognised organisation has failed to comply with any obligation to which it is subject by virtue of this Act; or

(c) that the continued recognition of the organisation is undesirable having regard to the existence of one or more other organisations which have been or are to be recognised under paragraph 3 above.

(2) Subsections (2) to (9) of section 11 of this Act shall have effect in relation to the revocation of a recognition order under this paragraph as they have effect in relation to the revocation of a recognition order under subsection (1) of that section but with the substitution—

(a) for references to the Secretary of State of references to the Registrar;

(b) for the reference in subsection (3) to members of a reference to members of the organisation which are member societies in relation to it; and

(c) for the reference in subsection (6) to investors of a reference to members of the societies which are member societies in relation to the organisation.

Compliance orders

6.—(1) If at any time it appears to the Registrar—

(a) that any requirement mentioned in paragraph 3 above is not satisfied in the case of a recognised self-regulating organisation for friendly societies; or

(b) that such an organisation has failed to comply with any obligation to which it is subject by virtue of this Act,

he may, instead of revoking the recognition order under paragraph 5 above, make an application to the court under this paragraph.

(2) If on any such application the court decides that the requirement in question is not satisfied or, as the case may be, that the organisation has failed to comply with the obligation in question it may order the organisation concerned to take such steps as the court directs for securing that that requirement is satisfied or that that obligation is complied with.

(3) The jurisdiction conferred by this paragraph shall be exercisable by the High Court and the Court of Session.

7.—(1) If at any time it appears to the Registrar that the rules of a recognised self-regulating organisation for friendly societies do not satisfy the requirements of paragraph 3(1) of Schedule 2 to this Act as modified by paragraph 4(4) above he may, instead of revoking the recognition order or making an application under paragraph 6 above, direct the organisation to alter, or himself alter, its rules in such manner as he considers necessary for securing that the rules satisfy those requirements.

(2) Before giving a direction or making any alteration under this paragraph the Registrar shall consult the organisation concerned.

(3) Any direction given under sub-paragraph (1) above shall, on the application of the Registrar, be enforceable by mandamus or, in Scotland, by an order for specific performance under section 91 of the Court of Session Act 1868.

(4) A recognised self-regulating organisation for friendly societies whose rules have been altered by or pursuant to a direction given by the Registrar under sub-paragraph (1) above may apply to the court and if the court is satisfied—

(*a*) that the rules without the alteration satisfied the requirements mentioned in that sub-paragraph; or

(*b*) that other alterations proposed by the organisation would result in the rules satisfying those requirements,

the court may set aside the alteration made by or pursuant to the direction given by the Registrar and, in a case within paragraph (*b*) above, order the organisation to make the alterations proposed by it; but the setting aside of an alteration under this sub-paragraph shall not affect its previous operation.

(5) The jurisdiction conferred by sub-paragraph (4) above shall be exercisable by the High Court and the Court of Session.

(6) Subsections (2) to (7) and (9) of section 11 of this Act shall, with the modifications mentioned in paragraph 5(2) above and any other necessary modifications, have effect in relation to any direction given or alteration made by the Registrar under sub-paragraph (1) above as they have effect in relation to an order revoking a recognition order.

(7) The fact that the rules of an organisation have been altered by or pursuant to a direction given by the Registrar, or pursuant to an order made by the court, under this paragraph shall not preclude their subsequent alteration or revocation by that organisation.

8.—(1) The Registrar or the Secretary of State may make regulations requiring a recognised self-regulating organisation for friendly societies to give the Registrar or, as the case may be, the Secretary of State forthwith notice of the occurrence of such events relating to the organisation or its members as are specified in the regulations and such information in respect of those events as is so specified.

(2) The Registrar or the Secretary of State may make regulations requiring a recognised self-regulating organisation for friendly societies to furnish the Registrar or, as the case may be, the Secretary of State at such times or in respect of such periods as are specified in the regulations with such information relating to the organisation or its members as is so specified.

(3) The notices and information required to be given or furnished under the foregoing provisions of this paragraph shall be such as the Registrar or, as the case may be, the Secretary of State may reasonably require for the exercise of his functions under this Act.

(4) Regulations under the foregoing provisions of this paragraph may require information to be given in a specified form and to be verified in a specified manner.

(5) A notice or information required to be given or furnished under the foregoing provisions of this paragraph shall be given in writing or such other manner as the Registrar or, as the case may be, the Secretary of State may approve.

(6) Where a recognised self-regulating organisation for friendly societies amends, revokes or adds to its rules or guidance it shall within seven days give the Registrar written notice of the amendment, revocation or addition; but notice need not be given of the revocation of guidance other than such as is mentioned in paragraph 2(6) above or of any amendment of or addition to guidance which does not result in or consist of such guidance as is there mentioned.

(7) The Registrar shall send the Secretary of State a copy of any notice given to him under sub-paragraph (6) above.

(8) Contravention of or of regulations under this paragraph shall not be an offence.

9.—(1) A recognised self-regulating organisation for friendly societies shall not exercise any powers for purposes corresponding to those of the powers exercisable by the Registrar by virtue of paragraph 23 below in relation to a regulated friendly society unless it has given reasonable notice of its intention to do so to the Registrar and informed him—

(*a*) of the manner in which and the date on or after which it intends to exercise the power; and

(*b*) in the case of a proposal to impose a prohibition or requirement, of the reason why it proposes to act and its reasons for considering that that reason exists and that it is necessary to impose the prohibition or requirement.

(2) A recognised self-regulating organisation for friendly societies shall not exercise any power to which sub-paragraph (1)(*a*) above applies if before the date given in the notice in pursuance of that sub-paragraph the Registrar has served on it a notice in writing directing

it not to do so; and the Registrar may serve such a notice if he considers it is desirable for protecting members or potential members of the society against the risk that it may be unable to meet its liabilities or to fulfil the reasonable expectations of its members or potential members.

Prevention of restrictive practices

10.—(1) The powers conferred by sub-paragraph (2) below shall be exercisable by the Secretary of State if at any time it appears to him that—
   (a) any rules made or guidance issued by a recognised self-regulating organisation for friendly societies;
   (b) any practices of any such organisation; or
   (c) any practices of persons who are members of, or otherwise subject to the rules made by, any such organisation,
have, or are intended or likely to have, to a significant extent the effect of restricting, distorting or preventing competition and that that effect is greater than is necessary for the protection of investors.

(2) The powers exercisable under this sub-paragraph are to direct the Registrar—
   (a) to revoke the recognition order of the organisation;
   (b) to direct the organisation to take specified steps for the purpose of securing that the rules, guidance or practices in question do not have the effect mentioned in sub-paragraph (1) above;
   (c) to make alterations in the rules for that purpose;
and subsections (2) to (5), (7) and (9) of section 11 of this Act, as applied by sub-paragraph (2) of paragraph 5 above, shall have effect in relation to the revocation of a recognition order by virtue of a direction under this sub-paragraph as they have effect in relation to the revocation of such an order under sub-paragraph (1) of that paragraph.

(3) The practices referred to in paragraph (b) of sub-paragraph (1) above are practices of the organisation in its capacity as such; and the practices referred to in paragraph (c) of that sub-paragraph are practices in relation to business in respect of which the persons in question are subject to the rules of the organisation and which are required or contemplated by its rules or guidance or otherwise attributable to its conduct in its capacity as such.

(4) Subsections (3) to (8) of section 122 of this Act shall apply for the purposes of this paragraph as if—
   (a) the reference to a notice in subsection (3) included a notice received under paragraph 8(7) above or 33(4) below;
   (b) the references to rules and guidance in subsection (4) included such rules and guidance as are mentioned in sub-paragraph (1) above;
   (c) the reference to practices in subsection (6) included such practices as are mentioned in sub-paragraph (1) above; and
   (d) the reference to the Secretary of State's powers in subsection (7) included his powers under sub-paragraph (2) above.

(6) Section 128 of this Act shall apply for the purposes of this paragraph as if—
   (a) the powers referred to in subsection (1) of that section included the powers conferred by sub-paragraph (2)(b) and (c) above;
   (b) the references to Chapter XIV of Part I included references to this paragraph; and
   (c) the reference to a recognised self-regulating organisation included a reference to a recognised self-regulating organisation for friendly societies.

Fees

11.—(1) An applicant for a recognition order under paragraph 3 above shall pay such fees in respect of his application as may be required by a scheme made and published by the Registrar; and no application for such an order shall be regarded as duly made unless this sub-paragraph is complied with.

(2) Subsections (2) to (4) of section 112 of this Act apply to a scheme under sub-paragraph (1) above as they apply to a scheme under subsection (1) of that section.

(3) Every recognised self-regulating organisation for friendly societies shall pay such periodical fees to the Registrar as he may by regulations prescribe.

Application of provisions of this Act

12.—(1) Subject to the following provisions of this paragraph, sections 44(7), 102(1)(c), 124, 125, 126, 180(1)(n), 181, 187, 192 and 200(4) of this Act shall apply in relation to recognised self-regulating organisations for friendly societies as they apply in relation to recognised self-regulating organisations.

(2) In its application by virtue of sub-paragraph (1) above section 126(1) of this Act shall have effect as if the reference to section 119(2) were a reference to paragraph 10(1) above.

(3) In its application by virtue of sub-paragraph (1) above subsection (2) of section 187 of this Act shall have effect as if—

(a) the reference in paragraph (a) to paragraphs 1 to 6 of Schedule 2 were to paragraphs 2 to 6 of that Schedule (as they apply by virtue of paragraph 4 above) and to sub-paragraph (2) of paragraph 4 above; and

(b) paragraph (d) referred to the powers of the organisation under paragraph 23(4) below.

(4) A direction under subsection (1) of section 192 of this Act as it applies by virtue of sub-paragraph (1) above shall direct the Registrar to direct the organisation not to take or, as the case may be, to take the action in question; and where the function of making or revoking a recognition order in respect of a self-regulating organisation for friendly societies is exercisable by a transferee body any direction under that subsection as it applies as aforesaid shall be a direction requiring the Registrar to direct the transferee body to give the organisation such a direction as is specified in the direction given by the Secretary of State.

(5) Subsection (5) of that section shall not apply to a direction given to the Registrar by virtue of this paragraph.

Part III

Registrar's Powers in Relation to Regulated Friendly Societies

Special provisions for regulated friendly societies

13. Paragraphs 14 to 25 below shall have effect in connection with the exercise of powers for the regulation of regulated friendly societies in relation to regulated business, but nothing in this Part of this Schedule shall affect the exercise of any power conferred by this Act in relation to a regulated friendly society which is an authorised person by virtue of section 25 of this Act to the extent that the power relates to other investment business.

Conduct of investment business

14.—(1) The rules under section 48 of this Act shall not apply to a regulated friendly society but the Registrar may, with the consent of the Secretary of State, make such rules as may be made under that section regulating the conduct of any such society other than a member society as respects the matters mentioned in sub-paragraph (2) below.

(2) The matters referred to in sub-paragraph (1) above are—

(a) procuring persons to transact regulated business with it and advising persons as to the exercise of rights conferred by investments acquired from the society in the course of such business;

(b) managing the investments of pension funds, procuring persons to enter into contracts for the management of such investments and advising persons on such contracts and the exercise of the rights conferred by them;

(c) matters incidental to those mentioned in paragraphs (a) and (b) above.

(3) Section 50 of this Act shall apply in relation to rules under this paragraph as it applies in relation to rules under section 48 except that—

(a) for the reference to the Secretary of State there shall be substituted a reference to the Registrar; and

(b) the Registrar shall not exercise the power under subsection (1) to alter the requirement of rules made under this paragraph without the consent of the Secretary of State.

15.—(1) The rules under section 51 of this Act shall not apply to any investment agreement which a person has entered or offered to enter into with a regulated friendly society if, as respects the society, entering into the agreement constitutes the carrying on of regulated business but the Registrar may, with the consent of the Secretary of State, make rules for enabling a person who has entered or offered to enter into such an agreement to rescind the agreement or withdraw the offer within such period and in such manner as may be specified in the rules.

(2) Subsection (2) of section 51 of this Act shall apply in relation to rules under this paragraph as it applies in relation to rules under that section but with the substitution for the reference to the Secretary of State of a reference to the Registrar.

16.—(1) Regulations under section 52 of this Act shall not apply to any regulated friendly society but the Registrar may, with the consent of the Secretary of State, make such regulations as may be made under that section imposing requirements on regulated friendly societies other than member societies.

(2) Any notice or information required to be given or furnished under this paragraph shall be given in writing or in such other manner as the Registrar may approve.

17.—(1) Rules under section 53 of this Act shall not apply to any regulated friendly society but the Registrar may, with the consent of the Secretary of State make rules concerning indemnity against any claim in respect of any description of civil liability incurred by a regulated friendly society in connection with any regulated business.

(2) Such rules shall not apply to a member society of a recognised self-regulating organisation for friendly societies unless that organisation has requested that such rules should apply to it; and any such request shall not be capable of being withdrawn after rules giving effect to it have been made but without prejudice to the power of the Registrar to revoke the rules if he and the Secretary of State think fit.

(3) Subsections (3) and (4) of section 53 of this Act shall apply in relation to such rules as they apply to rules under that section but with the substitution for references to the Secretary of State of references to the Registrar.

18.—(1) No scheme established by rules under section 54 shall apply in cases where persons who are or have been regulated friendly societies are unable, or likely to be unable, to satisfy claims in respect of any description of civil liability incurred by them in connection with any regulated business by the Registrar may, with the consent of the Secretary of State, by rules establish a scheme for compensating investors in such cases.

(2) Subject to sub-paragraph (3) below, subsections (2) to (4) and (6) of that section shall apply in relation to such rules as they apply to rules under that section but with the substitution for the references to the Secretary of State, authorised persons, members and a recognised self-regulating organisation of references respectively to the Registrar, regulated friendly societies, member societies and a recognised self-regulating organisation for friendly societies.

(3) Subsection (3) of that section shall have effect with the substitution for the words "the Secretary of State is satisfied" of the words "the Registrar and the Secretary of State are satisfied".

(4) The references in section 179(3)(*b*) and 180(1)(*e*) of this Act to the body administering a scheme established under section 54 of this Act shall include the body administering a scheme established under this paragraph.

19.—(1) Regulations under section 55 of this Act shall not apply to money held by regulated friendly societies but the Registrar may, with the consent of the Secretary of State, make regulations with respect to money held by a regulated friendly society in such circumstances as may be specified in the regulations.

(2) Regulations under this paragraph shall not provide that money held by a regulated friendly society shall be held as mentioned in paragraph (*a*) of subsection (2) of that section but paragraphs (*b*) to (*f*) of that subsection and subsections (3) and (4) of that section shall apply in relation to regulations made under this paragraph as they apply in relation to regulations under that section (but with the substitution for the reference in paragraphs (*b*) and (*e*) of subsection (2) to a member of a recognised self-regulating organisation of a reference to a member society of a recognised self-regulating organisation for friendly societies and for the reference in paragraph (*e*) of that subsection to the Secretary of State of a reference to the Registrar).

20. Regulations under section 56(1) of this Act shall not permit anything to be done by a regulated friendly society but that section shall not apply to anything done by such a society in the course of or in consequence of an unsolicited call which, as respects the society constitutes the carrying on of regulated business, if it is permitted to be done by the society in those circumstances—

(*a*) in the case of a member society, by the rules of the recognised self-regulating organisation for friendly societies of which it is a member; and

(*b*) in any other case, by regulations made by the Registrar with the consent of the Secretary of State.

21.—(1) If it appears to the Registrar that a regulated friendly society other than a member society has contravened—

(*a*) any provision of rules or regulations made under this Schedule or of section 56 or 59 of this Act;

(*b*) any condition imposed under section 50 of this Act as it applies by virtue of paragraph 14(3) above;

(*c*) any prohibition or requirement imposed under Chapter VI of Part I of this Act as it applies by virtue of paragraph 23 below; or

(*d*) any requirement imposed under paragraph 24 below;

he may publish a statement to that effect.

(2) Subsections (2) to (5) of section 60 above shall apply in relation to the power under sub-paragraph (1) above as they apply in relation to the power in subsection (1) of that section but with the substitution for the references to the Secretary of State of references to the Registrar.

22.—(1) If on the application of the Registrar the court is satisfied—

(*a*) that there is a reasonable likelihood that any regulated friendly society will contravene any provision of—

   (i) any prohibition or requirement imposed under Chapter VI of Part I of this Act as it applies by virtue of paragraph 23 below;

   (ii) the rules or regulations made under this Schedule;

   (iii) any requirement imposed under paragraph 24 below;

   (iv) section 47, 56 or 59 of this Act;

   (v) the rules of a recognised self-regulating organisation for friendly societies in relation to which it is a member society,

   or any condition imposed under section 50 of this Act as it applies by virtue of paragraph 14(3) above;

(*b*) that any regulated friendly society has contravened any such provision or condition and that there is a reasonable likelihood that the contravention will continue or be repeated; or

(*c*) that any person has contravened any such provision or condition and that there are steps that could be taken for remedying the contravention,

the court may grant an injunction restraining the contravention or, in Scotland, an interdict prohibiting the contravention or, as the case may be, make an order requiring the society and any other person who appears to the court to have been knowingly concerned in the contravention to take steps to remedy it.

(2) No application shall be made by the Registrar under sub-paragraph (1) above in respect of any such rules as are mentioned in paragraph (*a*)(v) of that sub-paragraph unless it appears to him that the organisation is unable or unwilling to take appropriate steps to restrain the contravention or to require the society concerned to take such steps as are mentioned in sub-paragraph (1) above.

(3) Subsections (3) to (9) of section 61 of this Act apply to such a contravention as is mentioned in sub-paragraph (1)(*a*) above as they apply to such a contravention as is mentioned in subsection (3) of that section, but with the substitution for the references to the Secretary of State of references to the Registrar.

(4) Without prejudice to the preceding provisions of this paragraph—

(*a*) a contravention of any rules or regulations made under this Schedule;

(*b*) a contravention of any prohibition or requirement imposed under Chapter VI of Part I of this Act as it applies by virtue of paragraph 23 below;

(*c*) a contravention of any requirement imposed under paragraph 24 below;

(*d*) a contravention by a member society of any rules of the recognised self-regulating organisation for friendly societies of which it is a member relating to a matter in respect of which rules or regulations have been or could be made under this Schedule or of any requirement or prohibition imposed by the organisation in the exercise of powers for purposes corresponding to those of the said Chapter VI or paragraph 24;

shall be actionable at the suit of a person who suffers loss as a result of the contravention subject to the defences and other incidents applying to actions for breach of statutory duty, but no person shall be guilty of an offence by reason of any such contravention and no such contravention shall invalidate any transaction.

(5) This paragraph is without prejudice to any equitable remedy available in respect of property which by virtue of a requirement under section 67 of this Act as it applies by virtue of paragraph 23 below is subject to a trust.

Intervention, information and investigations

23.—(1) The powers conferred by Chapter VI of Part I of this Act shall not be exercisable in relation to a regulated friendly society or the appointed representative of such a society by the Secretary of State but instead shall be exercisable by the Registrar; and accordingly references in that Chapter to the Secretary of State shall as respects the exercise of powers in relation to a regulated friendly society or such a representative be taken as references to the Registrar.

(2) Section 64 of this Act shall not apply to the exercise of those powers by virtue of sub-paragraph (1) above but those powers shall only be exercisable by the Registrar if it appears to him—

(a) that the exercise of the powers is desirable in the interests of members or potential members of the regulated friendly society; or

(b) that the society is not a fit person to carry on regulated business of a particular kind or to the extent to which it is carrying it on or proposing to carry it on; or

(c) that the society has contravened any provision of this Act or of any rules or regulations made under it or in purported compliance with any such provision has furnished him with false, inaccurate or misleading information or has contravened any prohibition or requirement imposed under this Act.

(3) For the purposes of sub-paragraph (2)(b) above the Registrar may take into account any matters that could be taken into account in deciding whether to withdraw or suspend an authorisation under Chapter III of Part I of this Act.

(4) The powers conferred by this paragraph shall not be exercisable in relation—

(a) to a member society which is subject to the rules of a recognised self-regulating organisation for friendly societies in carrying on all the investment business carried on by it; or

(b) to an appointed representative of a member society if that member society, and each other member society which is his principal, is subject to the rules of such an organisation in carrying on the investment business in respect of which it has accepted responsibility for his activities;

except that the powers conferred by virtue of section 67(1)(b) of this Act may on any of the grounds mentioned in sub-paragraph (2) above be exercised in relation to a member society or appointed representative at the request of the organisation in relation to which the society or, as the case may be, the society which is the representative's principal is a member society.

24.—(1) The Registrar may by notice in writing require any regulated friendly society (other than a member society) or any self-regulating organisation for friendly societies to furnish him with such information as he may reasonably require for the exercise of his functions under this Act.

(2) The Registrar may require any information which he requires under this paragraph to be furnished within such reasonable time and verified in such manner as he may specify.

25.—(1) Where a notice or copy of a notice is served on any person under section 60 or section 70 of this Act as they apply by virtue of paragraph 21(2) or 23 above, Chapter IX of Part I of this Act (other than section 96) shall, subject to sub-paragraph (2) below, have effect—

(a) with the substitution for the references to the Secretary of State of references to the Registrar; and

(b) as if for the references in section 98(4) to sections 28, 33 and 60 of this Act there were substituted references to paragraphs 21, 23, 24, 26 and 27 of this Schedule.

(2) Where the friendly society in question is an authorised person by virtue of section 25 of this Act the provisions mentioned in sub-paragraph (1) above shall have effect as if the references substituted by that sub-paragraph had effect in addition to rather than in substitution for the references for which they are there substituted.

(3) Where the Tribunal reports that the appropriate decision is to take action under paragraph 26 or 27 of this Schedule the Registrar shall take the report into account but shall not be bound to act on it.

Exercise of powers under enactments relating to friendly societies

26.—(1) If it appears to the Chief Registrar of friendly societies that a regulated friendly society which is an authorised person by virtue of section 23(1) of this Act—

(a) has contravened any provision of—

(i) this Act or any rules or regulations made under it;

(ii) any requirement imposed under paragraph 24 above;

(iii) the rules of a recognised self-regulating organisation for friendly societies in relation to which it is a member society; or

(b) in purported compliance with any such provision has furnished false, inaccurate or misleading information,

he may exercise any of the powers mentioned in sub-paragraph (2) below in relation to that society.

(2) The powers mentioned in sub-paragraph (1) above are those under subsection (1) of section 87 (inspection and winding up of registered friendly societies), subsection (1)

of section 88 (suspension of business of registered friendly societies), subsections (1) and (2) of section 89 (production of documents) and subsections (1) and (2) of section 91 (cancellation and suspension of registration) of the Friendly Societies Act 1974; and subject to sub-paragraph (3) below the remaining provisions of those sections shall apply in relation to the exercise of those powers by virtue of this paragraph as they do in relation to their exercise in the circumstances mentioned in those sections.

(3) In its application by virtue of this paragraph—

(*a*) section 88 of the said Act of 1974 shall have effect with the omission of subsections (3), (5) and (9); and

(*b*) section 89 of that Act shall have effect with the omission of subsection (7).

27.—(1) If it appears to the Registrar of Friendly Societies for Northern Ireland that a regulated friendly society which is an authorised person by virtue of section 23(2) of this Act—

(*a*) has contravened any provision of—

    (i) this Act or any rules or regulations made under it;

    (ii) any requirement imposed under paragraph 24 above;

    (iii) the rules of a recognised self-regulating organisation for friendly societies in relation to which it is a member society; or

(*b*) in purported compliance with any such provision has furnished false, inaccurate or misleading information,

he may exercise any of the powers mentioned in sub-paragraph (2) below in relation to that society.

(2) The powers mentioned in sub-paragraph (1) above are those under subsection (1) of section 77 (inspection and winding up of registered friendly societies), subsection (1) of section 78 (suspension of business of registered friendly societies), subsections (1) and (2) of section 79 (production of documents) and subsections (1) and (2) of section 80 (cancellation and suspension of registration) of the Friendly Societies Act (Northern Ireland) 1970; and subject to sub-paragraph (3) below the remaining provisions of those sections shall apply in relation to the exercise of those powers by virtue of this paragraph as they do in relation to their exercise in the circumstances mentioned in those sections.

(3) In its application by virtue of this paragraph section 78 of the said Act of 1970 shall have effect with the omission in subsection (2) of the words from "and such notice" onwards and of subsection (4).

PART IV

TRANSFER OF REGISTRAR'S FUNCTIONS

28.—(1) If it appears to the Registrar—

(*a*) that a body corporate has been established which is able and willing to discharge all or any of the functions to which this paragraph applies; and

(*b*) that the requirements of Schedule 7 to this Act (as it has effect by virtue of sub-paragraph (3) below) are satisfied in the case of that body,

he may, with the consent of the Secretary of State and subject to the following provisions of this paragraph and paragraphs 29 and 30 below, make an order transferring all or any of those functions to that body.

(2) The body to which functions are transferred by the first order made under sub-paragraph (1) above shall be the body known as The Securities and Investments Board Limited if the Secretary of State consents to the making of the order and it appears to the Registrar that that body is able and willing to discharge those functions, that the requirements mentioned in paragraph (*b*) of that sub-paragraph are satisfied in the case of that body and that he is not precluded from making the order by the following provisions of this paragraph or paragraph 29 or 30 below.

(3) For the purposes of sub-paragraph (1) above Schedule 7 shall have effect as if—

(*a*) for references to a designated agency there were substituted references to a transferee body; and

(*b*) for the reference to complaints in paragraph 4 there were substituted a reference to complaints arising out of the conduct by regulated friendly societies of regulated business.

(4) An order under sub-paragraph (1) above is in this Act referred to as a transfer order and a body to which functions are transferred by a transfer order is in this Act referred to as a transferee body.

(5) Subject to sub-paragraphs (6) and (8) below, this paragraph applies to the functions of the Registrar under section 113(3) of this Act and paragraph 38 below and any functions

conferred on him by virtue of paragraphs 2 to 25 above other than the powers under sections 66 and 68 of this Act and, so far as applicable to assets belonging to a regulated friendly society, the power under section 67 of this Act.

(6) If the Registrar transfers his functions under Chapter VI of Part I of this Act they shall not be exercisable by the transferee body if the only reasons by virtue of which it appears to the body as mentioned in paragraph 23(2) above relate to the sufficiency of the funds of the society to meet existing claims or of the rates of contribution to cover benefits assured.

(7) Any function may be transferred by an order under this paragraph either wholly or in part and a function may be transferred in respect of all societies or only in respect of such societies as are specified in the order.

(8) A transfer order—

(*a*) may reserve to the Registrar the function of revoking a recognition order in respect of a self-regulating organisation for friendly societies on the ground that the requirement mentioned in paragraph 4(2) above is not satisfied; and

(*b*) shall not transfer to a transferee body the function of revoking any such recognition order on the ground that the organisation has contravened the provisions of paragraph 9 above.

(9) No transfer order shall be made unless a draft of it has been laid before and approved by a resolution of each House of Parliament.

29. The Registrar shall not make a transfer order transferring any function of making rules or regulations to a transferee body unless—

(*a*) the body has furnished him and the Secretary of State with a copy of the rules or regulations which it proposes to make in the exercise of those functions; and

(*b*) they are both satisfied that those rules or regulations will—

    (i) afford investors an adequate level of protection,

    (ii) in the case of rules and regulations corresponding to those mentioned in Schedule 8 to this Act, comply with the principles set out in that Schedule, and

    (iii) take proper account of the supervision of the friendly societies by the Registrar under the enactments relating to friendly societies.

30.—(1) The Registrar shall also before making a transfer order transferring any functions to a transferee body require it to furnish him and the Secretary of State with a copy of any guidance intended to have continuing effect which it proposes to issue in writing or other legible form and they may take such guidance into account in determining whether they are satisfied as mentioned in paragraph 29(*b*) above.

(2) In this Act references to guidance issued by a transferee body are references to guidance issued or any recommendation made by it which is issued or made to regulated friendly societies or self-regulating organisations for friendly societies generally or to any class of regulated friendly societies or self-regulating organisations for friendly societies, being societies which are or may be subject to rules or regulations made by it or organisations which are or may be recognised by it in the exercise of its functions under a transfer order.

31.—(1) Subject to the provisions of this paragraph, sections 115, 116, 117(3) to (5) and 118 of this Act shall apply in relation to the transfer of functions under paragraph 28 above as they apply in relation to the transfer of functions under section 114 of this Act.

(2) Subject to sub-paragraphs (5) and (6)(*b*) below, for references in those provisions to the Secretary of State, a designated agency and a delegation order there shall be substituted respectively references to the Registrar, a transferee body and a transfer order.

(3) The Registrar may not exercise the powers conferred by subsections (1) and (2) of section 115 except with the consent of the Secretary of State.

(4) In subsection (3) of section 115 for the reference to Schedule 7 to this Act there shall be substituted a reference to that Schedule as it has effect by virtue of paragraph 28(3) above and in subsection (5) of that section for the reference to section 114(9)(*b*) of this Act there shall be substituted a reference to paragraph 29(*b*) above.

(5) Section 118(3)(*b*) shall have effect as if the reference to any provision applying to the Secretary of State were a reference to any provision applying to the Secretary of State or the Registrar.

(6) In Schedule 9 to this Act—

(*a*) paragraph 1(2) and (3) shall be omitted;

(*b*) paragraph 4 shall have effect as if the references to the Secretary of State were references to the Secretary of State and the Registrar;

(*c*) paragraph 5 shall have effect as if the reference to section 205(2) were a reference to paragraph 45(1) below;

(*d*) paragraph 12(3) shall have effect as if the reference to section 114(9) were a reference to paragraph 29 above.

(7) The power mentioned in paragraph 2(3) of Schedule 9 to this Act shall not be exercisable on the ground that the company has ceased to be a designated agency or, as the case may be, a transferee body if the company remains a transferee body or, as the case may be, a designated agency.

32. A transferee body shall at least once in each year for which the transfer order is in force make a report to the Registrar on the discharge of the functions transferred to it by the order and on such other matters as the order may require and the Registrar shall send a copy of each report received by him under this paragraph to the Secretary of State who shall lay copies of the report before Parliament.

33.—(1) This paragraph applies where the function of making or revoking a recognition order in respect of a self-regulating organisation for friendly societies is exercisable by a transferee body.

(2) Paragraph 3(2) above shall have effect as if the first reference to the Secretary of State included a reference to the Registrar.

(3) The transferee body shall not regard the requirement mentioned in paragraph 4(2) as satisfied unless the Registrar has certified that he also regards it as satisfied.

(4) A transferee body shall send the Registrar and the Secretary of State a copy of any notice received by it under paragraph 8(6) above.

(5) Where the Secretary of State exercises any of the powers conferred by paragraph 10(2) above in relation to an organisation the Registrar shall direct the transferee body to take the appropriate action in relation to that organisation and such a direction shall, on the application of the Registrar, be enforceable by mandamus or, in Scotland, by an order for specific performance under section 91 of the Court of Session Act 1868.

34. A transferee body to which the Registrar has transferred any function of making rules or regulations may make those rules or regulations without the consent of the Secretary of State.

35.—(1) A transferee body shall not impose any prohibition or requirement under section 65 or 67 of this Act on a regulated friendly society or vary any such prohibition or requirement unless it has given reasonable notice of its intention to do so to the Registrar and informed him—

(a) of the manner in which and the date on or after which it intends to exercise the power; and

(b) in the case of a proposal to impose a prohibition or requirement, on which of the grounds specified in paragraph 23(2) above it proposes to act and its reasons for considering that the ground in question exists and that it is necessary to impose the prohibition or requirement.

(2) A transferee body shall not exercise any power to which sub-paragraph (1) above applies if before the date given in the notice in pursuance of sub-paragraph (1)(a) above the Registrar has served on it a notice in writing directing it not to do so; and the Registrar may serve such a notice if he considers it is desirable for protecting members or potential members of the regulated friendly society against the risk that it may be unable to meet its liabilities or to fulfil the reasonable expectations of its members or potential members.

36.—(1) The Secretary of State shall not consent to the making of an order by the Registrar under paragraph 28 above transferring any functions to a transferee body unless he is satisfied that any rules, regulations, guidance and recommendations of which copies are furnished to him under paragraphs 29(a) and 30(1) above do not have, and are not intended or likely to have, to any significant extent the effect of restricting, distorting or preventing competition or, if they have or are intended or likely to have that effect to any significant extent, that the effect is not greater than is necessary for the protection of investors.

(2) Section 121(2) and (4) and sections 122 to 128 above shall have effect in relation to transferee bodies and transfer orders as they have effect in relation to designated agencies and designation orders but subject to the following modifications.

(3) Those provisions shall have effect as if the powers exercisable under section 121(3) were—

(a) to make an order transferring back to the Registrar all or any of the functions transferred to the transferee body by a transfer order; or

(b) to direct the Registrar to direct the transferee body to take specified steps for the purpose of securing that the rules, regulations, guidance or practices in question do not have the effect mentioned in sub-paragraph (1) above.

(4) No order shall be made by virtue of sub-paragraph (3) above unless a draft of it has been laid before and approved by a resolution of each House of Parliament.

(5) For the decisions referred to in section 122(1) there shall be substituted a reference to the Secretary of State's decision whether he is precluded by sub-paragraph (1) above from giving his consent to the making of a transfer order.

(6) Section 128 shall apply as if—

(a) the powers referred to in subsection (1) of that section included the power conferred by sub-paragraph (3)(b) above; and

(b) the references to Chapter XIV of Part I included references to this paragraph.

37.—(1) If a transferee body has reasonable grounds for believing that any regulated friendly society has failed to comply with an obligation to which it is subject by virtue of this Act it shall forthwith give notice of that fact to the Registrar so that he can take it into consideration in deciding whether to exercise in relation to the society any of the powers conferred on him by sections 87 to 89 and 91 of the Friendly Societies Act 1974 or, as the case may be, sections 77 to 80 of the Friendly Societies Act (Northern Ireland) 1970 (inspection, winding up, suspension of business and cancellation and suspension of registration).

(2) A notice under sub-paragraph (1) above shall contain particulars of the obligation in question and of the transferee body's reasons for considering that the society has failed to satisfy that obligation.

(3) A transferee body need not give a notice under sub-paragraph (1) above in respect of any matter unless it considers that that matter (either alone or in conjunction with other matters) would justify the withdrawal of authorisation under section 28 of this Act in the case of a person to whom that provision applies.

PART V

MISCELLANEOUS AND SUPPLEMENTAL

38.—(1) The Registrar may publish information or give advice, or arrange for the publication of information or the giving of advice, in such form and manner as he considers appropriate with respect to—

(a) the operation of this Schedule and the rules and regulations made under it in relation to registered friendly societies, including in particular the rights of their members, the duties of such societies and the steps to be taken for enforcing those rights or complying with those duties;

(b) any matters relating to the functions of the Registrar under this Schedule or any such rules or regulations;

(c) any other matters about which it appears to him to be desirable to publish information or give advice for the protection of those members or any class of them.

(2) The Registrar may offer for sale copies of information published under this paragraph and may, if he thinks fit, make reasonable charges for advice given under this paragraph at any person's request.

(3) This paragraph shall not be construed as authorising the disclosure of restricted information within the meaning of section 179 of this Act in any case in which it could not be disclosed apart from the provisions of this paragraph.

39. In the case of an application for authorisation under section 26 of this Act made by a society which is registered under the Friendly Societies Act 1974 within the meaning of that Act or is registered or deemed to be registered under the Friendly Societies Act (Northern Ireland) 1970 ("a registered society"), section 27(3)(c) of this Act shall have effect as if it referred only to any person who is a trustee manager or member of the committee of the society.

40. Where the other person mentioned in paragraph (c) of the definition of "connected person" in section 105(9) of this Act is a registered society that paragraph shall have effect with the substitution for the words from "member" onwards of the words "trustee, manager or member of the committee of the society".

41. In relation to any such document as is mentioned in subsection (1) of section 204 of this Act which is required or authorised to be given to or served on a registered society—

(a) subsection (3)(c) of that section shall have effect with the substitution for the words from "member" onwards of the words "trustee, manager or member of the committee of the society"; and

(b) subsection (4)(c) of that section shall have effect as if for the words from "member" onwards there were substituted the words "trustee, manager or member of the committee of the society, the office which is its registered office in accordance with its rules".

42. Rules under paragraphs 14, 15, 17 and 18 above and regulations under paragraphs 16, 19 and 20 above shall apply notwithstanding any provision to the contrary in the rules of any regulated friendly society to which they apply.

43.—(1) Where it appears to the Registrar, the assistant registrar for Scotland, the Industrial Assurance Commissioner or the Industrial Assurance Commissioner for Northern Ireland that any such rules as are mentioned in section 48(2)(*j*) of this Act which are made by virtue of paragraph 14 above (or any corresponding rules made by a self-regulating organisation for friendly societies) make arrangements for the settlement of a dispute referred to him under section 77 of the Friendly Societies Act 1974, section 65 of the Friendly Societies Act (Northern Ireland) 1970, section 32 of the Industrial Assurance Act 1923 or Article 36 of the Industrial Assurance (Northern Ireland) Order 1979 or that such rules relate to some of the matters in dispute he may, if he thinks fit, delegate his functions in respect of the dispute so as to enable it to be settled in accordance with the rules.

(2) If such rules provide that any dispute may be referred to such a person, that person may deal with any dispute referred to him in pursuance of those rules as if it were a dispute referred to him as aforesaid and may delegate his functions in respect of any such dispute to any other person.

44.—(1) In Part III of Schedule 1 to the House of Commons Disqualification Act 1975 (disqualifying offices) there shall be inserted at the appropriate place—

"Chairman of a transferee body within the meaning of Schedule 11 to the Financial Services Act 1986 if he is in receipt of remuneration."

(2) A corresponding amendment shall be made in Part III of Schedule 1 to the Northern Ireland Assembly Disqualification Act 1975.

. 45.—(1) Any power of the Chief Registrar of friendly societies to make regulations, rules or orders which is exercisable by virtue of this Act shall be exercisable by statutory instrument and the Statutory Instruments Act 1946 shall apply to any such power as if the Chief Registrar of friendly societies were a Minister of the Crown.

(2) Any such power of the Registrar of Friendly Societies for Northern Ireland shall be exercisable by statutory rule for the purposes of the Statutory Rules (Northern Ireland) Order 1979.

(3) Any regulations, rules or orders made under this Schedule by the Registrar may make different provision for different cases.

GENERAL NOTE

This schedule provides a framework for a régime for friendly societies parallel to the main investment business régime. The parallel régime applies to "regulated friendly societies," *i.e.* those authorised to carry on investment business by virtue of s.23 of the Act, and takes account of the pre-existing system of supervision by the Chief Registrar of Friendly Societies.

The schedule confers various powers upon the Chief Registrar of Friendly Societies and makes provision for the transfer of nearly all of them (with possible reservations) to a "transferee body"—in the first instance, the Securities and Investments Board: Part IV.

The Chief Registrar (and hence in practice the SIB) is empowered to recognise a self-regulating organisation for friendly societies: Part II. The Chief Registrar is also empowered (paras. 14–20) to lay down special provisions for the conduct by regulated friendly societies of that investment business for which they are authorised by virtue of s.23. In general, the rules and regulations made by the SIB under the main régime are not to apply to regulated friendly societies: the contemplated special provisions will apply instead. (But the regulation of any investment business for which a friendly society is *directly authorised* under s.25 remains a matter for the SIB's rules and regulations under the main régime: para. 13.) In particular, the mainstream Conduct of Business Rules are disapplied and instead the Chief Registrar is empowered to make rules regulating the marketing of friendly society policies, and the management by friendly societies of the investments of pension funds: para. 14.

Parallel powers of intervention are also conferred upon the Chief Registrar: paras. 23–25.

Section 172   SCHEDULE 12

TAKEOVER OFFERS:

PROVISIONS SUBSTITUTED FOR SECTIONS 428, 429 AND 430 OF COMPANIES ACT 1985

PART XIIIA

TAKEOVER OFFERS

"Takeover offers"

428.—(1) In this Part of this Act "a takeover offer" means an offer to acquire all the shares, or all the shares of any class or classes, in a company (other than shares which at the date of the offer are already held by the offeror), being an offer on terms which are the same in relation to all the shares to which the offer relates or, where those shares include shares of different classes, in relation to all the shares of each class.

(2) In subsection (1) "shares" means shares which have been allotted on the date of the offer but a takeover offer may include among the shares to which it relates all or any shares that are subsequently allotted before a date specified in or determined in accordance with the terms of the offer.

(3) The terms offered in relation to any shares shall for the purposes of this section be treated as being the same in relation to all the shares or, as the case may be, all the shares of a class to which the offer relates notwithstanding any variation permitted by subsection (4).

(4) A variation is permitted by this subsection where—

  (*a*) the law of a country or territory outside the United Kingdom precludes an offer of consideration in the form or any of the forms specified in the terms in question or precludes it except after compliance by the offeror with conditions with which he is unable to comply or which he regards as unduly onerous; and

  (*b*) the variation is such that the persons to whom an offer of consideration in that form is precluded are able to receive consideration otherwise than in that form but of substantially equivalent value.

(5) The reference in subsection (1) to shares already held by the offeror includes a reference to shares which he has contracted to acquire but that shall not be construed as including shares which are the subject of a contract binding the holder to accept the offer when it is made, being a contract entered into by the holder either for no consideration and under seal or for no consideration other than a promise by the offeror to make the offer.

(6) In the application of subsection (5) to Scotland, the words "and under seal" shall be omitted.

(7) Where the terms of an offer make provision for their revision and for acceptances on the previous terms to be treated as acceptances on the revised terms, the revision shall not be regarded for the purposes of this Part of this Act as the making of a fresh offer and references in this Part of this Act to the date of the offer shall accordingly be construed as references to the date on which the original offer was made.

(8) In this Part of this Act "the offeror" means, subject to section 430D, the person making a takeover offer and "the company" means the company whose shares are the subject of the offer.

Right of offeror to buy out minority shareholders

429.—(1) If, in a case in which a takeover offer does not relate to shares of different classes, the offeror has by virtue of acceptances of the offer acquired or contracted to acquire not less than nine-tenths in value of the shares to which the offer relates he may give notice to the holder of any shares to which the offer relates which the offeror has not acquired or contracted to acquire that he desires to acquire those shares.

(2) If, in a case in which a takeover offer relates to shares of different classes, the offeror has by virtue of acceptances of the offer acquired or contracted to acquire not less than nine-tenths in value of the shares of any class to which the offer relates, he may give notice to the holder of any shares of that class which the offeror has not acquired or contracted to acquire that he desires to acquire those shares.

(3) No notice shall be given under subsection (1) or (2) unless the offeror has acquired or contracted to acquire the shares necessary to satisfy the minimum specified in that subsection before the end of the period of four months beginning with the date of the offer; and no such notice shall be given after the end of the period of two months beginning with the date on which he has acquired or contracted to acquire shares which satisfy that minimum.

(4) Any notice under this section shall be given in the prescribed manner; and when the offeror gives the first notice in relation to an offer he shall send a copy of it to the company together with a statutory declaration by him in the prescribed form stating that the conditions for the giving of the notice are satisfied.

(5) Where the offeror is a company (whether or not a company within the meaning of this Act) the statutory declaration shall be signed by a director.

(6) Any person who fails to send a copy of a notice or a statutory declaration as required by subsection (4) or makes such a declaration for the purposes of that subsection knowing it to be false or without having reasonable grounds for believing it to be true shall be liable to imprisonment or a fine, or both, and for continued failure to send the copy or declaration, to a daily default fine.

(7) If any person is charged with an offence for failing to send a copy of a notice as required by subsection (4) it is a defence for him to prove that he took reasonable steps for securing compliance with that subsection.

(8) Where during the period within which a takeover offer can be accepted the offeror acquires or contracts to acquire any of the shares to which the offer relates but otherwise than by virtue of acceptances of the offer, then, if—

(a) the value of the consideration for which they are acquired or contracted to be acquired ("the acquisition consideration") does not at that time exceed the value of the consideration specified in the terms of the offer; or

(b) those terms are subsequently revised so that when the revision is announced the value of the acquisition consideration, at the time mentioned in paragraph (a) above, no longer exceeds the value of the consideration specified in those terms,

the offeror shall be treated for the purposes of this section as having acquired or contracted to acquire those shares by virtue of acceptances of the offer; but in any other case those shares shall be treated as excluded from those to which the offer relates.

Effect of notice under s.429

430.—(1) The following provisions shall, subject to section 430C, have effect where a notice is given in respect of any shares under section 429.

(2) The offeror shall be entitled and bound to acquire those shares on the terms of the offer.

(3) Where the terms of an offer are such as to give the holder of any shares a choice of consideration the notice shall give particulars of the choice and state—

(a) that the holder of the shares may within six weeks from the date of the notice indicate his choice by a written communication sent to the offeror at an address specified in the notice; and

(b) which consideration specified in the offer is to be taken as applying in default of his indicating a choice as aforesaid;

and the terms of the offer mentioned in subsection (2) shall be determined accordingly.

(4) Subsection (3) applies whether or not any time-limit or other conditions applicable to the choice under the terms of the offer can still be complied with; and if the consideration chosen by the holder of the shares—

(a) is not cash and the offeror is no longer able to provide it; or

(b) was to have been provided by a third party who is no longer bound or able to provide it,

the consideration shall be taken to consist of an amount of cash payable by the offeror which at the date of the notice is equivalent to the chosen consideration.

(5) At the end of six weeks from the date of the notice the offeror shall forthwith—

(a) send a copy of the notice to the company; and

(b) pay or transfer to the company the consideration for the shares to which the notice relates.

(6) If the shares to which the notice relates are registered the copy of the notice sent to the company under subsection (5)(a) shall be accompanied by an instrument of transfer executed on behalf of the shareholder by a person appointed by the offeror; and on receipt of that instrument the company shall register the offeror as the holder of those shares.

(7) If the shares to which the notice relates are transferable by the delivery of warrants or other instruments the copy of the notice sent to the company under subsection (5)(a) shall be accompanied by a statement to that effect; and the company shall on receipt of the statement issue the offeror with warrants or other instruments in respect of the shares and those already in issue in respect of the shares shall become void.

(8) Where the consideration referred to in paragraph (b) of subsection (5) consists of shares or securities to be allotted by the offeror the reference in that paragraph to the transfer of the consideration shall be construed as a reference to the allotment of the shares or securities to the company.

(9) Any sum received by a company under paragraph (b) of subsection (5) and any other consideration received under that paragraph shall be held by the company on trust for the person entitled to the shares in respect of which the sum or other consideration was received.

(10) Any sum received by a company under paragraph (b) of subsection (5), and any dividend or other sum accruing from any other consideration received by a company under that paragraph, shall be paid into a separate bank account, being an account the balance on which bears interest at an appropriate rate and can be withdrawn by such notice (if any) as is appropriate.

(11) Where after reasonable enquiry made at such intervals as are reasonable the person entitled to any consideration held on trust by virtue of subsection (9) cannot be found and

twelve years have elapsed since the consideration was received or the company is wound up the consideration (together with any interest, dividend or other benefit that has accrued from it) shall be paid into court.

(12) In relation to a company registered in Scotland, subsections (13) and (14) shall apply in place of subsection (11).

(13) Where after reasonable enquiry made at such intervals as are reasonable the person entitled to any consideration held on trust by virtue of subsection (9) cannot be found and twelve years have elapsed since the consideration was received or the company is wound up—

(*a*) the trust shall terminate;

(*b*) the company or, as the case may be, the liquidator shall sell any consideration other than cash and any benefit other than cash that has accrued from the consideration; and

(*c*) a sum representing—

(i) the consideration so far as it is cash;

(ii) the proceeds of any sale under paragraph (*b*) above; and

(iii) any interest, dividend ·or other benefit that has accrued from the consideration,

shall be deposited in the name of the Accountant of Court in a bank account such as is referred to in subsection (10) and the receipt for the deposit shall be transmitted to the Accountant of Court.

(14) Section 58 of the Bankruptcy (Scotland) Act 1985 (so far as consistent with this Act) shall apply with any necessary modifications to sums deposited under subsection (13) as that section applies to sums deposited under section 57(1)(*a*) of that Act.

(15) The expenses of any such enquiry as is mentioned in subsection (11) or (13) may be defrayed out of the money or other property held on trust for the person or persons to whom the enquiry relates.

Right of minority shareholder to be bought out by offeror

430A.—(1) If a takeover offer relates to all the shares in a company and at any time before the end of the period within which the offer can be accepted—

(*a*) the offeror has by virtue of acceptances of the offer acquired or contracted to acquire some (but not all) of the shares to which the offer relates; and

(*b*) those shares, with or without any other shares in the company which he has acquired or contracted to acquire, amount to not less than nine-tenths in value of all the shares in the company,

the holder of any shares to which the offer relates who has not accepted the offer may by a written communication addressed to the offeror require him to acquire those shares.

(2) If a takeover offer relates to shares of any class or classes and at any time before the end of the period within which the offer can be accepted—

(*a*) the offeror has by virtue of acceptances of the offer acquired or contracted to acquire some (but not all) of the shares of any class to which the offer relates; and

(*b*) those shares, with or without any other shares of that class which he has acquired or contracted to acquire, amount to not less than nine-tenths in value of all the shares of that class,

the holder of any shares of that class who has not accepted the offer may by a written communication addressed to the offeror require him to acquire those shares.

(3) Within one month of the time specified in subsection (1) or, as the case may be, subsection (2) the offeror shall give any shareholder who has not accepted the offer notice in the prescribed manner of the rights that are exercisable by him under that subsection; and if the notice is given before the end of the period mentioned in that subsection it shall state that the offer is still open for acceptance.

(4) A notice under subsection (3) may specify a period for the exercise of the rights conferred by this section and in that event the rights shall not be exercisable after the end of that period; but no such period shall end less than three months after the end of the period within which the offer can be accepted.

(5) Subsection (3) does not apply if the offeror has given the shareholder a notice in respect of the shares in question under section 429.

(6) If the offeror fails to comply with subsection (3) he and, if the offeror is a company, every officer of the company who is in default or to whose neglect the failure is attributable, shall be liable to a fine and, for continued contravention, to a daily default fine.

(7) If an offeror other than a company is charged with an offence for failing to comply with subsection (3) it is a defence for him to prove that he took all reasonable steps for securing compliance with that subsection.

Effect of requirement under s.430A

430B.—(1) The following provisions shall, subject to section 430C, have effect where a shareholder exercises his rights in respect of any shares under section 430A.

(2) The offeror shall be entitled and bound to acquire those shares on the terms of the offer or on such other terms as may be agreed.

(3) Where the terms of an offer are such as to give the holder of shares a choice of consideration the holder of the shares may indicate his choice when requiring the offeror to acquire them and the notice given to the holder under section 430A(3)—

(*a*) shall give particulars of the choice and of the rights conferred by this subsection; and

(*b*) may state which consideration specified in the offer is to be taken as applying in default of his indicating a choice;

and the terms of the offer mentioned in subsection (2) shall be determined accordingly.

(4) Subsection (3) applies whether or not any time-limit or other conditions applicable to the choice under the terms of the offer can still be complied with; and if the consideration chosen by the holder of the shares—

(*a*) is not cash and the offeror is no longer able to provide it; or

(*b*) was to have been provided by a third party who is no longer bound or able to provide it,

the consideration shall be taken to consist of an amount of cash payable by the offeror which at the date when the holder of the shares requires the offeror to acquire them is equivalent to the chosen consideration.

Applications to the court

430C.—(1) Where a notice is given under section 429 to the holder of any shares the court may, on an application made by him within six weeks from the date on which the notice was given—

(*a*) order that the offeror shall not be entitled and bound to acquire the shares; or

(*b*) specify terms of acquisition different from those of the offer.

(2) If an application to the court under subsection (1) is pending at the end of the period mentioned in subsection (5) of section 430 that subsection shall not have effect until the application has been disposed of.

(3) Where the holder of any shares exercises his rights under section 430A the court may, on an application made by him or the offeror, order that the terms on which the offeror is entitled and bound to acquire the shares shall be such as the court thinks fit.

(4) No order for costs or expenses shall be made against a shareholder making an application under subsection (1) or (3) unless the court considers—

(*a*) that the application was unnecessary, improper or vexatious; or

(*b*) that there has been unreasonable delay in making the application or unreasonable conduct on his part in conducting the proceedings on the application.

(5) Where a takeover offer has not been accepted to the extent necessary for entitling the offeror to give notices under subsection (1) or (2) of section 429 the court may, on the application of the offeror, make an order authorising him to give notices under that subsection if satisfied—

(*a*) that the offeror has after reasonable enquiry been unable to trace one or more of the persons holding shares to which the offer relates;

(*b*) that the shares which the offeror has acquired or contracted to acquire by virtue of acceptances of the offer, together with the shares held by the person or persons mentioned in paragraph (*a*), amount to not less than the minimum specified in that subsection; and

(*c*) that the consideration offered is fair and reasonable;

but the court shall not make an order under this subsection unless it considers that it is just and equitable to do so having regard, in particular, to the number of shareholders who have been traced but who have not accepted the offer.

Joint offers

430D.—(1) A takeover offer may be made by two or more persons jointly and in that event this Part of this Act has effect with the following modifications.

(2) The conditions for the exercise of the rights conferred by sections 429 and 430A shall be satisfied by the joint offerors acquiring or contracting to acquire the necessary shares jointly (as respects acquisitions by virtue of acceptances of the offer) and either jointly or separately (in other cases); and, subject to the following provisions, the rights and obligations

of the offeror under those sections and sections 430 and 430B shall be respectively joint rights and joint and several obligations of the joint offerors.

(3) It shall be a sufficient compliance with any provision of those sections requiring or authorising a notice or other document to be given or sent by or to the joint offerors that it is given or sent by or to any of them; but the statutory declaration required by section 429(4) shall be made by all of them and, in the case of a joint offeror being a company, signed by a director of that company.

(4) In sections 428, 430(8) and 430E references to the offeror shall be construed as references to the joint offerors or any of them.

(5) In section 430(6) and (7) references to the offeror shall be construed as references to the joint offerors or such of them as they may determine.

(6) In sections 430(4)(*a*) and 430B(4)(*a*) references to the offeror being no longer able to provide the relevant consideration shall be construed as references to none of the joint offerors being able to do so.

(7) In section 430C references to the offeror shall be construed as references to the joint offerors except that any application under subsection (3) or (5) may be made by any of them and the reference in subsection (5)(*a*) to the offeror having been unable to trace one or more of the persons holding shares shall be construed as a reference to none of the offerors having been able to do so.

Associates

430E.—(1) The requirement in section 428(1) that a takeover offer must extend to all the shares, or all the shares of any class or classes, in a company shall be regarded as satisfied notwithstanding that the offer does not extend to shares which associates of the offeror hold or have contracted to acquire; but, subject to subsection (2), shares which any such associate holds or has contracted to acquire, whether at the time when the offer is made or subsequently, shall be disregarded for the purposes of any reference in this Part of this Act to the shares to which a takeover offer relates.

(2) Where during the period within which a takeover offer can be accepted any associate of the offeror acquires or contracts to acquire any of the shares to which the offer relates, then, if the condition specified in subsection (8)(*a*) or (*b*) of section 429 is satisfied as respects those shares they shall be treated for the purposes of that section as shares to which the offer relates.

(3) In section 430A(1)(*b*) and (2)(*b*) the reference to shares which the offeror has acquired or contracted to acquire shall include a reference to shares which any associate of his has acquired or contracted to acquire.

(4) In this section "associate", in relation to an offeror means—

(*a*) a nominee of the offeror;

(*b*) a holding company, subsidiary or fellow subsidiary of the offeror or a nominee of such a holding company, subsidiary or fellow subsidiary;

(*c*) a body corporate in which the offeror is substantially interested; or

(*d*) any person who is, or is a nominee of, a party to an agreement with the offeror for the acquisition of, or of an interest in, the shares which are the subject of the takeover offer, being an agreement which includes provisions imposing obligations or restrictions such as are mentioned in section 204(2)(*a*).

(5) For the purposes of subsection (4)(*b*) a company is a fellow subsidiary of another body corporate if both are subsidiaries of the same body corporate but neither is a subsidiary of the other.

(6) For the purposes of subsection (4)(*c*) an offeror has a substantial interest in a body corporate if—

(*a*) that body or its directors are accustomed to act in accordance with his directions or instructions; or

(*b*) he is entitled to exercise or control the exercise of one-third or more of the voting power at general meetings of that body.

(7) Subsections (5) and (6) of section 204 shall apply to subsection (4)(*d*) above as they apply to that section and subsections (3) and (4) of section 203 shall apply for the purposes of subsection (6) above as they apply for the purposes of subsection (2)(*b*) of that section.

(8) Where the offeror is an individual his associates shall also include his spouse and any minor child or step-child of his.

Convertible securities

430F.—(1) For the purposes of this Part of this Act securities of a company shall be treated as shares in the company if they are convertible into or entitle the holder to subscribe for such shares; and references to the holder of shares or a shareholder shall be construed accordingly.

(2) Subsection (1) shall not be construed as requiring any securities to be treated—

(*a*) as shares of the same class as those into which they are convertible or for which the holder is entitled to subscribe; or

(*b*) as shares of the same class as other securities by reason only that the shares into which they are convertible or for which the holder is entitled to subscribe are of the same class.

GENERAL NOTE

This schedule substitutes new provisions for ss.428–30 of the Companies Act 1985 (formerly s.209 of the Companies Act 1948). The old provisions enabled an offeror company that had secured acceptances from the holders of at least nine-tenths in value of the target company's shares to divest the dissentients of their shares on the same terms. Conversely they enabled the dissentients to require the offeror company to acquire their shares once the 90 per cent. threshold was crossed.

The new provisions do not alter the essential features of the existing law. However, they strengthen the position of non-assenting shareholders in certain respects, supply a more detailed account of the procedure to be followed, and reflect modern developments in takeover practice.

Section 429(3): Under the old law the offeror company had to give notice of compulsory acquisition (if sought) during the two months after the four months after the making of the offer. Now notice is to be given during the two months after the reaching of the 90 per cent. threshold.

Section 429(8): The effect is that shares acquired in a private bargain at a price in excess of the offer price may be reckoned as contributing to the attainment of the 90 per cent. target, provided the offer price is revised upwards to bring it into line with the private bargain price.

Section 430C(4): This provision is designed to reduce the financial risk for a dissentient shareholder who applies to the court in the hope that it will disallow compulsory divestment or require it to proceed on terms different from those offered.

Section 430E(1): The effect of this provision is that shares acquired by an "associate" as defined in subs. (4)—not just a subsidiary—of the offeror are not to be reckoned as contributing to the attainment of the 90 per cent. target, unless the conditions laid down in s.429(8) are satisfied (*i.e.* the benefit of any higher price must be extended to dissentient shareholders).

Section 182   SCHEDULE 13

DISCLOSURE OF INFORMATION

1. In section 133(2)(*a*) of the Fair Trading Act 1973 after the words "the Telecommunications Act 1984" there shall be inserted the words "or Chapter XIV of Part I of the Financial Services Act 1986".

2. In section 41(1)(*a*) of the Restrictive Trade Practices Act 1976 after the words "the Telecommunications Act 1984" there shall be inserted the words "or Chapter XIV of Part I of the Financial Services Act 1986".

3.—(1) In section 19 of the Banking Act 1979 after subsection (2) there shall be inserted—

"(2A) Nothing in subsection (1) above prohibits the disclosure of information by the Bank to any person specified in the first column of the following Table if the Bank considers—

(*a*) that the disclosure would enable or assist the Bank to discharge its functions under this Act; or

(*b*) that it would enable or assist that person to discharge the functions specified in relation to him in the second column of that Table.

TABLE

Person	*Functions*
The Secretary of State.	Functions under the Insurance Companies Act 1982 or the Financial Services Act 1986.

Person	*Functions*
The Chief Registrar of friendly societies or the Registrar of Friendly Societies for Northern Ireland.	Functions under the Financial Services Act 1986 or under the enactments relating to friendly societies.
A designated agency or transferee body or the competent authority (within the meaning of the Financial Services Act 1986).	Functions under the Financial Services Act 1986.
A recognised self-regulating organisation, recognised professional body, recognised investment exchange, recognised clearing house or recognised self-regulating organisation for friendly societies (within the meaning of the Financial Services Act 1986).	Functions in its capacity as an organisation, body, exchange or clearing house recognised under the Financial Services Act 1986.
A person appointed or authorised to exercise any powers under section 94, 106 or 177 of the Financial Services Act 1986.	Functions arising from his appointment or authorisation under that section.
The body administering a scheme under section 54 of or paragraph 18 of Schedule 11 to the Financial Services Act 1986.	Functions under the scheme.

(2B) Nothing in subsection (1) above prohibits the disclosure by a person specified in the first column of the Table in subsection (2A) above of information obtained by him by virtue of a disclosure authorised by that subsection if he makes the disclosure with the consent of the Bank and for the purpose of enabling or assisting himself to discharge any functions specified in relation to him in the second column of that Table; and before deciding whether to give its consent to such a disclosure by any person the Bank shall take account of any representations made by him as to the desirability of or the necessity for the disclosure.".

(2) For subsection (6) of that section there shall be substituted—

"(6) Nothing in subsection (1) above prohibits the disclosure of information by or with the consent of the Bank for the purpose of enabling or assisting an authority in a country or territory outside the United Kingdom to exercise functions corresponding to those of the Bank under this Act, or to those of the Secretary of State under the Insurance Companies Act 1982 or the Financial Services Act 1986 or to those of the competent authority under the said Act of 1986 or any other functions in connection with rules of law corresponding to the provisions of the Company Securities (Insider Dealing) Act 1985 or Part VII of the said Act of 1986.".

4. In section 20(4) of that Act—

(a) for the words "in a country or territory outside the United Kingdom" there shall be substituted the words "in a member State other than the United Kingdom"; and

(b) in paragraph (b) for the words "subsections (4) to (6)" there shall be substituted the words "subsections (2A), (2B) and (4) to (6)".

5. At the end of section 19(3) of the Competition Act 1980 there shall be inserted—

"(h) Chapter XIV of Part I of the Financial Services Act 1986".

6. For subsections (1) and (2) of section 47A of the Insurance Companies Act 1982 there shall be substituted—

"(1) Subject to the following provisions of this section, no information relating to the business or other affairs of any person which has been obtained under section 44(2) to (4) above shall be disclosed without the consent of the person from whom the information was obtained and, if different, the person to whom it relates.

(2) Subsection (1) above shall not preclude the disclosure of information to any person who is a competent authority for the purposes of section 449 of the Companies Act 1985.

(2A) Subsection (1) above shall not preclude the disclosure of information as mentioned in any of the paragraphs except (m) of subsection (1) of section 180 of the Financial Services Act 1986 or in subsection (3) or (4) of that section or as mentioned in section 449(1) of the Companies Act 1985.

(2B) Subsection (1) above shall not preclude the disclosure of any such information as is mentioned in section 180(5) of the Financial Services Act 1986 by any person who by virtue of that section is not precluded by section 179 of that Act from disclosing it."

7. After subsection (1) of section 437 of the Companies Act 1985 there shall be inserted—

"(1A) Any persons who have been appointed under section 431 or 432 may at any time and, if the Secretary of State directs them to do so, shall inform him of any matters coming to their knowledge as a result of their investigations.";

and subsection (2) of section 433 of that Act shall be omitted.

8. In section 446 of that Act—

(a) in subsection (3) for the words "to 436" there shall be substituted the words "to 437"; and

(b) subsection (5) shall be omitted.

9.—(1) In subsection (1) of section 449 of that Act—

(a) for paragraphs (a) and (b) there shall be substituted—

"(a) with a view to the institution of or otherwise for the purposes of criminal proceedings;".

(b) for paragraph (d) there shall be substituted—

"(d) for the purpose of enabling or assisting the Secretary of State to exercise any of his functions under this Act, the Insider Dealing Act, the Prevention of Fraud (Investments) Act 1958, the Insurance Companies Act 1982, the Insolvency Act 1986, the Company Directors Disqualification Act 1986 or the Financial Services Act 1986.

(dd) for the purpose of enabling or assisting the Department of Economic Development for Northern Ireland to exercise any powers conferred on it by the enactments relating to companies or insolvency or for the purpose of enabling or assisting any inspector appointed by it under the enactments relating to companies to discharge his functions";

(c) after paragraph (e) there shall be inserted—

"(f) for the purpose of enabling or assisting the Bank of England to discharge its functions under the Banking Act 1979 or any other functions,

(g) for the purpose of enabling or assisting the Deposit Protection Board to discharge its functions under that Act,

(h) for any purpose mentioned in section 180(1)(b), (e), (h), (n) or (p) of the Financial Services Act 1986,

(i) for the purpose of enabling or assisting the Industrial Assurance Commissioner or the Industrial Assurance Commissioner for Northern Ireland to discharge his functions under the enactments relating to industrial assurance,

(j) for the purpose of enabling or assisting the Insurance Brokers Registration Council to discharge its functions under the Insurance Brokers (Registration) Act 1977,

(k) for the purpose of enabling or assisting an official receiver to discharge his functions under the enactments relating to insolvency or for the purpose of enabling or assisting a body which is for the time being a recognised professional body for the purposes of section 391 of the Insolvency Act 1986 to discharge its functions as such,

(l) with a view to the institution of, or otherwise for the purposes of, any disciplinary proceedings relating to the exercise by a solicitor, auditor, accountant, valuer or actuary of his professional duties,

(m) for the purpose of enabling or assisting an authority in a country or territory outside the United Kingdom to exercise corresponding supervisory functions.".

(2) After subsection (1) of that section there shall be inserted—

"(1A) In subsection (1) above 'corresponding supervisory functions' means functions corresponding to those of the Secretary of State or the competent authority under the Financial Services Act 1986 or to those of the Secretary of State under the Insurance Companies Act 1982 or to those of the Bank of England under the Banking Act 1979 or any other functions in connection with rules of law corresponding to the provisions of the Insider Dealing Act or Part VII of the Financial Services Act 1986.

(1B) Subject to subsection (1C), subsection (1) shall not preclude publication or disclosure for the purpose of enabling or assisting any public or other authority for the time being designated for the purposes of this section by the Secretary of State by an order in a statutory instrument to discharge any functions which are specified in the order.

(1C) An order under subsection (1B) designating an authority for the purpose of that subsection may—

(a) impose conditions subject to which the publication or disclosure of any information or document is permitted by that subsection; and (*b*) otherwise restrict the circumstances in which that subsection permits publication or disclosure.

    (1D) Subsection (1) shall not preclude the publication or disclosure of any such information as is mentioned in section 180(5) of the Financial Services Act 1986 by any person who by virtue of that section is not precluded by section 179 of that Act from disclosing it."

(3) For subsection (3) of that section (competent authorities) there shall be substituted—

    "(3) For the purposes of this section each of the following is a competent authority—

    (*a*) the Secretary of State,

    (*b*) the Department of Economic Development for Northern Ireland and any officer of that Department,

    (*c*) an inspector appointed under this Part by the Secretary of State,

    (*d*) the Treasury and any officer of the Treasury,

    (*e*) the Bank of England and any officer or servant of the Bank,

    (*f*) the Lord Advocate,

    (*g*) the Director of Public Prosecutions, and the Director of Public Prosecutions for Northern Ireland,

    (*h*) any designated agency or transferee body within the meaning of the Financial Services Act 1986 and any officer or servant of such an agency or body,

    (*i*) any person appointed or authorised to exercise any powers under section 94, 106 or 177 of the Financial Services Act 1986 and any officer or servant of such a person,

    (*j*) the body administering a scheme under section 54 of or paragraph 18 of Schedule 11 to that Act and any officer or servant of such a body,

    (*k*) the Chief Registrar of friendly societies and the Registrar of Friendly Societies for Northern Ireland and any officer or servant of either of them,

    (*l*) the Industrial Assurance Commissioner and the Industrial Assurance Commissioner for Northern Ireland and any officer of either of them,

    (*m*) any constable,

    (*n*) any procurator fiscal.

    (4) A statutory instrument containing an order under subsection (1B) is subject to annulment in pursuance of a resolution of either House of Parliament.".

10. After section 451 of that Act there shall be inserted—

"Disclosure of information by Secretary of State

    451A. The Secretary of State may, if he thinks fit, disclose any information obtained under this Part of this Act—

    (*a*) to any person who is a competent authority for the purposes of section 449, or

    (*b*) in any circumstances in which or for any purpose for which that section does not preclude the disclosure of the information to which it applies."

11. After Article 430(1) of the Companies (Northern Ireland) Order 1986 there shall be inserted—

    "(1A) Any persons who have been appointed under Article 424 or 425 may at any time and, if the Department directs them to do so shall, inform it of any matters coming to their knowledge as a result of their investigation.";

and Article 426(2) of that Order shall be omitted.

12. In Article 439 of that Order—

(*a*) in paragraph (3) for the words "to 429" there shall be substituted the words "to 430"; and

(*b*) paragraph (5) shall be omitted.

13.—(1) In paragraph (1) of Article 442 of that Order—

(*a*) for sub-paragraphs (*a*) and (*b*) there shall be substituted—

    "(*a*) with a view to the institution of or otherwise for the purposes of criminal proceedings;";

(*b*) for sub-paragraph (*d*) there shall be substituted—

    "(*d*) for the purpose of enabling or assisting the Department to exercise any of its functions under this Order, the Insider Dealing Order or the Prevention of Fraud (Investments) Act (Northern Ireland) 1940;

    (*dd*) for the purpose of enabling or assisting the Secretary of State to exercise any functions conferred on him by the enactments relating to companies or insolvency, the Prevention of Fraud (Investments) Act 1958, the Insurance Com-

panies Act 1982, or the Financial Services Act 1986, or for the purpose of
enabling or assisting any inspector appointed by him under the enactments
relating to companies to discharge his functions";

(*c*) after sub-paragraph (*e*) there shall be inserted—

"(*f*) for the purposes of enabling or assisting the Bank of England to discharge its
functions under the Banking Act 1979 or any other functions;

(*g*) for the purposes of enabling or assisting the Deposit Protection Board to
discharge its functions under that Act;

(*h*) for any purpose mentioned in section 180(1)(*b*), (*e*), (*h*), (*n*) or (*p*) of the
Financial Services Act 1986;

(*i*) for the purpose of enabling or assisting the Industrial Assurance Commissioner
for Northern Ireland or the Industrial Assurance Commissioner in Great Britain
to discharge his functions under the enactments relating to industrial assurance;

(*j*) for the purpose of enabling or assisting the Insurance Brokers Registration
Council to discharge its functions under the Insurance Brokers (Registration)
Act 1977;

(*k*) for the purpose of enabling or assisting the official assignee to discharge his
functions under the enactments relating to companies or bankruptcy;

(*l*) with a view to the institution of, or otherwise for the purposes of, any disciplinary
proceedings relating to the exercise by a solicitor, auditor, accountant, valuer or
actuary of his professional duties;

(*m*) for the purpose of enabling or assisting an authority in a country or territory
outside the United Kingdom to exercise corresponding supervisory functions.".

(2) After paragraph (1) of that Article there shall be inserted—

"(1A) In paragraph (1) "corresponding supervisory functions" means functions
corresponding to those of the Secretary of State or the competent authority under
the Financial Services Act 1986 or to those of the Secretary of State under the
Insurance Companies Act 1982 or to those of the Bank of England under the
Banking Act 1979 or any other functions in connection with rules of law corresponding to the provisions of the Insider Dealing Order or Part VII of the Financial
Services Act 1986.

(1B) Subject to paragraph (1C), paragraph (1) shall not preclude publication or
disclosure for the purpose of enabling or assisting any public or other authority for
the time being designated for the purposes of this Article by an order made by the
Department to discharge any functions which are specified in the order.

(1C) An order under paragraph (1B) designating an authority for the purpose of
that paragraph may—

(*a*) impose conditions subject to which the publication or disclosure of any
information or document is permitted by that paragraph; and

(*b*) otherwise restrict the circumstances in which that paragraph permits
publication or disclosure.

(1D) Paragraph (1) shall not preclude the publication or disclosure of any such
information as is mentioned in section 180(5) of the Financial Services Act 1986 by
any person who by virtue of that section is not precluded by section 179 of that Act
from disclosing it."

(3) For paragraph (3) of that Article (competent authorities) there shall be substituted—

"(3) For the purposes of this Article each of the following is a competent
authority—

(*a*) the Department and any officer of the Department,

(*b*) the Secretary of State,

(*c*) an inspector appointed under this Part by the Department,

(*d*) the Department of Finance and Personnel and any officer of that
Department;

(*e*) the Treasury and any officer of the Treasury,

(*f*) the Bank of England and any officer or servant of the Bank,

(*g*) the Lord Advocate,

(*h*) the Director of Public Prosecutions for Northern Ireland and the
Director of Public Prosecutions in England and Wales,

(*i*) any designated agency or transferee body within the meaning of the
Financial Services Act 1986 and any officer or servant of such an agency
or body,

(*j*) any person appointed or authorised to exercise any powers under
section 94, 106 or 177 of the Financial Services Act 1986 and any officer
or servant of such a person,

(k) the body administering a scheme under section 54 of or paragraph 18 of Schedule 11 to that Act and any officer or servant of such a body,

(l) the Registrar of Friendly Societies and the Chief Registrar of friendly societies in Great Britain and any officer or servant of either of them,

(m) the Industrial Assurance Commissioner for Northern Ireland and the Industrial Assurance Commissioner in Great Britain and any officer of either of them,

(n) any constable,

(o) any procurator fiscal.

(4) An order under paragraph (1B) is subject to negative resolution."

14. After Article 444 of that order there shall be inserted—

"Disclosure of information by Department

444A. The Department may, if it thinks fit, disclose any information obtained under this Part—

(a) to any person who is a competent authority for the purposes of Article 442, or

(b) in any circumstances in which or for any purpose for which that Article does not preclude the disclosure of the information to which it applies.".

Section 189   SCHEDULE 14

RESTRICTION OF REHABILITATION OF OFFENDERS ACT 1974

PART I

EXEMPTED PROCEEDINGS

1. Any proceedings with respect to a decision or proposed decision of the Secretary of State or a designated agency—

(a) refusing, withdrawing or suspending an authorisation;

(b) refusing an application under section 28(5) of this Act;

(c) giving a direction under section 59 of this Act or refusing an application for consent or for the variation of a consent under that section;

(d) exercising a power under Chapter VI of Part I of this Act or refusing an application for the rescission or variation of a prohibition or requirement imposed under that Chapter;

(e) refusing to make or revoking an order declaring a collective investment scheme to be an authorised unit trust scheme or a recognised scheme.

2. Any proceedings with respect to a decision or proposed decision of a recognised self-regulating organisation—

(a) refusing or suspending a person's membership of the organisation;

(b) expelling a member of the organisation;

(c) exercising a power of the organisation for purposes corresponding to those of Chapter VI of Part I of this Act.

3.—(1) Any proceedings with respect to a decision or proposed decision of a recognised professional body—

(a) refusing or suspending a person's membership of the body;

(b) expelling a member of the body.

(2) Any proceedings with respect to a decision or proposed decision of a recognised professional body or of any other body or person having functions in respect of the enforcement of the recognised professional body's rules relating to the carrying on of investment business—

(a) exercising a power for purposes corresponding to those of Chapter VI of Part I of this Act;

(b) refusing, suspending or withdrawing a certificate issued for the purposes of Part I of this Act.

4. Any proceedings with respect to a decision or proposed decision of the competent authority under Part IV of this Act refusing an application for listing or to discontinue or suspend the listing of any securities.

5. Any proceedings with respect to a decision or proposed decision of the Chief Registrar of friendly societies, the Registrar of Friendly Societies for Northern Ireland or a transferee body, exercising a power exercisable by virtue of paragraph 23 of Schedule 11 to this Act or

refusing an application for the rescission or variation of a prohibition or requirement imposed in the exercise of such a power.

6. Any proceedings with respect to a decision or proposed decision of a recognised self-regulating organisation for friendly societies—

(*a*) refusing or suspending a society's membership of the organisation;

(*b*) expelling a member of the organisation;

(*c*) exercising a power of the organisation for purposes corresponding to those for which powers are exercisable by the Registrar by virtue of paragraph 23 of Schedule 11 to this Act.

PART II

EXEMPTED QUESTIONS

Person putting question	Individual to whom question relates
1. The Secretary of State or a designated agency.	(*a*) An authorised person. (*b*) An applicant for authorisation under section 26 of this Act. (*c*) A person whose authorisation is suspended. (*d*) The operator or trustee of a recognised scheme or a collective investment scheme in respect of which a notice has been given by the operator under section 87(3) or an application made under section 88 of this Act. (*e*) An individual who is an associate of a person (whether or not an individual) described in paragraph (*a*), (*b*), (*c*) or (*d*) above.
2. A recognised self-regulating organisation or recognised professional body.	(*a*) A member of the organisation or body. (*b*) An applicant for membership of the organisation or body. (*c*) A person whose membership of the organisation or body is suspended. (*d*) An individual who is an associate of a person (whether or not an individual) described in paragraph (*a*), (*b*) or (*c*) above.
3. A recognised professional body.	(*a*) A person certified by the body. (*b*) An applicant for certification by the body. (*c*) A person whose certification by the body is suspended. (*d*) An individual who is an associate of a person (whether or not an individual) described in paragraph (*a*), (*b*) or (*c*) above.
4. A person (whether or not an individual) described in paragraph 1(*a*), (*b*), (*c*) or (*d*), paragraph 2(*a*), (*b*) or (*c*) or paragraph 3(*a*), (*b*) or (*c*) above.	An individual who is or is seeking to become an associate of the person in column 1.
5. The competent authority or any other person.	An individual from or in respect of whom information is sought in connection with an application for listing under Part IV of this Act.
6. The competent authority.	An individual who is or is seeking to become an associate of the issuer of securities listed under Part IV of this Act and from or in respect of whom information is sought which the issuer of the securities is required to furnish under listing rules.

Person putting question	*Individual to whom question relates*
7. The Chief Registrar of friendly societies, the Registrar of Friendly Societies for Northern Ireland or a transferee body.	An individual who is an associate of a society which is authorised under section 23 of this Act.
8. A recognised self-regulating organisation for friendly societies.	An individual who is an associate of a member or an applicant for membership of the organisation or of a society whose membership of the organisation is suspended.

PART III

EXEMPTED ACTIONS

Person taking action	*Exempted action*
1. The Secretary of State, a designated agency, a recognised self-regulating organisation, a recognised professional body, any other body or person mentioned in paragraph 3(2) of Part I of this Schedule or the competent authority.	Any such decision or proposed decision as is mentioned in Part I of this Schedule.
2. A person (whether or not an individual) described in paragraph 1(*a*), (*b*), (*c*) or (*d*), paragraph 2(*a*), (*b*) or (*c*) or paragraph 3(*a*), (*b*) or (*c*) of Part II of this Schedule.	Dismissing or excluding an individual from being or becoming an associate of the person in column 1.
3. The issuer of securities listed or subject to an application for listing under Part IV of this Act.	Dismissing or excluding an individual from being or becoming an associate of the issuer.
4. The Chief Registrar of friendly societies, the Registrar of Friendly Societies for Northern Ireland, a transferee body or a recognised self-regulating organisation for friendly societies.	Any such decision or proposed decision as is mentioned in Part I of this Schedule.

PART IV

SUPPLEMENTAL

1. In Part I of this Schedule "proceedings" includes any proceedings within the meaning of section 4 of the Rehabilitation of Offenders Act 1974.

2. In Parts II and III of this Schedule—
   (*a*) references to an applicant for authorisation, membership or certification are references to an applicant who has not yet been informed of the decision on his application;
   (*b*) references to an application for listing under Part IV of this Act are references to an application the decision on which has not yet been communicated to the applicant and which is not taken by virtue of section 144(5) of this Act to have been refused.

3. Paragraph 1(*d*) of Part II of this Schedule and so much of paragraph 1(*e*) as relates to it—
   (*a*) apply only if the question is put to elicit information for the purpose of determining whether the operator or trustee is a fit and proper person to act as operator or trustee of the scheme in question;
   (*b*) apply in the case of a scheme in respect of which a notice has been given under subsection (3) of section 87 only until the end of the period within which the operator may receive a notification from the Secretary of State under that subsection or, if earlier, the receipt by him of such a notification;

(*c*) apply in the case of a scheme in respect of which an application has been made under section 88 only until the applicant has been informed of the decision on the application.

SCHEDULE 15

TRANSITIONAL PROVISIONS

Interim authorisation

1.—(1) If before such day as is appointed for the purposes of this paragraph by an order made by the Secretary of State a person has applied—
   (*a*) for membership of any body which on that day is a recognised self-regulating organisation; or
   (*b*) for authorisation by the Secretary of State,
and the application has not been determined before the day on which section 3 of this Act comes into force, that person shall, subject to sub-paragraphs (2), (3) and (4) below, be treated until the determination of the application as if he had been granted an authorisation by the Secretary of State.

(2) Sub-paragraph (1) above does not apply to a person who immediately before the day on which section 3 of this Act comes into force is prohibited by the Prevention of Fraud (Investments) Act 1958 (in this Schedule referred to as "the previous Act") from carrying on the business of dealing in securities—
   (*a*) by reason of the refusal or revocation at any time before that day of a licence under that Act; or
   (*b*) by reason of the revocation at any time before that day of an order declaring him to be an exempted dealer.

(3) If a person who has made any such application as is mentioned in sub-paragraph (1) above has before the day on which section 3 of this Act comes into force been served with a notice under section 6 or 16(3) of the previous Act (proposed refusal or revocation of licence or proposed revocation of exemption order) but the refusal or revocation to which the notice relates has not taken place before that day—
   (*a*) the provisions of that Act with respect to the refusal or revocation of a licence or the revocation of an order under section 16 of that Act shall continue to apply to him until the application mentioned in sub-paragraph (1) above is determined; and
   (*b*) that sub-paragraph shall cease to apply to him if before the determination of the application mentioned in that sub-paragraph his application for a licence under that Act is refused, his licence under that Act is revoked or the order declaring him to be an exempted dealer under that Act is revoked.

(4) Notwithstanding sub-paragraph (1) above section 102(1)(*a*) of this Act shall not apply to a person entitled to carry on investment business by virtue of that sub-paragraph but the Secretary of State may make available for public inspection the information with respect to the holders of principal's licences mentioned in section 9 of the previous Act, any information in his possession by virtue of section 15(3) or (4) of that Act and the information mentioned in section 16(4) of that Act.

(5) Notwithstanding subsection (2) of section 3 of the previous Act a licence granted under that section before the day on which section 3 of this Act comes into force shall, unless revoked under section 6 of that Act, continue in force until that day.

Return of fees on pending applications

2. Any fee paid in respect of an application under section 3 of the previous Act which is pending on the day on which that Act is repealed shall be repaid to the applicant.

Deposits and undertakings

3. The repeal of section 4 of the previous Act shall not affect the operation of that section in a case where—
   (*a*) a sum deposited in accordance with that section has become payable as provided in subsection (2) of that section before the date on which the repeal takes effect; or
   (*b*) a sum has become payable before that date in pursuance of an undertaking given under subsection (4) of that section,

but, subject as aforesaid, any sum deposited under that section may be withdrawn by the depositor on application to the Accountant General of the Supreme Court and any undertaking given under that section shall be discharged.

Interim recognition of professional bodies

4.—(1) If on an application made under section 17 of this Act it appears to the Secretary of State that any of the requirements of section 18(3) of this Act or paragraphs 2 to 6 of Schedule 3 to this Act are not satisfied he may in accordance with this paragraph make a recognition order under section 18 of this Act ("an interim recognition order") notwithstanding that all or any of those requirements are not satisfied.

(2) The Secretary of State may, subject to sub-paragraphs (3) and (4) below, make an interim recognition order if he is satisfied—

   (a) that the applicant proposes to adopt rules and practices and to make arrangements which will satisfy such of the requirements mentioned in sub-paragraph (1) above as are not satisfied;

   (b) that it is not practicable for those rules, practices and arrangements to be brought into effect before the date on which section 3 of this Act comes into force but that they will be brought into effect within a reasonable time thereafter; and

   (c) that in the meantime the applicant will enforce its existing rules in such a way, and issue such guidance, as will in respect of investment business of any kind carried on by persons certified by it (or by virtue of paragraph 5 below treated as certified by it) afford to investors protection as nearly as may be equivalent to that provided as respects investment business of that kind by the rules and regulations under Chapter V of Part I of this Act.

(3) Where the requirements which are not satisfied consist of or include those mentioned in paragraph 2 of Schedule 3 to this Act an application for an interim recognition order shall be accompanied by—

   (a) a list of the persons to whom the applicant proposes to issue certificates for the purposes of Part I of this Act; and

   (b) particulars of the criteria adopted for determining the persons included in the list;

and the Secretary of State shall not make the order unless it appears to him that those criteria conform as nearly as may be to the conditions mentioned in that paragraph and that the applicant will, until the requirements of that paragraph are satisfied, have arrangements for securing that no person is certified by it (or by virtue of paragraph 5 below treated as certified by it) except in accordance with those criteria and for the effective monitoring of continued compliance by those persons with those criteria.

(4) Where the requirements which are not satisfied consist of or include that mentioned in paragraph 6 of Schedule 3 to this Act, the Secretary of State shall not make an interim recognition order unless it appears to him that the applicant will, until that requirement is satisfied, take such steps for complying with it as are reasonably practicable.

(5) An application for an interim recognition order shall be accompanied by a copy of the rules and by particulars of the practices and arrangements referred to in sub-paragraph (2)(a) above.

(6) An interim recognition order shall not be revocable but shall cease to be in force at the end of such period as is specified in it; and that period shall be such as will in the opinion of the Secretary of State allow a reasonable time for the rules, practices and arrangements mentioned in sub-paragraph (5) above to be brought into effect.

(7) The Secretary of State may on the application of the body to which an interim recognition order relates extend the period specified in it if that body satisfies him—

   (a) that there are sufficient reasons why the rules, practices and arrangements mentioned in sub-paragraph (5) above cannot be brought into effect by the end of that period; and

   (b) that those rules, practices and arrangements, or other rules, practices and arrangements which satisfy the requirements mentioned in sub-paragraph (2)(a) above and of which copies or particulars are furnished to the Secretary of State, will be brought into effect within a reasonable time thereafter;

but not more than one application shall be made by a body under this sub-paragraph.

(8) A recognition order under section 18 of this Act shall cease to be an interim recognition order if before it ceases to be in force—

   (a) the rules, practices and arrangements of which copies or particulars were furnished to the Secretary of State under sub-paragraph (5) or (7)(b) above are brought into effect; or

   (b) the Secretary of State certifies that other rules, practices and arrangements which have been brought into effect comply with the requirements mentioned in sub-paragraph (1) above.

(9) In this paragraph references to the adoption of rules or the making of arrangements include references to taking such other steps as may be necessary for bringing them into effect.

Interim authorisation by recognised professional bodies

5.—(1) If at the time when an interim recognition order is made in respect of a professional body that body is unable to issue certificates for the purposes of this Act, any person who at that time is included in the list furnished by that body to the Secretary of State in accordance with paragraph 4(3)(*a*) above shall be treated for the purposes of this Act as a person certified by that body.

(2) If at any time while an interim recognition order is in force in respect of a professional body and before the body is able to issue certificates as mentioned in sub-paragraph (1) above the body notifies the Secretary of State that a person not included in that list satisfies the criteria of which particulars were furnished by the body in accordance with paragraph 4(3)(*b*) above, that person shall, on receipt of the notification by the Secretary of State, be treated for the purposes of this Act as a person certified by that body.

(3) If at any time while an interim recognition order is in force in respect of a professional body it appears to the body—

(*a*) that a person treated by virtue of sub-paragraph (1) or (2) above as certified by it has ceased (after the expiration of such transitional period, if any, as appears to the body to be appropriate) to satisfy the criteria mentioned in sub-paragraph (2) above; or

(*b*) that any such person should for any other reason cease to be treated as certified by it,

it shall forthwith give notice of that fact to the Secretary of State and the person in question shall, on receipt of that notification by the Secretary of State, cease to be treated as certified by that body.

(4) Where by virtue of this paragraph a partnership is treated as certified by a recognised professional body section 15(3) of this Act shall apply as it applies where a certificate has in fact been issued to a partnership.

(5) Where by virtue of this paragraph any persons are treated as certified by a recognised professional body the requirements of paragraph 2 of Schedule 3 to this Act so far as relating to the retention by a person of a certificate issued by that body and the requirements of paragraph 4 of that Schedule shall apply to the body as if the references to persons certified by it included references to persons treated as certified.

Power of recognised professional body to make rules required by this Act

6.—(1) Where a recognised professional body regulates the practice of a profession in the exercise of statutory powers the matters in respect of which rules can be made in the exercise of those powers shall, if they would not otherwise do so, include any matter in respect of which rules are required to be made—

(*a*) so that the recognition order in respect of that body can cease to be an interim recognition order; or

(*b*) where the recognition order was not, or has ceased to be, an interim recognition order, so that the body can continue to be a recognised professional body.

(2) Rules made by virtue of this paragraph may in particular make provision for the issue, withdrawal and suspension of certificates for the purposes of this Act and the making of charges in respect of their issue and may accordingly apply to persons who are, or are to be, certified or treated as certified by the body in question whether or not they are persons in relation to whom rules could be made apart from this paragraph.

(3) Rules made by virtue of this paragraph may make different provision for different cases.

(4) The Secretary of State may at the request of a recognised professional body by order extend, modify or exclude any statutory provision relating to the regulation of the conduct, practice, or discipline of members of that body to such extent as he thinks necessary or expedient in consequence of the provisions of this paragraph; and any order made by virtue of this sub-paragraph shall be subject to annulment in pursuance of a resolution of either House of Parliament.

Notice of commencement of business

7. In the case of a person who is carrying on investment business in the United Kingdom on the day on which section 31 of this Act comes into force, section 32 of this Act shall have effect as if it required him to give the notice referred to in that section forthwith.

Advertisements

8.—(1) So long as Part III of the Companies Act 1985 remains in force section 57 of this Act shall not apply—
  (*a*) in relation to any distribution of a prospectus to which section 56 of that Act applies or would apply if not excluded by subsection (5)(*b*) of that section or to which section 72 of that Act applies or would apply if not excluded by subsection (6)(*b*) of that section or by section 76 of that Act, or in relation to any distribution of a document relating to securities of a corporation incorporated in Great Britain which is not a registered company, being a document which—
     (i) would, if the corporation were a registered company, be a prospectus to which section 56 of that Act applies or would apply if not excluded as aforesaid, and
     (ii) contains all the matters and is issued with the consents which, by virtue of sections 72 to 75 of that Act, it would have to contain and be issued with if the corporation were a company incorporated outside Great Britain and the document were a prospectus issued by that company;
  (*b*) in relation to any issue of a form of application for shares in, or debentures of, a corporation, together with—
     (i) a prospectus which complies with the requirements of section 56 of that Act or is not required to comply with them because excluded by subsection (5)(*b*) of that section, or complies with the requirements of Chapter II of Part III of that Act relating to prospectuses and is not issued in contravention of sections 74 and 75 of that Act, or
     (ii) in the case of a corporation incorporated in Great Britain which is not a registered company, a document containing all the matters and issued with the consents mentioned in sub-paragraph (*a*)(ii) of this paragraph, or in connection with a bona fide invitation to a person to enter into an underwriting agreement with respect to the shares or debentures.

(2) The provisions of this paragraph shall apply to Northern Ireland with the substitution for the references to Part III and Chapter II of Part III of the Companies Act 1985 of references to Part IV and Chapter II of Part IV of the Companies (Northern Ireland) Order 1986, for the references to sections 56, 56(5)(*b*), 72, 72(6)(*b*), 74, 76 and 72 to 75 of the Companies Act 1985 of references to Articles 66, 66(5)(*b*), 82, 82(6)(*b*), 84, 86 and 82 to 85 of the Companies (Northern Ireland) Order 1986, for the references to a corporation incorporated in Great Britain of references to a corporation incorporated in Northern Ireland and for the reference to a company incorporated outside Great Britain of a reference to a company incorporated outside the United Kingdom.

Authorised unit trust schemes

9.—(1) Where an order under section 17 of the previous Act (authorisation of unit trust schemes) is in force in respect of a unit trust scheme immediately before the coming into force of Chapter VIII of Part I of this Act the scheme shall be treated as an authorised unit trust scheme under that Part and the order as an order under section 78 of this Act.

(2) In relation to any such authorised unit trust scheme the reference in section 79(1)(*a*) of this Act to the requirements for the making of the order shall be construed as a reference to the requirements for the making of an order under section 78, but the scheme shall not be regarded as failing to comply with those requirements by reason of the manager or trustee not being an authorised person if he is treated as such a person by virtue of paragraph 1 above.

(3) If before the day on which Chapter VIII of Part I comes into force a notice in respect of a scheme has been served under subsection (2) of section 17 of the previous Act (proposed revocation of authorisation of unit trust scheme) but the revocation has not taken place before that day, the provisions of that subsection shall continue to apply in relation to the scheme and sub-paragraph (1) above shall cease to apply to it if the authorisation is revoked under that subsection.

Recognised collective investment schemes

10.—(1) If at any time before the coming into force of section 86 of this Act it appears to the Secretary of State that the law of a member State other than the United Kingdom confers rights on the managers and trustees of authorised unit trust schemes entitling them to carry on in that State on terms equivalent to those of that section—

(*a*) investment business which consists in operating or acting as trustee in relation to such schemes; and

(*b*) any investment business which is carried on by them in connection with or for the purposes of such schemes,

he may by order direct that schemes constituted in that State which satisfy such requirements as are specified in the order shall be recognised schemes for the purposes of this Act.

(2) Subsections (2) to (9) of section 86 of this Act shall have effect in relation to any scheme recognised by virtue of this paragraph; and the references in section 24 and 207(1) of this Act to a scheme recognised under section 86, and in section 76(1) of this Act to a scheme recognised under Chapter VIII of Part I of this Act, shall include references to any scheme recognised by virtue of this paragraph.

(3) In section 86(3)(*a*) as applied by sub-paragraph (2) above the reference to the rights conferred by any relevant Community instrument shall be construed as a reference to the rights conferred by virtue of an order made under this paragraph.

11.—(1) Subsection (7) of section 88 of this Act shall not apply to a scheme which is in existence on the date on which this Act is passed if—

(*a*) the units under the scheme are included in the Official List of The Stock Exchange and have been so included throughout the period of five years ending on the date on which this paragraph comes into force;

(*b*) the law of the country or territory in which the scheme is established precludes the participants being entitled or the operator being required as mentioned in that subsection; and

(*c*) throughout the period of five years ending on the date on which the application is made under that section, units under the scheme have in fact been regularly redeemed as mentioned in that subsection or the operator has in fact regularly ensured that participants were able to sell their units as there mentioned.

(2) The grounds for revoking an order made under section 88 of this Act by virtue of this paragraph shall include the ground that it appears to the Secretary of State that since the making of the order units under the scheme have ceased to be regularly redeemed or the operator has ceased regularly to ensure their sale as mentioned in sub-paragraph (1)(*c*) above.

Delegation orders

12.—(1) A delegation order may transfer a function notwithstanding that the provision conferring it has not yet come into force but no such function shall be exercisable by virtue of the order until the coming into force of that provision.

(2) Sub-paragraph (1) above applies also to a transfer order under paragraph 28(1) of Schedule 11 to this Act.

Disclosure of information

13. In determining for the purposes of section 180(6) of this Act and the enactments amended by paragraphs 3(2), 9(2) and 13(2) of Schedule 13 to this Act whether the functions of an authority in a country or territory outside the United Kingdom correspond to functions conferred by any of the provisions of this Act regard shall be had to those provisions whether or not they have already come into force.

Temporary exemptions for friendly societies

14.—(1) A registered friendly society which transacts no investment business after the date on which section 3 of this Act comes into force except for the purpose of making or carrying out relevant existing members' contracts shall be treated for the purposes of that section as if it were an exempted person under Chapter IV of Part I of this Act.

(2) Subject to sub-paragraph (3) below, for the purposes of this paragraph "relevant existing members' contracts", in relation to any society, means—

(*a*) contracts made by the society before that date; and

(*b*) in the case of a small income society—

(i) during the period of three years beginning with that date, tax exempt investment agreements made by it with persons who were members of the society before that date; and

(ii) after the expiry of that period, tax exempt investment agreements made by it with such persons before the expiry of that period.

(3) Paragraph (*b*) of sub-paragraph (2) above shall not apply to a registered friendly society after the expiry of the period of two years beginning with that date unless before the expiry of that period it has by special resolution (within the meaning of the Friendly Societies Act 1974 or, as the case may be, the Friendly Societies Act (Northern Ireland) 1970) determined—

(*a*) to transact no further investment business except for the purpose of carrying out contracts entered into before the expiry of the said period of three years; or

(*b*) to take such action as is necessary to procure the transfer of its engagements to another such society or a company or the amalgamation of the society with another such society under section 82 of the said Act of 1974 or, as the case may be, section 70 of the said Act of 1970,

and a copy of that resolution has been registered in accordance with section 86 of the said Act of 1974 or, as the case may be, section 75 of the said Act of 1970.

(4) For the purpose of sub-paragraph (2) above a society is a small income society if its income in 1985 from members' contributions did not exceed £50,000.

(5) For the purposes of sub-paragraph (2) above an investment agreement is a tax exempt investment agreement if the society by which it is made may obtain exemption from income and corporation tax on the profits from it under section 332 of the Income and Corporation Taxes Act 1970.

(6) A society to which sub-paragraph (1) or (2) above applies shall not be an authorised person for the purposes of this Act nor a regulated friendly society for the purposes of the provisions of Schedule 11 to this Act.

Dealings in course of non-investment business

15. If before the day on which section 3 of this Act comes into force a person has applied for permission under paragraph 23 of Schedule 1 to this Act and the application has not been determined before that day, that person shall, until the determination of the application and subject to his complying with such requirements as the Secretary of State may impose, be treated as if he had been granted a permission under that paragraph.

Northern Ireland

16. The foregoing provisions shall apply to Northern Ireland with the substitution for references to the previous Act or any provision of that Act of references to the Prevention of Fraud (Investments) Act (Northern Ireland) 1940 and the corresponding provision of that Act.

Section 212(2)　　　　　　　　SCHEDULE 16

CONSEQUENTIAL AMENDMENTS

1. In section 22 of the Charities Act 1960—
(*a*) subsection (10) shall be omitted; and
(*b*) in subsection (11) for the words "Subsections (9) and (10)" there shall be substituted the words "Subsection (9)".

2. In the Trustee Investments Act 1961—
(*a*) in section 11(3) for the words "the Prevention of Fraud (Investments) Act 1958 or the Prevention of Fraud (Investments) Act (Northern Ireland) 1940" there shall be substituted the words "the Financial Services Act 1986";
(*b*) for paragraph 3 of Part III of Schedule 1 there shall be substituted—
　　"3. In any units of an authorised unit trust scheme within the meaning of the Financial Services Act 1986";
(*c*) in paragraph 2(*a*) of Part IV of Schedule 1 for the words from "a recognised stock exchange" onwards there shall be substituted the words "a recognised investment exchange within the meaning of the Financial Services Act 1986";
(*d*) in the definition of "securities" in paragraph 4 of Part IV of that Schedule after the word "debentures" there shall be inserted the words "units within paragraph 3 of Part III of this Schedule".

3. In section 32 of the Clergy Pensions Measure 1961 No. 3—
(a) for paragraph (*t*) of subsection (1) there shall be substituted—
    "(*t*) in any units in any authorised unit trust scheme or a recognised scheme within the meaning of the Financial Services Act 1986"; and
(b) in subsection (5)(a) for the words from "a recognised stock exchange" onwards there shall be substituted the words "a recognised investment exchange within the meaning of the Financial Services Act 1986.".
4. In the Stock Transfer Act 1963—
(a) for paragraph (*e*) of section 1(4) there shall be substituted—
    "(*e*) units of an authorised unit trust scheme or a recognised scheme within the meaning of the Financial Services Act 1986"; and
(b) in the definition of "securities" in section 4(1) for the words from "unit trust scheme" to "scheme" there shall be substituted the words "collective investment scheme within the meaning of the Financial Services Act 1986".
5. In the Stock Transfer Act (Northern Ireland) 1963—
(a) for paragraph (*e*) of section 1(4) there shall be substituted—
    "(*e*) units of an authorised unit trust scheme or a recognised scheme within the meaning of the Financial Services Act 1986"; and
(b) in the definition of "securities" in section 4(1) for the words from "unit trust scheme" to "scheme" there shall be substituted the words "collective investment scheme within the meaning of the Financial Services Act 1986".
6. In section 25 of the Charities Act (Northern Ireland) 1964—
(a) subsection (16) shall be omitted; and
(b) in subsection (17) for the words "Subsections (15) and (16)" there shall be substituted the words "Subsection (15)".
7. In the Local Authorities' Mutual Investment Trust Act 1968—
(a) in section 1(2) for the words "recognised stock exchange within the meaning of the Prevention of Fraud (Investments) Act 1958" there shall be substituted the words "recognised investment exchange within the meaning of the Financial Services Act 1986"; and
(b) in the definition of "unit trust scheme" in section 2 for the words "Prevention of Fraud (Investments) Act 1958" there shall be substituted the words "Financial Services Act 1986".
8. In the Local Government Act 1972—
(a) in section 98(1) for the words from "and" onwards there shall be substituted the words "means—
    (a) investments falling within any of paragraphs 1 to 6 of Schedule 1 to the Financial Services Act 1986 or, so far as relevant to any of those paragraphs, paragraph 11 of that Schedule; or
    (b) rights (whether actual or contingent) in respect of money lent to, or deposited with, any society registered under the Industrial and Provident Societies Act 1965 or any building society within the meaning of the Building Societies Act 1986."; and
(b) for the definition of "securities" in section 146(2) there shall be substituted—
    " "securities" has the meaning given in section 98(1) above".
9. For subsection (1) of section 42 of the Local Government (Scotland) Act 1973 there shall be substituted—
    "(1) In sections 39 and 41 of this Act "securities" means—
        (a) investments falling within any of paragraphs 1 to 6 of Schedule 1 to the Financial Services Act 1986 or, so far as relevant to any of those paragraphs, paragraph 11 of that Schedule; or
        (b) rights (whether actual or contingent) in respect of money lent to, or deposited with, any society registered under the Industrial and Provident Societies Act 1965 or any building society within the meaning of the Building Societies Act 1986."
10. For paragraph 20 of Schedule 1 to the Industry Act 1975 there shall be substituted—
    "20. Section 57 of the Financial Services Act 1986 (restrictions on advertising) shall not apply to any investment advertisement within the meaning of that section which the Board issue or cause to be issued in the discharge of their functions."
11. For paragraph 20 of Schedule 1 to the Scottish Development Agency Act 1975 there shall be substituted—
    "20. Section 57 of the Financial Services Act 1986 (restrictions on advertising) shall not apply to any investment advertisement within the meaning of that section which the Agency issue or cause to be issued in the discharge of their functions."

12. For paragraph 21 of Schedule 1 to the Welsh Development Agency Act 1975 there shall be substituted—

> "21. Section 57 of the Financial Services Act 1986 (restrictions on advertising) shall not apply to any investment advertisement within the meaning of that section which the Agency issue or cause to be issued in the discharge of their functions.".

13. In section 3(5) of the Aircraft and Shipbuilding Industries Act 1977 the words "Sections 428 to 430 of the Companies Act 1985 and" shall be omitted and for the words "those sections" there shall be substituted the words "that section".

14. In paragraph 10(1)(*c*) of Part II of Schedule 10 to the Finance Act 1980 for the words "sections 428 to 430" there shall be substituted the words "sections 428 to 430F".

15. For the definition of "securities" in section 3(6) of the Licensing (Alcohol Education and Research) Act 1981 there shall be substituted—

> " "securities" means any investments falling within any of paragraphs 1 to 6 of Schedule 1 to the Financial Services Act 1986 or, so far as relevant to any of those paragraphs, paragraph 11 of that Schedule".

16. In section 97 of the Companies Act 1985—

(*a*) in subsection (1) after the word "conditions" there shall be inserted the words "and any conditions which apply in respect of any such payment by virtue of rules made under section 169(2) of the Financial Services Act 1986"; and

(*b*) in subsection (2)(*a*) for the words from "10 per cent." onwards there shall be substituted the words—

> "(i) any limit imposed on it by those rules or, if none is so imposed, 10 per cent. of the price at which the shares are issued; or
>
> (ii) the amount or rate authorised by the articles, whichever is the less".

17. In section 163 of the Companies Act 1985—

(*a*) for the words "a recognised stock exchange" in each place where they occur there shall be substituted the words "a recognised investment exchange";

(*b*) for the words "that stock exchange" in subsection (1) there shall be substituted the words "that investment exchange";

(*c*) in subsection (2) in paragraph (*a*) for the words "on that stock exchange" there shall be substituted the words "under Part IV of the Financial Services Act 1986" and in paragraph (*b*) for the words "that stock exchange" in both places where they occur there shall be substituted the words "that investment exchange";

(*d*) after subsection (3) of that section there shall be inserted—

> "(4) In this section "recognised investment exchange" means a recognised investment exchange other than an overseas investment exchange within the meaning of the Financial Services Act 1986."

18. In section 209(1)(*c*) of the Companies Act 1985 for the words "the Prevention of Fraud (Investments) Act 1958" there shall be substituted the words "the Financial Services Act 1986".

19. In section 265(4)(*a*) of the Companies Act 1985 for the words "recognised stock exchange" there shall be substituted the words "recognised investment exchange other than an overseas investment exchange within the meaning of the Financial Services Act 1986".

20. In section 329(1) of the Companies Act 1985 for the words "recognised stock exchange", "that stock exchange" and "the stock exchange" there shall be substituted respectively the words "recognised investment exchange other than an overseas investment exchange within the meaning of the Financial Services Act 1986", "that investment exchange" and "the investment exchange".

21. For paragraphs (*a*) to (*c*) of section 446(4) of the Companies Act 1985 there shall be substituted—

"(*a*) to any individual who is an authorised person within the meaning of the Financial Services Act 1986;

(*b*) to any individual who holds a permission granted under paragraph 23 of Schedule 1 to that Act;

(*c*) to any officer (whether past or present) of a body corporate which is such an authorised person or holds such a permission;

(*d*) to any partner (whether past or present) in a partnership which is such an authorised person or holds such a permission;

(*e*) to any member of the governing body or officer (in either case whether past or present) of an unincorporated association which is such an authorised person or holds such a permission".

22. At the end of sections 716(2) and 717(1) of the Companies Act 1985 there shall be inserted the words—

> "and in this subsection 'recognised stock exchange' means The Stock Exchange

and any other stock exchange which is declared to be a recognised stock exchange for the purposes of this section by an order in a statutory instrument made by the Secretary of State which is for the time being in force;".

23. In Schedule 4 to the Companies Act 1985—

(*a*) in paragraph 45 for the words "recognised stock exchange" there shall be substituted the words "recognised investment exchange other than an overseas investment exchange within the meaning of the Financial Services Act 1986"; and

(*b*) in paragraph 84 for the words from "on a recognised stock exchange" onwards there shall be substituted the words "on a recognised investment exchange other than an overseas investment exchange within the meaning of the Financial Services Act 1986 or on any stock exchange of repute outside Great Britain".

24. In Schedule 9 to the Companies Act 1985 in paragraphs 10(3) and 33 for the words "recognised stock exchange" there shall be substituted the words "recognised investment exchange other than an overseas investment exchange within the meaning of the Financial Services Act 1986".

25. In paragraph 11 of Schedule 13 to the Companies Act 1985 for paragraph (*a*) there shall be substituted—

(*a*) any unit trust scheme which is an authorised unit trust scheme within the meaning of the Financial Services Act 1986".

26. In Schedule 22 to the Companies Act 1985, in the second column of the entry relating to section 185(4) for the words "stock exchange" there shall be substituted the words "clearing house or".

27. In Schedule 24 to the Companies Act 1985—

(*a*) in the second column of the entry relating to section 329(3) for the words "stock exchange" there shall be substituted the words "investment exchange"; and

(*b*) after the entry relating to section 427(5) there shall be inserted—

| "429(6) | Offeror failing to send copy of notice or making statutory declaration knowing it to be false, etc. | 1. On indictment.

2. Summary. | 2 years or a fine; or both.

6 months or the statutory maximum; or both. | One-fiftieth of the statutory maximum. |
| 430A(6) | Offeror failing to give notice of rights to minority shareholder. | 1. On indictment

2. Summary. | A fine.

The statutory maximum. | One fiftieth of the statutory maximum". |

28. In section 16 of the Company Securities (Insider Dealing) Act 1985—

(*a*) in subsection (1) for the definition of "recognised stock exchange" there shall be substituted—

" 'recognised stock exchange' means The Stock Exchange and any other investment exchange which is declared by an order of the Secretary of State for the time being in force to be a recognised stock exchange for the purposes of this Act;"; and

(*b*) after that subsection there shall be inserted—

"(1A) The power to make an order under subsection (1) above shall be exercisable by statutory instrument.";

(*c*) in subsection (2) for the word "15" there shall be substituted the word "14".

29. For paragraph (*c*) of section 10(1) of the Bankruptcy (Scotland) Act 1985 there shall be substituted—

"(*c*) a petition is before a court for the winding up of the debtor under Part IV or V of the Insolvency Act 1986 or section 72 of the Financial Services Act 1986;".

30. In section 101 of the Building Societies Act 1986—

(*a*) for paragraph (1)(*a*) there shall be substituted—

"(*a*) offer for sale or invite subscription for any shares in or debentures of the company or allot or agree to allot any such shares or debentures with a view to their being offered for sale;";

(*b*) in subsection (1) after the words "the effect of the offer" there shall be inserted the words "the invitation"; and

(*c*) in subsection (2) for the words "the public" there shall be substituted the words ", invite subscription for,".

31. In Article 107 of the Companies (Northern Ireland) Order 1986—

(*a*) in paragraph (1) after the word "conditions" there shall be inserted the words "and any conditions which apply in respect of any such payment by virtue of rules made under section 169(2) of the Financial Services Act 1986";

(*b*) in sub-paragraph (2)(*a*) for the words from "10 per cent." onwards there shall be substituted the words—

"(i) any limit imposed on it by those rules or, if none is so imposed, 10 per cent. of the price at which the shares are issued; or

(ii) the amount or rate authorised by the articles, whichever is the less".

32. In Article 173 of the Companies (Northern Ireland) Order 1986—

(a) for the words "a recognised stock exchange", in each place where they occur, there shall be substituted the words "a recognised investment exchange";

(b) for the words "that stock exchange" in paragraph (1) there shall be substituted the words "that investment exchange";

(c) in paragraph (2), in sub-paragraph (a) for the words "on that stock exchange" there shall be substituted the words "under Part IV of the Financial Services Act 1986" and in sub-paragraph (b) for the words "that stock exchange" in both places where they occur there shall be substituted the words "that investment exchange";

(d) after paragraph (3) there shall be inserted—

"(4) In this Article "recognised investment exchange" means a recognised investment exchange other than an overseas investment exchange within the meaning of the Financial Services Act 1986."

33. In Article 217(1)(b) of the Companies (Northern Ireland) Order 1986 for the words "the Prevention of Fraud (Investments) Act (Northern Ireland) 1940 or of the Prevention of Fraud (Investments) Act 1958" there shall be substituted the words "the Financial Services Act 1986".

34. In Article 273(4)(a) of the Companies (Northern Ireland) Order 1986 for the words "recognised stock exchange" there shall be substituted the words "recognised investment exchange other than an overseas investment exchange within the meaning of the Financial Services Act 1986".

35. In Article 337(1) of the Companies (Northern Ireland) Order 1986 for the words "recognised stock exchange", "that stock exchange" and "the stock exchange" there shall be substituted respectively the words "recognised investment exchange", "that investment exchange" and "the investment exchange".

36. For sub-paragraphs (a) to (c) of Article 439(4) of the Companies (Northern Ireland) Order 1986 there shall be substituted—

"(a) to any individual who is an authorised person within the meaning of the Financial Services Act 1986;

(b) to any individual who holds a permission granted under paragraph 23 of Schedule 1 to that Act;

(c) to an officer (whether past or present) of a body corporate which is such an authorised person or holds such a permission;

(d) to any partner (whether past or present) in a partnership which is such an authorised person or holds such a permission;

(e) to any member of the governing body or officer (in either case whether past or present) of an unincorporated association which is such an authorised person or holds such a permission".

37. At the end of Article 665(2) and 666(1) of the Companies (Northern Ireland) Order 1986 there shall be inserted the words—

"and in this paragraph 'recognised stock exchange' means The Stock Exchange and any other stock exchange which is declared by an order of the Department for the time being in force to be a recognised stock exchange for the purposes of this Article;".

38. In Schedule 4 to the Companies (Northern Ireland) Order 1986—

(a) in paragraph 45 for the words "recognised stock exchange" there shall be substituted the words "recognised investment exchange other than an overseas investment exchange within the meaning of the Financial Services Act 1986";

(b) in paragraph 83 for the words from "on a recognised stock exchange" onwards there shall be substituted the words "on a recognised investment exchange other than an overseas investment exchange within the meaning of the Financial Services Act 1986 or on any stock exchange of repute outside Northern Ireland".

39. In Schedule 9 to the Companies (Northern Ireland) Order 1986, in paragraphs 10(3) and 33 for the words "recognised stock exchange" there shall be substituted the words "recognised investment exchange other than an overseas investment exchange within the meaning of the Financial Services Act 1986."

40. In paragraph 11 of Schedule 13 to the Companies (Northern Ireland) Order 1986 for paragraph (a) there shall be substituted—

"(a) any unit trust scheme which is an authorised unit trust scheme within the meaning of the Financial Services Act 1986".

41. In Schedule 21 to the Companies (Northern Ireland) Order 1986 in the second column of the entry relating to Article 195(4) for the words "stock exchange" there shall be substituted the words "clearing house or".

42. In Schedule 23 to the Companies (Northern Ireland) Order 1986 in the second column of the entry relating to Article 337(3) for the words "stock exchange" there shall be substituted the words "investment exchange".

43. In Article 2(1) of the Company Securities (Insider Dealing) (Northern Ireland) Order 1986, for the definition of "recognised stock exchange" there shall be substituted—

> " 'recognised stock exchange' means The Stock Exchange and any other investment exchange which is declared by an order of the Department for the time being in force to be a recognised stock exchange for the purposes of this Order;".

SCHEDULE 17

REPEALS AND REVOCATIONS

PART I

ENACTMENTS

Chapter	Short title	Extent of repeal
4 & 5 Geo. 6. c.9 (N.I.).	The Prevention of Fraud (Investments) Act (Northern Ireland) 1940.	The whole Act.
6 & 7 Eliz. 2. c.45.	The Prevention of Fraud (Investments) Act 1958.	The whole Act.
8 & 9 Eliz. 2. c.58.	The Charities Act 1960.	Section 22(10).
10 & 11 Eliz. 2. c.23.	The South Africa Act 1962.	In Schedule 4, the entry relating to the Prevention of Fraud (Investments) Act 1958.
1964 c.33 (N.I.).	The Charities Act (Northern Ireland) 1964.	Section 25(16).
1965 c.2.	The Administration of Justice Act 1965.	Section 14(1)(*e*) and (5)(*e*). In Schedule 1, the entry relating to the Prevention of Fraud (Investments) Act 1958.
1971 c.62.	The Tribunals and Inquiries Act 1971.	In Part I of Schedule 1, the entry relating to the tribunal constituted under section 6 of the Prevention of Fraud (Investments) Act 1958.
1972 c.71.	The Criminal Justice Act 1972.	In Schedule 5, the entry relating to the Prevention of Fraud (Investments) Act 1958.
1975 c.24.	The House of Commons Disqualification Act 1975.	In Part II of Schedule 1 the words "The Tribunal established under the Prevention of Fraud (Investments) Act 1958.
1975 c.68.	The Industry Act 1975.	In Schedule 1, paragraph 19.
1975 c.69.	The Scottish Development Agency Act 1975.	In Schedule 1, paragraph 19.
1975 c.70.	The Welsh Development Agency Act 1975.	In Schedule 1, paragraph 22.
1976 c.47.	The Stock Exchange (Completion of Bargains) Act 1976.	Section 7(2).
1977 c.3.	The Aircraft and Shipbuilding Industries Act 1977.	In section 3(5), the words "Sections 428 to 430 of the Companies Act 1985 and".
1978 c.23.	The Judicature (Northern Ireland) Act 1978.	Section 84(3)(*c*).
1979 c.37.	The Banking Act 1979.	Section 20(1) to (3). In Schedule 1, paragraph 9. In Schedule 6, paragraphs 4 and 5.
1982 c.50.	The Insurance Companies Act 1982.	Section 73. Section 79.
1982 c.53.	The Administration of Justice Act 1982.	Section 42(8).
1984 c.2.	The Restrictive Trade Practices (Stock Exchange) Act 1984.	The whole Act.

SCHEDULE 17—*continued*

Chapter	Short title	Extent of repeal
1985 c.6.	The Companies Act 1985.	Part III. Sections 81 to 83. In section 84(1) the words from "This" onwards. In section 85(1) the words "83 or". Sections 86 and 87. In section 97, subsection (2)(*b*) together with the word "and" immediately preceding it and subsections (3) and (4). Section 433(2). Section 446(5) and (6). In section 449(1)(*d*), the words "the Prevention of Fraud (Investments) Act 1958". In section 693, paragraph (*a*) and in paragraph (*d*) the words "in every such prospectus as above-mentioned and". Section 709(2) and (3). In section 744, the definitions of "recognised stock exchange" and "prospectus issued generally". Schedule 3. In Schedule 22, the entries relating to Parts III and IV. In Schedule 24, the entries relating to sections 56(4), 61, 64(5), 70(1), 78(1), 81(2), 82(5), 86(6), 87(4) and 97(4).
1985 c.8.	The Company Securities (Insider Dealing) Act 1985.	In section 3(1), the word "or" immediately preceding paragraph (*c*). In section 13, in subsection (1), the words from "and references" onwards and subsection (2). Section 15.
1985 c.9.	The Companies Consolidation (Consequential Provisions) Act 1985.	Section 7. In Schedule 2, the entries relating to the Prevention of Fraud (Investments) Act 1958, paragraph 19 of Schedule 1 to the Scottish Development Agency Act 1975, paragraph 22 of Schedule 1 to the Welsh Development Agency Act 1975, the Stock Exchange (Completion of Bargains) Act 1976, section 3(5) of the Aircraft and Shipbuilding Industries Act 1977 and section 20 of the Banking Act 1979.
1986 c.31.	The Airports Act 1986.	Section 10.
1986 c.44.	The Gas Act 1986.	Section 58.
1986 c.60.	The Financial Services Act 1986.	Section 195.

PART II

INSTRUMENTS

Number	Title	Extent of revocation
S.I. 1977/1254 (6 N.I. 21).	The Stock Exchange (Completion of Bargains) (Northern Ireland) Order 1977.	Article 2(2).
S.I. 1986/1032 (N.I. 6).	The Companies (Northern Ireland) Order 1986.	In Article 2(1), the definitions of "prospectus issued generally" and "recognised stock exchange". Part IV. Articles 91 to 93. In Article 94(1) the words from "This" onwards. In Article 95(1) the words "93 or". Articles 96 and 97. In Article 107, paragraph (2)(*b*) together with the word "and" immediately preceding it and paragraphs (3) and (4). Article 426(2). Article 439(5) and (6). In Article 442(1)(*d*), the words "the Prevention of Fraud (Investments) Act (Northern Ireland) 1940". In Article 643(1), sub-paragraph (*a*) and in sub-paragraph (*d*) the words "in every such prospectus as is mentioned in sub-paragraph (*a*) and". Article 658(2) and (3). Schedule 3. In Schedule 21, the entries relating to Parts IV and V. In Schedule 23, the entries relating to Articles 66(4), 71, 74(5), 80(1), 88(1), 91(2), 92(5), 96(6), 97(4) and 107(4).
S.I. 1986/1035 (N.I. 9).	The Companies (Consequential Provisions) (Northern Ireland) Order 1986.	In Schedule 2, the entries relating to the Prevention of Fraud (Investments) Act (Northern Ireland) 1940 and section 20 of the Banking Act 1979.
S.I. 1984/716.	The Stock Exchange (Listing) Regulations 1984.	The whole Regulations.

EDUCATION (No. 2) ACT 1986

(c.61)

An Act to amend the law relating to education.

[7th November 1986]

PARLIAMENTARY DEBATES
   Hansard: H.C. Vol. 97, col. 277; Vol. 99, col. 870; Vol. 101, col. 136; H.L. Vol. 478, cols. 270, 1076.
   This Bill was considered in the House of Commons Standing Committee F, on June 24, 1986.

PART I

INTRODUCTORY

Instruments of government and articles of government

1.—(1) For every county, voluntary and maintained special school there shall be—

(*a*) an instrument providing for the constitution of a governing body of the school (to be known as the instrument of government); and

(*b*) an instrument in accordance with which the school is to be conducted (to be known as the articles of government).

(2) The instrument of government and articles of government shall be made by order of the local education authority.

(3) The instrument of government shall contain such provisions as are required either by Part II of this Act (which is concerned, among other things, with the size and composition of governing bodies and the

procedures for electing members and filling vacancies) or by any other enactment.

(4) The articles of government shall contain such provisions as are required either by Part III of this Act (which is concerned, among other things, with the manner in which schools are to be conducted and the allocation of functions between the local education authority, the governing body and the head teacher) or by any other enactment.

(5) The instrument of government and articles of government shall—

(a) contain no provision which is inconsistent with any provision made by or under this Act or any other enactment; and

(b) comply with any trust deed relating to the school.

(6) This section is subject to the following provisions of this Act—

(a) section 9 (which provides for two or more schools to be grouped under a single governing body in certain circumstances); and

(b) section 12 (which provides for certain existing, or proposed, schools to have temporary governing bodies pending the constitution of governing bodies under instruments of government).

Procedure in relation to making etc. of instruments and articles

2.—(1) Before making any order under section 1 of this Act, a local education authority shall consult the governing body and the head teacher of the school concerned.

(2) Before making any such order in respect of a voluntary school, a local education authority shall—

(a) secure the agreement of the governing body to the terms of the proposed order;

(b) if it embodies or varies an instrument of government, secure the agreement of the foundation governors to any provisions which are of particular concern to those governors; and

(c) have regard to the way in which the school has been conducted.

(3) Where the governing body of any county, voluntary or maintained special school make a proposal to the local education authority for the alteration of the provision made by the instrument of government, or articles of government, for the school, it shall be the duty of the authority to consider their proposal.

(4) Where—

(a) the foundation governors of a voluntary school make a proposal to the local education authority for the alteration of the provision made by the instrument of government for the school; and

(b) the proposal relates solely to one or more matters which are of particular concern to those governors;

it shall be the duty of the authority to consider their proposal.

(5) Where a local education authority—

(a) propose to make an order under section 1 but cannot secure any agreement required by subsection (2) above;

    or

(b) refuse, in the case of a voluntary school, to make such an order in response to a proposal of a kind mentioned in subsection (3) or (4) above;

the authority or (as the case may be) the governing body or foundation governors may refer the matter to the Secretary of State.

(6) On any reference to him under subsection (5) above, the Secretary of State shall give such direction as he thinks fit having regard, in

particular, to the status of the school as a controlled, aided or (as the case may be) special agreement school.

(7) Where it appears to the Secretary of State—

(*a*) that an order, or proposed order, under section 1 is in any respect inconsistent with the provisions of any trust deed relating to the school; and

(*b*) that it is expedient in the interests of the school that the provisions of the trust deed should be modified for the purpose of removing the inconsistency;

he may by order make such modifications in the trust deed as appear to him to be just and expedient for that purpose.

PART II

SCHOOL GOVERNMENT

Governing bodies

Governing bodies for county, controlled and maintained special schools

3.—(1) This section applies in relation to any county, controlled or maintained special school.

(2) The instrument of government for such a school which has less than 100 registered pupils shall, subject to section 7 of this Act, provide for the governing body to consist of the following (and no others)—

(*a*) two parent governors;

(*b*) two governors appointed by the local education authority;

(*c*) one teacher governor;

(*d*) the head teacher, unless he chooses not to be a governor; and

(*e*) either—

(i) two foundation governors and one co-opted governor, in the case of a controlled school; or

(ii) three co-opted governors, in any other case.

(3) The instrument of government for such a school which has more than 99, but less than 300, registered pupils shall, subject to section 7, provide for the governing body to consist of the following (and no others)—

(*a*) three parent governors;

(*b*) three governors appointed by the local education authority;

(*c*) one teacher governor;

(*d*) the head teacher, unless he chooses not to be a governor; and

(*e*) either—

(i) three foundation governors and one co-opted governor, in the case of a controlled school; or

(ii) four co-opted governors, in any other case.

(4) The instrument of government for such a school which has more than 299, but less than 600, registered pupils shall, subject to section 7, provide for the governing body to consist of the following (and no others)—

(*a*) four parent governors;

(*b*) four governors appointed by the local education authority;

(*c*) two teacher governors;

(*d*) the head teacher, unless he chooses not to be a governor; and

(*e*) either—

(i) four foundation governors and one co-opted governor, in the case of a controlled school; or

(ii) five co-opted governors, in any other case.

(5) The instrument of government for such a school which has more than 599 registered pupils shall, subject to section 7, provide for the governing body to consist of the following (and no others)—

   (*a*) five parent governors;

   (*b*) five governors appointed by the local education authority;

   (*c*) two teacher governors;

   (*d*) the head teacher, unless he chooses not to be a governor; and

   (*e*) either—

      (i) four foundation governors and two co-opted governors, in the case of a controlled school; or

      (ii) six co-opted governors, in any other case.

(6) Where the instrument of government so provides, a school to which subsection (5) above would otherwise apply shall be treated for the purposes of this section as one to which subsection (4) above applies.

(7) Where the head teacher is a governor he shall be treated for all purposes as being an ex officio governor.

Governing bodies for aided and special agreement schools

4.—(1) This section applies in relation to any aided or special agreement school.

(2) The instrument of government for such a school shall provide for the governing body to include—

   (*a*) at least one governor appointed by the local education authority;

   (*b*) in the case of a school which is a primary school serving an area in which there is a minor authority, at least one governor appointed by the authority;

   (*c*) foundation governors;

   (*d*) at least one parent governor;

   (*e*) in the case of a school which has less than 300 registered pupils, at least one teacher governor;

   (*f*) in the case of a school which has 300 or more registered pupils, at least two teacher governors; and

   (*g*) the head teacher, unless he chooses not to be a governor.

(3) The instrument of government for such a school shall provide—

   (*a*) for such number of foundation governors as will lead to their outnumbering the other governors—

      (i) by two, if the governing body of the school will consist of eighteen or fewer governors; and

      (ii) by three, if it will consist of more than eighteen governors; and

   (*b*) for at least one of the foundation governors to be (at the time of his appointment) a parent of a registered pupil at the school.

(4) Where the head teacher of such a school has chosen not to be a governor, he shall nevertheless be counted as one for the purposes of calculating the required number of foundation governors.

(5) Subject to subsection (3) above, nothing in this section shall be taken to prevent the instrument of government for such a school from providing for the governing body to include governors in addition to those required by virtue of this section.

(6) Where the head teacher is a governor he shall be treated for all purposes as being an ex officio governor.

Governors

Appointment of parent governors by governing body

5.—(1) The instrument of government for any county or controlled school, or for any maintained special school which is not established in a hospital, may provide that if at the time when the instrument is made, or at any later time when there is a vacancy for a parent governor—

(*a*) at least fifty per cent. of the registered pupils at the school are boarders; and

(*b*) it would, in the opinion of the local education authority, be impracticable for there to be an election of parent governors;

the parent governors, or (as the case may be) the parent governor required to fill that vacancy, shall be appointed by the other members of the governing body.

(2) The instrument of government for every county, controlled and maintained special school at which parent governors are to be, or may be, elected shall provide for the required number of parent governors to be made up by parent governors appointed by the other members of the governing body if—

(*a*) one or more vacancies for parent governors are required to be filled by election; and

(*b*) the number of parents standing for election as parent governors is less than the number of vacancies.

(3) Where, in the opinion of the local education authority, it is likely to be impracticable for there to be elections of parent governors at any maintained special school which is established in a hospital, the instrument of government for that school may provide for the parent governors to be appointed by the other members of the governing body.

(4) The instrument of government for any school to which this section applies shall provide for it to be the duty of governors—

(*a*) in appointing any parent governor under any provision made by virtue of this section—

(i) to appoint a person who is the parent of a registered pupil at the school, where it is reasonably practicable to do so; and

(ii) where it is not, to appoint a person who is the parent of one or more children of compulsory school age;

(*b*) not to appoint any person as a parent governor, under any such provision, if that person is—

(i) an elected member of the local education authority;

(ii) an employee of the authority or of the governing body of any aided school maintained by the authority; or

(iii) a co-opted member of any education committee of the authority.

Connection with local business community

6. The instrument of government for any county, controlled or maintained special school shall provide for it to be the duty of the governors concerned, in co-opting any person to be a member of the governing body (otherwise than as a foundation governor)—

(*a*) to have regard—

(i) to the extent to which they and the other governors are members of the local business community; and

(ii) to any representations made to the governing body as to the desirability of increasing the connection between the governing body and that community; and

(*b*) where it appears to them that no governor of the school is a member of the local business community, or that it is desirable to increase the number of governors who are, to co-opt a person who appears to them to be a member of that community.

Appointment of representative governors in place of co-opted governors

7.—(1) The instrument of government for every primary school which is a county or controlled school serving an area in which there is a minor authority shall provide for one governor to be appointed by that authority.

(2) The instrument of government for every maintained special school which is established in a hospital shall provide for one governor to be appointed by the district health authority.

(3) The instrument of government for every maintained special school (other than one established in a hospital) shall, if the school has less than 100 registered pupils, provide for one governor to be appointed—

(a) by a voluntary organisation designated by the local education authority, in relation to the school, as the appropriate voluntary organisation concerned with matters in respect of which the school is specially organised;

or

(b) jointly by two or more voluntary organisations so designated;

and shall, if it has more than 99 registered pupils, provide for two governors to be so appointed.

(4) Where, by virtue of subsection (3) above, an instrument of government is required to provide for the appointment of two governors, it may make different provision in relation to the appointment of one governor to that made in relation to the appointment of the other.

(5) Where a local education authority are satisfied, in relation to any special school, that there is no voluntary organisation which it would be appropriate to designate for the purposes of subsection (3) above, that subsection shall not apply to its instrument of government.

(6) Where the instrument of government for any school is required by this section to provide for the appointment of any governor, the instrument—

(a) shall name the person or persons by whom the governor is to be appointed;

(b) shall not provide for a co-opted governor if the school is a controlled school with less than 600 registered pupils or is treated as such a school for the purposes of section 3 of this Act by virtue of subsection (6) of that section; and

(c) in any other case, shall provide for one or (as the case may be) two fewer co-opted governors than would otherwise be provided for.

(7) In subsection (6) above, references to co-opted governors are to governors required to be co-opted by virtue of section 3 of this Act and do not include references to co-opted foundation governors.

Governors' proceedings and tenure of office

8.—(1) The proceedings of the governing body of any county, voluntary or maintained special school shall not be invalidated by—

(a) any vacancy among their number; or

(b) any defect in the election or appointment of any governor.

(2) The instrument of government for every county, controlled and maintained special school shall provide for each governor, other than one who is an ex officio governor, to hold office for a term of four years.

(3) Subsection (2) above shall not be taken to prevent a governor from being elected or appointed for a further term, or from being disqualified, by virtue of regulations made under subsection (6) below, for continuing to hold office.

(4) Any governor of a county, voluntary or maintained special school may at any time resign his office.

(5) Any foundation governor of a voluntary school, or governor of a county, voluntary or maintained special school appointed otherwise than by being co-opted, may be removed from office by the person or persons who appointed him.

For the purposes of this subsection, a governor appointed in accordance with any provision made by virtue of section 5 of this Act shall be treated as having been co-opted.

(6) The Secretary of State may by regulations make provision as to the meetings and proceedings of the governing bodies of county, voluntary and maintained special schools (including provision modifying that made by subsection (1) above) and the circumstances in which persons are to be disqualified for holding office as governors of such schools.

(7) The regulations may, in particular, provide—

    (a) for the election by the governors of any such school of one of their number to be chairman, and one to be vice-chairman, of the school's governing body for such period as may be prescribed;

    (b) for the chairman of the governing body of any such school, or such other member of that body as may be prescribed, to have power in prescribed circumstances to discharge any of the functions of that body as a matter of urgency; and

    (c) as to the quorum required for the purposes of making appointments in accordance with any provision made by virtue of section 5 of this Act or when business is transacted by governors of a particular category.

(8) The minutes of the proceedings of the governing body of any county, voluntary or maintained special school shall be open to inspection by the local education authority.

(9) The instrument of government for every county, voluntary and maintained special school may make provision with respect to the matters mentioned in subsections (6) and (7) above.

(10) Any provision made by the instrument of government for any such school which relates to a matter dealt with by regulations under subsection (6) above (including any provision made by virtue of subsection (2) above) shall have effect subject to the regulations.

(11) No decision of a kind mentioned in subsection (12) below which is taken at a meeting of the governing body of any aided or special agreement school shall have effect unless it is confirmed at a second meeting of the governing body held not less than twenty-eight days after the first.

(12) The decisions are—

    (a) any decision that would result in the submission of proposals under section 13 of the 1980 Act (establishment and alteration of voluntary schools);

    (b) any decision to serve a notice under section 14(1) of the 1944 Act (discontinuance of school);

    (c) any decision that would result in an application under section 15(4) of the 1944 Act (revocation of order whereby school is an aided or special agreement school);

    (d) any decision to request the making of an order under subsection (2) of section 16 of the 1944 Act (discontinuance of school for which another school is substituted) or as to the submissions to be made to the Secretary of State in any consultations under subsection (3) of that section;

    (e) any decision to make an agreement under Schedule 2 to the

1944 Act (agreement for transfer of interest in school to local education authority).

Grouping of schools

Grouping of schools under single governing body

9.—(1) Subject to the requirements as to consent imposed by section 10 of this Act, a local education authority may resolve that any two or more schools maintained by them shall be grouped for the purposes of this Part of this Act.

(2) Where any schools are so grouped, they shall (subject to the following provisions of this section)—

(*a*) be treated for the purposes of this Part as a single school; and

(*b*) have a single governing body constituted under a single instrument of government.

(3) For the purposes of this Part of this Act, a group shall be treated—

(*a*) as an aided school, if it contains at least one such school;

(*b*) as a special agreement school, if it contains at least one such school and paragraph (*a*) above does not apply;

(*c*) as a controlled school, if it contains at least one such school and neither paragraph (*a*) nor paragraph (*b*) above applies;

(*d*) as a maintained special school, if it consists only of such schools; and

(*e*) as a county school, if none of the preceding paragraphs apply.

(4) Where any proposal or alteration of a kind mentioned in subsection (5) below relates to any school which is grouped with one or more other schools under this section, it shall be the duty of the local education authority—

(*a*) to review the grouping of those schools and to consider whether or not it should be brought to an end; and

(*b*) where the Secretary of State's consent to the grouping, or continued grouping, was at any time required by section 10 of this Act and the authority consider that the grouping should be continued—

(i) to report to him on the results of their review; and

(ii) to provide him with such information as he may reasonably require with a view to enabling him to consider whether or not the grouping should be brought to an end.

(5) The proposals and alterations referred to in subsection (4) above are—

(*a*) any proposal under—

(i) section 16 of the 1944 Act (transfer of schools to new sites and substitution of new for old schools);

(ii) sections 12 to 15 of the 1980 Act (establishment, discontinuance and alteration of schools); or

(iii) section 54 of this Act;

(*b*) any alteration made to arrangements approved by the Secretary of State in accordance with regulations made under section 12 of the 1981 Act (approval of special schools); and

(*c*) any alteration in the status of an aided or special agreement school effected by an order of the Secretary of State under section 15(4) of the 1944 Act (revocation of order by virtue of which school is an aided or special agreement school).

(6) The Secretary of State may by order bring to an end any grouping under this section in respect of which his consent was at any time required by section 10 of this Act.

(7) Any grouping under this section may also be brought to an end—

(a) if the group does not include any voluntary school, by resolution of the local education authority; and

(b) if it does include any such school—

(i) by resolution of the authority made with the agreement of the school's governing body; or

(ii) by one year's notice given either by the authority to the governing body or by the governing body to the authority.

(8) Any order under section 1 of this Act embodying an instrument of government for two or more schools which are grouped under this section shall be deemed to have been revoked—

(a) in the case of a group which was established for a specified period, at the end of that period; or

(b) on the bringing to an end of the group in accordance with subsection (6) or (7) above.

(9) Schedule 1 to this Act shall have effect for the purpose of making further provision in relation to schools grouped under this section.

Requirements as to consent to grouping

10.—(1) Before resolving to group any schools under section 9 of this Act, a local education authority shall obtain the consent of the Secretary of State to the proposed grouping unless—

(a) the group will consist only of two primary schools both of which serve substantially the same area;

(b) neither of the schools is a special school; and

(c) where they are in Wales, there is no significant difference between them in their use of the Welsh language.

(2) The Secretary of State's consent may be given subject to such conditions as he sees fit to impose with respect to the duration of the grouping to which his consent is given.

(3) Where two primary schools have been grouped under section 9 in circumstances in which the Secretary of State's consent was not required under subsection (1) above, his consent to their continuing to be so grouped shall be required if a change of circumstances occurs such that a proposal to group those schools under section 9 made after that change would require his consent under that subsection.

(4) Where the Secretary of State's consent is required to the grouping or continued grouping of any schools under section 9, sections 3 to 7 of this Act shall apply in relation to the group subject to such modifications (if any) as he may direct.

(5) No local education authority may pass a resolution under section 9 applying to any voluntary school without first obtaining the consent of its governing body.

(6) No local education authority may pass a resolution under section 9 applying to any county or maintained special school without first consulting its governing body.

(7) Any dispute as to whether, for the purposes of this section—

(a) two primary schools are to be regarded as serving substantially the same area; or

(b) there is any significant difference between two primary schools in their use of the Welsh language;

shall be determined by the Secretary of State.

Reviews

Review of constitution of governing bodies of county controlled and maintained special schools

11.—(1) The constitution of the governing body of every county, controlled and maintained special school shall be reviewed in accordance with the provisions of this section on, or as soon as is reasonably practicable after, the occurrence of any event which is a relevant event in relation to the school.

(2) In this section "relevant event", in relation to any school, means any of the following—

    (*a*) the implementation of any proposal under—

        (i) section 16(1) of the 1944 Act (transfer of schools to new sites);

        (ii) section 12(1)(*d*) of the 1980 Act (alteration of county schools); or

        (iii) section 13(1)(*b*) of the 1980 Act (alteration of voluntary schools);

      which provides for an increase in the number of registered pupils at the school;

    (*b*) in the case of a maintained special school, the implementation of any proposal to change approved arrangements which provides for an increase in the number of registered pupils at the school;

    (*c*) where no relevant event of a kind mentioned in paragraph (*a*) or (*b*) above has occurred in relation to the school before the fourth anniversary of the date on which the current instrument of government for the school was made, that anniversary;

    (*d*) where any relevant event has previously occurred in relation to the school, the fourth anniversary of the latest such event.

(3) Any review which is required by virtue of the occurrence of a relevant event of a kind mentioned in paragraph (*a*)(i), (ii) or (*b*) of subsection (2) above shall be carried out by the local education authority and any other review which is required by this section shall be carried out by the governing body.

(4) Whenever the local education authority or governing body of a school are required to carry out a review under this section they shall consider whether—

    (*a*) the governing body are properly constituted;

    (*b*) the provision made by the instrument of government for the school is in any respect different from that which a new instrument of government would be required to make.

(5) Where the governing body of a school have carried out a review under this section and have established that the provision made by the instrument of government for the school is in one or more respects different from that which a new instrument of government for the school would be required to make, they shall report the fact to the local education authority.

(6) Where a relevant event of a kind mentioned in paragraph (*a*)(i), (ii) or (*b*) of subsection (2) above has occurred in relation to any school, the local education authority shall determine the date on which, for the purposes of this section, that event is to be taken to have occurred, and shall notify the governing body accordingly.

(7) In this section "approved arrangements" means arrangements approved by the Secretary of State in accordance with regulations made under section 12 of the 1981 Act (approval of special schools).

Temporary governing bodies

Temporary governing bodies for new schools

    12.—(1) Where—

        (*a*) the Secretary of State has approved, under section 12 or 13 of the 1980 Act, any proposal of a kind mentioned in subsection (2) below; or (*b*) a local education authority making any such proposal have determined, under section 12(7) of that Act, that it should be implemented;

the local education authority shall make an arrangement for the constitution of a temporary governing body for the school (or proposed school) pending the constitution of its governing body under an instrument of government.

(2) The proposals referred to in subsection (1) above are—

    (*a*) any proposal made by a local education authority—

        (i) to establish a new county school; or

        (ii) to maintain as a county school any school which is neither a county school nor a voluntary school; and

    (*b*) any proposal that a relevant school should be maintained by a local education authority as a voluntary school.

(3) Where a local education authority propose to establish a new special school, they shall make an arrangement for the constitution of a temporary governing body for the school—

    (*a*) at least one year before the date on which the first pupils are expected to be admitted; or

    (*b*) on the day on which their resolution to establish the school is passed.

(4) Where a proposal of a kind mentioned in subsection (2) above has been duly published, the local education authority may make an arrangement for the constitution of a temporary governing body in anticipation of the approval of the proposal by the Secretary of State or (as the case may be) of the determination by the authority that it should be implemented.

(5) Where any proposal that a relevant school should be maintained by a local education authority as a controlled school has been duly published, the authority shall consult the promoters—

    (*a*) as to whether the power given to the authority by subsection (4) above should be exercised; and

    (*b*) if the authority propose to exercise it, as to the date on which it should be exercised.

(6) Where any proposal that a relevant school should be maintained by a local education authority as an aided school has been duly published, the authority and the promoters shall consider—

    (*a*) whether the power given to the authority by subsection (4) above should be exercised; and

    (*b*) where they agree that it should, on what date the authority should exercise it.

(7) Where, in a case falling within subsection (6) above, the authority and the promoters fail to agree on the question mentioned in paragraph (*a*) or on that mentioned in paragraph (*b*), either of them may refer the matter to the Secretary of State.

(8) On any reference under subsection (7) above, the Secretary of State shall give such direction as he thinks fit.

(9) In this section "relevant school", in relation to any proposal, means a school which—

    (*a*) was established by those making the proposal, or by persons whom they represent, and which is not a voluntary school; or

    (*b*) is proposed to be so established.

(10) Schedule 2 to this Act shall have effect for the purpose of supplementing this section.

Miscellaneous and supplemental

Effect of change of circumstances on instrument of government

13.—(1) Any instrument of government to which this Act applies shall (subject to subsection (2) below and paragraph 3(2) of Schedule 2 to this Act) make such provision as is appropriate having regard to all the circumstances of the school as at the date on which the instrument is made.

(2) Where a proposal of a kind mentioned in section 11(2)(*a*) or (*b*) of this Act has been implemented in relation to any school, the number of registered pupils at the school shall, for the purposes of subsection (1) above and until the number of registered pupils at the school reaches the maximum number of pupils provided for by the proposal, be deemed to be that maximum number.

(3) Where subsection (2) applies in relation to any school, the local education authority or (in the case of a proposal under section 13(1)(*b*) of the 1980 Act) the governing body may determine that it shall cease to apply (but without prejudice to its operation in relation to the implementation of any further proposal).

(4) Where the effect of any subsequent change in the circumstances of a school is that the provision made by the instrument of government for the school differs in any respect from the provision which a new instrument of government would be required to make, it shall be the duty of the local education authority (subject to subsection (7) below):—

(*a*) to vary the instrument of government in such manner as is required to remove any such difference; or

(*b*) to make a new instrument of government.

(5) Any instrument of government to which this Act applies may make provision which would be appropriate in the event of such a change in the circumstances of the school as is anticipated by that provision (including in particular a change in the number of registered pupils at the school).

(6) No provision made by any such instrument in anticipation of a change in the number of registered pupils at the school shall have effect before it is established, by a review under section 11 of this Act, that a new instrument of government for the school in question would be required to make that provision.

(7) For the purposes of subsection (4) above, any change in the number of registered pupils at a school occurring after the instrument of government for the school is made, or (as the case may be) varied, may be disregarded until a review under section 11 of this Act establishes that the provision made by the instrument differs in any respect from the provision which a new instrument of government for the school would be required to make.

(8) Where subsection (2) above has applied in relation to any school but the local education authority or (as the case may be) governing body have subsequently determined that it should cease to apply, subsections (4) and (7) above shall have effect as if a change in the number of registered pupils at the school had occurred at the time when that determination was made.

(9) Subsections (6) and (7) above do not apply to aided or special agreement schools.

Adjustment in number of governors

14.—(1) Where—

(*a*) any county, controlled or maintained special school has more governors of a particular category than are provided for by the instrument of government for the school; and

(b) the excess is not eliminated by the required number of governors of that category resigning;

such number of governors of that category as is required to eliminate the
excess shall cease to hold office.

(2) The governors who are to cease to hold office shall be selected on
the basis of seniority, the longest serving governor being the first to be
selected, and so on.

(3) Where it is necessary for the purpose of subsection (2) above to
select one or more governors from a group of equal seniority, it shall be
done by drawing lots.

(4) Subsections (2) and (3) above do not apply in relation to foundation
governors.

(5) The instrument of government for every controlled school shall
make provision for the procedure to be adopted whenever subsection (1)
above requires any foundation governor to cease to hold office.

Miscellaneous

15.—(1) Where a school to which section 3 or 4 of this Act applies has
more than one head teacher (whether or not as a result of two or more
schools being grouped under section 9 of this Act), each of them shall be
a governor unless he chooses not to be.

(2) It shall be for the local education authority, in the case of a county,
controlled or maintained special school, and for the governing body, in
the case of an aided or special agreement school—

(a) to determine, for the purposes of an election of parent governors
or teacher governors to the governing body, any question whether
a person is—
(i) a parent of a registered pupil at the school; or
(ii) a teacher at the school; and

(b) to make all necessary arrangements for, and to determine all other
matters relating to, any such election.

(3) The power conferred by subsection (2)(b) above includes power
to make provision as to qualifying dates but does not include power to
impose any requirement as to the minimum number of votes required to
be cast for a candidate to be elected.

(4) Any such election which is contested must be held by secret ballot.

(5) The arrangements made under subsection (2)(b) above shall, in the
case of any election of a parent governor, provide for every person who
is entitled to vote in the election to have an opportunity to do so by post
or, if he so prefers, by having his ballot paper returned to the school by
a registered pupil at the school.

(6) Where a vacancy for a parent governor of any county, voluntary or
maintained special school is required to be filled by election, it shall be
the duty of the appropriate authority to take such steps as are reasonably
practicable to secure that every person who is known to them to be a
parent of a registered pupil at the school is—

(a) informed of the vacancy and that it is required to be filled by
election;

(b) informed that he is entitled to stand as a candidate, and vote, at
the election; and

(c) given an opportunity to do so.

(7) The instrument of government for every voluntary school shall
name the person or persons (if any) who are entitled to appoint any
foundation governor.

(8) The instrument of government for any voluntary school may provide
for any foundation governorship to be held ex officio by the holder of an
office named in the instrument.

(9) The qualification of any person for election or appointment as a governor, of a particular category, of any county, voluntary or maintained special school, shall not have the effect of disqualifying him for election or appointment as a governor, of any other category, of that school.

(10) No person shall at any time hold more than one governorship of the same county, voluntary or maintained special school.

(11) Where the instrument of government for any county, voluntary or maintained special school provides for one or more governors to be appointed by persons acting jointly, any such appointment shall be made, in the event of failure on the part of those persons to make an agreed appointment—

(a) by the Secretary of State; or

(b) in accordance with any direction given by him.

(12) No instrument of government for any county, voluntary or maintained special school which provides for one or more persons to be co-opted, by governors, as members of the governing body of the school shall make any provision (otherwise than by virtue of section 6 of this Act) which has the effect of restricting those governors in their choice of person to co-opt.

(13) In subsection (12) above, references to co-opted governors are to governors required to be co-opted by virtue of section 3 of this Act and do not include references to co-opted foundation governors.

(14) No person shall be qualified for membership of the governing body of any county, voluntary or maintained special school unless he is aged eighteen or over, at the date of his election or appointment.

(15) In subsection (6) above, "appropriate authority" means—

(a) the local education authority, in the case of a county, controlled or maintained special school; and

(b) the governing body, in the case of an aided or special agreement school.

PART III

ORGANISATION AND FUNCTIONS

General

General responsibility for conduct of certain schools

16.—(1) The articles of government for every county, voluntary and maintained special school shall provide for the conduct of the school to be under the direction of the governing body, but subject to any provision of the articles conferring specific functions on any person other than the governing body, and to the provision made (otherwise than in the articles) by or under this Act or any other enactment.

(2) The Secretary of State may by regulations make provision as to the circumstances in which, in any case where—

(a) any provision of, or made under, this Act requires the governing body of a school to be consulted before a particular step is taken by the local education authority or the head teacher; and

(b) the authority or head teacher require to take that step as a matter of urgency but are unable to contact the chairman or vice-chairman of the governing body;

the authority or (as the case may be) the head teacher may proceed without consulting the governing body.

(3) Where a county, voluntary or maintained special school is organised in two or more separate departments, each with a head teacher, any

provision made by or under this Act which confers functions on, or in relation to, the head teacher of the school shall, except where the articles of government provide otherwise, have effect as if each department were a separate school.

School curriculum

Duty of local education authority to state policy

17.—(1) It shall be the duty of every local education authority—
   (a) to determine, and keep under review, their policy in relation to the secular curriculum for the county, voluntary and special schools maintained by them;
   (b) to make, and keep up to date, a written statement of that policy; and
   (c) to furnish the governing body and head teacher of every such school with a copy of the statement and publish it in such other manner as the authority consider appropriate.

(2) In discharging their duty under subsection (1) above, an authority shall consider, in particular—
   (a) the range of the secular curriculum; and
   (b) the balance between its different components.

(3) In carrying out their functions under this Act or any other enactment, a local education authority shall have regard to their policy in relation to the secular curriculum for their schools, as expressed in their statement.

(4) Every head teacher to whom any copy of a statement is furnished under this section shall make it available, at all reasonable times, to persons wishing to inspect it.

County, controlled and maintained special schools

18.—(1) The articles of government for every county, controlled and maintained special school shall provide for it to be the duty of the governing body to consider—
   (a) the policy of the local education authority as to the secular curriculum for the authority's schools, as expressed in the statement made by the authority under section 17 of this Act;
   (b) what, in their opinion, should be the aims of the secular curriculum for the school; and
   (c) how (if at all) the authority's policy with regard to matters other than sex education should in their opinion be modified in relation to the school;
and to make, and keep up to date, a written statement of their conclusions.

(2) The articles of government for every such school shall provide for it to be the duty of the governing body—
   (a) to consider separately (while having regard to the local education authority's statement under section 17 of this Act) the question whether sex education should form part of the secular curriculum for the school; and
   (b) to make, and keep up to date, a separate written statement—
      (i) of their policy with regard to the content and organisation of the relevant part of the curriculum; or
      (ii) where they conclude that sex education should not form part of the secular curriculum, of that conclusion.

(3) The articles of government for every such school shall provide for it to be the duty of the governing body—
   (a) when considering the matters mentioned in subsections (1) and (2) above, to do so in consultation with the head teacher and to have regard—

    (i) to any representations which are made to them, with regard to any of those matters, by any persons connected with the community served by the school; and

    (ii) to any such representations which are made to them by the chief officer of police and which are connected with his responsibilities;

  (*b*) to consult the authority before making or varying any statement under subsection (1) above; and

  (*c*) to furnish the authority and head teacher with an up to date copy of any statement under this section.

(4) The articles of government for every such school shall provide for it to be the duty of the head teacher to make any statement furnished to him under this section available at all reasonable times, to persons wishing to inspect it.

(5) The articles of government for every such school shall provide for the determination and organisation of the secular curriculum for the school to be the responsibility of the head teacher and for it to be his duty to secure that that curriculum is followed within the school.

(6) The articles of government for every such school shall provide for it to be the duty of the head teacher, in discharging his duties in relation to the secular curriculum for the school—

  (*a*) to consider the statement of the local education authority under section 17 of this Act and those of the governing body under this section;

  (*b*) to have regard—

    (i) to any representations which are made to him, with regard to the determination or organisation of the secular curriculum, by any persons connected with the community served by the school; and

    (ii) to any such representations which are made to him by the chief officer of police and which are connected with that officer's responsibilities; and

  (*c*) to ensure that that curriculum—

    (i) so far as it relates to sex education, is compatible with the governing body's policy (as expressed in their statement under subsection (2) above) except where that policy is incompatible with any part of the syllabus for a course which forms part of that curriculum and leads to a public examination;

    (ii) so far as it relates to other matters, is compatible with the authority's policy (as expressed in their statement) or, to the extent to which it is incompatible, is compatible with that policy as modified by the governing body's statement under subsection (1) above; and

    (iii) is compatible with the enactments relating to education (including, in particular, those relating to children with special educational needs).

(7) The articles of government for every such school shall provide for the governing body to have power to review their conclusions about the matters mentioned in subsections (1) and (2) above whenever they think fit, and for it to be their duty to do so immediately following—

  (*a*) the implementation of any proposal under—

    (i) section 16 of the 1944 Act (transfer of schools to new sites);

    (ii) section 12 or 13 of the 1980 Act (establishment, alteration and discontinuance of schools); or

    (iii) section 15 of the 1980 Act (reduction of school places);

    which materially affects the school; or

  (*b*) in the case of a maintained special school, any change in any of the arrangements made for pupils at the school and their special educational needs which must be complied with (by virtue of regulations made under section 12 of the 1981 Act) for the school to be approved as a maintained special school under section 9(5) of the 1944 Act.

(8) The article of government for every such school shall provide for it to be the duty of the governing body, where—

(a) they have completed such a review; and

(b) they consider it appropriate to make a fresh written statement of their conclusions;

to do so and to furnish the local education authority and the head teacher with a copy of it.

Aided and special agreement schools

19.—(1) The articles of government for every aided and special agreement school shall provide—

(a) for the content of the secular curriculum for the school to be under the control of the governing body;

(b) for the governing body to have regard to the policy of the local education authority as to the curriculum for the authority's schools, as expressed in the statement made by the authority under section 17 of this Act; and

(c) for the head teacher to be allocated by the governing body such functions as will, subject to the resources available, enable him to determine and organise the curriculum and secure that it is followed within the school.

(2) The articles of government for every such school shall provide for it to be the duty of the governing body, when considering the content of the secular curriculum for the school, to have regard—

(a) to any representations which are made to them, with regard to that curriculum, by any persons connected with the community served by the school; and

(b) to any such representations which—

    (i) are made to them by the chief officer of police; and

    (ii) are connected with his responsibilities.

(3) Where the governing body of any such school make any statement in writing of their policy as to the secular curriculum for the school they shall furnish a copy of it to the head teacher; and the head teacher shall make it available, at all reasonable times, to persons wishing to inspect it.

Information for parents

20. The Secretary of State shall make regulations requiring the governing body of every county, voluntary and maintained special school to make available to parents of registered pupils at the school, in such form and manner and at such times as may be prescribed—

(a) such information as to any syllabuses to be followed by those pupils; and

(b) such other information as to the educational provision made for them by the school;

as may be prescribed.

School terms etc.

Terms, sessions and holidays

21.—(1) The articles of government for every county, controlled and maintained special school shall provide for it to be the duty of the local education authority to determine—

(*a*) the times at which the school session is to begin and end on any
day; and

(*b*) the dates and times at which the school terms and holidays are to
begin and end.

(2) The articles of government for every such school shall provide for
the local education authority to have power to require pupils in attendance
at the school to attend at any place outside the school premises for the
purpose of receiving any instruction or training included in the secular
curriculum for the school.

(3) The articles of government for every aided and special agreement
school shall make the same provision as is required by subsections (1) and
(2) above, but in relation to the governing body in place of the local
education authority.

Discipline

Discipline: general duties

22. The articles of government for every county, voluntary and maintained special school shall provide:—

(*a*) for it to be the duty of the head teacher to determine measures
(which may include the making of rules and provision for enforcing
them) to be taken with a view to—

(i) promoting, among pupils, self-discipline and proper regard
for authority;

(ii) encouraging good behaviour on the part of pupils;

(iii) securing that the standard of behaviour of pupils is acceptable; and

(iv) otherwise regulating the conduct of pupils;

(*b*) for it to be the duty of the head teacher, in determining any such
measures—

(i) to act in accordance with any written statement of general
principles provided for him by the governing body; and

(ii) to have regard to any guidance that they may offer in relation
to particular matters;

(*c*) for it to be the duty of the head teacher to make any such measures
generally known within the school;

(*d*) for the standard of behaviour which is to be regarded as acceptable
at the school to be determined by the head teacher, so far as it is
not determined by the governing body;

(*e*) for it to be the duty of the governing body and the head teacher to
consult the local education authority, before determining any such
measures, on any matter arising from the proposed measures which
can reasonably be expected—

(i) to lead to increased expenditure by the authority; or

(ii) to affect the responsibilities of the authority as an employer;

(*f*) for the power to exclude a pupil from the school (whether by
suspension, expulsion or otherwise) to be exercisable only by the
head teacher.

Exclusion of pupils: duty to inform parents etc.

23. The articles of government for every county, voluntary and maintained special school shall provide—

(*a*) for it to be the duty of the head teacher—

(i) where he excludes from the school a pupil who is under
eighteen, to take (without delay) reasonable steps to inform
a parent of the pupil of the period of the exclusion and the
reasons for it;

(ii) where he decides that any exclusion of such a pupil from the school which was originally for a fixed or indefinite period should be made permanent, to take (without delay) reasonable steps to inform a parent of the pupil of his decision and of the reasons for it; and

(iii) where he excludes any pupil from the school to take (without delay) reasonable steps to inform the pupil, if he is aged eighteen or over, or a parent of his, if he is under eighteen, that the pupil or (as the case may be) parent may make representations about the exclusion to the governing body and the local education authority;

(*b*) for it to be the duty of the head teacher, where he excludes a pupil from the school—

(i) for more than five school days (in the aggregate) in any one term; or

(ii) in circumstances in which the pupil would, as a result of his exclusion from the school, lose an opportunity to take any public examination;

to inform the local education authority and the governing body (without delay) of the period of the exclusion and of the reasons for it and where he decides that any exclusion of a pupil from the school which was originally for a fixed or indefinite period should be made permanent, to inform them (without delay) of his decision and of the reasons for it.

Reinstatement of excluded pupils: county, controlled and maintained special schools

24. The articles of government for every county, controlled and maintained special school shall provide—

(*a*) for it to be the duty of the local education authority, where they have been informed of the permanent exclusion of a pupil from the school—

(i) to consider, after consulting the governing body, whether he should be reinstated immediately, reinstated by a particular date or not reinstated;

(ii) where they consider that he should be reinstated, to give the appropriate direction to the head teacher; and

(iii) where they consider that he should not be reinstated, to inform the pupil (if he is aged eighteen or over) or a parent of his (if he is under eighteen) of their decision;

(*b*) for it to be the duty of the head teacher, where he has excluded a pupil from the school—

(i) for more than five school days (in the aggregate) in any one term; or

(ii) in circumstances in which the pupil would, as a result of his exclusion from the school, lose an opportunity to take any public examination;

to comply with any direction for the reinstatement of the pupil given by the governing body or the local education authority, in the case of an exclusion for a fixed period, or by the governing body, in the case of an exclusion which is for an indefinite period or is permanent;

(*c*) for it to be the duty of the local education authority, where they have been informed of the indefinite exclusion of a pupil from the school, to consult the governing body and, where the governing body do not intend to direct the head teacher to reinstate the pupil or the authority consider that he should be reinstated by a date

which is earlier than that determined by the governing body as the
date by which he is to be reinstated—
  (i) to direct that he be reinstated immediately; or
  (ii) to direct that he be reinstated within such period as may be
       specified in the direction;
  (*d*) for it to be the duty of the local education authority where—
       (i) they have been informed of the exclusion of a pupil from the
           school for a fixed period; and
       (ii) they propose to give a direction for his reinstatement;
       to consult the governing body before doing so;
  (*e*) for any direction given by virtue of paragraph (*c*) above to cease to
       have effect (without prejudice to any subsequent direction given
       by virtue of any other provision made by the articles in accordance
       with this section) if the head teacher decides that the exclusion of
       the pupil concerned should be made permanent;
  (*f*) for it to be the duty of the head teacher to comply with any
       direction given in exercise of the duty imposed on the local
       education authority by virtue of paragraph (*a*) or (*c*) above;
  (*g*) for it to be the duty of the head teacher, where conflicting directions
       for the reinstatement of a pupil are given by the governing body
       and the local education authority, to comply with that direction
       which will lead to the earlier reinstatement of the pupil; and
  (*h*) for it to be the duty of the governing body and the local education
       authority to inform each other and—
       (i) the pupil concerned, if he is aged eighteen or over; or
       (ii) a parent of his, if he is under eighteen;
       of any direction, of a kind mentioned in this section, which is given
       by them.

Reinstatement of excluded pupils: aided and special agreement schools

25. The articles of government for every aided and special agreement
school shall provide—
  (*a*) for it to be the duty of the governing body, where they have been
       informed of the permanent exclusion of a pupil from the school—
       (i) to consider whether he should be reinstated immediately,
           reinstated by a particular date or not reinstated;
       (ii) where they consider that he should be reinstated, to give
            the appropriate direction to the head teacher; and
       (iii) where they consider that he should not be reinstated, to
             inform (without delay) the local education authority and
             either the pupil, if he is aged eighteen or over, or a parent
             of his, if he is under eighteen, of their decision;
  (*b*) for it to be the duty of the head teacher where he has excluded a
       pupil from the school—
       (i) for more than five school days (in the aggregate) in any one
           term; or
       (ii) in circumstances in which the pupil would, as a result of his
            exclusion from the school, lose an opportunity to take any
            public examination;
       to comply with any direction for the reinstatement of the pupil
       given by the governing body or, in the case of an exclusion for a
       fixed period, by the governing body or the local education
       authority;
  (*c*) for it to be the duty of the local education authority to consult the
       governing body before giving any direction by virtue of paragraph
       (*b*) above;
  (*d*) for it to be the duty of the local education authority, where they

have been informed of the indefinite exclusion of a pupil from the school, to consult the governing body and, where the governing body do not intend to direct the head teacher to reinstate the pupil or the authority consider that he should be reinstated by a date which is earlier than that determined by the governing body as the date by which he is to be reinstated—

    (i) to direct that he be reinstated immediately; or

    (ii) to direct that he be reinstated within such period as may be specified in the direction;

(*e*) for any direction given by virtue of paragraph (*d*) above to cease to have effect (without prejudice to any direction given by virtue of any other provision made by the articles in accordance with this section) if the head teacher decides that the exclusion of the pupil concerned should be made permanent;

(*f*) for it to be the duty of the head teacher to comply with any direction given in exercise of the duty imposed on the local education authority by virtue of paragraph (*d*) above;

(*g*) for it to be the duty of the head teacher, where conflicting directions for the reinstatement of a pupil are given by the governing body and the local education authority, to comply with that direction which will lead to the earlier reinstatement of the pupil; and

(*h*) for it to be the duty of the governing body and the local education authority to inform each other and—

    (i) the pupil concerned, if he is aged eighteen or over; or

    (ii) a parent of his, if he is under eighteen;

of any direction, of a kind mentioned in this section, which is given by them.

Appeals

26.—(1) Every local education authority shall make arrangements for enabling—

(*a*) a registered pupil at a county, controlled or maintained special school who is aged eighteen or over, or a parent of his, in the case of a pupil at such a school who is under eighteen, to appeal against any decision not to reinstate the pupil following his permanent exclusion from the school; and

(*b*) any governing body of such a school, the head teacher of which has been directed by the authority to reinstate any registered pupil at the school who has been permanently excluded, to appeal against the direction.

(2) The governing body of every aided or special agreement school shall make arrangements for enabling a registered pupil at the school who is aged eighteen or over, or a parent of a pupil at such a school who is under eighteen to appeal against any decision not to reinstate the pupil following his permanent exclusion from the school.

(3) Joint arrangements may be made under subsection (2) above by the governing bodies of two or more aided or special agreement schools maintained by the same local education authority.

(4) Any appeal by virtue of this section shall be to an appeal committee constituted in accordance with Part I of Schedule 2 to the 1980 Act; and Schedule 3 to this Act shall have effect, in place of Part II of Schedule 2 to the 1980 Act, in relation to any such appeal.

(5) The decision of an appeal committee on any such appeal shall be binding on the persons concerned; and where the committee determines that the pupil in question should be reinstated it shall direct that he be reinstated immediately or direct that he be reinstated by such date as is specified in the direction.

Exclusion: additional provision for appeals

27. Where the articles of government for any county, voluntary or maintained special school provide—
  (a) for the parents of any pupil who is excluded from the school in circumstances in which no right of appeal is given by section 26 of this Act to have the right to appeal against his exclusion to a person specified by the articles; and
  (b) for the procedure to be followed on such an appeal;
any decision on such an appeal that the pupil should be reinstated, or that he should be reinstated earlier than would otherwise be the case, shall be binding on the head teacher.

Local education authority's reserve power

28.—(1) Every local education authority shall have power, in the circumstances mentioned in subsection (3) below, to take such steps in relation to any county, controlled or special school maintained by them as they consider are required to prevent the breakdown, or continuing breakdown, of discipline at the school.

(2) The governing body and the head teacher of every aided and special agreement school shall, in the circumstances mentioned in subsection (3) below, consider any representations made to them by the local education authority.

(3) The circumstances are that—
  (a) in the opinion of the authority—
       (i) the behaviour of registered pupils at the school; or
       (ii) any action taken by such pupils or their parents;
      is such that the education of any such pupils is, or is likely in the immediate future to become, severely prejudiced; and
  (b) the governing body have been informed in writing of the authority's opinion.

(4) Steps taken by an authority under subsection (1) above may include the giving of any direction to the governing body or head teacher.

Finance

Finance

29.—(1) The articles of government for every county, voluntary and maintained special school shall provide—
  (a) for it to be the duty of the local education authority (with a view to assisting the governing body to judge whether expenditure in relation to their school represents the economic, efficient and effective use of resources) to furnish the governing body, once in every year, with a statement of—
       (i) expenditure incurred or proposed to be incurred by the authority in meeting the day to day cost of running the school (itemised as the authority think appropriate); and
       (ii) such expenditure of a capital nature, incurred or proposed to be incurred by the authority, as they consider appropriate;
  (b) for it to be the duty of the local education authority to make available, in every year, a sum of money which the governing body are to be entitled to spend at their discretion (but subject to paragraph (c) below) on books, equipment, stationery and such other heads of expenditure (if any) as may be specified by the authority or prescribed by the Secretary of State;
  (c) for it to be the duty of the governing body, in spending any such sum, to comply with such reasonable conditions as the authority think fit to impose;

(d) for the governing body to have power to delegate to the head teacher, to such extent as they may specify, their powers in relation to the sum so made available; and

(e) for it to be the duty of the governing body not to incur any expenditure under any of the heads of expenditure mentioned in paragraph (b) above which, in the opinion of the head teacher, would be inappropriate in relation to the curriculum for the school.

(2) Before making any regulations under subsection (1)(b) above, the Secretary of State shall consult such associations of local authorities as appear to him to be concerned and any local authority with whom consultation appears to him to be desirable.

Reports and meetings

Governors' annual report to parents

30.—(1) The articles of government for every county, voluntary and maintained special school shall provide for it to be the duty of the governing body to prepare, once in every school year, a report ("the governors' report") containing—

(a) a summary of the steps taken by the governing body in the discharge of their functions during the period since their last report; and

(b) such other information as the articles may require.

(2) The articles of government for every such school shall, in particular, require the governors' report—

(a) to be as brief as is reasonably consistent with the requirements as to its contents;

(b) where there is an obligation on the governing body (by virtue of section 31 of this Act) to hold an annual parents' meeting—

　　(i) to give details of the date, time and place for the next such meeting and its agenda;

　　(ii) to indicate that the purpose of that meeting will be to discuss both the governors' report and the discharge by the governing body, the head teacher and the local education authority of their functions in relation to the school; and

　　(iii) to report on the consideration which has been given to any resolutions passed at the previous such meeting;

(c) to give the name of each governor and indicate whether he is a parent, teacher or foundation governor or was co-opted or otherwise appointed as a governor or is an ex officio governor;

(d) to say, in the case of an appointed governor, by whom he was appointed;

(e) to give, in relation to each governor who is not an ex officio governor, the date on which his term of office comes to an end;

(f) to name, and give the address of, the chairman of the governing body and their clerk;

(g) to give such information as is available to the governing body about arrangements for the next election of parent governors;

(h) to contain a financial statement—

　　(i) reproducing or summarising the latest financial statement provided for the governing body by the local education authority (by virtue of paragraph (a) of section 29(1) of this Act);

　　(ii) indicating, in general terms, how any sum made available to the governing body by the authority (by virtue of paragraph (b) of that section), in the period covered by the report, was used; and

(iii) giving details of the application of any gifts made to the
school in that period;

(*i*) to give, in the case of a secondary school, such information in
relation to public examinations as is required to be published by
virtue of section 8(5) of the 1980 Act;

(*j*) to describe what steps have been taken by the governing body to
develop or strengthen the school's links with the community
(including links with the police); and

(*k*) to draw attention to the information made available by the governing body in accordance with the regulations made under section 20
of this Act.

(3) The articles of government for every such school shall—

(*a*) enable the governing body to produce their report in such
language or languages (in addition to English) as they consider
appropriate; and

(*b*) require them to produce it in such language or languages (in
addition to English and any other language in which the
governing body propose to produce it) as the local education
authority may direct.

(4) The articles of government for every such school shall provide for
it to be the duty of the governing body of any such school to take such
steps as are reasonably practicable to secure that—

(*a*) the parents of all registered pupils at the school and all persons
employed at the school are given (free of charge) a copy of the
governors' report;

(*b*) copies of the report are available for inspection (at all reasonable
times and free of charge) at the school; and

(*c*) where there is an obligation on the governing body (by virtue of
section 31 of this Act) to hold an annual parents' meeting, copies
of the report to be considered at that meeting are given to parents
not less than two weeks before that meeting.

Annual parents' meetings

31.—(1) Subject to subsections (7) and (8) below, the articles of
government for every county, voluntary and maintained special school
shall provide for it to be the duty of the governing body to hold a meeting
once in every school year ("the annual parents' meeting") which is open
to—

(*a*) all parents of registered pupils at the school;

(*b*) the head teacher; and

(*c*) such other persons as the governing body may invite.

(2) The purpose of the meeting shall be to provide an opportunity for
discussion of—

(*a*) the governors' report; and

(*b*) the discharge by the governing body, the head teacher and the
local education authority of their functions in relation to the school.

(3) No person who is not a parent of a registered pupil at the school
may vote on any question put to the meeting.

(4) The articles of government for every such school shall provide—

(*a*) for the proceedings at any annual parents' meeting to be under
the control of the governing body;

(*b*) for any annual parents' meeting, at which the required number
of parents of registered pupils at the school are present, to be
entitled to pass (by a simple majority) resolutions on any
matters which may properly be discussed at the meeting;

(*c*) for it to be the duty of the governing body—

(i) to consider any resolution which is duly passed at such a meeting and which they consider is a matter for them;

(ii) to send to the head teacher a copy of any such resolution which they consider is a matter for him; and

(iii) to send to the local education authority a copy of any such resolution which they consider is a matter for the authority; and

(d) for it to be the duty of the head teacher, and of the local education authority, to consider any such resolution a copy of which has been sent to him, or them, by the governing body and to provide the governing body with a brief comment on it (in writing) for inclusion in their next governors' report.

(5) The articles of government for every county, controlled and maintained special school shall provide for any question whether any person is to be treated as the parent of a registered pupil at the school, for the purposes of any provision of the articles relating to the annual parents' meeting, to be determined by the local education authority.

(6) The articles of government for every aided or special agreement school shall provide for any such question to be determined by the governing body.

(7) The articles of government for every special school established in a hospital shall provide that where the governing body are of the opinion that it would be impracticable to hold an annual parents' meeting in a particular school year they may refrain from holding such a meeting in that year.

(8) The articles of government for every county, voluntary and maintained special school (other than a special school established in a hospital), the proportion of registered pupils at which who are boarders is, or is likely to be, at least fifty per cent., shall provide that where—

(a) the governing body are of the opinion that it would be impracticable to hold an annual parents' meeting in a particular school year; and

(b) at least fifty per cent. of the registered pupils at the school are boarders at the time when the governing body form that opinion; they may refrain from holding such a meeting in that year.

(9) In subsection (4)(b) above "the required number", in relation to any school, means any number equal to at least twenty per cent. of the number of registered pupils at the school.

Reports by governing body and head teacher

32.—(1) The articles of government for every county, voluntary and maintained special school shall provide—

(a) for the governing body to furnish to the local education authority such reports in connection with the discharge of their functions as the authority may require (either on a regular basis or from time to time); and

(b) for the head teacher to furnish to the governing body or (as the case may be) local education authority such reports in connection with the discharge of his functions as the governing body or authority may so require.

(2) The articles of government for every aided school shall provide—

(a) for the local education authority to notify the governing body of any requirement of a kind mentioned in subsection (1)(b) above which is imposed by them on the head teacher; and

(b) for the head teacher to furnish the governing body with a copy of any report which he makes in complying with the requirement.

Admissions

Admissions

33.—(1) Where the governing body of any county or voluntary school are responsible for determining the arrangements for admitting pupils to the school, they shall—

(a) at least once in every school year, consult the local education authority as to whether those arrangements are satisfactory; and

(b) consult the authority before determining, or varying, any of them.

(2) Where the local education authority are responsible for determining the arrangements for admitting pupils to any such school they shall—

(a) at least once in every school year, consult the governing body as to whether those arrangements are satisfactory; and

(b) consult the governing body before determining, or varying, any of them.

Appointment and dismissal of staff

Determination of staff complement for schools

34.—(1) Every county, controlled, special agreement and maintained special school shall have a complement of teaching and non-teaching posts determined by the local education authority.

(2) The complement for any such school shall include—

(a) all full-time teaching posts; and

(b) all part-time teaching posts which are to be filled by persons whose only employment with the authority will be at the school.

(3) The complement for any such school shall not include any staff employed by the authority solely in connection with either or both of the following—

(a) the provision of meals;

(b) the supervision of pupils at midday.

Appointment and dismissal of staff: introductory

35.—(1) The appointment and dismissal of staff (including teachers) at every county, controlled, special agreement and maintained special school shall be under the control of the local education authority, but—

(a) the appointment of a head teacher shall be subject to the provision made by the articles of government for the school in accordance with section 37 of this Act;

(b) the appointment of a deputy head teacher shall be subject to the provision made by the articles in accordance with section 39 of this Act;

(c) the appointment and dismissal of the clerk to the governing body shall be subject to section 40 of this Act and to any provision made by the articles in accordance with that section;

(d) the appointment of any other staff (including any teacher), to a post which is part of the school's complement, shall be subject to the provision made by the articles in accordance with section 38 of this Act;

(e) the dismissal of staff shall be subject to the provision made by the articles in accordance with section 41 of this Act;

(f) the appointment and dismissal of staff at any school for which there is a temporary governing body shall be subject to the provisions of Schedule 2 to this Act; and

(g) this section is subject to the provisions of sections 27 and 28 of the 1944 Act (which relate to religious education).

(2) The articles of government for every such school shall provide for it to be the duty of the local education authority to consult the governing body and the head teacher before appointing any person to work solely at the school otherwise than—

(a) in a teaching post;

(b) in a non-teaching post which is part of the complement of the school; or

(c) solely in connection with either or both of the following—
  (i) the provision of meals;
  (ii) the supervision of pupils at midday.

The selection panel

36.—(1) The articles of government for every county, controlled, special agreement and maintained special school shall provide—

(a) for the constitution of a selection panel whenever such a panel is required, by virtue of section 37 or 39 of this Act, in relation to the appointment of a head teacher or deputy head teacher;

(b) for the selection panel to consist of a specified number of persons appointed to it by the local education authority and a specified number of governors appointed to it by the governing body, the number so specified being—
  (i) in each case, not less than three; and
  (ii) in relation to appointments made by the governing body, not less than the number specified in relation to appointments made by the authority; and

(c) for the governing body and the authority to have power to replace, at any time, any member of the selection panel whom they have appointed.

(2) The Secretary of State may by regulations make provision as to the meetings and proceedings of selection panels.

Appointment of head teacher

37.—(1) The articles of government for every county, controlled, special agreement and maintained special school shall provide—

(a) for it to be the duty of the local education authority not to appoint a person to be the head teacher of the school unless his appointment has been recommended by a selection panel constituted in accordance with the articles;

(b) for it to be the duty of the authority, in the event of the post of head teacher being vacant, to appoint an acting head teacher after consulting the governing body;

(c) for it to be the duty of the authority, before appointing a head teacher, to advertise the vacancy in such publications circulating throughout England and Wales as they consider appropriate;

(d) for it to be the duty of the selection panel constituted in relation to the appointment of a head teacher to interview such applicants for the post as they think fit;

(e) in the event of a failure of the panel to agree on the applicants whom they wish to interview—
  (i) for those members of the panel appointed by the governing body to have the right to nominate not more than two applicants to be interviewed by the panel; and
  (ii) for the other members of the panel to have the right to nominate not more than two other applicants to be so interviewed;

(f) for it to be the duty of the panel, where they consider that it is

appropriate to do so, to recommend to the authority for appointment as head teacher one of the applicants interviewed by them;
   (g) for it to be the duty of the panel, where they are unable to agree
on a person to recommend to the authority—
      (i) to repeat (with a view to reaching agreement) such of the
steps which they are required to take by virtue of paragraphs
(*d*) to (*f*) above as they think fit;
      (ii) where they have repeated any of those steps and remain
unable to agree, or have decided that it is not appropriate
to repeat any of them, to require the authority to re-
advertise the vacancy; and
      (iii) where the vacancy is re-advertised, to repeat all of those
steps;
   (h) for it to be the duty of the panel, where the authority decline to
appoint a person recommended by them—
      (i) where there are applicants for the post whom they have not
interviewed, to interview such of those applicants (if any) as
they think fit;
      (ii) to recommend another of the applicants interviewed by
them, if they think fit;
      (iii) to ask the authority to re-advertise the vacancy, if they
consider that it should be re-advertised; and
      (iv) where the vacancy is re-advertised, to repeat the steps which
they are required to take by virtue of paragraphs (*d*) to (*f*);
   (i) for it to be the duty of the authority to re-advertise the post of
head teacher where they are required to do so by the panel; and
for the authority to have power to do so, where—
      (i) the post has been duly advertised;
      (ii) the selection panel have failed to make either a recommen-
dation which is acceptable to the authority or a request that
the post be re-advertised; and
      (iii) the authority are of the opinion that the panel have had
sufficient time in which to carry out their functions; and
   (j) for the chief education officer of the authority, or a member of his
department nominated by him, to have the right to attend all
proceedings of the panel (including interviews) for the purpose of
giving advice to members of the panel.
  (2) In this section "head teacher" does not include an acting head
teacher.

Appointment of certain other staff

  38.—(1) The articles of government for every county, controlled,
special agreement and maintained special school shall provide for it to be
the duty of the local education authority, where there is a vacancy in any
post which is part of the complement of the school—
   (a) to decide whether, in the case of a post which is not a new one, it
should be retained;
   (b) to advertise the vacancy, and fill it in accordance with the procedure
laid down by virtue of subsection (3) below, unless they have the
intention mentioned in paragraph (c) below; and
   (c) to fill the vacancy in accordance with the procedure laid down by
virtue of subsection (4) below, if they intend to appoint a person
who, at the time when they form that intention, is an employee of
theirs or has been appointed to take up employment with them at
a future date.

(2) This section does not apply in relation to the appointment of a head teacher or deputy head teacher or to any temporary appointment made pending—

(*a*) the return to work of the holder of the post in question; or

(*b*) the taking of any steps required by the articles of government in relation to the vacancy in question.

(3) The articles of government for every such school shall provide—

(*a*) for it to be the duty of the authority, where they decide to advertise the vacancy, to do so in a manner likely in their opinion to bring it to the notice of persons (including employees of theirs) who are qualified to fill the post;

(*b*) for it to be the duty of the governing body, where the vacancy is advertised—

(i) to interview such applicants for the post as they think fit; and

(ii) where they consider that it is appropriate to do so, to recommend to the authority for appointment to the post one of the applicants interviewed by them;

(*c*) for it to be the duty of the governing body, where they are unable to agree on a person to recommend to the authority—

(i) to repeat the steps which they are required to take by virtue of paragraph (*b*) above, if they consider that to do so might lead to their reaching agreement;

(ii) where they have repeated those steps and remain unable to agree, or have decided that it is not appropriate to repeat them, to ask the authority to re-advertise the vacancy; and

(iii) where the vacancy is re-advertised, to repeat those steps;

(*d*) for it to be the duty of the governing body, where the authority decline to appoint a person recommended by them—

(i) where there are applicants for the post whom they have not interviewed, to interview such of those applicants (if any) as they think fit;

(ii) to recommend another of the applicants interviewed by them, if they think fit;

(iii) to ask the authority to re-advertise the vacancy, if they consider that it should be re-advertised; and

(iv) where the vacancy is re-advertised, to repeat the steps which they are required to take by virtue of paragraph (*b*) above;

(*e*) for it to be the duty of the authority, where they are asked by the governing body to re-advertise the vacancy, to do so unless they decide—

(i) that the post is to be removed from the complement of the school; or

(ii) to appoint a person who, at the time when that decision is made, is an employee of theirs or has been appointed to take up employment with them at a future date; and

(*f*) for—

(i) the head teacher, where he would not otherwise be entitled to be present; and

(ii) such person (if any) as the authority appoint to represent them,

to be entitled to be present, for the purpose of giving advice, whenever governors meet to discuss the appointment or an applicant is interviewed.

(4) The articles of government for every such school shall provide—

(*a*) in the event of the vacancy not being advertised, for the governing body to be entitled to determine a specification for the post in consultation with the head teacher;

(b) where the governing body have determined such a specification, for it to be their duty to send a copy of it to the authority;

(c) for it to be the duty of the authority—

    (i) to have regard to the specification, and consult the governing body and the head teacher, when considering whom to appoint to the post; and

    (ii) if they make an appointment to a teaching post with which the governing body disagree, to report the fact to the next meeting of their appropriate education committee.

(5) No local education authority shall appoint a person to a post which they have advertised in accordance with requirements imposed by virtue of subsection (3) above unless—

(a) his appointment has been recommended in accordance with those requirements; or

(b) the authority decide to appoint a person who, at the time when that decision is made, is an employee of theirs or has been appointed to take up employment with them at a future date.

(6) The articles of government for every such school shall provide—

(a) for the governing body to have power to delegate any of the functions which are theirs by virtue of this section, in relation to the filling of a particular vacancy or a vacancy of a kind specified by them, to—

    (i) one or more governors;

    (ii) the head teacher; or

    (iii) one or more governors and the head teacher acting together; and

(b) for the provision made in the articles by virtue of subsection (3)(e) or (4)(c)(ii) to apply in such a case with the substitution of references to the person or persons to whom the functions are delegated for references to the governing body.

Appointment of deputy head teacher

39.—(1) The articles of government for every county, controlled, special agreement and maintained special school shall, in relation to the appointment of a deputy head teacher for the school, make—

(a) the same provision, modified in accordance with subsections (2) and (3) below, as that made by the articles (in accordance with section 37 of this Act) in relation to the appointment of a head teacher for the school; or

(b) the same provision as that made by the articles (in accordance with section 38 of this Act) in relation to the appointment of other teachers at the school.

(2) Articles of government which, in accordance with subsection (1) above, provide for the appointment of a deputy head teacher for the school to be on the recommendation of a selection panel shall provide for the head teacher, where he is not a member of the panel—

(a) to be entitled to be present, for the purpose of giving advice, at any proceedings of the panel (including interviews); and

(b) whether or not he attends any such proceedings, to be consulted by the panel before it makes any recommendation to the local education authority.

(3) No provision shall be required in the articles of government similar to that mentioned in section 37(1)(b) of this Act.

(4) In subsection (1) above "head teacher" does not include an acting head teacher.

Appointment and dismissal of clerk to governing body

40.—(1) The articles of government for every county and maintained special school shall provide for the clerk to the governing body to be appointed by the local education authority in accordance with arrangements to be determined by them in consultation with the governing body.

(2) The clerk to the governing body of any controlled or special agreement school shall be appointed—

(a) where the articles of government make provision in relation to his appointment, in accordance with that provision;

(b) in every other case, by the authority in accordance with arrangements determined by them in consultation with the governing body.

(3) Arrangements determined in respect of any school under subsections (1) or (2)(b) above may be varied by the authority in consultation with the governing body.

(4) The articles of government for every county and maintained special school shall provide for it to be the duty of the authority not to dismiss the clerk except in accordance with arrangements determined by them in consultation with the governing body.

(5) The articles of government for every county, controlled, special agreement and maintained special school shall provide for the governing body to have power, where the clerk fails to attend any meeting of theirs, to appoint one of their number to act as clerk for the purposes of that meeting, but without prejudice to his position as a governor.

(6) The clerk to the governing body of any controlled or special agreement schools may not be dismissed except—

(a) where the articles of government make provision in relation to his dismissal, in accordance with that provision; or

(b) in any other case, in accordance with arrangements determined by the local education authority in consultation with the governing body.

(7) The articles of government for every county, controlled, special agreement and maintained special school shall provide for it to be the duty of the local education authority to consider any representations made to them by the governing body as to the dismissal of their clerk.

Dismissal, etc. of staff

41.—(1) The articles of government for every county, controlled, special agreement and maintained special school shall provide—

(a) for it to be the duty of the local education authority to consult the governing body and the head teacher (except where he is the person concerned) before—

(i) dismissing (otherwise than under section 27(5) or 28(4) of the 1944 Act, which allow foundation governors to require the authority to dismiss a reserved teacher) any person to whom subsection (3) below applies;

(ii) otherwise requiring any such person to cease to work at the school; or

(iii) permitting any such person to retire in circumstances in which he would be entitled to compensation for premature retirement;

(b) for it to be the duty of the local education authority, where a teacher at the school is required to complete an initial period of probation, to consult the governing body and the head teacher before—

    (i) extending his period of probation; or

    (ii) deciding whether he has completed it successfully;

(c) for it to be the duty of the local education authority, where the governing body recommend to them that a person should cease to work at the school, to consider their recommendation;

(d) for both the governing body and the head teacher to have power to suspend any person employed to work at the school where, in the opinion of the governing body or (as the case may be) the head teacher, his exclusion from the school is required; and

(e) for it to be the duty of the governing body, or head teacher, when exercising that power—

    (i) to inform the local education authority and the head teacher or (as the case may be) governing body forthwith; and

    (ii) to end the suspension if directed to do so by the authority.

(2) In this section "suspend" means suspend without loss of emoluments.

(3) This subsection applies to any person who is employed—

(a) in a post which is part of the complement of the school in question; or

(b) to work solely at the school in any other post, otherwise than solely in connection with either or both of the following—

    (i) the provision of meals;

    (ii) the supervision of pupils at midday.

School premises

School premises

42. The articles of government for every county and maintained special school shall provide—

(a) for the use of the school premises at all times other than during any school session, or break between sessions on the same day, to be under the control of the governing body;

(b) for the governing body to exercise control subject to any direction given to them by the local education authority and in so doing to have regard to the desirability of the premises being made available (when not required by or in connection with the school) for use by members of the community served by the school.

PART IV

MISCELLANEOUS

Freedom of speech in universities, polytechnics and colleges

43.—(1) Every individual and body of persons concerned in the government of any establishment to which this section applies shall take such steps as are reasonably practicable to ensure that freedom of speech within the law is secured for members, students and employees of the establishment and for visiting speakers.

(2) The duty imposed by subsection (1) above includes (in particular) the duty to ensure, so far as is reasonably practicable, that the use of any premises of the establishment is not denied to any individual or body of persons on any ground connected with—

(a) the beliefs or views of that individual or of any member of that body; or

(b) the policy or objectives of that body.

(3) The governing body of every such establishment shall, with a view to facilitating the discharge of the duty imposed by subsection (1) above in relation to that establishment, issue and keep up to date a code of practice setting out—

(*a*) the procedures to be followed by members, students and employees of the establishment in connection with the organisation—

(i) of meetings which are to be held on premises of the establishment and which fall within any class of meeting specified in the code; and

(ii) of other activities which are to take place on those premises and which fall within any class of activity so specified; and

(*b*) the conduct required of such persons in connection with any such meeting or activity;

and dealing with such other matters as the governing body consider appropriate.

(4) Every individual and body of persons concerned in the government of any such establishment shall take such steps as are reasonably practicable (including where appropriate the initiation of disciplinary measures) to secure that the requirements of the code of practicc for that establishment, issued under subsection (3) above, are complied with.

(5) The establishments to which this section applies are—

(*a*) any university;

(*b*) any establishment which is maintained by a local education authority and for which section 1 of the 1968 (No. 2) Act (government and conduct of colleges of education and other institutions providing further education) requires there to be an instrument of government; and

(*c*) any establishment of further education designated by or under regulations made under section 27 of the 1980 Act as an establishment substantially dependent for its maintenance on assistance from local education authorities or on grants under section 100(1)(*b*) of the 1944 Act.

(6) In this section—

"governing body", in relation to any university, means the executive governing body which has responsibility for the management and administration of its revenue and property and the conduct of its affairs (that is to say the body commonly called the council of the university);

"university" includes a university college and any college, or institution in the nature of a college, in a university.

(7) Where any establishment—

(*a*) falls within subsection (5)(*b*) above; or

(*b*) falls within subsection (5)(*c*) above by virtue of being substantially dependent for its maintenance on assistance from local education authorities;

the local education authority or authorities maintaining or (as the case may be) assisting the establishment shall, for the purposes of this section, be taken to be concerned in its government.

(8) Where a students' union occupies premises which are not premises of the establishment in connection with which the union is constituted, any reference in this section to the premises of the establishment shall be taken to include a reference to the premises occupied by the students' union.

Political indoctrination

44.—(1) The local education authority by whom any county, voluntary or special school is maintained, and the governing body and head teacher of the school shall forbid—

(*a*) the pursuit of partisan political activities by any of those registered pupils at the school who are junior pupils; and

(*b*) the promotion of partisan political views in the teaching of any subject in the school.

(2) In the case of activities which take place otherwise than on the premises of the school concerned, subsection (1)(*a*) above applies only where arrangements for junior pupils to take part in the activities are made by any member of the staff of the school (in his capacity as such) or by anyone acting on his, or the school's behalf.

Duty to secure balanced treatment of political issues

45. The local education authority by whom any county, voluntary or special school is maintained, and the governing body and head teacher of the school, shall take such steps as are reasonably practicable to secure that where political issues are brought to the attention of pupils while they are—

(*a*) at the school; or

(*b*) taking part in extra-curricular activities which are provided or organised for registered pupils at the school by or on behalf of the school;

they are offered a balanced presentation of opposing views.

Sex education

46. The local education authority by whom any county, voluntary or special school is maintained, and the governing body and head teacher of the school, shall take such steps as are reasonably practicable to secure that where sex education is given to any registered pupils at the school it is given in such a manner as to encourage those pupils to have due regard to moral considerations and the value of family life.

Abolition of corporal punishment

47.—(1) Where, in any proceedings, it is shown that corporal punishment has been given to a pupil by or on the authority of a member of the staff, giving the punishment cannot be justified on the ground that it was done in pursuance of a right exercisable by the member of the staff by virtue of his position as such.

(2) Subject to subsection (3) below, references in this section to giving corporal punishment are references to doing anything for the purposes of punishing the pupil concerned (whether or not there are also other reasons for doing it) which, apart from any justification, would constitute battery.

(3) A person is not to be taken for the purposes of this section as giving corporal punishment by virtue of anything done for reasons that include averting an immediate danger of personal injury to, or an immediate danger to the property of, any person (including the pupil concerned).

(4) A person does not commit an offence by reason of any conduct relating to a pupil which would, apart from this section, be justified on the ground that it is done in pursuance of a right exercisable by a member of the staff by virtue of his position as such.

(5) In this section "pupil" means a person—

(*a*) for whom education is provided—

(i) at a school maintained by a local education authority;

(ii) at a special school not so maintained; or

(iii) at an independent school which is maintained or assisted by a Minister of the Crown (including a school of which a government department is the proprietor) or assisted

by a local education authority and which falls within a
prescribed class;

(b) for whom primary or secondary education, or education which
would be primary or secondary education if it were provided
full-time, is provided by a local education authority otherwise
than at a school; or

(c) to whom subsection (6) below applies and for whom education
is provided at an independent school which does not fall within
paragraph (a)(iii) above;

but does not include any person who is aged eighteen or over.

(6) This subsection applies to a person if—

(a) he holds an assisted place under a scheme operated by the
Secretary of State under section 17 of the 1980 Act;

(b) any of the fees or expenses payable in respect of his attendance
at school are paid by the Secretary of State under section 100
of the 1944 Act or by a local education authority under section
6 of the Education (Miscellaneous Provisions) Act 1953;

(c) any of the fees payable in respect of his attendance at school
are paid by a local education authority under section 81 of the
1944 Act; or

(d) he falls within a prescribed category of persons.

(7) The Secretary of State may prescribe, for the purposes of subsection
(6)(d) above, one or more categories of persons who appear to him to be
persons in respect of whom any fees are paid out of public funds.

(8) A person shall not be debarred from receiving education (whether
by refusing him admission to a school, suspending his attendance or
otherwise) by reason of the fact that this section applies in relation to
him, or if he were admitted might so apply.

(9) The power conferred on the Secretary of State by paragraph 4 of
Schedule 4 to the 1980 Act to terminate a participation agreement under
section 17 of that Act if he is not satisfied that appropriate educational
standards are being maintained includes power to do so if he is not
satisfied that subsection (8) above is being complied with.

(10) In this section "member of the staff" means—

(a) in relation to a person who is a pupil by reason of the provision
of education for him at any school, any teacher who works at
the school and any other person who has lawful control or
charge of the pupil and works there; and

(b) in relation to a person who is a pupil by reason of the provision
of education for him by a local education authority at a place
other than a school, any teacher employed by the authority
who works at that place and any other person employed by the
authority who has lawful control or charge of the pupil and
works there.

(11) An Order in Council under paragraph 1(1)(b) of Schedule 1 to the
Northern Ireland Act 1974 (legislation for Northern Ireland in the interim
period) which states that it is made only for the purposes corresponding
to those of this section—

(a) shall not be subject to paragraph 1(4) and (5) of that Schedule
(affirmative resolution of both Houses of Parliament); but

(b) shall be subject to annulment in pursuance of a resolution of either
House.

Abolition of corporal punishment: Scotland

48. After section 48 of the Education (Scotland) Act 1980, there shall
be inserted the following new section—

"Corporal Punishment

Abolition of corporal punishment of pupils

48A.—(1) Where, in any proceedings, it is shown that corporal punishment has been given to a pupil by or on the authority of a member of the staff, giving the punishment cannot be justified on the ground that it was done in pursuance of a right exercisable by the member of the staff by virtue of his position as such.

(2) Subject to subsection (3) below, references in this section to giving corporal punishment are references to doing anything for the purposes of punishing the pupil concerned (whether or not there are also other reasons for doing it) which, apart from any justification, would constitute physical assault upon the person.

(3) A person is not to be taken for the purposes of this section as giving corporal punishment by virtue of anything done for reasons which include averting an immediate danger of personal injury to, or an immediate danger to the property of, any person (including the pupil concerned).

(4) A person does not commit an offence by reason of any conduct relating to a pupil which would, apart from this section, be justified on the ground that it was done in pursuance of a right exercisable by a member of the staff by virtue of his position as such.

(5) In this section 'pupil' means a person—

    (a) for whom education is provided—

        (i) at a public school,

        (ii) at a grant-aided school, or

        (iii) at an independent school, maintained or assisted by a Minister of the Crown, which is a school prescribed by regulations made under this section or falls within a category of schools so prescribed.

    (b) for whom school education is provided by an education authority otherwise than at a school, or

    (c) to whom subsection (6) below applies and for whom education is provided at an independent school which does not fall within paragraph (a)(iii) above.

(6) This subsection applies to a person if—

    (a) he holds an assisted place under a scheme operated by the Secretary of State under section 75A of this Act.

    (b) any of the fees or expenses payable in respect of his attendance at school are paid by the Secretary of State under section 73(f) of this Act.

    (c) any of the fees payable in respect of his attendance at school are paid by an education authority under section 24(1)(c), 49(2)(b), 50(1) or 64(3) of this Act, or

    (d) he falls within a category, prescribed by regulations made under this section, of persons appearing to the Secretary of State to be persons in respect of whom any fees are paid out of public funds.

(7) In this section 'member of the staff' means—

    (a) in relation to a person who is a pupil by reason of the provision of education for him at any school, any teacher who works at the school and any other person who has lawful control or charge of the pupil and works there, and

    (b) in relation to a person who is a pupil by reason of the provision of school education for him by an education authority at a place other than a school, any teacher employed by the authority who works at that place and any other person employed by the authority who has lawful control or charge of the pupil and works there.

(8) The Secretary of State may, by order made by statutory instrument, prescribe—

(a) schools or categories of school for the purposes of subsection (5)(a)(iii) above; and

(b) categories of persons for the purposes of subsection (6)(d) above.

(9) A person shall not be debarred from receiving education (whether by refusing him admission to, or excluding him from, a school or otherwise) by reason of the fact that this section applies in relation to him, or if he were admitted might so apply.

(10) The power conferred on the Secretary of State by paragraph 4 of Schedule 1A to this Act to revoke a determination under section 75A of this Act if he is not satisfied that appropriate educational standards are being maintained includes power to do so if he is not satisfied that subsection (9) above is being complied with.".

Appraisal of performance of teachers

49.—(1) The Secretary of State may by regulations make provision requiring local education authorities, or such other persons as may be prescribed, to secure that the performance of teachers to whom the regulations apply—

(a) in discharging their duties; and

(b) in engaging in other activities connected with the establishments at which they are employed;

is regularly appraised in accordance with such requirements as may be prescribed.

(2) The regulations may, in particular, make provision—

(a) requiring the governing bodies of such categories of schools or other establishments as may be prescribed—

(i) to secure, so far as it is reasonably practicable for them to do so, that any arrangements made in accordance with the regulations are complied with in relation to their establishments; and

(ii) to provide such assistance to the local education authority as the authority may reasonably require in connection with their obligations under the regulations;

(b) with respect to the disclosure to teachers of the results of appraisals and the provision of opportunities for them to make representations with respect to those results; and

(c) requiring local education authorities to have regard to the results of appraisals in the exercise of such of their functions as may be prescribed.

(3) The regulations may be expressed to apply to any of the following categories of teacher, that is to say teachers employed—

(a) at any school maintained by a local education authority;

(b) at any special school (whether or not so maintained);

(c) at any further education establishment provided by a local education authority;

(d) at any further education establishment designated by regulations made under section 27 of the 1980 Act as an establishment substantially dependent for its maintenance—

(i) on assistance from local education authorities; or

(ii) on grants under section 100(1)(b) of the 1944 Act;

(e) at any school or other establishment which falls within any prescribed class of school, or other establishment, of a kind mentioned in any of paragraphs (*a*) to (*d*) above; or

(*f*) by a local education authority otherwise than at a school or further education establishment.

(4) Before making any regulations under subsection (1) above, the Secretary of State shall consult—

(*a*) such associations of local authorities, and representatives of teachers, as appear to him to be concerned; and

(*b*) any other person with whom consultation appears to him to be desirable.

Grants for teacher training, etc.

50.—(1) The Secretary of State may by regulations make provision for the payment by him to local education authorities and other persons of grants to facilitate and encourage the training of—

(*a*) teachers;

(*b*) youth and community workers;

(*c*) education welfare officers;

(*d*) educational psychologists;

(*e*) local education authority inspectors;

(*f*) education advisers employed by such authorities; and

(*g*) such other classes of person, employed in connection with the discharge of any of the functions of such authorities, as may be prescribed.

(2) For the purposes of this section "training" includes—

(*a*) further training, whether or not the person undergoing it is already qualified;

(*b*) the provision of experience (whether or not within education) which is likely to benefit a person in his capacity as an employee of the kind in question;

(*c*) training a person with a view to his continuing to be employed in education but in a different capacity; and

(*d*) the study of matters connected with, or relevant to, education.

(3) Regulations under this section may, in particular—

(*a*) provide for grants to be payable only in respect of training approved by the Secretary of State for the purposes of the regulations;

(*b*) make provision whereby the making of payments by the Secretary of State in pursuance of the regulations is dependent on the fulfilment of such conditions as may be prescribed or otherwise determined by the Secretary of State; and

(*c*) make provision requiring local education authorities, and other persons, to whom payments have been made in pursuance of the regulations to comply with such requests as may be prescribed or so determined.

(4) In this section—

"education welfare officer" means any person who is employed by a local education authority, or employed by any other authority in connection with education, and whose duties include securing the regular attendance at school of pupils of compulsory school age;

"leisure-time facilities" means facilities of a kind which local education authorities are under the duty imposed by sections 41(*b*) and 53(1) of the 1944 Act (provision of facilities for leisure-time occupation, recreation and social and physical training) to secure are provided within their areas; and "youth and community worker" means any person who is employed (whether or not by a local education authority) in such category of employment connected with leisure-time facilities as may be prescribed.

Recoupment

51.—(1) Subject to subsection (2) below, where any provision for primary, secondary or further education is made by a local education authority in respect of a pupil who belongs to the area of another such authority, the providing authority shall, on making a claim within the prescribed period, be entitled to be paid by the other authority—

(a) such amount as the authorities may agree; or

(b) failing agreement, such amount as may be determined in accordance with a direction given by the Secretary of State under this subsection.

(2) Subsection (1) above does not apply to provision for—

(a) primary education made (otherwise than in a hospital) in respect of a pupil who has not attained the age of five years; or

(b) further education made in respect of pupils who do not fall within a prescribed category;

unless it is made with the consent of the authority from whom payment is claimed.

(3) Any direction under subsection (1) above may—

(a) be a general direction applying to all cases to which it is expressed to apply or a direction applying to a particular case;

(b) be designed to provide for the amounts payable by one authority to another to reflect average costs incurred by local education authorities in the provision of education (whether in England and Wales as a whole or in any particular area or areas); and

(c) be based on figures for average costs determined by such body or bodies representing local education authorities, or on such other figures relating to costs so incurred, as the Secretary of State considers appropriate.

(4) A direction applying to a particular case may be given notwithstanding that a general direction would otherwise apply to that case.

(5) It shall not be a ground for refusing to admit a pupil to or excluding a pupil from, a further education establishment that he does not belong to the area of a local education authority maintaining or assisting that establishment ("a responsible authority").

(6) Subsection (5) above does not apply—

(a) in relation to pupils who do not fall into a prescribed category; or

(b) to any refusal to admit a pupil to a further education establishment where his admission would cause a pupil belonging to the area of a responsible authority to be refused admission to that establishment.

(7) References in this section to provision for education include references to provision of any benefits or services for which provision is made by or under the enactments relating to education.

(8) References in subsections (1) to (6) above to further education do not include references to further education of a kind such that expenditure on its provision would fall within paragraph 6 of Schedule 10 to the Local Government, Planning and Land Act 1980.

(9) A local education authority may make a payment to another such authority under subsection (1) above notwithstanding that no claim has been made by the other authority under that subsection.

(10) For the purposes of this section any question whether a pupil belongs, or does not belong, to the area of a particular local education authority shall be decided, as it would for the purposes of the 1980 Act, in accordance with section 38(5) of that Act and the regulations made under that section.

(11) Any dispute between local education authorities as to whether one of them is entitled to be paid any amount by another under this section shall be determined by the Secretary of State.

(12) Section 31(8) of the London Government Act 1963 (obligations in relation to pupils from outside the area of local education authority) shall cease to have effect.

Recoupment: cross-border provisions

52.—(1) The Secretary of State may make regulations requiring or authorising payments of amounts determined by or under the regulations to be made by one authority to another where—

(a) the authority receiving the payment makes, in such cases or circumstances as may be specified in the regulations, provision for education in respect of a pupil having such connection with the area of the paying authority as may be so specified; and

(b) one of the authorities is a local education authority and the other an education authority in Scotland.

(2) The basis on which amounts payable under the regulations are to be determined shall be such as the Secretary of State sees fit to specify in the regulations and may, in particular, be similar to that adopted by him in relation to directions given under section 51(1) of this Act.

(3) Any question concerning the connection of any pupil with the area of a particular local education authority or education authority shall be decided in accordance with the provisions of the regulations.

(4) The reference in subsection (1) above to provision for education includes a reference to provision of any benefits or services for which provision is made by or under the enactments relating to education.

School transport

53. In section 55 of the 1944 Act (provision of transport and other facilities), the following subsection shall be added at the end—

"(3) In considering whether or not they are required by subsection (1) above to make arrangements in relation to a particular pupil, the local education authority shall have regard (amongst other things) to the age of the pupil and the nature of the route, or alternative routes, which he could reasonably be expected to take."

Change of status of controlled school to aided school

54.—(1) On an application duly made to him by the governing body of any controlled school, the Secretary of State may by order direct that as from the date specified in the order the school shall be an aided school.

(2) The Secretary of State shall not make an order under this section unless he is satisfied that the governing body will be able and willing—

(a) with the assistance of any maintenance contribution payable by him under the 1944 Act, to defray the expenses which would fall to be borne by them under section 15(3)(a) of that Act; and

(b) to pay to the local education authority any compensation payable by the governing body under section 55 of this Act.

(3) Where the governing body of a controlled school propose to apply for an order under this section they shall, after consulting the local education authority—

(a) publish their proposals in such manner as may be required by regulations made by the Secretary of State;

(b) submit a copy of the published proposals to him; and

(c) provide him with such information as he may reasonably require in order to enable him to give proper consideration to the proposals.

(4) The published proposals shall be accompanied by a statement which explains the effect of subsection (5) below and specifies the date on which the proposals are intended to be implemented.

(5) Before the end of the period of two months beginning with the day on which the proposals are first published, any of the following may submit objections to the proposals to the Secretary of State—

(a) any ten or more local government electors for the area;

(b) the governing body of any voluntary school affected by the proposals;

(c) any local education authority concerned.

(6) Where, in consequence of an order made under this section, an amount will be payable by a governing body by way of compensation under section 55 of this Act, the order—

(a) shall specify the amount so payable and the date by which it must be paid; and

(b) may impose such conditions in relation to its payment as the Secretary of State thinks fit.

(7) Where the Secretary of State proposes, in making an order under this section, to specify as the date from which the school is to be an aided school a different date to that proposed by the governing body, he shall first consult both that body and the local education authority as to the date which it would be appropriate to specify in the order.

(8) On the application of the local education authority or of the foundation governors of the school any such order may be varied, by order made by the Secretary of State, so as to specify—

(a) a different date to that specified under subsection (1) above; or

(b) a different amount to that specified under subsection (6) above.

(9) Before applying to the Secretary of State under subsection (8) above for the variation of an order, the foundation governors of the school shall consult the other governors.

(10) Before making any variation under subsection (8) above the Secretary of State shall consult—

(a) the local education authority, in the case of an application for variation made by foundation governors; and

(b) the foundation governors of the school, in the case of any application for variation made by the local education authority.

(11) Where foundation governors are consulted by the Secretary of State under subsection (10)(b) above, they shall, before giving him their views, consult the other governors of the school.

(12) Any order under this section may make such provision (including the modification of any provision made by or under this Act) as the Secretary of State considers appropriate in connection with the transition of the school in question from controlled to aided status and may, in particular, make provision—

(a) as to the circumstances in which, and purposes for which, the school is to be treated, before the specified date, as if it were an aided school;

(b) as to the time by which the new instrument of government and articles of government (appropriate for an aided school) are to be made for the school and the consent and consultation which is to be required before they are made;

(c) where the local education authority propose to pass a resolution (under section 9 of this Act) to group the school when it becomes an aided school, as to the consent required before that resolution is passed;

(d) as to the appointment and dismissal of staff for the school;

(e) as to the arrangements to be made in relation to the admission of pupils to the school;

(f) for the governing body of the school to continue, for such purposes as may be specified in the order, to act as the governing body after the school has become an aided school but before a new governing body has been constituted; and

(g) as to functions exercisable by, or in relation to, the governing body or the governors of any category so specified.

Compensation payable by governing body on change from controlled to aided status

55.—(1) Where a controlled school becomes an aided school by virtue of an order made under section 54 of this Act, the governing body shall pay to the local education authority (in accordance with the order) such sum, by way of compensation for capital expenditure on the school—

(a) as may be agreed by that body and the authority; or

(b) failing such agreement, as the Secretary of State thinks fit having regard to the current value of the property in question.

(2) In subsection (1) above "capital expenditure" means any expenditure incurred by the local education authority, or by any predecessor of theirs, in respect of the school under—

(a) section 2 of the Education (Miscellaneous Provisions) Act 1953 (power of Secretary of State, in certain circumstances, to require local education authority to defray expenses of establishing a controlled school);

(b) section 1 of the Education Act 1946 (power of Secretary of State, in certain circumstances, to require expenses incurred in enlarging controlled school to be paid by local education authority); or

(c) paragraph 1 of Schedule 1 to the Act of 1946 (provision of buildings etc. for voluntary schools);

other than expenditure which could have been so incurred in respect of the school if it had always been an aided school.

(3) The Secretary of State may, for the purpose of assisting him in any determination which he is required to make under subsection (1) above, appoint such person as he thinks competent to advise him on the valuation of property.

(4) No contribution, grant or loan shall be paid, or other payment made, by the Secretary of State to the governing body of any controlled school in respect of any compensation payable by them under this section.

Reports to Secretary of State

56. The governing body of every—

(a) county, voluntary and maintained special school; and

(b) establishment which is maintained by a local education authority and for which section 1 of the 1968 (No. 2) Act (government and conduct of colleges of education and other institutions providing further education) requires there to be an instrument of government;

shall make such reports and returns, and give such information, to the Secretary of State as he may require for the purpose of the exercise of his functions in relation to education.

Information and training for governors

57. Every local education authority shall secure—
> (a) that every governor of a county, voluntary or special school maintained by them is provided (free of charge) with—
>> (i) a copy of the instrument of government, and of the articles of government, for the school; and
>> (ii) such other information as they consider appropriate in connection with the discharge of his functions as a governor; and
> (b) that there is made available to every such governor (free of charge) such training as the authority consider necessary for the effective discharge of those functions.

Travelling and subsistence allowances for governors of schools and establishments of further education

58.—(1) A local education authority may, in accordance with the provisions of a scheme made by them for the purposes of this section, pay travelling and subsistence allowances to governors of—
> (a) county, voluntary and maintained special schools; and
> (b) any establishment which is maintained by a local education authority and for which section 1 of the 1968 (No. 2) Act (government and conduct of colleges of education and other institutions providing further education) requires there to be an instrument of government.

(2) Such a scheme may make different provision in relation to schools or other establishments of different categories (including provision for allowances not to be paid in respect of certain categories) but shall not make different provision in relation to different categories of governor of the same school or establishment.

(3) A local education authority shall not make any payment towards the cost of travelling or subsistence allowances for any governor of a designated establishment of further education if—
> (a) the authority have not made any scheme under subsection (1) above; or
> (b) the arrangements under which the allowance would otherwise be payable—
>> (i) provide for allowances which are to any extent more generous than the most generous payable by the authority under any such scheme; or
>> (ii) contain any provision which the authority would not have power to include in any such scheme.

(4) In this section "designated establishment of further education" means an establishment of further education designated by or under regulations made under section 27 of the 1980 Act as an establishment substantially dependent for its maintenance on assistance from local education authorities or on grants under section 100(1)(b) of the 1944 Act.

(5) Subject to subsection (6) below, a local education authority may pay travelling and subsistence allowances to persons appointed to represent them on the governing bodies of—
> (a) establishments of further education which are not maintained or assisted by them; or

(*b*) any independent school or special school which is not maintained by them.

(6) A local education authority shall not pay any allowance under subsection (5) above for expenses in respect of which the person incurring them is entitled to reimbursement by any person other than the authority or if—

(*a*) the authority have not made any scheme under subsection (1) above; or

(*b*) the arrangements under which the allowance would otherwise be payable—

   (i) provide for allowances which are to any extent more generous than the most generous payable by the authority under any such scheme; or

   (ii) contain any provision which the authority would not have power to include in any such scheme.

(7) No allowance may be paid to any governor of a school or establishment of a kind mentioned in subsection (1) above in respect of the discharge of his functions as such a governor, otherwise than under this section.

Repeal of section 4 of 1944 Act

59. Section 4 of the 1944 Act (which makes provision in relation to the two central advisory councils for education) shall cease to have effect.

Discontinuance of Secretary of State's duty to make annual reports

60.—(1) Section 5 of the 1944 Act (which requires the Secretary of State to make an annual report to Parliament) shall cease to have effect.

(2) The Secretary of State's report under that section for the year 1985 shall be the last such report that he is required to make.

Minimum age for governors of establishments of further education

61.—(1) No person shall be qualified for membership of the governing body of any institution—

(*a*) which is maintained by a local education authority; and

(*b*) for which section 1 of the 1968 (No. 2) Act (government and conduct of colleges of education and other institutions providing further education) requires there to be an instrument of government;

unless he is a student of the institution or is aged eighteen or over at the date of his election or appointment.

(2) The Secretary of State may by regulations make provision restricting—

(*a*) in relation to such matters or classes of matter as may be prescribed;

(*b*) in such circumstances as may be prescribed; and

(*c*) to such extent as may be prescribed;

the participation of any student of such an institution who is a member of its governing body in the proceedings of that body.

(3) The instrument of government for any such institution may make such provision in relation to restricting the participation of any such student in the proceedings of its governing body (in addition to that made by the regulations) as the regulations may authorise.

Access to papers etc. of governing bodies

62.—(1) The Secretary of State may make regulations requiring the governing body—

(*a*) of every county, voluntary and maintained special school; and

(b) of every institution of a kind mentioned in section 61 of this Act;
to make available, to such persons or classes of person as may be
prescribed, such documents and information relating to the meetings and
proceedings of the governing body as may be prescribed.

(2) Documents and information required by the regulations to be made
available shall be made available in such form and manner, and at such
times, as may be prescribed.

PART V

SUPPLEMENTAL

Orders and regulations

63.—(1) Any power of the Secretary of State to make orders or
regulations under this Act (other than under section 2(7), 9(6) or 54) shall
be exercised by statutory instrument.

(2) Any such statutory instrument (other than one made under section
66) shall be subject to annulment in pursuance of a resolution of either
House of Parliament.

(3) Regulations and orders under this Act may make different provision
for different cases or different circumstances and may contain such
incidental, supplemental or transitional provisions as the Secretary of
State thinks fit.

(4) Without prejudice to subsection (3) above, regulations under this
Act may make in relation to Wales provision different from that made in
relation to England.

Expenses

64. There shall be defrayed out of money provided by Parliament—
  (a) any expenses incurred by the Secretary of State under this Act;
      and
  (b) any increase attributable to this Act in the sums payable out of
      such money under any other Act.

Interpretation

65.— (1) In this Act—
  "the 1944 Act" means the Education Act 1944;
  "the 1968 (No. 2) Act" means the Education (No. 2) Act 1968;
  "the 1980 Act" means the Education Act 1980;
  "the 1981 Act" means the Education Act 1981;
  "boarder" includes a pupil who boards during the week but not at
      weekends;
  "co-opted governor", in relation to any school, means a person who
      is appointed to be a member of the governing body of the
      school by being co-opted by those governors of the school who
      have not themselves been so appointed but does not include a
      governor appointed in accordance with any provision made by
      virtue of section 5 of this Act;
  "exclude", in relation to the exclusion of any pupil from a school,
      means exclude on disciplinary grounds;
  "head teacher", except where provision to the contrary is made,
      includes an acting head teacher;
  "maintained special school" means a special school which is main-
      tained by a local education authority;
  "parent governor", in relation to any school, means (subject to
      section 5 of and Schedule 1 to this Act) a person who is elected
      as a member of the governing body of the school by parents of

registered pupils at the school and who is himself such a parent at the time when he is elected;

"promoters", in relation to any intended new school, or school which it is proposed should be maintained by a local education authority, means the persons who intend to establish the school or (as the case may be) who established the school which it is proposed should be so maintained, or their representatives;

"school day", in relation to any school, means any day on which at that school there is a school session; and

"teacher governor", in relation to any school, means (subject to Schedule 1 to this Act) a person who is elected as a member of the governing body of the school by teachers at the school and who is himself such a teacher at the time when he is elected.

(2) Except where otherwise provided, in this Act "governing body" and "governor" do not include a temporary governing body or any member of such a body.

Commencement

66.—(1) Sections 60 and 63 to 65, this section and section 67(1) to (3) and (7) of this Act shall come into force on the passing of this Act.

(2) Section 49 and 59 of this Act shall come into force at the end of the period of two months beginning with the day on which this Act is passed.

(3) The other provisions shall come into force on such date as the Secretary of State may by order appoint.

(4) Different dates may be appointed for different provisions or different purposes including, in particular, for the purpose of bringing particular provisions into force only in relation to particular schools or categories of school.

(5) Any order under this section may make such transitional provision as appears to the Secretary of State to be necessary or expedient in connection with the provisions brought into force by the order.

(6) Any such order may include such adaptations of the provisions which it brings into force, or of any other provisions of this Act then in force, as appear to him to be necessary or expedient for the purpose or in consequence of the operation of any provision of this Act (including, in particular, the provisions which the order brings into force) before the coming into force of any other provision.

Short title etc.

67.—(1) This Act may be cited as the Education (No. 2) Act 1986.

(2) This Act and the Education Acts 1944 to 1985 and the Education Act 1986 may be cited as the Education Acts 1944 to 1986.

(3) This Act shall be construed as one with the 1944 Act.

(4) Schedule 4 to this Act (which makes consequential amendments) shall have effect.

(5) This Act shall have effect subject to the transitional provisions set out in Schedule 5 to this Act.

(6) The enactments and instruments mentioned in Schedule 6 to this Act are hereby repealed or (as the case may be) revoked to the extent specified in the third column of that Schedule.

(7) In this Act—

    (*a*) sections 48, 52, 63(1) to (3) and 66(3) to (6), this section and so much of Schedule 6 as relates to any enactment which extends to Scotland, extend to Scotland; and

    (*b*) section 47(11) and this section extend to Northern Ireland;

but otherwise this Act extends only to England and Wales.

SCHEDULES

SCHEDULE 1

GROUPED SCHOOLS

General

1.—(1) In this Schedule—
"group" means two or more schools grouped under section 9 of this Act; and
"grouped school" means a school which forms part of a group.
(2) Any reference in any enactment to the governing body or governors of a school shall be construed, in relation to any grouped school, as a reference to the governing body or governors of the group.

Procedure in relation to making etc. of instrument of government

2.—(1) Before making an order under section 1 of this Act embodying the first instrument of government for any group; the local education authority shall consult the governing body and head teacher of each school within the group and, where the group contains one or more voluntary schools, shall—
(a) secure the agreement of the governing body of each such school to the terms of the proposed order;
(b) secure the agreement of the foundation governors of each such school to any provisions which will be of particular concern to the foundation governors of the group; and
(c) have regard to the way in which those schools have been conducted.
(2) Where such an order has been made, subsections (1) to (6) of section 2 of this Act shall apply in relation to any subsequent order embodying or varying the instrument of government for the group, or any proposal for the making of such an order—
(a) as if, in the case of a group which contains one or more voluntary schools, it were a single voluntary school; and
(b) as if, in any other case, it were a single county school.
(3) For the purposes of subsection (5) of section 2, any agreement required by sub-paragraph (1) above shall be deemed to have been required by subsection (2) of that section.

Election of parent and teacher governors

3. The instrument of government for any group—
(a) may provide for the local education authority to have power to determine, in relation to every election of parent or teacher governors, the school or schools within the group the parents of registered pupils at which, or (as the case may be) the teachers at which, are to be entitled to stand and vote at the election; and
(b) shall, where it does so, provide for it to be the duty of the authority to ensure that the position after any such election will be that there is no school within the group which will not have had an opportunity to have so participated in the election of at least one of the parent or (as the case may be) teacher governors of the group.

Governors' annual report to parents

4.—(1) In discharging their duty to prepare governors' reports; the governing body for a group shall prepare separate reports in relation to each of the schools within the group unless they decide to hold a joint annual parents' meeting, under paragraph 5 below.
(2) Where the governing body for a group prepare a single report covering all schools within the group, it shall be their duty to secure that any matters which they propose to report on and which are likely to be mainly of interest to the parents of registered pupils at a particular school within the group are treated separately in the report.

Annual parents' meeting

5.—(1) In discharging their duty to hold an annual parents' meeting for any grouped school the governing body for the group may, if they think fit, hold a joint meeting for all of the schools within the group.

(2) Where—

(*a*) a joint meeting is held; and

(*b*) the governing body have prepared separate governors' reports in relation to each of the schools within the group;

the governing body shall, when discharging the duty imposed on them by virtue of section 30(4) of this Act, attach to the report prepared in relation to any one school in the group copies of the reports prepared for each of the other schools within the group.

(3) Where at any joint meeting the question is put on any proposed resolution which concerns one or more, but not all, of the schools within the group—

(*a*) only parents of registered pupils at the school or schools which the proposed resolution concerns may vote on the question; and

(*b*) the registered pupils at the other schools shall be disregarded for the purposes of section 31(4)(*b*) of this Act as it applies in relation to the proposed resolution.

(4) Where at any joint meeting there is any disagreement as to which schools within the group a proposed resolution concerns, the matter shall be decided by the chairman of the governing body.

Section 12(10)   SCHEDULE 2

New Schools

Part I

General

1. In this Schedule—

"arrangement" means (except in paragraph 2(2)(*b*) or 19) an arrangement made under section 12 of this Act for the constitution of a temporary governing body for a new school;

"new school" means any school, or proposed school, which is required to have a temporary governing body or in respect of which the local education authority have power to make an arrangement under section 12(4);

"relevant proposal" means the proposal (of a kind mentioned in section 12) by reference to which the school in question is a new school; and

"temporary governor" means any member of a temporary governing body.

Constitution of temporary governing body

2.—(1) Subject to the provisions of this Schedule, every temporary governing body shall be constituted—

(*a*) in accordance with the provisions of sections 3 and 7 of this Act, in the case of a school whose governing body will be required to be constituted in accordance with those provisions; and

(*b*) in accordance with the provisions of section 4 of this Act, in the case of a school whose governing body will be required to be constituted in accordance with those provisions.

(2) For the purpose of the application of section 3, 4 or 7 of this Act in relation to the constitution of its temporary governing body, a new school shall be treated as having as registered pupils the maximum number of pupils referred to—

(*a*) in the relevant proposal; or

(*b*) in the case of a new school which will be a special school; in the arrangements for the school approved by the Secretary of State in accordance with regulations made under section 12 of the 1981 Act (approval of special schools).

(3) In co-opting any person (otherwise than as a temporary foundation or teacher governor) to be a member of a temporary governing body of a new school which will be a county, controlled or maintained special school, the temporary governors concerned shall—

(*a*) have regard—

(i) to the extent to which they and the other temporary governors are members of the local business community; and

(ii) to any representations made to the temporary governing body as to the desirability of increasing the connection between the temporary governing body and that community; and

(b) where it appears to them that no temporary governor of the new school is a member of the local business community, or that it is desirable to increase the number of temporary governors who are, co-opt a person who appears to them to be a member of that community.

(4) The first meeting of any temporary governing body shall be called—

(a) by their clerk; or

(b) where he fails to call it within such period as the local education authority consider reasonable, by the authority.

PART II

SCHOOL GOVERNMENT

Transition from temporary governing body to governing body

3.—(1) The requirement for there to be an instrument of government for a school to which section 1 of this Act applies shall take effect in relation to a new school from the date on which the relevant proposal is implemented.

(2) When that requirement takes effect, paragraph 2(2) above shall apply in relation to the governing body of the school as it applied in relation to its temporary governing body and shall continue to apply, for the purposes of determining (at any time after the governing body is first constituted) what provision would be required to be made by a new instrument of government for the school, until such time as—

(a) the number of registered pupils at the school reaches the maximum referred to in paragraph 2(2); or

(b) the local education authority exercise the power conferred on them by virtue of sub-paragraph (3) below.

(3) The instrument of government for every school to which paragraph 2(2) above applies at the time when it is made shall provide for the local education authority to have power to direct that that paragraph shall cease to apply in relation to the school.

(4) The local education authority shall secure that the governing body of any new school is constituted—

(a) as soon as is reasonably practicable after the requirement for there to be an instrument of government for the school takes effect; and

(b) in any event not later than the last day of the term in which pupils first attend the new school or (as the case may be) first attend the school after it becomes a maintained school.

(5) Where the requirement for there to be an instrument of government for a new school has taken effect, the temporary governing body of the school shall, until such time as the governing body is constituted—

(a) continue in existence (notwithstanding that the arrangement under which they were constituted has come to an end by virtue of paragraph 5 below); and

(b) be treated as if they were the governing body.

(6) Where a new school is grouped under section 9 of this Act, with effect from the time when an instrument of government is required for the school, any consent given by, or consultation with, the temporary governing body shall be treated for the purposes of section 10(5) and (6) of this Act as having been given by, or (as the case may be) held with, the governing body.

(7) Where any question arises as to the date which is to be taken to be the implementation date of any such proposal for the purposes of this paragraph, it shall be determined by the Secretary of State.

4.—(1) Before making any order under section 1 of this Act in respect of a new school, the local education authority shall consult the temporary governing body and head teacher.

(2) Before making any such order in respect of a new school which will be a voluntary school, the authority shall—

(a) secure the agreement of the temporary governing body to the terms of the proposed order; and

(b) if it embodies or varies an instrument of government, secure the agreement of the temporary foundation governors to any provisions which are of particular concern to those governors.

(3) Where a local education authority propose to make any such order in respect of a new school but cannot secure any agreement required by this paragraph, they or (as the case may be) the temporary governing body or temporary foundation governors may refer the matter to the Secretary of State.

(4) On any reference to him under this paragraph the Secretary of State shall give such direction as he thinks fit.

Duration of arrangement for temporary governing body

5.—(1) Every arrangement shall (if it has not been brought to an end under sub-paragraph (2) below) come to an end when the requirement for there to be an instrument of government for the new school first has effect.

(2) Where an arrangement has been made by virtue of section 12(3) or (4) of this Act and
    (a) the proposal in question is withdrawn;
    (b) the Secretary of State has decided not to approve that proposal or (as the case may be) not to approve the school as a special school; or
    (c) the local education authority have, under section 12(7) of the 1980 Act, determined not to implement that proposal;
the occurrence of that event shall bring the arrangement to an end.

Composition of temporary governing body

6.—(1) No local education authority shall make an arrangement in respect of a new school which will be a controlled school without the agreement of the promoters as to the provision which will be made in relation to the temporary foundation governors; and in the event of any disagreement between the authority and the promoters in respect of that provision, either of them may refer the matter to the Secretary of State.

(2) No local education authority shall make an arrangement in respect of a new school which will be an aided school without the agreement of the promoters as to the composition of the temporary governing body; and in the event of any disagreement between the authority and the promoters as to the composition of that body, either of them may refer the matter to the Secretary of State.

(3) On any reference under this paragraph, the Secretary of State shall give such direction as he thinks fit.

Appointment of temporary parent and teacher governors

7.—(1) The temporary parent governors for a new school shall, subject to sub-paragraph (2) below, be appointed—
    (a) where the school will be a county, controlled or maintained special school, by the local education authority; and
    (b) where it will be an aided school, by the promoters.

(2) Where—
    (a) two or more schools have been, or are to be, discontinued ("the discontinued schools"); and
    (b) the registered pupils at those schools, or a substantial number of those pupils, are expected to transfer to a new school;
the local education authority may (subject to sub-paragraph (3) below) provide for any of the governing bodies of the discontinued schools to appoint some or all of the temporary parent or teacher governors of the new school.

(3) No provision may be made under sub-paragraph (2) above for the appointment of temporary parent or teacher governors of a new school which will be an aided school without the agreement of the promoters; and in the event of any disagreement between the authority and the promoters as to whether any such provision should be made, either of them may refer the matter to the Secretary of State.

(4) On any reference under sub-paragraph (3) above, the Secretary of State shall give such direction as he thinks fit.

(5) Before making any provision under sub-paragraph (2) above for the appointment of temporary parent or teacher governors of a new school which will be a controlled school, the local education authority shall consult the promoters.

(6) No person shall be appointed under sub-paragraph (1) or (2) above as a temporary parent governor of a new school unless—
    (a) he is the parent of a child who is likely to become a registered pupil at the school; or

(*b*) where it is not reasonably practicable to appoint such a person, he is the parent of a child of compulsory school age.

(7) No person shall be appointed under sub-paragraph (1) as a temporary parent governor of a new school if he is—

(*a*) an elected member of the authority;

(*b*) an employee of the authority or of the governing body of any aided school maintained by the authority; or

(*c*) a co-opted member of any education committee of the authority.

Temporary teacher governors

8.—(1) Subject to paragraph 7(2) above, the temporary teacher governors of a new school shall be co-opted by a resolution passed at a meeting of those temporary governors who have not themselves been co-opted.

(2) No person shall be appointed as a temporary teacher governor of a new school unless he is employed as a teacher in a school maintained by a local education authority.

Duty to appoint suitably experienced members

9.—(1) Any person appointing a person as a temporary governor of a new school shall have regard to the desirability of that person being suitably experienced.

(2) For the purposes of this paragraph, a person is suitably experienced if he has served as a governor or temporary governor of a school and, in particular (in a case where registered pupils at another school which has been, or is to be, discontinued are expected to transfer to the new school), if he has served as a governor or temporary governor of that other school.

Proceedings etc.

10.—(1) The proceedings of a temporary governing body shall not be invalidated by—

(*a*) any vacancy among their number; or

(*b*) any defect in the appointment of any temporary governor.

(2) Any member of a temporary governing body may at any time resign his office, or be removed from office, in the same way as a member of a governing body constituted under an instrument of government.

(3) The minutes of the proceedings of any temporary governing body shall be open to inspection by the local education authority.

(4) The Secretary of State may by regulations make similar provision in relation to temporary governing bodies and their members as may be made in relation to governing bodies and their members under section 8 of this Act.

Miscellaneous

11.—(1) The qualification of any person for appointment as a temporary governor, of a particular category, of any new school shall not have the effect of disqualifying him for appointment as a temporary governor, of any other category, of that school.

(2) No person shall at any time hold more than one temporary governorship of the same school.

(3) Where any temporary governor is to be appointed by persons acting jointly, the appointment shall be made, in the event of failure on the part of those persons to make an agreed appointment—

(*a*) by the Secretary of State; or

(*b*) in accordance with any direction given by him.

(4) Subject to paragraph 2(3) above, where temporary governors are required to co-opt one or more persons to be temporary governors, the arrangement under which the temporary governing body are constituted shall not make any provision which has the effect of restricting those governors in their choice of person to co-opt.

(5) Sub-paragraph (4) above does not apply in relation to foundation governors.

(6) No person shall be qualified for membership of any temporary governing body unless he is aged eighteen or over at the date of his appointment.

PART III

ORGANISATION AND FUNCTIONS

General

12.—(1) The requirement for there to be articles of government for certain schools, which is imposed by section 1 of this Act, shall not apply in relation to a new school until such time as it is required to have an instrument of government (in accordance with section 1 as read with paragraph 3 of this Schedule).

(2) The determination of those matters relating to the conduct of any new school which require to be determined before a governing body is constituted for the school under an instrument of government shall be under the direction of the temporary governing body, but subject to any provision made by or under this Act (including, in particular, this Schedule) or any other enactment.

(3) The Secretary of State may by regulations make similar provision in relation to consultation with temporary governing bodies as he has power to make in relation to consultation with governing bodies under section 16(2) of this Act.

Reports and information to be provided by temporary governing body

13.—(1) Every temporary governing body shall furnish to the local education authority such reports in connection with the discharge of their functions as the authority may require (either on a regular basis or from time to time).

(2) Every temporary governing body shall make such reports and returns, and give such information, to the Secretary of State as he may require for the purpose of the exercise of his functions in relation to education.

(3) Every temporary governing body shall prepare—
    (*a*) immediately before the arrangement under which they are constituted comes to an end; and
    (*b*) for the purpose of assisting the governing body who will succeed them;
a brief report of the action which they have taken in the discharge of their functions; and shall recommend (with reasons) persons who belong to the community served by the new school and who are, in the opinion of the temporary governing body, suitable for appointment as co-opted members of the governing body.

(4) Before making any recommendations under sub-paragraph (3) above, a temporary governing body shall consult representatives of the local business community.

(5) All minutes and papers of any temporary governing body, including the report prepared under sub-paragraph (3) above, shall be made available to their successors.

Head teacher's reports

14.—(1) The head teacher of any new school for which a temporary governing body have been constituted shall furnish that body, or (as the case may be) the local education authority, with such reports in connection with the discharge of his functions as that body or authority may require (either on a regular basis or from time to time).

(2) Where, under sub-paragraph (1) above, any requirement is imposed by a local education authority on the head teacher of a new school which will be an aided school, the authority shall notify the temporary governing body of that requirement; and the head teacher of any such school shall furnish that body with a copy of any report which he makes in complying with any such requirement.

Preparation of curriculum

15.—(1) The head teacher of any new school for which a temporary governing body have been constituted shall, in preparing to discharge his functions in relation to the curriculum for the school, consult that body and the local education authority.

(2) Any authority who have been consulted under this paragraph shall inform the head teacher of the resources which are likely to be made available to the school; and the head teacher shall have regard to any information so given to him.

School terms etc.

16. Pending the coming into force of the articles of government for a new school, the times at which the school session is to begin and end on any day and the dates and times at which the school terms and holidays are to begin and end shall be determined—

(*a*) by the temporary governing body, in the case of a school which will be an aided school; and

(*b*) by the local education authority, in any other case.

Discipline

17. Pending the coming into force of the articles of government for a new school which will be a county, voluntary or maintained special school, the head teacher and the temporary governing body shall be under the same duties as will be required to be imposed on him and the governing body by virtue of section 22(*a*) to (*e*) of this Act.

Finance

18. Where a temporary governing body have been constituted for any new school, the local education authority shall consult that body and the head teacher on their proposed expenditure on books, equipment and stationery for the school.

Admission of pupils

19.—(1) The initial arrangements for the admission of pupils to a new school shall be made—

(*a*) where the school will be a county or controlled school, by the local education authority; and

(*b*) where it will be an aided school, by the temporary governing body or, where that body have not been constituted and the promoters consider that it is expedient for the arrangements to be determined without delay, by the promoters.

(2) Any person making any initial arrangements under this paragraph shall have regard to the arrangements in force for the admission of pupils to comparable schools in the area of the local education authority.

(3) Before making any such initial arrangements for a new school which will be a county school, the authority shall consult the temporary governing body unless—

(*a*) that body have not been constituted; and

(*b*) the authority consider that it is expedient for the initial arrangements to be determined without delay.

(4) Before making any such initial arrangements for a new school which will be a controlled schools, the authority shall consult—

(*a*) the temporary governing body; or

(*b*) where that body have not been constituted, the promoters.

(5) Before making any such initial arrangements for a new school which will be an aided school, the temporary governing body or (as the case may be) the promoters shall consult the authority.

(6) Sections 6 to 8 of the 1980 Act (admission to schools) shall have effect, in relation to any new school, as if the references to governors included references to the person responsible for the admission of pupils under the initial arrangements for that school.

Appointment of staff etc. at new aided schools

20.—(1) For the purposes of the appointment and dismissal of staff at any new school which will be an aided school, the local education authority and the temporary governing body shall (subject to sub-paragraph (2) below) have the same powers, and be under the same duties, as would the authority and the governing body for an aided school whose articles of government provided for—

(*a*) staff employed solely in connection with the provision of school meals to be appointed by the authority; and

(*b*) other staff employed at the school to be appointed by the governing body.

(2) The first appointment of a clerk to the temporary governing body of any such school shall be made by the promoters.

(3) Where the arrangement for the constitution of a temporary governing body of any such school comes to an end, the person who was the clerk to that body shall act as clerk to the governing body who succeed them, pending the appointment of their clerk.

(4) The authority shall, with a view to enabling staff to be appointed in good time, notify the temporary governing body of every such school of the steps (if any) which they intend to take in respect of the school under sections 22(4) and 24(2) of the 1944 Act (powers of authority in relation to certain staff).

(5) Paragraphs 21 to 25 and 26(1) and (2) below shall not apply in relation to any such school.

Determination of staff complement

21.—(1) Where a temporary governing body have been constituted for a new school, the complement of teaching and non-teaching posts for the school shall be determined by the local education authority.

(2) Section 34(2) and (3) of this Act shall apply in relation to any complement determined under this paragraph.

The selection panel

22.—(1) Whenever a selection panel is required by virtue of paragraph 23 or 25 below, it shall be constituted in accordance with this paragraph.

(2) A selection panel shall consist of such number of persons appointed to it by the local education authority, and such number of temporary governors appointed to it by the temporary governing body, as the authority shall determine.

(3) The number so determined shall—

    (*a*) in each case, be not less than three; and

    (*b*) in relation to appointments made by the temporary governing body, be not less than the number determined in relation to appointments made by the authority.

(4) The temporary governing body and the authority shall have power to replace, at any time, any member of a selection panel whom they have appointed.

(5) The Secretary of State may by regulations make provision, for the purposes of this paragraph, as to the meetings and proceedings of selection panels.

Appointment of head teacher and acting head teacher

23.—(1) Subject to sub-paragraphs (2) and (3) below, the same provision shall apply in relation to the appointment of a head teacher for a new school for which a temporary governing body have been constituted as is required to be made in relation to the appointment of a head teacher by the articles of government of a school to which section 37 of this Act applies.

(2) Where—

    (*a*) two or more schools are to be discontinued ("the discontinued schools"); and

    (*b*) the registered pupils at those schools, or a substantial number of those pupils, are expected to transfer to a new school;

the local education authority may, in consultation with the temporary governing body, appoint one of the head teachers of the discontinued schools as the first head teacher for the new school, instead of following the procedure mentioned in sub-paragraph (1) above.

(3) In the event of the post of head teacher for the new school being vacant, the authority may, if they think fit, appoint an acting head teacher after consulting the temporary governing body.

Appointment of certain other staff

24.—(1) Subject to sub-paragraph (3) below, the same provision shall apply in relation to the appointment of any person to a post which is part of the complement of a new school for which a temporary governing body have been constituted as is required to be made in relation to the appointment of any person to such a post by the articles of government of a school to which section 38 of this Act applies.

(2) The local education authority shall consult the temporary governing body and the head teacher before appointing any person to work solely at the school otherwise than—

    (*a*) in a teaching post;

    (*b*) in a non-teaching post which is part of the complement of the school; or

    (*c*) solely in connection with either or both of the following—

        (i) the provision of meals;

        (ii) the supervision of pupils at midday.

(3) This paragraph does not apply in relation to the appointment of a head teacher or deputy head teacher or to any temporary appointment pending—

    (*a*) the return to work of the holder of the post in question; or

    (*b*) the taking of any steps required by this Schedule in relation to the vacancy in question.

Appointment of deputy head teacher

25. Where a temporary governing body have been constituted for a new school, the provision which is to apply in relation to the appointment of a deputy head teacher of the school shall be—

(*a*) the same as that which may be made in the articles of government of a school to which section 39 of this Act applies by virtue of subsection (1)(*a*) of that section; or

(*b*) where the local education authority so decide, the same as that which may be made in the articles of government of such a school by virtue of subsection (1)(*b*) of section 39.

Appointment of clerk to temporary governing body

26.—(1) Where a temporary governing body have been constituted for a new school, the clerk to the temporary governing body shall be appointed by the local education authority.

(2) Where the arrangement for the constitution of a temporary governing body of any new school comes to an end, the person who was the clerk to that body shall act as clerk to the governing body who succeed them, pending the appointment of a clerk under section 40 of this Act.

(3) Where the clerk to a temporary governing body fails to attend any meeting of theirs, they may appoint one of their number to act as clerk for the purposes of that meeting, but without prejudice to his position as a temporary governor.

PART IV

MISCELLANEOUS

Travelling and subsistence allowances etc.

27. Section 58 of this Act shall apply in relation to the members of temporary governing bodies as it applies in relation to the members of governing bodies of county, voluntary and maintained special schools.

Expenses of temporary governing bodies, etc.

28. Where a temporary governing body are constituted for a new school, the local education authority shall be under the same duty to defray the expenses incurred in relation to the temporary governing body, and the staff appointed in accordance with the provisions of this Schedule, as they would be if the relevant proposal had been implemented and the temporary governing body were the governing body of the school.

Powers of Secretary of State

29. For the purposes of the following provisions of the 1944 Act—

(*a*) section 67(1) (determination of disputes);

(*b*) section 68 (prevention of unreasonable exercise of functions); and

(*c*) section 99(1) and (2) (default);

a temporary governing body shall be treated as if they were the governing body of the school in question.

Provision of information for temporary governing bodies

30.—(1) Every local education authority shall secure that the temporary governing body of each of the new schools which will be maintained by them are, on being constituted, provided (free of charge) with such explanatory and other information as the authority consider is required to enable that body to discharge their functions effectively.

(2) Where a new school will be a county, controlled or maintained special school, the authority shall, in discharging their duty under sub-paragraph (1) above, inform the temporary governing body, in particular—

(*a*) of the number of members of any selection panel required by virtue of paragraph 23 or 25 above who are to be appointed by the authority and the number who are to be appointed by the temporary governing body;

(*b*) whe.e the authority intend to exercise the power conferred on them by paragraph 23(2) above, of their intention to do so;

(*c*) of the provision which is to apply in relation to the appointment of the deputy head teacher of the school;

(*d*) of the complement of staff for the school; and

(*e*) of the authority's proposals with regard to the appointment of staff for the school and the timing of appointments.

(3) Where a new school will be an aided school, the authority shall, in discharging their duty under sub-paragraph (1) above, inform the temporary governing body, in particular, of

their proposals with regard to the appointment of staff for the school and the timing of appointments.

Section 26(4)   SCHEDULE 3

EXCLUSION ON DISCIPLINE GROUNDS: APPEALS

General

1. The articles of government for every county, controlled and maintained special school shall provide for it to be the duty of the local education authority, when (following the consideration which they are required to give to the case by virtue of section 24(*a*) of this Act) they inform a pupil, or a parent of his, of their decision that he should not be reinstated, to inform the pupil or (as the case may be) parent of his right to appeal against the decision.

2. The articles of government for every aided and special agreement school shall provide for it to be the duty of the governing body, when (following the consideration which they are required to give to the case by virtue of section 25(*a*) of this Act) they inform a pupil, or a parent of his, of their decision that he should not be reinstated, to inform the pupil or (as the case may be) parent of his right to appeal against the decision.

3.—(1) Where, in accordance with any provision of the articles of government of any school made by virtue of section 24(*a*) of this Act, the local education authority give a direction to the head teacher of the school for the reinstatement of any pupil who has been excluded, the direction shall not have effect for a period of seven days beginning with the day on which the governing body are informed of the direction by the authority unless, within that period, the governing body inform the authority that they do not intend to appeal against the direction.

(2) Where, before the end of that period, the governing body lodge an appeal against the direction in accordance with the relevant arrangements—

(*a*) the local education authority shall inform the pupil (if he is aged eighteen or over) or his parent (if he is under eighteen) of his right to make representations to the appeal committee; and

(*b*) the direction shall not have effect unless it is confirmed by the appeal committee or the appeal is withdrawn.

(3) No appeal against such a direction may be made by the governing body after the direction has taken effect.

4. Part I of Schedule 2 to the 1980 Act (constitution of appeal committees) shall have effect in relation to appeals with the necessary modifications.

5. The Secretary of State may by order amend this Schedule.

Procedure

6. An appeal shall be by notice in writing setting out the grounds on which it is made.

7. On an appeal by a pupil or parent, the appeal committee—

(*a*) shall afford the appellant an opportunity of appearing and making oral representations;

(*b*) may allow him to be accompanied by a friend or to be represented; and

(*c*) shall allow—

(i) the local education authority and the governing body to make written representations to the committee; or

(ii) an officer of the authority nominated by the authority, and a governor nominated by the governing body, to appear and make oral representations.

8. On an appeal by a governing body, the appeal committee—

(*a*) shall afford a governor nominated by the governing body an opportunity of appearing and making oral representations;

(*b*) shall afford the governing body an opportunity to be represented;

(*c*) shall allow the pupil, if he is aged eighteen or over, or a parent of his, if he is under eighteen, to make written representations to the committee or to appear and make oral representations; and

(*d*) shall allow the local education authority to make written representations or an officer of the authority nominated by them to appear and make oral representations.

9. The body responsible for making any arrangements under section 26 of this Act shall, in setting any time limits in connection with appeals, have regard to the desirability of securing that appeals are disposed of without delay.

10. In considering any appeal, the appeal committee shall take into account (amongst other things) any representations made to it by any of the persons whom it is required to afford an opportunity to make representations.

11. In the event of a disagreement between the members of an appeal committee the appeal under consideration shall be decided by a simple majority of the votes cast and in the case of an equality of votes the chairman of the committee shall have a second or casting vote.

12. The decision of an appeal committee and the grounds on which it is made shall be communicated by the committee in writing to the pupil (if he is aged eighteen or over) or a parent of his (if he is under eighteen) and to the local education authority and governing body.

13. All appeals shall be heard in private except when otherwise directed by the authority or governing body by whom the arrangements are made but, without prejudice to any of the provisions of this Schedule—

    (*a*) a member of the local education authority may attend any hearing of an appeal by an appeal committee, as an observer; and

    (*b*) any member of the Council on Tribunals may attend any meeting of any appeal committee at which an appeal is considered, as an observer.

14. Two or more appeals may be combined and dealt with in the same proceedings if the appeal committee consider that it is expedient to do so because the issues raised by the appeals are the same or connected.

15. Subject to the preceding provisions of this Schedule, all matters relating to the procedure on appeals, including the time within which they are to be brought, shall be determined by the authority or governing body by whom the arrangements are made; and neither section 106 of the Local Government Act 1972 nor paragraph 44 of Schedule 12 to that Act (procedure of committees of local authorities) shall apply to an appeal committee constituted in accordance with Part I of Schedule 2 to the Act of 1980.

16. In this Schedule references to appeals are to appeals under section 26 of this Act.

Section 67(4)   SCHEDULE 4

Consequential Amendments

The Education Act 1944 (c.31)

1. In section 15(2) of the Education Act 1944 (change of status of voluntary school), in the proviso—

    (*a*) the words "under this section" shall be inserted after "any application"; and

    (*b*) the words "or section 54 of the Education (No. 2) Act 1986" shall be inserted after "this section", where they last occur.

2. In section 22 of that Act, for subsection (4) (appointment and dismissal of certain staff) there shall be substituted—

    "(4) The local education authority may give directions to the governors of any aided school as to the number and conditions of service of persons employed at the school for the purposes of the care and maintenance of the school premises.".

The Education Act 1962 (c.12)

3. In section 4(5) of the Education Act 1962 (meaning of "training" in relation to grants for training of teachers) for "sections 2 and 3" there shall be substituted "section 2".

The Education (No. 2) Act 1968 (c.37)

4. In section 3(3) of the Education (No. 2) Act 1968 (application of enactment to certain establishments)—

    (*a*) after the words "applies" there shall be inserted the words "and special schools maintained by local education authorities"; and

    (*b*) after the word "establishments", in the second place where it occurs, there shall be inserted the words "and schools".

The Local Government Act 1974 (c.7)

5. In paragraph 5 of Schedule 5 to the Local Government Act 1974 (matters not subject to investigation by Local Commissioner) after the words "Act 1944" there shall be inserted the words "or sections 17 to 19 of the Education (No. 2) Act 1986".

The Sex Discrimination Act 1975 (c.65)

6. In section 51 of the Sex Discrimination Act 1975 (acts done under statutory authority) the following subsection shall be added at the end—
    "(3) This section shall apply in relation to instruments of government and articles of government for schools made under the Education (No. 2) Act 1986 as it applies in relation to instruments of government and articles of government for schools made by or under any Act passed before this Act.".

The Local Government, Planning and Land Act 1980 (c.65)

7. In paragraph 3(4) of Schedule 10 to the Local Government, Planning and Land Act 1980 (interpretation), for the words "31 of the Education Act 1980" there shall be substituted the words "51 of the Education (No. 2) Act 1986".

Section 67(5)   SCHEDULE 5

TRANSITIONAL PROVISIONS

Instruments of government for certain existing schools

1.—(1) Section 1 of this Act shall not require the making of an instrument of government for any aided or special agreement school in respect of which there is in force, at the time when that section comes into force, and continues in force, an instrument under which its governing body is constituted; but this paragraph shall cease to apply to any such school if it is grouped with another school under section 9 of this Act.
    (2) Any such instrument shall, after the commencement of section 1, be treated for the purposes of this Act as having been made by order under that section.

Grouping

2. Where a local education authority propose to group two or more schools which are subject to an arrangement under section 3 of the 1980 Act (the "section 3 schools"), the references in subsections (5) and (6) of section 10 of this Act to the governing body of each of the schools concerned shall be construed as references to the persons deemed to be governors of the section 3 schools by section 3(7) of the 1980 Act.

Recommendations by outgoing governing bodies

3.—(1) The governing body for any county, controlled or maintained special school which is constituted under an instrument of government or arrangement in force immediately before section 1 of this Act comes into force shall recommend (with reasons) to any governing body who will succeed them persons who belong to the community served by the school and who are, in their opinion, suitable for appointment as co-opted members of their successor.
    (2) Before making any recommendations under sub-paragraph (1) above, a governing body shall consult representatives of the local business community.

Section 67(6)

SCHEDULE 6

Repeals and Revocations

Part I

Enactments Repealed

Chapter	Short title	Extent of repeal
7 & 8 Gco. 6. c.31.	The Education Act 1944.	Section 4. Section 5. Sections 17 to 21. Section 23. Section 24(1). In section 27(3), from "but before" to end. In section 67(2), the words from "or whether" to "another".
1962 c.12.	The Education Act 1962.	In section 3, paragraph (*a*) and from "in the case of" to "this section". In section 4(3), "(*a*) or".
1963 c.33.	The London Government Act 1963.	In section 31, subsections (7)(*a*) and (8).
1966 c.42.	The Local Government Act 1966.	In Schedule 5, paragraph 6.
1968 c.37.	The Education (No. 2) Act 1968.	Section 2. In section 3(2), the words "or subsection (4) of section 2".
1980 c.20.	The Education Act 1980.	Section 2. Section 3. Section 4. Sections 31 and 32. In section 35(1), the words from "(other" to "(*b*))". Schedule 6.
1980 c.44.	The Education (Scotland) Act 1980.	Section 23(5) to (7).
1980 c.65.	The Local Government, Planning and Land Act 1980.	Section 68(5).

Part II

Instruments Revoked

Number	Name of instrument	Extent of revocation
S.I. 1970/1 536.	The Transfer of Functions (Wales) Order 1970.	Article 4.

SALMON ACT 1986*

(1986 c. 62)

ARRANGEMENT OF SECTIONS

PART I

ADMINISTRATION OF SALMON FISHERIES IN SCOTLAND

PART II

OTHER PROVISIONS APPLYING TO SCOTLAND

PART III

PROVISIONS APPLYING TO ENGLAND AND WALES

* Annotations by Donald R. MacLeod, Advocate.

PART IV

MISCELLANEOUS

SECT.
39. Review of certain salmon net fishing.
40. Interpretation.
41. Amendments and repeals.
42. Crown application.
43. Citation, commencement and extent.

An Act to make fresh provision for the administration of salmon fisheries in Scotland; to provide as to the licensing and regulation of salmon dealing in Scotland and in England and Wales; to provide for, and as respects, certain offences in the law of Scotland and in the law of England and Wales in connection with salmon; to amend the Salmon and Freshwater Fisheries Act 1975, section 5 of the Sea Fisheries Regulation Act 1966 and section 9 of the Diseases of Fish Act 1983; to provide for the review of salmon fishing by means of nets; and for connected purposes. [7th November 1986]

GENERAL NOTE

This Act, which is divided into four Parts, has several distinct purposes. It introduces a series of wide-ranging new provisions in the law relating to salmon fisheries and salmon fishing and reference is made to the annotation relating to each part for amplification of these reforms.

Pts. I and II of the Act apply only to Scotland while Pt. III introduces new provisions in respect of England and Wales. Pt. IV incorporates a directive to the Ministry of Agriculture, Fisheries and Food to prepare a report reviewing the nature and extent of salmon fishings in parts of Scotland and England as soon as practicable after a period of three years commencing with the passing of the Act. Other miscellaneous matters are also dealt with in Pt. IV.

The Act, with the exception of s.21. (Permitted methods of fishing for salmon), came into effect on January 7, 1987, having received the Royal Assent on November 17, 1986.

Reference will be made in these annotations to two major sources of information. These are:—

1. G. H. Tait, *A Treatise on the Law of Scotland as applied to the Game Laws and Trout and Salmon Fishing* (2nd edn. 1928) (hereinafter referred to as "Tait").

2. The Second Report on Scottish Salmon and Trout Fisheries chaired by the Honourable Lord Hunter. Presented to Parliament, August 1965. Cmnd. 2691 (hereinafter referred to as "the Hunter Report").

Certain statutes are referred to in these annotations, some of which appear with their full citations in Sched. 5. Of these it will be found that the Salmon Fisheries (Scotland) Act 1868 (31 & 32 Vict., c.13) and the Salmon and Freshwater Fisheries (Protection) (Scotland) Act 1951 (14 & 15 Geo. 6, c.26) predominate. These will be referred to respectively as "the 1868 Act" and "the 1951 Act."

Reference will also be made to the following statutes governing the River Tweed:—

1. The Tweed Fisheries Act 1857 (20 & 21 Vict., c.cxlviii);

2. The Tweed Fisheries Amendment Act 1859 (22 & 23 Vict., c.lxx).

Broadly speaking the Act has three main objectives. First, it seeks to modernise and improve the administration of salmon fisheries in Scotland. Second, an attempt has been made to introduce a greater degree of flexibility into the arrangements for the regulation of salmon fishing. Certain changes which before the passing of this Act required primary legislation may in future be made effective by statutory instrument, subject to parliamentary approval where appropriate. The intention is that this will enable proprietors and the Secretary of State to react more quickly to changing circumstances. Third, further measures have been introduced to combat poaching.

PARLIAMENTARY DEBATES
 Hansard: H.L. Vol. 469, cols. 350, 990; Vol. 470, cols. 545, 799; Vol. 471, cols. 295, 974; Vol. 481, col. 866. H.C. Vol. 93, col. 232; Vol. 102, col. 1340.
 The Bill was considered by Standing Committee D, April 22 to June 12, 1986.

PART I

ADMINISTRATION OF SALMON FISHERIES IN SCOTLAND

GENERAL NOTE
 Pt. I introduces major changes in the administration of salmon fisheries in Scotland. Before the passing of this Act the management of salmon stocks was the responsibility of district boards, which comprised an equal number of upper or rod proprietors and lower or netting proprietors, the person owning the fishery with the highest rateable value being elected as chairman. District boards in existence at the time of the passing of this Act numbered about half the salmon fishing districts in existence. The new provisions are intended to modernise and indeed democratise the arrangements for administration by providing for the chairman to be elected and for the co-option of representatives of salmon anglers and tenant netsmen. The policy of the Act however, is to provide proprietors with the majority of votes on the new salmon district fisheries boards and to provide also updated arrangements for weighted voting for the election of proprietors. In addition, the Act is intended to provide for the amalgamation of districts where proprietors consider this necessary in order to create a more viable management unit.
 Ss. 1 and 2 are concerned with the introduction of new salmon fishery districts and the Secretary of State is empowered to designate, by "designation order" any area as a salmon fishery district. Ss. 3 to 10 incorporate measures for the general regulation of salmon fishery, whilst ss. 11 to 13 deal with proprietors. Ss. 14 to 18 deal with salmon fishery boards and they are to be reconstituted while s.19 specifically excludes the application of Pt. I to that part of the River Esk which is situated in Scotland.
 Salmon fishery districts were originally introduced by Salmon Fisheries (Scotland) Act 1862 (25 & 26 Vict., c.97) and the Salmon Fisheries (Scotland) Act 1868 (31 & 32 Vict., c.123). A useful history of salmon fishery districts is contained in Tait at p. 194 *et seq.* The system has been subject to pointed criticism noteably in the Hunter Report, paras. 127–137. It should be noted in passing that the provisions of the new Act by no means meet the recommendations of the Hunter Report.

Salmon fishery districts

Salmon fishery districts

 1.—(1) A salmon fishery district shall be the area within the coastal limits of a district (within the meaning of the Salmon Fisheries (Scotland) Acts 1862 to 1868) and extending—
   (*a*) seaward for three miles from mean low water springs; and
   (*b*) landward to include the catchment area of each river which flows directly or indirectly into the sea within these limits
but excluding any area designated as a salmon fishery district by an order made under subsection (2) below.
 (2) Notwithstanding subsection (1) above, the Secretary of State may, in accordance with section 2 of this Act, by order designate any area as a salmon fishery district, whether or not it includes all or part of a salmon fishery district—
   (*a*) established by subsection (1) above; or
   (*b*) already designated as such by an order made under this subsection;
and such an order is referred to in this Act as a "designation order".
 (3) Districts within the meaning of the Salmon Fisheries (Scotland) Acts 1862 to 1868 shall cease to exist and, subject to subsection (6) below—

(*a*) any reference in any enactment to a particular district within that meaning shall be construed as a reference to the salmon fishery district established by subsection (1) above which has the same coastal limits as that district; and

(*b*) for references in any enactment, excluding this Act, to such districts in general there shall be substituted references to salmon fishery districts

and a salmon fishery district which has the same coastal limits as a district within the meaning of these Acts shall have the same name as that district.

(4) After consulting such persons as he thinks fit, the Secretary of State may, by order made by statutory instrument—

(*a*) where an island or part of an island is not within the area of a salmon fishery district by virtue of subsections (1) or (2) above, include in the area of a salmon fishery district—
  (i) that island or that part; and
  (ii) the sea within three miles from mean low water springs on that island or that part;

(*b*) where there is doubt as to whether a particular place is in a particular salmon fishery district, make provision for the purpose of removing that doubt; or

(*c*) change a reference used in describing a salmon fishery district where the suitability of that reference for that purpose has lessened or ceased

but such an order shall not create a salmon fishery district.

(5) The River Tweed shall not be a salmon fishery district except as otherwise provided in that Act.

(6) References in the Salmon and Freshwater Fisheries (Protection) (Scotland) Act 1951 and in any other enactment as amended by that Act to a district shall be construed as including references to the River Tweed.

DEFINITIONS
  "coastal limits": see s.40.
  "river": see s.40.
  "salmon fishery district": see s.40.

GENERAL NOTE
Subs. (1): This subsection redefines a district for the purpose of salmon legislation and rectifies an anomaly by providing that a district shall include not only the major rivers flowing into the sea between the existing coastal limits of the district but also all the rivers that do so.

Mean low water springs are marked on ordnance survey maps and accordingly were taken as the point of reference for the purposes of s.1(1)(*a*).

The phrase *catchment area* is not defined within the statute but it is thought not to be intended to convey anything other than the normal meaning which the words bear. The phrase has previously been used in the Land Drainage Acts 1930 and 1948.

Subs. (2): This section empowers the Secretary of State to designate any area as a salmon fishery district. When taken with s.2, this subsection gives power to amalgamate districts. It also establishes the concept of a "designation order" (see annotation to s.2 below).

Subs. (3): This subsection abolishes existing salmon fishery districts and reapplies existing legislation concerning a particular district to the new district for that area. There is also a directive that any new salmon fishery district within the same coastal limits as the pre-existing district shall have the same name as that district.

Subs. (4): This subsection is designed to allow the Secretary of State to classify the area which constitutes a salmon fishery district. It allows him to make minor adjustments to fishery district boundaries.

Subs. (6): The purpose of subss. (5) and (6) together with other references in the Act to the River Tweed is to preserve the unique administration of the fisheries there. At present this function is discharged by a body known as "The Tweed Commissioners" [see Tait p.204 *et seq.* and also the Tweed Fisheries Act 1969 (c.24).]

Designation orders

2.—(1) A designation order shall provide for the abolition of such salmon fishery districts as are superseded by the district so designated.

(2) A designation order shall provide for the application to the district so designated of such regulations—

(*a*) made under section 3 of this Act; or

(*b*) made under the Salmon Fisheries (Scotland) Acts 1862 to 1868 as respects the matters specified in section 6(6) of the Salmon Fisheries (Scotland) Act 1862

as the Secretary of State specifies in the order and he may, in such an order, amend regulations made under section 3(2)(*d*) of this Act or under section 6(6) of that Act in their application under this subsection.

(3) Subject to section 6(1) of this Act, a designation order shall specify for the district so designated the annual close time and the periods within that time when it is permitted to fish for and take salmon by rod and line; and the order may make different provision for different parts of the district.

(4) The power under section 1(2) of this Act to make a designation order shall not extend to the River Tweed.

(5) Schedule 1 shall have effect as to the procedure in the making of a designation order.

(6) The Secretary of State may by order vary the provisions of Schedule 1 to this Act.

(7) An order under subsection (6) above shall be made by statutory instrument which shall be subject to annulment in pursuance of a resolution of either House of Parliament.

DEFINITIONS

"annual close time": see s.6(1).

"designation order": see s.1(2), *supra.*

"rod and line": see the 1951 Act, s.24(1) as amended by s.8(6) of this Act.

GENERAL NOTE

This section, when taken together with s.1(2), effectively allows the amalgamation of districts in the interests of efficient management. It also makes provision for certain matters which shall be included within the designation order under s.1(2). The section is largely self explanatory and gives effect to Sched. 1 of the Act which specifies the procedure for making a designation order. The Schedule, which is designed to achieve flexibility, provides *inter alia* the making of a designation order on application by an existing district salmon fishery board or by the proprietors in the area in the absence of such a board and the orders are designed to alleviate problems to which attention is drawn in the Hunter Report about the non-existence of district boards in several areas.

The Schedule directs that an applicant shall submit with his application written proposals regarding certain matters after which the Secretary of State shall, after consulting such persons as he considers appropriate, set in motion the consultation and publication procedure or dismiss the application. In the event of his receiving objections, the Secretary of State may make the order, dismiss the application or cause a local enquiry to be held. The Schedule, which is in simple terms, is referred to for amplification of these provisions.

The power to make a designation order does not extend to the River Tweed (s.2(4)).

General regulation of salmon fisheries

Regulations

3.—(1) Subject to subsection (4) below, regulations made under the Salmon Fisheries (Scotland) Acts 1862 to 1868 as respects the matters specified in section 6(6) of the Salmon Fisheries (Scotland) Act 1862 shall have effect in relation to a salmon fishery district as they had effect, immediately before the commencement of this section, in relation to the part of that salmon fishery district which was a district within the meaning of these Acts and which had the same coastal limits as that salmon fishery district.

(2) The Secretary of State shall have power, after consulting such persons as he considers appropriate, to make regulations with respect to—

(*a*) the due observance of the weekly close time;

(*b*) the construction and use of cruives;

(*c*) the construction and alteration of dams, including mill dams, or lades or water wheels so as to afford a reasonable means for the passage of salmon;

(*d*) the meshes, materials and dimensions of nets used in fishing for or taking salmon;

(*e*) obstructions in rivers or estuaries to the passage of salmon;

(*f*) the construction, alteration and use for the control of the passage of salmon of—

    (i) screens in off-takes from inland waters; and

    (ii) structures associated with such screens.

(3) The Secretary of State shall have power, after consulting such persons as he considers appropriate, to make regulations amending section 13 of the Salmon and Freshwater Fisheries (Protection) (Scotland) Act 1951 (extent of the weekly close time and the period within which rod and line fishing is permitted); provided always that such regulations shall not shorten the periods specified in the said section 13.

(4) The power to make regulations under subsection (2) above includes power to revoke any regulations as described in subsection (1) above; and such regulations shall be treated as revoked insofar as they are inconsistent with the provisions of regulations made under this section.

(5) The power to make regulations under paragraphs (*c*) or (*f*) of subsection (2) above includes power to except from the application of a regulation or part of a regulation any works or any category of works; and section 11 of the Salmon Fisheries (Scotland) Act 1868 shall apply to regulations so made.

(6) The power to make regulations under subsection (2)(*d*) above includes power—

(*a*) to make different provision for different districts or different parts of a district;

(*b*) to except from the application of a regulation or part of a regulation a district or part of a district specified in the regulations.

(7) References in any enactment, other than in this Act or in section 36 of the Salmon Fisheries (Scotland) Act 1868, to—

(*a*) byelaws or regulations made under the Salmon Fisheries (Scotland) Acts 1862 to 1868 as respects the matters specified in section 6(6) of the Salmon Fisheries (Scotland) Act 1862; or

(*b*) the provisions of any of the Schedules to that Act of 1868 relating to such matters

shall be construed as including references to regulations made under subsection (2) above.

(8) Regulations under this section shall be made by statutory instrument which shall be subject to annulment in pursuance of a resolution of either House of Parliament.

DEFINITIONS

    "enactment": see s.40.

    "coastal limits": see s.40.

    "inland waters": see s.24(1) of the 1951 Act.

    "lade": see s.24(1) of the 1951 Act.

    "river": see s.40.

    "weekly close time": see s.13 of the 1951 Act.

GENERAL NOTE
Subs. (1): This subsection applies the regulations referred to therein to the new salmon fishery district which replaces pre-existing districts. See also subs. (4).

Subs. (2): The power given here may along with the power given in subs. (3) be exercised within the context of a designation order (see s.2(2) *supra*) but may also do so independently of such a designation order. Subhead (*f*) is a new provision.

Subs. (5) gives powers of exception in respect of regulations made under paras. (*c*) or (*f*) of subs. (2). The subsection is a virtual reincarnation of s.6(6) of the 1862 Act with the additional power to regulate the construction and alteration of dams other than mill dams although destruction and removal of such dams is not contemplated. This subsection, it should be noted, affects dams (although not generating stations) which produce electricity. See annotation to s.4.

The overall purpose of such regulations would of course be to ensure a provision of reasonable means of passage for salmon on an upstream migration.

There is no statutory definition of a "cruive" and the term has caused some degree of confusion which ought to be clarified. It consists of a dam erected on a river in such a way that it forms a trap into which the fish go and having done so are unable to escape therefrom. During the close season the restricting shutter is lifted and the fish can make their way upstream. See Tait p.172 for a full description of this ancient and rare device.

Subs. (3): The weekly close time for nets is from 12 noon each Saturday to 6 a.m. on the following Monday. In respect of rod fishing the restriction is confined to the twenty-four hour period of Sunday (see s.13 of the 1951 Act). The limits previously fixed are now a minimum and the idea is to provide versatility for each locality.

Subs. (6): This is an illustration of the versatile powers which the section is intended to give to the Secretary of State. In this case he has power to make varying specification appropriate to different districts with regard to nets used for fishing or of taking salmon.

Private generating stations

4.—(1) In subsection (2) of section 5 of the Electricity (Scotland) Act 1979 (formation of Fisheries Committee), after the words "Secretary of State" where they first occur there shall be inserted the words ", to a body or person who wishes to establish or extend a private generating station under section 35".

(2) After subsection (1) of section 35 (control of private hydro-electric generating stations), there shall be inserted the following subsections—

"(1A) A person or body wishing to establish or extend any such station shall prepare proposals with a view to the execution of the necessary works and paragraphs 2, 3 and 6 of Schedule 4 to this Act shall have effect in relation to such proposals as if they were constructional schemes proposed under section 10 of this Act and, for the purposes of this subsection, references in that Schedule to the Boards shall be construed as references to such a person or body.

(1B) The Secretary of State may make his consent under subsection (1) above conditional on the acceptance by the person or body of any recommendation made under paragraph 3 of Schedule 4 to this Act relating to the proposed establishment or extension; and such person or body shall be bound to implement such recommendation in executing the proposed works.".

(3) In paragraph 1 of Schedule 4 (constitution and functions of Fisheries Committee), after the words "Secretary of State" where they secondly occur there shall be inserted the words ", to a body or person who wishes to establish or extend a private generating station under section 35".

GENERAL NOTE
The Electricity (Scotland) Act 1979 (c.11), s.35(1) as amended by s.4 of the Energy Act 1983 (c.25) requires any person or body wishing to construct or extend a generating station without rating exceeding one megawatt (1 MW) or to extend an existing generating station by the installation of plant with such a rating to secure the consent of the Secretary of

State for Scotland. Effectively, what now has to happen is that anyone wishing to establish or extend such a generating station requires to consult the Fisheries Committee established by s.5(2) of the 1979 Act and the consent of the Secretary of State under s.35(1) of that Act may be made conditional on the acceptance of any recommendation of that Committee by a person seeking to establish or extend a station.

This provision affects only generating stations. Dams which produce electricity were formerly subject to the regulation Sched. G of the 1868 Act which is now replaced by s.3(2) above.

Enforcement of regulations

5.—(1) In section 15 of the Salmon Fisheries (Scotland) Act 1868 (offences related to regulations)—

(*a*) for the words from the beginning to "following offences" there shall be substituted the words "Any person";

(*b*) paragraph (7) shall be omitted; and

(*c*) for the words from "shall for every such offence" to the end there shall be substituted the words "shall be guilty of an offence; and section 19 of the Salmon and Freshwater Fisheries (Protection) (Scotland) Act 1951 (forfeiture of fish, instruments, articles, vehicles or boats) shall apply in relation to persons convicted of an offence under this section as it applies to those convicted of an offence under Part I or section 13 of that Act".

(2) Without prejudice to the generality of section 3(7) of this Act, in section 15 of that Act, "byelaw"—

(*a*) in paragraph (8), shall include regulations made under section 3(2) of this Act and the offence specified in that paragraph shall, as respects such regulations, extend to so much of the River Tweed as is situated outwith Scotland; and

(*b*) in paragraphs (2), (3) and (4), shall include such regulations except to the extent that they extend to the River Tweed.

GENERAL NOTE

Subs. (1): The effect of this subsection is to apply the forfeiture provisions of s.19 of the 1951 Act to the offences specified in s.15 of the 1868 Act. S.15(7) of the 1868 Act, which concerns the illegal discharge of sawdust or the shelling of corn into a river, is now repealed having been overtaken by the more comprehensive measures against pollution specified in s.31 of the Control of Pollution Act 1974, c.14.

Subs. (2)(a): This provision effectively makes it an offence to contravene any bye-laws including regulations made under s.3(2) of this Act even where the act complained of is committed in relation to that part of the River Tweed which is situated outside Scotland.

Subs. (2)(b): The effect of this provision is to include within the meaning of the word "bye-law", as it appears in paras. (2) (bye-laws in force regarding the observance of the weekly close time), (3) (fishing for salmon during the annual close time) or (4) (fishing with a net which has a mesh which contravenes the bye-laws) and regulations made under s.3(2) of this Act except to the extent that they extend to the River Tweed.

Annual close time

6.—(1) The annual close time for a salmon fishery district shall be a continuous period of not less than 168 days and shall apply to every mode of fishing for and taking salmon except to the extent that provision is made for periods within that time during which it is permitted to fish for and take salmon by rod and line.

(2) Subject to subsection (3) below, the dates of the annual close time and the periods within that time when it is permitted to fish for and take salmon by rod and line shall be, in the case of any particular district—

(*a*) the dates and periods specified in the designation order made in respect of that district; or

(*b*) where no designation order has been made in respect of that district, the dates and periods which were determined under section

6(5) of the Salmon Fisheries (Scotland) Act 1862, subject to any variation made under section 9 of the Salmon Fisheries (Scotland) Act 1868, which, immediately before the commencement of this section, were in force as respects the district within the meaning of the Salmon Fisheries (Scotland) Acts 1862 to 1868 which had the same coastal limits as that salmon fishery district.

(3) Notwithstanding subsection (2) above, the Secretary of State may, subject to subsection (1) above, by order prescribe for any district the dates of the annual close time and the periods within that time when it is permitted to fish for and take salmon by rod and line and he may make different provision for different parts of a district; and such an order is referred to in this Act as an "annual close time order."

(4) The Secretary of State may make an annual close time order in respect of a salmon fishery district only on application to him by—

(*a*) the district salmon fishery board for that district; or

(*b*) where there is no such board, two proprietors of salmon fisheries in that district.

(5) An application under subsection (4) above shall be accompanied by the applicant's written proposals which shall state—

(*a*) the proposed dates of the annual close time and the periods within that time when it shall be permitted to fish for and take salmon by rod and line in the district; and

(*b*) the general effect of the proposals

and the proposals may include different dates and periods for different parts of the district.

(6) Paragraphs 3 to 9 of Schedule 1 to this Act shall apply to the making of an annual close time order as they apply to the making of a designation order, and for this purpose—

(*a*) references to a designation order shall be construed as references to an annual close time order; and

(*b*) references to an applicant, and to an application, under paragraph 1 shall be construed respectively as references to an applicant, and to an application, under subsection (4) above.

(7) References in any enactment, other than in this Act, to—

(*a*) regulations or byelaws made under the Salmon Fisheries (Scotland) Acts 1862 to 1868 as respects the matters specified in section 6(5) of the Salmon Fisheries (Scotland) Act 1862; or

(*b*) the provisions of Schedule C to the Salmon Fisheries (Scotland) Act 1868 relating to such matters

shall be construed as including references to an annual close time order or to such part of a designation order as provides for the annual close time for a salmon fishery district.

GENERAL NOTE

This section has been designed to allow flexibility in fixing the annual close time. It permits the Secretary of State to bring into effect by regulation what would otherwise require primary legislation, so that different dates and periods may be specified in accordance with what are assessed to be the criteria applicable to the particular district.

If a designation order is made in respect of a particular district, it must contain the dates and periods of the annual close time (s.6(2)(*a*)). Where no such order is made the Secretary of State is empowered, on application to him, to make an "annual close time order," the making of which is governed by Sched. 1, paras. 3–9.

In the absence of a designation order or an annual close time order, the existing statutory provisions in respect of the original district within the same coastal limits as the new district are applied.

The period of the annual close time was previously fixed at 168 days. For the purpose of regulation, this is now the minimum period.

Reference is made to the separate legislation governing the River Tweed in this regard (see annotations to s.10 hereafter).

The annual close time applicable to any river is a period during which fishing is restricted or not permitted at all. Netting is not permitted during the annual close time but, dependent on the date, fishing by rod and line, using baits or flies according to the regulations of the particular river, may be permitted.

Estuary limits

7.—(1) Subject to subsection (2) below, the estuary limits of a river shall be the limits fixed by judicial decision or fixed and defined under section 6(1) of the Salmon Fisheries (Scotland) Act 1862.

(2) Whether or not a river has estuary limits as described in subsection (1) above, the Secretary of State may, by order, prescribe limits or, as the case may be, different limits which shall be the estuary limits for that river; and such an order is referred to in this Act as an "estuary limits order".

(3) The Secretary of State may make an estuary limits order only on application to him by—

    (a) the district salmon fishery board for the district in which the river is situated; or

    (b) where there is no such board, two proprietors of salmon fisheries in that district.

(4) An application under subsection (3) above shall be accompanied by the applicant's written proposals which shall state—

    (a) the proposed estuary limits; and

    (b) the general effect of the proposals.

(5) Paragraphs 3 to 9 of Schedule 1 to this Act shall apply to the making of an estuary limits order as they apply to the making of a designation order, and for this purpose—

    (a) references to a designation order shall be construed as references to an estuary limits order; and

    (b) references to an applicant, and to an application, under paragraph 1 shall be construed respectively as references to an applicant, and to an application, under subsection (3) above.

(6) For the purposes of this section—

    "estuary limits" means limits which divide each river including its mouth or estuary from the sea; and

    "river" does not include the River Tweed.

(7) References in any enactment, other than in this Act or in section 36 of the Salmon Fisheries (Scotland) Act 1868, to—

    (a) byelaws or regulations made under the Salmon Fisheries (Scotland) Acts 1862 to 1868 as respects the matters specified in section 6(1) of the Salmon Fisheries (Scotland) Act 1862; or

    (b) the provisions of Schedule B to the Salmon Fisheries (Scotland) Act 1868 relating to such matters

shall be construed as including references to an estuary limits order.

DEFINITIONS

"estuary limits": see subs. (6).

"river": see subs. (6).

GENERAL NOTE

This section preserves the estuary limits presently in existence but allows for variation thereof by order on application to the Secretary of State. Prior to the passing of this Act there was no power to make orders relating to estuary limits. The purpose is to allow flexibility so that estuary limits may be fixed for rivers where they have not previously been fixed and may be varied where they have become unsuitable because of topographical changes.

Paras. 3–9 of Sched. 1, governs the making of such an order.

The River Tweed has its own bye-laws relating to estuary limits.

Use of baits and lures

8.—(1) The Secretary of State may, subject to the provisions of this section, make regulations specifying baits and lures for the purposes of the definition of "rod and line" in section 24 of the Salmon and Freshwater Fisheries (Protection) (Scotland) Act 1951.

(2) The Secretary of State may make regulations under this section only on—

(*a*) application to him by a district salmon fishery board; or

(*b*) a joint application to him by more than one such board, and regulations made in respect of such application shall be made only in respect of the district of the applicant.

(3) Regulations under this section shall specify, subject to such exceptions as may be provided therein, all or any, or a combination of, the following—

(*a*) baits and lures or classes of baits and lures;

(*b*) times when the regulations apply;

(*c*) areas to which the regulations apply.

(4) An application under subsection (2) above shall be accompanied by the applicant's written proposals which shall state—

(*a*) the baits and lures which it is proposed should be specified;

(*b*) the places to which and the times during which the proposed regulations should apply; and

(*c*) the reasons for the proposals.

(5) Paragraphs 3 to 9 of Schedule 1 to this Act shall apply to the making of regulations under this section as they apply to the making of a designation order, and for this purpose—

(*a*) references to a designation order shall be construed as references to regulations under this section; and

(*b*) references to an applicant, and to an application, under paragraph 1 shall be construed respectively as references to an applicant, and to an application, under subsection (2) above.

(6) In section 24(1) of the Salmon and Freshwater Fisheries (Protection) (Scotland) Act 1951, at the end of the definition of "rod and line" there shall be inserted the following—"and, in the case of fishing for salmon in an area to which and at a time during which regulations made under section 8 of the Salmon Act 1986 apply, is not specified in such regulations in respect of that area and time".

GENERAL NOTE

This section is much in the style of s.7, allowing the Secretary of State to make regulations, on application to him by the district board or on the joint application to him of more than one board, in respect of baits and lures.

Subs. (6) is a consequential provision.

Limits of the Solway Firth

9.—References in any enactment to the limits of the Solway Firth shall be construed as references to the limits which were fixed under section 6(2) of the Salmon Fisheries (Scotland) Act 1862.

GENERAL NOTE

This section preserves and enforces the limits of the Solway Firth. These limits are important because they limit the use of fixed engines on the Scottish side of the Solway. Reference is made to the annotations relating to s.25 of this Act.

Application of regulations and annual close time orders to the River Tweed

10.—(1) The byelaw enacted by section 10 of the Salmon Fisheries (Scotland) Act 1868 as Schedule G to that Act, as amended by any other enactment, and so much of section 15 of that Act as relates thereto shall continue to have effect in relation to the River Tweed as it had effect before the commencement of this section.

(2) Regulations made under section 3 of this Act shall have effect in relation to the River Tweed but the power to make regulations under subsection (2)(*d*) of that section includes power to except the River Tweed from the application of any such regulation.

(3) Where such regulations have effect in relation to the River Tweed—

(*a*) references to a salmon fishery district shall include references to the River Tweed; and

(*b*) references to a district salmon fishery board shall include references to the River Tweed Council

unless the contrary intention appears.

(4) Subsections (3), (4)(*a*), (5) and (6) of section 6 and section 8 of this Act shall have effect in relation to the River Tweed with the following modifications—

(*a*) references to a salmon fishery district shall include references to the River Tweed;

(*b*) references to a district salmon fishery board shall include references to the River Tweed Council

and Schedule 1 to this Act shall, for the purposes of this subsection, be construed accordingly.

(5) In making an annual close time order in respect of the River Tweed, the Secretary of State may prescribe an annual close time, being a continuous period of not less than 153 days.

(6) The power to make regulations under—

(*a*) section 3(2)(*a*) of this Act includes power to amend section 12 of the Tweed Fisheries Amendment Act 1859;

(*b*) section 3(2)(*d*) of this Act includes power to amend sections 12 and 13 of that Act of 1859; and

(*c*) section 3(2)(*e*) of this Act includes power to amend section 57 of the Tweed Fisheries Act 1857; and

(*d*) section 8 of this Act includes power to amend section 6 of the Tweed Fisheries Amendment Act 1859

and the power to make an annual close time order in respect of the River Tweed includes power to amend section 6, 10 and 11 of that Act of 1859.

(7) This section extends to so much of the River Tweed as is situated outwith Scotland.

GENERAL NOTE

Subs. (1): The bye-law referred to herein which is set out as Sched. G of the 1868 Act relates to dams, sluices, lades and salmon ladders. The subsection continues to render the bye-law effective in relation to the River Tweed (see subs. (7)).

Subs. (2): This subsection provides for the application to the River Tweed of the regulations which the Secretary of State is empowered to make under s.3 of this Act. In the case of net regulations, the River Tweed may be excepted from the general provisions.

Subs. (5): This subsection reintroduces as a minimum the annual close time of 153 days in respect of the River Tweed which compares with the minimum time of 168 days now introduced by s.6 in respect of other rivers in Scotland. Both periods may now be extended but not reduced.

Subs. (6): This subsection effectively gives power to the Secretary of State to amend certain provisions of the Tweed Fisheries Acts of 1857 and 1859.

Reference is also made to s.38 of the Fisheries Act 1981 (c.29) which, for the purposes of s.6 of the Freshwater and Salmon Fisheries (Scotland) Act 1976 (c.22), treats the whole of the River Tweed as if it were situated in Scotland.

Proprietors

Qualified proprietors and upper and lower proprietors

11.—(1) A qualified proprietor shall be, for the purposes of this Act, a proprietor of a salmon fishery entered in the valuation roll.

(2) Where any salmon fishery is not entered or not entered separately in the valuation roll, the assessor shall, on the request of—

(*a*) the clerk to the district salmon fishery board for the district in which the fishery is situated; or

(*b*) where there is no such board for the district, the proprietor of that fishery,

value that fishery and enter it in the valuation roll.

(3) If a salmon fishery is situated in more than one salmon fishery district the assessor shall, on the request of—

(*a*) the clerk to the district salmon fishery board for either or any of these districts; or

(*b*) where there is no such board, the proprietor of that fishery

value that fishery and enter it in the valuation roll according to its value in each district.

(4) A qualified proprietor shall be an upper proprietor or a lower proprietor for the purposes of this Act according to whether his salmon fishery is, respectively, upstream or downstream of a division of a river as defined in subsection (7) below and, in this Act, "upper proprietor" and "lower proprietor" each mean a qualified proprietor.

(5) A qualified proprietor shall be both an upper proprietor and a lower proprietor if his is a qualified proprietor of one salmon fishery situated above and another situated below a division referred to in subsection (4) above, whether or not both fisheries are on the same river in the district, and he may act in either capacity or in both capacities in accordance with the provisions of this Act.

(6) Subject to subsection (5) above, a qualified proprietor in a salmon fishery district shall not be eligible for election, co-option or appointment to the district salmon fishery board for that district in respect of more than one salmon fishery.

(7) The division referred to in subsection (4) above shall be—

(*a*) a line across the river between points on either bank prescribed by the Secretary of State under subsection (8) below; or

(*b*) where the Secretary of State has not prescribed such points but a point of division has been fixed in accordance with section 6(4) of the Salmon Fisheries (Scotland) Act 1862, that point of division; or

(*c*) where no division has been effected under paragraphs (*a*) or (*b*) above, the normal tidal limit.

(8) When requested to do so by the district salmon fishery board for the district in which a river is situated, the Secretary of State may, by order made by statutory instrument, prescribe a point on each bank of the river to which the request relates.

(9) The clerk to a district salmon fishery board shall maintain a roll showing—

(*a*) the upper and lower proprietors in the district; and

(*b*) the values of their fisheries as entered in the valuation roll;

and the board may, if they are satisfied that a name should be added or removed, add or remove it.

(10) Subject to section 5 of the Sheriff Courts (Scotland) Act 1907 (jurisdiction as regards heritable property), the sheriff may, on summary application made to him by a person whose request to the board to add or remove a name has not been met, order the board to add or remove that name.

DEFINITIONS

"assessor": see s.40.

"proprietor": see s.40.

"valuation roll": see s.40.

GENERAL NOTE
This section effectively retains the system whereby the proprietors are divided into two groups—the "upper proprietors" and the "lower proprietors" depending on whether the proprietor's particular salmon fishery is upstream or downstream of a fixed dividing point. The Secretary of State is now empowered to fix such a dividing point. Historically the intention of doing so is to divide the netting proprietors from the angling proprietors. For details of how the voting of proprietors is weighted, see Sched. 2, para. 3(3).

Sole proprietor in a salmon fishery district

12.—(1) Where, after the commencement of this section, there is in a salmon fishery district only one proprietor of salmon fisheries, for references in this Act, except under paragraph 1 of Schedule 2 to this Act, to two proprietors of salmon fisheries in a salmon fishery district for which there is no board there shall be substituted references to that sole proprietor.

(2) Where, immediately before the commencement of this section, there is a sole proprietor in a district within the meaning of the Salmon Fisheries (Scotland) Acts 1862 to 1868, the powers of a district board conferred on him by section 19 of the Salmon Fisheries (Scotland) Act 1862 shall, on the commencement of this Act, cease to be exercisable by him.

(3) A person appointed as a water bailiff by a sole proprietor mentioned in subsection (2) above shall, on the commencement of this section, cease to have the powers and duties of a water bailiff conferred on him by or under any enactment to the extent that such powers and duties relate to that appointment.

GENERAL NOTE
The section removes the right of a sole proprietor to appoint a bailiff at his own hands. Bailiffs already appointed under the pre-existing legislation now cease to have that status. Sole proprietors may now apply to the Secretary of State for Scotland for the appointment of a water bailiff under the provisions of s.10(5) of the 1951 Act.

Mandatories

13.—(1) A qualified proprietor or an elected member or chairman of a district salmon fishery board may at any time authorise a person to act for him; and such a person is referred to in this Act as a "mandatory".

(2) A mandatory may as such be elected under Schedule 2 to this Act as a representative of qualified proprietors or as chairman but a person may not authorise another to act as a co-opted member under this Act nor shall a mandatory by co-opted under section 16(2) of this Act.

(3) A person who is both an upper and a lower proprietor by virtue of section 11(5) of this Act may authorise a person in accordance with this section in either or both of his capacities or may do so in each capacity.

GENERAL NOTE
This section provides a mandating power to proprietors of salmon fishings both in respect of the triennial election meeting or annual or other meetings of the district salmon fishery board.

District salmon fishery boards

District salmon fishery boards

14.—(1) If proprietors of salmon fisheries in a salmon fishery district—

    (*a*) form an association for the purpose of the protection or improvement of the fisheries within their district; and

    (*b*) elect, in accordance with Schedule 2 to this Act, a committee to act for them, that committee shall be the district salmon fishery board for that district; and the purpose of such a board shall be the purpose specified above in respect of the association.

(2) A district salmon fishery board shall have the powers and duties conferred—

(a) on them under this Act; and

(b) by any other enactment on a district board within the meaning of the Salmon Fisheries (Scotland) Acts 1862 to 1868;

and references in any enactment, other than in this Act, to a district board within the meaning of the Salmon Fisheries (Scotland) Acts 1862 to 1868 shall be construed as references to a district salmon fishery board.

(3) Subject to subsection (4) below, a committee mentioned in subsection (1) above shall cease to be the district salmon fishery board for a district on the expiry of a period of three years from the date of the last meeting of proprietors which elected, in accordance with Part I of Schedule 2 to this Act, such members as require to be elected under Part II of that Schedule.

(4) On the coming into force of a designation order—

(a) the transitional district board for; or

(b) the committee within the meaning of this section in respect of

a district superseded by the district so designated, as the case may be, shall cease to be a district salmon fishery board; and the committee within the meaning of this section which has been constituted in accordance with Schedule 2 to this Act in anticipation of the order and in respect of the district designated by the order shall be the district salmon fishery board for that district.

(5) If a committee ceases to be a district salmon fishery board, the assets and liabilities of that board shall be the assets and liabilities of the members of the association for which the committee acts; but, for the purposes of the winding-up of such an association, any assets of the former board remaining after the settlement of the liabilities of the former board shall be distributed amongst all the proprietors in the district who were liable to the fishery assessment immediately before the date on which the committee ceased to be such a board, according to the valuation of each fishery as entered in the valuation roll at that date.

(6) A district salmon fishery board shall not be bound by any direction given to them by the association for which the elected members of the board act as a committee.

(7) Nothing in this section shall affect the powers and duties of the River Tweed Council.

(8) The powers and duties under any enactment of district boards constituted in accordance with the Salmon Fisheries (Scotland) Acts 1862 to 1868 shall cease to have effect in relation to such boards and Schedule 3 to this Act shall have effect as respects such a board which was in office immediately before the commencement of this section; and such a board is referred to in this Act as a "transitional district board".

(9) There may be a district salmon fishery board for a district whether or not there are salmon in the waters of that district.

(10) The Secretary of State may by order vary the provisions of Schedule 2 or Schedule 3 to this Act.

(11) An order under subsection (10) above shall be made by statutory instrument which shall be subject to annulment in pursuance of a resolution of either House of Parliament.

DEFINITIONS
"district" and "salmon fishery district": see s.40.
"enactment": see s.40.
"fishery assessment": see s.15(2).

"River Tweed Council": see s.6 of the Tweed Fishery Act 1969, c.24.
"tenant netsman": see s.40.

GENERAL NOTE

Subs. (1) provides the means whereby a new district salmon fishery board may be created. The proprietors must first of all form themselves into an association for the purposes stated and elect a committee which shall become the district salmon fishery board for that district. Sched. 2 sets out the way in which the election is to proceed. Proprietors may form such an association even where there are no salmon in the waters of a particular district. This provision is intended to contemplate situations where endeavours are being made or are about to be made or may in future be made to restock the river with salmon, either naturally or artificially, in cases where the rivers have ceased to be salmon rivers by reason, say, of pollution.

The powers and duties conferred on a new district salmon fishery board are those which were previously in existence in relation to district boards together with those conferred on the new boards at ss.15 and 16 of this Act.

Transitional provisions are also incorporated within this section. Pre-existing district boards known as "transitional district boards" will continue in office and fall to be governed by Sched. 3 of the Act. They are meantime deemed to be the district salmon fishery board and shall, in terms of s.14(4), cease to be the salmon fishery board upon the coming into force of a designation order made under s.1(2) or upon the operation of para. 6 of Sched. 3, which provides for its cessation on the expiry of a period of three years from the last meeting of the proprietors properly constituted as the pre-existing district board, or six months from the date of commencement of s.14 of this Act whichever is the later. In practical terms this means that the former directive will be effective.

The major innovation which this section introduces is the direction to district salmon fishery boards to co-opt representatives of tenant netsmen and salmon anglers. S.14(1)(b) directs that the committee which is to form the new district salmon fishery board shall be elected in accordance with Sched. 2 to the Act and s.16(2) of the Act reinforces this direction. Sched. 2, at para. 6(3), directs that not more than three co-opted representatives in each category shall be members of the district salmon fishery board and there is detailed provision as to how representatives of tenant netsmen are to be chosen for co-option. When co-opting the representative of salmon anglers the board must look beyond the upper proprietors and must consult such organisations representing salmon anglers in the district as they see fit (Sched. 2, paras. 3 and 4). Para. 5(1) of the Schedule directs that the number of representatives of salmon anglers shall equal the number of representatives of tenant netsmen, and that that number shall be no more than three and shall not exceed whatever is the smaller number of qualified proprietors between the categories of upper and lower proprietors.

Financial powers and duties of district salmon fishery boards

15.—(1) Each year, a district salmon fishery board shall prepare—

(*a*) a report; and

(*b*) a statement of accounts, which shall be audited,

relating to the activities of the board; and the clerk of the board shall call an annual meeting of qualified proprietors in the district for the purposes of considering the report and the audited accounts.

(2) A district salmon fishery board shall have power to impose an assessment, to be known as the fishery assessment, on each salmon fishery in their district.

(3) The fishery assessment shall be assessed at such uniform rate or rates as are determined for all fisheries in the district by the board and shall be exigible according to the valuation of a fishery as entered in the valuation roll.

(4) Subsections (2) and (3) of section 11 of this Act shall apply for the purposes of this section as they apply for the purposes of that section.

(5) Arrears of fishery assessment may be recovered by—

(*a*) the district salmon fishery board which imposed the assessment; or

(*b*) the district salmon fishery board for a district created by a designation order in respect of an assessment imposed by a district salmon fishery board for a district superseded by that order; or

(*c*) the district salmon fishery board which replaced a transitional district board in respect of an assessment imposed by the transitional district board,
as the case may be, by action for payment of money.

(6) Any of the boards mentioned in subsection (5) above may recover arrears of fishery assessment which were due immediately before the commencement of this section under section 23 of the Salmon Fisheries (Scotland) Act 1862 in respect of any part of their district.

(7) The powers under subsections (5) and (6) above to recover arrears of fishery assessment include power to recover interest, chargeable at such rate as the Secretary of State shall, with the consent of the Treasury, determine, on such arrears from—

(*a*) in the case of recovery of arrears under subsection (5) above which have been outstanding for at least three months from the date of issue of a notice of assessment, that date; or

(*b*) in the case of recovery of arrears under subsection (6) above which have been outstanding for at least three months from the date of the coming into force of this section, that date,
until payment or the commencement of an action for payment, whichever is the earlier.

(8) A board may, in carrying out its purpose under this Act, borrow—

(*a*) an amount not exceeding twice the amount of the fishery assessment collected within the twelve month period immediately prior to the date of the decision to borrow; or

(*b*) such higher sum as is approved by the proprietors of fisheries which together amount to four fifths of the total value of fisheries in the district as entered in the valuation roll.

(9) In subsection (8)(*a*) above, "collected" means collected in—

(*a*) the district for which that board is the district salmon fishery board; and

(*b*) if that district has been designated in an order made under section 1(2) of this Act within that twelve month period, all the districts superseded by that order.

(10) In carrying out its purpose, a district salmon fishery board may authorise expenditure, including expenditure for the acquisition of heritable property, out of sums accruing to it from—

(*a*) the fishery assessment;

(*b*) the exercise of the power, under subsection (8) above, to borrow; or

(*c*) any other source;
but it shall not pay to any member of that board any salary or fees for his acting in any way as a member of or under that board.

DEFINITIONS
"collected": see subs. (9).
"qualified proprietor": see s.11(1), (4), (5), and (6).

GENERAL NOTE
This section outlines the financial powers and duties of district salmon fishery boards. A major innovation has been introduced in subs. (7) which permits the recovery of interest on arrears of fishery assessments.

The powers of the board to borrow are restricted in terms of subs. (8).

Subs. (10) allows the board in carrying out its purposes (which presumably include those objectives outlined in s.16(1)), to authorise expenditure for the acquisition of heritable property. This is a very important provision as it permits boards to acquire the salmon fishing rights of lower proprietors (*i.e.* netting rights) in order that these may be abandoned and the fisheries there managed for the advantage of the river as an angling concern. There are several existing district boards which have already carried out such purchases and subs. (10)(*c*) seems to envisage the possibility that the district salmon fishery board may receive funding from other sources to carry out such improvements.

General powers and duties of district salmon fishery boards

16.—(1) A district salmon fishery board may do such acts, execute such works and incur such expenses as may appear to them expedient for—
  (*a*) the protection or improvement of the fisheries within their district;
  (*b*) the increase of salmon; or
  (*c*) the stocking of the waters of the district with salmon.

(2) The elected members of a district salmon fishery board shall, in accordance with Part II of Schedule 2 to this Act, co-opt representatives of salmon anglers and tenant netsmen.

(3) On such terms and conditions as the board think fit, a district salmon fishery board—
  (*a*) shall appoint a person to act as clerk to the board; and
  (*b*) may appoint persons to act as water bailiffs, or in such other capacity as the board see fit.

(4) A district salmon fishery board may sue or be sued in the name of their clerk.

(5) References in any enactment to water bailiffs shall include references to water bailiffs appointed under this section.

GENERAL NOTE

The stated intention of the Government in introducing s.16(1) was that it would be the task of proprietors to attract anglers to the river by encouraging and improving facilities offered. Since however, the word "fisheries" where it appears in s.16(1)(*a*) clearly contemplates both netting fisheries and angling fisheries it seems arguable that improvement of the latter category could extend to the provision of such facilities. This is an important question because there are many areas where, because of awkward escarpments, backwaters and other difficult features of the landscape, paths and even footbridges may require to be constructed, not only for the benefit of the particular fishery which they immediately affect but to allow access to adjacent fisheries. It therefore seems sensible to suggest that a wide interpretation be given to the phrase "improvement of fisheries."

The board must appoint a person to act as its clerk but has a discretion as to whether or not to appoint water bailiffs and other employees.

During the passing of the Bill through Parliament, anxiety was expressed about the need for the district salmon fishery board governing the Solway to co-operate with English authorities. It certainly appears to have been intended that boards should be able to co-operate with water authorities. The reciprocal power of water authorities to co-operate with other bodies may be found in para. 2(1) of Sched. 3 to the Water Act 1973 (c.37) as amended by Sched. 1 to the Water Act 1980 (c.23). Particular concern arises on the Solway because the North West Water Autority is empowered, so far as the English side of the Firth is concerned, to issue licences for haaf-netting. The power to issue these licences so far as they affect the Scottish side of the Firth is vested in the Annan and Eskdale District Council which has for years restricted the issue of such licences. On the English side the issue is virtually uncontrolled because the water authority regards itself as having no discretion when an application is made to it. This, as can be imagined has been a bone of contention for some time.

The Act makes certain provisions in respect of the Solway and the annotations to ss.9 and 25 should be consulted.

Proceedings of district salmon fishery boards

17.—(1) The first meeting of a district salmon fishery board shall be at the date, time and place determined by the members of the board who were elected at the meeting of qualified proprietors called under paragraph 1 to Schedule 2 to this Act but in any case shall be no later than 21 days after that meeting.

(2) A district salmon fishery board shall determine the quorum for their meetings.

(3) At any meeting of the board, each member shall have one vote, subject to the following exceptions—
  (*a*) the chairman, in his capacity as such, shall have both a casting and a deliberative vote; and

(*b*) a person who is both an upper proprietor and a lower proprietor by virtue of section 11(5) of this Act shall have a vote in either capacity or in both capacities according to the capacity or capacities in which he has been elected or co-opted.

(4) No act or proceeding of a district salmon fishery board shall be questioned on account of any vacancy in their membership and no defect in the qualification or appointment of any person acting as a member shall vitiate any proceedings of the board in which that member has taken part.

(5) The minutes of proceedings of district salmon fishery boards shall be signed by the chairman and shall be conclusive evidence of the proceedings; and a meeting so minuted shall be presumed to have been duly convened and held and all members thereof to have been duly qualified.

(6) On the written request of any two members of the board, the chairman shall be bound to convene a meeting of the board within fourteen days of receiving the request and the clerk shall give notice to each member of the date, time and place of and the agenda for that meeting.

GENERAL NOTE

This section determines the proceedings of district salmon fishery boards. S.17(3)(*a*) gives to the chairman a casting and deliberative vote in order to remove the possibility of deadlock. Sched. 2 at para. 3(1) provides that the chairman shall be elected from amongst the qualified proprietors and co-optees are specifically excluded. Para. 6(1) of the Schedule declares that a person who is both an upper proprietor and a lower proprietor by virtue of s.11(5) of the Act may be elected as chairman.

Tenure of office

18.—(1) Before the expiry of a period of three years from—
(*a*) the first election of the members of the board; or
(*b*) the last meeting of qualifed proprietors called under this section
the clerk to that board shall call a meeting of qualified proprietors in that district for the purpose of electing or re-electing, in accordance with Part I of Schedule 2 to this Act, such members as require to be elected under Part II of that Schedule; and at that meeting each member of the board shall resign.

(2) The provisions of Schedule 2 to this Act, apart from paragraph 1, shall apply to further elections as they apply to the first election of the members.

(3) Without prejudice to subsection (1) above, a member of a district salmon fishery board may resign at any time and where a person ceases to meet the requirements of this Act for membership of a district salmon fishery board he shall cease to be a member of that board.

(4) Where a person is both an upper and lower proprietor by virtue of section 11(5) of this Act, subsection (3) above shall have effect as respects either or each such capacity.

(5) Where a vacancy in their number occurs, the board shall, so far and as soon as is reasonably practicable, fill that vacancy by—
(*a*) the electing by the elected members from amongst themselves of a new chairman;
(*b*) the appointing by the elected members of a qualified proprietor in the district as a representative of qualified proprietors according to the rules in Schedule 2 to this Act regarding the balance between upper and lower proprietors; and
(*c*) the co-opting by the board of a representative of salmon anglers or of tenant netsmen in accordance with that Schedule,

as the case may be, and a person appointed under paragraph (*b*) above shall be an elected representative of qualified proprietors for the purposes of this Act.

DEFINITION

"tenant netsman": see s.40.

GENERAL NOTE

This section provides for the triennial election or re-election of all members of the board at a meeting of qualified proprietors to be called by the clerk before the expiry of the *triennium*.

Questions have arisen with regard to the conduct of proceedings of the pre-existing district boards as to whether such meetings should be open to the public. In particular local journalists have often indicated their desire to attend these meetings but usually for the purpose of determining the votes of netting proprietors on matters affecting salmon angling and have been excluded by the chairman who may have been a netting proprietor. The Act does not make specific provision for the attendance of members of the public but co-opted members of the board consisting of representatives of salmon anglers and tenant netmen will be able to attend the annual meeting and the triennial election meeting and will be privy to the business of the meeting. Presumably it is implicit in their appointment that they will be expected to report back to the organisation which they represent and there does not seem to be any prohibition on the opportunity which is presented to them to publicise the business of such meetings. The only penalty may be a refusal by the board to co-opt of new such a member!

The remainder of the section is self-explanatory.

Application to the Esk

Application of Part I to the River Esk

19. The provisions of Part I of this Act shall not apply to so much of the River Esk, including its banks and tributary streams, as is situated in Scotland.

GENERAL NOTE

The River Esk has not hitherto been subject to Scottish legislation. This section preserves that practice so far as Pt. I is concerned. The 1951 Act has now been amended by s.26 of this Act to apply appropriate sections of that Act to that part of the river which is situated in Scotland. The annotation in respect of that section should be consulted together with s.29(1)(*d*) of this Act.

The governing statute in respect of other matters pertaining to that river—the Salmon and Freshwater Fisheries Act 1975 (c.51) should also be consulted.

PART II

OTHER PROVISIONS APPLYING TO SCOTLAND

GENERAL NOTE

This Part introduces miscellaneous provisions. S.20 enables a dealer licensing scheme to be introduced in Scotland. Dealer licensing will be designated and regulated by an order under s.44 of the Civic Government (Scotland) Act 1982, s.45. S.21 adds to s.2 of the 1951 Act permitted methods of fishing for salmon in the sea. S.22 introduces the new offence in Scotland of a person being in possession of salmon either believing that it had been unlawfully taken or possessing it in circumstances in which it would be reasonable for him so to suspect. Ss.23 to 30 make miscellaneous provision in respect of offences.

Additional powers in respect of licensing and regulation of salmon dealing

20.—(1) Without prejudice to the generality of section 44 of the Civic Government (Scotland) Act 1982 (power to designate additional activities as subject to licensing and regulation) an order as respects dealing in salmon made under that section may—

(*a*) define dealing in salmon and so define it as to—
    (i) include such acts preparatory to or connected with dealing in salmon;
    (ii) exclude dealing in such class or classes of salmon
as may be specified in the order;

(*b*) provide that the offence under section 7(1) of that Act (doing anything for which a licence is required without having one) shall be punishable—
    (i) on summary conviction, by imprisonment for a term not exceeding three months, or a fine not exceeding the statutory maximum or both;
    (ii) on conviction on indictment, by imprisonment for a term not exceeding two years, or a fine or both;

(*c*) provide that it shall be an offence for any person, other than a person holding a salmon dealer's licence, to buy salmon from or sell salmon to a person not having such a licence;

(*d*) provide that the offences under the said section 7(1) and any provision under paragraph (*c*) above shall be subject to such exceptions as may be specified in the order;

(*e*) provide that a licence shall be required only for such class or classes of dealing in salmon and dealing in such class or classes of salmon as may be specified in the order;

(*f*) provide as to the exercise of powers of entry and search by water bailiffs and persons appointed by the Secretary of State under section 10(5) of the Salmon and Freshwater Fisheries (Protection) (Scotland) Act 1951

but not so as to enable these powers to be exercised in any dwelling house or any yard, garden, outhouses and pertinents belonging thereto or usually enjoyed therewith.

(2) The Secretary of State shall have power, by order to prescribe, or to prescribe the maximum amounts of, the fees which the licensing authority may determine and charge under sub-paragraph (1) of paragraph 15 of Schedule 1 to the said Act of 1982 in respect of the licensing or dealing in salmon; and in that respect the licensing authority's powers under that paragraph shall be subject to the provisions of any such order.

(3) An order made under subsection (2) above shall be made by statutory instrument which shall be subject to annulment in pursuance of a resolution of either House of Parliament.

GENERAL NOTE

This section provides for the establishment of a dealer licensing system in Scotland. The intention is that district and islands councils will be the licensing authority.

Careful note should be taken of the fact that within this context the word "salmon" includes sea trout (see s.40) and until that fish is excluded for any order made under this section the order will apply with equal force to that species. Although the sea trout and the brown trout (the latter of which is not affected by this Act) have the same biological name—*salmo trutta*—they are quite distinguishable in that the sea trout is migratory while the brown trout normally remains resident in inland waters although it has been recorded in estuarial waters. The two fish are distinguishable by appearance.

It is clear from what was said in Parliament that the Government were anxious not to inhibit the fish-farming and re-stocking trade by applying licensing provisions to live salmon or indeed smoked salmon. S.20(1)(*a*)(ii) appears to allow such exceptions and s.20(1)(*c*) enables an order to be made creating *inter alia* the offence of an unlicensed person buying from or selling to an unlicensed person. It remains to be seen what the regulations will specify in this regard.

The scheme will be considerably reinforced in its effect by the provision of a reciprocal scheme in England (see s.31) which will do much to inhibit unlicensed trading across the border between the two countries.

Permitted methods of fishing for salmon

21. In section 2 of the Salmon and Freshwater Fisheries (Protection) (Scotland) Act 1951 (methods of fishing)—
> (*a*) after subsection (1) there shall be inserted the following subsection—
>> "(1A) No person shall fish for or take salmon in any waters in a salmon fishery district other than inland waters, except by rod and line, net and coble or bag net, fly net or other stake net."
> (*b*) after subsection (2) there shall be inserted the following subsections—
>> "(2A) After consulting such persons as he considers appropriate, the Secretary of State may, for the purposes of this section, by regulations define fishing for or taking salmon by—
>>> (*a*) net and coble;
>>> (*b*) bag net, fly net or other stake net,
>> whether by reference to anything used for the purpose, or to the circumstances in which or method by which it is so used, or to any combination thereof; and, in relation to net and coble, may make different provision as respects inland waters from that made as respects other waters.
>> (2B) The power to make regulations under this section includes power to amend or repeal section 62 of the Tweed Fisheries Act 1857 and section 12 and 13 of the Tweed Fisheries Amendment Act 1859.
>> (2C) Regulations made under this section shall be made by statutory instrument which shall be subject to annulment in pursuance of a resolution of either House of Parliament.".

DEFINITIONS
"inland waters": s.40 applies the definition contained in s.24(1) of the 1951 Act which declares that all rivers above estuary limits and their tributary streams, and all waters, watercourses and lochs whether natural or artificial draining into the sea are included in the definition.
"rod and line": see s.24(1) of the 1951 Act as amended by s.8(6) of this Act.

GENERAL NOTE
Subs. (1)(a): This subsection is to be read along with s.2(1) of the 1951 Act which specifies the only legal methods of fishing for taking salmon in any inland water. This subsection specifies the methods permitted in waters other than inland waters, that is to say, the waters specified in s.1(1)(*a*) of this Act.
Subs. (1)(b): This subsection introduces new subsections to s.2 of the 1951 Act. They empower the Secretary of State to define netting method and particularly empower him to amend or repeal redundant or suspersede provisions arising out of the Tweed Fisheries Act relating to netting.
For a very useful review of the law of what constitutes fishing by net and coble, see Tait p.178. The other methods of netting are discussed in the Hunter Report at paras. 75–78.

Offence of possessing salmon which have been illegally taken, killed or landed

22.—(1) After section 7 of the Salmon and Freshwater Fisheries (Protection) (Scotland) Act 1951 there shall be inserted the following section—
> **"Offence of possessing salmon which have been illegally taken, killed or landed**
>> 7A.—(1) A person who—
>>> (*a*) is in possession of salmon and believes; or
>>> (*b*) is in possession of salmon in circumstances in which it would be reasonable for him to suspect
>> that a relevant offence has at any time been committed in relation to the salmon shall be guilty of an offence and liable—

(i) on summary conviction to imprisonment for a term not exceeding three months, or to a fine not exceeding the statutory maximum or both;

(ii) on conviction on indictment to imprisonment for a term not exceeding two years, or to a fine or both.

(2) It shall be a defence in proceedings for an offence under this section to show that no relevant offence had in fact been committed in relation to the salmon.

(3) It shall be lawful to convict a person charged under this section on the evidence of one witness.

(4) For the purposes of this section an offence is a relevant offence in relation to a salmon if—

(*a*) it is committed by taking, killing or landing that salmon, either in Scotland or in England and Wales; or

(*b*) that salmon is taken, killed or landed, either in Scotland or in England and Wales in the course of the commission of the offence.

(5) In subsection (4) above, "offence", in relation to the taking, killing or landing of salmon either in Scotland or in England or Wales, means an offence under the law applicable to the place where the salmon is taken, killed or landed.

(6) A person shall not be guilty of an offence under this section in respect of conduct which constitutes a relevant offence in relation to any salmon or in respect of anything done in good faith for purposes connected with the prevention or detection of crime or the investigation or treatment of disease.

(7) Where an offence under this Act committed by a body corporate is proved to have been committed with the consent or connivance of, or to be attributable to any neglect on the part of, any director, manager, secretary or other similar officer of the body corporate, or any person who was purporting to act in any such capacity, he as well as the body corporate shall be guilty of the offence and shall be liable to be proceeded against and punished accordingly.

(8) Where the affairs of a body corporate are managed by its members, subsection (7) above shall apply in relation to the acts and defaults of a member in connection with his functions of management as if he were a director of the body corporate.".

(2) In section 11 of that Act (power of search)—

(*a*) in each of subsections (1) and (3) for the words "three and four" there shall be substituted "1 to 4, 7 and 7A";

(*b*) after the said subsection (3) there shall be inserted the following subsection—

"(3A) Where a constable has reasonable grounds for suspecting that an offence against section 7A of this Act is being committed and that evidence of the commission of the offence is to be found in any premises (other than a dwelling-house or any yard, garden, outhouses and pertinents belonging thereto or usually enjoyed therewith) but by reason of urgency or other good cause it is impracticable to apply for a warrant to search such premises, he may search them without warrant.";

(*c*) in subsection (4)—

(i) for the words "section three or section four" there shall be substituted "any of the provisions of sections 1 to 4, 7 and 7A";

(ii) after the word "thereon" there shall be inserted the words—

"or in any stationary vehicle on—

(*a*) a road within the meaning of the Roads (Scotland) Act 1984; or

(*b*) a highway within the meaning of the Highways Act 1980

adjoining such water or such land,".

DEFINITION

"water bailiff": see s.24(1) of the 1951 Act as amended by s.14(2) of this Act. This effectively means that the term includes any water bailiff or duly appointed officer of the district salmon fishery board.

GENERAL NOTE

Subs. (1): S.22 introduces perhaps the most important anti-poaching measure of the whole Act. It has been greeted with immense disappointment by the angling fraternity who regard it as only one of a series of measures which ought to have been introduced. Efforts were made to introduce a fish-tagging scheme such as is operated in other countries and it was even hoped that there might be a prohibition on wearing skin-diving equipment near salmon fisheries. At present skin divers who are poaching occasionally escape conviction by suggesting that they are seeking to find freshwater pearls.

The section provides for the insertion of a new section to be known as "7A" after s.7 of the 1951 Act. The section is designed to overcome the disadvantage which the original section certainly created for the prosecution in that the accused could not be convicted of the offence if he was able to prove that he himself did not commit the illegal act which allowed him to come into possession of the fish in question. (The case of *Aitchison* v. *Bartlett*, 1963 S.L.T. 65 is instructive in the interpretation of that original section). The offence created by the new section is complete however, when a person who is in possession of salmon and either believes or is in such possession in circumstances in which it would be reasonable to believe that a "relevant offence" had been committed in relation to the salmon. Subs. (4) specifies the extent of the phrase "relevant offence". The belief in question may be proved by way of confession and it is thought that it would be sufficient to prove circumstances in which it would reasonable for a person in possession of the salmon to have formed the suspicion that the relevant offence had been committed in relation to the salmon by the prosecutor's showing that the salmon was the subject of backdoor deals or the subject of sale below the market price or even displayed marked suggesting that it had been taken illegally. Caution should however be observed in relation to the last-mentioned matter since it may well be that the layman would not be able to distinguish net marks caused by legal nets such as stake nets from net marks caused by illegal nets such as monafilament gill nets.

Whereas the original s.7 applied to salmon, sea trout and brown trout the new s.7A applies only to salmon (*i.e.* salmon and sea trout). Reference is made to s.40 of this Act and s.24(1) of the 1951 Act. The explanation of the distinction between sea-trout and brown trout contained in the annotations to s.20 is referred to for its terms.

The common law crimes of theft or reset are inadequate to overcome the mischief which the new section seeks to outlaw because the wild salmon is *res nullius*. Different considerations would of course apply in respect of salmon which are the property of another, such as farmed salmon or salmon parr or smolts belonging to a stocking company whose trade it is to supply fishery authorities with stock.

Subs. (2) of the new section makes it a defence to show that no relevant offence had in fact been committed in relation to the salmon.

Subs. (3) continues the policy of the original s.7 which dispensed with the need for corroboration to secure conviction.

The wide scope of subs. (4)(*b*) and (5) should be carefully noted.

Subss. (7) and (8) make provision for the prosecution of officers of any body corporate who consent or connive at the commission of any offence under this Act.

Subs. (2): The effect of this subsection is first of all to allow a Sheriff or any Justice of the Peace to grant a warrant to any water bailiff, constable or other person to enter premises or any vehicle to secure evidence of an offence of contravening ss.1 to 4, 7 and 7A of the 1951 Act. Additionally, a constable may enter premises other than a dwellinghouse as specified in the new subsection without warrant in urgent circumstances or for other good reasons. To enter a dwellinghouse or other buildings within its curtilage a warrant is required by a constable or a water bailiff (subs. 11(1) of the 1951 Act). In order to search vehicles, constables and water bailiffs ought to have a warrant (s.11(2) of the 1951 Act). The power to a water bailiff to search a vehicle is now extended beyond the scope of s.11(4) of the 1951 Act, to include stationary vehicles on the public roads. A water bailiff of course does not have the power to stop a vehicle on the public roads. That power is confined to the police.

This section is primarily designed to allow entry to be made to enter premises such as a hotel without warrant where he has reason to suspect that evidence of illegally taken salmon is to be found. This provision poses a rather difficult question. Many anglers visiting rivers stay in small boarding houses which are not really hotels. They are effectively the residences or dwellinghouses of the owners and one is left wondering what would be the position about the powers of a constable seeking to act without a warrant in circumstances where he suspected that a visiting angler had taken fish by sniggering them or the like and had stored them, bearing the marks of such illegal activity, in a deep freeze in that house. The rule of strict construction in relation to a penal statute would seem to pose difficulties which the court will require to resolve as and when an appropriate case presents itself.

Power of court in trial of one offence to convict of another

23. If, upon a trial for an offence under—
 (*a*) section 10 of the Tweed Fisheries Amendment Act 1859 (having or selling salmon taken from the River Tweed during annual close time);
 (*b*) section 21 of the Salmon Fisheries (Scotland) Act 1868 (buying or selling salmon in close time);
 (*c*) section 7 of the Salmon and Freshwater Fisheries (Protection) (Scotland) Act 1951 (possessing illegally taken salmon or trout);
 (*d*) section 7A of the said Act of 1951 (possessing illegally taken salmon); or
 (*e*) any rule of law relating to reset;
the court is not satisfied that the accused is guilty of the offence charged but is satisfied that he is guilty of another of these offences, it may acquit him of the offence charged but find him guilty of the other offence and he shall then be liable to the same punishment as for that other offence.

GENERAL NOTE
The purpose of this section is to prevent people who have been charged under the new s.7A of the 1951 Act from avoiding conviction by explaining away suspicious circumstances through attributing them to an unlawful act which is not of itself a "relevant offence". Suppose that a person charged under that section maintained that the salmon had not been illegally taken in the sense envisaged by the section but had been stolen from a fish farm. If the explanation was accepted, the court could nevertheless convict the accused of reset although conviction of illegal possession would be impossible.

Unauthorised introduction of salmon or salmon eggs into certain waters

24.—(1) A person who intentionally introduces any salmon or salmon eggs into inland waters in a salmon fishery district for which there is a district salmon fishery board shall be guilty of an offence and liable on summary conviction to a fine not exceeding level 2 on the standard scale.

(2) A person shall not be guilty of an offence under this section in respect of an introduction of salmon or salmon eggs into such waters if—
 (*a*) he has the previous written consent of the district salmon fishery board for the salmon fishery district in which these waters are situated; or
 (*b*) the waters constitute or are included in a fish farm within the meaning of the Diseases of Fish Act 1937.

GENERAL NOTE
This is merely a precaution against someone who may decide to introduce salmon or salmon eggs into inland waters in a way that might not be compatible with the good

management of the fishery. It should be noticed in passing that the district salmon fishery board, being a body only concerned with the advancement of salmon interests, does not have power to consent to the introduction of other fish such as brown trout or rainbow trout or the eggs thereof.

The purpose of this section should not be misunderstood. It is not an anti-poaching provision. Confusion may arise because of a failure to recognise the biological distinction between salmon eggs and fish roe. The use of fish roe as a method of taking fish is a punishable offence (1951 Act, ss.2(1), 24(1) and (2), 25(2); 1868 Act, s.18 of, and Sched. 2 to, the Freshwater and Salmon Fisheries (Scotland) Act 1976 (c.22).)

Fixed engines in the Solway

25. After section 7 of the Salmon and Freshwater Fisheries (Protection) (Scotland) Act 1951, there shall be inserted the following section—
   "Fixed engines in the Solway
   7B.—(1) Any person who, for the purpose of taking or obstructing the free passage of salmon, places or uses an uncertificated fixed engine within the limits of the Solway Firth in Scotland shall be guilty of an offence and liable on summary conviction to a fine not exceeding level 4 on the standard scale.
      (2) In subsection (1) above—
         'fixed engine' includes any net or other implement for taking fish which is fixed to the soil or made stationary in any other way; and
         'uncertificated' means not having been certified as privileged under section 5 of the Solway Salmon Fisheries Commissioners (Scotland) Act 1877."

GENERAL NOTE
The annotations in respect of s.9 are referred to for their terms.

The new clause does nothing more than maintain the present ban on the use of uncertified fixed engines on the Scottish side of the Solway. It does not adversely affect existing salmon fishery rights. It has become necessary to make this provision because previous control of such engines was dependent upon s.33 of the 1862 Act which is now repealed by this Act. The matter was also affected by s.6(2) of the Salmon and Freshwater Fisheries Act 1975 (c.51) which is the governing English statute in respect of water authorities. The trouble is that no water authorities in Scotland were created under that section and thus this new provision required to be made in order to provide and maintain the pre-existing ban.

Poaching in the Esk

26.—(1) Section 21 of the Salmon and Freshwater Fisheries (Protection) (Scotland) Act 1951, (non-application of that Act to the River Esk in Scotland) shall be renumbered as subsection (1) of that section and—
   (*a*) at the beginning of that subsection there shall be inserted the words "Subject to subsection (2) below,"; and
   (*b*) after that subsection there shall be added the following subsection—
         "(2) Section 1 of this Act and sections 3 and 18 to 20 so far as relating to an offence under that section shall apply to so much of the River Esk, including its banks and tributary streams, as is situated in Scotland.".
   (2) In section 39 of the Salmon and Freshwater Fisheries Act 1975 (application of that Act to certain Border waters including the River Esk) there shall be inserted after subsection (1) the following subsection—
         "(1A) In the application of this Act, under subsection (1)(*b*) above, to the River Esk in Scotland, references to this Act in sections 31 to 33 and section 36 shall be construed as including references to sections 1, 3 and 18 to 20 of the Salmon and Freshwater Fisheries (Protection) (Scotland) Act 1951 as applied to that River by section 21 of that Act.".

(3) In section 43(3) of the said Act of 1975 (Scottish extent) after the words "39(1)" there shall be inserted the word ", (1A)".

(4) Section 9 of the Solway Act 1804 shall, so far as relating to salmon, cease to have effect in relation to so much of the River Esk, including its banks and tributary streams, as is situated in Scotland.

GENERAL NOTE

This is a technical provision to make it clear that an English water authority cannot prosecute directly for offences committed under the Salmon and Freshwater Fisheries Act 1975 in Scotland. The North West Water Authority is statutorily responsible for the River Esk. What happens as a matter of practice is that the authority makes reports of alleged offences to the Scottish Procurator-fiscal in the same way as other reporting agencies do. In fact the offence created by s.1 of the 1951 Act (fishing without permission) is imported into the 1975 Act thus closing down the loophole whereby that part of the River Esk which flows through Scotland was not subject to that jurisdiction in that respect.

For further provisions relating to the River Esk, see s.19.

Exemption from certain offences in respect of certain acts

27.—(1) A person shall not, in respect of any act or omission relating to fishing for or taking salmon, be guilty of a contravention of an enactment prohibiting or regulating that act or omission if the act or omission has been exempted by the Secretary of State.

(2) The Secretary of State may exempt an act or omission under subsection (1) above only if he is satisfied that—

(a) the proprietor of every affected salmon fishery in the salmon fishery district in which the act or omission is to take place, being a salmon fishery entered in the valuation roll; and

(b) if there is one, the district salmon fishery board for that district have previously consented to it; and, in this subsection, "salmon fishery district" includes the River Tweed and, in relation to that river, "district salmon fishery board" means the River Tweed Council.

(3) In subsection (2) above, "affected" means appearing to the Secretary of State to be likely to be affected by the exemption.

(4) An exemption under this subsection—

(a) may relate only to such person as may be specified in it;
(b) may be subject to such conditions as may be so specified;
(c) shall be in writing;
(d) shall specify—
    (i) the limits of the waters to which it relates;
    (ii) its duration; and
    (iii) the enactment to which it relates.

(5) In this section, "enactment" includes any instrument made after the passing of this Act under any enactment.

DEFINITION

"enactment": in this section this term is to be construed in accordance with subs. (5).

GENERAL NOTE

This section enables the Secretary of State to make exemptions from certain offences where all the affected proprietors in a salmon fishery district have consented to the exemptions. The provision will enable an otherwise illegal method of fishing to be used in specific instances such as, for example, salmon ranching and other developments.

Exemption from certain offences in respect of acts done for scientific etc. purposes

28.—(1) A person shall not, in respect of any act or omission relating to salmon or salmon roe or eggs, be guilty of a contravention of an enactment prohibiting or regulating that act or omission if—

    (*a*) the act or omission is for—
        (i) some scientific purpose;
        (ii) the purpose of protecting, improving or developing stocks
of fish; or
        (iii) the purpose of conserving any creature or other living
thing; and
    (*b*) he has obtained the previous permission in writing—
        (i) if the act or omission is one to which this sub-paragraph
applies, of the district salmon fishery board for the salmon
fishery district in which it takes place or of the Secretary of
State; and
        (ii) in any other case, of the Secretary of State for the act or
omission.
    (2) Sub-paragraph (i) of subsection (1)(*b*) above applies if the act or
omission referred to in that sub-paragraph—
    (*a*) takes place in a salmon fishery district for which there is a district
salmon fishery board; and
    (*b*) is a contravention of—
        (i) section 45 of the Tweed Fisheries Act 1857;
        (ii) section 6 of the Tweed Fisheries Amendment Act 1859;
        (iii) section 18, 19 or 20 of the Salmon Fisheries (Scotland)
Act 1868; or
        (iv) section 2 or 4(*c*) of the Salmon and Freshwater Fisheries
(Protection) (Scotland) Act 1951.
    (3) A permission under subsection (1) above shall specify the act or
omission permitted and the enactment to which the permission relates.
    (4) In this section—
    (*a*) references to a salmon fishery district and to a district salmon
fishery board include respectively references to the River Tweed
and to the River Tweed Council;
    (*b*) "enactment" includes any instrument made after the passing of this
Act under any enactment.

DEFINITIONS
    "enactment": This word is to be specially construed in terms of subs. (4)(*b*).
    "River Tweed" and "River Tweed Council": see s.40.

GENERAL NOTE
    This section makes provision to exempt from certain offences certain acts done for
scientific purposes or for the purpose of protecting and improving salmon stocks or other
conservation measures.

Application of sections 24 and 25 to River Esk and River Tweed

    29.—(1) Sections 27 and 28 of this Act, as respects any enactment—
    (*a*) which does not apply to so much of the River Esk, including its
banks and tributary streams, as is situated in Scotland but otherwise
extends to Scotland, shall likewise not apply to that part of that
River;
    (*b*) which applies to so much of the River Esk, with its banks and
tributary streams up to their source, as is situated in Scotland but
otherwise does not extend to Scotland, shall not apply to that part
of that River;
    (*c*) which extends to Scotland only but also applies to so much of the
River Tweed as is situated outwith Scotland, shall likewise apply to
that part of that River.

(2) In this section, "enactment" includes any instrument made after the passing of this Act under any enactment.

This section provides for the application of ss.27 and 28 to the River Esk and to the River Tweed in specific circumstances.

Prosecution of offences under the Act of 1868

30.—(1) Section 30 and sections 38 to 40 of the Salmon Fisheries (Scotland) Act 1868 (prosecution of offences at the instance of the clerk to a district board or of any other person) shall cease to have effect but any proceedings begun before the commencement of this section shall proceed as if this section had not been passed.

(2) A person who commits an offence under section 15 or sections 18 to 24 of that Act may be convicted on the evidence of one witness.

GENERAL NOTE
This section removes the right of a clerk to a district board or any other person to prosecute offences relating to salmon. This function will now be undertaken solely by the Procurator-fiscal.

Subs. (2) of this section extends the principle that the evidence of a single witness shall be sufficient to secure conviction. See the new s.7A of the 1951 Act introduced by s.22 of this Act.

PART II

PROVISIONS APPLYING TO ENGLAND AND WALES

GENERAL NOTE
This Part makes miscellaneous provisions relating to England and Wales. S.31 introduces for these countries a dealer licensing system similar but not quite the same as that introduced in Scotland under s.20. S.32 deals with the handling of salmon in suspicious circumstances while s.33 re-establishes what was thought to be the former position in law regarding fixed engines in England and Wales. S.34 removes the unnecessary requirement that under s.30 of the Salmon and Freshwater Fishery Act 1975, fish farms in England and Wales must obtain the consent of the water authority before they introduce fish or spawn into their waters. S.35 modifies the penalties under the 1975 Act for fishing with an illegal or unlicensed instrument, removing the distinction between acting alone and acting with another. S.36 amends the general provisions of the Salmon and Freshwater Fisheries Acts 1975 regarding the fishing of licensed nets by authorised servants or agents of the licensee. The effect will be that, in the areas where the number of licences issued is restricted under s.26 of the 1975 Act, the servants or agents must be accompanied by the licensee. S.37 enables local fisheries, committees to make bye-laws with the consent of the local water authority to protect salmon and to prevent interference with their migration. It also enables the local fisheries committee to make bye-laws with regard to the replacement and use of fixed engines within their sea fishing district which have become legal again because of the provision made by s.33. S.38 deals with the disclosure of information furnished under the Diseases of Fish Acts 1983 (c.30).

Dealer licensing in England and Wales

31.—(1) The Minister of Agriculture, Fisheries and Food and the Secretary of State may by order made by statutory instrument make provision for the purpose of prohibiting persons, in such cases as may be specified in the order, from—

(a) dealing in salmon otherwise than under and in accordance with a licence issued in pursuance of the order by such person as may be so specified; or

(b) buying salmon from a person who is not licensed to deal in salmon.

(2) Without prejudice to the generality of subsection (1) above, an order under this subsection may—

(a) prescribe the manner and form of an application for a licence to deal in salmon and the sum, or maximum sum, to be paid on the making of such an application;

(*b*) specify the circumstances in which such an application is to be granted or refused and the conditions that may be incorporated in such a licence;

(*c*) authorise the amendment, revocation or suspension of such a licence;

(*d*) create criminal offences consisting in the contravention of, or failure to comply with, provisions made under this section;

(*e*) provide for matters to be determined for the purposes of any such provision by a person authorised by any such provision to issue a licence; and

(*f*) make provision, whether by applying provisions of the Salmon and Freshwater Fisheries Act 1975 or otherwise, for the purpose of facilitating the enforcement of any provision made under this section.

(3) An order under this section may—

    (*a*) make different provision for different cases; and

    (*b*) contain such incidental, supplemental and transitional provision as appears to the Minister of Agriculture, Fisheries and Food and the Secretary of State to be necessary or expedient.

(4) Except in the case of an order to which subsection (5) below applies, no order shall be made under this section unless a draft of the order has been laid before, and approved by a resolution of, each House of Parliament.

(5) A statutory instrument containing an order under this section which relates exclusively to the sum, or maximum sum, to be paid on the making of an application for a licence to deal in salmon shall be subject to annulment in pursuance of a resolution of either House of Parliament.

(6) In this section "deal", in relation to salmon, includes selling any quantity of salmon, whether by way of business or otherwise, and acting on behalf of a buyer or seller of salmon.

GENERAL NOTE
See General Note to Pt. III.

Handling salmon in suspicious circumstances

32.—(1) Subject to subsections (3) and (4) below, a person shall be guilty of an offence if, at a time when he believes or it would be reasonable for him to suspect that a relevant offence has at any time been committed in relation to any salmon, he receives the salmon, or undertakes or assists in its retention, removal or disposal by or for the benefit of another person, or if he arranges to do so.

(2) For the purposes of this section an offence is a relevant offence in relation to a salmon if—

    (*a*) it is committed by taking, killing or landing that salmon, either in England and Wales or in Scotland; or

    (*b*) that salmon is taken, killed or landed, either in England and Wales or in Scotland, in the course of the commission of the offence.

(3) It shall be immaterial for the purposes of subsection (1) above that a person's belief or the grounds for suspicion relate neither specifically to a particular offence that has been committed nor exclusively to a relevant offence or to relevant offences; but it shall be a defence in proceedings for an offence under this section to show that no relevant offence had in fact been committed in relation to the salmon in question.

(4) A person shall not be guilty of an offence under this section in respect of conduct which constitutes a relevant offence in relation to any salmon or in respect of anything done in good faith for purposes connected

with the prevention or detection of crime or the investigation or treatment of disease.

(5) A person guilty of an offence under this section shall be liable—
>(*a*) on summary conviction, to imprisonment for a term not exceeding three months or to a fine not exceeding the statutory maximum or to both;
>(*b*) on conviction on indictment, to imprisonment for a term not exceeding two years or to a fine or to both.

(6) The Salmon and Freshwater Fisheries Act 1975 shall have effect as if—
>(*a*) in section 31(1)(*b*) and (*c*) (powers of search of water bailiffs), the references to a fish taken in contravention of that Act included references to a salmon in relation to which a relevant offence has been committed; and
>(*b*) in sections 33(2) (warrants to enter suspected premises), 36(1) (water bailiffs to be constables for the purpose of enforcing Act) and 39(1) (border rivers) and in paragraph 39(1)(*a*) of Schedule 3 (prosecution by water authorities) and Part II of Schedule 4 (procedure on prosecutions), the references to that Act included references to this section.

(7) In this section "offence", in relation to the taking, killing or landing of a salmon either in England and Wales or in Scotland, means an offence under the law applicable to the place where the salmon is taken, killed or landed.

GENERAL NOTE
See General Note to Pt. III.
As with the Scottish provision it is an offence to show that no relevant offence had in fact been committed in relation to the salmon in question (subs. (3)).
Subs. (4) similarly provides another defence which has its Scottish equivalent in s.22(6).

Placing and use of fixed engines

33.—(1) For subsection (1) of section 6 of the Salmon and Freshwater Fisheries Act 1975 (under which it is an offence to place a fixed engine in any inland or tidal waters or to use an unauthorised fixed engine for specified purposes) there shall be substituted the following subsection—
>"(1) Any person who places or uses an unauthorised fixed engine in any inland or tidal waters shall be guilty of an offence".

(2) In subsection (3) of the said section 6 (definition of unauthorised fixed engine), at the end of paragraph (*b*) there shall be inserted "; or
>(*c*) a fixed engine the placing and use of which is authorised by byelaws made by a water authority under this Act or by byelaws made by a local fisheries committee by virtue of section 37(2) of the Salmon Act 1986."

(3) In Part II of Schedule 3 to the said Act of 1975 (byelaws), after paragraph 21 there shall be inserted the following paragraph—
>"21A. Authorising the placing and use of fixed engines at such places in the water authority area (not being places within the sea fisheries district of a local fisheries committee), at such times and in such manner as may be prescribed by the byelaws and imposing requirements as to the construction, design, material and dimensions of such engines, including in the case of nets the size of mesh.".

GENERAL NOTE
Reference is made to the General Notes relating to Pt. III. This section is intended to overcome the difficulties posed by the interpretation placed by the court on s.6(1) of 1975 Act in the case of *Champion* v. *Maughan & Grove* [1984] 1 W.L.R. 469; [1984] 1 All E.R. 685. It became necessary to clarify the meaning of s.6 and to make provision for the use of

fixed engines for purpose of catching fish other than salmon or sea trout in the manner in which they had traditionally been used. This section taken together with s.37 cures these difficulties.

Introduction of fish into fish farms without consent

34. In section 30 of the Salmon and Freshwater Fisheries Act 1975 (prohibition of introduction of fish into inland waters without the consent of the water authority), at the end there shall be added the words "or the inland water is one which consists exclusively of, or of part of, a fish farm and which, if it discharges into another inland water, does so only through a conduit constructed or adapted for the purpose.

In this section "fish farm" has the same meaning as in the Diseases of Fish Act 1937.".

GENERAL NOTE

Reference is made to the General Note to Pt. III.

Removal of differential penalties under Salmon and Freshwater Fisheries Act 1975

35.—(1) In the Table in Part I of Schedule 4 to the Salmon and Freshwater Fisheries Act 1975 (mode of prosecution and punishment for offences), for the entries relating to sections 1 and 27 (being entries which make different provision according to whether the offender acted with another and do not provide for imprisonment on summary conviction) there shall be substituted the following entries, respectively—

Provision of Act creating the offence (1)	Description of offence (2)	Mode of prosecution (3)	Punishment (4)
"Section 1	Fishing with certain instruments for salmon, trout or freshwater fish and possessing certain instruments for fishing for such fish.	(*a*) Summarily .... (*b*) On indictment	Three months or the statutory maximum or both. Two years or a fine or both.
Section 27	Fishing for fish otherwise than under the authority of a licence and possessing an unlicensed instrument with intent to use it for fishing.	(*a*) If the instrument in question, or each of the instruments in question, is a rod and line, summarily. (*b*) In any other case— 　(i) summarily .... 　(ii) on indictment	Level 4 on the standard scale. three months or the statutory maximum or both; two years or a fine or both.".

(2) Subsection (1) above shall not affect any proceedings in respect of, or the punishment for, an offence committed before that subsection comes into force.

GENERAL NOTE

Reference is made to the General Note to Pt. III.

Servants and agents authorised by fishing licences

36.—(1) For paragraph 9 of Schedule 2 to the Salmon and Freshwater Fisheries Act 1975 (persons treated as servants and agents of licensee for the purpose of being entitled to use an instrument under the authority of the licence) there shall be substituted the following paragraph—

"9.—(1) A person who uses an instrument of any description for fishing in an area in relation to which an order under section 26 above limiting the number of licences for fishing with instruments of that description is in force shall not be treated for the purposes of section 25(3) above as the duly authorised servant or agent of any holder of a licence to use an instrument of that description unless, at the time that person uses the instrument—

  (a) his name and address are entered on the licence in accordance with the following provisions of this Schedule; and

  (b) he is not himself the holder of a licence to use an instrument of that description in that area; and

  (c) he is accompanied by the licensee or has the consent of the water authority to his use of the instrument in the absence of the licensee.

    (2) A person who uses an instrument of any description for fishing in an area in which no such order as is mentioned in sub-paragraph (1) above is in force shall not be treated for the purposes of section 25(3) above as the duly authorised servant or agent of any holder of a licence to use an instrument of that description unless, at the time that person uses the instrument—

  (a) his name and address are entered on the licence in accordance with the following provisions of this Schedule; or

  (b) he is accompanied by the licensee; or

  (c) he has the consent of the water authority to his use of the instrument otherwise than where there is compliance with paragraph (a) or (b) above.

    (3) The consent of a water authority shall not be given under this paragraph except—

  (a) in the case of a consent for the purposes of sub-paragraph (1)(c) above, in relation to a period which appears to the water authority to be a period throughout which the licensee will be unable through illness or injury to accompany his servant or agent;

  (b) in the case of a consent for the purposes of sub-paragraph (2)(c) above, where the giving of the consent appears to the water authority to be required by the special circumstances of the case."

    (2) Accordingly, in section 25(3) of that Act, for the words from "not exceeding" onwards there shall be substituted the words "subject to the provisions of paragraphs 9 to 13 of Schedule 2 to this Act".

GENERAL NOTE

Reference is made to the General Note to Pt. III.

The effect of this provision will be that, in areas where the number of licensees issued is restricted under s.26 of the 1975 Act, the servants or agents must be accompanied by the licensee when they fish. The only exception will be in the case of illness or injury.

In the parliamentary debate it was disclosed that the intention here was to restrict the activities of fishermen legally netting salmon in the area of sea off the Northumbrian coast. The intention is that they shall not fish for salmon over the week-end nor at night.

Byelaws under Sea Fisheries Regulation Act 1966

37.—(1) Subject to subsection (3) below, the power of a local fisheries committee to make byelaws under section 5 of the Sea Fisheries Regulation Act 1966 shall be exercisable for the purposes of protecting salmon and of preventing any interference with their migration and shall be so exercisable as if the references in that section to sea fish included references to salmon.

    (2) Subject to subsection (3) below, the power of a local fisheries committee to make byelaws under the said section 5 shall also include power to make byelaws which for the purposes of section 6 of the Salmon

and Freshwater Fisheries Act 1975 authorise the placing and use of fixed engines at such places in their sea fisheries district, at such times and in such manner as may be prescribed by the byelaws and impose requirements as to the construction, design, material and dimensions of such engines, including in the case of nets the size of mesh.

(3) A local fisheries committee shall not make byelaws for any purpose mentioned in subsection (1) or (2) above unless the water authority whose area for the purposes of functions relating to fisheries includes the whole or any part of the committee's sea fisheries district have consented to byelaws being made by the committee for that purpose.

(4) For the purposes of any byelaws made by virtue of this section the references to sea fish in sections 10(2)(*c*) and 12 of the said Act of 1966 (which include provision with respect to the seizure of, and searches for, sea fish taken in contravention of byelaws) shall be deemed to include references to salmon.

(5) In this section—
"fixed engine" has the same meaning as in the Salmon and Freshwater Fisheries Act 1975; and
"salmon" means fish of the salmon species and trout which migrate to and from the sea.

DEFINITIONS
"fixed engine" and "salmon": see subs. (5).

GENERAL NOTE
Reference is made to the General Note relating to Pt. III and to the annotation relating to s.33.
Subs. (3) requires the consent of the water authority which is responsible for the conservation of salmon within the particular sea fishery district.

Disclosure of information furnished under the Diseases of Fish Act 1983

38. In subsection (1) of section 9 of the Diseases of Fish Act 1983 (disclosure of information obtained in pursuance of section 7 of that Act), after paragraph (*c*) there shall be inserted the words "or
(*d*) for the purpose of enabling a water authority to carry out any of their functions under the 1937 Act".

GENERAL NOTE
This section makes provision for a new exemption to be added to the existing exemptions from the offence created by s.9 of the 1983 Act of disclosing information obtained in pursuance of s.7 thereof (Power to require information).

PART IV

MISCELLANEOUS

GENERAL NOTE
This part provides for the review of certain salmon net fishings as well as the conventional sections on interpretation, amendment and repeals, and citation and commencement.
The terms of s.42 should however be noted.

Review of certain salmon net fishing

39.—(1) The Minister of Agriculture, Fisheries and Food and the Secretary of State shall, as soon as practicable after the end of the period of three years beginning with the passing of this Act, prepare a report which, in the context of the need to ensure—

(*a*) that sufficient salmon return to spawn in the rivers wholly or partly situated in the areas and districts specified in subsection (3) below; and

(*b*) that fishing for salmon by means of nets is properly managed in those areas and districts,

reviews the nature and extent of all such fishing in those areas and districts.

(2) A copy of the report prepared under subsection (1) above shall be laid before each House of Parliament.

(3) The areas and districts referred to in subsection (1) above are the areas of the Yorkshire and Northumbrian water authorities and the salmon fishery districts from the River Forth to the River Ugie, the River Tweed being deemed for the purposes of this section to be included in those areas and districts.

GENERAL NOTE

The purpose of the review introduced by this section is to monitor the effect of the restriction which the Act introduces in respect of the North-East Drift Net Fishery on salmon stocks in English and Scottish rivers. It is well established that salmon migrating towards Scottish rivers do so through this area of the sea. The restriction referred to is contained in s.36.

Interpretation

40.—(1) In this Act, unless the context otherwise requires—

"annual close time order" has the meaning ascribed to it in section 6(3) of this Act;

"assessor" means the assessor or depute assessor for a valuation area appointed under section 116 of the Local Government (Scotland) Act 1973;

"board" and "district salmon fishery board" mean—

(*a*) the committee of an association of proprietors of salmon fisheries within the meaning of section 14 of this Act; or

(*b*) a transitional district board within the meaning of section 14(8) of this Act;

"coastal limits" means the limits of seacoast fixed for a district under section 6(3) of the Salmon Fisheries (Scotland) Act 1862;

"designation order" has the meaning ascribed to it in section 1(2) of this Act;

"district" and "salmon fishery district" mean an area described in section 1(1) of this Act or designated as such by a designation order;

"enactment" includes any Act of Parliament, whether public, general, local or private, and any instrument made under any enactment;

"fishery assessment" has the meaning ascribed to it in section 15(2) of this Act;

"fishery" and "salmon fishery" means a salmon fishery in any river or estuary or in the sea;

"inland waters" has the same meaning as in the Salmon and Freshwater Fisheries (Protection) (Scotland) Act 1951;

"proprietor" means, subject to subsection (3) below, any person, partnership, company or corporation which is the proprietor of a salmon fishery or which receives or is entitled to receive the rents of such fishery on its own account or as trustee, guardian or factor for any person, company or corporation;

"river" includes tributaries and any loch from or through which any river flows;

"River Tweed" means "the River" as defined by the Tweed Fisheries
    Amendment Act 1859, as amended by the byelaw made under
    section 4 of the Salmon Fisheries (Scotland) Act 1863;
"River Tweed Council" means the council constituted under section
    6 of the Tweed Fisheries Act 1969:
"salmon" means all migratory fish of the species *Salmo salar* and
    Salmo trutta and commonly known as salmon and sea trout
    respectively or any part of any such fish;
"tenant netsman" means a person in possession of a right, under a
    lease or sub-lease, of fishing for salmon with nets; and
"valuation roll" means a roll made up under section 1 of the Local
    Government (Scotland) Act 1975.

(2) In Part I of this Act, "the Salmon Fisheries (Scotland) Acts 1862 to
1868" means—

the Salmon Fisheries (Scotland) Act 1862;
the Salmon Fisheries (Scotland) Act 1864; and
the Salmon Fisheries (Scotland) Act 1868.

(3) In this Act, "proprietor" includes not more than one person
authorised by—

(a) in the case of a fishery in which more than one person has a *pro
    indiviso* share, such persons; or
(b) in the case of a fishery in which the rights to that fishery are shared
    by more than one person in any other way, such persons,

but in neither case does it include, except by virtue of this subsection, a
person whose right to that fishery is so shared.

Amendments and repeals

41.—(1) The enactments mentioned in Schedule 4 to this Act shall have
effect subject to the amendments there specified (being minor amendments
or amendments consequential on the preceding provisions of this Act).

(2) Subject to subsections (3) and (4) below, the enactments mentioned
in Schedule 5 to this Act are hereby repealed to the extent specified in the
third column of that Schedule.

(3) The repeal specified in Schedule 5 to this Act relating to section 13
of the Salmon Fisheries (Scotland) Act 1868 shall not extend to the River
Tweed.

(4) Notwithstanding the repeal specified in Schedule 5 to this Act
relating to the Salmon Fisheries (Scotland) Act 1863, the byelaw made
under section 4 of that Act in respect of the limits of the River Tweed
shall continue to have effect; and the repeal of that section shall not affect
the legality of any mode of fishing for or taking salmon at any place.

Crown application

42.—(1) Part I of this Act shall apply to land an interest in which
belongs to Her Majesty in right of the Crown and land an interest in
which belongs to a government department or is held in trust for Her
Majesty for the purposes of a government department, but otherwise this
Act shall not bind the Crown.

(2) In this section, "land" includes salmon fisheries.

Citation, commencement and extent

43.—(1) This Act, which may be cited as the Salmon Act 1986, shall,
with the exception of the provision mentioned in subsection (2) below,
come into force on the expiry of the period of two months beginning with
the date on which it is passed.

(2) Section 21 of this Act shall come into force on such date as the

Secretary of State may by order made by statutory instrument appoint, and such an order may include such transitional or saving provisions as appear to the Secretary of State to be necessary or expedient in connection with the provision brought into force by the order.

(3) The provisions of this Act modifying or repealing other enactments except section 38 have respectively the same extent as those other enactments.

(4) Subject to the application of section 39(1) of the Salmon and Freshwater Fisheries Act 1975 (border rivers) in relation to section 32 of this Act and the enactments amended by sections 33 to 36 of this Act, sections 31 to 38 of this Act extend to England and Wales only.

(5) Except as this Act otherwise provides, Parts I and II and section 42 of this Act extend to Scotland only.

SCHEDULES

Sections 2, 6, 7, 8 and 10   SCHEDULE 1

PROVISIONS AS RESPECTS THE MAKING OF DESIGNATION ORDERS

Proposals for a designation order

1. The Secretary of State may make a designation order only on the application to him by—

(a) a district salmon fishery board for a district which would be affected by the proposed order;

(b) where there is no such board, two proprietors of salmon fisheries in the area which would be affected by the proposed order; or

(c) any number of or combination of such boards or such proprietors in the area which would be affected by the proposed order

but the Secretary of State may act under this Schedule notwithstanding that the applicants do not represent the whole area which would be affected by the proposed order.

2. An application under paragraph 1 above shall be accompanied by the applicant's written proposals which shall state—

(a) the area which it is proposed should be designated as a salmon fishery district;

(b) the salmon fishery district or districts which are, at the time of the application, contained wholly or partly within that area;

(c) the reasons for the creation of the proposed salmon fishery district;

(d) the proposed dates of the annual close time and the periods within which it shall be permitted to fish for and take salmon by rod and line in the proposed district; and

(e) the general effect of the proposals.

Consultation and publication

3. On receiving an application under paragraph 1 above, the Secretary of State shall consult such persons as he considers appropriate and may—

(a) request from the applicant such additional information as he thinks fit;

(b) dismiss the application;

(c) proceed in accordance with the remaining provisions of this Schedule.

4.—(1) Before making a designation order, the Secretary of State shall direct that notice of the general effect of the proposals shall be given, specifying the time (not being less than 28 days from the date of the first publication of the notice) within which, and the manner in which, representations or objections with respect to the proposals may be made.

(2) Notice shall be given at least once in each of two successive weeks by advertising in a newspaper circulating in the district or districts affected by the proposals.

(3) The cost of giving notice shall be met by the applicant under paragraph 1 above.

5. At any time, the Secretary of State may alter the proposals in such way as he thinks fit and shall consider whether such alterations are sufficient to require—

(a) further consultation as mentioned in paragraph 3 above; and

(b) further notice to be given under paragraph 4 above.

Making of order

6. If no representations or objections are duly made, or if all so made are withdrawn, the Secretary of State may make a designation order.

7.—(1) If any representation or objection duly made is not withdrawn, the Secretary of State may, after considering the same—

(*a*) make a designation order;

(*b*) dismiss the application; or

(*c*) cause a local inquiry to be held.

(2) The Secretary of State shall appoint a person to hold the inquiry and to report thereon to him.

(3) Notification of the time when and the place where the inquiry is to be held shall be sent to any person who has duly made and has not withdrawn representations about or objections to the proposals, and shall be published at least once in each of two successive weeks in a newspaper circulating in the district or districts affected by the proposals.

(4) The person appointed to hold the inquiry may administer oaths and examine witnesses on oath and may accept, in lieu of evidence on oath by any person, a statement in writing by that person.

(5) The Secretary of State may make orders as to the expenses incurred by him in relation to the inquiry (including such reasonable sum as he may determine for the services of the person appointed to hold the inquiry) and as to the expenses incurred by the parties to the inquiry and as to the parties by whom such expenses shall be paid.

(6) Any order of the Secretary of State under sub-paragraph (5) above requiring any party to pay expenses may be enforced in like manner as a recorded decree arbitral.

8. After considering the report of the person appointed to hold the inquiry in pursuance of paragraph 7 above and any representations or objections which were duly made, the Secretary of State may make a designation order.

9. The power to make a designation order shall be exercisable by statutory instrument.

Sections 14, 16 and 18   SCHEDULE 2

ELECTION AND CO-OPTION OF MEMBERS OF DISTRICT SALMON FISHERY BOARDS

PART I

MEETING OF QUALIFIED PROPRIETORS

Calling of meeting

1.—(1) Where there is no district salmon fishery board or transitional district board for a district, the sheriff shall, on the application of two qualified proprietors of salmon fisheries in the district,—

(*a*) make up a roll of upper and lower proprietors in the district to which the application relates;

(*b*) call a meeting of these proprietors, at such time and place as he may direct, for the purpose of forming an association of proprietors of salmon fisheries for that district and electing a committee to become the district salmon fishery board for that district; and

(*c*) give notice at least once in each of two successive weeks by advertising in a newspaper circulating in the district of the date, time and place of that meeting.

(2) Where proposals for a designation order have been considered by the Secretary of State, in accordance with Schedule 1 to this Act, and he considers that a designation order should be made—

(*a*) the clerk or, acting jointly, the clerks to the district salmon fishery boards or transitional district boards for any district or districts which would be superseded by the proposed designation order shall perform, in respect of the proposed district, the duties specified in sub-paragraph (1) above; or

(*b*) where there is no district salmon fishery board for any district which would be superseded by the proposed designation order, the sheriff shall perform the duties specified in sub-paragraph (1) above on the application of two proprietors of salmon fisheries in the proposed district

and the following provisions of this Schedule shall have effect in respect of the proposed district as if it had been designated.

(3) Where the salmon fishery district lies in more than one sheriffdom, the sheriff in whose jurisdiction lies the major part of that district may, for the purposes of this Schedule, perform the duties specified in sub-paragraph (1) above in an adjacent sheriffdom.

(4) The sheriff may recover from the committee formed in accordance with this Schedule all expenses incurred by him in the performance of his duties under this paragraph, whether or not that committee becomes a district salmon fishery board, but if it does become such a board, these expenses may be met out of the fishery assessment.

2.—(1) At a meeting of proprietors called—

    (a) by the sheriff under paragraph 1 above;

    (b) by the clerk to a board in accordance with section 18(1) of this Act; or

    (c) by the clerk to a transitional district board in accordance with paragraph 7(a) of Schedule 3 to this Act,

the proprietors present shall elect or, as the case may be, re-elect a committee to act on behalf of the association.

(2) If—

    (a) the membership of that committee is in accordance with Part II of this Schedule; and

    (b) the requirements of this Part as respects eligibility are met

that committee shall be or continue to be the district salmon fishery board for that district.

(3) Membership of such a committee, whether or not it is a district salmon fishery board, shall not affect eligibility for membership of any other such committee or board.

Election of members

3.—(1) The meeting shall elect from amongst the qualified proprietors present a person to be chairman of the committee.

(2) In accordance with the following provisions of this Part of this Schedule, representatives of qualified proprietors shall then be elected by—

    (a) the upper proprietors from amongst themselves; and

    (b) the lower proprietors from amongst themselves

but an election under this sub-paragraph shall not be held invalid for the sole reason that there was only one upper or, as the case may be, lower proprietor present.

(3) A qualified proprietor shall have, in respect of each fishery he owns within the district, one vote in an election under this paragraph and shall have one additional vote for each £5,000 or part thereof by which the value of that fishery as entered in the valuation roll exceeds £5,000 but, subject to sub-paragraph (5) below, no proprietor shall have more than four votes in total as respects each fishery.

(4) A proprietor of a salmon fishery in the district which has been neither entered nor entered separately in the valuation roll shall, notwithstanding anything to the contrary, have one vote at the meeting and shall be eligible for election.

(5) A person who is both an upper and a lower proprietor by virtue of section 11(5) of this Act shall count as both an upper and as a lower proprietor for the purposes of this paragraph and he may both vote and be elected in each capacity.

Balance between upper and lower proprietors

4.—(1) In the election of representatives of qualified proprietors, not more than three may be elected by upper proprietors and not more than three may be elected by lower proprietors.

(2) Where there are less than three proprietors in the district qualified as upper proprietors or less than three qualified as lower proprietors, the number elected from either category shall not exceed the number eligible for election in the other category.

(3) If the person elected as chairman is—

    (a) an upper proprietor and there are less than four upper proprietors in that district; or

    (b) a lower proprietor and there are less than four lower proprietors in that district,

he shall also be eligible for election as a representative of qualified proprietors and, if elected, may act as such in addition to acting as chairman.

(4) In calculating the numbers of upper and lower proprietors, a person who is both an upper and a lower proprietor by virtue of section 11(5) of this Act shall be counted in each capacity in which he has been elected.

Co-optees

5.—(1) In the co-opting of representatives of salmon anglers and of tenant netsmen under Part II below, the number of representatives of salmon anglers shall equal the number of representatives of tenant netsmen but that number shall be no more than three and shall not exceed—

(*a*) the number of proprietors in the district qualified as upper proprietors; or

(*b*) the number of proprietors in the district qualified as lower proprietors,

whichever is the smaller number of qualified proprietors.

(2) A person who is both an upper and a lower proprietor by virtue of section 11(5) of this Act shall be counted in each capacity for the purposes of sub-paragraph (1) above.

(3) A representative of salmon anglers shall be a person whom the board consider to be representative of persons angling for salmon in the district but who is not himself an upper proprietor in that district.

(4) Before co-opting a person as a representative of salmon anglers, the board shall consult such organisations representing salmon anglers in the district as they think fit; but this requirement shall not apply to the filling of a vacancy in accordance with section 18(5) of this Act.

(5) A representative of tenant netsmen shall be—

(*a*) a tenant netsman in the district who is not a lower proprietor in that district;

(*b*) a tenant netsman in the district who is a lower proprietor in that district if—

(i) there are insufficient tenant netsmen who are qualified or willing to be co-opted and who are not also lower proprietors in that district; and

(ii) he has not been elected to the board of that district as a representative of lower proprietors or as chairman; or

(*c*) a lower proprietor in the district who is not a tenant netsman in that district if—

(i) there are insufficient tenant netsmen qualified or willing to be co-opted, whether or not they are also lower proprietors in that district; and

(ii) he has not been elected to the board of that district as a representative of lower proprietors or as chairman,

but a person shall not be disqualified under this sub-paragraph solely because he is an upper proprietor in that district or has been elected to the board of that district as a representative of upper proprietors.

PART II

MEMBERSHIP

6.—(1) The members of the committee shall be members of a district salmon fishery board if the committee consists of the following persons—

(*a*) an elected chairman; and

(*b*) in addition to the chairman, not more than six elected representatives of qualified proprietors in the district

and a person who is both an upper proprietor and a lower proprietor by virtue of section 11(5) of this Act may be elected in either capacity or in both capacities.

(2) As soon after the meeting of proprietors referred to in Part I above as is practicable, the chairman and the elected representatives of qualified proprietors shall, in accordance with the provisions of this Schedule co-opt representatives of salmon anglers and tenant netsmen in the district as required by section 16(2) of this Act.

(3) The members of a district salmon fishery board shall be—

(*a*) the persons mentioned in sub-paragraph (1) above;

(*b*) not more than three co-opted representatives of salmon anglers in the district; and

(*c*) not more than three co-opted representatives of tenant netsmen in the district

but a committee shall not fail to be a district salmon fishery board only by reason that no persons or not enough persons have been co-opted in accordance with this paragraph if—

(i) there has been insufficient time to co-opt such persons; or

(ii) no persons or not enough persons are willing to be co-opted.

Section 14(8)   SCHEDULE 3

TRANSITIONAL DISTRICT BOARDS

1. Subject to the provisions of this Schedule, a transitional district board within the meaning of section 14(8) of this Act shall be deemed to be a district salmon fishery board and have the powers and duties of such a board and references to a district salmon fishery

board shall, unless the context otherwise requires, include references to a transitional district board.

2.—(1) Sections 16(2) and 18 of this Act shall not apply to a transitional district board, which may retain the membership which it had at the commencement of section 14 of this Act.

(2) Subject to paragraph 3 below, vacancies on that board may be filled by the board by an upper or, as the case may be, lower proprietor within the meaning of this Act.

(3) The chairman or a member of a transitional district board may authorise a person to act for him as chairman or as such a member.

3. The chairman of a transitional district board shall be the proprietor whose salmon fishery or, taken together, fisheries in that district has or have the greatest value entered in the valuation roll.

4. The clerk to a transitional district board shall prepare a new roll of upper and lower proprietors in that district in accordance with section 11 of this Act so as to include in the roll any proprietors who were not proprietors of salmon fisheries in that district immediately before the commencement of section 14 of this Act.

5.—(1) A transitional district board may continue to collect the whole or any outstanding part of the fishery assessment imposed under section 23 of the Salmon Fisheries (Scotland) Act 1862 from proprietors of fisheries on which that assessment had been imposed before the commencement of section 14 of this Act.

(2) On the expiry of the period of the fishery assessment mentioned above, the board may levy a fishery assessment under section 15 of this Act but only in respect of fisheries in the district on which that assessment had been imposed before the commencement of section 14 of this Act.

(3) The board may recover arrears of fishery assessment, whether due before or after the commencement of section 14 of this Act, by action for payment of money.

(4) The power under subparagraph (3) above to recover arrears of fishery assessment includes power to recover interest, chargeable at such rate as the Secretary of State shall, with the consent of the Treasury, determine, on such arrears from—

(a) in the case of recovery of arrears due before the date of the coming into force of section 14 of this Act which have been outstanding for at least three months from that date, that date; or

(b) in the case of recovery of arrears due in respect of an assessment imposed by a transitional district board which have been outstanding for at least three months from the date of issue of a notice of assessment, that date

until payment or the commencement of an action for payment, whichever is the earlier.

6. A transitional district board shall cease to be deemed a district salmon fishery board and shall cease to have such powers and duties on the expiry of—

(a) three years from the date of the last meeting of proprietors within the meaning of sections 18 or 24 of the Salmon Fisheries (Scotland) Act 1862 or section 3 of the Salmon Fisheries (Scotland) Act 1868; or

(b) six months from the date of the commencement of section 14 of this Act, whichever is later.

7. At any time within the periods specified in paragraph 6 above, the clerk to a transitional district board shall, on the instructions of the board,—

(a) call a meeting of the upper and lower proprietors of the district, at such time and place as the board may direct, for the purpose of forming an association of proprietors of salmon fisheries for that district and electing a committee to become the district salmon fishery board for that district; and

(b) give notice at least once in two successive weeks by advertising in a newspaper circulating in the district of the date, time and place of that meeting.

8. Notwithstanding paragraph 6 above, a transitional district board shall cease to be deemed a district salmon fishery board and shall cease to have the powers and duties of a transitional district board on the election in accordance with Schedule 2 to this Act of a committee of an association of proprietors within the meaning of section 14 of this Act.

9. The assets and liabilities of a district board within the meaning of the Salmon Fisheries (Scotland) Acts 1862 to 1868 shall be transferred to the transitional district board for that district and, likewise, the assets and liabilities of a transitional district board shall be transferred to the district salmon fishery board for that district whenever such a board is elected.

Salmon Act 1986

SCHEDULE 4

MINOR AND CONSEQUENTIAL AMENDMENTS

Salmon Fisheries (Scotland) Act 1868 (c.123)

1. After section 1 of the Salmon Fisheries (Scotland) Act 1868 there shall be inserted the following section—
   "Expressions used in this Act
      1A. In this Act, unless the context otherwise requires the expressions "board" or "district salmon fishery board", "district" or "salmon fishery district", "fishery", "proprietor", "salmon" and "river" shall have the meanings ascribed to them in section 40(1) of the Salmon Act 1986 (interpretation).".

2. In section 11 of that Act (application to streams not frequented by salmon), for the words "mill dams" there shall be substituted the words "dams, including mill dams".

3.—(1) In section 18 of that Act (offence of buying, selling, possessing etc. of salmon roe), the words from "uses" to "purposes, or" shall be omitted.

(2) In section 19 (offences in relation to young salmon, salmon spawn, spawning beds etc.), the words from "for the purpose" in the second place where they occur to "purpose, or" shall be omitted.

(3) In section 20 (offences in relation to unclean or unseasonable salmon), the words from "or to any person" onwards shall be omitted.

4. In the said section 19, for the word "wilfully" there shall be substituted the word "knowingly".

5. In section 41 of that Act (extent), the words from "and Schedule G" to "Schedule" shall be omitted.

Diseases of Fish Act 1937 (c.33)

6. In subsection (3) of section 8 of the Diseases of Fish Act 1937 (penalties and legal proceedings) for the words after "be" there shall be substituted the words "proceeded against and punished in Scotland".

Salmon and Freshwater Fisheries (Protection) (Scotland) Act 1951 (c.26)

7. In section 1 of the Salmon and Freshwater Fisheries (Protection) (Scotland) Act 1951 (prohibition of poaching), for the words "low water mark" there shall be substituted the words "mean low water springs".

8. Section 9 of that Act (saving for acts done for scientific and other purposes) shall be renumbered as subsection (1) of that section and—
   (a) in that subsection the words from "or", where fourthly occurring, onwards shall cease to have effect; and
   (b) after that subsection there shall be added the following subsection
       "(2) This section does not apply to an act relating to salmon.".

9. In section 15(1)(c) of that Act (power of Secretary of State to conduct inquiries and to obtain information), the words from "so as to show" to the end of that subsection shall be omitted.

10. In section 19(2) of that Act (forfeitures) the words "on indictment" shall be omitted.

11. In section 22 of that Act (provisions as to River Tweed), for the reference to the Board of Commissioners of the River Tweed there shall be substituted a reference to the council constituted under section 6 of the Tweed Fisheries Act 1969.

12. In section 24 of that Act (interpretation), for the entries relating to "District" and "District Board" there shall be substituted the following entries—
       ""District" and "Salmon Fishery District" shall be deemed to include the River Tweed;
       "District Board" and "District Salmon Fishery Board" shall include the council constituted under section 6 of the Tweed Fisheries Act 1969;".

Salmon and Freshwater Fisheries Act 1975 (c.51)

13. In section 39 of the Salmon and Freshwater Fisheries Act 1975 (Border rivers and Solway Firth), after subsection (4) there shall be added the following subsection—
       "(5) Nothing in this section shall authorise a water authority to take legal proceedings in Scotland in respect of an offence against this Act.".

14. In section 43(3) of that Act (Scottish extent), for the words "and (4)" there shall be substituted the words "(4) and (5)".

Freshwater and Salmon Fisheries (Scotland) Act 1976 (c.22)

15.—(1) In section 7(5) of the Freshwater and Salmon Fisheries (Scotland) Act 1976 (fish farmers to be exempted from certain offences)—

(*a*) the word "4" shall be omitted; and

(*b*) after the word "8" there shall be inserted the words ", 8A".

(2) In Part I of Schedule 3 to that Act (offences from which fish farmers are to be exempted)—

(*a*) paragraph 4 shall be omitted; and

(*b*) after paragraph 8 there shall be inserted the following paragraph—

> "(8A) In the Salmon Act 1986, regulations made under section 3(2)(*a*) or (*d*) (general regulations).".

Section 41   SCHEDULE 5

REPEALS

Chapter	Short title	Extent of repeal
1696 c.35 (S.).	Salmon Act 1696.	The whole Act.
25 & 26 Vict. c.97.	Salmon Fisheries (Scotland) Act 1862.	The whole Act.
26 & 27 Vict. c.10.	Salmon Acts Amendment Act 1863.	The whole Act.
26 & 27 Vict. c.50.	Salmon Fisheries (Scotland) Act 1863.	The whole Act.
27 & 28 Vict. c.118.	Salmon Fisheries (Scotland) Act 1864.	The whole Act.
31 & 32 Vict. c.123.	Salmon Fisheries (Scotland) Act 1868.	The whole Act except sections 1, 11, 15, 18 to 24, 26, 27, 29, 31 to 36 and 41.
33 & 34 Vict. c.33.	Salmon Acts Amendment Act 1870.	The whole Act.
45 & 46 Vict. c.78.	Fishery Board (Scotland) Act 1882.	The whole Act.
14 & 15 Geo. 6 c.26.	Salmon and Freshwater Fisheries (Protection) (Scotland) Act 1951.	Section 14. In section 19(2) the words "on indictment,".

HOUSING AND PLANNING ACT 1986*

(1986 c.63)

ARRANGEMENT OF SECTIONS

PART I

HOUSING

The right to buy

PART II

SIMPLIFIED PLANNING ZONES

England and Wales

Scotland

---

* Annotations by Malcolm Grant, LL.D., Senior Lecturer in Law, University College London and Caroline Hunter, B.A., Barrister.

PART VII

GENERAL PROVISIONS

An Act to make further provision with respect to housing, planning and local inquiries; to provide financial assistance for the regeneration of urban areas; and for connected purposes.   [7th November, 1986]

PARLIAMENTARY DEBATES
    Hansard: H.C. Vol. 90, col. 467; Vol. 91, col. 152; Vol. 96, col. 458; Vol. 103, cols. 689, 964; H.L. Vol. 474, col. 410; Vol. 479, col. 850; Vol. 480, cols. 128, 358, 530; Vol. 481, cols. 274, 619, 1024.
    This Bill was considered in the House of Commons Standing Committee H between February 13 and April 10, 1986.

PART I

HOUSING

GENERAL NOTE TO PART I
    This Part of the Act contains its housing provisions and deals with a wide range of disparate issues principally involving amendment to the recent consolidation, the Housing Act 1985, which only came into force on April 1, 1986, accordingly allowing it less than a year before losing its comprehensiveness.
    Sections 1 to 5 deal with amendments to the "Right to Buy" provisions of Part V, Housing Act 1985. Most controversially, and in the face of government opposition, the House of Lords insisted on the inclusion of what is now s.1, substituting control by local authorities instead of the Secretary of State over the exemption from right to buy of "old people's dwellings". The other provisions relating to the right to buy reflect the continuing failure of the scheme in relation to flats. The discount for those who buy their flats is now increased (s.2)., and there are new provisions for the control of service charges after exercise of the right to buy (ss.4 & 5).
    While the right to buy remains a major arm of the government's housing policy, the government recognise that "however many public sector tenants we enable to buy the houses in which they live, a great many people will still need to rent their accommodation. The experience of thousands of them who are already tenants of local authorities has shown that some authorities are appallingly bad landlords", Lord Elton, July 30, 1986, *Hansard*, H.L. Vol. 479, col. 851 (second reading). Accordingly, ss.6 to 11 are concerned with the management of stock remaining in the public sector.
    Sections 6, 7 and 8 and Schedule 1 are intended to facilitate the disposal of tenanted local authority properties to other landlords (without prejudice to the tenants' right to buy and associated right to a mortgage). Section 9, on the other hand, enables a public sector

landlord to seek possession in order to sell into the private sector with vacant possession, in connection with a specific renovation or modernisation scheme.

"One way for a local authority to achieve more responsive local housing management is to delegate it. At present local authorities can delegate their housing management functions only to a tenant management co-operative and to no-one else", Lord Elton, *ibid*. Sections 11 and 12 enable local authorities—after consultation with tenants—to delegate housing management functions to *any* body or person and require authorities to *consider* the proposals of tenants' groups for the formation of management co-operatives actually to take over stock.

Sections 12 and 13 concern the assured tenancy scheme to be found in Part II, Housing Act 1980, and extends that scheme from new build dwellings, to existing dwellings which have been substantially improved or repaired. Of the "miscellaneous" sections, ss.14 to 24, the two most important in practice are likely to be ss.14 and 15. Section 14 is another House of Lords amendment opposed by the government. It seeks to "restore" (Baroness David, *Hansard* October 28, 1986, H.L. Vol. 481, col. 648, Third Reading), the position in homelessness law prior to the decision of the House of Lords in *Puhlhofer* v. *London Borough of Hillingdon* [1986] 1 A.C. 484, 18 H.L.R. 158. Section 15 provides for a new grant towards the cost of works required for the improvement and repair of the common parts of a building containing flats.

Apart from s.21 which relates to housing action and general improvement area resolutions, which comes into force on the date the Act was passed, none of the sections of this Part of the Act come into force until a day appointed by the Secretary of State by statutory instrument (s.57).

ABBREVIATIONS
1985 Act: Housing Act 1985.

The right to buy

Exception to the right to buy with respect to dwelling-houses for persons of pensionable age

1. In Schedule 5 to the Housing Act 1985 (exceptions to the right to buy: certain dwelling-houses for persons of pensionable age), there shall be substituted for paragraph 11—

"11.—(1) The right to buy does not arise if the dwelling-house—
(*a*) is particularly suitable for occupation by persons of pensionable age, having regard—
(i) to its location, and
(ii) to its size, design, heating system and other major features so far as those have been provided by the landlord, a predecessor of the tenant or a person qualified to succeed the tenant by virtue of Part IV of the Housing Act 1985,
(*b*) was let to the tenant or a predecessor in title of his for occupation by a person of pensionable age or a physically disabled person (whether the tenant or predecessor or another person).

(2) In determining whether a dwelling is particularly suitable, regard shall be had as to whether the dwelling—
(*a*) is easily accessible on foot;
(*b*) is on one level;
(*c*) being a flat located above ground floor, access by lift is available;
(*d*) has no more than two bedrooms;
(*e*) has a heating system serving the living room and at least one bedroom.".

DEFINITIONS
"right to buy": 1985 Act, s.118.

GENERAL NOTE

This section substitutes a new paragraph 11 in Schedule 5 to the 1985 Act (exceptions to the right to buy: certain dwelling-houses for persons of pensionable age). The previous paragraph gave landlord authorities the right to apply to the Secretary of State for exemption from the right to buy on the basis that the dwelling-house was "particularly suitable . . . for occupation by persons of pensionable age" (Sched. 5, para. 11(2), 1985 Act); application for exemption could be made once the tenant had served a notice claiming the right.

The new paragraph has two ends. First of all, it introduces new determinants governing what qualifies as a dwelling "particularly suitable" for occupation by persons of pensionable age—see subpara. (2). Secondly, it declares that the property is exempt once the test is fulfilled, *i.e.* there is no need for an "application" for exemption. As it is the landlord who decides this question, in practice this leaves the decision on exemption to each individual landlord.

Discount on right to buy and similar sales

2.—(1) In section 129 of the Housing Act 1985 (discount on exercise of right to buy), for subsections (1) and (2) substitute—

"(1) Subject to the following provisions of this Part, a person exercising the right to buy is entitled to a discount of a percentage calculated by reference to the period which is to be taken into account in accordance with Schedule 4 (qualifying period for right to buy and discount).

(2) The discount is, subject to any order under subsection (2A)—

    (*a*) in the case of a house, 32 per cent. plus one per cent. for each complete year by which the qualifying period exceeds two years, up to a maximum of 60 per cent.;

    (*b*) in the case of a flat, 44 per cent. plus two per cent. for each complete year by which the qualifying period exceeds two years, up to a maximum of 70 per cent.

(2A) The Secretary of State may by order made with the consent of the Treasury provide that, in such cases as may be specified in the order—

    (*a*) the minimum percentage discount,

    (*b*) the percentage increase for each complete year of the qualifying period after the first two, or

    (*c*) the maximum percentage discount,

shall be such percentage, higher than that specified in subsection (2), as may be specified in the order.

(2B) An order—

    (*a*) may make different provision with respect to different cases or descriptions of case,

    (*b*) may contain such incidental, supplementary or transitional provisions as appear to the Secretary of State to be necessary or expedient, and

    (*c*) shall be made by statutory instrument and shall not be made unless a draft of it has been laid before and approved by resolution of each House of Parliament.".

(2) The amendment made by subsection (1) does not apply where—

(*a*) the tenant's notice claiming to exercise the right to buy or, as the case may be, to acquire an additional share under a shared ownership lease was served before the commencement of that subsection, and

(*b*) the landlord has before commencement served its notice as to the terms of exercise of that right, that is, its notice under section 125 of, or paragraph 1(3) of Schedule 8 to, the Housing Act 1985,

but without prejudice to the tenant's right to withdraw the notice served before commencement and serve a new notice.

(3) In the following provisions (which in the case of disposals at a discount require a covenant for repayment of a proportion of the discount if the dwelling-house is disposed of within five years)—

    section 35(2) of the Housing Act 1985 (voluntary disposals by local authorities),

    section 155(2) of that Act (disposals in pursuance of the right to buy),

    section 155(3) of that Act (disposals in pursuance of the right to be granted a shared ownership lease), and

    paragraph 1(2) of Schedule 2 to the Housing Associations Act 1985 (voluntary disposals by registered housing associations),

for "five years" substitute "three years" and for "20 per cent." substitute "one-third".

(4) A conveyance or lease containing the covenant required by any of the provisions mentioned in subsection (3) which was executed before the amendments made by that subsection came into force shall, provided no amount was then or had previously been payable under the covenant, have effect with such modifications as may be necessary to bring it into conformity with the amendments.

DEFINITIONS

"commencement date": s.57(2).
"flat": 1985 Act, s.183.
"right to buy": 1985 Act, s.118.

GENERAL NOTE

This section makes major amendments to the discount provisions on exercise of the right to buy by a secure tenant under Part V, 1985 Act.

Subs. (1)

Although the wording has been altered, the effect is only to vary the discount so far as it relates to flats, and discount is unaffected so far as it relates to houses. Formerly, the discounts for houses and flats were calculated in the same way; now, the discount is increased to 44 per cent., plus two per cent. for each complete year by which the qualifying period exceeds two years, to a maximum of 70 per cent.

Any future alteration to the minimum percentage discount, the percentage increase for each complete year of the qualifying period after the first two, or the maximum percentage discount, can now be made by statutory instrument, instead of requiring amendment to the 1985 Act (new s.129(2B)). This applies to both flats and houses.

Subs. (2)

The amendment in subs. (1), above, will not benefit those who have already served a notice claiming to exercise the right to buy or acquire an additional share under a shared ownership lease and to whom the landlord has replied under 1985 Act, s.125 or 1985 Act Sched. 8, para. 1(3) (in the case of shared ownership leases) before commencement of the section. The tenant may, however, elect to withdraw his notice of exercise and recommence the process to take advantage of the increased discount. He will then be at risk of an increase in the purchase price resulting from a new valuation under s.127 of the 1985 Act.

Subss. (3), (4)

Where public sector properties are disposed of at a discount (not only under right to buy, but also on a voluntary disposal), there is a requirement that the disposal includes a covenant for repayment of the discount if the dwelling-house is disposed of within five years (ss.35(2) and 155 of the 1985 Act and Sched 2, para. 1(2), to the Housing Associations Act 1985). Under these provisions the purchaser had to covenant to repay 20 per cent. of the discount for each year less than the five years. The covenant is now reduced to three years, with a one-third repayment for each year less than three. All pre-existing covenants are automatically modified to the same effect, provided that at the date the new section comes into force no amount was then or had previously been payable under the covenant (subs. (4)).

Discount on exercise of right to purchase in Scotland

3.—(1) In section 1 (secure tenant's right to purchase) of the Tenants' Rights, Etc. (Scotland) Act 1980, in subsection (5), after "(*b*)" insert—

"subject to an order under subsection (5B) below,".

(2) After subsection (5A) of the said section 1 insert—

"(5B) The Secretary of State may by order made with the consent of the Treasury provide that, in such cases as may be specified in the order—

(a) the minimum percentage discount,

(b) the percentage increase for each complete year of the qualifying period after the first two, or

(c) the maximum percentage discount,

shall be such percentage, higher than that specified in subsection (5)(b), as may be specified in the order.

(5C) An order—

(a) may make different provision with respect to different cases or descriptions of case,

(b) may contain such incidental, supplementary or transitional provisions, including such amendments to the provisions of section 9A (application of Part I when dwelling-house is repurchased as defective) below, as appear to the Secretary of State to be necessary or expedient, and

(c) shall be made by statutory instrument and shall not be made unless a draft of it has been laid before and approved by resolution of each House of Parliament.".

GENERAL NOTE

While not amending the percentage discount for secure tenants exercising the right to purchase in Scotland a similar amendment to that found in s.2(1) above in relation to England and Wales is included, allowing change to be made by statutory instrument.

Service charges and other contributions payable after exercise of right to buy

4.—(1) In section 125 of the Housing Act 1985 (landlord's notice of purchase price and other matters), for subsection (4) (notice to include estimate of amount of service charges) substitute—

"(4) Where the notice states provisions which would enable the landlord to recover from the tenant—

(a) service charges, or

(b) improvement contributions,

the notice shall also contain the estimates and other information required by section 125A (service charges) or 125B (improvement contributions).".

(2) After that section insert—

"Estimates and information about service charges

125A.—(1) A landlord's notice under section 125 shall state as regards service charges (excluding, in the case of a flat, charges to which subsection (2) applies)—

(a) the landlord's estimate of the average annual amount (at current prices) which would be payable in respect of each head of charge in the reference period, and

(b) the aggregate of those estimated amounts,

and shall contain a statement of the reference period adopted for the purpose of the estimates.

(2) A landlord's notice under section 125 given in respect of a flat shall, as regards service charges in respect of repairs (including works for the making good of structural defects), contain—

(a) the estimates required by subsection (3), together with a statement of the reference period adopted for the purpose of the estimates, and

(b) a statement of the effect of—
    paragraph 16B of Schedule 6 (which restricts by reference to the estimates the amounts payable by the tenant), and section 450A and the regulations made under that section (right to a loan in respect of certain service charges).

(3) The following estimates are required for works in respect of which the landlord considers that costs may be incurred in the reference period—

(a) for works itemised in the notice, estimates of the amount (at current prices) of the likely cost of, and of the tenant's likely contribution in respect of, each item, and the aggregate amounts of those estimated costs and contributions, and

(b) for works not so itemised, an estimate of the average annual amount (at current prices) which the landlord considers is likely to be payable by the tenant.

Estimates and information about improvement contributions

125B.—(1) A landlord's notice under section 125 given in respect of a flat shall, as regards improvement contributions, contain—

(a) the estimates required by this section, together with a statement of the reference period adopted for the purpose of the estimates, and

(b) a statement of the effect of paragraph 16C of Schedule 6 (which restricts by reference to the estimates the amounts payable by the tenant).

(2) Estimates are required for works in respect of which the landlord considers that costs may be incurred in the reference period.

(3) The works to which the estimates relate shall be itemised and the estimates shall show—

(a) the amount (at current prices) of the likely cost of, and of the tenant's likely contribution in respect of, each item, and

(b) the aggregate amounts of those estimated costs and contributions.

Reference period for purposes of ss.125A and 125B

125C.—(1) The reference period for the purposes of the estimates required by section 125A or 125B is the period—

(a) beginning on such date not more than six months after the notice is given as the landlord may reasonably specify as being a date by which the conveyance will have been made or the lease granted, and

(b) ending five years after that date or, where the notice states that the conveyance or lease will provide for a service charge or improvement contribution to be calculated by reference to a specified annual period, with the end of the fifth such period beginning after that date.

(2) For the purpose of the estimates it shall be assumed that the conveyance will be made or the lease granted at the beginning of the reference period on the terms stated in the notice.".

(3) In section 127 of the Housing Act 1985 (valuation of dwelling-house for purposes of right to buy) in subsection (1) (basis of valuation), after paragraph (b) insert—

", and

(c) on the assumption that any service charges or improvement contributions payable will not be less than the amounts to be expected in accordance with the estimates contained in the landlord's notice under section 125.".

(4) In Part III of Schedule 6 to the Housing Act 1985 (terms of lease granted in pursuance of right to buy), after paragraph 16 insert—

"Service charges and other contributions payable by the tenant

16A.—(1) The lease may require the tenant to bear a reasonable part of the costs incurred by the landlord—

(a) in discharging or insuring against the obligations imposed by the covenants implied by virtue of paragraph 14(2) (repairs, making good structural defects, provision of services, etc.), or

(b) in insuring against the obligations imposed by the covenant implied by virtue of paragraph 14(3) (rebuilding or reinstatement, etc.),

and to the extent that by virtue of paragraph 15(3) (effect of provision of superior lease) such obligations are not imposed on the landlord, to bear a reasonable part of the costs incurred by the landlord in contributing to costs incurred by a superior landlord or other person in discharging or, as the case may be, insuring against obligations to the like effect.

(2) Where the lease requires the tenant to contribute to the costs of insurance, it shall provide that the tenant is entitled to inspect the relevant policy at such reasonable times as may be specified in the lease.

(3) Where the landlord does not insure against the obligations imposed by the covenant implied by virtue of paragraph 14(3), or, as the case may be, the superior landlord or other person does not insure against his obligations to the like effect, the lease may require the tenant to pay a reasonable sum in place of the contribution he could be required to make if there were insurance.

(4) Where in any case the obligations imposed by the covenants implied by virtue of paragraph 14(2) or (3) are modified in accordance with paragraph 14(4) (power of county court to authorise modification), the references in this paragraph are to the obligations as so modified.

(5) This paragraph has effect subject to paragraph 16B (restrictions in certain cases as regards costs incurred in the initial period of the lease).

16B.—(1) Where a lease of a flat requires the tenant to pay service charges in respect of repairs (including works for the making good of structural defects), his liability in respect of costs incurred in the initial period of the lease is restricted as follows.

(2) He is not required to pay in respect of works itemised in the estimates contained in the landlord's notice under section 125 any more than the amount shown as his estimated contribution in respect of that item, together with an inflation allowance.

(3) He is not required to pay in respect of works not so itemised at a rate exceeding—

(a) as regards parts of the initial period falling within the reference period for the purposes of the estimates contained in the landlord's notice under section 125, the estimated annual average amount shown in the estimates;

(b) as regards parts of the initial period not falling within that reference period, the average rate produced by averaging over the reference period all works for which estimates are contained in the notice;

together, in each case, with an inflation allowance.

(4) The initial period of the lease for the purposes of this paragraph begins with the grant of the lease and ends five years after the grant, except that—

(a) if the lease includes provision for service charges to be payable in respect of costs incurred in a period before the grant of the lease, the initial period begins with the beginning of that period;

(b) if the lease provides for service charges to be calculated by reference to a specified annual period, the initial period continues until the end of the fifth such period beginning after the grant of the lease; and

(c) if the tenant served notice under section 142 deferring completion, the initial period ends on the date on which it would have ended if the lease had been granted on the date on which the notice was served.

16C.—(1) Where a lease of a flat requires the tenant to pay improvement contributions, his liability in respect of costs incurred in the initial period of the lease is restricted as follows.

(2) He is not required to make any payment in respect of works for which no estimate was given in the landlord's notice under section 125.

(3) He is not required to pay in respect of works for which an estimate was given in that notice any more than the amount shown as his estimated contribution in respect of that item, together with an inflation allowance.

(4) The initial period of the lease for the purposes of this paragraph begins with the grant of the lease and ends five years after the grant, except that—

(a) if the lease includes provision for improvement contributions to be payable in respect of costs incurred in a period before the grant of the lease, the initial period begins with the beginning of that period;

(b) if the lease provides for improvement contributions to be calculated by reference to a specified annual period, the initial period continues until the end of the fifth such period beginning after the grant of the lease; and

(c) if the tenant served notice under section 142 deferring completion, the initial period ends on the date on which it would have ended if the lease had been granted on the date on which the notice was served.

16D.—(1) The Secretary of State may by order prescribe—

(a) the method by which inflation allowances for the purposes of paragraph 16B or 16C are to be calculated by reference to published statistics; and

(b) the information to be given to a tenant when he is asked to pay a service charge or improvement contribution to which the provisions of paragraph 16B or 16C are or may be relevant.

(2) An order—

(a) may make different provision for different cases or descriptions of case, including different provision for different areas;

(b) may contain such incidental, supplementary or transitional provisions as the Secretary of State thinks appropriate; and

(c) shall be made by statutory instrument which shall be subject to annulment in pursuance of a resolution of either House of Parliament.".

(5) For paragraph 18 of Schedule 6 to the Housing Act 1985 (avoidance of certain provisions relating to service charges) substitute—

"18. Where the dwelling-house is a flat, a provision of the lease or of an agreement collateral to it is void in so far as it purports—

(a) to authorise the recovery of such a charge as is mentioned in

paragraph 16A (contributions in respect of repairs, etc.) otherwise than in accordance with that paragraph and paragraph
16B (restrictions in initial period of lease); or
(b) to authorise the recovery of any charge in respect of costs
incurred by the landlord—
    (i) in discharging the obligations imposed by the covenant
    implied by paragraph 14(3) (rebuilding or reinstatement,
    &c.), or those obligations as modified in accordance with
    paragraph 14(4), or
    (ii) in contributing to costs incurred by a superior landlord
    or other person in discharging obligations to the like effect;
    or
(c) to authorise the recovery of an improvement contribution
otherwise than in accordance with paragraph 16C (restrictions
in initial period of lease).".
(6) The amendments in this section do not apply where—
(a) the tenant's notice claiming to exercise the right to buy was served
before the commencement of this section, and
(b) the landlord has before commencement served his notice under
section 125 of the Housing Act 1985 (notice of terms of exercise of
right);
but without prejudice to the tenant's right to withdraw the notice served
before commencement and serve a new notice.

DEFINITIONS
"commencement": s.57.
"dwelling-house": 1985 Act, ss.183, 184.
"flat": 1985 Act, s.183.
"right to buy": 1985 Act, s.118.

GENERAL NOTE
Under s.125 of the 1985 Act, a landlord is required to provide a tenant exercising the
right to buy with a notice of the purchase price and other matters within a defined period of
the tenant's notice of exercise of the right to buy. The information the landlord has to
provide includes (s.125(4)) an estimate of the service charges that the tenant will have to
pay (where the property is a flat or, albeit less commonly, where service charges are payable
in relation to a house). The recovery of service charges following disposal on right to buy of
a *flat* is specifically limited by Sched. 6, para. 18 to the 1985 Act and additionally subject to
the controls placed upon all landlords of flats in ss.18 to 31 of the Landlord and Tenant Act
1985. There are additional provisions governing recovery of service charges relating to a
house in ss.45 to 51 of the 1985 Act, although these are only applicable where a public
sector landlord was formerly the owner.
The new provisions added by this section and s.5 provide a far more comprehensive code
in relation to service charges following a disposal under the right to buy, some of it,
however, applicable only to flats. This is achieved first by requiring more detailed estimates
to be given to the tenant in the s.125 reply, then by limiting the amounts recoverable by the
landlord to those estimates for an initial period, and finally (s.5, below), by introducing the
right to a loan with which to pay for certain, specified, service charges.

Subs. (1)
Rather than simply stating an estimate of the average annual amount of service charges,
the s.125 notice must now include the estimates and other information required by the new
ss.125A and 125B.

Subs. (2)
This introduces the three new sections which now govern the s.125 notice.

New s.125A
A landlord must give an estimate of the annual amount of service charges during the
"reference period," for both flats and houses; service charges are defined in the new s.621A,
1985 Act, added by Sched 5, para. 39 below in identical terms to that formerly found in

s.46, 1985 Act, which is repealed by Sched. 12 below. In relation to flats those service charges which relate to repairs (including structural repairs) must be dealt with separately and must include estimates for works which the landlord considers may be incurred during the reference period.

The tenant must also be informed of the limitation on the recovery of service charges to those estimates contained in the new para. 16B of Sched. 6 to the 1985 Act, see subs. (4) below, and of the right to a loan in respect of some of those charges under the new s.450A of the 1985 Act, see s.5, below (subss. (2) and (3)). The *reference period* is defined in the new s.125C.

New s.125B

This introduces a new concept called the "improvement contribution," which is defined as "an amount payable by a tenant of a flat in respect of improvements to the flat, the building in which it is situated or any other building or land, other than works carried out in discharge of any such obligations as are referred to in paragraph 16A(1) of Schedule 6" of the 1985 Act, see Sched 5, para. 30(3) below. As to the obligations in para. 16A(1), see notes thereto below. The improvement contribution must of definition relate to improvements which the landlord is entitled to carry out and recover the cost of under the terms of the lease, since such sums would not otherwise be recoverable from a leaseholder. As to the distinction between improvement and repair see *Ravenseft Properties* v. *Davstone Holdings Limited* [1980] Q.B. 12, *Smedley* v. *Chumley & Hawkes Ltd.* (1981) 261 E.G. 775, C.A., *Halliard Property Co. Developments* v. *Nicholas Clarke Investments Ltd.* (1983) 269 E.G. 1257, Q.B.D. and *Elmcroft Developments* v. *Tankersley-Sawyer* (1984) 15 H.L.R. 63, C.A..

An estimate of improvement contributions in respect of which the landlord considers that costs may be incurred in the reference period must be given to the tenant, as must notice of the limitation of their recovery to those estimates under the new para. 16C of Sched. 6 to the 1985 Act, see subs. (4) below. The *reference period* is defined in the new s.125C.

New s.125C

This defines the reference period for which the estimates in ss.125A and 125B must be given. The period will generally be five years from a date, not later than six months after the service of the s.125 notice, specified by the landlord authority as one by which they consider that the conveyance will have been made or the lease granted. However, where the service charge or improvement contribution is calculated by reference to a specified annual period, the reference period will run to the end of the fifth such annual period after the chosen date.

Subs. (3)

S.127 of the 1985 Act dictates the principles upon which the purchase price of a property is to be ascertained for the purposes of the right to buy. The valuation is to be an open market value, subject to specified assumptions. A new assumption is now added, *viz.*, that any service charges or improvement contributions payable will not be less than the amounts contained in the estimates provided in the s.125 notice.

Subs. (4)

Part III of Sched. 6 to the 1985 Act governs the terms of a lease granted under the right to buy. Four new paragraphs are added governing the terms for the recovery of service charges and other contributions payable by the tenant. The law as unamended by these new paragraphs is described in the notes to a new para. 18 of Sched. 6 to the 1985 Act, see notes to subs. (5), below.

New para. 16A

The lease can enable the landlord to recover a reasonable part of the costs incurred in discharging or insuring against the obligations imposed upon the landlord by para. 14(2) of Sched. 6., *i.e.* repairing, making good structural defects and providing services, and in insuring against the obligation to reinstate or rebuild imposed by para. 14(3) (subpara. (1)). Where the landlord's obligation is not to do the works or to insure but to contribute towards a superior landlord's costs thereof the lease may require the tenant to bear a reasonable part of those contributions (subpara. (1)).

The tenant has the right to inspect any insurance policy towards which he is contributing (subpara. 2). Where no insurance is taken out against the obligation to rebuild or reinstate, the lease may require the tenant to pay a reasonable sum in place of the contribution he could be required to make if there were insurance (subpara. 3), but any costs above this are not recoverable, see new para. 18(*b*), below.

While this new paragraph provides the principal obligation on the tenant in regard to the recovery of service charges, the liability is further limited by para. 16B during the initial period of the lease.

New para. 16B
During the initial period of the lease, the landlord cannot recover more than the estimated costs of service charges for repairs given under s.125A(2), above, plus an allowance for inflation (as to the calculation of which, see para. 16D). The initial period is not necessarily the same as the reference period for the estimates (see s.125C) but will generally be a period of five years from the grant of the lease (subpara. (4)). If the landlord has correctly estimated the date of the grant of the lease for the commencement of the reference period then the two will generally be concurrent.

Note, however, that the commencement of the initial period is brought forward if the tenant is liable for service charges in respect of any period before the grant of the lease (subpara. (4)(*b*)). This refers to an unusual, but not unknown, cautious practice on the part of landlords concerned to ensure that tenants did not utilise the power of deferring purchase on account of the possibility of major, intervening works, which would increase the value of the property without the necessity for revaluation and accordingly at no cost to the tenant.

If the tenant chooses to defer completion under s.142 of the 1985 Act the initial period runs from the date of the tenant serving notice under s.142 rather than the date from which the lease is granted, *i.e.* the tenant cannot also defer the initial period (subpara. (4)(*c*)).

New para. 16C
Where a lease requires the payment of improvement contributions by the tenant (see notes to subs. (2), above) the liability is again limited during the initial period. No payments can be claimed for costs for which no estimate was given by notice under s.125B, (subpara. (2)). In relation to works for which an estimate was given, no more can be recovered than the estimate plus an allowance for inflation (as to the calculation of which see para. 16D) (subpara. (3)). The definition of initial period is identical to that in the new para. 16B, see notes thereto.

New para. 16D
The inflation allowance for paras. 16B and 16C is to be calculated by reference to published statistics. The method of calculation may be determined by statutory instrument. Provision may also be made for the information to be given to tenants when service charges or improvement contributions are demanded to which paras. 16B and 16C pertain.

Subs. (5)
The former para. 18 made all obligations to recover service charges prima facie void, but then allowed the recovery of certain reasonable costs. Recovery is now dealt with in the new para. 16A. The new para. 18 accordingly now simply provides for certain provisions to be void. Thus, a lease or any agreement collateral to it cannot authorise:

(a) the recovery of any of the charges mentioned in para. 16A, except in accordance with that paragraph and para. 16B;
(b) the recovery of reinstatement or rebuilding costs which the landlord may incur under the obligation imposed by para. 14(3) of Sched. 6 to the 1985 Act, or under an obligation to contribute towards a superior landlord's costs under a similar obligation; or
(c) the recovery of an improvement contribution otherwise than in accordance with para. 16C.

Subs. (6)
The amendments in this section do not apply where the landlord has before its commencement served a s.125 notice in response to the tenant's notice claiming the right to buy. There is no modification of existing leases or conveyances. A tenant whose grant or conveyance is not complete may opt to withdraw the right-to-buy notice before commencement of the section, but will then be at risk of an increased purchase price resulting from a new valuation under s.127 of the 1985 Act. As to commencement, see s.57(2), below.

Loans in respect of service charges

5. In Part XIV of the Housing Act 1985 (loans for acquisition or improvement of housing), after section 450 insert—

"Loans in respect of service charges

Right to a loan in certain cases after exercise of right to buy

450A.—(1) The Secretary of State may by regulations provide that where—

(a) a lease of a flat has been granted in pursuance of Part V (the right to buy), and

(b) the landlord is the housing authority who granted the lease or another housing authority,

the tenant has, in such circumstances as may be prescribed, a right to a loan in respect of service charges to which this section applies.

(2) This section applies to service charges in respect of repairs (whether to the flat, the building in which it is situated or any other building or land) which are payable in the period beginning with the grant of the lease and ending with the tenth anniversary of the grant or, where the lease provides for service charges to be payable by reference to a specified annual period, with the end of the tenth such period beginning after the grant of the lease.

(3) The regulations may provide that the right—

(a) arises only in respect of so much of a service charge as exceeds a minimum qualifying amount and does not exceed a maximum qualifying amount, and

(b) does not arise unless the amount thus qualifying for a loan itself exceeds a minimum amount,

the amounts being either prescribed or ascertained in a prescribed manner.

(4) The regulations shall provide that the right is—

(a) where the landlord is a housing association, a right to an advance from the Housing Corporation, and

(b) in any other case, a right to leave the whole or part of the service charge outstanding.

(5) The regulations may, as regards the procedure for exercising the right, provide—

(a) that a demand for service charges in respect of repairs shall inform the tenant whether, in the landlord's opinion, he is entitled to a loan and, if he is, what he must do to claim it;

(b) that the right must be claimed within a prescribed period of the demand; and

(c) that on the right being claimed the lender shall inform the tenant of the terms of the loan and of the prescribed period within which the tenant may accept the offer.

(6) In this section—

"housing authority" includes any housing association within section 80 (the landlord condition for secure tenancies); and

"repairs" includes works for making good a structural defect.

Power to make loans in other cases

450B.—(1) The Secretary of State may by regulations provide that where—

(a) a housing authority is the landlord of a flat under a long lease granted or assigned by the authority or by another housing authority, and

(b) the tenant is liable under the terms of the lease to pay service charges in respect of repairs (whether to the flat, the building in which it is situated or any other building or land), the landlord or, where the landlord is a housing association, the Housing Corporation may, in such circumstances as may be prescribed, make a loan to the tenant in respect of the service charges.

(2) The regulations shall provide that the power is—

(*a*) where the landlord is a housing association, a power of the Housing Corporation to make an advance, and

(*b*) in any other case, a power of the landlord to leave the whole or part of the service charge outstanding.

(3) Where the tenant is entitled to a loan in pursuance of regulations under section 450A, the power conferred by regulations under this section may be exercised in respect of any part of the service charge which does not qualify for a loan under that section.

(4) In this section—

"housing authority" includes any housing association within section 80 (the landlord condition for secure tenancies); and

"repairs" includes works for making good a structural defect.

(5) This section does not affect any other power of the landlord, or the Housing Corporation, to make loans.

Supplementary provisions as to regulations under s.450A or 450B

450C.—(1) This section applies to regulations under section 450A or 450B (regulations conferring right to loan, or power to make loan, in respect of service charges).

(2) The regulations may provide that the right or, as the case may be, the power does not arise in the case of any prescribed description of landlord.

(3) The regulations shall provide that the loan—

(*a*) in the case of a loan made in pursuance of regulations under section 450A (the right to a loan), shall be on such terms as may be prescribed, and

(*b*) in the case of a loan made by virtue of regulations under section 450B (power to make loan), shall be on such terms as the lender may determine subject to any provision made by the regulations;

and shall, in either case, be secured by a mortgage of the flat in question, but may be made whether or not the flat is adequate security for the loan.

(4) The regulations may—

(*a*) as regards the rate of interest payable on the loan, either prescribe the rate or provide that the rate shall be such reasonable rate as may be determined by the lender or, where the lender is a local authority, provide that Schedule 16 applies (local authority mortgage interest rates);

(*b*) as regards administrative expenses of the lender in connection with a loan, provide that the lender may charge such expenses to the borrower, to the extent that they do not exceed such amount as may be prescribed, and that the expenses so charged may, at the option of the borrower in the case of a loan under section 450A and at the option of the lender in the case of a loan under section 450B, be added to the amount of the loan.

(5) The regulations may apply whenever the lease in question was granted or assigned and whenever the service charge in question became payable.

(6) The regulations—

(*a*) may make different provision for different cases or descriptions of case, including different provision for different areas;

(*b*) may contain such incidental, supplementary and transitional provisions as the Secretary of State considers appropriate; and

(*c*) shall be made by statutory instrument which shall be subject to annulment in pursuance of a resolution of either House of Parliament.".

DEFINITIONS

"flat": 1985 Act, s.183.

"housing authority": 1985 Act, s.4.

"local authority": 1985 Act, s.4.

GENERAL NOTE

The new provisions contained in this section are enabling provisions permitting the introduction by regulations of a new right for secure tenants to set alongside the right to buy and the right to a mortgage contained in Part V of the 1985 Act. The new right is the right to a loan in respect of certain service charges. A new power is also given to housing authorities to make voluntary loans for service charges where the right to a loan does not arise.

New s.450A

The right to a loan under this section only arises where a lease of a flat has been granted in pursuance of the right to buy under Part V of the 1985 Act *and* the landlord is a housing authority. "Housing authority" is defined in s.4 of the 1985 Act, but is extended for this section to include housing associations which are secure landlords, see subs. (6).

The right to a loan arises in relation to service charges in respect of repairs payable over a ten-year period from the grant of the lease (subs. (2)). Such service charges will in any event have to fall within the provisions contained in paras. 16A and 16B of Sched. 6 to the 1985 Act (s.4, above) before they are recoverable by the landlord, see para. 18, *ibid.*, (s.4(5), above).

The regulations may provide for a minimum and maximum qualifying amount of service charge and for a minimum amount of loan and for the manner in which the amounts are to be ascertained (subs. (3)).

Where the landlord is a housing association, the right is to an advance from the Housing Corporation. In other cases the right is to leave the whole or part of the service charge outstanding (subs. (4)), *i.e.* by way of additional mortgage. Provisions for the terms of any loan under this section are contained in the new s.450C.

New s.450B

Where a loan under s.450A does not meet the whole of the service charge or, *e.g.* because the ten-year period has elapsed, the tenant is not entitled to a loan under that section as of right, the local authority (or as the case may be the Housing Corporation) may be given the power by regulations to make loans to the tenant (subs. (1)). In relation to the Housing Corporation the power is to make an advance and in other cases to leave the whole or part of the service charge outstanding (subs. (2)).

The power is additional to and does not affect other powers of the landlord or the Housing Corporation to make loans (subs. (5)), see, *e.g.* 1985 Act, s.435 and Housing Associations Act 1985, s.79.

New s.450C

This new section empowers the Secretary of State to make regulations regarding the terms of a loan under ss.450A or 450B.

The regulations *may*:

(a) provide that the right or power does not arise in the case of any prescribed description of landlord (subs. (2));

(b) prescribe the rate of interest, or provide that it shall be such reasonable rate as determined by the lender, or where the lender is a local authority provide that Sched. 16 to the 1985 Act applies (subs. (4));

(c) make provision as regards administrative expenses (subs. (4)); and,

(d) make different provision for different cases or descriptions of case, including different provision for different areas (subs. (6)).

The regulations *must* provide:

(a) in the case of a loan under s.450A that the loan is on such terms as may be prescribed (subs. (3)(*a*));

(b) in the case of a loan under s.450B that the loan is on such terms as the lender may determine, subject to the provisions of the regulations (subs. (3)(*b*));

(c) that in either case the loan be secured by a mortgage of the flat in question (subs. (3)); and

(d) that the loan be made whether or not the flat is adequate security for the loan (subs. (3)).

Other provisions with respect to public sector housing

Consultation before disposal to private sector landlord

6.—(1) In Part IV of the Housing Act 1985 (secure tenancies and rights of secure tenants), after section 106 insert—

"Consultation before disposal to private sector landlord

106A.—(1) The provisions of Schedule 3A have effect with respect to the duties of—

(*a*) a local authority proposing to dispose of dwelling-houses subject to secure tenancies, and

(*b*) the Secretary of State in considering whether to give his consent to such a disposal,

to have regard to the views of tenants liable as a result of the disposal to cease to be secure tenants.

(2) In relation to a disposal to which that Schedule applies, the provisions of that Schedule apply in place of the provisions of section 105 (consultation on matters of housing management).".

(2) After Schedule 3 to the Housing Act 1985 insert as Schedule 3A the Schedule set out in Schedule 1 to this Act (consultation before disposal to private sector landlord).

(3) The amendments made by this section apply to disposals after the commencement of this section.

DEFINITIONS
"commencement": s.57.
"local authority": 1985 Act, s.4.
"secure tenancy": 1985 Act, s.79.

GENERAL NOTE
Sections 7 and 8, below, are intended to encourage and facilitate the disposal to private sector landlords of *tenanted* properties held by local authorities. This section gives a corresponding right to those tenants liable as a result of such a disposal to lose their status as secure tenants to have their views considered beforehand, *i.e.* it is a consultation provision. Not only must the local authority consider their views, but so too must the Secretary of State when considering whether or not to consent to the disposal. There is no express provision empowering such disposals as consent under either s.32 or s.43 of the 1985 Act is all that is needed.

The mechanics of the consultation process are dealt with in Sched. 1, which inserts a new Sched. 3A to the 1985 Act. Consultation under this section applies in place of that required by the 1985 Act, s.105 (which would otherwise require consultation on such a disposal, see *Short* v. *London Borough of Tower Hamlets* (1985) 18 H.L.R. 171, C.A., see also *R.* v. *London Borough of Hammersmith and Fulham, ex p. Beddowes* (1986) 18 H.L.R. 458, C.A.). See further notes to Sched. 1, below.

Certificate of fair rent with a view to disposal by public sector body

7.—(1) In section 69 of the Rent Act 1977 (certificates of fair rent), after subsection (1) insert—

"(1A) A public sector body to which this subsection applies may, with a view to the disposal of an interest in a dwelling-house, apply to the rent officer for a certificate specifying a rent which in the opinion of the rent officer would be a fair rent under a regulated tenancy of the dwelling-house—

(*a*) in its present condition, or

(*b*) after the completion of works of improvement, conversion or repair.

(1B) In subsection (1A) "public sector body" means an authority or body within section 80(1) of the Housing Act 1985 (the landlord condition for secure tenancies) other than the Housing Corporation, a housing association or a housing trust which is a charity.

In this subsection "housing association", "housing trust" and "charity" have the same meaning as in Part IV of the Housing Act 1985.

(1C) A certificate under subsection (1) or (1A) shall be known as a certificate of fair rent.".

(2) In section 69(1) of the Rent Act 1977—

(*a*) after "improvements", in both places where it occurs, insert "or repairs", and

(*b*) at the end, add—

"No application shall be made under this subsection if an application could be made under subsection (1A) below.".

DEFINITIONS

"charity": 1985 Act, s.622.

"housing association": 1985 Act, s.5(1).

"housing trust": 1985 Act, s.6.

GENERAL NOTE

Under the Rent Act 1977, s.69, prospective landlords can make precautionary applications to the rent officer for a certificate of fair rent when they are contemplating improvements to or the letting of a dwelling-house which is or will be subject to a protected or statutory tenancy. This section amends s.69 by allowing applications for such a certificate to be made by public sector bodies who are contemplating disposing of tenanted stock into the private sector pursuant to the policy which this series of sections reflects. There is no express provision empowering such disposals as consent under either s.32 or s.43 of the 1985 Act is all that is needed.

On such a disposal, the former secure tenant will become the protected tenant of the new owner. The prospective rent payable after disposal is the type of information which should be supplied to the tenant during the consultation process which must precede disposal (see 1985 Act, Sched. 3A, para. 3(2) added by s.6 above and Sched. 1, below).

The application for a certificate of fair rent provides the mechanism whereby the prospective rent can be established. The effect of a certificate is to set a rent ceiling on the tenancy once it is within the Rent Act 1977. However, while normally a registration of fair rent lasts for two years (subject only to increase or decrease on the grounds of specified changes, *e.g.* improvements) (see 1977 Act, s.67(3)), when the ceiling has been set by *certificate*, the landlord can apply at any time for a new registration, *i.e.* an increase: 1977 Act, s.69(4).

Subs. (2)

As a wholly discrete amendment, and indeed one of the few purely private sector amendments to be found in this Part of this Act, the right to apply for a certificate of fair rent already available to private sector landlords who are contemplating improvements is now extended to landlords who are contemplating mere repairs.

Preservation of right to buy on disposal to private sector landlord

8.—(1) In Part V of the Housing Act 1985 (the right to buy), after section 171 insert—

"Preservation of right to buy on disposal to private sector landlord

Cases in which right to buy is preserved

171A.—(1) The provisions of this Part continue to apply where a person ceases to be a secure tenant of a dwelling-house by reason of the disposal by the landlord of an interest in the dwelling-house to a person who is not an authority or body within section 80 (the landlord condition for secure tenancies).

(2) In the following provisions of this Part—

 (*a*) references to the preservation of the right to buy and to a person having the preserved right to buy are to the continued application of the provisions of this Part by virtue of this section and to a person in relation to whom those provisions so apply;

 (*b*) "qualifying disposal" means a disposal in relation to which this section applies, and

 (*c*) the "former secure tenant" and the "former landlord" are the persons mentioned in subsection (1).

(3) This section does not apply—

 (*a*) where the former landlord was a person against whom the right to buy could not be exercised by virtue of paragraph 1, 2 or 3 of Schedule 5 (charities and certain housing associations), or

 (*b*) in such other cases as may be excepted from the operation of this section by order of the Secretary of State.

(4) Orders under subsection (3)(*b*)—

 (*a*) may relate to particular disposals and may make different provision with respect to different cases or descriptions of case, including different provision for different areas, and

 (*b*) shall be made by statutory instrument which shall be subject to annulment in pursuance of a resolution of either House of Parliament.

Extent of preserved right: qualifying persons and dwelling-houses

171B.—(1) A person to whom this section applies has the preserved right to buy so long as he occupies the relevant dwelling-house as his only or principal home, subject to the following provisions of this Part.

(2) References in this Part to a "qualifying person" and "qualifying dwelling-house", in relation to the preserved right to buy, are to a person who has that right and to a dwelling-house in relation to which a person has that right.

(3) The following are the persons to whom this section applies—

 (*a*) the former secure tenant, or in the case of a joint tenancy, each of them;

 (*b*) a qualifying successor as defined in subsection (4); and

 (*c*) a person to whom a tenancy of a dwelling-house is granted jointly with a person who has the preserved right to buy in relation to that dwelling-house.

(4) The following are qualifying successors for this purpose—

 (*a*) where the former secure tenancy was not a joint tenancy, a person who, on the death of the former secure tenant, becomes by virtue of paragraph 2 or 3 of Part I of Schedule 1 to the Rent Act 1977 (surviving spouse or member of deceased tenant's family) the statutory tenant of a dwelling-house in relation to which the former secure tenant had the preserved right to buy immediately before his death;

 (*b*) a person who becomes the tenant of a dwelling-house in pursuance of—

  (i) a property adjustment order under section 24 of the Matrimonial Causes Act 1973, or

        (ii) an order under Schedule 1 to the Matrimonial Homes Act 1983 transferring the tenancy,
in place of a person who had the preserved right to buy in relation to that dwelling-house.

(5) The relevant dwelling-house is in the first instance—

    (a) in relation to a person within paragraph (a) of subsection (3), the dwelling-house which was the subject of the qualifying disposal;

    (b) in relation to a person within paragraph (b) of that subsection, the dwelling-house of which he became the statutory tenant or tenant as mentioned in subsection (4)(a) or (b);

    (c) in relation to a person within paragraph (c) of subsection (3), the dwelling-house of which he became a joint tenant as mentioned in that paragraph.

(6) If a person having the preserved right to buy becomes the tenant of another dwelling-house in place of the relevant dwelling-house (whether the new dwelling-house is entirely different or partly or substantially the same as the previous dwelling-house) and the landlord is the same person as the landlord of the previous dwelling-house or, where that landlord was a company, is a connected company, the new dwelling-house becomes the relevant dwelling-house for the purposes of the preserved right to buy.

For this purpose "connected company" means a subsidiary or holding company within the meaning of section 736 of the Companies Act 1985.

Modifications of this Part in relation to preserved right

171C.—(1) Where the right to buy is preserved, the provisions of this Part have effect subject to such exceptions, adaptations and other modifications as may be prescribed by regulations made by the Secretary of State.

(2) The regulations may in particular provide—

    (a) that paragraphs 5 to 11 of Schedule 5 (certain exceptions to the right to buy) do not apply;

    (b) that the right to a mortgage is exercisable against the former landlord or, if the former landlord was a housing association, against the Housing Corporation;

    (c) that the provisions of this Part relating to the right to be granted a shared ownership lease do not apply; and

    (d) that the landlord is not required to but may include a covenant for the repayment of discount, provided its terms are no more onerous than those of the covenant provided for in section 155.

(3) The prescribed exceptions, adaptations and other modifications shall take the form of textual amendments of the provisions of this Part as they apply in cases where the right to buy is preserved; and the first regulations, and any subsequent consolidating regulations, shall set out the provisions of this Part as they so apply.

(4) The regulations—

    (a) may make different provision for different cases or descriptions of case, including different provision for different areas,

    (b) may contain such incidental, supplementary and transitional provisions as the Secretary of State considers appropriate, and

    (c) shall be made by statutory instrument which shall be

subject to annulment in pursuance of a resolution of either House of Parliament.

Subsequent dealings: disposal of landlord's interest in qualifying dwelling-house

171D.—(1) The disposal by the landlord of an interest in the qualifying dwelling-house, whether his whole interest or a lesser interest, does not affect the preserved right to buy, unless—

(*a*) as a result of the disposal an authority or body within section 80(1) (the landlord condition for secure tenancies) becomes the landlord of the qualifying person or persons, or

(*b*) paragraph 6 of Schedule 9A applies (effect of failure to register entry protecting preserved right to buy),

in which case the right to buy ceases to be preserved.

(2) The disposal by the landlord of a qualifying dwelling-house of less than his whole interest as landlord of the dwelling-house, or in part of it, requires the consent of the Secretary of State, unless the disposal is to the qualifying person or persons.

(3) Consent may be given in relation to a particular disposal or generally in relation to disposals of a particular description and may, in either case, be given subject to conditions.

(4) A disposal made without the consent required by subsection (2) is void, except in a case where, by reason of a failure to make the entries on the land register or land charges register required by Schedule 9A, the preserved right to buy does not bind the person to whom the disposal is made.

Subsequent dealings: termination of landlord's interest in qualifying dwelling-house

171E.—(1) On the termination of the landlord's interest in the qualifying dwelling-house—

(*a*) on the occurrence of an event determining his estate or interest, or by re-entry on a breach of condition or forfeiture, or

(*b*) where the interest is a leasehold interest, by notice given by him or a superior landlord, on the expiry or surrender of the term, or otherwise (subject to subsection (2)),

the right to buy ceases to be preserved.

(2) The termination of the landlord's interest by merger on his acquiring a superior interest, or on the acquisition by another person of the landlord's interest together with a superior interest, does not affect the preserved right to buy, unless—

(*a*) as a result of the acquisition an authority or body within section 80(1) (the landlord condition for secure tenancies) becomes the landlord of the qualifying person or persons, or

(*b*) paragraph 6 of Schedule 9A applies (effect of failure to register entry protecting preserved right to buy),

in which case the right to buy ceases to be preserved.

(3) Where the termination of the landlord's interest as mentioned in subsection (1) is caused by the act or omission of the landlord, a qualifying person who is thereby deprived of the preserved right to buy is entitled to be compensated by him.

Subsequent dealings: transfer of qualifying person to alternative accommodation

171F. The court shall not order a qualifying person to give up possession of the qualifying dwelling-house in pursuance of section 98(1)(*a*) of the Rent Act 1977 (suitable alternative accommodation) unless the court is satisfied—

(*a*) that the preserved right to buy will, by virtue of section 171B(6) (accommodation with same landlord or connected company), continue to be exercisable in relation to the dwelling-house offered by way of alternative accommodation and that the interest of the landlord in the new dwelling-house will be—

    (i) where the new dwelling-house is a house, not less than the interest of the landlord in the existing dwelling-house, or

    (ii) where the new dwelling-house is a flat, not less than the interest of the landlord in the existing dwelling-house or a term of years of which 80 years or more remain unexpired, whichever is the less; or

  (b) that the landlord of the new dwelling-house will be an authority or body within section 80(1) (the landlord condition for secure tenancies).

Land registration and related matters

171G. Schedule 9A has effect with respect to registration of title and related matters arising in connection with the preservation of the right to buy.

Disposal after notice claiming to exercise right to buy, etc.

171H.—(1) Where notice has been given in respect of a dwelling-house claiming to exercise the right to buy or the right to a mortgage and before the completion of the exercise of that right the dwelling-house is the subject of—

  (a) a qualifying disposal, or

  (b) a disposal to which section 171D(1)(a) or 171E(2)(a) applies (disposal to authority or body satisfying landlord condition for secure tenancies),

all parties shall, subject to subsection (2), be in the same position as if the disponee had become the landlord before the notice was given and had been given that notice and any further notice given by the tenant to the landlord and had taken all steps which the landlord had taken.

  (2) If the circumstances after the disposal differ in any material respect, as for example where—

  (a) the interest of the disponee in the dwelling-house after the disposal differs from that of the disponor before the disposal, or

  (b) the right to a mortgage becomes exercisable against the Housing Corporation rather than the former landlord, or *vice versa*, or

  (c) any of the provisions of Schedule 5 (exceptions to the right to buy) becomes or ceases to be applicable,

all those concerned shall, as soon as practicable after the disposal, take all such steps (whether by way of amending or withdrawing and re-serving any notice or extending any period or otherwise) as may be requisite for the purpose of securing that all parties are, as nearly as may be, in the same position as they would have been if those circumstances had obtained before the disposal.".

  (2) After Schedule 9 to the Housing Act 1985 insert as Schedule 9A the Schedule set out in Schedule 2 to this Act (land registration and related matters where right to buy preserved).

  (3) The amendments made by this section apply to qualifying disposals on or after the commencement of this section.

Definitions

  "commencement": s.57

  "dwelling-house": 1985 Act, ss.183, 184

  "right to buy": 1985 Act, s.118

  "secure tenant": 1985 Act, s.79

GENERAL NOTE

This section inserts no fewer than eight new sections (and a new Schedule) into Part V of the 1985 Act, preserving the "right to buy" for former secure tenants following disposal of their dwelling-houses into the private sector pursuant to the policy which this series of sections reflects. There is no express provision empowering such disposals as consent under either s.32 or s.43 of the 1985 Act is all that is needed.

Subs. (1)

New s.171A

This section defines those cases in which the "right to buy" is preserved, despite the fact that the tenant is no longer a secure tenant.

Subss. (1), (2) The right is preserved on a "qualifying disposal", *i.e.* a disposal by a secure landlord to a non-secure landlord, by reason of which the tenancy ceases to be secure.

Subss. (3), (4) Certain housing trusts and associations are in any event excluded from the "right to buy", by paras. 1, 2, and 3 of Sched. 5 to the 1985 Act. Disposals by such landlords are also excluded from these provisions. The Secretary of State has also reserved the right to exclude other landlords.

New s.171B

Subs. (1): The preserved right to buy only continues so long as the tenant continues to occupy the dwelling-house as his only or principal home. This test is the same as the relevant part of the definition of secure tenancy itself: see 1985 Act, s.81. There is no definition of the phrase "only or principal home" in the 1985 Act. It is similar to that used in the Leasehold Reform Act 1967, s.1(2): "only or main residence". By analogy, it would accordingly include a tenant who occupies part, but sublets the remainder of his home: see *Harris* v. *Swick Securities* [1969] 1 W.L.R. 1604. In *Poland* v. *Cadogan* [1980] 3 All E.R. 544, C.A., it was held that while long absences from a house may not prevent occupation, a long absence abroad with the premises sublet may indicate a lack of intention to occupy, sufficient to defeat the meaning of occupation for the purposes of that Act. In *Fowell* v. *Radford* (1970) 21 P. & C.R. 99, C.A., a claim by a husband and wife each to be entitled to be occupying a different house as the main home, although considered unusual, was upheld.

What is absolutely clear is that reliance cannot be placed on case law decided under the closest equivalent Rent Act phrase: "if and so long as he occupies the dwelling-house as his residence" (Rent Act 1977, s.2). This has been generously interpreted by the courts, in effect to mean occupation as *a* residence: see, *e.g. Bevington* v. *Crawford* (1974) 232 E.G. 191, C.A., *Gofor Investments* v. *Roberts* (1975) 119 S.J. 320, C.A.; see also *Langford Property Co. Ltd.* v. *Tureman* [1949] 1 K.B. 29, C.A., and *Beck* v. *Scholtz* [1953] 1 Q.B. 570, C.A. for two cases which usefully illustrate where the line is drawn. Thus, it may be the case that a tenant whose dwelling-house has been sold into the private sector may be a statutory tenant for Rent Act purposes, but still *not* be occupying the dwelling-house for the purposes of exercising the preserved "right to buy".

Subss. (2), (3), (4), (5): The preserved right does not only apply to the former secure tenant of the dwelling-house, but to "qualifying persons". These are:

(*a*) the former secure tenant, or in the case of a joint tenancy each of the tenants;

(*b*) a "qualifying successor", *i.e.* a person succeeding to the former secure tenancy under the succession provisions of the Rent Act 1977, or a spouse who becomes a tenant under a property adjustment order under s.24 of the Matrimonial Causes Act 1973, or an order under Matrimonial Homes Act 1983, in place of a person who had the preserved right;

(*c*) a joint tenant where that tenancy is granted to a person jointly with another person who has the preserved "right to buy".

Subs. (6): Once the former secure tenant becomes the tenant of a private landlord, the Rent Act 1977 will apply. Under s.98 of the 1977 Act, possession may be granted of a dwelling-house if suitable alternative accommodation is available. This subsection continues the preserved right to buy for tenants who either move voluntarily to other premises owned by the same private landlord or who are moved by court order, *i.e.* the preserved right to buy goes with the tenant (see further notes to s.171F, below). This provision cannot be circumvented by the landlord using a "connected company" as the new landlord.

New s.171C

Although the preserved right to buy operates in the same manner as the "right to buy" under Part V of the 1985 Act, the Secretary of State has reserved the right to make exceptions, adaptations and modifications to Part V for the purposes of the preserved right, *e.g.* governing from where the mortgage is to derive, the application of shared ownership leases, and covenants for the repayment of discount on further, onward sale by the purchasing tenant.

New s.171D

Subs. (1): The preserved right persists where the dwelling-house is sold to another landlord, unless that landlord is a secure landlord (in which case the tenancy will in any event fulfil the necessary conditions for the "right to buy" in its normal operation, *i.e.* under Part V of the 1985 Act) *if but only if* the right has been properly protected by registration of a land charge in accordance with the new Sched. 9A, inserted by s.8(2), below.

Subss. (2), (3), (4): A private sector landlord cannot dispose of *part* only of his interest without the approval of the Secretary of State. This is to ensure that a separation of interests is not used to defeat the tenant's preserved right to buy. Thus consent is required for the creation of an intermediate interest between the landlord and the tenant so as to limit the extent of exercise of the preserved right, *e.g.* to a leasehold instead of freehold.

New s.171E

This section deals with determination of the private landlord's interest other than disposal, which is governed by the new s.171D.

Subss. (1), (3): Where the landlord's interest is determined, *e.g.* by compulsory purchase or by re-entry on a breach of condition or on forfeiture, the preserved right is lost. Where the landlord's interest is leasehold, and comes to an end by notice to quit, effluxion of time, or surrender of the term, the right is similarly lost. However, if the loss of the right is caused by an act or omission on the part of the landlord (*e.g.* failure to apply for relief from forfeiture) the tenant is entitled to be compensated. No measure for the calculation of compensation is given, but it would obviously apply to the lost discount to which the tenant would otherwise have been entitled under s.129 of the 1985 Act.

Subs. (2): Where a person owns both a leasehold interest in property and a superior interest (either a longer lease or the freehold) those interests will merge into one, and continue as the superior interest. Where a landlord's interest is terminated by such a merger, either by acquisition by the landlord of the superior interest or by the acquisition by another person of both interests, it does not affect the preserved right. There are two exceptions to this, first where the acquisition is by a secure landlord, in which case the tenancy will in any event be subject to the "right to buy" (*i.e.* "normally", under Part V of the 1985 Act) or if the preserved right has not been properly protected by registration as a land charge in accordance with the new Schedule 9A, inserted by s.8(2), see notes to Sched. 2, below.

New s.171F

This section is in *effect* an amendment to the Rent Act 1977, although not so described. Disposal to the private sector will make former secure tenancies subject instead to the protection of the Rent Act 1977. Under s.98(1)(*a*) of the 1977 Act a court may make an order for possession if it considers it reasonable to do so and it is satisfied that suitable alternative accommodation is available. Where the tenant qualifies for the preserved right to buy possession may not be granted unless, additionally, the conditions of this section are satisfied.

New s.171G

See notes to Sched. 2, below.

New s.171H

This section deals with those cases where the tenant has before the disposal served a notice claiming to exercise his right to buy or to a mortgage. In these circumstances the purchasing private landlord steps into the shoes of the secure landlord (subs. (1)), *save* where the change of circumstances materially affects the rights involved, extraordinarily defined by illustration. If such circumstances arise, a wide and unspecific duty is placed on "all those concerned" to take "all such steps" as are necessary to secure that the position is the same as that which would have pertained if the change in circumstances had taken place prior to the disposal.

What this means, by reference to the first illustration given in subs. (2) of this opaque provision is that if, say, the purchasing private landlord buys a *leasehold* interest in a house (as distinct from flat) from a freeholding public landlord (who would, as freeholder, therefore be bound to sell the tenant a freehold), it is assumed that the freeholding public landlord had no greater interest than that which has been conveyed to the private landlord, *i.e.* the leasehold. On this example, the purchasing tenant will obtain a lesser (leasehold) interest.

Redevelopment of dwelling-house subject to secure tenancy

9.—(1) In Schedule 2 to the Housing Act 1985 (grounds for possession of dwelling-houses let under secure tenancies), in Part II (grounds on which court may order possession if suitable alternative accommodation is available), after ground 10 (redevelopment by landlord) insert—

"Ground 10A

The dwelling-house is in an area which is the subject of a redevelopment scheme approved by the Secretary of State or the Housing Corporation in accordance with Part V of this Schedule and the landlord intends within a reasonable time of obtaining possession to dispose of the dwelling-house in accordance with the scheme.
or
Part of the dwelling-house is in such an area and the landlord intends within a reasonable time of obtaining possession to dispose of that part in accordance with the scheme and for that purpose reasonably requires possession of the dwelling-house.".

(2) At the end of that Schedule insert—

"PART V

APPROVAL OF REDEVELOPMENT SCHEMES FOR PURPOSES OF GROUND 10A

1.—(1) The Secretary of State may, on the application of the landlord, approve for the purposes of ground 10A in Part II of this Schedule a scheme for the disposal and redevelopment of an area of land consisting of or including the whole or part of one or more dwelling-houses.
(2) For this purpose—
    (*a*) "disposal" means a disposal of any interest in the land (including the grant of an option), and
    (*b*) "redevelopment" means the demolition or reconstruction of buildings or the carrying out of other works to buildings or land;
and it is immaterial whether the disposal is to precede or follow the redevelopment.
(3) The Secretary of State may on the application of the landlord approve a variation of a scheme previously approved by him and may, in particular, approve a variation adding land to the area subject to the scheme.
2.—(1) Where a landlord proposes to apply to the Secretary of State for the approval of a scheme or variation it shall serve a notice in writing on any secure tenant of a dwelling-house affected by the proposal stating—
    (*a*) the main features of the proposed scheme or, as the case may be, the scheme as proposed to be varied,
    (*b*) that the landlord proposes to apply to the Secretary of State for approval of the scheme or variation, and
    (*c*) the effect of such approval, by virtue of section 84 and ground 10A in Part II of this Schedule, in relation to proceedings for possession of the dwelling-house,
and informing the tenant that he may, within such period as the landlord may allow (which shall be at least 28 days from service of the notice), make representations to the landlord about the proposal.

(2) The landlord shall not apply to the Secretary of State until it has considered any representations made to it within that period.

(3) In the case of a landlord to which section 105 applies (consultation on matters of housing management) the provisions of this paragraph apply in place of the provisions of that section in relation to the approval or variation of a redevelopment scheme.

3.—(1) In considering whether to give his approval to a scheme or variation the Secretary of State shall take into account, in particular—

(a) the effect of the scheme on the extent and character of housing accommodation in the neighbourhood,

(b) over what period of time it is proposed that the disposal and redevelopment will take place in accordance with the scheme, and

(c) to what extent the scheme includes provision for housing provided under the scheme to be sold or let to existing tenants or persons nominated by the landlord;

and he shall take into account any representations made to him and, so far as they are brought to his notice, any representations made to the landlord.

(2) The landlord shall give to the Secretary of State such information as to the representations made to it, and other relevant matters, as the Secretary of State may require.

4. The Secretary of State shall not approve a scheme or variation so as to include in the area subject to the scheme—

(a) part only of one or more dwelling-houses, or

(b) one or more dwelling-houses not themselves affected by the works involved in redevelopment but which are proposed to be disposed of along with other land which is so affected,

unless he is satisfied that the inclusion is justified in the circumstances.

5.—(1) Approval may be given subject to conditions and may be expressed to expire after a specified period.

(2) The Secretary of State, on the application of the landlord or otherwise, may vary an approval so as to—

(a) add, remove or vary conditions to which the approval is subject; or

(b) extend or restrict the period after which the approval is to expire.

(3) Where approval is given subject to conditions, the landlord may serve a notice under section 83 (notice of proceedings for possession) specifying ground 10A notwithstanding that the conditions are not yet fulfilled but the court shall not make an order for possession on that ground unless satisfied that they are or will be fulfilled.

6. Where the landlord is a registered housing association, the Housing Corporation, and not the Secretary of State, has the functions conferred by this Part of this Schedule.

7. In this Part of this Schedule references to the landlord of a dwelling-house include any authority or body within section 80 (the landlord condition for secure tenancies) having an interest of any description in the dwelling-house.".

(3) Section 29 of the Land Compensation Act 1973 (home loss payments) is amended as follows—

(a) in subsection (1) (circumstances in which, and persons by whom, payment to be made) after paragraph (d) insert—

"(e) the making of an order for possession on ground 10 or 10A in Part II of Schedule 2 to the Housing Act 1985;"; and

(b) in the same subsection, after paragraph (iv) insert—

"(v) where paragraph (e) applies, the landlord."; and

(*c*) in subsection (4) (interests and rights to which the section applies), after paragraph (*d*) insert—

"(*e*) a right to occupy the dwelling under a licence to which Part IV of the Housing Act 1985 (secure tenancies) applies.".

(4) In section 32 of the Land Compensation Act 1973 (supplementary provisions about home loss payments), after subsection (7A) insert—

"(7B) Where a landlord obtains possession by agreement of a dwelling subject to a secure tenancy within the meaning of Part IV of the Housing Act 1985 and—

(*a*) notice of proceedings for possession of the dwelling has been served, or might have been served, specifying ground 10 or 10A in Part II of Schedule 2 to that Act, or

(*b*) the landlord has applied, or could apply, to the Secretary of State or the Housing Corporation for approval for the purposes of ground 10A of a redevelopment scheme including the dwelling, or part of it,

the landlord may make to the person giving up possession a payment corresponding to any home loss payment which they would be required to make to him if an order for possession had been made on either of those grounds.".

DEFINITIONS
"dwelling-house": 1985 Act, s.112.
"secure tenancy": 1985 Act, s.79.

GENERAL NOTE
Under the 1985 Act, Ground 10 possession of a secure tenancy may be obtained if the *landlord* intends within a reasonable time to carry out demolition or construction works to the building in which the dwelling-house is situated. Suitable alternative accommodation must be provided. This section adds a new ground of possession which arises where it is intended to dispose of the property into the private sector in connection with a specific renovation or modernisation scheme, in which circumstances the works are unlikely to be carried out by the *landlord,* but will instead be carried out by the prospective purchaser.

Subs. (1)
New Ground 10A
The Ground is included in Part II of Sched. 2 to the 1985 Act. The landlord thus need not show that it is reasonable to make an order, simply that suitable alternative accommodation is available. As to the suitability of alternative accommodation see Part IV, *ibid.*

The landlord must satisfy the court that the terms of the Ground are fulfilled, *i.e.* there must be an *approved* redevelopment scheme, as defined by the new Part V of Sched. 2 to the 1985 Act (see subs. (2)), applicable to an area in which the dwelling-house is situated, *and* the landlord must intend to dispose of the property within a reasonable time of obtaining possession. If, however, only part of the dwelling-house is in the redevelopment area, possession of the property must *additionally* be reasonably required in order to dispose of that part.

Subs. (2)
A new Part V is added to Sched. 2 to the 1985 Act governing the approval by the Secretary of State of redevelopment schemes.

New Part V
Para. 1: The scheme must be for the disposal of an area of land which is to be redeveloped. Such redevelopment may take place before or after the disposal, although if the redevelopment is to take place prior to the disposal the landlord may be able to obtain possession under Ground 10, without the necessity of seeking approval, if it is the landlord who is to carry out the works. Approval may be sought for an area as small as part of a dwelling-house.

Para. 2: Before seeking approval for a scheme the landlord must consult with the tenants, as to both application for approval, and the details of the proposed scheme. Where the landlord would in any event have been under a duty to consult with the tenants under s.105 of the 1985 Act that duty is replaced by this. As to those landlords under such a duty, see 1985 Act, s.114.

Para. 3: Any decision of the Secretary of State would be open to challenge on judicial review principles, see generally *Associated Provincial Picture Houses* v. *Wednesbury Corporation* [1948] 1 K.B. 223, C.A. Such a challenge could be on the basis of failure to take into account relevant considerations, see, *e.g. R.* v. *Herefordshire County Council, ex p. NUPE* [1985] I.R.L.R. 258, C.A. This paragraph lays down certain statutory considerations which the Minister must take into account.

Para. 4: Where the area is of part only of a dwelling-house or the proposed works will not affect a particular dwelling-house, the Minister must not include them in the area unless he is satisfied that their inclusion is justified.

Subss. (3), (4)

A tenant against whom possession was obtained under Ground 10 of Sched. 2 to the 1985 Act had no right of compensation for the loss of his home. These subsections now add such a right under the Land Compensation Act 1973 for those displaced under *both* Ground 10 and 10A, *ibid.*

Management agreements

10. For section 27 of the Housing Act 1985 (agreements with housing co-operatives), and the heading preceding it, substitute—

"Management agreements

Management agreements

27.—(1) A local housing authority may, with the approval of the Secretary of State, agree that another person shall exercise as agent of the authority in relation to—

(a) such of the authority's houses as are specified in the agreement, and

(b) any other land so specified which is held for a related purpose, such of the authority's management functions as are so specified.

(2) In this Act "management agreement" and "manager", in relation to such an agreement, mean an agreement under this section and the person with whom the agreement is made.

(3) A management agreement shall set out the terms on which the authority's functions are exercisable by the manager.

(4) A management agreement may, where the manager is a body or association, provide that the manager's functions under the agreement may be performed by a committee or sub-committee, or by an officer, of the body or association.

(5) The Secretary of State's approval (which may be given unconditionally or subject to conditions) is required both for the terms of the agreement and the identity of the manager.

(6) References in this section to the management functions of a local housing authority in relation to houses or land include—

(a) functions conferred by any statutory provision, and

(b) the powers and duties of the authority as holder of an estate or interest in the houses or land in question.

Consultation required before management agreement can be approved

27A.—(1) A local housing authority who propose to enter into a management agreement shall serve notice in writing on the tenant of each house to which the proposal relates informing him of—

(a) such details of their proposal as the authority consider appropriate, but including the identity of the person who is to be the manager under the agreement,

(b) the likely consequences of the agreement for the tenant, and

(c) the effect of the provisions of this section,

and informing him that he may, within such reasonable period as may be specified in the notice, make representations to the authority.

(2) The authority shall consider any representations made to them within that period and shall serve a further written notice on the tenant informing him—

(*a*) of any significant changes in their proposal, and

(*b*) that he may within such period as is specified (which must be at least 28 days after the service of the notice) communicate to the Secretary of State his objection to the proposal,

and informing him of the effect of subsection (5) (approval to be withheld if majority of tenants are opposed).

(3) The Secretary of State shall not entertain an application for approval of a management agreement unless the local housing authority certify that the requirements of subsections (1) and (2) as to consultation have been complied with; and the certificate shall be accompanied by a copy of the notices given by the authority in accordance with those subsections.

(4) The Secretary of State may require the authority to carry out such further consultation with their tenants, and to give him such information as to the results of that consultation as he may direct.

(5) The Secretary of State shall not give his approval if it appears to him that a majority of the tenants of the houses to which the agreement relates do not wish the proposal to proceed; but this does not affect his general discretion to withhold his approval on grounds relating to whether the proposal has the support of the tenants or on any other ground.

(6) In making his decision the Secretary of State may have regard to any information available to him; and the local housing authority shall give him such information as to the representations made to them by tenants and others, and other relevant matters, as he may require.

(7) A management agreement made with the approval of the Secretary of State is not invalidated by a failure on his part or that of the local housing authority to comply with the requirements of this section.

(8) In the case of secure tenants the provisions of this section apply in place of the provisions of section 105 (consultation on matters of housing management) in relation to the making of a management agreement.

Agreements with housing co-operatives under superseded provisions

27B.—(1) In this section "housing co-operative" means a society, company or body of trustees with which a housing co-operative agreement was made, that is to say—

(*a*) an agreement to which paragraph 9 of Schedule 1 to the Housing Rents and Subsidies Act 1975 or Schedule 20 to the Housing Act 1980 applied or,

(*b*) an agreement made under section 27 above before the commencement of section 10 of the Housing and Planning Act 1986 (which substituted the present section 27).

(2) A housing co-operative agreement made with a local housing authority which is in force immediately before the commencement of section 10 of the Housing and Planning Act 1986 has effect as if made under the present section 27, so that, in particular, any terms of the agreement providing for the letting of land to the housing co-operative no longer have effect except in relation to lettings made before commencement.

(3) A housing co-operative agreement made with a new town corporation of the Development Board for Rural Wales which is in force immediately before the commencement of section 10 of the

Housing and Planning Act 1986 remains in force notwithstanding that the present section 27 does not apply to such authorities.

(4) In this Act (except in section 27) the expressions "management agreement" and "manager" in relation to such an agreement, include a housing co-operative agreement to which subsection (2) or (3) applies and the housing co-operative with whom the agreement is made.".

DEFINITIONS
"local housing authority": 1985 Act, ss.1, 2.

GENERAL NOTE
The "general management, regulation and control of a local housing authority's houses is vested in and shall be exercised by the authority": 1985 Act, s.21. However, under the former 1985 Act, s.27, management responsibilities could be transferred to housing co-operatives. The new s.27, substituted by this section, permits a wider delegation of powers to an unlimited range of persons, bodies or associations, subject only to approval from the Secretary of State and a new consultation requirement.

New s.27
An authority's management functions may be exercised by an agent: subs. (1). The identity of the agent and the terms of the agency are not statutorily controlled, save that the Secretary of State's approval must be obtained as to both: subs. (5).

New s.27A
Before a management agreement can be approved by the Secretary of State, the local housing authority must consult with those tenants who will be affected: subs. (3).
The consultation is a three-stage process:
(1) informing the tenants of the proposals and their effect: subs. (1);
(2) considering any representations made by the tenants: subs. (2);
(3) informing the tenants of any significant changes in the proposal and of the right to communicate any objections to the Secretary of State: subs. (2).

Subss. (5), (6) The Secretary of State's discretion is not wholly unfettered. He *must* refuse approval if it appears to him that a majority of the tenants of the properties affected do not wish the proposals to proceed. However, as the obligation is only to refuse "if it appears to" him that a majority oppose the proposals, it will be very important indeed for tenants opposing proposed agreements to make their objections known, since the Secretary of State will be making the decision on the basis of the information before him.

Subs. (7) A failure by either the Secretary of State or the local housing authority to comply with the requirements of this section does not invalidate an agreement. This would appear to prevent any challenge to a decision once the agreement has been entered into, on the grounds of no or inadequate consultation. However, it does not prevent the decision being challenged on other grounds, *e.g.* the decision has not been arrived at in good faith or is unreasonable: see generally *Associated Provincial Picture Houses* v. *Wednesbury Corporation* [1948] 1 K.B. 223, C.A., *Meade* v. *London Borough of Haringey* [1979] 1 W.L.R. 637, C.A. and *R.* v. *Secretary of State for the Environment, ex p. Nottinghamshire County Council* [1986] A.C. 240, H.L.

New s.27B
This section deals with those management co-operatives set up under the old s.27 of the 1985 Act or its predecessor legislation. All such agreements are now governed by the new s.27. Under the old s.27, a management agreement could extend to an actual letting of land, and it follows that no new land can be added to an existing management agreement (*i.e.* under the old legislation) after the commencement of this section: subs. (2). Any new arrangement, or new land, will have to fall within this new version of management agreement.

Subs. (3) By s.30(2) of the 1985 Act, the powers of the local housing authority under s.27 are extended to new town corporations and the Development Board for Rural Wales. The new s.27 does not apply to these other bodies, although their existing agreements are unaffected: see Sched. 12, below.

Proposals for co-operative management or ownership

11. In Part II of the Housing Act 1985, after the provisions inserted by section 10 above insert—

"Proposals for co-operative management or ownership

Proposals for co-operative management or ownership

27C.—(1) If a qualifying tenants' association serves written notice on the local housing authority—

(a) proposing that the authority should enter into a management agreement with the association with respect to houses and other land specified in the notice, or

(b) proposing that the association should acquire from the authority houses and other land specified in the notice at a specified price,

the authority shall take the proposal into consideration.

(2) If the authority have not, by the end of the period of six months after service of the notice, accepted the proposal in principle, they shall give the association a written statement of the reasons why they have not done so.

(3) A tenants' association is a qualifying association for the purposes of this section if—

(a) it is a housing association of which at least half the members are tenants of houses specified in the notice,

(b) it has at least 50 such members or is registered under the Industrial and Provident Societies Act 1965, and

(c) at least half the tenants of the specified houses are members of the association.".

DEFINITIONS
"local housing authority": 1985 Act, ss.1, 2.
"housing association": 1985 Act, s.5.

GENERAL NOTE
This new section gives a tenants' association which fulfils the conditions of subs. (3) the right to put up proposals to enter into a management agreement, or to acquire the properties in the area it covers, and to have such proposals considered by the local housing authority: subs. (1). If the authority do not wish to accept the proposal, they must serve a notice of their reasons for rejection within six months: subs. (2).

Assured tenancies

Extension of assured tenancies scheme to cases where works have been carried out

12.—(1) In section 56(1) of the Housing Act 1980 (tenancies which are assured tenancies), for paragraphs (a) and (b) substitute—

"(a) the conditions described in section 56A or 56B are satisfied,

(b) the interest of the landlord has, since the creation of the tenancy, belonged to an approved body, and

(c) the tenancy would, when created, have been a protected tenancy or, as the case may be, a housing association tenancy but for this section.".

(2) After that section insert—

"Conditions for assured tenancy: newly erected buildings

56A. The first set of conditions referred to in section 56(1)(a) above is that—

(*a*) the dwelling-house is, or forms part of, a building which was erected (and on which construction work first began) on or after 8th August 1980, and

(*b*) before the tenant first occupied the dwelling-house under the tenancy, no part of it had been occupied by any person as his residence except under an assured tenancy.

Conditions for assured tenancy: buildings to which works have been carried out

56B.—(1) The second set of conditions referred to in section 56(1)(*a*) above is that—

(*a*) qualifying works have been carried out (whether before or after the commencement of this section),

(*b*) the dwelling-house is (or was) fit for human habitation at the relevant date, and

(*c*) since the qualifying works were carried out no part of the dwelling-house has been occupied by any person as his residence except under an assured tenancy,

and, in the case of the first relevant tenancy, that the person (or persons) to whom the tenancy is granted is not (or do not include) a person who was a secure occupier of the dwelling-house before the works were carried out.

(2) Qualifying works means works involving expenditure attributable to the dwelling-house of not less than the prescribed amount which are carried out within the period of two years preceding the relevant date at a time when the premises constituting the dwelling-house at the relevant date either were not a dwelling-house or no part of them was occupied by a person as his residence.

(3) Expenditure is attributable to a dwelling-house if it is incurred on works carried out to the premises constituting the dwelling-house at the relevant date or to other land or buildings let with the dwelling-house under the first relevant tenancy.

(4) Where the dwelling-house is a flat, there is also attributable to the dwelling-house a proportion of any expenditure incurred on works carried out to the structure, exterior or common parts of, or to common facilities in, the building of which the dwelling-house forms part.

(5) The proportion so attributable shall be taken to be the amount produced by dividing the total amount of such expenditure by the number of units of occupation in the building at the relevant date.

(6) In this section—

'flat' means a separate set of premises, whether or not on the same floor, which—

(*a*) forms part of a building, and

(*b*) is divided horizontally from some other part of the building;

'the first relevant tenancy' means the first tenancy after the carrying out of the qualifying works under which a person is entitled to occupy the dwelling-house as his residence;

'the prescribed amount' means the amount which at the relevant date is prescribed for the purposes of this section by order of the Secretary of State;

'the relevant date' means the date of grant of the first relevant tenancy;

'secure occupier' means a person who, whether alone or jointly with others, occupied or was entitled to occupy the dwelling-house as—

(a) a protected or statutory tenant within the meaning of the Rent Act 1977,

(b) a secure tenant within the meaning of Part IV of the Housing Act 1985, or

(c) a protected occupier or statutory tenant within the meaning of the Rent (Agriculture) Act 1976.

Certification of fitness for purposes of s.56B

56C.—(1) An approved body having an interest in a dwelling-house which it proposes to let on an assured tenancy may—

(a) apply in writing to the local housing authority for a certificate that the dwelling-house is fit for human habitation, or

(b) submit to the local housing authority a list of works which it proposes to carry out to the dwelling-house with a request in writing for the authority's opinion whether the dwelling-house would, after the execution of the works, be fit for human habitation;

and the authority shall as soon as may be after receiving the application or request, and upon payment of such reasonable fee as they may determine, take the matter into consideration.

(2) If the authority are of opinion that the dwelling-house is fit for human habitation, they shall give the approved body a certificate to that effect.

(3) If the authority are of opinion that the dwelling-house will be fit for human habitation after the execution of the proposed works, they shall inform the approved body that they are of that opinion.

(4) In any other case, the authority shall give the approved body a list of the works which in their opinion are required to make the dwelling-house fit for human habitation.

(5) Where the authority have responded in accordance with subsection (3) or (4) and the works in question have been executed to their satisfaction, they shall, if the approved body applies in writing, and upon payment of such reasonable fee as the authority may determine, give the body a certificate that the dwelling-house is fit for human habitation.

(6) For the purpose of determining whether the condition in section 56B(1)(b) was satisfied in any case (fitness of dwelling-house on relevant date), but not for any other purpose, a certificate given under this section is conclusive evidence that the dwelling-house was fit for human habitation on the date on which the certificate was given.

(7) In this section 'the local housing authority' has the same meaning as in the Housing Act 1985.

Fitness for human habitation

56D. In determining for any of the purposes of section 56B or 56C whether a dwelling-house is, or would be, fit for human habitation, regard shall be had to its condition in respect of the following matters—

    repair,
    stability,
    freedom from damp,
    internal arrangement,
    natural lighting,
    ventilation,
    water supply,
    drainage and sanitary conveniences,
    facilities for the preparation and cooking of food and the disposal of waste water;

and the dwelling-house shall be deemed to be unfit only if it is, or would be, so far defective in one or more of those matters as to be not reasonably suitable for occupation in that condition.".

(3) In section 57 of the Housing Act 1980 (effect of interest of landlord ceasing to belong to approved body), in subsections (1) and (2) for "section 56(3)(*a*)" substitute "section 56(1)(*b*)".

DEFINITIONS
"local housing authority": 1985 Act, s.1.

GENERAL NOTE
The assured tenancy scheme was an experiment introduced in 1980 to try and revive building for rent, under which approved bodies can let newly-built homes subject to Part II of the Landlord and Tenant Act 1954 (as modified for the purpose), rather than under the Rent Act 1977. The essence of the distinction is that rents are open-market rather than registered by the Rent Officer. The scheme is now to be extended to properties which have been improved, repaired or converted. This is achieved by extending the conditions on which an assured tenancy may arise, through four new sections.

New s.56A
This repeats the conditions for newly-built dwellings previously found in the Housing Act 1980, s.56(3)(*b*) and (*c*).

New s.56B
This section extends the scheme to dwelling-houses fulfilling four conditions. First, qualifying works must have been carried out. These are defined in subss. (2), (3) and (4) by reference to the amount spent on the works. Secondly, the works have to achieve fitness for human habitation (as defined in s.56D) when the first assured tenancy is granted. Thirdly, since carrying out the works the dwelling-house must not have been occupied other than on assured tenancies. Fourthly, the grant of the first post-works assured tenancy must not be to a person who was a secure occupier of the dwelling-house (*i.e.* protected by the Rent Act 1977, Housing Act 1985 or Rent (Agriculture) Act 1976).

New s.56C
In order to establish fitness for human habitation for the purposes to s.56B, an approved body may obtain a certificate from the local housing authority that the dwelling-house is fit for human habitation as defined in s.56D. This certificate is conclusive evidence of compliance with that part of s.56B (subs. (6)).

New s.56D
The test for determining fitness for ss.56B and 56C is the same as that to be found in s.604 of the 1985 Act. In applying this test, the question asked is whether the property suffers from any one or more of the specified defects, and then whether or not the totality of the defects, taken in the round, means that the property is not reasonably suitable for occupation: *E.A. Wyse* v. *Secretary of State for the Environment* [1984] J.P.L. 256, Q.B.D.

Other amendments relating to assured tenancies

13.—(1) In section 19(5) of the Rent Act 1977 (contracts which are not restricted contracts), after paragraph (*e*) insert—
    ", or
    (*f*) it creates an assured tenancy within the meaning of section 56 of the Housing Act 1980;".

(2) In Schedule 15 to the Rent Act 1977 (grounds for possession), in Part IV (definition of suitable alternative accommodation), renumber paragraph 4 as sub-paragraph (1) of that paragraph and after it insert—
    "(2) For the purposes of sub-paragraph (1)(*b*) the terms of a tenancy shall not be treated as affording the required security by reason only of the fact that the tenancy is an assured tenancy within the meaning of section 56 of the Housing Act 1980.".

(3) In Schedule 4 to the Rent (Agriculture) Act 1976 (grounds for possession), in Case I (alternative accommodation not provided or

arranged by housing authority), renumber paragraph 2 as sub-paragraph (1) of that paragraph and after it insert—

"(2) For the purposes of sub-paragraph (1)(*b*) the terms of a tenancy shall not be treated as affording the required security by reason only of the fact that the tenancy is an assured tenancy within the meaning of section 56 of the Housing Act 1980.".

(4) In section 37 of the Landlord and Tenant Act 1954 (compensation where an order for new tenancy precluded on certain grounds), in subsection (2) (computation of compensation) as set out in paragraph 7 of Schedule 5 to the Housing Act 1980 (application of 1954 Act to assured tenancies), after "be" insert "the product of the appropriate multiplier and".

The above amendment applies notwithstanding that the application to the court under section 24 of the Landlord and Tenant Act 1954 was made before the commencement of this section, unless the application has been finally disposed of within the meaning of section 64(2) of that Act before commencement.

(5) In section 58 of the Housing Act 1980 (application of Landlord and Tenant Act 1954 to assured tenancies), at the end add—

"(3) In sections 56 to 58 of this Act 'tenancy' has the same meaning as in the Landlord and Tenant Act 1954 and references to the granting of a tenancy shall be construed accordingly.".

(7) In Schedule 5 to the Housing Act 1980 (application of Landlord and Tenant Act 1954 to assured tenancies), for paragraph 8 (modification of provisions relating to contracting out) substitute—

"8. Section 38 applies as if the following provisions were omitted—
   (*a*) in subsection (1), the words "(except as provided by subsection (4) of this section)";
   (*b*) in subsection (2), the words from the beginning to the end of paragraph (*b*);
   (*c*) subsections (3) and (4)."

The above amendment, so far as it relates to section 38(4) of the Landlord and Tenant Act 1954, does not apply to an agreement both approved by the court under that provision and entered into before the commencement of this section.

GENERAL NOTE
This contains a number of miscellaneous amendments relating to assured tenancies.

Subs. (1)
While s.56 of the Housing Act 1980, specifically amended the Rent Act 1977 to exclude assured tenancies from its ambit, there was no analogous exclusion relating to restricted contract tenancies, *e.g.* if furniture or services were provided by the landlord. This created an overlap between the Rent Tribunal's rent-fixing jurisdiction 1977 Act, s.77, and the market rent provisions in s.58 of the 1980 Act. This amendment now rectifies that oversight.

Subss. (2), (3)
Where a landlord seeks to obtain possession under the Rent Act 1977 or Rent (Agriculture) Act 1976 on the ground that suitable alternative accommodation will be available, the alternative accommodation has to be on a protected tenancy or otherwise provide equivalent security. The amendments in these two paragraphs assert that an assured tenancy will *not* provide equivalent security.

Miscellaneous

Housing the homeless

14.—(1) The Housing Act 1985 shall be amended in accordance with the following provisions.

(2) In section 58 (definition of homelessness) after subsection (2) there shall be inserted the following subsections—

"(2A) A person shall not be treated as having accommodation unless it is accommodation which it would be reasonable for him to continue to occupy.

(2B) Regard may be had, in determining whether it would be reasonable for a person to continue to occupy accommodation, to the general circumstances prevailing in relation to housing in the district of the local housing authority to whom he has applied for accommodation or for assistance in obtaining accommodation.".

(3) For section 69(1) (provisions supplementary to ss.63, 65 and 68) there shall be substituted the following subsection—

"(1) A local housing authority may perform any duty under section 65 or 68 (duties to persons found to be homeless) to secure that accommodation becomes available for the occupation of a person—

　(*a*) by making available suitable accommodation held by them under Part II (provision of housing) or any enactment, or

　(*b*) by securing that he obtains suitable accommodation from some other person, or

　(*c*) by giving him such advice and assistance as will secure that he obtains suitable accommodation from some other person,

and in determining whether accommodation is suitable they shall have regard to Part IX (slum clearance), X (overcrowding) and XI (houses in multiple occupation) of this Act.".

GENERAL NOTE

In *R.* v. *Hillingdon London Borough Council, ex p. Puhlhofer* [1986] A.C. 484, 18 H.L.R. 158, the House of Lords held that the adjectives "appropriate" or "reasonable" could not be imported into ss.58 and 65 of the 1985 Act, to qualify the word accommodation. The word appears in s.58 when defining whether or not a person is homeless. It appears in s.65, when defining the duties of an authority towards a person who is homeless (and in priority need of accommodation). This section is intended to "restore homeless people's rights to the situation existing before the *Puhlhofer* judgment," Baroness David, *Hansard*, October 28, 1986, Vol. 481, col. 648, Third Reading, by amendment to the 1985 Act.

Subs. (2)

Section 58 of the 1985 Act defines when a person is homeless for the purposes of Part II of the 1985 Act. A person is homeless "if he has no accommodation in England, Wales or Scotland", (s.58(1)). The current test of whether a person has accommodation is concerned to look at whether the applicant has legal rights of occupation, see s.58(2). The new subsections to be inserted into s.58 import concern with the quality of the accommodation occupied. The test is the same as that to be found when a local authority are considering whether an applicant is intentionally homeless under s.60, 1985 Act, *viz.* whether it is reasonable for the applicant to continue to occupy the accommodation.

This approach to the question of homelessness was adopted (in the minority) by Ackner L.J. in *Puhlhofer* (1985) 17 H.L.R. 588, in the Court of Appeal, following the decision of Woolf J. in *R.* v. *South Herefordshire District Council, ex p. Miles* (1983) 17 H.L.R. 82. At p. 92, Woolf J. said: "If the standard was lower than that required by section [60], an applicant would be entitled to leave accommodation, thus placing an obligation on the housing authority, without being regarded as intentionally homeless, when there would not be the same obligation to provide accommodation if the applicant did not move."

In determining whether it is reasonable for an applicant to continue to occupy accommodation, a local authority may have regard "to the general circumstances prevailing in relation to housing in the district of the local housing authority to whom he applied" (subs. 2B). Thus comparison may be made between the accommodation occupied and the conditions in the area of the authority to which the application is made. This element of the "reasonable to continue to occupy" test is also now to be imported in s.58.

For illustrations of when the courts have indicated that it was not reasonable for an applicant to continue to occupy property see: *Miles* (rat infested hut, 10 ft. by 20 ft., with no mains services, occupied by a couple and their three children, one of them newly born, but not *un*reasonable shortly before the birth of the third child); *R.* v. *Westminister City*

Council, ex p. Ali (1983) 11 H.L.R. 83, Q.B.D. (husband, wife and five children in 10ft. by 12 ft. room); and, *R.* v. *Preseli District Council, ex p. Fisher* (1984) 17 H.L.R. 147, Q.B.D. (one room boat, with no bath, shower, w.c., electricity, hot water or kitchen sink, occupied by the applicant, her children and two friends).

These cases clearly show that the conditions have to be extreme before there is a prospect of overturning a finding by an authority that it is reasonable for the applicant to continue to occupy accommodation. In *Puhlhofer*, the applicant his wife and two children occupied one room in a guest house with no cooking or laundry facilities. Applying the "reasonable to continue to occupy" test Ackner L.J. held that the applicant was not homeless, in the light of the authority's evidence that there were no fewer than 44 families on the council's waiting list for two-bedroomed accommodation considered to be of higher priority under their points system.

Grants for improvement or repair of common parts

15. Part XV of the Housing Act 1985 (grants for works of improvement, repair and conversion) is amended in accordance with Schedule 3 so as to provide for a new form of grant towards the costs of works required for the improvement or repair of the common parts of a building containing one or more flats.

GENERAL NOTE

D.O.E Circular 26/85 drew the attention of local authorities to the difficulties of making discretionary grants in relation to flats and common parts. Two particular problems arose. The first problem concerned the need on the part of an applicant to show that he has a freehold or leasehold interest of not less than five years in all parts of the building on which works are to be carried out, see s.463 of the 1985 Act. In many cases, long leaseholders in flats do not have the required proprietary interest in the common parts even although they may well be obliged under the terms of their leases to contribute towards their upkeep. Secondly, the certificate of future occupation required by s.464 of the 1985 Act, also had to extend to the common parts, and there would seem to be no qualifying occupation of those common parts by a grant-applicant leaseholder.

To overcome these problems a new common parts grant is provided for in Schedule 3. This introduces a new proprietary interest test and dispenses with the certificate of future occupation, subject however to occupation of a required proportion of flats in a building being in the occupation of tenants. In effect, the grant will not be available to a substantially void block. See further, notes to Schedule 3.

Housing management: financial assistance etc.

16. In Part XIII of the Housing Act 1985 (general financial provisions), after section 429 insert—

"**Housing management: financial assistance etc.**

429A.—(1) The Secretary of State may, with the consent of the Treasury, give financial assistance—

    (*a*) to persons managing public sector or former public sector housing, and

    (*b*) to persons seeking to facilitate or encourage improvements in, or providing services in connection with, the management of such housing;

and may, with the like consent, make payments otherwise than by way of financial assistance in pursuance of arrangements made with any such person.

(2) For this purpose—

    (*a*) "public sector housing" means housing accommodation in which an authority or body within section 80 (the landlord condition for secure tenancies) has an interest by virtue of which it receives a rack-rent, or would do so if the premises were let at a rack-rent; and

    (*b*) "former public sector housing" means housing accommodation in which such an authority, or a predecessor of

63–37

such an authority or an authority abolished by the Local Government Act 1985 formerly had such an interest.

(3) The Secretary of State may, with the consent of the Treasury, give financial assistance—

(*a*) to persons providing educational or training courses in housing management,

(*b*) to persons providing services for those providing such courses, and

(*c*) to persons providing financial or other assistance for those attending such courses;

and may, with the like consent, make payments otherwise than by way of financial assistance in pursuance of arrangements made with any such person.

(4) Financial assistance given by the Secretary of State under subsection (1) or (3) may be given in any form, and may in particular be given by way of grants, loans or guarantees or by incurring expenditure for the benefit of the person assisted; but the Secretary of State shall not in giving such assistance purchase loan or share capital in a company.

(5) Financial assistance may be given and other payments made on such terms as the Secretary of State, with the consent of the Treasury, considers appropriate; and the terms may, in particular, include provision as to the circumstances in which the assistance or other payment must be repaid or otherwise made good to the Secretary of State and the manner in which that is to be done.

(6) A person receiving financial assistance under this section shall comply with the terms on which it is given and compliance may be enforced by the Secretary of State.".

GENERAL NOTE

This section introduces a new housing subsidy, designed to encourage the involvement of the private sector in the ownership and management of public sector housing.

New s.429A

Subs. (1)

Financial assistance is available to "persons" managing public sector or former public sector housing or to those promoting such management. This will include housing associations, who will not be entitled to receive subsidy in the usual way under the Housing Associations Act 1985 on properties they manage under the new s.27 (see s.10, above) see Sched. 5, para. 42.

Subs. (2)

"*rack-rent,*" *i.e.* a rent which is not less than two-thirds of the full net annual value of the premises. The definition of the interest of the public sector landlord, *i.e.* that it receives the rack-rent or would do so if the premises were let at a rack-rent, is also to be found in s.207 of the 1985 Act. The second limb of the definition has recently been considered by the House of Lords in *Pollway Nominees Ltd* v. *London Borough of Croydon* (1986) 18 H.L.R. 443. It was held that where flats in a block were let on long leases the freeholder was not the person who would receive the rack-rent if the block were let at a rack-rent. Accordingly, assistance will not be available to those managing properties which are let on long-leases from public sector landlords.

Subs. (3)

Assistance is also available to those providing or promoting housing management education or training.

Matters to be taken into account in determining fair rent

17.—(1) Section 70 of the Rent Act 1977 (determination of fair rent) is amended as follows.

(2) In subsection (1) (matters to be taken into account), omit the word "and" before paragraph (*b*) and after that paragraph insert—
", and
   (c) any premium, or sum in the nature of a premium, which has been or may be lawfully required or received on the grant, renewal, continuance or assignment of the tenancy.".
(3) After subsection (4) insert—
   "(4A) In this section "premium" has the same meaning as in Part IX of this Act, and "sum in the nature of a premium" means—
      (*a*) any such loan as is mentioned in section 119 or 120 of this Act,
      (*b*) any such excess over the reasonable price of furniture as is mentioned in section 123 of this Act, and
      (*c*) any such advance payment of rent as is mentioned in section 126 of this Act.".
(4) The above amendments apply to every decision made by a rent officer or rent assessment committee after the commencement of this section, notwithstanding that the application was made before commencement or, in the case of a decision of a rent assessment committee, that the rent officer's decision was made before commencement.

GENERAL NOTE
In general it is unlawful to require the payment of a premium as a condition of the grant, renewal or continuance of a protected tenancy, see Part IX of the Rent Act 1977. However, for the grant, renewal or continuance of some tenancies a premium may lawfully be demanded, *e.g.* shared ownership leases granted by a housing association, certain long tenancies (see 1977 Act, s.127,) and certain tenancies granted by the Crown (see Housing Act 1980, s.73 and Sched. 8).
Until recently there had been some considerable doubt as to the effect on the rent which should be registered under Rent Act 1977, s.70, of either payment of a (lawful) premium, or the tenant's continuing right to receive a (lawful) premium on his departure. In *Crown Estates Commissioners* v. *Connor* (1986) 19 H.L.R. 35, Q.B.D., Mr Justice McCowan held that the right of a tenant of the Crown to charge a premium on assignment of a leasehold interest was a circumstance which could properly be taken into account when determining a fair rent. This amendment confirms that decision, and indeed *requires* such premiums to be taken into account.

Further provisions with respect to shared ownership leases

18. The provisions of Schedule 4 have effect to exclude certain shared ownership leases from the operation of the provisions of—
   (*a*) the Rent Act 1977 and the Rent (Agriculture) Act 1976, and
   (*b*) Part I of the Leasehold Reform Act 1967 (right of long leaseholder to enfranchisement or extension of lease).

GENERAL NOTE
Under Part V of the 1985 Act, a tenant exercising the right to buy has the right to a shared ownership lease where his mortgage entitlement is not sufficient to purchase the property outright (1985 Act, s.143). A shared-ownership lease is one under which the tenant purchases a "tranche" or "slice" of the equity in a long lease, with the right to purchase successive tranches until the whole has been acquired. Pending acquisition of the whole, the tenant will pay a rent reduced according to the slice of the equity he has already acquired.
This section, and Schedule 4, disapply specified provisions of the Leasehold Reform Act 1967, the Rent (Agriculture) Act 1976, and the Rent Act 1977, where shared ownership leases are involved, to ensure that reliance cannot be placed upon those provisions by a leaseholder in place of the terms of the lease, *e.g.* on default. See further notes to Sched. 4, below.

Extension of permitted objects of registered housing associations

19. In section 4 of the Housing Associations Act 1985 (eligibility for registration), in subsection (3) (permissible additional purposes or objects of association), after paragraph (*d*) insert—

"(*dd*) providing services of any description for owners or occupiers of houses in arranging or carrying out works of maintenance, repair or improvement, or encouraging or facilitating the carrying out of such works;".

GENERAL NOTE

To qualify for registration under the Housing Associations Act 1985, the objects or purposes of an association must be in accordance with those set out in s.4(2) of that Act. Any additional purposes or objects are limited to those set out in *ibid.*, s.4(3). This section adds a purpose to the s.4(3) schedule of "additional purposes." The amendment is designed to encourage housing associations to set up agency services to assist owner-occupiers with home improvements and repairs.

While several housing associations have already set up such agencies, primarily aimed at helping elderly owner-occupiers, it has been necessary for them to operate through separately constituted bodies. Such work will now be able to be undertaken under the direct auspices of the housing associations.

Disposal of dwellings in new towns

20.—(1) Part III of the New Towns Act 1981 (transfer of new town housing to district councils), is amended as follows.

(2) After section 57 insert—

"Savings for other powers of disposal

57A. The provisions of this Part as to the transfer of dwellings in a new town to a district council shall not be construed as restricting—

(*a*) the power of the Commission under section 36 above,

(*b*) the power of a development corporation under section 64 below, or

(*c*) the power of the Development Board for Rural Wales under section 4 of the Development of Rural Wales Act 1976,

to dispose of such dwellings to any person.".

(3) The following provisions (which relate to the initiation of consultations with a view to the transfer of new town housing to a district council) are repealed—

section 43(3) and (4),

section 49(*b*) and (*c*).

GENERAL NOTE

Part III of the New Towns Act 1981 is designed to encourage and facilitate the transfer of housing accommodation held by new town development corporations to their local district councils. By s.42 of that Act, the Secretary of State may direct that a transfer scheme is drawn up between the development corporation and the district council. This amendment to that Act is intended to "ensure that the choice between a local authority and a non-local authority option for the remaining new town housing is not restricted by any provisions in the legislation concerning statutory transfer to the local authority," Lord Skelmersdale, *Hansard*, H.L. Vol. 480, col. 430, October 10, 1986. In other words, the intention is that development corporations also consider disposal to private landlords and housing associations.

Effect of resolutions relating to housing action area or general improvement area

21.—(1) In Part VIII of the Housing Act 1985 (area improvement) before section 260, under the heading *"Supplementary provisions"* insert—

"Effect of resolutions relating to housing action area or general improvement area

259A.—(1) A resolution of a local housing authority passed after the commencement of this section—

(*a*) declaring an area to be a housing action area, excluding land from a housing action area or declaring that an area shall cease to be a housing action area, or

(*b*) declaring an area to be a general improvement area, excluding land from a general improvement area or declaring that an area shall cease to be a general improvement area,

has effect, subject to subsection (2), from the day on which the resolution is passed.

(2) A resolution declaring an area to be a general improvement area may be expressed to have effect from a future date, not later than four weeks after the passing of the resolution, on which the whole or part of that area will cease to be, or be included in, a housing action area.

Effect of certain resolutions passed before commencement of s.259A

259B.—(1) Where before the commencement of section 259A a local housing authority passed a resolution of any of the descriptions mentioned in the section expressed to have effect from a date after that on which it was passed—

(*a*) anything done before the commencement of this section in reliance on the view that the resolution was invalid shall have effect as if the resolution had not been passed, but

(*b*) otherwise, the resolution shall be taken for all purposes, both before and after the commencement of this section, to have been validly passed and to have had effect from the date on which it was expressed to have had effect;

subject to the following provisions

(2) A person shall not be proceeded against in respect of anything done or omitted before the commencement of this section which would not have been an offence if the resolution had not been passed.

(3) Where the resolution declared a housing action area or general improvement area and, before the commencement of this section, the local housing authority passed a further resolution making the like declaration in relation to the whole or part of the area to which the first resolution then related—

(*a*) both resolutions are effective, notwithstanding that they relate in whole or in part to the same area;

(*b*) the area covered by both resolutions is a housing action area or general improvement area by virtue of the joint effect of the two resolutions, and in the case of a housing action area shall continue to be such an area (subject to the provisions of this Part) until the end of the period of five years beginning with the date on which the second resolution was passed;

(*c*) it is immaterial whether steps taken before the commencement of this section were taken in reliance on the first resolution or the second, but steps taken in reliance on the first shall not be proceeded with to the extent that they have been superseded by, or are inconsistent with, steps taken in reliance on the second; and

(*d*) the areas declared by the two resolutions may be treated as one for the purposes of section 245(3) or 259(3) (limit on aggregate expenditure qualifying for contributions by Secretary of State).

(4) The provisions of subsection (3) do not affect the powers of the Secretary of State under section 241(2) (*a*) and (*b*) (power to overrule declaration of housing action area or exclude land from area) and, so far as they relate to the duration of a housing action

area, have effect subject to section 241(4) (effect of Secretary of State's decision in such a case).".

(2) In consequence of the above amendment, Part VIII of the Housing Act 1985 is further amended as follows—

(a) in section 239(4) (duration of housing action area), omit "beginning with the date on which the resolution is passed";

(b) in section 240(1) (steps to be taken after declaration of housing action area) omit "passing a resolution";

(c) in section 242(2) (incorporation into housing action area of land comprised in general improvement area), for "the resolution is passed declaring such an area" substitute "the area is declared";

(d) in section 250(1) (exclusion of land from, or termination of, housing action area), omit "on the date on which the resolution is passed";

(e) in section 257 (duty to publish information) for "have declared" substitute "have passed a resolution declaring" and for "assistance available" substitute "assistance which is or will be available";

(f) in section 258(1)(b) (resolution terminating general improvement area), for "an area to be no longer" substitute "that an area shall cease to be";

(g) in section 258(2) (effect of resolution excluding land from or terminating general improvement area) for "the date on which the resolution takes effect" substitute "the date on which the exclusion or cessation takes effect" and for "the exclusion or cessation" substitute "the resolution".

DEFINITIONS
"commencement": s.57
"general improvement area": 1985 Act, s.253
"housing action area": 1985 Act, s.239
"local housing authority": 1985 Act, ss.1, 2(2)

GENERAL NOTE
The amendments contained in this section to Part VIII of the 1985 Act, are prompted by the view that some declarations of housing action areas and general improvement areas are invalid because they do not take immediate effect, but purport to make a "future declaration", *i.e.* they are intended to come into effect at some point in the future.

New s.259A
This first part of the amendment establishes that all resolutions declaring an area (1985 Act ss.239 and 253) or terminating or excluding land from an area (1985 Act ss.250 and 258) have effect from the day on which they are passed (subs. (1)). However, an exception is available where an authority declare a general improvement area at the expiry of a housing action area (subs. (2)).

New s.259B
This section deals with those invalid resolutions which have already been passed. Prima facie they are to be treated as valid from the date on which they were expressed to have come into effect (subs. (1)). However, if anything was done in reliance on the view that the resolution was invalid, then the resolution shall be treated as if it had not been passed for —but only for—such act (or omission) (subs. (1)(b)). Furthermore, no prosecutions may be brought for offences (see, *e.g.* 1985 Act s.249) based on the passage of an invalid resolution (subs. (2)). Subs. (3) deals with the situation where an authority have already sought to rectify the situation by passing a further resolution.

Agreements with certain housing bodies exempt from Consumer Credit Act 1974

22.—(1) Section 16 of the Consumer Credit Act 1974 (exempt agreements) is amended as follows.

(2) In subsection (1) (which enables orders to be made exempting agreements with certain descriptions of creditor), after paragraph (f) insert—

"(ff) a body corporate named or specifically referred to in an order made under—

section 156(4), 444(1) or 447(2)(a) of the Housing Act 1985,

section 2 of the Home Purchase Assistance and Housing Corporation Guarantee Act 1978 or section 31 of the Tenants' Rights, &c. (Scotland) Act 1980, or

Article 154(1)(a) or 156AA of the Housing (Northern Ireland) Order 1981 or Article 10(6A) of the Housing (Northern Ireland) Order 1983; or";

and in subsection (3) (requirements as to consultation), in paragraph (d) (consultation with responsible Minister), for "or (f)" substitute ", (f) or (ff)".

(3) After subsection (6) insert—

"(6A) This Act does not regulate a consumer credit agreement where the creditor is a housing authority and the agreement is secured by a land mortgage of a dwelling.

(6B) In subsection (6A) "housing authority" means—

(a) as regards England and Wales, an authority or body within section 80(1) of the Housing Act 1985 (the landlord condition for secure tenancies), other than a housing association or a housing trust which is a charity;

(b) as regards Scotland, a development corporation established under an order made, or having effect as if made under the New Towns (Scotland) Act 1968, the Scottish Special Housing Association or the Housing Corporation;

(c) as regards Northern Ireland, the Northern Ireland Housing Executive.".

(4) The above amendments apply to agreements made after the commencement of this section.

DEFINITIONS
"commencement": s.57

GENERAL NOTE
The Consumer Credit Act 1974 provides protection for people to enter into credit transactions. A credit transaction includes arranging a mortgage loan. The Act presently provides (s.16) for local authorities, building societies and other specified bodies to be exempt from its provisions. For local authorities and building societies the exemption is automatic; the exemption of other bodies rests on (a) qualification under the Act, and (b) specification in an order made by the Secretary of State. The other bodies are insurance companies, friendly societies, organisations of employers or workers, charities, land improvement companies or bodies corporate named or specifically referred to in any public general Act.

In February 1986, the Joint Committee on Statutory Instruments took the view that the basis on which one of the statutory instruments made under s.16 was erroneous. This opinion cast doubt on the validity of several earlier orders.

Subs. (2)
A new category of specified bodies is added to s.16, allowing exemption orders to be made for a further category of corporate bodies, this will cover all those bodies who have been named in the negative orders on the validity of which doubt has now been cast.

Subs. (3)
The automatic exemption is extended to all housing authorities and not just local authorities.

Determination of price for leasehold enfranchisement

23.—(1) In section 9(1A) of the Leasehold Reform Act 1967 (determination of price payable for enfranchisement of higher value houses), in paragraph (*a*) (assumption that vendor is selling subject to existing tenancy) after "no right to acquire the freehold" insert "or an extended lease and, where the tenancy has been extended under this Part of this Act, that the tenancy will terminate on the original term date.".

(2) In section 23(5) of the Leasehold Reform Act 1967 (provisions as to tenancy granted in satisfaction of tenant's rights under Part I), in paragraph (*b*) (provisions which apply as if the tenancy were granted by way of extension) at the beginning insert "section 9(1) and (1A) above,".

(3) The above amendments do not apply—

(*a*) where the price for enfranchisement has been determined, by agreement or otherwise, before the commencement of this section; or

(*b*) where the notice under section 8 of the Leasehold Reform Act 1967 (notice of desire to have the freehold) was given before the passing of this Act; or

(*c*) where notice under section 14 of that Act (notice of desire to have extended lease) was given before 5th March 1986.

GENERAL NOTE

This section overturns the decision of the Court of Appeal in *Mosley* v. *Hickman* (1986) 18 H.L.R. 292, relating to the purchase price payable on enfranchisement of houses of higher value under the Leasehold Reform Act 1967. One of the assumptions on which the price is arrived at is "that the vendor was selling for an estate in fee simple, subject to the tenancy, but on the assumptions that this Part of this Act conferred no right to acquire the freehold", Leasehold Reform Act 1967, s.9(1A). In *Mosley* v. *Hickman* it was held that "subject to the tenancy" was not limited to the original tenancy but included a tenancy extended for fifty years under ss. 14 and 15 of the 1967 Act. The amendments in this section overturn this decision.

Minor and consequential amendments; repeals

24.—(1) The enactments relating to housing are amended in accordance with Part I of Schedule 5 with respect to the following matters—

(*a*) the effect of a covenant for repayment of discount given on the disposal of a dwelling-house;

(*b*) the acquisition by an authority or body within section 80 of the Housing Act 1985 (the landlord condition for secure tenancies) of a dwelling-house subject to a statutory tenancy;

(*c*) the contents of a landlord's notice under section 125 of that Act (notice of terms of exercise of right to buy);

(*d*) the steps to be taken where there is a change of landlord in the course of exercise of the right to buy;

(*e*) the deferment of completion in pursuance of the right to buy;

(*f*) the maximum penalty for voting in contravention of section 618(3) of the Housing Act 1985 (member of Common Council or committee voting on matter in which he is interested);

(*g*) the withholding of consent to the assignment by way of exchange of a secure tenancy of a dwelling-house managed by a certain description of housing association;

(*h*) grants for affording tax relief to housing associations;

(*i*) the recovery of service charges in respect of the cost of grant-aided works;

(*j*) miscellaneous corrections.

(2) Part II of Schedule 5 contains amendments consequential on the provisions of this Part.

(3) The enactments specified in Part I of Schedule 12 are repealed to the extent specified.

GENERAL NOTE

A number of errors were found in the 1985 consolidation Act and the amendments in subs.(1) and Sched. 5 are intended to correct them and make further minor amendments.

PART II

SIMPLIFIED PLANNING ZONES

GENERAL NOTE

This Part of the Act introduces simplified planning zones (S.P.Z.s). Separate provision is made for England and Wales (s.25) and Scotland (s.26).

The S.P.Z. idea is part of the Government's deregulation policy. Its purpose is to allow a local planning authority to grant a general planning permission for some part of its area, in a similar way to a special or general development order made by the Secretary of State. Developers will then be able to undertake development as of right, up to the tolerances specified by the S.P.Z. scheme, and without requiring further planning permission.

Background to the proposals

Government proposals for S.P.Z.s were first announced in a consultation paper issued by the Secretary of State in May 1984, which argued that experience with enterprise zones had indicated that a simplified planning regime could have positive advantages for the development of an area. Enterprise zones schemes had not led to a worsening of design standards or deterioration in the local environment. The advantages that were thought might come from an S.P.Z. were summed up as follows:

"S.P.Z.s could relieve local authorities of the burden of dealing with a substantial number of planning applications and relieve prospective developers of the complexity and expense of making such applications. The principal benefit of S.P.Z.s is more than this, however: viewed as an extension of the Enterprise Zone concept, although without the fiscal advantages of E.Z.s, they could be a means for local authorities to make more positive use of the planning system to attract developers by offering the certainty of a permission and prior knowledge of its terms, as well as relief from application fees. One value of the S.P.Z. approach is that local authority ownership of the land in question is not a prerequisite; an authority could use it actively to stimulate or accelerate development without first having to devote time and resources to assembling the site themselves. It could also be associated with other incentives such as loans to industry, Derelict Land Grant and Urban Development Grant."

Although the enterprise zone experiment may have inspired S.P.Z.s, Ministers became increasingly concerned as the Bill proceeded through Parliament to deny any further links between the two concepts. Thus, Lord Skelmersdale in the Committee stage in the House of Lords (*Hansard* H.L. Vol. 480, cols. 533–534):

"Whatever else S.P.Z.s may be, I cannot agree with the noble Lord that they are anything to do with enterprise zones. I agree when he says that their initial conception is a result of enterprise zones, but they are significantly different. What exactly are they? I hope that it will help the Committee when I say that I have come to see them as local general development orders made by planning authorities, taking account of the particular circumstances of their areas or parts of their areas. The essential point is that S.P.Z.s give planning permission for specified types of development without the need for a planning application or, of course, the payment of a fee. S.P.Z. schemes can be tailor made to suit a wide range of circumstances. They can vary in size and content. They could be for small areas, specifying a broad range of uses, say, for a central area site; or they could be larger but covering a more limited range of uses, for example, chimneys in a countryside area or whatever the local authority decides would be appropriate."

Exclusion of special areas

The 1984 consultation paper argued that an S.P.Z. would not be appropriate in National Parks, areas of outstanding natural beauty, green belts or conservation areas, but no such limitation appeared in the original Bill (H.C. Bill 63) other than an ambiguous provision that the powers to declare an S.P.Z. were exercisable by district planning authorities "except in a National Park." The Government initially argued that a specific statutory exclusion was unnecessary because "the vast majority of local planning authorities would not take steps which put at risk these very sensitive areas, which they normally seek to conserve, enhance and protect" (Standing Committee H; col. 333; March 13, 1986). But the Secretary of State eventually bowed to the strength of the public and Parliamentary opinion on the point and agreed to introduce an amendment (now s.24E(1) for England and Wales; 21E for Scotland) giving statutory effect to the restrictions suggested in the Consultation Paper.

The Secretary of State also has power at any time (s.24E(3) and (4) for England and Wales; s.21E(3) and (4) for Scotland) to order that an S.P.Z. scheme shall not have effect to grant planning permission in relation to any specified site or development, and in the case of an existing S.P.Z. scheme this will revoke permission accordingly, except where development has already begun.

Making an S.P.Z. scheme: the initial duty

All local planning authorities (excluding the English counties) are required by the new s.24A (s.21A for Scotland) to consider, as soon as practicable after the section comes into effect, the question for which part or parts of their area an S.P.Z. scheme is desirable, and thereafter keep that question under review; and to prepare an S.P.Z. scheme where it is thought desirable. The Act gives a deliberately wide measure of discretion to local planning authorities. It will be open to any authority to decide that an S.P.Z. scheme would not be desirable for its area, whether because they believe that the stimulus to development by relaxation of control under an S.P.Z. is not appropriate to the needs of their area, or because such a relaxation might be better achieved through other methods.

Right to seek Secretary of State's intervention

The new provisions confer a right on any person to ask the local planning authority to make or alter an S.P.Z. scheme. If they refuse, or do not decide to do so within three months from the date of the request, he may require them to refer the matter to the Secretary of State, unless an S.P.Z. scheme for all or part of the land, or an alteration to such an S.P.Z. scheme, has been adopted in the past 12 months (Act of 1971, Sched. 8A, para. 3 (for Scotland, Act of 1972, Sched. 6A, para.3), inserted by Sched. 6 to this Act).

The Secretary of State, upon considering the application and consulting, may decide to direct the local planning authority to make an S.P.Z. scheme (or alteration to an existing S.P.Z. scheme) which he thinks appropriate. Whatever decision he comes to, he is required to give written reasons for it.

This is the only means through which the Secretary of State is able to impose an S.P.Z. scheme on an unwilling local planning authority (although he does have power under para. 9 in all cases to call-in an S.P.Z. scheme for approval). The mechanism for enforcement is provided by the default powers in para. 11 of the Schedule. Where an S.P.Z. scheme or proposals for alteration are required (*i.e.* by direction of the Secretary of State) to be prepared, and the Secretary of State is satisfied (but only after holding a public local inquiry or other hearing) that the local planning authority are not taking the steps necessary to enable them to prepare or adopt the scheme or proposals within a reasonable period, he may himself make the scheme or alterations.

The planning framework for an S.P.Z. scheme

It is a notable feature of the S.P.Z. provisions that although the purpose of an S.P.Z. scheme is to grant planning permission for the development specified in the scheme, the legislation fails to tie an S.P.Z. scheme into the development plan for the area, or, indeed to any planning framework at all. An S.P.Z. scheme does not constitute a grant of planning permission under s.29 of the Act of 1971 (s.26 of the Scotland Act of 1972) so the duty imposed by the section on the local planning authority to have regard to the development plan and any other material considerations does not apply; nor does the obligation (which does not apply to Scotland) under s.86(3) of the Local Government, Planning and Land Act 1980 to seek the achievement of the general objectives of the structure plan.

It will be possible, therefore, for a local planning authority to promote an S.P.Z. scheme which conflicts with the established planning framework for the area. It must be assumed from the design of the legislation that it is intended that this should be so. There may be thought to be little point in some areas in having an S.P.Z. when the local plan already makes realistic allowance for development of the type the authority wish to promote. There are, nonetheless, some safeguards against S.P.Z. schemes being used to ride roughshod over the forward planning process. First, the S.P.Z. authority will, in most cases, be also the authority responsible for local plan preparation, and it is to be assumed that they will wish to maintain some constancy in planning policy. Secondly, there is also a requirement in the non-metropolitan counties (not Scotland) that the S.P.Z. authority consult with the county planning authority. Although the provisions do not expressly require the S.P.Z. authority to take the county's representations into account, it is now clear following *R.* v. *Secretary of State for Social Services, ex p. Association of Metropolitan Authorities* [1986] 1 All E.R. 164, that such an obligation is inherent in the very duty to consult. Thirdly, there is power for the Secretary of State to call-in the S.P.Z. scheme prior to its adoption by the local planning authority; and, in deciding whether or not to exercise that power, a representation from the county planning authority that the S.P.Z. scheme threatened their strategic policy would undoubtedly be a relevant consideration. Fourthly, objectors have the right to have their objections heard at a public local inquiry. But although this can be seen as an essential procedural safeguard, its substantive role is ambiguous. The inquiry is designed to be more like a local plan inquiry than a planning appeal. It is to be an inquiry not into an appeal against the refusal of planning permission, but into objections to a S.P.Z. and that must raise not only planning issues such as would arise on a planning appeal or local plan inquiry, but also the question of the desirability of the S.P.Z. as an instrument in pursuing the authority's particular policy objectives. The inspector reports to the authority themselves; and they have the power, acting within the procedural constraints and subject to the Secretary of State's power of call-in, to decline to accept his recommendations.

In the event that an S.P.Z. scheme proposes development that is not in accordance with the development plan, and the proposals survive the public local inquiry process and are adopted, it is clear that the S.P.Z. scheme must prevail over the local plan; although the Act does not, unlike in the case of enterprise zones, require the structure plan and local plan to be reviewed "as soon as practicable" and to be modified to the extent necessary to take account of the scheme (Local Government, Planning and Land Act 1980, Sched. 32, para. 23).

Moreover, the absence of any formal tie-in with local plans raises the prospects that an S.P.Z. scheme which does contain proposals which are directly in accordance with a recently adopted local plan, may simply re-open the debate as to the merits of the local plan. Objections may lawfully be made to the S.P.Z. scheme which are in essence objections to the local plan, and if made in accordance with the regulations (yet to be made) and not withdrawn, must be heard at a public local inquiry. It is surprising that this possibility was not blocked by provisions like those to be found in the main Act, such as s.16 (s.14 of the 1972 Scotland Act) which allows a local planning authority and the Secretary of State to disregard representations or objections to a local plan or structure plan if they are in substance objections to decisions or proposals under the Highways Acts or the New Towns Act; s.132(1) (s.121(1) of the 1972 Scotland Act), which similarly allows in the case of compulsory purchase under the 1971 Act, the disregard of any objection to a draft order which "amounts in substance to an objection to the provisions of the development plan defining the proposed use of that land or any land."

Concurrent consideration with local plan proposals

It is technically possible, and in principle may be highly desirable, for proposals for an S.P.Z. scheme and for a local plan (or alteration) to be prepared and adopted concurrently. The procedures for the two run parallel, and are in parts identical. But, as the Minister argued in Standing Committee (March 18, 1986; cols. 371–374) an S.P.Z. scheme is a quite different instrument from a local plan. It has a fixed life of 10 years, whereas a local plan is for an unfixed and possibly shorter period. It is envisaged that an S.P.Z. scheme would cover a smaller area than a local plan, and would be more precise, though less detailed. Concurrent handling may well result in unnecessary delays occurring in S.P.Z. scheme approval, if problems were to arise with some unrelated element of the local plan.

At the same time, there would be obvious difficulties if an authority proposed both a local plan and an S.P.Z. for an area but did not process the two concurrently. The S.P.Z. scheme would, particularly if it were processed more rapidly, override the local plan proposals and pre-empt objections to them.

Relationship with development control powers

It was held by the High Court in *R.* v. *City of London Corporation, ex p. Allan* (1980) 79 L.G.R. 223, that a planning authority were not disabled from considering a planning application for development merely because the same development was a proposal in a draft local plan that was still under consideration. That principle would seem to be *a fortiori* an S.P.Z. and an authority may grant planning permission on an application in accordance with the usual development control procedures for all or any of the development contained in a proposed S.P.Z.

Procedures for making an S.P.Z. scheme

The procedures for S.P.Z. scheme preparation in England and Wales are prescribed by Sched. 6, which inserts a new Sched. 8A into the Act of 1971. The procedures for Scotland are similar, but with some distinguishing characteristics which are considered further below. Much of the detail of the procedures is to be prescribed by regulations. The procedures are modelled closely on those for local plans, and in parts the wording is identical to that if the new local plan provision substituted by this Act for the original ss.11–15 of the 1971 Act.

There are seven principal stages:

(1) The decision by the authority to make a scheme, or the making of a directive against them by the Secretary of State requiring them to make a scheme. Having decided to make a scheme, the authority must notify the Secretary of State and determine the date on which they will begin. The reason for this latter formality is unclear. It is likely in many cases that preparatory work will already have begun, to test the feasibility of an S.P.Z. scheme prior to the authority resolving formally to proceed.

(2) Publicity and consultation: the authority are required to give adequate publicity to their proposals, to ensure that people are aware of their right to make representations and are given an adequate opportunity to make representations, and to take into account any representations made within the prescribed period. Similar requirements in the past relating to local plans have been interpreted as requiring the authority to have produced detailed proposals for consultation at this stage, and not merely an outline. But the Act suggests a more flexible approach here, since the next phase—placing the draft scheme on deposit for public inspection and objection—is required to take place only when the authority have "prepared the relevant documents, that is, the proposed scheme or alterations" (Act of 1971, Sched. 8A, para 5(3); inserted by Sched. 6 to this Act). This wording suggests that the preceding stage, of giving publicity to proposals, may take place before the preparation of a detailed scheme. Moreover, before preparing the scheme, the authority are required to consult with the Secretary of State for Transport and (in a non-metropolitan county) with the county council, both as highways authority and planning authority (Act of 1971, Sched. 8A para 5(5) and (6); as inserted by Sched. 6 to this Act).

(3) Placing of the draft scheme on deposit: the authority are next required to make copies of the scheme available for public inspection, indicating the time allowed for objections to be made; and to send a copy to the Secretary of State. Together with that copy must be forwarded a statement of the authority's handling of the publicity and consultation stage of the exercise, and the Secretary of State may, within 21 days of receipt, direct them to take further steps if he is not satisfied with those already taken (Act of 1971, Sched. 8A, para 7; as inserted by Sched. 6 to this Act). This requirement is also modelled on existing procedures for structure plans and local plans (Act of 1971, ss.8 and 12), where the Secretary of State's power of direction has proved to be very much a reserve power and has been rarely—if ever—used.

(4) Inquiry into objections: the authority must hold an inquiry into any objections which are made in accordance with regulations and have not been withdrawn; and they have discretion to hold an inquiry into other objections, such as late objections (Act of 1971, Sched. 8A, para. 8(1) and (2); as inserted by Sched. 6 to this Act.) The inspector reports to the authority, not to the Secretary of State.

(5) The authority are required to consider the objections. Although the Act itself imposes no obligation upon them to consider the inspector's report, this may be imposed by the regulations to be made under Sched. 8A, para.13, as in the case of local plans. Although this is not one of the issues mentioned specifically by that paragraph (which is modelled closely on s.18 of the Act of 1971), it falls within the general power to make regulations with respect to the adoption of an S.P.Z. scheme. The authority may then adopt the proposals as originally prepared, or as modified to take account of any objections or other material considerations. The Secretary of State has power to direct them to consider modifying the proposals, and they may then proceed to adopt the plan only if they satisfy him that they have made the necessary modifications, or if the direction has been withdrawn (Act of 1971, Sched. 8A, para 9; as inserted by Sched. 6 to this Act.) There is a separate power for the Secretary of State to call in the proposals for his own approval at any time after copies of the proposals have been sent to him, and before they have been adopted by the authority. He may approve the proposals, with or without modifications, or reject them.

(6) The adoption (by the authority) or approval (by the Secretary of State) of the proposals has effect to grant planning permission in accordance with the terms of the

scheme in respect of the land covered by the scheme (s.24A(2)), from the date of adoption or approval and for a period of 10 years (s.24C(1)).

(7) An existing S.P.Z. scheme may be altered at any time, whether at the authority's own initiative or at the request of any person or under direction for the Secretary of State, prompted by such a request. The procedures outlined above extend equally to alterations, except that:

(a) there is a more streamlined procedure available (modelled on that introduced for local plans by this Act) where it appears to the authority that the issues involved are not of sufficient importance to warrant the full procedure (Act of 1971, Sched. 8A, para.6(1); as inserted by Sched. 6 to this Act). The effect is to cut out entirely the preliminary publicity and consultation stage. The authority are required still to send copies to the Secretary of State for Transport and to the county council, but are not specifically required to consult with them. If objections are received and not withdrawn, the authority remain under a duty to arrange for a public local inquiry.

(b) the effect of adoption or approval of an alteration varies as to whether its purpose is to relax or extend control, or to include or exclude land from the zone: see further the notes to s.24D.

Procedures for preparation in Scotland

The corresponding provisions for Scotland are contained in the new ss.21A–21E inserted into the 1972 Act, and the new Sched. 6A inserted into that Act by Sched. 6 to this Act. The provisions correspond largely to those for England and Wales, but there are some differences:

(1) The function of preparation of S.P.Z. schemes is vested in Scotland in the "planning authority" which term is, by virtue of the Local Government (Scotland) Act 1973, s.172(3), to be construed as a reference to a general planning authority and to a district planning authority. The power, therefore, is not exercisable by the regional planning authorities.

(2) The Secretary of State does not have power to direct the S.P.Z. authority to undertake further publicity if dissatisfied with the steps already taken.

(3) The planning authority are required to consult with the Secretary of State and any local roads' authority as to the effect of their proposals on existing or proposed roads.

Public participation and consultation

The procedure for making an S.P.Z. scheme is far more complex, and involves more public participation, than that governing any other grant of planning permission. Even in enterprise zones the scheme is adopted under a comparatively straightforward procedure: the authority are invited by the Secretary of State to prepare a scheme in accordance with directions given by him, and to consider (without an inquiry) any objections made to it before adopting it. The Secretary of State may then proceed to designate the enterprise zone (Local Government, Planning and Land Act 1980, Sched. 32, paras. 1–5).

But the Government strenuously resisted attempts in Standing Committee to delete the requirement for a public inquiry into objections to an S.P.Z. scheme. The Parliamentary Under–Secretary of State (Mr R. Tracey M.P.) argued (Standing Committee H, March 18, 1986; col.376):

"I know that we may be open to some criticism on the point that the procedures are lengthy, but we must remember what the end product is, and that point has surely been exercising members of the Committee during our deliberations. The S.P.Z. scheme will give full planning permission for 10 years. Perhaps over a wide area it will affect the lives of those in or near it. We must be certain, before it becomes a reality, that it has been considered in depth beyond any criticism. The depth of consultation must be seen to be there.

Therefore, I make no apology for the fact that the procedures include a full public consultation exercise, a period for objections to be made and an opportunity for objectors to appear before a public inquiry. I cannot therefore concede that a public local inquiry, which can be a vital stage, can be dispensed with."

Challenge to the validity of an S.P.Z. scheme

S.P.Z. schemes are protected by the same privative provisions under the 1971 Act as extend to structure plans and local plans, by virtue of the amendments to those provisions made by Part II of Sched. 6 to this Act (Part IV for Scotland). The validity of a scheme may therefore be challenged only by application to the High Court made under s.244 of the 1971

Act (application to the Court of Session under s.232 of the Scotland Act) within six weeks of the date of adoption or approval of the scheme.

England and Wales

Simplified planning zones in England and Wales

25.—(1) In Part III of the Town and Country Planning Act 1971 (general planning control), after section 24 insert—

"Simplified planning zone schemes

Simplified planning zones

24A.—(1) A simplified planning zone is an area in respect of which a simplified planning zone scheme is in force.

(2) The adoption or approval of a simplified planning zone scheme has effect to grant in relation to the zone, or any part if it specified in the scheme, planning permission for development specified in the scheme or for development of any class so specified.

(3) Planning permission under a simplified planning zone scheme may be unconditional or subject to such conditions, limitations or exceptions as may be specified in the scheme.

(4) Every local planning authority—

    (*a*) shall consider, as soon as practicable after this section comes into operation, the question for which part or parts of their area a simplified planning zone scheme is desirable, and shall thereafter keep that question under review; and

    (*b*) shall prepare a scheme for any such part for which they decide, as a result of their original consideration or of any such review, that it is desirable to do so.

(5) The provisions of Schedule 8A to this Act have effect with respect to the making and alteration of simplified planning zone schemes and other related matters.

(6) The functions of local planning authorities under the provisions of this Act relating to simplified planning zone schemes shall be performed in non-metropolitan counties by the district planning authorities.

DEFINITIONS

"development": 1971 Act, s.290(1).
"district planning authority": 1971 Act, s.1(1).
"planning permission": 1971 Act, s.290(1).
"simplified planning zone": subs.(1).

ALLOCATION OF FUNCTIONS

The function of a local planning authority under this section is exercisable in a non-metropolitan county by the district planning authority.

GENERAL NOTE

This section lays the basis for S.P.Z. schemes by prescribing their content and effect, by imposing the initial duty on local planning authorities to consider whether to prepare an S.P.Z. scheme and by prescribing (through the insertion of a new Sched. 8A to the 1971 Act) the procedure for preparation and adoption of proposals for an S.P.Z. scheme. The details of procedure are to be prescribed by regulations, to be made under para. 13 of the new Sched. 8A. The principal steps in the process of making an S.P.Z. scheme are outlined above in the General Note to this Part of the Act.

Upon the commencement of these provisions, the local planning authority are under a duty to consider, as soon as practicable, the question for which part of their area an S.P.Z. scheme is desirable, and to keep that question under review thereafter. The duty is in broad terms: the legislation does not impose a duty on every authority to prepare an S.P.Z.

scheme, and it is likely that some authorities may decide that the concept is inapplicable to their area. The duty arising under this section is, however, reinforced by the right created in para. 3 of Sched. 8A for any person to request the authority to make an S.P.Z. scheme, and to have that request referred to the Secretary of State if the authority do not give a favourable response. The Secretary of State then has the power to direct the authority to prepare a scheme.

The adoption (by the local planning authority) or approval (by the Secretary of State) of an S.P.Z. scheme grants an immediate planning permission for a period of 10 years (s.24C(1)) for such development as is specified in the scheme. The permission has no effect on existing development rights (s.24B(2)), and the termination of the scheme results in the loss of the benefit of the planning permission where development has not begun (s.24C(2)).

Simplified planning zone schemes: conditions and limitations on planning permission

24B.—(1) The conditions and limitations on planning permission which may be specified in a simplified planning zone scheme may include—

    (*a*) conditions or limitations in respect of all development permitted by the scheme or in respect of particular descriptions of development so permitted, and

    (*b*) conditions or limitations requiring the consent, agreement or approval of the local planning authority in relation to particular descriptions of permitted development;

and different conditions or limitations may be specified for different cases or classes of case.

(2) Nothing in a simplified planning zone scheme shall affect the right of any person—

    (*a*) to do anything not amounting to development, or

    (*b*) to carry out development for which planning permission is not required or for which permission has been granted otherwise than by the scheme;

and no limitation or restriction subject to which permission has been granted otherwise than under the scheme shall affect the right of any person to carry out development for which permission has been granted under the scheme.

DEFINITIONS
"development": 1971 Act, s.290(1).
"local planning authority": 1971 Act, s.1(1).
"planning permission": 1971 Act, s.290(1).
"simplified planning zone scheme": 1971 Act, s.290(1).

GENERAL NOTE
Content of an S.P.Z. scheme
This section provides an outline of the permitted content of an S.P.Z. scheme, and it is supplemented by para. 1 of the new Sched. 8A to the 1971 Act, which requires an S.P.Z. scheme to consist of a map and a written statement, and such diagrams, illustrations and descriptive matter as the local planning authority think appropriate for explaining or illustrating the provisions of the scheme. It also requires that the scheme specify:

    "(a) the development or classes of development permitted by the scheme,

    (b) the land in relation to which permission is granted, and

    (c) any conditions, limitations or exceptions subject to which it is granted".

Finally, the scheme must contain such other matters as may be prescribed by the Secretary of State by regulations.

Conditions, limitations and exceptions
The section gives broad powers to design a system of conditions and limitations which may distinguish between different descriptions of development. Moreover, different permissions may, by virtue of s.24A(2), apply to different parts of the zone. This use of conditions and limitations is more akin to their role in the General Development Order than in relation to specific planning permissions. In the latter case, the only relevant limitations are usually

those contained in the description of the development in the planning application. In the case of an S.P.Z. scheme, the limitations must necessarily be more abstract, and set general limits on the scale of the development, such as the height, bulk and location of buildings. In accordance with the rules relating to development orders, any development which occurs in purported reliance upon an S.P.Z. scheme, but which exceeds a limitation contained in it, will be wholly outside the permission and not merely to the extent of the excess (though enforcement action may be limited to the extent of the excess, under s.87(9) (as amended) of the 1971 Act).

The Secretary of State does not propose to issue detailed guidance about the conditions and limitations that authorities may wish to use. The Parliamentary Under-Secretary stressed this in debate in Standing Committee, when urging the Committee to reject an amendment which would have required regulations to specify in advance what conditions or limitations an authority could apply in its S.P.Z. scheme (Standing Committee H, March 13, 1986; col. 339) that:

> "Again, I must emphasise that the S.P.Z.s are essentially a tool of and for the local planning authority. It will know best what developments to allow and what conditions, if any, are necessary. It would be difficult to set down in advance a full list of the possible conditions and limitations necessary to meet the requirements of all authorities and all circumstances.
>
> Moreover, I cannot see what advantage would be served by the amendment. My Department has already issued a circular advising authorities on the use of conditions on planning permissions. Authorities could draw on that if they wished when preparing S.P.Z.s, but I see no need for more advice on the subject."

But although the conditions contained in an S.P.Z. scheme are planning conditions, and are enforceable in the same way as any other planning conditions; they are imposed in a way which is distinguishable from conditions imposed on a grant of permission pursuant to an application. The question therefore arises whether they should be governed by the same rules relating to validity. It would be a relatively simple matter to translate to S.P.Z. schemes the test for validity of planning conditions which was endorsed by the House of Lords in *Newbury District Council* v. *Secretary of State for the Environment* [1981] A.C. 578. But there are some points of distinction. First, there is a difference of wording: there is no precondition requiring the authority only to include such conditions "as they think fit," although it may be thought that this was implicit in the exercise. Secondly, and more significantly, the status and purpose of an S.P.Z. scheme is different. It is more legislative in character, and the courts may, as in the case of a special development order (see, *e.g.* *Essex County Council* v. *Minister of Housing and Local Government* (1967) 18 P. & C.R. 531), be less willing to intervene. The different status of an S.P.Z. scheme is reflected in the provisions for legal challenge contained in the Act, which equate an S.P.Z. scheme with a development plan rather than with a grant of planning permission; and it may prove necessary for the court to strike down the whole S.P.Z. scheme where it is unable to disentangle an invalid condition. Thirdly, the privative provisions create a status of deemed validity, if no application to challenge an S.P.Z. scheme is made within the prescribed six-week period from the date of adoption or approval of the scheme. Finally, if the *Newbury* test were to be applied directly to S.P.Z. schemes, difficulties may arise in its application. To require that a condition relate reasonably and fairly to the permitted development, for example, may be a different matter when it is the S.P.Z. scheme itself which is defining the permitted development, rather than the developer's application. There is also the issue of the "exceptions" which an S.P.Z. scheme may contain, and which may be capable of imposing what are effectively negative conditions.

Whatever the appropriate test for the validity of conditions and exceptions, it will be open to the Secretary of State to intervene by way of call-in at any stage before adoption, and it is to be expected that central Government supervision of the content of S.P.Z. schemes will be undertaken through this mechanism.

Duration of simplified planning zone scheme

24C.—(1) A simplified planning zone scheme shall take effect on the date of its adoption or approval and shall cease to have effect at the end of the period of ten years beginning with that date.

(2) Upon the scheme's ceasing to have effect planning permission under the scheme shall also cease to have effect except in a case where the development authorised by it has been begun.

(3) The provisions of section 44(2) to (6) of this Act (which provide for the termination of planning permission if the completion of

development is unreasonably delayed) apply to planning permission under a simplified planning zone scheme where development has been begun but not completed by the time the area ceased to be a simplified planning zone.

(4) The provisions of section 43(1) to (3) of this Act apply in determining for the purposes of this section when development shall be taken to be begun.

DEFINITIONS
"development": 1971 Act, s.290(1).
"planning permission": 1971 Act, s.290(1)(*d*).
"simplified planning zone scheme": 1971 Act, s.290(1).

GENERAL NOTE
Planning permission granted by an S.P.Z. scheme runs for 10 years from the date of adoption or approval. It then terminates, but only in respect of development which has not by then begun. The Government resisted an attempt to have an absolute termination at the end of 10 years except in respect of development which had been completed, because this would, in their view, have effectively converted the 10-year life to an eight- or nine-year life. Under s.43(1) to (3) of the 1971 Act, which is applied by subs. (3), comparatively little is required to have occurred on the site in order for development to be taken to have begun. The digging of a trench, for example, may suffice to keep the permission alive, even though in the case of an S.P.Z. scheme there will be no plan of any building in the hands of the authority against which the beginning of development can be assessed. It may in practice be difficult therefore, to import the requirement stemming from *South Oxfordshire District Council* v. *Secretary of State for the Environment* [1981] J.P.L. 359 that the trench must be at least in the right place for the approved development, when development under an S.P.Z. scheme may be described in broad terms.

The authority do, however, have the ability to use the powers of s.44 of the Act of 1971, which are brought into play by subs. (3), to require that a planning permission shall cease to have effect at the end of the period specified in it (a minimum of 12 months.)

Alteration of simplified planning zone scheme
   24D.—(1) The adoption or approval of alterations to a simplified planning zone scheme has effect as follows.

(2) The adoption or approval of alterations providing for the inclusion of land in the simplified planning zone has effect to grant in relation to that land or such part of it as is specified in the scheme planning permission for development so specified or of any class so specified.

(3) The adoption or approval of alterations providing for the grant of planning permission has effect to grant such permission in relation to the simplified planning zone, or such part of it as is specified in the scheme, for development so specified or development of any class so specified.

(4) The adoption or approval of alterations providing for the withdrawal or relaxation of conditions, limitations or restrictions to which planning permission under the scheme is subject has effect to withdraw or relax the conditions, limitations or restrictions forthwith.

(5) The adoption or approval of alterations providing for—
   (*a*) the exclusion of land from the simplified planning zone,
   (*b*) the withdrawal of planning permission, or
   (*c*) the imposition of new or more stringent conditions, limitations or restrictions to which planning permission under the scheme is subject,
has effect to withdraw permission, or to impose the conditions, limitations or restrictions, with effect from the end of the period of twelve months beginning with the date of adoption or approval.

(6) The adoption or approval of alterations to a scheme does not affect planning permission under the scheme in any case where the development authorised by it has been begun.

The provisions of section 43(1) to (3) of this Act apply in determining for the purposes of this subsection when development shall be taken to be begun.

DEFINITIONS
"development": 1971 Act, s.290(1).
"planning permission": 1971 Act, 290(1).
"simplified planning zone scheme": 1971 Act, s.290(1).

GENERAL NOTE
The procedure for making alterations to an S.P.Z. scheme follows closely that for making a new S.P.Z. scheme, except that there is provision for expedited procedure in straightforward cases: see the General Note to this Part of the Act. An alteration may extend or reduce the extent of the zone, or relax or withdraw conditions, limitations or "restrictions" (a word not to be found in s.24A) or impose more stringent restrictions. Relaxations and extensions have immediate effect upon the adoption or approval of the alterations; but any unfavourable alteration has effect from 12 months following that date.

Alterations are not, by virtue of subs. (6), to affect development which has already begun, but the Act fails to specify whether the cut-off point is to be the date of adoption or approval, or the expiry of the 12-month period allowed by subs. (5). Although the opening words of subs. (6) imply that it is the adoption or approval of alterations which is the critical point, that interpretation would run counter to the broad principle of subs. (5) that the adoption or approval of unfavourable alterations has no effect until the expiry of the period. It must be the case therefore, that development may still be begun in that 12-month period, and it would be consistent with the overall design of the Act and of ss.41–43 that, once lawfully begun, it should lawfully be able to be completed.

Exclusion of certain descriptions of land or development
24E.—(1) The following descriptions of land may not be included in a simplified planning zone—
   (*a*) land in a National Park;
   (*b*) land in a conservation area;
   (*c*) land in an area designated under section 87 of the National Parks and Access to the Countryside Act 1949 as an area of outstanding natural beauty;
   (*d*) land identified in the development plan for the district as part of a green belt;
   (*e*) land in respect of which a notification or order is in force under section 28 or 29 of the Wildlife and Countryside Act 1981 (areas of special scientific interest).
(2) Where land included in a simplified planning zone becomes land of such a description, subsection (1) does not have effect to exclude it from the zone.
(3) The Secretary of State may by order provide that no simplified planning zone scheme shall have effect to grant planning permission—
   (*a*) in relation to an area of land specified in the order or to areas of land of a description so specified, or
   (*b*) for development of a description specified in the order.
(4) An order under subsection (3) has effect to withdraw such planning permission under a simplified planning zone scheme already in force with effect from the date on which the order comes into force, except in a case where the development authorised by the permission has been begun.
The provisions of section 43(1) to (3) of this Act apply in determining for the purposes of this subsection when development shall be taken to be begun.".
(2) After Schedule 8 to the Town and Country Planning Act 1971 insert as Schedule 8A the Schedule set out in Part I of Schedule 6 to this Act which contains provision with respect to the making and alteration of simplified planning zone schemes and other related matters.

(3) The Town and Country Planning Act 1971 also has effect subject to the consequential amendments specified in Part II of Schedule 6 to this Act.

<small>DEFINITIONS</small>
"area of outstanding natural beauty": National Parks and Access to the Countryside Act 1949, s.87.
"area of special scientific interest": Wildlife and Countryside Act 1981, ss.28, 29.
"development": Act of 1971, s.290(1).
"development plan": Act of 1971, s.290(1).
"land": Act of 1971, s.290(1).
"National Park": National Parks and Access to the Countryside Act 1949, ss.5(3), 114
"planning permission": 1971 Act, s.290(1).
"simplified planning zone scheme": 1971 Act, s.290(1).

<small>GENERAL NOTE</small>
This section prescribes the areas to be excluded from an S.P.Z. scheme. There are two categories: those that are mandatorily excluded by subs. (1), and those which may be excluded by the Secretary of State by order under subs. (3).

The discretionary power to exclude land or development was introduced by the Government so as to ensure that S.P.Z. schemes would not be allowed to override the EEC Directive on environmental assessment and to exclude minerals and waste disposal development altogether on the ground that they are often contentious, have a potentially severe impact on the environment and are frequently of long duration (Standing Committee H, March 13, 1986; col. 340). A further consideration must also be that these two forms of development are, in England, matters for county planning authorities, who are not S.P.Z. authorities under the Act. The Government has given an assurance (*op. cit.,* col. 341) that the necessary orders will be made before any S.P.Z. schemes are prepared.

Scotland

Simplified planning zones in Scotland

26.—(1) In Part III of the Town and Country Planning (Scotland) Act 1972 (general planning control), after section 21 insert—

"Simplified planning zone schemes

Simplified planning zones

21A.—(1) A simplified planning zone is an area in respect of which a simplified planning zone scheme is in force.

(2) The adoption or approval of a simplified planning zone scheme has effect to grant in relation to the zone, or any part of it specified in the scheme, planning permission for development specified in the scheme or for development of any class so specified.

(3) Planning permission under a simplified planning zone scheme may be unconditional or subject to such conditions, limitations or exceptions as may be specified in the scheme.

(4) Every planning authority—
(*a*) shall consider, as soon as practicable after this section comes into operation, the question for which part or parts of their district a simplified planning zone scheme is desirable, and shall thereafter keep that question under review; and
(*b*) shall prepare a scheme for any such part for which they decide, as a result of their original consideration or of any such review, that it is desirable to do so.

(5) The provisions of Schedule 6A to this Act have effect with respect to the making and alteration of simplified planning zone schemes and other related matters.

"development": 1972 Act, s.275(1).
"planning permission": 1972 Act, s.275(1).
"simplified planning zone": subs. (1).

GENERAL NOTE
This section lays the basis for S.P.Z. schemes in Scotland by prescribing their content and effect, by imposing the initial duty on planning authorities to consider whether to prepare an S.P.Z. scheme, and by prescribing (through the insertion of a new Sched. 6A to the 1972 Act) the procedure for preparation and adoption of proposals for an S.P.Z. scheme. The details of procedure are to be prescribed by regulations, to be made under para. 12 of the new Sched. 6A. The principal steps in the process of making an S.P.Z. scheme are outlined above in the General Note to this Part of the Act.

The provisions of this section are, without exception, identical to those of the new s.24A of the English Act (see generally the annotations to that section). The exception lies in the designation of planning authority, which is in Scotland to be the district and general planning authorities, by virtue of the Local Government (Scotland) Act 1973, s.172(3).

Simplified planning zone schemes: conditions and limitations on planning permission

21B.—(1) The conditions and limitations on planning permission which may be specified in a simplified planning zone scheme may include—

(a) conditions or limitations in respect of all development permitted by the scheme or in respect of particular descriptions of development so permitted, and

(b) conditions or limitations requiring the consent, agreement or approval of the planning authority in relation to particular descriptions of permitted development;

and different conditions or limitations may be specified for different cases or classes of case.

(2) Nothing in a simplified planning zone scheme shall affect the right of any person—

(a) to do anything not amounting to development, or

(b) to carry out development for which planning permission is not required or for which permission has been granted otherwise than by the scheme;

and no limitation or restriction subject to which permission has been granted otherwise than under the scheme shall affect the right of any person to carry out development for which permission has been granted under the scheme.

DEFINITIONS
"development": 1972 Act, s.275(1).
"planning permission": 1972 Act, s.275(1).
"simplified planning zone scheme": 1972 Act, s.275(1).

GENERAL NOTE
Content of an S.P.Z. scheme.
This section provides an outline of the permitted content of an S.P.Z. scheme, and it is supplemented by para. 1 of the new Sched. 6A to the 1972 Act, which requires an S.P.Z. scheme to consist of a map and a written statement, and such diagrams, illustrations and descriptive matter as the local planning authority think appropriate for explaining or illustrating the provisions of the scheme. It also requires that the scheme specify:

"(a) the development or classes of development permitted by the scheme,
(b) the land in relation to which permission is granted, and
(c) any conditions, limitations or exceptions subject to which it is granted".

Finally, the scheme must contain other matters as may be prescribed by the Secretary of State by regulations.

As to the question of validity of conditions and exceptions, see further the General Note to s.24B of the English Act.

Duration of simplified planning zone scheme

21C.—(1) A simplified planning zone scheme shall take effect on the date of its adoption or approval and shall cease to have effect at the end of the period of ten years beginning with that date.

(2) Upon the scheme's ceasing to have effect planning permission under the scheme shall also cease to have effect except in a case where the development authorised by it has been begun.

(3) The provisions of section 41(2) to (6) of this Act (which provide for the termination of planning permission if the completion of development is unreasonably delayed) apply to planning permission under a simplified planning zone scheme where development has been begun but not completed by the time the area ceases to be a simplified planning zone.

(4) The provisions of section 40(1) to (3) of this Act apply in determining for the purposes of this section when development shall be taken to be begun.

DEFINITIONS
"development": 1972 Act, s.275(1).
"planning permission": 1972 Act, s.275(1).
"simplified planning zone scheme": 1972 Act, s.275(1).

GENERAL NOTE
Planning permission granted by an S.P.Z. scheme runs for 10 years from the date of adoption or approval. It then terminates, but only in respect of development which has not by then begun. "Begun" is to be interpreted in accordance with s.40(1) to (3) of the 1972 Act. (See generally on this the annotations to s.24C of the English Act.)

The authority do, however, have the ability to use the powers of s.41 of the Act of 1972, which are brought into play by subs. (3), to require that a planning permission shall cease to have effect at the end of the period specified in it (a minimum of 12 months).

Alteration of simplified planning scheme

21D.—(1) The adoption or approval of alterations to a simplified planning zone scheme has effect as follows.

(2) The adoption or approval of alterations providing for the inclusion of land in the simplified planning zone has effect to grant in relation to that land or such part of it as is specified in the scheme planning permission for development so specified or of any class so specified.

(3) The adoption or approval of alterations providing for the grant of planning permission has effect to grant such permission in relation to the simplified planning zone, or such part of it as is specified in the scheme, for development so specified or development of any class so specified.

(4) The adoption or approval of alterations providing for the withdrawal or relaxation of conditions, limitations or restrictions to which planning permission under the scheme is subject has effect to withdraw or relax the conditions, limitations or restrictions forthwith.

(5) The adoption or approval of alterations providing for—
(*a*) the exclusion of land from the simplified planning zone,
(*b*) the withdrawal of planning permission, or
(*c*) the imposition of new or more stringent conditions, limitations or restrictions to which planning permission under the scheme is subject,
has effect to withdraw permission, or to impose the conditions, limitations or restrictions, with effect from the end of the period of twelve months beginning with the date of adoption or approval.

(6) The adoption or approval of alterations to a scheme does not affect planning permission under the scheme in any case where development authorised by it has been begun.

The provisions of section 40(1) to (3) of this Act apply in determining for the purposes of this subsection when development shall be taken to be begun.

DEFINITIONS
"development": 1972 Act, s.275(1).
"planning permission": 1972 Act, s.275(1).
"simplified planning zone scheme": 1972 Act, s.285(1).

GENERAL NOTE
The procedure for making alterations to an S.P.Z. scheme follows closely that for making a new S.P.Z. scheme, except that there is provision for expedited procedure in straightforward cases: see the General Note to this Part of the Act. An alteration may extend or reduce the extent of the zone, or relax or withdraw conditions, limitations or "restrictions" (a word not to be found in s.21A) or impose more stringent conditions, limitations or restrictions. As to the effect of these provisions, see the General Note to s.24D of the English Act.

Exclusion of certain descriptions of land or development
21E.—(1) The following descriptions of land may not be included in a simplified planning zone—
  (*a*) land in a conservation area;
  (*b*) land in a National Scenic Area;
  (*c*) land identified in the development plan for the area as part of a green belt;
  (*d*) land in respect of which a notification or order is in force under section 28 or 29 of the Wildlife and Countryside Act 1981 (areas of special scientific interest).
(2) Where land included in a simplified planning zone becomes land of such a description, subsection (1) does not have effect to exclude it from the zone.
(3) The Secretary of State may by order provide that no simplified planning zone scheme shall have effect to grant planning permission—
  (*a*) in relation to an area of land specified in the order or to areas of land of a description so specified; or
  (*b*) for development of a description specified in the order.
(4) An order under subsection (3) has effect to withdraw such planning permission under a simplified planning zone scheme already in force with effect from the date on which the order comes into force, except in a case where the development authorised by the permission has been begun.
The provisions of section 40(1) to (3) of this Act apply in determining for the purposes of this subsection when development shall be taken to be begun.".
(2) After Schedule 6 to the Town and Country Planning (Scotland) Act 1972 insert as Schedule 6A the Schedule set out in Part III of Schedule 6 to this Act which contains provision with respect to the making and alteration of simplified planning zone schemes and other related matters.
(3) The Town and Country Planning (Scotland) Act 1972 also has effect subject to the consequential amendments specified in Part IV of Schedule 6 to this Act.

DEFINITIONS
"area of special scientific interest": Wildlife and Countryside Act 1981, ss.28, 29.
"conservation area": 1972 Act, s.275(1).
"development": 1972 Act, s.275(1).
"development plan": 1972 Act, s.275(1).
"land": 1972 Act, s.275(1).
"National Scenic Area": 1972 Act, s.262C (inserted by para. 38 of Sched. 11 to this Act).

"planning permission": 1972 Act, s.275(1).
"simplified planning zone scheme": 1972 Act, s.275(1).

GENERAL NOTE
This section prescribes the areas to be excluded from an S.P.Z. scheme. There are two categories: those that are mandatorily excluded by subs. (1), and those which may be excluded by the Secretary of State by order under subs. (3). The mandatory categories are the same as for England and Wales, except that the National Scenic Areas, now provided with a statutory base by this Act, appear in place of the English National Parks and designated areas of outstanding natural beauty. National Scenic Areas are now to be statutorily designated under the new s.262C of the Town and Country Planning (Scotland) Act 1972, inserted by this Act, Sched.11, para. 38.
As to the discretionary exclusions, see further the General Note to s.24E of the English Act.

PART III

FINANCIAL ASSISTANCE FOR URBAN REGENERATION

GENERAL NOTE TO PART III
The provisions of this Part introduce a new form of Government grant for urban regeneration. It will supersede the existing informal arrangements for Urban Development Grant (U.D.G.), which have been in operation since 1983. In three years, 179 offers had been made of U.D.G. involving a maximum commitment of £85 million public money but levering private sector investment of £350 million as a result (Standing Committee H, March 20, 1986; cols. 429–430).
The Government propose that the new urban regeneration grant (U.R.G.) should similarly be used to underwrite private sector development, but that it should be used to improve areas rather than simply to promote individual developments. The areas to which it is proposed to apply the grant have three main characteristics (*Hansard*, H.C. Vol. 91, col. 159):
    (1) there is a lot of derelict land, which is disused, underused and obsolete;
    (2) they are too big to be regenerated or redeveloped by a single project supported by U.D.G.
    (3) individual buildings in the area cannot be dealt with because of surrounding conditions.
The areas would probably range from 5 to 100 acres, and U.R.G. will not normally be available in respect of individual buildings unless a particular project would have an important effect on the local economy and the environment (Standing Committee H, col. 430; March 25, 1986).
The amounts available in U.R.G., and whether they will come from existing urban programme resources or elsewhere, remain undecided. The Minister explained in Standing Committee that he was uncertain how quickly the scheme would take off, and was anxious not to over-estimate since the Treasury, if faced with under-spending, might insist upon a reduced allocation in subsequent years (*ibid.*, col. 394).
Assistance may take the form of grants, loans, guarantees and through incurring expenditure for the benefit of the recipient of the aid (s.27). The Act is open ended as to the terms upon which assistance may be made available (s.28), and the Minister in Standing Committee welcomed the flexibility, which he envisaged would allow conditions to be imposed on grants to require payment in appropriate cases, and to give interest free loans at low rates or commercial rates (*op. cit.*, col. 432). The Act forbids, however, the purchase by the Secretary of State of loan or share capital in a company (s.27(3)).
This Part of the Act extends to Scotland, as well as to England and Wales (s.57(1) and (2)).

Power to give assistance

27.—(1) The Secretary of State may, with the consent of the Treasury, give financial assistance to any person in respect of qualifying expenditure incurred in connection with activities contributing to the regeneration of an urban area by bringing land and buildings into effective use, creating an attractive environment, providing employment for people who live in the area or ensuring that housing and social facilities are available to encourage people to live and work in the area.

(2) Expenditure incurred in connection with any of the following qualifies for assistance—

(*a*) the acquisition of land or buildings;

(*b*) the reclamation, improvement or refurbishment of land or buildings;

(*c*) the development or the redevelopment of land, including the conversion or demolition of existing buildings;

(*d*) the equipment of fitting out of buildings or land;

(*e*) the provision of means of access, services or other facilities for buildings or land;

(*f*) environmental improvements.

Forms of assistance

28.—(1) Financial assistance under section 27 may be given in any form.

(2) Assistance may, in particular, be given by way of—

(*a*) grants,

(*b*) loans,

(*c*) guarantees, or

(*d*) incurring expenditure for the benefit of the person assisted.

(3) The Secretary of State shall not in giving financial assistance under section 27 purchase loan or share capital in a company.

Terms on which assistance is given

29.—(1) Financial assistance under section 27 may be given on such terms as the Secretary of State, with the consent of the Treasury, considers appropriate.

(2) The terms may, in particular, include provision as to—

(*a*) circumstances in which the assistance must be repaid, or otherwise made good, to the Secretary of State, and the manner in which that is to be done; or

(*b*) circumstances in which the Secretary of State is entitled to recover the proceeds or part of the proceeds of any disposal of land or buildings in respect of which assistance was provided.

(3) The person receiving assistance shall comply with the terms on which it is given and compliance may be enforced by the Secretary of State.

PART IV

HAZARDOUS SUBSTANCES

GENERAL NOTE TO PART IV

Background to the new controls

This Part of the Act introduces a new system of control over hazardous substances. The influence of planning control over the design and siting of new hazardous uses has been steadily increasing, reinforced by consultation on safety issues with the Health and Safety Executive. But the major drawback of the ordinary development control system in this context has been that it is limited to acts constituting "development" of land, whilst a new hazardous use may be introduced without any development occurring at all. An established industry might commence new hazardous operations, or intensify existing operations, without any further planning consent being required.

Planning arrangements have been strengthened over the years. Local planning authorities have, since 1972 (D.O.E. Circulars 1/72; 97/74), been urged to take safety factors into account on applications involving a major hazard, and to consult with the Health and Safety

Executive, particularly in cases involving the storage of large quantities of hazardous materials. But the comparative informality of these arrangements continued to cause concern, and the Advisory Committee on Major Hazards, in its *First Report* (H.M.S.O. 1976) urged that consultation with the Health and Safety Executive should be mandatory in all cases of applications involving, affecting or affected by, a notifiable installation. In its *Second Report* (H.M.S.O. 1979) the Committee proposed that development control should be extended by bringing within the statutory definition of "development" the introduction of a notifiable activity, so that planning permission would always be required. Although there were obvious problems in implementing this proposal and incorporating it into the overall structure of development control (should it, for example, be regarded as operational development or material change of use?), the Committee were firm in their preference for control to be exercised through the planning system rather than by a specialised licensing system administered by the H.S.E., since only the planning system would in their view give the community the opportunity of deciding whether they were prepared to accept the introduction of the hazard.

In 1983 the Government introduced amendments to the General Development Order and the Use Classes Order. Their effect was to take away the immunity from planning control (under the Use Classes Order) and the deemed planning permission (under the General Development Order) in cases of development involving a notifiable quantity of hazardous substances. But the changes still did not catch those cases where the introduction of hazardous substances did not involve any material change in the use of the land. Moreover, where development rights under the General Development Order were restricted by the amendment, and the local planning authority subsequently refused permission, a claim could be made for compensation under s.170 of the 1971 Act. Although the Town and Country Planning (Compensation) Act 1985 limited such claims to those based on applications for planning permission made within 12 months of the amendment to the General Development Order, it did not otherwise restrict the extent of local planning authorities' liability.

The present reforms were foreshadowed in a consultation paper issued by the Department of the Environment in 1984, "Planning Control over Hazardous Development", in which the Department argued against a straightforward extension of planning control, and suggested the setting up of a separate procedural regime, though still administered by local planning authorities. The procedures would be modelled on planning procedures, with comparable provision for applications, appeals and call-in.

Outline of hazardous substances control
Upon the coming into force of this Part of the Act, the presence on, over or under land of any hazardous substance in excess of the controlled quantity requires consent from the hazardous substances authority. In England and Wales this will be in Greater London and the metropolitan counties, the London boroughs and the district planning authorities. In the non-metropolitan counties, the district planning authorities will generally have the function, but it vests in the county planning authorities in relation to National Parks (outside the Peak Park and Lake District where the function vests in the Planning Board) and in relation to land used for mineral working or waste disposal. In Scotland the hazardous substances authority will be the planning authority, which by virtue of the Local Government (Scotland) Act 1973 means the district planning authority or general planning authority. In the case of operational land of statutory undertakers the function vests in "the appropriate Minister," and urban development corporations will have the function in their areas if they are the local planning authority in relation to all kinds of development. The Secretary of State has power to specify the control figures, and to carve out exceptions from control.

Applications for consent are made to the hazardous substances authority, who are to be required by regulations to consult with the Health and Safety Executive in prescribed cases (s.58C; s.56D in Scotland), and are empowered to grant consent either unconditionally or subject to such conditions as they think fit, or to refuse it, and in dealing with the application they are required to "have regard to any material considerations" (s.58D; s.56E in Scotland).

There is to be a right of appeal to the Secretary of State against refusal or conditions imposed on a grant of consent and a right of call-in (in Scotland, a right of reference to the regional planning authority) (s.58E; s.56F in Scotland), power to revoke or modify a grant of consent (s.58H; s.56J in Scotland) and special provision for emergencies (s.58L; s.56M in Scotland).

The new controls are to be phased in, with a transitional period during which consent may be claimed in respect of any hazardous substance which was present on land at any time within the 12 months immediately preceding the commencement date for this Part of the Act (s.33 of this Act; s.37 in Scotland).

Application of provisions to hazardous substances authorities
    The regime established by these provisions extends also to the grant of consent to
hazardous substances authorities themselves, but subject to such exceptions and modifications as may be prescribed by the Secretary of State. The regulations may require that any
such application should be made to him, rather than to the hazardous substances authority:
Act of 1971, s.271A, inserted by Sched. 7, para. 5, to this Act.

England and Wales

Hazardous substances authorities

30. The following sections shall be inserted after section 1 of the Town
and Country Planning Act 1971—

"Hazardous substances authorities—general

1A.—(1) Subject to subsections (2) to (4) below, in this Act
"hazardous substances authority", in relation to any land other than
land to which section 1B applies, means the council of the district or
London Borough in which it is situated.

(2) Subject to subsection (3) below, the county council are the
hazardous substances authority if the land is in a non-metropolitan
county and—

(*a*) is situated in a National Park;

(*b*) is used for the winning and working of minerals (including their
    extraction from a mineral-working deposit); or

(*c*) is situated in England and used for the disposal of refuse or
    waste materials.

(3) A joint planning board or special planning board for a National
Park are the hazardous substances authority for the Park.

(4) An urban development corporation are the hazardous substances authority for their area, if they are local planning authority in
relation to all kinds of development.

DEFINITIONS
    "development": 1971 Act, s.290(1).
    "hazardous substances authority": subss. (1) and (3).
    "joint planning board": 1971 Act, ss.1, 290(1).
    "land": 1971 Act, s.290(1).
    "National Park": National Parks and Access to the Countryside Act 1949, ss.5(3), 114.
    "urban development corporation": 1971 Act, s.290(1).
    "winning and working of minerals": 1971 Act, s.290(1).

GENERAL NOTE
    The function of hazardous substances authority vests in the London boroughs and the
metropolitan districts. In the non-metropolitan counties, it vests generally in the district
planning authorities, but in the county planning authorities in relation to National Parks
(outside the Peak Park and Lake District where the function vests in the Planning Board)
and in relation to land used for mineral working or waste disposal. In the case of operational
land of statutory undertakers the function vests in "the appropriate Minister" (new s.1B
below), and urban development corporations will have the function in their areas, if they
are the local planning authority, in relation to all kinds of development, which is presently
the case in relation to the urban development corporations in the London docklands and
Merseyside.

Hazardous substances authorities—statutory undertakers

1B.—(1) In this Act "hazardous substances authority", in relation
to land to which this section applies, means the appropriate Minister.

(2) This section applies—

(*a*) to operational land of statutory undertakers;

(*b*) to land in which statutory undertakers hold, or propose to acquire, an interest with a view to the land being used as operational land.

(3) For the purposes of this section any land to which this sub-section applies but which is not operational land of statutory under-takers authorised to carry on a harbour shall be treated as if it were such operational land.

(4) Subsection (3) above applies—

(a) to a wharf; and

(b) to harbour land,

as defined in the Harbours Act 1964.

(5) Any question whether subsection (3) above applies to land shall be determined by the Secretary of State and the Minister who is the appropriate Minister in relation to operational land of statutory undertakers who are authorised to carry on harbour undertakings.".

DEFINITIONS

"appropriate Minister": 1971 Act, s.290(1).

"hazardous substances authority": subs. (1); 1971 Act, s.1A.

"land": 1971 Act, s.290(1).

"operational land": 1971 Act, s.290(1).

"statutory undertakers": 1971 Act, s.290(1).

GENERAL NOTE

The hazardous substances authority in relation to operational land, or prospective operational land, of statutory undertakers is to be the "appropriate Minister", which is, by virtue of s.290(1) of the 1971 Act, to be the Minister to whom the function is assigned by s.224 of that Act. All wharves and harbour land are to be treated for the purposes of this section as if they were operational land of statutory undertakers.

Hazardous substances

31. The following shall be inserted after section 58A of the Town and Country Planning Act 1971—

"Hazardous substances

Requirement of hazardous substances consent

58B.—(1) Subject to the provisions of this Part of this Act, the presence of a hazardous substance on, over or under land requires the consent of the hazardous substances authority (in this Act referred to as "hazardous substances consent") unless the aggregate quantity of the substance—

(a) on, under or over the land;

(b) on, under or over other land which is within 500 metres of it and controlled by the same person; or

(c) in or on a structure controlled by the same person any part of which is within 500 metres of it,

is less than the controlled quantity.

(2) The temporary presence of a hazardous substance while it is being transported from one place to another is not to be taken into account unless it is unloaded.

(3) The Secretary of State—

(a) shall by regulations specify—

(i) the substances that are hazardous substances for the purposes of this Act;

(ii) the quantity which is to be the controlled quantity of any such substance;

(b) may by regulations provide that hazardous substances consent is not required or is only required—

(i) in relation to land of prescribed descriptions;

(ii) by reason of the presence of hazardous substances in prescribed circumstances;

(*c*) may by regulations provide that, except in such circumstances as may be prescribed, all hazardous substances falling within a group specified in the regulations are to be treated as a single substance for the purposes of this Act.

(4) Regulations which—

(*a*) are made by virtue of sub-paragraph (i) of subsection (3)(*a*) above; or

(*b*) are made by virtue of sub-paragraph (ii) of that paragraph and reduce the controlled quantity of a substance,

may make such transitional provision as appears to the Secretary of State to be appropriate.

(5) The power to make such transitional provision includes, without prejudice to its generality, power to apply section 23 of the Housing and Planning Act 1986 subject to such modifications as appear to the Secretary of State to be appropriate.

(6) Regulations under this section may make different provisions for different cases or descriptions of cases.

(7) Bodies corporate which are inter-connected for the purposes of the Fair Trading Act 1973 are to be treated as being one person for the purposes of this section and sections 58C to 58K and 101B below.

DEFINITIONS
"controlled quantity": 1971 Act, s.58B(3).
"hazardous substance": 1971 Act, s.58B(3).
"hazardous substances authority": 1971 Act, ss.1A, 1B, 290(1).
"hazardous substances consent": 1971 Act, ss.58B(1), 290(1).
"land": 1971 Act, s.290(1).

GENERAL NOTE
By virtue of this section the presence of a hazardous substance in excess of the controlled quantity requires hazardous substances consent, subject to the transitional provisions in s.34. The detail of control is to be provided in regulations to be made by the Secretary of State. Enforcement is provided for in the new s.101B (inserted into the 1971 Act by s.32 of this Act).

Applications for hazardous substances consent

58C.—(1) Provision may be made by regulations with respect to—

(*a*) the form and manner in which applications for hazardous substances consent are to be made;

(*b*) the particulars which they are to contain and the evidence by which they are to be verified;

(*c*) the manner in which they are to be advertised; and

(*d*) the time within which they are to be dealt with.

(2) Regulations may provide that an application for hazardous substances consent, or an appeal against the refusal of such an application or against the imposition of a condition on such a consent, shall not be entertained unless it is accompanied by a certificate in the prescribed form and corresponding to one or other of those described in section 27(1)(*a*) to (*d*) of this Act; and any such regulations may—

(*a*) include requirements corresponding to sections 27(2) and (4) and 29(3) of this Act; and

(*b*) make provision as to who is to be treated as the owner of land for the purposes of any provision of the regulations.

(3) If any person issues a certificate which purports to comply with the requirements of regulations made by virtue of subsection (2) above and which contains a statement which he knows to be false or

misleading in a material particular, or recklessly issues a certificate
which purports to comply with those requirements and which contains
a statement which is false or misleading in a material particular, he
shall be guilty of an offence and liable on summary conviction to a
fine of an amount not exceeding level 3 on the standard scale.

(4) Regulations—

(a) may require an applicant for hazardous substances consent or
the hazardous substances authority or both to give publicity to
an application for hazardous substances consent in such manner
as may be prescribed;

(b) may require hazardous substances authorities to conduct appropriate consultations before determining applications for hazardous substances consent;

(c) may provide for the manner in which such a consultation is to
be carried out and the time within which—

(i) such a consultation;

(ii) any stage in such a consultation,

is to be completed;

(d) may require hazardous substances authorities to determine
applications for hazardous substances consent within such time
as may be prescribed;

(e) may require hazardous substances authorities to give prescribed
persons or bodies prescribed information about applications
for hazardous substances consent, including information as to
the manner in which such applications have been dealt with.

(5) In subsection (4) above "appropriate consultations" means—

(a) consultations—

(i) in the case of a hazardous substances authority other than
the appropriate Minister, with the Health and Safety Executive;
and

(ii) in the case of the appropriate Minister, with the Health and
Safety Commission; and

(b) consultations with such persons or bodies as may be prescribed.

(6) Regulations under this section may make different provision for
different cases or descriptions of cases.

DEFINITIONS
"appropriate consultations": subs. (5).
"hazardous substances authority": 1971 Act, ss.1A, 1B, 290(1).
"hazardous substances consent": 1971 Act, ss.58B(1), 290(1).
"land": 1971 Act, s.290(1).

GENERAL NOTE
The detailed procedure for making applications for consent is to be prescribed by
regulations, but will be modelled closely on that for planning applications under the 1971
Act. The major difference lies in the consultation requirements: the authority must consult
with the Health and Safety Executive where so required by regulations, and the regulations
may lay down requirements for that consultation.

Determination of applications for hazardous substances consent
58D.—(1) Subject to the following provisions of this Act, where an
application is made to a hazardous substances authority for hazardous
substances consent, that authority, in dealing with the application,
shall have regard to any material considerations and—

(a) may grant hazardous substances consent, either unconditionally
or subject to such conditions as they think fit; or

(b) may refuse hazardous substances consent.

(2) Without prejudice to the generality of subsection (1) above, in
dealing with an application the authority shall have regard—

(*a*) to any current or contemplated use of the land to which the application relates;

(*b*) to the way in which land in the vicinity is being used or is likely to be used;

(*c*) to any planning permission that has been granted for development of land in the vicinity;

(*d*) to the provisions of the development plan; and

(*e*) to any advice which the Health and Safety Executive or Health and Safety Commission have given following consultations in pursuance of regulations under section 58C(4) above.

(3) If an application relates to more than one hazardous substance, the authority may make different determinations in relation to each.

(4) It shall be the duty of a hazardous substances authority, when granting hazardous substances consent, to include in that consent—

(*a*) a description of the land to which the consent relates;

(*b*) a description of the hazardous substance or substances to which it relates; and

(*c*) in respect of each hazardous substance to which it relates, a statement of the maximum quantity permitted by the consent to be present at any one time and of all conditions relating to that substance subject to which the consent is granted.

(5) Without prejudice to the generality of subsection (1) above, a hazardous substances authority may grant hazardous substances consent subject to conditions with respect to any of the following—

(*a*) how and where any hazardous substance to which the consent relates is to be kept or used;

(*b*) times between which any such substance may be present;

(*c*) the permanent removal of any such substance—

(i) on or before a date specified in the consent; or

(ii) before the end of a period specified in it and commencing on the date on which it is granted;

(*d*) the consent being conditional on the commencement or partial or complete execution of development on the land which is authorised by a specified planning permission;

but an authority who are a hazardous substances authority by virtue of section 1A above may only grant consent subject to conditions as to how a hazardous substance is to be kept or used if the conditions are conditions to which the Health and Safety Executive have advised the authority that any consent they might grant should be subject.

DEFINITIONS

"development plan": 1971 Act, s.290(1).
"hazardous substances authority": 1971 Act, ss.1A, 1B, 290(1).
"hazardous substances consent": 1971 Act, ss.58B(1), 290(1).
"land": 1971 Act, s.290(1).
"planning permission": 1971 Act, s.290(1).

GENERAL NOTE

This section lays the basis for decision making by the hazardous substances authority on applications for consent. Although modelled on s.29 of the 1971 Act, especially in its formulation of the requirement to have regard to material considerations and the power to impose conditions, it contains special provisions in subss. (2)–(5) which specifically require the authority to have regard to other land uses in the vicinity and any planning permission that may have been granted for other land in the vicinity. Special conditions which may be imposed are specified in subs. (5), though a local hazardous substances authority are permitted to impose conditions relating to how a hazardous substance is to be kept or used only if the Health and Safety Executive have advised them to.

Moreover, if there is any conflict between conditions imposed under these powers and the requirements of the Health and Safety Executive, then the latter take precedence (s.58N) and to the extent that any consent or notice issued by the hazardous substances authority requires or allows anything to be done in contravention of Part I of the Health and Safety at Work etc. Act 1974, or of any improvement notice or prohibition notice served under it, it is void.

References to Secretary of State and appeals

58E.—(1) Subject to subsections (2) and (3) below, sections 35 to 37 of this Act shall have effect in relation to applications for hazardous substances consent and to decisions on such applications as though they were applications for planning permission.

(2) In the application of sections 35 to 37 of this Act to hazardous substances consent—

(a) references to the local planning authority shall be construed as references to the hazardous substances authority;

(b) section 35(4) and section 36(5) and (7) shall be omitted;

(c) the words "and in such manner as may be prescribed" shall be substituted for the words in section 36(2) following "time";

(d) in section 37, the words "by the development order" shall be omitted from both places where they occur.

(3) Subsections (1) and (2) above do not have effect in relation to applications for hazardous substances consent relating to land to which section 1B of this Act applies or to decisions on such applications.

DEFINITIONS
"hazardous substances authority": 1971 Act, ss.1A, 1B, 290(1).
"hazardous substances consent": 1971 Act, ss.58B(1), 290(1).
"land": 1971 Act, s.290(1).
"planning permission": 1971 Act, s.290(1).

GENERAL NOTE
A right of appeal (including appeal in default of any decision from the hazardous substances authority within the prescribed time), and power for the Secretary of State to call in an application, are conferred by way of incorporation into these provisions of ss.35 to 37 of the 1971 Act, with appropriate modifications.

Deemed hazardous substances consent by virtue of authorisation of government department

58F.—(1) Where—

(a) the authorisation of a government department is required by virtue of an enactment in respect of development to be carried out by a local authority, or by statutory undertakers not being a local authority; and

(b) the development would involve the presence of a hazardous substance in circumstances requiring hazardous substances consent,

the department may, on granting that authorisation, also direct that hazardous substances consent shall be deemed to be granted subject to such conditions (if any) as may be specified in the directions.

(2) The department shall consult the Health and Safety Commission before issuing any such directions.

(3) The provisions of this Act (except Parts VII and XII) shall apply in relation to any hazardous substances consent deemed to be granted by virtue of directions under this section as if it had been granted by the Secretary of State on an application referred to him under section 35 of this Act, as applied by section 58E of this Act.

(4) The reference is subsection (1) above to the authorisation of a government department is to be construed in accordance with section 40(3) of this Act.

"authorisation of a government department": subs. (4).
"development": 1971 Act, s.290(1).
"hazardous substances consent": 1971 Act, ss.58B(1), 290(1).
"land": 1971 Act, s.290(1).
"local authority": 1971 Act, s.290(1).
"planning permission": 1971 Act, s.290(1).
"statutory undertakers": 1971 Act, s.290(1).

GENERAL NOTE
This section extends s.40 of the 1971 Act, which allows planning permission to be granted directly by a Government department where the development also requires authorisation under another enactment, to the new controls over hazardous substances. Hazardous substances consent may now also be deemed to be granted upon the issuing of such authorisation where the development is to be carried out by a local authority or statutory undertaker.

Grants of hazardous substances consent without compliance with conditions previously attached

58G.—(1) This section applies to an application for hazardous substances consent without a condition subject to which a previous hazardous substances consent was granted.

(2) On such an application the hazardous substances authority shall consider only the question of the conditions subject to which hazardous substances consent should be granted, and—

(a) if they determine that hazardous substances consent should be granted subject to conditions differing from those subject to which the previous consent was granted, or that it should be granted unconditionally, they shall grant hazardous substances consent accordingly; and

(b) if they determine that hazardous substances consent should be granted subject to the same conditions as those subject to which the previous consent was granted, they shall refuse the application.

(3) Where—

(a) hazardous substances consent has been granted or is deemed to have been granted for the presence on, over or under land of more than one hazardous substance; and

(b) an application under this section does not relate to all the substances,

the hazardous substances authority shall only have regard to any condition relating to a substance to which the application does not relate to the extent that it has implications for a substance to which the application does relate.

(4) Where—

(a) more than one hazardous substances consent has been granted or is deemed to have been granted in respect of the same land; and

(b) an application under this section does not relate to all the consents,

the hazardous substances authority shall only have regard to any consent to which the application does not relate to the extent that it has implications for consent to which the application does relate.

(5) Regulations may make provision in relation to applications under this section corresponding to any provision that may be made by regulations under section 58C above in relation to applications for hazardous substances consent.

DEFINITIONS
"hazardous substances authority": 1971 Act, ss.1A, 1B, 290(1).
"hazardous substances consent": 1971 Act, ss.58B(1), 290(1).
"land": 1971 Act, s.290(1).

GENERAL NOTE
This section confers power for the hazardous substances authority to review the conditions
subject to which consent has previously been granted, and corresponds to the new powers
introduced by this Act in relation to planning conditions generally (Sched. 11, para. 4) and
listed building consents (Sched. 9, para. 4).

Power to revoke or modify hazardous substances consent

58H.—(1) If it appears to the hazardous substances authority
that—
  (a) there has been a material change of use of land to which a
      hazardous substances consent relates; or
  (b) planning permission has been granted for development the
      carrying out of which would involve a material change of use
      of such land and the development to which the permission
      relates has been commenced,
they may by order—
  (i) if the consent relates only to one substance revoke it;
  (ii) if it relates to more than one, revoke it or revoke it so far as
      it relates to a specified substance.
  (2) The hazardous substances authority may by order—
  (a) revoke a hazardous substances consent which relates to only
      one substance if it appears to them that that substance has not
      for at least 5 years been present on, under or over the land to
      which the consent relates in a quantity equal to or exceeding
      the controlled quantity; and
  (b) revoke a hazardous substances consent which relates to a
      number of substances if it appears to them that none of those
      substances has for at least 5 years been so present.
  (3) The hazardous substances authority may by order revoke a
hazardous substances consent or modify it to such extent as they
consider expedient if it appears to them, having regard to any material
consideration, that it is expedient to revoke or modify it.
  (4) An order under this section shall specify the grounds on which
it is made.
  (5) An order under this section, other than an order relating to
land to which section 1B of this Act applies, shall not take effect
unless it is confirmed by the Secretary of State, and the Secretary of
State may confirm any such order submitted to him either without
modification or subject to such modification as he considers expedient.
  (6) Where a hazardous substances authority submit an order under
this section to the Secretary of State for his confirmation under this
section, the authority shall serve notice of the order—
  (a) on any person who is an owner of the whole or any part of the
      land to which the order relates;
  (b) on any person other than an owner who appears to them to be
      in control of the whole or any part of that land;
  (c) on any other person who in their opinion will be affected by
      the order;
and if within the period specified in that behalf in the notice (not
being less than 28 days from the service thereof) any person on whom
the notice is served so requires, the Secretary of State, before
confirming the order, shall afford to that person and to the hazardous
substances authority an opportunity of appearing before, and being

heard by, a person appointed by the Secretary of State for that purpose.

(7) Where an order under this section has been confirmed by the Secretary of State, the hazardous substances authority shall serve a copy of the order on every person who was entitled to be served with notice under subsection (6) above.

(8) Section 170 of this Act shall have effect where a hazardous substances consent is revoked or modified by an order made in the exercise of the power conferred by subsection (3) above as it has effect where an order is made under section 51 of this Act, but as if any reference in it to the local planning authority were a reference to the hazardous substances authority.

DEFINITIONS
"hazardous substance": 1971 Act, s.58B(3).
"hazardous substances authority": 1971 Act, ss.1A, 1B, 290(1).
"hazardous substances consent": 1971 Act, ss.58B(1), 290(1).
"land": 1971 Act, s.290(1).
"local planning authority": 1971 Act, s.290(1).
"owner": 1971 Act, s.290(1).

GENERAL NOTE
This section confers three separate powers of revocation of hazardous substances consent, for only one of which is there liability to pay compensation. A further power is conferred by s.58J. The powers are exercisable in different circumstances:
(1) material change of use: where there has been an actual material change of use of the land to which a consent relates, or planning permission has been granted for development involving such a change and the development to which it relates has commenced, then the hazardous substances authority may by order revoke the consent either in full, or so far as it relates to a specified substance (subs. (1)).
(2) less than five years' presence: the authority may also by order revoke a consent where the substance or substances have not been present in a controlled quantity for at least five years (subs. (2)).
(3) the general power: the authority may by order revoke any consent or modify it to such extent as they think expedient (subs. (3)). In this case, they may be liable to pay compensation, by virtue of the extension, by subs. (8), of s.170 of the 1971 Act to orders under subs. (3).
(4) change of person in control of part of the land: consent is automatically revoked without compensation if there is a change of person in control of any part of the land to which the consent relates, unless an application for continuance of the consent has previously been made to the hazardous substances authority (s.58J(2)); and where such an application is made, the authority may modify or revoke the consent (s.58J(4)) subject to compensation liability (s.58J(12)).
The purpose of the first two powers is apparently to allow non-compensable revocation of consent where it has, in effect, been abandoned. The Minister explained in Standing Committee (Standing Committee H, March 25, 1986; col. 437) that the possibility that hazardous uses may be kept on land often restricts the development permitted on neighbouring land, and if the use to which a consent relates has ceased the consent should therefore be revoked as soon as possible.
No order is to take effect without confirmation of the Secretary of State, and owners and other persons on whom notice of the order is served (subs. (6)) have the right to appear before and be heard by an inspector (subs. (6)) before any order is confirmed.

Provisions as to effect of hazardous substances consent and change of control of land

58J.—(1) Without prejudice to the provisions of this Part of this Act, any hazardous substances consent shall (except in so far as it otherwise provides) enure for the benefit of the land to which it relates and of all persons for the time being interested in the land.

(2) A hazardous substances consent is revoked if there is a change in the person in control of part of the land to which it relates, unless

an application for the continuation of the consent has previously been made to the hazardous substances authority.

(3) Regulations may make provision in relation to applications under subsection (2) above corresponding to any provision that may be made by regulations under section 58C of this Act in relation to applications for hazardous substances consent.

(4) When such an application is made, the authority, having regard to any material consideration—

(a) may modify the consent in any way they consider appropriate; or

(b) may revoke it.

(5) Without prejudice to the generality of subsection (4) above, in dealing with an application the authority shall have regard—

(a) to the matters to which a hazardous substances authority are required to have regard by section 58D(2)(a) to (d) above; and

(b) to any advice which the Health and Safety Executive or Health and Safety Commission have given following consultations in pursuance of regulations under subsection (3) above.

(6) If an application relates to more than one consent, the authority may make different determinations in relation to each.

(7) If a consent relates to more than one hazardous substance, the authority may make different determinations in relation to each.

(8) It shall be the duty of a hazardous substances authority, when continuing hazardous substances consent, to attach to the consent one of the following—

(a) a statement that it is unchanged in relation to the matters included in it by virtue of section 58D(4) above;

(b) a statement of any change in respect of those matters.

(9) The modifications which a hazardous substances authority may make by virtue of subsection (4)(a) above include, without prejudice to the generality of that paragraph, the making of the consent subject to conditions with respect to any of the matters mentioned in section 58D(5) above.

(10) Subject to subsection (11) below, sections 35 to 37 of this Act shall have effect in relation to applications under subsection (2) above and to decisions on such applications as though they were applications for planning permission.

(11) In the application of sections 35 to 37 of this Act by virtue of subsection (10) above—

(a) references to the local planning authority shall be construed as references to the hazardous substances authority;

(b) section 35(4) and section 36(5) and (7) shall be omitted;

(c) the words "and in such manner as may be prescribed" shall be substituted for the words in section 36(2) following "time";

(d) in section 37—

(i) the words "by the development order" shall be omitted from the first place where they occur; and

(ii) the words "the application shall be deemed to have been granted" shall be substituted for the words following paragraph (b).

(12) Where the authority modify or revoke the consent, they shall pay to the person in control of the whole of the land before the change compensation in respect of any loss or damage sustained by him and directly attributable to the modification or revocation.

Definitions
  "hazardous substances authority": 1971 Act, ss.1A, 1B, 290(1).
  "hazardous substances consent": 1971 Act, ss.58B(1), 290(1).

"land": 1971 Act, s.290(1).
"local planning authority": 1971 Act, s.290(1).
"planning permission": 1971 Act, s.290(1).

GENERAL NOTE

Although hazardous substances consent, like a planning permission, enures for the benefit of land unless it is expressly limited to a personal consent, it will be revoked automatically in the event of a change in the person in control of part of the land unless an application for the continuance of the consent has previously been made to the hazardous substances authority.

A change of control of the whole of the land does not trigger off the revocation, and the power seems intended to be directed at sub-division of the planning unit. But any change in control of part of the land will result in revocation of the whole of the relevant consent, unless there has been prior application. Moreover, the authority will have power on such application to modify or revoke the whole of the consent, though subject to payment of compensation to the person in control of the whole of the land before the change (subs. (12)).

Offences

58K.—(1) Subject to this Part of this Act, if there is a contravention of hazardous substances control, the appropriate person shall be guilty of an offence.

(2) There is a contravention of hazardous substances control—

(*a*) if a quantity of a hazardous substance equal to or exceeding the controlled quantity is or has been present on, under or over land and either—

(i) there is no hazardous substances consent for the presence of the substance; or

(ii) there is hazardous substances consent for its presence but the quantity present exceeds the maximum quantity permitted by the consent;

(*b*) if there is or has been a failure to comply with a condition subject to which a hazardous substances consent was granted.

(3) In subsection (1) above "the appropriate person" means—

(*a*) in relation to a contravention falling within paragraph (*a*) of subsection (2) above—

(i) any person knowingly causing the substance to be present on, over or under the land;

(ii) any person allowing it to be so present; and

(*b*) in relation to a contravention falling within paragraph (*a*) or (*b*) of that subsection, the person in control of the land.

(4) A person guilty of an offence under this section shall be liable—

(*a*) on summary conviction, to a fine not exceeding the statutory maximum; or

(*b*) on conviction on indictment, to a fine,

and if the contravention is continued after the conviction he shall be guilty of a further offence and liable on summary conviction to a fine not exceeding £200 for each day on which it continues, or on conviction on indictment to a fine.

(5) In any proceedings for an offence under this section it shall be a defence for the accused to prove—

(*a*) that he took all reasonable precautions and exercised all due diligence to avoid commission of the offence, or

(*b*) that commission of the offence could be avoided only by the taking of action amounting to a breach of a statutory duty.

(6) In any proceedings for an offence consisting of a contravention falling within subsection (2)(*a*) above, it shall be a defence for the accused to prove that at the time of the alleged commission of the offence he did not know, and had no reason to believe,—

(*a*) if the case falls within paragraph (*a*)(i)—
  (i) that the substance was present; or
  (ii) that it was present in a quantity equal to or exceeding the controlled quantity;
(*b*) if the case falls within paragraph (*a*)(ii), that the substance was present in a quantity exceeding the maximum quantity permitted by the consent.

(7) In any proceedings for an offence consisting of a contravention falling within subsection (2)(*b*) above, it shall be a defence for the accused to prove that he did not know, and had no reason to believe, that there was a failure to comply with a condition subject to which hazardous substances consent had been granted.

DEFINITIONS
"appropriate person": subs. (3).
"contravention of hazardous substances control": subs. (2).
"controlled quantity": 1971 Act, s.58B(3).
"hazardous substances consent": 1971 Act, ss.58B(1), 290(1).
"land": 1971 Act, s.290(1).

GENERAL NOTE
This section renders contravention of hazardous substances control a criminal offence. There is a contravention if there has been a quantity of hazardous substance equal to or exceeding the controlled quantity without consent, or in excess of consent; or if there has been any breach of a condition on a hazardous substances consent. In the special circumstances specified in s.58L, the Secretary of State is permitted to exclude certain contraventions from liability under this section for up to three months.
  Further enforcement powers are contained in s.32, which inserts a new s.101B in the 1971 Act allowing the authority to issue a special enforcement notice (a hazardous substances contravention notice) specifying the contravention and requiring specified steps to be taken to remedy it.

Emergencies
  58L.—(1) If it appears to the Secretary of State—
  (*a*) either—
      (i) that the community or part of it is being or is likely to be deprived of an essential service or commodity; or
      (ii) that there is or is likely to be a shortage of such a service or commodity affecting the community or part of it; and
  (*b*) that the presence of a hazardous substance on, over or under land specified in the direction in circumstances such that hazardous substances consent would be required, is necessary for the effective provision of that service or commodity,
he may direct that, subject to such conditions or exceptions as he thinks fit, the presence of the substance on, over or under the land is not to constitute a contravention of hazardous substances control so long as the direction remains in force.
  (2) A direction under this section—
  (*a*) may be withdrawn at any time;
  (*b*) shall in any case cease to have effect at the end of the period of three months beginning with the day on which it was given, but without prejudice to the Secretary of State's power to give a further direction.
  (3) Subject to subsection (4) below, the Secretary of State shall send a copy of any such direction to the authority which are the hazardous substances authority in relation to the land.

(4) Where the land is land to which section 1B of this Act applies, the Secretary of State shall send the copy to the authority which would be the hazardous substances authority in relation to the land but for that section.

"contravention of hazardous substances control": 1971 Act, s.58K(1).
"hazardous substance": 1971 Act, s.58B(3).
"hazardous substances authority": 1971 Act, ss.1A, 1B, 290(1).
"hazardous substances consent": 1971 Act, ss.58B(1), 290(1).
"land": 1971 Act, s.290(1).

GENERAL NOTE
This section confers on the Secretary of State a special power of exemption from criminal liability under the preceding section, and from enforcement action under s.101B, where an essential service or commodity is at stake and the presence of some hazardous substance requiring consent is necessary for the effective provision of the service or commodity. It is a temporary exemption, limited to a maximum period of three months, although with power for the Secretary of State to make further orders. If it is intended that the presence of the substance should continue beyond that period, then application for express consent may be made within the exemption period.

Registers, etc.
58M.—(1) Every authority which is a hazardous substances authority by virtue of section 1A of this Act shall keep, in such manner as may be prescribed, a register containing such information as may be prescribed with respect—
    (*a*) to applications for hazardous substances consent—
        (i) made to that authority; or
        (ii) made to the appropriate Minister with respect to land in relation to which, but for section 1B of this Act, that authority would be the hazardous substances authority;
        and including information as to the manner in which such applications have been dealt with;
    (*b*) to hazardous substances consent deemed to be granted under section 23 of the Housing and Planning Act 1986 with respect to land in relation to which that authority is, or but for section 1B of this Act would be, the hazardous substances authority;
    (*c*) to revocations or modifications of hazardous substances consent granted with respect to such land; and
    (*d*) to directions under section 58L of this Act sent to the authority by the Secretary of State.
(2) Where with respect to any land the appropriate Minister exercises any of the functions of a hazardous substances authority, he shall send to the authority which but for section 1B of this Act would be the hazardous substances authority in relation to the land any such information as appears to him to be required by them for the purposes of maintaining a register under this section.
(3) Every register kept under this section shall be available for inspection by the public at all reasonable hours.

"hazardous substances authority": 1971 Act, ss.1A, 1B, 290(1).
"hazardous substances consent": 1971 Act, ss.58B(1), 290(1).
"land": 1971 Act, s.290(1).

GENERAL NOTE
All hazardous substances authorities are required to keep a public register of applications, consents, revocations, modifications and directions under s.58L.

Health and safety requirements
58N.—(1) Nothing in—
(*a*) any hazardous substances consent granted or deemed to be granted under—
(i) the preceding provisions of this Act; or
(ii) section 34 of the Housing and Planning Act 1986; or
(*b*) any hazardous substances contravention notice issued under section 101B of this Act,
shall require or allow anything to be done in contravention of any of the relevant statutory provisions or any prohibition notice or improvement notice served under or by virtue of any of those provisions; and to the extent that such a consent or notice purports to require or allow any such thing to be done, it shall be void.
(2) Where it appears to a hazardous substances authority who have granted, or are deemed to have granted, a hazardous substances consent or who have issued a hazardous substances contravention notice that the consent or notice or part of it is rendered void by subsection (1) above, the authority shall, as soon as is reasonably practicable, consult the appropriate body with regard to the matter.
(3) If the appropriate body advise the authority that the consent or notice is rendered wholly void, the authority shall revoke it.
(4) If they advise that part of the consent or notice is rendered void, the authority shall so modify it as to render it wholly operative.
(5) In this section—
"the appropriate body" means—
(*a*) in relation to a hazardous substances authority other than the appropriate Minister, the Health and Safety Executive; and
(*b*) in relation to the appropriate Minister, the Health and Safety Commission; and
"relevant statutory provisions", "improvement notice" and "prohibition notice" have the same meanings as in Part I of the Health and Safety at Work etc. Act 1974.".

DEFINITIONS
"appropriate body": subs. (5).
"hazardous substances contravention notice": 1971 Act, s.101B(3).
"hazardous substances authority": 1971 Act, ss.1A, 1B, 290(1).
"hazardous substances consent": 1971 Act, ss.58B(1), 290(1).
"improvement notice": subs. (5).
"prohibition notice": subs. (5).
"relevant statutory provisions": subs. (5).

GENERAL NOTE
Where there is any conflict between action taken by a hazardous substances authority under these provisions, and any requirment of Part I of the Health and Safety at Work, etc. Act 1974, or an improvement notice or prohibition notice issued thereunder, then those requirements prevail.

Hazardous substances contravention notices
32. The following shall be inserted after section 101A of the Town and Country Planning Act 1971—

"Hazardous substances

Power to issue hazardous substances contravention notice
101B.—(1) Subject to subsection (2) below, where it appears to the hazardous substances authority that there is or has been a contravention of hazardous substances control, they may issue a hazardous substances contravention notice if they consider it expedient to do so having regard to any material consideration.

(2) A hazardous substances authority shall not issue a hazardous substances contravention notice where it appears to them that a contravention of hazardous substances control can be avoided only by the taking of action amounting to a breach of a statutory duty.

(3) In this Act "hazardous substances contravention notice" means a notice—

(*a*) specifying an alleged contravention of hazardous substances control; and

(*b*) requiring such steps as may be specified in the notice to be taken to remedy the contravention.

(4) A copy of a hazardous substances contravention notice shall be served—

(*a*) on the owner of the land to which it relates;

(*b*) on any person other than the owner who appears to the hazardous substances authority to be in control of that land; and

(*c*) on such other persons as may be prescribed.

(5) A hazardous substances contravention notice shall also specify—

(*a*) a date not less than 28 days from the date of service of copies of the notice as the date on which it is to take effect;

(*b*) in respect of each of the steps required to be taken to remedy the contravention of hazardous substances control, the period from the notice taking effect within which the step is to be taken.

(6) Where a hazardous substances authority issue a hazardous substances contravention notice the steps required by the notice may, without prejudice to the generality of subsection (3)(*b*) above, if the authority think it expedient, include a requirement that the hazardous substance be removed from the land.

(7) Where a notice includes such a requirement, it may also contain a direction that at the end of such period as may be specified in the notice any hazardous substances consent for the presence of the substance shall cease to have effect or, if it relates to more than one substance, shall cease to have effect so far as it relates to the substance which is required to be removed.

(8) The hazardous substances authority may withdraw a hazardous substances contravention notice (without prejudice to their power to issue another) at any time before it takes effect.

(9) If they do so, they shall forthwith give notice of the withdrawal to every person who was served with a copy of the notice.

(10) The Secretary of State may by regulations—

(*a*) specify matters which are to be included in hazardous substances contravention notices, in addition to those which are required to be included in them by this section;

(*b*) provide—

(i) for appeals to him against hazardous substances contravention notices;

(ii) for the persons by whom, grounds upon which and time within which such an appeal may be brought;

(iii) for the procedure to be followed on such appeals;

(iv) for the directions that may be given on such an appeal;

(v) for the application to such appeals, subject to such modifications as the regulations may specify, of any of the provisions of sections 88 to 88B, 243 and 246 of this Act;

(*c*) direct that any of the provisions of sections 89 to 93 of this Act shall have effect in relation to hazardous substances contravention notices subject to such modifications as he may specify in the regulations;

(d) make such other provision as he considers necessary or expedient in relation to hazardous substances contravention notices.

(11) If any person appeals against a hazardous substances contravention notice, the notice shall be of no effect pending the final determination or the withdrawal of the appeal.

(12) Regulations under this section may make different provision for different cases or descriptions of cases.".

DEFINITIONS
"appropriate body": subs. (5).
"contravention of hazardous substances control": 1971 Act, s.58K(2).
"hazardous substances contravention notice": subs. (3).
"hazardous substances authority": 1971 Act, ss.1A, 1B, 290(1).
"hazardous substances consent": 1971 Act, ss.58B(1), 290(1).
"land": 1971 Act, s.290(1).
"owner": 1971 Act, s.290(1).

GENERAL NOTE
This section makes provision for enforcement of hazardous substances control, through procedures modelled on those relating to the enforcement of planning control under the 1971 Act. Liability to enforcement action is independent from, and additional to, criminal liability under s.58K. The enforcement procedures in this section are intended to be remedial: the authority are empowered to serve a notice requiring the owner, or person otherwise in control, of the land to take such steps as are specified in the notice, within such time as may be specified, to remedy the contravention. The section does not impose any direct criminal liability for failure to comply with a notice, but the Secretary of State is empowered by subs. (10) to make regulations for the purpose, *inter alia*, of directing that the provisions of ss.89–93 (which deal with liability under, and the effect of, planning enforcement notices) shall extend to notices under this section, subject to such modifications as he may specify.

Consequential amendments

33. The enactments mentioned in Part I of Schedule 7 to this Act shall have effect with the amendments there specified, being amendments consequential on the provisions of this Part of this Act.

GENERAL NOTE
The amendments made in Sched. 7 are all consequential, and are intended principally to tie control of hazardous substances into the 1971 Act and other related legislation.

Transitional

34.—(1) Until the end of the transitional period—

(a) no offence is committed under section 58K of the Town and Country Planning Act 1971; and

(b) no hazardous substances contravention notice may be issued, in relation to a hazardous substance which is on, under or over any land,

if the substance was present on, under or over the land at any time within the establishment period and—

(i) in a case in which at the commencement date notification in respect of the substance was required by any of the Notification Regulations, both the conditions specified in subsection (2) below were satisfied; and

(ii) in a case in which at that date such notification was not so required, the condition specified in paragraph (b) of that subsection is satisfied.

(2) The conditions mentioned in subsection (1) above are—

(*a*) that notification required by the Notification Regulations was given before the commencement date; and

(*b*) that the substance has not been present during the transitional period in a quantity greater in aggregate than the established quantity.

(3) Where a hazardous substance was present on, under or over any land at any time within the establishment period, hazardous substances consent may be claimed in respect of its presence.

(4) A claim shall be made in the prescribed form before the end of the transitional period and shall contain the prescribed information as to the presence of the substance during the establishment period and as to how and where it was kept and used immediately before the commencement date.

(5) Subject to subsections (6) to (8) below, the hazardous substances authority shall be deemed to have granted any hazardous substances consent which is claimed under subsection (3) above.

(6) If at the commencement date notification in respect of the substance was required by regulation 3 or 5 of the Notification Regulations, hazardous substances consent is only to be deemed to be granted under this section if notification in respect of the substance was given before that date in accordance with those regulations.

(7) If at the commencement date such notification was not so required, hazardous substances consent is only to be deemed to be granted under this section if an aggregate quantity of the substance not less than the controlled quantity was present at any one time within the establishment period.

(8) If it appears to the hazardous substances authority that a claim for hazardous substances consent does not comply with subsection (4) above, it shall be their duty, before the end of the period of two weeks from their receipt of the claim,—

(*a*) to notify the claimant that in their opinion the claim is invalid; and

(*b*) to give him their reasons for that opinion.

(9) Hazardous substances consent which is deemed to be granted under this section is subject to the conditions that—

(*a*) the maximum aggregate quantity of the substance that may be present—

    (i) on, under or over the land to which the claim relates;

    (ii) on, under or over other land which is within 500 metres of it and controlled by the same person; or

    (iii) in or on a structure controlled by the same person any part of which is within 500 metres of it,

at any one time shall not exceed the established quantity; and

(*b*) the substance shall be kept and used in the place and manner in which information supplied in pursuance of regulations made by virtue of subsection (4) above shows that it was kept and used immediately before the commencement date, and

(*c*) none of the substance shall be kept or used in a container greater in capacity than the container, or the largest of the containers, in which the substance was kept or used immediately before the commencement date.

(10) In this section—

    "commencement date" means the date on which this Part of this Act comes into force;

    "the establishment period" means the period of 12 months immediately preceding the commencement date;

    "established quantity" means, in relation to any land—

(*a*) where before the commencement date there has been a notification in respect of a substance in accordance with any of the Notification Regulations—

    (i) the quantity notified or last notified before the commencement date; or

    (ii) a quantity equal to twice the quantity which was so notified or last notified before the start of the establishment period,

whichever is greater;

(*b*) where a notification was not required before that date by any of those regulations, a quantity exceeding by 50 per cent, the maximum quantity which was present on, under or over the land at any one time within the establishment period;

"Notification Regulations" means the Notification of Installations Handling Hazardous Substances Regulations 1982;

"the transitional period" means the period of 6 months beginning with the commencement date;

and other expressions have the same meanings as in the Town and Country Planning Act 1971.

DEFINITIONS
    "commencement date": subs. (10).
    "the establishment period": subs. (10).
    "established quantity": subs. (10).
    "hazardous substances authority": 1971 Act, ss.1A, 1B, 290(1).
    "hazardous substances consent": 1971 Act, ss.58B(1), 290(1).
    "land": 1971 Act, s.290(1).
    "Notification Regulations": subs. (10).
    "the transitional period": subs. (10).

GENERAL NOTE
    The transitional arrangements established by this section are important because the hazardous substances régime does not have a purely prospective effect. The new controls extend not only to the introduction of hazardous substances on to land in the future, but also to existing sites where hazardous substances are present. Consent must therefore be obtained where necessary for all existing sites, and the Act allows a six month transitional period following the commencement date of these provisions for consent to be obtained. During that period no offence is committed under s.58K, and no notice may be issued under s.101B, provided that the volume of the substance remains at or below the "established quantity" (subs. (10)), and that, if notification was required under the Notification Regulations, it had been given before the commencement date.

    Although hazardous substances consent is required for the future in all cases, there is an entitlement to receive consent if a hazardous substance was present at the land at any time within the period of 12 months preceding the commencement date (subs. (3)); and such consent is deemed to have been granted by the hazardous substances authority upon a valid claim being submitted under subs. (3). The deemed consent is, however, subject to the conditions imposed by subs. (9). The authority need not issue a consent as such, since it is deemed to be granted upon the making of the claim. Subs. (8) therefore requires the authority to notify a claimant within two weeks of the claim if they are of the opinion that the claim is invalid, and give their reasons.

Scotland

Hazardous substances—Scotland

35. The following shall be inserted after section 56AA of the Town and Country Planning (Scotland) Act 1972—

"Hazardous substances

Hazardous substances
56A.—(1) Subject to subsection (2) of this section and to section 56B below, it shall be the duty of the planning authority to control hazardous substances in accordance with the provisions of this Act.

(2) An urban development corporation shall control hazardous substances in their area if they are the planning authority in relation to all kinds of development.

DEFINITIONS
"planning authority": Local Government (Scotland) Act 1973, s.172(3).
"urban development corporation": 1972 Act, s.275(1).

GENERAL NOTE
Control over hazardous substances is in Scotland the function of the planning authority, and there is therefore no separate designation of "hazardous substances authority." In the case of operational land of statutory undertakers the function vests in "the appropriate Minister" (new s.56B below), and urban development corporations will have the function in their areas if they are the local planning authority in relation to all kinds of development.

Hazardous substances—statutory undertakers
56B.—(1) The appropriate Minister shall be the planning authority in respect of hazardous substances in relation to land to which this section applies.

(2) This section applies—
(*a*) to operational land of statutory undertakers;
(*b*) to land in which statutory undertakers hold, or propose to acquire, an interest with a view to the land being used as operational land.

(3) For the purposes of this section any land to which this subsection applies but which is not operational land of statutory undertakers authorised to carry on a harbour shall be treated as if it were such operational land.

(4) Subsection (3) above applies—
(*a*) to a wharf; and
(*b*) to harbour land,
as defined in the Harbours Act 1964.

(5) Any question whether subsection (3) above applies to land shall be determined by the Secretary of State and the Minister who is the appropriate Minister in relation to operational land of statutory undertakers who are authorised to carry on harbour undertakings.

DEFINITIONS
"appropriate Minister": 1972 Act, s.275(1).
"land": 1972 Act, s.275(1).
"operational land": 1972 Act, s.275(1).
"statutory undertakers": 1972 Act, s.275(1).

GENERAL NOTE
The hazardous substances authority in relation to operational land, or prospective operational land, of statutory undertakers is to be the "appropriate Minister," which is, by virtue of s.275(1) of the 1972 Act, to be the Minister to whom the function is assigned by s.213 of that Act. All wharves and harbour land are to be treated for the purposes of this section as if they were operational land of statutory undertakers.

Requirement of hazardous substances consent
56C.—(1) Subject to the provisions of this Part of this Act, the presence of a hazardous substance on, over or under land requires the consent of the planning authority (in this Act referred to as

"hazardous substances consent") unless the aggregate quantity of the substance—
  (*a*) on, under or over the land;
  (*b*) on, under or over other land which is within 500 metres of it and controlled by the same person; or
  (*c*) in or on a structure controlled by the same person any part of which is within 500 metres of it,
is less than the controlled quantity.

(2) The temporary presence of a hazardous substance while it is being transported from one place to another is not to be taken into account unless it is unloaded.

(3) The Secretary of State—
  (*a*) shall by regulations specify—
      (i) the substances that are hazardous substances for the purposes of this Act;
      (ii) the quantity which is to be the controlled quantity of any such substance;
  (*b*) may by regulations provide that hazardous substances consent is not required or is only required—
      (i) in relation to land of prescribed descriptions;
      (ii) by reason of the presence of hazardous substances in prescribed circumstances;
  (*c*) may by regulations provide that, except in such circumstances as may be prescribed, all hazardous substances falling within a group specified in the regulations are to be treated as a single substance for the purposes of this Act.

(4) Regulations which—
  (*a*) are made by virtue of sub-paragraph (i) of subsection (3)(*a*) above; or
  (*b*) are made by virtue of sub-paragraph (ii) of that paragraph and reduce the controlled quantity of a substance,
may make such transitional provision as appears to the Secretary of State to be appropriate.

(5) The power to make such transitional provision includes, without prejudice to its generality, power to apply section 38 of the Housing and Planning Act 1986 subject to such modifications as appear to the Secretary of State to be appropriate.

(6) Regulations under this section may make different provision for different cases or descriptions of cases.

(7) Bodies corporate which are inter-connected for the purposes of the Fair Trading Act 1973 are to be treated as being one person for the purposes of this section and sections 56D to 56L and 97B below.

DEFINITIONS
"controlled quantity": subs. (3).
"hazardous substance": subs. (3).
"hazardous substances consent": 1972 Act, ss.56C(1), 275(1).
"land": Act of 1972, s.275(1).

GENERAL NOTE
By virtue of this section the presence of a hazardous substance in excess of the controlled quantity requires hazardous substances consent, subject to the transitional provisions in s.38. The detail of control is to be provided in regulations to be made by the Secretary of State. Enforcement is provided for in the new s.97B (inserted into the 1972 Act by s.36 of this Act).

Applications for hazardous substances consent
  56D.—(1) Provision may be made by regulations with respect to—

(a) the form and manner in which applications for hazardous substances consent are to be made;

(b) the particulars which they are to contain and the evidence by which they are to be verified;

(c) the manner in which they are to be advertised; and

(d) the time within which they are to be dealt with.

(2) Regulations may provide that an application for hazardous substances consent, or an appeal against the refusal of such an application or against the imposition of a condition on such a consent, shall not be entertained unless it is accompanied by a certificate in the prescribed form and corresponding to one or other of those described in section 24(1)(a) to (d) of this Act and any such regulations may—

(a) include requirements corresponding to those mentioned in sections 23(1), 24(2) and (4) and 26(3) of this Act; and

(b) make provision as to who is to be treated as the owner of land for the purposes of any provision of the regulations.

(3) If any person issues a certificate which purports to comply with the requirements of regulations made by virtue of subsection (2) above and which contains a statement which he knows to be false or misleading in a material particular, or recklessly issues a certificate which purports to comply with those requirements and which contains a statement which is false or misleading in a material particular, he shall be guilty of an offence and liable on summary conviction to a fine not exceeding level 3 on the standard scale.

(4) Regulations—

(a) may require an applicant for hazardous substances consent or the planning authority or both to give publicity to an application for hazardous substances consent in such manner as may be prescribed;

(b) may require the planning authority to conduct appropriate consultations before determining applications for hazardous substances consent;

(c) may provide for the manner in which such a consultation is to be carried out and the time within which—

(i) such a consultation;

(ii) any stage in such a consultation,

is to be completed;

(d) may require the planning authority to determine applications for hazardous substances consent within such time as may be prescribed;

(e) may require the planning authority to give prescribed persons or bodies prescribed information about applications for hazardous substances consent including information as to the manner in which such applications have been dealt with.

(5) In subsection (4) above "appropriate consultations" means—

(a) consultations—

(i) in the case of a planning authority other than the appropriate Minister, with the Health and Safety Executive; and

(ii) in the case of the appropriate Minister, with the Health and Safety Commission; and

(b) consultations with such persons or bodies as may be prescribed.

(6) Regulations under this section may make different provision for different cases or descriptions of cases.

DEFINITIONS

"appropriate consultations": subs. (5).

"hazardous substances consent": 1972 Act, ss.56C(1), 275(1).

"land": 1972 Act, s.275(1).

GENERAL NOTE
The detailed procedure for making applications for consent is to be prescribed by regulations, but will be modelled closely on that for planning applications under the 1972 Act. The major difference lies in the consultation requirements: the authority must consult with the Health and Safety Executive where so required by regulations, and the regulations may lay down requirements for that consultation.

Determination of applications for hazardous substances consent

56E.—(1) Subject to the following provisions of this Act, where an application is made to a planning authority for hazardous substances consent, that authority, in dealing with the application, shall have regard to any material considerations, and—

(*a*) may grant hazardous substances consent, either unconditionally or subject to such conditions as they think fit; or

(*b*) may refuse hazardous substances consent.

(2) Without prejudice to the generality of subsection (1) above, in dealing with an application the authority shall have regard—

(*a*) to any current or contemplated use of the land to which the application relates;

(*b*) to the way in which land in the vicinity is being used or is likely to be used;

(*c*) to any planning permission that has been granted for development of land in the vicinity;

(*d*) to the provisions of the development plan; and

(*e*) to any advice which the Health and Safety Executive or Health and Safety Commission have given following consultations in pursuance of regulations under section 56D(4) above.

(3) If an application relates to more than one hazardous substance, the authority may make different determinations in relation to each.

(4) It shall be the duty of a planning authority, when granting hazardous substances consent, to include in that consent—

(*a*) a description of the land to which the consent relates;

(*b*) a description of the hazardous substance or substances to which it relates; and

(*c*) in respect of each hazardous substance to which it relates, a statement of the maximum amount permitted by the consent to be present at any one time and of all conditions relating to that substance subject to which the consent is granted.

(5) Without prejudice to the generality of subsection (1) above, a planning authority may grant hazardous substances consent subject to conditions with respect to any of the following—

(*a*) how and where any hazardous substance to which the consent relates is to be kept or used;

(*b*) times between which any such substance may be present;

(*c*) the permanent removal of any such substance—

(i) on or before a date specified in the consent; or

(ii) before the end of a period specified in it and commencing on the date on which it is granted;

(*d*) the consent being conditional on the commencement or partial or complete execution of development on the land which is authorised by a specified planning permission,

but a planning authority other than the appropriate Minister may only grant consent subject to conditions as to how a hazardous substance is to be kept or used if the conditions are conditions to which the Health and Safety Executive have advised the authority that any consent they might grant should be subject.

DEFINITIONS
"development plan": 1972 Act, s.275(1).
"hazardous substances consent": 1972 Act, ss.56C(1), 275(1).
"land": 1972 Act, s.275(1).
"planning permission": 1972 Act, s.275(1).

GENERAL NOTE
This section lays the basis for decision making by the planning authority on applications
for consent. Although modelled on s.26 of the 1972 Act, especially in its formulation of the
requirement to have regard to material considerations and the power to impose conditions,
it contains special provisions in subss. (2)–(5) which specifically require the authority to have
regard to other land uses in the vicinity and any planning permission that may have been
granted for other land in the vicinity. Special conditions which may be imposed are specified
in subs. (5), though a planning authority are permitted to impose conditions relating to how
a hazardous substance is to be kept or used only if the Health and Safety Executive have
advised them to.
Moreover, if there is any conflict between conditions imposed under these powers and the
requirements of the Health and Safety Executive; then the latter take precedence (s.56O)
and to the extent that any consent or notice issued by the planning authority requires or
allows anything to be done in contravention of Part I of the Health and Safety at Work, etc.
Act 1974, or of any improvement notice or prohibition notice served under it, it is void.

**References to regional planning authority and Secretary of State and
appeals**
56F.—(1) Subject to subsections (2) and (3) below, sections 32 to
34 of this Act and section 179 (reference of applications to regional
planning authority) of the Local Government (Scotland) Act 1973
shall have effect in relation to applications for hazardous substances
consent and to decisions on such applications as though they were
applications for planning permission.
(2) In the application of sections 32 to 34 of this Act to hazardous
substances consent—
   (*a*) section 32(4) and section 33(5) and (7) shall be omitted;
   (*b*) the words "and in such manner as may be prescribed" shall be
        substituted for the words in section 33(2) following "time";
   (*c*) in section 34, the words "by the development order" shall be
        omitted from both places where they occur.
(3) Subsections (1) and (2) above do not have effect in relation to
applications for hazardous substances consent relating to land to
which section 56B of this Act applies or to decisions on such
applications.

DEFINITIONS
"hazardous substances consent": 1972 Act, ss.56C(1), 275(1).
"land": 1972 Act, s.275(1).
"planning authority": Local Government (Scotland) Act 1973, s.172(3).
"planning permission": 1972 Act, s.275(1).

GENERAL NOTE
A right of appeal (including appeal in default of any decision from the planning authority
within the prescribed time), and power for the regional planning authority to call in an
application, are conferred by way of incorporation into these provisions of ss.32 to 34 of the
1972 Act and s.179 of the Local Government (Scotland) Act 1973, with appropriate
modifications.

**Deemed hazardous substances consent by virtue of authorisation of
government department**
56G.—(1) Where—
   (*a*) the authorisation of a government department is required by
        virtue of an enactment in respect of development to be carried
        out by a local authority, or by statutory undertakers not being
        a local authority; and

(*b*) the development would involve the presence of a hazardous
substance in circumstances requiring hazardous substances
consent,
the department may, on granting that authorisation, also direct that
hazardous substances consent for that development shall be deemed
to be granted subject to such conditions (if any) as may be specified
in the directions.

(2) The department shall consult the Health and Safety Commission
before issuing any such directions.

(3) The provisions of this Act (except Parts VII and XII) shall apply
in relation to any hazardous substances consent deemed to be granted
by virtue of directions under this section as if it had been granted by
the Secretary of State on an application referred to him under section
32 of this Act, as applied by section 56F of this Act.

(4) The reference in subsection (1) above to the authorisation of a
government department is to be construed in accordance with section
37(3) of this Act.

DEFINITIONS
  "authorisation of a government department": subs. (4).
  "development": 1972 Act, s.275(1).
  "hazardous substances consent": 1972 Act, ss.56C(1), 275(1).
  "land": 1972 Act, s.275(1).
  "local authority": 1972 Act, s.275(1).
  "planning permission": 1972 Act, s.275(1).
  "statutory undertakers": 1972 Act, s.275(1).

GENERAL NOTE
This section extends s.37 of the 1972 Act, which allows planning permission to be granted
directly by a Government department where the development also requires authorisation
under another enactment, to the new hazardous substances régime. Hazardous substances
consent may now also be deemed to be granted upon the issuing of such authorisation,
where the development is to be carried out by a local authority or statutory undertaker.

**Grants of hazardous substances consent without compliance with
    conditions previously attached**

56H.—(1) This section applies to an application for hazardous
substances consent without a condition subject to which a previous
hazardous substances consent was granted or is deemed to have been
granted.

(2) On such an application the planning authority shall consider
only the question of the conditions subject to which hazardous
substances consent should be granted, and—
  (*a*) if they determine that hazardous substances consent should be
      granted subject to conditions differing from those subject to
      which the previous consent was granted, or that it should be
      granted unconditionally, they shall grant hazardous substances
      consent accordingly; and
  (*b*) if they determine that hazardous substances consent should be
      granted subject to the same conditions as those subject to
      which the previous consent was granted, they shall refuse the
      application.

(3) Where—
  (*a*) hazardous substances consent has been granted or is deemed
      to have been granted for the presence on, over or under land
      of more than one hazardous substance; and
  (*b*) an application under this section does not relate to all the
      substances,
the planning authority shall only have regard to any condition relating
to a substance to which the application does not relate to the extent

that it has implications for a substance to which the application does relate.

(4) Where—

(*a*) more than one hazardous substances consent has been granted or is deemed to have been granted in respect of the same land; and

(*b*) an application under this section does not relate to all the consents,

the planning authority shall only have regard to any consent to which the application does not relate to the extent that it has implications for a consent to which the application does relate.

(5) Regulations may make provision in relation to applications under this section corresponding to any provision that may be made by regulations under section 56D of this Act in relation to applications for hazardous substances consent.

DEFINITIONS
"hazardous substances consent": 1972 Act, ss.56B(1), 275(1).
"land": 1972 Act, s.275(1).
"planning authority": Local Government (Scotland) Act 1973, s.172(3).

GENERAL NOTE
This section confers power for the planning authority to review the conditions subject to which consent has previously been granted, and corresponds to the new powers introduced by this Act in relation to planning conditions generally (Sched. 11, para. 31) and listed building consents (Sched. 9, para. 17).

Power to revoke or modify hazardous substances consent

56J.—(1) If it appears to the planning authority that—

(*a*) there has been a material change of use of land to which a hazardous substances consent relates; or

(*b*) planning permission has been granted for development the carrying out of which would involve a material change of use of such land and the development to which the permission relates has been commenced,

they may by order—

(i) if the consent relates only to one substance, revoke it;

(ii) if it relates to more than one, revoke it or revoke it so far as it relates to a specified substance.

(2) The planning authority may by order—

(*a*) revoke a hazardous substances consent which relates to only one substance if it appears to them that that substance has not for at least 5 years been present on, under or over the land to which the consent relates in a quantity equal to or exceeding the controlled quantity; and

(*b*) revoke a hazardous substances consent which relates to a number of substances if it appears to them that none of those substances has for at least 5 years been so present.

(3) The planning authority may by order revoke a hazardous substances consent or modify it to such extent as they consider expedient if it appears to them, having regard to any material consideration, that it is expedient to revoke or modify it.

(4) An order under this section shall specify the grounds on which it is being made.

(5) An order under this section, other than an order relating to land to which section 56B of this Act applies, shall not take effect unless it is confirmed by the Secretary of State, and the Secretary of State may confirm any such order submitted to him either without modification or subject to such modification as he considers expedient.

(6) Where a planning authority submit an order under this section to the Secretary of State for his confirmation under this section, the authority shall serve notice of the order on—

  (a) any person who is an owner, occupier or lessee of the whole or any part of the land to which the order relates; and

  (b) any other person who in their opinion will be affected by the order;

and if within the period specified in that behalf in the notice (not being less than 28 days from the service thereof) any person on whom the notice is served so requires, the Secretary of State, before confirming the order, shall afford to that person and to the planning authority an opportunity of appearing before, and being heard by, a person appointed by the Secretary of State for that purpose.

(7) Where an order under this section has been confirmed by the Secretary of State, the planning authority shall serve a copy of the order on every person who was entitled to be served with notice under subsection (6) of this section.

(8) Section 159 of this Act shall have effect where a hazardous substances consent is revoked or modified by an order made in the exercise of the power conferred by subsection (3) of this section as it has effect where an order is made under section 49 of this Act.

DEFINITIONS

  "hazardous substance": 1972 Act, s.56C(3).
  "hazardous substances consent": 1972 Act, ss.56C(1), 275(1).
  "land": 1972 Act, s.275(1).
  "owner": 1972 Act, s.275(1).
  "planning authority": Local Government (Scotland) Act 1973, s.172(3).

GENERAL NOTE

  This section confers three separate powers of revocation of hazardous substances consent, for only one of which is there liability to pay compensation. A further power is conferred by s.56K.

  See further the General Note to the corresponding section (s.58H) of the English provisions above.

Provisions as to effect of hazardous substances consent and change of control of land

56K.—(1) Without prejudice to the provisions of this Part of this Act, any hazardous substances consent shall (except in so far as it otherwise provides) enure for the benefit of the land to which it relates and of all persons for the time being interested in the land.

(2) A hazardous substances consent is revoked if there is a change in the person in control of part of the land to which it relates unless an application for the continuation of the consent has previously been made to the planning authority.

(3) Regulations may make provision in relation to applications under subsection (2) above corresponding to any provision that may be made by regulations under section 56D of this Act in relation to applications for hazardous substances consent.

(4) When such application is made, the authority, having regard to any material consideration—

  (a) may modify the consent in any way they consider appropriate; or

  (b) may revoke it.

(5) Without prejudice to the generality of subsection (4) above, in dealing with an application the authority shall have regard—

  (a) to the matters to which a planning authority are required to have regard by section 56E(2)(a) to (d) above; and

(b) to any advice which the Health and Safety Executive or Health and Safety Commission have given following consultations in pursuance of regulations under subsection (3) above.

(6) If an application relates to more than one consent, the authority may make different determinations in relation to each.

(7) If a consent relates to more than one hazardous substance, the authority may make different determinations in relation to each.

(8) It shall be the duty of a planning authority, when continuing hazardous substances consent, to attach to the consent one of the following—

(a) a statement that is unchanged in relation to the matters included in it by virtue of section 56E(4) above;

(b) a statement of any change in respect of those matters.

(9) The modifications which a planning authority may make by virtue of subsection (4)(a) above include, without prejudice to the generality of that paragraph, the making of the consent subject to conditions with respect to any of the matters mentioned in section 56E(5) above.

(10) Subject to subsection (11) below, sections 32 to 34 of this Act and section 179 of the Local Government (Scotland) Act 1973 shall have effect in relation to applications under subsection (2) above and to decisions on such applications as though they were applications for planning permission.

(11) In the application of sections 32 to 34 of this Act by virtue of subsection (10) above—

(a) section 32(4) and section 33(5) and (7) shall be omitted;

(b) the words "and in such manner as may be prescribed" shall be substituted for the words in section 33(2) following "time";

(c) in section 34—

(i) the words "by the development order" shall be omitted from the first place where they occur; and

(ii) the words "the application shall be deemed to have been granted" shall be substituted for the words following paragraph (b).

(12) Where the authority modify or revoke the consent, they shall pay to the person in control of the whole of the land before the change compensation in respect of any loss or damage sustained by him and directly attributable to the modification or revocation.

DEFINITIONS
"hazardous substances consent": 1972 Act, ss.56C(1), 275(1).
"land": 1972 Act, s.275(1).
"planning authority": Local Government (Scotland) Act 1973, s.172(3).
"planning permission": 1972 Act, s.275(1).

GENERAL NOTE
Although hazardous substances consent, like a planning permission, enures for the benefit of land unless it is expressly limited to a personal consent, it will be revoked automatically in the event of a change in the person in control of part of the land unless an application for the continuance of the consent has previously been made to the planning authority.

A change of control of the whole of the land does not trigger off the revocation, and the power thus seems to be directed at sub-division of the planning unit. But any change in control of part of the land will result in revocation of the whole of the relevant consent, unless there has been prior application. Moreover, the authority will have power to modify or revoke the whole of the consent, though subject to payment of compensation to the person in control of the whole of the land before the change (subs. (12)).

Offences

56L.—(1) Subject to this Part of this Act, if there is a contravention of hazardous substances control, the appropriate person shall be guilty of an offence.

(2) There is a contravention of hazardous substances control—

(*a*) if a quantity of a hazardous substance equal to or exceeding the controlled quantity is or has been present on, under or over land and either—

(i) there is no hazardous substances consent for the presence of the substance; or

(ii) there is hazardous substances consent for its presence but the quantity present exceeds the maximum quantity permitted by the consent;

(*b*) if there is or has been a failure to comply with a condition subject to which a hazardous substances consent was granted.

(3) In subsection (1) above "the appropriate person" means—

(*a*) in relation to a contravention falling within paragraph (*a*) of subsection (2) above—

(i) any person knowingly causing the substance to be present on, over or under the land;

(ii) any person allowing it to be so present; and

(*b*) in relation to a contravention falling within paragraph (*a*) or (*b*) of that subsection, the occupier of the land.

(4) A person guilty of an offence under this section shall be liable—

(*a*) on summary conviction, to a fine not exceeding the statutory maximum; or

(*b*) on conviction on indictment, to a fine,

and if the contravention is continued after the conviction he shall be guilty of a further offence and liable on summary conviction to a fine not exceeding £200 for each day on which it continues or on conviction on indictment to a fine.

(5) In any proceedings for an offence under this section it shall be a defence for the accused to prove—

(*a*) that he took all reasonable precautions and exercised all due diligence to avoid commission of the offence; or

(*b*) that commission of the offence could be avoided only by the taking of action amounting to a breach of a statutory duty.

(6) In any proceedings for an offence consisting of a contravention falling within subsection (2)(*a*) above, it shall be a defence for the accused to prove that at the time of the alleged commission of the offence he did not know, and had no reason to believe—

(*a*) if the case falls within paragraph (*a*)(i)—

(i) that the substance was present; or

(ii) that it was present in a quantity equal to or exceeding the controlled quantity;

(*b*) if the case falls within paragraph (*a*)(ii), that the substance was present in a quantity exceeding the maximum quantity permitted by the consent.

(7) In any proceedings for an offence consisting of a contravention falling within subsection (2)(*b*) above, it shall be a defence for the accused to prove that he did not know, and had no reason to believe, that he was failing to comply with a condition subject to which hazardous substances consent had been granted.

DEFINITIONS

"appropriate person": subs. (3).

"contravention of hazardous substances control": subs. (2).

"controlled quantity": 1972 Act, s.56C(3).

"hazardous substances consent": 1972 Act, ss.56C(1), 275(1).
"land": 1972 Act, s.275(1).

GENERAL NOTE
This section renders contravention of hazardous substances control a criminal offence. There is a contravention if there has been a quantity of hazardous substance equal to or exceeding the controlled quantity without consent, or in excess of consent; or if there has been any breach of a condition on a hazardous substance consent. In the special circumstances specified in s.56M, the Secretary of State is permitted to exclude certain contraventions from liability under this section for up to three months.

Further enforcement powers are contained in s.36, which inserts a new s.97B in the 1972 Act allowing the authority to issue a special enforcement notice (a hazardous substances contravention notice) specifying the contravention and requiring specified steps to be taken to remedy it.

Emergencies
    56M.—(1) If it appears to the Secretary of State—
    (*a*) either—
            (i) that the community or part of it is being or is likely to be deprived of an essential service or commodity; or
            (ii) that there is or is likely to be a shortage of such a service or commodity affecting the community or part of it; and
    (*b*) that the presence of a hazardous substance on, over or under land specified in the direction in circumstances such that hazardous substances consent would be required, is necessary for the effective provision of that service or commodity,
he may direct that, subject to such conditions or exceptions as he thinks fit, the presence of the substance on, over or under the land is not to constitute a contravention of hazardous substances control so long as the direction remains in force.
    (2) A direction under this section—
    (*a*) may be withdrawn at any time;
    (*b*) shall in any case cease to have effect at the end of the period of three months beginning with the day on which it was given, but without prejudice to the Secretary of State's power to give a further direction.
    (3) Subject to subsection (4) below, the Secretary of State shall send a copy of any such direction to the planning authority in relation to the land.
    (4) Where the land is land to which section 56B of this Act applies, the Secretary of State shall send the copy to the authority which would be the planning authority in relation to that land but for that section.

DEFINITIONS
"contravention of hazardous substances control": 1972 Act, s.56L(2).
"hazardous substance": 1972 Act, s.56C(3).
"hazardous substances consent": 1972 Act, ss.56C(1), 275(1).
"land": 1972 Act, s.275(1).
"planning authority": Local Government (Scotland) Act 1973, s.172(3).

GENERAL NOTE
This section confers on the Secretary of State a special power of exemption from criminal liability under the preceding section, and from enforcement action under s.97B, where an essential service or commodity is at stake and the presence of some hazardous substance requiring consent is necessary for the effective provision of the service or commodity. It is a temporary exemption, limited to a maximum period of three months, although with power for the Secretary of State to make further orders. If it were intended that the presence of the substance should continue beyond that period, then application for express consent may be made within the exemption period.

Registers, etc.

56N.—(1) Every planning authority shall keep, in such manner as may be prescribed, a register containing such information as may be so prescribed with respect—
 (*a*) to applications for hazardous substances consent—
   (i) made to that authority, or
   (ii) made to the appropriate Minister with respect to land in relation to which, but for section 56B of this Act, that authority would be the planning authority;
   and including information as to the manner in which such applications have been dealt with;
 (*b*) to hazardous substances consent deemed to be granted under section 38 of the Housing and Planning Act 1986 with respect to land in relation to which that authority is or but for section 56B of this Act would be, the planning authority;
 (*c*) to revocations or modifications of hazardous substances consent granted with respect to such land; and
 (*d*) to directions under section 56M above sent to the authority by the Secretary of State.

(2) Where with respect to any land the appropriate Minister exercises any of the functions of a planning authority for the purposes of hazardous substances control he shall send to the authority which, but for section 56B of this Act, would be the planning authority for those purposes in relation to that land any such information as appears to him to be required by them for the purposes of maintaining a register under this section.

(3) Every register kept under this section shall be available for inspection by the public at all reasonable hours.

DEFINITIONS
 "hazardous substances consent": 1972 Act, ss.56C(1), 275(1).
 "land": 1972 Act, s.275(1).
 "planning authority": Local Government (Scotland) Act 1973, s.172(3).

GENERAL NOTE
 All hazardous substances authorities are required to keep a public register of applications, consents, revocations or modifications and directions under s.56M.

Health and safety requirements

56O.—(1) Nothing in—
 (*a*) any hazardous substances consent granted or deemed to be granted under—
   (i) the preceding provisions of this Act; or
   (ii) section 38 of the Housing and Planning Act 1986; or
 (*b*) any hazardous substances contravention notice issued under section 97B of this Act,
shall require or allow anything to be done in contravention of any of the relevant statutory provisions or any prohibition notice or improvement notice served under or by virtue of any of those provisions; and to the extent that such a consent or notice purports to require or allow any such thing to be done, it shall be void.

(2) Where it appears to a planning authority who have granted or are deemed to have granted a hazardous substances consent or who have issued a hazardous substances contravention notice that the consent or notice or part of it is rendered void by subsection (1) above, the authority shall, as soon as is reasonably practicable, consult the appropriate body with regard to the matter.

(3) If the appropriate body advise the authority that the consent or notice is rendered wholly void, the authority shall revoke it.

(4) If they advise that part of the consent or notice is rendered void, the authority shall so modify it as to render it wholly operative.

(5) In this section—

"the appropriate body" means—

(a) in relation to a planning authority other than the appropriate Minister, the Health and Safety Executive; and

(b) in relation to the appropriate Minister, the Health and Safety Commission; and

"relevant statutory provisions", "improvement notice" and "prohibition notice" have the same meanings as in Part I of the Health and Safety at Work etc. Act 1974.".

DEFINITIONS

"appropriate body": subs. (5).

"hazardous substances contravention notice": 1972 Act, s.97B(3).

"hazardous substances consent": 1972 Act, ss.56C(1), 275(1).

"improvement notice": subs. (5).

"planning authority": Local Government (Scotland) Act 1973, s.172(3).

"prohibition notice": subs. (5).

"relevant statutory provisions": subs. (5).

GENERAL NOTE

Where there is any conflict between action taken by a planning authority under these provisions, and any requirement of Part I of the Health and Safety at Work, etc. Act 1974, or an improvement notice or prohibition notice issued thereunder, then those requirements prevail.

Hazardous substances contravention notices

36. The following shall be inserted after section 97A of the Town and Country Planning (Scotland) Act 1972—

"Hazardous substances

Power to issue hazardous substances contravention notice

97B.—(1) Subject to subsection (2) below, where it appears to the planning authority that there is or has been a contravention of hazardous substances control they may issue a hazardous substances contravention notice if they consider it expedient to do so having regard to any material consideration.

(2) A planning authority shall not issue a hazardous substances contravention notice where it appears to them that a contravention of hazardous substances control can be avoided only by the taking of action amounting to a breach of a statutory duty.

(3) In this Act "hazardous substances contravention notice" means a notice—

(a) specifying an alleged contravention of hazardous substances control; and

(b) requiring such steps as may be specified in the notice to be taken to remedy the contravention.

(4) A copy of a hazardous substances contravention notice shall be served—

(a) on the owner, the lessee and the occupier of the land to which it relates; and

(b) on such other persons as may be prescribed.

(5) A hazardous substances contravention notice shall also specify—

(a) a date not less than 28 days from the date of service of copies of the notice as the date on which it is to take effect;

(b) in respect of each of the steps required to be taken to remedy the contravention of hazardous substances control, the period from the notice taking effect within which the step is to be taken.

(6) Where a planning authority issue a hazardous substances contravention notice the steps required by the notice may, without prejudice to the generality of subsection (3)(*b*) above, if the authority think it expedient, include a requirement that the hazardous substance be removed from the land.

(7) Where a notice includes such a requirement, it may also contain a direction that at the end of such period as may be specified in the notice any hazardous substances consent for the presence of the substance shall cease to have effect or, if it relates to more than one substance, shall cease to have effect so far as it relates to the substance which is required to be removed.

(8) The planning authority may withdraw a hazardous substances contravention notice (without prejudice to their power to issue another) at any time before it takes effect.

(9) If they do so, they shall forthwith give notice of the withdrawal to every person who was served with a copy of the notice.

(10) The Secretary of State may by regulations—

(*a*) specify matters which are to be included in hazardous substances contravention notices, in addition to those which are required to be included in them by this section;

(*b*) provide—

   (i) for appeals to him against hazardous substances contravention notices;

   (ii) for the persons by whom, grounds upon which and time within which such an appeal may be brought;

   (iii) for the procedure to be followed on such appeals;

   (iv) for the directions that may be given on such an appeal;

   (v) for the application to such appeals, subject to such modifications as the regulations may specify, of any of the provisions of sections 85, 231(3) and 233 of this Act;

(*c*) direct that any of the provisions of sections 86 to 89A of this Act shall have effect in relation to hazardous substances contravention notices subject to such modifications as he may specify in the regulations;

(*d*) make such other provision as he considers necessary or expedient in relation to hazardous substances contravention notices.

(11) If any person appeals against a hazardous substances contravention notice, the notice shall be of no effect pending the final determination or the withdrawal of the appeal.

(12) Regulations under this section may make different provision for different cases or descriptions of cases.".

DEFINITIONS
"contravention of hazardous substances control": 1972 Act, s.58K(2).
"hazardous substances contravention notice": subs. (3).
"hazardous substances consent": 1972 Act, ss.56C(1), 275(1).
"land": 1972 Act, s.275(1).
"owner": 1972 Act, s.275(1).
"planning authority": Local Government (Scotland) Act 1973, s.172(3).

GENERAL NOTE
This section makes provision for enforcement of hazardous substances control, through procedures modelled on those relating to the enforcement of planning control under the 1972 Act.
Liability to enforcement action is independent from, and additional to, criminal liability under s.56J. The enforcement procedures in this section are intended to be remedial: the

authority are empowered to serve a notice requiring the owner, or person otherwise in control, of the land to take such steps as are specified in the notice, within such time as may be specified, to remedy the contravention. The section does not impose any direct criminal liability for failure to comply with a notice, but the Secretary of State is empowered by subs. (10) to make regulations for the purpose, *inter alia*, of directing that the provisions of ss.86 to 89A (which deal with liability under, and the effect of, planning enforcement notices) shall extend to notices under this section, subject to such modifications as he may specify.

Consequential amendments

37. The enactments mentioned in Part II of Schedule 7 to this Act shall have effect with the amendments there specified, being amendments consequential on the provisions of this Part of this Act.

GENERAL NOTE
The amendments made in Sched. 7 are all consequential, and are intended principally to tie control of hazardous substances into the 1972 Act and other related legislation.

Transitional (Scotland)

38.—(1) Until the end of the transitional period—
(*a*) no offence is committed under section 56L of the Town and Country Planning (Scotland) Act 1972; and
(*b*) no hazardous substances contravention notice may be issued, in relation to a hazardous substance which is on, under or over any land,
if the substance was present on, under or over the land at any time within the establishment period and—
  (i) in a case in which at the commencement date notification in respect of the substance was required by any of the Notification Regulations, both the conditions specified in subsection (2) below were satisfied; and
  (ii) in a case in which at that date such notification was not so required, the condition specified in paragraph (*b*) of that subsection is satisfied.
(2) The conditions mentioned in subsection (1) above are—
(*a*) that notification required by the Notification Regulations was given before the commencement date; and
(*b*) that the substance has not been present during the transitional period in a quantity greater in aggregate than the established quantity.
(3) Where a hazardous substance was present on, under or over any land at any time within the establishment period, hazardous substances consent may be claimed in respect of its presence.
(4) A claim shall be made in the prescribed form before the end of the transitional period and shall contain the prescribed information as to the presence of the substance during the establishment period and as to how and where it was kept and used immediately before the commencement date.
(5) Subject to subsections (6) to (8) below, the planning authority shall be deemed to have granted any hazardous substances consent which is claimed under subsection (2) above.
(6) If at the commencement date notification in respect of the substance was required by regulation 3 or 5 of the Notification Regulations, hazardous substances consent is only to be deemed to be granted under this section if notification in respect of the substance was given before that date in accordance with those regulations.
(7) If at the commencement date such notification was not so required, hazardous substances consent is only to be deemed to be granted under this section if an aggregate quantity of the substance not less than the

controlled quantity was present at any one time within the establishment period.

(8) If it appears to the planning authority that a claim for hazardous substances consent does not comply with subsection (4) above, it shall be their duty, before the end of the period of two weeks from their receipt of the claim,—

(a) to notify the claimant that in their opinion the claim is invalid; and

(b) to give him their reasons for that opinion.

(9) Hazardous substances consent which is deemed to be granted under this section is subject to the conditions that—

(a) the maximum aggregate quantity of the substance that may be present—

(i) on, under or over the land to which the claim relates;

(ii) on, under or over other land which is within 500 metres of it and controlled by the same person; or

(iii) in or on a structure controlled by the same person any part of which is within 500 metres of it,

at any one time shall not exceed the established quantity; and

(b) the substance shall be kept and used in the place and manner in which information supplied in pursuance of regulations made by virtue of subsection (4) above shows that it was kept and used immediately before the commencement date; and

(c) none of the substance shall be kept or used in a vessel or container greater in capacity than the container, or the largest of the containers, in which the substance was kept or used immediately before the commencement date.

(10) In this section—

"commencement date" means the date on which this Part of this Act comes into force;

"the establishment period" means the period of 12 months immediately preceding the commencement date;

"established quantity" means, in relation to any land—

(a) where before the commencement date there has been a notification in respect of a substance in accordance with any of the Notification Regulations—

(i) the quantity notified or last notified before the commencement date; or

(ii) a quantity equal to twice the quantity which was so notified or last notified before the start of the establishment period,

whichever is the greater;

(b) where a notification was not required before that date by any of those regulations, a quantity exceeding by 50 per cent. the maximum quantity which was present on, under or over the land at any one time within the establishment period;

"Notification Regulations" means the Notification of Installations Handling Hazardous Substances Regulations 1982;

"the transitional period" means the period of 6 months beginning with the commencement date;

and other expressions have the same meaning as in the Town and Country Planning (Scotland) Act 1972.

DEFINITIONS

"commencement date": subs. (10).

"the establishment period": subs. (10).

"established quantity": subs. (10).

"hazardous substances consent": 1972 Act, ss.56C(1), 275(1).

"land": 1972 Act, s.275(1).

"Notification Regulations": subs. (10).

"planning authority": Local Government (Scotland) Act 1973, s.172(3).
"the transitional period": subs. (10).

GENERAL NOTE

The transitional arrangements established by this section are important because the new régime does not have a purely prospective effect. The new controls extend not only to the introduction of hazardous substances on to land in the future, but also to existing sites where hazardous substances are present. Consent must therefore be obtained where necessary for all existing sites, and the Act allows a six-month transitional period following the commencement date of these provisions for consent to be obtained. During that period no offence is committed under s.56J, and no notice may be issued under s.97B, provided that the volume of the substance remains at or below the "established quantity" (subs. (10)), and that, if notification was required under the Notification Regulations, it had been given before the commencement date.

Although hazardous substances consent is required for the future in all cases, there is an entitlement to receive consent if a hazardous substance was present on the land at any time within the period of 12 months preceding the commencement date (subs. (3)); and such consent is deemed to have been granted by the planning authority upon a valid claim being submitted under subs. (3). The deemed consent is, however, subject to the conditions imposed by subs. (9). The authority need not issue a consent as such, since it is deemed to be granted upon the making of the claim. Subs. (8) therefore requires the authority to notify a claimant within two weeks of the claim if they are of the opinion that the claim is invalid, and give their reasons.

PART V

OPENCAST COAL

Abolition of Secretary of State's power to authorise opencast working, &c.

39.—(1) The following provisions of the Opencast Coal Act 1958 ("the 1958 Act") shall cease to have effect—

(a) sections 1 and 2 (authorisation by Secretary of State of opencast working of coal and associated provisions); and

(b) section 9(2) (buildings on land comprised in a compulsory rights order),

but this subsection does not affect a direction given under section 2 of the 1958 Act before the day on which the repeal of that section by paragraph (a) above comes into operation, and any repeal by this Act of an enactment which relates to directions under section 2 of the 1958 Act shall have no effect in relation to directions whose effect is continued by this subsection.

(2) The repeal of section 2(4) of the 1958 Act shall not prevent the felling of a tree that could not have been felled but for paragraph (a) of that subsection (which negatived tree preservation orders).

(3) The 1958 Act shall have effect with the amendments specified in Part I of Schedule 8 to this Act and section 29 of the Acquisition of Land Act 1981 shall have effect with the amendments specified in Part II of that Schedule.

(4) The enactments specified in Part II of Schedule 12 to this Act (which include enactments already obsolete or unnecessary) are repealed to the extent specified in the third column of that Schedule.

GENERAL NOTE

This section fulfils an undertaking given by the Government in 1984 (D.O.E. Circular 3/84) that it would repeal the exemptions from normal planning control that were conferred by the Opencast Coal Act 1958, and require for the future that all opencast coal applications should be made to mineral planning authorities, with the usual rights of appeal and call-in, rather than attract deemed consent under s.40 of the 1971 Act (in Scotland, s.37 of the 1972 Act). Under transitional arrangements in operation since March 1, 1984, the National Coal

Board has applied for planning permission under the usual provisions as well as for opencast mining authorisation under the 1958 Act.

Para. 1 of Sched. 8 imposes a new duty on the National Coal Board, in formulating proposals for opencast working, for incidental operations and for restoration of opencast sites, to have regard to the desirability of preserving natural beauty and of conserving natural features and buildings of special interest. The Board is also required to take into account any effect which the proposals would have on the natural beauty of the countryside or any such fauna, flora, features, buildings or objects.

This Part of the Act extends to Scotland as well as to England and Wales (s.57).

Part VI

Miscellaneous Provisions

England and Wales

Listed buildings and conservation areas

40. The enactments relating to listed buildings and conservation areas are amended in accordance with Part I of Schedule 9 with respect to the following matters—

(a) the treatment of free-standing objects and structures within the curtilage of a listed building;

(b) the scope of the exception for urgent works to a listed building;

(c) the grant of listed building consent subject to the subsequent approval of detail;

(d) applications for the variation or discharge of conditions attached to listed building consent;

(e) the extent of the exemption accorded to ecclesiastical buildings;

(f) dangerous structure orders in respect of listed buildings;

(g) the power of a local authority, the Secretary of State or the Historic Buildings and Monuments Commission for England to carry out urgent works for the preservation of a building;

(h) the control of demolition in a conservation area;

(i) the form of an application for listed building consent; and

(j) the powers of the Secretary of State with respect to applications for listed building consent.

GENERAL NOTE

This section gives effect to Sched. 9, Part I, which makes various amendments to the Act of 1971 relating to listed buildings and buildings in conservation areas. The principal changes are:

Free standing objects in curtilage (para. 1)

The definition of a listed building in s.54(9) of the Act of 1971 formerly included "any object or structure fixed to a building, or forming part of the land and comprised within the curtilage of a building." The decisions of the Court of Appeal in *Att.-Gen., ex rel Sutcliffe* v. *Calderdale Borough Council* [1983] J.P.L. 310, and *Debenhams* v. *Westminster City Council* [1986] J.P.L. 671 (since reversed on appeal [1987] 1 All E.R. 51), had demonstrated the breadth of this provision. It meant that, although listed building consent might not be necessary for the erection of a free standing structure in the curtilage of a listed building, consent would be required for its alteration or removal. The amendment therefore provides a narrower definition, under which protection will extend to free standing objects within the curtilage only where they form part of the land and have done so since before July 1, 1948 (the commencement date of the Town and Country Planning Act 1947).

Urgent works (para. 2)

This amendment narrows the scope of the exception from listed building control which existed in respect of urgent works. It had previously been a defence, to prosecution for carrying out unauthorised works to a listed building, that they were urgently necessary in the interests of safety or health, or for the preservation of the building, and that notice in writing of the need for the works had been given to the local planning authority as soon as reasonably practicable. The amendments restrict that defence. It will now be necessary to prove also that it was not practicable to have undertaken works of repair or works for providing temporary support or shelter, and to prove that the works were limited to the minimum measures immediately necessary. The requirement of written notice to the authority remains, but tightened up into a requirement that the notice should justify in detail the carrying out of the works.

Outline listed building consent (para. 3)

This amendment introduces the possibility of listed building consent being sought, and granted, in outline, with a condition reserving specified details of the works for subsequent approval by the planning authority. The procedure is modelled on that applicable to outline planning permission, but with improvements: the new subsection makes clear, for example, that approval may be reserved of details even where they have formed part of the application; and it leaves it to the authority in each case to specify which details they wish to reserve for subsequent approval, rather than following the outline planning permission model of specifying in the legislation a prescribed list of "reserved matters."

Modification or discharge of conditions (para. 4)

This is a new procedure allowing application to be made to vary or discharge any condition attached to a grant of listed building consent. A parallel procedure, though quite differently drafted, is also introduced by the Act (Sched. 11, para. 4) in respect of conditions on planning permissions. In the past, an applicant has had to apply for fresh consent.

An application for listed building consent may be made by any person, and not merely the landowner or lessee, although an applicant is required to notify any owners of interests in the land concerned. But under these provisions, the power to apply is limited to persons interested in the building concerned. This distinction is presumably deliberate. The wording of the new section implies that once a modification or discharge has been made, the pre-existing consent is supplanted by the new. But if an entirely fresh consent were granted it would not, unless it specifically so provided, override the previous consent, and the applicant would be entitled to implement either. It may therefore be that the intention of the section is to restrict the power to make applications, in cases where the existing consent is liable to be amended, to applicants who at least have some proprietary interest in the land.

But it is unfortunate that resort has been had to the ambiguous phrase "any person interested." In the context of planning agreements under s.52 of the Act of 1971, the word "interested" has been held to mean holding a proprietary interest in the land (*Jones* v. *Secretary of State for Wales* (1974) 28 P. & C.R. 280), though a wider view was mooted by Eveleigh L.J. in *Pennine Raceway Ltd.* v. *Kirklees Metropolitan District Council* [1982] 3 All E.R. 628. If the narrow view is the correct one under this section, than it must preclude any application being made by a potential purchaser of the property except through the present owner; yet, since there is no such restriction on applications for listed building consent itself, he could seek the same end through the alternative route of applying for a fresh consent.

Ecclesiastical exemption (para. 5)

The scope of the exemption from listed building controls of ecclesiastical buildings has provoked much controversy, particularly in light of the increasing number of redundant churches which are listed buildings. After some years of negotiations, agreement was reached in 1986 between the Government and representatives of the Church of England and other religious organisations, through the Churches Main Committee, to extend listed building control to include the partial demolition of non-Anglican buildings. Listed building consent is required already for total demolition, since the building can no longer at that stage be regarded as still being in ecclesiastical use; and demolition of churches of the Church of England is governed by the special requirements of the Pastoral Measure 1983. The terms of the agreement were announced in the House of Lords during the Committee stage of the Bill (*Hansard* H.L. Vol. 480, cols. 608–611) and these provisions were inserted into the Bill at the Report stage to give statutory effect where necessary to the agreement.

The new provisions allow the Secretary of State by order to restrict the scope of the ecclesiastical exemption, and to discriminate in doing so between different types of building and between different areas and the buildings of different denominations. The intention is that consent should be required for the partial demolition of a church if it would materially affect the architectural or historic interest of the building, such as the removal of a spire, tower or cupola, or if the works were otherwise to affect the interests of the building to such an extent that its value as a listed building, or the contribution an unlisted church makes to a conservation area, is brought into question. There is to be consultation as to how the necessary order will need to be drafted to achieve these ends (*Hansard* H.L. Vol. 481, col. 187).

The Minister also announced in the course of his statement at the Committee stage in the Lords, that the Church of England had further agreed to accept greater consultation with the Department of the Environment in relation to historic churches. In particular, when it is proposed to demolish a listed church (or a church in a conservation area), wholly or partly, under the Pastoral Measure 1983, the Church Commissioners have agreed always to ask the Secretary of State for the Environment whether he wishes to hold a non-statutory local public inquiry into the proposal if there are reasoned objections to it from the Historic Buildings and Monuments Commission, the Advisory Board for Redundant Churches, the local planning authority or a national amenity society. The Church Commissioners have undertaken to accept a recommendation from the Secretary of State, following such an inquiry, that the church is of sufficient importance to be vested in the Redundant Churches Fund or, in cases where the recommendation was not that the building should go to the Fund, to make further efforts to find an alternative use and to engage in further consultation with the Secretary of State before using the Pastoral Measure powers to demolish.

Dangerous structures orders (para. 6)

The amendment requires the local planning authority to consider whether to take other steps under the 1971 Act which may preserve a listed building (or a building in a conservation area or subject to a building preservation order) before making a dangerous structure order under the Building Act 1984 or London Building Acts (Amendment) Act 1939. They must consider first whether to exercise their powers to undertake urgent works under s.101, or the acquisition of the building under ss.114 and 115.

Urgent works for preservation (para. 7)

This amendment greatly strengthens the power of a local planning authority to undertake urgent works for the preservation of a building. First, it now extends to buildings which are occupied, though works may only be carried out to those parts which are not in use. Secondly, it will be possible to undertake works providing temporary support or shelter for the building and to recover the cost, including continuing expenses, from the owner. The Divisional Court had ruled, in *R.* v. *Secretary of State for the Environment, ex p. Hampshire County Council* [1981] J.P.L. 47, that the original power did not allow works which could involve the owner in continuing liability.

Control of demolition in conservation areas (para. 8)

These amendments translate across, to the conservation area provisions, certain provisions relating to listed buildings, including the amendments discussed above.

Local plans and unitary development plans

41.—(1) In Part II of the Town and Country Planning Act 1971 (development plans), the sections set out in Part I of Schedule 10 are substituted, except as to Greater London, for sections 10C to 15B (local plans), the main changes being—

(a) to provide for the co-ordination by county planning authorities, in conjunction with the district planning authorities, of the process of making, altering, repealing or replacing local plans;

(b) to provide a short procedure for altering a local plan where the issues are not of sufficient importance to warrant the full procedure; and

(c) to enable the Secretary of State to direct a local planning authority to reconsider proposals for making, altering, repealing or replacing a local plan; and

(d) to omit provisions which are spent in consequence of the approval of structure plans for the whole of England and Wales.

(2) The substituted sections have effect in relation to metropolitan counties until the coming into force of Part I of Schedule 1 to the Local Government Act 1985 (unitary development plans), but subject to the provisions of Part II of that Schedule.

(3) Part I of Schedule 1 to the Local Government Act 1985 (unitary development plans) is amended in accordance with Part II of Schedule 10 to this Act, so as to—

(a) provide a short procedure for altering a unitary development plan where the issues are not of sufficient importance to warrant the full procedure; and

(b) enable the Secretary of State to direct a local planning authority to reconsider proposals for making, altering or replacing a unitary development plan.

GENERAL NOTE

This section gives effect to Part I of Sched. 10 to the Act, which substitutes new provisions for local plans in the 1971 Act. The opportunity has been taken to redraft the provisions to take account of the fact that structure plans have now been approved for all of England and Wales, and also to take full account of the many amendments that had already been made to the original sections by the Local Government Act 1972, the Town and Country Planning (Amendment) Act 1972, the Local Government, Planning and Land Act 1980 and the Local Government (Miscellaneous Provisions) Act 1982.

The principal changes are:

(1) local plan schemes (s.11A): previously development plan schemes (old s.10C), these are now to be more specific instruments which will specify for each proposed local plan in the county the title and nature of the plan, and the area to which it is to apply, and give an indication of its scope. The schemes will apply not only to the preparation of local plans, but also to alterations, repeals and replacements.

(2) expedited procedures (s.12A): if the local planning authority are of the view that the issues involved in any proposals to alter, repeal or replace a local plan are not sufficiently important to warrant the full procedure, they may shorten the process by, effectively, omitting the pre-deposit stage and placing the proposals directly on deposit for public inspection. The duty to hold a public inquiry into any objections that may be made in accordance with the regulations is preserved. A similar power is contained in the procedures for simplified planning zones, and for unitary plans.

(3) Secretary of State's power to direct alterations, repeal or replacement (s.11B): the Secretary of State is to have power to direct a local planning authority to make, alter, replace or repeal a local plan. Previously his power was limited to directing an authority to prepare a local plan (old s.11(7)) and the power was not one of those which was extended to plan alterations by s.15.

(4) Secretary of State's power to direct modifications (s.14(4)): the Secretary of State is to have a new power to direct the local planning authority to consider making modifications to their local plan, prior to adopting it. This may allow him to oversee modifications without having to call in the plan for his own approval. The authority may not adopt the plan until the direction has been withdrawn or the modifications have been made.

The substituted sections have effect in the metropolitan areas (except Greater London) until the coming into force of the unitary plans provisions of the Local Government Act 1985 in the individual areas. In Greater London the old provisions continue to apply until the commencement of unitary planning. These are an amalgam of Sched. 4 to the 1971 Act, together with ss.13, 14 (except subss. (5)–(7)) and 15 of the 1971 Act.

Recovery of Minister's costs in connection with inquiries

42.—(1) The following provisions of this section apply where a Minister is authorised under or by virtue of any of the following statutory provisions to recover costs incurred by him in relation to an inquiry—

(a) section 250(4) of the Local Government Act 1972 (general provision as to costs of inquiries),

(b) section 96(5) of the Land Drainage Act 1976 (cost of inquiry under that Act),

(c) section 129(1)(d) of the Road Traffic Regulation Act 1984 (costs of inquiry under that Act),

(d) paragraph 9(2) of Schedule 22 to the Housing Act 1985 (costs of inquiry in connection with acquisition of land for clearance),

(e) any other statutory provision to which this section is applied by order of the Minister.

(2) What may be recovered by the Minister is the entire administrative cost of the inquiry, so that, in particular—

(a) there shall be treated as costs incurred in relation to the inquiry such reasonable sum as the Minister may determine in respect of the general staff costs and overheads of his department, and

(b) there shall be treated as costs incurred by the Minister holding the inquiry any costs incurred in relation to the inquiry by any other Minister or government department and, where appropriate, such reasonable sum as that Minister or department may determine in respect of general staff costs and overheads.

(3) The cost of an inquiry which does not take place may be recovered by the Minister from any person who would have been a party to the inquiry to the same extent, and in the same way, as the cost of an inquiry which does take place.

(4) The Minister may by regulations prescribe for any description of inquiry a standard daily amount and where an inquiry of that description does take place what may be recovered is—

(a) the prescribed standard amount in respect of each day (or an appropriate proportion of that amount in respect of a part of a day) on which the inquiry sits or the person appointed to hold the inquiry is otherwise engaged on work connected with the inquiry,

(b) costs actually incurred in connection with the inquiry on travelling or subsistence allowances or the provision of accommodation or other facilities for the inquiry,

(c) any costs attributable to the appointment of an assessor to assist the person appointed to hold the inquiry, and

(d) any legal costs or disbursements incurred or made by or on behalf of the Minister in connection with the inquiry.

(5) An order or regulations under this section shall be made by statutory instrument which shall be subject to annulment in pursuance of a resolution of either House of Parliament.

(6) An order applying this section to a statutory provision may provide for the consequential repeal of so much of that provision, or any other provision, as restricts the sum recoverable by the Minister in respect of the services of any officer engaged in the inquiry or is otherwise inconsistent with the application of the provisions of this section.

GENERAL NOTE

This section makes far reaching changes to the ability of the Secretary of State to recover his costs in relation to planning and other inquiries. He is to be entitled to include staff costs and departmental overheads and the costs of other Ministers and departments, and to recover his costs even where the inquiry has not gone ahead.

Further powers in relation to costs are conferred by Sched. 11, paras. 8 and 9, which extend to inspectors the power to award costs, and introduce a general power to award costs in appeals conducted by written representations.

Compulsory acquisition of land on behalf of parish or community councils

43. For section 125 of the Local Government Act 1972 (compulsory acquisition of land on behalf of parish or community councils) substitute—

"**Compulsory acquisition of land on behalf of parish or community councils**

125.—(1) If a parish or community council are unable to acquire by agreement under section 124 above and on reasonable terms suitable land for a purpose for which they are authorised to acquire land other than—

(*a*) the purpose specified in section 124(1)(*b*) above, or

(*b*) a purpose in relation to which the power of acquisition is by an enactment expressly limited to acquisition by agreement,

they may represent the case to the council of the district in which the parish or community is situated.

(2) If the district council are satisfied that suitable land for the purpose cannot be acquired on reasonable terms by agreement, they may be authorised by the Secretary of State to purchase compulsorily the land or part of it; and the Acquisition of Land Act 1981 shall apply in relation to the purchase.

(3) The district council in making and the Secretary of State in confirming an order for the purposes of this section shall have regard to the extent of land held in the neighbourhood by an owner and to the convenience of other property belonging to the same owner and shall, as far as practicable, avoid taking an undue or inconvenient quantity of land from any one owner.

(4) The order shall be carried into effect by the district council but the land when acquired shall be conveyed to the parish or community council; and accordingly in construing for the purposes of this section and of the order any enactment applying in relation to the compulsory acquisition, the parish or community council or the district council, or the two councils jointly, shall, as the case may require, be treated as the acquiring authority.

(5) The district council may recover from the parish or community council the expenses incurred by them in connection with the acquisition of land under this section.

(6) If a parish or community council make representations to a district council with a view to the making of an order under this section and the district council—

(*a*) refuse to make an order, or

(*b*) do not make an order within 8 weeks from the making of the representations or such longer period as may be agreed between the two councils,

the parish or community council may petition the Secretary of State who may make the order, and this section and the provisions of the Acquisition of Land Act 1981 shall apply as if the order had been made by the district council and confirmed by the Secretary of State.

(7) In the application of this section to a parish or community council for a group of parishes or communities—

(*a*) references to the parish or community shall be construed as references to the area of the group, and

(*b*) if different parts of the area of the group lie in different districts, references to the council of the district in which the parish or community is situated shall be construed as references to the councils of each of the districts acting jointly.".

GENERAL NOTE

The substituted section introduces a more straightforward procedure for compulsory purchase on behalf of parish councils. The previous procedure required that when a parish council represented to the district council that suitable land for their purpose could not be acquired by agreement on reasonable terms, the district council had, if they were satisfied that the circumstances justified them in proceeding, to arrange for a public local inquiry to be conducted by one or more of its members. Only when they had considered the matter in that way could they proceed to invoke compulsory purchase powers which might then, if there was objection, involve a further public inquiry. The new section omits altogether the requirement that the district council should hold a preliminary inquiry.

Overhead electricity lines

44.—(1) For section 21 of the Electricity (Supply) Act 1919 (overhead wires) substitute—

"**Overhead wires**

21.—(1) The Secretary of State shall before giving consent or authorisation for the placing of an electric line above ground give the local planning authority an opportunity of being heard.

(2) In subsection (1) "local planning authority" has the same meaning as in the Town and Country Planning Act 1971, except that in relation to a non-metropolitan county it includes the county planning authority only—

    (*a*) where the line is to be placed in a National Park; or

    (*b*) where the line is a high voltage line, that is, a line for conveying or transmitting electricity at or above a voltage of 132,000 volts.".

(2) In section 34 of the Electricity Act 1975 (public inquiries), after subsection (1) (inquiry to be held if local planning authority object) insert—

"(1A) In subsection (1) "local planning authority"—

    (*a*) in relation to an application for consent or authorisation under section 10(*b*) of the Schedule to the Act of 1899, means a local planning authority required to be given an opportunity of being heard under section 21 of the Electricity (Supply) Act 1919;

    (*b*) in relation to an application for consent under section 2 of the Electric Lighting Act 1909, means a local planning authority required to be given an opportunity of stating an objection under that section.".

(3) Section 149(3)(*a*) of the Local Government, Planning and Land Act 1980 (power of Secretary of State to confer functions of local planning authority on urban development corporation) has effect in relation to—

    section 21 of the Electricity (Supply) Act 1919, and

    section 34 of the Electricity Act 1957, so far as applying to an application for consent or authorisation under section 10(*b*) of the Schedule to the Electric Lighting (Clauses) Act 1899,

as it has effect in relation to the provisions listed in Part I of Schedule 29 to the 1980 Act.

GENERAL NOTE

The purpose of this amendment is to remove the obligation of electricity undertakers to consult county councils as well as district councils on the erection of power lines of less than 132KV.

Control of advertisements: experimental areas

45. In section 63 of the Town and Country Planning Act 1971 (control of advertisements), for subsection (3) (power to make different provision for different areas) substitute—

"(3) Regulations made for the purposes of this section may make different provision with respect to different areas, and in particular may make special provision—

    (*a*) with respect to conservation areas.

    (*b*) with respect to areas defined for the purposes of the regulations as experimental areas, and

    (*c*) with respect to areas defined for the purposes of the regulations as areas of special control.

(3A) An area may be defined as an experimental area for a prescribed period for the purpose of assessing the effect on amenity or public safety of advertisements of a prescribed description.

(3B) An area may be defined as an area of special control if it is—

(*a*) a rural area, or

(*b*) an area which appears to the Secretary of State to require special protection on grounds of amenity;

and, without prejudice to the generality of subsection (3), the regulations may prohibit the display in an area of special control of all advertisements except advertisements of such classes (if any) as may be prescribed.".

GENERAL NOTE

This amendment allows regulations to be made in relation to advertisement control which will allow special régimes to apply in conservation areas, experimental control areas, and areas of special control.

Land adversely affecting amenity of neighbourhood

46. For section 65 of the Town and Country Planning Act 1971 (proper maintenance of waste land), and the heading preceding it, substitute—

"Land adversely affecting amenity of neighbourhood

Power to require proper maintenance of land

65.—(1) If it appears to the local planning authority that the amenity of a part of their area, or of an adjoining area, is adversely affected by the condition of land in their area, they may serve on the owner and occupier of the land a notice under this section.

(2) The notice shall require such steps for remedying the condition of the land as may be specified in the notice to be taken within such period as may be so specified.

(3) Subject to the provisions of Part V of this Act, the notice shall take effect at the end of such period (not being less than 28 days after the service of the notice) as may be specified in the notice.

(4) In non-metropolitan counties the functions of the local planning authority under this section are exercisable by the district planning authorities.".

GENERAL NOTE

This amendment recasts the powers previously contained in s.65 so as to extend them to any land in the authority's area, and not merely to "any garden, vacant site or other open land." Moreover, for the previous test which required that it should appear to the local planning authority that the amenity of part of their area was "seriously injured" by the condition of the land, there is substituted the requirement that an amenity is "adversely affected."

The right of appeal, penalties for non-compliance and right for the authority themselves to carry out the required works (ss.104–107) remain unaltered.

Areas which may be designated urban development areas

47. In section 134 of the Local Government, Planning and Land Act 1980 (power to designate urban development areas), omit subsection (2) (which restricts the power to land in metropolitan districts and certain land in or adjacent to inner London).

GENERAL NOTE

The amendment is intended to allow an urban development corporation to be set up in a non-metropolitan area. The Secretary of State has announced proposals for four more corporations, of which one, in Teesside, would be outside a metropolitan area.

Repeal of unnecessary enactments

48.—(1) The following enactments are repealed—

(*a*) section 52 of the Requisitioned Land and War Works Act 1945 and paragraph 10 of the Schedule to the Requisitioned Land and War Works Act 1948 (reimbursement of expense of restoring land affected by war works, &c.);

(*b*) sections 66 to 72 of the Town and Country Planning Act 1971 (special control over industrial development);

(*c*) sections 250 to 252 of that Act (grants to local authorities for development of land, &c.).

(2) The repeal does not affect the operation—

(*a*) of section 52 of the Requisitioned Land and War Works Act 1945 or paragraph 10 of the Schedule to the Requisitioned Land and War Works Act 1948 in relation to undertakings given before the repeal;

(*b*) of sections 250 to 252 of the 1971 Act in relation to land for which approval for the purposes of regulations under section 250 was sought before 1st April 1986.

GENERAL NOTE

This section repeals enactments which are obsolete or superseded.

Minor and consequential amendments; repeals

49.—(1) The Town and Country Planning Act 1971, and certain related enactments, are amended in accordance with Part I of Schedule 11 with respect to the following matters—

(*a*) the operation of the Use Classes Order on the subdivision of the planning unit;

(*b*) the provision which may be made by development orders;

(*c*) the construction of references to certain documents relating to access for the disabled;

(*d*) applications to vary or revoke conditions attached to planning permission;

(*e*) the procedure on appeals and applications disposed of without a local inquiry or hearing;

(*f*) purchase notices;

(*g*) local inquiries;

(*h*) the determination of appeals by inspectors; and

(*i*) daily penalties for offences;

and that Part also contains amendments consequential on the provisions of this Part.

(2) The enactments specified in Part III of Schedule 12 are repealed to the extent specified.

GENERAL NOTE

Amongst the so-called "minor and consequential amendments" contained in Sched. 11 are some which are of considerable practical importance:

Use Classes Order and the planning unit (para. 1)

This is the first statutory acknowledgment of the idea of the planning unit, which is a concept developed by the courts as an aid to the application of the statutory definition of "development" as including the making of a material change in the use of any building or other land. In *Winton* v. *Secretary of State for the Environment* [1984] J.P.L. 188, the Divisional Court held that although the mere sub-division of the planning unit did not of itself constitute development, the exemptions conferred by the Use Classes Order did not extend to development occurring upon such a sub-division, because the "before and after" comparison which the Order required had to be made in relation to the same planning unit.

This amendment, which was recommended by the Property Advisory Group in their review of the Use Classes Order, allows the Order to be amended so as to extend its exemptions to sub-divisions of the planning unit.

Development orders (para. 2)

A separate régime of permitted development for the environmentally sensitive areas (National Parks, areas of outstanding natural beauty and conservation areas) has had, in the past, to be established by means of a separate special development order. The amendment allows the general development order to differentiate between areas, and thus to fulfil both functions. A new general development order is expected to be made early in 1987. A further amendment (para. 2(2)) allows the Secretary of State to remove the present power of direction exercisable by highway authorities in relation to planning applications. The intention is to replace it by a requirement merely that highway authorities should be consulted. The Government accept that the technical competence of local planning authorities has increased to the point where they should be entrusted to take decisions on highways matters in respect of classified roads if they have first taken the views of the highway authority (*Hansard* H.L.Vol. 401, col. 420).

Revocation or variation of planning conditions (para. 4)

The amendment introduces a new s.31A to the 1971 Act giving express power to apply for planning permission for the development of land without complying with conditions attached to an earlier permission. The amendment allows for a different procedure to be applied to such applications from that applying to applications for planning permission, and requires the local planning authority to consider only the question of the conditions subject to which planning permission should be granted.

Appeals and inquiries (paras. 8–12).

These amendments empower planning inspectors to make awards of costs, and permit costs to be awarded in written representation cases as well as those where an inquiry is held. A parallel power for the Secretary of State to recover his own costs in relation to an inquiry (including cases where for any reason the inquiry does not take place), is conferred by s.41, *post*. Para. 10 of the Schedule paves the way for the introduction by regulations of a statutory timetable for handling written representations cases.

Scotland

Listed buildings and conservation areas

50. The enactments relating to listed buildings and conservation areas are amended in accordance with Part II of Schedule 9 with respect to the following matters—

> (*a*) the treatment of free-standing objects and structures within the curtilage of a listed building;
> (*b*) late applications for listed building consent;
> (*c*) defence to proceedings under section 53;
> (*d*) the grant of listed building consent subject to subsequent approval of detail;
> (*e*) applications for the variation or discharge of conditions attached to listed building consent;
> (*f*) the extent of the exemption accorded to ecclesiastical buildings;
> (*g*) the effect of a listed building enforcement notice;
> (*h*) the power of a local authority or the Secretary of State to carry out urgent works for the preservation of a building;
> (*i*) the control of demolition in a conservation area;
> (*j*) the form of an application for listed building consent;
> (*k*) the calling in of applications for listed building consent; and
> (*l*) the application to planning authorities of provisions relating to listed buildings.

GENERAL NOTE

The amendments made by Part II of Sched. 9 follow closely in many respects those made by Part I to the English Act of 1971, as to which see the General Note to s.39. But there is one area of difference: the Scottish provisions introduce a power, which the English Act does not have, for late application for listed building consent. If consent is granted for the retention of works for the demolition, alteration or extension of a listed building which have been executed without consent, then the works are authorised from the date of the grant of consent on the late application (para. 14(2)) and such consent then overrides any relevant part of a listed building enforcement notice (para. 19).

Grants for repair of buildings in town schemes

51. After section 10B of the Town and Country Planning (Amendment) Act 1972 there shall be inserted the following section—

"Grants for repair of buildings in town schemes

10C.—(1) The Secretary of State may make grants for the purpose of defraying in whole or in part any expenditure incurred or to be incurred in the repair of a building which—

(*a*) is comprised in a town scheme; and

(*b*) appears to him to be of architectural or historic interest.

(2) For the purposes of this section a building is comprised in a town scheme if—

(*a*) it is in an area—

(i) designated as a conservation area under section 262 of the Act of 1972; and

(ii) appearing to the Secretary of State to be of outstanding architectural or historic interest; and

(*b*) it is included in a town scheme list or shown on a town scheme map.

(3) In subsection (2) above—

"town scheme list", means a list, compiled, after consultation with the Historic Buildings Council for Scotland, by the Secretary of State and one or more local authorities, of buildings which are to be the subject of a repair grant agreement; and

"town scheme map" means a map, prepared after such consultation by the Secretary of State and one or more local authorities, showing buildings which are to be the subject of such an agreement.

(4) In subsection (3) above—

"repair grant agreement" means an agreement between the Secretary of State and any authority who have participated in the compilation of a town scheme list or the preparation of a town scheme map under which the Secretary of State and the authority or authorities who have so participated have agreed that a specified sum of money shall be set aside for a specified period of years for the purpose of making grants for the repair of the buildings included in the town scheme list or shown on the town scheme map.

(5) A grant under this section may be made subject to conditions imposed by the Secretary of State for such purposes as he may think fit.

(6) Subject to subsection (7) below, before making any grant under this section the Secretary of State may consult with the Council, both as to the making of the grant and as to the conditions subject to which it should be made.

(7) Subsection (6) above shall not apply where the making of a grant appears to the Secretary of State to be a matter of immediate urgency.

(8) The Secretary of State may pay any grant under this section to an authority participating in a town scheme and may make arrangements with any such authority for the way in which the scheme is to be administered.

(9) Arrangements under subsection (8) above may include such arrangements for the offer and payment of grants under this section as may be agreed between the Secretary of State and any authority or authorities participating in a town scheme.

(10) Section 2 of the Local Authorities (Historic Buildings) Act 1962 (recovery of grants made by local authorities on disposal of property within three years) shall apply to a grant made by the Secretary of State under this section as it applies to a grant for the repair of property made by a local authority under that Act; and any reference to a local authority in that section shall accordingly be construed, in relation to a grant under this section, as a reference to the Secretary of State.

(11) In this section "local authority" means a regional, islands or district council.".

GENERAL NOTE
   This section corresponds closely to s.10B of the English Town and County Planning (Amendment) Act 1972, which was inserted by the Local Government, Planning and Land Act 1980. It makes provision for town scheme grants. Town schemes are arrangements under which the Secretary of State and a local authority (as defined in subs. (11)) agree to allocate a sum of money annually for the purpose of making grants towards the repair of buildings covered by the scheme.

Termination of grants for redevelopment etc.

52.—(1) No payment of grant under—
   (*a*) sections 237 to 239 of the Town and Country Planning (Scotland) Act 1972,
   (*b*) section 14 of the Housing and Town Development (Scotland) Act 1957, and
   (*c*) section 9 of the Local Government (Scotland) Act 1966
shall be made for the financial year 1986–87 or for any subsequent financial year.

(2) No claim for grant under the enactments mentioned in subsection (1)(*a*) and (*b*) above in respect of financial years prior to 1986–87 shall be entertained by the Secretary of State unless—
   (*a*) it is received by him before this Act is passed, and
   (*b*) any information reasonably required by him in relation to any such claim is received by him before the expiry of the period of two months after this Act is passed.

Minor and consequential amendments: repeals

53.—(1) The Town and Country Planning (Scotland) Act 1972, the Local Government (Scotland) Act 1973 and certain related enactments are amended in accordance with Part II of Schedule 11 with respect to the following matters—
   (*a*) directions as to modifications of local plans;
   (*b*) the operation of the Use Classes Order on the sub-division of the planning unit;
   (*c*) the provision that may be made by development orders;
   (*d*) applications to vary or revoke conditions attached to planning permission;
   (*e*) land adversely affecting the amenity of the neighbourhood;
   (*f*) purchase notices;
   (*g*) National Scenic Areas;
   (*h*) local inquiries;
   (*i*) procedure on applications and appeals disposed of without an inquiry or hearing;
   (*j*) the determination of appeals by appointed persons;

(*k*) daily penalties for offences;
and that Part also contains other minor amendments and amendments
consequential on the provisions of this Part.
   (2) The enactments mentioned in Part IV of Schedule 12 to this Act are
repealed to the extent specified.

GENERAL NOTE
   Part II of Sched. 11 amends the Act of 1972 along similar lines to the amendments made
by Part I to the English legislation (as to which see the General Note to s.49) but with the
following differences:

Directions to modify local plans (para. 28)
   The Secretary of State is to have power to direct a planning authority to consider
modifying a local plan prior to adopting it. The power is independent of the Secretary of
State's power to call-in the plan for his own approval, though if the planning authority are
unwilling to carry out a modification, the Secretary of State will need to consider whether
to exercise the call-in power.

National Scenic Areas (para. 38)
   National Scenic Areas have not previously had a statutory base. They were defined in a
publication of the Countryside Commission for Scotland, *Scotland's Scenic Heritage*, in 1978
(see further Young and Rowan-Robinson, *Scottish Planning Law and Procedure*, p.183) and
guidance in relation to the operation of planning controls in National Scenic Areas was
issued in S.D.D. Circular 20/1980. The Town and Country Planning (Restriction on
Permitted Development) (National Scenic Areas) (Scotland) Direction 1980 withdrew
permitted development status for certain types of development in the areas. The new
provision for formal designation carries with it a duty, in exercising any function under the
1972 Act, to pay special attention to the desirability of preserving or enhancing the character
or appearance of a designated area. That duty is modelled on the duty of planning authorities
in relation to conservation areas (Act of 1972, s.262(8)).

Provisions common to England and Wales and Scotland

Effect of modification or termination of enterprise zone scheme
   54.—(1) In Schedule 32 to the Local Government, Planning and Land
Act 1980 (enterprise zones), for paragraphs 21 and 22 (effect of modification or termination of scheme on planning permission) substitute—

   "*Effect on planning permission of modification or termination of scheme*

      21. Modifications to a scheme do not affect planning permission
   under the scheme in any case where the development authorised by
   it has been begun before the modifications take effect.
      22.—(1) Upon an area ceasing to be an enterprise zone planning
   permission under the scheme shall cease to have effect except in a
   case where the development authorised by it has been begun.
      (2) The following provisions (which provide for the termination of
   planning permission if the completion of development is unreasonably
   delayed) apply to planning permission under the scheme where
   development has been begun but not completed by the time the area
   ceases to be an enterprise zone—
         (*a*) in England and Wales, subsections (2) to (6) of section 44 of
            the 1971 Act;
         (*b*) in Scotland, subsections (2) to (6) of section 41 of the 1972
            Act.".
   (2) In paragraph 26 of that Schedule (interpretation of Part III of the
Schedule), after sub-paragraph (1) insert—
      "(1A) The following provisions apply in determining for the purposes
            of this Schedule when development shall be taken to be
            begun—

    (*a*) in England and Wales, subsections (1) to (3) of section 43 of the 1971 Act;

    (*b*) in Scotland, subsections (1) to (3) of section 40 of the 1972 Act.".

GENERAL NOTE

    This section amends the existing rules as to the termination of planning permission granted by an enterprise zone scheme. The 1980 Act provided originally that where a scheme was modified, operations which were started before the modification could lawfully be continued, but that the scheme did not authorise the carrying out of operations after the termination of an enterprise zone scheme; even if they started to be carried out before that date in accordance with the scheme. The new provisions allow development to be continued in either case, where it has already begun (using the criteria already established in the principal Act), and extend to this context the power of the planning authority to serve a completion notice. So far as termination of the scheme is concerned, the provisions are in line with the arrangements for simplified planning zones; but there are different provisions relating to the effect of approval of alterations to an S.P.Z. scheme.

    The amendments extend to Scotland.

Discrimination in exercise of planning functions

55.—(1) In Part III of the Race Relations Act 1976 (discrimination in fields other than employment), after section 19 insert—

"Planning

Discrimination by planning authorities

    19A.—(1) It is unlawful for a planning authority to discriminate against a person in carrying out their planning functions.

    (2) In this section "planning authority" means—

    (*a*) in England and Wales, a county, district or London borough council, a joint planning board, a special planning board or a National Park Committee, and

    (*b*) in Scotland, a planning authority or regional planning authority,

and includes an urban development corporation and a body having functions (whether as an enterprise zone authority or a body invited to prepare a scheme) under Schedule 32 to the Local Government, Planning and Land Act 1980.

    (3) In this section "planning functions" means—

    (*a*) in England and Wales, functions under the Town and Country Planning Act 1971, and such other functions as may be prescribed, and

    (*b*) in Scotland, functions under the Town and Country Planning (Scotland) Act 1972 or Part IX of the Local Government (Scotland) Act 1973, and such other functions as may be prescribed,

and includes, in relation to an urban development corporation, planning functions under Part XVI of the Local Government, Planning and Land Act 1980 and, in relation to an enterprise zone authority or body invited to prepare an enterprise zone scheme, functions under Part XVIII of that Act.".

GENERAL NOTE

    This section is designed to clarify the law relating to racial discrimination in planning. It is clear that such discrimination would not be a material consideration in the exercise of planning functions, and that decisions tainted by it could be set aside by the courts on a statutory appeal or application for judicial review. It was also widely assumed that planning functions were within the general prohibition against racial discrimination contained in the Race Relations Act 1976, as a "facility or service," but doubt was cast on that view by a decision of the House of Lords. In *Amin* v. *Entry Clearance Officer, Bombay* [1983] 2 All E.R. 864, the House held that although the Government's special voucher immigration scheme was discriminatory against women, the discrimination was not unlawful under the Sex Discrimination Act 1975, s.29 (which was in similar terms to the Race Relations Act 1976, s.19) because the prohibition extended to the provision of facilities or services, and not to grants of permission to use such facilities or services.

The new section therefore makes it clear that all planning functions, including the granting or refusal of permissions, are within the prohibition against racial discrimination.

PART VII

GENERAL PROVISIONS

Financial provisions

56.—(1) There shall be paid out of money provided by Parliament any expenses of the Secretary of State under this Act and any increase attributable to this Act in the sums so payable under any other enactment.

(2) Any sums received by the Secretary of State under this Act shall be paid into the Consolidated Fund.

(3) There shall be paid out of or into the Consolidated Fund or the National Loans Fund any increase attributable to this Act in the sums so payable under any other enactment.

Commencement

57.—(1) The following provisions of this Act come into force on the day this Act is passed—

> section 21 (effect of resolutions relating to housing action area or general improvement area);
>
> section 24(1)(*j*), paragraphs 10 to 13 of Schedule 5, the repeals specified in the first part of Part I of Schedule 12 and section 24(3) so far as relating to those repeals (miscellaneous corrections);
>
> section 52 (termination of grants for redevelopment in Scotland);
>
> this Part.

(2) The other provisions of this Act come into force on such day as may be appointed by the Secretary of State by order made by statutory instrument and—

> (*a*) different days may be appointed for different provisions or different purposes; and
>
> (*b*) an order may make such transitional provision as the Secretary of State thinks appropriate.

(5) For the purpose of any transitional provision in this Act or an order which refers to the date of service of a notice under the Housing Act 1985, no account shall be taken of any steps taken under section 177 of that Act (amendment or withdrawal and re-service of notice to correct mistakes).

Extent

58.—(1) The following provisions of this Act extend to England and Wales—

> Part I (housing), except section 3, paragraphs 10(7), 14 and 17 of Schedule 5 and the associated repeals in Part I of Schedule 12;
>
> in Part II (simplified planning zones), section 25 and Parts I and II of Schedule 6;
>
> Part III (financial assistance for urban regeneration);

> in Part IV (hazardous substances), sections 30 to 34 and Part I of
>   Schedule 7;
> Part V (opencast coal);
> in Part VI (miscellaneous provisions), sections 40 to 49, 54 and 55,
>   Part I of Schedule 9, Schedule 10, Part I of Schedule 11 and
>   Part III of Schedule 12.

(2) The following provisions of this Act extend to Scotland—

> in Part I (housing), sections 3, 19 and 22, paragraphs 8, 10(7), 13,
>   14, 17, 18 and 42 of Schedule 5 and the associated repeals in
>   Part I of Schedule 12;
> in Part II (simplified planning zones), section 26 and Parts III and
>   IV of Schedule 6;
> Part III (financial assistance for urban regeneration);
> in Part IV (hazardous substances), sections 35 to 38 and Part II of
>   Schedule 7;
> Part V (opencast coal) except so far as it repeals enactments which
>   extend to England and Wales only;
> in Part VI (miscellaneous provisions), sections 50 to 55, Part II of
>   Schedule 9, Part II of Schedule 11 and Part IV of Schedule 12;
> this Part.

(3) The following provisions of this Act extend to Northern Ireland—

> section 22 (amendments of Consumer Credit Act 1974), paragraph
>   18 of Schedule 5 (amendment relating to stamp duty),
> this Part.

Short title

59. This Act may be cited as the Housing and Planning Act 1986.

SCHEDULES

Section 6(2)   SCHEDULE 1

SCHEDULE TO BE INSERTED IN THE HOUSING ACT 1985

SCHEDULE 3A

CONSULTATION BEFORE DISPOSAL TO PRIVATE SECTOR LANDLORD

Disposals to which this Schedule applies

1.—(1) This Schedule applies to the disposal by a local authority of an interest in land as a result of which a secure tenant of the authority will become the tenant of a private sector landlord.

(2) For the purposes of this Schedule the grant of an option which if exercised would result in a secure tenant of a local authority becoming the tenant of a private sector landlord shall be treated as a disposal of the interest which is the subject of the option.

(3) Where a disposal of land by a local authority is in part a disposal to which this Schedule applies, the provisions of this Schedule apply to that part as to a separate disposal.

(4) In this paragraph "private sector landlord" means a person other than an authority or body within section 80 (the landlord condition for secure tenancies).

Application for Secretary of State's consent

2.—(1) The Secretary of State shall not entertain an application for his consent to a disposal to which this Schedule applies unless the authority certify either—

(*a*) that the requirements of paragraph 3 as to consultation have been complied with, or (*b*) that the requirements of that paragraph as to consultation have been complied with except in relation to tenants expected to have vacated the dwelling-house in question before the disposal;

and the certificate shall be accompanied by a copy of the notices given by the authority in accordance with that paragraph.

(2) Where the certificate is in the latter form, the Secretary of State shall not determine the application until the authority certify as regards the tenants not originally consulted—

(*a*) that they have vacated the dwelling-house in question, or

(*b*) that the requirements of paragraph 3 as to consultation have been complied with;

and a certificate under sub-paragraph (*b*) shall be accompanied by a copy of the notices given by the authority in accordance with paragraph 3.

(3) References in this Schedule to the Secretary of State's consent to a disposal are to the consent required by section 32 or 43 (general requirement of consent for disposal of houses or land held for housing purposes).

Requirements as to consultation

3.—(1) The requirements as to consultation referred to above are as follows.

(2) The authority shall serve notice in writing on the tenant informing him of—

(*a*) such details of their proposal as the authority consider appropriate, but including the identity of the person to whom the disposal is to be made,

(*b*) the likely consequences of the disposal for the tenant, and

(*c*) the effect of the provisions of this Schedule and of sections 171A to 171H (preservation of right to buy on disposal to private sector landlord),

and informing him that he may, within such reasonable period as may be specified in the notice, make representations to the authority.

(3) The authority shall consider any representations made to them within that period and shall serve a further written notice on the tenant informing him—

(*a*) of any significant changes in their proposal, and

(*b*) that he may within such period as is specified (which must be at least 28 days after the service of the notice) communicate to the Secretary of State his objection to the proposal,

and informing him of the effect of paragraph 5 (consent to be withheld if majority of tenants are opposed).

Power to require further consultation

4. The Secretary of State may require the authority to carry out such further consultation with their tenants, and to give him such information as to the results of that consultation, as he may direct.

Consent to be withheld if majority of tenants are opposed

5.—(1) The Secretary of State shall not give his consent if it appears to him that a majority of the tenants of the dwelling-houses to which the application relates do not wish the disposal to proceed; but this does not affect his general discretion to refuse consent on grounds relating to whether a disposal has the support of the tenants or on any other ground.

(2) In making his decision the Secretary of State may have regard to any information available to him; and the local authority shall give him such information as to the representations made to them by tenants and others, and other relevant matters, as he may require.

Protection of purchasers

6. The Secretary of State's consent to a disposal is not invalidated by a failure on his part or that of the local authority to comply with the requirements of this Schedule.

GENERAL NOTE

The new Sched. 3A to the 1985 Act, inserted by this Schedule, sets out the mechanics of the consultation process which must be undertaken prior to a disposal of local authority tenanted property into the private sector. The new schedule applies to disposals (including the grant of an option) by local authorities as a result of which a secure tenant will become the tenant of a "private sector landlord." A "private sector landlord" is defined as a body or authority not within s.80 of the 1985 Act, *i.e.* one to whom the landlord condition for secure tenancies does not apply: para. 1.

Applications for consent to the disposal under ss.32 or 43 of the 1985 Act must be accompanied by a certificate of consultation and a copy of the consultation notices: para. 2.

Consultation is a three stage process: para. 3.

(1) The authority must serve a notice on the tenant informing him—
  (*a*) of such details of the scheme as the authority consider appropriate,
  (*b*) the identity of the purchaser,
  (*c*) the likely consequences of the disposal for the tenant (this should surely include details in changes of security of tenure and any change in rent),
  (*d*) the effect of these consultation provisions,
  (*e*) the effect of the preserved right to buy,
  (*f*) the right to make representations to the authority within a reasonable, specified time;
(2) The authority must consider the representations;
(3) The authority must serve a further notice informing the tenant of any significant changes in the plan, of the right to make representations to the Secretary of State, and of the duty of the Secretary of State to withhold his consent if a majority of the tenants are opposed to the scheme.

The Secretary of State may require the authority to carry out further consultation and to give him the results of that consultation: para. 4.

The Secretary of State's discretion is not wholly unfettered. He *must* refuse approval if it appears to him that a majority of the tenants of the properties affected do not wish the proposals to proceed: para. 5. However, as the obligation is only to refuse "if it appears to" him that a majority opposes the proposals, it will be very important indeed for tenants opposing proposed agreements to make their objections known, since the Secretary of State will be making the decision on the basis of the information before him.

A failure by either the Secretary of State or the local housing authority to comply with the requirements of this schedule does not invalidate the giving of consent: para. 6. This would appear to prevent any challenge to the granting of consent on the grounds of no or inadequate consultation. However, it does not prevent the decision being challenged on other grounds, *e.g.* the decision has not been arrived at in good faith or is unreasonable: see generally *Associated Provincial Picture Houses* v. *Wednesbury Corporation* [1948] 1 K.B. 223, C.A., *Meade* v. *London Borough of Haringey* [1979] 1 W.L.R. 637, C.A. and *R.* v. *Secretary of State for the Environment, ex p. Nottinghamshire County Council* [1986] A.C. 240, H.L.

Section 8(2)   SCHEDULE 2

SCHEDULE TO BE INSERTED IN THE HOUSING ACT 1985

SCHEDULE 9A

LAND REGISTRATION AND RELATED MATTERS WHERE RIGHT TO BUY PRESERVED

Statement to be contained in instrument effecting qualifying disposal

1. On a qualifying disposal, the disponor shall secure that the instrument effecting the disposal—
  (*a*) states that the disposal is, so far as it relates to dwelling-houses occupied by secure tenants, a disposal to which section 171A applies (preservation of right to buy on disposal to private landlord), and
  (*b*) lists, to the best of the disponor's knowledge and belief, the dwelling-houses to which the disposal relates which are occupied by secure tenants.

Registration of title on qualifying disposal

2.—(1) Where on a qualifying disposal the disponor's title to the dwelling-house is not registered, section 123 of the Land Registration Act 1925 (compulsory registration of title) applies—
  (*a*) whether or not the dwelling-house is in an area in which an Order in Council under section 120 of that Act (areas of compulsory registration) is in force, and
  (*b*) whether or not, where the disposal takes the form of the grant or assignment of a lease, the lease is granted for a term of more than 21 years or, as the case may be, is a lease for a term of which more than 21 years are unexpired.

(2) In such a case the disponor shall give the disponee a certificate stating that the disponor is entitled to effect the disposal subject only to such incumbrances, rights and interests as are stated in the instrument effecting the disposal or summarised in the certificate.

(3) Where the disponor's interest in the dwelling-house is a lease, the certificate shall also state particulars of the lease and, with respect to each superior title—

(a) where it is registered, the title number;

(b) where it is not registered, whether it was investigated in the usual way on the grant of the disponor's lease.

(4) The certificate shall be—

(a) in a form approved by the Chief Land Registrar, and

(b) signed by such officer of the disponor or such other person as may be approved by the Chief Land Registrar,

and the Chief Registrar shall, for the purpose of registration of title, accept the certificate as sufficient evidence of the facts stated in it.

3. Where a qualifying disposal takes the form of the grant or assignment of a lease, sections 8 and 22 of the Land Registration Act 1925 (application for registration of leasehold land and registration of dispositions of leasehold) apply notwithstanding that it is a lease for a term of which not more than 21 years are unexpired or, as the case may be, a lease granted for a term not exceeding 21 years; and accordingly section 70(1)(k) of that Act (leases which are overriding interests) does not apply.

Entries on register protecting preserved right to buy

4. The Chief Land Registrar on application being made for registration of a disposition of registered land or, as the case may be, of the disponee's title under a disposition of unregistered land, shall, if the instrument effecting the disposal contains the statement required by paragraph 1, enter in the register—

(a) a notice protecting the rights of qualifying persons under this Part in relation to dwelling-houses comprised in the disposal, and

(b) a restriction stating the requirement of consent under section 171D(2) for certain subsequent disposals of the landlord's interest.

Change of qualifying dwelling-house

5.—(1) This paragraph applies where by virtue of section 171B(6) a new dwelling-house becomes the qualifying dwelling-house which—

(a) is entirely different from the previous qualifying dwelling-house, or

(b) includes new land,

and applies to the new dwelling-house or the new land, as the case may be.

(2) If the landlord's title is registered, the landlord shall apply for the entry on the register of—

(a) a notice protecting the rights of the qualifying person or persons under the provisions of this Part, and

(b) a restriction stating the requirement of consent under section 171D(2) for certain disposals of the landlord's interest.

(3) A qualifying person may apply for the entry of such a notice and restriction and section 64(1) of the Land Registration Act 1925 (production of land certificate) does not apply to the entry of a notice or restriction on such an application; but without prejudice to the power of the Chief Land Registrar to call for the production of the certificate by the landlord.

(4) If the landlord's title is not registered, the rights of the qualifying person or persons under the provisions of this Part are registrable under the Land Charges Act 1972 in the same way as an estate contract and the landlord shall, and a qualifying person may, apply for such registration.

Effect of non-registration

6.—(1) The rights of a qualifying person under this Part in relation to the qualifying dwelling-house—

(a) shall be treated as interests to which sections 20 and 23 of the Land Registration Act 1925 apply (under which the transferee or grantee under a registered disposition takes free from estates and interests which are not protected on the register and are not overriding interests), and

(b) shall not be treated as overriding interests for the purposes of that Act, notwithstanding that the qualifying person is in actual occupation of the land.

(2) Where by virtue of paragraph 5(4) the rights of a qualifying person under this Part in relation to the qualifying dwelling-house are registrable under the Land Charges Act 1972 in the same way as an estate contract, section 4(6) of that Act (under which such a contract may be void against a purchaser unless registered) applies accordingly, with the substitution for the reference to the contract being void of a reference to the right to buy ceasing to be preserved.

Statement required on certain disposals on which right to buy ceases to be preserved

7.—(1) A conveyance of the freehold or grant of a lease of the qualifying dwelling-house to a qualifying person in pursuance of the right to buy shall state that it is made in pursuance of the provisions of this Part as they apply by virtue of section 171A (preservation of the right to buy).

(2) Where on a conveyance of the freehold or grant of a lease of the qualifying dwelling-house to a qualifying person otherwise than in pursuance of the right to buy the dwelling-house ceases to be subject to any rights arising under this Part, the conveyance or grant shall contain a statement to that effect.

(3) Where on a disposal of an interest in a qualifying dwelling-house the dwelling-house ceases to be subject to the rights of a qualifying person under this Part by virtue of section 171D(1)(a) or 171E(2)(a) (qualifying person becoming tenant of authority or body satisfying landlord condition for secure tenancies), the instrument by which the disposal is effected shall state that the dwelling-house ceases as a result of the disposal to be subject to any rights arising by virtue of section 171A (preservation of the right to buy).

Removal of entries on land register

8. Where the registered title to land contains an entry made by virtue of this Schedule, the Chief Land Registrar shall, for the purpose of removing or amending the entry, accept as sufficient evidence of the facts stated in it a certificate by the registered proprietor that the whole or a specified part of the land is not subject to any rights of a qualifying person under this Part.

Liability to compensate or indemnify

9.—(1) An action for breach of statutory duty lies where—
(a) the disponor on a qualifying disposal fails to comply with paragraph 1 (duty to secure inclusion of statement in instrument effecting disposal), or
(b) the landlord on a change of the qualifying dwelling-house fails to comply with paragraph 5(2) or (4) (duty to apply for registration protecting preserved right to buy),
and a qualifying person is deprived of the preserved right to buy by reason of the non-registration of the matters which would have been registered if that duty had been complied with.

(2) If the Chief Land Registrar has to meet a claim under the Land Registration Acts 1925 to 1986 as a result of acting upon—
(a) a certificate given in pursuance of paragraph 2 (certificate of title on first registration),
(b) a statement made in pursuance of paragraph 7 (statements required on disposal on which right to buy ceases to be preserved), or
(c) a certificate given in pursuance of paragraph 8 (certificate that dwelling-house has ceased to be subject to rights under this Part),
the person who gave the certificate or made the statement shall indemnify him.

Meaning of "disposal" and "instrument effecting disposal"

10. References in this Schedule to a disposal or to the instrument effecting a disposal are to the conveyance, transfer, grant or assignment, as the case may be.

DEFINITIONS
    "qualifying disposal": s.8 (new s.171A).
    "qualifying person": s.8 (new s.171B).

GENERAL

The new Sched. 9A, inserted by this Schedule into the 1985 Act, sets out the details of the registration of the right to buy which is preserved upon the disposal of tenanted properties by public sector landlords to the private sector, see notes to s.8, above.

New Schedule 9A

Title to land has to be registered under the Land Registration Act 1925 in designated areas. On the first disposal of the land after its inclusion in a compulsory area title must be registered. Once registered all subsequent dispositions of the land must also be registered. Minor interests in the land can be protected by registration against the title of notices and restrictions, see s.3 of the 1925 Act. The preserved right to buy is fitted into this framework.

Para. 1

The disposal must include in the transfer documents a statement of those dwellings to which the preserved right applies.

Para. 2

If title to the premises has not previously been registered under the 1925 Act, it must now be registered whether or not the dwelling-house falls into an area of compulsory registration: subpara. (1).

Para. 4

The preserved right to buy will be entered as a notice on the register on application for registration of the disposal of title, *if* the disposal instrument contains the statement required in para. 1, above. The need for consent to disposal of a lesser interest under s.171D(2) (see notes to s.8, above) will be registered as a restriction.

Para. 5

Where the tenant, after disposal into the private sector, moves to new premises but continues to enjoy the preserved right under s.171B(6) (see notes to s.8, above), the landlord is under a duty to register a notice protecting the preserved rights and a restriction stating the requirement for consent under s.171D(2). If the new premises are not registered land then application must be made by the landlord under the Land Charges Act 1972. A tenant may himself seek registration of the notice and restriction.

Para. 6

Where the preserved right or the need for consent under s.171D(2) have not been registered they are not protected and any subsequent purchaser takes the property free of them.

Para. 7

This paragraph deals with those cases where the preserved right to buy ceases either because of sale to the tenant or because of sale to a secure landlord. The conveyance or grant must include a statement that the right has ceased.

Para. 9

Failure to make the required statement under para. 1 or to register the rights under para. 5 will have a drastic effect if the premises are subsequently disposed of, as the preserved right to buy will then be lost. Express provision is therefore made for the tenant to recover compensation for any loss caused by a breach of this statutory duty. Such compensation will presumably consist principally of the lost discount to which the tenant would otherwise have been entitled under s.129 of the 1985 Act: subpara. (1).

Section 15   SCHEDULE 3

COMMON PARTS GRANTS

PART I

AMENDMENTS OF PART XV OF THE HOUSING ACT 1985

1.—(1) Section 460 of the Housing Act 1985 (general description of main grants) is amended as follows.

(2) In subsection (1) omit the word "and" after the reference to special grants and after the reference to repairs grants insert "common parts grants (sections 498A to 498G)".

(3) In subsection (2) for paragraphs (*b*) and (*c*) substitute—

"(*b*) the improvement or repair of dwellings,

(*c*) the improvement or repair of the common parts of a building including one or more flats, and".

2. In section 462(1) of the Housing Act 1985 (preliminary condition for grants: the age of the property), after paragraph (*b*) insert ", or

(*c*) a common parts grant in respect of a building which was erected after 2nd October 1961,".

3. In section 463(1) of the Housing Act 1985 (preliminary condition for eligibility for grant: the interest of the applicant in the property) for "may entertain an application for a grant only if" substitute "shall not entertain an application for a grant, other than an application for a common parts grant, unless".

4. After section 464 of the Housing Act 1985 insert—

"Preliminary conditions for application for common parts grant

464A.—(1) A local housing authority shall not entertain an application for a common parts grant unless they are satisfied as regards the relevant works that the applicant either—

(*a*) has a duty to carry them out, or

(*b*) has power to carry them out and has a qualifying interest in the building or in a dwelling in the building,

and that, at the date of the application, at least the required proportion of the dwellings in the building is occupied by tenants.

(2) The following are qualifying interests for the purposes of subsection (1)(*b*)—

(*a*) an estate in fee simple absolute in possession;

(*b*) a term of years absolute of which not less than five years remains unexpired at the date of the application;

(*c*) a tenancy to which section 1 of the Landlord and Tenant Act 1954 applies (long tenancies at low rents);

(*d*) a protected tenancy, a secure tenancy, a protected occupancy or a statutory tenancy;

(*e*) a tenancy which satisfies such conditions as may be prescribed by order of the Secretary of State.

(3) The required proportion mentioned in subsection (1) is three-quarters or such other proportion as may be—

(*a*) prescribed for the purposes of this section by order of the Secretary of State, or

(*b*) approved by him, in relation to a particular case or description of case, on application by the local housing authority;

and "tenant" for the purposes of that requirement means a person who has an interest within any of paragraphs (*b*) to (*e*) of subsection (2) by virtue of which he occupies a dwelling in the building as his only or main residence.

(4) An order under this section—

(*a*) may make different provision with respect to different cases or descriptions of case, including different provision for different areas, and

(*b*) shall be made by statutory instrument which shall be subject to annulment in pursuance of a resolution of either House of Parliament.

(5) This section has effect subject to section 513 (parsonages, applications by charities, &c.).".

5. In section 466(1) of the Housing Act 1985 (grants requiring consent of the Secretary of State) for "or intermediate grant" substitute ", intermediate grant or common parts grant".

6. After section 498 of the Housing Act 1985 insert—

"Common parts grant

Works for which common parts grants may be given

498A.—(1) The works for which a common parts grant may be given are works required for the improvement or repair of the common parts of a building in which there are one or more flats, other than works for the provision of a dwelling.

(2) For this purpose—

(*a*) "flat" means a dwelling which is a separate set of premises, whether or not on the same floor, divided horizontally from some other part of the building, and

(*b*) "common parts" includes the structure and exterior of the building and common facilities provided, whether in the building or elsewhere, for persons who include the occupiers of one or more dwellings in the building.

Standard of repair to be attained

498B.—(1) The local housing authority shall not, without the consent of the Secretary of State, approve an application for a common parts grant in respect of a building unless they are satisfied that on completion of the relevant works the common parts of the building will be in reasonable repair.

(2) The Secretary of State's consent to the approval of applications where that standard will not be attained may be given in particular cases or in relation to descriptions of case.

(3) If in the opinion of the authority the relevant works are more extensive than is necessary for the purpose of securing that the common parts of the building will attain that standard, the authority may, with the consent of the applicant, treat the application as varied so that the relevant works include only such works as seem to the authority necessary for that purpose; and they may then approve the application as so varied.

Rateable value limit

498C.—(1) The local housing authority shall not approve an application for a common parts grant in respect of a building if, on the date of the application, the average rateable value of the dwellings in the building exceeds the limit specified for the purposes of this section by order of the Secretary of State.

(2) The consent of the Treasury is required for the making of an order.

(3) An order—

(*a*) may make different provision with respect to different cases or descriptions of case, including different provision for different areas, and

(*b*) shall be made by statutory instrument which shall be subject to annulment in pursuance of a resolution of either House of Parliament.

(4) For the purposes of this section—

(*a*) where a dwelling is a hereditament for which a rateable value is shown in the valuation list, the rateable value is the value shown;

(*b*) where a dwelling forms part only of such a hereditament, or consists of or forms part of more than one such hereditament, the rateable value is such value as the local housing authority, after consultation with the applicant as to an appropriate apportionment or aggregation, shall determine.

(5) This section does not apply to buildings in housing action areas.

Common parts grants are discretionary

498D.—(1) A local housing authority may approve an application for a common parts grant in such circumstances as they think fit.

(2) Subsection (1) has effect subject to the following provisions (which restrict the cases in which applications may be approved)—

section 465 (works already begun),

section 466 (cases in which consent of Secretary of State is required),

section 498B (standard of repair to be attained), and

section 498C (rateable value limit).

Common parts grants: estimated expense of works

498E.—(1) Where a local housing authority approve an application for a common parts grant, they shall determine the amount of the expenses which in their opinion are proper to be incurred for the execution of the relevant works and shall notify the applicant of that amount.

(2) If, after an application for a grant has been approved, the authority are satisfied that owing to circumstances beyond the control of the applicant the relevant works will not be carried out on the basis of the estimate contained in the application, they may, on receiving a further estimate, redetermine the estimated expense in relation to the grant.

(3) If the applicant satisfies the authority that—

(*a*) the relevant works cannot be, or could not have been, carried out without carrying out additional works, and

(*b*) this could not have been reasonably foreseen at the time the application was made,

the authority may determine a higher amount under subsection (1).

Common parts grant: limit on expense eligible for grant

498F.—(1) Except in a case or description of case in respect of which the Secretary of State approves a higher eligible expense, the eligible expense for the purposes of a common parts grant is so much of the estimated expense as does not exceed the prescribed amount.

(2) In subsection (1) "the prescribed amount" means an amount prescribed, or ascertained in a manner prescribed, by order of the Secretary of State.

(3) An order—

(*a*) may take different provision with respect to different cases or descriptions of case, including different provision for different areas, and

(*b*) shall be made by statutory instrument which shall be subject to annulment in pursuance of a resolution of the House of Commons.

Common parts grants: determination of amount

498G.—(1) The amount of a common parts grant shall be fixed by the local housing authority when they approve the application, and shall not exceed the appropriate percentage of the eligible expense.

(2) The authority shall notify the applicant of the amount of the grant together with the notification under section 498E(1) (notification of estimated expense of relevant works).

(3) Where the authority redetermine the amount of the estimated expense under section 498E(2) (new estimate where works cannot be carried out in accordance with original estimate), they shall make such other adjustments relating to the amount of the grant as appear to them to be appropriate; but the amount of the grant shall not be increased beyond the amount which could have been notified when the application was approved if the estimate contained in the application had been of the same amount as the further estimate.

(4) Where the authority redetermine the amount of the estimated expense under section 498E(3) (redetermination where additional works prove necessary), the eligible expense under section 498F shall be recalculated and if on the recalculation the amount of the eligible expense is greater than it was at the time when the application was approved, the amount of the grant shall be increased and the applicant notified accordingly.".

7. In section 499(3) of the Housing Act 1985 for "this Part" substitute "the following provisions of this Part down to section 507".

8. In section 511 of the Housing Act 1985 (payment of grants: general), in subsection (3)(*b*) for "or repairs grant" substitute ", repairs grant or common parts grant".

9. In section 513 of the Housing Act 1985 (special cases: parsonages, applications by charities, &c.), in subsection (2) (provisions disapplied) after the reference to section 464 omit the word "and" and insert—

"so much of section 464A(1)(*b*) (preliminary conditions for application for common parts grant) as requires the applicant to have a qualifying interest in the premises, and".

10.—(1) Section 514 of the Housing Act 1985 (power of local housing authority to carry out works with agreement of person by whom application for grant might be made) is amended as follows.

(2) For subsection (2) (definition of "requisite interest") substitute—

"(2) The reference in subsection (1) to a person having the requisite interest is, except in the case of a common parts grant, to a person who has an owner's interest in every parcel of land on which the relevant works are to be carried out; and in this subsection "owner's interest" has the same meaning as in section 463(1)(*a*).

(2A) The reference in subsection (1) to a person having the requisite interest is in the case of a common parts grant to a person who as regards the relevant works either—

(*a*) has a duty to carry them out, or

(*b*) has power to carry them out and has a qualifying interest in the building or in a dwelling in the building;

and in this subsection 'qualifying interest' has the same meaning as in section 464A(1)(*b*).".

11. In section 515 of the Housing Act 1985, for subsections (2) and (3) (effect on grant of disposal by applicant of his interest in the property) substitute—

"(2) Where an application for a grant is approved but before the certified date the applicant ceases to be a person entitled to apply for a grant of that description—

(*a*) in the case of an improvement grant, intermediate grant, special grant or repairs grant, no grant shall be paid or, as the case may be, no further instalments shall be paid, and

(*b*) in the case of a common parts grant, the local housing authority may refuse to pay the grant or any further instalment, and the authority may demand that any instalment of the grant which has been paid be repaid forthwith, together with interest from the date on which it was paid until repayment at such reasonable rate as the authority may determine.

(3) In subsection (2) 'the certified date' means the date certified by the local housing authority as the date on which the dwelling house or, as the case may be, the common parts of the building, first become fit for occupation or use after the completion of the relevant works to the satisfaction of the authority.

(4) For the purposes of subsection (2) an applicant ceases to be a person entitled to apply for a grant, other than a common parts grant, if he—

(*a*) ceases to have an owner's interest in every parcel of land on which the relevant works are to be or have been carried out, or

(*b*) ceases to be a tenant of the dwelling;

and in this subsection 'owner's interest' and 'tenant' have the same meaning as in section 463(1)(*a*) and (*b*).

(5) For the purposes of subsection (2) an applicant ceases to be a person entitled to apply for a common parts grant if he—

(*a*) ceases to have a duty to carry out the relevant works, or

(*b*) ceases to have power to carry them out or to have a qualifying interest in the building or in a dwelling in the building;

and in this subsection 'qualifying interest' has the same meaning as in section 464A(1)(*b*).".

12. In section 518 of the Housing Act 1985 (meaning of "dwelling for a disabled occupant" and related expressions), for subsection (3) substitute—

"(3) In this Part 'improvement'—

(*a*) in relation to a dwelling for a disabled occupant, includes the doing of works required for making the dwelling suitable for his accommodation, welfare or employment, and

(*b*) in relation to the common parts of a building which includes such a dwelling, includes the doing of works required for making the common parts suitable for use by a disabled occupant of a dwelling.".

13. Renumber section 519 of the Housing Act 1985 (meaning of "reasonable repair") as subsection (1) of that section and after it insert—

"(2) In determining what is 'reasonable repair' in relation to the common parts of a building, a local housing authority shall have regard to—

(*a*) the age and character of the building and the locality in which it is situated, and

(*b*) the character of the dwellings in the building and the period during which they are likely to be available for use as dwellings,

and shall disregard the state of internal decorative repair of the building and the dwellings in it.".

14.—(1) Section 526 of the Housing Act 1985 (the index to Part XV) is amended as follows.

(2) At the appropriate places insert—

"common parts (for the purposes of common parts grant)	section 498A(2)(*b*)"
"common parts grant	sections 460 and 498A"
"flat (for the purposes of common parts grant)	section 498A(2)(*a*)".

(3) In the second column of the entry relating to the expression "eligible expense" for "and 497" substitute ", 497 and 498F".

Part II

Amendment of Other Enactments

15. In section 116 of the Rent Act 1977 (consent of tenant to carrying out of works), in subsection (3) (cases in which county court may empower landlord to enter in absence of consent), for "improvement or intermediate grant" substitute "improvement grant, intermediate grant or common parts grant".

16.—(1) Part IV of the Housing Act 1985 (secure tenancies and rights of secure tenants) is amended as follows.

(2) In section 100 (power to reimburse cost of improvements carried out by tenant), in subsection (2) (cost to be net of grant), for "or repairs grant" substitute ", repairs grant or common parts grant".

(3) In section 101 (rent not to be increased on account of improvements carried out by tenant), in the second part of subsection (1) (application of provision where improvement grant-aided), for "or repairs grant" substitute ", repairs grant or common parts grant".

17. In section 244 of the Housing Act 1985 (powers of local housing authority with respect to environmental works in housing action area), in subsection (3) (no assistance for grant-aided works), for "or repairs grant" substitute ", repairs grant or common parts grant".

18. In section 255 of the Housing Act 1985 (powers of local housing authority in general improvement area), in subsection (2)(*b*) (no assistance for grant-aided works) for "or repairs grant" substitute ", repairs grant or common parts grant".

19. In section 535 of the Housing Act 1985 (exclusion of assistance under Part XVI (defective housing) where grant application pending under Part XV), in subsection (1)(*a*) for "or repairs grant" substitute, "repairs grant or common parts grant".

GENERAL NOTE

This Schedule adds to the 1985 Act the new common parts grant by amendment to the existing Act and the addition of several new sections. As to the purpose of this new grant, see the notes to s.15, above.

Para. 2

As with improvement and repair grants, applications will generally not be considered for a building erected after October 2, 1961.

Para. 3

Section 463 of the 1985 Act sets out the proprietory interest which an applicant must have before a grant can be considered. This condition is specifically excluded in the case of common parts grants, and a different condition applies, see para. 4, below.

Para. 4

This paragraph inserts the new s.464A of the 1985 Act, establishing the necessary preliminary conditions to applications for a common parts grant.

New s.464A

Two preliminary conditions must be satisfied. First, the applicant must show as regards the works to be carried out that he has either (a) a duty to carry them out or (b) both the power to carry them out *and* a qualifying interest in the property, as defined in subs. (2): subs. (1). In general where premises are let, one of the parties to the lease, more usually the landlord, has an express duty to carry out repairs to the common parts. Such a duty on the part of the landlord may also be implied into a lease in certain circumstances, see *Liverpool City Council* v. *Irwin* [1977] A.C. 239, H.L. Although unusual, a tenant may be under a duty to carry out works to the common parts, as, *e.g.* where the top floor flat leaseholder is responsible for the upkeep of the roof.

The second limb of the proprietory qualification (*i.e.* (b) in the last paragraph) is intended to cover the situation where no one is under a duty to maintain the common parts, an unusual but not unheard of situation. In these circumstances any tenant of a flat (whether under a long or short lease) is extremely unlikely to have the power to do the works to the common parts, as those parts will still be in the possession and control of the owner of the building.

Second, at the date of application at least three-quarters of the dwellings in the building must be occupied by tenants, as defined in subs. (2)(*b*)–(*e*): subss. (1), (3). The proportion may be altered by statutory instrument: subs. (3). In other words, the building must be no more than one-quarter vacant.

Para. 6

The new sections inserted by this para. set out the details of the grant.

New s.498A

The grant is available for works of improvement or repair to the common parts of a building which contain flats: subs. (1). "Common parts" is defined in subs. (2) as *including* the structure and exterior of the building, and the common facilities provided. The words "structure and exterior" are also to be found in s.11 of the Landlord and Tenant Act 1985, and have been held to include the partition wall between a house and the adjoining house (*Green* v. *Eales* (1841) 2 Q.B. 225), windows (*Quick* v. *Taff Ely Borough Council* [1985] 2

All E.R. 321, 18 H.L.R. 66, C.A.) and essential means of access to a house (*Brown* v. *Liverpool Corporation* [1969] 3 All E.R. 1345; 13 H.L.R. 1, C.A.).

New s.498B
The works to the common parts have to bring them up to a reasonable state of repair: subs. (1). Reasonable repair is defined in s.519 of the 1985 Act as amended by para. 13. This section is analogous to that to be found in s.468 of the 1985 Act (for improvement grants), s.476, *ibid* (for intermediate grants), s.493, *ibid* (for repairs grants) and s.485, *ibid*, for special grants. If more works are included than are needed to achieve the required standard, the authority can treat the application as varied so as to exclude the superfluous works, with the consent of the applicant: subs. (3). If the applicant does not consent, then (a) as the grant is discretionary it may be refused or reduced, and (b) only properly incurred expenditure is admissible under s.498E, below.

New s.498C
As with improvement grants to owner-occupied dwellings (see s.469 of the 1985 Act), rateable value limits are set, so that "high value" properties will not be eligible for a common parts grant. This section does not apply when the building is situated in a housing action area: subs. (5).
The rateable values (as defined in subs. (4)) are applied as at the date of the application. The limit is not to the building as a whole, but is to be calculated by reference to the average (presumably mean average) of the dwellings in the building.

New s.498D
Provided the authority are not prevented from approving the application for a common parts grant by one of the specified provisions, approval or refusal is entirely within their discretion. As anyone can make an application, it would seem that the authority are bound to consider each application, on its merits, but are perfectly entitled to formulate and adopt policies which will normally be applied, provided that the application of the policy is reconsidered in each case, and permits of exceptions where called for: see, *e.g. British Oxygen Co. Ltd.* v. *Board of Trade* [1971] A.C. 610, H.L., *Re Betts* [1983] 2 A.C. 613, 10 H.L.R. 97, H.L.
How far the grant proves successful will in large measure depend on the funding made available by central government, since expenditure on payment of grant is prescribed expenditure under s.71, and para. 1 of Sched. 12, to the Local Government, Planning and Land Act 1980.

New s.498E
The first stage in the calculation of a common parts grant is to establish the expense of the works. Not the whole of this expense will be eligible for grant-aid: s.498F, governs these limits. Even then, only a proportion of this eligible expense will be provided by way of grant: see s.498G.
The expenses to be taken into account are those which the authority consider "properly to be incurred", which clearly permits the authority to exclude estimates which in their judgment are exorbitant.

Subs. (2)
This meets the case where the applicant has to obtain a new estimate, *e.g.* if the builder who has provided the estimate withdraws, perhaps because of the length of time the authority take to reach a decision, a most common occurrence experienced in relation to the existing grants, and which the complexities of this new grant may exacerbate. If a new estimate is used, the authority must recalculate the estimated expense.

Subs. (3)
Normally, the expense is estimated as at the date the grant is approved. However, an applicant can apply for an increase on the grounds of "unforeseeable additional works", in which case the authority can increase the estimated expense, with consequential increase of the amount of grant under s.498G.

New s.498F
Not the whole of the eligible expense is admitted, only that which does not exceed the prescribed amount as defined in this section.

New s.498G

This is the last limb of the calculation. The amount payable is not to exceed the amount stated, so that authorities have a discretion (*cf.* s.498D) to pay as little as they wish.

Para. 8

Section 511 of the 1985 Act, governs the payment of grants and is applied to the common parts grant.

Para. 9

Section 513 disapplies certain conditions to parsonages and charities and is extended to common parts grant as set out in this para.

Para. 10

Section 514 permits "agency agreement" under which the authority "execute" grant-aided works or works which could have been grant-aided. They can only do this on behalf of a person with the "requisite interest" in the property. The amendments in this para. extend the definition of "requisite interest" to those who qualify for a common parts grant under s.464A, see para. 4, above.

Para. 11

Where a person disposes of his interest before the works are completed no grant is payable and any stage-payments made may be recovered: 1985 Act, s.515. This para. amends s.515 to bring in the common parts grant. However, rather than it being mandatory not to pay the grant, the local authority have a *discretion* not to pay it.

Para. 12

Secton 518 of the 1985 Act adapts the grant provisions to the needs of the disabled, and by this amendment a particular definition of "improvement" is included for the common parts grant for the same purpose.

Para. 13

The definition of reasonable repair (see notes to s.498B, above) is specially adapted for works to common parts by this amendment.

Paras. 14 to 19

These contain various consequential amendments.

Section 18　　　　　　　　　　SCHEDULE 4

FURTHER PROVISIONS WITH RESPECT TO SHARED OWNERSHIP LEASES

The Rent Act 1977 (c.42)

1.—(1) Part I of the Rent Act 1977 (preliminary provisions) is amended as follows.
(2) After section 5 insert—

"Certain shared ownership leases

5A.—(1) A tenancy is not a protected tenancy if it is a qualifying shared ownership lease, that is—
(a) a lease granted in pursuance of the right to be granted a shared ownership lease under Part V of the Housing Act 1985, or
(b) a lease granted by a housing association and which complies with the conditions set out in subsection (2) below.
(2) The conditions referred to in subsection (1)(b) above are that the lease—
(a) was granted for a term of 99 years or more and is not (and cannot become) terminable except in pursuance of a provision for re-entry or forfeiture;
(b) was granted at a premium, calculated by reference to the value of the dwelling-house or the case of providing it, of not less than 25 per cent., or such other percentage as may be prescribed, of the figure by reference to which it was calculated;
(c) provides for the tenant to acquire additional shares in the dwelling-house on terms specified in the lease and complying with such requirements as may be prescribed;

(*d*) does not restrict the tenant's powers to assign, mortgage or charge his interest in the dwelling-house;

(*e*) if it enables the landlord to require payment for outstanding shares in the dwelling-house, does so only in such circumstances as may be prescribed;

(*f*) provides, in the case of a house, for the tenant to acquire the landlord's interest on terms specified in the lease and complying with such requirements as may be prescribed; and

(*g*) states the landlord's opinion that by virtue of this section the lease is excluded from the operation of this Act.

(3) The Secretary of State may by regulations prescribe anything requiring to be prescribed for the purposes of subsection (2) above.

(4) The regulations may—

(*a*) make different provision for different cases or descriptions of case, including different provision for different areas, and

(*b*) contain such incidental, supplementary or transitional provisions as the Secretary of State considers appropriate,

and shall be made by statutory instrument which shall be subject to annulment in pursuance of a resolution of either House of Parliament.

(5) In any proceedings the court may, if of opinion that it is just and equitable to do so, treat a lease as a qualifying shared ownership lease notwithstanding that the condition specified in subsection (2)(*g*) above is not satisfied.

(6) In this section—

"house" has the same meaning as in Part I of the Leasehold Reform Act 1967;

"housing association" has the same meaning as in the Housing Associations Act 1985; and

"lease" includes an agreement for a lease, and references to the grant of a lease shall be construed accordingly.".

(3) In section 19(5) (contracts which are not restricted contracts), after paragraph (*c*) insert—

"(*cc*) it creates a qualifying shared ownership lease within the meaning of section 5A of this Act; or".

The Rent (Agriculture) Act 1976 (c.80)

2. In Schedule 2 to the Rent (Agriculture) Act 1976 (licences and tenancies giving rise to protected occupancy), in paragraph 3 (adaptation of provisions of Rent Act 1977 as they apply for the purposes of the 1976 Act), after sub-paragraph (2) insert—

"(2A) In section 5A (exclusion of certain shared ownership leases), in subsection (2)(*g*) (condition that lease states landlord's opinion that 1977 Act does not apply) for the reference to the 1977 Act substitute a reference to this Act.".

Part I of the Leasehold Reform Act 1967 (c.88)

3. In section 1 of the Leasehold Reform Act 1967 (tenants entitled to enfranchisement or extension), after subsection (1) insert—

"(1A) The references in subsection (1)(*a*) and (*b*) to a long tenancy at a low rent do not include a tenancy excluded from the operation of this Part by section 33A of and Schedule 4A to this Act.".

4. In section 3(2) of the Leasehold Reform Act 1967 after "long tenancy at a low rent" insert "(other than a lease excluded from the operation of this Part by section 33A of and Schedule 4A to this Act)".

5. After section 33 of the Leasehold Reform Act 1967 insert—

"Exclusion of certain shared ownership leases

33A. The provisions of Schedule 4A to this Act shall have effect to exclude certain shared ownership leases from the operation of this Part of this Act.".

6. After Schedule 4 to the Leasehold Reform Act 1967 insert—

"SCHEDULE 4A

EXCLUSION OF CERTAIN SHARED OWNERSHIP LEASES

Leases granted in pursuance of right to be granted a shared ownership lease

1. A lease granted in pursuance of the right to be granted a shared ownership lease under Part V of the Housing Act 1985 is excluded from the operation of this Part of this Act.

Certain leases granted by certain public authorities

2.—(1) A lease which—
   (*a*) was granted at a premium by a body mentioned in sub-paragraph (2), and
   (*b*) complies with the conditions set out in sub-paragraph (3),
is excluded from the operation of this Part at any time when the interest of the landlord belongs to such a body.
   (2) The bodies are—
   (*a*) a county, district or London borough council, the Common Council of the City of London or the Council of the Isles of Scilly;
   (*b*) the Inner London Education Authority or a joint authority established by Part IV of the Local Government Act 1985;
   (*c*) the Commission for the New Towns or a development corporation established by an order made, or having effect as made, under the New Towns Act 1981;
   (*d*) an urban development corporation within the meaning of Part XVI of the Local Government, Planning and Land Act 1980;
   (*e*) the Development Board for Rural Wales;
   (3) The conditions are that the lease—
   (*a*) provides for the tenant to acquire the freehold for a consideration which is to be calculated in accordance with the lease and which is reasonable, having regard to the premium or premiums paid by the tenant under the lease, and
   (*b*) states the landlord's opinion that by virtue of this paragraph the tenancy will be excluded from the operation of this Part of this Act at any time when the interest of the landlord belongs to a body mentioned in sub-paragraph (2) above.
   (4) If, in proceedings in which it falls to be determined whether a lease complies with the condition in sub-paragraph (3)(*a*), the question arises whether the consideration payable by the tenant on acquiring the freehold is reasonable, it is for the landlord to show that it is.

Certain leases granted by housing associations

3.—(1) A lease granted by a housing association and which complies with the conditions set out in sub-paragraph (2) is excluded from the operation of this Part of this Act, whether or not the interest of the landlord still belongs to such an association.
   (2) The conditions are that the lease—
   (*a*) was granted for a term of 99 years or more and is not (and cannot become) terminable except in pursuance of a provision for re-entry or forfeiture;
   (*b*) was granted at a premium, calculated by reference to the value of the house or the cost of providing it, of not less than 25 per cent., or such other percentage as may be prescribed, of the figure by reference to which it was calculated;
   (*c*) provides for the tenant to acquire additional shares in the house on terms specified in the lease and complying with such requirements as may be prescribed;
   (*d*) does not restrict the tenant's powers to assign, mortgage or charge his interest in the house;
   (*e*) if it enables the landlord to require payment for outstanding shares in the house, does so only in such circumstances as may be prescribed;
   (*f*) provides for the tenant to acquire the landlord's interest on terms specified in the lease and complying with such requirements as may be prescribed; and
   (*g*) states the landlord's opinion that by virtue of this paragraph the lease is excluded from the operation of this Part of this Act.
   (3) In any proceedings the court may, if of the opinion that it is just and equitable to do so, treat a lease as satisfying the conditions in sub-paragraph (2) notwithstanding that the condition specified in paragraph (*g*) of that sub-paragraph is not satisfied.

(4) In this paragraph "housing association" has the same meaning as in the Housing Associations Act 1985.

4.—(1) A lease for the elderly granted by a registered housing association and which complies with the conditions set out in sub-paragraph (2) is excluded from the operation of this Part of this Act at any time when the interest of the landlord belongs to such an association.

(2) The conditions are that the lease—

(*a*) is granted at a premium which is calculated by reference to a percentage of the value of the house or of the cost of providing it,

(*b*) complies, at the time when it is granted, with such requirements as may be prescribed, and

(*c*) states the landlord's opinion that by virtue of this paragraph the lease will be excluded from the operation of this Part of this Act at any time when the interest of the landlord belongs to a registered housing association.

(3) In this paragraph—

"lease for the elderly" has such meaning as may be prescribed; and

"registered housing association" has the same meaning as in the Housing Associations Act 1985.

Power to prescribe matters by regulations

5.—(1) The Secretary of State may by regulations prescribe anything requiring to be prescribed for the purposes of this Schedule.

(2) The regulations may—

(*a*) make different provision for different cases or descriptions of case, including different provision for different areas, and

(*b*) contain such incidental, supplementary or transitional provisions as the Secretary of State considers appropriate,

and shall be made by statutory instrument which shall be subject to annulment in pursuance of a resolution of either House of Parliament.

Interpretation

6. In this Schedule "lease" means a lease at law or in equity, and references to the grant of a lease shall be construed accordingly.".

Consequential amendments and repeals

7. In the Housing Act 1980, omit section 140.

8. In the Local Government, Planning and Land Act 1980, omit section 156(3).

9.—(1) The Local Government Act 1985 is amended as follows.

(2) In Schedule 13 (application of local authority provisions to residuary bodies), in paragraph 14, after sub-paragraph (*a*) insert—

"(*aa*) paragraph 2 of Schedule 4A to the Leasehold Reform Act 1967;".

and at the end of sub-paragraph (*b*) insert "and" and omit sub-paragraph (*d*) and the word "and" preceding it.

(3) In Schedule 14, omit paragraph 58(*e*).

10. In Part IV of the Housing Act 1985 (secure tenancies), in section 115 (meaning of "long tenancy"), in subsection (2)(*c*) after "1980" insert "or paragraph 3(2)(*b*) of Schedule 4A to the Leasehold Reform Act 1967".

Transitional provisions and savings

11.—(1) The amendments made by this Schedule apply only in relation to leases granted after the commencement of this Schedule.

(2) This Schedule does not affect the operation of section 140 of the Housing Act 1980, the enactments applying that section and regulations made under it, in relation to leases granted before the commencement of this Schedule.

GENERAL NOTE

This Schedule contains amendments to the Rent Act 1977, Rent (Agriculture) Act 1976 and the Leasehold Reform Act 1967 relating to shared ownership leases, see further notes to s.18 above.

Paras. 1, 2

The Rent Act 1977 and Rent (Agriculture) Act 1976 are amended to prevent shared ownership leases giving rise to a protected tenancy or a restricted contract tenancy, in the case of the 1977 Act, or a protected occupancy in the case of the 1976 Act. The exclusion only applies to "qualifying" shared ownership leases, as defined in subss. (1), (2) of new s.5A of the 1977 Act. These are limited to leases granted in pursuance of the right to a shared ownership lease under Part V of the 1985 Act and certain leases granted by housing associations.

Paras. 4, 5, 6

These paras. amend the Leasehold Reform Act 1967 so as to exclude certain leases from the right to extension or enfranchisement under the Act. The leases which are excluded are those set out in the new Sched. 4A to be added to the Act.

New Schedule 4A

The leases included are:

(1) those granted in pursuance of the right to a shared ownership lease under Part V, 1985 Act: para. 1;

(2) shared ownership leases granted voluntarily by certain public authorities: para. 2;

(3) shared ownership leases granted by housing associations: para. 3;

(4) shared ownership leases for the elderly granted by *registered* housing associations: para. (4). This para. is designed to include the schemes run by certain housing associations to provide sheltered accommodation for the elderly for which leases can be bought.

It should be noted that the definition of what constitutes a shared ownership lease differs in each case.

Section 24(1), (2)   SCHEDULE 5

HOUSING: MINOR AND CONSEQUENTIAL AMENDMENTS

PART I

MINOR AMENDMENTS

Effect of covenant for repayment of discount

1.—(1) In section 36 of the Housing Act 1985 (charge to secure repayment of discount given on voluntary disposal), after subsection (3) insert—

"(3A) The covenant required by section 35 (covenant for repayment of discount) does not, by virtue of its binding successors in title of the purchaser, bind a person exercising rights under a charge having priority over the charge taking effect by virtue of this section, or a person deriving title under him; and a provision of the conveyance, grant or assignment, or of a collateral agreement, is void in so far as it purports to authorise a forfeiture, or to impose a penalty or disability, in the event of any such person failing to comply with the covenant.".

(2) In section 156 of the Housing Act 1985 (charge to secure repayment of discount given on exercise of right to buy), after subsection (3) insert—

"(3A) The covenant required by section 155 (covenant for repayment of discount) does not, by virtue of its binding successors in title of the tenant, bind a person exercising rights under a charge having priority over the charge taking effect by virtue of this section, or a person deriving title under him; and a provision of the conveyance or grant, or of a collateral agreement, is void in so far as it purports to authorise a forfeiture, or to impose a penalty or disability, in the event of any such person failing to comply with that covenant.".

(3) In section 158 of the Housing Act 1985 (consideration for reconveyance or surrender of dwelling-house in National Park, etc. acquired in pursuance of right to buy) in subsection (3) (reduction of consideration where discount to be repaid or outstanding share to be paid for) after "shall be reduced" insert ", subject to subsection (4),", and after that subsection insert—

"(4) Where there is a charge on the dwelling-house having priority over the charge to secure payment of the sum due under the covenant mentioned in subsection (2), the consideration shall not be reduced under subsection (3) below the amount necessary to discharge the outstanding sum secured by the first-mentioned charge at the date of the offer to reconvey or surrender.".

(4) In paragraph 2 of Schedule 2 to the Housing Associations Act 1985 (charge to secure repayment of discount given on voluntary disposal by housing association), after sub-paragraph (3) insert—

"(3A) The covenant required by paragraph 1 (covenant for repayment of discount) does not, by virtue of its binding successors in title of the purchaser, bind a person exercising rights under a charge having priority over the charge taking effect by virtue of this paragraph, or a person deriving title under him; and a provision of the conveyance, grant or assignment, or of a collateral agreement, is void in so far as it purports to authorise a forfeiture, or to impose a penalty or disability, in the event of any such person failing to comply with that covenant.".

(5) The above amendments apply to covenants entered into before as well as after the commencement of this paragraph.

Acquisition of dwelling-house subject to statutory tenancy

2. In Part IV of the Housing Act 1985 (secure tenancies), before section 110 under the heading "*Supplementary provisions*" insert—

"Acquisition of dwelling-house subject to statutory tenancy
109A. Where an authority or body within section 80 (the landlord condition for secure tenancies) becomes the landlord of a dwelling-house subject to a statutory tenancy, the tenancy shall be treated for all purposes as if it were a contractual tenancy on the same terms, and the provisions of this Part apply accordingly.".

Landlord's notice to mention any structural defect

3. In section 125 of the Housing Act 1985 (exercise of right to buy: landlord's notice of purchase price and certain other matters), after subsection (4) insert—

"(4A) The notice shall contain a description of any structural defect known to the landlord affecting the dwelling-house or the building in which it is situated or any other building over which the tenant will have rights under the conveyance or lease.".

Re-service of notices, etc. on change of landlord in course of exercise of right to buy

4.—(1) Section 137 of the Housing Act 1985 (change of landlord after notice claiming right to buy or right to a mortgage) is amended as follows.

(2) Make the existing provision subsection (1) and in it after "all parties shall" insert ", subject to subsection (2),".

(3) After that subsection insert—

"(2) If the circumstances after the disposal differ in any material respect, as for example where—
(*a*) the interest of the disponee in the dwelling-house after the disposal differs from that of the disponor before the disposal, or
(*b*) the right to a mortgage becomes exercisable against the Housing Corporation rather than the landlord, or *vice versa*, or
(*c*) any of the provisions of Schedule 5 (exceptions to the right to buy) becomes or ceases to be applicable,
all those concerned shall, as soon as practicable after the disposal, take all such steps (whether by way or amending or withdrawing and re-serving any notice or extending any period or otherwise) as may be requisite for the purpose of securing that all parties are, as nearly as may be, in the same position as they would have been if those circumstances had obtained before the disposal.".

Deferment of completion in pursuance of right to buy

5.—(1) In sections 140(3)(*c*) and 152(3) of the Housing Act 1985 (period before notice to complete can be served where tenant entitled to defer completion) for "two years" substitute "three years".

(2) In sections 142(1)(*c*), (2) and (5) and 151(3) of that Act for "£100" (the amount which the tenant must deposit in order to be entitled to defer completion) substitute "£150".

(3) The above amendments apply where notice under section 142(1) of that Act claiming to be entitled to defer completion is served after the commencement of this paragraph.

(4) The above amendments to sections 140(3)(*c*), 142(5), 151(3) and 152(3) also apply where notice under section 142(1) of that Act claiming to be entitled to defer completion was served before the commencement of this paragraph if the tenant—

(*a*) serves a further notice on the landlord claiming the benefit of the longer period, and
(*b*) at the same time deposits with the landlord an additional £50;
and section 142(5) applies to the sum so deposited as if it had been deposited in pursuance of a notice under that section.

(5) No such further notice may be served if the landlord has already served a notice under section 140 or 152 of the Housing Act 1985 (landlord's first notice to complete).

(6) The following provisions of the Housing Act 1985 apply, as to provisions of Part V of that Act, to the provisions of this paragraph relating to a further notice or deposit—

section 170 (assistance in connection with legal proceedings),
section 176 (form and service of notices),
section 177 (errors and omissions in notices),
section 180 (statutory declarations),
section 181 (jurisdiction of county court).

Penalty for voting on certain housing matters

6.—(1) In section 618(4) of the Housing Act 1985 (penalty for member of Common Council or committee voting on housing matter relating to land in which he is interested), for "level 2 on the standard scale" substitute "level 4 on the standard scale".

(2) The above amendment does not apply to offences committed before the commencement of this paragraph.

Grounds for withholding consent to assignment of secure tenancy

7. In Schedule 3 to the Housing Act 1985 (grounds for withholding consent to assignment by way of exchange), after Ground 9 add—

"Ground 10

The dwelling-house is the subject of a management agreement under which the manager is a housing association of which at least half the members are tenants of dwelling-houses subject to the agreement, at least half the tenants of the dwelling-houses are members of the association and the proposed assignee is not, and is not willing to become, a member of the association.".

Grants for affording tax relief to housing associations

8.—(1) In section 62 of the Housing Associations Act 1985 (grants for affording relief from tax), after subsection (1) insert—

"(1A) In subsection (1)(*a*) 'letting' includes—
(*a*) in England and Wales, the grant of a shared ownership lease;
(*b*) in Scotland, disposal under a shared ownership agreement.".

(2) In section 73 of the Housing Associations Act 1985 (the index to Part II), at the appropriate place insert—

"shared ownership
agreement (in Scotland)
section 106."

Service charges in respect of the cost of grant-aided works

9.—(1) In the Landlord and Tenant Act 1985, after section 20 insert—

"Limitation of service charges: grant-aided works
"20A. Where relevant costs are incurred or to be incurred on the carrying out of works in respect of which a grant has been or is to be paid under Part XV of the Housing Act 1985 (grants for works of improvement, repair or conversion), the amount of the grant shall be deducted from the costs and the amount of the service charge payable shall be reduced accordingly.".

(2) In section 21 of the Landlord and Tenant Act 1985 (request or summary of relevant costs), in subsection (5) (contents of summary) after "shall" insert "state whether any of the costs relate to works in respect of which a grant has been or is to be paid under Part XV of the Housing Act 1985 (grants for works of improvement, repair or conversion) and".

(3) In section 47 of the Housing Act 1985 (limitation on service charges payable after disposal of house by public sector authority), after subsection (3) add—

"(4) Where relevant costs are incurred or to be incurred on the carrying out of works in respect of which a grant has been or is to be paid under Part XV (grants for works of improvement, repair or conversion), the amount of the grant shall be deducted from the costs and the amount of the service charge payable shall be reduced accordingly.".

(4) In section 48 of the Housing Act 1985 (request for summary of relevant costs), after subsection (3) (contents of summary) insert—

"(3A) The summary shall also state whether any of the costs relate to works in respect of which a grant has been or is to be paid under Part XV (grants for works of improvement, repair or conversion).".

Miscellaneous corrections

10.—(1) In section 73(5) of the Land Compensation Act 1973—

(*a*) in paragraph (*a*) for "Part I of Schedule 24 to the Housing Act 1985" substitute "Schedule 23 to the Housing Act 1985";

(*b*) in paragraph (*b*) for "Part II of that Schedule" substitute "Schedule 24 to that Act"; and

(*c*) in the closing words for "that Schedule" substitute "those Schedules".

(2) In sections 207 and 322 of the Housing Act 1985, in the definition of "person having control" for "house" substitute "premises".

(3) In section 251(5)(*b*) of the Housing Act 1985 after "housing action" insert "area".

(4) In section 256(4)(*b*) of the Housing Act 1985 for "to the local planning authority" substitute "of the local planning authority".

(5) In paragraph 1(2)(*c*) of Part I of Schedule 24 to the Housing Act 1985 for "demolished in pursuance of an undertaking given in accordance with section 264" substitute "vacated in pursuance of an undertaking for its demolition".

(6) In section 10(2)(*b*) of the Housing Associations Act 1985, for "Schedule 3 to the Housing Act 1985" substitute "Schedule 1 to the Housing Act 1985".

(7) In paragraph 27 of Schedule 2 to the Housing (Consequential Provisions) Act 1985 for "(4)", in both places where it occurs, substitute "(6)".

(8) In Schedule 3 to the Housing (Consequential Provisions) Act 1985, after paragraph 2 insert—

"2A. Any order made under section 115(11) of the Housing Act 1974 (form of notice of compensation where land in clearance area deemed appropriated for provision of housing) which was in force immediately before the repeal of that section by this Act may be revoked or amended by regulations under section 614 of the Housing Act 1985 (general power to prescribe forms, etc. by regulations).".

(9) The above amendments have effect from 1st April 1986.

11.—(1) In sections 80(1)(*a*) and 81(1)(*a*), (3)(*b*) and (4)(*b*) of the Building Act 1984 (service of notices in respect of proposed demolition), after "demolition order" insert "or obstructive building order".

(2) The above amendment to section 80 of the Building Act 1984 has effect from 1st April 1986.

12. In paragraph 14(2) of Schedule 11 and paragraph 8(2) of Schedule 22 to the Housing Act 1985 (procedure after compulsory purchase order has become operative), for "a copy of the notice" substitute "a copy of the order".

13. In Part II of the Housing Associations Act 1985 (housing association finance)—

(*a*) in section 67(1) (loans by Public Works Loan Commissioners: England and Wales), and

(*b*) in section 68(1) (loans by Public Works Loan Commissioners: Scotland), for "housing association" substitute "registered housing association".

PART II

CONSEQUENTIAL AMENDMENTS

Housing Rents and Subsidies (Scotland) Act 1975

14. In section 5 of the Housing Rents and Subsidies (Scotland) Act 1975 (agreements for exercise by housing co-operatives of certain local authority housing functions), omit subsection (6).

Rent Act 1977

15. In section 16 of the Rent Act 1977 (tenancy not protected if interest of landlord belongs to housing co-operative) for the words from "within the meaning of section 27" to the end substitute "within the meaning of section 27B of the Housing Act 1985 (agreements with housing co-operatives under certain superseded provisions) and the dwelling-house is comprised in a housing co-operative agreement within the meaning of that section".

16.—(1) Schedule 12 to the Rent Act 1977 (procedure on application for certificate of fair rent) is amended as follows.

(2) In paragraph (1)(*c*)—

(*a*)　after "section 69(1)(*a*)" insert "or (1A)(*b*)";

(*b*)　after "improvement" insert "or repair";

(*c*)　after "regulated" insert "or secure".

(3) In paragraph 3, after "If," insert—

"in the case of—

(*a*)　an application under section 69(1) of this Act where the dwelling-house is not subject to a regulated tenancy, or

(*b*)　an application under section 69(1A) of this Act where the dwelling-house is not subject to a secure tenancy,";

and omit "unless the dwelling-house is subject to a regulated tenancy".

(4) In paragraph 4, for the words from "an application" to "regulated tenancy" substitute "—

(*a*)　an application under section 69(1) of this Act where the dwelling-house is not subject to a regulated tenancy and which does not fall within paragraph 3 above, or

(*b*)　an application under section 69(1A) of this Act and which does not fall within paragraph 3 above and where the dwelling-house is not subject to a secure tenancy,".

(5) In paragraph 5(1), for "Where the dwelling-house is subject to a regulated tenancy" substitute "In the case of—

(*a*)　an application under section 69(1) of this Act where the dwelling-house is subject to a regulated tenancy, or

(*b*)　an application under section 69(1A) of this Act where the dwelling-house is subject to a secure tenancy,".

(6) In paragraphs 8(2) and 11, after "regulated" insert "or secure".

(7) After paragraph 11 add—

"12. In this Schedule 'secure tenancy' has the same meaning as in Part IV of the Housing Act 1985, but does not include such a tenancy where the landlord is the Housing Corporation, a housing association or a housing trust which is a charity.

In this paragraph 'housing association', 'housing trust' and 'charity' have the same meaning as in Part IV of the Housing Act 1985.".

Tenants' Rights, &c. (Scotland) Act 1980

17. In section 1(10) of the Tenants' Rights, &c. (Scotland) Act 1980 (landlords relevant to qualifying period for right to purchase and discount) in paragraph (*e*) for "section 27 of the Housing Act 1985" substitute "section 27B of the Housing Act 1985".

Finance Act 1981

18. In section 107 of the Finance Act 1981 (stamp duty payable on disposal of dwelling-house at a discount by certain authorities), after subsection (3A) insert—

"(3B) This section also applies to a conveyance or transfer on sale (including the grant of a lease) by a person against whom the right to buy under Part V of the Housing Act 1985 is exercisable by virtue of section 171A of that Act (preservation of right to buy on disposal to private sector landlord) to a person who is the qualifying person for the purposes of the preserved right to buy and in relation to whom that dwelling-house is the qualifying dwelling-house."

Local Government Act 1985

19. In paragraph 22 of Schedule 13 to the Local Government Act 1985 (provisions of Housing Act 1985 applying to residuary bodies) after "444," insert 450A to 450C,".

20. In section 4(*e*) of the Housing Act 1985 (general definition of "local authority" for the Act) for "444(4), 452(2), 453(2)" substitute "458".

21. In section 20 of the Housing Act 1985 (houses of local authority to which management provisions apply), for "down to section 26" substitute "down to section 27B".

22. In section 21 of the Housing Act 1985 (management powers to be exercised by local housing authority), in subsection (2) (general proposition subject to section 27), for "(agreements for exercise of housing management functions by co-operative)" substitute "(management agreements)".

23. In section 30 of the Housing Act 1985 (application of housing management provisions to new town corporations and the Development Board for Rural Wales), omit subsection (2) (which relates to section 27: management agreements).

24. Omit section 46 of the Housing Act 1985 (definition of "service charge" for the purposes of certain provisions of Part II).

25. In section 57 of the Housing Act 1985 (the index to Part II), in the entries relating to the expressions "payee and payer", "relevant costs" and "service charge" for "section 46" substitute "section 621A".

26. In section 80 of the Housing Act 1985 (the landlord condition for secure tenancies), for subsection (4) (housing co-operatives to which the section applies) substitute—

"(4) This section applies to a housing co-operative within the meaning of section 27B (agreements under certain superseded provisions) where the dwelling-house is comprised in a housing co-operative agreement within the meaning of that section.".

27. In section 117 of the Housing Act 1985 (the index to Part IV) at the appropriate places insert—

"consent (in Schedule 3A)	paragraph 2(3) of that Schedule"
"landlord (in Part V of Schedule 2)	paragraph 5 of that Part"
"management agreement and manager	sections 27(2) and 27B(4)".

28. In section 127(1) of the Housing Act 1985, omit the word "and" at the end of paragraph (*a*).

29. In section 130 of the Housing Act 1985 (reduction of discount where previous discount given), in subsection (2) (meaning of "previous discount") in paragraph (*a*) after "7" insert "or 7A" and after that paragraph insert—

"(*aa*) on conveyance of the freehold, or a grant or assignment of a long lease of a dwelling-house by a person against whom the right to buy was exercisable by virtue of section 171A (preservation of right to buy on disposal to private sector landlord) to a person who was a qualifying person for the purposes of the preserved right to buy and in relation to whom that dwelling-house was the qualifying dwelling-house, or".

30.—(1) Section 187 of the Housing Act 1985 (minor definitions for purposes of Part V (the right to buy)) is amended as follows.

(2) In the definition of "improvement"—

(*a*) after "means" insert ", in relation to a dwelling-house,",

(*b*) for "a dwelling-house", in both places, substitute "the dwelling-house", and

(*c*) at the end (full-out after paragraph (*c*)) insert "and shall be similarly construed in relation to any other building or land;".

(3) At the appropriate place insert—

" 'improvement contribution' means an amount payable by a tenant of a flat in respect of improvements to the flat, the building in which it is situated or any other building or land, other than works carried out in discharge of any such obligations as are referred to in paragraph 16A(1) of Schedule 6 (obligations to repair, reinstate, etc.);".

31. In section 188 of the Housing Act 1985 (the index to Part V) at the appropriate places insert—

"disposal and instrument effecting disposal (in Schedule 9A)	paragraph 10 of that Schedule"
"former landlord and former secure tenant (in relation to a qualifying disposal)	section 171A(2)(*c*)"
"improvement contribution	section 187"
"preserved right to buy	section 171A(2)(*a*)"

"qualifying disposal (in relation to the preserved right to buy)	section 171A(2)(*b*)"
"qualifying dwelling-house and qualifying person (in relation to the preserved right to buy)	section 171B(1)"
"reference period (for purposes of s.125A or 125B)	section 125C"
"service charge	section 621A".

32. In Part XIII of the Housing Act 1985 (general financial provisions), after section 427 insert—

"Entitlement to subsidy in case of land subject to management agreement

427A. The fact that a local housing authority or other body has entered into a management agreement, and any letting of land in connection with such an agreement—

(*a*) shall be disregarded in determining that authority or body's reckonable income or expenditure for the purposes of housing subsidy, and

(*b*) shall not be regarded as a ground for recovering, withholding or reducing any sum under section 427 (recoupment of housing subsidy).".

33. In section 434 of the Housing Act 1985 (the index to Part XIII) at the appropriate place insert—

"management agreement	sections 27(2) and 27B(4)".

34. In section 444(4) of the Housing Act 1985 (advances relevant to certain powers of local authority to give assistance), for the words from "by" to the end substitute "a housing authority".

35. In section 452 of the Housing Act 1985 (vesting of house in authority entitled to exercise power of sale), in subsection (2) omit the definition of "housing authority".

36. In section 453 of the Housing Act 1985 (power of authority which has granted shared ownership lease to make further advances), omit subsection (2) (which defines "housing authority").

37. In section 458 of the Housing Act 1985 (minor definitions), at the appropriate place insert—

" 'housing authority' includes any local authority, an urban development corporation, the Housing Corporation and a registered housing association;".

38. In section 459 of the Housing Act 1985 (the index to Part XIV), at the appropriate places insert—

"housing authority	sections 4(*a*) and 458"
"service charge	section 621A".

39. After section 621 of the Housing Act 1985 insert—

"Meaning of 'service charge' and related expressions

621A.—(1) In this Act 'service charge' means an amount payable by a purchaser or lessee of premises—

(*a*) which is payable, directly or indirectly, for services, repairs, maintenance or insurance or the vendor's or lessor's costs of management, and

(*b*) the whole or part of which varies or may vary according to the relevant costs.

(2) The relevant costs are the costs or estimated costs incurred or to be incurred by or on behalf of the payee, or (in the case of a lease) a superior landlord, in connection with the matters for which the service charge is payable.

(3) For this purpose—

(*a*) 'costs' includes overheads, and

(*b*) costs are relevant costs in relation to a service charge whether they are incurred, or to be incurred, in the period for which the service charge is payable or in an earlier or later period.

(4) In relation to a service charge—

(*a*) the 'payee' means the person entitled to enforce payment of the charge, and

(*b*) the 'payer' means the person liable to pay it.".

40.—(1) Schedule 4 to the Housing Act 1985 (the qualifying period for the right to buy) is amended as follows.

(2) After paragraph 5 insert—

"Periods during which right to buy is preserved

5A. A period qualifies under this paragraph if it is a period during which, before the relevant time—

(*a*) the secure tenant, or

(*b*) his spouse (if they are living together at the relevant time), or

(*c*) a deceased spouse of his (if they were living together at the time of the death), was a qualifying person for the purposes of the preserved right to buy or was the spouse of such a person and occupied the qualifying dwelling-house as his only or principal home.".

(3) In paragraph 7 (the landlord condition for qualifying period)—

(*a*) in sub-paragraph (1), in the opening words, after "subject to" insert "paragraph 7A and to", and omit the words from "a housing co-operative" to "management functions)";

(*b*) in sub-paragraph (2), omit the words from "a housing co-operative" to "1975".

(4) After paragraph 7 insert—

"7A.—(1) The landlord condition shall be treated as having been satisfied in the case of a dwelling-house comprised in a housing co-operative agreement made—

(*a*) in England and Wales, by a local housing authority, new town corporation or the Development Board for Rural Wales, or

(*b*) in Scotland, by an islands or district council,

if the interest of the landlord belonged to the housing co-operative.

(2) In sub-paragraph (1) "housing co-operative agreement" and "housing co-operative"—

(*a*) as regards England and Wales have the same meaning as in section 27B (agreements with housing co-operatives under superseded provisions), and

(*b*) as regards Scotland mean an agreement made under section 5 of the Housing Rents and Subsidies (Scotland) Act 1975 and a housing co-operative within the meaning of that section.".

41.—(1) Paragraph 14 of Schedule 6 to the Housing Act 1985 (terms of lease granted in pursuance of right to buy: implied covenants by landlord) is amended as follows.

(2) In sub-paragraph (2), omit the words following paragraph (*c*).

(3) In sub-paragraph (3), for the words from the beginning to "requirement" insert "There is an implied covenant".

(4) After sub-paragraph (3) insert—

"(3A) Sub-paragraphs (2) and (3) have effect subject to paragraph 15(3) (certain obligations not to be imposed, where landlord's title is leasehold, by reason of provisions of superior lease).".

Housing Associations Act 1985

42. In Part II of the Housing Associations Act 1985 (financial provisions), after section 69 insert—

"Land subject to housing management agreement

69A. A housing association is not entitled to a housing association grant, revenue deficit grant or hostel deficit grant in respect of land comprised in—

(*a*) a management agreement within the meaning of the Housing Act 1985 (see sections 27(2) and 27B(4) of that Act: delegation of housing management functions by certain authorities), or

(*b*) an agreement to which section 5 of the Housing Rents and Subsidies (Scotland) Act 1975 applies (agreements for exercise by housing co-operatives of certain local authority housing functions).".

GENERAL NOTE

See note to s.24, above.

     SCHEDULE 6

SIMPLIFIED PLANNING ZONES: FURTHER PROVISIONS

PART I

SCHEDULE TO BE INSERTED IN THE TOWN AND COUNTRY PLANNING ACT 1971

SCHEDULE 8A

SIMPLIFIED PLANNING ZONES

General

1. A simplified planning zone scheme shall consist of a map and a written statement, and such diagrams, illustrations and descriptive matter as the local planning authority think appropriate for explaining or illustrating the provisions of the scheme, and shall specify—
(a) the development or classes of development permitted by the scheme,
(b) the land in relation to which permission is granted, and
(c) any conditions, limitations or exceptions subject to which it is granted;
and shall contain such other matters as may be prescribed.

Proposals to make or alter scheme

2.—(1) A local planning authority may at any time decide to make a simplified planning zone scheme or to alter a scheme adopted by them or, with the consent of the Secretary of State, to alter a scheme approved by him.
(2) An authority who decide to make or alter a simplified planning zone scheme shall—
(a) notify the Secretary of State of their decision as soon as practicable, and
(b) determine the date on which they will begin to prepare the scheme or the alterations.

Power of Secretary of State to direct making or alteration of scheme

3.—(1) If a person requests a local planning authority to make or alter a simplified planning zone scheme but the authority—
(a) refuse to do so, or
(b) do not within the period of three months from the date of the request decide to do so,
he may, subject to sub-paragraph (2), require them to refer the matter to the Secretary of State.
(2) A person may not require the reference of the matter to the Secretary of State if—
(a) in the case of a request to make a scheme, a simplified planning zone scheme relating to the whole or part of the land specified in the request has been adopted or approved within the twelve months preceding his request;
(b) in the case of a request to alter a scheme, the scheme to which the request relates was adopted or approved, or any alteration to it has been adopted or approved, within that period.
(3) The Secretary of State shall, as soon as practicable after a matter is referred to him—
(a) send the authority a copy of any representations made to him by the applicant which have not been made to the authority, and
(b) notify the authority that if they wish to make any representations in the matter they should do so, in writing, within 28 days.
(4) The Secretary of State may, after—
(a) considering the matter and any written representations made by the applicant or the authority, and
(b) carrying out such consultations with such persons as he thinks fit,
give the authority a simplified planning zone direction.
(5) The Secretary of State shall notify the applicant and the authority of his decision and of his reasons for it.
4.—(1) A simplified planning zone direction is—
(a) if the request was for the making of a scheme, a direction to make a scheme which the Secretary of State considers appropriate; and

(*b*) if the request was for the alteration of a scheme, a direction to alter it in such manner as he considers appropriate.

(2) In either case the direction may extend to—

(*a*) the land specified in the request to the authority,

(*b*) any part of the land so specified, or

(*c*) land which includes the whole or part of the land so specified;

and, accordingly, may direct that land shall be added to or excluded from an existing simplified planning zone.

Publicity and consultation: general

5.—(1) A local planning authority who propose to make or alter a simplified planning zone scheme shall proceed in accordance with this paragraph, unless paragraph 6 applies (short procedure for certain alterations).

(2) They shall take such steps as will in their opinion secure—

(*a*) that adequate publicity for their proposals is given in the area to which the scheme relates,

(*b*) that persons who may be expected to wish to make representations about the proposals are made aware that they are entitled to do so, and

(*c*) that such persons are given an adequate opportunity of making such representations; and they shall consider any representations made to them within the prescribed period.

(3) They shall then, having prepared the relevant documents, that is, the proposed scheme or alterations—

(*a*) make copies of the documents available for inspection at their office, and

(*b*) send a copy of them to the Secretary of State.

(4) Each copy of the documents made available for inspection shall be accompanied by a statement of the time within which objections may be made.

(5) The local planning authority shall before preparing the proposed scheme or alterations consult the Secretary of State having responsibility for highways as to the effect of their proposals on existing or future highways; and when they have prepared the proposed scheme or alterations they shall send him a copy.

(6) A district planning authority in a non-metropolitan county shall also, before preparing the proposed scheme or alterations, consult the county council as planning authority and as to the effect of their proposals on existing or future highways; and when they have prepared the scheme or alterations they shall send the county council a copy.

Publicity and consultation: short procedure for certain alterations

6.—(1) Where a local planning authority propose to alter a simplified planning zone scheme and it appears to them that the issues involved are not of sufficient importance to warrant the full procedure set out in paragraph 5, they may proceed instead in accordance with this section.

(2) They shall prepare the proposed alterations and shall—

(*a*) make copies of them available for inspection at their office, and

(*b*) send a copy of them to the Secretary of State.

(3) Each copy of the documents made available for inspection shall be accompanied by a statement of the time within which representations or objections may be made.

(4) They shall then take such steps as may be prescribed for the purpose of—

(*a*) advertising the fact that the proposed alterations are available for inspection and the places and times at which, and the period during which, they may be inspected, and

(*b*) inviting the making of representations or objections in accordance with regulations; and they shall consider any representations made to them within the prescribed period.

(5) The local planning authority shall send a copy of the proposed alterations to the Secretary of State having responsibility for highways.

(6) A district planning authority in a non-metropolitan county shall also send a copy of the proposed alterations to the county council.

Powers of Secretary of State to secure adequate publicity and consultation

7.—(1) The documents sent by the local planning authority to the Secretary of State under paragraph 5(3) shall be accompanied by a statement—

(*a*) of the steps which the authority have taken to comply with paragraph 5(2), and

(*b*) of the authority's consultations with other persons and their consideration of the views of those persons.

(2) The documents sent by the local planning authority to the Secretary of State under paragraph 6(2) shall be accompanied by a statement of the steps which the authority are taking to comply with paragraph 6(4).

(3) If, on considering the statement and the proposals and any other information provided by the local planning authority, the Secretary of State is not satisfied with the steps taken by the authority, he may, within 21 days of the receipt of the statement, direct the authority not to take further steps for the adoption of the proposals without—

(a) if they have proceeded in accordance with paragraph 6, proceeding instead in accordance with paragraph 5, or

(b) in any case, taking such further steps as he may specify,

and satisfying him that they have done so.

(4) A local planning authority who are given directions by the Secretary of State shall—

(a) forthwith withdraw the copies of the documents made available for inspection as required by paragraph 5(3)(a) or 6(2)(a), and

(b) notify any person by whom objections to the proposals have been made to the authority that the Secretary of State has given such directions.

Objections: local inquiry or other hearing

8.—(1) The local planning authority may cause a local inquiry or other hearing to be held for the purpose of considering objections to their proposals for the making or alteration of a simplified planning zone scheme.

(2) They shall hold such a local inquiry or other hearing in the case of objections made in accordance with regulations unless all the persons who have made such objections have indicated in writing that they do not wish to appear.

(3) A local inquiry or other hearing shall be held by a person appointed by the Secretary of State or, in such cases as may be prescribed, by the authority themselves.

(4) Regulations may—

(a) make provision with respect to the appointment, and qualifications for appointment, of persons to hold a local inquiry or other hearing;

(b) include provision enabling the Secretary of State to direct a local planning authority to appoint a particular person, or one of a specified list or class of persons;

(c) make provision with respect to the remuneration and allowances of the person appointed.

(5) Subsections (2) and (3) of section 250 of the Local Government Act 1972 (power to summon and examine witnesses) apply to an inquiry held under this paragraph.

(6) The Tribunals and Inquiries Act 1971 applies to a local inquiry or other hearing held under this paragraph as it applies to a statutory inquiry held by the Secretary of State, with the substitution in section 12(1) (statement of reasons for decision) for the references to a decision taken by the Secretary of State of references to a decision taken by a local authority.

Adoption of proposals by local planning authority

9.—(1) After the expiry of the period afforded for making objections to proposals for the making or alteration of a simplified planning zone scheme or, if such objections were duly made within that period, after considering the objections so made, the local planning authority may, subject to the following provisions of this paragraph and to paragraph 10 (calling in of proposals by Secretary of State), by resolution adopt the proposals.

(2) They may adopt the proposals as originally prepared or as modified so as to take account of—

(a) any such objections as are mentioned in sub-paragraph (1) or any other objections to the proposals, or

(b) any other considerations which appear to the authority to be material.

(3) After copies of the proposals have been sent to the Secretary of State and before they have been adopted by the local planning authority, the Secretary of State may, if it appears to him that the proposals are unsatisfactory, direct the authority to consider modifying the proposals in such respects as are indicated in the direction.

(4) An authority to whom a direction is given shall not adopt the proposals unless they satisfy the Secretary of State that they have made the modifications necessary to conform with the direction or the direction is withdrawn.

Calling in of proposals for approval by Secretary of State

10.—(1) After copies of proposals have been sent to the Secretary of State and before they have been adopted by the local planning authority, the Secretary of State may direct that the proposals shall be submitted to him for his approval.

(2) In that event—

(*a*) the authority shall not take any further steps for the adoption of the proposals, and in particular shall not hold or proceed with a local inquiry or other hearing in respect of the proposals under paragraph 8; and

(*b*) the proposals shall not have effect unless approved by the Secretary of State and shall not require adoption by the authority.

Approval of proposals by Secretary of State

11.—(1) The Secretary of State may after considering proposals submitted to him under paragraph 10 either approve them, in whole or in part and with or without modifications, or reject them.

(2) In considering the proposals he may take into account any matters he thinks are relevant, whether or not they were taken into account in the proposals as submitted to him.

(3) Where on taking the proposals into consideration the Secretary of State does not determine then to reject them, he shall, before determining whether or not to approve them—

(*a*) consider any objections to them made in accordance with regulations,

(*b*) afford to any person who made such an objection which has not been withdrawn an opportunity of appearing before and being heard by a person appointed by him for the purpose, and

(*c*) if a local inquiry or other hearing is held, also afford such an opportunity to the authority and such other persons as he thinks fit,

except so far as objections have already been considered, or a local inquiry or other hearing into the objections has already been held, by the authority.

(4) In considering the proposals the Secretary of State may consult with, or consider the views of, any local planning authority or any other person; but he is under no obligation to do so, or to afford an opportunity for the making of representations or objections, or to cause a local inquiry or other hearing to be held, except as provided by sub-paragraph (3).

Default powers

12.—(1) Where by virtue of any of the preceding provisions of this Schedule—

(*a*) a simplified planning zone scheme or proposals for the alteration of such a scheme are required to be prepared, or

(*b*) steps are required to be taken for the adoption of any such scheme or proposals,

then, if the Secretary of State is satisfied, after holding a local inquiry or other hearing, that the local planning authority are not taking the steps necessary to enable them to prepare or adopt such a scheme or proposals within a reasonable period, he may make the scheme or the alterations, as he thinks fit.

(2) Where under this paragraph anything which ought to have been done by a local planning authority is done by the Secretary of State, the preceding provisions of this Schedule apply, so far as practicable, with any necessary modifications, in relation to the doing of that thing by the Secretary of State and the thing so done.

(3) Where the Secretary of State incurs expenses under this paragraph in connection with the doing of anything which should have been done by a local planning authority, so much of those expenses as may be certified by the Secretary of State to have been incurred in the performance of functions of that authority shall on demand be repaid by the authority to the Secretary of State.

Regulations and directions

13.—(1) Without prejudice to the preceding provisions of this Schedule, the Secretary of State may make regulations with respect to the form and content of simplified planning zone schemes and with respect to the procedure to be followed in connection with their preparation, withdrawal, adoption, submission, approval, making or alteration.

(2) Any such regulations may in particular—

(*a*) provide for the notice to be given of, or the publicity to be given to, matters included or proposed to be included in a simplified planning zone scheme and the adoption or approval of such a scheme, or of any alteration of it, or any other prescribed procedural step, and for publicity to be given to the procedure to be followed in these respects;

(*b*) make provision with respect to the making and consideration of representations as to matters to be included in, or objections to, any such scheme or proposals for its alteration;

(c) without prejudice to paragraph (b), provide for notice to be given to particular persons of the adoption or approval of a simplified planning zone scheme, or an alteration to such a scheme, if they have objected to the proposals and have notified the local planning authority of their wish to receive notice, subject (if the regulations so provide) to the payment of a reasonable charge;

(d) require or authorise a local planning authority to consult with, or consider the views of, other persons before taking any prescribed procedural step;

(e) require a local planning authority, in such cases as may be prescribed or in such particular cases as the Secretary of State may direct, to provide persons making a request in that behalf with copies of any document which has been made public for the purpose mentioned in paragraph 5(2) or 6(3) or has been made available for inspection under paragraph 5(3) or 6(2), subject (if the regulations so provide) to the payment of a reasonable charge;

(f) provide for the publication and inspection of a simplified planning zone scheme which has been adopted or approved, or any document adopted or approved altering such a scheme, and for copies of any such scheme or document to be made available on sale.

(3) Regulations under this paragraph may extend throughout England and Wales or to specified areas only and may make different provision for different cases.

(4) Subject to the preceding provisions of this Schedule and to any regulations under this paragraph, the Secretary of State may give directions to any local planning authority or to local planning authorities generally—

(a) for formulating the procedure for the carrying out of their functions under this Schedule;

(b) for requiring them to give him such information as he may require for carrying out any of his functions under this Schedule.

PART II

CONSEQUENTIAL AMENDMENTS—ENGLAND AND WALES

1. In section 34(1) of the Town and Country Planning Act 1971 (registers to be kept by local planning authorities) at the end add "and also containing such information as may be so prescribed with respect to simplified planning zone schemes relating to zones in the authority's area".

2. In section 41 of the Town and Country Planning Act 1971 (limit of duration of planning permission), in subsection (3) (exceptions) after paragraph (aa) insert—

    "(ab) to any planning permission granted by a simplified planning zone scheme;".

3. In section 53(1) of the Town and Country Planning Act 1971 (application to determine whether planning permission required) after "scheme" insert "or simplified planning zone scheme".

4. In section 242(1) of the Town and Country Planning Act 1971 (validity of certain instruments to be questioned under that Act and not otherwise), after paragraph (a) insert—

    "(aa) a simplified planning zone scheme or an alteration of such a scheme whether before or after the adoption or approval of the scheme or alteration;".

5. In section 244 of the Town and Country Planning Act 1971 (procedure for questioning certain instruments), after subsection (6) insert—

    "(7) Subsections (1) and (2) of this section apply to a simplified planning zone scheme or an alteration of such a scheme as they apply to a structure plan and an alteration of such a plan, with the following modifications—

        (a) for the references to Part II of this Act substitute references to Part III of this Act, and

        (b) for the reference to regulations under section 18(1) of this Act substitute a reference to regulations under paragraph 13 of Schedule 8A to this Act,

    and with any other necessary modifications.".

6. In section 287 of the Town and Country Planning Act 1971 (general provisions as to regulations and orders)—

    (a) in subsection (4) (orders to be made by statutory instrument) after "24," insert "24E,", and

    (b) in subsection (5)(b) (orders subject to negative resolution procedure), after "section" insert "24E,".

7. In section 290(1) of the Town and Country Planning Act 1971 (interpretation), at the appropriate place insert—

    "simplified planning zone" and "simplified planning zone scheme" shall be construed in accordance with section 24A of this Act;".

PART III

SCHEDULE TO BE INSERTED IN THE TOWN AND COUNTRY PLANNING (SCOTLAND) ACT 1972

SCHEDULE 6A

SIMPLIFIED PLANNING ZONE SCHEMES

General

1. A simplified planning zone scheme shall consist of a map and a written statement, and such diagrams, illustrations and descriptive matter as the planning authority think appropriate for explaining or illustrating the provisions of the scheme, and shall specify—
   (*a*) the development or classes of development permitted by the scheme,
   (*b*) the land in relation to which permission is granted; and
   (*c*) any conditions, limitations or exceptions subject to which it is granted;
and shall contain such other matters as may be prescribed.

Proposals to make or alter scheme

2.—(1) A planning authority may at any time decide to make a simplified planning zone scheme or to alter a scheme adopted by them or, with the consent of the Secretary of State, to alter a scheme approved by him.
   (2) An authority who decide to make or alter a simplified planning zone scheme shall—
   (*a*) notify the Secretary of State of their decision as soon as practicable, and
   (*b*) determine the date on which they will begin to prepare the scheme or the alterations.

Power of Secretary of State to direct making or alteration of scheme

3.—(1) If a person requests a planning authority to make or alter a simplified planning zone scheme but the authority—
   (*a*) refuse to do so, or
   (*b*) do not within the period of three months from the date of the request decide to do so,
he may, subject to sub-paragraph (2), require them to refer the matter to the Secretary of State.
   (2) A person may not require the reference of the matter to the Secretary of State if—
   (*a*) in the case of a request to make a scheme, a simplified planning zone scheme relating to the whole or part of the land specified in the request has been adopted or approved within the twelve months preceding his request;
   (*b*) in the case of a request to alter a scheme, the scheme to which the request relates was adopted or approved, or any alteration to it has been adopted, or approved within that period.
   (3) The Secretary of State shall, as soon as practicable after a matter is referred to him—
   (*a*) send the authority a copy of any representations made to him by the applicant which have not been made to the authority, and
   (*b*) notify the authority that if they wish to make any representations in the matter they should do so, in writing, within 28 days.
   (4) The Secretary of State may, after—
   (*a*) considering the matter and any written representations made by the applicant or the authority, and
   (*b*) carrying out such consultations with such persons as he thinks fit,
give the authority a simplified planning zone direction.
   (5) The Secretary of State shall notify the applicant and the authority of his decision and of his reasons for it.
4.—(1) A simplified planning zone direction is—
   (*a*) if the request was for the making of a scheme, a direction to make a scheme which the Secretary of State considers appropriate; and
   (*b*) if the request was for the alteration of a scheme, a direction to alter it in such manner as he considers appropriate.
   (2) In either case the direction may extend to—
   (*a*) the land specified in the request to the authority,
   (*b*) any part of the land so specified, or

(*c*) land which includes the whole or part of the land so specified;
and, accordingly, may direct that land shall be added to or excluded from an existing simplified planning zone.

Publicity and consultation: general

5.—(1) A planning authority who propose to make or alter a simplified planning zone scheme shall proceed in accordance with this paragraph.

(2) Subject to paragraph 6(2) below, they shall take such steps as will in their opinion secure—

(*a*) that adequate publicity for their proposals is given in the area to which the scheme relates,

(*b*) that persons who may be expected to wish to make representations about the proposals are made aware that they are entitled to do so, and

(*c*) that such persons are given an adequate opportunity of making such representations; and they shall consider any representations made to them within the prescribed period.

(3) They shall then, having prepared the relevant documents, that is, the proposed scheme or alterations—

(*a*) make copies of the documents available for inspection at their office, and

(*b*) send a copy of them to the Secretary of State.

(4) Each copy of the documents made available for inspection shall be accompanied by a statement of the time within which objections may be made.

(5) The planning authority shall before preparing the proposed scheme or alterations consult the Secretary of State and any local roads authority in whose district the proposed zone or any part of it lies as to the effect of their proposals on existing or future roads; and when they have prepared the proposed scheme or alterations they shall send a copy to the Secretary of State and any such local roads authority.

Publicity and consultation: expedited procedure

6.—(1) The documents sent by the planning authority to the Secretary of State under paragraph 5(3) shall be accompanied by a statement—

(*a*) of the steps which the authority have taken to comply with paragraph 5(2), and

(*b*) of the authority's consultations with other persons and their consideration of the views of those persons.

(2) Where a planning authority do not consider it appropriate to take the steps required by paragraph 5(2) of this Schedule in relation to proposals made by them under sub-paragraph (1) of that paragraph for the alteration of a simplified planning zone scheme, they may instead include, with the copies of those proposals made available for inspection and with the copy sent to the Secretary of State under paragraph (3) of that paragraph, a statement of their reasons for not taking such steps.

Objections: local inquiry or other hearing

7.—(1) The planning authority may cause a local inquiry or other hearing to be held for the purpose of considering objections to their proposals for the making or alteration of a simplified planning zone scheme.

(2) They shall hold such a local inquiry or other hearing in the case of objections made in accordance with regulations unless all the persons who have made such objections have indicated in writing that they do not wish to appear.

(3) A local inquiry or other hearing shall be held by a person appointed by the Secretary of State or, in such cases as may be prescribed, by the authority themselves.

(4) Regulations may—

(*a*) make provision with respect to the appointment, and qualifications for appointment, or persons to hold a local inquiry or other hearing;

(*b*) include provision enabling the Secretary of State to direct a planning authority to appoint a particular person, or one of a specified list or class of persons;

(*c*) make provision with respect to the remuneration and allowances of the person appointed.

(5) The Tribunals and Inquiries Act 1971 applies to a local inquiry or other hearing held under this paragraph as it applies to a statutory inquiry held by the Secretary of State, with the substitution in section 12(1) (statement of reasons for decision) for the references to a decision taken by the Secretary of State of references to a decision taken by a planning authority.

Adoption of proposals by planning authority

8.—(1) After the expiry of the period afforded for making objections to proposals for the making or alteration of a simplified planning zone scheme or, if such objections were duly made within that period, after considering the objections so made, the planning authority may, subject to the following provisions of this paragraph and to paragraph 9 (calling in of proposals by Secretary of State), by resolution adopt the proposals.

(2) They may adopt the proposals as originally prepared or as modified so as to take account of—

(*a*) any such objections as are mentioned in sub-paragraph (1) any other objections to the proposals, or

(*b*) any other considerations which appear to the authority to be material.

(3) After copies of the proposals have been sent to the Secretary of State and before they have been adopted by the planning authority, the Secretary of State may, if it appears to him that the proposals are unsatisfactory, direct the authority to consider modifying the proposals in such respects as are indicated in the direction.

(4) An authority to whom a direction is given shall not adopt the proposals unless they satisfy the Secretary of State that they have made the modification necessary to conform with the direction or the direction is withdrawn.

Calling in of proposals for approval by Secretary of State

9.—(1) After copies of proposals have been sent to the Secretary of State and before they have been adopted by the planning authority, the Secretary of State may direct that the proposals shall be submitted to him for his approval.

(2) In that event—

(*a*) the authority shall not take any further steps for the adoption of the proposals, and in particular shall not hold or proceed with a local inquiry or other hearing in respect of the proposals under paragraph 7; and

(*b*) the proposals shall not have effect unless approved by the Secretary of State and shall not require adoption by the authority.

Approval of proposals by Secretary of State

10.—(1) The Secretary of State may after considering proposals submitted to him under paragraph 9 either approve them, in whole or in part and with or without modifications, or reject them.

(2) In considering the proposals he may take into account any matters he thinks are relevant, whether or not they were taken into account in the proposals as submitted to him.

(3) Where on taking the proposals into consideration the Secretary of State does not determine then to reject them, he shall, before determining whether or not to approve them—

(*a*) consider any objections to them in accordance with regulations,

(*b*) afford to any person who made such an objection which has not been withdrawn an opportunity of appearing before and being heard by a person appointed by him for the purpose, and

(*c*) if a local inquiry or other hearing is held, also afford such an opportunity to the authority and such other persons as he thinks fit,

except so far as objections have already been considered, or a local inquiry or other hearing into the objections has already been held, by the authority.

(4) In considering the proposals the Secretary of State may consult with, or consider the views of, any planning authority or any other person; but he is under no obligation to do so, or to afford an opportunity for the making of representations or objections, or to cause a local inquiry or other hearing to be held, except as provided by sub-paragraph (3).

Default powers

11.—(1) Where by virtue of any of the preceding provisions of this Schedule—

(*a*) a simplified planning zone scheme or proposals for the alteration of such a scheme are required to be prepared, or

(*b*) steps are required to be taken for the adoption of any such scheme or proposals,

then, if the Secretary of State is satisfied, after holding a local inquiry or other hearing, that the planning authority are not taking the steps necessary to enable them to prepare or adopt such a scheme or proposals within a reasonable period, he may make the scheme, or the alterations, as he thinks fit.

(2) Where under this paragraph anything which ought to have been done by a planning authority is done by the Secretary of State, the preceding provisions of this Schedule apply, so far as practicable, with any necessary modifications in relation to the doing of that thing by the Secretary of State and the thing so done.

(3) Where the Secretary of State incurs expenses under this paragraph in connection with the doing of anything which should have been done by a planning authority, so much of those expenses as may be certified by the Secretary of State to have been incurred in the performance of functions of that authority shall on demand be repaid by the authority to the Secretary of State.

Regulations and directions

12.—(1) Without prejudice to the preceding provisions of this Schedule, the Secretary of State may make regulations with respect to the form and content of simplified planning zone schemes and with respect to the procedure to be followed in connection with their preparation, withdrawal, adoption, submission, approval, making or alteration.

(2) Any such regulations may in particular—

(*a*) provide for the notice to be given of, or the publicity to be given to, matters included or proposed to be included in a simplified planning zone scheme and the adoption or approval of such a scheme, or of any alteration of it, or any other prescribed procedural step, and for publicity to be given to the procedure to be followed in these respects;

(*b*) make provision with respect to the making and consideration of representations as to matters to be included in, or objections to, any such scheme or proposals for its alteration;

(*c*) without prejudice to paragraph (*b*), provide for notice to be given to particular persons of the adoption or approval of a simplified planning zone scheme, or an alteration to such a scheme, if they have objected to the proposals and have notified the planning authority of their wish to receive notice, subject (if the regulations so provide) to the payment of a reasonable charge;

(*d*) require or authorise a planning authority to consult with, or consider the views of, other persons before taking any prescribed procedural step;

(*e*) require a planning authority, in such cases as may be prescribed or in such particular cases as the Secretary of State may direct, to provide persons making a request in that behalf with copies of any document which has been made public for the purpose mentioned in paragraph 5(2) or has been made available for inspection under paragraph 5(3), subject (if the regulations so provide) to the payment of a reasonable charge;

(*f*) provide for the publication and inspection of a simplified planning zone scheme which has been adopted or approved, or any document adopted or approved altering such a scheme, and for copies of any such scheme or document to be made available on sale.

(3) Regulations under this paragraph may extend throughout Scotland or to specified areas only and may make different provision for different cases.

(4) Subject to the preceding provisions of this Schedule and to any regulations under this paragraph, the Secretary of State may give directions to any planning authority or to planning authorities generally—

(*a*) for formulating the procedure for the carrying out of their functions under this Schedule;

(*b*) for requiring them to give him such information as he may require for carrying out any of his functions under this Schedule.

PART IV

CONSEQUENTIAL AMENDMENTS—SCOTLAND

1. At the end of subsection (2) of section 31 of the Town and Country Planning (Scotland) Act 1972 (registers) insert "and also containing such information as may be so prescribed with respect to simplified planning zone schemes relating to zones in the authority's area".

2. In section 38 of the Town and Country Planning (Scotland) Act 1972 (limit of duration of planning permission), in subsection (3) (exceptions) after paragraph (*aa*) insert—

"(*ab*) to any planning permission granted by a simplified planning zone scheme;".

3. In section 51(1) of the Town and Country Planning (Scotland) Act 1972 (applications to determine whether planning permission required) after the word "scheme" insert "or simplified planning zone scheme".

4. After subsection (1)(*a*) of section 231 of the Town and Country Planning (Scotland) Act 1972 (validity of plans, &c.) insert—

"(*aa*) a simplified planning zone scheme or any alteration of any such scheme whether before or after the adoption or approval of the scheme or alteration; or".

5. In section 232 of the Town and Country Planning (Scotland) Act 1972 (proceedings for questioning plans, &c.), after subsection (3) insert—

"(4) Subsections (1) and (2) of this section apply to a simplified planning zone scheme or an alteration of such a scheme as they apply to a structure plan and an alteration of such a plan, with the following modifications—

(*a*) for the references to Part II of this Act substitute references to Part III of this Act, and

(*b*) for the reference to regulations under section 16(1) of this Act substitute a reference to regulations under paragraph 12 of Schedule 6A to this Act,

and with any other necessary modifications.".

6. In section 273 of the Town and Country Planning (Scotland) Act 1972 (orders)—

(*a*) in subsection (4), after "21," insert "21E,", and

(*b*) in subsection (5), after "1(3)," insert "21E,".

7. In section 275(1) of the Town and Country Planning (Scotland) Act 1972 after the definition of "road" insert—

" 'simplified planning zone' and 'simplified planning zone scheme' shall be construed in accordance with section 21A of this Act;".

Sections 33 and 37   SCHEDULE 7

HAZARDOUS SUBSTANCES: CONSEQUENTIAL AMENDMENTS

PART I

ENGLAND AND WALES

Radioactive Substances Act 1960 (c.34)

1. The following paragraph shall be inserted after paragraph 8A of Schedule 1 to the Radioactive Substances Act 1960 (duty of public and local authorities not to take account of any radioactivity in performing their functions)—

"8AA. Sections 58B to 58M and 101B of the Town and Country Planning Act 1971.".

Town and Country Planning Act 1971 (c.78)

2. In subsection (3) (action on the part of the Secretary of State that may be questioned in legal proceedings) of section 242 of the Town and Country Planning Act 1971, the following paragraph shall be inserted after paragraph (*d*)—

"(*dd*) any decision by the Secretary of State relating to an application for hazardous substances consent;".

3. In subsection (2)(*a*) of section 266 of that Act (orders which, in relation to Crown land, may only be made with consent of appropriate authority)—

(*a*) after "51B" there shall be inserted "58H"; and

(*b*) for "or 96" there shall be substituted "96 or 101B".

4. Section 269 of that Act (application to Isles of Scilly) shall have effect as if sections 58B to 58N and 101B were included among the provisions specified in Part III of Schedule 21 (provisions that may be applied to Isles as if they were a district).

5. The following section shall be inserted after section 271 of that Act—

"Application to certain hazardous substances authorities of provisions as to hazardous substances control

271A.—(1) The provisions of this Act relating to hazardous substances shall have effect subject to such exceptions and modifications as may be prescribed in relation to granting hazardous substances consent for authorities who are hazardous substances authorities by virtue of section 1A of this Act.

(2) Subject to the provisions of section 58F of this Act, any such regulations may in particular provide for securing—

(a) that any application by such an authority for hazardous substances consent in respect of the presence of a hazardous substance on, over, or under land shall be made to the Secretary of State and not to the hazardous substances authority;

(b) that any order or notice authorised to be made, issued or served under those provisions shall be made, issued or served by the Secretary of State and not by the hazardous substances authority."

6. In section 280 of that Act (rights of entry)—

(a) the following subsection shall be inserted after subsection (1)—

"(1A) Any person duly authorised in writing by the Secretary of State or by a hazardous substances authority may at any reasonable time enter any land for the purpose of surveying it in connection with—

(a) any application for hazardous substances consent;

(b) any proposal to issue a hazardous substances contravention notice.";

(b) at the end of subsection (4) there shall be added the words "and any person duly authorised in writing by the Secretary of State or by a hazardous substances authority may at any reasonable time enter any land for the purpose of ascertaining whether an offence appears to have been committed under section 58K of this Act.";

(c) the following subsection shall be inserted after subsection (6)—

"(6A) Subsection (6) above shall have effect for the purposes of a claim for compensation made by virtue of section 58H(8) or 58J(12) of this Act as if a reference to a local planning authority were a reference to a hazardous substances authority."; and

(d) in subsection (8), after the word "section" there shall be inserted the words "or a hazardous substances contravention notice has been issued".

7. In section 290(1) of that Act (Interpretation)—

(a) the following shall be inserted after the definition of "conservation area"—

" "contravention of hazardous substances control" has the meaning assigned to it by section 58K(2) of this Act;";

(b) the following shall be inserted after the definition of "the Greater London development plan"—

" "hazardous substances authority" is to be construed in accordance with sections 1A and 1B of this Act;

"hazardous substances consent" means consent required by section 58B of this Act;

"hazardous substances contravention notice" has the meaning assigned to it by section 101B(3) of this Act;"; and

(c) the following shall be inserted after the definition of "tree preservation order"—

" "urban development area" and "urban development corporation" have the same meaning as in Part XVI of the Local Government, Planning and Land Act 1980;".

Town and Country Planning Act 1984 (c.10)

8. In section 1 of the Town and Country Planning Act 1984 (applications in anticipation of disposal of Crown interest)—

(a) in subsection (1)(a), after the words "listed building consent" there shall be inserted the words ", hazardous substances consent"; and

(b) the following subsection shall be inserted after subsection (3)—

"(3A) Any hazardous substances consent granted by virtue of this section shall apply only—

(a) to the presence of the substance to which the consent relates after the land in question has ceased to be Crown land; and

(b) so long as that land continues to be Crown land, to the presence of the substance by virtue of a private interest in the land.".

Gas Act 1986 (c.44)

9. In sub-paragraph (1)(xxiv) of paragraph 2 of Schedule 7 to the Gas Act 1986 (enactments for the purposes of which a public gas supplier is deemed to be a statutory undertaker and his undertaking a statutory undertaking)—

(a) after "sections" there shall be inserted "1B,"; and

(b) after "49," there shall be inserted "58F,".

PART II

SCOTLAND

Radioactive Substances Act 1960 (c.34)

1. The following paragraph shall be inserted after the entry relating to the Sewerage (Scotland) Act 1968 in Part II of the first Schedule to the Radioactive Substances Act 1960 (duty of public and local authorities not to take account of any radioactivity in performing their functions)—

"17A. Sections 56A to 56N and 97B of the Town and Country Planning (Scotland) Act 1972.".

Town and Country Planning (Scotland) Act 1972 (c.52)

2. In subsection (3) (action on the part of the Secretary of State that may be questioned in legal proceedings) of section 231 of the Town and Country Planning (Scotland) Act 1972, the following paragraph shall be inserted after paragraph (*d*)—

"(*dd*) any decision by the Secretary of State relating to an application for hazardous substances consent;".

3. In subsection (2)(*a*) of section 253 of that Act (orders which, in relation to Crown land, may only be made with consent of appropriate authority)—

(*a*) after "49B" there shall be inserted "56J"; and

(*b*) for "or 92" there shall be substituted "92 or 97B".

4. The following section shall be inserted after section 257 of that Act—

"Application to planning authorities of provisions as to hazardous substances control

257A.—(1) The provisions of this Act relating to hazardous substances shall have effect subject to such exceptions and modifications as may be prescribed in relation to hazardous substances consent for planning authorities.

(2) Subject to the provisions of section 56G of this Act, any such regulations may in particular provide for securing—

(*a*) that any application by such an authority for hazardous substances consent in respect of the presence of a hazardous substance on, over or under such land shall be made to the Secretary of State and not to the planning authority;

(*b*) that any order or notice authorised to be made, issued or served under those provisions shall be made, issued or served by the Secretary of State and not by the planning authority.".

5. In section 265 of that Act (rights of entry)—

(*a*) the following subsection shall be inserted after subsection (1)—

"(1A) Any person duly authorised in writing by the Secretary of State or by a planning authority may at any reasonable time enter any land for the purpose of surveying it in connection with—

(*a*) any application for hazardous substances consent;

(*b*) any proposal to issue a hazardous substances contravention notice.";

(*b*) the following subsection shall be inserted after subsection (4)—

"(4A) Any person duly authorised in writing by the Secretary of State or by a planning authority may at any reasonable time enter any land for the purpose of ascertaining whether an offence appears to have been committed under section 56L of this Act."; and

(*c*) the following subsection shall be inserted after subsection (7)—

"(7A) Any person duly authorised in writing by the Secretary of State or a planning authority may at any reasonable time enter any land in respect of which a hazardous substances contravention notice has been served for the purpose of ascertaining whether the notice has been complied with.".

6. In section 275(1) of that Act (interpretation)—

(*a*) the following shall be inserted after the definition of "conservation area"—

" "contravention of hazardous substances control" has the meaning assigned to it by section 56L(2) of this Act;";

(*b*) the following shall be inserted after the definition of "government department"—

" "hazardous substances consent" means consent required by section 56C of this Act; "hazardous substances contravention notice" has the meaning assigned to it by section 97B(3) of this Act;"; and

(*c*) the following shall be inserted after the definition of "tree preservation order"—

" "urban development area" and "urban development corporation" have the same meaning as in Part XVI of the Local Government, Planning and Land Act 1980;".

Town and Country Planning Act 1984 (c.10)

7. In section 1 of the Town and Country Planning Act 1984 (applications in anticipation of disposal of Crown interests)—
   (a) in subsection (1)(a), after the words "listed building consent" there shall be inserted the words ", hazardous substances consent"; and
   (b) the following subsection shall be inserted after subsection (3)—
   "(3A) Any hazardous substances consent granted by virtue of this section shall apply only—
      (a) to the presence of the substance to which the consent relates after the land in question has ceased to be Crown land; and
      (b) so long as that land continues to be Crown land to the presence of the substance by virtue of a private interest in the land.".

Gas Act 1986 (c.44)

8. In sub-paragraph (1)(xxv) of paragraph 2 of Schedule 7 to the Gas Act 1986 after "46", there shall be inserted "56B, 56G,".

Section 39(3)　　　　　　　　SCHEDULE 8

OPENCAST COAL—MISCELLANEOUS AMENDMENTS

PART I

THE 1958 ACT

1. The following section shall be substituted for section 3—

"Preservation of amenity
   3.—(1) Where the Board are formulating any proposals as to the working of coal by opencast operations or the carrying out of operations incidental to such working, the Board, having regard to the desirability of preserving natural beauty, of conserving flora, fauna, and geological or physiographical features of special interests, and of protecting buildings and other objects of architectural or historic interest, shall take into account any effect which the proposals would have on the natural beauty of the countryside or on any such flora, fauna, features, buildings, or objects.
   (2) The provisions of the preceding subsection shall also apply, with the necessary modifications, where the Board are formulating any proposals as to the restoration of land affected by the working of coal by opencast operations or by operations incidental to such working.".
2.—(1) In section 4(1), for the words "the land comprised in an authorisation under section 1 of this Act" there shall be substituted the words "any land on which they desire to work coal by such operations or to carry out operations incidental to such working".
   (2) The following subsections shall be substituted for section 4(6)—
   "(6) A compulsory rights order may only be made if opencast planning permission has been applied for or granted in respect of the land comprised in the order or is deemed to have been granted in respect of it.
   (6A) Where a compulsory rights order is made before opencast planning permission has been granted in respect of the land comprised in the order, the Secretary of State shall not confirm it unless such permission in respect of that land has first been granted.
   (6B) Where a compulsory rights order is made in a case where opencast planning permission has been granted or is deemed to have been granted, the order, as from the time when it is made, shall include a reference to the permission.
   (6C) If opencast planning permission is granted in respect of land comprised in a compulsory rights order and the Secretary of State subsequently confirms the order, the order as confirmed shall include a reference to the permission.
   (6D) No compulsory rights order, as confirmed, shall extend to any land which is not comprised in the permission or deemed permission referred to in the order.".
3. In section 5(5)—

(*a*) for the word "authorisation" there shall be substituted the words "opencast planning permission"; and

(*b*) for the words "fulfilment of the authorised purposes" there shall be substituted the words "permitted activities".

4. In section 13, the words "in respect of which opencast planning permission has been granted" shall be substituted—

(*a*) in subsection (1)—

(i) for the words from "which", in the second place where it occurs, to "Act", in the second place where it occurs; and

(ii) for the words from "comprised", in the second place where it occurs, to "Act", in the third place where it occurs;

(*b*) in subsection (2), for the words from "which" to "Act";

(*c*) in subsection (4)—

(i) for the words from "which" to "Act"; and

(ii) for the words "comprised in such an authorisation"; and

(*d*) in subsection (5), for the words from "which", in the second place where it occurs, to the end of the subsection.

5. The following sections shall be substituted for section 14—

"Provisions as to agricultural tenancies in England and Wales

14.—(1) Without prejudice to the provisions of Part III of this Act as to matters arising between landlords and tenants in consequence of compulsory rights orders, the provisions of this section shall have effect where—

(*a*) opencast planning permission has been granted subject to a restoration condition and to an aftercare condition in which the use specified is use for agriculture or use for forestry, and

(*b*) immediately before that permission is granted, any of the land comprised therein consists of an agricultural holding or part of an agricultural holding,

whether any of that land is comprised in a compulsory rights order or not.

(2) For the purposes of the Agricultural Holdings Act 1986 (in this Act referred to as "the Act of 1986")—

(*a*) the holding shall not be taken to have ceased to be an agricultural holding; and

(*b*) where only part of the holding is comprised in opencast planning permission, that part shall not be taken to have ceased to form part of an agricultural holding,

by reason only that, while occupied or used for the permitted activities, the land is not being used for agriculture within the meaning of that Act.

(3) For the purposes of the Act of 1986, the tenant of the holding shall not be taken to have failed to fulfil his responsibilities to farm in accordance with the rules of good husbandry—

(*a*) by reason of his having permitted any of the land comprised in the opencast planning permission to be occupied for the purpose of carrying on any of the permitted activities, or by reason of any other thing done or omitted by him for facilitating the use of any of that land for that purpose;

(*b*) where any of that land is comprised in a compulsory rights order, by reason of the occupation or use of any of that land in the exercise of rights conferred by the order, in so far as that occupation or use was not permitted or facilitated by the tenant as mentioned in the preceding paragraph.

(4) For the purposes of the Act of 1986 nothing done or omitted by the tenant or by the landlord of the holding by way of permitting any of the land in respect of which opencast planning permission has been granted to be occupied for the purpose of carrying on any of the permitted activities, or by way of facilitating the use of any of that land for that purpose, shall be taken to be a breach of any term or condition of the tenancy, either on the part of the tenant or on the part of the landlord.

(5) For the purposes of subsections (1) to (3) of section 27 of the Act of 1986 (Agricultural Land Tribunal's consent to operation of notice to quit) the condition specified in paragraph (*f*) of subsection (3) of that section shall not be treated as satisfied if the use for the purpose for which the landlord proposes to terminate the tenancy is the use of the land for carrying on any of the permitted activities.

(6) On a reference to arbitration under section 12 of the Act of 1986 with respect to the rent which should be properly payable for the holding, in respect of any period for which the Board are in occupation of the holding, or of any part thereof, for the purpose of carrying on any of the permitted activities, the arbitrator shall not take into account any increase or diminution in the rental value of the holding in so far as that increase or diminution is attributable to the occupation of the holding, or of that part

of the holding, by the Board for the purpose of carrying on any of the permitted activities.

(7) For the purpose of the operation of section 13 of the Act of 1986 (increases of rent for landlord's improvements) in relation to improvements carried out on the holding, in a case where the improvements have been affected by anything done for the purpose of carrying on any of the permitted activities, the increase (if any) of the rental value of the holding attributable to the carrying out of the improvements shall be assessed as if it had not been done.

(8) This section does not extend to Scotland.

Provisions as to agricultural tenancies in Scotland

14A.—(1) Without prejudice to the provisions of Part III of this Act as to matters arising between landlords and tenants in consequence of compulsory rights orders, the provisions of this section shall have effect in Scotland where—

    (*a*) opencast planning permission has been granted subject to a restoration condition and to an aftercare condition in which the use specified is use for agriculture, and

    (*b*) immediately before that permission is granted, any of the land comprised therein consists of an agricultural holding or part of an agricultural holding,

whether any of that land is comprised in a compulsory rights order or not.

(2) In this section—

"aftercare condition" means a condition requiring that such steps shall be taken as may be necessary to bring land to the standard required for use for agriculture; and

"restoration condition" has the meaning given to it in section 27A(2) of the Town and Country Planning (Scotland) Act 1972.

(3) For the purposes of the Agricultural Holdings (Scotland) Act 1949 (in this Act referred to as "the Scottish Act of 1949")—

    (*a*) the holding shall not be taken to have ceased to be an agricultural holding; and

    (*b*) where only part of the holding is comprised in the opencast planning permission, that part shall not be taken to have ceased to form part of an agricultural holding,

by reason only that, while occupied or used for the permitted activities, the land is not being used for agriculture within the meaning of that Act.

(4) For the purposes of the Scottish Act of 1949, the tenant of the holding shall not be taken to have failed to fulfil his responsibilities to farm in accordance with the rules of good husbandry—

    (*a*) by reason of his having permitted any of the land comprised in the opencast planning permission to be occupied for the purpose of carrying on any of the permitted activities, or by reason of any other thing done or omitted by him for facilitating the use of any of that land for that purpose;

    (*b*) where any of that land is comprised in a compulsory rights order, by reason of the occupation or use of any of that land in the exercise of rights conferred by the order, in so far as that occupation or use was not permitted or facilitated by the tenant as mentioned in the preceding paragraph.

(5) For the purposes of the Scottish Act of 1949 nothing done or omitted by the tenant or by the landlord of the holding by way of permitting any of the land in respect of which opencast planning permission has been granted to be occupied for the purpose of carrying on any of the permitted activities, or by way of facilitating the use of any of that land for that purpose, shall be taken to be a breach of any term or condition of the tenancy, either on the part of the tenant or on the part of the landlord.

(6) For the purposes of section 25(2) of the Scottish Act of 1949, no account is to be taken of permission granted as mentioned in paragraph (*c*) of that subsection if the permission—

    (*a*) is granted on an application by the National Coal Board; and

    (*b*) relates to the working of coal by opencast operations; and

    (*c*) is granted subject to a restoration condition and an aftercare condition.

(7) For the purposes of section 26 of the Scottish Act of 1949 (in which subsection (1) specifies conditions for the giving of consent under section 25 of that Act to the operation of a notice to quit) the condition specified in paragraph (*e*) of subsection (1) shall not be treated as satisfied if the use for the purpose of which the landlord proposes to terminate the tenancy is the use of the land for carrying on any of the permitted activities.

(8) On a reference to arbitration under section 7 of the Scottish Act of 1949 with respect to the rent which should be properly payable for the holding, in respect of any

period for which the Board are in occupation of the holding, or of any part thereof, for the purpose of carrying on any of the permitted activities, the arbiter shall not take into account any increase or diminution in the rental value of the holding in so far as that increase or diminution is attributable to the occupation of the holding, or of that part of the holding, by the Board for the purpose of carrying on any of the permitted activities.

(9) For the purpose of the operation of section 8 of the Scottish Act of 1949 (which relates to increases of rent for improvements carried out by the landlord) in relation to an improvement carried out on the holding, in a case where the improvement has been affected by anything done for the purpose of carrying on any of the permitted activities, the increase (if any) of the rental value of the holding attributable to the carrying out of the improvement shall be assessed as if the improvement had not been so affected.

(10) The use of land for the working of coal by opencast operations shall not be a use for the purposes of which a landlord shall be entitled to resume the land.".

6. The following sections shall be substituted for section 15—

"Suspension of certain public rights of ways

15.—(1) Where—

   (*a*) the Board apply for opencast planning permission; and

   (*b*) over any part of the land to which the application relates there subsists a public right of way, not being a right enjoyed by vehicular traffic,

the Board may also apply to the Secretary of State for an order suspending the public right of way.

(2) The Secretary of State shall not make such an order unless—

   (*a*) opencast planning permission is granted; and

   (*b*) he is satisfied—

      (i) that a suitable alternative way will be made available by the Board (whether on land comprised in the opencast planning permission or on other land) for use by the public during the period for which the order remains in force; or

      (ii) that the provision of such an alternative way is not required.

(3) An order under this section shall specify the date, which shall not be earlier than the making of the order, with effect from which the right of way is suspended.

(4) Where an order has been made under this section the Secretary of State shall revoke it—

   (*a*) if—

      (i) no permitted activities have been carried on pursuant to the opencast planning permission on the land over which the right of way subsisted; and

      (ii) he is satisfied that there is no early prospect of such activities being so carried on; or

   (*b*) as soon after such permitted activities have been so carried on as he is satisfied that it is no longer necessary for the purpose of carrying on such permitted activities that the right of way should be suspended.

(5) An order under this section shall include such provisions as may appear to the Secretary of State to be appropriate for securing the reconstruction of the way on the restoration of the land over which the right of way subsisted immediately before the order was made.

(6) Where an order is made under this section then, in connection with the provision of such a suitable alternative way as is referred to in subsection (2) above,—

   (*a*) the order under this section may provide that, in so far as the carrying out of any operations, or any change in the use of land, involved in making the alternative way available or in permitting it to be used by the public, constitutes development within the meaning of the Act of 1971, permission for that development shall be deemed to be granted under Part III of that Act subject to such conditions (if any) as may be specified in the order;

   (*b*) where the order under this section includes provisions in accordance with paragraph (*a*) above, the Act of 1971 shall have effect as if they were conditions subject to which the opencast planning permission was granted;

   (*c*) if a compulsory rights order referring to the opencast planning permission is made, then, in the application to that order of section 5(5) above, the permitted activities shall be taken to include making an alternative way available for use by the public, and the right exercisable in accordance with that subsection, as against all persons directly concerned, shall include the right to permit the public to use any way so made available; and

   (*d*) if the land on which the alternative way is to be made available is specified in the order under this section and is land which does not form part of, but it contiguous with, the land to which the opencast planning permission relates, a compulsory rights order referring to the opencast planning permission may include that land as if it were part of the land comprised in the permission.

(7) In the application of this section to Scotland, it shall be read as if for "the Act of 1971" there were substituted "the Town and Country Planning (Scotland) Act 1972".

Suspension of public rights of way—supplementary

15A.—(1) Before submitting to the Secretary of State an application for an order under section 15 of this Act, the Board shall publish a notice in the prescribed form identifying the right of way and stating—

    (*a*) that the Board are proposing to apply for an order suspending it in connection with the working of coal by opencast operations;

    (*b*) that opencast planning permission has been applied for, or, as the case may be, has been granted; and

    (*c*) that objections to the application for the order may be made in writing to the Secretary of State within such time, not being less than 28 days from the publication of the notice, as may be specified.

(2) The duty to publish a notice imposed by subsection (1) above is a duty to publish it—

    (*a*) in two successive weeks in one or more local newspapers circulating in the locality in which the land over which the right of way subsists is situated; and

    (*b*) in the same or any other two successive weeks, in the appropriate Gazette.

(3) The period within which objections may be made expires when the period specified in the last publication of the notice expires; and any period specified in earlier publications is to be treated as extended accordingly.

(4) A notice under subsection (1) above shall name a place in the locality where a copy of the application and of a map showing the right of way can be inspected.

(5) The Board shall also, before submitting such an application to the Secretary of State,—

    (*a*) inform—

        (i) in England and Wales, the district council and, except in the case of a metropolitan district, the county council, and any parish or community council or parish meeting; and

        (ii) in Scotland, every local authority in whose area any part of the land over which the right of way subsists is situated of the right to object conferred by subsection (1) above;

    (*b*) send them a map showing the right of way and a copy of their notice under subsection (1) above; and

    (*c*) affix to some conspicuous object at either end of the right of way a notice giving in the prescribed form the prescribed particulars of their proposed application concerning it and of the right to object.

(6) If no objection is made by any such authority, other than a parish or community council or parish meeting, as is mentioned in subsection (5)(*a*) above, or if all objections which are made by any such authority are withdrawn, the Secretary of State, upon being satisfied that the Board have complied with subsections (1) to (5) above, may if he thinks fit make the order.

(7) The Secretary of State may, if he thinks fit, cause a public local inquiry to be held before determining whether to make an order, and shall cause such an inquiry to be held if an objection is made by any such authority and is not withdrawn.

(8) If the Secretary of State causes such an inquiry to be held, he shall consider all objections to the application which are duly made by any person and not withdrawn and the report of the person who held the inquiry before determining whether to make the order.

(9) An order under section 15 of this Act may be made either in accordance with the Board's application or subject to such modifications as the Secretary of State may determine.

(10) If the Secretary of State makes an order, the Board, as soon as may be after the order is made, shall publish a notice in the prescribed form that the order has been made, describing the right of way which is suspended, stating the date on which the order comes into operation and naming a place in the locality where a copy of the order and of any map to which it refers can be inspected at all reasonable hours, and shall serve a like notice and a copy of the order on any body required under this section to be informed of the application for the order.

(11) The duty to publish a notice imposed by subsection (10) above is a duty to publish it—

(*a*) in one or more local newspapers such as are mentioned in subsection (1) above; and

(*b*) in the appropriate Gazette.

(12) In this section "the appropriate Gazette" means—

(*a*) the London Gazette in a case where the land over which the right of way subsists is situated in England or Wales; and

(*b*) the Edinburgh Gazette in a case where it is situated in Scotland.".

7. In section 16—

(*a*) in subsections (1) and (2), for the words from "which" to "Act" there shall be substituted the words "in respect of which opencast planning permission has been granted";

(*b*) in subsection (3), for the words from "comprised" to "Act" there shall be substituted the words "in respect of which the permission was granted".

8. In sections 18(3)(*a*) and 19(4)(*a*)—

(*a*) for the word "authorisation", in the first place where it occurs, there shall be substituted the words "opencast planning permission"; and

(*b*) for the words "an authorisation" there shall be substituted the word "permission".

9. In section 38—

(*a*) in paragraph (*a*)—

(i) for the words from "which" to "Act" there shall be substituted the words "in respect of which opencast planning permission has been granted"; and

(ii) for the words "authorised purposes" there shall be substituted the words "purpose of carrying on the permitted activities";

(*b*) in paragraph (*b*), for the words "comprised in the authorisation" there shall be substituted the words "in respect of which the permission was granted and"; and

(*c*) for the words from "fulfilment" to the end of the subsection there shall be substituted the words "permitted activities".

10. In section 39(3)—

(*a*) in paragraph (*a*), for the words "an authorisation under section one of this Act" there shall be substituted the words "opencast planning permission";

(*b*) in paragraph (*b*)—

(i) for the words from "an" to "Act", in the first place where it occurs, there shall be substituted the words "opencast planning permission"; and

(ii) for the words "out of any authorised operations" there shall be substituted the words "on of any of the permitted activities"; and

(*c*) in paragraph (*d*), for the words "any of the provisions of the First" there shall be substituted the words "section 15A(4)(*c*) or any of the provisions of the".

11. In the proviso to section 39(5), for the words "any of the provisions of the First" there shall be substituted the words "section 15A(4)(*c*) or any of the provisions of the".

12. In section 45(2)—

(*a*) for the words from "an" to "Act" there shall be substituted the words "opencast planning permission has been granted"; and

(*b*) for the words "authorised operations", there shall be substituted the words "permitted activities".

13. In section 51(1)—

(*a*) the following definition shall be inserted after the definition of "National Trust"—

" "opencast planning permission" means planning permission which permits the Board to work coal by opencast operations or to carry out operations incidental to such working;";

(*b*) the following definition shall be inserted after the definition of "period of occupation"—

" "permitted activities" means—

(*a*) the working of coal by opencast operations pursuant to opencast planning permission and the carrying out of operations incidental to such working; and

(*b*) the carrying out of any conditions subject to which opencast planning permission has been granted;"; and

(*c*) the following definition shall be inserted after the definition of "persons directly concerned"—

" "planning permission" means planning permission under Part III of the Act of 1971;".

14. In section 52(2), the following definition shall be inserted after the definition of "owner"—

" "planning permission" means planning permission under Part III of the Act of 1972;".

15. In paragraph 5(1) of Part I of Schedule 2 (compulsory rights orders)—

(*a*) for the words "an authorisation under section one of this Act" there shall be substituted the words "opencast planning permission"; and

(*b*) for the words from "an authorisation", in the second place where those words occur, to "operations" there shall be substituted the words "opencast planning permission should be granted or should have been granted.".

16. In Schedule 6, in paragraph 18(2)(*c*), for the words from "purposes", in the first place where it occurs, to the end there shall be substituted the words "activities which, in relation to the opencast planning permission referred to in the order, constitute the permitted activities".

17. In Schedule 7, in paragraph 24(3)(*a*)—

(*a*) for the word "authorisation", in the first place where it occurs, there shall be substituted the words "opencast planning permission"; and

(*b*) for the words "had been made for such an authorisation" there shall be substituted the words "for opencast planning permission had been made".

PART II

ACQUISITION OF LAND ACT 1981 (*c*.67)

18. In section 29—

(*a*) in subsection (6)—

(i) for the words "an authorisation under section 1 of the Opencast Coal Act 1958" there shall be substituted the words "opencast planning permission"; and

(ii) for the words from "an authorisation", in the second place where they occur, to "operations" there shall be substituted the words "opencast planning permission should be granted or should have been granted"; and

(*b*) the following subsection shall be substituted for subsection (11)—

"(11) In this section "opencast planning permission" and "persons directly concerned" have the same meanings as in the Opencast Coal Act 1958.".

Sections 40 and 50   SCHEDULE 9

LISTED BUILDINGS AND CONSERVATION AREAS

PART I

ENGLAND AND WALES

Free-standing objects and structures within curtilage of listed building

1.—(1) In section 54(9) of the Town and Country Planning Act 1971 (definition of "listed building"), for the words from "and for the purposes" to the end substitute—

"and, for the purposes of the provisions of this Act relating to listed buildings and building preservation notices, the following shall be treated as part of the building—

(*a*) any object or structure fixed to the building;

(*b*) any object of structure within the curtilage of the building which, although not fixed to the building, forms part of the land and has done so since before 1st July 1948.".

(2) Where by virtue of this paragraph an object or structure ceases to be treated as part of a listed building—

(*a*) liabilities incurred before the commencement of this paragraph by reason of the object or structure being so treated cease to have effect, and

(*b*) a condition attached to a listed building consent ceases to have effect if, or to the extent that, it could not have been attached if this paragraph had been in force;

except for the purposes of criminal proceedings begun before the commencement of this paragraph.

Scope of exception for urgent works

2.—(1) In section 55 of the Town and Country Planning Act 1971 (control of works for demolition, alteration or extension of listed buildings), for subsection (6) (exception for certain urgent works) substitute—

"(6) In proceedings for an offence under this section it shall be a defence to prove the following matters—

(*a*) that works to the building were urgently necessary in the interests of safety or health or for the preservation of the building,

(*b*) that it was not practicable to secure safety or health or, as the case may be, the preservation of the building by works of repair or works for affording temporary support or shelter,

(*c*) that the works carried out were limited to the minimum measures immediately necessary, and

(*d*) that notice in writing justifying in detail the carrying out of the works was given to the local planning authority as soon as reasonably practicable.".

(2) In section 97 of the Town and Country Planning Act 1971 (appeal against listed building enforcement notice) in subsection (1) (grounds of appeal), for paragraph (*d*) substitute—

(*d*) that works to the building were urgently necessary in the interests of safety or health or for the preservation of the building, that it was not practicable to secure safety or health or, as the case may be, the preservation of the building by works of repair or works for affording temporary support or shelter, and that the works carried out were limited to the minimum measures immediately necessary;".

Grant of listed building consent subject to subsequent approval of detail

3.—(1) In section 56 of the Town and Country Planning Act 1971 (supplementary provisions with respect to listed building consent), after subsection (4A) insert—

"(4B) Listed building consent may be granted subject to a condition reserving specified details of the works (whether or not set out in the application) for subsequent approval by the local planning authority or, in the case of consent granted by the Secretary of State, specifying whether the reserved details are to be approved by the local planning authority or by him.".

(2) In paragraph 8(1) of Schedule 11 to the Town and Country Planning Act 1971 (listed building consent: appeal against decision), for the words from the beginning to "and the consent is refused" substitute—

"Where an application is made to the local planning authority—

(*a*) for listed building consent, or

(*b*) for approval of the authority required by a condition imposed on the granting of listed building consent with respect to details of the works,

and the consent or approval is refused".

(3) Renumber paragraph 9 of Schedule 11 to the Town and Country Planning Act 1971 (appeal in default of decision) as sub-paragraph (1) of that paragraph and after it insert—

"(2) Sub-paragraph (1) of this paragraph applies to an application to the local planning authority for approval by the authority required by a condition imposed on the granting of listed building consent with respect to details of the works as it applies to an application for listed building consent, with the following modifications—

(*a*) for references to the prescribed period substitute references to the period of eight weeks from the date of the receipt of the application, and

(*b*) omit paragraph (*b*) and the word 'or' preceding it.".

Application to modify or discharge conditions attached to listed building consent

4. After section 56A of the Town and Country Planning Act 1971 insert—

"Application for variation or discharge of conditions

56B.—(1) Any person interested in a listed building with respect to which listed building consent has been granted subject to conditions may apply to the local planning authority for the variation or discharge of the conditions.

(2) The application shall indicate what variation or discharge of conditions is applied for and the provisions of Part I of Schedule 11 to this Act apply to such an application as they apply to an application for listed building consent.

(3) On such an application the local planning authority or, as the case may be, the Secretary of State may vary or discharge the conditions attached to the consent, and

may add new conditions consequential upon the variation or discharge, as they or he thinks fit.".

Extent of exemption accorded to ecclesiastical buildings

5.—(1) After section 58A of the Town and Country Planning Act 1971 insert—

"Power to restrict exemption of certain ecclesiastical buildings

58AA.—(1) The Secretary of State may by order provide for restricting or excluding in such cases as may be specified in the order the operation in relation to ecclesiastical buildings of sections 56(1) and 58(2) of this Act (buildings excepted from provisions relating to listed buildings and building preservation notices).

(2) An order under this section may—

(*a*) make provision for buildings generally, for descriptions of building or for particular buildings;

(*b*) make different provision for buildings in different areas, for buildings of different religious faiths or denominations or according to the use made of the building;

(*c*) make such provision in relation to a part of a building (including, in particular, an object or structure falling to be treated as part of the building by virtue of section 54(9) of this Act) as may be made in relation to a building and make different provision for different parts of the same building;

(*d*) make different provision with respect to works of different descriptions or according to the extent of the works;

(*e*) make such consequential adaptations or modifications of the operation of any other provision of this Act, or of any instrument made under this Act, as appear to the Secretary of State to be appropriate.".

(2) In section 287 of the Town and Country Planning Act 1971 (regulations and orders)—

(*a*) in subsection (4) (orders to be made by statutory instrument), after "55(3)" insert "58AA";

(*b*) in subsection (5) (orders subject to negative resolution), after "section" insert "58AA";

(*c*) in subsection (9) (power to include supplementary and incidental provisions), after "section" insert "58AA".

Dangerous structure orders in respect of listed buildings

6.—(1) In the Town and Country Planning Act 1971, after the section inserted by paragraph 4 above insert—

"Dangerous structure orders in respect of listed buildings

56C.—(1) Before taking any steps with a view to the making of a dangerous structure order in respect of a listed building, a local planning authority shall consider whether they should instead exercise their powers under—

(*a*) section 101 of this Act (power to carry out urgent works for preservation of building), or

(*b*) sections 114 and 115 of this Act (power to acquire building in need of repair).

(2) In this section "dangerous structure order" means an order or notice under section 77(1)(*a*) or 79(1) of the Building Act 1984 or section 62(2), 65 or 69(1) of the London Building Acts (Amendment) Act 1939.".

(2) In sections 77 and 79 of the Building Act 1984 and in sections 62, 65 and 69 of the London Building Acts (Amendment) Act 1939 insert as the final subsection—

"( ) This section has effect subject to the provisions of the Town and Country Planning Act 1971 relating to listed buildings, buildings subject to building preservation orders and buildings in conservation areas.".

Works for preservation of buildings

7. For section 101 of the Town and Country Planning Act 1971 (urgent works for preservation of unoccupied buildings) substitute—

"Urgent works to preserve building

101.—(1) Where it appears to the local authority or the Secretary of State that works are urgently necessary for the preservation of—

(*a*) a listed building, or

(b) a building in respect of which a direction has been given by the Secretary of State that this section shall apply,

they or he may, subject to the following provisions of this section, execute the works, which may consist of or include works for affording temporary support or shelter for the building.

(2) The ground on which the Secretary of State may give a direction that this section shall apply to a building is that the building is in a conservation area and it appears to him that its preservation is important for maintaining the character or appearance of the conservation area.

(3) If the building is occupied works may be carried out only to those parts which are not in use; and no action may be taken in respect of an excepted building within the meaning of section 58(2) of this Act.

(4) The owner of the building shall be given not less than seven days' notice in writing of the intention to carry out the works and the notice shall describe the works proposed to be carried out.

(5) The Historic Buildings and Monuments Commission for England have the following functions under this section—

(a) as respects buildings in Greater London the Commission have concurrently with the relevant London borough council the functions of a local authority;

(b) the Secretary of State shall consult the Commission before giving a direction under subsection (1)(b) in respect of a building in England; and

(c) if it appears to the Secretary of State in accordance with subsection (1) that works are required for the preservation of a building in England, he shall not himself carry out the works but shall instead authorise the Commission to do so, specifying the works in the authorisation, and it shall be for the Commission to give notice to the owner under subsection (4).

Recovery of expenses of works under s.101

101A.—(1) This section has effect for enabling the expenses of works executed under section 101 of this Act to be recovered by the authority who carried out the works, that is, the local authority, the Historic Buildings and Monuments Commission for England or the Secretary of State or, in the case of works carried out by the Historic Buildings and Monuments Commission for England on behalf of the Secretary of State, by the Secretary of State.

(2) The authority or, as the case may be, the Secretary of State may give notice to the owner of the building requiring him to pay the expenses of the works.

(3) Where the works consist of or include works for affording temporary support or shelter for the building—

(a) the expenses which may be recovered include any continuing expenses involved in making available the apparatus or materials used, and

(b) notices under subsection (2) in respect of any such continuing expenses may be given from time to time.

(4) The owner may within 28 days of the service of the notice represent to the Secretary of State—

(a) that some or all of the works were unnecessary for the preservation of the building,

(b) in the case of works for affording temporary support or shelter, that the temporary arrangements have continued for an unreasonable length of time, or

(c) that the amount specified in the notice is unreasonable or that the recovery of it would cause him hardship,

and the Secretary of State shall determine to what extent the representations are justified.

(5) The Secretary of State shall give notice of his determination, the reasons for it and the amount recoverable—

(a) to the owner of the building, and

(b) to the local authority or the Historic Buildings and Monuments Commission for England, if they carried out the works.".

Control of demolition in conservation areas

8.—(1) Section 277A of the Town and Country Planning Act 1971 (control of demolition in conservation areas) is amended as follows.

(2) For subsection (8) (application of provisions relating to listed buildings) substitute—

"(8) The following provisions of this Act have effect in relation to buildings to which this section applies as they have effect in relation to listed buildings, subject to such exceptions and modifications as may be prescribed by regulations—

sections 55 to 56C and 58AA and Parts I and II of Schedule 11 (requirement of consent to works: application for and revocation of consent),

sections 96 to 100 (enforcement),

section 172 (compensation where consent revoked or modified),

section 190 and Schedule 19 (purchase notice on refusal of consent),

sections 242, 243, 245 and 246 (validity of orders, proceedings for review and appeals),

section 255 (contributions by local authorities and statutory undertakers);

section 266(1)(*b*), (4) and (5) (application to Crown land), and

section 271 and Part VI of Schedule 21 (application of provisions to works by local planning authority).".

(3) In subsection (11) (authorities exercising functions of local planning authority), in paragraph (*c*) (non-metropolitan counties, excluding areas in National Parks) omit "the county planning authority and".

Form of application for listed building consent

9. For paragraph 1(1) of Schedule 11 to the Town and Country Planning Act 1971 (regulations as to form and manner of application for listed building consent) substitute—

"(1) An application for listed building consent shall be made in such form as the local planning authority may require and shall contain—

(*a*) sufficient particulars to identify the building to which it relates, including a plan, and

(*b*) such other plans and drawings as are necessary to describe the works which are the subject of the application,

and such other particulars as may be required by the local planning authority.

(1A) Provision may be made by regulations under this Act with respect to the manner in which applications for listed building consent are to be made, the manner in which such applications are to be advertised and the time within which they are to be dealt with by local planning authorities or, as the case may be, by the Secretary of State.".

Listed building consent: consideration whether to call in application

10.—(1) In paragraph 5(2) of Schedule 11 to the Town and Country Planning Act 1971 (notice to local planning authority that Secretary of State requires further time to consider whether to call in an application for listed building consent), for the words from "and sub-paragraph (1)" to the end substitute "; and if he gives such a notice the authority shall not grant the listed building consent until he has notified them that he does not intend to require the reference of the application.".

(2) In paragraph 6(4) of Schedule 11 to the Town and Country Planning Act 1971 (notice to Historic Buildings and Monuments Commission that Secretary of State requires further time to consider whether to call in an application for listed building consent), for the words from "and sub-paragraph (3)" to the end substitute "; and if he gives such a notice the Commission shall not authorise the local planning authority as mentioned in sub-paragraph (2)(*a*) of this paragraph, nor under sub-paragraph (2)(*b*) of this paragraph direct them to grant listed building consent, until he has notified them that he does not intend to require the reference of the application.".

(3) In paragraph 6(6) of Schedule 11 to the Town and Country Planning Act 1971 (notice to local planning authority that Secretary of State requires further time to consider whether to call in application for listed building consent which the Historic Buildings and Monuments Commission have directed the authority to refuse), for the words from "and sub-paragraph (5)(*a*)" to the end substitute "; and if he gives such a notice the authority shall not give effect to the Commission's direction until he has notified them that he does not intend to require the reference of the application.".

Listed building consent: directions as to which applications need not be notified to the Secretary of State

11.—(1) Paragraph 7 of Schedule 11 to the Town and Country Planning Act 1971 (directions as to which applications need not be notified to Secretary of State) is amended as follows.

(2) In paragraph 7(1) (power to direct that certain descriptions of application need not be notified) omit, "other than such consent for the demolition of a building" and after that sub-paragraph insert—

"(1A) Before giving a direction under sub-paragraph (1) of this paragraph in respect of any description of application for consent to the demolition of a building in England, the Secretary of State shall consult the Historic Buildings and Monuments Commission for England.".

(3) For paragraph 7(1A) and (1B) (power to except applications from direction under sub-paragraph (1)) substitute—

"(1B) Where a direction is in force under sub-paragraph (1) of this paragraph, the Secretary of State may give to a local planning authority a direction that paragraph 5 or (as the case may be) paragraph 6 of this Schedule shall nevertheless apply—

(*a*) to a particular application for listed building consent, or

(*b*) to such descriptions of application for listed building consent as are specified in the direction;

and such a direction has effect in relation to any such application which has not been disposed of by the authority by their granting or refusing consent.".

(4) At the end of the paragraph add—

"(3) Directions under sub-paragraph (1) or (2) of this paragraph may be given to authorities generally or to particular authorities or descriptions of authority.".

Application to local planning authorities of provisions relating to listed buildings

12. In Part VI of Schedule 21 to the Town and Country Planning Act 1971 (provisions of Act applying to applications by local planning authorities with respect to listed buildings), at the appropriate place insert "Sections 242, 243, 245 and 246.".

PART II

SCOTLAND

Free-standing objects and structures within curtilage of listed building

13.—(1) In section 52(7) of the Town and Country Planning (Scotland) Act 1972 (definition of "listed building"), for the words from "and for the purposes" to the end substitute—

"and, for the purposes of the provisions of this Act relating to listed buildings and building preservation notices, the following shall be treated as part of the building—

(*a*) any object or structure fixed to the building;

(*b*) any object or structure within the curtilage of the building which, although not fixed to the building, forms part of the land and has done so much before 1st July 1948.".

(2) Where by virtue of this paragraph an object or structure ceases to be treated as part of a listed building—

(*a*) liabilities incurred before the commencement of this paragraph by reason of the object or structure being so treated cease to have effect, and

(*b*) a condition attached to listed building consent ceases to have effect if, or to the extent that, it could not have been attached if this paragraph had been in force;

except for the purposes of criminal proceedings begun before the commencement of this paragraph.

Late application for listed building consent

14.—(1) In subsection (1) of section 53 (control of works for demolition, alteration or extension of listed buildings) of the Town and Country Planning (Scotland) Act 1972, for the words "this Part of this Act" where they appear for the second time, substitute "subsection (2) of this section".

(2) After subsection (2) of the said section 53 insert—

"(2A) If written consent is granted by the planning authority or the Secretary of State for the retention of works for the demolition, alteration or extension of a listed building which have been executed without consent under subsection (2) of this section, the works are authorised under this Part of this Act from the grant of the consent under this subsection."

(3) After subsection (3) of the said section insert—

"(3A) Consent under subsection (2) or (2A) of this section is referred to in this Part of this Act as "listed building consent".".

(4) At the end of section 54A (limit on duration of listed building consent) of the Town and Country Planning (Scotland) Act 1972 there shall be added—

"(5) Nothing in this section applies to any consent to the retention of works granted under section 53(2A) of this Act.".

Defence to proceedings under section 53

15.—(1) In section 53 of the Town and Country Planning (Scotland) Act 1972 (control of works for demolition, alteration or extension of listed buildings), for subsection (6) (exception for certain urgent works) substitute—

"(6) In proceedings for an offence under this section it shall be a defence to prove the following matters—

(*a*) that works to the building were urgently necessary in the interest of safety or health or for the preservation of the building;

(*b*) that is was not practicable to secure safety or health or, as the case may be, the preservation of the building by works of repair or works for affording temporary support or shelter;

(*c*) that the works carried out were limited to the minimum measures immediately necessary, and

(*d*) that notice in writing justifying in detail the carrying out of the works was given to the planning authority as soon as reasonably practicable.".

(2) In section 93 of the Town and Country Planning (Scotland) Act 1972 (appeal against listed building enforcement notice), in subsection (1) (grounds of appeal), for paragraph (*c*) substitute—

(*c*) that works to the building were urgently necessary in the interests of safety or health or for the preservation of the building, that it was not practicable to secure safety or health or, as the case may be, the preservation of the building by works of repair or works for affording temporary support or shelter, and that the works carried out were limited to the minimum measures immediately necessary;".

Grant of listed building consent subject to subsequent approval of detail

16.—(1) In section 54 of the Town and Country Planning (Scotland) Act 1972 (supplementary provisions with respect to listed building consent), after subsection (4) insert—

"(4A) Listed building consent may be granted subject to a condition reserving specified details of the works (whether or not set out in the application) for subsequent approval by the planning authority or, in the case of consent granted by the Secretary of State, specifying whether the reserved details are to be approved by the planning authority or by him.".

(2) In paragraph 7(1) of the said Schedule 10 to the 1972 Act (listed building consent: appeal against decision), for the words from the beginning to "and the consent is refused" substitute—

"Where an application is made to the planning authority—

(*a*) for listed building consent, or

(*b*) for approval of the authority required by a condition imposed on the granting of listed building consent with respect to details of the works,

and the consent or approval is refused".

(3) Renumber paragraph 8 of that Schedule (appeal in default of decision) as subparagraph (1) of that paragraph and after it insert—

"(2) Sub-paragraph (1) of this paragraph applies to an application to the planning authority for approval by the authority required by a condition imposed on the granting of listed building consent with respect to details of the works as it applies to an application for listed building consent, with the following modifications—

(*a*) for references to the prescribed period substitute references to the period of two months from the date of the receipt of the application, and

(*b*) omit paragraph (*b*) and the word 'or' preceding it.".

Application to modify or discharge conditions attached to listed building consent

17. After section 54C of the Town and Country Planning (Scotland) Act 1972 insert—

"Application for variation or discharge of conditions

54D.—(1) Any person interested in a listed building with respect to which listed building consent has been granted subject to conditions may apply to the planning authority for the variation or discharge of the conditions.

(2) The application shall indicate what variation or discharge of conditions is applied for and the provisions of Part I of Schedule 10 to this Act apply to such an application as they apply to an application for listed building consent.

(3) On such an application the planning authority or, as the case may be, the Secretary of State may vary or discharge the conditions attached to the consent, and may add new conditions consequential upon the variation or discharge, as they or he think fit.".

Extent of exemption accorded to the ecclesiastical buildings

18.—(1) After section 56 of the Town and Country Planning (Scotland) Act 1972 insert—

"**Power to restrict exemption of certain ecclesiastical buildings**

56AA.—(1) The Secretary of State may by order provide for restricting or excluding in such areas as may be specified in the order the operation in relation to ecclesiastical buildings of sections 54(1) and 56(2) of this Act (buildings excepted from provisions relating to listed buildings and building preservation notices).

(2) An order under this section may—

(a) make provision for buildings generally, for descriptions of building or for particular buildings;

(b) make different provision for buildings in different areas, for buildings of different religious faiths or denominations or according to the use made of the building;

(c) make such provision in relation to a part of a building (including, in particular, an object or structure falling to be treated as part of the building by virtue of section 52(7) of this Act) as may be made in relation to a building and make different provision for different parts of the same building;

(d) make different provision with respect to works of different descriptions or according to the extent of the works;

(e) make such consequential adaptations or modifications of the operation of any other provision of this Act, or of any instrument made under this Act, as appear to the Secretary of State to be appropriate.

(3) This section is without prejudice to the Church of Scotland Act 1921.".

(2) In section 273 (regulations and orders) of the Town and Country Planning (Scotland) Act 1972—

(a) in subsection (4) (orders to be made by statutory instrument), after "53(3)" insert "56AA";

(b) in subsection (5) (orders subject to negative resolution), after "1(3)" insert "56AA";

(c) in subsection (9) (power to include supplementary and incidental provision), after "section" insert "56AA".

Effect of listed building enforcement notice

19. After section 95 of the Town and Country Planning (Scotland) Act 1972 insert—

"**Effect of listed building consent on listed building enforcement notice**

95A.—(1) If, after the issue of a listed building enforcement notice, consent is granted under section 53(2A) of this Act for the retention of any work to which the listed building enforcement notice relates, the notice shall cease to have effect in so far as it requires steps to be taken which would involve the works not being retained in accordance with the consent.

(2) If the consent is granted so as to permit the retention of works without complying with some condition subject to which a previous listed building consent was granted, the listed building enforcement notice shall cease to have effect in so far as it requires steps to be taken for complying with that condition.

(3) The preceding provisions of this section shall be without prejudice to the liability of any person for an offence in respect of a failure to comply with the listed building enforcement notice before the relevant provisions of that notice ceased to have effect.".

Works for preservation of buildings

20. For section 97 of the Town and Country Planning (Scotland) Act 1972 (urgent works for preservation of unoccupied buildings) substitute—

"Urgent works to preserve building

97.—(1) Where it appears to the planning authority or the Secretary of State that works are urgently necessary for the preservation of—

(*a*) a listed building, or

(*b*) a building in respect of which a direction has been given by the Secretary of State that this section shall apply,

they or he may, subject to the following provisions of this section, exclude the works, which may consist of or include works for affording temporary support or shelter for the building.

(2) The ground on which the Secretary of State may give a direction that this section shall apply to a building is that the building is in a conservation area and it appears to him that its preservation is important for maintaining the character or appearance of the conservation area.

(3) If the building is occupied works may be carried out only to those parts which are not in use; and no action may be taken in respect of an excepted building within the meaning of section 56(2) of this Act.

(4) The owner of the building shall be given not less than 7 days' notice in writing of the intention to carry out the works and the notice shall describe the works proposed to be carried out.

Recovery of expenses of works under s.97

97A.—(1) This section has effect for enabling the expenses of works executed under section 97 of this Act to be recovered.

(2) The planning authority or, as the case may be, the Secretary of State may give notice to the owner of the building requiring him to pay the expenses of the works.

(3) Where the works consist of or include works for affording temporary support or shelter for the building—

(*a*) the expenses which may be recovered include any continuing expenses involved in making available the apparatus or materials used, and

(*b*) notices under subsection (2) in respect of any such continuing expenses may be given from time to time.

(4) The owner may within 28 days of the service of the notice represent to the Secretary of State—

(*a*) that some or all of the works were unnecessary for the preservation of the building,

(*b*) in the case of works for affording temporary support or shelter, that the temporary arrangements have continued for an unreasonable length of time, or

(*c*) that the amount specified in the notice is unreasonable or that the recovery of it would cause him hardship,

and the Secretary of State shall determine to what extent the representations are justified.

(5) The Secretary of State shall give notice of his determination, the reasons for it and the amount recoverable—

(*a*) to the owner of the building, and

(*b*) to the planning authority, if they carried out the works.".

Control of demolition in conservation areas

21. Section 262A(8) of the Town and Country Planning (Scotland) Act 1972 (application to buildings in conservation areas of provisions relating to listed buildings) is amended as follows—

(*a*) for the words from "section 53" to "section 54C" substitute "sections 53 to 54D and 56AA";

(*b*) for "sections 92 to 95" substitute "sections 92 to 96";

(*c*) after "section 179" insert "sections 231 and 233, section 242";

(*d*) after "section 253(1)(*b*)" insert ", (4) and (5), section 257";

(*e*) after "Schedule 17" insert "Part IV of Schedule 19".

Form of application for listed building consent

22. For paragraph 1(1) of Schedule 10 of the Town and Country Planning (Scotland) Act 1972 (regulations as to form and manner of application for listed building consent) substitute—

"(1) An application for listed building consent shall be made in such form as the planning authority may require and shall contain—

(*a*) sufficient particulars to identify the building to which it relates, including a plan, and

(*b*) such other plans and drawings as are necessary to describe the works which are the subject of the application,

and such other particulars as may be required by the planning authority.

(1A) Provision may be made by regulations under this Act with respect to the manner in which applications for listed building consent are to be made, the manner in which such applications are to be advertised and the time within which they are to be dealt with by planning authorities or, as the case may be, by the Secretary of State.".

Calling in of application for listed building consent

23. In paragraph 5(2) of Schedule 10 to the Town and Country Planning (Scotland) Act 1972 (notice to planning authority that Secretary of State requires further time to consider whether to call in application for listed building consent), for the words from "and sub-paragraph (1)" to the end substitute ", and if he gives such a notice the authority shall not grant the listed building consent until he has notified them that he does not intend to require the reference of the application.".

Application to planning authorities of provisions relating to listed buildings

24. In Part IV of Schedule 19 to the Town and Country Planning (Scotland) Act 1972 (provisions of Act applying to applications by planning authorities with respect to listed buildings), at the appropriate place insert "Sections 231 and 233".

Section 41(1) and (3)   SCHEDULE 10

LOCAL PLANS AND UNITARY DEVELOPMENT PLANS

PART 1

SECTIONS 11 TO 158 OF THE TOWN AND COUNTRY PLANNING ACT 1971 (c.78),
AS SUBSTITUTED

ARRANGEMENT OF SECTIONS

Local Plans

*   *   *   *

Local plans

Local plans

11.—(1) A local plan shall consist of—

(*a*) a written statement formulating in such detail as the local planning authority think appropriate their proposals for the development or other use of land in their area, or for any description of development or other use of such land, including such measures as the authority think fit for the improvement of the physical environment and the management of traffic;

(*b*) a map showing those proposals; and

(c) such diagrams, illustrations or other descriptive matter as the authority think appropriate to explain or illustrate the proposals in the plan, or as may be prescribed.

(2) Different local plans may be prepared for different purposes for the same area.

(3) In formulating their proposals in a local plan the local planning authority shall have regard to any information and any other considerations which appear to them to be relevant or which may be prescribed or which the Secretary of State may in any particular case direct them to take into account.

(4) The proposals in a local plan shall be in general conformity with the structure plan.

(5) A local planning authority may prepare a local plan for a part of their area (an "action area") which they have selected for the commencement during a prescribed period of comprehensive treatment, by development, redevelopment or improvement of the whole or part of the area selected, or partly by one method and partly by another; and a local plan prepared for such an action area shall indicate the nature of the treatment selected for the area.

(6) For the purpose of discharging their functions with respect to local plans a district planning authority may, in so far as it appears to them necessary to do so having regard to the survey made by the county planning authority under section 6 of this Act, examine the matters mentioned in subsections (1) and (3) of that section so far as relevant to their area.

(7) In preparing a local plan a local planning authority shall take into account the provisions of any scheme under paragraph 3 of Schedule 32 to the Local Government, Planning and Land Act 1980 relating to land in their area which has been designated under that Schedule as an enterprise zone.

Local plan schemes

11A.—(1) A local plan scheme for each county shall be maintained in accordance with this section setting out a programme for the making, alteration, repeal or replacement of local plans for areas in the county, except any part of the county included in a National Park.

(2) The scheme shall, as regards each local plan for which it provides—

(a) specify the title and nature of the plan and the area to which it is to apply and give an indication of its scope,

(b) indicate where appropriate its relationship with the other local plans provided for by the scheme, and

(c) designate the local planning authority, whether county or district, responsible for the plan;

and may contain any appropriate incidental, consequential, transitional and supplementary provisions.

(3) The district planning authorities shall keep under review the need for, and adequacy of, local plans for their area and may make recommendations to the county planning authority for incorporation into the local plan scheme.

(4) The county planning authority shall, in the light of the recommendations of the district planning authorities and in consultation with those authorities, make and thereafter keep under review and from time to time amend the local plan scheme.

(5) As soon as practicable after making or amending a local plan scheme the county planning authority shall send a copy of the scheme, or the scheme as amended, to the Secretary of State.

(6) If a district planning authority make representation to the Secretary of State that they are dissatisfied with a local plan scheme, the Secretary of State may amend the scheme.

(7) A local planning authority may prepare proposals for the making, alteration, repeal or replacement of a local plan—

(a) in any case, except in the case of proposals relating only to land in a National Park, only where authorised to do so by the local plan scheme, and

(b) in the case of proposals for the alteration, repeal or replacement of a local plan approved by the Secretary of State, only with the consent of the Secretary of State;

but subject to any direction of the Secretary of State under section 11B.

Power of Secretary of State to direct making of local plan, &c.

11B.—(1) The Secretary of State may, after consulting a local planning authority, direct them to make, alter, repeal or replace a local plan with respect to their area or part of it.

(2) A direction for the making, alteration or replacement of a local plan shall specify the nature of the plan or, as the case may be, the nature of the alteration required.

(3) The authority shall comply with the direction as soon as possible.

(4) The county planning authority shall make such amendments of the relevant local plan scheme as appear to them appropriate in consequence of the direction.

Publicity and consultation: general

12.—(1) A local planning authority who propose to make, alter, repeal or replace a local plan shall proceed in accordance with this section, unless section 12A applies (short procedure for certain alterations, &c.).

(2) They shall take such steps as will in their opinion secure—

(*a*) that adequate publicity is given to the proposals in the area to which the plan relates,

(*b*) that persons who may be expected to wish to make representations about the proposals are made aware that they are entitled to do so, and

(*c*) that such persons are given an adequate opportunity of making such representations; and they shall consider any representations made to them within the prescribed period.

(3) They shall consult the county planning authority or, as the case may be, the district planning authority with respect to their proposals, shall afford that authority a reasonable opportunity to express their views and shall take those views into consideration.

(4) They shall then, having prepared the relevant documents, that is, the proposed plan, alterations, instrument of repeal or replacement plan, as the case may be, and having obtained any certificate required by section 15 (certificate of conformity with structure plan)—

(*a*) make copies of the documents available for inspection at their office,

(*b*) send a copy of them to the Secretary of State, and

(*c*) send a copy of them to the district or county planning authority, as the case may require.

(5) Each copy of the documents made available for inspection shall be accompanied by a statement of the time within which objections may be made.

Publicity and consultation: short procedure for certain alterations, &c.

12A.—(1) Where a local planning authority propose to alter, repeal or replace a local plan and it appears to them that the issues involved are not of sufficient importance to warrant the full procedure set out in section 12, they may proceed instead in accordance with this section.

(2) They shall prepare the relevant documents, that is, the proposed alterations, instrument of repeal or replacement plan, as the case may be, and, having obtained any certificate required by section 15 (certificate of conformity with structure plan) shall—

(*a*) make copies of the documents available for inspection at their office,

(*b*) send a copy of them to the Secretary of State, and

(*c*) send a copy of them to the county or district planning authority, as the case may require.

(3) Each copy of the documents made available for inspection shall be accompanied by a statement of the time within which representation or objections may be made.

(4) They shall then take such steps as may be prescribed for the purpose of—

(*a*) advertising the fact that the documents are available for inspection and the places and times which, and period during which, they may be inspected, and

(*b*) inviting the making of representations or objections in accordance with regulations; and they shall consider any representations made to them within the prescribed period.

Powers of Secretary of State to secure adequate publicity and consultation

12B.—(1) The documents sent by the local planning authority to the Secretary of State under section 12 shall be accompanied by a statement—

(*a*) of the steps which the authority have taken to comply with subsection (2) of that section, and

(*b*) of the authority's consultations with other persons and their consideration of the views of those persons.

(2) The documents sent by the local planning authority to the Secretary of State under section 12A shall be accompanied by a statement of the steps which the authority are taking to comply with subsection (4) of that section.

(3) If, on considering the statement and the proposals and any other information provided by the local planning authority, the Secretary of State is not satisfied with the steps taken by the authority, he may, within 21 days of the receipt of the statement, direct the authority not to take further steps for the adoption of the proposals without—

(*a*) if they have proceeded in accordance with section 12A, proceeding instead in accordance with section 12, or

(*b*) in any case, taking such further steps as he may specify,

and satisfying him that they have done so.

(4) A local planning authority who are given directions by the Secretary of State shall—

(*a*) forthwith withdraw the copies of the documents made available for inspection as required by section 12(4) or 12A(2), and

(*b*) notify any person by whom objections to the proposals have been made to the authority that the Secretary of State has given such directions.

Objections local inquiry or other hearing

13.—(1) The local planning authority may cause a local inquiry or other hearing to be held for the purpose of considering objections to their proposals for the making, alteration, repeal or replacement of a local plan.

(2) They shall hold such a local inquiry or other hearing in the case of objections made in accordance with regulations unless all the persons who have made such objections have indicated in writing that they do not wish to appear.

(3) A local inquiry or other hearing shall be held by a person appointed by the Secretary of State or, in such cases as may be prescribed, by the authority themselves.

(4) Regulations may—

(*a*) make provision with respect to the appointment, and qualifications for appointment, of persons to hold a local inquiry or other hearing;

(*b*) include provision enabling the Secretary of State to direct a local planning authority to appoint a particular person, or one of a specified list or class of persons;

(*c*) make provision with respect to the remuneration and allowances of the person appointed.

(5) Subsections (2) and (3) of section 250 of the Local Government Act 1972 (power to summon and examine witnesses) apply to an inquiry held under this section.

(6) The Tribunals and Inquiries Act 1971 applies to a local inquiry or other hearing under this section as it applies to a statutory inquiry held by the Secretary of State, with the substitution in section 12(1) (statement of reasons for decision) for the references to a decision taken by the Secretary of State of references to a decision taken by a local authority.

Adoption of proposals

14.—(1) After the expiry of the period afforded for making objections to proposals for the making, alteration, repeal or replacement of a local plan or, if such objections were duly made within that period, after considering the objections so made, the local planning authority may, subject to the following provisions of this section and to section 14A (calling in of proposals by Secretary of State), by resolution adopt the proposals.

(2) They may adopt the proposals as originally prepared or as modified so as to take account of—

(*a*) any such objections as are mentioned in subsection (1) or any other objections to the proposals, or

(*b*) any other considerations which appear to the authority to be material.

(3) The authority shall not adopt any proposals which do not conform generally to the structure plan.

(4) After copies of the proposals have been sent to the Secretary of State and before they have been adopted by the local planning authority, the Secretary of State may, if it appears to him that the proposals are unsatisfactory, direct the authority to consider modifying the proposals in such respects as are indicated in the direction.

(5) An authority to whom a direction is given shall not adopt the proposals unless they satisfy the Secretary of State that they have made the modifications necessary to conform with the direction or the direction is withdrawn.

(6) Where an objection to the proposals has been made by the Minister of Agriculture, Fisheries and Food and the local planning authority do not propose to modify their proposals to take account of the objection—

(*a*) the authority shall send particulars of the objection to the Secretary of State, together with a statement of their reasons for not modifying their proposals to take account of it, and

(*b*) they shall not adopt the proposals unless the Secretary of State authorises them to do so.

Calling in of proposals for approval by Secretary of State

14A.—(1) After copies of proposals have been sent to the Secretary of State and before they have been adopted by the local planning authority, the Secretary of State may direct that the proposals shall be submitted to him for his approval.

(2) In that event—

(a) the authority shall not take any further steps for the adoption of the proposals, and in particular shall not hold or proceed with a local inquiry or other hearing in respect of the proposals under section 13; and

(b) the proposals shall not have effect unless approved by the Secretary of State and shall not require adoption by the authority.

(3) Where particulars of an objection made by the Minister of Agriculture, Fisheries and Food have been sent to the Secretary of State under section 14(6), then, unless the Secretary of State is satisfied that that Minister no longer objects to the proposals, he shall give a direction in respect of the proposals under this section.

Approval of proposals by Secretary of State

14B.—(1) The Secretary of State may after considering proposals submitted to him under section 14A either approve them, in whole or in part and with or without modifications or reservations, or reject them.

(2) In considering the proposals he may take into account any matters he thinks are relevant, whether or not they were taken into account in the proposals as submitted to him.

(3) Where on taking the proposals into consideration the Secretary of State does not determine then to reject them, he shall, before determining whether or not to approve them—

(a) consider any objections to them made in accordance with regulations,

(b) afford to any person who made such an objection which has not been withdrawn an opportunity of appearing before and being heard by a person appointed by him for the purpose, and

(c) if a local inquiry or other hearing is held, also afford such an opportunity to the authority and such other persons as he thinks fit,

except so far as the objections have already been considered, or a local inquiry or other hearing into the objections has already been held, by the authority.

(4) In considering the proposals the Secretary of State may consult with, or consider the views of, any local planning authority or any other person; but he is under no obligation to do so, or to afford an opportunity for the making of representations or objections, or to cause a local inquiry or other hearing to be held, except as provided by subsection (3).

Conformity between plans: certificate of conformity

15.—(1) A district planning authority who have prepared proposals for the making, alteration, repeal or replacement of a local plan shall not take the steps mentioned in section 12(4) or 12A(2) (deposit of documents for inspection, &c.) unless a certificate that the proposals conform generally to the structure plan has been issued in accordance with this section.

(2) The district planning authority shall request the county planning authority to certify that their proposals so conform and that authority shall, within a month of receiving the request, or such longer period as may be agreed between the authorities, consider the matter and, if satisfied that the proposals do so conform, issue a certificate to that effect.

(3) If it appears to the county planning authority that the proposals do not so conform in any respect, they shall, during or as soon as possible after the end of that period, refer the question whether they so conform in that respect to the Secretary of State to be determined by him.

(4) The Secretary of State may in any case by direction to a county planning authority reserve for his own determination the question whether proposals for the making, alteration, repeal or replacement of a local plan conform generally to the structure plan.

(5) On determining a question so referred to or reserved for him, the Secretary of State—

(a) if he is of opinion that the proposals do so conform, may issue, or direct the county planning authority to issue, a certificate to that effect, and

(b) if he is of the contrary opinion, may direct the district planning authority to revise their proposals in such respects as he thinks appropriate so that they will so conform.

Conformity between plans: alteration of structure plan

15A.—(1) Where proposals for the alteration or replacement of a structure plan have been prepared and submitted to the Secretary of State, he may, on the application of a local planning authority proposing to make, alter, repeal or replace a local plan, direct that it shall be assumed for that purpose that the structure plan proposals have been approved by him, subject to such modifications as may from time to time be proposed by him and notified to the county planning authority.

(2) A direction ceases to have effect if the Secretary of State rejects the proposals for the alteration or replacement of the structure plan.

(3) Before giving a direction the Secretary of State shall consult—

(a) in the case of an application by a county planning authority, any district planning authority whose area is affected by the relevant local plan proposals;

(b) in the case of an application by a district planning authority, the county planning authority.

(4) A county planning authority shall, on the approval of proposals for the alteration or replacement of a structure plan, consider whether the local plans for areas affected conform generally to the structure plan as altered or to the new plan, as the case may be.

(5) Within the period of one month from the date on which they receive notice of the Secretary of State's approval of the proposals, the county planning authority shall send—

(a) to the Secretary of State, and

(b) to every district planning authority responsible for such a local plan,

lists of the local plans so affected which, in their opinion, do and do not so conform.

Conformity between plans: local plan prevails

15B.—(1) Where there is a conflict between any of the provisions of a local plan in force for an area and the provisions of the relevant structure plan, the provisions of the local plan shall be taken to prevail for all purposes.

(2) Where the structure plan is altered or replaced and the local plan is specified in a list under section 15A(5) as a plan which does not conform to the structure plan as altered or replaced, subsection (1) above does not apply until a proposal for the alteration of the local plan, or for its repeal and replacement, has been adopted or approved by the Secretary of State and the alteration, or replacement plan, has come into force.

PART II

UNITARY DEVELOPMENT PLANS

1. Part I of Schedule 1 to the Local Government Act 1985 (unitary development plans) is amended as follows.

2. After paragraph 6 insert—

"Direction to reconsider proposals

6A.—(1) After a copy of a unitary development plan has been sent to the Secretary of State and before it is adopted by the local planning authority, the Secretary of State may, if it appears to him that the plan is unsatisfactory, direct the authority to consider modifying the proposals in such respects as are indicated in the direction.

(2) An authority to whom a direction is given shall not adopt the plan unless they satisfy the Secretary of State that they have made the modifications necessary to conform with the direction or the direction is withdrawn.".

3. In paragraph 10(2) (provisions applicable to making of unitary development plan also apply to alteration or replacement of plan), at the beginning insert "Subject to paragraph 10A below,".

4. After paragraph 10 insert—

"Short procedure for certain alterations

10A.—(1) Where a local planning authority propose to alter or replace a unitary development plan and it appears to them that the issues involved are not of sufficient importance to warrant the full procedure set out in paragraph 3(1) and (2), they may instead proceed as follows.

(2) They shall prepare the relevant documents, that is, the proposed alterations or replacement plan, and shall make a copy of them available for inspection at their office

and at such other places as may be prescribed and send a copy to the Secretary of State.

(3) Each copy of the documents made available for inspection shall be accompanied by a statement of the time within which representations or objections may be made.

(4) They shall then take such steps as may be prescribed for the purpose of—

(a) advertising the fact that the documents are available for inspection, and the places and times at which and period during which they may be inspected, and

(b) inviting the making of representations or objections in accordance with regulations;

and they shall consider any representations made to them within the prescribed period.

(5) The documents sent by the local planning authority to the Secretary of State under sub-paragraph (2) above shall be accompanied by a statement of the steps which the authority are taking to comply with sub-paragraph (4) above.

(6) If, on considering the statement submitted with and the matters contained in the documents sent to him under sub-paragraph (2) above and any other information provided by the local planning authority, the Secretary of State is not satisfied with the steps taken by the authority he may, within twenty-one days of the receipt of the statement, direct the authority not to take further steps for the adoption of their proposals without—

(a) proceeding in accordance with paragraph 3(1) and (2) above, or

(b) taking such further action as he may specify,

and satisfying him that they have done so.

(7) A local planning authority who are given directions by the Secretary of State under sub-paragraph (6) above shall—

(a) forthwith withdraw the copies of documents made available for inspection as required by sub-paragraph (2) above; and

(b) notify any person by whom objections to the proposals have been made to the authority that the Secretary of State has given such directions as aforesaid.

(8) Where a local planning authority proceed in accordance with this paragraph, the references in paragraphs 4(2)(a) and (4) and 7(1) to copies made available or sent to the Secretary of State under paragraph 3(2) shall be construed as references to copies made available or sent to the Secretary of State under sub-paragraph (2) of this paragraph.".

Sections 49 and 53   SCHEDULE 11

PLANNING: MINOR AND CONSEQUENTIAL AMENDMENTS

PART I

ENGLAND AND WALES

Operation of Use Classes Order on subdivision of planning unit

1. In section 22(2) of the Town and Country Planning Act 1971 (operations and changes of use not amounting to development), in paragraph (*f*) (use of same prescribed class as existing use) for "the use thereof" substitute "the use of the buildings or other land or, subject to the provisions of the order, of any part thereof".

Development orders

2.—(1) In section 24 of the Town and Country Planning Act 1971 (development orders), for subsection (3) (general and special orders) substitute—

"(3) A development order may be made either—

(a) as a general order applicable, except so far as the order otherwise provides, to all land, but which may make different provision with respect to different descriptions of land, or

(b) as a special order applicable only to such land or descriptions of land as may be specified in the order.".

(2) In paragraph 17 of Schedule 16 to the Local Government Act 1972 (inclusion of provision in development orders empowering local highway authority to impose restrictions on grant of planning permission in certain cases) for "shall include in a development order under section 24 provision" substitute "may include in a development order under section 24 such provision as he thinks fit".

Disabled persons: construction of references to certain documents

3.—(1) In section 29A of the Town and Country Planning Act 1971 (duty to draw attention to certain provisions for the benefit of the disabled: public buildings and places of work), in subsection (1) for paragraph (ii) substitute—

"(ii) the Code of Practice for Access of the Disabled to Buildings (British Standards Institution code of practice BS 5810: 1979) or any prescribed document replacing that code.".

(2) In section 29B of the Town and Country Planning Act 1971 (duty to draw attention to certain provisions for the benefit of the disabled: educational buildings), in subsection (1) for paragraph (ii) substitute—

"(ii) to Design Note 18 'Access for Disabled People to Educational Buildings' published in 1984 on behalf of the Secretary of State, or any prescribed document replacing that Note.".

Applications to vary or revoke conditions attached to planning permission

4. After section 31 of the Town and Country Planning Act 1971 insert—

"Permission to develop land without compliance with conditions previously attached

31A.—(1) This section applies to applications for planning permission for the development of land without complying with conditions subject to which a previous planning permission was granted.

(2) Special provision may be made with respect to such applications—

(*a*) by regulations under section 25 of this Act as regards the form and content of the application, and

(*b*) by a development order as regards the procedure to be followed in connection with the application.

(3) On such an application the local planning authority shall consider only the question of the conditions subject to which planning permission should be granted, and—

(*a*) if they decide that planning permission should be granted subject to conditions differing from those subject to which the previous permission was granted, or that it should be granted unconditionally, they shall grant planning permission accordingly, and

(*b*) if they decide that planning permission should be granted subject to the same conditions as those subject to which the previous permission was granted, they shall refuse the application.

(4) This section does not apply where the application is made after the previous planning permission has become time-expired, that is to say, the previous permission having been granted subject to a condition as to the time within which the development to which it related was to be begun, that time has expired without the development having been begun.".

Purchase notices: transmission of documents to Secretary of State

5.—(1) In section 181 of the Town and Country Planning Act 1971 (action by council on whom purchase notice is served)—

(*a*) in subsection (1)(*c*) (notice of unwillingness to comply with purchase notice: contents of notice) for the words from "and that they have transmitted" to the end substitute "and that they have transmitted to the Secretary of State a copy of the purchase notice and of the notice under this subsection";

(*b*) in subsection (3) (duty of council to transmit documents to Secretary of State) for the words from "they shall transmit" to the end substitute "then, before they take steps to serve that notice, they shall transmit to the Secretary of State a copy of the purchase notice together with a copy of the notice which they propose to serve".

(2) In paragraph 1 of Schedule 19 to the Town and Country Planning Act 1971 (action by council on whom listed building purchase notice is served)—

(*a*) in sub-paragraph (1)(*c*) (notice of unwillingness to comply with purchase notice: contents of notice) for the words from "and that they have transmitted" to the end substitute "and that they have transmitted to the Secretary of State a copy of the purchase notice and of the notice under this sub-paragraph";

(*b*) in sub-paragraph (3) (duty of council to transmit documents to Secretary of State) for the words from "they shall transmit" to "reasons" substitute "then, before they take steps to serve that notice, they shall transmit to the Secretary of State a copy of the purchase notice together with a copy of the notice which they propose to serve under sub-paragraph (1)(*c*)".

Purchase notice relating to land where use restricted by virtue of previous planning permission

6. In section 184 of the Town and Country Planning Act 1971 (power to refuse to confirm purchase notice where land has restricted use by virtue of previous planning permission)—
  (*a*) in subsection (1) (cases to which the section applies) for "land which has a restricted use" substitute "land which consists in whole or in part of land which has a restricted use"; and
  (*b*) in subsection (3) (power of Secretary of State to refuse to confirm purchase notice), for the words "the land ought, in accordance with the previous planning permission", substitute "the land having a restricted use by virtue of a previous planning permission ought, in accordance with that permission,".

Consideration of purchase notice concurrently with related planning appeal

7.—(1) In section 186(3) of the Town and Country Planning Act 1971 (relevant period at end of which purchase notice is deemed to have been confirmed) after "relevant period is" insert ", subject to subsection (3A) of this section,", and after that subsection insert—
  "(3A) The relevant period does not run if the Secretary of State has before him at the same time both a copy of the purchase notice transmitted to him under section 181(3) of this Act and an appeal notice under any of the following provisions of this Act relating to any of the land to which the purchase notice relates—
    section 36 (appeal against refusal of planning permission, &c.),
    section 88 (appeal against enforcement notice),
    section 95 (appeal against refusal of established use certificate),
    section 97 (appeal against listed building enforcement notice), or
    paragraph 8 or 9 of Schedule 11 (appeal against refusal of listed building consent, &c.).".
(2) In paragraph 3(3)(*b*) of Schedule 19 to the Town and Country Planning Act 1971 (relevant period at end of which listed building purchase notice is deemed to have been confirmed) after " 'the relevant period' is" insert ", subject to sub-paragraph (3A) of this paragraph,", and after that sub-paragraph insert—
  "(3A) The relevant period does not run if the Secretary of State has before him at the same time both a copy of the listed building purchase notice transmitted to him under paragraph 1(3) of this Schedule and an appeal notice under any of the following provisions of this Act relating to any of the land to which the purchase notice relates—
    section 97 (appeal against listed building enforcement notice), or
    paragraph 8 or 9 of Schedule 11 (appeal against refusal of listed building consent, &c.).".

Local inquiries: application of general provisions of Local Government Act

8.—(1) In section 282 of the Town and Country Planning Act 1971 (local inquiries held by Secretary of State), for subsection (2) substitute—
  "(2) The provisions of subsections (2) to (5) of section 250 of the Local Government Act 1972 (local inquiries: evidence and costs) apply to an inquiry held by virtue of this section.".
(2) In Schedule 9 to the Town and Country Planning Act 1971 (determination of certain appeals by person appointed by the Secretary of State), in paragraph 5 (local inquiries and hearings held by appointed person) for sub-paragraph (3) substitute—
  "(3) The provisions of subsections (2) to (5) of section 250 of the Local Government Act 1972 (local inquiries: evidence and costs) apply to an inquiry held by virtue of this paragraph, with the following adaptations—
    (*a*) for the references in subsection (4) (recovery of costs of holding the inquiry) to the Minister causing the inquiry to be held, substitute the Secretary of State; and
    (*b*) for the reference in subsection (5) (orders as to the costs of the parties) to the Minister causing the inquiry to be held, substitute a reference to the person appointed to determine the appeal or the Secretary of State.".

Orders as to costs of parties where no local inquiry held

9.—(1) After section 282 of the Town and Country Planning Act 1971 (local inquiries: application of general provisions of Local Government Act) insert—

"Orders as to costs of parties where no local inquiry held
    282A.—(1) The Secretary of State has the same power to make orders under section 250(5) of the Local Government Act 1972 (orders with respect to the costs of the parties) in relation to proceedings to which this section applies which do not give rise to a local inquiry as he has in relation to a local inquiry.
    (2) This section applies to proceedings under this Act where the Secretary of State is required, before reaching a decision, to afford any person an opportunity of appearing before and being heard by a person appointed by him.".
(2) In Schedule 9 to the Town and Country Planning Act 1971 (determination of certain appeals by persons appointed by the Secretary of State), in paragraph 5 (local inquiries and hearings held by appointed person) at the end add—
    "(4) The person appointed to determine the appeal or the Secretary of State has the same power to make orders under section 250(5) of the Local Government Act 1972 (orders with respect to the costs of the parties) in relation to proceedings under this Schedule which do not give rise to an inquiry under this paragraph as he has in relation to such an inquiry.".

Procedure on applications and appeals disposed of without inquiry or hearing

10. After section 282A of the Town and Country Planning Act 1971 insert—

"Procedure on certain appeals and applications
    282B.—(1) The Secretary of State may by regulations prescribe the procedure to be followed in connection with proceedings under this Act where he is required, before reaching a decision, to afford any person an opportunity of appearing before and being heard by a person appointed by him and which are to be disposed of without an inquiry or hearing to which rules under section 11 of the Tribunals and Inquiries Act 1971 apply.
    (2) The regulations may in particular make provision as to the procedure to be followed—
        (*a*) where steps have been taken with a view to the holding of such an inquiry or hearing which does not take place, or
        (*b*) where steps have been taken with a view to the determination of any matter by a person appointed by the Secretary of State and the proceedings are the subject of a direction that the matter shall instead be determined by the Secretary of State, or
        (*c*) where steps have been taken in pursuance of such a direction and a further direction is made revoking that direction,
    and may provide that such steps shall be treated as compliance, in whole or in part, with the requirements of the regulations.
    (3) The regulations may also—
        (*a*) provide for a time limit within which any party to the proceedings must submit representations in writing and any supporting documents;
        (*b*) prescribe the time limit (which may be different for different classes of proceedings) or enable the Secretary of State to give directions setting the time limit in a particular case or class of case;
        (*c*) empower the Secretary of State to proceed to a decision taking into account only such written representations and supporting documents as were submitted within the time limit; and
        (*d*) empower the Secretary of State after giving the parties written notice of his intention to do so, to proceed to a decision notwithstanding that no written representations were made within the time limit, if it appears to him that he has sufficient material before him to enable him to reach a decision on the merits of the case.".

Power to return appeal for determination by inspector

11. In Schedule 9 to the Town and Country Planning Act 1971 (determination of certain appeals by persons appointed by the Secretary of State), after paragraph 3 (power of Secretary of State to direct that appeal should be determined by him) insert—

"3A—(1) The Secretary of State may by a further direction revoke a direction under paragraph 3 of this Schedule at any time before the determination of the appeal.

(2) A direction under this paragraph shall state the reasons for which it is given and shall be served on the person, if any, previously appointed to determine the appeal, the applicant or appellant, the local planning authority and any person who has made representations relating to the subject matter of the appeal which the authority are required to take into account under section 29(3)(*a*) of this Act.

(3) Where a direction under this paragraph has been given, the provisions of this Schedule relevant to the appeal shall apply, subject to sub-paragraph (4), as if no direction under paragraph 3 had been given.

(4) Anything done by or on behalf of the Secretary of State in connection with the appeal which might have been done by the person appointed to determine the appeal (including any arrangements made for the holding of a hearing or local inquiry) shall, unless that person directs otherwise, be treated as having been done by him.".

Appointment of assessors

12. In Schedule 9 to the Town and Country Planning Act 1971 (determination of certain appeals by persons appointed by the Secretary of State), in paragraph 5 (local inquiries and hearings) after sub-paragraph (1) insert—

"(1A) Where a person appointed under this Schedule to determine an appeal—

(*a*) holds a hearing by virtue of paragraph 2(2)(*b*) of this Schedule, or

(*b*) holds an inquiry by virtue of this paragraph,

an assessor may be appointed by the Secretary of State to sit with the appointed person at the hearing or inquiry to advise him on any matters arising notwithstanding that the appointed person is to determine the appeal.".

Increase of daily penalties for offences

13.—(1) In the provisions of the Town and Country Planning Act 1971 listed in column 1 of the following Table, which impose daily penalties for certain offences whose general nature is indicated in column 2, for the amount shown in column 3 substitute the amount shown in column 4.

TABLE

Provision of 1971 Act	Nature of offence	Present maximum daily fine	New maximum daily fine
Section 57(3)	Damage to listed building.	£20	£40
Section 89(4)	Non-compliance with enforcement notice.	£100	£200
Section 89(5)	Use of land in contravention of enforcement notice.	£100	£200
Section 90(7)	Non-compliance with stop notice.	£100	£200
Section 98(4)	Failure to secure compliance with listed building enforcement notice.	£100	£200
Section 104(7)	Failure to secure compliance with notice as to condition of land.	£20	£40
Section 109(2)	Contravention of advertisement control regulations.	£20	£40

(2) The increased amounts applicable by virtue of sub-paragraph (1) apply to every day after the commencement of this paragraph, notwithstanding that the offence began before.

Consequential amendments of the Town and Country Planning Act 1971

14. In section 1 of the Town and Country Planning Act 1971 for subsection (2A) substitute—

"(2A) References in this Act to a local planning authority in relation to a non-metropolitan county shall be construed, subject to any express provision to the contrary as references to both the county planning authority and the district planning authorities.".

15. In section 18(1)(*f*) of that Act, except as respect Greater London—

(*a*) for "section 12(1)(*a*)" substitute "section 12(2)(*a*)", and

(*b*) for "section 12(2)" substitute "section 12(4) or 12A(2)".

16. In section 29(1)(*a*) of that Act for "sections 41, 42, 70 and 77 to 80" substitute "sections 41 and 42".

17. In sections 35(4) and 36(5) of that Act for "and 30A" substitute ", 30A and 31A".

18. In sections 36(7) of that Act for "sections 29(1), 30(1), 67 and 74" substitute "sections 29(1) and 30(1)".

19. In section 55(4) of that Act omit "under section 56 of this Act".

20. In section 105 of that Act—

(*a*) in paragraph (*a*) for "seriously injure" substitute "adversary affect",

(*b*) omit paragraph (*c*), and

(*c*) in paragraph (*d*) for "seriously injuring" substitute "adversely affecting".

21. In Schedule 21, in Parts I and V for "Sections 63 to 68" substitute "Sections 63 to 65".

Consequential amendments of other enactments

22. In section 182(5) of the Local Government Act 1972 (functions exercisable in National Park concurrently by county planning authority and district planning authority), for the words "(waste land)", which describe the subject-matter of section 65 of the Town and Country Planning Act 1971, substitute "(power to require proper maintenance of land)".

23.—(1) Part I of Schedule 16 to the Local Government Act 1972 (functions under and modification of Town and Country Planning Act 1971) is amended as follows.

(2) For paragraphs 10 to 12 (joint local plans) substitute, except as respects Greater London—

"10.—(1) This paragraph applies where two or more local planning authorities jointly prepare proposals for the making, alteration, repeal or replacement of a local plan.

(2) The local planning authorities are jointly responsible for taking the steps required by section 12 or 12A, except that they each have the duty imposed by section 12(4)(*a*) or 12A(2)(*a*) of making copies of the relevant documents available for inspection and objections to the proposals may be made to any of those authorities and the statement required by section 12(5) or 12A(3) to accompany the relevant documents shall state that objections may be so made.

(3) It shall be for each of the local planning authorities to adopt the proposals under section 14(1) and they may do so as respects any part of their area to which the proposals relate, but any modifications subject to which the proposals are adopted must have the agreement of all those authorities.

11. Where in a non-metropolitan county—

(*a*) a structure plan has been jointly prepared by two or more county planning authorities, or

(*b*) a local plan has been jointly prepared by two or more district planning authorities,

a request for a certificate under section 15 that the local plan conforms generally to the structure plan shall be made by each district planning authority to the county planning authority for the area comprising the district planning authority's area and it shall be for that county planning authority to deal with the request.

12. Where a local plan has been made jointly, the power of making proposals for its alteration, repeal or replacement may be exercised as respects their respective areas by any of the authorities by whom it was made, in accordance with the provisions of the relevant local plan scheme, and the Secretary of State may under section 11B direct any of them to make proposals as respects their respective areas.".

(3) In paragraph 19(2) (planning applications subject to duty to consult county planning authority)—

(*a*) in sub-paragraph (vi), for the words from "section 12" to the end substitute "section 12 or 12A (publicity and consultation regarding local plans)", and

(*b*) in sub-paragraph (vii), for the words from "the said section 12" to the end substitute "section 12 or 12A (publicity and consultation regarding local plans)".

24. In section 8(3) of the Refuse Disposal (Amenity) Act 1978 (application of general provisions of Town and Country Planning Act 1971 relating to local inquiries and service of notices) for "to 284" substitute "283 and 284".

25.—(1) The Industrial Development Act 1982 is amended as follows.

(2) In section 14 (power of Secretary of State to provide premises and sites), in subsection (2) (restriction on acquisition of buildings) for "section 66 of the Town and Country Planning Act 1971" substitute "section 14A of this Act".

(3) After that section insert—

"Meaning of 'industrial buildings'

14A.—(1) In section 14(2) of this Act 'industrial building' means a building which is used or designed for use for carrying on, in the course of a trade or business, a process for or incidental to any of the following purposes—

(*a*) the making of any article or part of any article,

(*b*) the altering, repairing, ornamenting, finishing, cleaning, washing, freezing, packing or canning, or adapting for sale, or breaking up or demolition, of any article, or

(*c*) the getting, dressing or preparation for sale of minerals or the extraction or preparation for sale of oil or brine,

or which is used or designed for use for carrying on, in the course of a trade or business, scientific research.

(2) For the purposes of subsection (1) premises which—

(*a*) are used or designed for use of providing services or facilities ancillary to the use of other premises for the carrying on of any such process or research as is mentioned in that subsection, and

(*b*) are or are to be comprised in the same building or the same curtilage as those other premises,

shall themselves be treated as used or designed for use for the carrying on of such a process or, as the case may be, of such research.

(3) In this section—

'article' means an article of any description, including a ship or vessel;

'building' includes part of a building;

'minerals' includes all minerals and substances in or under land of a kind ordinarily worked for removal by underground or surface working, except that it does not include peat cut for purposes other than sale;

'scientific research' means any activity in the fields of natural or applied science for the extension of knowledge.".

26. In Part I of Schedule 1 to the Local Government Act 1985 (unitary development plans), in paragraph 12 (joint plans), for sub-paragraph (7) substitute—

"(7) In relation to any proposals made jointly under paragraph 10 above, the references—

(*a*) in sub-paragraph (2) of that paragraph to paragraphs 2 to 9 above, and

(*b*) in paragraph 10A(1) above to paragraph 3(1) above,

shall include a reference to sub-paragraph (2) above.

(7A) In relation to such joint proposals the references in paragraph 10A above to the local planning authority shall be construed as references to the authorities acting jointly, except that—

(*a*) each of the authorities shall have the duty under sub-paragraph (2) of making copies of the relevant documents available for inspection, and

(*b*) representations or objections may be made to any of the authorities, and the statement required by sub-paragraph (3) of that paragraph shall state that objections may be so made.

27.—(1) In Part II of Schedule 1 to the Local Government Act 1985 (transitional provisions), paragraph 20 (local plans between abolition date and commencement of unitary planning provisions) is amended as follows.

(2) In sub-paragraph (2) (application of provisions of Part II of Town and Country Planning Act 1971) omit the words from "and in respect of those matters" to the end.

(3) After that sub-paragraph insert—

"(2A) In respect of the matters referred to in sub-paragraph (2) the following provisions (which relate to county planning authorities) do not apply to metropolitan district councils, namely, sections 11A, 11B(4), 12(3) and (4)(*c*), 12A(2)(*c*), 15, 15A and 15B(2).".

(4) For sub-paragraph (3) substitute—

"(3) In section 15(1) and (2) (alteration of local plans), as applying in Greater London, the reference to a local plan adopted by a local planning authority includes, in the case of a London borough council, a local plan adopted by the Greater London Council and in force in respect of the area of that authority on the abolition date.

(3A) A metropolitan district council may at any time—

(*a*) make proposals for the preparation, alteration, repeal or replacement of a local plan adopted by them or adopted by the metropolitan county council and in force in the area of that authority on the abolition date;

(*b*) with the consent of the Secretary of State, make proposals for the alteration, repeal or replacement of a local plan approved by him.".

PART II

SCOTLAND

Directions as to modifications of local plans

28.—(1) After subsection (2) of section 12 of the Town and Country Planning (Scotland) Act 1972 (adoption and approval of local plans) insert—

"(2A) After copies of a local plan have been sent to the Secretary of State and before it has been adopted by the planning authority, the Secretary of State may, if it appears to him that any part of it is unsatisfactory, and without prejudice to his power to make a direction under subsection (3) below, direct the authority to consider modifying the plan in such respects as are indicated in the direction.

(2B) An authority to whom a direction is given shall not adopt the plan unless they satisfy the Secretary of State that they have made the modifications necessary to confirm with the direction or the direction is withdrawn.".

(2) In subsection (1) of that section for the words "(2) and (3)" substitute "(2), (2A), (2B) and (3)".

Operation of Use Classes Order on subdivision of planning unit

29. In section 19(2) of the Town and Country Planning (Scotland) Act 1972 (operations and changes of use not amounting to development), in paragraph (*f*) (use of same prescribed class as existing use) for "the use thereof" substitute "the use of the buildings or other land or, subject to the provisions of the order, of any part thereof".

Development orders

30. In section 21 of the Town and Country Planning (Scotland) Act 1972 (development orders), for subsection (3) (general and special orders) substitute—

"(3) A development order may be made either—

(*a*) as a general order applicable, except so far as the order otherwise provides, to all land, but which may make different provision with respect to different descriptions of land, or

(*b*) as a special order applicable only to such land or descriptions of land as may be specified in the order.".

Applications to vary or revoke conditions attached to planning permission

31. After section 28 of the Town and Country Planning (Scotland) Act 1972 insert—

"Permission to develop land without compliance with conditions previously attached

28A.—(1) This section applies to applications for planning permission for the development of land without complying with conditions subject to which a previous planning permission was granted.

(2) Special provision may be made with respect to such applications—

(*a*) by regulations under section 22 of this Act as regards the form and content of the application, and

(*b*) by a development order as regards the procedure to be followed in connection with the application.

(3) On such an application the planning authority shall consider only the question of the conditions subject to which planning permission should be granted, and—

(*a*) if they decide that planning permission should be granted subject to conditions differing from those subject to which the previous permission was granted, or that it should be granted unconditionally, they shall grant planning permission accordingly, and

(*b*) if they decide that planning permission should be granted subject to the same conditions as those subject to which the previous permission was granted, they shall refuse the application.

(4) This section does not apply where the application is made after the previous planning permission has become time-expired, that is to say, the previous permission having been granted subject to a condition as to the time within which the development to which it related was to have begun, that time has expired without the development having been begun.".

Land adversely affecting amenity of neighbourhood

32.—(1) For subsection (1) of section 63 of the Town and Country Planning (Scotland) Act 1972 (proper maintenance of waste land) substitute—
"(1) If it appears to a planning authority that the amenity of any part of their district, or an adjoining district, is adversely affected by the condition of any land in their district, they may serve on the owner, lessee and occupier of the land a notice under this section requiring such steps for abating the adverse effect as may be specified in the notice to be taken within such period as may be so specified.".
(2) In subsections (1B) and (1C) of the said section, for the words "waste land notice" substitute "notice under this section".
33.—(1) In subsections (1) and (5) of section 63A (appeals against waste land notices) of the Town and Country Planning (Scotland) Act 1972, for the words "waste land notice" substitute "notice under section 63 of this Act."
(2) For paragraph (*a*) of the said subsection (1) substitute—
"(*a*) that neither the amenity of any part of the planning authority's district nor that of any adjoining district has been adversely affected;".
(3) In paragraph (*b*) of the said subsection (1), for the word "injury" substitute "adverse effect".

Appeals against notices under section 63A

34.—(1) After subsection (6) of section 63A insert—
"(7) Subject to section 279 of this Act, Schedule 7 to this Act applies to appeals under this section.".
(2) After sub-paragraph (1)(*a*) of paragraph 2 of Schedule 7 (determination of appeals by person appointed by Secretary of State) to the Town and Country Planning (Scotland) Act 1972, insert—
"(*aa*) in relation to appeals under section 63A, subsections (4) and (6);".

Purchase notices: transmission of documents to the Secretary of State

35.—(1) In section 170 of the Town and Country Planning (Scotland) Act 1972 (action by planning authority on whom purchase notice is served)—
(*a*) in subsection (1)(*c*) (notice of unwillingness to comply with purchase notice: contents of notice) for the words from "and that they have transmitted" to the end substitute "and that they have transmitted to the Secretary of State a copy of the purchase notice and of the notice under this subsection";
(*b*) in subsection (3) (duty of planning authority to transmit documents to Secretary of State) for the words from "they shall transmit" to the end substitute "then, before they take steps to serve that notice, they shall transmit to the Secretary of State a copy of the purchase notice together with a copy of the notice which they propose to serve".
(2) In paragraph 1 of Schedule 17 to the Town and Country Planning (Scotland) Act 1972 (action by planning authority on whom listed building purchase notice is served)—
(*a*) in sub-paragraph (1)(*c*) (notice of unwillingness to comply with purchase notice: contents of notice) for the words from "and that they have transmitted" to the end substitute "and that they have transmitted to the Secretary of State a copy of the purchase notice and of the notice under this sub-paragraph.";
(*b*) in sub-paragraph (3) (duty of planning authority to transmit documents to Secretary of State) for the words from "they shall transmit" to "reasons" substitute "then, before they take steps to serve that notice, they shall transmit to the Secretary of State a copy of the purchase notice together with a copy of the notice which they propose to serve under sub-paragraph (1)(*c*)".

Purchase notice relating to land where use restricted by virtue of previous planning permission

36. In section 173 of the Town and Country Planning (Scotland) Act 1972 (power to refuse to confirm purchase notice where land has restricted use by virtue of previous planning permission)—

(a) in subsection (1) (cases to which the section applies) for "land which has a restricted use" substitute "land which consists in whole or in part of land which has a restricted use"; and

(b) in subsection (3) (power of Secretary of State to refuse to confirm purchase notice), for the words "the land ought, in accordance with the previous planning permission," substitute "the land having a restricted use by virtue of a previous planning permission ought, in accordance with that permission,".

Consideration of purchase notice concurrently with related planning appeal

37.—(1) In section 175(3) of the Town and Country Planning (Scotland) Act 1972 (relevant period at end of which purchase notice is deemed to have been confirmed) after "relevant period is" insert ", subject to subsection (3A) of this section,", and after that subsection insert—

"(3A) The relevant period does not run if the Secretary of State has before him at the same time both a copy of the purchase notice transmitted to him under section 170(3) of this Act and an appeal notice under any of the following provisions of this Act relating to any of the land to which the purchase notice relates—

section 33 (appeal against refusal of planning permission, &c.),

section 85 (appeal against enforcement notice),

section 91 (appeal against refusal of established use certificate),

section 93 (appeal against listed building enforcement notice), or

paragraph 7 or 8 of Schedule 10 (appeal against refusal of listed building consent, &c.).".

(2) In paragraph 3(3)(b) of Schedule 17 to the Town and Country Planning (Scotland) Act 1972 (relevant period at end of which listed building purchase notice is deemed to have been confirmed) after " "the relevant period" is" insert ", subject to sub-paragraph (3A) of this paragraph,", and after that sub-paragraph insert—

"(3A) The relevant period does not run if the Secretary of State has before him at the same time both a copy of the listed building purchase notice transmitted to him under paragraph 1(3) of this Schedule and an appeal notice under any of the following provisions of this Act relating to any of the land to which the purchase notice relates—

section 93 (appeal against listed building enforcement notice), or

paragraph 7 or 8 of Schedule 10 (appeal against refusal of listed building consent, &c.).".

National Scenic Areas

38. After section 262B of the Town and Country Planning (Scotland) Act 1972 insert—

"National Scenic Areas

262C.—(1) Where it appears to the Secretary of State, after such consultation with the Countryside Commission for Scotland and such other persons or bodies as he thinks fit, that an area is of outstanding scenic value and beauty in a national context, and that special protection measures are appropriate for it, he may designate the area by a direction under this section as a National Scenic Area; and any such designation may be varied or cancelled by a subsequent direction.

(2) Notice of any such designation, variation, or cancellation as is mentioned in subsection (1) above shall be published in the Edinburgh Gazette and in at least one newspaper circulating in the vicinity of the Area by the Secretary of State.

(3) Every planning authority shall compile and make available for inspection free of charge at reasonable hours and at a convenient place a list containing such particulars as the Secretary of State may determine of any area in their district which has been designated as a National Scenic Area.

(4) Where any area is for the time being designated as a National Scenic Area, special attention shall be paid to the desirability of preserving or enhancing its character or appearance in the exercise, with respect to any land in that area, of any powers under this Act.".

Recovery of expenses of local inquiry

39.—(1) For subsection (7) of section 267 (local inquiries) of the Town and Country Planning (Scotland) Act 1972 and subsections (7) and (8) of section 210 (power to direct inquiries) of the Local Government (Scotland) Act 1973 substitute—

"(7) The Minister may make orders as to the expenses incurred—
   (*a*) by the Minister in relation to—
      (i) the inquiry;
      (ii) arrangements made for an inquiry which does not take place; and
   (*b*) by the parties to the inquiry,

and as to the parties by whom any of the expenses mentioned in paragraphs (*a*) and (*b*) above shall be paid.

(7A) What may be recovered by the Minister is the entire administrative expense of the inquiry, so that, in particular—
   (*a*) there shall be treated as expenses incurred in relation to the inquiry such reasonable sum as the Minister may determine in respect of the general staff expenses and overheads of his department, and
   (*b*) there shall be treated as expenses incurred by the Minister holding the inquiry any expenses incurred in relation to the inquiry by any other Minister or Government department and, where appropriate, such reasonable sum as that Minister or department may determine in respect of general staff expenses and overheads.

(7B) The Minister may by regulations prescribe for any description of inquiry a standard daily amount and where an inquiry of that description does take place what may be recovered is—
   (*a*) the prescribed standard amount in respect of each day (or an appropriate proportion of that amount in respect of a part of a day) on which the inquiry sits or the person appointed to hold the inquiry is otherwise engaged on work connected with the inquiry,
   (*b*) expenses actually incurred in connection with the inquiry on travelling or subsistence allowances or the provision of accommodation or other facilities for the inquiry, and
   (*c*) any expenses attributable to the appointment of an assessor to assist the person appointed to hold the inquiry, and
   (*d*) any legal expenses or disbursements incurred or made by or on behalf of the Minister in connection with the inquiry.".

(2) After subsection (7B) of the said section 210 of the Local Government (Scotland) Act 1973 insert—

"(8) Where the Minister has made an order under subsection (7) of this section requiring any party to pay expenses to him he shall certify the amount of the expenses, and any amount so certified shall be a debt due by that party to the Crown and shall be recoverable accordingly.".

(3) In subsection (1) of section 233 of the Local Government (Scotland) Act 1973 (orders, rules and regulations), after "104(1)" insert "210(7)".

(4) After section 210 of the Local Government (Scotland) Act 1973 insert—

"Recovery of expenses of local inquiry
210A.—(1) The following provisions of this section apply where a Minister is authorised under or by virtue of any of the following statutory provisions to recover expenses incurred by him in relation to an inquiry—

   section 129(1)(*d*) of the Road Traffic Regulation Act 1984 (expenses of inquiry under that Act),

any other statutory provision to which this section is applied by order of the Minister.

(2) What may be recovered by the Minister is the entire administrative expense of the inquiry, so that, in particular—
   (*a*) there shall be treated as expenses incurred in relation to the inquiry such reasonable sum as the Minister may determine in respect of the general staff expenses and overheads of his department, and
   (*b*) there shall be treated as expenses incurred by the Minister holding the inquiry any expenses incurred in relation to the inquiry by any other Minister or Government department and, where appropriate, such reasonable sum as that Minister or department may determine in respect of general staff expenses and overheads.

(3) The expense of an inquiry which does not take place may be recovered by the Minister from any person who would have been a party to the inquiry to the same extent, and in the same way, as the expense of an inquiry which does take place.

(4) The Minister may by regulations prescribe for any description of inquiry a standard daily amount and where an inquiry of that description does take place what may be recovered is—

(*a*) the prescribed standard amount in respect of each day (or an appropriate proportion of that amount in respect of a part of a day) on which the inquiry sits or the person appointed to hold the inquiry is otherwise engaged on work connected with the inquiry,

(*b*) expenses actually incurred in connection with the inquiry on travelling or subsistence allowances or the provision of accommodation or other facilities for the inquiry,

(*c*) any expenses attributable to the appointment of an assessor to assist the person appointed to hold the inquiry, and

(*d*) any legal expenses or disbursements incurred or made by or on behalf of the Minister in connection with the inquiry.

(5) An order or regulation under this section shall be made by statutory instrument which shall be subject to annulment in pursuance of a resolution of either House of Parliament.

(6) An order applying this section to a statutory provision may provide for the consequential repeal of so much of that provision, or any other provision, as restricts the sum recoverable by the Minister in respect of the services of any officer engaged in the inquiry or is otherwise inconsistent with the application of the provisions of this section.".

Orders as to expenses of parties where no local inquiry held

40.—(1) After the said section 267 of the Town and Country Planning (Scotland) Act 1972 insert—

"Orders as to expenses of parties where no local inquiry held

267A.—(1) The Secretary of State has the same power to make orders under section 267(7) above in relation to proceedings to which this section applies which do not give rise to a local inquiry as he has in relation to a local inquiry.

(2) This section applies to proceedings under this Act where the Secretary of State is required, before reaching a decision, to afford any person an opportunity of appearing before and being heard by a person appointed by him.".

(2) In Schedule 7 to the Town and Country Planning (Scotland) Act 1972 (determination of certain appeals by person appointed by the Secretary of State), in paragraph 5 (local inquiries and hearings)—

(*a*) in sub-paragraph (3) after the word "shall" insert "subject to sub-paragraph (4) below".

(*b*) after sub-paragraph (3) insert—

"(4) The person appointed to determine the appeal has the same power to make orders under section 267(7) of this Act in relation to proceedings under this Schedule which do not give rise to an inquiry as he has in relation to such an inquiry.

(5) For the purposes of this paragraph, references to the Minister in subsections (7) and (8) of section 267 shall be read as references to the person appointed by the Secretary of State to determine the appeal.".

Procedure on applications and appeals disposed of without inquiry or hearing

41. After section 267A of the Town and Country Planning (Scotland) Act 1972 insert—

"Procedure on certain appeals and applications

267B.—(1) The Secretary of State may by regulations prescribe the procedure to be followed in connection with proceedings under this Act where he is required, before reaching a decision, to afford any person an opportunity of appearing before and being heard by a person appointed by him and which are to be disposed of without an inquiry or hearing to which rules under section 11 of the Tribunals and Inquiries Act 1971 apply.

(2) The regulations may in particular make provision as to the procedure to be followed—

(*a*) where steps have been taken with a view to the holding of such an inquiry or hearing which does not take place, or

(*b*) where steps have been taken with a view to the determination of any matter by a person appointed by the Secretary of State and the proceedings are the subject of a direction that the matter shall instead be determined by the Secretary of State, or

(*c*) where steps have been taken in pursuance of such a direction and a further direction is made revoking that direction,

and may provide that such steps shall be treated as compliance, in whole or in part, with the requirements of the regulations.

(3) The regulations may also—

(*a*) provide for a time limit within which any party to the proceedings must lodge written submissions and any supporting documents;

(*b*) prescribe the time limit (which may be different for different classes of proceedings) or enable the Secretary of State to give directions setting the time limit in a particular case or class of case;

(*c*) empower the Secretary of State to proceed to a decision taking into account only such written submissions and supporting documents as were lodged within the time limit; and

(*d*) empower the Secretary of State, after giving the parties written notice of his intention to do so, to proceed to a decision notwithstanding that no written submissions were lodged within the time limit, if it appears to him that he has sufficient material before him to enable him to reach a decision on the merits of the case.".

Power to return appeal for determination by appointed person

42. In Schedule 7 to the Town and Country Planning (Scotland) Act 1972 (determination of certain appeals by persons appointed by the Secretary of State), after paragraph 3 (power of Secretary of State to direct that appeal should be determined by him) insert—

"3A.—(1) The Secretary of State may by a further direction revoke a direction under paragraph 3 of this Schedule at any time before the determination of the appeal.

(2) A direction under this paragraph shall state the reasons for which it is given and shall be served on the person, if any, previously appointed to determine the appeal, the applicant or appellant, the planning authority and any person who has made representations relating to the subject matter of the appeal which the authority are required to take into account under section 26(3)(*a*) of this Act.

(3) Where a direction under this paragraph has been given, the provisions of this Schedule relevant to the appeal shall apply, subject to sub-paragraph (4), as if no direction under paragraph 3 had been given.

(4) Anything done by or on behalf of the Secretary of State in connection with the appeal which might have been done by the person appointed to determine the appeal (including any arrangements made for the holding of a hearing or local inquiry) shall, unless that person directs otherwise, be treated as having been done by him.".

Appointment of assessors

43. In Schedule 7 to the Town and Country Planning (Scotland) Act 1972 (determination of certain appeals by persons appointed by the Secretary of State), in paragraph 5 (local inquiries and hearings), after sub-paragraph (1) insert—

"(1A) Where a person appointed under this Schedule to determine an appeal—

(*a*) holds a hearing by virtue of paragraph 2(2)(*b*) of this Schedule, or

(*b*) holds an inquiry by virtue of this paragraph,

an assessor may be appointed by the Secretary of State to sit with the appointed person at the hearing or inquiry to advise him on any matters arising notwithstanding that the appointed person is to determine the appeal.".

Increase of daily penalties for offences

44.—(1) In the provisions of the Town and Country Planning (Scotland) Act 1972 listed in column 1 of the following Table, which imposes daily penalties for certain offences whose general nature is indicated in column 2, for the amount shown in column 3 substitute the amount shown in column 4.

Table

Provision of 1972 Act	Nature of offence	Present maximum daily fine	New maximum daily fine
Section 55(3)	Damage to listed building.	£20	£40
Section 86	Non-compliance with enforcement notice.	£100	£200
Section 87(8)(*b*)	Non-compliance with stop notice.	£100	£200
Section 94(2)(*a*)	Failure to secure compliance with listed building enforcement notice.	£100	£200
Section 98(3)	Failure to secure compliance with tree preservation order.	£50	£100
Section 100(1)(*a*)	Non-compliance with discontinuance order.	£100	£200
Section 101(2)	Contravention of advertisement control regulations.	£20	£40

(2) The increased amounts applicable by virtue of sub-paragraph (1) apply to every day after the commencement of this paragraph, notwithstanding that the offence began before.

Other minor amendments of the Town and Country Planning (Scotland) Act 1972

45. In section 84(7) of the Town and Country Planning (Scotland) Act 1972 (power to serve enforcement notice) after "place" insert "or, (according to the particular circumstances of the breach) to secure compliance with the conditions or limitations subject to which planning permission was granted".

46. In section 99 (enforcement of duties as to replacement of trees) of the Town and Country Planning (Scotland) Act 1972, in subsection (3), after "85(2)" insert "to (2D)".

47. In section 158(6)(*b*) of the Town and Country Planning (Scotland) Act 1972 (compensation for planning decisions restricting development other than new development) for the word "7" there shall be substituted the word "8".

48. In section 205(3)(*a*) and 205A(3)(*a*) of the Town and Country Planning (Scotland) Act 1972 (procedure in anticipation of planning permission, &c.) after "authority" insert "or".

49. In section 205(5) of the Town and Country Planning (Scotland) Act 1972 for "204(5)" substitute "204(4)".

50. In section 231 of the Town and Country Planning (Scotland) Act 1972 (validity of development plans and certain orders, decision and directions)—

(*a*) at the end of subsection (2)(*a*) insert "or as applied under section 181 of the Local Government (Scotland) Act 1973", and

(*b*) at the end of subsection (2)(*b*) insert "or under the provisions of that section as applied by or under any other provision of this Act or as applied under section 181 of the Local Government (Scotland) Act 1973.".

51. In section 260 of the Town and Country Planning (Scotland) Act 1972 (default powers of the Secretary of State), at the end of subsection (1) insert "or, in the case of a tree preservation order under section 58 of this Act, as if it had been made and confirmed by the planning authority".

52. In section 270 of the Town and Country Planning (Scotland) Act 1972 (power to require information as to interest in land) insert—

"(*d*) the time when that use began;,

(*e*) the name and address of any person known to the person on whom the notice is served as having used the premises for those purposes;

(*f*) the time when any activities being carried out on the premises began.".

53. In sub-paragraph 2(2) of Schedule 7 (determination of certain appeals by person appointed by Secretary of State) of the Town and Country (Scotland) Act 1972, for "85(2)" substitute "85(2D)".

Consequential amendments of the Town and Country Planning (Scotland) Act 1972

54. In section 26(1)(*a*) of the Town and Country Planning (Scotland) Act 1972, for the words "sections 38, 39, 68 and 75 to 78" there shall be substituted the words "sections 38 and 39".

55. In sections 32(4) and 33(5) of the Town and Country Planning (Scotland) Act 1972 for the words "and 27A" substitute "27A and 28A".

56. In section 33(7) of the Town and Country Planning (Scotland) Act 1972 for the words ", 27(1) and 65" there shall be substituted the words "and 27(1)".

57. In section 53(4) of the Town and Country Planning (Scotland) Act 1972 omit "under section 54 of this Act".

58. In section 267 (local inquiries) of the Town and Country Planning (Scotland) Act 1972, in subsection (9), after "section" insert ", except where the context otherwise requires,".

59. In section 275(1) of the Town and Country Planning (Scotland) Act 1972 (interpretation) the following shall be inserted after the definition of "Minister"—

" 'National Scenic Area' has the meaning assigned to it by section 262C of this Act.".

60. In Parts I and III of Schedule 19 to the Town and Country Planning (Scotland) Act 1972 for "Sections 61 to 66" substitute "Sections 61 to 63A".

Consequential amendments of other enactments

61. In subsection (5) of section 179 (reference of applications to regional planning authority) of the Local Government (Scotland) Act 1973, after "27A" insert "28A".

62. In subsection 8(4) of the Refuse Disposal (Amenity) Act 1978 (application of general provisions of the Town and Country Planning (Scotland) Act 1972 relating to local inquiries and services of notices) for "to 270" substitute "and 268 to 270".

Sections 24(3), 39(4), 49(2) and 53(2)

SCHEDULE 12

REPEALS

PART I

HOUSING

Repeals coming into force on passing of Act

Chapter	Short title	Extent of Repeal
1985 c.71.	Housing (Consequential Provisions) Act 1985.	In Schedule 2, in paragraph 24(8)— (a) in sub-paragraph (d), the words from "for 'section 60" to "1985' and"; (b) in sub-paragraph (e), the words from "for the" to "Schedule' and"; (c) sub-paragraph (f).

Repeals coming into force on appointed day

Chapter	Short title	Extent of repeal
1975 c.28.	Housing Rents and Subsidies (Scotland) Act 1975.	Section 5(6).
1977 c.42.	Rent Act 1977.	In section 69(1), the words "(to be known as a certificate of fair rent)". In section 70(1), the word "and" before paragraph (b). In Schedule 12, in paragraph 3, the words "unless the dwelling-house is subject to a regulated tenancy".
1980 c.51.	Housing Act 1980.	Section 56(3). Section 140.

Chapter	Short title	Extent of Repeal
1980 c.65.	Local Government, Planning and Land Act 1980.	Section 156(3).
1981 c.64.	New Towns Act 1981.	Section 43(3) and (4). Section 49(b) and (c).
1985 c.51.	Local Government Act 1985.	In Schedule 13, in paragraph 14, subparagraph (d) and the word "and" preceding it. In Schedule 14, paragraph 58(e).
1985 c.68.	Housing Act 1985.	Section 30(2). Section 46. In section 127, the word "and" at the end of paragraph (a). In section 452(2), the definition of "housing authority". Section 453(2). In Schedule 4, in paragraph 7(1), the words from "a housing co-operative" to "management functions)". In Schedule 6, in paragraph 14(2), the words following paragraph (c).
1985 c.71.	Housing (Consequential Provisions) Act 1985.	In Schedule 2, paragraphs 27, 35(3), 44(3), and 45(2).

PART II

OPENCAST COAL

Chapter	Short title	Extent of repeal
6 & 7 Eliz. 2 c.69.	Opencast Coal Act 1958.	Sections 1 and 2. Section 9(2). In section 18(2), the words "(apart from this Act)". In section 39(10), the words "First or". Section 46(2). Section 48. In section 51, in subsection (1), the definitions of "the authorised purposes" and "authorised operations". Section 53(2). Schedule 1. In Schedule 9, in paragraph 3(2), the words "under the First Schedule to this Act, or". Schedule 10.
1971 c.78.	Town and Country Planning Act 1971.	In section 216(3), in paragraph (a), the words "or the National Coal Board" and in paragraph (b), the words from "or" to "1958".
1972 c.52.	Town and Country Planning (Scotland) Act 1972.	Section 58(10)(a). In section 205(3) and 205A(3), in paragraph (a) the words "or the National Coal Board" and in paragraph (b) the words from "or" to "1958".
1975 c.56.	Coal Industry Act 1975.	Section 5. In Schedule 3, paragraphs 3 and 11. Schedule 4.
1981 c.67.	Acquisition of Land Act 1981.	In Schedule 4, paragraph 11(5).
1986 c.5.	Agricultural Holdings Act 1986.	In Schedule 14, paragraph 25.

PART III

MISCELLANEOUS (ENGLAND AND WALES)

Chapter	Short title	Extent of repeal
62 & 63 Vict. c.19.	Electric Lighting (Clauses) Act 1899.	In the Schedule, in section 10(*b*), the words "and the express consent of the local authority also".
16 & 17 Geo. 5 c.51.	Electricity (Supply) Act 1926.	In Schedule 6, the entry relating to section 21 of the Electricity (Supply) Act 1919.
8 & 9 Geo. 6 c.43.	Requisitioned Land and War Works Act 1945.	Section 52.
10 & 11 Geo. 6 c.51.	Town and Country Planning Act 1947.	In Schedule 8, the entry relating to section 21 of the Electricity (Supply) Act 1919.
10 & 11 Geo. 6 c.54.	Electricity Act 1947.	In Part I of Schedule 4, the entry relating to section 21 of the Electricity (Supply) Act 1919.
11 & 12 Geo. 6 c.17.	Requisitioned Land and War Works Act 1948.	In the Schedule, paragraph 10.
5 & 6 Eliz. 2 c.48.	Electricity Act 1957.	In section 33(3), the words "and the next following".
1968 c.14.	Public Expenditure and Receipts Act 1968.	In Schedule 3, in paragraph 6, the entry relating to section 290(4) of the Local Government Act 1933.
1971 c.78.	Town and Country Planning Act 1971.	In section 29A— (*a*) in subsection (2), the definition of "the Code of Practice for Access of the Disabled to Buildings"; (*b*) subsection (3). Section 29B(2) and (3). In section 32(2), in the proviso, the words "of sections 66 to 86". In section 55(4), the words "under section 56 of this Act". Sections 66 to 86. Section 88B(4). Section 105(1)(*c*). Section 110(1). In section 147(3), the words from "or in respect of" to the end. Section 151. Section 165(4). In section 169— (*a*) subsection (5); (*b*) in subsection (7), the words from "and no compensation" to the end. In section 180(4), the words from "and no account" to the end. Section 185. Section 191(2). In section 237(5), the words from "and no compensation" to the end. Sections 250 to 252. In section 260(1)(*d*), the words "grants in accordance with regulations made under section 250 of this Act or". In section 287— (*a*) in subsection (4), the words "69, 73(6), 74(4), 75(8)"; (*b*) in subsection (5)(*b*), the words "69, 73(6), 75(8) or" and the words from "or an order under section 74(4)" to the end;

Chapter	Short title	Extent of Repeal
1971 c.78—*cont.*	Town and Country Planning Act 1971—*cont.*	(*c*) subsection (7); (*d*) subsection (9). In section 290(1)— (*a*) in the definition of "building", the words in parenthesis; (*b*) the definition of "industrial development certificate". Schedules 12 and 13. In Schedule 21— (*a*) in Part I, the references to sections 250, 251(1) and 252; (*b*) in Part II, the references to sections 79 to 81; (*c*) in Part III, the references to sections 72 and 251(2) to (5); (*d*) in Part V, the references to sections 72 and 73 to 86. In Schedule 24, paragraphs 20A, 26 to 30 and 70.
1972 c.42.	Town and Country Planning (Amendment) Act 1972.	Sections 5 and 6.
1972 c.70.	Local Government Act 1972.	In section 182(1), the words from "(2A)" to the end. Section 183(2). In section 250(4), the words from "(including" to "in the inquiry)". In Schedule 16, paragraphs 1 to 3.
1974 c.7.	Local Government Act 1974.	In Schedule 6, paragraph 25(4).
1974 c.32.	Town and Country Amenities Act 1974.	Section 3(1). Section 5.
1976 c.70.	Land Drainage Act 1976.	In section 96(5), the words from "including" to "in the inquiry)".
1977 c.40	Control of Office Development Act 1977.	The whole Act.
1980 c.65.	Local Government, Planning and Land Act 1980.	Section 88. In section 134— (*a*) in subsection (1), the words "Subject to subsection (2) below,"; (*b*) subsection (2). In Schedule 14, paragraphs 6 to 8. In Schedule 15, paragraphs 1 and 16. In Part I of Schedule 29, in the entry relating to section 65, the word "waste".
1981 c.67.	Acquisition of Land Act 1981.	In Schedule 4, in paragraph 1, in the entry relating to the Local Government Act 1972, the words "section 125(4) and (7)".
1982 c.30.	Local Government (Miscellaneous Provisions) Act 1981.	In Schedule 6, in the Table in paragraph 7(*b*) the entries relating to ss.15 and 15A of the Town and Country Planning Act 1971.
1982 c.52.	Industrial Development Act 1982.	Section 15(1)(*b*). In Part II of Schedule 2, paragraph 7(1).
1983 c.47.	National Heritage Act 1983.	In Schedule 4, paragraph 18. Schedule 5, paragraph 6.
1984 c.27.	Road Traffic Regulation Act 1984.	In section 129(1)(*d*), the words from "(including" to "in the inquiry)".
1985 c.51.	Local Government Act 1985.	Section 3(2). In Schedule 2, paragraph 1(8).

PART IV

MISCELLANEOUS (SCOTLAND)

Chapter	Short title	Extent of repeal
1968 c.14.	Public Expenditure and Receipts Act 1968.	In Schedule 3, in paragraph 6, the entry relating to section 355(8) of the Local Government (Scotland) Act 1947.
1972 c.52.	Town and Country Planning (Scotland) Act 1972.	In section 29(2), in the proviso, the words "of sections 64 to 83".
		In section 53(2), the word "only" and the words "(in this Act referred to as listed building consent)".
		In section 53(4) the words "under section 54 of this Act,".
		In section 63(1A), the words from "; and references" to "construed".
		Sections 64 to 83.
		Section 85(8).
		In section 136(3) the words from "or in respect of" to the end.
		Section 140.
		Section 154(4).
		In section 158—
		(*a*) Subsection (5).
		(*b*) In subsection (7) the words from "and no compensation" to the end.
		In section 169(4) the words from "and no account" to the end.
		Section 174.
		Section 180(2).
		In section 226(5) the words from "and no compensation" to the end.
		Section 231(2)(*e*).
		In section 233(3), the words "(other than an order under section 203(1)(*a*) of this Act)".
		Sections 237 to 239.
		In section 247(1)(*d*), the words from "in accordance" to "grants".
		In section 273—
		(*a*) In subsection (4), the words "67, 71(6), 72(4), 73(8)".
		(*b*) In subsection (5) the words "67, 71(6), 73(8)".
		(*c*) Subsections (7) to (9).
		In section 275(1)—
		(*a*) In the definition of "building", the words ", except in sections 71 to 83 of this Act,".
		(*b*) the definition of "industrial development certificate".
		In Schedule 19—
		(*a*) in Part I, the reference to sections 237, 238(1) and 239;
		(*b*) in Part II, the references to sections 77 to 79 and 83;
		(*c*) in Part III, the reference to section 70.
		In Schedule 22, paragraphs 22 to 25 and 60.
1974 c.32.	Town and Country Amenities Act 1974.	Section 5.

Chapter	Short title	Extent of Repeal
1980 c.65.	Local Government, Planning and Land Act 1980.	In section 134(1) the words "Subject to subsection (2) below,". In Part I of Schedule 30, in the entry relating to section 63, the word "waste".
1982 c.52.	Industrial Development Act 1982.	Section 15(1)(*b*). Paragraph 10 of Part II of Schedule 2.
1984 c.27.	Road Traffic Regulation Act 1984.	In section 129(1)(*d*) the words from "(including" to "in the inquiry)".

PUBLIC ORDER ACT 1986*

(1986 c. 64)

---

* Annotations by Thomas Gibbons, Faculty of Law, University of Newcastle Upon Tyne.

PART IV

EXCLUSION ORDERS

PART V

MISCELLANEOUS AND GENERAL

An Act to abolish the common law offences of riot, rout, unlawful
assembly and affray and certain statutory offences relating to public
order; to create new offences relating to public order; to control public
processions and assemblies; to control the stirring up of racial hatred;
to provide for the exclusion of certain offenders from sporting events;
to create a new offence relating to the contamination of or interference
with goods; to confer power to direct certain trespassers to leave land;
to amend section 7 of the Conspiracy and Protection of Property Act
1875, section 1 of the Prevention of Crime Act 1953, Part V of the
Criminal Justice (Scotland) Act 1980 and the Sporting Events (Control
of Alcohol etc.) Act 1985; to repeal certain obsolete or unnecessary
enactments; and for connected purposes.   [7th November 1986]

PARLIAMENTARY DEBATES
    Hansard: H.C. Vol. 88, col. 457; Vol. 89, col. 794; Vol. 96, cols. 957, 1038; Vol. 103, col.
818; H.L. Vol. 474, col. 448; Vol. 476, col. 513; Vol. 478, col. 910; Vol. 479, col. 458; Vol.
480, col. 9; Vol. 481, cols. 167, 237, 441, 745.
    This Bill was considered in the House of Commons Standing Committee G, January 23
to April 10, 1986.

INTRODUCTION AND GENERAL NOTE
    This Act represents the culmination of a prolonged debate about the law's capacity to
deal with public disturbances. Common law offences have been modernised, following the
Law Commission's recommendations. The provision for regulating public assembly has been
extended, including a new power to deal with mass trespass. In addition, the scope of
offences against racial hatred has been increased. In general, the effect is to tighten control
of public dissent; dissent which has been evidenced in recent years by more frequent
marches, rallies, sit-ins and lengthy demonstrations, and by more acrimonious and unyielding
industrial disputes. Although free assembly has featured strongly in the rhetoric of the
debate, no effective protection is offered in this legislation; indeed, the trend is in the other

direction. At the same time, there has been much concern about sheer rowdy behaviour, especially that connected with football matches, and the Act is intended to provide some remedy in that field.

OFFICIAL PUBLICATIONS
  Home Affairs Committee, *Law Relating to Public Order*, 5th Report, (1979–80) H.C. 756.
  Home Office, *Review of the Public Order Act 1936 and Related Legislation* (1980) Cmnd. 7891 (Green Paper).
  Home Office & Scottish Office, *Review of Public Order Law* (1985) Cmnd. 9510 (White Paper).
  Law Commission, *Offences against Public Order* (1982) Working Paper No. 82 (Working Paper).
  Law Commission, *Offences Relating to Public Order* (1983) H.C. 85, Law Com. No. 123 (Final Report).
  (Lord Scarman) Home Office, *The Brixton Disorders* (1981) Cmnd. 8427.

OTHER LITERATURE
  M. D. A. Freeman, Law and Order in 1984, (1984) *Current Legal Problems* 175.
  A. T. H. Smith, Public Order Law 1974–1983: Developments and Proposals, [1984] *Criminal Law Review* 643.
  M. Supperstone, *Brownlie's Law of Public Order and National Security* (1981) 2nd ed.

PART I

NEW OFFENCES

GENERAL NOTE
  Much of this part is based upon the Law Commission's examination of the common law and some statutory offences relating to serious offences committed in connection with disturbances to public order. The Commission's report, *Offences Relating to Public Order* (1983) H.C. 85 (Law Com. 123), recommended new offences of riot, violent disorder, fear or provocation of violence by a group and affray, to replace the common law offences of riot, rout, unlawful assembly and affray. The Commission's terms of reference did not extend to offences contained in legislation dealing with minor public disorder but it decided to adopt the criteria used in s.5, Public Order Act 1936 as a threshold for criminal liability when formulating its new offences and it commented extensively upon the operation and effect of s.5.
  The Home Office's White Paper, *Review of Public Order* (1985), Cmnd. 9510, represented an attempt to rationalise both serious and less serious offences in this area. It sought to remove an overlap which existed between the Commission's proposals and s.5 of the 1936 Act by revamping the latter and floating a new offence of disorderly conduct which would apply at the more trivial end of the spectrum. In doing so, it drew upon many of the Law Commission's recommendations.
  The provisions of Part I closely reflect the substance of the White Paper. They create a range of offences graded according to seriousness: the worst kinds of group violence are dealt with in riot, whilst quite minor examples of nuisance or offensiveness are encompassed in disorderly conduct. Additional provision is made for alternative verdicts to be reached in proceedings under this Part and there are new powers of arrest. Powers to deal with or prevent a breach of the peace at common law are unaffected: s.40(4).
  The result is a comprehensive package of measures which will greatly facilitate the prosecution of those involved in public disorder. Whether it will serve to increase public tranquility is another matter, of course. The quality and efficiency of law enforcement policy are much more important in that regard but they are not, and perhaps cannot be, addressed in an Act of this type. Similarly, the roots of the passion and antagonism which are manifested in disorder cannot be tackled in the formulation of offences, yet they remain a crucial context for evaluating the efficiency and significance of this legislation.

Riot

1.—(1) Where 12 or more persons who are present together use or threaten unlawful violence for a common purpose and the conduct of them (taken together) is such as would cause a person of reasonable firmness present at the scene to fear for his personal safety, each of the persons using unlawful violence for the common purpose is guilty of riot.

(2) It is immaterial whether or not the 12 or more use or threaten unlawful violence simultaneously.

(3) The common purpose may be inferred from conduct.

(4) No person of reasonable firmness need actually be, or be likely to be, present at the scene.

(5) Riot may be committed in private as well as in public places.

(6) A person guilty of riot is liable on conviction on indictment to imprisonment for a term not exceeding ten years or a fine or both.

DEFINITION
"violence": s.8.

GENERAL NOTE
This section creates a new offence of riot, replacing the common law offence which is abolished in s.9(1). At common law, the necessary elements of riot consisted of:

> "(1) number of persons, three at least; (2) common purpose; (3) execution or inception of the common purpose; (4) an intent to help one another by force if necessary against any person who may oppose them in the execution of their common purpose; (5) force or violence not merely used in [demolishing a brick wall, the common purpose here], but displayed in such a manner as to alarm at least one person of reasonable firmness and courage": *Field* v. *Metropolitan Police Receiver* [1907] 2 K.B. 853 *per* Phillimore J. at 860.

Any person who actively encouraged or promoted the riot, or who participated in it, would be guilty of an offence: *R.* v. *Caird* (1970) 54 Cr.App.R. 499.

The principal differences between the new offence and the common law are as follows:

(*a*) twelve or more persons rather than three are required;

(*b*) there is no specific need to show an intention to resist any opposition by force;

(*c*) no person need actually feel alarmed by the display of violence;

(*d*) action falling short of the use of violence will not render a person guilty.

Adopting comments in *Caird*, the Law Commission noted that the gravity of riotous behaviour is to be seen in, "the threat that lies in the power of numbers . . . and using those numbers to achieve their purpose." The sum is thus greater than the parts and this was a major reason for the Commission's considering that the existence of an offence of riot continued to be justified. In addition, it argued that, "without replacement, the law would not be able to deal adequately with those who provoke or lead wide-scale public disturbances" but who cannot be prosecuted for offences against persons or property: Final Report, paras. 6.8 and 6.9.

The Law Commission's view was formed notwithstanding difficulties which existed at common law in specifying the nature of common purpose and its execution or inception and in then proving it. These problems may persist in relation to the new offence, not least because of the increase in numbers. In addition, the Standing Committee's difficulty in understanding the components of the offence may cast doubt on a jury's ability to cope with it. Neither the Law Commission nor the Government envisaged that the offence would be frequently charged, however. Rather, riot is to be seen as being reserved for the most serious and widespread examples of public disorder. It is most likely that violent disorder, in s.2, will be used for dealing with most group violence, whether actual or threatened.

This section is modelled upon the Law Commission's Draft Bill, Clause 1.

Subs. (1)

This subsection states the circumstances and conduct required for riot. A number of expressions in this definition are elaborated in subsequent subsections and are discussed in relation to them below. The mental element required is to be found in s.6(1), (5)–(7). By s.7(1), the Director of Public Prosecutions must consent to any prosecution.

Riot is an offence committed by an individual but which takes place in a group context. That context is set out in the first part of this subsection. It involves the use or threat of unlawful violence for a common purpose by the group in such a way as to arouse fear in a notional bystander of reasonable firmness. There is no limit on the duration of the climate of fear thus produced, provided that it involves 12 or more present together, and it might include, for example, continued and concerted shouting of threats over a period of some hours. Within the general context, it is only when a participating individual uses violence with the necessary mental element and for the common purpose, that the offence is committed. It is not necessary to show any injury to persons or damage to property for violence to have been used. By s.8, other violent conduct, such as that section's example of throwing a missile which falls short, or hammering with a fist on a vehicle or aiming a punch which misses, will suffice. This broad meaning of violence is intended to serve the same purpose as the concept of participation in riot at common law. A mere threat of violence, although relevant to the existence of the context, will not ground liability, however.

"Unlawful" violence is not defined but it was envisaged by the Law Commission as including any general defence, self-defence, or the use of force in law enforcement under s.3, Criminal Law Act 1967: Final Report, para. 3.40. If sufficient persons were to be acquitted of a charge of riot on the basis of such defences, it might be that there would be less than the 12 persons needed to establish the general context for the offence. In such a case, nobody could be convicted of riot, although it might be open to the jury to find members of the group guilty of violent disorder, by virtue of s.6(3), Criminal Law Act 1967.

"Threaten" is an ordinary word in the language: see *Brutus* v. *Cozens* [1973] A.C. 854 at 862 *per* Lord Reid. It includes threats in the form of words in the offences of riot and violent disorder but not affray. Gestures will also be included. Clearly, there will be much scope for disagreement about the borderline between displays of emotion or anger and the communication of a desire to inflict violence.

Subs. (2)

In determining whether the appropriate context exists, at the time that the accused uses violence, it is not necessary to show that all 12 or more of the group are using or threatening violence at exactly the same time. The Law Commission envisaged only the continuous presence of 12 or more at a continuing event or set of circumstances, during which they use or threaten such violence for a common purpose; otherwise the prosecution's burden would be too onerous: Final Report, para. 6.21. In determining whether the group does constitute 12 or more, the mental element of each person using or threatening violence is not required, by s.6(7). However unlikely in practice, it would be possible for every member of the group but one to engage in violence or threaten violence but to show that he neither intended to use or threaten violence nor was aware that his conduct might be violent or threaten violence, yet create a sufficient context for the exceptional member to be convicted where he had used violence for the group's common purpose. To put the point differently, only the person charged with riot needs to have the mental element proved against him.

The figure 12 was settled by the Law Commission following responses to its Working Paper in which it had suggested that a group of three or more would suffice. It had been concerned about the difficulties of proof that the higher number would entail. As it acknowledged, both the rationale in *R.* v. *Caird* and the ordinary meaning of riot, suggested that three was inadequate. The figure of 12 is inevitably arbitrary but there is an historical link with the repealed Riot Act 1714. See Final Report, para. 6.19.

Subs. (3)

The common purpose may be inferred from conduct. At common law, the concept seems to have been confused with motivation but it has been pointed out that the crucial factor is what appears to be a common purpose from the general behaviour of the persons involved, given the nature of riot as an especially alarming breach of the peace: see *Supperstone*, p. 131. The Law Commission endorsed this view in its Working Paper, para. 2.27, and Final Report. It also noted that a prior plan or agreement is unnecessary to prove common purpose. All that is required is, "an accurate assessment of what the rioters are actually doing": Final Report, para. 6.24. The behaviours which manifest the purpose may be different, however; for example, stone throwing, damaging pavements, or brandishing weapons may all be involved.

The common purpose may be lawful, however improbably, or unlawful. It need not be confined to an objective unrelated to some general political purpose: see *Supperstone*, p. 132; Final Report, para. 6.25.

Where a group can be shown to have a common purpose, that in itself is not sufficient to create the general context for riot. The common purpose must be the object of any violence, actual or threatened, which the members are using. It cannot be assumed, however, that violence which occurs in connection with any group must be directed towards the group's common purpose. One of the difficulties in proving the objects of such violence is that there may be many overlapping or parallel layers of purpose. The general principles of interpretation applicable to a criminal statute suggest, however, that it is the purpose which is most proximate to the activity in question which is relevant for the offence. Thus, acts of violence by groups of two or three who are close to each other and part of a larger crowd, otherwise peacefully demonstrating or picketing in support of some cause, would not appear to be linked by that broader purpose but by the particular circumstances of the violence, for example, an attack on a police vehicle or breaking a shop window. This appears to have been the Government's objective, too: see Standing Committee, col. 71.

Absence of common purpose means that an accused cannot be found guilty of riot. If that absence is caused by intoxication, the same will apply; as the Law Commission suggests, common purpose "amounts in substance to a further mental element of intent": Final Report, para. 6.28.

Subs. (4)

At common law, it was established that a bystander did not actually have to be put in fear but it was unclear whether the presence of somebody of reasonable firmness and courage who would have been put in fear was required or whether it was sufficient that it would be likely that such a person would experience such fear, if present: see Working Paper, para. 2.32 and *Kamara* v. *D.P.P.* [1974] A.C. 104 at 116. A similar issue arose in relation to the common law offence of affray, now abolished by s.9(1), where there was a requirement of violence of a degree, "as to be calculated to terrify a person of reasonably firm character": *Taylor* v. *D.P.P.* [1973] A.C. 964 at 987 *per* Lord Hailsham. In that case, however, Lord Hailsham suggested, *obiter*, that in a private place the actual presence of a bystander would be needed (at p. 988) although it had been held, in *R.* v. *Mapstone* [1963] 3 All E.R. 930, that the likelihood that such a person would be terrified was sufficient. See Final Report, para. 3.28.

The Law Commission decided that the uncertainty should be resolved in favour of the objective test which it considered should be applied to riot, violent disorder and affray and which is contained in this section and in ss.2 and 3. The discussion here applies equally, therefore, to the reasonable firmness test in those sections. The arguments in favour of an objective test are that actual bystanders may be difficult to find, having already fled and it would only confuse a jury to expect it to speculate on the likelihood of a bystander's presence and likely fear. In addition, reliance upon an actual bystander leaves the success of the prosecution open to chance, depending upon his fortitude; a conviction would depend upon the timidity or temerity of those who happen to be there.

Against these arguments, it was maintained in debate upon the Bill that the absence of an actual victim gave too much leeway to prosecutors and left too much discretion to the police in forming a judgment that the degree of violence was sufficiently serious. In the event, the Law Commission's view prevailed.

The "person of reasonable firmness" is not envisaged as the reasonable person, who presumably might bring the standards of the reasonable man to bear in judging the propriety of the violence witnessed: Final Report, para. 3.38 (but *cf.* para. 3.37: the test of the reaction of the hypothetical reasonable person). The concern is with how the hypothetical bystander would respond, given reasonable firmness, not whether he approves or disapproves or whether he ought to have felt fear or not. The function of the test is to provide a measure of the requisite degree of violence.

"Present at the scene" is elaborated as referring to, "anyone who would have been in real danger of becoming involved in the disturbance": Final Report, para. 3.38. It does not imply any necessary degree of physical proximity to the disturbance.

"Personal safety" was envisaged as emphasising the fear for physical safety. The conduct must be such as "would" give rise to such fear, not might; this is seen, rightly, as limiting the breadth of the offence. Violence against property is not precluded from giving rise to such fear. See generally, Final Report, paras. 3.36, 5.35 and 6.26.

Subs. (5)

At common law, a riot could take place anywhere and the new offence makes similar provision. Dwellings are not excluded, since there is a public interest in preventing such serious disorder and, in any event, it may not always be confined to one type of territory rather than another. The same considerations apply to violent disorder and affray.

Subs. (6)

The offence is an arrestable offence under s.24, Police and Criminal Evidence Act 1984.

Violent disorder

2.—(1) Where 3 or more persons who are present together use or threaten unlawful violence and the conduct of them (taken together) is such as would cause a person of reasonable firmness present at the scene to fear for his personal safety, each of the persons using or threatening unlawful violence is guilty of violent disorder.

(2) It is immaterial whether or not the 3 or more use or threaten unlawful violence simultaneously.

(3) No person of reasonable firmness need actually be, or be likely to be, present at the scene.

(4) Violent disorder may be committed in private as well as in public places.

(5) A person guilty of violent disorder is liable on conviction on indictment to imprisonment for a term not exceeding 5 years or a fine or both, or on summary conviction to imprisonment for a term not exceeding 6 months or a fine not exceeding the statutory maximum or both.

DEFINITION
"violence": s.8.

GENERAL NOTE
This section creates a new offence of violent disorder which replaces the common law offence of unlawful assembly, repealed by s.9(1). Unlawful assembly was characterised by uncertainty and disagreement about its nature and scope. The Law Commission identified four different ways of defining it: Working Paper, paras. 2.43–50. One view, following Lambard, was that unlawful assembly was an incipient riot. Another, following Hawkins, was that it consisted of three or more persons gathering for purposes forbidden by law or with the intention of carrying out a lawful or unlawful purpose in such a way as to create, or cause firm persons to apprehend, a breach of the peace. A third view, that of Smith and Hogan, was that unlawful assembly consisted of an assembly of three or more with the common purpose of committing a crime of violence or of achieving another purpose, lawful or not, in a manner causing reasonable men to apprehend a breach of the peace. Fourthly, Brownlie's view was that an assembly of three or more is unlawful when it occurs in a way that gives persons of ordinary firmness reasonable grounds to fear a breach of the peace, and where the accused intends or abets the use of violence or other acts which he knows to be likely to cause a breach of the peace.

At common law, problems were caused in the following situations. There was difficulty in identifying the moment when an assembly became unlawful, illustrated by the explanation offered in *R.* v. *Caird* (1970) 50 Cr.App.R. 449. There was uncertainty as to what constituted breach of the peace, illustrated by the differences between *R.* v. *Howell* [1981] 3 W.L.R. 501 and *R.* v. *Chief Constable of Devon & Cornwall, ex p. C.E.G.B.* [1981] 3 W.L.R. 967. There was ambiguity about the responsibility of members of an assembly for unlawful acts which are likely to be committed by others, illustrated by the apparent strain entailed in reconciling *Beatty* v. *Gillbanks* (1889) 9 Q.B.D. 308 and *Wise* v. *Dunning* [1902] 1 K.B. 167.

In seeking to reflect the nuances of defining unlawful assembly, the Law Commission produced, in its Working Paper, a proposed statutory offence which it conceded in its Final Report to be "undeniably complex": para. 5.6. In reworking that proposal, the Commission emphasised two broad situations with which a new offence would have to deal; first, there was conduct undertaken by persons in combination, in such a way as to create an apprehension that a breach of the peace would occur; secondly, there was conduct undertaken by a combination of persons who intended to provoke others to break the peace. In both situations, the fact of combination was considered to be a significant contribution to the gravity of the offending behaviour. In the second situation, however, the claim to freedom of assembly competed with the need for public order. Here, the Law Commission decided that the threshold of the criminal sanction should lie at the point where there is threatened disorder and where it is demonstrated by the use of threatening, abusive or insulting words or behaviour. Adopting Lord Reid's observations in *Brutus* v. *Cozens* [1973] A.C. 854 at 862, it argued that, "these terms are acceptable and appropriate for defining the limits within which public protest may take place without incurring serious penalties": Final Report, para. 5.12. Finally, the Law Commission accepted the need to find an alternative formulation to the concept of breach of the peace. Not only was its present meaning unclear, but it did not embrace the intimidation falling short of violence which the use of threatening, abusive or insulting words might produce, as illustrated in *Parkin* v. *Norman* [1983] Q.B. 92 explaining the operation of s.5, Public Order Act 1936.

The new offence in this section consists substantially of one limb of the Law Commission's proposals for replacing unlawful assembly, namely its provision for group violence falling short of riot. The second limb of the Commission's proposals consisted of an offence, triable either way, of conduct intended or likely to cause fear or provoke violence where threatening, abusive or insulting behaviour was used in a group. That second limb has not been incorporated into this Act but many of its features have been accepted as a basis for reforming s.5, Public Order Act 1936, with which it overlapped, and which has been replaced with the summary offence contained in s.4 of this Act. The Law Commission sought to distinguish the two limbs of its proposals on the basis that the seriousness of the use of violence in a group should be marked by a separate offence differentiating it from threats of violence made in a group. The offence of violent disorder in this section makes no such distinction, however, applying to both the use and threat of violence; in this respect, it is closer to unlawful assembly. The effect is to facilitate the group trial of both users and threateners of violence: White Paper, para. 3.14. The corollary is that threateners may be subject to trial upon indictment and more severe penalties.

Violent disorder is envisaged as being used as the normal charge for serious outbreaks of public order: the Home Secretary, *Hansard*, H.C. Vol. 89, col. 795. The inclusion of threats in its definition creates a wider offence than the Law Commission suggested, and the absence of common purpose creates a wider offence than the first three meanings of unlawful assembly in that casual association will suffice. On the other hand, the prohibited behaviour is restricted to that of a violent nature. The general effect, however, will be to make more readily available a serious public order offence which can be proved more easily and will be a much more attractive option than unlawful assembly for the prosecution.

Subs. (1)

This subsection follows the pattern established in s.1(1) establishing the conduct required for violent disorder and leaving further elaboration of its components to subsequent subsections. The mental element that is required is to be found in s.6(2), (5)–(7). Here, there is a group context but without the requirement of common purpose found in riot. Thus, a casual or opportunist participant will be caught, provided that his behaviour is sufficiently associated with others for them to be present together. Another distinguishing feature from riot is the creation of liability for both the use and threat of violence in the general context.

For discussion of "unlawful" violence and the meaning of "threatens," see the note to s.1(1).

Provision for an alternative verdict of guilt under s.4 is made in s.7(3); although more logical within a sliding scale of liability, the Law Commission's suggested alternative verdict of affray was felt by the Government to be too complicated for juries to manage.

Subs. (2)

The figure 3 reflects the common law condition for unlawful assembly. As with the case of riot, the use or threats of violence need not occur at the same time; all that is envisaged is a continuing set of circumstances. *Cf. R.* v. *Jones* (1974) Cr.App.R. 120. Similarly, as with the case of riot, only the person charged with violent disorder need have the mental element proved against him; it is irrelevant to establishing the context of the conduct: s.6(7).

Subs. (3)

See the discussion in the note to s.1(4).

Subs. (4)

This provision reflects the common law position.

Subs. (5)

This is an arrestable offence under s.24, Police and Criminal Evidence Act 1984.

Affray

3.—(1) A person is guilty of affray if he uses or threatens unlawful violence towards another and his conduct is such as would cause a person of reasonable firmness present at the scene to fear for his personal safety.

(2) Where 2 or more persons use or threaten the unlawful violence, it is the conduct of them taken together that must be considered for the purposes of subsection (1).

(3) For the purposes of this section a threat cannot be made by the use of words alone.

(4) No person· of reasonable firmness need actually be, or be likely to be, present at the scene.

(5) Affray may be committed in private as well as in public places.

(6) A constable may arrest without warrant anyone he reasonably suspects is committing affray.

(7) A person guilty of affray is liable on conviction on indictment to imprisonment for a term not exceeding 3 years or a fine or both, or on summary conviction to imprisonment for a term not exceeding 6 months or a fine not exceeding the statutory maximum or both.

DEFINITION
"violence": s.8.

GENERAL NOTE
This section creates a new offence of affray which replaces the common law offence abolished by s.9(1). Affray at common law was reformulated in recent years by two decisions of the House of Lords, *Button* v. *D.P.P.* [1966] A.C. 591 and *Taylor* v. *D.P.P.* [1973] A.C. 964. Their effect is summarised in Smith & Hogan, *Criminal Law* (1985), 5th ed., p. 738, as requiring:

"(1) unlawful fighting or unlawful violence used by one or more persons against another or others; or an unlawful display of force by one or more persons without actual violence;

(2) in a public place or, if on private premises, in the presence of at least one innocent person who was terrified; and

(3) in such a manner that a bystander of reasonably firm character might reasonably be expected to be terrified."

The Law Commission emphasised that the purpose of charging affray at common law was to mark the serious implications that street-fighting, brawling, and concerted attacks have for public order when they are conducted in an especially terrifying manner. The concern is not so much with the injury caused to particular victims, for which offences against the person may be charged in addition, but with the impact that fighting and violence has upon public tranquility, whatever its specific effects. As a result, affray could be charged without evidence of an assault against an identified victim. See Final Report, paras. 3.1–5. The White Paper noted that, numerically, affray was the "most useful" of the common law public order offences: para. 3.15.

The Law Commission's proposals are, in substance, a statutory restatement of the common law offence with some minor modifications and are reflected in this section.

Subs. (1)
This subsection sets out the conduct required for affray. It consists of the behaviour, subject to subs. (3), that is embraced by the offences of riot and violent disorder but without their general contexts, including the existence of a group. The mental element that is required is to be found in s.6(2), (5) and (6). Although the purpose of the offence is to deal with fighting, it could apply to situations where no fighting occurs but only a display of violence. This reflects the common law position.

One person may be found guilty of affray; his victim may not retaliate or his assailant may not be prosecuted or may successfully establish self defence. Not any assault will suffice, however: a more pervasive public fear is required.

For discussion of "unlawful" violence, and the meaning of "threatens" see the note to s.1(1).

In the event of failure to convict, an alternative finding of guilt under s.4 is possible, by s.7(3).

Subs. (2)
The fear that the actual or threatened violence produces must be judged by reference to the totality of the situation. If a simple fight is unlikely to involve others it may be alarming or offensive but may not be capable of reasonably inducing fear for personal safety. Where

64–9

fighting is likely to spread or is fast-moving and generally disruptive, such fear may be well grounded.

Subs. (3)

The common law position is followed here; in *Taylor* v. *D.P.P.* [1973] A.C. 964 at 987, Lord Hailsham stated that affray cannot be based upon "mere words, unaccompanied by the brandishing of a weapon or actual violence". Such words may be caught by s.4 and that establishes an acceptable basis for the threshold of the criminal sanction. The relationship between affray and violent disorder should not be forgotten, however. A large affray is likely to constitute violent disorder, so the significance of the nature of the threat depends upon the size of the group. There is a strong incentive for prosecutors to charge the more serious offence for substantially the same behaviour whenever possible. At the same time, the absence of a rationale for not giving preferential treatment to speech in violent disorder is highlighted, although neither the Law Commission nor Lord Hailsham addressed themselves to the basis for the common law rule in affray.

Subs. (4)

See the discussion in the note to s.1(4). It reflects the position recently confirmed in *Attorney-General's Reference No. 3 of 1983* [1985] 2 W.L.R. 253.

Subs. (5)

This reflects the common law position.

Subs. (6)

The arrest power may be needed because the offence is not arrestable under s.24, Police and Criminal Evidence Act 1984. Section 25 of that Act does provide for a conditional arrest power, however, and that would appear to overlap with the power here, insofar as it is a preventive power.

Fear or provocation of violence

4.—(1) A person is guilty of an offence if he—
  (*a*) uses towards another person threatening, abusive or insulting words or behaviour, or
  (*b*) distributes or displays to another person any writing, sign or other visible representation which is threatening, abusive or insulting,
with intent to cause that person to believe that immediate unlawful violence will be used against him or another by any person, or to provoke the immediate use of unlawful violence by that person or another, or whereby that person is likely to believe that such violence will be used or it is likely that such violence will be provoked.

(2) An offence under this section may be committed in a public or a private place, except that no offence is committed where the words or behaviour are used, or the writing, sign or other visible representation is distributed or displayed, by a person inside a dwelling and the other person is also inside that or another dwelling.

(3) A constable may arrest without warrant anyone he reasonably suspects is committing an offence under this section.

(4) A person guilty of an offence under this section is liable on summary conviction to imprisonment for a term not exceeding 6 months or a fine not exceeding level 5 on the standard scale or both.

DEFINITIONS
  "dwelling": s.8.
  "violence": s.8.

GENERAL NOTE

In this section, a new offence is created to replace s.5, Public Order Act 1936 which is abolished by s.9(2)(*d*). By s.5, "any person who in any public place or at any public meeting (a) uses threatening, abusive or insulting words or behaviour, or (b) distributes or displays any writing, sign or visible representation which is threatening, abusive or insulting, with intent to provoke a breach of the peace or whereby a breach of the peace is likely to be occasioned, shall be guilty of an offence." The new offence is substantially similar to the old but incorporates features of the second limb of the Law Commission's proposals to replace unlawful assembly: see the General Note to s.2.

The Law Commission wanted an offence which dealt with threats in private as well as public circumstances, which was not dependent upon breach of the peace, and which applied to damage to property not only in the owner's presence. These latter objectives were to be achieved by using the concept of unlawful violence and emphasising the fear which it engenders. The White Paper adopted these suggestions as the basis for the new threatening behaviour offence but included a specific exception for dwellings: *cf.* Final Report, para. 5.46. It did, however, reject a requirement that violence should be immediate, on the expedient ground that it was not to be found in the old s.5, but that found its way back into the package by the time the Bill was first published: see White Paper, paras. 3.7–3.12.

This offence will enhance an already extensive range of measures available to the police for dealing with disorder by providing a ready if not necessarily simple means of tackling intimidation. The Association of Chief Police Officers was frequently mentioned in Parliament as pressing the need for such additional power. The dangers of what could be seen as an all-embracing, speculative, even complex offence were not entertained as a serious possibility. In particular, the problems which arose with unlawful assembly, concerning the responsibility of the law-abider for others' unlawful reactions to his behaviour, have not been resolved.

Subs. (1)

This subsection establishes the conduct and circumstances required for the offence of causing fear or provocation of violence. The mental element is to be found in s.6(3)(5)(6).

The relevant words and behaviour must be used towards another person. Their use in isolation, whilst possibly leading to the consequences mentioned, would not pose a danger to the public peace: Final Report, para. 5.45. Arguably, this requirement only states explicitly what was implicit in the old s.5 offence.

"Threatening, abusive or insulting" are ordinary words of the language: *Brutus* v. *Cozens* [1973] A.C. 854 at 862 *per* Lord Reid. They are to be regarded as strong words, however, and do not include merely vigorous, distasteful or unmannerly speech. In *Jordan* v. *Burgoyne* [1963] 2 Q.B. 744, insult was taken to imply a sense of hitting with words. Nevertheless, some dilution, as the Law Commission puts it, has occurred in the magistrates courts in relation to the old s.5 offence: see Final Report, para. 5.12 n.45, quoting Brownlie. The Commission's view that appellate supervision will overcome this problem, however, seems rather optimistic.

Visible representations would include graffiti, placards and printed material. In addition, film or video would appear to be included; the special provision in Part III, for racial hatred, was made in order to clarify such a policy in an earlier draft of s.18.

Under the old s.5, a major component of the offence was concerned with the likely effect of conduct upon those who witnessed it. That conduct had to be such as to bring about a breach of the peace as a natural and probable result: *Parkin* v. *Norman* [1983] Q.B. 92; *Marsh* v. *Arscott* (1982) 75 Cr.App.R. 211. If the potential offender happened to choose a victim who was unlikely to respond with violence, such as a police officer, an elderly person or a pacifist, the s.5 offence could not be committed. The Law Commission considered that this was an unacceptable loophole and suggested a formulation directed at the fear which threatening, abusive or insulting conduct can produce: Final Report, paras. 5.14–18. This subsection incorporates this proposal, so that threats which intimidate are expressly prohibited.

Immediacy connotes a causing of fear or provoking of violence which occurs at the same time that the conduct takes place. A fear that violence will occur at another location would appear to be insufficient. It is to be hoped that the broad meaning given to an imminent breach of the peace in *Moss* v. *McLachlan* [1985] I.R.L.R. 76 will not find favour in interpreting this subsection (*cf. R.* v. *Howell* [1982] Q.B. 416). The Law Commission thought that conduct remote in place, but not in time, might attract liability, but the Minister in Standing Committee thought not: col. 193. Fear does not have to be experienced by the observer, however, nor does violence have to be directed against him. Likely does not mean liable: *Parkin* v. *Norman* above.

Subs. (2)

This provision follows the policy adopted for riot, violent disorder and affray. Back and front gardens are included; *cf. R.* v. *Edwards and Roberts* (1978) 67 Cr.App.R. 228. Conduct taking place across a street of dwellings does not appear to be covered, however.

Subs. (3)

This is a narrow power but s.25, Police and Criminal Evidence Act 1984 will also apply.

Subs. (4)

The standard scale is defined in s.75, Criminal Justice Act 1982.

Harassment, alarm or distress

5.—(1) A person is guilty of an offence if he—

     (*a*) uses threatening, abusive or insulting words or behaviour, or disorderly behaviour, or

     (*b*) displays any writing, sign or other visible representation which is threatening, abusive or insulting,

within the hearing or sight of a person likely to be caused harassment, alarm or distress thereby.

(2) An offence under this section may be committed in a public or a private place, except that no offence is committed where the words or behaviour are used, or the writing, sign or other visible representation is displayed, by a person inside a dwelling and the other person is also inside that or another dwelling.

(3) It is a defence for the accused to prove—

     (*a*) that he had no reason to believe that there was any person within hearing or sight who was likely to be caused harassment, alarm or distress, or

     (*b*) that he was inside a dwelling and had no reason to believe that the words or behaviour used, or the writing, sign or other visible representation displayed, would be heard or seen by a person outside that or any other dwelling, or

     (*c*) that his conduct was reasonable.

(4) A constable may arrest a person without warrant if—

     (*a*) he engages in offensive conduct which the constable warns him to stop, and

     (*b*) he engages in further offensive conduct immediately or shortly after the warning.

(5) In subsection (4) "offensive conduct" means conduct the constable reasonably suspects to constitute an offence under this section, and the conduct mentioned in paragraph (*a*) and the further conduct need not be of the same nature.

(6) A person guilty of an offence under this section is liable on summary conviction to a fine not exceeding level 3 on the standard scale.

GENERAL NOTE

Despite broad support from the Opposition, this was one of the more controversial sections of the Bill in its passage through Parliament. It first surfaced in the White Paper, although the Chief Constable of Essex was credited as its progenitor in Standing Committee, cols. 179, 181 and 195. The White Paper identified the mischief to be remedied as including the following: the creation of noise or disturbances on housing estates; the nuisance caused by groups of youths shouting abuse and obscenities or pestering bus queues; turning out dance hall lights to cause panic; rowdy behaviour in the streets late at night, alarming residents of a locality: White Paper, paras. 3.21–26. In Parliament, further elaborations included loutish, abusive and rowdy behaviour directed at the elderly, ethnic groups, shoppers and dwellers in housing estates. The offence was intended to include blowing whistles, banging dustbin lids and other similar noise. Indeed, it was to cover "anti-social behaviour" in general: *Hansard*, H.C. Vol. 89, cols. 796 and 863.

On the other hand, the Government did not want to include boisterous, excitable behaviour; it was to be a law against hooliganism, perhaps directed at nobody in particular, but not against high spirits: *Hansard*, H.C., Vol. 89 col. 796 and Standing Committee, cols. 216 and 293. The problem, as the Government frequently admitted in drawing these distinctions, was to draft a clause that would differentiate between the two types of behaviour. At one point, the Minister of State put it in terms of broadly knowing what he was aiming at—a broadly nefarious or malicious purpose, ill-motivated rather than light-hearted: Standing Committee, cols. 216 and 218.

In the White Paper, the suggested offence of disorderly behaviour consisted of threatening, abusive or insulting or disorderly words or behaviour in or within view of a public place which causes substantial alarm, harassment or distress, with conviction to result in a maximum fine of £100. The offence in this section differs from that by not having the requirement of "causing" "substantial" consequences, by attracting a special power of arrest and by attracting a maximum fine of £400. In the first Bill, in addition, the likelihood of such consequences was to be assessed without the actual presence of a victim. Despite doubts about the need for a new offence of this kind and about the breadth and vagueness of the formulation of many of its elements in the White Paper, the present offence is even wider. In addition, the attached power of arrest has raised fears that a new "sus" law has been created, providing opportunities for harassment and discrimination against minority and racial groups and reducing the basis for sound relations in general between the police and the public.

Subs. (1)

This subsection sets out the conduct and consequences necessary for the offence of causing harassment, alarm or distress. The required mental element is to be found in s.6(4)–(6).

For discussion of threatening, abusive or insulting words or behaviour, and visible representations of such a nature, see the note to s.4(1). Subs. (1)(*b*) differs from its counterpart in s.4 by not including the distribution of visible representations. Thus, letters are not included, the outcome of the Law Commission's proposals on poison pen letters being awaited in this respect.

"Disorderly" behaviour is not a concept new to the law. Drunk and disorderly behaviour is prohibited by s.91, Criminal Justice Act 1967. The expression, disorderly manner, appears in s.1, Public Meetings Act 1908, although it is specifically directed to preventing the transaction of business. Much local legislation, now expired under the timetable under the Local Government Act 1972, prohibited disorderly behaviour where it was likely to occasion a breach of the peace. In the context of such a consequence, Brownlie suggests that it may include profane, obscene and probably indecent language. He continues, "It may be that the term 'disorderly' involves a somewhat liberal view of what may occasion a breach of the peace. Indeed, in Scotland, South Australia and New Zealand it has been held that the term involves conduct which offends right-thinking members of the public," at p. 193. Inevitably, there will be a tendency to define disorderliness by reference to the consequences, rather than establishing a standard of behaviour and requiring the perpetrator to take his audience as he finds them. The unfortunate result will be that anybody whose behaviour produces harassment, alarm or distress will be deemed to be acting in a disorderly manner however vulnerable the audience. The attempt to objectify the victim in this subsection will not serve to clarify the standard of behaviour that is sought. In ordinary conversation, disorderly implies unruliness, confusion or violating conventional notions of tranquility and that may extend to the offensive or the annoying, depending upon the circumstances. It is submitted that within the context of this public order statute in general and the other, strong, components of this subsection, disorderly behaviour should not go so far but should be interpreted to include only such activity as gives rise to an apprehension that violence, as defined in s.8, is a real possibility. That test would satisfy the mischief that the section was intended to meet, whilst avoiding unjustifiably officious intrusions by the criminal law.

"Harassment" suggests repeated behaviour which worries or pesters. "Alarm" suggests the sudden arousing of fear, of a sense of danger. "Distress" implies that grief, anxiety or suffering are being experienced. Clearly, the unconventional, the inconvenient and the exuberant may all arouse these states of feeling and to varying degrees. As a safeguard, the White Paper had included the condition "substantial" to qualify these consequences but that was dropped on presentation of the Bill, on the grounds that it would create unresolvable measurement difficulties; the Law Society had pointed to the vulnerability of witnesses to cross-examination on the point, for example: see Standing Committee, cols. 235, 247 and 294; *Hansard*, H.L. Vol. 478, col. 933. Instead, reliance was placed upon the hope and confidence that magistrates would not be concerned with "trifling" matters. Of all the criteria, distress is the most subjective and might include varying degrees of affront, upset or anger, and at incidents as diverse as swearing, silly walking, taking part in a student rag or carrying a controversial banner. Without some guidance from the courts, especially in respect of the level of disorderly behaviour required, the offence could develop excessive scope. *Cf.* Brownlie's comments upon s.5, Public Order Act 1936 at pp. 5–14.

"Within the hearing or sight of a person" was inserted, following discussion in Standing Committee, as a compromise between those who wished the offence to be directed at a particular victim, in order to secure evidence of a harm caused, and those, including the Government, who wanted an element of objectivity and were also doubtful of any victims' willingness to come to court as witnesses. The result is a condition by which it is unnecessary to produce any victim in court but evidence must be adduced as to the characteristics and circumstances of those who were around when the incident occurred. Nevertheless, it will, typically, be the police evidence of the incident which will be the primary basis for a prosecution and some concern at this was expressed during debate. The fact that the offence is described as "offensive conduct" in subs. (5) for the purposes of arrest will not allay fears that its scope may be broadened in practice. It will be noted that the relevant person does not have to actually experience harassment, alarm or distress; but likely does not mean liable.

Subs. (2)
  See the note to s.4(2).

Subs. (3)
  These defences, for which there are no counterparts in s.4, must be established by the accused on the balance of probabilities. The accused's beliefs about the relevant circumstances are to be measured by an objective standard of knowledge. The defence of reasonableness is unusual, given the nature of the conduct and consequences required for the offence. It would appear to facilitate argument about the appropriate social standards to be adopted by the court and, in particular, might include the conduct of a householder attempting to disperse noisy revellers or, as mentioned in Standing Committee, a fireman using strong language to clear people away from an incident!

Subss. (4), (5)
  The arrest power contained in this subsection provides much scope for heavy-handed policing and produced extensive debate in Parliament. The power is primarily envisaged as a preventive one and the possibility that it will be used without charges being pressed subsequently gave rise to some concern.
  In practical terms, the absence of any indication that time should be allowed to comply with a warning, combined with the possibility that different types of conduct may be involved, means that the safeguard represented by the warning will often be worthless. In any event, the conditional power of arrest in s.25, Police and Criminal Evidence Act 1984, will apply to this offence. This arrest power was included to close the possible and, arguably, remote gap that might exist if an arrest is sought in relation to a past offence under that latter section.
  As an additional safeguard, the Home Office will be issuing a circular to the police, explaining the operation of this power: *Hansard*, H.C. Vol. 96, col. 994. Perhaps it will also explain why the offence is described as "offensive conduct" in these subsections.

Mental element: miscellaneous

  6.—(1) A person is guilty of riot only if he intends to use violence or is aware that his conduct may be violent.

  (2) A person is guilty of violent disorder or affray only if he intends to use or threaten violence or is aware that his conduct may be violent or threaten violence.

  (3) A person is guilty of an offence under section 4 only if he intends his words or behaviour, or the writing, sign or other visible representation, to be threatening, abusive or insulting, or is aware that it may be threatening, abusive or insulting.

  (4) A person is guilty of an offence under section 5 only if he intends his words or behaviour, or the writing, sign or other visible representation, to be threatening, abusive or insulting, or is aware that it may be

threatening, abusive or insulting or (as the case may be) he intends his behaviour to be or is aware that it may be disorderly.

(5) For the purposes of this section a person whose awareness is impaired by intoxication shall be taken to be aware of that of which he would be aware if not intoxicated, unless he shows either that his intoxication was not self-induced or that it was caused solely by the taking or administration of a substance in the course of medical treatment.

(6) In subsection (5) "intoxication" means any intoxication, whether caused by drink, drugs or other means, or by a combination of means.

(7) Subsections (1) and (2) do not affect the determination for the purposes of riot or violent disorder of the number of persons who use or threaten violence.

GENERAL NOTE
This section adopts the approach taken by the Law Commission: see Final Report, paras. 3.41–54. It concedes that, in practice, the mental element may not be of great importance. Nevertheless, consistency and a desire to avoid unnecessary complexity led it to recommend a mental element based upon the common law of assault and battery and statutory offences against the person. In doing so, the Commission preferred the description of recklessness used in *R.* v. *Cunningham* [1957] 2 Q.B. 396 to that in *M.P.C.* v. *Caldwell* [1982] A.C. 341. The expression "aware that his conduct may be" represents this choice. "It emphasises that the prohibited conduct . . . does not here necessarily imply a particular result": para. 3.52; the risk must be actually foreseen by the accused.

Subs. (3)
This subsection reverses the position which existed under s.5, Public Order Act 1936. There, intention or awareness as to the threatening, abusive or insulting nature of the conduct was irrelevant: *Parkin* v. *Norman* [1983] Q.B. 92. The speaker had to take his audience as he found it: *Jordan* v. *Burgoyne* [1963] 2 Q.B. 744.

Subss.(5), (6)
These subsections follow the Law Commission's approach in seeking to clarify that the principle applied to self-induced intoxication in relation to recklessness applies equally to the new concept of awareness. In addition, the defence's burden of proof is clarified, as is the nature of intoxication. See Final Report, paras. 3.53–54.

Procedure: miscellaneous

7.—(1) No prosecution for an offence of riot or incitement to riot may be instituted except by or with the consent of the Director of Public Prosecutions.

(2) For the purposes of the rules against charging more than one offence in the same count or information, each of sections 1 to 5 creates one offence.

(3) If on the trial on indictment of a person charged with violent disorder or affray the jury find him not guilty of the offence charged, they may (without prejudice to section 6(3) of the Criminal Law Act 1967) find him guilty of an offence under section 4.

(4) The Crown Court has the same powers and duties in relation to a person who is by virtue of subsection (3) convicted before it of an offence under section 4 as a magistrates' court would have on convicting him of the offence.

Subs. (2)
The reference is to the Indictment Rules 1971, r.7, which facilitate the avoidance of charges in single counts or informations being held bad for duplicity.

Subss. (3), (4)
These subsections provide for greater flexibility in situations where the jurisdictions of the Crown and Magistrates' Courts would otherwise be exclusive. The alternative verdict

provision represents a simplification of the Law Commission's proposals for escalators of alternatives: Final Report, paras. 7.5ff.

By virtue of s.6(3), Criminal Law Act 1967, violent disorder may be an "essential ingredient" of riot and may provide an alternative verdict; specific provision is not required in subs. (3), therefore.

Interpretation

8. In this Part—

"dwelling" means any structure or part of a structure occupied as a person's home or as other living accommodation (whether the occupation is separate or shared with others) but does not include any part not so occupied, and for this purpose "structure" includes a tent, caravan, vehicle, vessel or other temporary or movable structure;

"violence" means any violent conduct, so that—

(*a*) except in the context of affray, it includes violent conduct towards property as well as violent conduct towards persons, and

(*b*) it is not restricted to conduct causing or intended to cause injury or damage but includes any other violent conduct (for example, throwing at or towards a person a missile of a kind capable of causing injury which does not hit or falls short).

GENERAL NOTE

"Violence" is defined in the same terms as the Law Commission's draft Clause 8(1), drawing upon its Final Report, paras. 5.30–33. Violence means the use of physical force causing injury or damage but it has broader connotations indicating actions done with great strength or intensity. The Law Commission considered that it should be made clear that violence can be directed to property as much as to persons, following *R.* v. *Howell* [1982] Q.B. 416, but that, in both cases, actual injury or damage need not occur. The emphasis, then, was on the nature of the conduct rather than its consequences.

The Law Commission envisaged that violence would, however, be such, "that it can be regarded as violence towards property and the jury must be sure that it was of such a nature": para. 5.33. The definition which it produced, and which is adopted in this section, does not clarify that position, however. "Any" violent conduct is the starting point and the Law Commission's objectives are inclusive features of it. Their examples, of wielding a lethal instrument or discharging a firearm in the direction of another, do not meet the objection that "violent conduct" could be interpreted to include relatively minor incidents, such as raising a fist or slapping a car roof on a picket line. Some attempts to tighten up the definition were made in Standing Committee but it was thought that some conduct might be lost and that the question of what was violent could be left to the jury: Standing Committee, col. 376. In practice, the inclusion of trivial conduct is unlikely to be significant for ss.1–3 because violent conduct always falls to be examined in the context of fear for personal safety, but it could add further scope to s.4. Any safeguard lies in the emphasis which should be given to the excessive force, the vehemence and the roughness, which characterises "violence" in its ordinary meaning.

Offences abolished

9.—(1) The common law offences of riot, rout, unlawful assembly and affray are abolished.

(2) The offences under the following enactments are abolished—

(*a*) section 1 of the Tumultuous Petitioning Act 1661 (presentation of petition to monarch or Parliament accompanied by excessive number of persons),

(*b*) section 1 of the Shipping Offences Act 1793 (interference with operation of vessel by persons riotously assembled),

(*c*) section 23 of the Seditious Meetings Act 1817 (prohibition of certain meetings within one mile of Westminster Hall when Parliament sitting), and (*d*) section 5 of the Public Order Act 1936 (conduct conducive to breach of the peace).

GENERAL NOTE

Subs. (2)(*b*), (*c*) and (*d*) apply in Scotland, by s.42(2).

Construction of other instruments

10.—(1) In the Riot (Damages) Act 1886 and in section 515 of the Merchant Shipping Act 1894 (compensation for riot damage) "riotous" and "riotously" shall be construed in accordance with section 1 above.

(2) In Schedule 1 to the Marine Insurance Act 1906 (form and rules for the construction of certain insurance policies) "rioters" in rule 8 and "riot" in rule 10 shall, in the application of the rules to any policy taking effect on or after the coming into force of this section, be construed in accordance with section 1 above unless a different intention appears.

(3) "Riot"and cognate expressions in any enactment in force before the coming into force of this section (other than the enactments mentioned in subsections (1) and (2) above) shall be construed in accordance with section 1 above if they would have been construed in accordance with the common law offence of riot apart from this Part.

(4) Subject to subsections (1) to (3) above and unless a different intention appears, nothing in this Part affects the meaning of "riot" or any cognate expression in any enactment in force, or other instrument taking effect, before the coming into force of this section.

GENERAL NOTE

A change in the definition of riot is unlikely to affect claims for compensation brought under the Riot (Damages) Act 1886. There, eligibility applies where persons are riotously and "tumultuously" assembled and that has been held to signify an assembly of considerable size: *Dwyer* v. *Metropolitan Police Commissioner* [1967] 2 Q.B. 970.

The effect of the change might be to broaden the scope of some insurance policies but the insurance market is not precluded from substituting violent disorder for riot where relevant, and assuming that the market would bear such exclusions.

PART II

PROCESSIONS AND ASSEMBLIES

GENERAL NOTE

In this part, a lengthy debate about the regulation of free assembly has come to some fruition. The impetus for reform developed after 1979, when a change of administration occurred, and a new will to tackle perceived inadequacies of existing provisions for maintaining public order was manifested. In particular, disturbances at Grunwick in 1976–77, at Lewisham and Ladywood in 1977, and at Leicester and Southall in 1979 were all mentioned as being of some significance in the Green Paper of 1980. By the time the White Paper was published in 1985, the Select Committee on Home Affairs had added its weight to the calls for overhaul, Lord Scarman had reported upon the Brixton riots of 1981 and the miners' strike of 1985 had precipitated an unprecedented change in police tactics and organisation for dealing with intense and sustained picketing. Other activities mentioned in the White Paper included those of animal rights protestors, the National Front, and members of the anti-nuclear movement: paras. 1.3–1.6.

In general, however, the main issues which fell to be discussed in the White Paper remained the same as those first mooted in the Green Paper or the almost contemporaneous report of the Select Committee. Apart from the undesirability of increased public disorder, the questions centred round the strain upon police resources, the cost of policing, and upheaval caused to the community by public demonstrations and protests. Although public order was the primary concern, and the Green Paper had established the principle that; "The freedom to demonstrate peacefully under the law is, in a democracy, essential to the health of the community as a whole," in the Preface, it emerged that other concerns about cost and inconvenience were also important, although often presented as elements of the case in favour of further and earlier preventive measures to forestall actual outbreaks of disorder during processions and assemblies.

Formerly, processions were regulated by s.3, Public Order Act 1936. Since they are prima facie lawful uses of the highway, that section facilitated some control of their incidence and organisation, the test being the likelihood that serious public disorder would be occasioned. No such preventive powers existed in relation to stationary meetings. For both processions and meetings, of course, other provisions under statute and at common law could be used to penalise actual outbreaks of violence or to prevent them from immediately occurring; for example, those relating to obstruction of the highway or breach of the peace. Neither of these is affected by this Act; on the latter, see s.40(4).

Discussing the provisions of s.3, Public Order Act 1936, the Green Paper raised a number of possibilities for reform. The serious public disorder test was thought to continue to be the proper criterion for banning processions and the White Paper confirmed that; but it created possibly too high a hurdle for justifying the imposition of conditions. There, the removal of the "serious" requirement and the addition of the effect of the procession on the policing of the area as a whole appeared to be the favoured option; the White Paper did not entertain it, however. Other criteria which were mooted were: the nature of the participating organisations; the objects of the procession, for example, political; and the offensiveness of the message conveyed. These were rejected on the grounds that they would involve invidious or controversial choices which would reflect badly upon the police. A test of disruption was rejected as being too imprecise but it reappeared in strengthened form in the White Paper! The power to ban particular marches, rather than a class of them, was favoured, as was a power for the senior police officer on the spot to re-route; the White Paper agreed. Greater powers of arrest associated with control were considered desirable as was advance notice of processions; again, the White Paper agreed. The idea that demonstrators should bear the cost of policing their marches, however, was thought to be unfair on the peaceful organiser and inconsistent with the general principle that taxation finances law enforcement and, indirectly, freedom. On the question of controlling static meetings, the Government was open-minded but it was favourably disposed by the time of the White Paper.

This part substantially reflects the White Paper's proposals. The emphasis is upon improved preventive measures which are capable of being enforced by the police. Inevitably, they will have an effect on free assembly well in advance of behaviour at the criminal threshold. It will be more difficult to demonstrate: the lawfulness of protest activity will be more difficult to predict; greater dependence will be placed upon police discretion; and in general the official control of public behaviour will be more pervasive. The implications for free speech are not so easy to identify, however. The value of the demonstration as a means of persuasion is not absolute. In many cases, arguments are furthered by the discussion of the relevant issues which may follow media coverage of the event. Often, displays of solidarity and commitment are guided towards gaining the media's attention rather than seeking to influence directly the object of their discontent. Nevertheless, this is not always so, and there will continue to be an important role for the spontaneous outcry or the well-focussed petition or vigil. Furthermore, it is not a matter of indifference that news values require some interest to be taken in mass activities. The balance seems to have shifted now, however, in favour of those who prefer not only public order but also tranquility: see the Green Paper, para. 13 and the White Paper, para. 1.7.

Advance notice of public processions

11.—(1) Written notice shall be given in accordance with this section of any proposal to hold a public procession intended—

    (*a*) to demonstrate support for or opposition to the views or actions of any person or body of persons,

    (*b*) to publicise a cause or campaign, or

    (*c*) to mark or commemorate an event,

unless it is not reasonably practicable to give any advance notice of the procession.

(2) Subsection (1) does not apply where the procession is one commonly or customarily held in the police area (or areas) in which it is proposed to be held or is a funeral procession organised by a funeral director acting in the normal course of his business.

(3) The notice must specify the date when it is intended to hold the procession, the time when it is intended to start it, its proposed route, and the name and address of the person (or of one of the persons) proposing to organise it.

(4) Notice must be delivered to a police station—

(a) in the police area in which it is proposed the procession will start, or

(b) where it is proposed the procession will start in Scotland and cross into England, in the first police area in England on the proposed route.

(5) If delivered not less than 6 clear days before the date when the procession is intended to be held, the notice may be delivered by post by the recorded delivery service; but section 7 of the Interpretation Act 1978 (under which a document sent by post is deemed to have been served when posted and to have been delivered in the ordinary course of post) does not apply.

(6) If not delivered in accordance with subsection (5), the notice must be delivered by hand not less than 6 clear days before the date when the procession is intended to be held or, if that is not reasonably practicable, as soon as delivery is reasonably practicable.

(7) Where a public procession is held, each of the persons organising it is guilty of an offence if—

(a) the requirements of this section as to notice have not been satisfied, or

(b) the date when it is held, the time when it starts, or its route, differs from the date, time or route specified in the notice.

(8) It is a defence for the accused to prove that he did not know of, and neither suspected nor had reason to suspect, the failure to satisfy the requirements or (as the case may be) the difference of date, time or route.

(9) To the extent that an alleged offence turns on a difference of date, time or route, it is a defence for the accused to prove that the difference arose from circumstances beyond his control or from something done with the agreement of a police officer or by his direction.

(10) A person guilty of an offence under subsection (7) is liable on summary conviction to a fine not exceeding level 3 on the standard scale.

DEFINITION
"public processions": s.16.

GENERAL NOTE
The White Paper presented the case for advance notice of processions in the terms mentioned by the Select Committee at para. 35: negotiation between police and organisers is stimulated; the organiser's responsibility is underlined; additional pressure and expense to discover information about processions is avoided: White Paper, para. 4.2

The Select Committee recommended a notice period of 72 hours as a minimum and that was reflected in some local legislation passed around 1980, but now repealed by s.40(3) and Sch. 3. This section incorporates a longer period which was considered to be administratively more convenient. As many as 92 local authority areas in England and Wales have had local requirements for advance notice, although most will lapse under the timetable established under the Local Government Act 1972. The Government suggested that this section will make little practical difference to the planning of processions, since the police experience is that most organisers consult with them in any event. Only one prosecution has been mounted under previous advance notice provisions: against a National Front march in 1982 in the West Midlands.

The section does not require organisers to seek permission to march from the police. Notice of intention to march may lead the police to impose conditions under s.12, however, not necessarily because public disorder is anticipated but for operational convenience.

Subs. (1)
Written notice, in a form specified in subs.(3), is required. Oral, including telephoned, notice was considered to be administratively unworkable; some record of the details of the

procession is needed to make them foolproof and verifiable: Standing Committee, col. 416. Failure to provide notice will render the organiser liable under subs.(7).

A "public procession" is a procession in a public place, by s.16 which also defines "public place." "Procession" is not defined but in *Flockart* v. *Robinson* [1950] 2 K.B. 498, a case under s.3, Public Order Act 1936, Lord Goddard said at p. 502: "A procession is not a mere body of persons: it is a body of persons moving along a route. Therefore the person who organises the route is the person who organises the procession."

The purposes mentioned are intended to exclude trivial or uncontroversial processions such as school crocodiles or a group of tourists following a guide. Yet a wedding procession appears to be included in para. (*c*), as does a pre-arranged, celebratory pub crawl. Sponsored walks will be caught by para. (*b*), as will a group of ramblers setting out to reclaim a right of way. In these situations, only the common sense of the police will prevent absurdity.

"Unless not reasonably practicable to give any advance notice" is intended to allow spontaneous events to escape the requirement of advance notice. The phrase is ambiguous, however. "Any" might refer to unwritten notice, so as to imply that if a telephone call could have been made then written notice should have been given. That interpretation would be oppressive and almost absurd, however, and the better view must be to treat "any" as qualifying "written notice" in the opening words of the subsection. There is no requirement to delay a spontaneous procession in order to give notice. Reasonable practicability will be judged according to the availability of writing materials and the distance to the nearest police station. Yet, despite the Government's dismissal of Opposition fears, in Standing Committee at col. 480, the position in respect of delay is not clear. Some balance between the urgency of the protest and the possibility of notifying the police may be involved in deciding what is "reasonable," but the requirement of practicability suggests that the actual feelings of those involved in the procession rather than some objective inhibition upon their expression should be the dominant consideration.

Subs. (2)

It is not clear for how many times a procession must be held before it becomes common or customary. Armistice Day parades, the Lord Mayor of London's parade, and other traditional carnivals appear to be included. Much may depend upon whether the police may be expected to anticipate them and plan for them, although that would not be a satisfactory basis for grounding criminal liability.

Subss. (4)–(6)

"Police area" is defined in s.62, Police Act 1964. Until a late amendment in the House of Lords, notice had to be delivered in every police area through which the procession passed. If it cannot be expected that postal notice will arrive at the relevant police station not less than six clear days before the date of the procession, hand delivery is required. The effect is to place the onus upon the organiser to check whether postal notice has arrived and to be prepared to deliver by hand. A defence is open to the organiser under the first limb of subs.(8), but it will only assist him for as long as he labours under the misapprehension built into subs.(5) that the recorded delivery service guarantees a minimum delivery time; in fact, it only guarantees that a record of delivery will be made, as and when, if ever, delivery occurs.

Subss. (7)–(9)

The organiser must give notice in which he elects to specify the occasion of the procession, and he must then ensure that he can meet his representations as to date, time and route precisely, in order to avoid liability. The defences, involving an objective state of knowledge, must be established on the balance of probabilities; they enable an organiser to escape liability for the effects of post office inefficiency, an inability to exert authority over the procession, or new arrangements acceptable to the police, or to possibly escape the burden imposed by another organiser's representations. Apart from these defences, the offence could operate fairly rigidly and whether or not trivial deviations might be caught will depend upon the good will of the police.

The offence may attract a conditional power of arrest under s.25, Police and Criminal Evidence Act 1984. The standard scale is defined in s.75, Criminal Justice Act 1982.

Imposing conditions on public processions

12.—(1) If the senior police officer, having regard to the time or place at which and the circumstances in which any public procession is being held or is intended to be held and to its route or proposed route, reasonably believes that—

> (*a*) it may result in serious public disorder, serious damage to property or serious disruption to the life of the community, or
>
> (*b*) the purpose of the persons organising it is the intimidation of others with a view to compelling them not to do an act they have a right to do, or to do an act they have a right not to do,

he may give directions imposing on the persons organising or taking part in the procession such conditions as appear to him necessary to prevent such disorder, damage, disruption or intimidation, including conditions as to the route of the procession or prohibiting it from entering any public place specified in the directions.

(2) In subsection (1) "the senior police officer" means—

> (*a*) in relation to a procession being held, or to a procession intended to be held in a case where persons are assembling with a view to taking part in it, the most senior in rank of the police officers present at the scene, and
>
> (*b*) in relation to a procession intended to be held in a case where paragraph (*a*) does not apply, the chief officer of police.

(3) A direction given by a chief officer of police by virtue of subsection (2)(*b*) shall be given in writing.

(4) A person who organises a public procession and knowingly fails to comply with a condition imposed under this section is guilty of an offence, but it is a defence for him to prove that the failure arose from circumstances beyond his control.

(5) A person who takes part in a public procession and knowingly fails to comply with a condition imposed under this section is guilty of an offence, but it is a defence for him to prove that the failure arose from circumstances beyond his control.

(6) A person who incites another to commit an offence under subsection (5) is guilty of an offence.

(7) A constable in uniform may arrest without warrant anyone he reasonably suspects is committing an offence under subsection (4), (5) or (6).

(8) A person guilty of an offence under subsection (4) is liable on summary conviction to imprisonment for a term not exceeding 3 months or a fine not exceeding level 4 on the standard scale or both.

(9) A person guilty of an offence under subsection (5) is liable on summary conviction to a fine not exceeding level 3 on the standard scale.

(10) A person guilty of an offence under subsection (6) is liable on summary conviction to imprisonment for a term not exceeding 3 months or a fine not exceeding level 4 on the standard scale or both, notwithstanding section 45(3) of the Magistrates' Courts Act 1980 (inciter liable to same penalty as incited).

(11) In Scotland this section applies only in relation to a procession being held, and to a procession intended to be held in a case where persons are assembling with a view to taking part in it.

DEFINITION
  "public processions": s.16.

GENERAL NOTE
  This section replaces s.3(1), Public Order Act 1936, which is repealed by s.40(3) and Sch. 3. It builds upon the reports of Lord Scarman on the Red Lion Square disorders and that of the Select Committee. An increased number of criteria for imposing conditions are now available, in terms similar to the former subsection, and including the test of serious public disorder. They are serious damage to property, serious disruption to the life of the community, and intimidation. The requirement that a risk of breach of the peace should exist before flags, banners or emblems should be restricted is omitted. The description of

the range of conditions remains the same, however, although the police are given greater flexibility in imposing them. This section applies to Scotland by s.42(2).

Subs. (1)

The senior police officer is defined in subs.(2). Where a procession exists or is taking place, the senior officer on the spot is responsible for imposing conditions. There will not usually be any incentive for chief officers to postpone decisions in order to surprise organisers, although that will be possible, because the normal practice is for arrangements to be discussed well in advance. The senior officer could be of quite subordinate rank but that is unlikely because the police will generally make contingency arrangements and an inspector or above can be expected to be present: see Standing Committee, col. 543ff.

Conditions can be imposed either before or during processions. This was true of s.3(1), Public Order Act 1936 but *cf. Brownlie*, p.54. The conditions can be quite wide-ranging since their scope is defined by very broad purposes. An outright ban would be inconsistent with s.13 but the result of conditions directed to the time, route and even date might be that a procession would be so marginalised as to be effectively neutralised. A procession postponed, broken into small groups, required to take a scenic route through the suburbs, and prohibited from displaying banners may not amount to much of a protest. The justifications for the conditions might well not be apparent to the organisers or participants since the circumstances which the police can take into account appear to be unlimited.

The safeguard against oppressive use of conditions lies in the requirement that they be reasonable. Both the necessity for imposing them and their contents will be subject to judicial review on the basis of the principle in *Associated Picture Houses* v. *Wednesbury Corporation* [1948] 1 K.B. 223. For an example in the context of policing, see *Holgate-Mohammed* v. *Duke* [1984] A.C. 437. In practical terms, however, contemporaneous conditions are unlikely to be scrutinised, if at all, before the point of the procession will have been lost. In any event, the merits of the case are not reviewable.

"Serious" public disorder or damage to property is not defined. It can refer to both the scope and intensity of law-breaking. In theory, it should be specified independently of the effect upon police resources but, in practice, that is likely to be an important consideration for the relevant officer, together with his experience of previous disorder; and the courts will be reluctant to interfere.

"Serious disruption to the life of the community" is a criterion fraught with difficulties. What is the life of the community? What disrupts it, and seriously? In practice, it appears to involve matters such as traffic congestion or blocking shopping streets; during debate, Lord Denning reported that a procession had once caused him to miss a train. Essentially, however, the phrase reflects a view that everyday, commercial considerations are more valuable than democratic aims and practices. Lord Scarman argued that the expression should be measured by reference to the normal life of a democratic community (*Hansard*, H.L. Vol. 476, col. 541), but that would entail a degree of protection to free assembly which neither Parliament nor the courts have been prepared to offer in the past.

"Intimidation" is not defined but the courts have been disposed to give it a very broad meaning in recent cases involving picketing; it encompasses both weight of numbers or even glowering: see *Thomas* v. *National Union of Mineworkers* [1986] 1 Ch. 20. A similar approach may be anticipated here, since this provision was made with picketing in mind.

Subss. (4)–(6)

These offences reflect the former provisions of s.3(4), Public Order Act 1936. Certain defences are established, however, and mere participants are subject to a lesser penalty than organisers or inciters. The offences depend, in effect, upon knowledge of the relevant condition but the burden of proof is reversed.

Subs. (7)

This power is new. The power under s.25, Police and Criminal Evidence Act 1984 will also apply.

Subss. (8)–(10)

The standard scale is defined in s.75, Criminal Justice Act 1982.

Prohibiting public processions

13.—(1) If at any time the chief officer of police reasonably believes that, because of particular circumstances existing in any district or part of a district, the powers under section 12 will not be sufficient to prevent the holding of public processions in that district or part from resulting in serious public disorder, he shall apply to the council of the district for an order prohibiting for such period not exceeding 3 months as may be specified in the application the holding of all public processions (or of any class of public procession so specified) in the district or part concerned.

(2) On receiving such an application, a council may with the consent of the Secretary of State make an order either in the terms of the application or with such modifications as may be approved by the Secretary of State.

(3) Subsection (1) does not apply in the City of London or the metropolitan police district.

(4) If at any time the Commissioner of Police for the City of London or the Commissioner of Police of the Metropolis reasonably believes that, because of particular circumstances existing in his police area or part of it, the powers under section 12 will not be sufficient to prevent the holding of public processions in that area or part from resulting in serious public disorder, he may with the consent of the Secretary of State make an order prohibiting for such period not exceeding 3 months as may be specified in the order the holding of all public processions (or of any class of public procession so specified) in the area or part concerned.

(5) An order made under this section may be revoked or varied by a subsequent order made in the same way, that is, in accordance with subsections (1) and (2) or subsection (4), as the case may be.

(6) Any order under this section shall, if not made in writing, be recorded in writing as soon as practicable after being made.

(7) A person who organises a public procession the holding of which he knows is prohibited by virtue of an order under this section is guilty of an offence.

(8) A person who takes part in a public procession the holding of which he knows is prohibited by virtue of an order under this section is guilty of an offence.

(9) A person who incites another to commit an offence under subsection (8) is guilty of an offence.

(10) A constable in uniform may arrest without warrant anyone he reasonably suspects is committing an offence under subsection (7), (8) or (9).

(11) A person guilty of an offence under subsection (7) is liable on summary conviction to imprisonment for a term not exceeding 3 months or a fine not exceeding level 4 on the standard scale or both.

(12) A person guilty of an offence under subsection (8) is liable on summary conviction to a fine not exceeding level 3 on the standard scale.

(13) A person guilty of an offence under subsection (9) is liable on summary conviction to imprisonment for a term not exceeding 3 months or a fine not exceeding level 4 on the standard scale or both, notwithstanding section 45(3) of the Magistrates' Courts Act 1980.

DEFINITIONS
   "the City of London": s.16.
   "the metropolitan police district": s.16.
   "public procession": s.16.

GENERAL NOTE
   This section reflects s.3(2) and (3), Public Order Act 1936 which is repealed by s.40(3) and Sch. 3. The White Paper proposed a power to ban just one procession but the Government was persuaded that this would place a difficult burden upon the police in tackling evasionary tactics, such as changing the name of the event or group, and in rendering them open to charges of political bias. This section retains, then, the problems associated with the old law. A ban reaches far beyond the behaviour which might justify its imposition in the first place, both in terms of the period of time involved and the number of

groups which might otherwise want to process. As the White Paper conceded, the threat of only one counter-demonstration can result in a procession's being stopped.

It should be noted that a ban can only be justified on the grounds of serious public disorder, not the broader criteria which apply to the imposing of conditions in s.12. Judicial review is available, as formerly, with "reasonably" being included only to confirm that, but it does not extend to the merits of the council's or Commissioner's decision: see *Kent* v. *M.P.C.* (1981) *The Times*, May 15, 1986 and the note to s.12(1). As under the previous law, too, provision for revocation is made in subs. (5). It was pointed out in Standing Committee that the Home Secretary does not normally use the full three months available when confirming a ban; the period will be as short as possible: col. 630.

The offence of participation is new. For all offences, knowledge of the ban is required. Assisting an organiser is no longer an offence, however. Other new features are the provision for records in subs.(6) and the power of arrest, albeit by a constable in uniform, in subs.(10). The standard scale is defined in s.75, Criminal Justice Act 1982.

Imposing conditions on public assemblies

14.—(1) If the senior police officer, having regard to the time or place at which and the circumstances in which any public assembly is being held or is intended to be held, reasonably believes that—

(*a*) it may result in serious public disorder, serious damage to property or serious disruption to the life of the community, or

(*b*) the purpose of the persons organising it is the intimidation of others with a view to compelling them not to do an act they have a right to do, or to do an act they have a right not to do,

he may give directions imposing on the persons organising or taking part in the assembly such conditions as to the place at which the assembly may be (or continue to be) held, its maximum duration, or the maximum number of persons who may constitute it, as appear to him necessary to prevent such disorder, damage, disruption or intimidation.

(2) In subsection (1) "the senior police officer" means—

(*a*) in relation to an assembly being held, the most senior in rank of the police officers present at the scene, and

(*b*) in relation to an assembly intended to be held, the chief officer of police.

(3) A direction given by a chief officer of police by virtue of subsection (2)(*b*) shall be given in writing.

(4) A person who organises a public assembly and knowingly fails to comply with a condition imposed under this section is guilty of an offence, but it is a defence for him to prove that the failure arose from circumstances beyond his control.

(5) A person who takes part in a public assembly and knowingly fails to comply with a condition imposed under this section is guilty of an offence, but it is a defence for him to prove that the failure arose from circumstances beyond his control.

(6) A person who incites another to commit an offence under subsection (5) is guilty of an offence.

(7) A constable in uniform may arrest without warrant anyone he reasonably suspects is committing an offence under subsection (4), (5) or (6).

(8) A person guilty of an offence under subsection (4) is liable on summary conviction to imprisonment for a term not exceeding 3 months or a fine not exceeding level 4 on the standard scale or both.

(9) A person guilty of an offence under subsection (5) is liable on summary conviction to a fine not exceeding level 3 on the standard scale.

(10) A person guilty of an offence under subsection (6) is liable on summary conviction to imprisonment for a term not exceeding 3 months or a fine not exceeding level 4 on the standard scale or both, notwithstanding section 45(3) of the Magistrates' Courts Act 1980.

DEFINITION
"public assembly": s.16.

GENERAL NOTE
This section draws upon the provisions of s.12 and allows conditions to be imposed on almost exactly the same terms as in relation to processions. See generally, therefore, the notes to s.12.

Some differences do exist, however. The conditions mentioned in subs. (1) are limited to restricting the place, the duration and the number of participants. The date or time of an assembly cannot be altered by the police, therefore. It will be possible to reduce the impact of a gathering however, by allowing only a small group to meet for a very short time at a remote venue. Although not allowed, a ban could effectively occur. Again, judicial review can provide a remedy in theory: see the note to s.12(1).

Following discussion in Parliament, the definition of public assembly was altered to mean, eventually, one of 20 or more persons. The venue must be wholly or partly open to the air; sports stadiums or parks are envisaged. Thus, meetings in halls, conference rooms or churches are excluded. So, too, are small groups engaged in, for example, vigils or pickets. Larger outdoor prayer meetings are unlikely to involve serious disorder, damage or disruption, but rival groups could cause conditions to be imposed. The general powers available for maintaining the peace will continue to apply: see s.40(4).

In connection with the power of arrest in subs. (7), note that Sch. 2, para. 1, creates a similar power in respect of intimidation under s.7, Conspiracy and Protection of Property Act 1875.

This section applies to Scotland, by s.42(2).

Delegation

15.—(1) The chief officer of police may delegate, to such extent and subject to such conditions as he may specify, any of his functions under sections 12 to 14 to a deputy or assistant chief constable; and references in those sections to the person delegating shall be construed accordingly.

(2) Subsection (1) shall have effect in the City of London and the metropolitan police district as if "a deputy or assistant chief constable" read "an assistant commissioner of police".

DEFINITIONS
"the City of London": s.16.
"the metropolitan police district": s.16.

GENERAL NOTE
This section applies to Scotland, by s.42(2).

Interpretation

16. In this Part—
  "the City of London" means the City as defined for the purposes of the Acts relating to the City of London police;
  "the metropolitan police district" means that district as defined in section 76 of the London Government Act 1963;
  "public assembly" means an assembly of 20 more persons in a public place which is wholly or partly open to the air;
  "public place" means—
          (a) any highway, or in Scotland any road within the meaning of the Roads (Scotland) Act 1984, and
          (b) any place to which at the material time the public or any section of the public has access, on payment or otherwise, as of right or by virtue of express or implied permission;
  "public procession" means a procession in a public place.

GENERAL NOTE

The definition of "public place" confirms that the relevant time is the occasion of the procession or assembly. Tortious occupation of property is outside the scope of this Part. This section applies to Scotland, by s.42(2).

PART III

RACIAL HATRED

GENERAL NOTE

In this part, all the former offences relating to racial hatred have been brought together and rationalised to incorporate improved and common features in conjunction with a number of new offences. This followed some extremely cooperative debate in Parliament during which many constructive criticisms from the Opposition were acted upon by the Government.

The principal provision in the old law was s.5A, Public Order Act 1936. An offence would be committed if threatening, abusive or insulting words or written matter were used, published or distributed in a case where, in all the circumstances, hatred was likely to be stirred up against a racial group in Great Britain. This offence has been extended in ss.18 and 19 to include behaviour and the display of written material; it applies to private as well as public places and includes the private circulation of material; and it now applies to such conduct where the intention is to stir up racial hatred. In addition, a new offence of possessing racially inflammatory material has been created with related powers of entry, search and forfeiture in ss.23–25. By s.5, Theatres Act 1968, the presenter or director of a play which involved the use of threatening, abusive or insulting words would be guilty of an offence if he intended to stir up racial hatred and that was a likely consequence. This is now incorporated into s.20 which includes, however, the strict liability element as an alternative basis for conduct. In addition, s.20 contains the extensions mentioned above, together with provisions modelled upon s.27, Cable and Broadcasting Act 1984. That offence is also modified to create consistency and is brought into this Act as s.22. For completeness, a new offence of distributing, playing or showing a recording is created in s.21.

These reforms are a response to continued criticism that racial harmony remains as elusive as ever and that racial discrimination is being actively fostered by individuals and political groups who appear to be untouched by any attempts by the law to suppress their activities. For examples of the latter, see Standing Committee, pp. 880–4. For a critical review, see P. Gordon, *Incitement to Racial Hatred* (1982) Runnymede Trust. Part of the problem has been that a narrow scope was selected as suitable for legal intervention because of concern about interference with free speech. In addition, there have been difficulties in proving offences, either because evidence has been hard to find or because courts have been reluctant or unwilling to convict.

The measures contained in this Part do have greater potential for success than the offences which they replace. The ambit of behaviour is wider; intentional conduct, regardless of the result, is punishable; racialist propaganda will be subject to control. Nevertheless, obstacles remain. The use of threatening, abusive or insulting conduct remains as the criminal threshold and will not extend to "less blatantly bigoted . . . more apparently rational and moderate" messages (former Government's White Paper prior to the Race Relations Act 1976: Cmnd. 6234, para. 126). The object of the conduct still must be to stir up racial "hatred," a strong expression which may be difficult to establish. An attempt to couch the offence in terms of intimidation was rejected in debate: Standing Committee, col. 835ff. Furthermore, the action or consent of the Attorney-General is still required in order to mount a prosecution. On the other hand, these obstacles represent sensitivity to the dangers of encroaching upon free expression however unacceptable the content. "It is arguable that false and evil publications of this kind may well be more effectively defeated by public education and debate than by prosecution and that in practice the criminal law would be ineffective to deal with such material": *ibid.* Yet it may be that such arguments are most persuasive only when new moral orthodoxies are in the process of being created; such inhibitions have not noticeably influenced the prohibition of obscenity, blasphemy or defamation, for example. Possibly, Part III marks another stage in establishing such consensus against discriminating attitudes, although its effectiveness will remain open to doubt.

For the restriction on prosecutions without the Attorney-General's permission, and for sentences, see s.27.

By s.42(2), this section applies to Scotland.

Meaning of "racial hatred"

Meaning of "racial hatred"

17. In this Part "racial hatred" means hatred against a group of persons in Great Britain defined by reference to colour, race, nationality (including citizenship) or ethnic or national origins.

GENERAL NOTE

By s.29, racial hatred in Part III has the meaning given in this section. It is based upon the definition of racial group in s.3, Race Relations Act 1976. That definition has been discussed in *Mandla* v. *Lee* [1983] 2 A.C. 548. The House of Lords explained the nature of ethnic origins in terms of a group's regarding itself and being regarded by others as a distinct community by virtue of certain characteristics such as: a long shared history, a cultural tradition of its own, a common ancestry, a common language and literature, a common religion, and being a minority. On that basis, Sikhs were held to be racial group by reference to ethnic origins. On the same basis, Jews and Romany gypsies can be defined as such. The Attorney-General indicated that he will consider prosecutions for offences under Part III against such gypsies in exactly the same way as in respect of other ethnic groups: *Hansard*, H.C., Vol. 481, col. 463.

"Hatred" is not defined but connotes intense dislike, animosity or enmity. It implies sufficient dislike to be manifested in active demonstration of ill-will. Such hatred must be manifested against a group living in Great Britain but it can be the result of threatening, abusive or insulting conduct directed at persons outside Great Britain.

Acts intended or likely to stir up racial hatred

Use of words or behaviour or display of written material

18.—(1) A person who uses threatening, abusive or insulting words or behaviour, or displays any written material which is threatening, abusive or insulting, is guilty of an offence if—

(a) he intends thereby to stir up racial hatred, or

(b) having regard to all the circumstances racial hatred is likely to be stirred up thereby.

(2) An offence under this section may be committed in a public or a private place, except that no offence is committed where the words or behaviour are used, or the written material is displayed, by a person inside a dwelling and are not heard or seen except by other persons in that or another dwelling.

(3) A constable may arrest without warrant anyone he reasonably suspects is committing an offence under this section.

(4) In proceedings for an offence under this section it is a defence for the accused to prove that he was inside a dwelling and had no reason to believe that the words or behaviour used, or the written material displayed, would be heard or seen by a person outside that or any other dwelling.

(5) A person who is not shown to have intended to stir up racial hatred is not guilty of an offence under this section if he did not intend his words or behaviour, or the written material, to be, and was not aware that it might be, threatening, abusive or insulting.

(6) This section does not apply to words or behaviour used, or written material displayed, solely for the purpose of being included in a programme broadcast or included in a cable programme service.

DEFINITIONS

"cable programme service": s.2, Cable and Broadcasting Act 1984, by s.29.
"dwelling": s.29.

"programme": s.29.
"racial hatred": s.17, by s.29.
"written material": s.29.

GENERAL NOTE

This section replaces part of s.5A, Public Order Act 1936 which is repealed by s.40(3) and Sch. 3.

Subs. (1)

On the use of threatening, abusive or insulting words, behaviour or displays, see the note to s.4(1). The old s.5A(1)(*b*) did not include displays.

The intentional limb in para. (*a*) is new. The intention is to be assessed regardless of the actual consequence of the prohibited conduct; under s.6, Race Relations Act 1965, and also s.5, Theatres Act 1968, liability depended upon the intention's being coupled with a likelihood that racial hatred would be stirred. Intention will be proved on the basis of inferences drawn from conduct and the surrounding circumstances. For the purposes of para. (*a*), s.18 creates a strict liability offence: see subs. (5).

Subs. (2)

See the note to s.4(2).

Subs. (4)

This is similar to s.5(3)(*b*).

Subs. (5)

The effect of this statement of the required mental element is that a person who intends to stir up racial hatred must take responsibility for conduct which turns out to be threatening, abusive or insulting, whether or not it was intended to be so. In cases where racial hatred is a natural and probable result of the conduct, the mental element of intention or awareness is required. See the General Note to s.6 and the note to s.6(3).

Subs. (6)

For conduct solely related to inclusion in a programme, see s.22. Conduct which is not so included, for example, taking place in a studio, will be covered by this section.

Publishing or distributing written material

19.—(1) A person who publishes or distributes written material which is threatening, abusive or insulting is guilty of an offence if—

(*a*) he intends thereby to stir up racial hatred, or

(*b*) having regard to all the circumstances racial hatred is likely to be stirred up thereby.

(2) In proceedings for an offence under this section it is a defence for an accused who is not shown to have intended to stir up racial hatred to prove that he was not aware of the content of the material and did not suspect, and had no reason to suspect, that it was threatening, abusive or insulting.

(3) References in this Part to the publication or distribution of written material are to its publication or distribution to the public or a section of the public.

DEFINITIONS

"racial hatred": s.17, by s.29.
"written material": s.29.

GENERAL NOTE

This section replaces part of s.5A, Public Order Act 1936 which is repealed by s.40(3) and Sch. 3. Graffiti, including swastikas, is included. Written material, as defined in s.29 was originally envisaged as covering video and film but s.21 was introduced to put the matter beyond doubt.

Subs. (1)
See the note to s.18(1).

Subs. (2)
In relation to the publication and distribution, the offence is strict liability; *cf.* note to s.18(5). In the case of unintended stirring of racial hatred, lack of awareness as to the content of the material must be proved on the balance of probabilities in order to establish a defence; but there is a further objective requirement as to the state of knowledge which is acceptable. Writing such material is not, in itself, an offence.

Subs. (3)
The notion of publishing itself connotes making available to the public. By s.5A(6), Public Order Act 1936, members of an association, of which the person publishing or distributing was a member, were excluded. The absence of such an exemption here is a significant change. Delivery of material to particular individuals will continue to fall outside the ambit of the offence, however: see *R.* v. *Britton* [1967] 2 Q.B. 51.

Public performance of play

20.—(1) If a public performance of a play is given which involves the use of threatening, abusive or insulting words or behaviour, any person who presents or directs the performance is guilty of an offence if—
   (*a*) he intends thereby to stir up racial hatred, or
   (*b*) having regard to all the circumstances (and, in particular, taking the performance as a whole) racial hatred is likely to be stirred up thereby.
   (2) If a person presenting or directing the performance is not shown to have intended to stir up racial hatred, it is a defence for him to prove—
   (*a*) that he did not know and had no reason to suspect that the performance would involve the use of the offending words or behaviour, or
   (*b*) that he did not know and had no reason to suspect that the offending words or behaviour were threatening, abusive or insulting, or
   (*c*) that he did not know and had no reason to suspect that the circumstances in which the performance would be given would be such that racial hatred would be likely to be stirred up.
   (3) This section does not apply to a performance given solely or primarily for one or more of the following purposes—
   (*a*) rehearsal,
   (*b*) making a recording of the performance, or
   (*c*) enabling the performance to be broadcast or included in a cable programme service;
but if it is proved that the performance was attended by persons other than those directly connected with the giving of the performance or the doing in relation to it of the things mentioned in paragraph (*b*) or (*c*), the performance shall, unless the contrary is shown, be taken not to have been given solely or primarily for the purposes mentioned above.
   (4) For the purposes of this section—
   (*a*) a person shall not be treated as presenting a performance of a play by reason only of his taking part in it as a performer,
   (*b*) a person taking part as a performer in a performance directed by another shall be treated as a person who directed the performance if without reasonable excuse he performs otherwise than in accordance with that person's direction, and
   (*c*) a person shall be taken to have directed a performance of a play given under his direction notwithstanding that he was not present during the performance;

and a person shall not be treated as aiding or abetting the commission of an offence under this section by reason only of his taking part in a performance as a performer.

(5) In this section "play" and "public performance" have the same meaning as in the Theatres Act 1968.

(6) The following provisions of the Theatres Act 1968 apply in relation to an offence under this section as they apply to an offence under section 2 of that Act—

section 9 (script as evidence of what was performed),
section 10 (power to make copies of script),
section 15 (powers of entry and inspection).

DEFINITIONS
"play": s.18(1), Theatres Act 1968, by subs. (5).
"public performance": s.18(1).
"racial hatred": s.17, by s.29.
"recording": s.21(2).

GENERAL NOTE
This section replaces s.5, Theatres Act 1968 which is repealed by s.40(3) and Sch. 3. The offence follows the broad pattern established in this Part but contains more elaborate defences to take account of the amount of responsibility that various parties involved have over the presentation of the offending conduct.

Subs. (1)
See the note to s.18(1). In para. (*b*), the reference to "the performance as a whole" was inserted to ensure that "all the circumstances" would not be interpreted so as to allow isolated parts of a performance to be used as a basis for prosecution. The offence only applies to presenters and directors.

Subs. (2)
These defences to a strict liability offence must be established on the balance of probabilities. They refer to: knowledge of the content of the performance, to take account of ad-libbing, for example; knowledge of the nature of the performance despite knowledge of the conduct, to take account of the impact on the audience; knowledge of the effect of the performance, to take account of the consequences of the performance for the audience or for the wider community. See the note to s.19(2); disproving knowledge is easier than disproving awareness but the objective conditions as to the state of knowledge render the distinction indiscernable.

Subs. (3)
This is based upon s.7(2), Theatres Act 1968. Either the possibility of prosecution is too inhibiting for artistic freedom or it is assumed that the company and technical supporting staff are immune from the mischief of the Act.

Subs. (4)
This section is based upon s.18(2), Theatres Act 1968. It is intended to protect the interests of actors.

Distributing, showing or playing a recording

21.—(1) A person who distributes, or shows or plays, a recording of visual images or sounds which are threatening, abusive or insulting is guilty of an offence if—

(*a*) he intends thereby to stir up racial hatred, or
(*b*) having regard to all the circumstances racial hatred is likely to be stirred up thereby.

(2) In this Part "recording" means any record from which visual images or sounds may, by any means, be reproduced; and references to the distribution, showing or playing of a recording are to its distribution, showing or playing to the public or a section of the public.

(3) In proceedings for an offence under this section it is a defence for an accused who is not shown to have intended to stir up racial hatred to prove that he was not aware of the content of the recording and did not suspect, and had no reason to suspect, that it was threatening, abusive or insulting.

(4) This section does not apply to the showing or playing of a recording solely for the purpose of enabling the recording to be broadcast or included in a cable programme service.

DEFINITIONS
"distributes": subs. (2), by s.29.
"racial hatred": s.17, by s.29.
"recording": subs. (2), by s.29.

GENERAL NOTE
This section is concerned with the effects of video and film, although it was conceded in Parliament that a particular problem of racial hatred has not yet arisen in respect of such materials. The broad pattern of this Part is again followed. See generally, notes to s.18(1), (5), (6).

Broadcasting or including programme in cable programme service

22.—(1) If a programme involving threatening, abusive or insulting visual images or sounds is broadcast, or included in a cable programme service, each of the persons mentioned in subsection (2) is guilty of an offence if—
  (*a*) he intends thereby to stir up racial hatred, or
  (*b*) having regard to all the circumstances racial hatred is likely to be stirred up thereby.
(2) The persons are—
  (*a*) the person providing the broadcasting or cable programme service,
  (*b*) any person by whom the programme is produced or directed, and
  (*c*) any person by whom offending words or behaviour are used.
(3) If the person providing the service, or a person by whom the programme was produced or directed, is not shown to have intended to stir up racial hatred, it is a defence for him to prove that—
  (*a*) he did not know and had no reason to suspect that the programme would involve the offending material, and
  (*b*) having regard to the circumstances in which the programme was broadcast, or included in a cable programme service, it was not reasonably practicable for him to secure the removal of the material.
(4) It is a defence for a person by whom the programme was produced or directed who is not shown to have intended to stir up racial hatred to prove that he did not know and had not reason to suspect—
  (*a*) that the programme would be broadcast or included in a cable programme service, or
  (*b*) that the circumstances in which the programme would be broadcast or so included would be such that racial hatred would be likely to be stirred up.
(5) It is a defence for a person by whom offending words or behaviour were used and who is not shown to have intended to stir up racial hatred to prove that he did not know and had no reason to suspect—
  (*a*) that a programme involving the use of the offending material would be broadcast or included in a cable programme service, or
  (*b*) that the circumstances in which a programme involving the use of the offending material would be broadcast, or so included, or in

which a programme broadcast or so included would involve the use of the offending material, would be such that racial hatred would be likely to be stirred up.

(6) A person who is not shown to have intended to stir up racial hatred is not guilty of an offence under this section if he did not know, and had no reason to suspect, that the offending material was threatening, abusive or insulting.

(7) This section does not apply—

    (*a*) to the broadcasting of a programme by the British Broadcasting Corporation or the Independent Broadcasting Authority, or

    (*b*) to the inclusion of a programme in a cable programme service by the reception and immediate re-transmission of a broadcast by either of those authorities.

(8) The following provisions of the Cable and Broadcasting Act 1984 apply to an offence under this section as they apply to a "relevant offence" as defined in section 33(2) of that Act—

    section 33 (scripts as evidence),

    section 34 (power to make copies of scripts and records),

    section 35 (availability of visual and sound records);

and sections 33 and 34 of that Act apply to an offence under this section in connection with the broadcasting of a programme as they apply to an offence in connection with the inclusion of a programme in a cable programme service.

DEFINITIONS

    "broadcast": s.29.

    "cable programme service": s.2, Cable and Broadcasting Act 1984, by s.29.

    "programme": s.29.

    "racial hatred": s.17, by s.29.

GENERAL NOTE

    This subsection replaces s.27, Cable and Broadcasting Act 1984 which is repealed by s.40(3) and Sch. 3. It applies the general pattern of this Part to cable and direct broadcasting by satellite; the BBC's and IBA's broadcasts, and their programmes which are subject to the "must carry" requirement, are not included: see subs. (7). See generally, the note to s.18(1). As in the case of s.20, there are a series of defences to take account of the amount of control that the various parties involved have over the transmission of the offending images and sounds.

Racially inflammatory material

Possession of racially inflammatory material

23.—(1) A person who has in his possession written material which is threatening, abusive or insulting, or a recording of visual images or sounds which are threatening, abusive or insulting, with a view to—

    (*a*) in the case of written material, its being displayed, published, distributed, broadcast or included in a cable programme service, whether by himself or another, or

    (*b*) in the case of a recording, its being distributed, shown, played, broadcast or included in a cable programme service, whether by himself or another,

is guilty of an offence if he intends racial hatred to be stirred up thereby or, having regard to all the circumstances, racial hatred is likely to be stirred up thereby.

(2) For this purpose regard shall be had to such display, publication, distribution, showing, playing, broadcasting or inclusion in a cable pro-

gramme service as he has, or it may reasonably be inferred that he has, in view.

(3) In proceedings for an offence under this section it is a defence for an accused who is not shown to have intended to stir up racial hatred to prove that he was not aware of the content of the written material or recording and did not suspect, and had no reason to suspect, that it was threatening, abusive or insulting.

(4) This section does not apply to the possession of written material or a recording by or on behalf of the British Broadcasting Corporation or the Independent Broadcasting Authority or with a view to its being broadcast by either of those authorities.

DEFINITIONS
"broadcast": s.29.
"cable programme service": s.2, Cable and Broadcasting Act 1984, by s.29.
"distribution": s.19(3), by s.29.
"publication": s.19(3), by s.29.
"racial hatred": s.17, by s.29.
"recording": s.21(2), by s.29.
"written material": s.29.

GENERAL NOTE
In this section, a new offence is created to deal with the accumulation and storing of materials which are to be used to foment racial hatred. The possessor of the materials does not need to be the one who disseminates it. Possession appears to involve both a degree of control over the material and knowledge that such control is being exercised: see *Warner* v. *Metropolitan Police Commissioner* [1969] 2 A.C. 256. Knowledge about the threatening, abusive or insulting nature of the material is irrelevant but there is a defence for innocent possession in subs. (3), following the general approach adopted in this Part. The BBC and IBA are exempted by subs. (4); their duties under the BBC's Licence and the Independent Broadcasting Act 1981 are considered to be adequate to deal with any problem which might be likely to arise.

The section is not intended to stifle the genuine pursuit of research. However, the risk that dissemination of research findings will stimulate racial hatred must be borne by the person storing the material, for example, the researcher or a library. Persons engaging upon race-related research will have a difficult burden to discharge when raising any defence under subs. (3); for a library it may be a little easier.

Powers of entry and search

24.—(1) If in England and Wales a justice of the peace is satisfied by information on oath laid by a constable that there are reasonable grounds for suspecting that a person has possession of written material or a recording in contravention of section 23, the justice may issue a warrant under his hand authorising any constable to enter and search the premises where it is suspected the material or recording is situated.

(2) If in Scotland a sheriff or justice of the peace is satisfied by evidence on oath that there are reasonable grounds for suspecting that a person has possession of written material or a recording in contravention of section 23, the sheriff or justice may issue a warrant authorising any constable to enter and search the premises where it is suspected the material or recording is situated.

(3) A constable entering or searching premises in pursuance of a warrant issued under this section may use reasonable force if necessary.

(4) In this section "premises" means any place and, in particular, includes—

(*a*) any vehicle, vessel, aircraft or hovercraft,
(*b*) any offshore installation as defined in section 1(3)(*b*) of the Mineral Workings (Offshore Installations) Act 1971, and
(*c*) any tent or movable structure.

DEFINITIONS
"recording": s.21(2), by s.29.
"written material": s.29.

GENERAL NOTE
This section provides the grounds for obtaining a warrant to enter and search premises in order to discover unlawfully possessed written or recorded material. In England and Wales, the procedure for applying for the warrant and for executing it is contained in ss.15 and 16, Police and Criminal Evidence Act 1984 and Code D, under that Act, relating to the Search and Seizure of Persons and Property. The necessity of using reasonable force, authorised by subs. (3), will be assessed by reference to that Code. Seizure of material is governed by s.19 of the 1984 Act.

Power to order forfeiture

25.—(1) A court by or before which a person is convicted of—
   (*a*) an offence under section 18 relating to the display of written material, or
   (*b*) an offence under section 19, 21 or 23,
shall order to be forfeited any written material or recording produced to the court and shown to its satisfaction to be written material or a recording to which the offence relates.
   (2) An order made under this section shall not take effect—
   (*a*) in the case of an order made in proceedings in England and Wales, until the expiry of the ordinary time within which an appeal may be instituted or, where an appeal is duly instituted, until it is finally decided or abandoned;
   (*b*) in the case of an order made in proceedings in Scotland, until the expiration of the time within which, by virtue of any statute, an appeal may be instituted or, where such an appeal is duly instituted, until the appeal is finally decided or abandoned.
   (3) For the purposes of subsection (2)(*a*)—
   (*a*) an application for a case stated or for leave to appeal shall be treated as the institution of an appeal, and
   (*b*) where a decision on appeal is subject to a further appeal, the appeal is not finally determined until the expiry of the ordinary time within which a further appeal may be instituted or, where a further appeal is duly instituted, until the further appeal is finally decided or abandoned.
   (4) For the purposes of subsection (2)(*b*) the lodging of an application for a stated case or note of appeal against sentence shall be treated as the institution of an appeal.

DEFINITIONS
"recording": s.21, by s.29.
"written material": s.29.

Supplementary provisions

Savings for reports of parliamentary or judicial proceedings

26.—(1) Nothing in this Part applies to a fair and accurate report of proceedings in Parliament.
   (2) Nothing in this Part applies to a fair and accurate report of proceedings publicly heard before a court or tribunal exercising judicial authority where the report is published contemporaneously with the proceedings or, if it is not reasonably practicable or would be unlawful to

publish a report of them contemporaneously, as soon as publication is reasonably practicable and lawful.

Procedure and punishment

27.—(1) No proceedings for an offence under this Part may be instituted in England and Wales except by or with the consent of the Attorney General.

(2) For the purposes of the rules in England and Wales against charging more than one offence in the same count or information, each of sections 18 to 23 creates one offence.

(3) A person guilty of an offence under this Part is liable—
  (*a*) on conviction on indictment to imprisonment for a term not exceeding two years or a fine or both;
  (*b*) on summary conviction to imprisment for a term not exceeding six months or a fine not exceeding the statutory maximum or both.

Subs. (1)
  The Attorney-General's approval was considered necessary to protect against mischievous, frivolous or unsupported prosecutions, whether they are used in order to harass individuals or to bring discredit to the legislation. Counter-principles of free expression, including free elections and a free media, were also considered to be more appropriate for the Attorney-General. It was indicated in Standing Committee, however, that if the new Crown Prosecution Service were to establish a reputation for probity and action, then this constraint upon prosecutions might be reconsidered. In practice, in any event, the Director of Public Prosecutions will already be closely involved in any such decisions.

Subs. (2)
  The relevant rules are the Indictment Rules 1971, r.7, which facilitate the avoidance of charges in single counts or information being held bad for duplicity.

Subs. (3)
  "Statutory maximum" is defined in s.75, Criminal Justice Act 1982.

Offences by corporations

28.—(1) Where a body corporate is guilty of an offence under this Part and it is shown that the offence was committed with the consent or connivance of a director, manager, secretary or other similar officer of the body, or a person purporting to act in any such capacity, hc as well as the body corporate is guilty of the offence and liable to be proceeded against and punished accordingly.

(2) Where the affairs of a body corporate are managed by its members, subsection (1) applies in relation to the acts and defaults of a member in connection with his functions of management as it applies to a director.

Interpretation

29. In this Part—
  "broadcast" means broadcast by wireless telegraphy (within the meaning of the Wireless Telegraphy Act 1949) for general reception, whether by way of sound broadcasting or television;
  "cable programme service" has the same meaning as in the Cable and Broadcasting Act 1984;
  "distribute", and related expressions, shall be construed in accordance with section 19(3) (written material) and section 21(2) (recordings);
  "dwelling" means any structure or part of a structure occupied as a person's home or other living accommodation (whether the occupation is separate or shared with others) but does not

include any part not so occupied, and for this purpose "structure" includes a tent, caravan, vehicle, vessel or other
temporary or movable structure;
"programme" means any item which is broadcast or included in a
cable programme service;
"publish", and related expressions, in relation to written material,
shall be construed in accordance with section 19(3);
"racial hatred" has the meaning given by section 17;
"recording" has the meaning given by section 21(2), and "play" and
"show", and related expressions, in relation to a recording,
shall be construed in accordance with that provision;
"written material" includes any sign or other visible representation.

PART IV

EXCLUSION ORDERS

GENERAL NOTE
In this Part, a framework is established for the purpose of assisting with the quelling of
football hooliganism. It was introduced at a late stage of the general discussion about public
order which preceded this Act, although a similar scheme was the subject of a Private
Members Bill in 1981. It was not mentioned in the White Paper and neither was it suggested
directly in the Report of the Home Office's *Committee of Inquiry into Crowd Safety and
Control at Sports Grounds*, chaired by Mr. Justice Popplewell, (1986), Cmnd. 9585 (Interim)
and 9710 (Final).
In considering various proposals for dealing with football hooliganism, however, the
Government has been strongly disposed, as had Popplewell—Interim Report, para. 6.48, to
the idea of football clubs' organising a voluntary scheme for issuing membership cards to
supporters; although the clubs have been equally strongly reluctant to comply. This Part
contains legislative teeth in the event of any such scheme's being implemented. It does
depend, however, upon the creation of an adequate base of information about football
supporters' attendance at matches and that will depend upon the cooperation of the clubs.
In the absence of some methodical scrutiny of attendance, the enforcement of the provisions
of this Part will depend upon chance recognitions or surveillance, neither very practicable.
The Government regards the exclusion order as part of a general package of measures
including other public order offences and especially the control of alcohol in connection with
matches under the Sporting Events (Control of Alcohol etc.) Act 1985. Football matches
from which sentenced hooligans will be excluded are anticipated to be closely related to
matches designated under the 1985 Act, in other words, focuses of trouble: see generally,
Hansard, H.C. Vol. 89, col. 863 and Standing Committee, cols. 972–6. In passing this
legislation, however, the opportunity has been taken to modify some of the provisions of the
1985 Act in relation to alcohol consumed in clubhouses at football grounds, following
discussion by Popplewell—Final Report, para. 4.91. Schedule 1 makes provision for the
relaxation of restrictions upon the consumption of alcohol in directors' or companies' private
viewing boxes at designated sporting events. On the other hand, there is a tightening of
controls in respect of the use of fireworks at such events. In addition, minibuses will now be
included in the Act's purview.

Exclusion orders

30.—(1) A court by or before which a person is convicted of an offence
to which section 31 applies may make an order (an exclusion order)
prohibiting him from entering any premises for the purpose of attending
any prescribed football match there.
(2) No exclusion order may be made unless the court is satisfied that
making such an order in relation to the accused would help to prevent
violence or disorder at or in connection with prescribed football matches.
(3) An exclusion order may only be made—

(*a*) in addition to a sentence imposed in respect of the offence of which the accused is convicted, or

(*b*) in addition to a probation order or an order discharging him absolutely or conditionally.

(4) An exclusion order may be made as mentioned in subsection (3)(*b*) notwithstanding anything in sections 2, 7 and 13 of the Powers of Criminal Courts Act 1973 (which relate to orders there mentioned and their effect).

GENERAL NOTE

The general scheme is as follows. Upon convicting a person of an offence connected with football, described in s.31, a court may make an order prohibiting him from entering premises for the purposes of attending a prescribed football match. The court is not involved in identifying which matches are to be subject to the prohibition. Instead, it makes a general prohibition dependent upon the Home Secretary's selection of matches from which he would want all excluded persons to be banned, under s.36. The court can determine the maximum length for which a person can be liable to be prohibited although it must be for at least three months but, if it is for longer than one year, the offender can apply to terminate the order: ss.32 and 33.

Exclusion orders have rather draconian connotations associated with the Prevention of Terrorism (Temporary Provisions) Act 1976 but they are known elsewhere in the law, for example, the Licensed Premises (Exclusion of Certain Persons) Act 1980. One of their principal drawbacks is that they tend to displace or divert the prohibited conduct rather than remove it. Under s.37, the Home Secretary can extend the provisions of this Part to any other sporting event.

Subs. (2)

The implication is that the offender must be a regular hooligan. The court needs to be able to predict that future violence will be carried out or organised by him and, in order to do that, his previous pattern of behaviour in relation to football matches will be crucial evidence. Isolated acts of hooliganism should not qualify for an exclusion order, therefore, unless it can be demonstrated that a repetition of that type of offending is likely.

Offences connected with football

31.—(1) This section applies to any offence which fulfils one or more of the following three conditions.

(2) The first condition is that the offence was committed during any period relevant to a prescribed football match (as determined under subsections (6) to (8)), while the accused was at, or was entering or leaving or trying to enter or leave, the football ground concerned.

(3) The second condition is that the offence—

(*a*) involved the use or threat of violence by the accused towards another person and was committed while one or each of them was on a journey to or from an association football match,

(*b*) involved the use or threat of violence towards property and was committed while the accused was on such a journey, or

(*c*) was committed under section 5 or Part III while the accused was on such a journey.

(4) The third condition is that the offence was committed under section 1(3) or (4) or 1A(3) or (4) of the Sporting Events (Control of Alcohol etc.) Act 1985 (alcohol on journeys to or from certain sporting events) and the designated sporting event concerned was an association football match.

(5) For the purposes of subsection (3) a person's journey includes breaks (including overnight breaks).

(6) The period beginning 2 hours before the start of the match or (if earlier) 2 hours before the time at which it is advertised to start, and ending 1 hour after the end of it, is a period relevant to it.

(7) Where the match is advertised to start at a particular time on a particular day and is postponed to a later day, the period in the advertised

day beginning 2 hours before and ending 1 hour after that time is also a period relevant to it.

(8) Where the match is advertised to start at a particular time on a particular day and does not take place, the period in that day beginning 2 hours before and ending 1 hour after that time is a period relevant to it.

GENERAL NOTE

This section sets out the required relationship between an offence and association football, or any other sport included by virtue of s.37. The presence of any one of three conditions is sufficient. First, any offence, however trivial or unrelated to football hooliganism, will qualify if it was committed during any period relevant to a prescribed football match as set out in subs. (6)–(8). Dropping litter would be included, although that would hardly seem to be within the objects of the legislation and of prescribing football matches. Secondly, if the offence takes place on a journey to or from a football match and involves the use or threat of violence to persons or property, or conduct causing harassment, alarm or distress, or the stirring up of racial hatred, it will qualify. Thirdly, if the offence involves the use of alcohol on a journey to or from a designated association football match, under the 1985 Act, it will also qualify.

Subs. (5) has the effect of including long, extended journeys. Subss. (6)–(8) define the period relevant to a prescribed match as the period extending from two hours before the beginning of an actual match, or its advertised time and date whether played or not, to one hour after the match or that time and date.

Effect of order

32.—(1) An exclusion order shall have effect for such period as is specified in the order.

(2) The period shall be not less than three months or, in the case of a person already subject to an exclusion order, not less than three months plus the unexpired period of the earlier order or, if there is more than one earlier order, of the most recent order.

(3) A person who enters premises in breach of an exclusion order is guilty of an offence and liable on summary conviction to imprisonment for a term not exceeding 1 month or a fine not exceeding level 3 on the standard scale or both.

(4) A constable who reasonably suspects that a person has entered premises in breach of an exclusion order may arrest him without warrant.

GENERAL NOTE

"Standard scale" has the meaning given by s.75, Criminal Justice Act 1982. In the first Bill, a constable was given a power of expulsion which, it was anticipated, would be used in conjunction with s.25, Police and Criminal Evidence Act 1984. The Association of Chief Police Officers considered that a loophole might have been created in cases of re-entry to a match where no injury or damage was anticipated: see Standing Committee, col. 1059. Hence, the power in subs. (4) was inserted. No power of entry to a ground is given to the constable but in most cases he is likely to be on club premises by consent.

Application to terminate order

33.—(1) A person in relation to whom an exclusion order has had effect for at least one year may apply to the court by which it was made to terminate it.

(2) On such an application the court may, having regard to the person's character, his conduct since the order was made, the nature of the offence which led to it and any other circumstances of the case, either by order terminate the order (as from a date specified in the terminating order) or refuse the application.

(3) Where an application under this section is refused, a further application in respect of the exclusion order shall not be entertained if made within the period of six months beginning with the day of the refusal.

(4) The court may order the applicant to pay all or any part of the costs of an application under this section.

(5) In the case of an exclusion order made by a magistrates' court, the reference in subsection (1) to the court by which it was made includes a reference to any magistrates' court acting for the same petty sessions area as that court.

(6) Section 63(2) of the Magistrates' Courts Act 1980 (power to suspend or rescind orders) does not apply to an exclusion order.

Information

34.—(1) Where a court makes an exclusion order, the clerk of the court (in the case of a magistrates' court) or the appropriate officer (in the case of the Crown Court)—
  (*a*) shall give a copy of it to the person to whom it relates,
  (*b*) shall (as soon as reasonably practicable) send a copy of it to the chief officer of police for the police area in which the offence leading to the order was committed, and
  (*c*) shall (as soon as reasonably practicable) send a copy of it to any prescribed person.

(2) Where a court terminates an exclusion order under section 28, the clerk of the court (in the case of a magistrates' court) or the appropriate officer (in the case of the Crown Court)—
  (*a*) shall give a copy of the terminating order to the person to whom the exclusion order relates,
  (*b*) shall (as soon as reasonably practicable) send a copy of the terminating order to the chief officer of police for the police area in which the offence leading to the exclusion order was committed, and
  (*c*) shall (as soon as reasonably practicable) send a copy of the terminating order to any prescribed person.

(3) References in this section to the clerk of a magistrates' court shall be construed in accordance with section 141 of the Magistrates' Courts Act 1980, reading references to that Act as references to this section.

(4) In this section "prescribed" means prescribed by order made by the Secretary of State.

(5) The power to make an order under this section shall be exercisable by statutory instrument subject to annulment in pursuance of a resolution of either House of Parliament.

GENERAL NOTE
  This section facilitates the establishment of a procedure for exchanging information between the courts, the police and football clubs. The type of person whom the Home Secretary expects to prescribe was indicated in Standing Committee, cols. 172–6: it will be somebody nominated by the football authorities who will be responsible for circulating the relevant details to clubs and other football organisations. This exchange of information will operate against the background of the collection of photographs, under s.35, and intelligence network organised by the police to deal with football hooliganism: see references in Standing Committee at cols. 953 and 987.

Subs. (2)
  The reference to s.28 appears to be a mistake. It ought to read s.33(2).

Photographs

35.—(1) The court by which an exclusion order is made may make an order which—
  (*a*) requires a constable to take a photograph of the person to whom the exclusion order relates or to cause such a photograph to be taken, and

(*b*) requires that person to go to a specified police station not later than 7 clear days after the day on which the order under this section is made, and at a specified time of day or between specified times of day, in order to have his photograph taken.

(2) In subsection (1) "specified" means specified in the order made under this section.

(3) No order may be made under this section unless an application to make it is made to the court by or on behalf of the person who is the prosecutor in respect of the offence leading to the exclusion order.

(4) If the person to whom the exclusion order relates fails to comply with an order under this section a constable may arrest him without warrant in order that his photograph may be taken.

GENERAL NOTE

There was uncertainty in Parliament as to how this section would assist in enforcement. The problems of circulating photographs, the memory that a police officer would need, the probability that the police already gather sufficient photographs for their needs, all featured amongst the doubts. In respect of the latter point, the absence of a mandatory power here is a recognition of existing police intelligence gathering: see Standing Committee, col. 987. It is not envisaged that photographs will be circulated in connection with information under s.34; Standing Committee, col. 990.

Prescribed football matches

36.—(1) In this Part "prescribed football match" means an association football match of any description prescribed by order made by the Secretary of State.

(2) The power to make an order under this section shall be exercisable by statutory instrument subject to annulment in pursuance of a resolution of either House of Parliament.

GENERAL NOTE

The Home Secretary's present policy was explained in Standing Committee, col. 972: international matches and the major league, cup and other competitions will be prescribed, in other words, the same types of match as those designated under the 1985 Act.

Extension to other sporting events

37.—(1) The Secretary of State may by order provide for sections 30 to 35 to apply as if—
(*a*) any reference to an association football match included a reference to a sporting event of a kind specified in the order, and
(*b*) any reference to a prescribed football match included a reference to such a sporting event of a description specified in the order.

(2) An order under subsection (1) may make such modifications of those sections, as they apply by virtue of the order, as the Secretary of State thinks fit.

(3) The power to make an order under this section shall be exercisable by statutory instrument, and no such order shall be made unless a draft of the order has been laid before and approved by resolution of each House of Parliament.

GENERAL NOTE

It may be observed that this section gives the Secretary of State potentially very broad powers. He could virtually recast the whole scheme in relation to different sporting events, under subs. (2). The affirmative procedure in subs. (3) does provide a certain amount of Parliamentary scrutiny, however.

PART V

MISCELLANEOUS AND GENERAL

Contamination of or interference with goods with intention of causing public alarm or anxiety, etc.

38.—(1) It is an offence for a person, with the intention—
  (a) of causing public alarm or anxiety, or
  (b) of causing injury to members of the public consuming or using the goods, or
  (c) of causing economic loss to any person by reason of the goods being shunned by members of the public, or
  (d) of causing economic loss to any person by reason of steps taken to avoid any such alarm or anxiety, injury or loss,
to contaminate or interfere with goods, or make it appear that goods have been contaminated or interfered with, or to place goods which have been contaminated or interfered with, or which appear to have been contaminated or interfered with, in a place where goods of that description are consumed, used, sold or otherwise supplied.

(2) It is also an offence for a person, with any such intention as is mentioned in paragraph (a), (c) or (d) of subsection (1), to threaten that he or another will do, or to claim that he or another has done, any of the acts mentioned in that subsection.

(3) It is an offence for a person to be in possession of any of the following articles with a view to the commission of an offence under subsection (1)—
  (a) materials to be used for contaminating or interfering with goods or making it appear that goods have been contaminated or interfered with, or
  (b) goods which have been contaminated or interfered with, or which appear to have been contaminated or interfered with.

(4) A person guilty of an offence under this section is liable—
  (a) on conviction on indictment to imprisonment for a term not exceeding 10 years or a fine or both, or
  (b) on summary conviction to imprisonment for a term not exceeding six months or a fine not exceeding the statutory maximum or both.

(5) In this section "goods" includes substances whether natural or manufactured and whether or not incorporated in or mixed with other goods.

(6) The reference in subsection (2) to a person claiming that certain acts have been committed does not include a person who in good faith reports or warns that such acts have been, or appear to have been committed.

GENERAL NOTE

These offences were added to the Bill by the Government at a late stage in Committee in the House of Lords. There was little discussion of the provision but general agreement that some such reform was necessary. Poisoning, marking or otherwise contaminating goods has been reported more often in recent years although it has yet to become a frequent occurrence. The Government considered, however, that existing provisions, such as s.1(1), Criminal Damage Act 1971 or s.23, Offences against the Person Act 1861, were inadequate to cover the mischief here, namely the sense of widespread alarm that campaigns of contamination can cause.

Subs. (1)

It is an offence, having the intention set out in paras. (a)–(d), either to contaminate or interfere with goods, or to make it appear that goods have been contaminated or interfered with, or to put goods which have been thus tampered with in a place relevant for the purposes of the section. That place is one where goods of the type which have been actually or apparently tampered with are consumed, used, sold or otherwise supplied. Thus, a shop selling for example food, perfume, or furs would be covered, as would a restaurant. A lorry or a transit warehouse would not appear to be included, however. The offence applies to tampering at some other place as well as at the point of supply as, for example, when goods are brought into a shop and placed on a shelf. In this context, "description" must refer to the genus of the goods rather than the brand name in order for the spirit of the section to be advanced.

An ulterior intention must be proved, perhaps by evidence that it was anticipated by the accused that customers would be turned away or that proprietors would feel constrained to empty shelves. Deciding what public alarm or anxiety is for the purpose of establishing such an intention will not be easy; see the note to s.5(1). The mere likelihood of the consequences will not ground liability.

Subs. (2)
There is a limited but apparently otiose defence in subs. (6).

Subs. (3)
On possession, see the note to s.23.

Power to direct trespassers to leave land

39.—(1) If the senior police officer reasonably believes that two or more persons have entered land as trespassers and are present there with the common purpose of residing there for any period, that reasonable steps have been taken by or on behalf of the occupier to ask them to leave and—

(*a*) that any of those persons has caused damage to property on the land or used threatening, abusive or insulting words or behaviour towards the occupier, a member of his family or an employee or agent of his, or

(*b*) that those persons have between them brought twelve or more vehicles on to the land,

he may direct those persons, or any of them, to leave the land.

(2) If a person knowing that such a direction has been given which applies to him—

(*a*) fails to leave the land as soon as reasonably practicable, or

(*b*) having left again enters the land as a trespasser within the period of three months beginning with the day on which the direction was given.

he commits an offence and is liable on summary conviction to imprisonment for a term not exceeding three months or a fine not exceeding level 4 on the standard scale, or both.

(3) A constable in uniform who reasonably suspects that a person is committing an offence under this section may arrest him without warrant.

(4) In proceedings for an offence under this section it is a defence for the accused to show—

(*a*) that his original entry on the land was not as a trespasser, or

(*b*) that he had a reasonable excuse for failing to leave the land as soon as reasonably practicable or, as the case may be, for again entering the land as a trespasser.

(5) In this section—

"land" does not include—

(*a*) buildings other than—

(i) agricultural buildings within the meaning of section 26(4) of the General Rate Act 1967, or

(ii) scheduled monuments within the meaning of the Ancient Monuments and Archaeological Areas Act 1979;

(*b*) land forming part of a highway;
"occupier" means the person entitled to possession of the land by
  virtue of an estate or interest held by him;
"property" means property within the meaning of section 10(1) of
  the Criminal Damage Act 1971;
"senior police officer" means the most senior in rank of the police
  officers present at the scene;
"trespasser", in relation to land, means a person who is a trespasser
  as against the occupier of the land;
"vehicle" includes a caravan as defined in section 29(1) of the
  Caravan Sites and Control of Development Act 1960;
and a person may be regarded for the purposes of this section as having
the purpose of residing in a place notwithstanding that he has a home
elsewhere.

DEFINITIONS
  "land": subs. (5).
  "occupier": subs. (5).
  "property": s.10(1), Criminal Damage Act 1971, by subs. (5).
  "senior police officer": subs. (5).
  "trespasser": subs. (5).
  "vehicle": subs. (5).

GENERAL NOTE
  This section represents the culmination of a number of attempts to deal with mass trespass,
which were only formulated during the passage of the Bill. A clause concerning disorder and
damage to property by trespassers was debated but withdrawn in the House of Lords in
connection with s.5: *Hansard*, H.C. Vol. 478, col. 967. The debate on s.14 was used as an
opportunity to raise the issue, too, although the Home Office agreed with the Association
of Chief Police Officers that any additional powers for the police to deal with trespassers
was unnecessary and undesirable: Standing Committee, col. 719ff. The spectacle of a convoy
of hippies attempting a pilgrimage to Stonehenge in the summer of 1986, and invading
private farmland in the process, had an effect where a lengthy encampment at Greenham
Common had had none, however, and was enough to change the Government's mind.
Nevertheless, drafting such an offence was not easy because a narrow path had to be traced
between the oppressive effects of using the criminal law against harmless and inadvertent
trespassers and the practical advantages of a quick and costless remedy, to the occupier,
against those who were deliberately trading on the inefficiency of the civil law in order to
cause nuisance or damage with impunity. Some years earlier, the Law Commission had
experienced similar difficulties in Part II of their *Report on Conspiracy and Criminal Law
Reform* (1976) Law Com. No. 76. The solution to the problem here has been to give yet
another preventive power to the police, and one which overlaps with other powers under
this Act or for breach of the peace. The great advantage of this power is that it facilitates
a peaceful resolution to potential public disorder by providing an authority to act which does
not depend upon an offence's having been committed. Its great disadvantage is that it
requires judgments to be made by the police upon matters of civil law with which they are
traditionally uneasy and which provide much scope for misunderstanding and counterprod-
uctive resentment.

Subs. (1)
  A number of conditions are required before this power can be invoked, rendering it rather
complex to operate. It cannot be used against one person. Two or more must have entered
land as trespassers. That means that it cannot be used where a licence has been revoked.
Land does not include a highway, for which s.137, Highways Act 1980 and s.25, Police and
Criminal Evidence Act 1984 is appropriate. Nor does it include buildings, except certain
agricultural ones or certain scheduled monuments, hardly information at even a senior police
officer's hand.
  The trespassers must be on the land with a common purpose (on which, see the note to
s.1) to reside there for any period. That phrase is taken from s.10, Caravan Sites Act 1968.
The existence of a home elsewhere is irrelevant to its determination, by subs. (5), but some
evidence of a willingness to remain on the land as a substitute or replacement for any other
home would be required; a person resides where in common parlance he lives: *R.* v. *St.*

Leonard, Shoreditch (Inhabitants) (1865) L.R. 1 Q.B. 21. Day visitors, with no indication of any ability or inclination to stay overnight, cannot be asked to leave under this power, therefore.

The occupier must have taken reasonable steps, either himself or through his agents, to ask the trespassers to leave. Unreasonable indications of his attitude, such as the use of violence or setting dogs on them, will apparently invalidate the use of the power.

When all these conditions have been met, two further, alternative, aggravating conditions are required. Either damage to property on the land or the use of threatening, abusive or insulting behaviour to the occupier or his family, employees or agents must be shown. On the latter, see the note to s.4. Alternatively, the trespassers must have brought twelve or more vehicles on the land. Some thought this number too high but the Government was anxious not to be seen as acting oppressively towards gypsies.

None of these matters can be resolved easily. They involve issues of land, employment and contract law as well as questions of fact. When the senior police officer makes up his mind on them, however, he may be able to invoke his power to direct any of the trespassers to leave. The only consolation for him is that he need only form a reasonable belief about them, although that would be subject to judicial review, in theory.

Subs. (2)
Only when the trespassers refuse to leave reasonably or re-enter again within three months is an offence committed. Limited defences are available under subs. (4), in relation to just one of the conditions mentioned in subs. (1) or compliance with the direction. The accused must have known that a direction existed and applied to him, however.

Amendments, repeals and savings

40.—(1) Schedule 1, which amends the Sporting Events (Control of Alcohol etc.) Act 1985 and Part V of the Criminal Justice (Scotland) Act 1980, shall have effect.

(2) Schedule 2, which contains miscellaneous and consequential amendments, shall have effect.

(3) The enactments mentioned in Schedule 3 (which include enactments related to the subject matter of this Act but already obsolete or unnecessary) are repealed to the extent specified in column 3.

(4) Nothing in this Act affects the common law powers in England and Wales to deal with or prevent a breach of the peace.

(5) As respects Scotland, nothing in this Act affects any power of a constable under any rule of law.

Commencement

41.—(1) This Act shall come into force on such day as the Secretary of State may appoint by order made by statutory instrument, and different days may be appointed for different provisions or different purposes.

(2) Nothing in a provision of this Act applies in relation to an offence committed or act done before the provision comes into force.

(3) Where a provision of this Act comes into force for certain purposes only, the references in subsection (2) to the provision are references to it so far as it relates to those purposes.

Extent

42.—(1) The provisions of this Act extend to England and Wales except so far as they—
    (*a*) amend or repeal an enactment which does not so extend, or
    (*b*) relate to the extent of provisions to Scotland or Northern Ireland.
(2) The following provisions of this Act extend to Scotland—
    in Part I, section 9(2) except paragraph (*a*);
    in Part II, sections 12 and 14 to 16;
    Part III;

Part V, except sections 38, 39, 40(4), subsections (1) and (3) of this
section and any provision amending or repealing an enactment
which does not extend to Scotland.

(3) The following provisions of this Act extend to Northern Ireland—
sections 38, 41, this subsection, section 43 and paragraph 6 of
Schedule 2.

Short title

43. This Act may be cited as the Public Order Act 1986.

SCHEDULES

SCHEDULE 1

SPORTING EVENTS

PART I

ENGLAND AND WALES

Introduction

1. The Sporting Events (Control of Alcohol etc.) Act 1985 shall be amended as mentioned
in this Part.

Vehicles

2. The following shall be inserted after section 1 (offences in connection with alcohol on
coaches and trains)—

"Alcohol on certain other vehicles

1A.—(1) This section applies to a motor vehicle which—

(*a*) is not a public service vehicle but is adapted to carry more than 8 passengers,
and

(*b*) is being used for the principal purpose of carrying two or more passengers for
the whole or part of a journey to or from a designated sporting event.

(2) A person who knowingly causes or permits intoxicating liquor to be carried on a
motor vehicle to which this section applies is guilty of an offence—

(*a*) if he is its driver, or

(*b*) if he is not its driver but is its keeper, the servant or agent of its keeper, a
person to whom it is made available (by hire, loan or otherwise) by its keeper
or the keeper's servant or agent, or the servant or agent of a person to whom it
is so made available.

(3) A person who has intoxicating liquor in his possession while on a motor vehicle to
which this section applies is guilty of an offence.

(4) A person who is drunk on a motor vehicle to which this section applies is guilty of
an offence.

(5) In this section—

"keeper", in relation to a vehicle, means the person having the duty to take out a
licence for it under section 1(1) of the Vehicles (Excise) Act 1971,

"motor vehicle" means a mechanically propelled vehicle intended or adapted for use
on roads, and

"public service vehicle" has the same meaning as in the Public Passenger Vehicles
Act 1981.".

Fireworks etc.

3. The following shall be inserted after section 2 (offences in connection with alcohol, containers etc. at sports grounds)—

"**Fireworks etc.**

2A.—(1) A person is guilty of an offence if he has an article or substance to which this section applies in his possession—

(*a*) at any time during the period of a designated sporting event when he is in any area of a designated sports ground from which the event may be directly viewed, or

(*b*) while entering or trying to enter a designated sports ground at any time during the period of a designated sporting event at the ground.

(2) It is a defence for the accused to prove that he had possession with lawful authority.

(3) This section applies to any article or substance whose main purpose is the emission of a flare for purposes of illuminating or signalling (as opposed to igniting or heating) or the emission of smoke or a visible gas; and in particular it applies to distress flares, fog signals, and pellets and capsules intended to be used as fumigators or for testing pipes, but not to matches, cigarette lighters or heaters.

(4) This section also applies to any article which is a firework.".

Licensing etc.

4. The following shall be inserted after section 5—

"**Private facilities for viewing events**

5A.—(1) In relation to a room in a designated sports ground—

(*a*) from which designated sporting events may be directly viewed, and

(*b*) to which the general public are not admitted,

sections 2(1)(*a*) and 3(1)(*a*) of this Act have effect with the substitution for the reference to the period of a designated sporting event of a reference to the restricted period defined below.

(2) Subject to any order under subsection (3) below, the restricted period of a designated sporting event for the purposes of this section is the period beginning 15 minutes before the start of the event or (if earlier) 15 minutes before the time at which it is advertised to start and ending 15 minutes after the end of the event, but—

(*a*) where an event advertised to start at a particular time on a particular day is postponed to a later day, the restricted period includes the period in the day on which it is advertised to take place beginning 15 minutes before and ending 15 minutes after that time, and

(*b*) where an event advertised to start at a particular time on a particular day does not take place, the period is the period referred to in paragraph (*a*) above.

(3) The Secretary of State may by order provide, in relation to all designated sporting events or in relation to such descriptions of event as are specified in the order—

(*a*) that the restricted period shall be such period, shorter than that mentioned in subsection (2) above, as may be specified in the order, or

(*b*) that there shall be no restricted period.

(4) An order under this section shall be made by statutory instrument which shall be subject to annulment in pursuance of a resolution of either House of Parliament.

Occasional licences

5B.—(1) An occasional licence which is in force for any place situated in the area of a designated sports ground, and which would (apart from this section) authorise the sale of intoxicating liquor at the place during the whole or part of the period of a designated sporting event at the ground, shall not authorise such sale.

(2) Where the sale of intoxicating liquor would (apart from this section) be authorised by an occasional licence, its holder is guilty of an offence if he sells or authorises the sale of such liquor and by virtue of this section the licence does not authorise the sale.

(3) A person is guilty of an offence if he consumes intoxicating liquor at a place, or takes such liquor from a place, at a time when an occasional licence which would (apart from this section) authorise the sale of the liquor at the place does not do so by virtue of this section.

Clubs

5C.—(1) Subsections (3) and (5) of section 39 of the Licensing Act 1964 (clubs), and subsection (4) of that section as it applies to subsection (3), shall not apply as regards the supply of intoxicating liquor in the area of a designated sports ground during the period of a designated sporting event at the ground or as regards the keeping of intoxicating liquor for such supply; but subsections (2) to (5) below shall apply.

(2) During the period of such an event at the ground, intoxicating liquor shall not be supplied by or on behalf of a registered club to a member or guest in the area of the ground except at premises in respect of which the club is registered.

(3) A person supplying or authorising the supply of intoxicating liquor in contravention of subsection (2) above is guilty of an offence.

(4) A person who, during the period of such an event, obtains or consumes intoxicating liquor supplied in contravention of subsection (2) above is guilty of an offence.

(5) If intoxicating liquor is kept in any premises or place by or on behalf of a club for supply to members or their guests in contravention of subsection (2) above, every officer of the club is guilty of an offence unless he shows that it was so kept without his knowledge or consent.

Non-retail sales

5D.—(1) During the period of a designated sporting event at a designated sports ground, intoxicating liquor shall not be sold in the area of the ground except by sale by retail.

(2) A person selling or authorising the sale of intoxicating liquor in contravention of subsection (1) above is guilty of an offence.

(3) A person who, during the period of such an event, obtains or consumes intoxicating liquor sold in contravention of subsection (1) above is guilty of an offence.".

Supplementary

5. In sections 2 and 3, after subsection (1) insert—

"(1A) Subsection (1)(*a*) above has effect subject to section 5A(1) of this Act."

6. In section 7(3) (power to stop and search vehicles), after "public service vehicle (within the meaning of section 1 of this Act)" insert "or a motor vehicle to which section 1A of this Act applies".

7.—(1) Section 8 (penalties) shall be amended as follows.

(2) In paragraph (*a*) after "1(2)" there shall be inserted "or 1A(2)".

(3) In paragraph (*b*) after "1(3)" there shall be inserted ", 1A(3)", after "2(1)" there shall be inserted ", 2A(1)" and after "3(10)" there shall be inserted ", 5B(2), 5C(3), 5D(2)".

(4) In paragraph (*c*) after "1(4)" there shall be inserted ", 1A(4)".

(5) At the end there shall be inserted—

"(*d*) in the case of an offence under section 5B(3), 5C(4) or 5D(3), to a fine not exceeding level 3 on the standard scale, and

(*e*) in the case of an offence under section 5C(5), to a fine not exceeding level 1 on the standard scale.".

Minor amendment

8. Section 3(9) (notice varying order about sale or supply of intoxicating liquor) shall have effect, and be taken always to have had effect, as if in paragraph (*b*) "order" read "notice".

PART II

SCOTLAND

Introduction

9. Part V of the Criminal Justice (Scotland) Act 1980 (sporting events: control of alcohol etc.) shall be amended as mentioned in this Part.

Vehicles

10. After section 70 there shall be inserted the following—
"Alcohol on certain other vehicles

70A.—(1) This section applies to a motor vehicle which is not a public service vehicle but is adapted to carry more than 8 passengers and is being operated for the principal purpose of conveying two or more passengers for the whole or part of a journey to or from a designated sporting event.

(2) Any person in possession of alcohol on a vehicle to which this section applies shall be guilty of an offence and liable on summary conviction to imprisonment for a period not exceeding 60 days or a fine not exceeding level 3 on the standard scale or both.

(3) Any person who is drunk on a vehicle to which this section applies shall be guilty of an offence and liable on summary conviction to a fine not exceeding level 2 on the standard scale.

(4) Any person who permits alcohol to be carried on a vehicle to which this section applies and—

    (*a*) is the driver of the vehicle, or

    (*b*) where he is not its driver, is the keeper of the vehicle, the employee or agent of the keeper, a person to whom it is made available (by hire, loan or otherwise) by the keeper or the keeper's employee or agent, or the employee or agent of a person to whom it is so made available,

shall, subject to section 71 of this Act, be guilty of an offence and liable on summary conviction to a fine not exceeding level 3 on the standard scale.".

11. In section 71 (defences in connection with carriage of alcohol) for "or 70" there shall be substituted ", 70 or 70A(4)".

12. In section 75 (police powers of enforcement) for "or 70" there shall be substituted ", 70 or 70A".

13. In section 77 (interpretation of Part V)—

    (*a*) the following definitions shall be inserted in the appropriate places alphabetically—

        " "keeper", in relation to a vehicle, means the person having the duty to take out a licence for it under section 1(1) of the Vehicles (Excise) Act 1971;

        "motor vehicle" means a mechanically propelled vehicle intended or adapted for use on roads;"; and

    (*b*) in the definition of "public service vehicle" for the words "Part I of the Transport Act 1980" there shall be substituted the words "the Public Passenger Vehicles Act 1981";".

Fireworks etc.

14.—(1) After section 72 there shall be inserted the following—
"Possession of fireworks etc. at sporting events

72A.—(1) Any person who has entered the relevant area of a designated sports ground and is in possession of a controlled article or substance at any time during the period of a designated sporting event shall be guilty of an offence.

(2) Any person who, while in possession of a controlled article or substance, attempts to enter the relevant area of a designated sports ground at any time during the period of a designated sporting event at the ground shall be guilty of an offence.

(3) A person guilty of an offence under subsection (1) or (2) above shall be liable on summary conviction to imprisonment for a period not exceeding 60 days or to a fine not exceeding level 3 on the standard scale or both.

(4) It shall be a defence for a person charged with an offence under subsection (1) or (2) above to show that he had lawful authority to be in possession of the controlled article or substance.

(5) In subsections (1) and (2) above "controlled article or substance" means—

    (*a*) any article or substance whose main purpose is the emission of a flare for purposes of illuminating or signalling (as opposed to igniting or heating) or the emission of smoke or a visible gas; and in particular it includes distress flares, fog signals, and pellets and capsules intended to be used as fumigators or for testing pipes, but not matches, cigarette lighters or heaters; and

    (*b*) any article which is a firework.".

(2) In section 75 (police powers of enforcement) at the end of subparagraph (ii) of paragraph (*e*) there shall be inserted—
"; or
(iii) a controlled article or substance as defined in section 72A(5) of this Act.".

SCHEDULE 2

OTHER AMENDMENTS

Conspiracy and Protection of Property Act 1875 (c.86)

1.—(1) In section 7 of the Conspiracy and Protection of Property Act 1875 (offence to intimidate etc. with a view to compelling another to abstain from doing or to do an act) for the words from "shall" to the end there shall be substituted "shall be liable on summary conviction to imprisonment for a term not exceeding 6 months or a fine not exceeding level 5 on the standard scale or both.".
(2) And the following shall be added at the end of that section—
"A constable may arrest without warrant anyone he reasonably suspects is committing an offence under this section.".

Prevention of Crime Act 1953 (c.14)

2. In section 1 of the Prevention of Crime Act 1953 (offence to have offensive weapon) at the end of subsection (4) (offensive weapon includes article intended by person having it for use by him) there shall be added "or by some other person".

Civic Government (Scotland) Act 1982 (c.45)

3.—(1) Part V of the Civic Government (Scotland) Act 1982 (public processions) shall be amended in accordance with this paragraph.
(2) In section 62 (notification of processions)—
  (*a*) in subsection (1)—
        (i) after "below" there shall be inserted "(*a*)"; and
        (ii) at the end there shall be inserted—
     "; and
        (*b*) to the chief constable.";
  (*b*) in subsection (2)—
        (i) in paragraph (*a*), after "council" there shall be inserted "and to the office of the chief constable";
        (ii) in paragraph (*b*), for "that office" there shall be substituted "those offices";
  (*c*) in subsection (4)—
        (i) after "area" there shall be inserted "(*a*)"; and
        (ii) after "them" there shall be inserted—
     "; and
        (*b*) intimated to the chief constable,"; and
  (*d*) in subsection (12), in the definition of "public place", for "the Public Order Act 1936" there shall be substituted "Part II of the Public Order Act 1986".
(3) In section 63 (functions of regional and islands councils in relation to processions)—
  (*a*) after subsection (1) there shall be inserted—
        "(1A) Where notice of a proposal to hold a procession has been given or falls to be treated as having been given in accordance with section 62(1) of this Act—
              (*a*) if a regional or islands council have made an order under subsection (1) above they may at any time thereafter, after consulting the chief constable, vary or revoke the order and, where they revoke it, make any order which they were empowered to make under that subsection;

      (*b*) if they have decided not to make an order they may at any time thereafter, after consulting the chief constable, make any order which they were empowered to make under that subsection.";

  (*b*) in subsection (2) after "(1)" there shall be inserted "or (1A)";

  (*c*) in subsection (3)—

      (i) in paragraph (*a*)(i), after "(1)" there shall be inserted or (1A) above";

      (ii) in paragraph (*a*)(ii), for "such an order" there shall be substituted "an order under subsection (1) above or to revoke an order already made under subsection (1) or (1A) above";

      (iii) at the end of paragraph (*a*)(ii), for "and" there shall be substituted—

        "(iii) where they have, under subsection (1A) above, varied such an order, a copy of the order as varied and a written statement of the reasons for the variation; and";

      (iv) in paragraph (*b*), after "(1)" there shall be inserted "or (1A)", and after "made" where third occurring there shall be inserted "and, if the order has been varied under subsection (1A) above, that it has been so varied"; and

      (v) at the end of paragraph (*b*) there shall be inserted "; and

      (*c*) where they have revoked an order made under subsection (1) or (1A) above in relation to a proposal to hold a procession, make such arrangements as will ensure that persons who might take or are taking part in that procession are made aware of the fact that the order has been revoked.".

  (4) In section 64 (appeals against orders under section 63)—

    (*a*) in subsection (1) for the words from "against" to the end there shall be substituted—

      "against—

      (*a*) an order made under section 63(1) or (1A) of this Act; or

      (*b*) a variation under section 63(1A) of this Act of an order made under section 63(1) or (1A),

    in relation to the procession.";

    (*b*) in subsection (4) after "make" there shall be inserted "or, as the case may be, to vary"; and

    (*c*) in subsection (7) after "order" there shall be inserted "or, as the case may be, the variation of whose order".

  (5) In section 65 (offences and enforcement)—

    (*a*) in paragraphs (*b*) and (*c*) of subsection (1), after "(1)" there shall be inserted "or (1A)"; and

    (*b*) in paragraphs (*b*) and (*c*) of subsection (2), after "(1)" there shall be inserted "or (1A)".

  (6) In section 66 (relationship with Public Order Act 1936)—

    (*a*) for "the Public Order Act 1936" there shall be substituted "Part II of the Public Order Act 1986";

    (*b*) in paragraph (*a*), for "or order made under section 3" there shall be substituted "under section 12", and "or that order" shall be omitted; and

    (*c*) in paragraph (*b*), "or order under the said section 3" shall be omitted.

Criminal Justice Act 1982 (c.48)

  4. The following shall be inserted at the end of Part II of Schedule 1 to the Criminal Justice Act 1982 (statutory offences excluded from provisions for early release of prisoners)—

PUBLIC ORDER ACT 1986

  27. Section 1 (riot).

  28. Section 2 (violent disorder).

  29. Section 3 (affray).".

Cable and Broadcasting Act 1984 (c.46)

  5.—(1) The Cable and Broadcasting Act 1984 as it extends to England and Wales and Scotland is amended as follows.

  (2) Omit section 27 (inclusion of programme in cable programme service likely to stir up racial hatred).

(3) In section 28 (amendment of the law of defamation), at the end add—

"(6) In this section "words" includes pictures, visual images, gestures and other methods of signifying meaning.".

(4) In section 33(2), in the definition of "relevant offence" omit "an offence under section 27 above or".

6.—(1) Section 27 of the Cable and Broadcasting Act 1984 as it extends to Northern Ireland is amended as follows.

(2) For subsections (1) to (5) substitute—

"(1) If a programme involving threatening, abusive or insulting visual images or sounds is included in a cable programme service, each of the persons mentioned in subsection (2) below is guilty of an offence if—

(*a*) he intends thereby to stir up racial hatred, or

(*b*) having regard to all the circumstances racial hatred is likely to be stirred up thereby.

(2) The persons are—

(*a*) the person providing the cable programme service,

(*b*) any person by whom the programme is produced or directed, and

(*c*) any person by whom offending words or behaviour are used.

(3) If the person providing the service, or a person by whom the programme was produced or directed, is not shown to have intended to stir up racial hatred, it is a defence for him to prove that—

(*a*) he did not know and had no reason to suspect that the programme would involve the offending material, and

(*b*) having regard to the circumstances in which the programme was included in a cable programme service, it was not reasonably practicable for him to secure the removal of the material.

(4) It is a defence for a person by whom the programme was produced or directed who is not shown to have intended to stir up racial hatred to prove that he did not know and had no reason to suspect—

(*a*) that the programme would be included in a cable programme service, or

(*b*) that the circumstances in which the programme would be so included would be such that racial hatred would be likely to be stirred up.

(5) It is a defence for a person by whom offending words or behaviour were used and who is not shown to have intended to stir up racial hatred to prove that he did not know and had no reason to suspect—

(*a*) that a programme involving the use of the offending material would be included in a cable programme service, or

(*b*) that the circumstances in which a programme involving the use of the offending material would be so included, or in which a programme so included would involve the use of the offending material, would be such that racial hatred would be likely to be stirred up.

(5A) A person who is not shown to have intended to stir up racial hatred is not guilty of an offence under this section if he did not know, and had no reason to suspect, that the offending material was threatening, abusive or insulting.

(5B) A person guilty of an offence under this section is liable—

(*a*) on conviction on indictment to imprisonment for a term not exceeding two years or a fine or both;

(*b*) on summary conviction to imprisonment for a term not exceeding six months or a fine not exceeding the statutory maximum or both.".

(3) In subsection (8) (consents to prosecutions), for the words from "shall not be instituted" to the end substitute "shall not be instituted except by or with the consent of the Attorney General for Northern Ireland.".

(4) In subsection (9) (interpretation) for " 'racial group' means a group of persons" substitute " 'racial hatred' means hatred against a group of persons in Northern Ireland".

(5) After subsection (10) insert—

"(11) This section extends to Northern Ireland only.".

Police and Criminal Evidence Act 1984 (c.60)

7. In section 17(1)(*c*) of the Police and Criminal Evidence Act 1984 (entry for purpose of arrest for certain offences) in sub-paragraph (i) the words from "4" to "peace)" shall be omitted and after sub-paragraph (ii) there shall be inserted—

"(iii) section 4 of the Public Order Act 1986 (fear or provocation of violence);".

             SCHEDULE 3

REPEALS

Chapter	Short title	Extent of repeal
13 Chas. 2. Stat. 1. c.5.	Tumultuous Petitioning Act 1661.	The whole Act.
33 Geo. 3. c.67.	Shipping Offences Act 1793.	The whole Act.
57 Geo. 3. c.19.	Seditious Meetings Act 1817.	The whole Act.
5 Geo. 4. c.83.	Vagrancy Act 1824.	In section 4, the words from "every person being armed" to "arrestable offence" and from "and every such gun" to the end.
2 & 3 Vict. c.47.	Metropolitan Police Act 1839.	In section 54, paragraph 13.
2 & 3 Vict. c.xciv.	City of London Police Act 1839.	In section 35, paragraph 13.
3 Edw. 7. c.ccl.	Erith Tramways and Improvement Act 1903.	Section 171.
1 Edw. 8 & 1 Geo. 6. c.6.	Public Order Act 1936.	Section 3. Section 4. Section 5. Section 5A. In section 7, in subsection (2) the words "or section 5 or 5A" and in subsection (3) the words ", four or five". Section 8(6). In section 9, in subsection (1) the definition of "public procession" and in subsection (3) the words "by the council of any borough or district or".
7 & 8 Geo. 6. c.xxi.	Middlesex County Council Act 1944.	Section 309.
1967 c.58.	Criminal Law Act 1967.	Section 11(3). In Schedule 2, paragraph 2(1)(*b*).
1968 c.54.	Theatres Act 1968.	Section 5. In sections 7(2), 8, 9(1), 10(1)(*a*) and (*b*), 15(1)(*a*) and 18(2) the references to section 5.
1976 c.74.	Race Relations Act 1976.	Section 70. Section 79(6).
1976 c.xxxv.	County of South Glamorgan Act 1976.	Section 25. In Part I of Schedule 3, the entry relating to section 25.
1980 c.62.	Criminal Justice (Scotland) Act 1980.	In section 75(*e*)(i), the word "or" at the end.
1980 c.x.	County of Merseyside Act 1980.	In section 30(2), paragraph (*b*), the word "and" preceding that paragraph and the words from "and may make" to the end. In section 30(5), the words "in the said section 31 or". Section 31. In section 137(2), the reference to section 31.
1980 c.xi.	West Midlands County Council Act 1980.	Section 38, except subsection (4). In section 116(2), the reference to section 38.
1980 c.xiii.	Cheshire County Council Act 1980.	Section 28, except subsection (4). In section 108(2), the reference to section 28.

Chapter	Short title	Extent of repeal
1980 c.xv.	Isle of Wight Act 1980.	Section 26, except subsection (4). In section 63(2), the reference to section 26.
1981 c.ix.	Greater Manchester Act 1981.	Section 56, except subsection (4). In section 179(2), the reference to section 56.
1981 c.xxv.	East Sussex Act 1981.	Section 29. In section 102(2), the reference to section 29.
1982 c.45.	Civic Government (Scotland) Act 1982.	Section 62(10). In section 63(3)(*a*)(i), the word "or" at the end. In section 66, in paragraph (*a*), the words "or that order", and in paragraph (*b*) the words "or order under the said section 3".
1982 c.48.	Criminal Justice Act 1982.	In Part I of Schedule 1, the entries relating to riot and affray.
1984 c.46.	Cable and Broadcasting Act 1984.	Section 27. In section 33(2), the words "an offence under section 27 above or".
1984 c.60.	Police and Criminal Evidence Act 1984.	In section 17(1)(*c*)(i) the words from "4" to "peace)".
1985 c.57.	Sporting Events (Control of Alcohol etc.) Act 1985.	In section 8, the word "and" at the end of paragraph (*b*).

HOUSING (SCOTLAND) ACT 1986*

(1986 c.65)

ARRANGEMENT OF SECTIONS

---

* Annotations by C. M. G. Himsworth, B.A., LL.B., Senior Lecturer in Law, University of Edinburgh.

An Act to amend the Tenants' Rights, Etc. (Scotland) Act 1980, the Housing Associations Act 1985 in its application to Scotland and the Building (Scotland) Act 1959; to make further provision as regards housing in Scotland; and for connected purposes.

[7th November 1986.]

PARLIAMENTARY DEBATES
Hansard: H.C. Vol. 86, col. 712; Vol. 87, col. 1046; Vol. 92, col. 1137; Vol. 93, col. 174; Vol. 100, col. 1059; H.L. Vol. 472, cols. 226, 926; Vol. 474, col. 1052; Vol. 476, col. 312; Vol. 481, col. 716.
The Bill was considered in Committee by the first Scottish Standing Committee, December 10 to February 11, 1986.

INTRODUCTION AND GENERAL NOTE

The purpose of this Act is to make a number of amendments to the Tenants' Rights, Etc. (Scotland) Act 1980. Probably the most significant (and also the most controversial) is the extension of the right to purchase to tenants of most housing associations and of regional councils (and other police and fire authorities). The Act increases the amount of discount to be paid to a tenant who purchases a flat and makes other miscellaneous amendments. There are also amendments to, *inter alia*, the Housing Associations Act 1985 (many of them consequential upon the extension of the right to purchase) to the Building (Scotland) Act 1959, and to the Land Compensation (Scotland) Act 1973. A late addition was the amendment made to the Housing (Homeless Persons) Act 1977 in s.21.

The Act had an interesting passage through Parliament and produced considerable conflict between the two Houses. The Bill having been passed by the Commons with some amendments, the Lords made further amendments (to produce an earlier version of what is now s.21 and to amend Sched. 1 as it affects housing associations) against the wishes of the Government. The Commons rejected the first amendment but proposed alternatives to the others. These Commons amendments were accepted by the Lords subject to a further amendment with certain consequential amendments added. The Lords also proposed an amendment to produce a different version of s.21 (the one now incorporated into the Act) and, with time running out at the end of the Session, the Government recommended to the Commons that the final Lords package should be accepted.

The Housing and Planning Act 1986, which, so far as it relates to housing, contains provisions for England and Wales in parallel with those enacted for Scotland in the Housing (Scotland) Act, also ran into difficulties at the end of the Session. It should be noted that that Act contains a number of provisions which extend to Scotland—many of them being amendments to the Housing Associations Act 1985. Special mention should, however, be made of s.3 of the Housing and Planning Act 1986. This inserts into s.1 of the Tenants' Rights, Etc. (Scotland) Act 1980 new subsections (5B) and (5C) which enable the Secretary of State to prescribe by order (statutory instrument subject to approval of draft by each House) different percentage discounts (minimum, maximum and intermediate) on the purchase of houses by tenants.

COMMENCEMENT AND EXTENT

In accordance with s.26 the Act, with the exception of that section, comes into force on days to be appointed by the Secretary of State. In terms of S.I. 1986 No. 2137 the whole Act comes into force on January 7, 1987.

The Act applies to Scotland only.

Amendment of Tenants' Rights, Etc. (Scotland) Act 1980

Extension of right to purchase and of "secure tenancy"

1.—(1) In section 1(3) of the 1980 Act (dwelling-houses to which right to purchase applies), for the words "of paragraphs (*a*), (*b*), (*c*) or (*f*)" there shall be substituted the words "paragraph, other than (*g*),".

(2) In section 10(2) of the 1980 Act (landlords in secure tenancies)—
(*a*) after paragraph (*a*) there shall be inserted the following paragraph—

"(aa) a regional council, or a joint board or joint committee
of two or more regional councils, or any trust under the
control of a regional council;"; and
(b) after paragraph (g) there shall be inserted the following
paragraphs—
"(h) a police authority within the meaning of section 2(1),
as read with subsection (9)(b) of section 19, of the Police
(Scotland) Act 1967 or a joint police committee constituted
by virtue of subsection (2)(b) of the said section 19; and
(i) a fire authority in Scotland for the purposes of the Fire
Services Acts 1947 to 1959 (or a joint committee constituted
by virtue of section 36(4)(b) of the Fire Services Act 1947).".

General Note
This section, with which should be read Sched. 1, para. 1(e), (f) and (g) and parts of
Sched. 3, makes the most significant changes contained in the Act affecting the right of
secure tenants to purchase their houses. That right is established by four provisions in the
Tenants' Rights, Etc. (Scotland) Act 1980. S.10(2) defines the landlords whose tenants are
prima facie secure; Sched. 1 excludes from security certain of those tenants; s.1(3) lists those
secure tenants who have the right to purchase; and s.1(11) restricts further that list. All four
provisions are amended.

Subs. (1)
Subject to what is said below, the effect of this subsection is to extend the right to
purchase to virtually all categories of public sector secure tenants (the only exception being
tenants of housing trusts in existence on November 13, 1953, or of societies within the
meaning of the Housing Act 1914). In particular the tenants of housing associations (but see
below) and of the Housing Corporation now have the right to purchase.

Subs. (2)
By amending s.10(2) to the 1980 Act, this subsection adds to the list of public sector
landlords, whose tenants are secure, regional councils, police authorities and fire authorities.
The terms of the amended s.1(3) define such tenants as tenants with the right to purchase
(but, in relation to tenants of police and fire authorities, see too the amendments to Sched.
1 to the 1980 Act made by Sched. 1, para. 18 to this Act).
The amendments to s.1(11) of the 1980 Act are made by Sched. 1, para. 1(f) and (g) to
this Act and qualify in important ways the new rights of housing association tenants to
purchase their houses. See also ss.15 and 16 of this Act which amend the Housing
Associations Act 1985 in ways which are largely consequential upon the amendments in this
section. For further consequential amendments see Sched. 1, paras. 1(e), 2, 6 and 18. For
the amendment to Sched. 1 to the 1980 Act, see s.10.

Increased discount where dwelling-house purchased is a flat

2.—(1) Subject to subsection (3) below, in section 1(5)(b) of the 1980
Act (discount for purposes of calculation of purchase price of dwelling-
house)—
(a) in sub-paragraph (i), after the words "32 per cent." there shall be
inserted the words ", or where the dwelling-house is a flat 44 per
cent.,";
(b) in sub-paragraph (ii), after the words "one per cent." there shall
be inserted the words ", or where the dwelling-house is a flat two
per cent.,";
(c) after the words "60 per cent." there shall be inserted the words
", or where the dwelling-house is a flat 70 per cent.,"; and
(d) at the end there shall be added the words "For the purposes of the
foregoing provisions of this paragraph a "flat" is a separate and
self-contained set of premises, whether or not on the same floor,
forming part of a building from some other part of which it is
divided horizontally.".

(2) Subject to subsection (3) below, in section 9A of the 1980 Act (application of Part I of that Act when dwelling-house is repurchased as defective), after the words " '30 per cent.';" there shall be inserted the words "(AA) for the words '44 per cent.' there shall be substituted the words '40 per cent.';".

(3) Subsections (1) and (2) above shall have no effect as regards the exercise of a right to purchase by application under section 2(1) of the 1980 Act if the offer to sell has been duly served (whether by the landlord or, under section 7(3)(*a*) of that Act, by the Lands Tribunal for Scotland) before the date of coming into force of this section.

GENERAL NOTE

One of the most fundamental characteristics of the rules governing the right to purchase is the purchaser's entitlement to a discount in the calculation of the price to be paid. The details are contained in s.1(5)(*b*) of the 1980 Act as amended by the Tenants' Rights, Etc. (Scotland) Amendment Act 1984 and provide for a minimum discount of 32 per cent. based on two years' occupation of the house to be bought rising by 1 per cent. per year of occupation to a maximum discount of 60 per cent. The rules prior to amendment by this Act made no distinction between houses which are "flats" and other houses but now that distinction is introduced in order to give a higher entitlement to discount to the occupants of flats. The Government had been concerned (see H.C. Standing Committee, col. 247; H.L. Standing Committee, col. 77) by the low rate of purchase by such tenants—probably because of fears about future liabilities as owners. The amendments made to s.1(5)(*b*) (the original clause was amended at Committee stage in the Lords) now provide for a higher initial discount of 44 per cent. rising in 2 per cent. (instead of 1 per cent.) stages to a maximum of 70 per cent. (based on 15 years occupation instead of the normal 30 years needed to qualify for maximum discount).

With this section should now be read the further amendments made by s.3 of the Housing and Planning Act 1986.

Subs. (1)

This makes (in (*a*)–(*c*)) the amendments already referred to. Para. (*d*) defines a flat for the purposes of this provision. See also s.208(1) of the Housing (Scotland) Act 1966.

Subs. (2)

This makes an amendment to s.9A of the 1980 Act (inserted by the Housing Defects Act 1984) consequential upon the changes in subs. (1). It provides a minimum discount of 40 per cent. rather than the normal 30 per cent. for those tenants immediately eligible to buy their house or flat in terms of the Housing Defects Act.

Subs. (3)

This ensures that changes in the section do not have retrospective application to offers made prior to the commencement of the section. A relevant tenant who has received (but not yet accepted) an offer on that date would be able to withdraw his application and reapply with a right to a new offer under the revised and more generous discount rules.

Amendment of date after which certain restrictions may apply as regards price fixed for purchase of dwelling-house; and extension of those restrictions

3.—(1) Subject to subsection (6) below, in subsection (7) of section 1 of the 1980 Act (fixing of price at which tenant entitled to purchase dwelling-house)—

    (*a*) for the words "15 May 1975" there shall be substituted the words "31 December 1978"; and

    (*b*) in paragraph (*a*), for the words "in providing the dwelling-house" there shall be substituted the words—

        "after that date (either or both)—

          (i) in providing;

          (ii) in making improvements (other than by way of repair or maintenance) to,

        the dwelling-house".

(2) Subject to subsection (6) below, after the said subsection (7) there shall be inserted the following subsection—

"(7A) Where the dwelling-house was first let under a tenancy which, if Part II of this Act had then been in force, would have been a secure tenancy, on or before the date mentioned in subsection (7) above but an outstanding debt has been incurred after that date in making improvements (other than by way of repair or maintenance) to the dwelling-house, the price fixed under subsection (5) above shall not be less than—

(*a*) that outstanding debt; or

(*b*) the market value of the dwelling-house determined under subsection (5)(*a*) above,

whichever is the lesser except in such cases as the Secretary of State may, by order made as is mentioned in subsection (7) above, prescribe.".

(3) Subject to subsection (6) below, in subsection (8) of the said section 1 (interpretation of "outstanding debt")—

(*a*) after the word "means" there shall be inserted the words ", in relation to paragraph (*a*)(i) of that subsection,"; and

(*b*) at the end there shall be added the words "; and

(*e*) where the landlord is a body mentioned in paragraph (*d*) or (*e*) of section 10(2) of this Act, any proportion or capital grants which it must repay on the dwelling-house being sold;

but in relation to paragraph (*a*)(ii) of that subsection and in subsection (7A) above its meaning is confined to any undischarged debt arising from the cost of the works of improvement together with—

(i) administrative costs attributable to those works; and

(ii) where the landlord is such body as is mentioned in paragraph (*e*) above, any such proportion as is there mentioned.".

(4) With the consent of the Treasury the Secretary of State may by order made by statutory instrument—

(*a*) amend subsection (7) of the said section 1 so as to substitute a later date for—

(i) the words substituted by subsection (1) above; or

(ii) words substituted by virtue of this subsection; or

(*b*) provide that subsections (7)(*a*)(ii), (7A) and (8) of the said section 1 shall apply with such modifications as he may specify in the order;

and such order may make different provision in relation to different areas, cases or classes of case and may exclude certain areas, cases or classes of case.

(5) A statutory instrument under subsection (4) above shall be subject to annulment in pursuance of a resolution of either House of Parliament.

(6) The foregoing provisions of this section shall have no effect as regards the exercise of a right to purchase by application under section 2(1) of the 1980 Act if the offer to sell has been duly served (whether by the landlord or, under section 7(3)(*a*) of that Act, by the Lands Tribunal for Scotland) before the date of coming into force of this section.

GENERAL NOTE

Subss. (7) and (8) of s.1 of the 1980 Act were designed to reduce a purchasing tenant's entitlement to discount where he was buying a newer house (first let after May 15, 1975) and where the discounted price would be less than what was defined in subs. (8) as the amount of the outstanding debt on the house. The rule was to protect landlords from major losses incurred by compulsory large discounts on these newer properties.

The amendments made by this section change those rules and make them rather more sophisticated and flexible. In particular the relevant date is changed to December 31, 1978; the cost of improvements since that date on a house originally let before it may now also be taken into account; and most aspects of the scheme now become amendable by order.

See also Sched. 1, paras. 3, 7 and 8.

Subs. (1)

This substitutes (by para. (*a*)) the new date in s.1(7) of the 1980 Act. For discussion of the choice of this date see H.C. Standing Committee, col. 262. In terms of subs. (4) the date becomes further amendable by order.

Thereafter in para. (*b*) the subsection extends the scope of the amount to include within the "outstanding debt" for the house not only the costs of provision but also the costs of improvement after December 31, 1978. This parallels the provision made in subs. (2) concerning the improvement of older houses. Is there a paradox in the new formula's reference to "the outstanding debt *incurred after that date* [December 31, 1978] (either or both)—(1) in providing; . . . the dwelling house."? At what point is the debt *incurred* on a house provided before but first let after December 31, 1978? Presumably before that date?

Subs. (2)

The purpose of the new subs. (7A) is to add to the landlord's protection against too expensive a discount, the situation in which it does not provide a new house but makes improvements to an older (pre December 31, 1978) house. This is in part to remove a landlord's reluctance to carry out extensive improvements to a house which might then be sold at a substantial discount. For a provision designed to prevent landlords from negotiating agreements that the tenant of a house to be improved will not seek to exercise his right to purchase, see Sched. 1, para. 1.

Notice again that the new subs. (7A) is amendable by order.

Subs. (3)

The amendments made to s.1(8) of the 1980 Act are largely consequential upon those made above. Subs. (8) defines "outstanding debt" and the original formula is now confined to debts arising from the *provision* of a house. In relation to debts arising from *improvement* (whether of a pre- or post- 1978 house) these are defined to relate to the cost of the work plus administrative costs.

Both definitions are also adjusted to allow for this Act's admission of the Housing Corporation and housing associations (bodies mentioned in paras. (*d*) and (*e*) of s.10(2) of the 1980 Act) as landlords subject to the tenant's right to purchase. The outstanding debt for these landlords is extended to include the amount of capital grants to be repaid.

Subss. (4) and (5)

The power further to amend the date in s.1(7) has already been mentioned. The formula seems, however, a little inelegant especially in so far as it provides for the substitution of a "later date" for "words substituted" by subs. (1)—a term which could apply both to para. (*a*) and para. (*b*).

Para. (*b*) of this subsection permits further modification of the "improvement" provisions and of the definitions of outstanding debt in s.1(8) of the 1980 Act.

Why were these provisions not drafted as further amendments to s.1 of the 1980 Act? It seems an unnecessary complexity to detach them from it.

Subs. (6)

This makes similar provision in relation to the amendments made by this section, as is made by s.2(3).

Secretary of State's power to give directions as to conditions in offers to sell

4. After section 4 of the 1980 Act there shall be inserted the following section—

"Further limitations on conditions of sale

4A.—(1) Where it appears to the Secretary of State that the inclusion of conditions of a particular kind in offers to sell would be unreasonable he may by direction require landlords generally, landlords of a particular description, or particular landlords not to include conditions of that kind (or not to include conditions of that kind unless modified in such manner as may be specified in the direction) in offers to sell served on or after a date so specified.

(2) Where a condition's inclusion in an offer to sell—

(*a*) is in contravention of a direction under subsection (1) above; or

(*b*) in a case where the tenant has not by the date specified in such a direction served a relative notice of acceptance on the landlord, would have been in such contravention had the offer to sell been served on or after that date,

the condition shall have no effect as regards the offer to sell.

(3) A direction under subsection (1) above may—

(*a*) make different provision in relation to different areas, cases or classes of case and may exclude certain areas, cases or classes of case; and

(*b*) be varied or withdrawn by a subsequent direction so given.

(4) Section 211 of the Local Government (Scotland) Act 1973 (provision for default of local authority) shall apply as regards a failure to comply with a requirement in a direction under subsection (1) above as that section applies as regards such failure as is mentioned in subsection (1) thereof.".

GENERAL NOTE

Subject to some important qualifications contained in the section, s.4 of the 1980 Act permits and, in some cases, requires offers to sell which are made by landlords to their tenants to contain "such conditions as are reasonable". If a tenant complains that a condition included by the landlord is unreasonable, he takes that complaint to the Lands Tribunal for Scotland under s.2(3) of the Act and quite a substantial number of decisions on unreasonableness have been issued (see Himsworth *Public Sector Housing Law in Scotland*, 2nd ed. 1986, pp.66–71). However, the Government considered it unsatisfactory to leave questions of unreasonableness to be resolved on an individual basis by the Lands Tribunal. If landlords engaged in the repeated insertion of unreasonable conditions, this was a problem better addressed by blanket action by the Secretary of State. In debate (see H.C. Standing Committee, col. 276), the minister referred to unreasonable conditions relating to common ground, rights of access, responsibility for common services and obligations to pay for repairs.

S.4 of this Act is aimed (by the insertion of a new s.4A in the 1980 Act) at these problems and enables the Secretary of State to direct in advance that certain kinds of condition shall not be included in an offer with the sanction that, if included, they shall have no effect and with the further possibility of default action taken by the Secretary of State under s.211 of the Local Government (Scotland) Act 1973. The Secretary of State's directions may be addressed to individual landlords or to landlords of a particular description (subs. (1)); they may differ from area to area, case to case, and may be subsequently varied or withdrawn.

Financial and other assistance for tenants involved in proceedings under Part I of 1980 Act etc.

5. After section 9A of the 1980 Act there shall be inserted the following section—

"Financial and other assistance for tenants involved in proceedings under Part I etc.

9B.—(1) Where, in relation to any proceedings, or prospective proceedings, to which this section applies, a tenant or purchaser is an actual or prospective party, the Secretary of State may on written application to him by the tenant or purchaser give financial or other assistance to the applicant, if the Secretary of State thinks fit to do so:

Provided that assistance under this section shall be given only where the Secretary of State considers—

(*a*) that the case raises a question of principle and that it is in the public interest to give the applicant such assistance; or

(b) that there is some other special consideration.

(2) This section applies to—

(a) any proceedings under this Part of this Act; and

(b) any proceedings to determine any question arising under or in connection with this Part of this Act other than a question as to market value for the purposes of section 1(5) of this Act.

(3) Assistance by the Secretary of State under this section may include—

(a) giving advice;

(b) procuring or attempting to procure the settlement of the matter in dispute;

(c) arranging for the giving of advice or assistance by a solicitor or counsel;

(d) arranging for representation by a solicitor or counsel;

(e) any other form of assistance which the Secretary of State may consider appropriate.

(4) In so far as expenses are incurred by the Secretary of State in providing the applicant with assistance under this section, any sums recovered by virtue of an award of expenses, or of an agreement as to expenses, in the applicant's favour with respect to the matter in connection with which the assistance is given shall, subject to any charge or obligation for payment in priority to other debts under the Legal Aid and Advice (Scotland) Acts 1967 and 1972 and to any provision of those Acts for payment of any sum into the legal aid fund, be paid to the Secretary of State in priority to any other debts.

(5) Any expenses incurred by the Secretary of State in providing assistance under this section shall be paid out of money provided by Parliament; and any sums received by the Secretary of State under subsection (4) above shall be paid into the Consolidated Fund.".

GENERAL NOTE

This section which inserts a new s.9B into the 1980 Act (s.9A is an unrelated section inserted by the Housing Defects Act 1984) reflects the Government's view that, whilst local authorities can afford to take disputed questions under Part I of the Act to the Lands Tribunal for Scotland and thereafter on appeal to the Court of Session, a tenant may not have the resources to do so (see, *e.g,* H.C. Standing Committee, col. 301). The new s.9B gives the Secretary of State the power to provide to actual or prospective purchasers various forms of assistance.

The case has to be one raising a question of principle and one where it is in the public interest to provide assistance or, alternatively, where there is some other special consideration. The Secretary of State may give the assistance on application by the tenant and then only if he thinks fits to do so.

Provision is made in subss. (4) and (5) for the financing of assistance out of the Consolidated Fund and for the recovery of the Secretary of State's expenses in appropriate cases.

Information from landlords in relation to Secretary of State's powers under Part I of 1980 Act

6. After the section inserted into the 1980 Act by section 5 of this Act there shall be inserted the following section—

"Information from landlords in relation to Secretary of State's powers under this Part

9C.—(1) Without prejudice to section 199 of the Local Government (Scotland) Act 1973 (reports and returns by local authorities etc.), where it appears to the Secretary of State necessary or expedient, in relation to the exercise of his powers under this Part of this Act, he may by notice in writing to a landlord require it—

(*a*) at such time and at such place as may be specified in the notice, to produce any document; or

(*b*) within such period as may be so specified or such longer period as the Secretary of State may allow, to furnish a copy of any document or supply any information.

(2) Any officer of the landlord designated in the notice for that purpose or having custody or control of the document or in a position to give that information shall, without instructions from the landlord, take all reasonable steps to ensure that the notice is complied with.".

GENERAL NOTE

The Secretary of State's powers under the 1980 Act are expanded by the amendments made by earlier sections of this Act. The justification given for this new s.9C is that, to enable him to exercise those powers, the Secretary of State will, from time to time, require information held by landlords.

In relation to local authorities he already has the power to request such information under s.199 of the Local Government (Scotland) Act 1973. This new section extends to all public sector landlords subject to the right to purchase under Part I of the 1980 Act. A further substantial extension of the minister's powers is conferred by subs. (2) which authorises the designation of an officer who will be required to take all reasonable steps to ensure compliance. Do such reasonable steps include the supply of information against the declared wishes of an officer's employing authority? What are the consequences for the officer if he (*a*) supplies the information or (*b*) refuses?

Contributions towards the cost of transfers and exchanges

7. After section 25 of the 1980 Act there shall be inserted the following cross-heading and section—

"*Transfers and Exchanges*

Contributions towards the cost of transfers and exchanges

25A.—(1) The Secretary of State may with the consent of the Treasury make out of money provided by Parliament grants or loans towards the cost of arrangements for facilitating moves to and from homes by which—

(*a*) a secure tenant of one landlord (the "first landlord") becomes, at his own request, the secure tenant of a different landlord (whether or not by means of an exchange whereby a secure tenant of the different landlord becomes the secure tenant of the first landlord); or

(*b*) each of two or more tenants of dwelling-houses, one at least of which is let under a secure tenancy, becomes the tenant of the other dwelling-house (or, as the case may be, of one of the other dwelling-houses).

(2) The grants or loans may be made subject to such conditions as the Secretary of State may determine, and may be made so as to be repayable (or, as the case may be, repayable earlier) if there is a breach of such a condition.

(3) In subsection (1) above, the reference to a "secure tenant" is to a tenant under a secure tenancy within the meaning of this Act or of the Housing Act 1985 or of Chapter II of Part II of the Housing (Northern Ireland) Order 1983.".

GENERAL NOTE

This section inserts a new s.25A at the end of the "Tenants' Charter" provisions in Part II of the 1980 Act to enable the Secretary of State to promote tenant mobility in the public sector. Explaining the provision, the minister referred to existing Government support for two schemes—the national mobility scheme and the tenants' exchange scheme—with financing approved under the Parliamentary vote and Appropriation Act procedure (H.C.

Standing Committee, col. 329). The new section gives specific statutory authority for the grants and loans made.

Duty of housing association to make rules governing housing list etc.

8. For subsection (1A) of section 27 of the 1980 Act (publication of rules as to housing lists etc.) there shall be substituted the following subsections—

"(1A) It shall be the duty of every registered housing association (within the meaning of the Housing Associations Act 1985)—

   (*a*) within the period of six months commencing with the date of coming into force of section 8 of the Housing (Scotland) Act 1986 to make rules governing the matters mentioned in paragraphs (*a*) to (*d*) of subsection (1) above (unless it has, in accordance with subsections (2) and (2A) below, published such rules before that date and those rules remain current);

   (*b*) within six months of the making of rules under paragraph (*a*) above, and within six months of any alteration of such rules (whether or not made under that paragraph)—

      (i) to send a copy of them to each of the bodies mentioned in subsection (1B) below; and

      (ii) to publish them in accordance with subsections (2) and (2A) below.

   (1B) The bodies referred to in subsection (1A)(*b*)(i) above are—

      (i) the Housing Corporation; and

      (ii) every islands or district council within whose area there is a dwelling-house let, or to be let, by the association under a secure tenancy.".

GENERAL NOTE

S.27 of the 1980 Act imposed upon public sector landlords, other than housing associations, a requirement to publish any rules they had governing the allocation of their houses including rules about transfers and exchanges. The obligation was extended to registered housing associations by the insertion of a new subsection (1A) by Sched. 3, para. 44 to the Local Government (Miscellaneous Provisions) (Scotland) Act 1981.

These new subss. (1A) and (1B) replace and strengthen that provision by the introduction of a positive obligation upon housing associations to make allocation rules. Although permissive only, these rules had in practice been made by local authorities and other landlords. Some 40 per cent. of housing associations had failed to do so (see H.C. Standing Committee, col. 335) and this, in the Government's view, required change. The new subs. (1A) requires those associations who have not already published the rules to do so within six months of the commencement of the section (for that, see s.26(2)).

Extension of power of islands and district councils to indemnify certain heritable creditors

9. In section 31 of the 1980 Act (local authority indemnities for building societies)—

   (*a*) in subsection (1)—

      (i) after the words "(Northern Ireland) 1967)" and, at the second and third places where they occur, "building society" there shall in each case be inserted the words "or recognised body";

      (ii) for the words "the standard security" there shall be substituted the words "a heritable security";

   (*b*) in subsection (2) for the words "under the standard security" there shall be substituted the words ", or recognised body, under the heritable security";

   (*c*) in subsection (5) after the words "building societies" there shall be inserted the words "or recognised bodies"; and (*d*) after subsection (5) there shall be inserted the following subsections—

> "(5A) In this section "recognised body" means a body designated, or of a class or description designated, in an order made under this subsection by statutory instrument by the Secretary of State with the consent of the Treasury.
>
> (5B) Before making an order under subsection (5A) above varying or revoking an order previously so made, the Secretary of State shall give an opportunity for representations to be made on behalf of a recognised body which, if the order were made, would cease to be such a body.".

GENERAL NOTE

Under s.31 of the 1980 Act, local authorities have the power to indemnify building societies against losses incurred on home loans. This section extends that power to authorise indemnities for other bodies referred to in paras. (*a*)–(*c*) and defined in the new subs. (5A) inserted by para. (*d*) as "recognised bodies" designated by the Secretary of State.

The substitution of "standard security" by "heritable security" in paras. (*a*) and (*b*) was required because of the need to accommodate those forms of "heritable security" current prior to the Conveyancing and Feudal Reform (Scotland) Act 1970.

Removal of restriction on security of tenure

10. In Schedule 1 to the 1980 Act, paragraph 1 (tenancy not to be secure tenancy if for period exceeding 20 years) shall cease to have effect.

GENERAL NOTE

This section was introduced as a new clause at the Lords Report stage (see Report, col. 1063). Sched. 1 to the 1980 Act lists the types of tenancy which are not secure tenancies— the first of which is the tenancy for a period exceeding 20 years.

As explained by the minister, the specific reason for the deletion of the exclusion was the Government's wish to circumvent the device adopted by at least one regional council (whose tenants were to become secure and entitled to buy under this Act) which was to renegotiate long leases for their tenants to prevent the creation of their right to buy.

Restoration of ground for recovery of possession of dwelling-house

11. In Schedule 2 to the 1980 Act (grounds for recovery of possession of dwelling-houses let under secure tenancies), after paragraph 5 there shall be inserted the following paragraph—

> "6. The landlord wishes to transfer the secure tenancy of the dwelling-house to—
>
> (*a*) the tenant's spouse (or former spouse); or
> (*b*) a person with whom the tenant has been living as husband and wife,
>
> who has applied to the landlord for such transfer; and either the tenant or the (as the case may be) spouse, former spouse or person, no longer wishes to live together with the other in the dwelling-house.".

GENERAL NOTE

Sched. 2 to the 1980 Act lists the grounds on which, under ss.14–15, the landlord may take proceedings to end a secure tenancy. In its original version, para. 6 enabled the landlord to secure the transfer from one spouse (or former spouse or person who has lived with another as man and wife) to the other.

That paragraph was, however, repealed by the Matrimonial Homes (Family Protection) (Scotland) Act 1981 as a part of the package of new provisions introduced by the Act. As the minister explained, however, the need for the landlord's own power to intervene to be restored had been brought to the attention of the Government by housing pressure groups (see H.C. Standing Committee, col. 355). What the Government had not adopted was the further suggestion that the "occupancy rights" (under the 1981 Act) of the spouse from whom the tenancy is transferred should be automatically terminated.

Note that, under the amended terms of s.15 of the 1980 Act (Sched. 1, para. 15 to this Act) the ground for recovery of possession under para. 6 is one which requires the court to be satisfied both as to the ground itself, that it is reasonable to make the possession order and that suitable alternative accommodation for the tenant will be available.

Further amendment of 1980 Act

12. The 1980 Act shall have effect subject to the amendments specified in Schedule 1 to this Act.

GENERAL NOTE
Many of this Act's most significant adjustments to the 1980 Act are contained in Sched. 1 where separate notes are added.

Amendment of Housing Associations Act 1985

Shared ownership agreements

13.—(1) In section 4 of the 1985 Act (eligibility of housing associations for registration), at the end of subsection (3) there shall be added the following paragraph—
  "(*h*) in Scotland, acquiring, or repairing and improving, or building, or creating by the conversion of dwellings or other property, dwellings to be disposed of under shared ownership agreements.".
(2) In section 106(2) of the 1985 Act (interpretation for purposes of application to Scotland), for the definition of "shared ownership lease" there shall be substituted the following definition—
  ' "shared ownership agreement" means an agreement whereby a registered housing association—
  (*a*) sells a *pro indiviso* right in a dwelling to a person and leases the remaining *pro indiviso* rights therein to him subject to his being entitled, from time to time, to purchase those remaining rights until he has purchased the entire dwelling; or
  (*b*) conveys *pro indiviso* rights in dwellings to trustees to hold on behalf of persons each of whom, by purchasing a share in those dwellings, becomes entitled to exclusive occupancy of one of the dwellings but with any such person who wishes to sell or otherwise dispose of his share being required to do so through the agency of the trustees,
  or such other agreement as may be approved whereby a person acquires from a registered housing association a *pro indiviso* right in a dwelling or dwellings and thereby becomes entitled to exclusive occupancy of the dwelling or, as the case may be, of one of the dwellings;'.

GENERAL NOTE
The point of the amendments made by this section to ss.4 and 106(2) of the Housing Associations Act 1985 is to extend the permissible purposes or objects of associations eligible for registration under that Act. The new purpose is the provision of houses to be disposed of under shared ownership agreements.

Subs. (1)
This makes the necessary addition to s.4 of the 1985 Act.

Subs. (2)
This amends s.106(2) of the 1985 Act to supply a definition of the meanings of "shared ownership agreement" used in s.4.
In para. (*a*) is the "normal" version of shared ownership agreement under which the person acquires a house from a housing association in part as purchaser and in part as lessee but with the right to purchase those remaining rights in the house—as the purchaser's financial position improves.

Para. (*b*) provides for the "equity-sharing" model of shared ownership (frequently used by elderly persons) under which the rights in the housing association's housing development are held by trustees on behalf of occupants who have each bought a share in the houses and become entitled to exclusive occupation of one house. When that occupation ceases, the person is normally entitled to the market value of his or her "share" of the development.

There is the possibility of further variants on the model of shared ownership provided that the agreements are approved. Approval is by the Housing Corporation. See the new subs. (3) added to s.106 of the 1985 Act by Sched. 2, para. 7 to this Act.

Payments etc. in community-based housing associations

14. After section 15 of the 1985 Act there shall be inserted the following section—

"Payments etc. in community-based housing associations in Scotland

15A.—(1) In relation to a community-based housing association in Scotland the following are also permitted, notwithstanding section 15(1) of this Act—
(*a*) payments made by the association in respect of the purchase of a dwelling, or part of a dwelling, owned and occupied by a person described in subsection (2) below who is not an employee of the association; but only if—
(i) such payments constitute expenditure in connection with housing projects undertaken for the purpose of improving or repairing dwellings, being expenditure in respect of which housing association grants may be made under section 41(1) of this Act; and
(ii) the purchase price does not exceed such value as may be placed on the dwelling, or as the case may be part, by the district valuer;
(*b*) the granting of the tenancy of a dwelling, or part of a dwelling, to such a person; but only if the person—
(i) lives in the dwelling or in another dwelling owned by the association; or
(ii) has at any time within the period of twelve months immediately preceding the granting of the tenancy lived in the dwelling (or such other dwelling) whether or not it belonged to the housing association when he lived there.
(2) The persons mentioned in subsection (1) above are—
(*a*) a committee member or voluntary officer of the association; or
(*b*) a person who at any time in the twelve months preceding the payment (or as the case may be the granting of the tenancy) has been such a member or officer; or
(*c*) a close relative of a person described in paragraph (*a*), or (*b*), above.
(3) For the purposes of subsection (1) above, a housing association is "community-based" if it is designated as such by the Housing Corporation.
(4) The Housing Corporation—
(*a*) shall make a designation under subsection (3) above only if it considers that the activities of the housing association relate wholly or mainly to the improvement of dwellings, or the management of improved dwellings, within a particular community (whether or not identified by reference to a geographical area entirely within any one administrative area); and
(*b*) may revoke such a designation if it considers, after giving the association an opportunity to make representations

to it as regards such revocation, that the association's activities have ceased so to relate.".

GENERAL NOTE

In order to discourage situations in which an undesirable conflict of interest might arise, s.15 of the Housing Associations Act 1985 imposes on registered housing associations a general prohibition upon the making of payments or granting of other benefits to persons who are their committee members, officers or employees—whether at the time or during the preceding 12 months. There are limited statutory exemptions from this rule in s.15(2) including payments to employees under their contracts of employment.

This new s.15A which applies only to community-based associations as defined in subs. (3) and (4) permits payments/benefits to the persons other than employees listed in subs. (2) of the two types listed in subss. (1)(*a*) and (*b*). The purpose is to enable such associations then to enter into what are, for them, necessary arrangements with persons within their communities who are also closely connected with the association.

Subss. (1)(*a*) and (*b*) restricts the transactions concerned to the purchase of a house (subject to conditions (i) and (ii)) and the grant of a tenancy (again subject to further conditions (i) and (ii)).

The term "close relative" in new s.15A(2)(*c*) also appears in s.15(1)(*c*) of the 1985 Act but is not defined in that Act although, in s.105, "members of a person's family" are.

Extension of sections 44 and 45 of 1985 Act to Scotland

15. Sections 44 (projects qualifying for housing association grant; repair or improvement after exercise of right to buy etc.) and 45 (projects qualifying for such grant: disposal to tenant of charitable housing association etc.) of the 1985 Act shall apply to Scotland; and accordingly—
    (*a*) in the said section 44—
        (i) in subsection (1), after the words "exercise" there shall be inserted the word "—(*a*)"; and after the words "1985" there shall be inserted the following paragraph—
            "; or
                (*b*) in Scotland, his right to purchase under section 1 of the Tenants' Rights, Etc. (Scotland) Act 1980,";
        (ii) in subsection (2), after the word "exercised" there shall be inserted the word "—(*a*)"; and after the word "lease" there shall be inserted the following paragraph—
            "; or
                (*b*) in Scotland, the right to purchase,"; and
        (iii) for subsection (3) there shall be substituted the following subsection—
            "(3) "Dwelling-house", in the application of this section to—
                (*a*) England and Wales, has the same meaning as in Part V of the Housing Act 1985; and
                (*b*) Scotland, means a house."; and
    (*b*) in the said section 45—
        (i) in subsection (2), after the word "for" there shall be inserted the word "—(*a*)" and at the end there shall be added the following words—
            "; or
                (*b*) subsection (11)(*e*) or (*f*) of section 1 of the Tenants' Rights, Etc. (Scotland) Act 1980 (analogous Scottish provision) would have a right to purchase under that section.";
        (ii) in subsection (3), at the end there shall be added the words "; and a dwelling is also publicly funded for this purpose if it is in Scotland and housing association grant has been paid in respect of a project which included its improvement or repair or, where it and another dwelling are both provided for letting

under the project, the improvement or repair of that other
dwelling.";

(iii) in subsection (4), at the beginning there shall be inserted the
words "In England and Wales,"; and

(iv) after subsection (4) there shall be added the following
subsection—

"(5) In Scotland, where a registered housing association
concludes missives for the acquisition of a house and,
without taking title, disposes of its interest to a tenant to
whom this section applies, subsection (1) and the following
provisions have effect as if the association first acquired the
house and then disposed of it to the tenant—

section 8 (disposal of land by registered housing
associations),

section 9 (consent of Housing Corporation to disposals),

section 79(2) (power of Housing Corporation to lend to
person acquiring interest from registered housing
association), and

section 6 of the Tenants' Rights, Etc. (Scotland) Act 1980
(recovery of discount on early re-sale).".

GENERAL NOTE

Ss.41–53 of the Housing Associations Act 1985 deal with the Secretary of State's powers
to make housing association grants to registered associations. Ss.42 and 43 define the
projects which qualify for grant—in the main projects for the provision of accommodation
including provision by improvement or repair.

S.44, as originally enacted, dealt with the situation (then liable to arise in England and
Wales only) in which projects involved houses to be sold to their tenants under the Housing
Act 1985 (which is the consolidating Act containing provisions equivalent to the Tenants'
Rights, Etc. (Scotland) Act 1980). The section enabled such projects to qualify for grant
save that, in cases where the grant was made after the tenant had exercised his right to buy,
the Secretary of State might reduce the amount of grant.

A consequence of the passing of s.1(1) of this Act (extending the right to purchase to
tenants of housing associations) is that s.44 of the 1985 Act should be extended to Scotland
and this is achieved by the amendments contained in para. (a) of s.14. The term "house" is
defined in s.106(2) of the 1985 Act.

S.45 is extended (subject to the error referred to in the next paragraph) to Scotland by the
amendments made in para. (b). It is a section which provides for the situation (by permitting
payment of housing association grant) where a registered association arranges for the sale
of one of its houses to the tenant of a housing association (see 1980 Act s.10(2)(e)) which
is a charity and which is, therefore, a category of landlord not bound to sell to its tenants
under the 1980 Act. The new s.45(5) permits the same rules to apply where the "acquiring"
housing association does not take title before disposal to the tenant.

Because of adjustments to the Bill in the House of Lords affecting Sched. 1 to this Act
and inserting, in particular, a new para. (e) in s.1(11) of the 1980 Act (small housing
associations) and because of an apparent failure to take consequential account of these in
s.15, this section does not have its intended effect and the above account of para. (b) could,
therefore, be misleading. The section mistakenly refers to "subsection (11)(e) or (f) of
section 1" instead of "subsection (11)(f) or (g) of section 1". No doubt a small further
amendment will have to be made.

N.B. Sched. 3 to this Act deletes "ss.44 and 45" from the list of provisions in the 1985 Act
applying to England and Wales only.

Repayment of housing association grant

16.—(1) In section 52 of the 1985 Act (reduction, suspension or
reclamation of housing association grant), at the end of subsection (1)
there shall be added the following words—

"or

(f) there is paid to the association, in respect of land to which the
grant relates, an amount payable in pursuance of section 6 of

the Tenants' Rights, Etc. (Scotland) Act 1980 (recovery of discount on early re-sale), or
(g) in Scotland, there is paid to the association, in respect of land to which the grant relates, an amount payable as regards the purchase, under a shared ownership agreement, of a *pro indiviso* share in a dwelling by a person who already has such a share in the dwelling under that agreement.".
(2) In subsection (3)(*b*) of the said section 52, for the words "or (*e*)" there shall be substituted the words "(*e*), (*f*) or (*g*)".

GENERAL NOTE
This section has the effect of extending to Scotland those provisions in s.52 of the Housing Associations Act 1985 which authorise the Secretary of State to reduce, suspend or reclaim housing association grant where payments are made to an association when discount is refunded or on purchase under a shared ownership agreement (see s.13 above).
This is achieved by the insertion of new paras. (*f*) and (*g*) in s.52(1) and the consequential adjustment of s.52(3)(*b*) (supply of information). There is another consequential amendment in Sched. 3 (repeals). The 1985 Act is not amended to ensure expressly that the new paras. (*f*) and (*g*) apply only in Scotland (see 1985 Act, s.107).

Housing Expenditure and Grants

Precondition as regards use of renewal and repairs fund for certain housing expenditure

17. In paragraph 22(2) of Schedule 3 to the Local Government (Scotland) Act 1975 (restrictions on use of capital and renewal and repair funds), after the word "restaurant" there shall be inserted the words "; and if the renewal and repair fund is used so to meet expenditure incurred by the authority in relation to any house, or other property, to which their housing revenue account relates, the amount in question shall, subject to paragraph 1(7) of Schedule 4 to the Housing (Financial Provisions (Scotland) Act 1972, first to be carried to the credit of that account".

GENERAL NOTE
The effect of this small amendment is to ensure that where expenditure is incurred by a housing authority on a house to which its housing revenue account relates and that expenditure is to be met out of its renewal and repair fund, the amount must first be carried to the credit of the housing revenue account. Making the transfer subject to para. 1(7) of Sched. 4 to the 1972 Act further ensures that such a transfer requires the consent of the Secretary of State.

Grants to Scottish Special Housing Association and development corporations

18.—(1) In section 4 of the Housing (Financial Provisions) (Scotland) Act 1978 (grants to Scottish Special Housing Association and development corporations)—
(*a*) for subsection (1) there shall be substituted the following subsection—
"(1) The Secretary of State may each year make grants, of such amount and subject to such conditions as he may determine, to the Scottish Special Housing Association (in this Act referred to as "the Association") and to development corporations in accordance with the provisions of this section."; and
(*b*) in subsection (2), for the words from "calculated" to "State" there shall be substituted the words "approved by the Secretary of State and calculated in accordance with rules made by him".
(2) After the said section 4 there shall be inserted the following section—

"Grants for affording tax relief to Scottish Special Housing Association

4A.—(1) The Secretary of State may, on the application of the Association, make grants to the Association for affording relief from—

(*a*) income tax (other than income tax which the Association is entitled to deduct on making any payment); and

(*b*) corporation tax.

(2) A grant under this section shall be of such amount, shall be made at such times and shall be subject to such conditions as the Secretary of State thinks fit.

(3) The conditions mentioned in subsection (2) above may include conditions for securing the repayment in whole or in part of a grant made to the Association in the event of tax in respect of which the grant was made subsequently being found not to be chargeable or in such other events as the Secretary of State may determine.

(4) An application under this section shall be made in such manner and shall be supported by such evidence as the Secretary of State may direct.

(5) The Commissioners of Inland Revenue and their officers may disclose to the Secretary of State such particulars as he may reasonably require for determining whether a grant should be made under this section or whether a grant so made should be repaid or the amount of such grant or repayment.".

GENERAL NOTE

This section makes adjustments to the provisions in the Housing (Financial Provisions) (Scotland) Act 1978 relating to the making of grants by the Secretary of State to the S.S.H.A. and to new town development corporations.

Subs. (1)

This first provides a substitute s.4(1) of the 1978 Act but does not alter the Secretary of State's powers to make grants. The adjustment to s.4(2) makes explicit the power of the Secretary of State to determine the total net annual expenditure on which grant is payable.

Subs. (2)

This inserts a new s.4A to make provision for the Secretary of State to make grants to the S.S.H.A. to afford relief from income tax and corporation tax to which it is liable. S.4A is similar to s.62 of the Housing Associations Act 1985.

Amendment of Building (Scotland) Act 1959

Amendment of Building (Scotland) Act 1959

19.—(1) The Building (Scotland) Act 1959 shall be amended in accordance with the following provisions of this section.

(2) In section 3(4)(*b*) (circumstances in which building standards regulations are not to apply), after the words "exempted classes" there shall be inserted the words ", to such extent as may be specified in the regulations".

(3) For section 4B (power of Secretary of State to approve types of building, etc.), there shall be substituted the following section—

"Class warrants

4B.—(1) The following provisions of this section shall have effect with a view to enabling the Secretary of State, on an application being made to him under this section, to issue a certificate (to be known as a "class warrant") that a particular design (including specification of materials) of building conforms, either generally or in any class of case, to particular provisions of the building standards regulations.

(2) A person intending to apply for a class warrant under this section shall send a copy of the prospective application in the prescribed manner to a body designated by the Secretary of State which, if it is satisfied that the design in respect of which the warrant is sought conforms to the building standards regulations, shall recommend that the class warrant be issued.

(3) An application to the Secretary of State for a class warrant under this section shall be made in the prescribed manner and shall be accompanied by a relevant recommendation made under subsection (2) above.

(4) The Secretary of State may, where a recommendation under subsection (2) above is made in respect of a design of building, issue a class warrant in respect of that design; and a class warrant so issued shall be accepted by a local authority as conclusive of the matters stated therein.

(5) A body designated under subsection (2) above may charge such fee for considering a design in respect of which a copy application has been sent to it under that subsection as may be agreed between the applicant and the body.

(6) A class warrant shall, if it so provides, cease to have effect at the end of such period as may be specified in it.

(7) The Secretary of State may at any time vary or revoke a class warrant; but before doing so he shall give the person on whose application it was issued reasonable notice that he proposes so to do.

(8) Where the Secretary of State varies or revokes a class warrant he shall publish notice of that fact in such manner as he thinks fit.

(9) There may be prescribed—

    (*a*) the type, part or parts of building to which the provisions of this section shall apply;

    (*b*) the terms and conditions on which a class warrant may be issued;

    (*c*) procedures incidental to any provisions of this section;

    (*d*) the fee, if any, to be charged for issuing a class warrant;

    (*e*) any variations in the design of building which will be permitted.

(10) Where a fee is chargeable by virtue of subsection (9)(*d*) above, the regulations under which it is chargeable may make different provision (which, without prejudice to the generality of this subsection, may include provision for remission of the fee in whole or in part) for—

    (*a*) different cases or classes of case; or

    (*b*) different circumstances or classes of circumstances,

(difference being determined by reference to any factor or factors whatsoever).".

(4) After section 6 there shall be inserted the following section—

"Self-certification of design

6AA.—(1) On making an application for a warrant under section 6 of this Act, an applicant may submit a certificate issued under this section certifying that the design (including the specification of material to be used) of the building complies with building standards regulations prescribed under paragraph (*a*) of subsection (2) below; and in determining whether to issue the warrant, the local authority shall accept the certificate as conclusive of the facts to which it relates.

(2) There may be prescribed—

    (*a*) the part or parts of the building standards regulations in relation to which a certificate under this section may be submitted and different provision may be made in respect of different parts of the regulations and in respect of different types of building;

(*b*) whether or not by reference to specific criteria, such person or persons as shall be entitled to issue such certificate;

(*c*) the form of such certificate;

(*d*) the drawings, plans, specifications or other material which shall be submitted with the certificate.".

(5) In section 9 (certificate of completion), after subsection (2) there shall be inserted the following subsection—

"(2A) Where the Secretary of State has issued a relevant class warrant, a local authority shall grant a certificate of completion in respect of any building unless—

(i) the approved design (or an approved variation) has not been complied with whether by reason of faulty workmanship or otherwise; or

(ii) the building standards regulations in relation to any part of the building to which section 4B of this Act does not apply have not been complied with.".

(6) For section 20 (fees chargeable by local authorities) there shall be substituted the following section—

"Fees chargeable by local authorities

20.—(1) A local authority may in respect of the performance of their functions under this Act charge such fees as may be prescribed; but there may also be prescribed cases or classes of case for which, or circumstances or classes of circumstances where, no fee shall be chargeable.

(2) Where a fee is chargeable by virtue of subsection (1) above, the regulations under which it is so chargeable may make different provision (which, without prejudice to the generality of this subsection, may include provision for remission of the fee in whole or in part) for—

(*a*) different cases or classes of case;

(*b*) different circumstances or classes of circumstances;

(*c*) different items or classes of business,

(difference being determined by reference to any factor or factors whatsoever).".

GENERAL NOTE

This section contains a number of amendments to the system of building control operated under the Building (Scotland) Act 1959. They derive from proposals announced as a Statement of Intent by the Secretary of State on November 29, 1984.

Subs. (2)

S.3(4)(*b*) of the 1959 Act enables the Secretary of State to exempt classes of buildings from the building standards regulations. This amendment will allow the exemption of parts of buildings (the remainder of which stay subject to control) rather than requiring the exemption of the entire building as previously.

Subs. (3)

This substitutes as new s.4B for that originally inserted by the Health and Safety at Work etc., Act 1974, s.75 and Sched. 7, para. 3. It introduces a new and more flexible system of class warrants in place of the unused system of "type approvals" created by that Act. Bodies (probably including, for houses, the National House Builders Council) are to be designated by the Secretary of State under the new subs. (2) to which applications for a class warrant are to be made under subss. (2), (3) and, in relation to fees, (5). If a designated body recommends the issue of a class warrant the Secretary of State may issue it under subs. (4), (6), (7) and, by regulations, under subss. (9) and (10). Once issued a class warrant must be accepted by a local authority as conclusive of matters stated in it. Notice too the terms of s.19(5) of this Act inserting a new s.9(2A) into the 1959 Act relating to the obligation of local authorities to grant certificates of completion in respect of buildings covered by class warrants.

In passing, it is interesting to note the extremely broad terminology in the final two lines of new subs. (10) (see also new s.20(2) in subs. (6) below). Despite the language used, which factors could be struck down as irrelevant by a court in judicial review proceedings?

Subs. (4)

This provides statutory authority for the Secretary of State to prescribe parts of the building standards as areas where an applicant may, at the point of application for a warrant, self-certify the design of a building as being in compliance with the regulations. In contrast with the position of class warrants (see subss. (3) above and (5) below), self-certification of design does not also compel an authority to issue a (nearly) automatic certificate of completion.

Subs. (5)

See note to subs. (3) above.

Subs. (6)

This substitutes a new s.20 for the previous version in the 1959 Act. It provides greater flexibility to the Secretary of State especially as to the rules for the remission of fees.

Amendment of Land Compensation (Scotland) Act 1973

Compensation for person displaced from dwelling-house let under secure tenancy

20.—(1) The Land Compensation (Scotland) Act 1973 shall be amended in accordance with the following provisions of this section.

(2) In section 27(1) (right to home loss payment where person displaced from dwelling)—

(*a*) after paragraph (*e*) there shall be inserted the following paragraph—

"(*f*) an order for recovery of possession of the dwelling under section 15(2) of the Tenants' Rights, Etc. (Scotland) Act 1980, on the ground set out in paragraph 10 of Part I of Schedule 2 to that Act,"; and

(*b*) after sub-paragraph (v) there shall be inserted the following sub-paragraph—

"(vi) where paragraph (*f*) above applies, the landlord.".

(3) In section 29 (supplementary provisions about home loss payments), after subsection (7) there shall be inserted the following subsection—

"(7AA) If a landlord recovers possession of a dwelling by agreement—

(*a*) after serving notice under section 14 of the Tenants' Rights, Etc. (Scotland) Act 1980 on the tenant specifying the ground set out in paragraph 10 of Part I of Schedule 2 to that Act; or

(*b*) where, but for that agreement, it would have served such notice on him specifying that ground,

it may, in connection with the recovery, make to him a payment corresponding to any home loss payment which it would be required to make to him if the recovery were by order under section 15(2) of that Act.".

GENERAL NOTE

This section makes a number of amendments to s.27 (and s.29) of the Land Compensation (Scotland) Act 1973 under which home loss payments (for personal upset and the like) are made when compulsory purchase and various housing orders are implemented. The amendments ensure that such payments are to be made when possession of a house is recovered from a secure tenant in reliance upon para. 10 of Part I of Sched. 2 to the 1980 Act (recovery to enable demolition or substantial works to take place). The new s.29(7AA) permits the making of the equivalent of a home loss payment when possession is given up to the landlord (by agreement) in advance of court proceedings and an order under s.15(2) of the 1980 Act.

Amendment of Housing (Homeless Persons) Act 1977

Functions of local authorities with respect to persons who are homeless or threatened with homelessness

21.—(1) The Housing (Homeless Persons) Act 1977 shall be amended in accordance with the following provisions of this section.

(2) In section 1(2) (homeless persons and persons threatened with homelessness) after paragraph (c) there shall be inserted the following paragraph—

"(d) it is overcrowded as defined in section 89 of the Housing (Scotland) Act 1966 and may endanger the health of the occupants."

(3) In section 4 (duties of housing authorities to homeless persons and persons threatened with homelessness) after subsection (6) there shall be inserted the following subsection—

"(7) Where a local authority has a duty under subsections (4) and (5) above "accommodation" shall be defined as accommodation that shall not be overcrowded as defined in section 89 of the Housing (Scotland) Act 1966 and which does not pose a threat to the health of the occupants.".

GENERAL NOTE

Apart from the rights of housing association tenants to purchase their houses, this section was probably the most hotly contested as the Bill passed through Parliament. There were unsuccessful attempts to amend the Bill to introduce a clause of this sort in the Commons. It was raised again in the Lords at Report Stage and an amendment was passed at Third Reading. When the Bill returned to the Commons the clause was rejected and it was only when the Lords (with reluctant acquiescence by the Government) insisted yet again upon a revised version that the Commons yielded and the clause was finally incorporated into the Act as passed.

The purpose of the section is, in the view of its proponents, to undo the effect of the decision of the House of Lords in *Puhlhofer* v. *Hillingdon London Borough Council* [1986] 1 All E.R. 467 and to restore what they claimed to be the original intention of the Housing (Homeless Persons) Act 1977 which, since the Housing Act 1985, applies in Scotland only. It was argued that the interpretation of the word "accommodation" in ss.1 and 4 of the 1977 Act adopted by the court had been so narrow as to allow a local authority legitimately to decline to take action to provide housing under the Act where the house occupied by the applicant for assistance was overcrowded. So long as the house was, in some sense, capable of constituting accommodation, the fact that it was "inappropriate" (through overcrowding) for a particular occupier did not oblige the authority to act.

Subs. (2)

S.1(2) of the 1977 Act expands the definition of homelessness in subs. (1) by providing that a person is still homeless despite having accommodation if (a) he cannot secure entry to it; (b) occupation of it would lead to violence; or (c) it is a movable structure and there is no place to put it. This subsection provides a new such category of accommodation which is both overcrowded and endangers health. S.89 of the Housing (Scotland) Act 1966 defines a house as overcrowded if either (a) it is necessary for occupants aged 10 or over of the opposite sex (other than persons living as husband and wife) to sleep in the same room or (b) if the number of persons sleeping in the house exceeds the number permitted (in terms of the number of rooms and their floor area) by a formula prescribed in Sched. 5 to the 1966 Act.

Subs. (3)

S.4 of the 1977 Act lays down the duties of housing authorities under the Act and the circumstances in which they arise. This additional subs. (7) ensures that the "accommodation" to be provided by an authority (or which it must ensure continues to be available if homelessness is threatened rather than actual) is again not overcrowded. A slightly different formula concerning the health of occupants is used (in comparison with that inserted into s.1

of the Act). The difference was not referred to in debate and does not appear to be significant.

Supplemental

Interpretation

22. In this Act—
   "the 1980 Act" means the Tenants' Rights, Etc. (Scotland) Act 1980; and
   "the 1985 Act" means the Housing Associations Act 1985.

Consequential, transitional and supplementary provision

23.—(1) The Secretary of State may by order made by statutory instrument make such incidental, consequential, transitional or supplementary provision as appears to him to be necessary or proper for giving full effect to, or in consequence of any of the provisions of, this Act.

(2) A statutory instrument made under subsection (1) above shall be subject to annulment in pursuance of a resolution of either House of Parliament.

(3) Paragraph 7(*a*)(ii) and (*b*)(ii) of Schedule 1 to this Act shall have no effect as regards any case in which repayment has become exigible under subsection (1) of section 6 of the 1980 Act before the coming into force of that paragraph; but in any other case the terms of any standard security, offer to sell or concluded missives shall, in so far as they are inconsistent with the period of years specified in that subsection, or with the proportions specified in subsection (3) of that section, have effect as if so modified as to obviate that inconsistency.

Expenses

24. There shall be paid out of the money provided by Parliament any—
   (*a*) sums required by the Secretary of State for making grants, loans or other payments by virtue of this Act;
   (*b*) administrative expenses incurred by him by virtue of this Act;
   (*c*) increase attributable to the provisions of this Act in the sums which under any other enactment are paid out of money so provided.

Minor amendments and repeals

25.—(1) The enactments specified in Schedule 2 to this Act shall have effect subject to the amendments there specified, (being minor amendments or amendments consequential on the provisions of this Act).

(2) The enactments specified in Schedule 3 to this Act are repealed to the extent specified in the third column of that Schedule.

Citation, commencement and extent

26.—(1) This Act may be cited as the Housing (Scotland) Act 1986.

(2) This Act, except this section, shall come into force on such day as the Secretary of State may appoint by order made by statutory instrument; and different days may be so appointed for different provisions and for different purposes.

(3) This Act applies to Scotland only.

SCHEDULES

SCHEDULE 1

AMENDMENT OF 1980 ACT

1. In section 1 (secure tenant's right to purchase)—
   (*a*) in subsection (1A)—
       (i) after the word "Act" there shall be inserted the word "—(*a*)";
       (ii) in the proviso, for the word "subsection" there shall be substituted the word "paragraph"; and
       (iii) after the proviso there shall be added the following paragraph—
             "(*b*) a landlord mentioned in paragraph (*a*) or (*aa*) of section 10(2) of this Act is required neither to enter into, nor to induce (or seek to induce) any person to enter into, such agreement as is mentioned in paragraph (*a*) above or into any agreement which purports to restrict that person's rights under this Act";
   (*b*) in subsection (4)(*a*), for the words "over the age of 18 years and at the relevant date the dwelling-house has been their only or principal home for a continuous period of 6 months, and" there shall be substituted the words "at least 18 years of age, that they have, during the period of 6 months ending with the relevant date, had their only or principal home with the tenant and that";
   (*c*) in subsection (5)—
       (i) for the words "subsection (7)" there shall be substituted the words "subsections (7) and (7A)"; and
       (ii) in paragraph (*b*)(ii), for the words "tenant or by any one of the joint tenants or by his spouse" there shall be substituted the words "appropriate person";
   (*d*) after subsection (5) there shall be inserted the following subsection—
             "(5A) for the purposes of subsection (5)(*b*)(ii) above, the "appropriate person" is the tenant or, if it would result in a higher discount and if she is cohabiting with him as at the relevant date, his spouse; and where joint tenants are joint purchasers the "appropriate person" shall be whichever tenant (or as the case may be spouse) has the longer or longest such occupation.";
   (*e*) in subsection (10)—
       (i) after paragraph (*d*) there shall be inserted the following paragraphs—
             "(*dd*) a registered housing association within the meaning of the Housing Associations Act 1985;
             (*ddd*) the Housing Corporation;";
       (ii) in paragraph (*h*), for the words "or section 19(9)(*b*) of the Police (Scotland) Act 1967" there shall be substituted the words ", as read with subsection (9)(*b*) of section 19, of the Police (Scotland) Act 1967 or a joint police committee constituted by virtue of subsection (2)(*b*) of the said section 19";
       (iii) in paragraph (*i*), after the words "1959" there shall be inserted the words "(or a joint committee constituted by virtue of section 36(4)(*b*) of the Fire Services Act 1947)"; and
       (iv) in paragraph (*l*), for the words "by the tenant or occupier" there shall be substituted the words ", whether by the tenant or his spouse,";
   (*f*) in subsection (11)—
       (i) in paragraph (*a*), for the words "of paragraphs (*a*), (*b*) or (*c*)" there shall be substituted the words "paragraph, other than (*g*),"; and
       (ii) at the end of paragraph (*c*) there shall be added the following paragraphs—
             ";
             (*d*) where a landlord mentioned in paragraph (*e*) of section 10(2) of this Act has at no time received a grant under—
                 (i) any enactment mentioned in paragraph 2 of Schedule 1 to the Housing Associations Act 1985 (grants under enactments superseded by the Housing Act 1974);
                 (ii) section 31 of the Housing Act 1974 (management grants);
                 (iii) section 41 of the Housing Associations Act 1985 (housing association grants);

65-23

     (iv) section 54 of that Act (revenue deficit grants);

     (v) section 55 of that Act (hostel deficit grants); or

     (vi) section 59(2) of that Act (grants by local authorities); or

(*e*) where a landlord so mentioned has at no time let (or had available for letting) more than 100 dwellings; or

(*f*) where a landlord so mentioned is a charity—

     (i) entered in the register of charities maintained under the Charities Act 1960 by the Charity Commissioners for England and Wales; or

     (ii) which but for section 4(4) of, and paragraph (*g*) of the Second Schedule to, that Act (exempt charities) would require to be so entered; or

(*g*) where by virtue of section 49(2) of the said Act of 1960 (extent) a landlord so mentioned is not one to which Part II of that Act (registration of charities etc.) applies, but—

     (i) the landlord has, in respect of all periods from 14th November 1985, or from the date of first being registered by the Housing Corporation (whichever is the later), claimed and been granted (whether or not retrospectively) under section 360(1) of the Income and Corporation Taxes Act 1970 (special exemptions for charities) exemption from tax; and

     (ii) where such exemption has not been claimed and granted in respect of all periods from the said date of registration, the rules of the landlord, registered under the Industrial and Provident Societies Act 1965 and in force at that date were such as would have admitted of such exemption had it been claimed as at that date; or

(*h*) where, within a neighbourhood, the dwelling-house is one of a number (not exceeding 14) of dwelling-houses with a common landlord, being a landlord so mentioned, and it is the practice of that landlord to let at least one half of those dwelling-houses for occupation by any or all of the following—

     (i) persons who have suffered from, or are suffering from, mental disorder (as defined in the Mental Health (Scotland) Act 1984), physical handicap or addiction to alcohol or other drugs;

     (ii) persons who have been released from prison or other institutions;

     (iii) young persons who have left the care of a local authority,

and a social service is, or special facilities are, provided wholly or partly for the purpose of assisting those persons.";

(*g*) after subsection (11) there shall be inserted the following subsections—

"(11A) The Secretary of State may by order amend, or add to, the list of classes set out in sub-paragraphs (i) to (iii) of paragraph (*h*) of subsection (11) above.

(11B) The Commissioners of Inland Revenue shall, as regards any registered housing association, at the request of the Secretary of State, provide him and the Housing Corporation with such information as will enable them to determine whether that association is a landlord in respect of which this section will not, by virtue of subsection (11)(*g*) above, apply; and where a registered housing association is refused exemption on a claim under section 360(1) of the Income and Corporation Taxes Act 1970 the Commissioners shall forthwith inform the Secretary of State and the Housing Corporation of that fact.

(11C) Where information has been received by the Housing Corporation under subsection (11B) above and having regard to that information the Corporation is satisfied that the housing association to which it relates is not a landlord in respect of which this section applies, they shall make an entry to that effect in the register of housing associations maintained by them under section 3(1) of the Housing Associations Act 1985; and they shall cancel that entry where subsequent information so received in relation to that housing association is inconsistent with their being so satisfied."; and

(*h*) in subsection (12), in the definition of "occupation"—

(i) for paragraph (iii) there shall be substituted the following
paragraphs—

"(iii) as a child, or as the spouse of a child, of a person mentioned
in paragraph (i) above who has succeeded, directly or indirectly, to
the rights of that person in a dwelling-house occupation of which
would be reckonable for the purposes of this section; but only in
relation to any period when the child, or as the case may be spouse
of the child, is at least 16 years of age;
or

(iv) in the discretion of the landlord, as a member of the family
of a person mentioned in paragraph (i) above who, not being that
person's spouse or child (or child's spouse), has succeeded, directly
or indirectly, to such rights as are mentioned in paragraph (iii)
above; but only in relation to any period when the member of the
family is at least 16 years of age, and";

(ii) for the word "disregarded" there shall be substituted the words
"regarded as not affecting continuity";

(iii) for the word "subsection" there shall be substituted the words "subsections (3) and"; and

(iv) for the words "in connection with service by the tenant or occupier as
a member of the regular armed forces of the Crown" there shall be
substituted the words "as is mentioned in subsection (10)(*l*) above".

2. In section 1A(2) (restriction on order vesting in landlord heritable proprietor's interest),
for the words "of paragraphs (*a*), (*b*), (*c*) and (*f*)" there shall be substituted the words
"paragraph, other than (*g*),".

3. After section 1A there shall be inserted the following section—

"Provision of information to secure tenants

1B.—(1) Whenever a new secure tenancy is to be created, if—

(*a*) by virtue of subsection (11) of section 1 of this Act, the dwelling-house is not
one to which that section applies; or

(*b*) subsection (7) or (7A) of that section may (assuming no change in the date for
the time being specified in the former subsection and disregarding any order
made, or which might be made, by the Secretary of State under section 3(4)(*b*)
of the Housing (Scotland) Act 1986) affect any price fixed, as regards the
dwelling-house, under subsection (5) of that section,

the landlord shall so inform the prospective tenant by written notice.

(2) Where in the course of a secure tenancy the dwelling-house, by virtue of
subsection (11) of the said section 1, ceases to be one to which that section applies, the
landlord shall forthwith so inform the tenant by written notice.".

4. In section 2(6) (time for serving notice of acceptance), after sub-paragraph (iii*a*) there
shall be inserted the following sub-paragraph—

"(iii*b*) a finding or determination by the Lands Tribunal for Scotland in a matter
referred to it under subsection (2)(*d*) of the said section 7 where no order is
made under the said subsection (3)(*b*);".

5. In section 4—

(*a*) in subsection (7)(*a*) (order affecting right of pre-emption where unreasonable
proportion of dwelling-houses in rural area sold other than as principal homes),
for the words "the number of dwelling-houses of which the council concerned is
the landlord at the date of commencement of this Part of this Act" there shall
be substituted the words "all relevant dwelling-houses"; and

(*b*) after subsection (7) there shall be inserted the following subsection—

"(7A) For the purposes of subsection (7)(*a*) above, a "relevant dwelling-
house" is one of which, at the date of—

(*a*) commencement of this Part of this Act, the council concerned; or

(*b*) coming into force of paragraph 5 of Schedule 1 to the Housing (Scotland)
Act 1986, a registered housing association,

is landlord.".

6. In section 5(1) (loan to purchase dwelling-house), after the word "body;" there shall
be inserted the following paragraph—

"(*aa*) in the case where the landlord is the Housing Corporation or a registered
housing association, to the Housing Corporation;".

7. In section 6 (recovery of discount on early re-sale)—

(*a*) in subsection (1), for the words—
  (i) from "(otherwise than" to "compulsory purchase)" there shall be substituted the words—
  "(except as provided for in section 6A of this Act)";
  (ii) "5 years" there shall be substituted the words "3 years"; and
  (iii) "a proportion of the discount under section 1(5)(*b*) of this Act in accordance with subsection (3) below" there shall be substituted the words ", in accordance with subsection (3) below, a proportion of the difference between the market value determined, in respect of the dwelling-house, under section 1(5)(*a*) of this Act and the price at which the dwelling-house was so purchased";

(*b*) in subsection (3)—
  (i) for the word "discount" there shall be substituted the word "difference";
  (ii) for the words from "80" to the end there shall be substituted the words "66 per cent where it occurs in the second such year and 33 per cent where it occurs in the third such year.";

(*c*) in subsection (5), at the end there shall be added the words "For the avoidance of doubt, paragraph (*a*) above applies to a standard security granted in security both for the purpose mentioned in sub-paragraph (i) and for that mentioned in sub-paragraph (ii) thereof as it applies to a standard security so granted for but one of those purposes."; and

(*d*) in each of subsections (5) and (6), for the words "repay a proportion of discount under this section" there shall be substituted the words "make a repayment under subsection (1) above".

8. After section 6 there shall be inserted the following section—

"Cases where discount etc. is not recoverable
6A.—(1) There shall be no liability to make a repayment under section 6(1) of this Act where the disposal is made—
(*a*) by the executor of the deceased owner acting in that capacity; or
(*b*) as a result of a compulsory purchase order; or
(*c*) in the circumstances specified in subsection (2) below.
(2) The circumstances mentioned in subsection (1)(*c*) above are that the disposal—
(*a*) is to a member of the owner's family who has lived with him for a period of 12 months before the disposal; and
(*b*) is for no consideration:
Provided that, if the disponee disposes of the house before the expiry of the 3 year period mentioned in subsection (1) of section 6 of this Act, the provisions of that section will apply to him as if this was the first disposal and he was the original purchaser.".

9. In section 8(1) (powers of local authorities to sell houses), for the words "Notwithstanding anything contained in any" there shall be substituted the words "Subject to section 74(2) of the Local Government (Scotland) Act 1973 (restriction on disposal of land) but notwithstanding anything contained in any other".

10. In section 10(4)(*b*) (application of certain provisions to tenancies which are not secure tenancies), after the word "2" there shall be inserted the words "or 9".

11. In section 13(2) (succession to secure tenancy)—
(*a*) for paragraph (*a*) there shall be substituted the following paragraph—
  "(*a*) a person whose only or principal home at the time of the tenant's death was the dwelling-house and who was at that time either—
  (i) the tenant's spouse; or
  (ii) living with the tenant as husband and wife;"; and
(*b*) in paragraph (*c*), for the word "over" there shall be substituted the words "who has attained".

12. In section 15 (power of court to adjourn proceedings for possession of dwelling-house)—
(*a*) in subsection (1), for the words from "1 to" to "Part I" there shall be substituted the words "1 to 7 and 16 of Part I";
(*b*) for subsection (2) there shall be substituted the following subsection—
  "(2) Subject to subsection (1) above, in proceedings under the said section 14 the court shall make an order for recovery of possession if it appears to the court that the landlord has a ground for recovery of possession, being—
  (*a*) a ground set out in any of paragraphs 1 to 5, 7 and 16 of the said Part

I and specified in the notice required by the said section 14 and that it is reasonable to make the order; or

   (*b*) a ground set out in any of paragraphs 8 to 15 of the said Part I and so specified and that other suitable accommodation will be available for the tenant when the order takes effect; or

   (*c*) the ground set out in paragraph 6 of the said Part I and so specified and both that it is reasonable to make the order and that other suitable accommodation will be available as aforesaid,"; and

   (*c*) in subsection (3), after the words "(2)(*b*)" there shall be inserted the words "or (*c*)".

13. For section 26 (restriction on residential requirements) there shall be substituted the following sections—

"Admission to housing list

26.—(1) In considering whether an applicant for local authority housing is entitled to be admitted to a housing list, an islands or district council shall take no account of—

   (*a*) the age of the applicant provided that he has attained the age of 16 years; or

   (*b*) the income of the applicant and his family; or

   (*c*) whether, or to what value, the applicant or any of his family owns or has owned (or any of them own or have owned) heritable or moveable property; or

   (*d*) any outstanding liability (for payment of rent or otherwise) attributable to the tenancy of any dwelling-house of which the applicant is not, and was not when the liability accrued, a tenant; or

   (*e*) whether the applicant is living with, or in the same dwelling-house as—

      (i) his spouse; or

      (ii) a person with whom he has been living as husband and wife.

(2) Where an applicant—

   (*a*) is employed in the area of the islands or district council; or

   (*b*) has been offered employment in the area of the council; or

   (*c*) wishes to move into the area of the council and the council is satisfied that his purpose in doing so is to seek employment; or

   (*d*) has attained the age of 60 years and wishes to move into the area of the council to be near a younger relative; or

   (*e*) has special social or medical reasons for requiring to be housed within the area of the council,

admission to a housing list shall not depend on the applicant being resident in the area.

(3) Where an islands or district council has rules which give priority to applicants on its housing list it shall apply those rules to an applicant to whom subsection (2) above applies no less favourably than it applies them to a tenant of the council whose housing needs are similar to those of the applicant and who is seeking a transfer to another dwelling-house belonging to the council.

(4) In this section and in section 27 of this Act "housing list" means a list of applicants for local authority housing which is kept by an islands or district council in connection with allocation of housing.

Allocation of local authority housing

26A. In the allocation of local authority housing an islands or district council—

   (*a*) shall take no account of—

      (i) the length of time for which an applicant has resided in its area; or

      (ii) any of the matters mentioned in paragraphs (*a*) to (*d*) of section 26(1) of this Act; and

   (*b*) shall not impose a requirement—

      (i) that an application must have remained in force for a minimum period; or

      (ii) that a divorce or judicial separation be obtained; or

      (iii) that the applicant no longer be living with, or in the same dwelling-house as, some other person,

before the applicant is eligible for the allocation of housing.".

14. In section 27(2A) (certain registered housing association rules to be available for perusal), for the words "(1A)(*a*)(ii)" there shall be substituted the words "(1A)(*b*)(i)".

15. In section 30—

(*a*) in subsection (4) (home loan interest rate chargeable) at the beginning there shall be inserted the words "Subject to subsection (8) below,"; and

(*b*) for subsection (8) (variation of home loan interest rate), there shall be substituted the following subsections—

"(8) Where the declaration of a new standard rate or, as the case may be, the determination of a new locally determined rate, affects the rate of interest chargeable under subsection (4) above by an islands or district council the council shall, as soon as practicable after such declaration or determination, serve in respect of each of its variable interest home loans a notice on the borrower which shall, as from the appropriate day—

(*a*) vary the rate of interest payable by him; and

(*b*) where, as the result of the variation, the amount outstanding under the advance or security would increase if the periodic repayments were not increased, increase the amount of the periodic repayments to such an amount as will ensure that the said outstanding amount will not increase.

(8A) In subsection (8) above, "the appropriate day" means such day as shall be specified in the notice, being—

(*a*) in the case of a new standard rate, a day not less than 2 weeks, nor more than 6 weeks, after service of the notice; and

(*b*) in the case of a new locally determined rate, the first day of the relevant period of 6 months.".

16. In section 82 (interpretation), for the definition of "family" there shall be substituted the following definition—

' "family", and any reference to membership thereof, shall be construed in accordance with section 82A of this Act;'.

17. After section 82 there shall be inserted the following section—

"Members of a person's family

82A.—(1) A person is a member of another's family for the purposes of this Act if—

(*a*) he is the spouse of that person or he and that person live together as husband and wife; or

(*b*) he is that person's parent, grandparent, child, grandchild, brother, sister, uncle, aunt, nephew or niece.

(2) For the purposes of subsection (1)(*b*) above—

(*a*) a relationship by marriage shall be treated as a relationship by blood;

(*b*) a relationship of the half-blood shall be treated as a relationship of the whole blood;

(*c*) the stepchild of a person shall be treated as his child; and

(*d*) an illegitimate child shall be treated as the legitimate child of his mother and reputed father.".

18. At the end of Schedule 1 (tenancies which are not secure tenancies) there shall be added the following cross-headings and paragraphs—

"Police and fire authorities

8. A tenancy shall not be a secure tenancy if the landlord is an authority or committee mentioned in—

(*a*) section 10(2)(*h*) of this Act and the tenant—

(i) is a constable of a police force, within the meaning of the Police (Scotland) Act 1967, who in pursuance of regulations under section 26 of that Act occupies the dwelling-house without obligation to pay rent or rates; or

(ii) in a case where head (i) above does not apply, is let the dwelling-house expressly on a temporary basis pending its being required for the purposes of such a police force; or

(*b*) section 10(2)(*i*) of this Act and the tenant—

(i) is a member of a fire brigade, maintained in pursuance of the Fire Services Act 1947, who occupies the dwelling-house in consequence of a condition in his contract of employment that he live in close proximity to a particular fire station; or

(ii) in a case where head (i) above does not apply, is let the dwelling-house expressly on a temporary basis pending its being required for the purposes of such a fire brigade.

Dwelling-houses part of, or within curtilage of, certain other buildings

9. A tenancy shall not be a secure tenancy if the dwelling-house forms part of, or is within the curtilage of, a building which mainly—

(*a*) is held by the landlord for purposes other than the provision of housing accommodation; and

(*b*) consists of accommodation other than housing accommodation.".

19. In Part I of Schedule 2 (grounds on which courts may order recovery of possession of dwelling-house)—

(*a*) in paragraph 10—

(i) for the words "The landlord intends" there shall be substituted the words "It is intended";

(ii) for the word "it" there shall be substituted the words "such demolition or work"; and

(iii) for the words "do so without" there shall be substituted the words "take place without the landlord"; and

(*b*) at the end there shall be added the following paragraph—

"16. The tenant is the person, or one of the persons, to whom the tenancy was granted and the landlord was induced to grant the tenancy by a false statement made knowingly or recklessly by the tenant.".

GENERAL NOTE

The Schedule contains the numerous amendments to the 1980 Act authorised by s.12.

Para. 1(a)

S.1(1A) of the 1980 Act was inserted by the Local Government and Planning (Scotland) Act 1982 to prohibit landlords from requiring payments or deposits in advance of house purchase by tenants. This further amendment prohibits local authorities from trying to restrict a tenant's rights by entering into the agreements referred to. See also note to s.3(2).

Para. 1(b)

This removes the former need for members of the family wishing to be joint purchasers to have occupied with the applicant the house *which is the subject of the application.*

Para. 1(c)

These changes are consequential upon s.3 of this Act and upon para. 1(*d*) below.

Para. 1(d)

See para. 1(*c*) above. These changes are designed to clarify the basis upon which the greatest discount of the price can be claimed, *i.e.* in reliance upon the longest period of occupation of the person now defined as the "appropriate person".

Para. 1(e)

S.1(10) of the 1980 Act lists the landlords, the occupation of whose houses qualifies tenants for the right to purchase and for discount. Sub-paras. (i)–(iii) are "consequential" upon s.1 of this Act although sub-paras. (ii)–(iii) do appear to duplicate the material in s.1 which already appeared to be an inelegant insertion (see note to that section). Sub-para. (iv) contains a substantive amendment to allow spouses as well as members of the armed forces themselves to count their occupation of Crown accommodation.

Paras. 1(f) and (g)

S.1(11) of the 1980 Act excludes certain categories of tenant from the general right of secure tenants to purchase their houses. The adjustments that subsection and the addition of subs. (11A), (11B) and (11C) which are made by these paragraphs are, in part, consequential upon the extensions of the right to purchase made by s.1 of this Act and, at other points, qualify those extensions in important ways.

Sub-para. (i) is a technical adjustment consequential upon s.1(1).

Sub-para. (ii) adds to the list of tenants excluded from the right to buy some categories of housing association tenants who would otherwise have gained that right by virtue of s.1(1):—

Section 1(11)(d)

A landlord mentioned in para. (*e*) of s.10(2) is a registered housing association. By virtue of this para. (*d*), tenants of registered associations which have not been in receipt of public funds (*i.e.* under the Housing Associations Act 1985 and earlier legislation) are excluded.

Section 1(11)(e)

This para. excludes tenants of registered associations which are small and have never let more than 100 dwellings. The exclusion was not contained in the original Bill but was introduced by the Lords at Third Reading when the number of dwellings was fixed at 250. This was reduced to 100 when the Bill returned to the Commons. Note the unfortunate effect of this late amendment upon the terms of s.15 of this Act (and thus s.45 of the Housing Associations Act 1985).

Section 1(11)(f)

In the Bill, as originally published, there was a simple exclusion from the right to buy of registered housing associations which are charities entered in the register maintained by the Charity Commissioners for England and Wales. In the course of the Bill's passage, however, this simple exclusion was expanded.

In the main the additions, represented by s.1(11)(*f*)(ii), and (*g*) and s.(11B) and (11C) (introduced by para. 1(*g*) of this Schedule) expand the definition of charities to include Scottish charitable housing associations exempt from registration under the 1960 Act. The mechanisms are established for the identification of such associations by reference to their claims to exemption from taxation.

These additions were largely in place by the time the Bill first left the Commons but the terms of s.1(11)(*g*) were further adjusted. As the Bill left the Commons the words from "all periods from 14th November 1985 . . . (whichever is the later)" read "all periods from 3 October 1980". The Lords deleted the whole of (i) and (ii) and inserted "is, by virtue of section 360(1) of the Income and Corporation Taxes Act 1970 (special exemptions for charities), exempt from tax; or". On return to the Commons the Lords amendments were undone but the date in the Bill was changed to November 14, 1985, which allowed associations achieving charitable status before that date to claim exemption under the Act. The Bill was further amended by the Lords to include the reference to later registration to permit charitable associations established after November 14, 1985, to be exempt from the Act. This was not changed further by the Commons. The debates reflect the fierce disagreements within and between the two Houses on the question of charitable status associations. A point which attracted much attention (most explicitly in the Commons) was that only one charitable association, the Link Housing Association, is compelled to sell to its tenants since it achieved its charitable status *after* November 1985 and is not exempt on the grounds of either size or special needs provision.

The addition of s.1(11) and the new s.1(11A), were achieved at Commons Report Stage. These provisions exempt from the right to buy provisions the tenants of certain small housing associations serving special needs "within a neighbourhood". Three categories of special need are listed but these are variable by order.

Para. 1(h)

S.1(12) of the 1980 Act defines, for the purposes of the section, a number of terms including the fundamental "occupation". Sub-para. (*i*) has the effect of extending occupation to include (*a*) that of fathers—and mothers-in-law and (*b*), at the discretion of the landlord, other members of the family of a former tenant. For "members of the family", see paras. 16 and 17 below.

Sub-para. (ii) removes an ambiguity in the former term "disregarded". The remaining sub-paras. correct small anomalies in the meaning of "dwelling-house" in this context.

Para. 2

S.1A of the 1980 Act was inserted by the Local Government (Miscellaneous Provisions) (Scotland) Act 1981 and authorises the vesting in the landlord by order of a heritable proprietor's interest. The amendment is consequential upon the extended list of selling landlords introduced by s.1.

Para. 3

This places a new duty upon a landlord to inform a prospective tenant (or in subs. (2) continuing tenant) of either a restriction of the right to purchase (because of the application of s.1(11) of the 1980 Act) or restriction of entitlement to discount (because of the amended ss.1(7)–7(A) of the 1980 Act—see s.3 of this Act).

Para. 4

This amendment removes an anomaly to give a tenant unsuccessful in obtaining an order from the Lands Tribunal under s.7(2)(*d*) (introduced by the Local Government and Planning (Scotland) Act 1982), a further two months within which to accept the original offer.

Para. 5

These amendments restructure the rules under s.4 by which a local authority may apply to the Secretary of State for an order allowing the insertion of a right of pre-emption on houses in rural areas. The extension to "all relevant dwelling houses" as defined allows the houses of not only the authority itself but also of housing associations to be included in the calculation.

Para. 6

New purchasers of housing association houses have the right to a loan enjoyed by other tenants under s.5. Application is to be made to the Housing Corporation.

Paras. 7 and 8

These amendments recast the rules under which a purchaser may be obliged to repay discount in the event of an early re-sale. Notice also, however, the important qualification to 7(*a*)(ii) and (*b*)(ii) in s.23(3) of the Act.

The amendments in para. 7 reduce the period within which resale will require payment from five years to three years and, accordingly, the percentages to be repaid after one and two years (*i.e.* 100 per cent. within first year, 66 per cent. in second year, and 33 per cent. in third year). The point of para. 7(*a*)(iii) is to ensure that, in the event that discount is reduced by s.1(7)–(7A), the amount repayable is calculated in relation to the actual amount of discount allowed.

Para. 8, inserting the new s.6A, recasts the rules which exempt from repayment and, in particular, introduces the exemption for certain disposals to members of the owner's family (see para. 17, below).

Para. 9

This amendment is designed to make quite clear that the power of local authorities to sell houses under s.8 of the 1980 Act is subject to the need, *if the sale is at less than the best price obtainable*, to get the consent of the Secretary of State under s.74(2) of the Local Government (Scotland) Act 1973.

Para. 10

Prior to this change, tenants who were not secure simply because they occupied their houses "under contract of employment" nevertheless obtained many of the benefits (not including the right to buy) of secure tenants. To this group are added those tenants who are not secure by virtue of the exclusion in para. 18 below (houses within the curtilage of other buildings). No doubt many tenants excluded from security by para. 2 of Sched. 1 (employment) will also be excluded by new para. 9 (curtilage). If a tenant *is* excluded by both, will he be excluded "by reason only of the operation of paragraph 2 or 9" as required by the amended s.10(4)(*b*)?

Para. 11

The amendment in (*a*) extends the right to succeed to a secure tenancy to the other of two persons living as husband and wife in addition to a spouse.

Amendment (*b*) removes the ambiguity in the expression "over the age of 16 years" (did that mean 17 years?) by substituting the phrase "who has attained".

Para. 12

The amendment in (*a*) extends to proceedings based on new ground 16 (see para. 19 below), the power of the court to adjourn under s.15(1). It also confirms the inclusion of reinstated ground 6 (see s.11 of this Act). For an illustration of the very slight use in practice of s.15(1) outwith Glasgow and Edinburgh, see Adler, Himsworth and Kerr *Public Housing, Rent Arrears and the Sheriff Court* Scottish Office 1985.

Amendment (*b*) restructures s.15(2) and, in so doing, removes an odd anomaly that, in the case of grounds 8–15, the court did not have to find the ground for possession established;

it places the new ground 16 (as a "conduct" rather than "management" ground) in the 2(*a*) category; and places new ground 6 in a new bridging category in which both reasonableness and the availability of other accommodation will have to be established. For "suitable accommodation" see Sched. 2, Part II to the 1980 Act.

Amendment (*c*) is simply consequential upon (*b*).

Para. 13

The existing s.26 of the 1980 Act lays down certain ground rules for local authorities in admitting applicants to a housing list and thereafter in allocating houses.

The main effect of this paragraph is to separate rules of admission to housing lists from rules for allocation in the new ss.26 and 26A. In the new s.26, however, the duty to take no account of the matters in (1)(*b*) (income); (1)(*c*) (value of property); (1)(*d*) (outstanding liability from a tenancy when the applicant was not the tenant); and (1)(*e*) (marital status) are new. The age in (1)(*a*) is lowered from 18 to 16. Subs. (1)(*e*) (which was added at the Commons Report stage) comes close to requiring that the very presence of a spouse (or person) and thus the size of the family unit has to to ignored. It presumably tolerates, however, the taking into account (and thus exclusion where relevant) of a homosexual relationship.

The new s.26A (which was heavily amended in the Commons on Report) deals, on its face, with allocation and, for this purpose, the matters in (*a*) which are new are, by reference to new s.26, those in subs. (1)(*a*) (age reduced from 18 to 16), (*c*); and (*d*). The obligation not to impose the requirements in s.26A, para. (*b*) is also new.

Para. 14

This is a technical amendment consequential upon s.8 of this Act.

Para. 15

S.30 of the 1980 Act established the rules for the new "variable interest home loans" made by local authorities. One aspect of the rules was the mechanism contained in subs. (8) for affecting a variation in the interest rate and notifying relevant borrowers. In practice, problems arose as to the dates of service of notice and the dates of change of rate thereafter. The device of "the appropriate day" used in the new s.8 and defined in the new s.8A is intended to remove these problems by detaching the procedure from any fixed period after the date of a declaration or determination which triggers the change in rate to be charged.

"Standard rate," "locally determined rate," and "relevant period of 6 months" are all defined in s.30(4)–(7).

Paras. 16 and 17

Relationship within a "family" are important at a number of different points in the 1980 Act where it deals with the right to purchase and with security of tenure and the term "family" is defined in s.82.

The amendments in these paragraphs produce a more comprehensive version of the "family." Presumably, however, the person who, for instance, lives as husband or wife with one's grandparent is not a member of one's family?

Para. 18

Sched. 1 to the 1980 Act excludes some tenancies from the security created by s.10 and thus from the right to buy. The addition by s.1 of this Act of regional councils, police and fire authorities required (by new para. 8) the further exclusion from security of tenure of "operational" or potentially "operational" houses which might not be adequately excluded otherwise.

The new para. 9 excludes from security those houses which are parts of other buildings (or within their curtilage) used for other purposes. It clarifies the exclusion of the houses of *e.g.* school janitors if so attached. This would not itself exclude a park-keeper's house if there were no other dominant "building" in the park. "Curtilage" is not defined in the Act. See, however, the dicta of Lord Mackintosh in *Sinclair Lockhart's Trustees* v. *Central Land Board*, 1951 S.C. 258 at p.264, where he said that the "ground which is used for the comfortable enjoyment of a house or other building may be regarded as being within the curtilage of that house or building and thereby is an integral part of the same although it has not been marked off or enclosed in any way. It is enough that it serves the purposes of the house or building in some necessary or reasonably useful way". See also *Paul* v. *Ayrshire County Council*, 1964 S.L.T. 207, at p.111, and *Assessor for Lothian Region* v. *B.P. Oil Grangemouth Refinery Ltd.*, 1985 S.L.T. 453.

Para. 19

Sched. 2, Pt. 1 to the 1980 Act lists the grounds for recovery of possession of a secure tenancy. The amendments in this paragraph alter the terms of ground 10 and add a new ground 16 (ground 6 is reinstated by s.11 of this Act).

Ground 10 is now amended (by para. (*a*)) to allow possession to be recovered where demolition or substantial works affecting the house can be those of someone other than the landlord itself. See also s.20 of this Act concerning the payment of compensation.

Para. (*b*) creating ground 16 allows for recovery on the basis of a false statement by the tenant.

See also the note on para. 12 above.

Section 25(1)   SCHEDULE 2

MINOR AND CONSEQUENTIAL AMENDMENTS

The Building (Scotland) Act 1959 (c.24)

1. In section 17(2) of the Building (Scotland) Act 1959 (restriction on effect of requirement to demolish, or carry out operations in relation to, a building), after paragraph (*b*) there shall be inserted the following paragraph—
   "(*bb*) a building to which section 262A of the said Act of 1972 (control of demolition in conservation areas) applies;".

The Housing (Financial Provisions) (Scotland) Act 1972 (c.46)

2. In the proviso to paragraph 2 of Schedule 4 to the Housing (Financial Provisions) (Scotland) Act 1972 (debits to housing revenue account in respect of loan charges payable as regards certain sold, or demolished, houses), for the words "to which the account relates and which is demolished after the coming into force of this Act or in respect of any house to which the account relates and which is" there shall be substituted the words "which, being a house to which the account related—
   (*a*) was demolished after the coming into force of this Act; or
   (*b*) was".

The Land Tenure Reform (Scotland) Act 1974 (c.38)

3. In section 8(7) of the Land Tenure Reform (Scotland) Act 1974 (saving)—
   (*a*) for the words "1971" there shall be substituted the words "1984 or a secure tenancy within the meaning of the Tenants' Rights, Etc. (Scotland) Act 1980"; and
   (*b*) for the words "that Act" there shall be substituted the words "either of those Acts".

The Housing Associations Act 1985 (c.69)

4.—(1) The Housing Associations Act 1985 shall be amended in accordance with this paragraph.

(2) In section 8(1) (power of registered housing associations to dispose of land), after the word "buy)" there shall be inserted the words "and Part I of the Tenants' Rights, Etc. (Scotland) Act 1980 (analogous Scottish provisions)".

(3) In section 15(1) (prohibition on payments etc. by certain registered housing associations), at the end there shall be added the words "or by section 15A of this Act".

(4) In section 40 (index of defined expressions), after the entry relating to a shared ownership lease there shall be inserted the following entry—
   "shared ownership agreement (in relation to   section 106".
       Scotland)

(5) In section 42 (projects qualifying for housing association grant: accommodation for letting, hostels), in subsection (2)(*a*)—
   (*a*) after the word "includes" there shall be inserted the words
       "—(i) In England and Wales,"; and
   (*b*) after the word "lease," there shall be inserted the following sub-paragraph—
       "(ii) in Scotland, disposal under a shared ownership agreement,".

(6) In section 86 (Housing Corporation indemnities for building societies)—
   (*a*) in subsection (1)—

    (i) after the words "building society" in each of the three places where they occur there shall be inserted the words "or recognised body"; and

    (ii) in paragraph (*b*), for the word "the" where it last occurs there shall be substituted the word "a";

  (*b*) in subsection (2), after the words "building society" there shall be inserted the words "or recognised body";

  (*c*) in subsection (5), after the words "building societies" there shall be inserted the words "or recognised bodies"; and

  (*d*) at the end there shall be added the following subsections—

    "(6) In this section, "recognised body" means a body designated, or of a class or description designated, in an order made under this subsection by statutory instrument by the Secretary of State with the consent of the Treasury.

    (7) Before making an order under subsection (6) above varying or revoking an order previously so made, the Secretary of State shall give an opportunity for representations to be made on behalf of a recognised body which, if the order were made, would cease to be such a body.".

(7) In section 106 (interpretation), at the end there shall be added the following subsection—

  "(3) In the definition of "shared ownership agreement" in subsection (2) above, "approved" means approved by the Secretary of State after consultation with the Housing Corporation.".

(8) In section 107—

  (*a*) in subsection (3) (list of provisions of Act applying to England and Wales only), for the words "4(3)(*g*)" there shall be substituted the words "4(3)(*d*)"; and

  (*b*) in subsection (4) (list of provisions of Act applying to Scotland only), after the word "only—" there shall be inserted the words—

    "section 4(3)(*h*),

    section 15A,".

GENERAL NOTE

This Schedule contains the amendments authorised by s.25 of the Act.

Para. 1

This adjustment takes account of an amendment made to the Town and Country Planning (Scotland) Act 1972 by the Town and Country Amenities Act 1974.

Para. 2

This is designed to revoke an apparent conflict between s.23 and Sched. 4 to the Housing (Financial Provisions) (Scotland) Act 1972.

Para. 3

Technical amendments to the 1974 Act.

Paras. 4–8

These amendments are consequential upon other provisions in the Act affecting housing associations and their tenants.

Section 25(2)   SCHEDULE 3

Repeals

Chapter	Short title	Extent of repeal
10 & 11 Eliz. 2. c.37.	The Building Societies Act 1962.	In Schedule 3.3(2)(*b*), the word "and" where it first occurs.
1968 c.31.	The Housing (Financial Provisions) (Scotland) Act 1968.	Section 25(1)(*d*).
1980 c.52.	The Tenants' Rights, Etc. (Scotland) Act 1980.	In section 1(8), the word "and" at the end of paragraph (*c*). In section 1(11), the word "nor" at the end of paragraph (*b*). In section 10(2), the word "and" at the end of paragraph (*f*). In section 30(5), the words "and the standard rate shall be effective from the date when it is declared by the Secretary of State". In Schedule 1, paragraph 1.
1985 c.69.	The Housing Associations Act 1985.	Section 100. In section 106(2), the definition of "heritable security". In section 107(3), the words "17(4),"; the words "sections 44 and 45,"; the word "(3)" where it occurs in the entry relating to section 52; and the words "section 105,".

General Note

Most of these repeals are consequential and technical. Note, however, the repeal of s.100 of the Housing Associations Act 1985 which removes the power of the Housing Corporation to appoint the Scottish Special Housing Association as its agent in relation to certain of its functions carried out in Scotland.

NATIONAL HEALTH SERVICE (AMENDMENT) ACT 1986

(c.66)

An Act to apply certain enactments, orders and regulations relating to food and health and safety to certain health service bodies and premises; to make further provision as to pharmaceutical services under the National Health Service Act 1977 and the National Health Service (Scotland) Act 1978 and the remuneration of persons providing those services, general medical services, general dental services or general ophthalmic services under those Acts; to provide further, as respects Scotland, as to co-operation among certain bodies in securing and advancing the health of disabled persons, the elderly and others; and for connected purposes.   [7th November 1986]

PARLIAMENTARY DEBATES
Hansard: H.C. Vol. 94, col. 799; Vol. 95, col. 704; Vol. 99, col. 26; Vol. 103, col. 976; H.L. Vol. 476, col. 126; Vol. 479, col. 910; Vol. 480, col. 815; Vol. 481, cols. 677, 939.
The Bill was considered in the House of Commons Standing Committee E, April 29 to May 13, 1986.

Application of food legislation to health authorities and health service premises

1.—(1) For the purposes of the food legislation—

(a) a health authority shall not be regarded as the servant or agent of the Crown, or as enjoying any status, immunity or privilege of the Crown; and

(b) premises used by a health authority shall not be regarded as property of or property held on behalf of the Crown.

(2) The appropriate authority may by regulations—

(a) provide who is to be treated as the occupier or owner of any such premises for any of those purposes; and

(b) make such modifications of the food legislation, in its application to health authorities, as appear to the authority to be necessary for its effective operation in relation to them.

(3) The powers to make regulations conferred by subsection (2) above shall be exercisable by statutory instrument.

(4) A statutory instrument containing regulations made in the exercise of the power conferred by paragraph (a) of that subsection shall be subject to annulment in pursuance of a resolution of either House of Parliament.

(5) A statutory instrument containing regulations made in the exercise of the power conferred by paragraph (*b*) shall not be made unless a draft of the instrument has been laid before Parliament and approved by a resolution of each House.

(6) Section 125 of the 1977 Act and section 101 of the 1978 Act shall have no effect in relation to any action, liability, claim or demand arising out of the food legislation.

(7) In this section—

(*a*) as respects England and Wales—

   (i) "the appropriate authority" means the Ministers, as defined in section 132(1) of the Food Act 1984;

   (ii) "the food legislation" means the Food Act 1984 and any regulations or order made under it;

   (iii) "health authority" has the meaning assigned to it by section 128 of the 1977 Act;

(*b*) as respects Scotland—

   (i) "the appropriate authority" means the Secretary of State;

   (ii) "the food legislation" means the Milk and Dairies (Scotland) Acts 1914 to 1949, the Food and Drugs (Scotland) Act 1956 and the Control of Food Premises (Scotland) Act 1977 and any regulations or order made under those Acts;

   (iii) "health authority" means a Health Board constituted under section 2 of the 1978 Act, the Common Services Agency constituted under section 10 of that Act or a State Hospital Management Committee constituted under section 91 of the Mental Health (Scotland) Act 1984.

(8) This section shall have no effect in relation to anything done or omitted before its commencement.

Health and safety legislation

2.—(1) For the purposes of health and safety legislation—

(*a*) a health authority shall not be regarded as the servant or agent of the Crown, or as enjoying any status, immunity or privilege of the Crown; and

(*b*) premises used by a health authority shall not be regarded as property of or property held on behalf of the Crown.

(2) In this section—

"health authority"—

(*a*) as respects England and Wales, has the meaning assigned to it by section 128 of the 1977 Act; and

(*b*) as respects Scotland, means a Health Board constituted under section 2 of the 1978 Act, the Common Services Agency constituted under section 10 of that Act or a State Hospital Management Committee constituted under section 91 of the Mental Health (Scotland) Act 1984; and

"the health and safety legislation" means—

(*a*) the Health and Safety at Work etc. Act 1974 and the regulations, orders and other instruments in force under it; and

(*b*) the enactments specified in the third column of Schedule 1 to that Act and the regulations, orders and other instruments in force under those enactments.

(3) Section 125 of the 1977 Act and section 101 of the 1978 Act shall have no effect in relation to any action, liability, claim or demand arising out of the health and safety legislation.

(4) This section shall have no effect in relation to anything done or omitted before its commencement.

Pharmaceutical services

3.—(1) The following section shall be substituted for section 42 of the 1977 Act—

"**Regulations as to pharmaceutical services**

42.—(1) Regulations shall provide for securing that arrangements made by a Family Practitioner Committee under section 41 above will enable persons in the Committee's locality for whom drugs, medicines or appliances mentioned in that section are ordered as there mentioned to receive them from persons with whom such arrangements have been made.

(2) The regulations shall include provision—

(a) for the preparation and publication by a Committee of one or more lists of persons, other than medical practitioners and dental practitioners, who undertake to provide pharmaceutical services from premises in the Committee's locality;

(b) that an application to a Committee for inclusion in such a list shall be made in the prescribed manner and shall state—

   (i) the services which the applicant will undertake to provide and, if they consist of or include the supply of appliances, which appliances he will undertake to supply; and

   (ii) the premises from which he will undertake to provide those services;

(c) that, except in prescribed cases—

   (i) an application for inclusion in such a list by a person not already included; and

   (ii) an application by a person already included in such a list for inclusion also in respect of services or premises other than those already listed in relation to him,

shall be granted only if the Committee is satisfied, in accordance with the regulations, that it is necessary or desirable to grant it in order to secure in the neighbourhood in which the premises are located the adequate provision by persons included in the list of the services, or some of the services, specified in the application; and

(d) for the removal of an entry in respect of premises from a list if it has been determined in the prescribed manner that the person to whom the entry relates—

   (i) has never provided from those premises; or

   (ii) has ceased to provide from them,

the services, or any of the services, which he is listed as undertaking to provide from them.

(3) The regulations may include provision—

(a) that an application to a Committee may be granted in respect of some only of the services specified in it;

(b) that an application to a Committee relating to services of a prescribed description shall be granted only if it appears to the Committee that the applicant has satisfied such conditions with regard to the provision of those services as may be prescribed;

(c) that the inclusion of a person in a list in pursuance of such an application may be for a fixed period;

(d) that, where the premises from which an application states that the applicant will undertake to provide services are in an area of a prescribed description, the applicant shall not be included in the list unless his inclusion is approved by a prescribed body and by reference to a prescribed criterion; and

(e) that the prescribed body may give its approval subject to conditions.

(4) The regulations shall include provision conferring on such persons as may be prescribed rights of appeal from decisions made by virtue of this section.

(5) The regulations shall be so framed as to preclude—

(*a*) a person included in a list published under subsection (2)(*a*) above; and

(*b*) an employee of such a person;

from taking part in the decision whether an application such as is mentioned in subsection (2)(*c*) above should be granted or an appeal against such a decision brought by virtue of subsection (4) above should be allowed.".

(2) Regulations purporting to be made under section 42(*b*) of the 1977 Act and made before the passing of this Act shall be treated as being and always having been valid.

(3) The following subsections shall be substituted for subsection (2) of section 27 of the 1978 Act—

"(2) Regulations shall provide for securing that arrangements made by a Health Board under subsection (1) will enable persons in the Board's area for whom drugs, medicines or appliances mentioned in that subsection are ordered as there mentioned to receive them from persons with whom such arrangements have been made.

(3) The regulations shall include provision—

(*a*) for the preparation and publication by a Health Board of one or more lists of persons, other than medical practitioners and dental practitioners, who undertake to provide pharmaceutical services from premises in the Board's area;

(*b*) that an application to a Health Board for inclusion in such a list shall be made in the prescribed manner and shall state—

   (i) the services which the applicant will undertake to provide and, if they consist of or include the supply of appliances, which appliances he will undertake to supply; and

   (ii) the premises from which he will undertake to provide those services;

(*c*) that, except in prescribed cases—

   (i) an application for inclusion in such a list by a person not already included; and

   (ii) an application by a person already included in such a list for inclusion also in respect of services or premises other than those already listed in relation to him,

shall be granted only if the Health Board is satisfied, in accordance with the regulations, that it is necessary or desirable to grant it in order to secure in the neighbourhood in which the premises are located the adequate provision by persons included in the list of the services, or some of the services, specified in the application; and

(*d*) for the removal of an entry in respect of premises from a list if it has been determined in the prescribed manner that the person to whom the entry relates—

   (i) has never provided from those premises;

     or

   (ii) has ceased to provide from them,

the services, or any of the services, which he is listed as undertaking to provide from them.

(4) The regulations may include provision—

(*a*) that an application to a Health Board may be granted in respect of some only of the services specified in it;

(*b*) that an application to a Health Board relating to services of a prescribed description shall be granted only if it appears to the Board that the applicant has satisfied such conditions with regard to the provision of those services as may be prescribed;

(*c*) that the inclusion of a person in a list in pursuance of such an application may be for a fixed period;

(*d*) that, where the premises from which an application states that the applicant will undertake to provide services are in an area of a prescribed description, the applicant shall not be included in the list unless his inclusion is approved by a prescribed body and by reference to a prescribed criterion; and

(*e*) that the prescribed body may give its approval subject to conditions.

(5) The regulations shall include provision conferring on such persons as may be prescribed rights of appeal from decisions made by virtue of subsection (3) or (4).

(6) The regulations shall be so framed as to preclude—

(*a*) a person included in a list published under subsection (3)(*a*) above; and

(*b*) an employee of such a person;

from taking part in the decision whether an application such as is mentioned in subsection (3)(*c*) above should be granted or an appeal against such a decision brought by virtue of subsection (5) above should be allowed.".

(4) In section 28 of the 1978 Act, after the word "by" where it first occurs in each of subsections (1) and (2) there shall be inserted the words "or under".

Remuneration of persons providing general medical services etc.

4.—(1) On a determination of remuneration for any of the descriptions of services mentioned in section 43A(1) of the 1977 Act or section 28A(1) of the 1978 Act or any category of services falling within such a description the determining authority may adjust the amount of the remuneration in either or both of the following ways—

(*a*) by deducting an amount to take account of any overpayment;

(*b*) by adding an amount to take account of any underpayment,

if it appears to the authority that an earlier determination was unsatisfactory.

(2) An earlier determination is to be taken to have been unsatisfactory only if, had it fallen to the authority to make it at the time of the later determination, the authority would have made it on the basis of different information.

(3) If an amount falls to be deducted by virtue of subsection (1)(*a*) above, the determining authority, in fixing amounts of remuneration for persons to whom the determination relates, may have regard to the period within which they first provided services of the description to which it relates.

(4) In this section—

"earlier determination" means an earlier determination of remuneration of the same or other persons for services of the same description or any category of services falling within that description and includes such a determination made before the passing of this Act;

"overpayment" means the aggregate of any amounts which were properly paid under the earlier determination but which in the authority's opinion were paid because that determination was unsatisfactory, exclusive of any portion of that aggregate in respect of which a deduction under subsection (1) above has already been made; and

"underpayment" means the aggregate of any amounts which in the authority's opinion would have been paid under the earlier determination if that determination had not been unsatisfactory, exclusive of any portion of that aggregate in respect of which an addition under subsection (1) above has already been made.

(5) If the later determination is of remuneration for a category of services falling within one of the descriptions of services mentioned in section 43A(1) of the 1977 Act or section 28A(1) of the 1978 Act, it is immaterial whether the earlier determination was of remuneration for the same category of services or for any other category of services falling within the same description.

(6) In subsection (7) of section 43B of the 1977 Act and of section 28B of the 1978 Act—

(*a*) in paragraph (*a*), for the words "a kind to which the determination will relate" there shall be substituted the words "the description to which the determination will relate or of any category falling within that description"; and

(*b*) the following paragraph shall be substituted for paragraph (*d*)—

"(*d*) the extent to which it is desirable to encourage the provision, either generally or in particular places, of the description or category of services to which the determination will relate;".

(7) The following subsection shall be inserted after each of those subsections—

"(8) If the determination is of remuneration for a category of services falling within one of the descriptions of services mentioned in subsection (1) of the preceding section, the reference in subsection (7)(*a*) above to a category of services is a reference to the same category of services or to any other category of services falling within the same description.".

Co-operation and advice in relation to disabled persons, the elderly and others

5.—(1) After section 13 of the 1978 Act there shall be inserted the following sections—

"Co-operation in planning of services for disabled persons, the elderly and others

13A.—(1) The duty under section 13, in relation to persons to whom this section applies, includes—

(*a*) joint planning of—

(i) services for those persons; and

(ii) the development of those services,

being services which are of common concern to Health Boards and either or both of the authorities mentioned in that section;

(*b*) such consultation with voluntary organisations providing services similar to those mentioned in paragraph (*a*) as might be expected to contribute substantially to the joint planning of the services mentioned in that paragraph;

(*c*) the publication, at such times and in such manner as the bodies who have made joint plans under paragraph (*a*) consider appropriate, of those joint plans.

(2) This section applies to—

(*a*) disabled persons within the meaning of the Disabled Persons (Services, Consultation and Representation) Act 1986;

(b) persons aged 65 or more; and
(c) such other categories of persons as the Secretary of State may by order specify.

Joint Liaison Committees

13B.—(1) The Secretary of State may, after consultation with such Health Boards, local authorities, education authorities, associations of such authorities and other organisations and persons as appear to him to be appropriate, by order provide for the formation and as to the functions of committees, to be known as joint liaison committees, to advise Health Boards and local and education authorities on the performance of such of their duties under section 13 as consist of co-operation in the planning and operation of services of common concern to Health Boards and such authorities.

(2) An order under subsection (1) may contain provisions relating to the role of voluntary organisations in joint liaison committees.".

(2) Section 15 of the Disabled Persons (Services, Consultation and Representation) Act 1986 is hereby repealed.

Expenses

6. There shall be paid out of money provided by Parliament any increase attributable to this Act in sums so provided under any other Act.

Orders in Council making corresponding provision for Northern Ireland

7. An Order in Council under paragraph 1(1)(b) of Schedule 1 to the Northern Ireland Act 1974 (legislation for Northern Ireland in the interim period) which states that it is made for purposes corresponding to those of this Act—
(a) shall not be subject to paragraph 1(4) and (5) of that Schedule (affirmative resolution of both Houses of Parliament); but
(b) shall be subject to annulment in pursuance of a resolution of either House.

Short title, etc.

8.—(1) This Act may be cited as the National Health Service (Amendment) Act 1986.

(2) In this Act—
    "the 1977 Act" means the National Health Service Act 1977; and
    "the 1978 Act" means the National Health Service (Scotland) Act 1978.

(3) Section 21(1) of the Health Services Act 1980 and paragraph 54 of Schedule 1 to that Act shall cease to have effect.

(4) Sections 1 and 2 above shall come into force at the end of the period of three months beginning with the day on which this Act is passed.

(5) Each of the following provisions of this Act—
    (a) section 3 above; and
    (b) to the extent that it inserts section 13B of the 1978 Act into that Act, section 5 above,
shall come into force on such day as the Secretary of State may by order made by statutory instrument appoint in relation to it.

(6) Section 7 above extends to Northern Ireland only, but apart from that section, subsection (1) above and this subsection, this Act does not extend to Northern Ireland.

CONSOLIDATED FUND (No. 2) ACT 1986

(1986 c. 67)

Apply certain sums out of the Consolidated Fund to the service of the years ending on 31st March 1987 and 1988.   [18th December 1986]

PARLIAMENTARY DEBATES
Hansard: H.C. Vol. 107, cols. 442, 871. H.L. Vol. 483, col. 105.

Issue out of the Consolidated Fund for the year ending 31st March 1987

1. The Treasury may issue out of the Consolidated Fund of the United Kingdom and apply towards making good the supply granted to Her Majesty for the service of the year ending on 31st March 1987 the sum of £2,206,135,000.

Issue out of the Consolidated Fund for the year ending 31st March 1988

2. The Treasury may issue out of the Consolidated Fund of the United Kingdom and apply towards making good the supply granted to Her Majesty for the service of the year ending on 31st March 1988 the sum of £44,907,033,000.

Short title

3. This Act may be cited as the Consolidated Fund (No. 2) Act 1986.

ADVANCE PETROLEUM REVENUE TAX ACT 1986

(1986 c. 68)

An Act to provide for the repayment of certain amounts of advance petroleum revenue tax.   [18th December 1986]

PARLIAMENTARY DEBATES
Hansard: H.C. Vol. 105, col. 566; Vol. 106, cols. 633, 1090. H.L. Vol. 482, col. 1062; Vol. 483, col. 108.

Repayment of APRT where net profit period not yet reached

1.—(1) In accordance with the provisions of this Act, advance petroleum revenue tax shall be repaid to a participator in an oil field—
  (a) in respect of whom none of the chargeable periods ending before 1st July 1986 is his net profit period for the purposes of this Act; and
  (b) who was a participator in that field on 6th November 1986 and who, on that date, was entitled to a share of the oil won from that field during the chargeable period ending on 31st December 1986; and the Schedule to this Act shall have effect for determining whether any chargeable period is for the purposes of this Act a participator's net profit period in relation to a particular oil field.

(2) In this section "relevant participator" means any such participator as is referred to in subsection (1) above; and other expressions used in this Act have the same meaning as in Chapter II of Part VI of the Finance Act 1982 (advance petroleum revenue tax).

(3) There shall be determined in the case of every relevant participator the amount by which his APRT credit for the chargeable period ending on 31st December 1986 exceeds his provisional liability for petroleum revenue tax for that period in respect of the field in question and, subject to subsection (5) below, on a claim made in that behalf, there shall be repaid to the participator so much of that excess as does not exceed £15 million.

(4) The reference in subsection (3) above to a participator's provisional liability for petroleum revenue tax for a chargeable period is a reference to the amount of tax shown to be payable by him for that period in the statement delivered under section 1(1)(a) of the Petroleum Revenue Tax Act 1980.

(5) A claim under subsection (3) above shall be made in such form as the Board may prescribe (whether before or after the passing of this Act) and shall be made not later than 28th February 1987 and, for the purposes of this Act, the Board may have regard to claims made before as well as after the passing of this Act.

(6) Paragraph 10(4) of Schedule 19 to the Finance Act 1982 (interest on certain repayments of APRT) shall not apply to any amount of APRT which is repayable only by virtue of this Act.

(7) A repayment of APRT made to a relevant participator pursuant to this Act,—
  (a) shall be presumed to be a repayment of APRT which was paid later in priority to APRT which was paid earlier; and
  (b) shall be disregarded in computing his income for the purposes of income tax or corporation tax.

Short title and construction

2.—(1) This Act may be cited as the Advance Petroleum Revenue Tax Act 1986.

(2) This Act shall be construed as one with Part I of the Oil Taxation Act 1975.

Section 1(1)   SCHEDULE

NET PROFIT PERIOD

1. In this Schedule—
  (*a*) "the principal Act" means the Oil Taxation Act 1975;
  (*b*) "statement", in relation to an oil field and a chargeable period, means the statement delivered by a participator in that oil field in respect of that period under section 1(1)(*a*) of the Petroleum Revenue Tax Act 1980;
  (*c*) "the material date", in relation to a participator in an oil field, means the date on which he delivers his statement in respect of that field for the chargeable period ending on 31st December 1986; and
  (*d*) "section 111" means section 111 of the Finance Act 1981 (restriction of expenditure supplement).

2. Subject to the following provisions of this Schedule, if a chargeable period is a participator's net profit period for the purposes of section 111, that period is also his net profit period for the purposes of this Act.

3.—(1) If, before the material date, no notice of assessment or determination under paragraph 10 of Schedule 2 to the principal Act has been given to a participator with respect to any of the chargeable periods ending before 1st July 1986, the question whether one of those periods is his net profit period for the purposes of this Act shall be determined, subject to sub-paragraphs (2) and (3) below, on the assumption that, before making any modifications under subsections (3) to (5) of section 111, the amount of the assessable profit or allowable loss which accrued to the participator in each of the chargeable periods ending before 1st July 1986 was as set out in the statement delivered in respect of that period.

(2) If the expenditure treated as allowed in determining the assessable profit or allowable loss set out in the statement delivered in respect of any of the chargeable periods referred to in sub-paragraph (1) above is less than could have been treated as so allowed by virtue of paragraph 2(4) of the Schedule to the Petroleum Revenue Tax Act 1980, the assessable profit or allowable loss set out in that statement shall be taken for the purposes of sub-paragraph (1) above to be what it would have been if account had been taken of all the expenditure which could have been treated as so allowed.

(3) In any case where—
  (*a*) by virtue of sub-paragraph (2) above, any amount of expenditure is treated as allowed in determining the assessable profit or allowable loss which is taken to be set out in the statement for any chargeable period, and
  (*b*) the whole or any part of that amount is in fact treated as allowed in determining the assessable profit or allowable loss set out in the statement delivered in respect of any subsequent period,

the assessable profit or allowable loss of that subsequent period as set out in the statement delivered in respect of that period shall be taken for the purposes of sub-paragraph (1) above to be adjusted so as to prevent any amount of expenditure being taken into account more than once.

4.—(1) If, in a case where paragraph 3(1) above does not apply in relation to a participator,—
  (*a*) one of the chargeable periods ending before 1st July 1986 is the participator's net profit period for the purposes of section 111, and
  (*b*) a claim has been made under Schedule 5 or Schedule 6 to the principal Act in respect of expenditure incurred before 1st July 1986, and
  (*c*) as to the whole or any part of that expenditure, at the material date either the Board have not notified their decision on the claim or an appeal against their decision on the claim has not been finally determined or abandoned (or treated as abandoned),

the question whether one of the periods referred to in paragraph (*a*) above is the participator's net profit period for the purposes of this Act shall be determined on the assumptions in sub-paragraph (2) below.

(2) The assumptions referred to in sub-paragraph (1) above are—
  (*a*) that so much of any expenditure as falls within paragraph (*c*) of that sub-paragraph has been allowed and, in the case of expenditure claimed as qualifying

    for supplement under paragraph (*b*)(ii) or paragraph (*c*)(ii) of section 2(9) of the principal Act, has been allowed as so qualifying; and

(*b*) that the participator's share of any of that expenditure which is the subject of a claim under Schedule 5 to the principal Act is the share proposed in the claim under paragraph 2(4)(*b*) of that Schedule.

  5. Any reference in paragraph 3 or paragraph 4 above to a question whether a chargeable period is a participator's net profit period being determined on particular assumptions is a reference to that question being determined (on the basis of those assumptions) in accordance with sections 111 and 112 of the Finance Act 1981.

BISHOPS (RETIREMENT) MEASURE 1986

(1986 No. 1)

A Measure passed by the General Synod of the Church of England to make fresh provision with respect to the resignation or retirement of archbishops and bishops and for purposes connected therewith.

[18th March 1986]

PART I

Bishops

Resignation of bishop

1.—(1) Where a person holding the office of diocesan bishop or suffragan bishop wishes to resign his office he shall, after consultation with the archbishop, tender his resignation to the archbishop in a written instrument in the prescribed form.

(2) If the archbishop decides to accept the resignation, he shall, within 28 days of receiving the instrument, by endorsement upon the instrument in the prescribed form declare the bishopric vacant as from a date specified in the endorsement (which shall subject to the provisions of sections 1(3) and 3 of the Ecclesiastical Offices (Age Limit) Measure 1975, be the date proposed by the bishop in the instrument or such later date as may be agreed by the archbishop and bishop concerned); and the instrument shall be filed in the provincial registry.

M1–1

Retirement of bishop on reaching age-limit

2.—(1) Not less than six months before the date on which a person holding the office of diocesan bishop or suffragan bishop is required to vacate his office in accordance with section 1 of the Ecclesiastical Offices (Age Limit) Measure 1975, the archbishop shall by written instrument in the prescribed form declare the bishopric vacant as from that date or, if his continuance in office beyond that date is authorised under section 3(1) of that Measure, from the later date so authorised.

(2) Where after the making of an instrument under subsection (1) above—

> (*a*) in the case of an instrument relating to a diocesan bishop, the archbishop authorises his continuance in office under section 3(1) of the Ecclesiastical Offices (Age Limit) Measure 1975, or
>
> (*b*) in the case of an instrument relating to a suffragan bishop, the diocesan bishop authorises his continuance in office under that section,

the archbishop may by written instrument in the prescribed form substitute for the date specified in the instrument made under subsection (1) above the date of the expiration of the period for which continuance in office is so authorised.

(3) Any instrument made under this section shall be filed in the provincial registry.

Retirement of bishop in case of disability

3.—(1) Where it appears to the archbishop that a person holding the office of diocesan bishop or suffragan bishop is incapacitated by physical or mental disability from the due performance of his episcopal duties, the archbishop may, with the concurrence of the two senior diocesan bishops of the province, and subject to subsection (2) below, request the bishop to tender his resignation to the archbishop in a written instrument in the prescribed form.

(2) Before making any such request the archbishop shall send to the bishop notice of his intention to do so, and if within 15 days after receiving such notice or within such extended period as the archbishop may allow the bishop sends to the archbishop a demand for a medical examination, the archbishop shall not request the bishop to tender his resignation until the report of the medical examination has been considered by the archbishop and the said senior bishops.

(3) The expenses of the medical examination shall be defrayed by the Church Commissioners.

(4) On receiving an instrument of resignation under subsection (1) above, the archbishop shall by endorsement on the instrument in the prescribed form declare the bishopric vacant as from a date specified in the endorsement.

(5) If the bishop to whom a request has been made by the archbishop under this section refuses or fails within 2 months of the receipt of the request to tender his resignation or is prevented by his infirmity from so doing, the archbishop may by written instrument in the prescribed form declare the bishopric vacant as from a date specified in the instrument.

(6) The date from which a bishopric may be declared vacant under this section shall not be earlier than the date of the endorsement under subsection (4) above or the date of the instrument under subsection (5) above, as the case may be; and any instrument made under this section shall be filed in the provincial registry.

PART II

Archbishops

Resignation of archbishop

4. Where an archbishop wishes to resign his archbishopric he shall tender his resignation to Her Majesty in a written instrument in the prescribed form and Her Majesty may by Order in Council declare the archbishopric vacant as from a date specified in the Order (which date shall not be earlier than the date of the Order).

Retirement of archbishop on reaching age-limit

5. Not less than six months before the date on which an archbishop is required to vacate his office in accordance with section 1 of the Ecclesiastical Offices (Age Limit) Measure 1975, the archbishop shall tender his resignation to Her Majesty in a written instrument in the prescribed form and Her Majesty may by Order in Council declare the archbishopric vacant as from that date or, if Her Majesty decides to exercise Her discretion under section 2 thereof, as from such later date as Her Majesty may determine under that section.

Retirement of archbishop in case of disability

6.—(1) Where it appears to the two senior bishops of the province that the archbishop of that province is incapacitated by physical or mental disability from the due performance of his duties, the two senior bishops may, with the concurrence of the archbishop of the other province and subject to subsection (2) below, request the archbishop to tender his resignation to Her Majesty in a written instrument in the prescribed form, and Her Majesty, on receiving the resignation, may by Order in Council declare the archbishopric vacant as from a date specified in the Order.

(2) Before making any such request the two senior bishops shall send to the archbishop notice of their intention to do so, and if within 15 days after receiving such notice or within such extended period as the two senior bishops may allow the archbishop sends to the two senior bishops a demand for a medical examination, the two senior bishops shall not request the archbishop to tender his resignation until the report of the medical examination has been considered by the two senior bishops and the archbishop of the other province.

(3) The expenses of the medical examination shall be defrayed by the Church Commissioners.

(4) If the archbishop to whom a request has been made by the two senior bishops under this section refuses or fails within two months of the receipt of the request to tender his resignation or is prevented by his infirmity from so doing, the two senior bishops may with the concurrence of the archbishop of the other province petition Her Majesty to declare the archbishopric vacant.

(5) Upon receiving any such petition Her Majesty may by Order in Council declare the archbishopric vacant as from a date specified in the Order.

(6) The date from which an archbishopric may be declared vacant by an Order in Council under subsection (1) or (5) above shall not be earlier than the date of the Order.

PART III

General provisions

Provisions as to pensions

7. Where a bishopric is declared vacant under section 3 or an archbishopric is declared vacant under section 6 of this Measure, the bishop or archbishop shall be treated for the purposes of sections 1 of the Clergy Pensions Measure 1961 as having retired on the ground of infirmity on the date from which the bishopric or archbishopric is declared vacant.

Effect of declaration of vacancy

8.—(1) Where a bishopric or archbishopric has been declared vacant under this Measure, any other preferment held by the bishop or archbishop shall also be vacated unless in the case of a bishopric the archbishop, or in the case of an archbishopric Her Majesty, declares that it shall not be vacated.

(2) Any such declaration shall be made in the written instrument, endorsement or Order in Council declaring the bishopric or archbishopric vacant.

Fee for legal officers

9. No fee shall be prescribed under the Ecclesiastical Fees Measure 1962 in respect of any specific duty imposed on any legal officer by virtue of the provisions of this Measure; in this section "legal officer" has the same meaning as in the Ecclesiastical Fees Measure 1962.

Interpretation

10.—(1) In this Measure the following expressions have the meanings hereby respectively assigned to them unless the context otherwise requires, that is to say:—

"archbishop" in relation to any diocesan bishop means the archbishop of the province in which his diocese is situated and in relation to any suffragan bishop means the archbishop of the province in which the diocese of the bishop to whom he is suffragan is situated;

"medical examination" means an examination into the physical or mental abilities of the person demanding the examination by a medical practitioner agreed on between that person and the person or persons requesting his resignation or, failing such agreement, appointed by the President of the Royal College of Physicians;

"preferment" includes an archbishopric, a bishopric, archdeaconry, deanery or office in a cathedral or collegiate church, and a benefice, and every curacy, lectureship, readership, chaplaincy, office or place which requires the discharge of any spiritual duty;

"prescribed" means prescribed by the Vicars-General of the provinces of Canterbury and York acting jointly.

(2) In this Measure the expression "diocesan bishop" shall not include an archbishop.

(3) The powers exercisable by an archbishop under this Measure shall, during the absence abroad or incapacity through illness of the archbishop or a vacancy in the see, be exercisable by the archbishop of the other province.

(4) For the purposes of this Measure, the seniority of a diocesan bishop after the Bishops of London and Winchester in the province of Canterbury and after the Bishop of Durham in the province of York shall be determined by length of service as a diocesan bishop within the provinces except that any diocesan bishop who by reason of illness or absence is unable to act or whose retirement is in question shall be disregarded.

Minor and consequential amendments

11.—(1) In section 3(1) of the Ecclesiastical Offices (Age Limit) Measure 1975 there shall be added at the end the words "except that a diocesan bishop may exercise his powers under this subsection in relation to a suffragan bishop only after consultation with the archbishop of the province."

(2) In subsections (1), (9) and (13) of section 8 of the Church of England (Miscellaneous Provisions) Measure 1983 for any reference to a deed there shall be substituted a reference to an instrument.

Repeals

12.—(1) Any rule of law or custom with respect to the resignation or retirement of an archbishop or a bishop is hereby abrogated.

(2) The enactments specified in the Schedule to this Measure are hereby repealed to the extent specified in column 3 of that Schedule.

Short title, extent and commencement

13.—(1) This Measure may be cited as the Bishops (Retirement) Measure 1986.

(2) This Measure shall extend to the whole of the provinces of Canterbury and York.

(3) This Measure shall come into force on such day as the Archbishops of Canterbury and York may jointly appoint.

S.12(2)   SCHEDULE

REPEALS

Provision	Short title	Extent of repeal
1951 No. 2.	The Bishops (Retirement) Measure 1951.	The whole Measure
1961 No. 3.	The Clergy Pensions Measure 1961.	In Schedule 2, the amendments to the Bishops (Retirement) Measure 1951.
1975 No. 2.	The Ecclesiastical Offices (Age Limit) Measure 1975.	Section 4.
1983 No. 2.	The Church of England (Miscellaneous Provisions) Measure 1983.	Section 7.

ECCLESIASTICAL FEES MEASURE 1986

(1986 No. 2)

A Measure passed by the General Synod of the Church of England to make further provision with respect to ecclesiastical fees and for purposes connected therewith.   [18th March 1986]

PART I

Parochial Fees

Preparation of draft Parochial Fees Orders

1.—(1) The Church Commissioners may prepare a draft of an order (to be known as a "Parochial Fees Order") which prescribes the amount of the parochial fees to be paid to the persons specified in that order in relation to the matters so specified.

(2) A draft order prepared under subsection (1) above may contain such incidental provisions as the Church Commissioners consider necessary or desirable.

Procedure for making Parochial Fees Orders

2.—(1) Every draft Parochial Fees Order shall be laid before the General Synod and if it is approved by the General Synod, whether with or without amendment, the draft order as so approved shall be referred to the Church Commissioners.

(2) Where a draft order is referred to the Church Commissioners under subsection (1) above then—

(*a*) if it has been approved by the General Synod without amendment, the Church Commissioners shall, by applying their seal, make the order;

(*b*) if it has been approved by the General Synod with amendment, the Church Commissioners may either—

(i) by applying their seal make the order as so amended, or

(ii) withdraw the draft order for further consideration in view of any amendment made by the General Synod;

and a Parochial Fees Order shall not come into force until it has been sealed by the Church Commissioners.

(3) Where the Standing Committee of the General Synod determines that a draft Parochial Fees Order does not need to be debated by the General Synod, then, unless—

(*a*) notice is given by a member of the General Synod in accordance with its Standing Orders that he wishes the draft order to be debated, or

(*b*) notice is so given by any such member that he wishes to move an amendment to the draft order and at least twenty-five other members of the Synod indicate when the amendment is called that they wish the amendment to be moved,

the draft order shall for the purposes of subsections (1) and (2) above be deemed to have been approved by the General Synod without amendment.

(4) The Statutory Instruments Act 1946 shall apply to a Parochial Fees Order sealed by the Church Commissioners under subsection (2) above as if it were a statutory instrument and were made when sealed by the Commissioners and as if this Measure were an Act providing that any such order shall be subject to annulment in pursuance of a resolution of either House of Parliament.

Provisions as to persons to whom parochial fees are to be paid

3.—(1) During a vacancy in a benefice parochial fees which, but for the vacancy, would be paid to the incumbent of the benefice shall be paid to the diocesan board of finance or to such other person as the said board, after consultation with the bishop, may direct.

(2) Where a licence of a chapel includes a provision fixing a fee for the solemnization of a marriage or any other matter for which a parochial fee is prescribed by a Parochial Fees Order then, notwithstanding anything in the licence, the fee to be paid in respect of that matter shall be the fee prescribed by the order, but any provision of the licence as to the person to whom the fee in respect of that matter is to be paid shall continue to apply and where the licence provides for the fee to be paid to two or more persons the fee prescribed by the order shall be payable to those persons in the same proportions as under the provisions of the licence.

PART II

Ecclesiastical Judges' and Legal Officers' Fees

Constitution of Fees Advisory Commission

4.—(1) After every ordinary election to the General Synod the Archbishops of Canterbury and York shall jointly request—

(a) the Lord Chancellor to appoint a person who is or has been a judge of the Court of Appeal or of the High Court of Justice, a circuit judge or a recorder;

(b) the chairman of the Bar Council to appoint a barrister; and

(c) the president of the Law Society to appoint a solicitor;

and the three persons so appointed together with—

(d) the person who holds the appointments of First Church Estates Commissioner and Chairman of the Central Board of Finance, and

(e) a member of the Standing Committee of the General Synod appointed for the purposes of this Measure by that Committee,

shall constitute the Fees Advisory Commission.

(2) If at any time the appointments of First Church Estates Commissioner and Chairman of the Central Board of Finance are not both held by the same person, subsection (1) above shall have effect as if for paragraphs (d) and (e) there were substituted the following paragraphs—

"(d) the First Church Estates Commissioner and

(e) the Chairman of the Central Board of Finance."

(3) The members of the Fees Advisory Commission appointed under paragraphs (a) to (c) of subsection (1) above and (unless the appointments of First Church Estates Commissioner and Chairman of the Central Board of Finance are not held by the same person) the member appointed under paragraph (e) of that subsection (the "appointed members") shall hold office until, after the next following ordinary election to the General Synod, further appointments are made under this section.

(4) If an appointed member of the Fees Advisory Commission dies or resigns, then—

(a) if he was appointed under paragraph (a), (b) or (c) of subsection (1) above, the Archbishops of Canterbury and York shall jointly request the person who appointed him to appoint as a member of the Commission another person who is qualified for appointment under the paragraph in question;

(b) if he was appointed under paragraph (e) of that subsection, the Standing Committee of the General Synod shall appoint as a member of the Commission another member of that Committee,

and a person appointed under this subsection shall hold office for the period for which the person who has died or resigned would have held office.

(5) The Fees Advisory Commission shall be entitled to act notwithstanding any temporary vacancy caused by the death or resignation of any of its members.

(6) An appointed member of the Fees Advisory Commission whose term of office comes to an end shall be eligible for reappointment.

Legal Officers (Annual Fees) Orders

5.—(1) The Fees Advisory Commission may make recommendations as to the annual fees to be paid to legal officers in respect of such of the duties of their office as are specified by the Commission, and the Commission may make an order (to be known as a "Legal Officers (Annual Fees) Order") to give effect to their recommendations.

(2) Any order made under subsection (1) above may contain such incidental provisions as the Fees Advisory Commission considers necessary or desirable.

(3) Any order made under subsection (1) above shall be laid before the General Synod and shall not come into force until it has been approved by the General Synod.

(4) Where the Standing Committee of the General Synod determines that a Legal Officers (Annual Fees) Order does not need to be debated by the General Synod, then, unless notice is given by a member of the General Synod in accordance with its Standing Orders that he wishes the order to be debated, the order shall for the purposes of subsection (3) above be deemed to have been approved by the General Synod.

(5) The Statutory Instruments Act 1946 shall apply to a Legal Officers (Annual Fees) Order approved by the General Synod as if it were a statutory instrument and were made when so approved and as if this Measure were an Act providing that any such order shall be subject to annulment in pursuance of a resolution of either House of Parliament.

Ecclesiastical Judges and Legal Officers (Fees) Orders

6.—(1) The Fees Advisory Commission may make recommendations as to the fees to be paid in respect of such duties performed by ecclesiastical judges and legal officers as are specified by the Commission (not, in the case of legal officers, being duties covered by the annual fees payable under a Legal Officers (Annual Fees) Order), and the Commission may make an order (to be known as an "Ecclesiastical Judges and Legal Officers (Fees) Order") to give effect to their recommendations.

(2) Any order made under subsection (1) above may contain such incidental provisions as the Fees Advisory Commission considers necessary or desirable.

(3) Any order made under subsection (1) above shall be laid before the General Synod and shall not come into force until it has been approved by the General Synod, whether with or without amendment.

(4) Where the Standing Committee of the General Synod determines that an Ecclesiastical Judges and Legal Officers (Fees) Order does not need to be debated by the General Synod, then, unless—

(*a*) notice is given by a member of the General Synod in accordance with its Standing Orders that he wishes the order to be debated, or

(*b*) notice is so given by any such member that he wishes to move an amendment to the order and at least twenty-five other members of the Synod indicate when the amendment is called that they wish the amendment to be moved,

the order shall for the purposes of subsection (3) above be deemed to have been approved by the General Synod without amendment.

(5) The Statutory Instruments Act 1946 shall apply to an Ecclesiastical Judges and Legal Officers (Fees) Order approved by the General Synod as if it were a statutory instrument and were made when so approved and as if this Measure were an Act providing that any such order shall be subject to annulment in pursuance of a resolution of either House of Parliament.

Part III

Miscellaneous and General

Recovery of fees

7. Any fee payable by virtue of an order made under this Measure shall be recoverable as a debt.

Reimbursement of archbishops or bishops

8. Where an archbishop or bishop has paid any sum by virtue of any order made or deemed to be made under this Measure and the liability to pay that sum was imposed on him as archbishop or bishop, the Church Commissioners shall reimburse that sum to the archbishop or bishop.

Private, local and personal Acts which are inconsistent with Parochial Fees Orders

9. Schedule 1 to this Measure which relates to private, local and personal Acts which are inconsistent with a Parochial Fees Order shall have effect.

Interpretation

10. In this Measure the following expressions have the meanings hereby respectively assigned to them—

"ecclesiastical judges" means the Dean of the Court of Arches and the Auditor of the Chancery Court of York, the Vicars General of the provinces of Canterbury and York, the Commissary General and Diocesan Chancellors;

"legal officers" means the provincial registrars, diocesan registrars, bishops' legal secretaries and chapter clerks;

"parish" means any ecclesiastical parish or other place the incumbent or minister whereof either is entitled to retain for his own benefit or is under a duty to pay over to any other person the parochial fees chargeable;

"parochial fees" mean any fees payable to a parochial church council, to a clerk in Holy Orders, or to any other person performing duties in connection with a parish for, or in respect of, the solemnization or performance of church offices or the erection of monuments in churchyards or such other services or matters as may by law or custom be included in a Parochial Fees Order and such other services or matters for which, in the opinion of the Church Commissioners, the payment of fees is appropriate, except fees or other charges payable under section 214 of, and Schedule 26 to, the Local Government Act 1972 (burial fees) or fees payable under section 62 of the Cremation Act 1902 (cremation service fees).

Repeals, consequential amendments and transitional provisions

11.—(1) The Ecclesiastical Fees Measure 1962 is hereby repealed.

(2) In section 63 of the Ecclesiastical Jurisdiction Measure 1963 for the words from "Ecclesiastical Fees" to the end of the section there shall be substituted the words "Ecclesiastical Fees Measure 1986" and in section 6(3) of the Faculty Jurisdiction Measure 1964 for the words "Ecclesiastical Fees Measure 1962" there shall be substituted the words "Ecclesiastical Fees Measure 1986."

(3) The transitional provisions in Schedule 2 to this Measure shall have effect.

Short title, extent and commencement

12.—(1) This Measure may be cited as the Ecclesiastical Fees Measure 1986.

(2) This Measure shall extend to the whole of the provinces of Canterbury and York except the Channel Islands and the Isle of Man, but may be applied to the Channel Islands, as defined by the Channel Islands (Church Legislation) Measures 1931 and 1957, or either of them, in accordance with the provisions of those Measures and may be extended to the Isle of Man by or under Act of Tynwald.

(3) This Measure shall come into force on such day as the Archbishops of Canterbury and York may jointly appoint and different days may be so appointed for different provisions.

SCHEDULES

SCHEDULE 1

PRIVATE, LOCAL AND PERSONAL ACTS WHICH ARE INCONSISTENT WITH PAROCHIAL FEES ORDERS

1. Where a Parochial Fees Order is inconsistent with a private, local or personal Act which affects a parish, the parochial church council or, if there is no parochial church council, the incumbent or minister may apply to the Church Commissioners requesting them to prepare an order providing for the amendment or repeal of that Act in order to permit the Parochial Fees Order to apply to the parish; and, on receiving such an application, the Church Commissioners may prepare a draft order accordingly.

2. Where the Church Commissioners prepare a draft order under paragraph 1 above, they shall—

(a) send a copy of that order to the bishop of the diocese in which the parish is situated, the parochial church council (if any) and the incumbent or minister of the parish, and any person whose power of fixing fees or whose right to receive fees is affected by the order, together with a notice that consideration will be given to any representations sent in writing to them before such date (which shall not be less than one month from the date of the sending of the notice) as may be specified in the notice; and

(b) cause a copy of the order to be posted for a period of not less than one month on or near the principal door of the church of the parish, or at least one of such churches if there be more than one, together with a notice that consideration will be given to any representations sent in writing to them before such date (which shall not be less than one month from the date when the copy of the order was first posted), as may be specified in the notice; and

(c) publish an advertisement in at least one local newspaper circulating in the parish stating the purport of the draft order and at what place in the parish it may be inspected (which may be on or near the church door mentioned in sub-paragraph (b) above or such other place as the Church Commissioners may decide) and that consideration will be given to any representations sent in writing to them before such date (which shall not be less than one month from the date when the advertisement was published) as may be specified in the advertisement.

3. The Church Commissioners shall consider all representations made to them under paragraph 2 above and may make such amendments in the order as they think fit.

4. When the periods during which representations may be made under paragraph 2 above have all expired and the Church Commissioners have considered all representations made to them, they may, by applying their seal, make the order or, as the case may be, the order as amended under paragraph 3 above.

5. The Statutory Instruments Act 1946 shall apply to an order sealed by the Church Commissioners under paragraph 4 above as if it were a statutory instrument and were made when sealed by the Commissioners and as if this Measure were an Act providing that the order shall be subject to annulment in pursuance of a resolution of either House of Parliament.

6. The Church Commissioners shall send copies of any order made under this Schedule to every person or body specified in sub-paragraph 2(a) above and shall publish in the London Gazette a notice stating they have made the order and specifying a place where copies of the order may be obtained.

SCHEDULE 2

TRANSITIONAL PROVISIONS

1. No order made under Part I of this Measure shall be binding on a clerk in Holy Orders or other person performing duties in connection with a parish to whom the provisions of section 2(4) of the Ecclesiastical Fees Measure 1962 applied immediately before the coming into force of this provision without his consent in writing; but such consent when given shall be irrevocable.

2. Until the Fees Advisory Commission is constituted under this Measure, the members of the Fees Committee appointed under section 1(3) of the Ecclesiastical Fees Measure 1962 shall, notwithstanding the repeal of that Measure by this Measure, continue to hold office and may perform any of the functions of the Fees Advisory Commission under this Measure.

3. Notwithstanding the repeal by this Measure of the Ecclesiastical Fees Measure 1962, any order made under that Measure relating to legal officers' fees or parochial fees shall be deemed to have been made under this Measure; and any fee payable at the coming into force of this Measure under an existing order relating to legal officers' fees or parochial fees shall be deemed to be payable under this Measure.

4. Any sum payable to any person under the provisions of section 5 of the Ecclesiastical Fees Measure 1962 shall, if reimbursible by the Church Commissioners at the coming into force of this provision, be deemed to be reimbursible under this Measure.

5. Nothing in this Schedule shall be taken as prejudicing the application of sections 16 and 17 of the Interpretation Act 1978.

PATRONAGE (BENEFICES) MEASURE 1986

(1986 No. 3)

PART III

MISCELLANEOUS PROVISIONS AS TO PATRONAGE

A Measure passed by the General Synod of the Church of England to amend the law relating to patronage of benefices.

[18th July 1986]

PART I

REGISTRATION AND TRANSFER OF RIGHTS OF PATRONAGE

Registration of patrons

1.—(1) Subject to the provisions of this Measure, the registrar of each diocese shall compile and maintain a register indicating in relation to every benefice in the diocese the person who is the patron of the benefice and containing such other information as may be prescribed.

(2) Except as provided by this Measure, no person shall be entitled, after the expiration of the period of fifteen months beginning with the date on which this section comes into force, to exercise any of the functions of a patron of a benefice unless he is registered as patron of that benefice, and the said period is in this Measure referred to as the "registration period".

(3) The provisions of Schedule 1 to this Measure shall have effect with respect to the registration of patrons of benefices and other matters relating thereto.

(4) The registration under this Measure of any person as a patron of a benefice shall be conclusive evidence of the matters registered.

(5) Any register maintained under this Measure shall be open to inspection by the public at all reasonable times.

Registration of patronage belonging to an office

2. In the case of a right of patronage of a benefice which belongs to an office, the duty of the registrar of the diocese under section 1(1) of this Measure to register in relation to that benefice the person who is the patron thereof shall be construed as a duty to register that office as a patron of that benefice; and section 1(4) shall apply in relation to an office which is registered as a patron as it applies in relation to a person who is so registered.

Transfer of rights of patronage

3.—(1) No right of patronage of a benefice shall be capable of sale and any transfer thereof for valuable consideration shall be void.

(2) Subject to the provisions of this section, a right of patronage vested in an ecclesiastical corporation shall not be transferred to any body or person unless—

    (*a*) the consent of the bishop or, if the bishop is the proposed transferor, the consent of the archbishop has been obtained; or

    (*b*) the transfer is made by a pastoral scheme or order.

(3) Where a right of patronage of a benefice is proposed to be transferred otherwise than by a pastoral scheme or order, the proposed transferor shall send to the bishop (or, if the bishop is the proposed transferor, to the archbishop) and to the registrar of the diocese a notice stating— .

    (*a*) his intention to transfer that right;

    (*b*) the name and address of the proposed transferee; and

    (*c*) particulars of the terms of the proposed transfer.

(4) On receiving a notice under subsection (3) above, the registrar shall send to the secretary of the parochial church council of the parish concerned a notice informing him of the proposed transfer and stating that before the expiration of the period of one month beginning with the date on which the notice is sent to him representations with respect to the proposed transfer may be made to the registrar by the parochial church council; and the registrar shall notify the bishop and the proposed transferor, or, if the bishop is the proposed transferor, the bishop and the archbishop, of any representations made to him within that period.

(5) After the expiration of the period of one month mentioned in subsection (4) above, the bishop or, if the bishop is the proposed transferor, the archbishop shall consider any representations made under that subsection and, whether or not any such representations have been made, the bishop or archbishop may request the proposed transferor (either personally or through some person appointed by the proposed transferor) to confer with him (or with some person appointed by the

bishop or, as the case may be, the archbishop) as to the proposed transfer; and the bishop or, as the case may be, the archbishop shall not give any consent required under this section until after any such representations have been considered and any such request has been complied with.

(6) Any transfer of a right of patronage otherwise than by a pastoral scheme or order shall be in the prescribed form.

(7) Where a right of patronage of a benefice is transferred otherwise than by a pastoral scheme or order, the registrar shall not register the transferee as a patron of that benefice unless—

(*a*) he is satisfied that the requirements of this section have been complied with; and

(*b*) an application for registration is made in accordance with Schedule 1 to this Measure before the expiration of the period of twelve months from the date of the execution of the transfer;

and if no such application for registration is made before the expiration of that period of twelve months the transfer shall be of no effect.

(8) No transfer of a right of patronage of a benefice shall take effect during the period of a vacancy in that benefice.

(9) In this section "transfer" means a transfer *inter vivos* including a transfer by way of exchange; but it does not include a transfer by operation of law, a transfer upon the appointment of a new trustee or a transfer by the personal representatives of a deceased person.

Rectification of register

4.—(1) The registrar of a diocese may rectify an entry in the register of patrons in any case—

(*a*) where all the persons interested agree to the rectification of the entry; or

(*b*) where the registrar decides that the entry should be rectified—

(i) because a person is, or is not, entitled to be registered as patron of a benefice, or

(ii) because information registered as to the exercise of a right of presentation to a benefice is incorrect,

and, in either case, no appeal against the registrar's decision has been brought within the period specified in paragraph 8 of Schedule 1 to this Measure or the appeal has been dismissed; or

(*c*) where any rectification of the entry is required by reason of a decision of the chancellor of the diocese under that Schedule.

(2) Where in the case of an entry in the register relating to any benefice—

(*a*) the entry has been adverse to the claim of any person for a period of more than thirty years, or

(*b*) if the period of thirty years from the end of the registration period has not expired, the benefice has been held adversely to the claim of any person for a period of more than thirty years,

then, notwithstanding anything in subsection (1) above or in paragraph 5 of Schedule 1 to this Measure, no rectification of that entry may be made in favour of that person unless all the persons interested agree to that rectification.

(3) Section 25 of the Limitation Act 1980 (time limits for actions to enforce advowsons) shall cease to have effect at the end of the registration period.

Rights of patronage exercisable otherwise than by registered patron

5.—(1) Where an office is registered as a patron of a benefice, the person who is for the time being the holder of that office shall, subject to the provisions of Part II of this Measure, be entitled to discharge all the functions of a patron of that benefice.

(2) Where a registered patron of a benefice dies then, until the person to whom the right of patronage is to be transferred is registered as a patron of that benefice, the personal representatives of the deceased patron shall, subject to the provisions of Part II of this Measure, be entitled to discharge all the functions of a patron of that benefice.

(3) A registered patron of a benefice may by an instrument creating a power of attorney confer on the donee of the power authority to discharge on his behalf all the functions of a patron of that benefice, and where such a power is created the donee shall, subject to the provisions of Part II of this Measure, be entitled to discharge those functions until the power is revoked.

(4) Any person entitled to discharge any functions in relation to a benefice by virtue of this section shall be entitled to discharge those functions notwithstanding that he is not registered in the register of patrons in relation to that benefice.

Abolition of registration of advowsons at Land Registry

6.—(1) After the date on which section 1 of this Measure comes into force, no advowson shall be registered in the register of title to freehold and leasehold land kept at Her Majesty's Land Registry, and after the expiration of the registration period under this Measure all titles to advowsons registered in that register shall be deemed, by operation of this Measure and without any entry being made in the register, to have been closed and removed from that register.

(2) In section 3 of the Land Registration Act 1925 in paragraph (viii) (definition of "land") the words "an advowson" shall cease to have effect at the end of the registration period.

PART II

EXERCISE OF RIGHTS OF PRESENTATION

General provisions as to filling of vacancies

Notification of vacancies

7.—(1) Subject to section 70 of the Pastoral Measure 1983, where a benefice becomes vacant by reason of the death of the incumbent, the bishop shall, as soon as practicable after he becomes aware of the vacancy, give notice of that fact to the designated officer of the diocese.

(2) Subject to section 70 of the Pastoral Measure 1983, where the bishop is aware that a benefice is shortly to become vacant by reason of resignation or cession, the bishop shall give such notice of that fact as he considers reasonable in all the circumstances to the designated officer of the diocese.

(3) Any notice required to be given to the designated officer under subsection (1) or (2) above shall also be given to the registrar of the diocese, unless he is the designated officer.

(4) As soon as practicable after receiving a notice under subsection (1) or (2) above the designated officer shall send notice of the vacancy to the registered patron of the benefice and to the secretary of the parochial church council of the parish belonging to the benefice; and any such notice shall include such information as may be prescribed.

(5) In this Measure "the designated officer", in relation to a diocese, means such person as the bishop, after consulting the bishop's council,

may designate or, if no person is designated, the secretary of the pastoral committee of the diocese.

Provisions as to declarations of membership

8.—(1) Where the registered patron of a benefice is an individual and is not a clerk in Holy Orders, he shall on receiving notice of a vacancy in the benefice under section 7(4) of this Measure—

(*a*) if able to do so, make a written declaration (in this Measure referred to as "the declaration of membership") declaring that he is an actual communicant member of the Church of England or of a Chuch in communion with that Church; or

(*b*) if unable to make the declaration himself, appoint some other person, being an individual who is able and willing to make it or is a clerk in Holy Orders or one of the bodies mentioned in subsection (7) below, to act as his representative to discharge in his place the functions of a registered patron.

(2) Where the registered patron of a benefice is a body of persons corporate or unincorporate then, on receiving notice of a vacancy in the benefice under section 7(4) of this Measure, that body shall appoint an individual who is able and willing to make the declaration of membership or is a clerk in Holy Orders to act as its representative to discharge in its place the functions of a registered patron.

(3) Notwithstanding anything in subsection (1) above, where the registered patron of a benefice who is an individual and is not the bishop of a diocese is of the opinion, on receiving notice of a vacancy in the benefice under section 7(4) of this Measure, that he will be unable for any reason to discharge his functions as a patron of that benefice he may, notwithstanding that he is able to make the declaration of membership, appoint such a representative as is mentioned in subsection (1)(*b*) above to discharge those functions in his place.

(4) Where a benefice the right of presentation to which belongs to an office (other than an ecclesiastical office) becomes vacant, the person who holds that office on the date on which the benefice becomes vacant shall be entitled to present on that vacancy and shall as soon as practicable after that date—

(*a*) if able to do so, make the declaration of membership, or

(*b*) if unable to make the declaration himself, appoint some other person, being a person who may be appointed as a representative under subsection (1)(*b*) above, to act as his representative to discharge in his place the functions of a registered patron.

(5) Where the right of presentation to a benefice is exercisable by the donee of a power of attorney, the donee shall as soon as practicable after receiving notice of the vacancy in the benefice (or, if the power is created during the vacancy, as soon as practicable after it is created)—

(*a*) if able to do so, make the declaration of membership, or

(*b*) if unable to make the declaration himself, appoint some other person, being a person who may be appointed as a representative under subsection (1)(*b*) above, to act as his representative to discharge in his place the functions of a registered patron.

(6) Where under the preceding provisions of this section a body mentioned in subsection (7) below is appointed to discharge the functions of a registered patron, that body shall as soon as practicable after being so appointed appoint as its representative an individual who is able and willing to make the declaration of membership or is a clerk in Holy Orders.

(7) The bodies referred to in subsection (1)(*b*) above are—
  (*a*) the dean and chapter or the cathedral chapter of the cathedral church of the diocese;
  (*b*) the dean and chapter of the collegiate church of St. Peter in Westminster;
  (*c*) the dean and canons of the collegiate church of St. George, Windsor;
  (*d*) any diocesan board of patronage;
  (*e*) any patronage board constituted by a pastoral scheme;
  (*f*) any university in England or any college or hall in such a university; and
  (*g*) the colleges of Eton and Winchester.

Information to be sent to designated officer

9.—(1) Before the expiration of the period of two months beginning with the date on which a benefice becomes vacant, a registered patron who is an individual shall send to the designated officer of the diocese—
  (*a*) the declaration of membership made by him, or
  (*b*) the name and address of his representative and the declaration of membership made by that representative.

(2) Before the expiration of the said period of two months, a registered patron which is a body of persons corporate or unincorporate shall send to the designated officer of the diocese the name and address of the individual who is to act as its representative and the declaration of membership made by that representative.

(3) Where the functions of a registered patron are to be discharged by the holder of an office, subsection (1) above shall apply to the person who holds that office on the date on which the benefice becomes vacant as it applies to the registered patron.

(4) Where the functions of a registered patron are to be discharged by the donee of a power of attorney, subsection (1) above shall apply to the donee as it applies to the registered patron except that, if the power is created during the vacancy concerned, there shall be substituted for the period of two months mentioned in that subsection the period of two months beginning with the date on which the power is created, and the information required to be sent under that subsection shall include information as to that date.

(5) Where the registered patron or his representative is a clerk in Holy Orders, the registered patron shall, before the expiration of the period during which the declaration of membership is required to be sent to the designated officer under the preceding provisions of this section, notify the designated officer of that fact, and a declaration of membership made by that clerk shall not be required to be sent to the designated officer under this section.

(6) As soon as practicable after receiving information under this section as to the appointment of a representative, the designated officer shall send to the secretary of the parochial church council the name and address of that representative.

Disqualification for presentation

10. Where the registered patron of a benefice or the representative of that patron, is a clerk in Holy Orders or is the wife of such a clerk, that clerk shall be disqualified for presentation to that benefice.

Requirements as to meetings of parochial church council

11.—(1) Before the expiration of the period of four weeks beginning with the date on which the notice under section 7(4) of this Measure is sent to the secretary of the parochial church council, one or more meetings of that council shall be held for the purposes of—

(*a*) preparing a statement describing the conditions, needs and traditions of the parish;

(*b*) appointing two lay members of the council to act as representatives of the council in connection with the selection of an incumbent;

(*c*) deciding whether to request the registered patron to consider advertising the vacancy;

(*d*) deciding whether to request a meeting under section 12 of this Measure; and

(*e*) deciding whether to request a statement in writing from the bishop describing in relation to the benefice the needs of the diocese and the wider interests of the Church.

(2) A meeting of the parochial church council for which subsection (1) above provides shall be convened by the secretary thereof, and no member of that council who is—

(*a*) the outgoing incumbent or the wife of the outgoing incumbent, or

(*b*) the registered patron, or

(*c*) the representative of the registered patron,

shall attend that meeting.

(3) None of the following members of the parochial church council, that is to say—

(*a*) any person mentioned in subsection (2) above, and

(*b*) any deaconess or lay worker licensed to the parish,

shall be qualified for appointment under subsection (1)(*b*) above.

(4) If before the vacancy in the benefice is filled any person appointed under subsection (1)(*b*) above dies or becomes unable for any reason to act as the representative of, or ceases to be a member of, the council by which he was appointed, then, except where he ceases to be such a member and the council decides that he shall continue to act as its representative, his appointment shall be deemed to have been revoked and the council shall appoint another lay member of the council (not being a member disqualified under subsection (3) above) to act in his place for the remainder of the proceedings under this Part of this Measure.

(5) If a parochial church council holds a meeting under subsection (1) above but does not appoint any representatives at that meeting, then, subject to subsection (6) below, two churchwardens who are members of that council (or, if there are more than two churchwardens who are members of the council, two churchwardens chosen by all the churchwardens who are members) shall act as representatives of the council in connection with the selection of an incumbent.

(6) A churchwarden who is the registered patron of a benefice shall not be qualified under subsection (5) above to act as a representative of the parochial church council or to choose any other churchwarden so to act, and in any case where there is only one churchwarden qualified to act as such a representative that churchwarden may act as the sole representative of that council in connection with the selection of the incumbent.

(7) Any representative of the parochial church council appointed under subsection (1) or (4) above and any churchwarden acting as such a representative by virtue of subsection (5) or (6) above is in this Part of this Measure referred to as a "parish representative", and where a churchwarden is entitled to act as the sole parish representative any reference in this Part to the parish representatives shall be construed as a reference to that churchwarden.

(8) A copy of the statement prepared under subsection (1)(*a*) above together with the names and addresses of the parish representative shall,

as soon as practicable after the holding of the meeting under that subsection, be sent by the secretary of the parochial church council to the registered patron and, unless the bishop is the registered patron, to the bishop.

Joint meeting of parochial church council with bishop and patron

12.—(1) where a request for a meeting under this section is made—
 (a) by a notice sent by the registered patron or the bishop to the secretary of the parochial church council, or
 (b) by a resolution of the parochial church council, passed at a meeting held under section 11 of this Measure,
a joint meeting of the parochial church council with the registered patron and (if the bishop is not the registered patron) the bishop shall be held for the purpose of enabling those present at the meeting to exchange views on the statement prepared under section 11(1)(a) of this Measure (needs of the parish) and the statement presented under subsection (2) below (needs of the diocese).

(2) At any meeting held under this section the bishop shall present either orally or, if a request for a statement in writing has been made by the registered patron or the parochial church council, in writing a statement describing in relation to the benefice the needs of the diocese and the wider interests of the Church.

(3) Any notice given under subsection (1)(a) above shall be of no effect unless it is sent to the secretary of the parochial church council not later than ten days after a copy of the statement prepared under subsection (1)(a) of section 11 of this Measure is received by the persons mentioned in subsection (8) of that section.

(4) The outgoing incumbent and the wife of the outgoing incumbent shall not be entitled to attend a meeting held under this section.

(5) A meeting requested under this section shall be held before the expiration of the period of six weeks beginning with the date on which the request for the meeting was first made (whether by the sending of a notice as mentioned in subsection (1)(a) above or by the passing of a resolution as mentioned in subsection (1)(b) above), and at least fourteen days' notice (unless a shorter period is agreed by all the persons concerned) of the time and place at which the meeting is to be held shall be given by the secretary of the parochial church council to the registered patron, the bishop (if he is not the registered patron) and the members of the parochial church council.

(6) If either the registered patron or the bishop is unable to attend a meeting held under this section, he shall appoint some other person to attend on his behalf.

(7) The chairman of any meeting held under this section shall be such person as the persons who are entitled to attend and are present at the meeting may determine.

(8) No meeting requested under this section shall be treated for the purposes of this Measure as having been held unless there were present at the meeting—
 (a) the bishop or the person appointed by the bishop to attend on his behalf, and
 (b) the registered patron or the person appointed by the patron to attend on his behalf, and
 (c) at least one third of the members of the parochial church council who were entitled to attend.

(9) The secretary of the parochial church council shall invite both the rural dean of the deanery in which the parish is (unless he is the outgoing

incumbent) and the lay chairman of the deanery synod of that deanery to attend a meeting held under this section.

Provisions with respect to the selection of incumbent

13.—(1) The registered patron of a vacant benefice shall not make to any priest an offer to present him to a benefice until—

(*a*) if a request for a meeting under section 12 of this Measure has been made, either—
    (i) that meeting has been held, or
    (ii) all the parties concerned have agreed that no such meeting should be held, or
    (iii) the period of six weeks mentioned in section 12(5) has expired; and

(*b*) (whether or not such a request has been made) the making of the offer to the priest in question has been approved—
    (i) by the parish representatives, and
    (ii) if the registered patron is a person other than the bishop of the diocese in which the benefice is, by that bishop.

(2) If, before the expiration of the period of four weeks beginning with the date on which the registered patron sent to the bishop a request for him to approve under paragraph (*b*) of subsection (1) above the making of the offer to the priest named in the request, no notice is received from the bishop of his refusal to approve the making of the offer, the bishop shall be deemed to have given his approval under that paragraph.

(3) If, before the expiration of the period of two weeks beginning with the date on which the registered patron sent to the parish representatives a request for them to approve under paragraph (*b*) of subsection (1) above the making of the offer to the priest named in the request, no notice is received from any representative of his refusal to approve the making of the offer, the representatives shall be deemed to have given their approval under that paragraph.

(4) If—

(*a*) the bishop refuses to approve under paragraph (*b*) of subsection (1) above the making of the offer to the priest named in the request, or

(*b*) any parish representative refuses to approve under that paragraph the making of that offer,

the bishop or the representative, as the case may be, shall notify the registered patron in writing of the grounds on which the refusal is made.

(5) Where approval of an offer is refused under subsection (4) above, the registered patron may request the archbishop to review the matter and if, after review, the archbishop authorises the registered patron to make the offer in question, the patron may make that offer accordingly.

(6) Where a priest accepts an offer made in accordance with the provisions of this section to present him to a benefice and the registered patron is a person other than the bishop, the patron shall send the bishop a notice presenting the priest to him for admission to the benefice.

Failure of registered patron to comply with section 9

14.—(1) Where any declaration of membership or other information required to be sent to the designated officer under section 9 of this Measure is not sent to that officer before the expiration of the period during which it is required to be so sent and the registered patron is a person other than the bishop then, after the expiration of that period—

(*a*) no meeting shall be held under section 12 of this Measure by reason of any request made by the registered patron and subsections

(2), (5), (6) and (8) of that section shall not apply in relation to that patron; and

(b) no offer shall be made to any priest under section 13 of this Measure;

but the bishop may, subject to subsection (2) below, make to such a priest as he thinks fit an offer to collate him to the benefice.

(2) The bishop shall not make an offer under subsection (1) above unless the making of the offer has been approved by the parish representatives, and subsections (3), (4)(b) and (5) of section 13 of this Measure shall apply in relation to a request sent by the bishop to those representatives by virtue of this subsection as if for any reference to the registered patron there were substituted a reference to the bishop.

(3) Where under subsection (1) above the bishop makes to a priest an offer to collate him to a benefice in respect of which there is more than one person registered under this Measure, the registered patron whose turn it was to present to the benefice shall be treated for the purposes of this Measure as having exercised that turn.

Failure of council to comply with section 11 or 12

15. If a copy of the statement prepared under section 11(1)(a) of this Measure is not sent under subsection (8) of that section to the persons mentioned in that subsection or if notice is not given under section 12(5) of this Measure of any joint meeting requested under subsection (1)(a) of the said section 12 then—

(a) if the bishop is the registered patron, he may, without making any request for the approval of the parish representatives, make to such priest as he thinks fit an offer to collate him to the benefice; and

(b) if the bishop is not the registered patron, that patron shall be entitled to proceed under section 13 of this Measure as if paragraphs (a) and (b)(i) of subsection (1), subsection (3) and paragraph (b) of subsection (4) thereof had not been enacted.

Provisions which apply where benefice remains vacant for nine months

Presentation to benefices remaining vacant for nine months

16.—(1) If at the expiration of the period of nine months beginning with the date on which a benefice becomes vacant—

(a) no notice of presentation under section 13(6) of this Measure has been received by the bishop, or

(b) where the bishop is the registered patron, he has not received an acceptance of any offer made by him to collate a priest to the benefice,

the right of presentation to that benefice shall be exercisable by the archbishop in accordance with the provision of this section; and a notice to that effect shall be sent by the bishop to the archbishop.

(2) In calculating the period of nine months mentioned in subsection (1) above, no account shall be taken of any of the following periods, that is to say—

(a) a period during which the decision of the bishop to refuse to approve the making to a priest of an offer to present him to a benefice is under review by an archbishop,

(b) a suspension period within the meaning of the Pastoral Measure 1983, and

(c) a period during which the exercise of rights of presentation is restricted under section 24 or 69 of that Measure.

(3) As soon as practicable after a right of presentation becomes exercisable by an archbishop under this section, the archbishop shall send to the secretary of the parochial church council of the parish concerned a notice requiring him within three weeks after receiving the notice to send to the archbishop copies of the statement describing the conditions, needs and traditions of the parish prepared in accordance with section 11 of this Measure together with copies of any additional observations which the council wishes the archbishop to consider.

(4) The bishop may, and if the archbishop so requests shall, send to the archbishop a statement describing in relation to the benefice the needs of the diocese and the wider interests of the Church.

(5) Before the archbishop decides on the priest to whom an offer to present him to the benefice is to be made he shall consult the bishop, the parish representatives and such other persons as he thinks fit, including other persons who in his opinion can also represent the views of the parishioners and, if during the period of nine months mentioned in subsection (1) above the approval of the bishop or the parish representatives to the making of an offer to a priest by the registered patron of the vacant benefice has been refused under section 13 of this Measure, the archbishop shall not make any offer to that priest under this section unless the consent of the bishop or, as the case may be, the parish representatives has been obtained.

(6) Where a priest accepts an offer to present him to a benefice made in accordance with the provisions of this section, the archbishop shall send to the bishop a notice presenting the priest to him for admission to the benefice.

Institution and collation

Provisions to have effect where bishop refuses to institute presentee

17.—(1) Nothing in the preceding provisions of this Measure shall be taken as affecting the power of a bishop under section 2(1)(*b*) of the Benefices Act 1898 or section 1 of the Benefices Measure 1972 or any rule of law to refuse to institute or admit a presentee to the benefice.

(2) Where in exercise of any such power a bishop refuses to institute or admit a presentee to a benefice, and either no legal proceedings in respect of the refusal are brought or the refusal of the bishop is upheld in such proceedings, the presentation to the benefice affected shall be made by the registered patron whose turn it was to present when the vacancy first occurred; and for the purposes of sections 7, 9, 11 and 12 of this Measure a new vacancy shall not be treated as having occurred by virtue of this section.

Amendment of Benefices Act 1898

18.—(1) Section 3 of the Benefices Act 1898 (appeal against refusal to institute) shall have effect subject to the following amendments—

  (*a*) in subsection (1) for the words from "require that the matter" to the end of the subsection there shall be substituted the words "appeal to the archbishop and the Dean of the Arches and Auditor who shall decide whether to uphold the bishop's refusal or direct him to institute or admit the presentee".

  (*b*) for subsections (2) and (3) there shall be substituted the following subsection—

    "(2) Any proceedings on an appeal under this section shall be held in public and any party to such proceedings shall be entitled to appear by counsel or a solicitor."

(c) in subsection (4) for the words "judgment of the court" there shall be substituted the words "decision of the archbishop and Dean";

(d) for subsection (6) there shall be substituted the following subsections—

"(6) The Dean of the Arches and Auditor may nominate a chancellor to hear, in his place, an appeal under this section with the archbishop, and where any such nomination is made any reference in subsection (1) or (4) above to the Dean shall be construed accordingly.

(7) In this section 'the archbishop' means the archbishop of the province in which the benefice is or, where the benefice is in the diocese of the archbishop of that province or the archbishopric of that province is vacant or the archbishop is patron of that benefice, the archbishop of the other province."

(2) For section 11 of that Act (rules) there shall be substituted the following section—

"Rules

11. The Patronage (Appeals) Committee constituted under Schedule 1 to the Patronage (Benefices) Measure 1986 shall have power to make rules—

(a) prescribing anything to be prescribed under this Act,

(b) regulating the procedure and practice on or in connection with proceedings on an appeal under section 3 of this Act including, without prejudice to the generality of the preceding provision, rules regulating matters relating to costs, fees and expenses in respect of any such proceedings."

Notice of intention of bishop to institute or collate person to benefice

19.—(1) Subject to subsection (3) below, a bishop shall not on a vacancy in a benefice institute or collate any person to the benefice unless after the occurrence of the vacancy a notice in the prescribed form, signed by or on behalf of the bishop, is served on the secretary of the parochial church council of the parish concerned informing him of the bishop's intention to institute or collate that person to the benefice specified in the notice and a period of three weeks has expired since the date of the service of the notice.

(2) As soon as practicable after receiving a notice under subsection (1) above the secretary shall cause the notice or a copy thereof to be fixed on or near the principal door of every church in the parish and every building licensed for public worship in the parish and to remain affixed thereon for two weeks.

(3) Subsection (1) above shall not apply in relation to a person designated by or selected under a pastoral scheme or order as the incumbent of any benefice.

Provisions relating to benefice of which an incumbent is patron

Bishop to act in place of incumbent patron in certain cases

20. Where a benefice ("the ancillary benefice") becomes vacant and it is the turn of the incumbent of another benefice ("the principal benefice"), being the registered patron of the ancillary benefice, to present to that benefice, then if, when the ancillary benefice becomes vacant or at any time during the vacancy thereof and before a notice of presentation under section 13(6) of this Measure is sent to the bishop by the incumbent of the principal benefice—

(*a*) the principal benefice is or becomes vacant, or
(*b*) the principal benefice is under sequestration, or
(*c*) the incumbent of the principal benefice is suspended or inhibited
from discharging all or any of the duties attached to his preferment,
the bishop shall discharge in his place the functions of a registered patron.

Exercise of patronage by personal representatives

Exercise of patronage by personal representatives

21. Where a benefice becomes vacant and either—
(*a*) the registered patron who would have been entitled to present
upon the vacancy is dead and the person to whom the right of
patronage is to be transferred has not before the vacancy
occurs been registered as a patron of that benefice, or
(*b*) the registered patron dies during the vacancy,
then, notwithstanding anything in section 3(8) of this Measure the right of
presentation to that benefice upon that vacancy shall be exercisable by
that patron's personal representatives; but, before they exercise that right,
they shall comply with the requirements of sections 8 and 9 of this
Measure as if they were the registered patron.

Exchange of benefices

Exchange of benefices

22.—(1) Two incumbents may by instrument in writing agree to
exchange their benefices if the agreement of the following persons has
been obtained—
(*a*) the bishop of the diocese in which each benefice is,
(*b*) any registered patron whose turn it is to present to either of the
benefices, and
(*c*) the parochial church council of the parish of each benefice, the
agreement having in each case been given by resolution of the
council.
(2) Where a registered patron whose turn it is to present to a benefice
has given his agreement under subsection (1) above to an exchange by the
incumbent of that benefice, he shall be treated for the purposes of this
Measure as having exercised that turn.

Special provisions as to certain benefices

Special provisions applicable to certain benefices

23. The provisions of this Part of this Measure shall in their application
to—
(*a*) a benefice which comprises two or more parishes,
(*b*) a benefice of which the parochial church council of the parish
belonging to the benefice is the registered patron, and
(*c*) benefices held in plurality,
have effect subject to the provisions of Schedule 2 to this Measure.

Interpretation of Part II

Interpretation of Part II

24.—(1) Subject to subsections (2) and (3) below, in this Part of this
Measure, except in sections 7(4) and 10, any reference to a registered

patron, in relation to any vacancy in a benefice in respect of which there is more than one patron registered under this Measure, shall be construed as a reference to the registered patron whose turn it is, according to the information in the register of patrons on the date on which the vacancy occurs, to present on that vacancy.

(2) In a case where the functions of the registered patron of a benefice in relation to a vacancy in the benefice are to be discharged by the holder of an office or the donee of a power of attorney, any reference in this Part of this Measure (except in sections 8, 9(1) to (4) and 21) to the registered patron shall (subject to subsection (3) below) be construed as a reference to that office-holder or donee as the case may be.

(3) In sections 11 and 12 of this Measure any reference to the registered patron of a benefice (except the reference in section 11(2)(b) shall in a case where the functions of the patron in relation to a vacancy in the benefice are to be discharged by a representative be construed as a reference to that representative, and in section 13 of this Measure any reference to the registered patron of a benefice shall, in a case where the registered patron, being an individual, has appointed a body mentioned in section 8(7) of this Measure or another individual to discharge those functions, be construed as a reference to that body or that other individual, as the case may be.

(4) In this Part of this Measure, except in section 8, "representative", in relation to a registered patron, means—

(a) in the case of a registered patron who is an individual, the individual appointed under section 8(1)(b), (3) or (6);

(b) in the case of a registered patron which is a body of persons, the individual appointed under section 8(2);

(c) in the case of a registered patron which is an office, the individual appointed under section 8(4) or (6);

(d) in a case where the functions of a registered patron are to be discharged by the donee of a power of attorney, the individual appointed under section 8(5) or (6).

(5) In this Part of this Measure "parish representative" has the meaning assigned to it by section 11(7) of this Measure.

PART III

MISCELLANEOUS PROVISIONS AS TO PATRONAGE

Appointment of patron of benefice which has no registered patron

Appointment of patron of benefice which has no registered patron

25. Where at the expiration of the registration period or at any subsequent time no person is registered as the patron of a benefice, then unless in relation to that benefice—

(a) a notice under paragraph 7 of Schedule 1 to this Measure has been served on any person by the registrar of the diocese in which the benefice is and either the period mentioned in paragraph 8 of that Schedule has not expired or an appeal under paragraph 9 thereof has not been determined; or

(b) the right of presentation to the benefice is exercisable by the personal representatives of a deceased patron,

the Diocesan Board of Patronage for the diocese shall become the patron of that benefice, and the registrar of the diocese shall register that Board as patron accordingly.

Diocesan Boards of Patronage

Diocesan Board of Patronage

26.—(1) There shall continue to be a body corporate in every diocese called the Diocesan Board of Patronage.

(2) The constitution and rules of procedure of Diocesan Boards of Patronage shall be those set out in Schedule 3 to this Measure.

Powers of Diocesan Boards of Patronage

27.—(1) Subject to subsection (2) below, a Diocesan Board of Patronage shall have power to acquire, hold and transfer any right of patronage and to exercise any right of presentation or other right incident to a right of patronage held by the Board.

(2) Subject to subsection (3) below, a Diocesan Board of Patronage shall not transfer any right of patronage held by it to any other person without the consent of the parochial church council of the parish or each of the parishes belonging to the benefice concerned unless the transfer is authorised by or under any enactment.

(3) If a parish is transferred from a benefice in one diocese to a benefice in another diocese, the Diocesan Board of Patronage for the first-mentioned diocese may transfer its right of patronage to the Diocesan Board of Patronage of that other diocese without the consent of the parochial church council of that parish.

(4) Where the transfer of a right of patronage requires the consent of a parochial church council under this section, any transfer of the right effected without that consent shall be void.

Presentation by Diocesan Board of Patronage in case of void benefice

28. Where a benefice becomes void under section 4 of the Simony Act 1588 (simoniacal presentation etc. to a benefice declared void and the presentation to be made by the Crown for that turn) the presentation to that benefice upon that vacancy shall be made by the Diocesan Board of Patronage.

Benefices affected by pastoral re-organisation

Provisions as to patronage affected by pastoral schemes

29.—(1) In section 32 of the Pastoral Measure 1983 (provisions as to patronage) in subsection (1) for the word "patron" there shall be substituted the words "registered patron" and for subsection (3) there shall be substituted the following subsections—

"(3) Without prejudice to the generality of subsections (1) and (2) above, a pastoral scheme (whether it relates only to an existing benefice or provides for the creation of a new benefice) may with the consent of the registered patron or patrons of any benefice affected by the scheme provide for the transfer of existing rights of patronage to, or for the vesting of new rights of patronage in, a special patronage board constituted by the scheme.

(3A) A special patronage board constituted by a pastoral scheme by virtue of subsection (3) shall consist of such members as the scheme may provide, and the scheme may designate the member who is to be chairman of the board; and the following provisions of paragraph 1 of Schedule 3 shall apply to such a patronage board as they apply to a patronage board constituted by a pastoral scheme establishing a team ministry, that is to say—

(*a*) sub-paragraph (6) so far as it relates to any member of a board;

(b) sub-paragraph (7) so far as it relates to the entitlement to votes
of any member of a board;
(c) sub-paragraph (8), and
(d) sub-paragraph (10) so far as it relates to the transfer of the
rights to be members of a board."

(2) Where any right of patronage of a benefice is transferred to or
becomes vested in any person by virtue of a pastoral scheme the registrar
of the diocese in which that benefice is shall, on receiving a copy of the
Order in Council confirming the scheme, register him as the patron of
that benefice.

(3) Subject to any provision for the designation or selection of the first
incumbent of a new benefice created by a pastoral scheme, sections 7 to
16 of this Measure shall apply to the making of the first presentation to
the benefice as if the coming into operation of the scheme were the
occurrence of a vacancy in the benefice.

Other amendments of the law relating to rights of patronage etc.

Removal of certain disabilities

30.—(1) The following enactments (which impose disabilities on patrons
practising the Roman Catholic religion etc.) that is to say—
(a) section 13 of the Presentation of Benefices Act 1605;
(b) section 2 of the Presentation of Benefices Act 1688; and
(c) section 1 of the Presentation of Benefices Act 1713,
shall cease to have effect

(2) Section 15 of the Roman Catholic Relief Act 1829 (Roman Catholic
member of lay body corporate not to vote in election, presentation or
appointment of persons to ecclesiastical benefice, etc., in the gift, patronage or disposal of that body) shall cease to have effect in so far as it
relates to benefices.

(3) Section 17 of the Roman Catholic Relief Act 1829 (right of
presentation to benefice to devolve upon the Archbishop of Canterbury
for the time being where right belongs to office which is held by person
professing the Roman Catholic religion) and, in section 4 of the Jews
Relief Act 1858, the words from the beginning to "being; and" (similar
provision relating to right of presentation belonging to office held by
person professing the Jewish religion) shall cease to have effect.

Abrogation of rules as to lapse

31.—(1) Without prejudice to the provisions of section 16 of this
Measure, any rule of law whereby the right of patronage of a benefice
lapses to a bishop or archbishop or to Her Majesty in right of Her Crown
shall cease to have effect.

(2) Nothing in this section shall affect any right of presentation which
on a vacancy in a benefice is exercisable by Her Majesty—
(a) by reason of the appointment to a diocesan bishopric of the
incumbent of the benefice concerned, or
(b) by reason of a vacancy in the see of a diocesan bishop who is a
registered patron of the benefice concerned.

Advowsons appendant to become advowsons in gross

32.—(1) Every advowson which immediately before the date on which
this section comes into force is appendant to any land or any manor shall
by virtue of this section be severed from that land or manor and become
an advowson in gross which—

(a) in the case of land belonging at that date to a charity, shall belong to that charity;

(b) in any other case, shall belong in his personal capacity to the person who at that date is the owner in fee simple of that land or the lord of that manor, as the case may be.

(2) Every advowson which immediately before the said date is appendant to any rectory, not being a rectory with cure of souls, shall by virtue of this section be severed from that rectory and become an advowson in gross belonging in his personal capacity to the person who at that date is the rector of that rectory.

(3) Nothing in this section shall affect the trusts, if any, on which any advowson is held.

Transfer of advowson held on trust for sale or comprised in settled land

33.—(1) Where any advowson is held by any trustee on trust for sale, or on a trust which would be a trust for sale if the advowson were capable of sale, it shall be lawful for the trustees to transfer the advowson gratuitously to any person who has agreed to accept it and—

(a) being an individual—
    (i) is an ecclesiastical corporation sole, or
    (ii) is an actual communicant member of the Church of England, or

(b) being a body of persons, corporate or unincorporate,—
    (i) is one of the bodies mentioned in section 8(7) of this Measure, or
    (ii) has the furtherance of the work of the Church of England as one of its objects.

(2) Where the consent of any person is by any instrument containing such a trust, or by any statutory provision, made requisite to the execution of the trust, then, subject to section 26(1) and (2) of the Law of Property Act 1925 (consents to the execution of a trust for sale), the trustees shall obtain the consent of that person to the execution of a transfer made lawful by subsection (1) above.

(3) The tenant for life of settled land may make a grant in fee simple of any advowson comprised in the settled land gratuitously to any such person as is referred to in subsection (1) above.

(4) Subsection (3) above shall be construed as one with the Settled Land Act 1925, and that Act shall apply as if the power conferred by subsection (3) had been conferred by that Act.

(5) Nothing in any local Act or trust deed shall prevent the transfer *inter vivos* by trustees of an advowson which is the subject of a trust.

Abolition of certain rights etc. of patronage

34.—(1) The right of pre-emption of the patron of a benefice under section 4 of the Parsonages Measure 1938 over any property belonging to the benefice in respect of which it is proposed to exercise a power of sale conferred by that Measure is hereby abolished.

(2) The requirement to obtain the consent of the patron of a benefice to the exercise of the power conferred by—

(a) section 2A of the Parsonages Measure 1938 (power of bishop during vacancy in benefice to divide, enlarge or improve parsonage house); or

(b) section 9(1) of the Church Property (Miscellaneous Provisions) Measure 1960 (power of incumbent or bishop to take or grant easements over land belonging to benefice), or

(c) section 11(1) of the Measure (power of incumbent to dedicate
    certain land belonging to benefice for purpose of a highway),
is hereby abolished.

(3) The requirement to obtain the consent of the patron of a church to
the exercise of the power conferred by section 20(1) of the Marriage Act
1949 (power of bishop to license chapel for publication of banns and
solemnisation of marriages) is hereby abolished.

(4) The obligation imposed by section 4 of the Army Chaplains Act
1868 to transmit to the patron or patrons of a church or chapel affected
a copy of the draft of a scheme for constituting a precinct or district an
extra parochial district for the purpose of that Act in order that he or they
may have an opportunity of making observations or objections is hereby
abolished.

(5) The Parsonages Board within the meaning of the Repair of Benefice
Buildings Measure 1972 shall consult the registered patron, if any, of the
benefice affected before—

(a) determining on the alterations (if any) with which damage to the
    parsonage house is to be made good under section 12(3) of that
    Measure, or

(b) determining that the whole or part of the damage be not made
    good,

but shall not, in either case, be prohibited from making its determination
without the consent of that patron.

(6) No incumbent shall be prohibited under section 21(1) of the Repair
of Benefice Buildings Measure 1972 from making additions or alterations
to the buildings of the parsonage house without the consent of the patron,
but before making any such addition or alteration he shall consult the
registered patron, if any, of the benefice.

PART IV

GENERAL AND SUPPLEMENTARY PROVISIONS

*Benefices in the patronage of the Crown, Duke of Cornwall or Lord
Chancellor*

Provisions with respect to benefices in the patronage of the Crown or Duke of Cornwall

35.—(1) Without prejudice to the application of sections 28 and 31 of
this Measure to the Crown and except as provided by this section, nothing
in this Measure shall apply in relation to any benefice the patronage or
any share in the patronage of which is vested in or exercisable by Her
Majesty, whether in right of Her Crown or Her Duchy of Lancaster or
otherwise, or is vested in or exercisable by the possessor for the time
being of the Duchy of Cornwall, whether Her Majesty or a Duke of
Cornwall (in this Measure referred to as a "Crown benefice").

(2) Where it appears to the registrar of a diocese that a benefice is a
Crown benefice, the registrar shall, as soon as practicable after the date
on which section 1 of this Measure comes into force, notify Her Majesty
or the possessor for the time being of the Duchy of Cornwall that he
proposes to register Her Majesty or the possessor for the time being of
the Duchy of Cornwall, as the case may be, as patron of the benefice
specified in the notice.

(3) Where in the case of a Crown benefice a share only in the patronage
is vested in Her Majesty or the possessor for the time being of the Duchy

of Cornwall (in this section referred to as a "shared benefice") sections 1 and 2 of this Measure shall apply for the purpose of enabling any patron other than Her Majesty or the possessor for the time being of the Duchy of Cornwall to be registered as a patron of that benefice and sections 5 and 21 of this Measure shall apply in relation to a registered patron of a shared benefice other than Her Majesty or the possessor for the time being of the Duchy of Cornwall.

(4) Where a right of patronage in a Crown benefice is transferred to any person other than Her Majesty or the Duke of Cornwall the registrar shall not register the transferee as patron of the benefice unless the application for transfer is made in accordance with Schedule 1 to this Measure before the expiration of the period of twelve months beginning with the date of execution of the transfer.

(5) Where a right of patronage of a benefice is proposed to be transferred to Her Majesty or to the possessor for the time being of the Duchy of Cornwall, section 3(2) to (7) of this Measure shall not apply but the transferor shall send a notice to the registrar to inform him of the transfer and the registrar shall notify Her Majesty or the possessor for the time being of the Duchy of Cornwall that he proposes to register Her Majesty or, as the case may be, the possessor of the Duchy of Cornwall as patron of that benefice.

(6) Section 3(1) of this Measure shall apply to the transfer of a right of patronage of a Crown benefice.

(7) Section 7 of this Measure shall apply in relation to a Crown benefice, and where the designated officer of a diocese receives a notice under that section in respect of a Crown benefice then—

(a) if the patronage is vested wholly in Her Majesty or the possessor for the time being of the Duchy of Cornwall or, in the case of a shared benefice, if the right of presentation upon the vacancy in question is exercisable by Her Majesty or the Duke of Cornwall, any parochial church council to which notice is given under section 7(4) of this Measure may send to Her Majesty or the Duke of Cornwall, as the case may be, a statement describing the conditions, needs and traditions of the parish, and a copy of any such statement shall be sent to the bishop;

(b) if the benefice is a shared benefice and the right of presentation upon the vacancy in question is exercisable by a person other than Her Majesty or the Duke of Cornwall, sections 8 to 21 of this Measure shall apply in relation to the benefice.

(8) Section 22 of this Measure shall apply in relation to a Crown benefice and where the consent of Her Majesty or the possessor for the time being of the Duchy of Cornwall is required by that section that consent may be given in accordance with the provisions of paragraphs (a) to (d) of section 81(2) of the Pastoral Measure 1983 and those provisions shall have effect accordingly with the necessary modifications.

(9) Section 34 of this Measure shall apply in relation to a Crown benefice.

Provisions with respect to benefices in patronage of Lord Chancellor

36. Without prejudice to the provisions of the Lord Chancellor (Tenure of Office and Discharge of Ecclesiastical Functions) Act 1974, the provisions of section 35 of this Measure shall apply in relation to a benefice the patronage or a share of the patronage of which is vested in the Lord Chancellor as it applies in relation to a Crown benefice, and accordingly any reference in that section to Her Majesty shall in relation to any benefice the patronage or a share of the patronage of which is so vested by construed as including a reference to the Lord Chancellor.

Supplementary provisions

Provisions as to notices and other documents

37.—(1) All notices, agreements, approvals, consents and requests required or authorised by this Measure to be served, sent, given or made shall be in writing, and all such notices, other than notices under paragraphs 7 and 8 of Schedule 1 to this Measure shall be in the prescribed form.

(2) Any notice or other document required or authorised by this Measure to be served on or sent or given to any person may be served, sent or given by delivering it to him, or by leaving it at his proper address, or by post.

(3) Any notice or other document required or authorised to be served, sent or given to a corporation or to an unincorporated body having a secretary or clerk or to a firm, shall be duly served, sent or given if it is served on or sent or given to, as the case may be, the secretary or clerk of the corporation or body or a partner of the firm.

(4) Subject to subsection (5) below, for the purposes of this section and of section 7 of the Interpretation Act 1978 in its application to this section, the proper address of the person on or to whom any such notice or other document is required or authorised to be served, sent or given shall be his last known address, except that in the case of the secretary or clerk of a corporation, it shall be that of the registered or principal office of the corporation, and in the case of the secretary or clerk of an unincorporated body or a partner of a firm, it shall be that of the principal office of the body or firm.

(5) If the person on or to whom any such notice or other document is to be served, sent or given has specified an address within the United Kingdom for the serving, sending or giving of the notice or other document, his proper address for the said purposes shall be that address.

Patronage (Procedure) Committee

38.—(1) There shall be a committee, to be known as the Patronage (Procedure) Committee, which shall consist of a chairman and four other members appointed by the Standing Committee.

(2) The Patronage (Procedure) Committee shall have power to make rules with regard to any matter of procedure arising under this Measure and in particular with regard to any matter to be prescribed thereunder, except that no rules may be made under this subsection with regard to any matter in respect of which rules may be made by the Patronage (Appeals) Committee under paragraph 11 of Schedule 1 to this Measure.

(3) Any three members of the Patronage (Procedure) Committee may exercise all the powers of the Committee.

(4) Any rules made by the Patronage (Procedure) Committee shall be laid before the General Synod and shall not come into force until approved by the General Synod, whether with or without amendment.

(5) Where the Standing Committee determines that the rules do not need to be debated by the General Synod, then, unless—

(a) notice is given by a member of the General Synod in accordance with its Standing Orders that he wishes the rules to be debated, or

(b) notice is so given by any such member that he wishes to move an amendment to the rules and at least twenty-five other members of the Synod indicate when the amendment is called that they wish the amendment to be moved,

the rules shall for the purposes of subsection (4) above be deemed to have been approved by the General Synod without amendment.

(6) The Statutory Instruments Act 1946 shall apply to rules approved by the General Synod under this section as if they were statutory

instruments and were made when so approved, and as if this Measure were an Act providing that any such rules shall be subject to annulment in pursuance of a resolution of either House of Parliament.

Interpretation

39.—(1) In this Measure, unless the context otherwise requires—
"actual communicant member of the Church of England" means a member of the Church of England who is confirmed or ready and desirous of being confirmed and has received Communion according to the use of the Church of England or of a Church in communion with the Church of England at least three times during the twelve months preceding the date on which he makes the declaration of membership;

"actual communicant member of a Church in communion with the Church of England" means a communicant member of a Church in communion with the Church of England who has received Communion according to the use of the Church of England or of a Church in communion with the Church of England at least three times during the twelve months preceding the date on which he makes the declaration of membership;

"archbishop" means the archbishop of the province in which the benefice is or, where the benefice is in the diocese of the archbishop of that province or the archbishopric of that province is vacant or the archbishop is the patron of that benefice, the archbishop of the other province;

"benefice" means the office of rector or vicar of a parish or parishes, with cure of souls, but not including the office of vicar in a team ministry or any office in a cathedral church;

"the bishop" means the bishop of the diocese concerned;

"clerk in Holy Orders" means a priest or deacon of the Church of England and "priest" includes a bishop;

"the declaration of membership" has the meaning assigned to it by section 8(1);

"the designated officer" has the meaning assigned to it by section 7(5);

"parish" means a parish constituted for ecclesiastical purposes and does not include a conventional district;

"pastoral committee", "pastoral order" and "pastoral scheme" have the same meanings respectively as in the Pastoral Measure 1983;

"patron", in relation to any benefice, means the person or persons entitled, otherwise than by virtue of section 16, to present to that benefice upon a vacancy, including—
   (a) in any case where the right to present is vested in different persons jointly, every person whose concurrence would be required for the exercise of the joint right, and
   (b) in any case where the patronage is vested in different persons by way of alternate or successive right of presentation, every person who would be entitled to present on the next or any subsequent turn;

"register of patrons" means a register compiled and maintained under section 1;

"registered" means registered under this Measure in a register of patrons;

"registered patron", in relation to a benefice, means any person who or office which is for the time being registered as a patron of that benefice;

"registration period" has the meaning assigned to it by section 1(2);
"the Standing Committee" means the Standing Committee of the
    General Synod.

(2) Where a pastoral scheme or pastoral order provides for the holding
of benefices in plurality any reference in this Measure to a benefice shall
be construed as including a reference to benefices held in plurality.

(3) If any question arises whether a Church is a Church in communion
with the Church of England, it shall be conclusively determined for the
purposes of this Measure by the Archbishops of Canterbury and York.

Temporary provision with respect to filling of certain vacancies

40. Where a benefice is vacant at the date on which section 1 of this
Measure comes into force, or becomes vacant after that date and before
the end of the registration period, the vacancy shall be filled in accordance
with the law in force immediately before that date, except that if a
suspension period has been declared in respect of the benefice under
section 67 of the Pastoral Measure 1983 or any restriction has been
imposed by section 69 of that Measure in respect of the benefice and the
suspension period does not come to an end, or the restriction does not
cease to be in force, until after the end of the registration period, the
vacancy shall be filled in accordance with the provisions of this Measure.

Amendments and repeals

41.—(1) The enactments specified in Schedule 4 to this Measure shall
have effect subject to the amendments specified in that Schedule, being
minor amendments or amendments consequential on the provisions of this
Measure.

(2) Subject to section 40 of this Measure, the enactments specified in
Schedule 5 to this Measure (which include enactments which were obsolete, spent or unnecessary before the passing of this Measure) and the
instrument there specified are hereby repealed to the extent specified in
column 3 of that Schedule.

Short title, extent and commencement

42.—(1) This Measure may be cited as the Patronage (Benefices)
Measure 1986.

(2) This Measure shall extend to the whole of the provinces of
Canterbury and York, except the Channel Islands and the Isle of Man,
but may be applied to the Channel Islands, as defined in the Channel
Islands (Church Legislation) Measures 1931 and 1957, or either of them,
in accordance with those Measures, and may be extended to the Isle of
Man by or under Act of Tynwald.

(3) This Measure shall come into operation on such date as the
Archbishops of Canterbury and York may jointly appoint; and different
dates may be appointed for different provisions.

SCHEDULES

Section 1   SCHEDULE 1

REGISTRATION OF PATRONS

Preparation of list of patrons

1. The registrar of each diocese shall before the expiration of the period of one month
beginning with the date on which section 1 of this Measure comes into force prepare a list
of all the benefices in the diocese which shall specify in relation to each benefice the person

who in the opinion of the registrar is entitled to be registered under this Measure as the patron thereof and shall contain, in a case where he considers that more than one person is entitled to be so registered, such information as may be prescribed as to the exercise of the right to present to that benefice upon a vacancy.

2.—(1) Before the expiration of the period of six weeks beginning with the date on which section 1 of this Measure comes into force the registrar shall—

    (*a*) send to each person who is named in the list prepared under paragraph 1 above a notice specifying the benefice or benefices in respect of which the registrar considers he is entitled to be registered and containing such information as may be prescribed (including, in the case of patronage vested in more than one person, prescribed information as to the exercise of the right of presentation),

    (*b*) advertise in the prescribed manner such information concerning the list prepared by the registrar and the provisions of this Measure as may be prescribed.

(2) Any notice under sub-paragraph (1)(*a*) above shall inform the person to whom the notice is sent that the registrar proposes at the end of the registration period to register that person as a patron of the benefice specified in the notice and also to register the information contained in the notice unless before that date some other person applies to be registered in respect of the same right of patronage or expresses disagreement with that information; and the person to whom the notice is sent shall be required to acknowledge in the prescribed form the receipt of the notice.

(3) The registrar shall send to the incumbent of the benefice concerned and to the secretary of the parochial church council concerned a copy of any notice sent by him under sub-paragraph (1)(*a*) above.

Application for registration

3. Any person who claims to be a patron of a benefice at the date on which section 1 of this Measure comes into force may before the end of the registration period apply to the registrar of the diocese in which the benefice is situated to be registered as a patron of that benefice, notwithstanding that he is not named on the list prepared by that registrar under paragraph 1 above.

4. Any person to whom a right of patronage of a benefice is transferred after the date on which section 1 of this Measure comes into force shall before the expiration of the period of twelve months beginning with the date on which the transfer takes effect apply to the registrar of the diocese to be registered as a patron of that benefice.

5. Any person who claims in relation to any benefice—

    (*a*) that he is entitled to be registered as a patron of that benefice in place of, or in addition to, any person who is so registered, or

    (*b*) that any information registered as to the exercise of a right of presentation to that benefice is incorrect,

may at any time apply to the registrar of the diocese for the register to be rectified under section 4 of this Measure.

6. Any application made under paragraph 3, 4 or 5 above shall be accompanied by such documents and other information as may be prescribed.

Determination of disputes

7. Where the registrar—

    (*a*) decides that any person—

        (i) who is named in a list prepared under paragraph 1 above, or

        (ii) who has made an application under paragraph 3, 4 or 5 above,

    is not entitled to be registered as a patron of the benefice concerned; or

    (*b*) decides that information which any patron of a benefice wishes to be registered as to the exercise of his right to present to that benefice ought not to be registered; or

    (*c*) decides that any person who is registered as a patron of a benefice was not entitled to be so registered; or

    (*d*) decides that any information which is registered as to the exercise of a right to present to a benefice is incorrect,

he shall serve a notice on that person informing him of his decision and of the effect of paragraphs 8 and 9 below.

8. A person on whom a notice is served under paragraph 7 above may, before the expiration of the period of twenty-eight days beginning with the date of the notice, appeal against the registrar's decision by sending him a notice of appeal.

9.—(1) On receiving a notice of appeal under paragraph 8 above the registrar shall refer the appeal to the chancellor of the diocese and the chancellor shall decide whether to uphold the appeal or dismiss it and shall inform the registrar and the appellant of his decision.

(2) Any proceedings on an appeal to the chancellor of a diocese under this paragraph shall be held in public and any party to such proceedings shall be entitled to appear by counsel or a solicitor.

Rules

10.—(1) There shall be a committee to be known as the Patronage (Appeals) Committee which shall consist of—

> the Dean of the Arches and Auditor or, if the Dean nominates the Vicar-General of the Province of Canterbury or the Vicar-General of the Province of York to act in his place, the Vicar-General so nominated;

> one chancellor and one diocesan registrar nominated jointly by the Archbishops of Canterbury and York; and

> two persons nominated by the Standing Committee.

(2) Any three members of the Patronage (Appeals) Committee, one of whom shall be the Dean of the Arches and Auditor or the Vicar-General nominated by the Dean under sub-paragraph (1) above, may exercise all the powers of the Committee.

11. The Patronage (Appeals) Committee shall have power to make rules regulating the procedure and practice on or in connection with proceedings on an appeal under this Schedule including, without prejudice to the generality of the preceding provision, rules regulating matters relating to costs, fees and expenses in respect of any such proceedings.

12.—(1) Any rules made by the Patronage (Appeals) Committee shall be laid before the General Synod and shall not come into force until approved by the General Synod, whether with or without amendment.

(2) Where the Standing Committee determines that the rules do not need to be debated by the General Synod, then, unless—

(a) notice is given by a member of the General Synod in accordance with its Standing Orders that he wishes the rules to be debated, or

(b) notice is so given by any such member that he wishes to move an amendment to the rules and at least twenty-five other members of the Synod indicate when the amendment is called that they wish the amendment to be moved,

the rules shall for the purposes of sub-paragraph (1) above be deemed to have been approved by the General Synod without amendment.

(3) The Statutory Instruments Act 1946 shall apply to rules approved by the General Synod under this paragraph as if they were statutory instruments and were made when so approved, and as if this Measure were an Act providing that any such rules shall be subject to annulment in pursuance of a resolution of either House of Parliament.

Registration

13.—(1) In the case of any disagreement as to the person entitled to be registered as patron of a benefice or as to the exercise of the right of presentation, the registrar as soon as practicable after he—

(a) has determined that a person is entitled to be registered as a patron of a benefice (and has determined the information, if any, to be registered as to the exercise of the right of presentation) and either the period mentioned in paragraph 8 above has expired or the appeal has been dismissed; or

(b) has been informed of the decision of the chancellor on an appeal brought under paragraph 9 above, being a decision as to the person entitled to be registered as a patron of that benefice or as to any information to be registered in respect of the exercise of right of presentation,

shall register that person as a patron of that benefice in the register of patrons accordingly (together with any information to be registered as to the exercise of the right of presentation) and shall inform him that he has done so.

(2) Unless the person entitled to the right of patronage in question has already been registered under sub-paragraph (1) above, the registrar shall at the end of the registration period register in the register of patrons as a patron of the benefice specified in a notice

under paragraph 2 above the person to whom the notice was sent (and the information in that notice) and shall inform him that he has done so.

Notices to parishes

14. After the registrar has registered any person as a patron of a benefice he shall within one month from the end of the registration period or, in the case of a right of patronage registered after the end of that period, as soon as practicable after the registration, send to the secretary of the parochial church council of the parish, or of each of the parishes, belonging to the benefice a notice stating that that person has been registered and giving the name and address of that person and particulars of the benefice and of the information which has been registered in relation thereto.

Benefices held in plurality

15. The preceding provisions of this Schedule shall have effect for the purpose of enabling any person who is a patron of two or more benefices which are for the time being held in plurality, to be registered as a patron of those benefices while so held subject to the modification that for references to a benefice there shall be substituted references to benefices so held.

Rights of patronage belonging to an office

16. Where a right of patronage of a benefice belongs to, or is claimed to belong to, an office, the provisions of this Schedule shall have effect subject to the following modifications—

(a) the notice required to be sent under paragraph 2(1)(a) shall be sent to the person who then holds that office and shall state the intention of the registrar to register that office as a patron of that benefice;

(b) any person who is a patron at the time of the application holds that office, and claims that on the date on which section 1 of this Measure comes into force a right of patronage of that benefice belonged to that office, may apply under paragraph 3 for that office to be registered as a patron of that benefice;

(c) any person who at the time of the application holds that office (being an office to which a right of patronage has been transferred after the said date) may apply under paragraph 4 for that office to be registered as a patron of that benefice;

(d) any notice required to be served under paragraph 7 or information required to be given under paragraph 9 or 13 shall be served on or given to the person who then holds that office.

Section 23   SCHEDULE 2

MODIFICATION OF PART II IN ITS APPLICATION TO CERTAIN BENEFICES

Benefice comprising two or more parishes

1. Where a benefice comprises two or more parishes then, except in a case in which paragraph 19 or 20 below applies, the provisions of Part II of this Measure shall have effect subject to the modifications for which paragraphs 2 to 18 below provide.

2. In section 7(4), for the words "the parish" there shall be substituted the words "each of the parishes".

3. In section 9(6) for the words "secretary of the parochial church council" there shall be substituted the words "secretaries of the parochial church councils".

4. For section 11(1) there shall be substituted:—

"(1) Before the expiration of the period of four weeks beginning with the date on which the notice under section 7(4) of this Measure is sent to the secretaries of the parochial church councils concerned one or more joint meetings of those councils shall be held for the purposes of—

(a) discharging the duties imposed on them by subsection (1A) below;

(b) appointing such number of persons, but not less than four, as will enable each of those councils to have at least one representative, to act as representatives of those councils in connection with the selection of an incumbent;

(c) deciding whether to request the registered patron to consider advertising the vacancy;

(*d*) deciding whether to request a meeting under section 12 of this Measure;

(*e*) deciding whether to request a statement in writing from the bishop describing in relation to the benefice the needs of the diocese and the wider interests of the church;

and each person appointed under paragraph (*b*) shall be a member of one of the parochial church councils concerned.

(1A) At the meeting, or the first meeting, convened under this section, the parochial church councils shall decide whether they will join in preparing a statement describing the conditions, needs and traditions of the parishes belonging to the benefice or whether the parochial church council of each parish will prepare such a statement in relation to that parish, and that decision having been made, the parochial church councils of those parishes or the parochial church council of each parish, as the circumstances require, shall prepare such a statement."

5. In section 11(2), for the words from the beginning to "council", in the second place where it occurs; there shall be substituted the words "A joint meeting of the parochial church councils for which subsection (1) above provides shall be convened by the secretaries of those councils, and no member of any of those councils".

6. In section 11(3), for the words "the parochial church council" there shall be substituted the words "any of the parochial church councils" and for the words "the parish" there shall be substituted the words "any of the parishes".

7. In section 11(4), for the words from "the council by which he was appointed" to the end there shall be substituted the words "any of the councils by which he was appointed then, except where he ceases to be such a member and those councils decide that he shall continue to act as their representative, his appointment shall be deemed to have been revoked and those councils shall appoint another lay member of any of those councils in his place".

8. For section 11(5) there shall be substituted—

"(5) If the parochial church councils concerned hold a joint meeting under subsection (1) above but do not appoint representatives under paragraph (*b*) of that subsection, all the churchwardens who are members of any of the councils concerned shall appoint not more than five of those churchwardens to act as representatives of those councils in connection with the selection of an incumbent."

9. In section 11(8) for "1(*a*)" there shall be substituted "(1A)" and for the words "secretary of the parochial church council" there shall be substituted the words "secretaries of the parochial church councils".

10. For section 12(1) there shall be substituted—

"(1) Where a request for a meeting under this section is made—

(*a*) by a notice sent by the registered patron or the bishop to the secretaries of the parochial church councils concerned or

(*b*) by a resolution of those councils passed at a joint meeting held under section 11 of this Measure,

a joint meeting of those councils with the registered patron and (if the bishop is not the registered patron) the bishop shall be held for the purpose of enabling those present at the meeting to exchange views on the statement or statements prepared under section 11(1A) of this Measure (needs of the parish) and the statement presented under subsection (2) below (needs of the diocese)."

11. In section 12(2) for the word "council" there shall be substituted the word "councils".

12. In section 12(3) for the words "the parochial church council" there shall be substituted the words "each of the parochial church councils concerned" and for "(1)(*a*)" there shall be substituted "(1A)."

13. In section 12(5) for the words "secretary of the parochial church council" there shall be substituted the words "secretaries of the parochial church councils" and for the words "parochial church council" in the second place where those words occur there shall be substituted the words "parochial church councils concerned".

14. In section 12(8)(*c*) for the word "council" there shall be substituted the words "councils concerned".

15. In section 12(9) for the words "The secretary of the parochial church council shall invite both the rural dean of the deanery in which the parish is" there shall be substituted the words "The secretaries of the parochial church councils concerned shall invite both the rural dean of the deanery which comprises the parishes concerned."

16. In section 16(3) for the words "of the parish", in the first place where those words occur, there shall be substituted the words "of each of the parishes belonging to the benefice".

17. In section 19(1) for the words "of the parish" there shall be substituted the words "of each of the parishes".

18. In section 22(1) for the words "the parish of each benefice" there shall be substituted the words "every parish belonging to each benefice".

Benefices having team council or joint parochial church council

19. Where, by a pastoral scheme or by a scheme made under the Church Representation Rules, a team council is established in respect of a benefice which comprises more than one parish, the functions under Part II of this Measure of the parochial church councils of those parishes shall be exercisable by the team council.

20. Where, by a pastoral scheme or by a scheme made under the Church Representation Rules, a joint parochial church council is established for all the parishes of a benefice, the functions under Part II of this Measure of the parochial church councils of those parishes shall be exercisable by the joint parochial church council.

Benefice of which parochial church council is the registered patron

21. Where the parochial church council of the parish belonging to a benefice is the registered patron of the benefice, Part II of this Measure shall have effect in relation to that benefice as if the provisions thereof requiring the appointment of parish representatives and the approval of such representatives to the making of an offer to present a priest to the benefice, and any other provisions thereof referring to such representatives, were omitted.

Benefices held in plurality

22. Where two or more benefices are held in plurality, the provision of Part II of this Measure shall have effect in relation to them as if they were a single benefice comprising two or more parishes.

Section 26 SCHEDULE 3

CONSTITUTION AND PROCEDURE OF A DIOCESAN BOARD OF PATRONAGE

1.—(1) A Diocesan Board of Patronage (hereinafter referred to as "the Board") shall consist of—
  (*a*) the bishop of the diocese;
  (*b*) three clerks in Holy Orders beneficed in or licensed to any parish in the diocese elected by the house of clergy of the diocesan synod by the method of the single transferable vote;
  (*c*) five lay persons elected by the house of laity of that synod by the method of the single transferable vote; and
  (*d*) for the purpose of transacting any business relating to a particular benefice, the archdeacon in whose archdeaconry, and both chairmen of the deanery synod of the deanery in which, that benefice is.

(2) An archdeacon shall not be qualified to be elected under subparagraph (1)(*b*).

2. The bishop of the diocese may nominate any suffragan bishop or assistant bishop holding office in the diocese to act in his place as a member of the Board on such occasions as he may determine.

3. The Board shall elect one of its members other than the bishop to be the chairman of the Board.

4.—(1) The election of members of the Board shall take place every six years in the same year as, but after, the election of members of the diocesan synod, and the elected members of the Board shall hold office for a term of six years beginning with 1st January next following their election.

(2) Where a casual vacancy occurs among the elected members of the Board, then—
    (*a*) if the vacancy is among the members elected under paragraph 1(1)(*b*) above, the vacancy shall be filled by the election by the elected clerical members of the Bishop's Council of a person qualified to be elected under that paragraph,
    (*b*) if the vacancy is among the members elected under paragraph 1(1)(*c*) above, the vacancy shall be filled by the election by the elected lay members of the Bishop's Council of a lay person.

(3) Any person elected to fill a casual vacancy shall hold office only for the unexpired portion of the term of office of the person in whose place he is elected.

(4) An elected member of the Board, if qualified for election, shall be eligible for re-election on the termination of any period of office.

5.—(1) The quorum of the Board shall be six.

(2) Subject to sub-paragraph (1), the Board may act notwithstanding any vacancy in its membership.

6. A clerical member of the Board shall not take part in any proceedings of the Board connected with the exercise of a right of presentation in favour of himself.

7. Subject to the preceding provisions and to any directions as to procedure given by the diocesan synod, the Board shall have power to regulate its own procedure.

8. No election shall be held under this Schedule until after the election of members of the diocesan synod to be held in the year 1988 and any member of a diocesan board of patronage who holds office on the date on which this Schedule comes into force shall, subject to paragraph 4(2) and (3) above, continue in office until the 31st December 1988.

Section 41   SCHEDULE 4

MINOR AND CONSEQUENTIAL AMENDMENTS

Pluralities Act 1838

1. In section 58 of the Pluralities Act 1838 for the words from "upon any such" to the end there shall be substituted the words "no offer of any benefice which becomes void under this section shall be made under any provision of the Patronage (Benefices) Measure 1986 or otherwise to the person by reason of whose non-residence the benefice so became void".

Parsonages Measure 1938

2. In section 2A of the Parsonages Measure 1938 for the words "the Diocesan Dilapidations Board and the patron of the benefice" there shall be substituted the words "and the Diocesan Dilapidations Board".

3. In section 3(1) of that Measure for the words "the patron", where first occurring, there shall be substituted the words "the registered patron", and the words from "Provided" to the end shall be omitted.

4. In section 7 of that Measure immediately before the word "patron" wherever occurring, there shall be inserted the word "registered".

5. In section 13 of that Measure immediately before the word "patron", wherever occurring, there shall be inserted the word "registered".

6. In section 15(1) of that Measure paragraph (i) shall be omitted and in paragraphs (ii) and (iii) immediately before the word "patron" there shall be inserted the word "registered".

7. In section 16 of that Measure immediately before the word "patron", where first occurring, there shall be inserted the word "registered", and at the end of that section there shall be inserted the words "and for the purposes of this Measure Her Majesty shall be deemed to be the registered patron of a benefice the patronage of which is vested in the Crown or is part of the possessions of the Duchy of Lancaster, and the possessor for the time being of the Duchy of Cornwall shall be deemed to be the registered patron of a benefice the patronage of which is part of the possessions of that Duchy".

8. At the end of section 20 of that Measure there shall be inserted the words "and 'registered patron' has the same meaning as in the Patronage (Benefices) Measure 1986".

New Parishes Measure 1943

9. In section 28 of the New Parishes Measure 1943 for the words "parochial church council or patron" there shall be substituted the words "or parochial church council".

Parsonages (Amendment) Measure 1947

10. In section 1 of the Parsonages (Amendment) Measure 1947 immediately before the word "patron" there shall be inserted the word "registered", and at the end of that section there shall be added the following paragraph—

"In this section 'registered patron' has the same meaning as in the Patronage (Benefices) Measure 1986."

City of London (Guild Churches) Act 1952

11. In section 9(6) of the City of London (Guild Churches) Act 1952 for the words from the beginning to "1931" there shall be substituted the words "The Patronage (Benefices) Measure 1986".

12. In section 10(1) of that Act for the word "is" there shall be substituted the words "was at the passing of this Act".

Synodical Government Measure 1969

13. In Schedule 3 of the Synodical Government Measure 1969 (Church Representation Rules)—

(a) in rule 16(3) there shall be inserted at the end the words "or the functions of a parochial church council under Part II of the Patronage (Benefices) Measure 1986";

(b) in rule 17—

(i) in paragraph (1)(c) there shall be inserted at the beginning the words "subject to paragraph 20 of Schedule 2 to the Patronage (Benefices) Measure 1986";

(ii) in paragraph (2) after the words "said Measure" there shall be inserted the words "and to paragraph 20 of Schedule 2 to the Patronage (Benefices) Measure 1986";

(c) in rule 17A—

(i) in paragraph (1)(c) there shall be inserted at the beginning the words "subject to paragraph 19 of Schedule 2 to the Patronage (Benefices) Measure 1986";

(ii) in paragraph (2) after the words "the said Measure" there shall be inserted the words "and to paragraph 19 of Schedule 2 to the Patronage (Benefices) Measure 1986";

(d) in rule 17B—

(i) in paragraph (1)(c) after "1983" there shall be inserted the words "and its functions under Part II of the Patronage (Benefices) Measure 1986";

(ii) at the end of paragraph 3 there shall be added the words "except that the functions of a parochial church council under Part II of the Patronage (Benefices) Measure 1986 may not be delegated to a group council".

Repair of Benefice Buildings Measure 1972

14. In the proviso to section 12(3) of the Repair of Benefice Buildings Measure 1972 for the words "the patron" there shall be substituted the words "after consulting the registered patron", and after the word "consent", where last occurring, there shall be inserted the words "and after such consultation".

15. In section 21(1) of that Measure for the words from "without" to "patron" there shall be substituted the words "until after he has consulted the registered patron, and obtained the consent of the Board".

16. In section 31(1) of that Measure for the definition of "patron" there shall be substituted the words "'registered patron' has the same meaning as in the Patronage (Benefices) Measure 1986".

Pastoral Measure 1983

17. In section 18(2) of the Pastoral Measure 1983—

(a) in the proviso for the words "section 1 of the Benefices (Exercise of Rights of Presentation) Measure 1931" there shall be substituted the words "section 7 of the Patronage (Benefices) Measure 1986";

(b) in paragraph (b) of the proviso for the words "section 1" there shall be substituted the words "section 7".

18. In section 67 of that Measure—

(a) in subsection (1) for the word "patron", in each place where it occurs, there shall be substituted the words "registered patron";

(b) in subsection (6) for paragraph (b) there shall be substituted—

"(b) the registered patron of the benefice, unless the only registered patron is the bishop;".

19. In section 68(2) of that Measure for the word "patron" there shall be substituted the words "registered patron".

20. In section 69 of that Measure—
    (*a*) in subsection (1) for the word patron, in both places where that word occurs, there shall be substituted the words "registered patron";
    (*b*) in subsection (2) for paragraph (*a*) there shall be substituted—
        "(*a*) the registered patron, unless the only registered patron is the bishop;"; for the word "patron" in the second place where it occurs there shall be substituted the words "registered patron" and for the words from "and the requirement" to the end of the subsection there shall be substituted the words "and the provisions of section 7 of the Patronage (Benefices) Measure 1986 shall, subject to the modifications made by section 70 of this Measure, apply".

21. In section 70 of that Measure—
    (*a*) in paragraph (*a*) for the words "section 1 of the Benefices (Exercise of Rights of Presentation) Measure 1931" there shall be substituted the words "section 7 of the Patronage (Benefices) Measure 1986";
    (*b*) in paragraph (*d*) for the words "section 1" there shall be substituted the words "section 7(4)".

22. For section 80(1) of that Measure there shall be substituted the following subsection—
    "(1) Where it is necessary for the purposes of this Measure or any scheme or order made thereunder to find the registered patron of a benefice and it appears to the Commissioners that it is not possible or is not reasonably practicable to find that patron, the Commissioners may direct that the diocesan board of patronage shall be treated for those purposes as the registered patron of that benefice, and any such direction shall be conclusive for the said purposes."

23. In section 82 of that Measure for the word "patron" there shall be substituted the words "registered patron".

24. In section 87(1) of that Measure the following definition shall be inserted after the definition of "redundancy scheme"—
    "registered patron", in relation to a benefice or to benefices held in plurality, means every person who is for the time being registered under the Patronage (Benefices) Measure 1986 in a register of patrons as a patron of that benefice or those benefices."

25. In Schedule 3 to that Measure—
    (*a*) in paragraph 1—
        (i) in sub-paragraph (3) for the words from the beginning to "any other enactment" there shall be substituted the words "Any enactment";
        (ii) in sub-paragraph (6) there shall be inserted at the end of the words "being a person who has made the declaration of membership within the meaning of the Patronage (Benefices) Measure 1986";
        (iii) in sub-paragraph (9) for the words "presentation of the rector by" there shall be substituted the words "patron to be";
    (*b*) for paragraph 3 there shall be substituted the following paragraph—
        "3. Where a group ministry is established by a pastoral scheme for a group of benefices, the registered patron of a benefice in the group shall consult the other incumbents and any priests in charge in the group before he makes a request under section 13 of the Patronage (Benefices) Measure 1986 for the approval of the parish representatives (as defined in section 11(7) of that Measure), and (unless the registered patron is the bishop) of the bishop, to the making to a priest of an offer to present him to the benefice";
    (*c*) in paragraph 4(3)(*c*) there shall be inserted at the beginning the words "subject to paragraph 19 of Schedule 2 to the Patronage (Benefices) Measure 1986,";
    (*d*) in paragraph 13(1)(*c*) there shall be inserted at the beginning the words "subject to paragraph 20 of Schedule 2 to the Patronage (Benefices) Measure 1986,".

Section 41 SCHEDULE 5

REPEALS

Acts

Chapter	Short title	Extent of repeal
31 Eliz. 1. c. 6.	The Simony Act 1588.	In section 4, the words from "And that it shall" to "turne onlye". In section 5, the words from "and that the patron" to the end. Section 6. In section 9, the words from "and that the patron" to "notwithstandinge".
3 Jas. 1. c. 5.	The Presentation of Benefices Act 1605.	Section 13.
1 Will. & Mar. c. 26.	The Presentation of Benefices Act 1688.	The whole Act.
13 Anne c. 13.	The Presentation of Benefices Act 1713.	The whole Act except sections 9 and 11.
1 Geo. 1 stat. 2. c.10	The Queen Anne's Bounty Act 1714.	In section 6, the words from the beginning to "benefices, and" in the second place where those words occur. Sections 7 and 8.
11 Geo. 2. c. 17.	The Church Patronage Act 1737.	The whole Act.
44 Geo. 3. c. 43.	The Clergy Ordination Act 1804.	In section 1, the words from "Provided" to the end.
10 Geo. 4. c. 7	The Roman Catholic Relief Act 1829.	Section 15 insofar as it relates to ecclesiastical benefices. In section 16, the words from "Provided", where last occurring, to the end. Section 17.
1 & 2 Vict. c. 106.	The Pluralities Act 1838.	In section 31, the word "benefice", where it occurs for the second and sixth time, and the words "or benefice". In section 58, the words from "and it shall be lawful" to "second publication thereof as aforesaid".
3 & 4 Vict. c. 20.	The Queen Anne's Bounty Act 1840.	Sections 2 to 4.
3 & 4 Vict. c. 113.	The Ecclesiastical Commissioners Act 1840.	Sections 42, 48 and 73.
4 & 5 Vict. c. 39.	The Ecclesiastical Commissioners Act 1841.	Section 22.
9 & 10 Vict. c. 88.	The Church Patronage Act 1846.	The whole Act.
16 & 17 Vict. c. 50.	The Ecclesiastical Commissioners (Exchange & Patronage) Act 1953.	The whole Act.
19 & 20 Vict. c. 50.	The Sale of Advowsons Act 1856.	The whole Act.
21 & 22 Vict. c. 49.	The Jews Relief Act 1858.	In section 4, the words from the beginning to "being; and".
23 & 24 Vict. c. 124.	The Ecclesiastical Commissioners Act 1860.	Section 42.
31 & 32 Vict. c. 83.	The Army Chaplains Act 1868.	In section 4, the words "and to the patron or patrons", the words "patron or patrons" in the second place where they occur and the words "and patron or patrons".

Chapter	Short title	Extent of repeal
31 & 32 Vict. c. 114.	The Ecclesiastical Commission Act 1868.	Section 12.
33 & 34 Vict. c. 39.	The Church Patronage Act 1870.	The whole Act.
34 & 35 Vict. c. 45.	The Sequestration Act 1871.	Section 6.
61 & 62 Vict. c. 48.	The Benefices Act 1898.	Section 1. In section 2, paragraph (*a*) of subsection (1) and subsection (2). Sections 5 and 6.
12 & 13 Geo. 6. c. 76.	The Marriage Act 1949.	In section 20, in subsections (1) to (3) and (6), the words "patron and" and the words "patron or", wherever they occur, and in subsection (7) the words " 'patron' and" and the words "patron or" and the words, "as the case may be".

Measures

Chapter	Short title	Extent of repeal
14 & 15 Geo. 5. No. 1.	The Benefices Act 1898 (Amendment) Measure 1923.	The whole Measure.
20 & 21 Geo. 5. No. 8.	The Benefices (Transfer of Rights of Patronage) Measure 1930.	The whole Measure except as applied by section 6(3) of the City of London (Guild Churches) Act 1960.
21 & 22 Geo. 5. No. 3.	The Benefices (Exercise of Rights of Presentation) Measures 1931.	The whole Measure.
22 & 23 Geo. 5. No. 1.	The Benefices (Diocesan Boards of Patronage) Measure 1932.	The whole Measure.
23 Geo. 5. No. 1.	The Benefices (Purchase of Rights of Patronage) Measure 1933.	The whole Measure.
1 & 2 Geo. 6. No. 3.	The Parsonages Measure 1938.	In section 3(1), the proviso. Section 4. In section 15(1), paragraph (i). Section 19.
6 & 7 Geo. 6. No. 1.	The New Parishes Measure 1943.	Section 29(2).
7 & 8 Eliz. 2. No. 2.	The Vacancies in Sees Measure 1959.	Section 1 and the Schedule.
8 & 9 Eliz. 2. No. 1.	The Church Property (Miscellaneous Provisions) Measure 1960.	In section 3(2), the words from "and at" to the end. In section 9(1), the words "the patron", In section 11(1), the words "the patron".
1972 No. 2.	The Repair of Benefice Buildings Measure 1972.	Section 27(2).
1978 No. 1.	The Dioceses Measure 1978.	In the Schedule, in paragraph 10, the words from "and for" to the end.
1983 No. 1.	The Pastoral Measure 1983.	Section 32(10). Sections 71 and 72. In section 81(1) the words from the beginning to "Crown", where it first occurs. In Schedule 3, paragraphs 5(4) and 6.

Instrument

Number	Title	Extent of repeal
1938 No. 636.	Rules made by Queen Anne's Bounty pursuant to section 15 of the Parsonages Measure 1938.	Rule 1. In rule 2, the words "as defined by these Rules". In rule 3, the words "(as defined by these Rules)". Rule 7. In the Schedule, Form No. 4.

DEACONS (ORDINATION OF WOMEN) MEASURE 1986

(1986 No. 4)

ARRANGEMENT OF SECTIONS

A Measure passed by the General Synod of the Church of England to make provision for the ordination of women as deacons, and for connected purposes. [7th November 1986]

Provision for ordination of women as deacons

1.—(1) It shall be lawful for the General Synod to make provision by Canon for enabling a woman to be ordained to the office of deacon if she otherwise satisfies the requirements of Canon Law as to the persons who may be ordained as deacons.

(2) In the case of a deaconess who is licensed or holds a bishop's permission to officiate, a Canon made in pursuance of subsection (1) above may make provision for enabling the deaconess to be ordained to the office of deacon notwithstanding—

(*a*) that she has not after applying to be so ordained been further examined concerning her knowledge of holy scripture or of the doctrine, discipline and worship of the Church of England, or

(*b*) that she has not exhibited to the bishop of the diocese any certificate or other document which is required to be so exhibited by every person who is to be made a deacon.

(3) In section 1(1) of the Clergy (Ordination and Miscellaneous Provisions) Measure 1964 there shall be inserted at the beginning the words "Subject to the provisions of section 1(2) of the Deacons (Ordination of Women) Measure 1986".

(4) Nothing in this Measure shall make it lawful for a woman to be ordained to the office of priest.

Provisions as to the order of deaconesses

2.—(1) It shall be lawful for the General Synod to provide by Canon that no woman shall be admitted to the order of deaconesses unless before the date on which this Measure comes into force she has been accepted for training for admission to that order.

(2) Nothing in this Measure shall affect the rights of a deaconess who does not become a deacon.

Provisions as to pensions etc.

3.—(1) Subject to subsection (2) below, the provisions of Parts I, III and IV of the Clergy Pensions Measure 1961 (in this section referred to as "the 1961 Measure") shall, so far as material, apply in relation to a woman who becomes a clerk in Holy Orders within the meaning of that Measure by virtue of being ordained to the office of deacon, and in relation to the husband or widower of any such woman, as they apply in relation to a male clerk in Holy Orders and the wife or widow of any such clerk.

(2) For the purposes of section 46 of the 1961 Measure the retiring age of a woman shall be the age of sixty years or such other age as the General Synod may by resolution from time to time determine.

(3) In consequence of the foregoing provisions of this section the 1961 Measure shall have effect subject to the amendments specified in the Schedule to this Measure.

Interpretation

4. In any Canon, order, rule or regulation relating to deacons, words importing the masculine gender include the feminine, unless the contrary intention appears.

Short title, commencement and extent

5.—(1) This Measure may be cited as the Deacons (Ordination of Women) Measure 1986.

(2) This Measure shall come into force on such day as the Archbishops of Canterbury and York may jointly appoint.

(3) This Measure shall extend to the provinces of Canterbury and York except that it shall only extend to the Isle of Man and the Channel Islands in accordance with the following provisions of this section.

(4) Sections 1, 2, 4 and 5 shall extend to the Isle of Man and section 3 may by or under Act of Tynwald be extended to the Isle of Man with such exceptions, adaptations and modifications as may be specified in such Act or instrument thereunder.

(5) This Measure may be applied to the Channel Islands as defined in the Channel Islands (Church Legislation) Measures 1931 and 1957, or either of them, in accordance with those Measures.

SCHEDULE

Amendments of Clergy Pensions Measure 1961

1. In section 2(3) for the words "his wife", in both places where those words occur, there shall be substituted the words "his spouse".

2. In section 19 for paragraph (*b*) there shall be substituted the following paragraph—
   "(*b*) for the provision of homes of residence for retired clerks and their spouses, and for the widows, widowers and dependants of deceased clerks, in accordance with the provisions of section twenty-six of this Measure;".

3. In section 26—
   (*a*) in subsection (1)(*a*) for the words "wives and for the widows" there shall be substituted the words "spouses and for the widows, widowers";
   (*b*) in subsection (3A)—
     (i) for paragraph (*a*) there shall be substituted the following paragraph—
        "(*a*) a retired clerk or retired church worker or the spouse of a retired clerk or retired church worker;";
     (ii) in paragraph (*b*) for the words "wife of such clerk or the spouse of such church worker" there shall be substituted the words "spouse of such clerk or such church worker";
     (iii) for paragraph (*c*) there shall be substituted the following paragraph—
        "(*c*) the widow or widower of a deceased clerk or deceased church worker;";
     (iv) in the definition of "the retiring age" for the words "a clerk" there shall be substituted the words "a male clerk" and for the words "female church worker" there shall be substituted the words "female clerk or female church worker".

4. In section 46 for the definition of "retiring age" there shall be substituted the following definition—

> " 'retiring age' means in the case of a man the age of 65 years or such earlier age as the General Synod may by resolution from time to time determine and in the case of a woman the age of 60 years or such other age as the General Synod may so determine;".

CURRENT LAW
STATUTE CITATOR 1986

This is the third part of the Current Law Statute Citator 1986 and is up to date to December 31, 1986.
It comprises in a single table:
  (i) Statutes passed between January 1 and December 31,1986;
 (ii) Statutes affected during this period by Statutory Instrument;
(iii) Statutes judicially considered during this period;
 (iv) Statutes repealed and amended during this period.

 (S.) Amendments relating to Scotland only.

ACTS OF THE PARLIAMENT OF SCOTLAND

CAP.

12. Removings Act 1555.
see *Middleton* v. *Booth* (O.H.), 1986 S.L.T. 450.

15. Incest Act 1567.
repealed: 1986, c.36, sch. 2.
See *H.M. Advocate* v. *J.M.R.*, 1985 S.C.C.R. 330.

CAP.

27. Ejection Caution Act 1594.
see *Middleton* v. *Booth* (O.H.), 1986 S.L.T. 450.

5. Bankruptcy Act 1696.
Grant's Tr. v. *Grant* (O.H.), 1986 S.L.T. 220.

35. Salmon Act 1696
repealed: 1986, c.62, sch.5.

ACTS OF THE PARLIAMENTS OF ENGLAND, GREAT BRITAIN, AND THE UNITED KINGDOM

CAP.

32 Hen. 8 (1540)

42. Barbers and Chirurgians Act 1540.
repealed: S.L.R. 1986.

21 Jac. 1 (1623)

16. Limitation Act 1623.
repealed: S.L.R. 1986.

13 Car. 2, Stat. 1 (1661)

5. Tumultous Petitioning Act 1661.
repealed: 1986, c.64, sch.3.

29 Car. 2 (1677)

3. Statute of Frauds 1677.
s. 4, see *Perrylease* v. *Imecar AG* (1986) New L.J. 987, Scott J.

5 Geo. 1 (1718)

20. Revenue of Scotland Act 1718.
repealed: S.L.R. 1986.

10 Geo. 1 (1723)

19. Court of Session Act 1723.
repealed: S.L.R. 1986.

11 Geo. 2 (1737)

19. Distress for Rent Act 1737.
s. 20, repealed: S.L.R. 1986.

18 Geo. 2 (1744)

15. London Barbers and Surgeons Act 1744.
repealed, except ss.12, 15–18; S.L.R. 1986.

CAP.

20 Geo. 2 (1746)

43. Heritable Jurisdictions (Scotland) Act 1746.
s. 34, repealed in pt.: S.L.R. 1986.

24 Geo. 2 (1750)

23. Calendar (New Style) Act 1750.
s. 4, repealed in pt.: S.L.R. 1986.

15 Geo. 3 (1775)

52. Porcelain Patent Act 1775.
repealed: S.L.R. 1986.

17 Geo. 3 (1776)

11. Worsted Act 1776.
repealed: S.L.R. 1986.

33 Geo. 3 (1793)

67. Shipping Offences Act 1793.
repealed: 1986, c.64, sch. 3

39 & 40 Geo. 3 (1800)

67. Union with Ireland Act 1800.
art. 6, see *Ex p. Molyneux* [1986] 1 W.L.R. 331, Taylor J.

41 Geo. 3 (1801)

32. Irish Charges Act 1801.
repealed: S.L.R. 1986.

103. Malta Act 1801.
repealed: S.L.R. 1986.

CAP.

54 Geo. 3 (1814)
67. **Justiciary Courts (Scotland) Act 1814.**
repealed: S.L.R. 1986.

57 Geo. 3 (1817)
19. **Seditious Meetings Act 1817.**
repealed: 1986, c.64, sch. 3.

5 Geo. 4 (1824)
83. **Vagrancy Act 1824.**
s. 4, see *Wood* v. *Comr. of Police of the Metropolis* [1986] 1 W.L.R. 796, C.A.
s. 4, repealed in pt: 1986, c.64, sch. 3.

6 Geo. 4 (1825)
23. **Sheriff Courts (Scotland) Act 1825.**
repealed: S.L.R. 1986.

9 Geo. 4 (1828)
83. **Australian Courts Act 1828.**
s. 15, repealed: 1986, c.2, s.11.

10 Geo. 4 (1829)
44. **Metropolitan Police Act 1829.**
ss. 14–16, repealed: S.L.R. 1986.

11 Geo. 4 & 1 Will. 4 (1830)
68. **Carriers Act 1830.**
s. 10, repealed: S.L.R. 1986.
69. **Court of Session Act 1830.**
s. 33, repealed in pt. (S): 1986, c.9, sch. 2.
70. **Law Terms Act 1830.**
repealed: S.L.R. 1986.

1 & 2 Will. 4 (1831)
37. **Truck Act 1831.**
repealed: 1986, c.48, schs. 1, 5.

2 & 3 Will. 4 (1832)
71. **Prescription Act 1832.**
s.3, see *Carr-Saunders* v. *McNeil (Dick) Associates* [1986] 1 W.L.R. 922, Millett J.

6 & 7 Will. 4 (1836)
22. **Bastards (Scotland) Act 1836.**
repealed: 1986, c.9, sch. 2.
114. **Trials for Felony Act 1836.**
repealed: S.L.R. 1986.

7 Will. 4 & 1 Vict. (1837)
26. **Wills Act 1837.**
s. 18A, amended: 1986, c.55, s.53.

1 & 2 Vict. (1837–38)
119. **Sheriff Courts (Scotland) Act 1838.**
repealed: S.L.R. 1986.

CAP.

2 & 3 Vict. (1839)
47. **Metropolitan Police Act 1839.**
ss. 32, 74, repealed: S.L.R. 1986.
s. 54, see *Grant* v. *Taylor* [1986] Crim.L.R. 252, D.C.: *Masterson* v. *Holden* [1986] 1 W.L.R. 1017, D.C.
s. 54, repealed in pt: 1986, c.64, sch. 3.
s. 66, see *R.* v. *Hamilton* [1986] Crim.L.R. 187, C.A.
71. **Metropolitan Police Courts Act 1839.**
ss. 39, 40, 51, sch. A, repealed: S.L.R. 1986.

6 & 7 Vict. (1843)
85. **Evidence Act 1843.**
repealed: S.L.R. 1986.

7 & 8 Vict. (1844)
69. **Judicial Committee Act 1844.**
s. 1, repealed in pt.: S.L.R. 1986.

8 & 9 Vict. (1845)
16. **Companies Clauses Consolidation Act 1845.**
s. 143, repealed: S.L.R. 1986.
17. **Companies Clauses Consolidation (Scotland) Act 1845.**
s. 145, repealed: S.L.R. 1986.
19. **Lands Clauses Consolidation (Scotland) Act 1845.**
ss. 129, 132, repealed: S.L.R. 1986.
20. **Railways Clauses Consolidation Act 1845.**
s. 139, repealed: S.L.R. 1986.
33. **Railways Clauses Consolidation (Scotland) Act 1845.**
s. 131, repealed: S.L.R. 1986.
72. **Rothwell Gaol Act 1845.**
repealed: S.L.R. 1986.
109. **Gaming Act 1845.**
see *Foster* v. *Attard* [1986] Crim.L.R. 627, D.C.
s. 18, see *Lipkin Gorman* v. *Karpnale and Lloyds Bank* [1986] F.L.R. 271, Alliott J.

10 & 11 Vict. (1847)
89. **Town Police Clauses Act 1847.**
s. 40, see *Challoner* v. *Evans, The Times,* November 22, 1986, D.C.

12 & 13 Vict. (1849)
51. **Judicial Factors Act 1849.**
s. 25, amended (S.): 1986, c.9, sch. 1.

13 & 14 Vict. (1850)
59. **Australian Constitutions Act 1850.**
s. 28, repealed: 1986, c.2, s.11.

14 & 15 Vict. (1851)
26. **Herring Fishery Act 1851.**
repealed: S.L.R. 1986.

CAP.

14 & 15 Vict. (1851)—cont.

99. Evidence Act 1851.
s. 7, see *R.* v. *McGlinchey* [1985] 9 N.I.J.B. 62, C.A.

100. Criminal Procedure Act 1851.
repealed: S.L.R. 1986.

16 & 17 Vict. (1853)

107. Customs Consolidation Act 1853.
repealed: S.L.R. 1986.

129. Pilotage Law Amendment Act 1853.
repealed: S.L.R. 1986.

17 & 18 Vict. (1854)

91. Lands Valuation (Scotland) Act 1854.
ss. 20 (in pt.), 28, 29, repealed: S.L.R. 1986.
s. 42, see *Assessor for Central Region* v. *Independent Broadcasting Authority*, 1986 S.L.T. 307; *Assessor for Dumfries and Galloway* v. *Independent Broadcasting Authority*, 1986 S.L.T. 111; *Assessor for Lothian Region* v. *Blue Circle Industries*, 1986, S.L.T. 537.

112. Literary and Scientific Institutions Act 1854.
ss. 22, 23 (in pt.), repealed: S.L.R. 1986.

18 & 19 Vict. (1855)

68. Burial Grounds (Scotland) Act 1855.
s. 5, repealed in pt.: S.L.R. 1986.

19 & 20 Vict. (1856)

2. Metropolitan Police Act 1856.
s. 2, amended: 1986, c.32, s.35.

97. Mercantile Law Amendment Act 1856.
s. 5, see *Brown* v. *Cork* [1986] P.C.C. 78, C.A.

20 & 21 Vict. (1857)

60. Irish Bankrupt and Insolvent Act 1857.
s. 343, see *JP and AP (Bankrupts), Re* [1985] 11 N.I.J.B. 9, Hutton J.

81. Burial Act 1857.
ss. 10, 23, repealed in pt.: S.L.R. 1986.

21 & 22 Vict. (1858)

90. Medical Act 1858.
ss. 48–51, repealed: S.L.R. 1986.

23 & 24 Vict. (1860)

5. Indian Securities Act 1860.
repealed: S.L.R. 1986.

66. Medical Act 1860.
s. 2, repealed in pt.: S.L.R. 1986.

154. Landlord and Tenant Law Amendment Act Ireland 1960.
s. 3, see *Northern Ireland Housing Executive* v. *Duffin* [1985] 8 N.I.J.B. 62, Carswell J.

CAP.

24 & 25 Vict. (1861)

86. Conjugal Rights (Scotland) Amendment Act 1861.
s. 9, substituted: 1986, c. 9, sch. 1; amended: 1986, c.55, sch. 1

100. Offences against the Person Act 1861.
s. 16, see *R.* v. *Williams (Clarence Ivor)*, *The Times*, October 28, 1986, C.A.
s. 20, see *R.* v. *Knight (D.)* (1985) 7 Cr.App.R.(S.) 5, C.A.; *R.* v. *Dume (Constantine)*, *The Times*, October 16, 1986, C.A.
s. 24, see *R.* v. *Hill (Frederick)*, *The Times*, July 28, 1986, H.L.
s. 34, see *R.* v. *Criminal Injuries Compensation Board, ex p. Webb*, *The Times*, May 9, 1986, C.A.
ss. 44, 45, see *Saeed* v. *Greater London Council (I.L.E.A.)* [1986] I.R.L.R. 23, Popplewell J.

124. Metropolitan Police (Receiver) Act 1861.
ss. 5 (in pt.), 8, repealed: S.L.R. 1986.

25 & 26 Vict. (1862)

97. Salmon Fisheries (Scotland) Act 1862.
repealed: 1986, c.62, sch. 5.

26 & 27 Vict. (1863)

10. Salmon Acts Amendment Act 1863.
repealed: 1986, c.62, sch. 5.

50. Salmon Fisheries (Scotland) Act 1863.
repealed: 1986, c.62, s.41, sch. 5.

27 & 28 Vict. (1864)

24. Naval Agency and Distribution Act 1864.
s. 26, repealed in pt.: S.L.R. 1986.

25. Naval Prize Act 1864.
s. 54, repealed in pt.: S.L.R. 1986.

58. Hartlepool Pilotage Order Confirmation Act 1864.
repealed: S.L.R. 1986.

118. Salmon Fisheries (Scotland) Act 1864.
repealed: 1986, c.62, sch. 5.

28 & 29 Vict. (1865)

89. Greenwich Hospital Act 1865.
s. 60, repealed in pt.: S.L.R. 1986.

100. Harbours Transfer Act 1865.
repealed: S.L.R. 1986.

111. Navy and Marines (Property of Deceased) Act 1865.
s. 18, repealed in pt.: S.L.R. 1986.

125. Dockyard Ports Regulation Act 1865.
ss. 7 (in pt.), 8–10, 26 (in pt.), repealed: S.L.R. 1986.

30 & 31 Vict. (1867)

17. Lyon King of Arms Act 1867.
s. 11, repealed in pt.: S.L.R. 1986.

80. Valuation of Lands (Scotland) Amendment Act 1867.
ss. 6 (in pt.), 8, repealed: S.L.R. 1986.

CAP.

31 & 32 Vict. (1868)

20. **Legitimacy Declaration Act (Ireland) 1868.**
s. 2, repealed: 1986, c.55, sch. 2.
37. **Documentary Evidence Act 1868.**
sch. 1, functions transferred: order 86/600.
101. **Titles to Land Consolidation (Scotland) Act 1868.**
ss. 3, 157, see *Leeds Permanent Building Society* v. *Aitken Malone & Mackay* (O.H.), 1986 S.L.T. 338.
s. 162, repealed in pt.: S.L.R. 1986.
123. **Salmon Fisheries (Scotland) Act 1868.**
repealed except ss. 1, 11, 15, 18–24, 26, 27, 29, 31–36, 41: 1986, c.62, s.41, sch. 5.
s. 1A, added: *ibid.*, sch. 4.
s. 11, amended: *ibid.*
s. 15, amended and repealed in pt.: *ibid.*, s.5.
s. 18, repealed in pt: *ibid.*, sch. 4.
s. 19, amended and repealed in pt.: *ibid.*
s. 20, repealed in pt: *ibid.*
ss. 30, 38–40, repealed: *ibid.*, s.30.
ss. 41, repealed in pt: *ibid.*, sch. 4.

32 & 33 Vict. (1869)

62. **Debtors Act 1869.**
s. 6, see *Al Nahkel for Contracting and Trading* v. *Lowe, The Times*, December 21, 1985, Tudor Price J.
115. **Metropolitan Public Carriage Act 1869.**
s. 9, order 86/857.

33 & 34 Vict. (1870)

33. **Salmon Acts Amendment Act 1870.**
repealed: 1986, c.62, sch. 5.
52. **Extradition Act 1870.**
s. 2, orders 85/1989–1993; 86/220, 766, 1300, 2011–2016, 2020.
s. 3, see *R.* v. *Governor of Pentonville Prison, ex p. Herbage (No. 3), The Times*, November 15, 1986, D.C.
ss. 7, 10, 14, see *R.* v. *Secretary of State for the Home Department, ex p. Rees* [1986] 2 W.L.R. 1024, H.L.
s. 10, see *R.* v. *Governor of Pentonville Prison, ex p. Voets* [1986] 1 W.L.R. 470, D.C.
ss. 10, 14, 15, 26, see *R.* v. *Bow Street Magistrates, ex p. Van der Holst* (1986) 83 Cr.App.R. 114, D.C.
s. 15, see *Espinosa, Re* [1986] Crim.L.R. 684, D.C
s. 17, orders 85/1989–1993, 2011–2016, 2020.
s. 21, orders 85/1989–1993; 86/220, 1300, 2011–2016, 2020.
69. **Statute Law Revision Act 1870.**
repealed: S.L.R. 1986.
71. **National Debt Act 1870.**
ss. 2, 4, Pts. IV, V (ss. 22–42), s. 73, sch. 2, repealed: S.L.R. 1986.
78. **Tramways Act 1870.**
s. 64, repealed in pt.: S.L.R. 1986.

CAP.

34 & 35 Vict. (1871)

3. **Parliamentary Costs Act 1871.**
s. 4, repealed in pt.: S.L.R. 1986.
70. **Local Government Board Act 1871.**
repealed: S.L.R. 1986.
96. **Pedlars Act 1871.**
s. 5, amended: order 85/2027.

36 & 37 Vict. (1873)

57. **Consolidated Fund (Permanent Charges Redemption) Act 1873.**
s. 8, repealed in pt.: S.L.R. 1986.
59. **Slave Trade (East African Courts) Act 1873.**
repealed: S.L.R. 1986.
60. **Extradition Act 1873.**
R. v. *Secretary of State for the Home Department, ex p. Spermacet Whaling and Shipping Co. S.A., The Times*, November 14, 1986, D.C.
88. **Slave Trade Act 1873.**
ss. 2, 29, repealed in pt.: S.L.R. 1986.

37 & 38 Vict. (1874)

42. **Building Societies Act 1874.**
ss. 1, 4, 32, repealed: 1896, c.53, sch. 19.
48. **Hosiery Manufacture (Wages) Act 1874.**
repealed: 1986, c.48, schs. 1, 5

38 & 39 Vict. (1875)

17. **Explosives Act 1875.**
s. 83, repealed in pt.: S.L.R. 1986.
18. **Seal Fishery Act 1875.**
s. 1, repealed in pt.: S.L.R. 1986.
43. **Medical Act (Royal College of Surgeons of England) 1875.**
repealed: S.L.R. 1986.
51. **Pacific Islanders Protection Act 1875.**
repealed: S.L.R. 1986.
86. **Conspiracy and Protection of Property Act 1875.**
s. 7, amended: 1986, c.64, sch. 2.
89. **Public Works Loans Act 1875.**
s. 41, repealed in pt.: S.L.R. 1986.

39 & 40 Vict. (1876)

18. **Treasury Solicitor Act 1876.**
s. 5, repealed in pt.: S.L.R. 1986.
36. **Customs Consolidation Act 1876.**
s. 42, see *Conegate* v. *H.H. Customs and Excise* [1986] Crim.L.R. 562, D.C.
s. 43, repealed: S.L.R. 1986.
70. **Sheriff Courts (Scotland) Act 1876.**
Pt. VII, repealed: S.L.R. 1986.
s. 54, Act of Sederunt 86/267.
77. **Cruelty to Animals Act 1876.**
repealed: 1986, c.14, s.27.

40 & 41 Vict. (1877)

2. **Treasury Bills Act 1877.**
s. 9, repealed in pt.: S.L.R. 1986.
41. **Crown Office Act 1877.**
ss. 3, 5, repealed in pt.: S.L.R. 1986.

CAP.

41 & 42 Vict. (1878)

33. Dentists Act 1878.
repealed: S.L.R. 1986.

42 & 43 Vict. (1879)

11. Bankers' Books Evidence Act 1879.
ss. 7, 10, see *Carmichael* v. *Sexton,* 1986
S.L.T. 16.
s. 9, amended: 1986, c.53, sch. 18.
17. House of Commons Costs Taxation Act 1879.
ss. 1, 2, repealed in pt.: S.L.R. 1986.
21. Customs and Inland Revenue Act 1879.
s. 8, repealed: S.L.R. 1986.
38. Slave Trade (East African Courts) Act 1879.
repealed: S.L.R. 1986.
58. Public Offices Fees Act 1879.
s. 2, order 86/2030.
ss. 2, 3, order 86/1399; S.R. 1986 No. 232.
ss. 2, 3, repealed in pt.: S.L.R. 1986.

44 & 45 Vict. (1881)

24. Summary Jurisdiction (Process) Act 1881.
s. 6, repealed in pt.: S.L.R. 1986.

45 & 46 Vict. (1882)

50. Municipal Corporations Act 1882.
s. 257, repealed in pt.: S.L.R. 1986.
61. Bills of Exchange Act 1882.
ss. 27, 29, see *Mackenzie Mills* v. *Buono, The Times,* July 31, 1986, C.A.
s. 29, see *Lipkin Gorman* v. *Karpnale and Lloyds Bank* [1986] F.L.R. 271, Alliott J.
78. Fishery Board (Scotland) Act 1882.
repealed: 1986, c.62, sch. 5.

46 & 47 Vict. (1883)

3. Explosive Substances Act 1883.
s. 2, see *Rellew* v. *Secretary of State* [1985] 6 N.I.J.B. 86, Hutton J.
31. Payment of Wages in Public-houses Prohibition Act 1883.
repealed: 1986, c.48, schs. 1, 5.

47 & 48 Vict. (1884)

20. Greek Marriages Act 1884.
repealed: 1986, c.55, s.62, sch. 2.
23. National Debt (Conversion of Stock) Act 1884.
ss. 1 (in pt.), 6, 7, 9 (in pt.), repealed: S.L.R. 1986.
31. Colonial Prisoners Removal Act 1884.
ss. 4, 13, repealed in pt.: S.L.R. 1986.
55. Pensions and Yeomanry Pay Act 1884.
s. 2, repealed in pt.: S.L.R. 1986.

48 & 49 Vict. (1885)

49. Submarine Telegraph Act 1885.
s. 6, repealed in pt.: S.L.R. 1986.

CAP.

49 & 50 Vict. (1886)

27. Guardianship of Infants Act 1886.
repealed: 1986, c.9, sch. 2.
s. 9, amended: 1986, c.55, sch.1; repealed in pt.: *ibid.,* sch. 2.
38. Riot (Damages) Act 1886.
s. 3, regs. 86/76.
41. Customs Amendment Act 1886.
repealed: S.L.R. 1986.
48. Medical Act 1886.
repealed: S.L.R. 1986.
53. Sea Fishing Boats (Scotland) Act 1886.
s. 14, repealed in pt.: S.L.R. 1986.

50 & 51 Vict. (1887)

43. Stanneries Act 1887.
ss. 12, 13, repealed: 1986, c.48, sch. 5.
45. Metropolitan Police Act 1887.
s. 4, repealed: S.L.R. 1986.
46. Truck Amendment Act 1887.
repealed: 1986, c.48, schs. 1, 5.
53. Escheat (Procedure) Act 1887.
s. 2, repealed in pt.: S.L.R. 1986.
54. British Settlements Act 1887.
s. 7, repealed: S.L.R. 1986.
58. Coal Mines Regulation Act 1887.
repealed: 1986, c.48, sch. 5.
ss. 12–14, repealed: *ibid.,* sch. 1.
71. Coroners Act 1887.
s. 6, see *R.* v. *Central Cleveland Coroner, ex p. Dent, The Times,* February 17, 1986, D.C.; *Inquest into the Death of Adam Bithell (Decd), Re,* (1986) 150 J.P.N. 348, D.C.; *Rapier, Decd, Re* [1986] 3 W.L.R. 830, D.C.

51 & 52 Vict. (1888)

2. National Debt (Conversion) Act 1888.
ss. 2 (in pt.), 19, 25, 27, 28, 32, repealed: S.L.R. 1986.
15. National Debt (Supplemental) Act 1888.
repealed: S.L.R. 1986.
25. Railway and Canal Traffic Act 1888.
s. 40, repealed in pt.: S.L.R. 1986.
64. Law of Libel Amendment Act 1888.
s. 9, repealed in pt.: S.L.R. 1986.

52 & 53 Vict. (1889)

6. National Debt Act 1889.
s. 2, repealed in pt.: S.L.R. 1986.
30. Board of Agriculture Act 1889.
ss. 2 (in pt.), 9, 11 (in pt.), 13, sch. 1 (in pt.), repealed: S.L.R. 1986.
45. Factors Act 1889.
s. 9, see *Martin* v. *Duffy* [1985] 11 N.I.J.B. 80, Lord Lowry L.C.J.
53. Paymaster General Act 1889.
s. 1, repealed in pt.: S.L.R. 1986.
69. Public Bodies Corrupt Practices Act 1889.
s. 1, see *R.* v. *Parker* (1985) 82 Cr.App.R. 69, C.A.

CAP.

53 & 54 Vict. (1890)

8. **Customs and Inland Revenue Act 1890.**
repealed: S.L.R. 1986.
21. **Inland Revenue Regulation Act 1890.**
s. 8, repealed: S.L.R. 1986.
27. **Colonial Courts of Admiralty Act 1890.**
ss. 7 (in pt.), 9 (in pt.), 13 (in pt.), 14 (in pt.), 16–18, schs. 1, 2, repealed: S.L.R. 1986.
37. **Foreign Jurisdiction Act 1890.**
ss. 11, 13, 18, repealed in pt.: S.L.R. 1986.

54 & 55 Vict. (1891)

39. **Stamp Act 1891.**
sch. 1, amended: 1986, c.41, s.64; repealed in pt.: *ibid.*, s.80, sch. 23.
40. **Brine Pumping (Compensation for Subsidence) Act 1891.**
s. 28, repealed in pt.: S.L.R. 1986.

55 & 56 Vict. (1892)

6. **Colonial Probates Act 1892.**
s. 4, repealed in pt.: S.L.R. 1986.
17. **Sheriff Courts (Scotland) Extracts Act 1892.**
s. 2, repealed in pt.: S.L.R. 1986.
23. **Foreign Marriage Act 1892.**
s. 21, repealed in pt.: S.L.R. 1986.
39. **National Debt (Stockholders Relief) Act 1892.**
s. 7, repealed: S.L.R. 1986.

56 & 57 Vict. (1893–94)

44. **Sheriff Courts Consignations (Scotland) Act 1893.**
ss. 2 (in pt.), 6, 7 (in pt.), 8 (in pt.), 9 (in pt.), repealed: S.L.R. 1986.
s. 7, amended: *ibid.*

57 & 58 Vict. (1894)

2. **Behring Sea Award Act 1894.**
s. 3, repealed in pt.: S.L.R. 1986.
28. **Notice of Accidents Act 1894.**
ss. 2, 7, 8, repealed in pt.: S.L.R. 1986.
30. **Finance Act 1984.**
s. 8, amended: order 86/1942, 1943.
47. **Building Societies Act 1894.**
ss. 8 (in pt.), 29, repealed: 1986, c.53, sch. 19.
52. **Coal Mines (Check Weigher) Act 1894.**
repealed: 1986, c.48, schs. 1, 5.
60. **Merchant Shipping Act 1894.**
ss. 369, 417, repealed in pt.: S.L.R. 1986.
s. 418, order 86/1892.
s. 421, order 86/1983.
s. 427, regs. 86/1072; rules 86/1258.
s. 466, see *The European Gateway, The* [1986] 3 W.L.R. 756, Steyn J.
ss. 479, 489, repealed in pt: S.L.R. 1986.
ss. 510, 518, 523, see *Pierce* v. *Bernis; The Lusitania* [1986] 2 W.L.R. 501; [1986] 1 Lloyd's Rep. 132, Sheen J.
ss. 683 (in pt.), 738 (in pt.), 740, repealed: S.L.R. 1986
s. 738, orders 86/1892, 1893.

CAP.

58 & 59 Vict. (1895)

14. **Courts of Law Fees (Scotland) Act 1895.**
s. 2, orders 85/2072; 86/449–451.
21. **Seal Fisheries (North Pacific) Act 1895.**
s. 6, repealed in pt.: S.L.R. 1986.
44. **Judicial Committee Amendment Act 1895.**
s. 1, order 86/1161.
s. 1, repealed in pt.: S.L.R. 1986.

59 & 60 Vict. (1896)

35. **Judicial Trustees Act 1896.**
s. 4, repealed in pt.: S.L.R. 1986.
44. **Truck Act 1896.**
repealed: 1986, c.48, schs. 1, 5.
s. 1, see *Sealand Petroleum* v. *Barratt* [1986] 1 W.L.R. 700, C.A.
48. **Light Railways Act 1896.**
s. 3, orders 86/174(S.), 277.
s. 5, repealed: S.L.R. 1986.
ss. 7, 9–11, orders 86/174(S.), 277, 343, 690, 1000.
s. 10, repealed in pt.: S.L.R. 1986.
s. 12, orders 86/174(S), 277, 343, 1000.
s. 18, order 86/277.
s. 24, order 86/690.

61 & 62 Vict. (1898)

36. **Criminal Evidence Act 1898.**
s. 1, see *R.* v. *Powell* [1985] 1 W.L.R. 1364, C.A.: *R.* v. *Burke* [1985] Crim.L.R. 660, C.A.; *R.* v. *Owen (A. C.)* (1986) 83 Cr.App.R. 100, C.A.
44. **Merchant Shipping (Mercantile Marine Fund) Act 1898.**
s. 5, regs. 86/334.

62 & 63 Vict. (1899)

19. **Electric Lighting (Clauses) Act 1899.**
s. 57, regs. 86/1627.
sch., repealed in pt.: 1986, c.63, sch. 12.

63 & 64 Vict. (1900)

44. **Exportation of Arms Act 1900.**
repealed: S.L.R. 1986.

2 Edw. 7 (1902)

7. **Finance Act 1902.**
s. 11, repealed: S.L.R. 1986.
21. **Shop Clubs Act 1902.**
repealed: 1986, c.48, schs. 1, 5.
41. **Metropolis Water Act 1902.**
s. 18, repealed in pt.: S.L.R. 1986.

3 Edw. 7 (1903)

30. **Railways (Electrical Power) Act 1903.**
s. 1, repealed in pt.: S.L.R. 1986.
31. **Board of Agriculture and Fisheries Act 1903.**
s. 1 (in pt.), sch., repealed: S.L.R. 1986.

CAP.

5 Edw. 7 (1905)

9. Coal Mines (Weighing of Minerals) Act 1905.
repealed: 1986, c.48, schs. 1, 5.

6 Edw. 7 (1906)

25. Open Spaces Act 1906.
s. 15, repealed in pt.: order 86/1.
41. Marine Insurance Act 1906.
s. 55, see *Lloyd (J.J.) Instruments* v. *Northern Star Insurance Co., Financial Times*, October 21, 1986, C.A.
s. 57, see *ICI Fibres* v. *Mat Transport, The Financial Times*, December 2, 1986, Staughton J.
48. Merchant Shipping Act 1906.
s. 72, see *Pierce* v. *Bernis: The Lusitania* [1986] 2 W.L.R. 501, Sheen J.
50. National Galleries of Scotland Act 1906.
s. 8, repealed: S.L.R. 1986.
55. Public Trustee Act 1906.
s. 8, amended: 1986, c.57, sch.

7 Edw. 7 (1907)

24. Limited Partnerships Act 1907.
s. 4, see *Reed (Inspector of Taxes)* v. *Young* [1986] 1 W.L.R. 649, H.L.
29. Patents and Designs Act 1907.
ss. 62, 63, amended: 1986, c.39, sch. 2.
s. 82, repealed: S.L.R. 1986.
ss. 88, 91, 91A, repealed: 1986, c.39, sch. 3.
51. Sheriff Courts (Scotland) Act 1907.
s. 5, amended: 1986, c.9, sch. 1; repealed in pt.: *ibid.*, sch. 2.
s. 6, see *City of Glasgow District Council* v. *Hamlet Textiles*, 1986 S.L.T. 415; *R.I. Combined Parkinson Services* v. *Barneston*, 1986 S.L.T. (Sh.Ct.) 63.
s. 6, amended: 1986, c.55, sch. 1.
s. 27(B), see *Cassidy* v. *Cassidy*, 1986 S.L.T.(Sh.Ct.) 17.
s. 29, see *Rediffusion* v. *McIlroy*, 1986 S.L.T.(Sh.Ct.) 33.
s. 40, Acts of Sederunt 86/266, 978, 1129.
sch. 1, see *Cadzow* v. *White*, 1986 S.L.T.(Sh.Ct.) 21; *Haliburton Manufacturing and Services* v. *Picts (Construction) Co.*, 1986 S.L.T.(Sh.Ct.) 24; *Guardian Royal Exchange Group* v. *Moffat*, 1986 S.L.T. 262; *Borland* v. *Lochwinnoch Golf Club*, 1986 S.L.T.(Sh.Ct.) 13; *Cunningham* v. *Rowe*, 1985 S.L.C.R. 154; *R.I. Combined Parkinson Services* v. *Barneston*, 1986 S.L.T. (Sh.Ct.) 63.
55. London Cab and Stage Carriage Act 1907.
s. 1, order 86/857.

8 Edw. 7 (1908)

36. Small Holdings and Allotments Act 1908.
s. 39, repealed in pt.: S.L.R. 1986.
ss. 47, 58, sch. 1, amended: 1986, c.5, sch.14.

CAP.

8 Edw. 7 (1908)—cont.

51. Appellate Jurisdiction Act 1908.
s. 3, sch., repealed in pt.: S.L.R. 1986.
53. Law of Distress Amendment Act 1908.
s. 4, amended: 1986, c.5, sch. 14.
57. Coal Mines Regulation Act 1908.
s. 2, repealed in pt.: 1986, c.48, schs. 4, 5.
s. 8, repealed: *ibid.*, sch. 4.
62. Local Government (Scotland) Act 1908.
repealed: S.L.R. 1986.

9 Edw. 7 (1909)

8. Trawling in Prohibited Areas Prevention Act 1909.
repealed: S.L.R. 1986.

1 & 2 Geo. 5 (1911)

6. Perjury Act 1911.
s. 3, amended: 1986 c.16, s.4.
s. 13, see *R.* v. *Rider* [1986] Crim.L.R. 626: (1986) 83 Cr.App.R. 207, C.A.
27. Protection of Animals Act 1911.
s. 1, amended: 1986, c.14, sch. 3.
s. 15, see *Hudnott* v. *Campbell, The Times*, June 27, 1986, D.C.
28. Official Secrets Act 1911.
s. 2, see *Loat* v. *Andrews, The Times*, June 3, 1986, D.C.; *Loat* v. *James* [1986] Crim.L.R. 744, D.C.
s. 11, repealed in pt.: S.L.R. 1986.
42. Merchant Shipping Act 1911.
repealed: S.L.R. 1986.
46. Copyright Act 1911.
ss. 1, 35, see *Computer Edge Pty.* v. *Apple Computer Inc.* [1986] F.S.R. 537, High Ct. of Australia.
s. 15, amended: order 86/600.
ss. 34, 37 (in pt.), repealed: S.L.R. 1986.
49. Small Landholders (Scotland) Act 1911.
sch. 1, repealed in pt.: S.L.R. 1986.

2 & 3 Geo. 5 (1912–13)

14. Protection of Animals (Scotland) Act 1912.
s. 1, amended: 1986, c.14, sch. 3.
31. Pilotage Act 1913.
repealed (Isle of Man): S.L.R. 1986.

3 & 4 Geo. 5 (1913)

17. Fabrics (Misdescription) Act 1913.
s. 2, repealed in pt.: S.L.R. 1986.
20. Bankruptcy (Scotland) Act 1913.
s. 4, see *Grant's Tr.* v. *Grant* (O.H.), November 15, 1985.
s. 29, see *James Finlay Corporation* v. *McCormack* (O.H.), 1986 S.L.T. 106.
s. 98, see *Grindall* v. *John Mitchell (Grangemouth)* (O.H.), 1987 S.L.T. 137.

4 & 5 Geo. 5 (1914)

18. Patents and Designs Act 1914.
repealed: 1986, c.39, sch. 3.
47. Deeds of Arrangement Act 1914.
ss. 3, 11, 15, 16, 23, 30, amended: 1986, c.45, sch. 14.

CAP.

4 & 5 Geo. 5 (1914)—cont.

48. Feudal Casualties (Scotland) Act 1914.
s. 23, repealed in pt.: S.L.R. 1986.

59. Bankruptcy Act 1914.
see *Eyre* v. *Hall* (1986) 280 E.G. 193, C.A.
s. 1, see *James* v. *Amsterdam-Rotterdam Bank N.V.* [1986] 3 All E.R. 179, D.C.
ss. 4, 5, see *Patel (A Debtor), Re* [1986] 1 W.L.R. 221, D.C.
s. 31, see *Unit 2 Windows (in Liquidation), Re* [1985] 1 W.L.R. 1383, Walton J.
ss. 82, 105, see *Colgate (A Bankrupt), Re, ex p. Trustee of the Property of the Bankrupt* [1986] 2 W.L.R. 137, C.A.
s. 96, order 86/1361.
s. 133, order 86/2030.

61. Special Constables Act 1914.
s. 1, S.R. 1986 No. 279.

64. Customs (Exportation Prohibition) Act 1914.
repealed: S.L.R. 1986.

5 & 6 Geo. 5 (1914–15)

2. Customs (Exportation Restriction) Act 1914.
repealed: S.L.R. 1986.

18. Injuries in War Compensation Act (Session 2) 1914.
s. 1, scheme 86/1095.

48. Fishery Harbours Act 1915.
s. 2, repealed in pt.: S.L.R. 1986.

89. Finance (No. 2) Act 1915.
s. 48, repealed in pt.: S.L.R. 1986.

6 & 7 Geo. 5 (1916)

9. Pacific Islands Regulations (Validation) Act 1916.
repealed: S.L.R. 1986.

24. Finance Act 1916.
s. 66, repealed in pt.: S.L.R. 1986.

31. Police, Factories, etc. (Miscellaneous Provisions) Act 1916.
s. 5, regs. 86/1696

52. Trading with the Enemy and Export of Prohibited Goods Act 1916.
repealed: S.L.R. 1986.

7 & 8 Geo. 5 (1917–18)

31. Finance Act 1917.
s. 35, repealed: S.L.R. 1986.

55. Chequers Estate Act 1917.
sch., amended: 1986, c.5, sch. 14.

8 & 9 Geo. 5 (1918)

15. Finance Act 1918.
repealed: S.L.R. 1986.

24. Flax Companies (Financial Assistance) Act 1918.
repealed: S.L.R. 1986.

9 & 10 Geo. 5 (1919)

37. War Loan Act 1919.
repealed: S.L.R. 1986.

CAP.

9 & 10 Geo. 5 (1919)—cont.

51. Checkweighing in Various Industries Act 1919.
repealed: 1986, c.48, schs. 1, 5.

53. War Pensions (Administrative Provisions) Act 1919.
s. 8, sch., repealed in pt.: S.L.R. 1986.

59. Land Settlement (Facilities) Act 1919.
ss. 2, 11, 27, amended: 1986, c.5, sch. 14.

100. Electricity (Supply) Act 1919.
s. 21, substituted: 1986, c.63, s.44.

10 & 11 Geo. 5 (1920)

16. Imperial War Museum Act 1920.
ss. 2, 3, sch., functions transferred: order 86/600.

18. Finance Act 1920.
s. 42, repealed in pt.: 1986, c.41, s.85, sch. 23.

27. Nauru Island Agreement Act 1920.
repealed: S.L.R. 1986.

55. Emergency Powers Act 1920.
s. 2, repealed in pt.: S.L.R. 1986.

75. Official Secrets Act 1920.
s. 7, see *Loat* v. *Andrews, The Times,* June 3, 1986, D.C.

11 & 12 Geo. 5 (1921)

32. Finance Act 1921.
s. 17, repealed: S.L.R. 1986.

49. War Pensions Act 1921.
ss. 1 (in pt.), 2 (in pt.), 3 (in pt.), 4, 6 (in pt.), 9 (in pt.), repealed: S.L.R. 1986.

55. Railways Act 1921.
s. 70, repealed: S.L.R. 1986.

58. Trusts (Scotland) Act 1921.
s. 2, amended: 1986, c.9, sch. 1.

12 & 13 Geo. 5 (1922)

51. Allotments Act 1922.
ss. 3, 11, amended: 1986, c.5, sch. 14.

54. Milk and Dairies (Amendment) Act 1922.
ss. 3, 6, order 86/788(S.).

13 & 14 Geo. 5 (1923)

8. Industrial Assurance Act 1923.
s. 43, regs. 86/608.
s. 43, repealed in pt.: S.L.R. 1986.

20. Mines (Working Facilities and Support) Act 1923.
s. 3, see *BP Development , Re, Financial Times,* February 26, 1986, Warner J.

15 & 16 Geo. 5 (1924–25)

18. Settled Land Act 1925.
s. 73, amended: 1986, c.5, sch. 14.

20. Law of Property Act 1925.
ss. 2, 14, see *City of London Building Society* v. *Flegg* [1986] 2 W.L.R. 616, C.A.
s. 52, amended: 1986, c.45, sch. 14.
s. 53, see *Midland Bank* v. *Dobson and Dobson* (1986) 1 F.L.R. 171, C.A.

CAP.

15 & 16 Geo. 5 (1924–25)—cont.

20. Law of Property Act 1925—cont.
s. 62, see *Deen* v. *Andrews* (1986) 52 P. & C.R. 17, Hirst J.
s. 84, see *Da Costa's Application, Re* (1986) 52 P. & C.R. 99, Lands Tribunal (Ref. No. LP/40/1983), V. G. Wellings Esq., Q.C.
ss. 141, 142, see *Pettiward Estates* v. *Shephard*, April 11, 1986; Assistant Recorder Rice; West London County Ct.
s. 146, see *Smith* v. *Metropolitan Properties* (1985) 277 E.G. 753, Walton J.; *Church Comrs. for England* v. *Nodjoumi* (1986) 51 P. & C.R. 155, Hirst J.
s. 149, see *Bass Holdings* v. *Lewis* (1986) 280 E.G. 771, C.A.
s. 198, see *Barber* v. *Shah* (1985) 17 H.L.R. 584, D.C.
s. 199, see *Kingsnorth Finance* v. *Tizard* [1986] 2 All E.R. 54, Judge Finlay Q.C.

21. Land Registration Act 1925.
ss. 3, 20, see *City of London Building Society* v. *Flegg* [1986] 2 W.L.R. 616, C.A.
s. 8, amended: 1986, c.26, ss. 2, 3.
ss. 18, 19, 21, 22, repealed in pt.: *ibid.*, s.4.
s. 25, amended: 1986, c.53, sch. 18.
s. 42, amended: 1986, c.45, sch. 14.
s. 49, amended: 1986, c.32, s.39.
s. 54, see *Clayhope Properties* v. *Evans* [1986] 2 All E.R. 795, C.A.
s. 54, repealed in pt.: 1986, c.26, s.5.
s. 59, see *Clayhope Properties* v. *Evans* [1986] 2 All E.R. 795, C.A.
s. 70, see *City of London Building Society* v. *Flegg* [1986] 2 W.L.R. 616, C.A.; *Winkworth* v. *Baron (Edward) Development Company, The Times*, December 10, 1986, H.L.; *Kingsnorth Finance* v. *Tizard* (1986) 83 L.S.Gaz. 1231, Judge Finlay Q.C.
s. 70, amended. 1986, c.26, s.4.
s. 77, substituted: *ibid.*, s.1.
ss. 82, 123, see *Proctor* v. *Kidman* (1986) 51 P. & C.R. 67, C.A.
s. 102, repealed in pt.: 1986, c.26, s.5.
s. 112AA, amended: 1986, c.45, sch.14.
s. 123, amended: 1986, c.26, s.2.
ss. 126, 137, repealed in pt.: S.L.R. 1986.
s. 144, rules 86/1534, 1536, 1537.
s. 144, repealed in pt.: 1986, c.26, s.5.
s. 145, order 86/1399.

22. Land Charges Act 1925.
s. 6, see *Clayhope Properties* v. *Evans* [1986] 2 All E.R. 795, C.A.

23. Administration of Estates Act 1925.
s. 46, see *Collens, Decd., Re; Royal Bank of Canada (London)* v. *Krogh* [1986] 1 All E.R. 611, Browne-Wilkinson V.-C.

24. Universities and College Estates Act 1925.
s. 26, amended: 1986, c.5, sch. 14.
s. 33, repealed in pt.: S.L.R. 1986.

CAP.

15 & 16 Geo. 5 (1924–25)—cont.

29. Gold Standard Act 1925.
repealed: S.L.R. 1986.

45. Guardianship of Infants Act 1925.
repealed (S.): 1986, c.9, sch. 2.

71. Public Health Act 1925.
s. 7, repealed in pt.: 1986, c.44, sch. 9.

16 & 17 Geo. 5 (1926)

16. Execution of Diligence (Scotland) Act 1926.
s. 6, Acts of Sederunt 86/255, 266.

36. Parks Regulation (Amendment) Act 1926.
s. 2, see *Burgess* v. *McCracken, The Times*, June 26, 1986, D.C.

40. Indian and Colonial Divorce Jurisdiction Act 1926.
repealed: 1986, c.55, sch. 2.

51. Electricity (Supply) Act 1926.
sch. 6, repealed in pt: 1986, c.63, sch. 12.

59. Coroners (Amendment) Act 1926.
s. 12, repealed in pt.: S.L.R. 1986.
s. 13, see *R.* v. *H.M. Coroner of the Eastern District of the Metropolitan County of West Yorkshire, ex p. National Union of Mineworkers, Yorkshire Area* (1985) 150 J.P. 58, D.C.
s. 19, see *R.* v. *Central Cleveland Coroner, ex p. Dent, The Times*, February 17, 1986, D.C.; *Rapier, Decd, Re* [1986] 3 W.L.R. 830, D.C.

60. Legitimacy Act 1926.
s. 10, see *Dunbar of Kilconzie, Petr.*, 1986 S.L.T. 463, H.L.

17 & 18 Geo. 5 (1927)

10. Finance Act 1927.
s. 55, amended: 1986, c.41, s.73; repealed in pt.: *ibid.*; repealed (prosp.): *ibid.*, s.74, sch. 23.

36. Landlord and Tenant Act 1927.
ss. 17, 19, amended: 1986, c.5, sch. 14.
s. 25, repealed in pt.: 1986, c.44, sch. 9.

18 & 19 Geo. 5 (1928)

3. Patents and Designs (Convention) Act 1928.
repealed: 1986, c.39, sch. 3.

17. Finance Act 1928.
s. 26, repealed: S.L.R. 1986.
s. 31, repealed: 1986, c.41, sch. 23.
s. 35, repealed in pt.: S.L.R. 1986.

26. Administration of Justice Act 1928.
s. 16, repealed (S.): 1986, c.9, sch. 2.

43. Agricultural Credits Act 1928.
s. 5, amended: 1986, c.5, sch. 14.

19 & 20 Geo. 5 (1929)

25. Local Government (Scotland) Act 1929.
ss. 20, 47, 48, 77 (in pt.), repealed: S.L.R. 1986.

CAP.

20 & 21 Geo. 5 (1929–30)

25. Third Parties (Rights against Insurers) Act 1930.
ss. 1, 2, 4, amended: 1986, c.45, sch. 14.
33. Illegitimate Children (Scotland) Act 1930.
repealed: 1986, c.9, sch. 2.

21 & 22 Geo. 5 (1930–31)

46. Gold Standard (Amendment) Act 1931.
repealed: S.L.R. 1986.

22 & 23 Geo. 5 (1931–32)

4. Statute of Westminster 1931.
ss. 4, 9, 10, amended: 1986, c.2, s.12.
32. Patents and Designs Act 1932.
repealed: S.L.R. 1986.
47. Children and Young Persons (Scotland) Act 1932.
repealed: 1986, c.9, sch. 2.
53. Ottawa Agreements Act 1932.
repealed: S.L.R. 1986.

23 & 24 Geo. 5 (1932–33)

12. Children and Young Persons Act 1933.
s. 1, see *R.* v. *Lane and Lane* [1985] Crim.L.R. 789; (1985) 82 Cr.App.R. 5, C.A.
s. 7, amended and repealed in pt.: 1986, c.34, s.1.
s. 53, see *R.* v. *Horrocks, The Times,* February 8, 1986, C.A.; *R.* v. *Burrowes* (1985) 7 Cr.App.R.(S.) 106, C.A.; *R.* v. *Gaskin* (1985) 7 Cr.App.R.(S.) 28, C.A.; *R.* v. *Fairhurst, The Times,* August 2, 1986, C.A.
s. 107, repealed in pt.: S.L.R. 1986.
13. Foreign Judgments (Reciprocal Enforcement) Act 1933.
ss. 1, 3, order 86/2027.
14. London Passenger Transport Act 1933.
s. 93, repealed in pt.: 1986, c.44, sch. 9.
33. Metropolitan Police Act 1933.
repealed: 1986, c.32, s.35.
36. Administration of Justice (Miscellaneous Provisions) Act 1933.
sch. 2, repealed in pt.: S.L.R. 1986.
41. Administration of Justice (Scotland) Act 1933.
s. 4, Act of Sederunt 86/543.
s. 16, Acts of Sederunt 86/255, 341, 514, 515, 694, 799, 967, 1128, 1231, 1937, 1941, 1955.
53. Road and Rail Traffic Act 1933.
s. 42, order 86/277.

24 & 25 Geo. 5 (1933–34)

22. Assessor of Public Undertakings (Scotland) Act 1934.
ss. 2, 3, repealed: S.L.R. 1986.
32. Finance Act 1934.
s. 24, repealed: S.L.R. 1986.

CAP.

24 & 25 Geo. 5 (1933–34)—cont.

36. Petroleum (Production) Act 1934.
ss. 3, 11, 12, see *BP Development, Re, Financial Times,* February 26, 1986, Warner J.
s. 6, regs. 86/1021.
41. Law Reform (Miscellaneous Provisions) Act 1934.
s. 1, see *R. (Deceased), Re; R.* v. *O.* (1986) 16 Fam.Law 58, Mr. Registrar Garland; *Lane (Deceased), Re, Lane* v. *Lane* (1986) 16 Fam.Law 74, C.A.; *Whytte* v. *Ticehurst* [1986] 2 W.L.R. 700, Booth J.
s. 3, see *Knibb and Knibb* v. *National Coal Board* (1986) 26 R.V.R. 123, C.A.
43. National Maritime Museum Act 1934.
ss. 2, 4, 6, functions transferred: 86/600.
45. Solicitors Act 1934.
repealed: S.L.R. 1986.

25 & 26 Geo. 5 (1935)

30. Law Reform (Married Women and Joint Tortfeasors) Act 1935.
s. 6, see *Fortes Service Areas* v. *Department of Transport* (1984) 31 Build.L.R. 5, C.A.

26 Geo. 5 & 1 Edw. 8 (1935–36)

22. Hours of Employment (Conventions) Act 1936.
s. 1, sch. 1 (in pt.), repealed: 1986, c.59, s.7, sch.
s. 4, repealed in pt: *ibid.*, sch.
36. Pilotage Authorities (Limitation of Liability) Act 1936.
repealed (Isle of Man): S.L.R. 1986.
40. Midwives Act 1936.
repealed: S.L.R. 1986.
44. Air Navigation Act 1936.
repealed: S.L.R. 1986.
49. Public Health Act 1936.
s. 64, see *Investors in Industry Commercial Properties* v. *South Bedfordshire District Council (Ellison & Partners (A Firm), Third Party)* [1986] 1 All E.R. 787, C.A.
ss. 72–74, see *Mattison* v. *Beverley Borough Council, The Times,* July 8, 1986, MacPherson J.
s. 99, see *Birmingham City Council* v. *Kelly* (1985) 17 H.L.R. 573, D.C.
s. 100, see *Bradford Metropolitan City Council* v. *Brown, The Times,* March 18, 1986, C.A.
s. 324, functions transferred: order 86/600.
s. 343, repealed in pt.: 1986, c.44, sch. 9.

1 Edw. 8 & 1 Geo. 6 (1936–37)

6. Public Order Act 1936.
ss. 3–5A, 7 (in pt.)–9 (in pt.), repealed: 1986, c.64, sch. 3.
s. 5, see *G.* v. *Chief Superintendent of Police, Stroud, The Times,* November 29, 1986, D.C.

CAP.
1 Edw. 8 & 1 Geo. 6 (1936–37)—cont.

33. Diseases of Fish Act 1937.
s. 1, order 86/283.
s. 8, amended: 1986, c.62, sch. 4.
s. 9, regs. 86/538.
s. 13, order 86/213 (S.).

37. Children and Young Persons (Scotland) Act 1937.
s. 12, see *Kennedy* v. *S.,* 1986 S.L.T. 679.
s. 18, amended and repealed in pt.: 1986, c.34, s.2.

40. Public Health (Drainage of Trade Premises) Act 1937.
s. 14, repealed in pt.: S.L.R. 1986.

48. Methylated Spirits (Sale by Retail) (Scotland) Act 1937.
ss. 2 (in pt.), 3, repealed: S.L.R. 1986.

54. Finance Act 1937.
s. 29, repealed: S.L.R. 1986.

70. Agriculture Act 1937.
repealed: S.L.R. 1986.

1 & 2 Geo. 6 (1937–38)

22. Trade Marks Act 1938.
see *Coca-Cola Co.'s Applications, Re* [1986] 2 All E.R. 274, H.L.
s. 1, substituted: 1986, c.39, sch. 1.
s. 4, see *CPC (United Kingdom)* v. *Keenan* [1986] F.S.R. 527, Peter Gibson J.
s. 5, see *Williams & Humbert* v. *International Distillers and Vintners* [1986] F.S.R. 150, Whitfield J.
ss. 9, 10, see *Telecheck Trade Mark* [1986] R.P.C. 77, Board of Trade; *A.D.D.-70 Trade Mark* [1986] R.P.C. 89, Trade Marks Registry; *VEW Trade Mark* [1986] R.P.C. 82, Board of Trade; *Always Trade Mark* [1986] R.P.C. 93, Falconer J.; *GI Trade Mark* [1986] R.P.C. 100, Board of Trade.
s. 17, see *Telecheck Trade Mark* [1986] R.P.C. 77; *VEW Trade Mark* [1986] R.P.C. 82, Board of Trade; *Always Trade Mark* [1986] R.P.C. 93, Falconer J.
s. 19, amended: 1986, c.39, sch. 2; repealed in pt.: *ibid.,* sch. 3.
s. 26, see *Williams & Humbert* v. *International Distillers and Vintners* [1986] F.S.R. 150, Whitfield J.
s. 26, amended: 1986, c.39, sch. 2.
s. 36, rules 86/1319.
s. 39A, orders 86/1303, 1890.
s. 39A, added: 1986, c.39, sch. 2.
s. 40, rules 86/691, 1319, 1367, 1447.
s. 40, repealed in pt.: S.L.R. 1986.
s. 40A, rules 86/1319.
s. 40A, added: S.L.R. 1986.
s. 41, rules 86/691, 1447.
s. 43, see *Always Trade Mark* [1986] R.P.C. 93, Falconer J.

CAP.
1 & 2 Geo. 6 (1937–38)—cont.

22. Trade Marks Act 1938—*cont.*
s. 53, see *Telecheck Trade Mark* [1986] R.P.C. 77, Board of Trade; *VEW Trade Mark* [1986] R.P.C. 82, Board of Trade.
ss. 57, 58, repealed: 1986, c.39, sch. 3.
s. 61, amended: *ibid.,* sch. 2.
s. 68, see *A.D.D.-70 Trade Mark* [1986] R.P.C. 89, Trade Marks Registry.

29. Patents &c. (International Conventions) Act 1938.
repealed: 1986, c.39, sch. 3.

34. Leasehold Property (Repairs) Act 1938.
s. 7, amended: 1986, c.5, sch. 14.

48. Criminal Procedure (Scotland) Act 1938.
repealed: 1986, c.36, sch. 2.

52. Coal Act 1938.
s. 45, repealed in pt.: S.L.R. 1986.

69. Young Persons (Employment) Act 1938.
s. 7, repealed in pt.: S.L.R. 1986.

2 & 3 Geo. 6 (1938–39)

4. Custody of Children (Scotland) Act 1939.
repealed: 1986, c.9, sch. 2.

13. Cancer Act 1939.
ss. 4, 5, 7, repealed in pt.: S.L.R. 1986.

21. Limitation Act 1939.
s. 2, see *Yorkshire Electricity Board* v. *British Telecommunications: Igoe (P.) & Son (A Firm) (Third Party)* (1985) 83 L.G.R. 760, C.A.
s. 2A, see *Arnold* v. *Central Electricity Generating Board, The Times,* January 24, 1986, Mr. Michael Ogden Q.C.
s. 21, see *Arnold* v. *Central Electricity Generating Board, The Times,* October 20, 1986, C.A.

31. Civil Defence Act 1939.
s. 83, repealed in pt.: S.L.R. 1986.
s. 90, repealed in pt.: 1986, c.44, sch.9.

32. Patents and Designs (Limits of Time) Act 1939.
repealed: S.L.R. 1986.

41. Finance Act 1939.
s. 38, repealed in pt.: S.L.R. 1986.

44. House to House Collections Act 1939.
ss. 1, 11, see *Cooper* v. *Coles* [1986] 3 W.L.R. 888, D.C.

48. Agricultural Development Act 1939.
repealed: S.L.R. 1986.

69. Import, Export and Customs Powers (Reference) Act 1939.
s. 1, orders 86/82, 1446, 1934.
s. 2, repealed in pt.: S.L.R. 1986.

82. Personal Injuries (Emergency Provisions) Act 1939.
ss. 1, 2, scheme 86/628.

107. Patents, Designs, Copyright and Trade Marks (Emergency) Act 1939.
s. 4, amended: 1986, c.39, sch. 2.
s. 6, amended: S.L.R. 1986.; c.39, sch. 2.
ss. 7, 10, amended: *ibid.*

CAP.

3 & 4 Geo. 6 (1939–40)

14. Agriculture (Miscellaneous War Provisions) Act 1940.
s. 27, repealed: S.L.R. 1986.
23. National Loans (No. 2) Act 1940.
repealed: S.L.R. 1986.
35. Indian and Colonial Divorce Jurisdiction Act 1940.
repealed: 1986, c.55, sch. 2.
38. Truck Act 1940.
repealed: 1986, c.48, schs. 1, 5.
42. Law Reform (Miscellaneous Provisions) (Scotland) Act 1940.
s. 3, see *Comex Houlder Diving* v. *Colne Fishing Co.* 1987 S.L.T. 13.

4 & 5 Geo. 6 (1940–41)

50. Agriculture (Miscellaneous Provisions) Act 1941.
ss. 1, 12–14, repealed: S.L.R. 1986.

5 & 6 Geo. 6 (1941–42)

9. Restoration of Pre-War Trade Practices Act 1942.
repealed: S.L.R. 1986.
10. Securities (Validation) Act 1942.
repealed: S.L.R. 1986.
21. Finance Act 1942.
sch. 11, repealed in pt.: S.L.R. 1986.

6 & 7 Geo. 6 (1942–43)

16. Agriculture (Miscellaneous Provisions) Act 1943.
repealed, except ss.18, 24, sch. 3: S.L.R. 1986.
21. War Damage Act 1943.
s. 2, see *South Herefordshire District Council and Morris* (Ref: APP/V1830/G/84/70) (1986) 1 P.A.D. 294.
39. Pensions Appeal Tribunals Act 1943.
s. 10, rules 86/366.
s. 13, sch., rules 86/373(S.).

7 & 8 Geo. 6 (1943–44)

10. Disabled Persons (Employment) Act 1944.
s. 9, see *Hobson* v. *G.E.C. Telecommunications* [1985] I.C.R. 777, E.A.T.
28. Agriculture (Miscellaneous Provisions) Act 1944.
s. 1, sch. 1, repealed: 1986, c.49, sch. 4.
31. Education Act 1944.
s. 4, repealed: 1986, c.61, s.59, sch. 6.
s. 5, repealed: *ibid.*, s.60, sch. 6.
s. 6, see *R.* v. *Brent London Borough Council, ex p. Gunning* (1985) 84 L.E.R. 168, Hodgson J.
ss. 8, 17, see *Honeyford* v. *City of Bradford Metropolitan Council* [1986] I.R.L.R. 32, C.A.
s. 15, amended: 1986, c.61, sch. 4.
ss. 17–21, repealed: *ibid.*, sch. 6.

CAP.

7 & 8 Geo. 6 (1943–44)—cont.

31. Education Act 1944—*cont.*
ss. 17, 24, see *McGoldrick* v. *Brent London Borough Council, The Times*, November 20, 1986, C.A.
s. 22, amended: 1986, c.61, sch. 4.
ss. 23, 24, 27, see *Honeyford* v. *City of Bradford Metropolitan Council* [1986] I.R.L.R. 32, C.A.
ss. 23, 24 (in pt.), 27 (in pt.), repealed: 1986, c.61, sch. 6.
s. 37, see *Enfield London Borough Council* v. *Forsyth, The Times*, November 19, 1986, C.A.
s. 39, see *Rogers* v. *Essex County Council* [1986] 3 W.L.R. 689, H.L.
s. 55, amended: 1986, c.61, s.53.
s. 67, repealed in pt.: *ibid.*, sch. 6.
s. 81, see *R.* v. *Oxfordshire Education Authority, ex p. W, The Times*, November 22, 1986, D.C.
s. 99, see *R.* v. *Northampton County Council, ex p. Gray, The Times*, June 10, 1986, D.C.
s. 100, regs. 86/989.
sch. 1, see *R.* v. *Brent London Borough Council, ex p. Gunning* (1985) 84 L.E.R. 169, Hodgson J.; *R.* v. *Kirklees Metropolitan Borough Council, ex p. Molloy, The Times*, November 5, 1986, Mann J.; *R.* v. *Croydon London Borough Council, ex p. Leney, The Times*, November 27, 1986, D.C.
43. Matrimonial Causes (War Marriages) Act 1944.
repealed: 1986, c.55, sch. 2.

8 & 9 Geo. 6 (1944–45)

28. Law Reform (Contributory Negligence) Act 1945.
s. 1, see *A.B. Marintrans* v. *Comet Shipping Co.; Shinjitsu Maru No. 5, The* [1985] 3 All E.R. 442, Neill, L.J.
42. Water Act 1945.
s. 19, orders 86/1618, 1733, 1776.
s. 23, orders 86/2, 13, 136, 245–247, 401, 740, 1277, 1532, 1986.
s. 32, orders 86/2, 13, 136, 249, 401, 1733.
s. 33, orders 86/136, 249, 401, 1532, 1733.
s. 41, repealed in pt.: S.L.R. 1986.
s. 50, orders 86/2, 13, 136, 249, 401, 1277, 1532, 1733.
s. 59, repealed in pt.: S.L.R. 1986.
sch. 3, amended: order 86/1; repealed in pt.: 1986, c.44, sch. 9.
43. Requisitioned Land and War Works Act 1945.
s. 52, repealed: 1986, c.63, s.48, sch. 12.
s. 53, repealed in pt.: S.L.R. 1986.

9 & 10 Geo. 6 (1945–46)

17. Police (Overseas Service) Act 1945.
ss. 1–3, repealed in pt.: S.L.R. 1986.

CAP.
9 & 10 Geo. 6 (1945–46)—cont.

36. Statutory Instruments Act 1946.
s. 6, order 86/2239.
s. 9, repealed in pt.: S.L.R. 1986.

44. Patents and Designs Act 1946.
repealed: S.L.R. 1986.

58. Borrowing (Control and Guarantees) Act 1946.
ss. 1, 3, order 86/770.
s. 3, repealed in pt.: S.L.R. 1986.

59. Coal Industry Nationalisation Act 1946.
s. 46, see *R.* v. *National Coal Board, ex p. National Union of Mineworkers, The Times*, March 8, 1986, D.C.; *National Coal Board* v. *National Union of Mineworkers, The Times*, June 21, 1986, Scott J.
ss. 50, 62 (in pt.), 64 (in pt.), repealed: S.L.R. 1986.

73. Hill Farming Act 1946.
s. 9, repealed: 1986, c.5, sch. 15.
ss. 12 (in pt.), 13–17, repealed: S.L.R. 1986.
s. 20, regs. 86/428.
s. 28, order 86/1823(S.)
ss. 32, 37, 39, repealed in pt.: S.L.R. 1986.

10 & 11 Geo. 6 (1946–47)

14. Exchange Control Act 1947.
s. 36, repealed in pt.: S.L.R. 1986.
sch. 4, amended: 1986, c.45, sch. 14.
sch. 5, repealed in pt.: S.L.R. 1986.

30. Indian Independence Act 1947.
s. 17, repealed: 1986, c.55, sch. 2.

35. Finance Act 1947.
s. 58, repealed: S.L.R. 1986.

40. Industrial Organisation and Development Act 1947.
ss. 1–6, order 86/1110.
s. 8, order 86/1372.
s. 9, order 86/995.
s. 14, order 86/1110.

41. Fire Services Act 1947.
s. 14, see *York City Council and York Rugby League Football Club* (Ref. T/APP/F2740/A/85/30349/P2) (1986) 1 P.A.D. 303.
s. 17, regs. 85/1758(S.).
s. 26, order 86/1663.
s. 36, repealed in pt.: S.L.R. 1986.

42. Acquisition of Land (Authorisation Procedure) (Scotland) Act 1947.
s. 7, repealed in pt.: 1986, c.44, sch. 9.

43. Local Government (Scotland) Act 1947.
s. 216, regs. 86/411.

44. Crown Proceedings Act 1947.
s. 2, see *O'Neill* v. *Department of Health and Social Services* [1986] 5 N.I.J.B. 60, Carswell J.
s. 3, amended: 1986, c.39, sch. 2.
s. 10, see *Bell* v. *Secretary of State for Defence* [1985] 3 All E.R. 661, C.A.
s. 21, 38, see *R.* v. *Secretary of State for the Home Department, ex p. Herbage* [1986] 3 W.L.R. 504, Hodgson J.

CAP.
10 & 11 Geo. 6 (1946–47)—cont.

44. Crown Proceedings Act 1947—*cont.*
s. 40, see *R.* v. *Secretary of State for Foreign and Commonwealth Affairs, ex p. Trawnick, The Times*, February 21, 1986, C.A.

46. Wellington Museum Act 1947.
functions transferred: order 86/600.

48. Agriculture Act 1947.
s. 73, amended: 1986, c.5, sch. 14.
s. 78, repealed in pt. (S.): S.L.R. 1986.
s. 97, repealed: *ibid.*
s. 103, repealed: 1986, c.49, sch. 4.
sch. 2, amended: 1986, c.5, sch. 14.

51. Town and Country Planning Act 1947.
sch. 8, repealed in pt.: 1986, c.36, sch. 12.

54. Electricity Act 1947.
s. 64, repealed in pt.: S.L.R. 1986.
sch. 4, repealed in pt.: 1986, c.63, sch. 12.

11 & 12 Geo. 6 (1947–48)

3. Burma Independence Act 1947.
s. 4, repealed in pt.: 1986, c.55, sch. 2.

7. Ceylon Independence Act 1947.
s. 3, sch. 2 (in pt.), repealed: 1986, c.55, sch. 2.

17. Requisitioned Land and War Works Act 1948.
sch., repealed in pt.: 1986, c.63, s.48, sch. 12.

22. Water Act 1948.
s. 15, repealed in pt.: 1986, c.44, sch. 9.

29. National Assistance Act 1948.
s. 22, regs. 86/861, 1050(S).
s. 22, amended: 1986, c.50, sch. 10.
s. 26, regs. 86/1050(S).
s. 36, see *R.* v. *Kent County Council, ex p. Bruce, The Times*, February 8, 1986, D.C.
s. 42, amended (S.): 1986, c.9, sch. 1.
s. 43, repealed in pt.: 1986, c.50, schs. 10, 11.
s. 44, repealed (S.): 1986, c.9, sch. 2.
ss. 50 (in pt.), 53, repealed: 1986, c.50, sch. 11.

36. House of Commons Members' Fund Act 1948.
s. 3, resolution 85/2082.
s. 6, repealed: S.L.R. 1986.

37. Radioactive Substances Act 1948.
s. 5, S.R. 1986 No. 61.

38. Companies Act 1948.
s. 66, see *Barry Artist, Re* [1985] 1 W.L.R. 1305, Nourse J.
s. 94, see *G. L. Saunders, Re* [1986] 1 W.L.R. 215, Nourse J.
ss. 95, 98, see *R.* v. *Registrar of Companies, ex p. Central Bank of India* [1986] 1 All E.R. 105, C.A.
s. 188, see *Arctic Engineering, Re* [1986] 1 W.L.R. 686, Hoffmann J.
s. 212, see *Holliday (L.B.) & Co., Re* [1986] 2 All E.R. 367, Mervyn Davies J.

CAP.
11 & 12 Geo. 6 (1947–48)—cont.
38. Companies Act 1948—*cont.*
Pt. V(ii) (iii), (ss.218–310), ss. 245, 307, see *Ross* v. *Smith*, 1986 S.L.T. (Sh.Ct.) 59.
s. 223, see *Byblos Bank* v. *Al Khudhairy, Financial Times*, November 7, 1986, C.A.; *Trendworthy Two* v. *Islington London Borough Council* (1986) 26 R.V.R. 153, Michael Wheeler Q.C.
s. 322, see *Mace Builders (Glasgow)* v. *Lunn* [1986] 3 W.L.R. 921, C.A.
s. 332, see *Rossleigh* v. *Carlaw*, 1986 S.L.T. 204; *R.* v. *Lockwood* [1986] Crim.L.R. 244, C.A.; *Augustus Barnett and Son, Re* [1986] P.C.C. 167, Hoffmann J.
s. 353, see *Aga Estate Agencies, Re, The Times*, June 4, 1986, Harman J.
s. 369, see *Nicholl* v. *Cutts*, 1985 P.C.C. 311, C.A.
s. 371, see *Potters Oils, Re* [1986] 1 W.L.R. 201, Hoffman J.
s. 437, see *Blake* v. *Charles Sullivan Cars, The Times*, June 26, 1986, D.C.
s. 447, see *Speed Up Holdings* v. *Gouch* [1986] F.S.R. 330, Evans-Lombe Q.C.
41. Law Reform (Personal Injuries) Act 1948.
s. 2, see *Foster* v. *Tyne and Wear County Council* [1986] 1 All E.R. 567, C.A.
44. Merchant Shipping Act 1948.
s. 5, order 86/2220.
45. Agriculture (Scotland) Act 1948.
schs. 5, 6, see *Jedlitschka* v. *Fuller*, 1985 S.L.C.R. 90.
52. Veterinary Surgeons Act 1948.
repealed: S.L.R. 1986.
63. Agricultural Holdings Act 1948.
repealed: 1986, c.5, sch. 15.
s. 8, see *Buckinghamshire County Council* v. *Gordon* (1986) 279 E.G. 853, H.H. Judge Barr.
65. Representation of the People Act 1948.
repealed: 1986, c.56, sch. 4.

12, 13 & 14 Geo. 6 (1948–49)
2. Debts Clearing Offices Act 1948.
repealed: S.L.R. 1986.
5. Civil Defence Act 1948.
ss. 3, 6, repealed in pt.: S.L.R. 1986.
10. Administration of Justice (Scotland) Act 1948.
s. 2, Act of Sederunt 86/543.
16. National Theatre Act 1949.
functions transferred: order 86/600.
26. Public Works (Festival of Britain) Act 1949.
repealed: S.L.R. 1986.
29. Consular Conventions Act 1949.
s. 6, order 86/216.
34. Milk (Special Designations) Act 1949.
ss. 10, 11, order 86/788(S.).
35. British Film Institute Act 1949.
s. 1, functions transferred: order 86/600.

CAP.
12, 13 & 14 Geo. 6 (1948–49)—cont.
37. Agriculture (Miscellaneous Provisions) Act 1949.
s. 10, repealed: 1986, c.5, sch. 15.
s. 12, repealed: S.L.R. 1986.
sch. 1, repealed in pt.: 1986, c.5, sch. 15.
41. Ireland Act 1949.
s. 2, see *ex p. Molyneaux* [1986] 1 W.L.R. 331, Taylor J.
s. 3, see *R.* v. *McGlinchey* [1985] 9 N.I.J.B. 62, C.A.
42. Lands Tribunal Act 1949.
s. 3, rules 86/1322.
43. Merchant Shipping (Safety Convention) Act 1949.
s. 23, regs. 86/1069.
s. 33, regs. 86/837.
47. Finance Act 1949.
s. 40, repealed in pt.(S.): S.L.R. 1986.
s. 48, repealed in pt.: *ibid.*
54. Wireless Telegraphy Act 1949.
s. 1, see *Rudd* v. *Department of Trade and Industry* [1986] Crim.L.R. 455, C.A.; *Walkingshaw* v. *McIntyre*, 1985 S.C.C.R. 389.
s. 2, regs. 86/1039.
s. 14, see *Rudd* v. *Department of Trade and Industry* [1986] Crim.L.R. 455, C.A.
62. Patents and Designs Act 1949.
repealed: 1986, c.39, sch. 3.
66. House of Commons (Redistribution of Seats) Act 1949.
repealed: 1986, c.56, sch. 4.
s. 3, order 86/597.
74. Coast Protection Act 1949.
s. 5, see *Thanet District Council and Nature Conservancy Council* (Ref.: SE/5283/42/12) (1985) 1 P.A.D. 99.
75. Agricultural Holdings (Scotland) Act 1949.
s. 7, see *Dunbar and Anderson, Joint Applicants*, 1985 S.L.C.R. 1; *Kinnaird Trust and Boyne, Joint Applicants*, 1985 S.L.C.R. 19.
s. 7, repealed in pt.: S.L.R. 1986.
s. 24. see *Morrison's Exrs.* v. *Rendall*, 1986 S.L.T. 227.
s. 26, see *Clamp* v. *Sharp*, 1985 S.L.C.R. 95.
s. 28, see *Jedlitschka* v. *Fuller*, 1985 S.L.C.R. 90.
s.75, see *Macgregor* v. *Glencruitten Trust*, 1985 S.L.C.R. 77.
sch. 6, see *Suggett* v. *Shaw*, 1985 S.L.C.R. 80.
76. Marriage Act 1949.
ss. 1, 5, amended: 1986, c.16, sch. 1.
s. 5A, added: *ibid.*, s.3.
s. 16, amended: *ibid.*, sch. 1.
s. 23, repealed in pt.: 1986, c.7, s.1.
ss. 27, 27A, 27B, regs. 86/1442, 1445.
ss. 27B, 27C, added: 1986, c.16, sch. 1.
ss. 31, 32, 35, regs. 86/1442, 1445.
s. 39, amended: 1986, c.16, sch. 1.
s. 55, regs. 86/1442, 1445.

CAP.

12, 13 & 14 Geo. 6 (1948–49)—cont.

76. Marriage Act 1949—cont.
s. 57, regs. 86/1442.
s. 74, regs. 86/1442, 1444, 1445.
s. 76, regs. 86/1442.
s. 78, amended: 1986, c.16, sch. 1.
sch. 1, amended and repealed in pt.: *ibid.*
sch. 6, repealed in pt.: 1986, c.7, s.1.

84. War Damaged Sites Act 1949.
repealed: S.L.R. 1986.

87. Patents Act 1949.
s. 13, see *Sevcon* v. *Lucas CAV* [1986] 1 W.L.R. 462, H.L.
ss. 29, 31, see *Donaldson Co. Inc's Patent* [1986] R.P.C. 1, Falconer J.

88. Registered Designs Act 1949.
s. 13, repealed in pt.: S.L.R. 1986.
s. 17, substituted: 1986, c.39, sch. 1.
s. 24, repealed: *ibid.*, sch. 3.
ss. 36, 40, rules 86/584.

102. Festival of Britain (Supplementary Provisions) Act 1949.
repealed: S.L.R. 1986.

103. Parliament Act 1949.
s. 1, repealed in pt.: S.L.R. 1986.

14 Geo. 6 (1950)

12. Foreign Compensation Act 1950.
s. 7, order 86/219.

17. Agriculture (Miscellaneous Provisions) Act 1950.
repealed: S.L.R. 1986.

20. Colonial and Other Territories (Divorce Jurisdiction) Act 1950.
repealed: 1986, c.55, sch. 2.

21. Miscellaneous Financial Provisions Act 1950.
repealed: S.L.R. 1986.

27. Arbitration Act 1950.
s. 1, see *Property Investments (Development)* v. *Byfield Building Services* (1985) 31 Build.L.R. 47, Steyn J.
s. 3, amended: 1986, c.45, sch. 14.
s. 7, see *Ministry of Food Government of Bangladesh* v. *Bengal Liner; The Bengal Pride* [1986] 1 Lloyd's Rep. 167, Leggatt J.
ss. 18, 19, see *Kurkjian (SN) (Commodity Brokers)* v. *Marketing Exchange for Africa, Financial Times*, June 11, 1986, Staughton J.
s. 19A, see *Food Corporation of India* v. *Marastro Cia. Naviera S.A.: the Trade Fortitude* (1986) 136 New L.J. 607, C.A.
s. 20, see *Knibb and Knibb* v. *National Coal Board* (1986) 26 R.V.R. 123, C.A.
ss. 20, 26, see *Coastal States Trading (U.K.)* v. *Niebro Minaeroloel GmbH* [1986] 1 Lloyd's Rep. 465, Hobhouse J.
s. 22, see *Compagnie Nationale Algerienne de Navigation* v. *Hecate Shipping Co.* [1985] 2 Lloyd's Rep. 588, Leggatt J.

CAP.

14 Geo. 6 (1950)—cont.

27. Arbitration Act 1950—cont.
s. 27, see *European Grain & Shipping* v. *Dansk Landbrugs Grovvareslskab* [1985] 1 Lloyd's Rep. 163, Leggatt J.; *Pittallis* v. *Sherefettin* (1986) 278 E.G. 153, C.A.

37. Maintenance Orders Act 1950.
ss. 3, 4, amended: 1986, c.50, sch. 10.
s. 7, repealed: 1986, c.55, sch. 2.
ss. 9, 11, 12, amended: 1986, c.50, sch. 10.
s. 16, see *Tayside Regional Council* v. *Thaw*, 1987 S.L.T. 69.
s. 16, amended: 1986, c.50, sch. 10.

39. Public Utilities Street Works Act 1950.
s. 26, see *Yorkshire Electricity Board* v. *British Telecom* [1986] 2 All E.R. 961, H.L.

14 & 15 Geo. 6 (1950–51)

9. Restoration of Pre-War Trade Practices Act 1950.
repealed: S.L.R. 1986.

18. Livestock Rearing Act 1951.
s. 8, repealed in pt.: S.L.R. 1986.

26. Salmon and Freshwater Fisheries (Protection) (Scotland) Act 1951.
s. 1, amended; 1986, c.62, sch. 4.
s. 2, amended; *ibid.*, s.21.
s. 7A, added: *ibid.*, s.22.
s. 7B, added: *ibid.*, s.25.
s. 9, amended and repealed in pt.: *ibid.*, sch. 4.
s. 11, amended: *ibid.*, s.22.
s. 14, repealed: *ibid.*, sch. 5.
s. 15, repealed in pt.: *ibid.*, sch. 4.
s. 19, repealed in pt.: *ibid.*, schs. 4, 5.
s. 21, amended: *ibid.*, s.26.
s. 22, amended: *ibid.*, sch. 4.
s. 24, amended: *ibid.*, s.8, sch. 4.

39. Common Informers Act 1951.
sch., repealed in pt.: 1986, c.48, sch. 5.

65. Reserve and Auxiliary Forces (Protection of Civil Interests) Act 1951.
s. 27, amended: 1986, c.5, sch. 14.

15 & 16 Geo. 6 & 1 Eliz. 2 (1951–52)

10. Income Tax Act 1952.
s. 430, see *"B": Sun Life Assurance Co. of Canada* v. *Pearson* [1986] S.T.C. 335, C.A.

13. Festival Pleasure Gardens Act 1952.
repealed: S.L.R. 1986.

15. Agriculture (Fertilisers) Act 1952.
repealed: S.L.R. 1986.

35. Agriculture (Ploughing Grants) Act 1952.
repealed: S.L.R. 1986.

47. Rating and Valuation (Scotland) Act 1952.
s. 6, Act of Sederunt 86/641.

52. Prison Act 1952.
ss. 13, 39, see *Nicoll* v. *Catron* (1985) 81 Cr.App.R. 339, D.C.; *R.* v. *Moss and Harte* [1986] Crim.L.R. 659; (1985) 82 Cr.App.R. 116, C.A.

CAP.

15 & 16 Geo. 6 & 1 Eliz. 2 (1951–52)—cont.

52. Prison Act 1952—*cont.*
s. 43, see *Nicoll* v. *Catron* (1985) 81 Cr.App.R. 339, D.C.
s. 47, see *R.* v. *Secretary of State for the Home Department, ex p. Hickling* (1986) 16 Fam. Law 140, C.A.

62. Agriculture (Calf Subsidies) Act 1952.
repealed: S.L.R. 1986.

66. Defamation Act 1952.
s. 5, see *Polly Peck (Holdings)* v. *Trelford* [1986] 2 W.L.R. 845, C.A.

1 & 2 Eliz. 2 (1952–53)

14. Prevention of Crime Act 1953.
s. 1, see *R.* v. *Flynn* [1986] Crim.L.R. 239; (1986) 82 Cr.App.R. 319, C.A.; *Coull* v. *Guild*, 1986 S.L.T. 184; *Houghton* v. *Chief Constable of Greater Manchester, The Times*, July 24, 1986, C.A.
s. 1, amended: 1986, c.64, sch. 2.
s. 4, see *R.* v. *Flynn (James)* (1986) 82 Cr.App.R. 319, C.A.

34. Finance Act 1953.
s. 30, functions transferred: order 86/600.

36. Post Office Act 1953.
s. 16, regs. 86/260; order 86/1019.

37. Registration Service Act 1953.
s. 17, repealed: S.L.R. 1986.
s. 20, regs. 86/1442, 1445.

2 & 3 Eliz. 2 (1953–54)

17. Royal Irish Constabulary (Widows' Pensions) Act 1954.
s. 1, regs. 86/1381.

21. Rights of Entry (Gas and Electricity Boards) Act 1954.
ss. 1, 2, amended: 1986, c.44, sch. 7.
s. 3, amended: *ibid.*; repealed in pt.: *ibid.*, schs. 7, 9.

32. Atomic Energy Authority Act 1954.
s. 1, amended and repealed in pt.: 1986, c.3, s.7.

39. Agriculture (Miscellaneous Provisions) Act 1954.
s. 2, repealed: S.L.R. 1986.

46. Protection of Animals (Anaesthetics) Act 1954.
sch. 1, amended: 1986, c.14, sch. 3.

48. Summary Jurisdiction (Scotland) Act 1954.
sch. 2, see *Anderson* v. *Allan*, 1985 S.C.C.R. 399.

56. Landlord and Tenant Act 1954.
s. 23, see *Linden* v. *Department of Health and Social Security* [1986] 1 W.L.R. 164, Scott J.; *Trans-Britannia Properties* v. *Darby Properties* (1986) 278 E.G. 1254, C.A.
s. 24A, see *Thomas* v. *Hammond-Lawrence* [1986] 1 W.L.R. 456, C.A.; *Charles Follett* v. *Cabtell Investment Co.* (1986) 280 E.G. 639, Mr. T. L. G. Cullen Q.C.

CAP.

2 & 3 Eliz. 2 (1953–54)—cont.

56. Landlord and Tenant Act 1954—*cont.*
s. 25, see *Aireps* v. *Bradford City Metropolitan Council* (1985) 267 E.G. 1067; *Morrow* v. *Nadeem* [1986] 1 W.L.R. 1381, C.A.
s. 28, see *Stratton (R. J.)* v. *Wallis Tomlin & Co.* (1985) 277 E.G. 409, C.A.
s. 29, see *Sharma* v. *Knight, The Times*, January 30, 1986, C.A.
s. 30, see *Mulareczyk* v. *Azralnove Investments* (1985) 276 E.G. 1064, C.A.; *Aireps* v. *Bradford City Metropolitan Council* (1985) 267 E.G. 1067; *Leathwoods* v. *Total Oil Great Britain* (1986) 51 P. & C.R. 20, C.A.; *Jones* v. *Jenkins* (1985) 277 E.G. 644, C.A.; *Cerex Jewels* v. *Peachey Property Corp., The Times*, May 12, 1986, C.A.; *Beard (Formerly Coleman)* v. *Williams* (1986) 278 E.G. 1087, C.A.; *Thornton (J.W.)* v. *Blacks Leisure Group* (1986) 279 E.G. 588, C.A.
s. 31A, see *Mularczyk* v. *Azralnove Investments* (1985) 276 E.G. 1064, C.A.; *Cerex Jewels* v. *Peachey Property Corp., The Times*, May 12, 1986, C.A.
s. 34, see *Brett* v. *Brett Essex Golf Club, The Times*, May 12, 1986, H.L.
s. 37, amended: 1986, c.63, s.13.
s. 38, see *Cardiothoracic Institute* v. *Shrewdcrest* [1986] 1 W.L.R. 368, Ch.D., Knox J.
s. 43, amended: 1986, c.5. sch. 14.
s. 56, see *Linden* v. *Department of Health and Social Security* [1986] 1 W.L.R. 164, Scott J.
s. 69, see *Stratton (R. J.)* v. *Wallis Tomlin & Co.* (1985) 277 E.G. 409, C.A.
s. 69, amended: 1986, c.5, sch. 14.

57. Baking Industry (Hours of Work) Act 1954.
repealed: 1986, c.59, s.8, sch.

61. Pharmacy Act 1954.
s. 8, see *R.* v. *Pharmaceutical Society of Great Britain, ex p. Sokoh, The Times*, December 4, 1986, Webster J.

68. Pests Act 1954.
s. 12, amended: 1986, c.14, sch. 3.

70. Mines and Quarries Act 1954.
s. 51, repealed in pt.: 1986, c.48, schs. 1, 5.
s. 88, see *England* v. *Cleveland Potash, The Times*, July 1, 1986, C.A.
ss. 125, 126, 128, 131, repealed in pt.: 1986, c.59, s.7, sch.
s. 185, repealed: 1986, c.48, sch. 5.
s. 187, amended: *ibid.*, sch. 4; repealed in pt.: *ibid.*, sch. 5.
sch. 4, repealed in pt.: 1986, c.59, sch.

3 & 4 Eliz. 2 (1954–55)

7. Fisheries Act 1955.
s. 3, repealed: S.L.R. 1986.

14. Imperial War Museum Act 1955.
s. 2, functions transferred: order 86/600.

3 & 4 Eliz. 2 (1954–55)—cont.

18. Army Act 1955.
continued in force: 1986, c.21, s.1.
ss. 28, 29, 33, repealed in pt.: *ibid.*, s.4, sch. 2.
s. 44B, added: *ibid.*, s.2.
s. 55, repealed in pt.: *ibid.*, s.4, sch. 2.
s. 62, amended: *ibid.*, s.3.
s. 65, repealed in pt.: *ibid.*, s.4, sch. 2.
s. 69, amended: *ibid.*, s.4.
ss. 71, 71AA, amended: *ibid.*, sch. 1.
s. 71B, amended: *ibid.*, s.5; repealed in pt.: *ibid.*, sch. 2.
ss. 107, 108, 113, amended: *ibid.*, sch. 1.
s. 114, repealed: *ibid.*, s.6, sch. 2.
s. 120, repealed in pt.: *ibid.*, sch. 2.
s. 133A, amended: *ibid.*, sch. 1; repealed in pt.: *ibid.*, sch. 2.
s. 134, see *R.* v. *Amos, The Times*, March 18, 1986, Courts-Martial Appeal Court.
s. 203, see *Roberts* v. *Roberts* [1986] 1 W.L.R. 437, Wood J.
s. 205, repealed in pt.: 1986, c.21, sch. 2.
s. 209, amended: *ibid.*, s.8.
s. 213, repealed in pt.: *ibid.*, s.14, sch. 2.
s. 225, amended: *ibid.*, sch. 1.
sch. 3, repealed in pt.: *ibid.*, sch. 2.
sch. 5A, regs. 86/1241.
sch. 5A, amended: 1986, c.21, ss.9–11, sch. 1; repealed in pt.: *ibid.*, s.10, sch.2.
sch. 6, amended: *ibid.*, sch. 1.

19. Air Force Act 1955.
continued in force: 1986, c.21, s.1.
ss. 12, 13, see *R.* v. *Garth* [1986] 2 W.L.R. 80, H.L.
ss. 28, 29, 33, repealed in pt.: 1986, c.21, s.4, sch. 2.
s. 44B, added: *ibid.*, s.2.
s. 55, repealed in pt.: *ibid.*, s.4, sch. 2.
s. 62, amended: *ibid.*, s.3.
s. 65, repealed in pt.: *ibid.*, s.4, sch. 2.
s. 69, amended: *ibid.*, s.4.
ss. 71, 71AA, amended: *ibid.*, sch. 1.
s. 71B, amended: *ibid.*, s.5; repealed in pt.: *ibid.*, sch. 2.
ss. 107, 108, 113, amended: *ibid.*, sch. 1.
s. 114, repealed: *ibid.*, s.6, sch. 2.
s. 120, repealed in pt.: *ibid.*, sch. 2.
s. 132, amended; *ibid.*, s.7.
s. 133A, amended: *ibid.*, sch. 1; repealed in pt.: *ibid.*, sch. 2.
s. 205, repealed in pt.: *ibid.*
s. 209, amended: *ibid.*, s.8.
s. 223, amended: *ibid.*, sch. 1.
sch. 3, repealed in pt.: *ibid.*, sch. 2.
sch. 5A, regs. 86/1241.
sch. 5A, amended: 1986, c.21, ss.9–11, sch. 1; repealed in pt.: *ibid.*, s.10, sch. 2.
sch. 6, amended: *ibid.*, sch. 1.

21. Crofters (Scotland) Act 1955.
s. 12, see *Fountain Forestry* v. *W. H. Ross*, 1985 S.L.C.R. 115.
s.16A, see *MacColl* v. *Crofters Commission*, 1985 S.L.C.R. 142.

3 & 4 Eliz. 2 (1954–55)—cont.

21. Crofters (Scotland) Act 1955—cont.
ss. 25, 26, see *Sikorski* v. *Noble*, 1985 S.L.C.R. 139.

27. Public Libraries (Scotland) Act 1955.
s. 1, repealed: S.L.R. 1986.

4 & 5 Eliz. 2 (1955–56)

6. Miscellaneous Financial Provisions Act 1955.
s. 5, repealed in pt.: S.L.R. 1986.

16. Food and Drugs Act 1955.
s. 2, see *R.* v. *Uxbridge JJ., ex p. Gow; R.* v. *Uxbridge JJ., ex p. Cooperative Retail Services* [1986] Crim.L.R. 177, D.C.; *Shearer* v. *Rowe* (1986) 84 L.G.R. 296, D.C.
ss. 2, 91, 92, 108, see *Arun District Council* v. *Argyle Stores* [1986] Crim.L.R. 685, D.C.
s. 135, see *Fleming* v. *Edwards, The Times*, March 15, 1986, D.C.

20. Agriculture (Improvement of Roads) Act 1955.
repealed: S.L.R. 1986.

23. Leeward Islands Act 1956.
repealed: S.L.R. 1986.

30. Food and Drugs (Scotland) Act 1956.
s. 4, regs. 86/789–791, 836, 1288.
s. 7, regs. 86/789, 790, 836, 1288.
s. 13, regs. 85/1856; 86/789, 790, 1808.
s. 26, regs. 86/836.
s. 56, regs. 85/1856; 86/789–791, 836, 1288, 1808.

49. Agriculture (Safety, Health and Welfare Provisions) Act 1956.
s. 24, amended: 1986, c.5, sch. 14.

52. Clean Air Act 1956.
s. 11, order 86/638.
ss. 33, 34, regs. 86/162, 892(S.), 1480.

54. Finance Act 1956.
s. 34, functions transferred: order 86/600.

60. Valuation and Rating (Scotland) Act 1956.
s. 7, see *Assessor for Tayside Region* v. *D. B. Marshall (Newbridge)*, 1983 S.C. 54.

62. Hotel Proprietors Act 1956.
see *Bradford City Metropolitan Council and Shellbridge Holdings* (Ref. T/APP/W4705/C/84/2296/P6) (1986) 1 P.A.D. 181.

63. British Caribbean Federation Act 1956.
repealed: S.L.R. 1986.

69. Sexual Offences Act 1956.
s. 13, see *Chief Constable of Hampshire* v. *Mace, The Times*, June 20, 1986, C.A.
s. 14, see *R.* v. *Court, The Times*, October 20, 1986, C.A.
ss. 14, 15, 46, see *R.* v. *Thomas (E.)* (1985) 81 Cr.App.R. 331, C.A.

74. Copyright Act 1956.
ss. 1, 18, see *Amstrad Consumer Electronics* v. *British Phonographic Industry* [1986] F.S.R. 159, C.A.
s. 4, see *Plix Products* v. *Winstone (Frank M.)* [1985] F.S.R. 63, H.Ct. of N.Z.

CAP.

4 & 5 Eliz. 2 (1955–56)—cont.

74. Copyright Act 1956—*cont.*
ss. 16, 18, 19, see *Columbia Picture Industries* v. *Robinson* [1986] F.S.R. 367, Scott J.
ss. 17, 18, see *Besson (A. P.)* v. *Fulleon and Amlani* [1986] F.S.R. 319, Harman J.
s. 21, see *CBS Songs* v. *Amstrad Consumer Electronics, The Times*, May 9, 1986, Whitford J.; *Amstrad Consumer Electronics* v. *British Phonographic Industry* [1986] F.S.R. 159, C.A.; *Reid* v. *Kennett* [1986] Crim.L.R. 456, D.C.: *Musa* v. *Le Maitre, The Times*, December 11, 1986, D.C.
ss. 31, 47, order 86/1299.
ss. 45, 46, see *Rickless* v. *United Artists Corp.* [1986] F.S.R. 502, Hobhouse J.
sch. 7, repealed in pt.: S.L.R. 1986.

5 & 6 Eliz. 2 (1957)

11. Homicide Act 1959.
s. 2, see *R.* v. *Campbell, The Times*, November 4, 1986, C.A.
s. 3, see *R.* v. *Doughty* [1986] Crim.L.R. 625, C.A.
16. Nurses Agencies Act 1957.
ss. 2, 7, regs. 86/1414.
36. Cheques Act 1957.
s. 4, see *Thackwell* v. *Barclays Bank* [1986] 1 All E.R. 676, Hutchison J.
48. Electricity Act 1957.
s. 33, repealed in pt.: 1986, c.63, sch. 12.
s. 34, amended: *ibid.*, s.44.
53. Naval Discipline Act 1957.
continued in force: 1986, c.21, s.1.
ss. 6, 11, 24, repealed in pt.: *ibid.*, s.4, sch. 2.
s. 29B, added: *ibid.*, s.2.
s. 33B, repealed in pt.: *ibid.*, s.4, sch. 2.
s. 35, amended: *ibid.*, s.3.
s. 36A, repealed in pt.: *ibid.*, s.4, sch. 2.
s. 38, amended: *ibid.*, sch. 1.
s. 39, amended: *ibid.*, s.4.
s. 42, repealed in pt.: *ibid.*, schs. 1, 2.
ss. 43, 43AA, amended: *ibid.*, sch. 1.
s. 43B, amended: *ibid.*, s.5; repealed in pt.: *ibid.*, sch. 2.
s. 52, amended: *ibid.*, s.7.
ss. 70, 117, 128A, 128D, amended: *ibid.*, sch. 1.
s. 128F, repealed in pt.: *ibid.*, sch. 2.
sch. 4, amended: *ibid.*, s.8.
sch. 4A, regs. 86/1241.
sch. 4A, amended: 1986, c.21, ss.10, 11, sch. 1; repealed in pt.: *ibid.*, s.10, sch. 2.
55. Affiliation Proceedings Act 1957.
s. 4, see *Turner* v. *Blunden* [1986] 2 W.L.R. 491, D.C.
56. Housing Act 1957.
see *R.* v. *Hillingdon London Borough Council, ex p. Pulhofer, The Times*, February 7, 1986, H.L.

CAP.

5 & 6 Eliz. 2 (1957)—cont.

56. Housing Act 1957—*cont.*
ss. 9, 11, 37, 39, see *Pollway Nominees* v. *Croydon London Borough Council* [1986] 2 All E.R. 849, H.L.
s. 27, see *Barber* v. *Shah* (1985) 17 H.L.R. 584, D.C.
s. 111, see *R.* v. *Secretary of State for Health and Social Security, ex p. Sheffield* (1985) 18 H.L.R. 6, Forbes J.
57. Agriculture Act 1957.
sch. 1, repealed in pt.: 1986, c.49, sch. 4.
59. Coal-Mining (Subsidence) Act 1957.
s. 10, amended: 1986, c.5, sch. 14.
s. 13, see *Knibb and Knibb* v. *National Coal Board* (1986) 26 R.V.R. 123, C.A.

6 & 7 Eliz. 2 (1957–58)

26. House of Commons (Redistribution of Seats) Act 1958.
repealed: 1986, c.56, sch. 4.
32. Opticians Act 1958.
sch., order 86/309.
39. Maintenance Orders Act 1958.
s. 4, see *Berry* v. *Berry* [1986] 3 W.L.R. 257, C.A.
s. 18, see *R.* v. *Cardiff JJ., ex p. Salter* (1986) 1 F.L.R. 162, Wood J.; *R.* v. *Horseferry Road Magistrates' Court, ex p. Bernstein, The Times*, November 4, 1986, Arnold J.
40. Matrimonial Proceedings (Children) Act 1958.
s. 7, repealed; 1986, c.9, sch. 2.
s. 8, amended: 1986, c.55, sch. 1; repealed in pt.: 1986, c.9, sch. 2.
s. 9, amended (S.): *ibid.*, sch. 1.
ss. 9, 10, amended: 1986, c.55, sch. 1.
s. 11, amended: *ibid.*, sch. 1; repealed in pt.: 1986, c.9, sch. 2.
s. 13, repealed: 1986, c.55, sch. 2.
s. 14, repealed: 1986, c.9, sch. 2.
44. Dramatic and Musical Performers' Protection Act 1958.
see *Rickless* v. *United Artists Corporation, The Times*, December 12, 1986, C.A.
45. Prevention of Fraud (Investments) Act 1958.
repealed: 1986, c.60, sch. 17.
47. Agricultural Marketing Act 1958.
s. 2, amended: 1986, c.49, sch. 3.
s. 2, sch. 1, order 86/83.
sch. 1, amended: 1986, c.49, s.11.
sch. 2, amended: 1986, c.45, sch. 14.
51. Public Records Act 1958.
s. 2, regs. 86/697.
53. Variation of Trusts Act 1958.
s. 1, see *Knocker* v. *Youle* [1986] 1 W.L.R. 934, Warner J.
64. Local Government and Miscellaneous Financial Provisions (Scotland) Act 1958.
sch. 4, repealed in pt.: S.L.R. 1986.
67. Water Act 1958.
repealed: S.L.R. 1986.

CAP.

6 & 7 Eliz. 2 (1957–58)—cont.

69. Opencast Coal Act 1958.
ss. 1, 2, repealed: 1986, c.63, s.39, sch. 12.
s. 3, substituted: *ibid.*, sch. 8.
ss. 4, 5, amended: *ibid.*
s. 9, repealed in pt.: *ibid.*, s.39, sch. 12.
s. 13, amended: *ibid.*
ss. 14, 14A, 15, 15A, substituted: *ibid.*
s. 16, amended: *ibid.*
s. 18, amended: *ibid.*; repealed in pt.: *ibid.*, sch. 12.
ss. 24–28, amended: 1986, c.5, sch. 14.
s. 38, amended: 1986, c.63, sch. 8.
s. 39, amended: *ibid.*; repealed in pt.: *ibid.*, sch. 12.
s. 45, amended: *ibid.*, sch. 8.
s. 46, repealed in pt.: *ibid.*, sch. 12.
s. 48, repealed: *ibid.*
s. 51, amended: 1986, c.5, sch. 14; c.63, sch. 8; repealed in pt.: 1986, c.44, sch. 9; c.63, sch. 12.
s. 52, amended: *ibid.*, sch. 8.
s. 53, repealed in pt.: *ibid.*, sch. 12.
sch. 1, repealed: *ibid.*
sch. 2, amended: *ibid.*, sch. 8.
schs. 6, 7, amended: 1986, c.5, sch. 14; c.63, sch. 8.
schs. 9 (in pt.), 10, repealed: *ibid.*, sch. 12.

71. Agriculture Act 1958.
ss. 4, 9 (in pt.), schs. 1 (in pt.), 4 (in pt.), repealed: 1986, c.5, sch. 15.

7 & 8 Eliz. 2 (1958–59)

5. Adoption Act 1958.
s. 29, see *Gatehouse* v. *R.* [1986] 1 W.L.R. 18, D.C.
s. 34, see *T. (A Minor) (Adoption: Parental Consent), Re* [1986] 1 All E.R. 817, C.A.

12. Agriculture (Small Farmers) Act 1959.
repealed: S.L.R. 1986.

24. Building (Scotland) Act 1959.
s. 3, regs. 86/1278.
s. 3, amended: 1986, c.65, s.19.
s. 4B, substituted: *ibid.*
s. 6AA, added: *ibid.*
s. 9, amended: *ibid.*
s. 13, see *City of Edinburgh District Council* v. *Co-operative Wholesale Society*, 1986 S.L.T. (Sh.Ct.) 57.
s. 17, amended: 1986, c.65, sch. 2.
s. 20, substituted: *ibid.*
sch. 4, regs. 86/1278.

49. Chevening Estate Act 1959.
sch., amended: 1986, c.5, sch. 14.

52. Town and Country Planning Act 1959.
s. 26, see *Freeman* v. *Plymouth City Council, The Times*, March 11, 1986, Hodgson J.

72. Mental Health Act 1959.
s. 90, see *R.* v. *Secretary of State for the Home Department, ex p. Alghali, The Times*, July 22, 1986, D.C.

73. Legitimacy Act 1959.
s. 2, see *Dunbar of Kilconzie, Petr.*, 1986 S.L.T. 463, H.L.

CAP.

8 & 9 Eliz. 2 (1959–60)

1. Mr. Speaker Morrison's Retirement Act 1959.
repealed: S.L.R. 1986.

22. Horticulture Act 1960.
s. 1, amended: 1986, c.5, sch. 14.

34. Radioactive Substances Act 1960.
s. 2, order 86/1002; S.R.s 1986 Nos. 10–12.
s. 4, S.R. 1986 No. 12.
ss. 6, 7, order 86/1002; S.R.s 1986 Nos. 10–12.
s. 21, S.R.s 1986 Nos. 10–12.
sch. 1, amended: 1986, c.36, sch. 7.
sch. 1, amended (S.): *ibid.*

37. Payment of Wages Act 1960.
repealed: 1986, c.48, schs. 1, 5.
ss. 1, 2, 7, amended: 1986, c.53, sch. 18.

42. Merchant Shipping (Minicoy Lighthouse) Act 1960.
repealed: S.L.R. 1986.

52. Cyprus Act 1960.
sch., repealed in pt.: 1986, c.55, sch. 2.

55. Nigeria Independence Act 1960.
sch. 2, repealed in pt.: 1986, c.55, sch. 2.

58. Charities Act 1960.
s. 9, amended: 1986, c.41, s.33.
s. 19, order 86/2003.
s. 22, amended: 1986, c.60, sch. 16; repealed in pt.: *ibid.*, schs. 16, 17.
s. 28, see *Brooks* v. *Richardson* [1986] 1 W.L.R. 385, Warner J.
s. 30, amended: 1986, c.45, sch. 14.
sch. 2, amended: order 86/452.
sch. 6, repealed in pt.: S.L.R. 1986.

62. Caravan Sites and Control of Development Act 1960.
see *R.* v. *Beaconsfield JJ., ex p. Stubbings, The Times*, May 7, 1986, D.C.
ss. 1, 3, see *Balthasar* v. *Mullane* (1986) 84 L.G.R. 55, C.A.
s. 24, see *West Glamorgan County Council* v. *Rafferty: R.* v. *Secretary of State for Wales, ex p. Gilhaney, The Times*, June 4, 1986, C.A.

64. Building Societies Act 1960.
ss. 72, 73 (in pt.), 77, sch. 5 (in pt.), repealed: 1986, c.53, sch. 19.

65. Administration of Justice Act 1960.
s. 13, see *Linnett* v. *Coles* [1986] 3 W.L.R. 843, D.C.

66. Professions Supplementary to Medicine Act 1960.
s. 2, order 86/660.
s. 10, order 86/630.

9 & 10 Eliz. 2 (1960–61)

16. Sierra Leone Independence Act 1961.
sch. 3, repealed in pt.: 1986, c.55, sch. 2.

27. Carriage by Air Act 1961.
s. 4, order 86/1778.
sch. 1, see *Swiss Bank Corp.* v. *Brink's-MAT* [1986] 2 All E.R. 188, Bingham J.

31. Printer's Imprint Act 1961.
s. 1, amended: 1986, c.39, sch. 2.

CAP.

9 & 10 Eliz. 2 (1960–61)—cont.

33. Land Compensation Act 1961.
s. 5, see *Harrison & Hetherington* v. *Cumbria County Council* (1985) 50 P. & C.R. 396, H.L.; *Palatine Graphic Art Co.* v. *Liverpool City Council* [1986] 2 W.L.R. 285, C.A.
s. 20, order 86/435.

34. Factories Act 1961.
s. 5, see *Davis* v. *Massey Ferguson Perkins* [1986] I.C.R. 580, Evans J.
s. 14, see *TBA Industrial Products* v. *Laine, The Times*, June 23, 1986, D.C.
s. 28, see *Allen* v. *Avon Rubber Co., The Times*, May 20, 1986, C.A.
ss. 28, 29, see *Hemmings* v. *British Aerospace*, May 2, 1986, Swinton-Thomas J., Bristol.
s. 29, see *Darby* v. *G.K.N. Screws and Fasteners* [1986] I.C.R. 1, Pain J.; *Allen* v. *Avon Rubber Co., The Times*, May 20, 1986, C.A.; *Davies* v. *Massey Ferguson Perkins* [1986] I.C.R. 580, Evans J.
ss. 86, 88, 89, repealed in pt.: 1986, c.59, s.7, sch.
s. 90, repealed in pt.: *ibid.*, sch.
ss. 91–94, repealed in pt.: *ibid.*, s.7, sch.
ss. 95, 96 (in pt.)–102 (in pt.), 106 (in pt.)–109 (in pt.), 110, 111, 112 (in pt.)–115 (in pt.), repealed: *ibid.*, sch.
ss. 135, 135A, repealed: 1986, c.48, schs. 1, 5.
sch. 6, repealed in pt.: S.L.R. 1986.

36. Finance Act 1961.
s. 34, repealed: 1986, c.41, sch. 23.

39. Criminal Justice Act 1961.
s. 22, see *Nicoll* v. *Catron* (1985) 81 Cr.App.R. 339, D.C.
s. 29, see *R.* v. *Secretary of State for the Home Department, ex p. Greenwood, The Times*, August 2, 1986, Macpherson J.

54. Human Tissue Act 1961.
s. 1, amended: 1986, c.18, s.1.

62. Trustee Investments Act 1961.
s. 11, amended: 1986, c.60, sch. 16.
s. 12, order 86/601.
sch. 1, amended: 1986, c.53, schs. 18, 19; c.60, sch. 16.

64. Public Health Act 1961.
see *Investors in Industry Commercial Properties* v. *South Bedfordshire District Council, The Times*, December 31, 1985, C.A.
s. 4, see *Hertsmere Borough Council* v. *Dunn (Alan) Building Contractors* (1985) 84 L.G.R. 214, D.C.
s. 17, see *Rotherham Metropolitan Borough Council* v. *Dodds* [1986] 2 All E.R. 867, C.A.

65. Housing Act 1961.
ss. 15, 19, see *R.* v. *Hackney London Borough Council, ex p. Thrasyvoulou, The Times*, May 30, 1986, C.A.

CAP.

9 & 10 Eliz. 2 (1960–61)—cont.

65. Housing Act 1961—cont.
s. 32, see *Fraser* v. *Hopewood Properties*, October 29, 1985: H.H. Judge Parker: West London County Ct.
ss. 32, 33, see *Department of Transport* v. *Egoroff* (1986) 278 E.G. 1361, C.A.

10 & 11 Eliz 2 (1961–62)

1. Tanganyika Independence Act 1961.
sch. 2, repealed in pt.: 1986, c.55, sch. 2.

9. Local Government (Financial Provisions, etc.) (Scotland) Act 1962.
s. 5, repealed: S.L.R. 1986.

12. Education Act 1962.
see *R.* v. *Hertfordshire County Council, ex p. Cheung; R.* v. *Sefton Metropolitan Borough Council, ex p. Pau, The Times*, April 4, 1986, C.A.
s. 1, see *R.* v. *West Glamorgan County Council, ex p. Gheissary; R.* v. *East Sussex County Council, ex p. Khatibshahidi, The Times*, December 18, 1985, Hodgson J.; *R.* v. *Lancashire County Council, ex p. Huddleston* [1986] 2 All E.R. 941, C.A.
s. 1, regs. 86/1306, 1397.
s. 3, regs. 86/1324, 1346.
s. 3, repealed in pt.: 1986, c.61, sch. 6.
s. 4, regs. 86/1306, 1324, 1346, 1397.
s. 4, amended: 1986, c.61, sch. 4; repealed in pt.: *ibid.*, sch. 6.
sch. 1, regs. 86/1306.

19. West Indies Act 1962.
s. 5, order 86/1157.

23. South Africa Act 1962.
sch. 3, repealed in pt.: 1986, c.55, sch. 2.
sch. 4, repealed in pt.: 1986, c.60, sch. 17.

35. Shops (Airports) Act 1962.
s. 1, order 86/981.
s. 1, amended: 1986, c.31, s.70.

37. Building Societies Act 1962.
repealed: 1986, c.53, sch. 19.
s. 25, see *Martin* v. *Bell-Ingram*, 1986 S.L.T. 575.
s. 58, order 86/406.
s. 123, regs. 86/609.
sch. 3, repealed in pt. (S.): 1986, c.65, sch. 3.

40. Jamaica Independence Act 1962.
sch. 2, repealed in pt.: 1986, c.55, sch. 2.

54. Trinidad and Tobago Independence Act 1962.
sch. 2, repealed in pt.: 1986, c.55, sch.2.

56. Local Government (Records) Act 1962.
s. 2, order 86/803.

57. Uganda Independence Act 1962.
sch. 3, repealed in pt.: 1986, c.55, sch. 2.

58. Pipe-lines Act 1962.
s. 57, see *BP Development, Re, Financial Times*, February 26, 1986, Warner J.
s. 58, amended: 1986, c.44, sch. 7.
s. 66, repealed in pt.: *ibid.*, sch. 9.
s. 67, repealed in pt.: S.L.R. 1986.

11 Eliz. 2 (1962)

4. Foreign Compensation Act 1962.
s. 3, order 86/219.

1963

2. Betting, Gaming and Lotteries Act 1963.
s. 10, regs. 86/103, 120(S.).
s. 55, regs. 86/120(S.).

11. Agriculture (Miscellaneous Provisions) Act 1963.
ss. 4, 5, 9, 10, 12, repealed: S.L.R. 1986.
s. 20, repealed in pt.: 1986, c.5, sch. 15.
s. 22, amended: *ibid.*, sch. 14.

12. Local Government (Financial Provisions) (Scotland) Act 1963.
s. 9, order 86/140; regs. 86/407.
s. 19, see *Trustees of Paisley Golf Club* v. *Assessor for Strathclyde Region*, 1986 S.L.T. 493; *Hamilton District Council* v. *Assessor for Strathclyde Region*, 1986 S.L.T. 370; *East Kilbride Sports Club* v. *Assessor for Strathclyde Region*, 1986 S.L.T. 379.

18. Stock Transfer Act 1963.
s. 1, amended: 1986, c.53, sch. 18; c.60, sch. 16.

24. British Museum Act 1963.
ss. 1, 10, functions transferred: order 86/600.

25. Finance Act 1963.
s. 55, amended: 1986, c.41, s.64.
s. 59, amended: *ibid.*, s.65.
s. 62, repealed in pt.: *ibid.*, s.79, sch. 23.
ss. 71 (in pt.), 73 (in pt.), schs. 12, 14 (in pt.): S.L.R. 1986.

31. Weights and Measures Act 1963.
s. 11, see *Evans* v. *Clifton Inns, The Times*, March 18, 1986, D.C.
ss. 14, 24, 26, see *North Yorkshire County Council* v. *Holmesterne Farm Co.* (1985) 150 J.P.N. 111, D.C.
s. 22, sch. 6, see *Church* v. *Lee & Co-operative Retail Services*, (1986) 150 J.P.N. 335, D.C.

33. London Government Act 1963.
ss. 4, 8, repealed in pt.: 1986, c.56, sch. 4.
s. 23, see *Fleming* v. *Wandsworth London Borough Council, The Times*, December 23, 1985, C.A.; *R.* v. *Secretary of State for the Environment, ex p. Newham London Borough Council, The Times*, December 23, 1985, Taylor J.
s. 31, repealed in pt.: 1986, c.61, sch. 6.
ss. 84, 85, order 86/918.
sch. 3, repealed in pt.: 1986, c.56, sch. 4.

34. Children and Young Persons Act 1963.
sch. 3, repealed in pt.: S.L.R. 1986.

38. Water Resources Act 1963.
s. 67, order 86/1575.
s. 93, repealed in pt.: S.L.R. 1986.
s. 133, orders 86/58, 1670.
ss. 134, 137, repealed in pt.: S.L.R. 1986.

1963—cont.

41. Offices, Shops and Railway Premises Act 1963.
s. 16, see *Mackay* v. *Dryborough & Co.* 1986 S.L.T. 624.

54. Kenya Independence Act 1963.
s. 7, repealed: 1986, c.55, sch. 2.

1964

7. Shipbuilding Credit Act 1964.
repealed: S.L.R. 1986.

14. Plant Varieties and Seeds Act 1964.
s. 9, regs. 86/339.
s. 16, regs. 86/338, 1114.
s. 16, amended: 1986, c.49, s.2.
s. 36, regs. 86/339.

24. Trade Union (Amalgamations, etc.) Act 1964.
s. 7, regs. 86/302.

26. Licensing Act 1964.
ss. 8, 10, amended: 1986, c.45, sch. 14.
s. 87, orders 86/525, 971.
s. 169, see *Woby* v. *B. and O.* [1986] Crim.L.R. 183, D.C.

28. Agriculture and Horticulture Act 1964.
ss. 19, 20, repealed in pt.: 1986, c.20, s.7.

40. Harbours Act 1964.
s. 14, orders 86/124, 137, 301, 1038(S.), 1626.
sch. 3, repealed in pt.: 1986, c.44, sch. 9.

41. Succession (Scotland) Act 1964.
ss. 4, 6 (in pt.), 9 (in pt.), 10A, 11 (in pt.), 13 (in pt.), repealed: 1986, c.9, sch. 2.
s. 30, see *Marshall* v. *Marshall's Exr.* (O.H.), 1987 S.L.T. 49.
ss. 33, 36, amended: 1986, c.9, sch. 1; repealed in pt.: *ibid.*, sch. 2.

46. Malawi Independence Act 1964.
s. 6, repealed: 1986, c.55, sch. 2.

48. Police Act 1964.
s. 15, see *Harris* v. *Sheffield United Football Club, The Times*, April 4, 1986, Boreham J.
s. 31, order 86/455.
s. 33, regs. 86/784, 2032.
s. 35, regs. 86/2033.
s. 37, see *Calveley* v. *Merseyside Police* [1986] I.R.L.R. 177, C.A.
s. 44, regs. 86/1846.
ss. 48, 49, see *Peach* v. *Comr. of Police for the Metropolis* [1986] 2 All E.R. 129, C.A.
s. 51, see *Liepins* v. *Spearman* [1986] R.T.R. 24, D.C.; *Bennett* v. *Bale* [1986] Crim.L.R. 404, D.C.; *Smith* v. *Reynolds* [1986] Crim.L.R. 559, D.C.; *Smith* v. *Hancock* [1986] Crim.L.R. 560, D.C.; *Smith* v. *Lowe* [1986] Crim.L.R. 561, D.C.; *Weight* v. *Long* [1986] Crim.L.R. 746, D.C.

51. Universities and College Estates Act 1964.
sch. 3, repealed in pt.: 1986, c.5, sch. 15.

60. Emergency Laws (Re-enactments and Repeals) Act 1964.
ss. 4, 7, regs. 85/1932.

CAP.
1964—cont.

65. Zambia Independence Act 1964.
s. 7, repealed: 1986, c.55, sch. 2.

75. Public Libraries and Museums Act 1964.
functions transferred: order 86/600.
see *R.* v. *Ealing, Hammersmith and Fulham, and Camden London Borough Councils, ex p. Times Newspapers, The Times*, November 6, 1986, D.C.
s. 2, amended: order 86/600.

92. Finance (No. 2) Act 1964.
repealed: S.L.R. 1986.

1965

2. Administration of Justice Act 1965.
s. 7, rules 86/1142.
s. 14, sch. 1, repealed in pt.: 1986, c.60, sch. 17.

3. Remuneration of Teachers Act 1965.
s. 2, orders 86/176, 559.
s. 7, order 86/559.
s. 8, amended: 1986, c.1, s. 2.

12. Industrial and Provident Societies Act 1965.
s. 31, amended: 1986, c.53, sch. 18.
s. 55, amended: 1986, c.45, sch. 14.
ss. 70, 71, regs. 86/621, 622.

14. Cereals Marketing Act 1965.
s. 1, amended: 1986, c.49, s.4, sch. 3.
ss. 2–5, repealed: *ibid.*, s.4, sch. 4.
s, 6, amended: *ibid.*, s.4.
s. 7, amended: *ibid.*, sch. 3.
Pt. II, repealed: *ibid.*, s.4, sch. 4.
s. 12, repealed in pt.: *ibid.*, sch. 4.
s. 13, order 86/138.
ss. 13 (in pt.), 14, 15, repealed: 1986, c.49, sch. 4.
s. 16, amended: *ibid.*, s.5, sch. 3.
ss. 18, 19, repealed in pt.: *ibid.*, sch. 4.
s. 20, amended: *ibid.*, s.5.
s. 23, repealed in pt.: *ibid.*, sch. 4.
s. 24, amended: *ibid.*, ss.5, 6; repealed in pt.: *ibid.*, s.5, sch. 4.
sch. 1, amended: *ibid.*, s.4, sch. 3.
sch. 2, repealed: *ibid.*, sch. 4.
sch. 3, amended: 1986, c.49, s.5, sch. 3; repealed in pt.: *ibid.*, sch. 4.

17. Museum of London Act 1965.
functions transferred: order 86/600.
s. 1, repealed in pt.: 1986, c.8, sch.
ss. 3, 8, substituted: *ibid.*, s. 2.
s. 9, amended: *ibid.*
s. 13, repealed: *ibid.*, sch.
s. 14, amended: *ibid.*, s. 4; repealed in pt.: *ibid.*, sch.
s. 15, amended: *ibid.*, s. 3.

19. Teaching Council (Scotland) Act 1965.
s. 5, regs. 86/1353.

24. Severn Bridge Tolls Act 1965.
ss. 1, 3, 4, sch. 2, see *R.* v. *Secretary of State for Transport, ex p. Gwent County Council* [1986] 2 All E.R. 18, Webster J.

CAP.
1965—cont.

25. Finance Act 1965.
s. 22, see *Kirby* v. *Thorn E.M.I* [1986] 1 W.L.R. 851, Ch.D.; [1986] S.T.C. 200, Knox J.
s. 56, see *Elliss* v. *B.P. Oil Northern Ireland Refinery; Elliss* v. *B.P. Tyne Tanker Co., The Times*, December 16, 1986, C.A.
schs. 1–4, repealed: S.L.R. 1986.
sch. 6, see *Passant* v. *Jackson* [1986] S.T.C. 164, C.A.
sch. 7, see *Westcott* v. *Woolcombers* [1986] S.T.C. 182, Hoffman J.; *Powlson* v. *Welbeck Securities* [1986] S.T.C. 423, Hoffman J.

32. Administration of Estates (Small Payments) Act 1965.
s. 6, repealed in pt.: S.L.R. 1986.
schs. 1, 3, repealed in pt.: 1986, c.53, sch. 19.

33. Control of Office and Industrial Development Act 1965.
repealed: S.L.R. 1986.

36. Gas Act 1965.
s. 4, repealed in pt.: 1986, c.44, schs. 7, 9.
Pt. II (ss. 4–28), amended: *ibid.*, sch. 7.
ss. 5, 6, 13, 15–17, 19, amended: *ibid.*
s. 21, amended and repealed in pt.: *ibid.*
ss. 22, 27, amended: *ibid.*
s. 28, amended: *ibid.*; repealed in pt.: *ibid.*, schs. 7, 9.
s. 32, schs. 2, 6, amended: *ibid.*, sch. 7.

37. Carriage of Goods by Road Act 1965.
s. 1, sch., see *Arctic Electronics Co. (U.K.)* v. *McGregor Sea and Air Services* [1986] R.T.R. 207, Hobhouse J.
ss. 9, 12, order 86/1882.

45. Backing of Warrants (Republic of Ireland) Act 1965.
s. 2, see *Simpson* v. *McLeod*, 1986 S.C.C.R. 237.
s. 8, repealed in pt.: S.L.R. 1986.

46. Highlands and Islands Development (Scotland) Act 1965.
s. 1, order 86/1956.

49. Registration of Births, Deaths and Marriages (Scotland) Act 1965.
s. 14, amended: 1986, c.9, sch. 1.
s. 18, amended: *ibid.*; repealed in pt.: *ibid.*, sch. 2.
s. 18A, added: *ibid.*, sch. 1.
s. 20, amended: *ibid.*
s. 28A, regs. 85/2005; 86/21.
s. 32, regs. 82/21.
ss. 37, 38, 40, 43, regs. 85/1890.
s. 43, amended: 1986, c.9, sch. 1; repealed in pt.: *ibid.*, sch. 2.
s. 47, regs. 85/1890.
s. 54, regs. 85/1890, 2005; 86/21.
s. 56, amended: 1986, c.9, sch. 1.

51. National Insurance Act 1965.
s. 110, regs. 86/24.

55. Statute Law Revision (Consequential Repeals) Act 1965.
repealed: 1986, c.50, sch. 11.

1965—cont.

56. Compulsory Purchase Act 1965.
s. 30, see *Fagan* v. *Knowsley Metropolitan Borough Council* (1985) 50 P. & C.R. 363, C.A.
s. 36, order 86/1575.

57. Nuclear Installations Act 1965.
s. 28, order 86/2018.

1966

9. Rating Act 1966.
repealed: S.L.R. 1986.

19. Law Reform (Miscellaneous Provisions) (Scotland) Act 1966.
s. 8, amended: 1986, c.55, sch. 1; repealed in pt.: *ibid.*, sch. 2.

20. Supplementary Benefit Act 1966.
s. 26, repealed: 1986, c.50, sch. 11.

29. Singapore Act 1966.
s. 2, repealed: 1986, c.55, sch. 2.

34. Industrial Development Act 1966.
sch. 2, repealed in pt.: 1986, c.31, sch. 6.

36. Veterinary Surgeons Act 1966.
s. 19, amended: 1986, c.14, sch. 3.

38. Sea Fish Regulation Act 1966.
s. 1, orders 86/647, 648, 1201.
s. 2, order 86/1201.
s. 18, order 86/647, 1201.

42. Local Government Act 1966.
ss. 35, 40, sch. 3, order 85/2027.
sch. 5, repealed in pt.: 1986, c.61, sch. 6.

45. Armed Forces Act 1966.
s. 2, regs. 86/2072–2074.
s. 29, repealed: 1986, c.21, sch. 2.

51. Local Government (Scotland) Act 1966.
s. 2, order 86/140.
ss. 3, 4, orders 86/140, 1965.
s. 5, see *Lord Advocate* v. *Stirling District Council,* 1986 S.L.T. 179.
s. 15, see *Assessor for Borders Region* v. *A.M.S. Leisure,* 1986 S.L.T. 689.
s. 18, amended: 1986, c.44, sch. 7.
s. 25, regs. 86/342.
s. 42, order 85/2054.
s. 45, orders 85/2054; 86/140, 1965.
sch. 1, order 86/140, 1965.
sch. 4, order 85/2054.

1967

4. West Indies Act 1967.
repealed, except ss. 6, 8, 17 (in pt.), 19, 21: S.L.R. 1986.
s. 13, amended: order 86/948.

7. Misrepresentation Act 1967.
s. 2, see *Highland Insurance Company* v. *Continental Insurance Company, The Times,* May 6, 1986, Steyn J.

8. Plant Health Act 1967.
s. 2, orders 86/195, 196, 1135.
s. 3, orders 86/194–197, 476, 1135, 1342.
s. 4A, added: 1986, c.49, s.3.
s. 5, order 86/1342.

1967—cont.

9. General Rate Act 1967.
ss. 1–5, 11, 12, 50, see *Smith* v. *Skinner: Gladden* v. *McMahon* (1986) 26 R.V.R. 45, D.C.
ss. 6, 7, see *Trendworthy Two* v. *Islington London Borough* (1985) 277 E.G. 539, Mervyn Davies J.
s. 7, see *Investors in Industry Commerical Properties* v. *Norwich City Council* [1986] 2 W.L.R. 925, H.L.
ss. 7, 9, see *Rialto Builders* v. *Barnet London Borough Council* (1986) 26 R.V.R. 120, Wood Green Crown Court.
ss. 12, 14, rules 86/1236.
s. 19, amended: 1986, c.44, sch. 7; repealed in pt.: *ibid.*, sch. 9.
s. 26, see *Hemens (Valuation Officer)* v. *Whitsbury Farm and Stud, The Times,* November 10, 1986, C.A.
s. 33, order 86/1365.
s. 33, substituted: 1986, c.44, sch. 7.
s. 33A, added: *ibid.*
s. 79, see *MacFarquhar* v. *Phillimore; Marks* v. *Phillimore* (1986) 279 E.G. 584, C.A.
s. 97, see *Ratford* v. *Northavon District Council* [1986] 3 All E.R. 193, C.A.
ss. 102, 103, see *R.* v. *Lambeth Borough Council, ex p. Sterling (Ahijah)* (1986) 26 R.V.R. 27, C.A.
s. 113, rules 86/1236.
s. 114, rules 86/1236; order 86/1365.
sch. 1, see *Trendworthy Two* v. *Islington London Borough* (1985) 277 E.G. 539, Mervyn Davies J.; *London Merchant Securities* v. *Islington London Borough Council, The Times,* March 29, 1986, C.A.; *Debenhams* v. *Westminster City Council* (1986) 83 L.S.Gaz. 1479; (1986) 278 E.G. 974, C.A.; *Investors in Industry Commercial Properties* v. *Norwich City Council* [1986] 2 W.L.R 925, H.L.; *London Merchant Securities* v. *Islington London Borough Council* [1986] R.A. 81, C.A.; *Rialto Builders* v. *Barnet London Borough Council* (1986) 26 R.V.R. 120, Wood Green Crown Court; *Hailbury Investments* v. *Westminster City Council* [1986] 1 W.L.R. 1232, H.L.; *Trendworthy Two* v. *Islington London Borough Council* (1986) 26 R.V.R. 15, Michael Wheeler, Q.C.
sch. 3, amended: 1986, c.44, sch. 7.
sch. 6, substituted: *ibid.*
sch. 10, see *Smith* v. *Skinner; Gladden* v. *McMahon* (1986) 26 R.V.R. 45, D.C.

10. Forestry Act 1967.
s. 9, regs. 85/1958.
s. 17, see *Cullen* v. *Jardine* [1985] Crim.L.R. 668, D.C.
ss. 17A–17C, added: 1986, c.30, s.1.
s. 27, amended: *ibid.*
s. 32, regs. 85/1958.
s. 35, amended: 1986, c.30, s.1.
s. 40, repealed in pt.: 1986, c.44, sch. 9.

CAP.
1967—cont.

13. Parliamentary Commissioner Act 1967.
s. 4, order 86/1889.
s. 5, order 86/1168.
sch. 2, amended: order 86/600; 1986, c.44,
sch. 1; c.53, sch. 1; c.57, sch.
sch. 3, amended: order 86/1168.

22. Agriculture Act 1967.
s. 1, amended: 1986, c.49, s.7.
ss. 10–12, repealed: S.L.R. 1986.
s. 13, amended: 1986, c.49, s.7; repealed
in pt.: *ibid.*, s.7, sch. 4.
s. 26, amended: 1986, c.5, sch. 14,
repealed in pt.: S.L.R. 1986.
ss. 27–29, amended: 1986, c.5, sch. 14.
ss. 43, 44, repealed: S.L.R. 1986.
s. 48, amended: 1986, c.5, sch. 14.
s. 61, order 86/817.
s. 61, amended: *ibid.*; repealed in pt.:
S.L.R. 1986.
s. 62, order 86/817; amended: *ibid.*
s. 69, repealed in pt.: S.L.R. 1986.
sch. 3, amended: 1986, c.5, sch. 14.

24. Slaughter of Poultry Act 1967.
s. 1, amended: 1986, c.14, sch. 3.
s. 2, see *Malins* v. *Cole & Attard*, Knightsbridge Crown Court.

32. Development of Inventions Act 1967.
s. 1, sch., regs. 86/431.

**41. Marine, etc., Broadcasting (Offences) Act
1967.**
s. 3, amended: order 86/948.

43. Legal Aid (Scotland) Act 1967.
repealed: 1986, c.47, sch. 5.
s. 2, regs. 85/1859.
s. 3, regs. 85/1859; 86/1358.
s. 4, regs. 86/253, 254.
s. 14A, regs. 86/673, 674, 681.
s. 15, regs. 85/1859, 1860, 86/673, 674, 681,
1154, 1358, 1359.

47. Decimal Currency Act 1967.
repealed: S.L.R. 1986.

**48. Industrial and Provident Societies Act
1967.**
s. 7, regs. 86/621, 622.

54. Finance Act 1967.
s. 29, repealed: 1986, c.41, s.79, sch. 23.
s. 40, orders 86/1181, 1832.

58. Criminal Law Act 1967.
s. 2, see *Ward* v. *Chief Constable of Avon
and Somerset Constabulary, The Times,*
June 26, 1986, C.A.; *Houghton* v. *Chief
Constable of Greater Manchester, The
Times,* July 24, 1986, C.A.
s. 3, see *R.* v. *Renouf* [1986] 1 W.L.R.
522, C.A.
s. 4, see *R.* v. *Donald and Donald* [1986]
Crim.L.R. 535, C.A.
s. 6, see *R.* v. *Saunders* [1986] 1 W.L.R.
1163, C.A..
s. 11, sch. 2, repealed in pt.: 1986, c.64,
sch. 3.

65. Antarctic Treaty Act 1967.
s. 1, amended: order 86/948.

CAP.
1967—cont.

66. Welsh Language Act 1967.
s. 2, rules 86/1079; regs. 86/1445, 1460.
s. 3, regs. 86/1445.

68. Fugitive Offenders Act 1967.
s. 2, order 86/2022.

75. Matrimonial Homes Act 1967.
s. 2, see *Baggott* v. *Baggott* (1986) 16
Fam.Law 129, C.A.

76. Road Traffic Regulation Act 1967.
ss. 71, 72, 78A, see *Spittle* v. *Kent County
Constabulary* [1986] R.T.R. 142, D.C.
s. 85, see *Lowe* v. *Lester* [1986] Crim.L.R.
339, D.C.

77. Police (Scotland) Act 1967.
s. 26, regs. 86/576.
s. 27, regs. 86/121.
s. 32, order 86/390.
s. 41, see *Kinney* v. *Tudhope,* 1985
S.C.C.R. 393.

80. Criminal Justice Act 1967.
s. 10, see *R.* v. *Horseferry Road Metropolitan Stipendiary Magistrate, ex p.
O'Regan, The Times,* May 17, 1986,
D.C.
ss. 60, 62, see *R.* v. *McKinnon (William
Harold), The Times,* November 26,
1986.
s. 67, see *R.* v. *McIntyre* (1985) 7
Cr.App.R.(S.) 196, C.A.

83. Sea Fisheries (Shellfish) Act 1967.
s. 1, order 86/1896, 1901.

84. Sea Fish (Conservation) Act 1967.
s. 1, order 86/497.
s. 4, orders 86/1438, 1439.
s. 5, orders 86/988, 1115, 1620, 1936, 1982.
s. 6, orders 86/496, 1437.
s. 15, orders 86/497, 988, 1115, 1437–1439,
1620, 1936, 1982.
s. 20, orders 86/497, 988, 1437–1439.

86. Countryside (Scotland) Act 1967.
s. 60, repealed in pt.: S.L.R. 1986.

88. Leasehold Reform Act 1967.
see *James* v. *U.K.* (1986) 26 R.V.R. 139,
European Ct. of Human Rights.
s. 1, see *MacFarquhar* v. *Phillimore;
Marks* v. *Phillimore* (1986) 27 E.G. 584,
C.A.
s. 1, amended: 1986, c.5, sch. 14; c.63,
sch. 4.
s. 3, amended: *ibid.*
s. 4, see *Johnston* v. *Duke of Westminster*
[1986] 3 W.L.R. 18, H.L.
s. 9, see *Mosley* v. *Hickman; Same* v.
Hagan; Same v. *Francis* (1986) 278 E.G.
728, C.A.
ss. 9, 23, amended: 1986, c.63, s.23.
s. 33A, sch. 4, added: *ibid.*, sch. 4.

1968

2. Provisional Collection of Taxes Act 1968.
s. 1, amended: 1986, c.41, s.86.

3. Capital Allowances Act 1968.
s. 14, amended: 1986, c.41, s.56, sch. 13.
ss. 51–66, repealed: *ibid.*, sch. 23.

CAP.
1968—cont.

3. Capital Allowances Act 1968—*cont.*
s. 68, repealed: *ibid.*, s.56, sch. 23; substituted: *ibid.*, s.56.
s. 69, amended: *ibid.*
ss. 70, 74, 75, 78, 79, 83, repealed in pt.: *ibid.*, sch. 23.
s. 84, order 86/539.
s. 85, amended: 1986, c.41, s.56: repealed in pt.: *ibid.*, sch. 23.
ss. 87, 93, amended: *ibid.*, sch. 13.
s. 95, order 86/539.
schs. 5, 6, repealed: 1986, c.41, sch. 23.
sch. 7, amended: *ibid.*, sch. 13; repealed in pt.: *ibid.*, sch. 23.

8. Mauritius Independence Act 1968.
see *R.* v. *Secretary of State for the Home Department, ex p. Bibi (Mahaboob)* [1985] Imm. A.R. 134, Mann J.

11. Revenue Act 1968.
repealed: S.L.R. 1986.

13. National Loans Act 1968.
s. 4, order 86/129; amended: *ibid.*; 1986, c.41, s.112.
schs. 1, 5, repealed in pt.: S.L.R. 1986.

14. Public Expenditure and Receipts Act 1968.
s. 5, sch. 3, orders 86/368, 408(S.), 977(S.).
sch. 3, repealed in pt.: 1986, c.63, sch. 12.
sch. 3, repealed in pt. (S.): *ibid.*

16. New Towns (Scotland) Act 1968.
s. 47, repealed in pt.: 1986, c.44, sch. 9.

18. Consular Relations Act 1968.
s. 1, amended: order 86/948.
ss. 4, 16, order 86/217.

19. Criminal Appeal Act 1968.
s. 2, see *R.* v. *Khan* [1985] R.T.R. 365, C.A.; *R.* v. *Grant* [1986] Crim.L.R. 235, C.A.
s. 4, see *R.* v. *Fairhurst, The Times,* August 2, 1986, C.A.
ss. 18, 31, see *R.* v. *Suggett* (1985) 81 Cr.App.R. 243, C.A.
s. 42. see *Gooch* v. *Ewing (Allied Irish Bank, Garnishee)* [1985] 3 All E.R. 654, C.A.

22. Legitimation (Scotland) Act 1968.
ss. 2, 4, 7, 8, see *Dunbar of Kilconzie, Petr.,* 1986 S.L.T. 463, H.L.

25. Local Authorities' Mutual Investment Trust Act 1968.
ss. 1, 2, amended: 1986, c.60, sch. 16.

27. Firearms Act 1968.
ss. 2, 3, 57, see *Hall* v. *Cotton* [1986] 3 W.L.R. 681, D.C.
ss. 5, 57, see *R.* v. *Clarke (Frederick)* [1986] 1 W.L.R. 209, C.A.
s. 32, amended and repealed in pt.: order 86/986.
s. 35, amended: *ibid.*
s. 43, orders 86/986, 996(S.).

29. Trade Descriptions Act 1968.
see *R.* v. *Gupta (Kuldip)* (1985) 7 Cr.App.R.(S.) 172, C.A.
ss. 8, 9, order 86/193.

CAP.
1968—cont.

29. Trade Descriptions Act 1968—*cont.*
s. 14, see *R.* v. *Bow Street Magistrates' Court, ex p. Joseph* (1986) 130 S.J. 593, D.C.; *Smith* v. *Dixons,* 1986 S.C.C.R. 1.
s. 19, see *R.* v. *Pain, Jory and Hawkins* (1986) 82 Cr.App.R. 141, C.A.
s. 20, see *R.* v. *Burridge* (1985) 7 Cr.App.R.(S.) 125, C.A.
s. 23, see *Olgeirsson* v. *Kitching* [1986] 1 W.L.R. 304, D.C.
s. 24, see *Amos* v. *Melcon (Frozen Foods)* (1985) 4 T.L.R. 247, D.C.
s. 38, order 86/193.

31. Housing (Financial Provisions) (Scotland) Act 1968.
s. 25, repealed in pt.: 1986, c.65, sch. 3.

32. Industrial Expansion Act 1968.
s. 9, repealed: S.L.R. 1986.

34. Agriculture (Miscellaneous Provisions) Act 1968.
s. 1, amended: 1986, c.14, sch. 3.
ss. 9, 10, repealed: 1986, c.5, sch. 15.
ss. 12, 13, amended: *ibid.*, sch. 14.
s. 15, repealed in pt.: *ibid.*, sch. 15.
s. 17, amended: *ibid.*, sch. 14; repealed in pt.: *ibid.*, sch. 15.
ss. 38–40, repealed: S.L.R. 1986.
s. 42, sch. 3, amended: 1986, c.5, sch. 14.

37. Education (No. 2) Act 1968.
s. 2, repealed: 1986, c.61, sch. 6.
s. 3, amended: *ibid.*, sch. 4; repealed in pt.: *ibid.*, sch. 6.

41. Countryside Act 1968.
ss. 11, 49, see *Thanet District Council and Nature Conservancy Council* (Ref: SE2/5283/42/12) (1985) 1 P.A.D. 99.

46. Health Services and Public Health Act 1968.
s. 60, sch. 5, repealed in pt.: S.L.R. 1986.

48. International Organisations Act 1968.
s. 1, order 86/2017.

49. Social Work (Scotland) Act 1968.
s. 2, amended: 1986, c.33, s.12.
s. 5, regs. 85/1798, 1799.
ss. 15, 16, see *Lothian Regional Council* v. *S.,* 1986 S.L.T.(Sh.Ct.) 37.
ss. 16, 18, amended: 1986, c.9, sch. 1.
s. 28, repealed in pt.: 1986, c.50, sch. 11.
s. 32, see *Kennedy* v. *S.,* 1986 S.L.T. 679.
s. 35, rules 85/1724; 86/518.
s. 37, see *Humphries* v. *S.,* 1986 S.L.T. 683.
s. 44, rules 86/518.
s. 48, rules 85/1724.
s. 53, repealed: 1986, c.47, sch. 5.
s. 78, amended: 1986, c.50, sch. 10.
ss. 78, 80, 82, see *Tayside Regional Council* v. *Thaw,* 1987 S.L.T. 69.
s. 81, amended: 1986, c.9, sch. 1; repealed in pt.: *ibid.*, schs. 1, 2.
s. 87, amended: 1986, c.50, sch. 10.

CAP.

1968—cont.

49. Social Work (Scotland) Act 1968—cont.
ss. 88, 94, amended: 1986, c.9, sch. 1.
sch. 4, repealed: 1986, c.47, sch. 5.

52. Caravan Sites Act 1968.
see *R.* v. *Beaconsfield JJ., ex p. Stubbings, The Times*, May 7, 1986, D.C.
s. 1, see *Balthasar* v. *Mullane* (1985) 17 H.L.R. 561; (1986) 84 L.G.R. 55, C.A.
Pt. II (ss. 6–12), see *West Glamorgan County Council* v. *Rafferty; R.* v. *Secretary of State for Wales ex p. Gilhaney* (1986) 18 H.L.R. 375, C.A.
s. 12, orders 86/688, 1145, 1170, 1572, 2048.

54. Theatres Act 1968.
s. 5, repealed: 1986, c.64, sch. 3.
ss. 7–10, 15, 18, repealed in pt.; *ibid.*

59. Hovercraft Act 1968.
s. 1, order 86/1305.

60. Theft Act 1968.
s. 3, see *R.* v. *Navvabi* [1986] 3 All E.R. 120, C.A.
s. 5, see *Att.-Gen.'s Ref. (No. 1 of 1985)* [1986] 2 W.L.R. 733, C.A.
s. 6, see *R.* v. *Sobel* [1986] Crim.L.R. 261, C.A.
s. 9, see *Norfolk Constabulary* v. *Seekings and Gould* [1986] Crim.L.R. 167, Norwich Crown Court; *R.* v. *O'Neill, McMullen and Kelly, The Times*, October 17, 1986, C.A.
s. 12, see *Chief Constable of Avon and Somerset Constabulary* v. *Jest* [1986] R.T.R. 372, D.C.
s. 15, see *R.* v. *Cooke* [1986] 3 W.L.R. 327, H.L.
s. 16, see *R.* v. *McNiff* [1986] Crim.L.R. 57, C.A.; *R.* v. *Bevan, The Times*, October 24, 1986, C.A.
s. 22, see *R.* v. *Hall* (1985) 81 Cr.App.R. 260, C.A.; *R.* v. *Roberts* [1986] Crim.L.R. 122, C.A.
s. 25, see *R.* v. *Cooke* [1986] 3 W.L.R. 327, H.L.
s. 27, see *R.* v. *Rasini, The Times,* March 20, 1986, C.A.; *R.* v. *Simmons* [1986] Crim.L.R. 397, C.A.

63. Domestic and Appellate Proceedings (Restriction of Publicity) Act 1968.
s. 2, amended: 1986, c.55, sch. 1; repealed in pt.: *ibid.*, schs. 1, 2.

64. Civil Evidence Act 1968.
ss. 2, 4, see *D. (A Minor) (Wardship: Evidence) Re,* (1986) Fam.Law 263; (1986) 2 F.L.R. 189, Wood J.
sch., repealed in pt.: 1986, c.59, sch.

65. Gaming Act 1968.
ss. 6–8, repealed in pt.: S.L.R. 1986.
s. 16, amended: 1986, c.11, s.7.
s. 22, amended: *ibid.*, s.2.
s. 34, see *J. E. Sheeran (Amusement Arcades)* v. *Hamilton District Council,* 1986 S.L.T. 289.

CAP.

1968—cont.

65. Gaming Act 1968—cont.
s. 34, order 86/1981; amended: *ibid.*
s. 51, order 86/1981.
sch. 9, repealed in pt.: S.L.R. 1986.

67. Medicines Act 1968.
s. 13, order 86/228.
s. 15, orders, 86/228, 1180.
s. 35, order 86/1180.
s. 57, orders 86/982, 1997.
s. 58, see *Pharmaceutical Society of Great Britain* v. *Storkwain* [1986] 2 All E.R. 635, H.L.
s. 58, order 86/586.
s. 62, order 86/1368.
s. 72, amended: 1986, c.45, sch. 14.
s. 103, regs. 86/26, 144.
s. 129, orders 86/982, 1997.
s. 130, orders 86/2177.

69. Justices of the Peace Act 1968.
s. 1, see *R.* v. *Kingston Crown Court, ex p. Guarino* [1986] Crim.L.R. 325, D.C.

70. Law Reform (Miscellaneous Provisions) (Scotland) Act 1968.
ss. 1–6, repealed: 1986, c.9, sch. 2.
s. 7, amended: *ibid.*, sch. 1; repealed in pt.: *ibid.*, sch. 2.
s. 10, see *Guardian Royal Exchange Group* v. *Moffat,* 1986 S.L.T. 262.
s. 11 (in pt.), sch. 1, repealed: 1986, c.9, sch. 2.

73. Transport Act 1968.
s. 60, see *Creek* v. *Fossett, Eccles and Supertents* [1986] Crim.L.R. 256; *Smith* v. *Holt Brothers,* 1986 S.L.T. (Sh.Ct.) 49; *Kennet* v. *Holding & Barnes; Harvey (T. L.)* v. *Hall* [1986] R.T.R. 334, D.C.
s. 69, regs. 86/1391.
s. 89, regs. 86/666.
s. 91, regs. 86/666, 1391.
s. 95, regs. 86/1458.
ss. 95, 96, see *Carter* v. *Walton* [1985] R.T.R. 378, D.C.
s. 96, see *Williams* v. *Boyd* [1986] R.T.R. 185; [1986] Crim.L.R. 564, D.C.
s. 96, order 86/1459; regs. 86/1492.
ss. 96, 97, see *Brown* v. *W. Burns Tractors,* 1986 S.C.C.R. 146.
s. 97, see *Creek* v. *Fossett, Eccles and Supertents* [1986] Crim.L.R. 256; *Ross-Taylor* v. *Houston,* 1986 S.C.C.R. 210.
s. 98, regs. 86/1493.
s. 99, see *R.* v. *Parkinson* (1984) 6 Cr.App.R.(S.) 423, C.A.
s. 101, order 86/1459; regs. 86/1493.
s. 103, see *Carter* v. *Walton* [1985] R.T.R. 378, D.C.
s. 109, amended: 1986, c.44, sch. 7.
s. 113, order 86/870.
s. 121, orders 86/277, 343.
s. 157, order 86/1459.

1969

29. Tanzania Act 1969.
ss. 2, 4 (in pt.), 7 (in pt.), repealed: 1986, c.55, sh. 2.

37. Employer's Liability (Defective Equipment) Act 1969.
s. 1, see *Coltman* v. *Bibby Tankers; Derbyshire, The* [1986] 2 All E.R. 65, Sheen J.

46. Family Law Reform Act 1969.
s. 7, see *S. W. (A Minor) (Wardship: Jurisdiction), Re*, (1985) 15 Fam.Law 322, Sheldon J.; *M. (A Minor), Re, The Times*, January 24, 1986, C.A.
s. 22, regs. 86/1357.
sch. 1, repealed in pt.: 1986, c.53, sch. 19.

48. Post Office Act 1969.
s. 7, amended: 1986, c.44, sch. 7.
sch. 4, repealed in pt.: S.L.R. 1986; 1986, c.48, sch. 5.

54. Children and Young Persons Act 1969.
s. 1, see *A.* v. *Wigan Metropolitan Borough Council* (1986) 16 Fam.Law 162, Ewbank J.; *D. (A Minor), Re* [1986] 3 W.L.R. 85, C.A.; *Berkshire County Council* v. *D.-P.* (1986) Fam.Law 264; (1986) 2 F.L.R. 276, C.A.
s. 2, amended: 1986, c.28, s.2.
s. 15, see *W.* v. *Nottinghamshire County Council* (1986) 16 Fam.Law 185, C.A.
s. 16, amended: 1986, c.28, s.2.
s. 21, see *R.* v. *Salisbury and Tilsbury and Mere Combined Juvenile Court, ex p. Ball* (1985) 15 Fam.Law 313, Kennedy J.
ss. 21, 22, amended: 1986, c.28, s.2.
s. 28, see *R.* v. *Bristol JJ., ex p. Broome, The Times*, December 6, 1986, Booth J.
s. 32A, see *R.* v. *Plymouth Juvenile Court, ex p. F, The Times*, August 8, 1986, Waterhouse J.
s. 32A, amended: 1986, c.28, s.3.
s. 32C, added: *ibid.*
s. 70, see *D. (A Minor), Re* [1986] 3 W.L.R. 85, C.A.; *Berkshire County Council* v. *D.-P.* (1986) 16 Fam.Law 264; (1986) 2 F.L.R. 276, C.A.

59. Law of Property Act 1969.
s. 28, rules 86/1322.

1970

8. Insolvency Services (Accounting and Investment) Act 1970.
repealed: 1986, c.45, sch. 12.

9. Taxes Management Act 1970.
s. 20, see *Monarch Assurance Co.* v. *Special Commissioners* [1986] S.T.C. 311, Ch.D.
ss. 21, 25, amended: 1986, c.41, sch. 18.
s. 34, see *Honig* v. *Sarsfield* [1986] S.T.C. 246, C.A.
s. 35, see *Bray* v. *Best, The Times*, January 21, 1986, Walton J.
s. 40, see *Honig* v. *Sarsfield* [1986] S.T.C. 246, C.A.
s. 47B, added: 1986, c.41, sch. 9.

1970—cont.

9. Taxes Management Act 1970—cont.
s. 49, see *Bye* v. *Coren* [1986] S.T.C. 393, C.A.
s. 89, orders 86/1181, 1832.
ss. 93, 95, see *Jolley* v. *Bolton General Comrs. and I.R.C.* [1986] S.T.C. 414, Scott J.
s. 95, see *Lear* v. *Leek General Comrs. and I.R.C* [1986] S.T.C. 542, Vinelott J.
.s. 98, amended: 1986, c.41, s.28, schs. 9, 11, 12.
s. 114, see *Bayliss* v. *Gregory* [1986] 1 All E.R. 289, Vinclott J.

10. Income and Corporation Taxes Act 1970.
s. 1, see *Wilson* v. *Alexander* [1986] S.T.C. 365, Harman J.
s. 8, amended: order 86/529.
s. 54, see *Halton Properties* v. *McHugh, The Times*, December 16, 1986, Peter Gibson J.
s. 55, amended: 1986, c.41, s.30.
s. 65, order 86/328; amended: *ibid.*
ss. 108, 109, see *Aspin* v. *Estill* [1986] S.T.C. 323, Ch.D.
s. 130, see *Bott (E.)* v. *Price, The Times*, December 8, 1986, Hoffmann J.
s. 132, amended: 1986, c.39, sch. 2.
s. 134, amended: 1986, c.41, sch. 13.
s. 155, amended: *ibid.*, s.56.
s. 168, see *Reed* v. *Young* [1986] 1 W.L.R. 649, H.L.
s. 174, amended: 1986, c.41, sch. 13.
s. 180, amended: *ibid.*, s.56.
s. 181, see *Bray* v. *Best* [1986] S.T.C. 96, Walton J.; *Hamblett* v. *Godfrey* [1986] 2 All E.R. 513, Knox J.; *Wilson* v. *Alexander* [1986] S.T.C. 365, Harman J.
s. 183, see *Hamblett* v. *Godfrey (Inspector of Taxes)* [1986] 2 All E.R. 513, Knox J.; *Wilson* v. *Alexander* [1986] S.T.C. 365, Harman J.
s. 184, amended: 1986, c.41, s.34.
s. 186, amended: *ibid.*, s.26.
s. 195, see *Wilson* v. *Alexander* [1986] S.T.C. 365, Harman J.
s. 204, see *I.R.C.* v. *Findlay McClure & Co.* (O.H.), 1986 S.L.T. 417.
ss. 219, 219A, amended: 1986, c.50, sch. 10; repealed in pt.: *ibid.*, sch. 11.
s. 227, amended: 1986, c.41, s.56.
s. 247, amended: 1986, c.45, sch. 14.
s. 248, amended: 1986, c.41, s.30.
s. 252, amended: *ibid.*, ss.42, 56, sch. 10.
s. 253, amended: *ibid.*, s.42, sch. 10.
s. 265, amended: 1986, c.45, sch. 14.
s. 286, amended: 1986, c.41, s.43.
s. 316, see *"B": Sun Life Assurance Co. of Canada* v. *Pearson* [1986] S.T.C. 335, C.A.
s. 343, regs. 86/482.
s. 343, amended: 1986, c.41, s.47; c.53, sch. 18; repealed in pt.: *ibid.*, sch. 19.
s. 350, repealed in pt.: 1986, c.44, sch. 9.
s. 352, amended: 1986, c.41, s.56.

CAP.

1970—cont.

10. Income and Corporation Taxes Act 1970—cont.
s. 377, substituted: *ibid.*, s.51.
s. 415, amended: 1986, c.53, sch. 18.
s. 457, amended: 1986, c.41, s.32; repealed in pt.: *ibid.*, s.32, sch. 23.
ss. 469, 471, 472, amended: *ibid.*, sch. 18.
s. 475, repealed in pt.: *ibid.*, sch. 23.
s. 477, amended: *ibid.*, sch. 18.
s. 478, see *I.R.C.* v. *Brackett; Brackett* v. *Chater* [1986] S.T.C. 521, Hoffmann J.
s. 497, see *Padmore* v. *I.R.C., The Times*, December 3, 1986, Peter Gibson J.
s. 497, order 86/224.
ss. 497, 501, 505, see *Collard* v. *Mining & Industrial Holdings* [1986] S.T.C. 230, Walton J.
s. 526, amended: 1986, c.41, s.56.
sch. 8, amended: *ibid.*, s.45; repealed in pt.: *ibid.*, sch. 23.

17. Proceedings against Estates Act 1970.
repealed: S.L.R. 1986.

24. Finance Act 1970.
s. 30, order 86/1942.
s. 33, amended: 1986, c.41, s.83.

27. Fishing Vessels (Safety Provisions) Act 1970.
s. 2, amended: 1986, c.23, s.5.
s. 3, amended and repealed in pt.: *ibid.*

31. Administration of Justice Act 1970.
sch. 8, amended and repealed in pt.: 1986, c.50, sch. 10.

32. Riding Establishments Act 1970.
s. 4, repealed in pt.: S.L.R. 1986.

33. Law Reform (Miscellaneous Provisions) Act 1970.
s. 3, see *Simmons* v. *Polak*, March 26, 1986; H.H. Judge Lowe; Willesden County Ct.

34. Marriage (Registrar General's Licence) Act 1970.
ss. 2, 7, 18, regs. 86/142.

35. Conveyancing and Feudal Reform (Scotland) Act 1970.
s. 1, see *MacDonald* v. *Stornoway Trust*, First Division, May 20, 1986.
ss. 20, 24, 27, sch. 3, see *Skipton Building Society* v. *Wain* (O.H.), 1986 S.L.T. 96.
ss. 24, 29, sch. 3, see *National & Provincial Building Society* v. *Riddell*, 1986 S.L.T.(Sh.Ct.) 6.
sch. 3, repealed in pt.: 1986, c.45, sch. 14.

36. Merchant Shipping Act 1970.
Commencement order: 86/2006.
s. 28, amended: 1986, c.23, s.10.
ss. 43, 68, regs. 86/1935.
s. 84, regs. 86/680.
s. 101, orders 86/2066.

37. Republic of Gambia Act 1970.
s. 2, repealed in pt.: S.L.R. 1986.

CAP.

1970—cont.

40. Agriculture Act 1970.
Commencement order: 86/707.
ss. 1–24, repealed: 1986, c.49, sch. 4.
s. 13, order 86/441.
ss. 25, 26, repealed: 1986, c.49, s.10, sch. 4.
s. 27, repealed: *ibid.*, sch. 4.
s. 28, amended: *ibid.*, s.22.
ss. 28, 29, scheme 86/57.
ss. 29 (in pt.), 34 (in pt.), 35, 36 repealed: S.L.R. 1986.
s. 66, regs. 86/177, 1735; S.Rs. 1986 Nos. 67, 334.
s. 66, amended: regs. 86/1735.
ss. 68–70, 73, 74, 74A, regs. 86/177, 1735; S.Rs. 1986 Nos. 67, 334.
s. 82, amended: regs. 86/1735.
s. 84, regs. 86/177, 1735; S.Rs. 1986 Nos. 67, 334.
s. 86, S.Rs. 1986 Nos. 67, 334.
ss. 103, 107, repealed: 1986, c.49, sch. 4.
s. 113, order 86/707.
sch. 1, repealed: 1986, c.49, sch. 4.
sch. 4, repealed in pt.: 1986, c.5, sch. 15.
sch. 5, order 86/707.
sch. 5, repealed in pt.: S.L.R. 1986.

41. Equal Pay Act 1970.
s. 1, see *Hayward* v. *Cammell Laird Shipbuilders; Forex Neptune (Overseas)* v. *Miller, The Times*, November 18, 1986, E.A.T.; *Rainey* v. *Greater Glasgow Health Board*, 1987 S.L.T. 146, H.L.
s. 2A, see *Forex Neptune (Overseas)* v. *Miller, The Times*, November 18, 1986, E.A.T.
s. 3, repealed: 1986, c.59, sch.
s. 4, repealed: 1986, c.48, sch. 5.
s. 6, amended: 1986, c.59, ss.2, 9: repealed in pt.: *ibid.*, sch.
s. 10, repealed: *ibid.*

44. Chronically Sick and Disabled Persons Act 1970.
s. 1, amended: 1986, c.33, s.9.
s. 2, see *R.* v. *Kent County Council, ex p. Bruce, The Times*, February 8, 1986, D.C.
s. 14, amended: 1986, c.44, sch. 7.
s. 21, regs. 86/178.
s. 29, amended (S.): 1986, c.44, s.12.

55. Family Income Supplements Act 1970.
repealed: 1986, c.50, sch. 11.
see *Decision No. R(FIS)* 2/85.
s. 1, see *Taylor* v. *Supplementary Benefit Officer* (1986) 1 F.L.R. 16, C.A.
ss. 2, 3, regs. 86/1120.
s. 6, see *Decision No. R(FIS)* 3/85.
s. 10, regs. 86/1120.

1971

3. Guardianship of Minors Act 1971.
see *Ainsbury* v. *Millington* [1986] 1 All E.R. 73, C.A.; *Essex County Council* v. *T., The Times*, March 15, 1986, C.A.

1971—cont.

3. Guardianship of Minors Act 1971—*cont.*
s. 9, see *T. D. (A Minor) (Wardship: Jurisdiction), Re* (1986) 16 Fam.Law 18, Sheldon J.; *R.* v. *Oxford JJ., ex p. D.* [1986] 3 W.L.R. 447, Waite J.
s. 15, amended: 1986, c.55, sch. 1; repealed in pt.: *ibid.*, schs. 1, 2.
s. 15A, added: *ibid.*, sch. 1.
s. 17, repealed in pt.: *ibid.*, schs. 1, 2.

10. Vehicles (Excise) Act 1971.
s. 2A, order 86/1428.
ss. 2A, 4, 7, amended: 1986, c.41, sch. 2.
s. 7, regs. 86/1467.
s. 8, see *Algar* v. *Shaw* [1986] Crim.L.R. 750, D.C.
ss. 8, 12, 16, see *Kennet* v. *Holding & Barnes; Harvey (T. L.)* v. *Hall* [1986] R.T.R. 334, D.C.
s. 12, regs. 86/607.
s. 16, see *Smith* v. *Holt Brothers,* 1986 S.L.T. (Sh.Ct.) 49.
s. 16, regs. 86/1177, 2100, 2101.
s. 16, amended: 1986, c.41, s.3, sch. 2.
s. 17, repealed in pt.: *ibid.*, sch. 2.
s. 23, regs. 86/607, 1177.
s. 23, repealed in pt.: 1986, c.41, schs. 2, 23.
s. 28, see *Algar* v. *Shaw* [1986] Crim.L.R. 750, D.C.
s. 29, see *Walkingshaw* v. *McLaren,* 1985 S.C.C.R. 293.
s. 37, regs. 86/607, 1177, 2100.
s. 39, regs. 86/607.
schs. 2, 4, amended: 1986, c.41, sch. 2.
sch. 7, regs. 86/607.
sch. 7, repealed in pt.: 1986, c.41, sch. 23.

17. Industry Act 1971.
repealed: S.L.R. 1986.

23. Courts Act 1971.
s. 9, see *R.* v. *Croydon Crown Court, ex p. Claire, The Times,* April 3, 1986, D.C.
s. 57, see *R.* v. *Maidstone Crown Court, ex p. Grill, The Times,* July 15, 1986, C.A.
sch. 8, repealed in pt.: S.L.R. 1986.
sch. 9, repealed in pt.: 1986, c.5, sch. 15.

29. National Savings Bank Act 1971.
s. 4, order 86/1217.

32. Attachment of Earnings Act 1971.
s. 24, sch. 1, amended: 1986, c.50, sch. 10.
sch. 3, amended: 1986, c.48, sch. 4.
sch. 4, repealed: 1986, c.50, sch. 10.

33. Armed Forces Act 1971.
ss. 26, 33, 54, sch. 1, repealed in pt.: 1986, c.21, sch. 2.

34. Water Resources Act 1971.
s. 1, orders 86/774, 775, 1531, 1575, 1690, 1739.

38. Misuse of Drugs Act 1971.
see *R.* v. *Hunt (Richard), The Times,* December 13, 1986, H.L.
s. 2, order 86/2230.

1971—cont.

38. Misuse of Drugs Act 1971—*cont.*
s. 3, see *R.* v. *Ellis and Street; R.* v. *Smith (Gloria Marie), The Times,* August 12, 1986, C.A.
s. 4, see *R.* v. *Hughes* (1985) 81 Cr.App.R. 344, C.A.; *R.* v. *Dempsey and Dempsey* (1986) 82 Cr.App.R. 291, C.A.; *Kerr* v. *H.M. Advocate,* 1986 S.C.C.R. 81; *R.* v. *Taylor* [1986] Crim.L.R. 680, St. Alban's Crown Court.
s. 5, see *Miller* v. *H.M. Advocate,* 1985 S.C.C.R. 314; *Kerr* v. *H.M. Advocate,* 1986 S.C.C.R. 81; *R.* v. *Dempsey and Dempsey* [1986] Crim.L.R. 171; (1986) Cr.App.R. 291, C.A.; *R.* v. *Maginnis* [1986] 2 W.L.R. 767, C.A.; *Guild* v. *Ogilvie,* 1986 S.L.T. 343; *R.* v. *Martindale* [1986] 1 W.L.R. 1042, C.A.; *Allan* v. *Taylor,* 1986 S.C.C.R. 202.
s. 7, regs. 85/2066; 86/52.
s. 9A, added: 1986, c.32, s.34.
s. 10, regs. 85/2066, 2067; 86/52, 53.
s. 22, regs. 85/2066; 86/52.
s. 23, see *Foster* v. *Attard, The Times,* January 4, 1986, D.C.; *Allan* v. *Tant,* 1986 S.C.C.R. 175.
s. 27, see *R.* v. *Marland and Jones* (1986) 82 Cr.App.R. 134, C.A.; *R.* v. *Maidstone Crown Court, ex p. Gill* [1986] Crim.L.R. 737; [1986] 1 W.L.R. 1405, D.C.
s. 28, see *R.* v. *Ellis and Street; R.* v. *Smith (Gloria Marie), The Times,* August 12, 1986, C.A.
s. 30, regs. 86/416.
s. 31, regs. 85/2066, 2067; 86/52, 53, 416.
s. 38, regs. 86/52, 53.
sch. 2, see *R.* v. *Cunliffe* [1986] Crim.L.R. 547, C.A.
sch. 4, see *Kerr* v. *H.M. Advocate,* 1986 S.C.C.R. 81.
sch. 4, amended: 1986, c.32, s.34.

39. Rating Act 1971.
s. 2, see *Hemens (Valuation Officer)* v. *Whitsbury Farm and Stud, The Times,* November 10, 1986, C.A.
ss. 5, 7, see *Assessor for Tayside Region* v. *D. B. Marshall (Newbridge),* 1983 S.C. 54.

40. Fire Precautions Act 1971.
s. 27, repealed in pt.: S.L.R. 1986.

48. Criminal Damage Act 1971.
s. 1, see *R.* v. *Appleyard* (1985) 81 Cr.App.R. 319, C.A.; *Hardman* v. *Chief Constable of Avon & Somerset Constabulary* [1986] Crim.L.R. 330, Bristol Crown Court; *R.* v. *Steer* [1986] 1 W.L.R. 1286, C.A.
ss. 1, 10, see *Cox* v. *Riley* [1986] Crim.L.R. 460; (1986) 83 Cr.App.R. 54, D.C.

1971—cont.

53. Recognition of Divorces and Legal Separations Act 1971.
repealed: 1986, c.55, sch. 2.
ss. 2, 3, see *R.* v. *Secretary of State for the Home Department, ex p. Fatima* [1986] 2 W.L.R. 693, H.L.

55. Law Reform (Jurisdiction in Delict) (Scotland) Act 1971.
s. 1, see *Comex Houlder Diving* v. *Colne Fishing Co.*, 1987 S.L.T. 13.

56. Pensions (Increase) Act 1971.
s. 5, regs. 86/391.
sch. 2, repealed in pt.: S.L.R. 1986.

57. Pool Competitions Act 1971.
continued in force: order 86/1234.
s. 8, order 86/1234.

58. Sheriff Courts (Scotland) Act 1971.
s. 32, Acts of Sederunt 85/1976; 86/513, 517, 545, 692, 1230, 1946, 1947, 1966.
s. 37, amended: 1986, c.9, sch. 1.
s. 38, see *Rediffusion* v. *McIlroy*, 1986 S.L.T.(Sh.Ct.) 33.

60. Prevention of Oil Pollution Act 1971.
s. 2, amended: 1986, c.6, s.1.

62. Tribunals and Inquiries Act 1971.
s. 10, rules 86/366, 952.
s. 11, rules 86/420, 1700(S.), 1761, 1957.
s. 12, see *R.* v. *Secretary of State for Social Services, ex p. Connolly* [1986] 1 W.L.R. 421, C.A.
s. 14, see *R.* v. *Registrar of Companies, ex p. Central Bank of India* [1986] 1 All E.R. 105, C.A.; *R.* v. *Secretary of State for Foreign and Commonwealth Affairs, ex p. Trawnick, The Times*, February 21, 1986, C.A.
sch. 1, amended: 1986, c.5, sch. 14; repealed in pt.: S.L.R. 1986; c.45, sch. 14; s.60, sch. 17.

65. Licensing (Abolition of State Management) Act 1971.
repealed: S.L.R. 1986.

68. Finance Act 1971.
s. 32, order 86/529.
s. 32, amended: 1986, c.41, s.16.
ss. 44, 50, amended: *ibid.*, s.55.
s. 52, repealed: *ibid.*, sch. 23.
sch. 8, repealed in pt.: *ibid.*, ss.55, 57.
sch. 10, see *Magnavox Electronics Co. (in liquidation)* v. *Hall*, [1986] S.T.C. 561, C.A.

77. Immigration Act 1971.
s. 2, see *Brahmbhatt* v. *Chief Immigration Officer at Heathrow Airport* [1984] Imm.A.R. 202, C.A.
s. 3, see *Genec* v. *Secretary of State for the Home Department* [1984] Imm.A.R. 180, Immigration Appeal Tribunal; *R.* v. *Immigration Appeal Tribunal, ex p. Singh (Bakhtaur), The Times*, June 27, 1986, H.L.; *R.* v. *Secretary of State for the Home Office, ex p. Erdogan, The Times*, June 30, 1986, Nolan J.

1971—cont.

77. Immigration Act 1971—*cont.*
s. 4, see *R.* v. *Secretary of State for the Home Department, ex p. Bugdaycay* [1986] 1 W.L.R. 155, C.A.; *R.* v. *Secretary of State for the Home Department, ex p. Patel, The Times*, October 27, 1986, C.A.
s. 5, see *R.* v. *Secretary of State for the Home Department, ex p. Alghali, The Times*, July 22, 1986, D.C.
s. 13, see *R.* v. *Secretary of State for the Home Department, ex p. Swat* [1986] 1 All E.R. 717, C.A.
s. 15, see *R.* v. *Immigration Appeal Tribunal, ex p. Chumun and Bano-Ovais, The Times*, December 3, 1986, Hodgson J.
s. 22, see *R.* v. *Immigration Appeal Tribunal, ex p. Jones (Ross), The Times*, October 10, 1986, Simon Brown J.
s. 24, see *Manickavasagar* v. *Comr. of Police for the Metropolis, The Times*, July 16, 1986, D.C.; *Enaas* v. *Dovey, The Times*, November 25, 1986, D.C.
s. 26, see *R.* v. *Secretary of State for the Home Department, ex p. Patel, The Times*, October 27, 1986, C.A.
s. 28, see *Enaas* v. *Dovey, The Times*, November 25, 1986, D.C.
s. 30, see *R.* v. *Secretary of State for the Home Department, ex p. Alghali, The Times*, July 22, 1986, D.C.
s. 33, see *R.* v. *Secretary of State for the Home Department, ex p. Rouse, The Times*, November 25, 1985, Woolf J.: *R.* v. *Secretary of State for the Home Department, ex p. Bugdaycay* [1986] 1 W.L.R. 155, C.A.; *R.* v. *Secretary of State for the Home Department, ex p. Khaled, The Times*, November 13, 1986, Otton J.
s. 35, repealed in pt.: S.L.R. 1986.
sch. 2, see *R.* v. *Secretary of State for the Home Department, ex p. Swat* [1986] 1 All E.R. 717, C.A.; *Singh (Baljinder)* v. *Hammond, The Times*, November 10, 1986, D.C.; *R.* v. *Secretary of State for the Home Department, ex p. Patel, The Times*, October 27, 1986, C.A.

78. Town and Country Planning Act 1971.
s. 1, amended: 1986, c.63, sch. 11.
ss. 1A, 1B, added: *ibid.*, s.30.
s. 9, see *Barnham* v. *Secretary of State for the Environment* (1986) 52 P. & C.R. 10, Farquharson J.
ss. 11–15B, substituted: (exc. G.L.): 1986, c.63, s.41, sch. 10.
s. 12, see *Vaughan* v. *Secretary of State for the Environment and Mid-Sussex District Council* [1986] J.P.L. 840, McNeill J.
s. 18, amended: 1986, c.63, sch. 11.

1971—cont.

78. Town and Country Planning Act 1971—cont.

s. 22, see *Chiltern and Dacorum District Councils and London Ultralight Flying Club* (Refs. APP/XO4/15/A/83/009764, APP/A 1910/A/009807) (1985) 1 P.A.D. 61; *Canterbury City Council and Noding* (Ref. APP/J2210/A/85/025910) (1986) 1 P.A.D. 237; *Hereford and Worcester County Council and Newbould* (Ref: LW/APP/HE/202) (1986) 1 P.A.D. 281.

s. 22, amended: 1986, c.63, sch. 11.

s. 23, see *Hereford and Worcester County Council and Newbould* (Ref. LW/APP/HE/202) (1986) 1 P.A.D. 281; *Cynon Valley Borough Council v. Secretary of State for Wales* (1986) 280 E.G. 195, C.A.

s. 24, orders 86/8, 435, 812, 1176.

s. 24, amended: 1986, c.63, sch. 11.

ss. 24A–24E, added: *ibid.*, s.25.

s. 25, order 86/435.

s. 27, repealed in pt.: 1986, c.5, sch. 14.

s. 29, see *Gransden (E.C.) & Co. and Falkbridge* v. *Secretary of State for the Environment and Gillingham Borough Council* [1986] J.P.L. 519, Woolf J.

s. 29, amended: 1986, c.63, sch. 11.

ss. 29A, 29B, amended: *ibid.*, repealed in pt.: *ibid.*, sch. 12.

s. 31, order 86/435.

s. 31A, added: 1986, c.63, sch. 11.

s. 32, see *Dacorum District Council and Berkhampstead Tool Hire* (Ref. T/APP/A1910/A/84/023290/P5) (1986) 1 P.A.D. 153; *Derbyshire County Council and Kelly (D.P.) (Sheffield)* (Ref. T/APP/D1000/A/84/20223/P7) (1986) 1 P.A.D. 207; *Basildon District Council and Marshall* (Ref: T/APP/U1505/A/85/028060/P2) (1986) 1 P.A.D. 289.

s. 32, repealed in pt.: 1986, c.63, sch. 12.

s. 33, see *Chiltern and Dacorum District Councils and London Ultralight Flying Club* (Refs. APP/XO4/15/A/83/009764, APP/A 1910/A/009807) (1985) 1 P.A.D. 61.

s. 34, order 86/435.

s. 34, amended: 1986, c.63, sch. 6.

s. 35, see *Lichfield District Council and Wetenhall Cooper* (Ref. WMR/P/5370/219/1) (1985) P.A.D. 10; *Thanet District Council and Nature Conservancy Council* (Ref. SE2/5283/42/12) (1985) 1 P.A.D. 99.

s. 35, amended: 1986, c.63, sch. 11.

s. 36, see *Birmingham City Council and Bridgens (E.) and Co.* (Ref. T/APP/P4605/A/84/20649/P5) (1985) 1 P.A.D. 53; *Wyre Borough Council and Broseley Estates* (Ref. APP/U2370/A/84/012076) (1985) 1

1971—cont.

78. Town and Country Planning Act 1971—cont.

P.A.D. 47; *Surrey Heath Borough Council and VDU Installation* (Ref. T/APP/D3640/A/84/25692/P2)(1985) 1 P.A.D. 31; *Richmond-upon-Thames and C. & A. Pension Trustees* (Ref. T/APP/25810/A/84/18543/P5) (1985) 1 P.A.D. 44; *Westminster City Council and Eagle Star Properties* (Ref. T/APP/X5990/A/84/14192/P7) (1985) 1 P.A.D. 41; *Kensington and Chelsea Royal Borough Council and Legal and General Assurance Society* (Ref. T/APP/K5600/A/84/20971/P5) (1984) 1 P.A.D. 35; *Salisbury District Council and Lewis* (Ref. T/APP/T3915/A/84/023625/P4) (1985) 1 P.A.D. 29; *Wigan Metropolitan Borough Council and Broseley Estates* (Ref. T/APP/5089/A/83/3093/P5) (1985) 1 P.A.D. 5; *Stratford-on-Avon District Council and Sequoia Properties* (Ref. T/APP/J.3720/A/83/3136) (1985) 1 P.A.D. 14; *Dudley Metropolitan Borough Council and Davies and Firmstone* (Ref. T/APP/C4615/A/84/020675/P2) (1985) 1 P.A.D. 1; *Barnet London Borough Council and Happy Eater* (Ref. T/APP/N5090/A/84/022152/P5) (1985) 1 P.A.D. 50; *Ipswich Borough Council and Charles Manning Amusement Park* (Ref. T/APP/R3515/A/84/023608/P7) (1985) 1 P.A.D. 56; *Windsor and Maidenhead District Council and Walton Masters* (Ref. T/APP/DO325/A/84/20012/P2) (1985) 1 P.A.D. 67; *Greenwich London Borough Council and Trident Builders Merchants* (Refs: APP/5012/C/83/3323, APP/E5330/C84/286, APP/E5330/A/83/7343 (PLUP 4C)) (1985) 1 P.A.D. 94; *Chiltern and Dacorum District Councils and London Ultralight Flying Club* (Refs. APP/XO4/15/A/83/009764, APP/A 1910/A/009807) (1985) 1 P.A.D. 61; *Chiltern District Council and Gibbs* (Ref: T/APP/XO4015/A/84/020070/P5) (1985) 1 P.A.D. 96; *Bracknell District Council and Society of Licensed Victuallers* (Ref. APP/C0305A/84/12718) (1985) 1 P.A.D. 90; *Darlington Borough Council and Gibbon* (Ref. T/APP/L1310/A/84/21736/P2) (1985) 1 P.A.D. 59; *Northumberland County Council and Northern Aggregates* (Ref. T/APP/R2900/A/84/18860) (1985) 1 P.A.D. 76; *Merseyside County Council and Odgen (A) and Sons* (Ref. APP/5093/A/82/106489) (1985) 1 P.A.D. 72; *Metropolitan Borough of Solihull and Newcombe Estate Co.* (Ref. T/APP/Q4625/A/84/14314–5/P7 and

1971—cont.

78. Town and Country Planning Act 1971—cont.

T/APP/Q4625/A/85/28864–5/P7) (1985) 1 P.A.D. 69; *Hereford and Worcester County Council and Dubberley* (Ref. APP/5058/D/83/75 and APP/F1800/A/84/14233) (1985) 1 P.A.D. 85; *Basingstoke and Dean Borough Council and Church* (Ref. T/APP/H1705/A/84/019340/P3) (1985) 1 P.A.D. 65; *Taunton Deane Borough Council and Gillards Farms and Transport* (Ref. APP/D3315/A/84/U19906) (1986) 1 P.A.D. 124: *Stafford Borough Council and Midland Counties Securities* (Ref. T/APP/Y3425/A/84/018365–8/P5) (1986) 1 P.A.D. 108; *Richmondshire District Council and Markendale-Lancashire* (Ref. T/APP/E2720/A/84/24672/P2) (1986) 1 P.A.D. 130; *Kirklees Metropolitan Borough Council and Williams (Hounslow)* (Ref. T/APP/J4715/A/23376/P7) (1986) 1 P.A.D. 145; *North Devon District Council and B.E.P.* (Ref. T/AA/G1115/A/84/025282/P2) (1986) 1 P.A.D. 141; *East Hertfordshire District Council and Raynham House Investments* (Ref. T/APP/J1915/A/85/028356/P5) (1986) 1 P.A.D. 128; *Buckinghamshire County Council and Firmin* (Ref. APP/5123/A/83/003033) (1986) 1 P.A.D. 136; *Lancaster City Council and Rushworth* (Ref. T/APP/A2335/A/84/022747/P5) (1986) 1 P.A.D. 102; *Wealden District Council and Broad Oak United Football and Boys Club* (Ref. T/APP/E1435/A/84/017949/P6) (1986) 1 P.A.D. 111; *Mid-Sussex District Council and Charles Church Developments* (Ref. APP/D3830/A/84/017196) (1986) 1 P.A.D. 120; *Guildford Borough Council and Downland General Housing Association* (Ref. T/APP/Y3615/A/84/17956/P5) (1986) 1 P.A.D. 116; *Barnet London Borough and Ashton Homes* (Ref. T/APP/N5090/A/84/023447/P2 and 025940/P2) (1986) 1 P.A.D. 105; *Bath City Council and Anglia Building Society* (Ref. T/APP/P0105/A/85/028040/P7) (1986) 1 P.A.D. 175; *New Forest District Council and Messrs. Austin and Wyatt* (Ref. T/APP/B1740/A/85/028722/P4) (1986) 1 P.A.D. 172; *Brentwood District Council and Trust House Forte Catering* (Ref. APP/H1515/A/84/020808 (1986) 1 P.A.D. 185; *Chelmsford Borough Council and Bartella* (Ref. T/APP/W1525/A/84/023883/P5) (1986) 1 P.A.D. 187; *Colchester Borough Council and Mecca Bookmakers* (Ref.

1971—cont.

78. Town and Country Planning Act 1971—cont.

T/APP/A1530/A/84/19893/P7) (1986) 1 P.A.D. 178; *Derbyshire County Council and Kelly (D.P.) (Sheffield)* (Ref. T/APP/D1000/A/84/20223/P7) (1986) 1 P.A.D. 207; *Surrey County Council and Conoco (U.K.)* (Ref. APP/B3600/A/84/20896/Part 2) (1986) 1 P.A.D. 197; *Bromley London Borough Council and Jackson* (Ref. T/APP/G5180/A/85/025913/P2) (1986) 1 P.A.D. 144; *Hillingdon London Borough Council and Black (W.E.)* (Ref. T/APP/R5510/A/84/25735/P5) (1986) 1 P.A.D. 156: *Windsor and Maidenhead Royal Borough Council and Lambart Computing* (Ref. T/APP/D0325/A/84/16136/P2) (1986) 1 P.A.D. 162; *South Bucks District Council and Holland Automation International (U.K.)* (Ref. T/APP/N0410/A/85/027035/P2) (1986) 1 P.A.D. 159; *Windsor and Maidenhead Royal Borough Council and City and Northern* (Ref. APP/D0325/A/84/021226) (1986) 1 P.A.D. 169; *Westminster City Council and McDonalds Hamburgers* (Ref. T/APP/X5990/A/84/0254265/P5) (1986) 1 P.A.D. 191; *Chester City Council and Proven Chemicals* (Ref. T/APP/X0605/A/85/028950/P5) (1986) 1 P.A.D. 252; *Hertfordshire County Council and Tarmac Topmix* (Ref. T/APP/Y1945/A/84/21382/P7) (1986) 1 P.A.D. 246; *Canterbury City Council and Noding* (Ref. APP/J2210/A/85/025910) (1986) 1 P.A.D. 237; *Cherwell District Council and Faccenda Chicken* (Ref. T/APP/C3105/A/84/24404/P5) (1986) 1 P.A.D. 241; *Lake District Special Planning Board and Carey* (Ref. APP/5941/A/82/01842) (1986) 1 P.A.D. 224; *Guildford Borough Council and Martin Grant Homes* (Refs. APP/5386/A/82/012131 and APP/Y3615/A/021620) (1986) 1 P.A.D. 231; *Sheffield (City) Metropolitan District Group and Wiggins Group* (Ref. A/44420/A/84/018093) (1986) 1 P.A.D. 210; *Crewe and Nantwich Borough Council and Need and Beecroft* (Ref. APP/K0615/A/84/023059) (1986) 1 P.A.D. 228; *Kettering Borough Council and Burton Latimer Settled Estates and Springfer Estates* (Ref. T/APP/L2820/A/2631/P6) (1986) 1 P.A.D. 214; *Staffordshire Moorlands District Council and Machin Developments* (Ref. T/APP/L3435/A/84/014722/P7) (1986) 1

1971—cont.

78. Town and Country Planning Act 1971—
cont.

P.A.D. 221; *Horsham District Council and Bramber Parish Council* (Ref. T/APP/Z3285/A/85/028692/P2 and A/85/033593/P2) (1986) 1 P.A.D. 300; *Carrick District Council and Probus Burial Board* (Ref. APP/P0810/A/016464) (1986) 1 P.A.D. 297; *Rochester-upon-Medway City Council and Marina Services Medway* (Ref. T/APP/Y2240/A/85/27198/P5) (1986) 1 P.A.D. 276; *Torbay Borough Council and Coughlan* (Ref. T/APP/MH140/A/85/030786/P5) (1986) 1 P.A.D. 269; *Salisbury District Council and Trafalgar Fisheries* (Ref. T/APP/T3915/A/85/29345/P2) (1986) 1 P.A.D 272; *Breckland District Council and Dereham Congregation of Jehovah's Witnesses* (Ref. T/APP/F2605/A/85/31220/P3) (1986) 1 P.A.D 286; *Sheffield City Council and Alderoak* (Ref. T/APP/U4420/A/85/28855/P7) (1986) 1 P.A.D. 263; *Grimsby Borough Council and Latimer* (Ref. T/APP/T2025/A/84/25178/P7) (1986) 1 P.A.D. 284; *Torbay Borough Council and South Western Electricity Board* (Ref. SW/APP/M1140/84/02001 and A/85/020911) (1986) 1 P.A.D. 266; *Enfield London Borough Council and Limebear* (Ref. T/APP/Q5300/C/85/1127/P6) (1986) 1 P.A.D. 289; *Basildon District Council and Marshall* (Ref. T/APP/U1505/A/85/028060/P2) (1986) 1 P.A.D. 289; *South Staffordshire District Council and Smith* (Refs. T/APP/C3430/C/84/2825/P6 and A/84/29841/P6) (1986) 1 P.A.D. 289; *York Rugby League Football Club* (Ref. T/APP/F2740/A/85/30349/P2) (1986) 1 P.A.D. 303; *Macclesfield Borough Council and Ripper* (Ref. T/APP/C0630/A/85/28013/P2) (1986) 1 P.A.D. 306: *Rochford District Council and McCarthy and Stone (Developments)* (Ref. T/APP/B1550/A/85/032721/P2) (1986) 1 P.A.D. 311; *Brent London Borough Council and Ashton Homes* (Ref. T/APP/T5150/A/85031344/P3) (1986) 1 P.A.D. 314; *Tamworth Borough Council and Simpson (R.A.) and Son (Tamworth)* Ref. T/APP/Z3445/A/85/032993/P4) (1986) 1 P.A.D. 318; *Lewes District Council and Rendell and Aldous* (Ref. T/APP/P1425/A/85/036484/P2) (1986) 1 P.A.D. 321; *Fareham Borough Council and Truryn Leisure Services (U.K.)* (Ref. T/APP/A1720/A/85/033780/P5)

1971—cont.

78. Town and Country Planning Act 1971—
cont.

(1986) 1 P.A.D. 324: *Salford City Council and Avanti Engineering* (Ref. T/APP/V4230/A/85/36430/P2) (1986) 1 P.A.D. 328; *Tunbridge Wells Borough Council and Boulding* (Ref. T/APP/M2270/A/85/036704/P4) (1986) 1 P.A.D. 331; *Luton Borough Council and Firbank (C.) and Son* (Ref. T/APP/A0210/A/85/035525/P5) (1986) 1 P.A.D. 334; *Erewash Borough Council and Lucking (C.J. & D.J.)* (Ref. T/APP/N1025/A/85/34832/P2) (1986) 1 P.A.D. 338; *Walsall Metropolitan Borough Council and Robert M. Douglas Holdings* (Ref. T/APP/V4630/A/85/026623/P7) (1986) 1 P.A.D. 341; *Stafford Borough Council and Trustees Savings Bank* (Ref. T/APP/T3425/A/85/036134/P4) (1986) 1 P.A.D. 344; *Wealdon District Council and Mortlake* (Ref. T/APP/C1435/A/85/033119/P3) (1986) 1 P.A.D. 347.

s. 36, order 86/435.

s. 36, amended: 1986, c.63, sch. 11.

s. 37, see *Wyre Borough Council and Broseley Estates* (Ref. APP/U2370/A/84/012076) (1985) 1 P.A.D. 47: *Borough of Richmond-upon-Thames and C. & A. Pension Trustees* (Ref. T/APP/25810/A/84/18543/P5) (1985) 1 P.A.D. 44; *Westminster City Council and Eagle Star Properties* (Ref. T/APP/X5990/A/84/14192/P7) (1985) 1 P.A.D. 41; *Kensington and Chelsea Royal Borough Council and Legal and General Assurance Society* (Ref. T/APP/K5600/A/84/20971/P5) (1984) 1 P.A.D. 35; *Barnet London Borough and Ashton Homes* (Ref. T/APP/N5090/A/84/023447/P2 and 025940/P2) (1986) 1 P.A.D. 105.

s. 37, order 86/435.

s. 41, amended: 1986, c.63, sch. 6.

s. 42, order 86/435.

s. 43, see *Macclesfield Borough Council and Ripper* (Ref. T/APP/C0630/A/85/28013/P2) (1986) 1 P.A.D. 306.

s. 45, see *Hertsmere District Council and Deem* (Ref. E1/5254/28/2) (1985) 1 P.A.D. 20; *Islington London Borough Council and Katsiaounis* (Ref. GLP/5020/28/12) (1985) 1 P.A.D. 22.

s. 51, see *Islington London Borough Council and Katsiaounis* (Ref. GLP/5020/28/12) (1985) 1 P.A.D. 22.

s. 52, see *Kensington and Chelsea Royal Borough Council and Legal and General Assurance Society* (Ref. T/APP/K5600/A/84/20971/P5) (1984) 1 P.A.D. '

1971—cont.

78. Town and Country Planning Act 1971—
cont.

35; *Lichfield District Council and Wetenhall Cooper* (Ref. WMR/P/5370/219/1) (1985) 1 P.A.D. 10; *Buckinghamshire County Council and Firmin* (Ref. APP/5123/A/83/003033) (1986) 1 P.A.D. 136; *City of Bradford Metropolitan Council* v. *Secretary of State for the Environment and McLean Homes Northern* [1986] J.P.L. 292, Farquarson J.; *Wealden District Council and Broad Oak United Football and Boys Club* (Ref. T/APP/E1435/A/84/017949/P6) (1986) 1 P.A.D. 111; *Abbey Homesteads (Developments)* v. *Northamptonshire County Council* (1986) 278 E.G. 1249, C.A.; *Cherwell District Council and Faccenda Chicken* (Ref. T/APP/C3105/A/84/24404/P5) (1986) 1 P.A.D. 241; *Staffordshire Moorlands District Council and Machin Developments* (Ref. T/APP/L3435/A/84/014722/P7) (1986) 1 P.A.D. 221; *Rochester-upon-Medway City Council and Marina Services Medway* (Ref. T/APP/Y2240/A/85/27198/P.5) (1986) 1 P.A.D. 276; *City of Bradford Metropolitan Council* v. *Secretary of State for the Environment and McLean Homes Northern* [1986] J.P.L. 598, C.A.; *Rochford District Council and McCarthy and Stone (Developments)* Ref. T/APP/B1550/A/85/032721/P2) (1986) 1 P.A.D. 311.

s. 53, see *Chiltern and Dacorum District Councils and London Ultralight Flying Club* (Refs. APP/XO4/15/A/83/009764, APP/A 1910/A/009807) (1985) 1 P.A.D. 61; *Stafford Borough Council and Midland Counties Securities* (Ref. T/APP/Y3425/A/84/018365–8/P5) (1986) 1 P.A.D. 108; *Lancaster City Council and Rushworth* (Ref. T/APP/A2335/A/84/022747/P5) (1986) 1 P.A.D. 102; *Canterbury City Council and Noding* (Ref. APP/J2210/A/85/025910) (1986) 1 P.A.D. 237; *South Herefordshire District Council and Morris* Ref. APP/U1830/G/84/70) (1986) 1 P.A.D. 294; *South Oxfordshire District Council* v. *Secretary of State for the Environment* (1986) 52 P. & C.R. 1, McCullough J.

s. 53, order 86/435.

s. 53, amended: 1986, c.63, sch. 6.

s. 54, see *Debenhams* v. *Westminster City Council* (1986) 83 L.S.Gaz. 1479; (1986) 278 E.G. 974, C.A.; *Cotswold District Council* v. *Secretary of State for the Environment* (1986) 61 P. & C.R. 139, D.C.

s. 54, amended: 1986, c.63, sch. 9.

s. 55, see *Cotswold District Council* v. *Secretary of State for the Environment*

1971—cont.

78. Town and Country Planning Act 1971—
cont.

(1986) 61 P. & C.R. 139, D.C.; *R.* v. *Wells Street Stipendiary Magistrate, ex p. Westminster City Council* [1986] 1 W.L.R. 1046, D.C.

s. 55, amended: 1986, c.63, sch. 9; repealed in pt.: *ibid.*, schs. 11, 12.

s. 56, see *Harrow London Borough Council and Bovis Homes* (Ref. T/APP/M5450/A/85/31367/P2) (1986) 1 P.A.D. 217.

s. 56, amended: 1986, c.63, sch. 9.

ss. 56A, 56C, added: *ibid.*

s. 57, amended: *ibid.*, sch. 11.

s. 58AA, added: *ibid.*, sch. 9.

s. 58B–58N, added: *ibid.*, s.31.

s. 60, repealed in pt.: *ibid.*, sch. 12.

s. 63, amended: *ibid.*, s.45.

s. 64, see *Islington London Borough Council and Katsiaounis* (Ref. GLP/5020/28/12) (1985) 1 P.A.D. 22.

s. 65, substituted: 1986, c.63, s.46.

ss. 66–72, repealed: *ibid.*, s.48, sch. 12.

ss. 73–80, repealed: *ibid.*, sch. 12.

s. 81, see *R.* v. *Secretary of State for the Environment, ex p. Hillingdon London Borough Council* [1986] (Note) 2 All E.R. 273, C.A.

ss. 81–83, repealed: 1986, c.63, sch. 12.

s. 84, see *Harper's Application, Re* (1986) 52 P. & C.R. 104, Lands Tribunal (Ref. No. LP/43/1984), V.G. Wellings Esq. Q.C.

ss. 84–86, repealed: 1986, c.63, sch. 12.

s. 87, see *R.* v. *Secretary of State for the Environment, ex p. Hillingdon London Borough Council* [1986] 1 W.L.R. 192, Woolf J.; *R.* v. *Greenwich London Borough Council, ex p. Patel* (1986) 84 L.G.R. 241, C.A.

s. 88, see *Pearcy (John) Transport* v. *Secretary of State for the Environment, The Times*, January 31, 1986, Mr. David Widdicombe Q.C., sitting as a deputy High Court Judge: *Greenwich London Borough Council and Trident Builders Merchants* (Refs: APP/5012/C/83/3323, APP/E5330/C84/286, APP/E5330/A/83/7343(PLUP 4C)) (1985) 1 P.A.D. 93; *R.* v. *Greenwich London Borough Council, ex p. Patel* (1986) 84 L.G.R. 241, C.A.; *Bradford City Metropolitan Council and Shellbridge Holdings* (Ref. T/APP/W4705/C/84/2296/P6) (1986) 1 P.A.D. 181; *Cambridge City Council and Hadjioannou* (Ref. T/APP/Q0505/C/84/3679/P6) (1986) 1 P.A.D. 256; *Enfield London Borough Council and Limebear* (Ref. T/APP/Q5300/C/85/1127/P6) (1986) 1 P.A.D. 289; *South Staffordshire District*

1971—cont.

78. Town and Country Planning Act 1971—
cont.
Council and Smith (Refs.
T/APP/C3430/C/84/2825/P6 and
A/84/29841/P6) (1986) 1 P.A.D. 289;
Vaughan v. *Secretary of State for the
Environment and Mid-Sussex District
Council* [1986] J.P.L. 840, McNeill J.

s. 88A, see *Hughes (H.T.) & Sons* v. *Secretary of State for the Environment*
(1986) 51 P. & C.R. 134, D.C.

s. 88B, repealed in pt.: 1986, c.63, sch. 12.

s. 89, amended: *ibid.*, sch. 11.

ss. 89, 91, see *R.* v. *Greenwich London
Borough Council, ex p. Patel* (1986) 84
L.G.R. 241, C.A.

s. 90, see *Runnymede Borough Council* v.
Smith [1986] J.P.L. 592, Millett J.

s. 90, amended: 1986, c.63, sch. 11.

s. 92A, order 86/435.

s. 94, see *Vaughan* v. *Secretary of State for
the Environment and Mid-Sussex District
Council* [1986] J.P.L. 840, McNeill J.

ss. 94, 95, see *Hereford and Worcester
County Council and Dubberley* Ref.
APP/5058/D/83/75 and APP/F1800/A/
84/14233) (1985) 1 P.A.D. 85.

s. 97, amended: 1986, c.63, sch. 9.

s. 98, amended: *ibid.*, sch. 11.

ss. 101, 101A, substituted: *ibid.*, sch. 9.

s. 101B, added: *ibid.*, s.32.

s. 104, amended: *ibid.*, sch. 11.

s. 105, amended: *ibid.*; repealed in pt.:
ibid., schs. 11, 12.

s. 109, amended: *ibid.*, sch. 11.

s. 110, repealed in pt.: *ibid.*, sch. 12.

s. 119, repealed in pt.: order 86/452.

ss. 147 (in pt.), 151, repealed: 1986, c.63,
sch. 12.

s. 164, see *Hertsmere District Council and
Deem* (Ref. E1/5254/28/2) (1985) 1
P.A.D. 20.

ss. 165, 169, repealed in pt.: 1986, c.63,
sch. 12.

s. 177, see *Texas Homecare* v. *Lewes District Council* (1986) 51 P. & C.R. 205,
Lands Tribunal.

s. 180, see *Balco Transport Services* v.
Secretary of State for the Environment
[1985] 3 All E.R. 689, C.A.

ss. 181, 184, amended: 1986, c.63, sch. 11.

s. 185, repealed: *ibid.*, sch. 12.

s. 186, amended: *ibid.*, sch. 11.

s. 191, repealed in pt.: *ibid.*, sch. 12.

s. 195, see *Binns* v. *Secretary of State for
Transport* (1985) 50 P. & C.R. 468,
Lands Tribunal.

s. 210, see *Guildford Borough Council and
Downland General Housing Association*
(Ref. T/APP/Y3615/A/84/17956/P5)
(1986) 1 P.A.D. 116.

s. 216, repealed in pt.: 1986, c.63, sch. 12.

s. 223, amended: 1986, c.31, sch. 4; c.44,
sch. 7.

1971—cont.

78. Town and Country Planning Act 1971—
cont.
s. 224, repealed in pt.: 1986, c.31, sch. 6;
c.44, sch. 9.

s. 225, see *Torbay Borough Council and
South Western Electricity Board* (Ref.
SW/APP/M1140/84/02001 and
A/85/020911) (1986) 1 P.A.D. 266.

s. 237, repealed in pt.: 1986, c.63, sch. 12.

s. 242, amended: *ibid.*, schs. 6, 7.

s. 243, see *R.* v. *Greenwich London Borough Council, ex p. Patel* (1986) 84
L.G.R. 241, C.A.; *Vaughan* v. *Secretary
of State for The Environment and Mid-
Sussex District Council* [1986] J.P.L.
840, McNeill J.

s. 244, amended: 1986, c.63, sch. 6.

s. 245, see *G.L.C.* v. *Secretary of State for
the Environment and Harrow London
Borough Council* [1985] J.P.L. 868,
Woolf J.; *Penwith District Council* v.
Secretary of State for the Environment
(1985) 277 E.G. 194, Woolf J.; *Chelmsford Borough Council* v. *Secretary of
State for the Environment and Alexander
(E.R.)* [1985] J.P.L. 112, Glidewell J.;
Gransden (E.C.) & Co. and Falkbridge
v. *Secretary of State for the Environment
and Gillingham Borough Council* [1986]
J.P.L. 519, Woolf J.; *Surrey Heath Borough Council* v. *Secretary of State for
the Environment, The Times,* November
3, 1986, Kennedy J.; *Centre 21* v. *Secretary of State for the Environment*
(1986) 280 E.G. 889, C.A.

s. 246, see *Pearcy (John) Transport* v. *Secretary of State for the Environment, The
Times,* January 31, 1986, Mr. David
Widdicombe Q.C., sitting as a deputy
High Court Judge; *London Parachuting*
v. *Secretary of State for the Environment
and South Cambridgeshire District
Council* [1986] J.P.L. 428, Mann J.;
Miah v. *Secretary of State for the
Environment and Hillingdon Borough
Council* [1986] J.P.L. 756, Woolf J.

ss. 250–252, repealed: 1986, c.63, s.48,
sch. 12.

s. 260, repealed in pt.: *ibid.*

s. 266, amended: *ibid.*, sch. 7.

s. 271A, added: *ibid.*

s. 277A, see *Rochford District Council and
McCarthy and Stone (Developments)*
(Ref. T/APP/B1550/A/85/032721/P2)
(1986) 1 P.A.D. 311.

s. 277A, amended and repealed in pt.:
1986, c.63, sch. 9.

s. 280, amended: *ibid.*, sch. 7.

s. 282, amended: *ibid.*, sch. 11.

ss. 282A, 282B, added: *ibid.*, sch. 11.

s. 287, amended: *ibid.*, schs. 6, 9; repealed
in pt.: *ibid.*, sch. 12.

s. 287, regs. 86/623; orders 86/8, 435, 812,
1176.

1971—cont.

78. Town and Country Planning Act 1971—
cont.
s. 290, see *Canterbury City Council and Noding* (Ref. APP/J2210/A/85/025910) (1986) 1 P.A.D. 237; *South Herefordshire District Council and Morris* (Ref. APP/U1830/G/84/70) (1986) 1 P.A.D. 294.
s. 290, amended: 1986, c.63, schs. 6, 7; repealed in pt.: 1986, c.44, sch. 9; c.63, sch. 12.
sch. 7, see *R.* v. *Secretary of State for the Environment, ex p. Great Grimsby Borough Council, The Times,* May 12, 1986, Russell J.
sch. 8A, added: 1986, c.63, s.25, sch. 6.
sch. 9, see *Birmingham City Council and Bridgens (E.) and Co.* (Ref. T/APP/P4605/A/20649/P5) (1985) 1 P.A.D. 53; *Surrey Heath Borough Council and VDU Installation* (Ref. T/APP/D3640/A/84/25692/P2) (1985) 1 P.A.D. 31; *Kensington and Chelsea Royal Borough Council and Legal and General Assurance Society* (Ref. T/APP/K5600/A/84/20971/P5) (1984) 1 P.A.D. 35; *Salisbury District Council and Lewis* (Ref. T/APP/T3915/A/84/023625/P4) (1985) 1 P.A.D. 29; *Wigan Metropolitan Borough Council and Broseley Estates* (Ref. T/APP/5089/A/83/3093/P5) (1985) 1 P.A.D. 5; *Stratford-on-Avon District Council and Sequoia Properties* (Ref. T/APP/J.3720/A/83/3136) (1985) 1 P.A.D. 14; *Dudley Metropolitan Borough Council and Davies and Firmstone* (Ref. T/APP/C4615/A/84/020675/P2) (1985) 1 P.A.D. 1; *Barnet London Borough Council and Happy Eater* (Ref. T/APP/N5090/A/84/022152/P5) (1985) 1 P.A.D. 50; *Greenwich London Borough Council and Trident Builders Merchants* (Ref. APP/5012/C/83/3323, APP/E5330/C84/286, APP/E5330/A/83/7343 (PLUP 4C)) (1985) 1 P.A.D. 93; *Chiltern District Council and Gibbs* (Ref. T/APP/XO4015/A/84/020070/P5) (1985) 1 P.A.D. 96; *Bracknell District Council and Society of Licensed Victuallers* (Ref. APP/C0305A/84/12718) (1985) 1 P.A.D. 90; *Northumberland County Council and Northern Aggregates* (Ref. T/APP/R2900/A/84/18860) (1985) 1 P.A.D. 76; *Hereford and Worcester County Council and Dubberley* (Ref. APP/5058/D/83/75 and APP/F1800/A/84/14233) (1985) 1 P.A.D. 85; *Stafford Borough Council and Midland Counties Securities* (Ref. T/APP/Y3425/A/84/018365–8/P5) (1986) 1 P.A.D. 108; *Lancaster City Council and Rushworth* (Ref.

1971—cont.

78. Town and Country Planning Act 1971—
cont.
T/APP/A2335/A/84/022747/P5) (1986) 1 P.A.D. 102; *Wealden District Council and Broad Oak United Football and Boys Club* (Ref. T/APP/E1435/A/84/017949/P6) (1986) 1 P.A.D. 111; *Guildford Borough Council and Downland General Housing Association* (Ref. T/APP/Y3615/A/84/17956/P5) (1986) 1 P.A.D. 116; *Barnet London Borough and Ashton Homes* (Ref. T/APP/N5090/A/84/023447/P2 and 025940/P2) (1986) 1 P.A.D. 105; *Chelmsford Borough Council and Bartella* (Ref. T/APP/W1525/A/84/023883/P5) (1986) 1 P.A.D. 187; *Derbyshire County Council and Kelly (D.P.) (Sheffield)* (Ref. T/APP/D1000/A/84/20223/P7) (1986) 1 P.A.D. 207; *Bromley London Borough Council and Jackson* (Ref. T/APP/G5180/A/185/025913/P2) (1986) 1 P.A.D. 144; *Bradford City Metropolitan Council and Shellbridge Holdings* (Ref. T/APP/W4705/C/84/2296/P6) (1986) 1 P.A.D. 181; *Westminster City Council and McDonalds Hamburgers* (Ref. T/APP/X5990/A/84/0254265/P5) (1986) 1 P.A.D. 191; *Horsham District Council and Bramber Parish Council* (Ref. T/APP/Z3825/A/85/028692/P2 and A/85/033593/P2) (1986) 1 P.A.D. 300; *Carrick District Council and Probus Burial Board* (Ref. APP/P0810/A/84/016464) (1986) 1 P.A.D. 297; *Rochester-upon-Medway City Council and Marina Services Medway* (Ref. T/APP/Y2240/A/85/27198/P5) (1986) 1 P.A.D. 276; *Torbay Borough Council and Coughlan* (Ref. T/APP/MH140/A/85/030786/P5) (1986) 1 P.A.D. 269; *Salisbury District Council and Trafalgar Fisheries* (Ref. T/APP/T3915/A/85/29345/P2) (1986) 1 P.A.D. 272; *Breckland District Council and Dereham Congregation of Jehovah's Witness* (Ref. T/APP/F2605/A/85/031220/P3) (1986) 1 P.A.D. 286; *Sheffield City Council and Alderoak* (Ref. T/APP/U4420/A/85/28855/P7) (1986) 1 P.A.D. 263; *Grimsby Borough Council and Latimer* (Ref. T/APP/T2025/A/84/25178/P7) (1986) 1 P.A.D. 284: *Torbay Borough Council and South Western Electricity Board* (Ref. SW/APP/M1140/84/02001 and A/85/020911) (1986) 1 P.A.D. 266; *Enfield London Borough Council and Limebear* (Ref. T/APP/Q5300/C/85/1127/P6) (1986) 1

1971—cont.

78. Town and Country Planning Act 1971— *cont.*

P.A.D. 289; *Basildon District Council and Marshall* (Ref. T/APP/U1505/A/85/028060/P2) (1986) 1

P.A.D. 289; *South Staffordshire District Council and Smith* (Refs. T/APP/C3430/C/84/2825/P6 and A/84/29841/P6) (1986) 1 P.A.D. 289; *York City Council and York Rugby League Football Club* (Ref. T/APP/F2740/A/85/30349/P2) (1986) 1

P.A.D. 303; *Macclesfield Borough Council and Ripper* (Ref. T/APP/C0630/A/85/28013/P2) (1986) 1

P.A.D. 306; *Rochford District Council and McCarthy and Stone (Developments)* (Ref. T/APP/B1550/A/85/032721/P2) (1986) 1

P.A.D. 311; *Brent London Borough Council and Ashton Homes* (Ref. T/APP/T5150/A/85031344/P3) (1986) 1

P.A.D. 314; *Tamworth Borough Council and Simpson (R.A.) and Son (Tamworth)* Ref. T/APP/Z3445/A/85/032993/P4) (1986) 1

P.A.D. 318; *Lewes District Council and Rendell and Aldous* (Ref. T/APP/P1425/A/85/036484/P2) (1986) 1

P.A.D. 321; *Fareham Borough Council and Truryn Leisure Services (U.K.)* (Ref. T/APP/A1720/A/85/033780/P5) (1986) 1 P.A.D. 324; *Salford City Council and Avanti Engineering* (Ref. T/APP/V4230/A/85/36430/P2) (1986) 1

P.A.D. 328; *Tunbridge Wells Borough Council and Boulding* (Ref. T/APP/M2270/A/85/036704/P4) (1986) 1

P.A.D. 331; *Luton Borough Council and Firbank (C.) and Son* (Ref. T/APP/A0210/A/85/035525/P5) (1986) 1

P.A.D. 334; *Erewash Borough Council and Lucking (C.J & D.J.)* (Ref. T/APP/N1025/A/85/34832/P2) (1986) 1

P.A.D. 338; *Walsall Metropolitan Borough Council and Robert M. Douglas Holdings* (Ref. T/APP/V4630/A/85/026623/P7) (1986) 1

P.A.D. 341; *Stafford Borough Council and Trustee Savings Bank* (Ref. T/APP/T3425/A/85/036134/P4) (1986) 1

P.A.D. 344; *Wealdon District Council and Mortlake* (Ref. T/APP/C1435/A/85/033119/P3) (1986) 1

P.A.D. 347.

sch. 9, regs. 86/623.

sch. 9, amended: 1986, c.63, sch. 11.

sch. 11, amended: *ibid.*, schs. 7, 9; repealed in pt.: *ibid.*, sch. 9.

schs. 12, 13, repealed: *ibid.*, sch. 12.

sch. 14, order 86/435.

sch. 19, amended: 1986, c.63, sch. 11.

1971—cont.

78. Town and Country Planning Act 1971— *cont.*

sch. 21, amended: *ibid.*, schs. 9, 11; repealed in pt.: *ibid.*, sch. 12.

sch. 24, repealed in pt.: *ibid.*

80. Banking and Financial Dealings Act 1971.

s. 2, amended: 1986, c.53, sch. 11.

1972

6. Summer Time Act 1972.

s. 2, order 86/223.

11. Superannuation Act 1972.

s. 1, order 86/2119.

s. 5, repealed in pt.: 1986, c.45, sch. 14.

s. 7, regs. 86/24, 214 (S.), 380, 1449.

s. 10, regs. 86/199, 587 (S.), 701 (S.).

s. 12, regs. 86/24, 199, 214 (S.), 380, 587 (S.), 701 (S.), 1449.

s. 18, repealed in pt. (S.): 1986, c.47, sch. 5.

s. 24, regs. 85/2036 (S.); 86/151, 409 (S.), 412 (S.).

sch. 1, amended: 1986, c.51, s.1.

sch. 3, regs. 86/199.

sch. 6, repealed in pt.: S.L.R. 1986.

sch. 7, regs. 86/24.

18. Maintenance Orders (Reciprocal Enforcement) Act 1972.

s. 31, amended (S.): 1986, c.47, sch. 3.

s. 32, amended (S.): *ibid.*; repealed in pt. (S.): *ibid.*, schs. 3, 5.

ss. 34, 43A, amended (S.): *ibid.*, sch. 3.

20. Road Traffic Act 1972.

see *Penman* v. *Parker, The Times*, April 14, 1986, D.C.

s. 1, see *R.* v. *Khan* [1985] R.T.R. 365, C.A.; *R.* v. *Crossman* [1986] R.T.R. 49, C.A.

s. 2, see *R.* v. *Hazell* [1985] R.T.R. 369, C.A.; *O'Toole* v. *MacDougall*, 1986 S.C.C.R. 56.

s. 3, see *R.* v. *Hazell* [1985] R.T.R. 369, C.A.; *McCallum* v. *Hamilton*, 1986 S.L.T. 156; *McLean* v. *Annan*, 1986 S.C.C.R. 52; *R.* v. *Bristol Crown Court, ex p. Jones; Jones* v. *Chief Constable of Avon and Somerset Constabulary* [1986] R.T.R. 259, D.C..

s. 5, see *Oxford* v. *Baxendale, The Times*, April 28, 1986, D.C.; *Archbold* v. *Jones* [1986] R.T.R. 178, D.C.; *Redmond* v. *Parry* [1986] R.T.R. 146, D.C.; *Thompson* v. *Thynne* [1986] R.T.R. 293, D.C.

s. 6, see *Graham* v. *Albert* [1985] R.T.R. 352, D.C.; *Duddy* v. *Gallagher* [1985] R.T.R. 401, D.C.; *Broadbent* v. *High* [1985] R.T.R. 359, D.C.; *Reid* v. *Tudhope*, 1986 S.L.T. 136; *Anderton* v. *Kinnard* [1986] R.T.R. 11, D.C.; *Chief Constable of the Avon and Somerset Constabulary* v. *Creech* [1986] Crim.L.R. 62, D.C.; [1986] R.T.R. 18, D.C.; *Walton* v. *Rimmer* [1986] R.T.R.

1972—cont.

20. Road Traffic Act 1972—*cont.*
31, D.C.; *Chief Constable of Gwent* v. *Dash* [1986] R.T.R. 41, D.C.; *Gilligan* v. *Tudhope*, 1986 S.L.T. 299; *Denneny* v. *Harding* [1986] Crim.L.R. 254, D.C.; *Oxford* v. *Baxendale, The Times*, April 28, 1986, D.C.; *Blake* v. *Pope, The Times*, May 15, 1986, D.C.; *Rawlins* v. *Brown, The Times*, June 6, 1986, D.C.; *Woodburn* v. *McLeod*, 1986 S.L.T. 325; *Ross* v. *Allan*, 1986 S.L.T. 349; *Sivyer* v. *Parker* [1986] Crim.L.R. 410, D.C.; *Johnson* v. *West Yorkshire Metropolitan Police* [1986] R.T.R. 167, D.C.; *Owen* v. *Morgan* [1986] R.T.R. 151, D.C.; *Waite* v. *Smith* [1986] Crim.L.R. 405, D.C.; *Price* v. *Nicholls* [1986] R.T.R. 155, D.C.; *McKoen* v. *Ellis, The Times*, July 11, 1986, D.C.; *Burditt* v. *Roberts* (1986) 150 J.P.344, D.C.; *Davidson* v. *Aitchison*, 1986 S.L.T. 402; *Harvie* v. *Cardle*, 1986 S.C.C.R. 41; *Smith* v. *Geraghty* [1986] R.T.R. 222, D.C.; *Perry* v. *McGovern* [1986] R.T.R. 240, D.C.; *Dawson* v. *Lunn* [1986] R.T.R. 234, D.C.; *Valentine* v. *McPhail*, 1986 S.L.T. 598; *Lang* v. *Hindhaugh* [1986] R.T.R. 271, D.C.; *Lloyd* v. *Morris* [1986] R.T.R. 299, D.C.; *Blake* v. *Pope* [1986] 1 W.L.R. 1152, D.C.; *Rynsard* v. *Spalding* [1986] R.T.R. 303, D.C.; *Jones* v. *Thomas (John Barrie), The Times*, November 5, 1986, D.C.; *McGrath* v. *Field, The Times*, November 20, 1986, D.C.; *Chief Constable of Kent* v. *Berry* [1986] R.T.R. 321, D.C.; *Burridge* v. *East* [1986] R.T.R. 328, D.C.; *Gordon* v. *Thorpe* [1986] R.T.R. 338, D.C.; *Denneny* v. *Harding* [1986] R.T.R. 350, D.C.; *R.* v. *Kingston upon Thames JJ., ex p. Khanna* [1986] R.T.R. 364, D.C.; *Fawcett* v. *Gasparics* [1986] R.T.R. 375, D.C.; *Burditt* v. *Roberts* (Note) [1986] R.T.R. 391, D.C.; *Wakely* v. *Hyams, The Times*, November 11, 1986, D.C.
s. 7, see *Graham* v. *Albert* [1985] R.T.R. 352, D.C.; *Bunyard* v. *Hayes* (Note) [1985] R.T.R. 348, D.C.; *Chief Constable of the Avon and Somerset Constabulary* v. *Creech* [1986] Crim.L.R. 62, D.C.; *Redmond* v. *Parry* [1986] R.T.R. 146, D.C.; *Teape* v. *Godfrey* [1986] R.T.R. 213, D.C.; *Blake* v. *Pope* [1986] 1 W.L.R. 1152, D.C.
s. 8, see *Bunyard* v. *Hayes* (Note) [1985] R.T.R. 348, D.C.; *Graham* v. *Albert* [1985] R.T.R. 352, D.C.; *Duddy* v. *Gallagher* [1985] R.T.R. 401, D.C.; *Broadbent* v. *High* [1985] R.T.R. 359, D.C.; *Reid* v. *Tudhope*, 1986 S.L.T. 136; *Harris* v. *Tudhope*, 1985 S.C.C.R. 305; *Anderton* v. *Kinnard* [1986] R.T.R. 11, D.C.; *Patterson* v. *Charlton* [1986]

1972—cont.

20. Road Traffic Act 1972—*cont.*
R.T.R. 18, D.C.; *Walton* v. *Rimmer* [1986] R.T.R. 31, D.C.; *Chief Constable of Kent* v. *Mather* [1986] R.T.R. 36, D.C.; *Chief Constable of Gwent* v. *Dash* [1986] R.T.R. 41, D.C.; *Oldfield* v. *Anderton* [1986] Crim.L.R. 189, D.C.; *Bain* v. *Tudhope*, 1985 S.C.C.R. 412; *Gilligan* v. *Tudhope*, 1986 S.L.T. 299; *Chief Constable of the Avon and Somerset Constabulary* v. *Creech* [1986] Crim.L.R. 62; [1986] R.T.R. 87, D.C.; *Denneny* v. *Harding* [1986] Crim.L.R. 254, D.C.; *Burridge* v. *East, The Times*, May 6, 1986, D.C.; *Clarke* v. *Hegarty, The Times*, May 19, 1986, D.C.; *Dye* v. *Manns* [1986] Crim.L.R. 337, D.C.; *Rawlins* v. *Brown, The Times*, June 6, 1986, D.C.; *Woodburn* v. *McLeod*, 1986 S.L.T. 325; *Ross* v. *Allan*, 1986 S.L.T. 349; *Sivyer* v. *Parker* [1986] Crim.L.R. 410, D.C.; *Archbold* v. *Jones* [1986] R.T.R. 178, D.C.; *Johnson* v. *West Yorkshire Metropolitan Police* [1986] R.T.R. 167, D.C.; *Owen* v. *Morgan* [1986] R.T.R. 151, D.C.; *Waite* v. *Smith* [1986] Crim.L.R. 405, D.C.; *Price* v. *Nicholls* [1986] R.T.R. 155, D.C.; *Burditt* v. *Roberts* (1986) 150 J.P. 344, D.C.; *Davidson* v. *Aitchison*, 1986 S.L.T. 402; *Smith* v. *Geraghty* [1986] R.T.R. 222, D.C.; *Perry* v. *McGovern* [1986] R.T.R. 240, D.C.; *Horrocks* v. *Binns* [1986] R.T.R. 202, D.C.; *Dempsey* v. *Catton* [1986] R.T.R. 194, D.C.; *Teape* v. *Godfrey* [1986] R.T.R. 213, D.C.; *McCormick* v. *Hitchins* (1986) 83 Cr.App.R. 11, D.C.; *R.* v. *Brentford Magistrates' Court, ex p. Clarke* [1986] Crim.L.R. 633, D.C.; *Oxford* v. *Baxendale* [1986] Crim.L.R. 631, D.C.; *Thompson* v. *Thynne* [1986] R.T.R. 293; [1986] Crim.L.R. 629, D.C.; *Chief Constable of Avon and Somerset Constabulary* v. *Kelliher* [1986] Crim.L.R. 635, D.C.; *Valentine* v. *McPhail*, 1986 S.L.T. 598; *Houston* v. *McLeod*, 1986 S.C.C.R. 219; *Manuel* v. *Stewart*, 1986 S.L.T. 593; *Smith* v. *Hand* [1986] R.T.R. 265, D.C.; *Oldfield* v. *Anderton* [1986] R.T.R. 314, D.C.; *McGrath* v. *Field, The Times*, November 20, 1986, D.C.; *Chief Constable of Kent* v. *Berry* [1986] R.T.R. 321; *Burridge* v. *East* [1986] R.T.R. 328, D.C.; *Gordon* v. *Thorpe* [1986] R.T.R. 338, D.C.; *Denneny* v. *Harding* [1986] R.T.R. 350, D.C.; *R.* v. *Kingston upon Thames JJ, ex p. Khanna* [1986] R.T.R. 364, D.C.; *Fawcett* v. *Gasparics* [1986] R.T.R. 375, D.C.; *Slender* v. *Boothby* [1986] R.T.R. 385, D.C.; *Wright* v. *Taplin* (Note) [1986] R.T.R. 388, D.C.; *Burditt* v. *Roberts* (Note) [1986] R.T.R. 391, D.C.

1972—cont.

20. Road Traffic Act 1972—*cont.*

s. 9, see *Chief Constable of Kent* v. *Mather* [1986] R.T.R. 36, D.C.

s. 10, see *Duddy* v. *Gallagher* [1985] R.T.R. 401, D.C.; *Perry* v. *McGovern, The Times*, December 20, 1985, D.C.; *Reid* v. *Tudhope*, 1986 S.L.T. 136; *Anderton* v. *Kinnard* [1986] R.T.R. 11, D.C.; *Patterson* v. *Charlton* [1986] R.T.R. 18, D.C.; *Walton* v. *Rimmer* [1986] R.T.R. 31, D.C.; *Rynsard* v. *Spalding* [1985] Crim.L.R. 795, D.C.; *Beck* v. *Scammell* [1985] Crim.L.R. 794, D.C.; *Chief Constable of the Avon and Somerset Constabulary* v. *Creech* [1986] Crim.L.R. 62; [1986] R.T.R. 87, D.C.; *Newton* v. *Woods, The Times*, June 16, 1986, D.C.; *Archbold* v. *Jones* [1986] R.T.R. 178, D.C.; *Johnson* v. *West Yorkshire Metropolitan Police* [1986] R.T.R. 167, D.C.; *Beck* v. *Scammell* [1986] R.T.R. 162, D.C.; *Price* v. *Nicholls* [1986] R.T.R. 155, D.C.; *Penman* v. *Parker* [1986] 1 W.L.R. 882, D.C.; *O'Brien* v. *Ferguson*, 1986 S.C.C.R. 155; *Toovey* v. *Chief Constable of Northumbria* [1986] Crim.L.R. 475, D.C.; *Smith* v. *Geraghty* [1986] R.T.R. 222, D.C.; *Perry* v. *McGovern* [1986] R.T.R. 240, D.C.; *R.* v. *Brentford Magistrates' Court, ex p. Clarke* [1986] Crim.L.R. 633, D.C.; *Dawson* v. *Lunn* [1986] R.T.R. 234, D.C.; *Lloyd* v. *Morris* [1986] R.T.R. 299, D.C.; *Rynsard* v. *Spalding* [1986] R.T.R. 303, D.C.; *Burridge* v. *East* [1986] R.T.R. 328, D.C.; *Denneny* v. *Harding* [1986] R.T.R. 350, D.C.; *Fawcett* v. *Gasparics* [1986] R.T.R. 375, D.C.; *Wright* v. *Taplin* (Note) [1986] R.T.R. 388, D.C.; *Burditt* v. *Roberts* (Note) [1986] R.T.R. 391, D.C.

s. 12, see *Duddy* v. *Gallagher* [1985] R.T.R. 401, D.C.; *Patterson* v. *Charlton* [1986] R.T.R. 18, D.C.; *Anderton* v. *Waring* [1986] R.T.R. 74, D.C.; *Johnson* v. *West Yorkshire Metropolitan Police* [1986] R.T.R. 167, D.C.; *Price* v. *Nicholls* [1986] R.T.R. 155, D.C.; *Smith* v. *Geraghty* [1986] R.T.R. 222, D.C.; *Thompson* v. *Thynne* [1986] R.T.R. 293, D.C.; *Lloyd* v. *Morris* [1986] R.T.R. 299, D.C.; *Rynsard* v. *Spalding* [1986] R.T.R. 303, D.C.; *Denneny* v. *Harding* [1986] R.T.R. 350, D.C.; *R.* v. *Kingston upon Thames JJ., ex p. Khanna* [1986] R.T.R. 364, D.C.

s. 25, see *McNamee* v. *Carmichael*, 1985 S.C.C.R. 289; *Bentley* v. *Mullen* [1986] R.T.R. 7, D.C.

ss. 32, 33, regs. 86/472.

s. 34, regs. 86/1078.

1972—cont.

20. Road Traffic Act 1972—*cont.*

s. 40, see *Simpson* v. *Vant* [1986] Crim.L.R. 473; [1986] R.T.R. 247, D.C.; *Percy* v. *Smith* [1986] R.T.R. 252, D.C.

s. 40, regs. 85/2051; 86/1078, 1597, 1812, 1813.

s. 41, regs. 86/1597.

s. 42, order 86/313.

s. 43, regs. 86/372, 904.

s. 44, see *Thomas* v. *Hooper* [1986] R.T.R. 1, D.C.

ss. 45, 46, see *Kennet* v. *Holding & Barnes; Harvey (T.L.)* v. *Hall* [1986] R.T.R. 334, D.C.

s. 45, regs. 86/371, 1090.

s. 46, see *Creek* v. *Fossett, Eccles and Supertents* [1986] Crim.L.R. 256.

ss. 47, 50, regs. 86/427, 739, 1089.

s. 63, regs. 86/369.

s. 88, regs. 86/748.

s. 93, see *Redmond* v. *Parry* [1986] R.T.R. 146, D.C.; *Chatters* v. *Burke* [1986] 3 All E.R. 168, D.C.; *McLean* v. *Annan*, 1986 S.C.C.R. 52; *Harvie* v. *Cardle*, 1986 S.C.C.R. 41; *Denneny* v. *Harding* [1986] R.T.R. 350, D.C.

s. 99, see *Lang* v. *Hindhaugh* [1986] R.T.R. 271, D.C.

s. 101, see *R.* v. *Preston* [1986] R.T.R. 136, C.A.; *Simpson* v. *Vant* [1986] R.T.R. 247, D.C.

s. 107, regs. 86/748.

s. 119, regs. 86/752, 868.

ss. 120, 124, regs. 86/868.

s. 126, regs. 86/1338.

ss. 131, 135, regs. 86/882, 1338.

s. 143, see *Thomas* v. *Hooper* [1986] R.T.R. 1, D.C.; *MacDonald* v. *MacGillivray*, 1986 S.C.C.R. 28; *Chief Constable of Avon and Somerset Constabulary* v. *Jest* [1986] R.T.R. 372, D.C..

s. 150, amended: 1986, c.45, sch. 14.

ss. 154, 155, amended: order 86/368.

s. 159, see *Chief Constable of Gwent* v. *Dash* [1986] R.T.R. 41, D.C.

s. 161, see *Sparks* v. *Worthington* [1986] R.T.R. 64, C.A.

s. 168, see *Blake* v. *Charles Sullivan Cars, The Times*, June 26, 1986, D.C.

s. 172, regs. 86/1078.

s. 177, see *Bentley* v. *Mullen* [1986] R.T.R. 7, D.C.

s. 179, see *Sage* v. *Townsend, The Times*, May 27, 1986, D.C.

s. 182, see *Taylor* v. *Comr. of Police of the Metropolis, The Times*, November 3, 1986, D.C.

s. 190, see *Percy* v. *Smith* [1986] R.T.R. 252, D.C.; *Chief Constable of Avon and Somerset* v. *F, The Times*, November 3, 1986, D.C.

1972—cont.

20. **Road Traffic Act 1972**—*cont.*
 s. 196, see *Lang* v. *Hindhaugh* [1986]
 R.T.R. 271, D.C.
 s. 199, regs. 86/371.
 s. 203, see *Spittle* v. *Kent County Constabulary* [1986] R.T.R. 142, C.A.
 sch. 4, see *Cardle* v. *Campbell*, 1985
 S.C.C.R. 309; *Bentley* v. *Mullen* [1986]
 R.T.R. 7, D.C.; *R.* v. *Preston* [1986]
 R.T.R. 136, C.A.; *Redmond* v. *Parry*
 [1986] R.T.R. 146, D.C.; *Simpson* v.
 Vant [1986] Crim.L.R. 473; [1986]
 R.T.R. 247, D.C.; *Aird* v. *Valentine*,
 1986 S.C.C.R. 353; *Denneny* v. *Harding*
 [1986] R.T.R. 350, D.C.

38. **Matrimonial Proceedings (Polygamous Marriages) Act 1972.**
 s. 2, repealed in pt.: S.L.R. 1986.

41. **Finance Act 1972.**
 s. 38, see *R.* v. *Asif* [1985] Crim.L.R. 679;
 (1985) 82 Cr.App.R. 123, C.A.
 ss. 53, 54, repealed: S.L.R. 1986.
 s. 79, amended: 1986, c.41, s.26.
 s. 84, amended: *ibid.*, s.17.
 ss. 84, 85, 100, see *Collard* v. *Mining & Industrial Holdings* [1986] S.T.C. 230,
 Walton J.
 s. 100, amended: 1986, c.41, s.49; repealed
 in pt.: *ibid.*, s.49, sch. 23.
 s. 103, repealed in pt.: *ibid.*, s.17, sch. 23.
 s. 107, repealed in pt.: *ibid.*, s.49, sch. 23.
 s. 122, repealed: S.L.R. 1986.
 sch. 16, see *R.* v. *H.M. Inspector of Taxes,
 ex p. Lansing Bagnall* [1986] S.T.C. 453,
 C.A.
 sch. 16, amended: 1986, c.41, s.32; c.45,
 sch. 14.
 schs. 27, 28 (in pt.), repealed: S.L.R.
 1986.

42. **Town and Country Planning (Amendment) Act 1972.**
 ss. 5, 6, repealed: 1986, c.63, sch. 12.
 s. 10C, added: *ibid.*, s.51.

46. **Housing (Financial Provisions) (Scotland) Act 1972.**
 s. 23A, see *Lord Advocate* v. *Stirling District Council*, 1986 S.L.T. 179.
 s. 23A, order 86/7.
 ss. 24, 25, amended: 1986, c.50, sch. 10.
 sch. 4, repealed in pt.: 1986, c.65, sch. 2.

47. **Housing Finance Act 1972.**
 s. 91A, see *Yorkbrook Investments* v.
 Batten (1986) 52 P. & C.R. 51, C.A.

50. **Legal Advice and Assistance Act 1972.**
 repealed (S.): 1986, c.47, sch. 5.
 ss. 1, 11, regs. 85/1860 (S.).
 s. 5, regs. 86/1359 (S.).

52. **Town and Country Planning (Scotland) Act 1972.**
 ss. 12, 19, amended: 1986, c.63, sch. 11.
 ss. 19, 20, see *City of Aberdeen District Council* v. *Secretary of State for Scotland*, 1986 S.L.T. 458.

1972—cont.

52. **Town and Country Planning (Scotland) Act 1972**—*cont.*
 s. 21, order 85/2007.
 s. 21, amended: 1986, c.63, sch. 11.
 ss. 21A–21E, added: *ibid.*, s.26.
 s. 26, amended: *ibid.*, sch. 11.
 s. 28A, added: *ibid.*
 s. 29, repealed in pt.: *ibid.*, sch. 12.
 s. 31, amended: *ibid.*, sch. 6.
 ss. 32, 33, amended: *ibid.*, sch. 11.
 s. 38, amended: *ibid.*, sch. 6.
 s. 51, amended: *ibid.*
 s. 52, amended: *ibid.*, sch. 9.
 s. 53, amended: *ibid.*; repealed in pt.:
 ibid., schs. 11, 12.
 ss. 54, 54A, amended: *ibid.*, sch. 9.
 ss. 54D, 56 AA, added: *ibid.*
 s. 55, amended: *ibid.*, sch. 11.
 ss. 56A–56O, added: *ibid.*, s.35.
 s. 58, repealed in pt.: *ibid.*, sch. 12.
 s. 63, amended: *ibid.*, sch. 11; repealed in
 pt.: *ibid.*, sch. 12.
 s. 63A, amended: *ibid.*, sch. 11.
 ss. 64–83, repealed: *ibid.*, sch. 12.
 s. 84, amended: *ibid.*, sch. 11.
 s. 85, repealed in pt.: *ibid.*, sch. 12.
 ss. 86, 87, amended: *ibid.*, sch. 11.
 s. 93, amended: *ibid.*, sch. 9.
 s. 94, amended: *ibid.*, sch. 11.
 s. 95A, amended: *ibid.*, sch. 9.
 ss. 97, 97A, substituted: *ibid.*
 s. 97B, added: *ibid.*, s.36.
 s. 98, amended: *ibid.*, sch. 11.
 ss. 99–101, amended: *ibid.*
 s. 120, repealed in pt.: S.L.R. 1986.
 ss. 136 (in pt.), 140, 154 (in pt.):
 repealed: 1986, c.63, sch. 12.
 s. 158, amended: *ibid.*, sch. 11; repealed
 in pt.: *ibid.*, sch. 12.
 s. 169, repealed in pt.: *ibid.*
 ss. 170, 173, amended: *ibid.*, sch. 11.
 s. 174, repealed: *ibid.*, sch. 12.
 s. 175, amended: *ibid.*, sch. 11.
 s. 180, repealed in pt.: *ibid.*, sch. 12.
 ss. 205, 205A, amended: *ibid.*, sch. 1;
 repealed in pt.: *ibid.*, sch. 12.
 s. 212, amended: 1986, c.31, sch. 4; c.44,
 sch. 7.
 s. 213, repealed in pt.: 1986, c.31, sch. 6;
 c.44, sch. 9.
 s. 226, repealed in pt.: 1986, c.63, sch. 12.
 s. 231, amended: *ibid.*, schs. 6, 7, 11.
 s. 232, amended: *ibid.*, sch. 6.
 ss. 233 (in pt.), 237–239, 247 (in pt.),
 repealed: *ibid.*, sch. 12.
 s. 253, amended: *ibid.*, sch. 7.
 s. 257A, added: *ibid.*
 s. 260, amended: *ibid.*, sch. 11.
 s. 262A, amended: *ibid.*, sch. 9.
 s. 262C, added: *ibid.*, sch. 11.
 s. 265, amended: *ibid.*, sch. 7.
 s. 267, amended: *ibid.*, sch. 11.
 ss. 267A, 267B, added: *ibid.*
 s. 270, amended: *ibid.*

1972—cont.

52. Town and Country Planning (Scotland) Act 1972—cont.
s. 273, order 85/2007.
s. 273, amended: 1986, c.63, schs. 6, 9; repealed in pt.: *ibid.*, sch. 12.
s. 275, amended: *ibid.*, schs. 6, 7, 11; repealed in pt.: S.L.R. 1986; c.44, sch. 9; c.63, sch. 12.
sch. 6A, added: *ibid.*, s.26, sch. 6.
sch. 7, amended: *ibid.*, sch. 11.
sch. 10, amended: *ibid.*, sch. 9.
sch. 17, amended: *ibid.*, sch. 11.
sch. 19, amended: *ibid.*, schs. 9, 11; repealed in pt.: *ibid.*, sch. 12.
sch. 22, repealed in pt.: *ibid.*

54. British Library Act 1972.
functions transferred: order 86/600.

60. Gas Act 1972.
ss. 1 (in pt.), 2 (in pt.), 3–5, 6 (in pt.), 7–13, Pts. II, III (ss.14–31), 32–50, schs. 1–8, repealed: 1986, c.44, sch. 9.

61. Land Charges Act 1972.
s. 16, amended: 1986, c.45, sch. 14.
sch. 2, amended, 1986, c.5, sch. 14; repealed in pt.: *ibid.*, sch. 15.

62. Agriculture (Miscellaneous Provisions) Act 1972.
s. 15, repealed: 1986, c.5, sch. 15.
s. 16, repealed in pt.: 1986, c.49, sch. 4.
s. 20, order 86/1342.

66. Poisons Act 1972.
s. 2, order 86/9.
s. 7, rules 86/10, 1704.

67. Companies (Floating Charges and Receivers) (Scotland) Act 1972.
s. 17, see *Mace Builders (Glasgow)* v. *Lunn, The Times*, October 11, 1986, C.A.

68. European Communities Act 1972.
s. 1, amended: 1986, c.58, s.1.
s. 2, regs. 85/2075; 86/23, 68, 560, 666, 890, 938, 947, 1082, 1233, 1272, 1295, 1352, 1373, 1391, 1447, 1456, 1457, 1500, 1501, 1542, 1611, 1613(S.), 1669, 1735, 1795, 1876, 1894, 1980, 2076; S.Rs. 1986 Nos. 188, 299, 334.
s. 3, amended: 1986, c.58, s.2.
s. 5, order 85/2019; 86/346–348, 813.
s. 9, see *TCB* v. *Gray* [1986] 1 All E.R. 587, Browne-Wilkinson V.-C.
s. 11, amended: 1986, c.58, s.2.
s. 24, regs, 86/470.
sch. 2, order 86/813.

70. Local Government Act 1972.
order 86/1190.
s. 13, see *Taylor* v. *Masefield, The Times*, May 22, 1986, C.A.
s. 51, orders 85/2061; 86/281, 321, 1619, 1909.
s. 58, orders 86/526, 533, 535, 556.
s. 67, orders 85/2061–2064; 86/4, 281, 321, 526, 533, 535, 556, 1364, 1619, 1909, 2008.

1972—cont.

70. Local Government Act 1972—cont.
s. 94, see *R.* v. *Newham London Borough Council, ex p. Haggerty, The Times*, April 11, 1986, Mann J.
s. 98, amended: 1986, c.60, sch. 16.
s. 100G, order 86/854.
s. 101, see *R.* v. *Secretary of State for the Environment, ex p. Hillingdon London Borough Council* [1986] (Note) 2 All E.R. 273, C.A.
s. 101, repealed in pt.: S.L.R. 1986.
s. 109, order 86/854.
s. 111, see *Smith* v. *Skinner; Gladden* v. *McMahon* (1986) 26 R.V.R. 45, D.C.; *Westminster City Council, Re* [1986] 2 W.L.R. 807, H.L.; *R.* v. *Oxfordshire Education Authority, ex p. W, The Times*, November 22, 1986, D.C.
s. 112, see *R.* v. *District Auditor for Leicester, ex p. Leicester City Council* (1985) 25 R.V.R. 191, Woolf J.
s. 119, repealed in pt.: 1986, c.50, sch. 11.
s. 123, see *R.* v. *Doncaster Metropolitan Borough Council, ex p. Braim, The Times*, October 11, 1986, McCullough J.
s. 125, see *Wealden District Council and Broad Oak United Football and Boys Club* (Ref. T/APP/E1435/A/84/017949/P6) (1986) 1 P.A.D. 111.
s. 125, substituted: 1986, c.63, s.43.
s. 137, see *R.* v. *District Auditor for Leicester, ex p. Leicester City Council* (1985) 25 R.V.R. 191, Woolf J.; *R.* v. *District Auditor No. 3 Audit District of West Yorkshire Metropolitan County Council, ex p. West Yorkshire Metropolitan County Council* [1986] 26 R.V.R. 24, D.C.
s. 137, amended: 1986, c.10, s.3.
s. 142, see *R.* v. *Inner London Education Authority, ex p. Westminster City Council* [1986] 1 All E.R. 19, Glidewell J.
s. 142, amended: 1986, c.10, s.3.
s. 146, amended: 1986, c.60, sch. 16.
s. 147, see *R.* v. *District Auditor for Leicester, ex p. Leicester City Council* (1985) 25 R.V.R. 191, Woolf J.
s. 151, see *Smith* v. *Skinner; Gladden* v. *McMahon* (1986) 26 R.V.R. 45, D.C.
s. 161, see *Wilkinson* v. *Doncaster Metropolitan Borough Council* (1986) 84 L.G.R. 257, C.A.
ss. 173, 177, regs. 86/724.
s. 177, amended: 1986, c.10, s.11.
ss. 177A, 178, regs. 86/299, 724.
s. 182, amended: 1986, c.63, sch. 11; repealed in pt.: *ibid.*, sch. 12.
s. 183, repealed in pt.: *ibid.*
s. 214, order 86/1782.
s. 222, see *Runnymede Borough Council* v. *Ball* [1986] 1 All E.R. 629, C.A.; *London Docklands Corp.* v. *Rank Hovis* (1985) 84 L.G.R. 101, C.A.
s. 241, order 86/561.

CAP.
1972—cont.
70. Local Government Act 1972—*cont.*
s. 250, see *Greenwich London Borough Council and Trident Builders Merchants* (Refs. APP/5012/C/83/3323, APP/E5330 /C84/286, APP/E5330/A/83/7343 (PLUP 4C) (1985) 1 P.A.D. 93.
s. 250, repealed in pt.: 1986, c.63, sch. 12.
s. 262, orders 86/114, 1133, 1190, 1461, 2068, 2106.
s. 266, regs. 86/299; orders 86/561, 854.
s. 270, see *London Docklands Corp.* v. *Rank Hovis* (1985) 84 L.G.R. 101, C.A.
sch. 10, orders 85/2063, 2064; 86/4, 1364, 2008.
sch. 12, amended: 1986, c.10, s.10.
sch. 12A, amended: 1986, c.24, s.2; c.53, sch. 18.
sch. 13, regs. 86/282, 345.
sch. 16, order 86/435; amended: order 86/452; repealed in pt.: 1986, c.63, sch. 12.
sch. 17, order 86/561.
71. Criminal Justice Act 1972.
sch. 5, repealed in pt.: 1986, c.60, sch. 17.
75. Pensioners and Family Income Supplement Act 1972.
repealed: 1986, c.50, sch. 11.
80. Pensioners' Payments and National Insurance Contributions Act 1972.
repealed: 1986, c.50, sch. 11.

1973
2. National Theatre and Museum of London Act 1973.
repealed: 1986, c.8, sch.
14. Costs in Criminal Cases Act 1973.
s. 2, see *R.* v. *Nottingham JJ., ex p. Fohmann, The Times,* October 27, 1986, D.C.
16. Education Act 1973.
s. 3, regs. 86/1325.
17. Northern Ireland Assembly Act 1973.
ss. 2, 5, order 86/1811.
18. Matrimonial Causes Act 1973.
s. 1, see *Quoraishi* v. *Quoraishi* (1985) 15 Fam. Law 308, C.A.; *Cahill* v. *Cahill* (1986) 16 Fam. Law 102, C.A.
s. 11, amended: 1986, c.16, s.6.
s. 23, see *Sherdley* v. *Sherdley* [1986] 2 All E.R. 202, C.A.; *Collins* v. *Collins, The Times,* August 12, 1986, C.A.; *R.* v. *Rushmoor Borough Council, ex p. Barrett, The Times,* September 5, 1986, Reeve J.
ss. 23, 25, see *Roberts* v. *Roberts* [1986] 1 W.L.R. 437, Wood J.
ss. 24, 24A, see *R.* v. *Rushmoor Borough Council, ex p. Barrett, The Times,* September 5, 1986, Reeve J.
s. 25, see *Michael* v. *Michael, The Times,* May 28, 1986, C.A.; *Sherdley* v. *Sherdley* [1986] 2 All E.R. 202, C.A.; *Collins* v. *Collins, The Times,* August 12, 1986, C.A.

CAP.
1973—cont.
18. Matrimonial Causes Act 1973—*cont.*
s. 25A, see *Morris* v. *Morris* (1986) 16 Fam. Law 24, C.A.; *Seaton* v. *Seaton, The Times,* February 24, 1986, C.A.
s. 31, see *Morris* v. *Morris* (1986) 16 Fam. Law 24, C.A.; *Sandford* v. *Sandford* (1986) 16 Fam. Law 104, C.A.; *S.* v. *S., The Times,* July 9, 1986, Walker J.; *S.* v. *S.* [1986] 3 W.L.R. 518, Waite J.
s. 39, amended: 1986, c.45, sch. 14.
s. 41, amended: 1986, c.55, sch. 1.
s. 43, see *J.* v. *Devon County Council (Wardship: Jurisdiction)* (1986) 16 Fam. Law 162, Swinton Thomas J.
s. 43, amended: 1985, c.28, s.1.
s. 45, see *Williams* v. *Att.-Gen., The Times,* October 29, 1986, Latey J.
s. 45, repealed: 1986, c.55, sch. 2.
s. 47, amended: *ibid.,* sch. 1.
s. 49, see *Bradley* v. *Bradley (Queen's Proctor Intervening* (1986) 16 Fam. Law 25, Eastham J.
s. 50, rules 86/634, 1096.
s. 50, amended: 1986, c.55, sch. 1; repealed in pt.: *ibid.,* schs. 1, 2.
s. 51, order 86/696.
26. Land Compensation Act 1973.
s. 29, see *Greater London Council* v. *Holmes* [1986] 1 All E.R. 739, C.A.; *Casale* v. *Islington, London Borough of* (1985) 18 H.L.R. 146, Taylor J.
ss. 29, 32, amended: 1986, c.63, s.9.
s. 34, amended: 1986, c.5, sch. 14.
s. 44, amended: 1986, c.44, sch. 7.
ss. 48, 56, amended: 1986, c.5, sch. 14.
s. 58, amended: 1986, c.44, sch. 7.
ss. 59, 87, amended: 1986, c.5, sch. 14.
s. 73, amended: 1986, c.63, sch. 5.
27. Bahamas Independence Act 1973.
s. 5, repealed: S.L.R. 1986.
29. Guardianship Act 1973.
see *Essex County Council* v. *T, The Times,* March 15, 1986, C.A.
s. 1, amended: 1986, c.55, sch. 1; repealed in pt.: *ibid.,* schs. 1, 2.
ss. 2, 5, repealed in pt.: *ibid.*
s. 10, amended: *ibid.,* sch. 1.
ss. 10, 11 (in pt.), 12 (in pt.), repealed (S.): 1986, c.9, sch. 2.
s. 13, amended (S.): *ibid.,* sch. 1.
s. 15 (in pt.), schs. 4, 5 (in pt.), repealed (S.): *ibid.,* sch. 2.
sch. 2, repealed in pt.: 1986, c.55, schs. 1, 2.
33. Protection of Wrecks Act 1973.
s. 1, order 86/1441.
ss. 1, 3, order 86/1020.
36. Northern Ireland Constitution Act 1973.
s. 21, see *French's Application, Re* [1985] 7 N.I.J.B. 48, Carswell J.
s. 26, order 86/222.
s. 28, amended: 1986, c.56, sch. 3; repealed in pt.: *ibid.,* sch. 4.

1973—cont.

37. Water Act 1973.
s. 29, order 86/1952.
s. 30, see *South West Water Authority* v. *Rumbles, The Times,* May 7, 1986, C.A.; *South West Water Authority* v. *Rumbles (No. 2)* (1986) 26 R.V.R. 144, C.A.
s. 34, see *London Electricity Board* v. *Redbridge London Borough Council* (1985) 84 L.G.R. 146, Stocker J.
s. 38, amended: order 86/208.

38. Social Security Act 1973.
s. 58, amended: 1986, c.50, sch. 10.
s. 64, amended: *ibid.,* s.12, sch. 10.
s. 65, orders 86/111, 465, 940, 946.
s. 66, regs. 86/1716.
s. 66, amended: 1986, c.50, sch. 10.
s. 67, amended: *ibid.,* schs. 5, 10.
ss. 68, 69, amended: *ibid.,* sch. 10.
s. 70, repealed: 1986, c.48, sch. 5
s. 92, repealed in pt.: 1986, c.50, sch. 11.
s. 99, regs. 86/1716.
s. 99, amended: 1986, c.50, sch. 10; repealed in pt.: *ibid.,* sch. 11.
sch. 16, regs. 86/1716.
sch. 16, amended: 1986, c.50, s.10, sch. 10.
sch. 23, amended: *ibid.,* sch. 11.

41. Fair Trading Act 1973.
s. 43, repealed in pt. (S.): 1986, c.47, sch. 5.
Pt. 5 (ss.57–77), see *R.* v. *Monopolies and Mergers Commission, ex p. Matthew Brown, The Times,* July 18, 1986, Macpherson J.
s. 75, see *R.* v. *Monopolies and Mergers Commission, ex p. Argyll Group* [1986] 2 All E.R. 257, C.A.
s. 133, amended: 1986, c.31, sch. 4; c.44, sch. 7; c.60, sch. 13.
sch. 5, amended: 1986, c.44, sch. 7.
sch. 7, repealed in pt.: 1986, c.31, sch. 6.

43. Hallmarking Act 1973.
s. 4, regs. 86/1757.
s. 4, amended: *ibid.*
s. 21, regs. 86/1757.
sch. 1, order 86/1758; amended: *ibid.*
sch. 2, amended: order 86/1757.

45. Domicile and Matrimonial Proceedings Act 1973.
ss. 2, 15, 16, repealed: 1986, c.55, sch. 2.
sch. 2, amended (S.): 1986, c.9, sch. 1; repealed in pt. (S.): *ibid.,* sch. 2.

48. Pakistan Act 1973.
s. 4, repealed in pt.: 1986, c.55, sch. 2.

50. Employment and Training Act 1973.
s. 12, amended: 1986, c.50, sch. 10.

51. Finance Act 1973.
s. 17, see *Stevenson* v. *Wishart* [1986] 1 All E.R. 404, Knox J.
s. 31, repealed in pt.: 1986, c.41, sch. 23.
s. 46, functions transferred: order 86/600.
s. 56, regs. 86/589, 831, 1043.

1973—cont.

51. Finance Act 1973—*cont.*
sch. 19, see *National Smokeless Fuels* v. *I.R.C.* [1986] S.T.C. 300, Ch.D.
sch. 21, repealed in pt.: 1986, c.41, sch. 23.

52. Prescription and Limitation (Scotland) Act 1973.
s. 6, see *Fyfe* v. *Croudace* (O.H.), 1986 S.L.T. 528; *Grindall* v. *John Mitchell (Grangemouth)* (O.H.), 1987 S.L.T. 137.
ss. 6, 9, see *Barclay* v. *Chief Constable, Northern Constabulary* (O.H.), 1986 S.L.T. 562.
s. 17, see *Sellars* v. *I.M.I. Yorkshire Imperial,* 1986 S.L.T. 629; *Barclay* v. *Chief Constable, Northern Constabulary* (O.H.), 1986 S.L.T. 562; *Grindall* v. *John Mitchell (Grangemouth)* (O.H.), 1987 S.L.T. 137
s. 22, see *Barclay* v. *Chief Constable, Northern Constabulary* (O.H.), 1986 S.L.T. 562.

56. Land Compensation (Scotland) Act 1973.
ss. 27, 29, amended: 1986, c.65, s.20.
ss. 41, 54, amended: 1986, c.44, sch. 7.

57. Badgers Act 1973.
s. 8, amended: 1986, c.14, sch. 3.

61. Pensioners' Payments and National Insurance Act 1973.
repealed: 1986, c.50, sch. 11.

62. Powers of Criminal Courts Act 1973.
s. 13, see *R.* v. *Secretary of State for the Home Department, ex p. Thornton* [1986] 3 W.L.R. 158, C.A.; *R.* v. *Barnes (W.T.)* (1986) 83 Cr.App.R. 58, C.A.
s. 14, see *Thorpe* v. *Griggs* (1984) 6 Cr.App.R.(S.) 286, D.C.
s. 16, see *R.* v. *Worcester Crown Court, ex p. Lamb* (1985) 7 Cr.App.R.(S.) 44, D.C.
s. 21, see *R.* v. *Cardiff JJ., ex p. Salter* (1986) 1 F.L.R. 162, Wood J.
ss. 22, 23, 26, see *R.* v. *Barnes (W.T.)* (1986) 83 Cr.App.R. 58, C.A.
s. 36, see *Gooch* v. *Ewing (Allied Irish Bank, Garnishee)* [1985] 3 All E.R. 654, C.A.
s. 39, see *R.* v. *Mayer* (1984) 6 Cr.App.R.(S.) 193, C.A.; *R.* v. *Cannon* (1986) 82 Cr.App.R. 286, C.A.
s. 39, amended: 1986, c.45, sch. 14.
s. 40, see *R.* v. *Prefas, The Times,* November 12, 1986, C.A.
s. 43, see *R.* v. *Slater (J.K.)* [1986] 1 W.L.R. 1340, C.A.
s. 44, see *R.* v. *Powell (M. B.)* (1984) 6 Cr.App.R.(S.) 354, C.A.; *R.* v. *Arif Mohammed* (1985) 7 Cr.App.R.(S.) 92, C.A.; *R.* v. *Parrington* (1985) 7 Cr.App.R. (S.) 18, C.A.
s. 54, sch. 3, orders 85/2031; 86/464, 945, 1280, 1713.

CAP.

1973—cont.

65. Local Government (Scotland) Act 1973.
s. 17, orders 86/209, 210.
s. 42, amended: 1986, c.60, sch. 16.
ss. 45, 49A, regs. 86/588.
s. 50G, order 86/1433.
ss. 83, 88, amended: 1986, c.10, s.3.
ss. 108, 108A, 211, see *Lord Advocate* v. *Stirling District Council*, 1986 S.L.T. 179.
s. 111, regs. 86/407, 411.
s. 117, repealed: S.L.R. 1986.
ss. 179, 210, amended: 1986, c.63, sch. 11.
s. 210A, added: *ibid.*
s. 233, regs. 86/407; order 86/1433.
s. 223, amended: 1986, c.63, sch.11.
sch. 27, repealed in pt.: 1986, c.49, sch. 4.
67. Fuel and Electricity (Control) Act 1973.
s. 10, order 86/1885.

1974

4. Legal Aid Act 1974.
s. 1, regs. 86/643.
s. 1, amended: *ibid.*; 1986, c.50, sch. 10.
s. 2, see *Parry* v. *Parry* [1986] 16 Fam. Law 211, C.A
s. 4, amended: 1986, c.50, sch 10.
s. 11, regs. 86/274, 276.
s. 11, amended: 1986, c.50, sch. 10.
s. 13, see *Landau* v. *Purvis, The Times*, August 12, 1986, G. Godfrey Q.C.
s. 20, regs. 86/272, 275, 276, 445, 643, 1186, 1559.
s. 28, amended: 1986, c.28, s.3.
ss. 28, 31, see *R.* v. *Huntingdon Magistrates' Court, ex p. Yapp* [1986] Crim.L.R. 689, D.C.
s. 30, regs. 86/273.
s. 39, regs. 86/273, 274, 444, 1515, 1835.
sch. 1, amended: 1986, c.50, sch. 10.
7. Local Government Act 1974.
s. 15, see *Investors in Industry Commercial Properties* v. *Norwich City Council* [1986] 2 W.L.R. 925, H.L.
sch. 3, amended: 1986, c.44, sch. 7.
sch. 5, amended: 1986, c.61, sch. 4.
sch. 6, repealed in pt.: 1986, c.63, sch. 12.
14. National Insurance Act 1974.
s. 6, amended: 1986, c.50, sch. 10; repealed in pt.: *ibid.*, sch. 11.
23. Juries Act 1974.
s. 18, see *R.* v. *Bliss* [1986] Crim.L.R. 467, C.A.
24. Prices Act 1974.
s. 2, order 86/175.
28. Northern Ireland Act 1974.
s. 1, order 86/1047.
sch. 1, S.R.s. 1986 Nos. 107, 124, 169.
30. Finance Act 1974.
ss. 2, 22, repealed in pt.: 1986, c.41, sch. 23.
s. 37, repealed in pt.: *ibid.*, s.17, sch. 23.

CAP.

1974—cont.

30. Finance Act 1974—*cont.*
s. 53, repealed: S.L.R. 1986.
schs. 11, 12, repealed in pt.: 1986, c.41, sch. 23.
schs. 13, 14 (in pt.), repealed: S.L.R. 1986.
32. Town and Country Planning Amenities Act 1974.
ss. 3 (in pt.), 5, repealed: 1986, c.63, sch. 12.
s. 5, repealed (S.): *ibid.*
37. Health and Safety at Work etc., Act 1974.
s. 2, see *Tudhope* v. *City of Glasgow District Council*, 1986, S.C.C.R. 168.
s. 2, regs. 86/890.
s. 3, see *R.* v. *Mara, The Times*, November 13, 1986, C.A.
ss. 10, 11, 15, 18, see *Hadley* v. *Hancox, The Times*, November 18, 1986, D.C.
s. 15, regs. 85/2023; 86/890, 1709, 1922, 1951.
s. 33, see *Kemp* v. *Liebherr—Great Britain, The Times*, November 5, 1986, D.C.
s. 34, amended: 1986, c.44, sch. 7.
s. 37, see *Dutton & Clark* v. *Daly* [1985] I.C.R. 780, E.A.T.
s. 43, regs. 86/392, 669.
s. 60, repealed in pt.: S.L.R. 1986.
s. 82, regs. 86/392, 1922, 1951.
sch. 3, regs. 85/2023; 86/890.
sch. 1, repealed in pt.: 1986, c.59, sch.
sch. 3, regs. 86/1951.
sch. 4, repealed in pt.: S.L.R. 1986.
38. Land Tenure Reform (Scotland) Act 1974.
s. 8, repealed in pt.: 1986, c.65, sch. 2.
39. Consumer Credit Act 1974.
ss. 11, 12, see *U.D.T.* v. *Whitfield*, June 12, 1986; Judge Vos, Newcastle County Ct.
ss. 9, 15, 56, see *Moorgate Mercantile Leasing* v. *Isobel Gell and Ugolini Dispensers (U.K.)*, October 21, 1985; H.H. Judge Rice; Grays Thurrock County Court.
s. 16, order 86/1105.
s. 16, amended: 1986, c.53, sch. 18; c.63, s.22; repealed in pt.: 1986, c.53, sch. 19.
s. 22, regs. 86/1016.
s. 39, see *Brookes* v. *Retail Credit Cards* [1986] Crim.L.R. 327, D.C.
s. 138, see *Davies* v. *Directloans* [1986] 1 W.L.R. 823, Edward Nugee Q.C. sitting as a deputy High Court judge; *Coldunell* v. *Gallon* [1986] 1 All E.R. 429, C.A.
ss. 145, 147, see *Brookes* v. *Retail Credit Cards* [1986] Crim.L.R. 327, D.C.
s. 147, regs. 86/1016.
s. 165, see *Aitchison* v. *Rizza*, 1985 S.C.C.R. 297.
s. 174, amended: 1986, c.31, sch. 4; c.44, sch. 7.
s. 182, order 86/1105.
s. 189, regs. 86/1016.
s. 189, amended: 1986, c.53, sch. 18.

CAP.

1974—cont.

40. Control of Pollution Act 1974.
see *Dudley Metropolitan Borough Council and Davies and Firmstone* (Ref. T/APP/C4615/A/84/020675/P2) (1985) 1 P.A.D. 1; *Hereford and Worcester County Council and Dubberley* (Ref. APP/5058/D/83/75 and APP/F1800/A/84/14233) (1985) 1 P.A.D. 85.
ss. 5, 10, see *Hereford and Worcester County Council and Newbould* (Ref. LW/APP/HE/202) (1986) 1 P.A.D. 281.
s. 32, order 86/1623.
s. 73, repealed in pt.: 1986, c.44, sch. 9.
s. 100, regs. 86/902, 1992.
s. 104, regs. 86/902, 1992; order 86/1623.

43. Merchant Shipping Act 1974.
s. 1, orders 86/1777, 2038.
s. 5, order 86/296.
s. 14, order 86/310.
s. 24, repealed in pt.: S.L.R. 1986.

46. Friendly Societies Act 1974.
s. 42, regs. 85/1919.
s. 87, amended: 1986, c.45, sch. 14.
s. 104, regs. 86/620.
s. 109, regs. 85/1919.
sch. 10, repealed in pt.: 1986, c.53, sch. 19.

47. Solicitors Act 1974.
s. 32, amended: 1986, c.53, sch. 18; repealed in pt.: *ibid.*, schs. 18, 19.
s. 33, amended: *ibid.*, sch. 18.
s. 74, see *Tarrant* v. *Speechly Bircham*, May 19, 1986, H.H. Judge Birks, Slough County Ct.
s. 85, see *Lipkin Gorman* v. *Karpaule and Lloyds Bank* [1986] F.L.R. 271, Alliott J.
ss. 85, 87, amended: 1986, c.53, sch. 18.

48. Railways Act 1974.
s. 3, order 86/1891.

49. Insurance Companies Act 1974.
ss. 2, 11, see *Phoenix General Insurance Co. of Greece SA* v. *Halvanon Insurance Co.; Same* v. *Administratia Asigurarilor de Stat, Financial Times*, October 15, 1986, C.A.

50. Road Traffic Act 1974.
s. 24, sch. 6, see *Bentley* v. *Mullen* [1986] R.T.R. 7, D.C.

52. Trade Union and Labour Relations Act 1974.
s. 1, repealed in pt.: S.L.R. 1986.
s. 2, see *Burnley Nelson Rossendale and District Textile Workers' Union* v. *Amalgamated Textile Workers' Union* [1986] 1 All E.R. 885, Tudor Price J.
ss. 2, 14, see *News Group Newspapers* v. *Society of Graphical and Allied Trades 1982* [1986] I.R.L.R. 227, C.A.
s. 8, regs. 86/302; amended: *ibid.*
s. 13, see *Barretts & Baird (Wholesale)* v. *Institution of Professional Civil Servants, Financial Times*, November 26, 1986, Henry J.

CAP.

1974—cont.

52. Trade Union and Labour Relations Act 1974—cont.
s. 15, see *News Group Newspapers* v. *Sogat 1982, The Times*, August 1, 1986, Stuart-Smith J.
s. 17, see *Scotsman Publications* v. *Society of Graphical and Allied Trades* (O.H.), 1986 S.L.T. 646.
s. 18, see *Marley* v. *Forward Trust Group* [1986] I.R.L.R. 43, E.A.T.; *National Coal Board* v. *National Union of Mineworkers, The Times*, June 21, 1986, Scott J.
ss. 20–24, sch. 4 (in pt.), repealed: S.L.R. 1986.

53. Rehabilitation of Offenders Act 1974.
see *D.* v. *Yates, The Times*, December 3, 1986, C.A.
s. 4, orders 86/1249.

54. Pensioners' Payments Act 1974.
repealed: 1986, c.50, sch. 11.

1975

3. Arbitration Act 1975.
s. 1, see *S.I. Sethia Liners* v. *State Trading Corp. of India* [1985] 1 W.L.R. 1398, C.A.
s. 7, see *Zambia Steel & Buildings Supplies* v. *James Clark & Eaton, Financial Times*, August 15, 1986, C.A.
s. 7, order 86/949.

7. Finance Act 1975.
s. 6, amended: 1986, c.41, s.47.
sch. 4, functions transferred: order 86/600.
sch. 5, see *Cholmondeley* v. *I.R.C.* [1986] S.T.C. 384, Scott J.

14. Social Security Act 1975.
s. 1, repealed in pt.: 1986, c.50, sch.11.
s. 4, amended: order 86/25; 1986, c.50, s.74, sch. 10.
ss. 7, 8, amended: order 86/25.
s. 9, amended: *ibid.*; 1986, c.41, s.41.
s. 12, repealed in pt.: 1986, c.50, sch. 11.
s. 13, amended: *ibid.*, sch. 8; repealed in pt.: *ibid.*, schs. 8, 11.
s. 14, amended: *ibid.*, sch. 10.
ss. 15A, 16, regs. 86/484.
s. 17, regs. 86/1011, 1118.
s. 18, amended: 1986, c.50, s.43.
s. 19, see *Cartlidge* v. *Chief Adjudication Officer* [1986] 2 W.L.R. 558, C.A.
s. 19, amended: 1986, c.50, s.44.
s. 20, amended: *ibid.*, s.43.
s. 21, repealed: *ibid.*, s.38, sch. 11.
s. 22, regs. 86/903.
ss. 22, 23, substituted: 1986, c.50, sch. 4.
s. 24, substituted: *ibid.*, s.36.
ss. 25, 26, repealed in pt.: *ibid.*, sch. 11.
s. 27, regs. 86/903.
s. 28, repealed in pt.: 1986, c.50, schs. 10, 11.
s. 32, repealed: *ibid.*, sch. 11.
s. 33. repealed in pt.: *ibid.*, s.42, sch. 11.
s. 34, repealed in pt.: *ibid.*, sch. 11.

(45)

CAP.

1975—cont.

14. Social Security Act 1975—cont.

s. 36, see *White* v. *Chief Adjudication Officer* [1986] 2 All E.R. 905, C.A.

s. 36, regs. 86/1933.

s. 37, see *Drake* v. *Chief Adjudication Officer (No. 150/85)* [1986] 3 All E.R. 65, European Ct.

s. 37, repealed in pt.: 1986, c.50, s.37, sch. 11.

s. 37A, regs. 86/1541.

s. 37A, amended: 1986, c.50, s.71; repealed in pt.: *ibid.*, sch. 11.

s. 38, amended: *ibid.*, s.45.

s. 41, amended: *ibid.*, sch. 11.

s. 49A, added; *ibid.*, s.44.

s. 50, amended: *ibid.*, sch. 3; repealed in pt.: *ibid.*, schs. 3, 11.

s. 51, regs. 86/1545.

s. 57, repealed in pt.: 1986, c.50, sch. 11.

s. 58, regs. 86/1118.

ss. 58, 59, repealed: 1986, c.50, schs. 3, 11.

s. 59A, added; *ibid.*, sch. 31.

s. 60, repealed: *ibid.*, sch. 11.

ss. 62, 64–75, amended: *ibid.*, schs. 3, 11.

s. 77, amended: *ibid.*, sch. 3.

s. 79, regs. 86/1772.

ss. 79–81, repealed: 1986, c.50, sch. 11.

s. 82, see *White* v. *Chief Adjudication Officer* [1986] 2 All E.R. 905, C.A.

ss. 82 (in pt.), 84 (in pt.), repealed: 1986, c.50, sch. 11.

s. 85, regs. 86/903.

ss. 86, 88 (in pt.), repealed: 1986, c.50, sch. 11.

s. 90, amended: 1986, c.50, sch. 10; repealed in pt.: *ibid.*, sch. 11.

s. 92, repealed: *ibid.*, s.69, sch. 11.

s. 95, repealed: *ibid.*, schs. 5, 11.

ss. 96, 98, amended: *ibid.*, sch. 5.

s. 100, amended: *ibid.*, sch. 5; repealed in pt.: *ibid.*, schs. 5, 11.

s. 101, amended: *ibid.*, sch. 5; repealed in pt.: *ibid.*, sch. 11.

s. 102, amended: *ibid.*, sch. 5.

s. 103, substituted: *ibid.*

s. 104, amended: *ibid.*; repealed in pt.: *ibid.*, schs. 5, 11.

s. 106, see *R.* v. *Secretary of State for Social Services, ex p. Connolly* (1986) 83 L.S.Gaz. 786, C.A.

s. 106, amended: 1986, c.50, sch. 5; repealed in pt.: *ibid.*, sch. 11.

s. 107, see *Fraser* v. *Secretary of State for Social Services*, 1986 S.L.T. 386.

s. 107, amended: 1986, c.50, sch. 5; repealed in pt.: *ibid.*, sch. 11.

s. 108, amended: *ibid.*, sch. 3.

s. 109, amended: *ibid.*, sch. 5.

s. 110, amended: *ibid.*; repealed in pt.: *ibid.*, schs. 5, 11.

s. 112, amended: *ibid.*, sch. 5.

s. 114, regs. 86/1541.

CAP.

1975—cont.

14. Social Security Act 1975—cont.

s. 114, amended: 1986, c.50, sch. 5; repealed in pt.: *ibid.*, schs. 5, 11.

s. 115, regs. 86/1933.

ss. 117, 119, repealed in pt.: 1986, c.50, sch. 11.

ss. 120, 121, order 86/25.

s. 122, amended: 1986, c.50, sch. 10; repealed in pt.: *ibid.*, sch. 11.

s. 123A, order 86/25.

s. 123A, amended: 1986, c.50, s.74.

s. 124, order 86/1117.

ss. 124–126A, repealed: 1986, c.50, sch. 11.

s. 126A, order 86/1117.

s. 129, regs. 86/198.

ss. 131, regs. 86/485, 486, 1118, 1545.

s. 134, amended: 1986, c.50, s.74; repealed in pt.: *ibid.*, sch. 11.

ss. 135 (in pt.), 136, repealed: *ibid.*

s. 141, amended: *ibid.*, sch. 10; repealed in pt.: *ibid.*, sch.11.

s. 142, amended: *ibid.*, s.65.

s. 143, amended: *ibid.*; repealed in pt.: *ibid.*, s.65, sch. 11.

ss. 144, 145, 146 (in pt,), 147, repealed: *ibid.*, sch. 11.

s. 149, see *I.R.C.* v. *Findlay McClure & Co.* (O.H.), 1986 S.L.T. 417.

ss. 151 (in pt.), 152 (in pt.), 164, repealed: 1986, c.50, sch. 11.

s. 165A, regs. 86/903.

s. 165A, amended: 1986, c.50, sch. 10; substituted: *ibid.*

s. 166, regs. 86/485, 486, 903, 1009, 1011, 1259, 1961.

s. 166, amended: 1986, c.50, s.62, sch. 5.

s. 167, amended: *ibid.*, ss.43, 62, 74, sch. 10.

s. 168, regs. 86/198, 317, 485, 715, 1046, 1545, 1716, 1717.

sch. 1, amended: 1986, c.50, sch. 8.

sch. 3, amended: *ibid.*, schs. 4, 8, 10; repealed in pt.: *ibid.*, sch. 11.

sch. 4, amended: *ibid.*, s.36; repealed in pt.: *ibid.*, s.38, sch. 11.

sch. 5, repealed: *ibid.*

sch. 8, amended: *ibid.*, sch. 3; repealed in pt.: *ibid.*, sch. 11.

sch. 9, repealed: *ibid.*, schs. 3, 11.

schs. 12, 13, amended: *ibid.*, sch. 5.

sch. 13, regs. 86/1933.

sch. 14, regs. 86/1118.

sch. 14, repealed: 1986, c.50, sch. 11.

sch. 16, amended: *ibid.*, sch. 10; repealed in pt.: *ibid.*, sch. 11.

sch. 20, regs. 86/198, 317, 485, 486, 751, 1011, 1046, 1118, 1541, 1545, 1716, 1717, 1772.

sch. 20, amended: 1986, c.50, sch. 5.

15. Social Security (Northern Ireland) Act 1975.

s. 9, amended: 1986, c.41, s.41.

ss. 15A, 16, S.R. 1986 No. 82.

s. 17, S.Rs. 1986 Nos. 212, 266, 275.

ss. 22, 27, S.R. 1986 No. 157.

CAP.

1975—cont.

15. Social Security (Northern Ireland) Act 1975—cont.

s. 51, S.R. 1986 No. 303.
s. 58, S.R. 1986 No. 212.
ss. 76, 77, S.Rs. 1986 Nos. 179, 270.
s. 78, S.R. 1986 No. 179.
s. 85, S.R. 1986 No. 157.
s. 112A, added: 1986, c.50, sch. 9.
s. 113, S.Rs. 1986 Nos. 179, 270.
s. 120, S.R.s 1986 Nos. 16, 211.
s. 124, S.R. 1986 No. 45.
s. 126, S.R.s 1986 Nos. 71, 72, 212, 303.
s. 146, S.R. 1986 No. 179.
s. 154A, S.R. 1986 No. 157.
sch. 10, amended: 1986, c.50, sch. 9.
sch. 14, S.R. 1986 No. 212.

16. Industrial Injuries and Diseases (Old Cases) Act 1975.

s. 2, scheme 86/1174.
s. 2, repealed in pt.: 1986, c.50, sch. 10.
s. 4, scheme 86/1174.
s. 4, amended: 1986, c.50, sch. 10; repealed in pt.: ibid., sch. 11.
s. 7, amended and repealed in pt.: ibid., sch. 10.
ss. 9 (in pt.), 10, repealed: ibid., sch. 11.

17. Industrial Injuries and Diseases (Northern Ireland Old Cases) Act 1975.

ss. 2, 4, S.R. 1986 No. 222.

18. Social Security (Consequential Provisions) Act 1975.

schs. 2, 3, repealed in pt.: 1986, c.50, sch. 11.

20. District Courts (Scotland) Act 1975.

s. 1A, order 86/1836.
s. 21, repealed: 1986, c.47, sch. 5.

21. Criminal Procedure (Scotland) Act 1975.

s. 1, see MacDougall v. Russell, 1986 S.L.T. 403.
s. 28, see Tin Fan Lau, Petr., 1986 S.L.T. 535.
s. 67, see H.M. Advocate v. J.M.R., 1985 S.C.C.R. 330; Varey v. H.M. Advocate, 1986 S.L.T. 321.
s. 75, see Welsh v. H.M. Advocate, 1986 S.L.T. 664.
s. 83, see MacNeil v. H.M. Advocate, 1986 S.C.C.R. 288.
s. 101, see Welsh v. H.M. Advocate, 1986 S.L.T. 664; MacDougall v. Russell, 1986 S.L.T. 403; Dobbie v. H.M. Advocate, 1986 S.L.T. 648.
s. 114, Act of Adjournal 86/1687.
s. 141, see Upton v. H.M. Advocate, 1986 S.L.T. 594.
s. 153, see MacKenzie v. H.M. Advocate, 1986 S.L.T. 389; 1986 S.C.C.R. 94.
s. 160, see Varey v. H.M. Advocate, 1986 S.L.T. 321.
s. 171, amended: 1986, c.36, sch. 1.
s. 218, see Muir v. H.M. Advocate, 1985 S.C.C.R. 402.
s. 228, see Morland v. H.M. Advocate, 1985 S.C.C.R. 316; Allison v. H.M. Advocate, 1985 S.C.C.R. 408.

CAP.

1975—cont.

21. Criminal Procedure (Scotland) Act 1975—cont.

s. 252, see Morland v. H.M. Advocate, 1985 S.C.C.R. 316; McCadden v. H.M. Advocate, 1986 S.L.T. 138; Allison v. H.M. Advocate, 1985 S.C.C.R. 408.
s. 254, see King v. H.M. Advocate, 1985 S.C.C.R. 322; Grant v. H.M. Advocate, 1985 S.C.C.R. 431.
s. 263A, see Lord Advocate's References (No. 1 of 1985), 1987 S.L.T. 187.
s. 290, see Sharp v. Tudhope, 1986 S.C.C.R. 64.
s. 311, see Cardle v. Campbell, 1985 S.C.C.R. 309; Geddes v. Hamilton, 1986 S.L.T. 536.
s. 312, see Anderson v. Allan, 1985 S.C.C.R. 399; Davidson v. Aitchison, 1986 S.L.T. 402; Allan v. McGraw, 1986 S.C.C.R. 257.
s. 314, see Tudhope v. Buckner, 1985 S.C.C.R. 352.
s. 331, see Tudhope v. Buckner, 1985 S.C.C.R. 352; McCartney v. Tudhope, 1986 S.L.T. 159; Stagecoach v. McPhail, 1986 S.C.C.R. 184.
s. 331, amended: 1986, c.36, sch. 1.
s. 334, see Jessop v. Christie, 1986 S.C.C.R. 7.
s. 336, see Milne v. Guild, 1986 S.L.T. 431.
s. 346, see Templeton v. MacLeod, 1986 S.L.T. 149; Conner v. Lockhart, 1986 S.C.C.R. 360.
s. 368, amended: 1986, c.36, sch. 1.
s. 444, see Durant v. Lockhart, 1986 S.L.T. 312; MacDougall, Petr. 1986 S.C.C.R. 128.
s. 452, see Aitchison v. Rizza, 1985 S.C.C.R. 297.
s. 457, Acts of Adjournal 86/1191, 1686.
sch. 1, repealed in pt.: 1986, c.36, sch. 1.
sch. 7A, repealed in pt.: 1986, c.48, sch. 5.

22. Oil Taxation Act 1975.

s. 19, amended: 1986, c.41, s.54.
sch. 3, amended: 1986, c.44, sch. 7.

23. Reservoirs Act 1975.

Commencement orders: 86/466, 2202.
s. 4, regs. 86/853.
s. 5, regs. 86/468, 853.
s. 19, rules 86/467.
ss. 20, 21, regs. 86/468.
s. 23, regs. 86/468; rules 86/467.
s. 29, orders 86/466, 2202.

24. House of Commons Disqualification Act 1975.

s. 5, order 86/2219.
sch. 1, amended: 1986, c.31, s.2; c.39, sch. 2; c.44, s.49, schs. 1, 2; c.47, sch. 3(S.); c.48, sch. 4; c.49, sch. 4; c.53, sch. 1; 56, sch. 3; c.60, sch. 11; order 86/2219; repealed in pt.: 1986, c.31, sch. 6; c.44, sch. 9; c.60, sch. 17; order 86/2219.

CAP.

1975—cont.

25. Northern Ireland Assembly Disqualification Act 1975.
sch. 1, amended: 1986, c.31, s.2; c.44, s.49, schs. 1, 2; c.45, sch. 3(S.); c.48, sch. 4; c.49, sch. 4; c.53, sch. 1; c.56, sch. 3; c.60, sch. 11.

26. Ministers of the Crown Act 1975.
s. 1, order 86/600.

27. Ministerial and other Salaries Act 1975.
s. 1, order 86/1169; amended: *ibid.*

28. Housing Rents and Subsidies (Scotland) Act 1975.
s. 5, repealed in pt.: 1986, c.63, schs. 5, 12.

30. Local Government (Scotland) Act 1975.
s. 2, see *Assessor for Strathclyde Region* v. *Scottish Special Housing Association,* 1986 S.L.T. 421; *Assessor for Borders Region* v. *A.M.S. Leisure,* 1986 S.L.T. 689.
ss. 2 (in pt.), 5 (in pt.), repealed: S.L.R. 1986.
s. 8, amended: 1986, c.50, sch. 10.
s. 15, order 86/672.
sch. 1, amended: 1986, c.44, sch. 7; repealed in pt.: *ibid.,* sch. 9.
sch. 3, amended: 1986, c.65, s.17.

33. Referendum Act 1975.
repealed: S.L.R. 1986.

34. Evidence (Proceedings in Other Jurisdictions) Act 1975.
see *Jahre (Anders), Re* [1986] 1 Lloyd's Rep. 496, C.A.; *Barber (J.) & Sons (A Firm)* v. *Lloyd's Underwriters* (1986) 2 All E.R. 845, Evans J; *R.* v. *Secretary of State for the Home Department, ex p. Spermacet Whaling and Shipping Co. S.A., The Times,* November 14, 1986, D.C.
ss. 1, 2, 9, see *State of Norway's Application, Re* [1986] 3 W.L.R. 452, C.A.
s. 10, order 86/218.

36. Air Travel Reserve Fund Act 1975.
s. 6, order 86/155.

45. Finance (No. 2) Act 1975.
ss. 47, 48, orders 86/1181, 1832.
s. 69, amended: 1986, c.41, s.21.
s. 70, sch. 12, regs. 86/1240.

51. Salmon and Freshwater Fisheries Act 1975.
s. 6, amended: 1986, c.62, s.33.
s. 25, amended: *ibid.,* s.36.
s. 30, amended: *ibid.,* s.34.
ss. 39, 43, amended: *ibid.,* sch. 4.
ss. 39, 43, amended (S.): *ibid.,* s.26.
sch. 2, amended: *ibid.,* s.36.
sch. 3, amended: *ibid.,* s.33.
sch. 4, amended: *ibid.,* s.35.

52. Safety of Sports Grounds Act 1975.
s. 1, order 86/1243(S.), 1296.
s. 6, regs. 86/1045.
s. 15, order 86/1044.
s. 18, orders 86/1044, 1296.

CAP.

1975—cont.

54. Limitation Act 1975.
s. 1, see *Arnold* v. *Central Electricity Generating Board* [1986] 3 W.L.R. 171, Mr. Michael Ogden Q.C.

55. Statutory Corporations) Financial Provisions) Act 1975.
s. 6, sch. 3, repealed in pt.: 1986, c.44, sch. 9.

56. Coal Industry Act 1975.
s. 5, schs. 3 (in pt.), 4, repealed: 1986, c.63, sch. 12.
sch. 1, amended: 1986, c.44, sch. 7.

60. Social Security Pensions Act 1975.
s. 1, amended: 1986, c.50, s.74.
ss. 3, 5, amended: *ibid.,* sch. 8.
s. 6, amended: *ibid.,* s.18, sch. 8; repealed in pt.: *ibid.,* schs. 8, 11.
ss. 13, 15, amended: *ibid.,* sch. 10.
s. 19, repealed in pt.: *ibid.,* sch. 11.
s. 21, order 86/809.
s. 22, repealed in pt.: 1986, c.50, sch. 11.
s. 23, amended: *ibid.,* sch. 10; repealed in pt.: *ibid.,* sch. 11.
s. 24, amended: *ibid.,* sch. 10.
s. 26, amended: *ibid.,* s.9, schs. 2, 10.
s. 27, amended: *ibid.,* sch. 10.
s. 29, amended: *ibid.,* schs. 2, 10.
s. 30, amended: *ibid.;* repealed in pt.: *ibid.,* sch. 11.
ss. 31, 32, regs. 86/1716.
s. 32, amended: 1986, c.50, s.9, schs. 2, 10; repealed in pt.: *ibid.,* sch. 11.
s. 33, amended: *ibid.,* sch. 2, 10; repealed in pt.: *ibid.,* sch. 11.
s. 34, repealed: *ibid.*
s. 35, regs. 86/1716.
s. 35, amended: 1986, c.50, s.9, sch. 8.
s. 36, amended: *ibid.,* s.9, sch. 2; repealed in pt.: *ibid.,* sch. 11.
s. 37, amended: *ibid.*
s. 37A, added: *ibid.,* s.9.
s. 38, regs. 86/317, 1716.
s. 38, amended: 1986, c.50, s.9, sch. 10.
s. 39, amended: *ibid.,* s.9; repealed in pt.: *ibid.,* sch. 11.
s. 40, amended: *ibid.,* sch. 2.
s. 41, repealed in pt.: *ibid.,* schs. 10, 11.
s. 41A, amended: *ibid.,* schs. 2, 10.
s. 41B, amended: *ibid.,* sch. 9.
s. 41E, amended: *ibid.,* sch. 2.
s. 42, regs. 86/317.
s. 42, amended: 1986, c.50, schs. 2, 10.
s. 43, regs. 86/317.
s. 43, amended: 1986, c.50, sch. 10.
s. 44, amended: *ibid.,* s.9, schs. 2, 10; repealed in pt.: *ibid.,* sch. 11.
s. 44ZA, added: *ibid.,* sch. 2.
s. 45, regs. 86/317, 1716.
s. 45, amended: 1986, c.50, schs. 2, 8.
s. 46, repealed: *ibid.,* sch. 11.
s. 47, regs. 86/317.
s. 48, amended: 1986, c.50, sch. 2.
s. 49, amended: *ibid.,* s.9, schs. 2, 10; repealed in pt.: *ibid.,* schs. 10, 11.

CAP.

1975—cont.

60. Social Security Pensions Act 1975—*cont.*
s. 50, amended: *ibid.*, s.9, schs. 2, 10.
s. 51, amended: *ibid.*, sch. 2.
s. 52, regs. 86/317, 1716.
s. 52A, order 86/2070.
s. 52C, amended: 1986, c.50, sch. 10.
s. 52D, amended: *ibid.*, s.9, sch. 10; repealed in pt.: *ibid.*, sch. 11.
ss. 56A, 56E, regs. 86/1046, 1717.
s. 56K, repealed in pt.: 1986, c.50, sch. 11.
s. 56P, added: *ibid.*, s.11.
s. 58, amended: 1986, c.45, sch. 14.
s. 59, order 86/1116.
s. 59, amended: 1986, c.50, s.9, sch. 10.
s. 59A, amended: *ibid.*, s.9.
s. 61, amended: *ibid.*, sch. 10.
s. 62, regs. 86/1046.
s. 66, regs. 86/317, 1046.
s. 66, amended: 1986, c.50, schs. 2, 10; repealed in pt.: *ibid.*, sch. 11.
sch. 1, amended: *ibid.*, s.18, sch. 10.
sch. 1A, regs. 86/751.
sch. 1A, amended: 1986, c.50, sch. 10: repealed in pt.: *ibid.*, schs. 10, 11.
sch. 2, regs. 86/317, 1716.
sch. 2, amended: 1986, c.50, sch. 2; repealed in pt.: *ibid.*, sch. 11.
sch. 3, amended: 1986, c.45, sch. 14; c.50, sch. 2.
sch. 4, repealed in pt.: *ibid.*

61. Child Benefit Act 1975.
s. 2, amended: 1986, c.50, s.70.
s. 5, repealed in pt.: *ibid.*, sch. 11.
s. 6, amended: *ibid.*, sch. 10; repealed in pt.: *ibid.*, sch. 11.
ss. 7, 8, 9 (in pt.), 10, 11, repealed: *ibid.*
s. 15, repealed in pt.: *ibid.*, s.65, sch. 11.
s. 17, repealed in pt.: *ibid.*, sch. 11.
s. 22, regs. 86/1172.
s. 22, amended: 1986, c.50, s.62
s. 24, repealed in pt.: *ibid.*, sch. 11.
sch. 3, amended: *ibid.*, sch. 10.
sch. 5, repealed in pt.: *ibid.*, sch. 11.

63. Inheritance (Provision for Family and Dependants) Act 1975.
s. 1, see *Whytte* v. *Ticehurst* [1986] 2 W.L.R. 700, Booth J.; *Debenham Decd., Re* (1986) 16 Fam. Law 101, Ewbank J.
s. 2, see *Debenham Decd., Re* (1986) 16 Fam. Law 101, Ewbank J.
s. 3, see *R. (Deceased), Re; R.* v. *O.* (1986) 16 Fam. Law 58; Mr. Registrar Garland; *Debenham Decd., Re* (1986) 16 Fam. Law 101, Ewbank J.

65. Sex Discrimination Act 1975.
s. 1, see *Hayes* v. *Malleable Working Men's Club and Institute; Maughan* v. *North East London Magistrates' Court Committee* [1985] I.C.R. 703, E.A.T.; *Greencroft Social Club and Institute* v. *Mullen* [1985] I.C.R. 796, E.A.T.; *Por-*

CAP.

1975—cont.

65. Sex Discrimination Act 1975—*cont.*
celli v. *Strathclyde Regional Council* [1986] I.C.R.564, Court of Session, First Division; *Rainey* v. *Greater Glasgow Health Board*, 1987 S.L.T. 146.
s. 6, see *Hayes* v. *Malleable Working Men's Club and Institute; Maughan* v. *North East London Magistrates' Court Committee* [1985] I.C.R. 703, E.A.T.; *Gunning* v. *Mirror Group Newspapers* [1986] 1 All E.R. 385, C.A.; *Haughton* v. *Olau Line (U.K.)* [1986] 1 W.L.R. 504, C.A.; *Porcelli* v. *Strathclyde Regional Council* [1986] I.C.R. 564, Court of Session, First Division: *Gloucester Working Men's Club & Institute* v. *James* [1986] I.C.R. 603, E.A.T.
s. 6, amended: 1986, c.59, s.2; repealed in pt.: *ibid.*, s.1, sch.
s. 7, see *Willliams* v. *Dyfed County Council* [1986] I.C.R. 449, E.A.T.
s. 7, amended: 1986, c.59, s.1.
s. 10, see *Haughton* v. *Olau Line (U.K.)* [1986] 1 W.L.R. 504, C.A.
s. 11, amended: 1986, c.59, s.2; repealed in pt.: *ibid.*, s.1, sch.
s. 47, amended: *ibid.*, s.4.
s. 51, amended: 1986, c.61, sch. 4.
s. 75, amended (S.): 1986, c.47, sch. 3.
s. 76, see *Gloucester Working Men's Club & Institute* v. *James* [1986] I.C.R. 603, E.A.T.
ss. 80, 81, repealed in pt.: 1986, c.59, sch.
s. 82, see *Gunning* v. *Mirror Group Newspapers* [1986] 1 All E.R. 385, C.A.
s. 82, amended: 1986, c.59, s.2.
schs. 1 (in pt.), 2, repealed: *ibid.*, sch.

66. Recess Elections Act 1975.
s. 1, amended: 1986, c.45, sch. 14.

68. Industry Act 1975.
sch. 1, amended: 1986, c.60, sch. 16; repealed in pt.: *ibid.*, sch. 17.

69. Scottish Development Agency Act 1975.
sch. 1, amended: 1986, c.60, sch. 16; repealed in pt.: *ibid.*, sch. 17.

70. Welsh Development Agency Act 1975.
s. 27, repealed in pt.: 1986, c.44, sch. 9.
sch. 1, amended: 1986, c.60, sch. 16; repealed in pt.: *ibid.*, sch. 17.

71. Employment Protection Act 1975.
s. 8, regs. 86/302; amended: *ibid.*
s. 40, repealed in pt.: 1986, c.50, sch. 11.
ss. 99, 101, see *T.G.W.U.* v. *Ledbury Preserves (1928), The Times*, July 24, 1986, E.A.T.
sch. 16, repealed in pt.: 1986, c.48, sch. 5; c.59, sch.

72. Children Act 1975.
s. 3, see *V. (A Minor) (Adoption: Consent), Re* [1986] 1 All E.R. 752, C.A.

(49)

1975—cont.

72. Children Act 1975—cont.
s. 8, see *M. (A Minor) (Adoption Order: Access), Re* (1985) 15 Fam. Law 321, C.A.; *V. (A Minor) (Adoption: Consent), Re* [1986] 1 All E.R. 752, C.A.; *C. (A Minor) (Adoption Order: Condition), Re* (1986) 1 F.L.R. 315, C.A.
s. 12, see *G.B. (Adoption: Parental Agreement) Re* (1985) 15 Fam. Law 314, C.A.; *V. (A Minor) (Adoption: Consent), Re* [1986] 1 All E.R. 752, C.A.; *S. (A Minor) (Adoption: Procedure), Re* (1986) 1 F.L.R. 302, C.A.
ss. 12, 33, 37, see *M. (A Minor), Re, The Times*, October 13, 1986, C.A.
s. 14, see *T.D. (A Minor) (Wardship: Jurisdiction), Re* (1986) 16 Fam. Law 18, Sheldon J.
s. 19, see *O. (A Minor) (Adoption by Grandparents), Re* (1985) 15 Fam. Law 305, D.C.
s. 33, repealed in pt.: 1986, c.55, schs. 1, 2.
s. 47, amended (S.): 1986, c.9, sch. 1; repealed in pt. (S.): *ibid.*, sch. 2.
ss. 47, 48, Acts of Sederunt 86/513, 515.
s. 48, repealed in pt. (S.): 1986, c.9, sch. 2.
s. 49, amended: *ibid.*, sch. 1.
s. 53, repealed in pt. (S.): *ibid.*, sch. 2.
ss. 53 (in pt.), 54, repealed: 1986, c.55, sch. 2.
s. 55, amended (S.): 1986, c.9, sch. 1.
s. 100, amended: 1986, c.55, sch. 1; repealed in pt.: *ibid.*, schs. 1, 2.
s. 103, regs. 86/3.
schs. 1, 2, amended: order 86/948.

74. Petroleum and Submarine Pipe-Lines Act 1975.
ss. 26, 27, 32, regs. 86/1985.

75. Policyholders Protection Act 1975.
ss. 5, 15, 16, amended: 1986, c.45, sch. 14.

76. Local Land Charges Act 1975.
s. 74, rules 86/424.
sch. 1, see *Barber* v. *Shah* (1985) 17 H.L.R. 584, D.C.

78. Airports Authority Act 1975.
repealed: 1986, c.31, sch. 6.

1976

3. Road Traffic (Drivers' Ages and Hours of Work) Act 1976.
s. 2, see *Carter* v. *Walton* [1985] R.T.R. 378, D.C.

4. Trustee Savings Bank Act 1976.
Commencement order: 86/1221.
s. 38, order 86/1221.

13. Damages (Scotland) Act 1976.
s. 1, see *Donald* v. *Strathclyde Passenger Transport Executive*, 1986 S.L.T. 625.
sch. 1, amended: 1986, c.9, sch. 1.

19. Seychelles Act 1976.
s. 6, repealed: S.L.R. 1986.

1976—cont.

21. Crofting Reform (Scotland) Act 1976.
see *Macphee* v. *South Uist Estates*, 1985 S.L.C.R. 108.
s. 4, see *MacLugash* v. *Islay Estates Co.*, 1985 S.L.C.R. 99.
s. 9, see *Wester Ross Salmon* v. *Maclean*, 1985 S.L.C.R. 124; *Trustees of Tenth Duke of Argyll* v. *MacKay*, 1985 S.L.C.R. 121.

22. Freshwater and Salmon Fisheries (Scotland) Act 1976.
s. 1, orders 86/469, 473, 474, 1590.
s. 7, sch. 3, amended and repealed in pt.: 1986, c.62, sch. 4.

24. Development Land Tax Act 1976.
s. 33, amended: 1986, c.45, sch. 14.

27. Theatres Trust Act 1976.
sch., functions transferred: order 86/600.

34. Restrictive Trade Practices Act 1976.
s. 2, see *National Daily and Sunday Newspapers Proprietors' Agreement, Re* [1986] I.C.R. 44, Restrictive Practices Ct.
s. 9, order 86/614.
ss. 11, 16, see *Royal Institution of Chartered Surveyors' Application, Re; Royal Institution of Chartered Surveyors* v. *Director General of Fair Trading* [1986] I.C.R. 551, C.A.
s. 41, amended: 1986, c.31, sch. 4; c.44, sch. 7; c.60, sch. 13.
s. 42, order 86/614.
sch. 1, amended: 1986, c.45, sch. 14.
sch. 3, amended: 1986, c.39, sch. 2.
sch. 5, repealed in pt.: 1986, c.49, sch. 4.

35. Police Pensions Act 1976.
ss. 1, 3, regs. 85/2029; 86/1379, 1380.
s. 4, regs. 86/1379.
s. 5, regs. 86/1380.

36. Adoption Act 1976.
s. 47, amended: order 86/948; repealed in pt.: 1986, c.50, sch. 11.

38. Dangerous Wild Animals Act 1976.
s. 5, amended: 1986, c.14, sch. 3.

39. Divorce (Scotland) Act 1976.
s. 5, see *Brodie* v. *Brodie* (O.H.), 1986 S.L.T. 640.

40. Finance Act 1976.
s. 64, see *Wilson* v. *Alexander* [1986] S.T.C. 365, Harman J.
s. 64, order 86/703.
s. 64A, order 86/702; amended: *ibid.*
s. 126, repealed: 1986, c.41, s.79, sch. 23.
s. 127, repealed in pt.: *ibid.*, s.84, sch. 23.
sch. 7, amended: order 86/703.

44. Drought Act 1976.
s. 5 (in pt.), sch. 3, repealed: S.L.R. 1986.

45. Rating (Charity Shops) Act 1976.
s. 1, repealed in pt.: S.L.R. 1986.

46. Police Act 1976.
s. 11, see *R.* v. *Secretary of State for the Home Department, ex p. Thornton* [1986] 3 W.L.R. 158, C.A.

1976—cont.

47. Stock Exchange (Completion of Bargains) Act 1976.
s. 5, amended: 1986, c.60, s.194.
s. 7, repealed in pt.: *ibid.*, sch. 17.

50. Domestic Violence and Matrimonial Proceedings Act 1976.
s. 2, see *Newman* v. *Benesch, The Times,* September 22, 1986, C.A.

52. Armed Forces Act 1976.
s. 7, amended: 1986, c.21, s.7; repealed in pt.: *ibid.*, s.7, sch. 2.
sch. 3, amended: *ibid.*, ss.9, 12.

54. Trinidad and Tobago Republic Act 1976.
s. 2, repealed in pt.: S.L.R. 1986.

55. Agriculture (Miscellaneous Provisions) Act 1976.
ss. 17–24, 27 (in pt.), repealed: 1986, c.5, sch. 15.
s. 18, see *Bailey* v. *Sitwell* (1986) 279 E.G. 1092, Hodgson J.
sch. 3, repealed in pt.: 1986, c.5, sch.15; S.L.R. 1986.
sch. 3A, repealed: 1986, c.5, sch. 15.

57. Local Government (Miscellaneous Provisions) Act 1976.
s. 15, repealed in pt.: 1986, c.31, sch. 6.
s. 33, amended: 1986, c.44, sch. 7.
s. 55, see *Challoner* v. *Evans, The Times,* November 22, 1986, D.C.

60. Insolvency Act 1976.
s. 3, repealed: 1986, c.45, sch. 12.

63. Bail Act 1976.
s. 6, see *Schiavo* v. *Anderton* [1986] 3 W.L.R. 177, D.C.; *Laidlaw* v. *Atkinson, The Times,* August 2, 1986, D.C.

66. Licensing (Scotland) Act 1976.
s. 68, see *Wilson* v. *Allied Breweries,* 1986 S.L.T. 549.
ss. 68, 127, 139, see *Tudhope* v. *McDonald,* 1986 S.C.C.R. 32.

67. Sexual Offences (Scotland) Act 1976.
ss. 2A–2D, added: 1986, c.36, s.1.
s. 4, amended: *ibid.*, sch. 1.

69. Companies Act 1976.
s. 12, see *Taylor* v. *McGirr* [1986] Crim.L.R. 544, D.C.
s. 28, see *Arctic Engineering, Re* [1986] 1 W.L.R. 686, Hoffman J.

70. Land Drainage Act 1976.
s. 2, amended and repealed in pt.: order 86/208.
s. 3, amended: orders 86/613, 615.
s. 5, amended: order 86/208.
s. 11, orders 86/1266, 1919.
s. 43, amended: 1986, c.49, sch. 3.
s. 45, amended: order 86/208.
s. 49, order 86/447.
s. 96, repealed in pt.: 1986, c.63, sch. 12.
s. 98, repealed in pt.: order 86/208.
s. 104A, added: order 86/208.
s. 109, order 86/1919.
s. 112, amended: 1986, c.44, sch. 7; repealed in pt.: 1986, c.31, sch. 6.

1976—cont.

70. Land Drainage Act 1976—*cont.*
s. 116, amended: order 86/208.
sch. 5, amended and repealed in pt.: *ibid.*

71. Supplementary Benefits Act 1976.
s. 1, regs. 86/1292.
ss. 1, 3, see *Vaughan* v. *Social Security Adjudication Officer, The Times,* July 17, 1986, C.A.; *Kelly* v. *Supplementary Benefits Commission,* 1983, S.C. 32.
ss. 1–21, repealed: 1986, c.50, sch. 11.
s. 2, see *R.* v. *Secretary of State for Social Services, ex p. Cotton, The Times,* December 14, 1985, C.A.
s. 2, regs. 86/1259, 1292, 1293.
s. 3, regs. 86/1259, 1961.
s. 4, regs. 86/1259.
s. 5, regs. 86/1010.
s. 6, see *Decisions Nos. R(SB)* 22/85; *R(SB)* 34/85.
s. 8, amended: 1986, c.50, sch. 10.
ss. 11, 14, regs. 86/562, 1259.
s. 17, amended (S.): 1986, c.9, sch. 1; repealed in pt. (S.): *ibid.*, sch. 2.
s. 18, see *Tayside Regional Council* v. *Thaw,* 1987 S.L.T. 69.
s. 18, amended (S): 1986, c.9, sch. 1.
s. 19, repealed (S.): *ibid.*, sch. 2.
ss. 24–27, repealed: 1986, c.50, sch. 11.
s. 25, see *R.* v. *Davis, The Times,* May 20, 1986, D.C.
ss. 31–34, repealed: 1986, c.50, sch. 11.
s. 33, see *R.* v. *D.H.S.S., ex p. London Borough of Camden, The Times,* March 5, 1986, D.C.
s. 33, regs. 86/1259, 1292.
s. 34, regs. 86/562, 1010, 1259, 1292, 1293, 1961.
sch. 1, regs. 86/562, 1293.
schs. 1, 5 (in pt.), 7 (in pt.), repealed: 1986, c.50, sch. 11.

74. Race Relations Act 1976.
s. 1, see *Raval* v. *D.H.S.S.* [1985] I.C.R. 685, E.A.T.; *R.* v. *Commission for Racial Equality, ex p. Westminster City Council* [1985] I.C.R. 827, C.A.; *Singh* v. *British Rail Engineering* [1986] I.C.R. 22, E.A.T.; *McAlister* v. *Labour Party, The Times,* June 5, 1986, E.A.T.; *Tejani* v. *Superintendent Registrar for the District of Peterborough, The Times,* June 10, 1986, C.A.; *Gwynedd County Council* v. *Jones, The Times,* July 28, 1986, E.A.T.
s. 4, see *Raval* v. *D.H.S.S.* [1985] I.C.R. 685, E.A.T.: *R.* v. *Commission for Racial Equality, ex p. Westminster City Council* [1985] I.C.R. 827, C.A.; *Deria* v. *General Council of British Shipping* [1986] I.C.R. 172, C.A.; *De Souza* v. *The Automobile Association* [1986] I.C.R. 514, C.A.
ss. 8, 14, see *Deria* v. *General Council of British Shipping* [1986] I.C.R. 172, C.A.
s. 19A, added: 1986, c.63, s.55.

1976—cont.

74. Race Relations Act 1976—*cont.*
s. 58, see *R.* v. *Commission for Racial Equality, ex p. Westminster City Council* [1985] I.C.R. 827, C.A.
s. 66, amended (S.): 1986, c.47, sch. 8.
ss. 70, 79 (in pt.), repealed: 1986, c.64, sch. 3.

75. Development of Rural Wales Act 1976.
s. 13A, order 86/1509.
s. 34, repealed in pt.: 1986, c.31, sch. 6; c.44, sch. 9.
sch. 3, repealed in pt.: *ibid.*

76. Energy Act 1976.
ss. 9, 12, amended: 1986, c.44, sch. 7.
s. 18, repealed in pt.: *ibid.*, sch. 9.

80. Rent (Agriculture) Act 1976.
s. 9, amended: 1986, c.5, sch. 14.
sch. 2, amended: *ibid.*, c.63, sch. 4.
sch. 4, amended: *ibid.*, s.13.

82. Sexual Offences (Amendment) Act 1976.
s. 2, see *R.* v. *Cox (David), The Times*, June 18, 1986, C.A.

86. Fishery Limits Act 1976.
ss. 2, 6, order 86/382.

1977

3. Aircraft and Shipbuilding Industries Act 1977.
s. 3, amended: 1986, c.60, sch. 16; repealed in pt.: *ibid.*, schs. 16, 17.
s. 11, order 86/2258.
s. 11, amended: 1986, c.19, s.1.

5. Social Security (Miscellaneous Provisions) Act 1977.
s. 9, repealed: 1986, c.50, sch. 11.
s. 12, order 86/592.
s. 17, repealed in pt.: 1986, c.50, sch. 11.
s. 18, amended: *ibid.*, sch. 10; repealed in pt.: *ibid.*, sch. 11.
s. 19, repealed: *ibid.*
s. 21, amended: *ibid.*, sch. 8.
ss. 21, 22, regs. 86/1716.
s. 22, repealed in pt.: 1986, c.50, sch. 11.

8. Job Release Act 1977.
s. 1, order 86/1291.
s. 1, continued in force: *ibid.*

12. Agricultural Holdings (Notices to Quit) Act 1977.
repealed: 1986, c.5, sch. 15.
s. 2, see *Featherstone* v. *Staples* [1986] 2 All E.R. 461, C.A.

15. Marriage (Scotland) Act 1977.
s. 2, see *H.M. Advocate* v. *J.M.R.*, 1985, S.C.C.R. 330.
s. 2, amended: 1986, c.9, sch. 1; c.16, sch. 2; repealed in pt.: 1986, c.9, sch. 2.
s. 3, regs. 85/1889; 86/1622, 1954.
s. 3, amended: 1986, c.16, sch. 2; c.55, sch. 1.
ss. 5–7, amended: 1986, c.16, sch. 2.
ss. 19, 25, regs. 85/1889.
s. 26, regs. 85/1889; 86/1622, 1954.
s. 26, amended: 1986, c.55, sch. 1.
sch. 1, amended: 1986, c.16, sch. 2.

1977—cont.

32. Torts (Interference with Goods) Act 1977.
s. 6, see *Highland Leasing* v. *Paul Field (T/A Field Machinery)*, December 6, 1985; R. M. Stewart Q.C.

36. Finance Act 1977.
s. 32, amended: 1986, c.41, s.34; repealed in pt.: *ibid.*, s.34, sch. 23.
sch. 7, see *Platten* v. *Brown* [1986] S.T.C. 514, Hoffmann J.

37. Patents Act 1977.
ss. 2, 5, see *L'Oreal's Application* [1986] R.P.C. 19, Whitford J.
s. 15, see *Ogawa Chemical Industries* [1986] R.P.C. 63, Falconer J; *Kiwi Coders Corporation's Application* [1986] R.P.C. 106, Whitford J.
ss. 18, 19, see *Ogwa Chemical Industries* [1986] R.P.C. 63, Falconer J.
ss. 19, 27, amended: 1986, c.39, sch. 2.
s. 32, substituted: *ibid.*, sch. 1.
s. 35, repealed: *ibid.*, sch. 3.
s. 46, see *R.* v. *Comptroller-General of Patents, Designs and Trade Marks, ex p. Gist-Brocades* [1986] 1 W.L.R. 51, H.L.
s. 50, see *An Application by Generics (U.K.), Re, Financial Times*, March 26, 1986, Whitford J.
s. 70, see *Neild* v. *Rockley* [1986] F.S.R. 3, Falconer J.; *Johnston Electric Industrial Manufactory* v. *Mabuchi-Motor K.K.* [1986] F.S.R. 280, Whitfield J.
s. 78, see *L'Oreal's Application* [1986] R.P.C. 19, Whitford J.
s. 90, repealed in pt.: S.L.R. 1986.
s. 123, amended: 1986, c.39, sch. 2.
sch. 1, see *R.* v. *Comptroller-General of Patents, Designs and Trade Marks, ex p. Gist-Brocades* [1986] 1 W.L.R. 51, H.L.
ss. 105, 127, see *Santa Fe International Corp.* v. *Napier Shipping S.A.* [1986] R.P.C. 22, Court of Session.
sch. 2, see *Santa Fe International Corp.* v. *Napier Shipping S.A.* [1986] R.P.C. 22, Court of Session.

38. Administration of Justice Act 1977.
s. 1, sch. 1, repealed in pt. (S.): 1986, c.47, sch. 5.

39. Coal Industry Act 1977.
s. 7, order 86/625; amended: order 86/631.

40. Control of Office Development Act 1977.
repealed: 1986, c.63, sch. 12.

42. Rent Act 1977.
s. 1, see *R.*, v. *Rent Officer of the Nottinghamshire Registration Area, ex p. Allen* (1986) 52 P. & C.R. 41, Farquharson J.
s. 2, see *Duke* v. *Porter* (1986) 280 E.G. 633, C.A.
s. 5A, added: 1986, c.63, sch. 4.
s. 10, amended: 1986, c.5, sch. 14.
s. 16, amended: 1986, c.63, sch. 5.
s. 19, amended: *ibid.*, s.13, sch. 4.
s. 25, see *MacFarquhar* v. *Phillimore: Marks* v. *Phillimore* (1986) 279 E.G. 584, C.A.

CAP.
1977—cont.

42. Rent Act 1977—cont.
s. 67, see *R. v. Chief Rent Officer for Kensington and Chelsea London Borough Council, ex p. Moberly* (1986) 278 E.G. 305, C.A.
s. 69, amended: 1986, c.63, s.7; repealed in pt.: *ibid.*, sch. 12.
s. 70, see *Crown Estates Comrs. v. Connor* (1986) 280 E.G. 532, McCowan J.
s. 70, amended: 1986, c.63, s.17; repealed in pt.: *ibid.*, s.17, sch. 12.
s. 98, see *Alexander v. Mohamedzadeh* (1985) 276 E.G. 1258, C.A.; *Minchburn v. Fernandez* (1986) 280 E.G. 770, C.A.
s. 116, amended: 1986, c.63, sch. 3.
s. 137, amended: 1986, c.5, sch. 14.
sch. 12, amended: 1986, c.63, sch. 5; repealed in pt.: *ibid.*, sch. 12.
sch. 15, see *Manaton v. Edwards* (1985) 276 E.G. 1257, C.A.; *Alexander v. Mohamedzadeh* (1985) 276 E.G. 1258; (1986) 51 P. & C.R. 41, C.A.; *Hewitt v. Lewis* [1986] 1 All E.R. 927, C.A.; *Naish v. Curzon* (1986) 51 P. & C.R. 229, C.A.
sch. 15, amended: 1986, c.63, s.13.

43. Protection from Eviction Act 1977.
s. 1, see *Schon v. Camden London Borough Council, The Times,* May 6, 1986, C.A.; *R. v. Ahmad* [1986] Crim.L.R. 739, C.A.
ss. 1, 4, see *Costelloe v. London Borough of Camden* [1986] Crim.L.R. 249, D.C.
s. 3, see *Schon v. Camden London Borough Council* (1986) 279 E.G. 859, D.C.
s. 8, amended: 1986, c.5, sch. 14.

45. Criminal Law Act 1977.
s. 1, see *R. v. Elghazal* [1986] Crim.L.R. 52, C.A.; *R. v. James and Ashford* [1986] Crim.L.R. 118, C.A.; *R. v. Grant* (1986) 82 Cr.App.R. 324, C.A.; *R. v. Cooke* [1986] 3 W.L.R. 327, H.L.
s. 5, see *R. v. Grant (Alexander), The Times,* December 24, 1985, C.A.; *R. v. Cooke* [1986] 3 W.L.R. 327, H.L.: *R. v. Evans* [1986] Crim.L.R. 470, C.A.; *R. v. Sirat (Mohammed)* (1986) 83 Cr.App.R. 41; [1986] Crim.L.R. 245, C.A.
s. 47, see *R. v. Taylor (J.S.)* (1984) 6 Cr.App.R.(S.) 448, C.A.; *R. v. Hannell* (1985) 82 Cr.App.R. 41, C.A.
s. 50, see *R. v. Hazell* [1985] R.T.R. 369, C.A.; *R. v. Khan* [1985] R.T.R. 365, C.A.
sch. 1, repealed in pt.: 1986, c.48, sch. 5.

46. Insurance Brokers (Registration) Act 1977.
ss. 12, 15, amended: 1986, c.60, s.138.

48. Housing (Homeless Persons) Act 1977.
s. 1, see *R. v. Purbeck District Council, ex p. Cadney* (1985) 17 H.L.R. 534, Nolan J.; *R. v. Hillingdon London Borough*

CAP.
1977—cont.

48. Housing (Homeless Persons) Act 1977—cont.
Council, ex p. Pulhofer [1986] 1 All E.R. 467, H.L.; *R. v. Hammersmith and Fulham London Borough Council, ex p. O'Brian* (1985) 84 L.G.R. 202, Glidewell J.
s. 1, amended (S.): 1986, c.65, s.21.
s. 2, see *Kelly v. Monklands District Council* (O.H.), 1986 S.L.T. 169; *R. v. Hammersmith and Fulham London Borough Council, ex p. O'Brian* (1985) 84 L.G.R. 202, Glidewell J.
s. 4, see *R. v. Ealing London Borough Council, ex p. McBain* [1985] 1 W.L.R. 1351, C.A.; *Kelly v. Monklands District Council* (O.H.), 1986 S.L.T. 169; *R. v. Hillingdon London Borough Council* [1986] 1 All E.R. 467, H.L.; *R. v. East Hertfordshire District Council, ex p. Hunt,* (1985) 18 H.L.R. 51, Mann J.; *R. v. Hammersmith and Fulham London Borough Council, ex p. O'Brian* (1985) 84 L.G.R. 202, Glidewell J.; *R. v. Camden London Borough Council, ex p. Wait, The Times,* July 12, 1986, McCowan J.
s. 4, amended (S.): 1986, c.65, s.21.
s. 5, see *R. v. Hammersmith and Fulham London Borough Council, ex p. O'Brian* (1985) 84 L.G.R. 202, Glidewell J.
s. 12, see *Kelly v. Monklands District Council* (O.H.), 1986 S.L.T. 169.
s. 16, see *R. v. Wimbourne District Council, ex p. Curtis,* (1985) 18 H.L.R. 79, Mann J.
s. 17, see *R. v. Eastleigh Borough Council, ex p. Evans* (1984) 17 H.L.R. 515, McNeil J.; *R. v. Penwith District Council, ex p. Trevena* (1984) 17 H.L.R. 527, McNeil J.; *R. v. Wimbourne District Council, ex p. Curtis,* (1985) 18 H.L.R. 79, Mann J.: *R. v. Hammersmith and Fulham London Borough Council, ex p. O'Brian* (1985) 84 L.G.R. 202, Glidewell J.

49. National Health Service Act 1977.
s. 11, orders 86/440, 963, 1015.
ss. 12, 13, regs. 86/964.
ss. 13, 14, see *Linden v. D.H.S.S.* [1986] 1 W.L.R. 164, Scott J.
s. 29, regs. 86/381, 916, 1846.
s. 32, regs. 86/1642.
ss. 35, 36, regs. 86/1499.
s. 38, regs. 86/975.
s. 39, regs. 86/975, 976.
s. 40, regs. 86/975.
ss. 41, 42, regs. 86/381, 916, 1486.
s. 42, substituted: 1986, c.66, s.3.
s. 43B, amended: *ibid.*, s.4.
s. 50, regs. 86/975.
s. 77, regs. 86/432.
s. 78, regs. 86/976, 1136.
ss. 81, 82, regs. 86/976.

CAP.

1977—cont.

49. National Health Service Act 1977—cont.
s. 83, regs. 86/432.
s. 121, regs. 86/459, 950.
ss. 126–128, regs. 86/975.
sch. 4, regs. 86/458.
sch. 5, see *R.* v. *Trent Regional Health Authority, ex p. Jones, The Times*, June 19, 1986, Macpherson J.
sch. 5, regs. 86/331, 524, 964, 1014.
sch. 10, see *Kerr* v. *Morris* [1986] 3 W.L.R. 662, C.A.
sch. 12, regs. 86/976, 1136.
sch. 15, repealed in pt.: S.L.R. 1986.
50. Unfair Contract Terms Act 1977.
s. 28, order 86/1777.
sch. 1, amended: 1986, c.39, sch. 2.
51. Pensioners' Payments Act 1977.
repealed: 1986, c.50, sch. 11.

1978

2. Commonwealth Development Corporation Act 1978.
ss. 2, 9, amended: 1986, c.25, s.1.
s. 9A, repealed in pt.: *ibid.*
s. 10A, added: *ibid.*
ss. 11, 12, amended: *ibid.*
s. 17, amended and repealed in pt.: *ibid.*
3. Refuse Disposal (Amenity) Act 1978.
ss. 3, 4, regs. 86/183.
s. 8, amended: 1986, c.63, sch. 11.
s. 12 (in pt.), sch. 1, repealed: 1986, c.31, sch. 6.
5. Northern Ireland (Emergency Provisions) Act 1978.
continued in force, exc. s.12, sch. 1: order 86/74.
s. 14, see *Murray* v. *Ministry of Defence* [1985] 12 N.I.J.B. 1, Murray J.
s. 30, order 86/75.
s. 33, orders 86/74, 1146.
sch. 4, amended: order 86/75.
8. Civil Aviation Act 1978.
s. 8, sch. 1 (in pt.), repealed: 1986, c.31, sch. 6.
10. European Assembly Elections Act 1978.
s. 1, repealed in pt.: 1986, c.58, sch.
sch. 1, regs. 86/2209.
sch. 2, amended: 1986, c.56, sch. 3.
14. Housing (Financial Provisions) (Scotland) Act 1978.
ss. 1, 2, orders 86/388, 389, 678.
s. 3, orders 86/389, 678.
s. 4, amended: 1986, c.65, s.18.
s. 4A, added: *ibid.*
15. Solomon Islands Act 1978.
s. 8, repealed: S.L.R. 1986.
17. Internationally Protected Persons Act 1978.
ss. 3, 4, order 86/2013.
22. Domestic Proceedings and Magistrates' Courts Act 1978.
ss. 3, 20, see *Blower* v. *Blower* (1986) 16 Fam.Law 56, Heilbron J.

CAP.

1978—cont.

22. Domestic Proceedings and Magistrates' Courts Act 1978—cont.
ss. 8, 30 amended: 1986, c.55, sch. 1.
s. 29, see *Berry* v. *Berry, The Times*, May 2, 1986, C.A.
23. Judicature (Northern Ireland) Act 1978.
s. 55, S.Rs. 1986 Nos. 128, 184, 203.
ss. 62, see *Kelly* v. *Quartey-Papafio* [1985] 5 N.I.J.B. 84, Hutton J.; *Coubrough* v. *Short Brothers* [1985] 13 N.I.J.B. 20, C.A.
s. 84, repealed in pt.: 1986, c.60, sch. 17.
s. 94A, amended: 1986, c.39, sch. 2.
s. 116, S.Rs. 1986 Nos. 103, 140, 195, 232, 233.
sch. 5, repealed in pt.: 1986, c.53, sch. 19.
26. Suppression of Terrorism Act 1978.
s. 5, order 86/2146.
s. 7, order 86/2019.
s. 8, orders 86/271, 1137.
27. House Purchase Assistance and Housing Corporation Guarantee Act 1978.
ss. 1, 2, order 86/1511.
s. 3, amended: 1986, c.53, sch. 18; repealed in pt.: *ibid.*, sch. 19.
28. Adoption (Scotland) Act 1978.
s. 18, see *Borders Regional Council* v. *M.*, 1986 S.L.T. 222.
ss. 18, 39, amended: 1986, c.9, sch. 1.
s. 41, amended: 1986, c.36, sch. 1; order 86/948.
s. 46, amended: 1986, c.9, sch. 1.
s. 65, amended: *ibid.*; repealed in pt.: *ibid.*, sch. 2.
29. National Health Service (Scotland) Act 1978.
ss. 13A, 13B, added: 1986, c.66, s.5.
ss. 19, regs. 86/303, 925, 1507.
s. 22, regs. 86/1657.
s. 25, regs. 86/1571.
s. 26, regs. 86/965, 966.
s. 27, regs. 86/303, 925, 1507.
ss. 27, 28, amended: 1986, c.66, s.3.
s. 28B, amended: *ibid.*, s.4.
s. 34, regs. 86/965.
s. 69, regs. 86/488.
s. 70, regs. 86/966, 1192.
ss. 73, 74, regs. 86/966.
s. 75, regs. 86/488.
s. 98, regs. 86/516, 924.
ss. 105, 106, regs. 86/965.
s. 108, regs. 86/303, 448, 516, 924, 965, 1507, 1571, 1657.
schs. 1, 5, regs. 86/944.
sch. 11, regs. 86/965, 966, 1192.
sch. 16, repealed in pt.: S.L.R. 1986.
30. Interpretation Act 1978.
s. 7, see *Austin Rover Group* v. *Crouch Butler Savage Associates, The Times*, April 1, 1986, C.A.
s. 16, see *Taylor* v. *McGirr* [1986] Crim.L.R. 544, D.C.

CAP.

1978—cont.

31. Theft Act 1978.
s. 1, see *R.* v. *Widdowson, The Times,* January 7, 1986, C.A.

33. State Immunity Act 1978.
s. 4, amended: order 86/948.
s. 7, amended: 1986, c.39, sch. 2.
s. 21, see *R.* v. *Secretary of State for Foreign and Commonwealth Affairs, ex p. Trawnik, The Times,* February 21, 1986, C.A.

38. Consumer Safety Act 1978.
Commencement order: 86/1297.
s. 1, regs. 86/758, 1323.
ss. 2–4, repealed in pt.: 1986, c.29, sch. 2.
s. 5, amended: *ibid.,* s.16; repealed in pt.: *ibid.,* sch. 2.
ss. 9–11, repealed in pt.: *ibid.*
s. 12, order 86/1297.
sch. 1, repealed in pt.: 1986, c.29, sch. 2.
sch. 2, substituted: *ibid.,* s.14, sch. 1.

40. Rating (Disabled Persons) Act 1978.
s. 1, amended: 1986, c.50, sch. 10.
s. 2, see *Samaritans of Tyneside* v. *Newcastle Upon Tyne City Council* [1985] R.A. 219, C.A.
s. 4, amended: 1986, c.50, sch. 10.

42. Finance Act 1978.
s. 39, repealed: 1986, c.41, sch. 23.
s. 54, amended: *ibid.,* s.24.
sch. 9, amended: *ibid.,* ss. 22–24.

44. Employment Protection (Consolidation) Act 1978.
see *Notcutt* v. *Universal Equipment Co. (London), The Times,* March 26, 1986, C.A.
s. 4, see *Igbo* v. *Johnson Matthey Chemicals* [1986] I.C.R. 82, E.A.T.
ss. 8, 11, see *Coales* v. *Wood (John) & Co.* [1986] I.C.R. 71, E.A.T.
s. 15, order 86/2283.
s. 15, amended: *ibid.*
s. 18, amended: 1986, c.48, sch. 4.
s. 23, see *National Coal Board* v. *Ridgeway, The Times,* August 14, 1986, E.A.T.
ss. 23, 24, see *Adlam* v. *Salisbury and Wells Theological College* [1985] I.C.R. 786, E.A.T.
s. 33, see *Community Task Force* v. *Rimmer* [1986] I.R.L.R. 203, E.A.T.
s. 33, amended: 1986, c.50, sch. 10; repealed in pt.: *ibid.,* sch. 11.
ss. 34–44, repealed: *ibid.*
s. 45, see *Community Task Force* v. *Rimmer* [1986] I.C.R. 491, E.A.T.
s. 50, scc *Notcutt* v. *Universal Equipment Co. (London)* [1986] 1 W.L.R. 641, C.A.
s. 55, see *Dutton & Clark* v. *Daly* [1985] I.C.R. 780, E.A.T.; *Lewis* v. *Motorworld Garages* [1986] I.C.R. 157, C.A.; *Newham London Borough* v. *Ward* [1985] I.R.L.R. 509, C.A.; *Shook* v.

CAP.

1978—cont.

44. Employment Protection (Consolidation) Act 1978—*cont.*
London Borough of Ealing [1986] I.R.L.R. 46, E.A.T.; *Fay* v. *North Yorkshire County Council* [1986] I.C.R. 133, C.A.; *Lewis* v. *Surrey County Council, The Times,* August 15, 1986, C.A.
s. 57, see *Rolls Royce Motors* v. *Dewhurst* [1985] I.C.R. 869, E.A.T.; *Pink* v. *White; Pink* v. *White & Co. (Earls Barton)* [1985] I.R.L.R. 489, E.A.T.; *Stacey* v. *Babcock Power* [1986] 2 W.L.R. 207, E.A.T.; *Holden* v. *Bradville* [1985] I.R.L.R. 483, E.A.T.; *Lafferty (F.) Construction* v. *Duthie* [1985] I.R.L.R. 487, E.A.T.; *West Midlands Co-operative Society* v. *Tipton* [1986] 2 W.L.R. 306, H.L.; *Saeed* v. *G.L.C. (I.L.E.A.)* (1986) I.R.L.R. 23, Popplewell J.; *Pritchett and Dyjasek* v. *J. McIntyre* [1986] I.R.L.R. 97, E.A.T.; *R.S.P.C.A.* v. *Cruden* [1986] I.R.L.R. 83, E.A.T.; *Wadley* v. *Eager Electrical* [1986] I.R.L.R. 93, E.A.T.; *MDH* v. *Sussex* [1986] I.R.L.R. 123, E.A.T.; *Graham* v. *ABF* [1986] I.R.L.R. 90, E.A.T.; *Fay* v. *North Yorkshire County Council* [1986] I.C.R. 133, C.A.; *Fenton* v. *Stablegold (t/a Chiswick Court Hotel)* [1986] I.R.L.R. 64, E.A.T.; *Hereford and Worcester County Council* v. *Neale* [1986] I.R.L.R. 168, C.A.; *Adams* v. *Derby City Council* [1986] I.R.L.R. 163, E.A.T.; *Shook* v. *Ealing London Borough Council* [1986] I.C.R. 314, E.A.T.; *Laughton and Hawley* v. *BAP Industrial Supplies* [1986] I.R.L.R. 245, E.A.T.; *Pritchett* v. *J. McIntyre, The Times,* October 24, 1986, C.A.
s. 60, see *Stockton-on-Tees Borough Council* v. *Brown, The Times,* August 18, 1986, E.A.T.
s. 64, see *Hyland* v. *Barker (J. H.) (North West)* [1985] I.C.R. 861, E.A.T.; *South West Launderettes* v. *Laidler* [1986] I.R.L.R. 68, E.A.T.; *Highlands and Islands Development Board* v. *MacGillivray,* 1986 S.L.T. 363; [1986] I.R.L.R. 210, Court of Session; *Secretary of State for Scotland* v. *Meikle* [1986] I.R.L.R. 208, E.A.T.; *Swaine* v. *Health and Safety Executive* [1986] I.C.R. 498, E.A.T.
s. 64, amended: 1986, c.59, s.3.
s. 64A, see *Keabeech* v. *Mulcahay* [1985] I.C.R. 791, E.A.T.
s. 67, see *Hennessey* v. *Craigmyle & Co. and A.C.A.S.* [1985] I.R.L.R. 446, E.A.T.; *Croydon Health Authority* v. *Jaufurally* [1986] I.C.R. 4, E.A.T.; *Lang* v. *Devon General, The Times,* August 19, 1986, E.A.T.

1978—cont.

44. Employment Protection (Consolidation) Act 1978—cont.

s. 68, see *Artisan Press* v. *Strawley and Parker* [1986] I.R.L.R. 126, E.A.T.

s. 69, see *Boots Co.* v. *Lees-Collier, The Times*, January 24, 1986, E.A.T.; *Electronic Data Processing* v. *Wright* [1986] I.C.R. 76, E.A.T.

ss. 69, 71, see *Artisan Press* v. *Strawley* [1986] I.C.R. 328, E.A.T.

s. 72, see *Fenton* v. *Stablegold (t/a Chiswick Court Hotel)* [1986] I.R.L.R. 64, E.A.T.

s. 73, see *R.S.P.C.A.* v. *Cruden* [1986] I.C.R. 205, E.A.T.; *Artisan Press* v. *Strawley and Parker* [1986] I.R.L.R. 126, E.A.T.; *Fenton* v. *Stablegold (t/a Chiswick Court Hotel)* [1986] I.R.L.R. 64, E.A.T.

s. 73, amended: 1986, c.59, s.3.

s. 74, see *Boots Co.* v. *Lees-Collier, The Times*, January 24, 1986, E.A.T.; *R.S.P.C.A.* v. *Cruden* [1986] I.C.R. 205, E.A.T.; *Scottish & Newcastle Breweries* v. *Halliday* [1986] I.C.R. 577, E.A.T.

s. 75, order 86/2284; amended: *ibid.*

ss. 75, 75A, see *Artisan Press* v. *Strawley* [1986] I.C.R. 328, E.A.T.

s. 81, see *Pink* v. *White; Pink* v. *White & Co. (Earls Barton)* [1985] I.R.L.R. 489, E.A.T.; *Marley* v. *Forward Trust Group* [1986] I.R.L.R. 43, E.A.T.; *Flack* v. *Kodak* [1986] I.R.L.R. 255, C.A.; *Secretary of State for Employment* v. *Spence* [1986] I.R.L.R. 248, C.A.

s. 82, amended: regs. 86/151.

s. 84, see *Mckindley* v. *Hill (William) (Scotland)* [1985] I.R.L.R. 492, E.A.T.; *Lucas* v. *Henry Johnson (Packers & Shippers)* [1986] I.C.R. 384, E.A.T.; *Hempell* v. *W.H. Smith & Sons* [1986] I.C.R. 365, E.A.T.

s. 87, see *Spinpress* v. *Turner* [1986] I.C.R. 433, E.A.T.

s. 104, amended: 1986, c.48, s.27; repealed in pt.: *ibid.*, sch. 5.

s. 104A, added: *ibid.*, s.27.

s. 106, see *Secretary of State for Employment* v. *Spence* [1986] I.R.L.R. 248, C.A.

s. 106, amended: 1986, c.45, sch. 14; repealed in pt.: 1986, c.48, sch. 5.

s. 108, amended: *ibid.*, sch. 4.

s. 113, repealed: *ibid.*, sch. 5.

s. 117, amended: *ibid.*, s.27.

s. 122, order 86/2283.

s. 122, amended: 1986, c.45, sch. 14; order 86/2283; repealed in pt.: 1986, c.50, sch. 11.

s. 123, amended: 1986, c.45, sch. 14; c.50, sch. 10; repealed in pt.: *ibid.*, sch. 11.

s. 124, amended: *ibid.*, sch. 10.

1978—cont.

44. Employment Protection (Consolidation) Act 1978—cont.

s. 125, amended: 1986, c.45, sch. 14; c.50, sch. 10.

s. 126, amended: *ibid.*

s. 127, amended: 1986, c.45, sch. 14; c.50, sch. 10; repealed in pt.: *ibid.*, sch. 11.

s. 132, amended: *ibid.*, sch.10; repealed in pt.: *ibid.*, sch. 11.

s. 133, amended: 1986, c.48, sch. 4; repealed in pt.: 1986, c.50, sch. 11.

ss. 134, see *Hennessy* v. *Craigmyle & Co.* [1986] I.C.R. 461.

s. 136, amended: 1986, c.48, sch. 4.

ss. 138, 139, repealed in pt.: 1986, c.50, sch. 11.

s. 140, see *Hennessy* v. *Craigmyle & Co.* [1986] I.C.R. 461, C.A.; *Igbo* v. *Johnson Matthey Chemicals* [1986] I.C.R. 505, C.A.

s. 148, order 86/2283.

s. 151, see *Flack* v. *Kodak, The Times*, May 31, 1986, C.A.

s. 153, see *South West Launderettes* v. *Laidler* [1986] I.C.R. 455, E.A.T.; *The Highlands and Islands Development Board* v. *MacGillivray*, 1986 S.L.T. 363; [1986] I.R.L.R. 210, Court of Session.

s. 153, amended: 1986, c.48, sch. 4; repealed in pt.: 1986, c.50, sch. 11.

s. 154, orders 86/2283, 2284.

ss. 155–157, repealed in pt.: 1986, c.50, sch. 11.

sch. 2, see *Community Task Force* v. *Rimmer* [1986] I.R.L.R. 203, E.A.T.

sch. 3, see *Notcutt* v. *Universal Equipment Co. (London)* [1986] 1 W.L.R. 641, C.A.

sch. 4, amended: regs. 86/151.

sch. 6, repealed in pt.: 1986, c.48, sch. 5.

sch. 13, see *Flack* v. *Kodak* [1986] 2 All E.R. 1003, C.A.; *Express and Star* v. *Bunday, The Times*, October 20, 1986, E.A.T.; *Surrey County Council* v. *Lewis* (1986) 130 S.J. 785, C.A.

sch. 14, order 86/2283.

sch. 14, amended: *ibid.*; repealed in pt.: regs. 86/151; 1986, c.50, sch. 11.

sch. 15, repealed in pt.: *ibid.*

sch. 16, repealed in pt.: 1986, c.48, sch. 5.

49. Community Service by Offenders (Scotland) Act 1978.

s. 1, see *McQueen* v. *Lockhart*, 1986 S.C.C.R. 20.

1979

2. Customs and Excise Management Act 1979.

s. 22, order 86/525, 971.

ss. 35, 42, regs. 86/1819.

s. 50, see *McNeil* v. *H.M. Advocate*, 1986 S.C.C.R. 288.

s. 68, see *R.* v. *Uxbridge JJ., ex p. Sofaer, The Times*, December 4, 1986, D.C.

1979—cont.

2. **Customs and Excise Management Act 1979**—cont.
   s. 93, see *R.* v. *Customs and Excise Comrs., ex p. Hedges and Butler* [1986] 2 All E.R. 164, D.C.
   s. 93, regs. 86/79, 910.
   s. 93, amended: 1986, c.41, sch. 3.
   s. 100A, order 86/1643.
   ss. 101, 102, 104, amended: 1986, c.41, sch. 5.
   s. 127A, regs. 86/910.
   s. 161, see *McNeil* v. *H.M. Advocate*, 1986 S.C.C.R. 288.
   s. 170, see *R.* v. *Shivpuri* [1986] 2 W.L.R. 988, H.L.; *R.* v. *Ellis and Street; R.* v. *Smith (Gloria Marie), The Times,* August 12, 1986, C.A.
   ss. 171, 177, sch. 4, repealed in pt.: S.L.R. 1986.
3. **Customs and Excise Duties (General Reliefs) Act 1979.**
   s. 1, orders 85/2041; 86/787.
   s. 4, orders 85/2041; 86/495, 1102.
   s. 13, order 86/2105.
4. **Alcoholic Liquor Duties Act 1979.**
   s. 4, repealed in pt.: 1986, c.41, sch. 23.
   s. 12, amended: *ibid.*, sch. 5; repealed in pt.: *ibid.*, s.8, sch. 23.
   s. 15, regs. 86/79.
   s. 15, repealed in pt.: 1986, c.41, schs. 3, 23.
   s. 18, repealed in pt.: *ibid.*, s.8, sch. 23.
   s. 25, repealed in pt.: *ibid.*, sch. 23.
   s. 46, amended: *ibid.*, s.4; repealed in pt.: *ibid.*, s.4, sch. 23.
   ss. 47, 48, repealed in pt.: *ibid.*, s.8, sch. 23.
   s. 49A, added: *ibid.*, s.4.
   ss. 54–56, repealed in pt.: *ibid.*, sch. 23.
   s. 75, repealed in pt.: *ibid.*, s.8, sch. 23.
   s. 81, repealed: *ibid.*
   s. 82, regs. 86/1820.
   s. 83, repealed: 1986, c.41, sch. 23.
5. **Hydrocarbon Oil Duties Act 1979.**
   ss. 6, 11, amended: 1986, c.41, s.2.
   sch. 3, amended: *ibid.*, sch. 5.
6. **Matches and Mechanical Lighters Duties Act 1979.**
   s. 2, repealed in pt.: 1986, c.41, s.8, sch. 23.
   s. 7, amended: *ibid.*, sch. 5.
7. **Tobacco Products Duty Act 1979.**
   sch. 1, amended: 1986, c.41, s.1.
8. **Excise Duties (Surcharges or Rebates) Act 1979.**
   sch. 1, repealed in pt.: S.L.R. 1986.
10. **Public Lending Right Act 1979.**
   functions transferred: order 86/600.
   s. 3, order 86/2103.
11. **Electricity (Scotland) Act 1979.**
   ss. 5, 35, sch. 4, amended: 1986, c.62, s.4.
12. **Wages Councils Act 1979.**
   repealed: 1986, c.48, s.12, sch. 5.

1979—cont.

14. **Capital Gains Tax Act 1979.**
   s. 5, order 86/527.
   s. 31, amended: 1986, c.41, s.56.
   s. 32, see *Chaney* v. *Watkis* [1986] S.T.C. 89, Nicholls J.
   s. 34, amended: 1986, c.41, s.56.
   s. 67, substituted: *ibid.*, s.59.
   s. 101, see *Moore* v. *Thompson* [1986] S.T.C. 170, Millett J.
   s. 107, amended: 1986, c.41, s.59.
   sch. 2, order 86/12.
   sch. 2, repealed in pt.: 1986, c.44, sch. 9.
15. **House of Commons (Redistribution of Seats) Act 1979.**
   repealed: 1986, c.56, sch. 4.
26. **Legal Aid Act 1979.**
   Pt. II (ss. 6–10). ss. 12 (in pt.), 14(in pt.), sch. 1 (in pt.), repealed (S): 1986, c.47, sch. 5.
27. **Kiribati Act 1979.**
   s. 6, repealed in pt.: S.L.R. 1986.
30. **Exchange Equalisation Account Act 1979.**
   s. 3, amended: 1986, c.41, s.113.
34. **Credit Unions Act 1979.**
   s. 6, amended: 1986, c.45, sch. 14.
   s. 31, regs. 86/622.
36. **Nurses, Midwives and Health Visitors Act 1979.**
   s. 22, orders 86/786, 1345, 1897.
37. **Banking Act 1979.**
   s. 1, see *SCF Finance Co.* v. *Masri (No. 2)* [1986] 1 All E.R. 40, Leggatt J.; *SCF Finance Co.* v. *MASRI, The Times,* August 12, 1986, C.A.
   s. 2, regs. 86/769, 1712.
   s. 6, amended: 1986, c.45, sch. 14.
   s. 8, amended: 1986, c.60, s.185.
   s. 18, amended: 1986, c.45, sch. 14.
   s. 19, amended: *ibid.*; c.60, sch. 13.
   s. 20, amended: *ibid.*; repealed in pt.: *ibid.*, sch. 17.
   s. 23, order 86/772.
   ss. 28, 31, amended: 1986, c.45, sch. 14.
   ss. 34, 36, 41, 50, amended: 1986, c.53, sch. 18.
   sch. 1, repealed in pt.: order 86/100; 1986, c.53, sch. 19; c.60, sch. 17.
   sch. 6, repealed in pt.: 1986, c.53, sch. 19; c.60, sch. 17.
38. **Estate Agents Act 1979.**
   s. 10, amended: 1986, c.31, sch. 4; c.44, sch. 7.
39. **Merchant Shipping Act 1979.**
   Commencement order: 86/1052.
   s. 21, regs. 86/144, 837, 1066–1075, 1935.
   s. 21, amended: 1986, c.23, s.11.
   s. 22, regs. 86/144, 1066–1074.
   s. 32, order 86/1052.
   s. 34, order 86/2285.
   s. 47, order 86/1163.
   s. 49, amended and repealed in pt.: 1986, c.23, s.11.
   s. 52, order 86/1052.

CAP.

1979—cont.

39. Merchant Shipping Act 1979—*cont.*
sch. 3, order 86/1777.
sch. 4, orders 86/1040, 1932, 2224.

41. Pneumoconiosis etc. (Workers' Compensation) Act 1979.
ss. 1, 4, 7, regs. 85/2035.
s. 2, amended: 1986, c.50, sch. 3; repealed in pt.: *ibid.*, sch. 11.

42. Arbitration Act 1979.
s. 1, see *Norwich Union Life Insurance Society* v. *Trustee Savings Bank Central Board* (1986) 278 E.G. 162, Hoffman J.; *Trave Schiffahrtsgesellschaft mbh* v. *Ninemia Maritime Corp.* [1986] 2 W.L.R. 773, C.A.; *Lucas Industries* v. *Welsh Development Agency* [1986] 3 W.L.R. 80, Browne-Wilkinson V.-C.; *Gebr. Van Weelde Sch. b.v.* v. *Société Industrielle D'acide Phosphorique Et Déngrais; Dynashinky, The* [1986] 1 Lloyd's Rep. 435, Hobhouse J.; *Aden Refinery Co.* v. *Ugland Management Co.* [1986] 3 W.L.R. 949, C.A.

43. Crown Agents Act 1979.
s. 17, amended and repealed in pt.: 1986, c.43, s.1.

46. Ancient Monuments and Archaeological Areas Act 1979.
s. 61, repealed in pt.: 1986, c.31, sch. 6; c.44, sch. 9.

48. Pensioners' Payments and Social Security Act 1979.
repealed: 1986, c.50, sch. 11.
s. 4, order 86/1119.

50. European Assembly (Pay and Pensions) Act 1979.
s. 8, repealed in pt.: 1986, c.58, sch.

53. Charging Orders Act 1979.
ss. 1, 3, see *Harman* v. *Glencross* [1986] 1 All E.R. 545, C.A.
s. 6, amended: 1986, c.53, sch. 18.

54. Sale of Goods Act 1979.
s. 14, see *Wormwell* v. *R.H.M. Agricultural (East)* [1986] 1 W.L.R. 336, Piers Ashworth Q.C.; *M/S Aswan Engineering Establishment* v. *Lupdine, The Times*, August 4, 1986, C.A.; *Bernstein* v. *Pamsons Motors, The Times*, October 25, 1986, Rougier J.; *Rogers* v. *Parish (Scarborough), The Times*, November 8, 1986, C.A.
s. 25, see *Martin* v. *Duffy* [1985] 11 N.I.J.B. 80, Lord Lowry L.C.J.

55. Justices of the Peace Act 1979.
s. 18, rules 86/923.
s. 23, orders 86/231, 765, 1057.
s. 44, see *R.* v. *Cardiff JJ., ex p. Salter* (1986) 1 F.L.R. 162, Wood J.
s. 52, see *Waltham Forest JJ., ex p. Solanke* [1986] 3 W.L.R. 315, C.A.

CAP.

1980

4. Bail, etc. (Scotland) Act 1980.
s. 2, see *Welsh* v. *H.M. Advocate*, 1986 S.L.T. 664.

5. Child Care Act 1980.
ss. 2, 3, 12A, see *W.* v. *Nottinghamshire County Council* (1986) 12 Fam. Law 185, C.A.
ss. 12A–12G, see *T.D. (A Minor) (Wardship: Jurisdiction), Re,* (1986) 16 Fam. Law 18, Sheldon J.
s. 12B, see *R.* v. *Bolton Metropolitan Borough Council, ex p. B.* (1986) 84 L.G.R. 78, Wood J.
ss. 12B–12D, see *Devon County Council* v. *C.* (1986) 16 Fam. Law 20, C.A.
s. 12C, see *Hereford and Worcester County Council* v. *Jah* (1985) 15 Fam. Law 324, C.A.; *A.* v. *Wigan Metropolitan Borough Council* (1986) 16 Fam. Law 162, Ewbank J.
s. 18, see *R.* v. *Avon County Council, ex p. K.* [1986] 1 F.L.R. 443, Heilbron J.
s. 21, see *Kininmonth* v. *Chief Adjudication Officer, The Times*, October 17, 1986, C.A.
s. 21A, see *M. (A Minor), Re, The Times*, January 24, 1986, C.A.; *M.* v. *Lambeth Borough Council (No. 3)* (1986) 16 Fam. Law 23, Sheldon J.; *Liverpool City Council* v. *H.K.* (1985) 83 L.G.R. 421, Heilbron J.
s. 21A, regs. 86/1591.
s. 22A, amended: 1986, c.28, s.1.
s. 25, repealed in pt.: 1986, c.50, sch. 11.
s. 39, regs. 86/1591.
s. 45, amended: 1986, c.50, sch. 10.
s. 46, see *R.* v. *Essex County Council, ex p. Washington, The Times*, July 12, 1986, C.A.
s. 85, regs. 86/1591.
s. 85, amended: 1986, c.28, s.1.
s. 87, see *T.D. (A Minor) (Wardship: Jurisdiction), Re,* (1986) 16 Fam. Law 18, Sheldon J.

9. Reserve Forces Act 1980.
ss. 6, 117, repealed in pt.: 1986, c.21, sch. 2.
s. 158, order 86/2026.

15. National Health Service (Invalid Direction) Act 1980.
repealed: S.L.R. 1986.

16. New Hebrides Act 1980.
s. 3, repealed: S.L.R. 1986.

17. National Heritage Act 1980.
functions transferred: order 86/600.

20. Education Act 1980.
ss. 2–4, repealed: 1986, c.61, sch. 6.
s. 17, regs. 86/991.
s. 18, regs. 86/990.
s. 22, amended: 1986, c.50, s.77.
s. 27, regs. 86/542.
ss. 31, 32, repealed: 1986, c.61, sch. 6.
s. 35, regs. 86/542, 990, 991.
s. 35 (in pt.), sch. 6, repealed: 1986, c.61, sch. 6.

1980—cont.

21. Competition Act 1980.
s. 19, amended: 1986, c.31, sch. 4; c.44, sch. 7; c.60, sch. 13.

22. Domestic Proceedings and Magistrates' Courts Act 1980.
s. 29, see *Berry* v. *Berry* [1986] 3 W.L.R. 257, C.A.

23. Consular Fees Act 1980.
s. 1, order 86/1881.

25. Insurance Companies Act 1980.
sch. 3, repealed (N.I.): 1986, c.53, sch. 19.

26. British Eurospace Act 1980.
s. 7, order 86/848.
s. 9, amended: 1986, c.45, sch. 14.

30. Social Security Act 1980.
ss. 1, 4 (in pt.), repealed: 1986, c.50, sch. 11.
s. 5, repealed in pt.: *ibid.*, s.38, sch. 11.
ss. 7, 8 (in pt.), repealed: *ibid.*, sch. 11.
ss. 9, 10, amended: *ibid.*, sch. 10; repealed in pt.: *ibid.*, sch. 11.
s. 14, see *White* v. *Chief Adjudication Officer* [1986] 3 All E.R. 905, C.A.
s. 14, amended: 1986, c.50, sch. 9; repealed in pt.: *ibid.*, sch. 11.
ss. 15, 17 (in pt.), repealed: *ibid.*
s. 18, amended: *ibid.*, sch. 10; repealed in pt.: *ibid.*, sch. 11.
s. 20, schs. 1, 2, repealed in pt.: *ibid.*
sch. 3, amended: *ibid.*, sch. 10; repealed in pt.: *ibid.*, sch. 11.
sch. 4, repealed in pt. (S.): 1986, c.47, sch. 5.

37. Gas Act 1980.
repealed: 1986, c.44, sch. 9.

39. Social Security (No. 2) Act 1980.
ss. 1, 2, 4 (in pt.), 6, repealed: 1986, c.50, sch. 11.

42. Employment Act 1980.
s. 4, see *McGhee* v. *Transport and General Workers Union* (1985) 82 L.S.Gaz. 3696, C.A.; *Clark* v. *Society of Graphical and Allied Trades 1982* [1986] I.C.R. 12, E.A.T.
ss. 4, 5, see *Day* v. *Society of Graphical and Allied Trades 1982* [1986] I.C.R. 640, E.A.T.
s. 5, see *Saunders* v. *Bakers Food and Allied Workers Union* [1986] I.R.L.R. 16, E.A.T.

43. Magistrates' Courts Act 1980.
s. 6, see *R.* v. *Horseferry Road Metropolitan Stipendiary Magistrate, ex p. O'Regan, The Times*, May 17, 1986, D.C.
s. 10, see *Arthur* v. *Stringer, The Times*, October 11, 1986, D.C.
s. 22, see *R.* v. *Salisbury Magistrates' Court, ex p. Mastin* [1986] Crim.L.R. 545, D.C.
s. 24, see *R.* v. *Newham Juvenile Court, ex p. F. (A Minor)* [1986] 1 W.L.R. 939, D.C.; see *R.* v. *Doncaster Crown Court, ex p. C.P.S., The Times*, December 2, 1986, D.C.

1980—cont.

43. Magistrates' Courts Act 1980—*cont.*
s. 25, see *Gillard, Re (sub nom. R.* v. *Dudley JJ., ex p. Gillard)* [1985] 3 W.L.R. 936, H.L.; *R.* v. *Southend JJ., ex p. Wood, The Times*, March 8, 1986, D.C.
ss. 34, 35, see *Chief Constable of Kent* v. *Mather* [1986] R.T.R. 36, D.C.
s. 44, see *Bentley* v. *Mullen* [1986] R.T.R. 7, D.C.
s. 49, See *R.* v. *Tottenham JJ., ex p. M.L.* (1986) 82 Cr.App.R. 277, C.A.
s. 64, see *R.* v. *Salisbury and Tilsbury and Mere Combined Juvenile Court, ex p. Ball* (1985) 15 Fam. Law 313, Kennedy J.
s. 65, amended: 1986, c.50, sch. 10.
s. 87, see *Gooch* v. *Ewing (Allied Irish Bank, Garnishee)* [1985] 3 All E.R. 654, C.A.
s. 95, see *Parry* v. *Meugens* (1986) 1 F.L.R. 125, Reeve J.; *Berry* v. *Berry* [1986] 3 W.L.R. 257, C.A.
s. 97, see *R.* v. *Sheffield JJ., ex p. Wrigley* [1985] R.T.R. 78, D.C.
s. 111, see *Berry* v. *Berry* [1986] 3 W.L.R. 257, C.A.
s. 114, see *R.* v. *Newcastle upon Tyne JJ., ex p. Skinner, The Times*, October 27, 1986, D.C.
s. 115, see *Howley* v. *Oxford* (1985) 81 Cr.App.R. 246, D.C.; *Lanham* v. *Bernard, The Times*, June 23, 1986, D.C.
s. 120, see *R.* v. *Bow Street Magistrates' Court, ex p. Hall, The Times*, October 27, 1986, C.A.
s. 122, see *R.* v. *Croydon Crown Court, ex p. Claire, The Times*, April 3, 1986, D.C.
s. 144, rules 86/367, 1079, 1141, 1332, 1333, 1498, 1962.
s. 145, rules 86/1498, 1962.
s. 150, see *Chief Constable of Kent* v. *Mather* [1986] R.T.R. 36, D.C.
sch. 1, repealed in pt.: 1986, c.48, sch. 5.

44. Education (Scotland) Act 1980.
s. 1, see *Walker* v. *Strathclyde Regional Council (No. 1)* (O.H.), 1986 S.L.T. 523.
s. 4, amended and repealed in pt.: 1986, c.33, s.14.
s. 23, repealed in pt.: 1986, c.61, sch. 6.
ss. 28, 28A, see *Keeney* v. *Strathclyde Regional Council* (O.H.), 1986 S.L.T. 490.
s. 48A, added: 1986, c.61, s.48.
s. 49, regs. 86/1227.
s. 53, amended: 1986, c.50, s.77.
ss. 61–64, amended: 1986, c.33, s.14.
s. 70, see *Walker* v. *Strathclyde Regional Council (No. 1)* (O.H.), 1986 S.L.T. 523.
ss. 73, 74, regs. 86/410, 510, 1103.
ss. 75A, 75B, regs. 86/1104.

1980—cont.

44. Education (Scotland) Act 1980—cont.
s. 77, regs. 86/1353.
s. 87, see *Connor* v. *Strathclyde Regional Council* (O.H.), 1986 S.L.T. 530.
s. 88, see *Nahar* v. *Strathclyde Regional Council* (O.H.), 1986 S.L.T. 570.

45. Water (Scotland) Act 1980.
s. 17, order 86/693.
ss. 41, 60, 85, regs. 86/411.
s. 107, order 86/693.

46. Solicitors (Scotland) Act 1980.
ss. 25, 51, amended: 1986, c.47, sch. 3.

48. Finance Act 1980.
s. 24, order 86/529.
s. 24, amended: 1986, c.41, s.19.
ss. 64, 65, amended: *ibid.*, s.57, sch. 16; repealed in pt.: *ibid.*, sch. 16.
ss. 66, 67, repealed: *ibid.*
s. 68, amended and repealed in pt.: *ibid.*
s. 69, amended: *ibid.*
s. 79, amended: *ibid.*, s.101.
ss. 96, 100, repealed: *ibid.*, sch. 23.
sch. 10, amended: *ibid.*, ss.22, 23, 25; c.60, sch. 16; repealed in pt.: 1986, c.41, s.25, sch. 23.
sch. 18, amended: *ibid.*, s.73; repealed in pt.: *ibid.*, s.74, sch. 23.

51. Housing Act 1980.
ss. 2, 5, 10, 16, schs. 1, 4, see *Enfield London Borough Council* v. *McKeon* [1986] 2 All E.R. 730, C.A.
s. 28, see *Freeman* v. *Plymouth City Council, The Times*, March 11, 1986, Hodgson J.
ss. 30, 50, see *Harrogate Borough Council* v. *Simpson* [1986] 2 F.S.R. 91, C.A.
s. 33, see *Torridge District Council* v. *Jones* (1985) 276 E.G. 1253, C.A.
s. 56, orders 86/864, 866, 1208, 1209, 1729.
s. 56, amended: 1986, c.63, s.12; repealed in pt.: *ibid.*, sch. 12.
s. 56A–56D, added: *ibid.*, s.12.
s. 56B, order 86/2180.
s. 58, amended: 1986, c.63, s.13.
s. 140, repealed: *ibid.*, schs. 4, 12.
sch. 5, amended: *ibid.*, s.13.

52. Tenants' Rights, Etc. (Scotland) Act 1980.
s. 1, see *Motherwell District Council* v. *Gliori*, 1986 S.L.T. 444; *Campbell* v. *City of Edinburgh District Council*, 1987 S.L.T. 51; *McGroarty* v. *Stirling District Council* (O.H.), 1987 S.L.T. 85.
s. 1, amended: 1986, c.63, s.3, sch. 5; c.65, ss.1–3, sch. 1; repealed in pt.: *ibid.*, sch. 3.
s. 1A, amended: 1986, c.65, sch. 1.
s. 1B, added: *ibid.*, sch. 1.
s. 2, see *Neave* v. *City of Dundee District Council*, 1986 S.L.T. (Lands Tr.) 18; *McGroarty* v. *Stirling District Council* (O.H.), 1987 S.L.T. 85.
s. 2, amended: 1986, c.65, sch. 1.

1980—cont.

52. Tenants' Rights, Etc. (Scotland) Act 1980—cont.
s. 3, see *Thomson* v. *City of Glasgow District Council*, 1986 S.L.T. (Lands Tr.) 6.
s. 4, amended: 1986, c.65, sch. 1.
s. 4A, added: *ibid.*, s.4.
ss. 5, 6, amended: *ibid.*, sch. 1.
s. 6A, added: *ibid.*
s. 7, see *Neave* v. *City of Dundee District Council*, 1986 S.L.T. (Lands Tr.) 18.
s. 8, see *McGroarty* v. *Stirling District Council* (O.H.), 1987 S.L.T. 85.
s. 8, amended: 1986, c.65, sch. 1.
s. 9A, amended: *ibid.*, s.2.
s. 9B, added: *ibid.*, s.5.
s. 9B, amended: 1986, c.47, sch. 3.
s. 9C, added: 1986, c.65, s.6.
s. 10, see *Campbell* v. *City of Edinburgh District Council*, 1987 S.L.T. 51; *Thomson* v. *City of Glasgow District Council*, 1986 S.L.T. (Lands Tr.) 6.
s. 10, amended: 1986, c.65, s.1, sch. 1; repealed in pt.: *ibid.*, sch. 3.
ss. 12, 14, 15, see *Charing Cross and Kelvingrove Housing Association* v. *Kraska*, 1986 S.L.T.(Sh.Ct.) 42.
ss. 13, 15, amended: 1986, c.65, sch. 1.
s. 25A, added: *ibid.*, s.7.
s. 26, substituted: *ibid.*, sch. 1.
s. 26A, added: *ibid.*
s. 27, amended: *ibid.*, s.8.
s. 30, amended: 1986, c.65, sch. 1; repealed in pt.: *ibid.*, sch. 3.
s. 31, amended: *ibid.*, s.9.
s. 82, see *Thomson* v. *City of Glasgow District Council*, 1986 S.L.T. (Lands Tr.) 6; *Neave* v. *City of Dundee District Council*, 1986 S.L.T. (Lands Tr.) 18.
s. 82, amended: 1986, c.65, sch. 1.
s. 82A, added: *ibid.*
sch. 1, see *Campbell* v. *City of Edinburgh District Council*, 1987 S.L.T. 51.
sch. 1, amended: 1986, c.65, sch. 1; repealed in pt., *ibid.*, s.10.
sch. 2, see *Charing Cross and Kelvingrove Housing Association* v. *Kraska*, 1986 S.L.T. (Sh.Ct.) 42.
sch. 2, amended: 1986, c.65, s.11, schs. 1, 3.

53. Health Services Act 1980.
s. 21, sch. 1, repealed in pt.: 1986, c.66, s.8.

55. Law Reform (Miscellaneous Provisions) (Scotland) Act 1980.
s. 2, repealed in pt.: S.L.R. 1986.
s. 26, repealed: 1986, c.47, sch. 5.

58. Limitation Act 1980.
s. 2, see *Sevcon* v. *Lucas CAV* [1986] 1 W.L.R. 462, H.L.
ss. 11, 14, see *Pilmore* v. *Northern Trawlers* [1986] 1 Lloyd's Rep. 552, Eastham J.

1980—cont.

58. Limitation Act 1980—cont.
s. 14, see *Fowell* v. *National Coal Board, The Times*, May 28, 1986, C.A.
ss. 1A, 14B, added: 1986, c.37, s.1.
s. 14, see *Bristow* v. *Grout, The Times*, November 3, 1986, Jupp J.
ss. 28A, added: 1986, c.37, s.2.
s. 32, amended: *ibid.*
s. 33, see *Pilmore* v. *Northern Trawlers* [1986] 1 Lloyd's Rep. 552, Eastham J.; *Bradley* v. *Hanseatic Shipping* [1986] 2 Lloyd's Rep. 34, C.A.
s. 35, see *Grimsby Cold Stores* v. *Jenkins & Potter* (1985) 5 Const.L.J. 362, C.A.; *Steamship Mutual Underwriting Association* v. *Trollope & Colls (City)* (1985) 2 Const. L.J. 75, H.H. Judge Newey, Q.C., O.R.

60. Civil Aviation Act 1980.
ss. 24, 25, repealed: 1986, c.31, sch. 6.

62. Criminal Justice (Scotland) Act 1980.
s. 9, see *Brady* v. *Lockhart*, 1985 S.C.C.R. 349; *Cirignaco, Petr.*, 1986 S.L.T. (Sh.Ct.) 11.
s. 10, see *Wilson* v. *Tudhope*, 1985 S.C.C.R. 339.
s. 10, repealed in pt.: 1986, c.47, sch. 5.
s. 14, see *MacDougall* v. *Russell*, 1986 S.L.T. 403.
s. 26, see *Allan* v. *Taylor*, 1986 S.C.C.R. 202.
s. 37, see *Lord Advocate's Reference (No. 1 of 1985)*, 1987 S.L.T. 187.
s. 70A, added: 1986, c.64, sch. 1.
s. 71, amended: *ibid.*
s. 72A, added: *ibid.*
s. 75, amended: *ibid.*; repealed in pt.: *ibid.*, sch. 3.
s. 80, see *Glover* v. *Tudhope*, 1986 S.C.C.R. 49.
sch. 1, see *Allan* v. *Taylor*, 1986 S.C.C.R. 202.
sch. 2, see *Morland* v. *H.M. Advocate*, 1985 S.C.C.R. 316; *King* v. *H.M. Advocate*, 1985 S.C.C.R. 322; *Allison* v. *H.M. Advocate*, 1985 S.C.C.R. 408.
sch. 3, see *Aitchison* v. *Rizza*, 1985 S.C.C.R. 297.
sch. 8, repealed in pt.: S.L.R. 1986.

63. Overseas Development and Co-operation Act 1980.
s. 4, order 86/1587.
s. 7, order 86/286; amended: *ibid.*
sch. 1, repealed in pt.: 1986, c.44, sch. 9.

65. Local Government, Planning and Land Act 1980.
s. 20, see *Wilkinson* v. *Doncaster Metropolitan Borough Council* (1986) 84 L.G.R. 257, C.A.
s. 54, amended: 1986, c.50, sch. 10.
ss. 56, 59, see *Smith* v. *Skinner; Gladden* v. *McMahon* (1986) 26 R.V.R. 45, D.C.
s. 57, amended: 1986, c.54, sch. 1.

1980—cont.

65. Local Government, Planning and Land Act 1980—cont.
s. 59, see *Nottinghamshire County Council* v. *Secretary of State for the Environment; City of Bradford Metropolitan Council* v. *The Same* [1986] 2 W.L.R. 1, H.L.; *R.* v. *Secretary of State for the Environment, ex p. Hackney London Borough Council* (1986) 84 L.G.R. 32, C.A.
s. 59, amended: 1986, c.54, sch.1; repealed in pt.: *ibid.*, schs. 1, 2.
ss. 60, 61, amended: *ibid.*, sch. 1.
s. 62, substituted: *ibid.*
s. 65, amended: *ibid.*
s. 68, repealed in pt.: 1986, c.61, sch. 4.
Pt. VIII (ss.71–85), see *R.* v. *Secretary of State for the Environment, ex p. Newham London Borough Council, The Times*, December 23, 1985, Taylor J.
s. 72, repealed in pt.: 1986, c.31, sch. 6.
ss. 72, 78, see *Smith* v. *Skinner; Gladden* v. *McMahon* (1986) 26 R.V.R. 45, D.C.
s. 88, repealed: 1986, c.63, sch. 12.
ss. 108, 120, repealed in pt.: 1986, c.31, sch. 6; c.44, sch. 9.
s. 134, repealed in pt.: 1986, c.63, s.47, sch. 12.
s. 134, repealed in pt. (S.): *ibid.*, sch. 12.
s. 136, see *London Docklands Corp.* v. *Rank Hovis* (1985) 84 L.G.R. 101, C.A.
s. 154, amended: 1986, c.50, s.10.
s. 156, repealed in pt.: 1986, c.63, schs. 4, 12.
s. 170, repealed in pt.: 1986, c.31, sch. 6; c.44, sch. 9.
sch. 10, regs. 85/2030; 86/314.
sch. 10, amended: 1986, c.61, sch. 4.
schs. 14, 15, repealed in pt.: 1986, c.63, sch. 12.
sch. 16, repealed in pt.: 1986, c.31, sch. 6; c.44, sch. 9.
sch. 19, repealed in pt.: 1986, c.44, sch. 9.
sch. 29, repealed in pt.: 1986, c.63, sch. 12.
sch. 30, repealed in pt. (S.): *ibid.*
sch. 32, order 86/1557.
sch. 32, amended: 1986, c.63, s.54.

66. Highways Act 1980.
s. 16, scheme 86/1646.
s. 39, repealed: S.L.R. 1986.
s. 90C, regs. 86/1858.
s. 106, instruments 85/731, 1429.
s. 131, see *Greenwich London Borough Council* v. *Millcroft Construction, The Times*, July 26, 1986, D.C.
s. 135, amended: 1986, c.49, s.21.
s. 137, see *Cooper* v. *Metropolitan Police Comr.* (1986) 82 Cr.App.R. 238, D.C.; *Hirst* v. *Chief Constable of West Yorkshire, The Times*, November 19, 1986, C.A.
s. 161, amended: 1986, c.13, s.1.
s. 161A, added: *ibid.*

CAP.

1980—cont.

66. Highways Act 1980—cont.
sch. 23, order 86/610.
sch. 24, repealed in pt.: S.L.R. 1986.

1981

3. Gas Levy Act 1981.
s. 1, amended: 1986, c.44, sch. 6.
s. 3, substituted: *ibid.*
ss. 4, 5, amended: *ibid.*
s. 5A, added: *ibid.*
ss. 6, 7, amended: *ibid.*

7. House of Commons Members' Fund and Parliamentary Pensions Act 1981.
s. 2, resolution 85/2082.

14. Public Passenger Vehicles Act 1981.
s. 5, regs. 86/1030, 1629, 1691.
s. 6, regs. 86/1812.
ss. 14, 16, regs. 86/1668.
s. 18, regs. 86/994, 1668.
s. 19, amended: 1986, c.45, sch. 14.
s. 44, regs. 86/1813.
s. 52, regs. 86/370, 869, 972, 1245, 1668, 1671, 1691.
ss. 54, 56, regs. 86/1629.
s. 57, regs. 86/1668, 1691.
s. 58, regs. 86/1628.
s. 59, regs. 86/994, 1668, 1691.
s. 60, regs. 86/370, 753, 869, 972, 1030, 1245, 1629, 1668, 1671, 1691.
s. 61, regs. 86/370, 567, 1030, 1628, 1779.
s. 78, order 86/1504.
ss. 81, 82, regs. 86/1668.

20. Judicial Pensions Act 1981.
s. 21, order 86/814.

22. Animal Health Act 1981.
s. 1, orders 86/5, 498, 862, 1290, 2061, 2062.
s. 7, orders 86/5, 862, 1290, 1755.
s. 8, orders 86/498, 862, 1755.
s. 10, order 86/2062.
s. 11, orders 86/1528, 1734.
s. 14, order 86/862.
ss. 15, 17, orders 86/862, 1755.
s. 21, order 86/2061.
s. 23, orders 86/5, 862, 1290, 1755.
s. 25, orders 86/498, 862, 1755.
s. 72, order 86/1755.
s. 87, orders 86/498, 1755.
s. 88, order 86/1755.
s. 95, order 86/2062.

23. Local Government (Miscellaneous Provisions) (Scotland) Act 1981.
s. 23, orders 86/388, 389.

28. Licensing (Alcohol Education and Research) Act 1981.
s. 3, amended: 1986, c.60, sch. 16.

29. Fisheries Act 1981.
s. 30, orders 86/110, 250, 251, 779, 926, 2090.
sch. 4, repealed in pt.: S.L.R. 1986.

33. Social Security Act 1981.
ss. 1, 4, sch. 1 (in pt.), repealed: 1986, c.50, sch. 11.

CAP.

1981—cont.

35. Finance Act 1981.
s. 55, amended: 1986, c.45, sch. 14.
s. 107, amended: 1986, c.63, sch. 5.
s. 109, repealed: 1986, c.41, sch. 23.
s. 111, see *I.R.C.* v. *Mobil North Sea, The Times,* November 21, 1986, C.A.
sch. 8, repealed in pt.: 1986, c.41, sch. 23.
sch. 9, amended: *ibid.,* sch. 10.

36. Town and Country Planning (Minerals) Act 1981.
Commencement order: 86/760.
see *Northumberland County Council and Northern Aggregates (Ref. T/APP/R2900/A/84/18860)* (1985) 1 P.A.D. 76.
s. 35, order 86/760.

45. Forgery and Counterfeiting Act 1981.
ss. 3, 10, see *R.* v. *Tobierre* [1986] 1 W.L.R. 125, C.A.
s. 9, see *R.* v. *Moore* [1986] Crim.L.R. 552, C.A.

47. Criminal Attempts Act 1981.
s. 1, see *R.* v. *Widdowson, The Times,* January 7, 1986, C.A.; *R.* v. *Webster,* February 12, 1986, Turner J.; *Bullivant (Roger)* v. *Ellis, Financial Times,* April 16, 1986, Falconer J.; *Chief Constable of Hampshire* v. *Mace* [1986] Crim.L.R. 725, D.C.; *R.* v. *Shivpuri* [1986] 2 W.L.R. 988, H.L.; *R.* v. *Gullefer, The Times,* November 25, 1986, C.A.
s. 5, see *R.* v. *Grant* (1986) 82 Cr.App.R. 324, C.A.

49. Contempt of Court Act 1981.
s. 2, see *Bullivant (Roger)* v. *Ellis, Financial Times,* April 16, 1986, Falconer J.; *Att.-Gen.* v. *News Group Newspapers* [1986] 2 All E.R. 833, C.A.
s. 4, see *R.* v. *Rhuddlan JJ., ex p. H.T.V.* [1986] Crim.L.R. 329, D.C.
ss. 6, 7, see *Bullivant (Roger)* v. *Ellis, Financial Times,* April 16, 1986, Falconer J.
s. 8, see *McCadden* v. *H.M. Advocate,* 1986 S.L.T. 138.
s. 10, see *Handmade Films (Productions)* v. *Express Newspapers* [1986] F.S.R. 463, Browne-Wilkinson V.C.; *Maxwell* v. *Pressdram, The Times,* November 12, 1986, C.A.
s. 12, see *R.* v. *Havant Magistrates' Court and Portsmouth Crown Court, ex p. Palmer* [1985] Crim.L.R. 658, D.C.
s. 13, repealed in pt. (S.): 1986, c.47, sch. 5.
s. 14, see *H (A Minor) (Injunction: Breach), Re,* (1986) 16 Fam. Law 139, C.A.; *C. (A Minor) (Wardship: Contempt), Re,* (1986) 16 Fam. Law 187, C.A.; *Linnett* v. *Coles* [1986] 3 W.L.R. 843, D.C.
sch. 2, repealed in pt. (S.): 1986, c.47, sch. 5.

CAP.

1981—cont.

53. Deep Sea Mining (Temporary Provisions) Act 1981.
s. 1, amended: order 86/948.

54. Supreme Court Act 1981.
rules 86/632.
s. 18, see *Gooch* v. *Ewing (Allied Irish Bank, Garnishee)* [1985] 3 All E.R. 654, C.A.; *Aiden Shipping Co.* v. *Interbulk* [1985] 1 W.L.R. 1222, C.A.; *R.* v. *Bolton JJ., ex p. Graeme, The Times*, March 14, 1986, C.A.: *McCarney* v. *McCarney* (1986) 1 F.L.R. 312, C.A.; *Smith* v. *Middleton* [1986] 1 W.L.R. 598, C.A.; *Parry* v. *Parry* [1986] 16 Fam. Law 211, C.A.
s. 26, repealed in pt.: 1986, c.55, schs. 1, 2.
s. 29, see *R.* v. *Central Criminal Court, ex p. Raymond* [1986] 1 W.L.R. 710, C.A.; *R.* v. *Maidstone Crown Court, ex p. Gill* [1986] 1 W.L.R. 1405, D.C.
s. 31, see *R.* v. *Secretary of State for the Environment, ex p. G.L.C., The Times*, December 30, 1985, Woolf J.; *R.* v. *Stratford-on-Avon District Council, ex p. Jackson* [1985] 1 W.L.R. 1319, C.A.; *R.* v. *Secretary of State for the Environment, ex p. Nottinghamshire County Council, The Times*, November 10, 1986, D.C.; *R.* v. *Secretary of State for the Home Department, ex p. Herbage* [1986] 3 W.L.R. 504, Hodgson J.
s. 33, see *Taylor* v. *Anderton, The Times*, October 21, 1986, Scott J.
s. 35A, see *Edmunds* v. *Adas, Financial Times*, February 12, 1986, C.A.; *Edmunds* v. *Lloyds Italico & L'Ancora Compagnia di Assicurazione e Riassicurazione S.p.A.* [1986] 1 W.L.R. 492, C.A.; *Coastal States Trading (U.K.)* v. *Mebro Minaeraloel GmbH* [1986] 1 Lloyd's Rep. 465, Hobhouse J.
s. 37, see *Ainsbury* v. *Millington* [1986] 1 All E.R. 73, C.A.; *Daiches* v. *Bluelake Investments* (1986) 51 P. & C.R. 51, Harman J.; *Bayer AG* v. *Winter* [1986] 1 All E.R. 733, C.A.; *South Carolina Insurance Co.* v. *Assurantie Maatschappij "De Zeven Provincien" N.V.* [1986] 3 W.L.R. 398, H.L.
s. 40A, amended: 1986, c.45, sch. 14.
s. 47, see *R.* v. *Nodjoumi* (1985) 7 Cr.App.R. (S.) 183, C.A.
s. 48, see *R.* v. *Plymouth JJ., ex p. Hart* [1986] 2 W.L.R. 976, D.C.; *Dutta* v. *Westcott* [1986] 3 W.L.R. 746, D.C.; *Arthur* v. *Stringer, The Times*, October 11, 1986, D.C.
s. 51, see *Aiden Shipping Co.* v. *Interbulk* [1986] 2 W.L.R. 1051, H.L.
s. 72, see *Charles of the Ritz Group* v. *Jory* [1986] F.S.R. 14, Scott J.
s. 72, amended: 1986, c.39, sch. 2.

CAP.

1981—cont.

54. Supreme Court Act 1981—*cont.*
s. 79, see *R.* v. *Croydon Crown Court, ex p. Claire, The Times*, April 3, 1986, D.C.
s. 84, rules 86/1187.
ss. 93, 97, amended: 1986, c.57, sch.
s. 99, order 86/1361.
s. 130, orders 86/637, 705.
s. 138, see *Bankers Trust Co.* v. *Galadari, The Times*, October 15, 1986, C.A.
sch. 1, amended: 1986, c.16, s.5; c.39, sch. 2; c.55, sch. 1.

55. Armed Forces Act 1981.
ss. 1, 6 (in pt.), repealed: 1986, c.21, sch. 2.
s. 14, amended: *ibid.*, s.13.

56. Transport Act 1981.
s. 19, see *R.* v. *Yates* [1986] R.T.R. 68, C.A.; *Allan* v. *Barclay*, 1986 S.C.C.R. 111; *Middleton* v. *Tudhope*, 1986 S.C.C.R. 241.
s. 25, see *Graham* v. *Albert* [1985] R.T.R. 352, D.C.; *Bunyard* v. *Hayes* [1985] R.T.R. 348, D.C.; *Duddy* v. *Gallagher* [1985] R.T.R. 401, D.C.; *Broadbent* v. *High* [1985] R.T.R. 359, D.C.; *Sivyer* v. *Parker, The Times*, January 23, 1986, D.C.; *Anderton* v. *Kinnard* [1986] R.T.R. 11, D.C.; *Patterson* v. *Charlton* [1986] R.T.R. 18, D.C.; *Walton* v. *Rimmer* [1986] R.T.R. 31, D.C.; *Archbold* v. *Jones* [1986] R.T.R. 178, D.C.; *Johnson* v. *West Yorkshire Metropolitan Police* [1986] R.T.R. 167, D.C.; *Beck* v. *Scammell* [1986] R.T.R. 162, D.C.; *Price* v. *Nicholls* [1986] R.T.R. 155, D.C.; *Owen* v. *Morgan* [1986] R.T.R. 151, D.C.; *Redmond* v. *Parry* [1986] R.T.R. 146, D.C.
s. 30, see *R.* v. *Preston* [1986] R.T.R. 136, C.A.; *Redmond* v. *Parry* [1986] R.T.R. 146, D.C.
sch. 8, see *Graham* v. *Albert* [1985] R.T.R. 352, D.C.; *Bunyard* v. *Hayes* [1985] R.T.R. 348, D.C.; *Duddy* v. *Gallagher* [1985] R.T.R. 401, D.C.; *Broadbent* v. *High* [1985] R.T.R. 359, D.C.; *Sivyer* v. *Parker, The Times*, January 23, 1986, D.C.; *Anderton* v. *Kinnard* [1986] R.T.R. 11, D.C.; *Patterson* v. *Charlton* [1986] R.T.R. 18, D.C.; *Walton* v. *Rimmer* [1986] R.T.R. 31, D.C.; *Harris* v. *Tudhope*, 1985 S.C.C.R. 305; *Bain* v. *Tudhope*, 1985 S.C.C.R. 412; *Archbold* v. *Jones* [1986] R.T.R. 178, D.C.; *Johnson* v. *West Yorkshire Metropolitan Police* [1986] R.T.R. 167, D.C.; *Owen* v. *Morgan* [1986] R.T.R. 151, D.C.; *Beck* v. *Scammell* [1986] R.T.R. 162, D.C.; *Price* v. *Nicholls* [1986] R.T.R. 155, D.C.; *Redmond* v. *Parry* [1986] R.T.R. 146, D.C.; *O'Brien* v. *Ferguson*, 1986 S.C.C.R. 155; *Houston* v. *McLeod*, 1986 S.C.C.R. 219.

CAP.
1981—cont.

56. Transport Act 1981—*cont.*
sch. 9, see *Cardle* v. *Campbell*, 1985 S.C.C.R. 309; *R.* v. *Preston* [1986] R.T.R. 136, C.A.; *Redmond* v. *Parry* [1986] R.T.R. 146, D.C.; *Aird* v. *Valentine,* 1986 S.C.C.R. 353.

59. Matrimonial Homes (Family Protection) (Scotland) Act 1981.
s. 4, see *Matheson* v. *Matheson,* 1986 S.L.T. (Sh.Ct.) 2; *McCafferty* v. *McCafferty,* 1986 S.L.T. 650; *Boyle* v. *Boyle* (O.H.), 1986 S.L.T. 656.
s. 7, see *Dunsmore* v. *Dunsmore,* 1986 S.L.T. (Sh.Ct.) 9.
s. 14, see *Boyle* v. *Boyle* (O.H.), 1986 S.L.T. 656.
s. 19, see *Crow* v. *Crow* (O.H.), 1986 S.L.T. 270.
ss. 5, 7, see *R.* v. *Hereford and Worcester County Council, ex p. Lashford, The Times,* November 10, 1986, C.A.
s. 7, see *R.* v. *Oxfordshire Education Authority, ex p. W., The Times,* November 22, 1986, D.C.

61. British Nationality Act 1981.
see *R.* v. *Secretary of State for the Home Department, ex p. Bibi (Mahaboob)* [1985] Imm.A.R. 134, Mann J.
ss. 4, 37, amended: order 86/948.
s. 8, see *R.* v. *Secretary of State for the Home Department, ex p. Dinesh, The Times,* December 11, 1986, Russell J.
s. 41, regs. 86/378.
ss. 41–43, 45–48, 50, 51, amended: order 86/948.
sch. 6, repealed in pt. (prosp.): order 86/948.

63. Betting and Gaming Duties Act 1981.
ss. 1, 6, amended: 1986, c.41, sch. 4.
ss. 9, 12, amended: *ibid.*; repealed in pt.: *ibid.*, schs. 4, 23.
s. 12, regs. 86/400, 404.
s. 17, amended: 1986, c.41, sch. 4.
ss. 19, 20, amended: *ibid.*; repealed in pt.: *ibid.*, schs. 4, 23.
s. 22, order 86/2069; amended: *ibid.*
ss. 28, 29, amended: 1986, c.41, sch. 4.
s. 29A, added: *ibid.*, s.7.
s. 35, amended: *ibid.*, sch. 4; repealed in pt.: *ibid.*, schs. 4, 23.
sch. 1, regs. 86/400, 404.
schs. 1, 3, amended: 1986, c.41, sch. 4.
sch. 4, order 86/2069; amended: *ibid.*

64. New Towns Act 1981.
s. 7, order 86/435.
s. 41, order 86/502.
ss. 43, 49, repealed in pt.: 1986, c.63, s.20, sch. 12.
s. 57A, added: *ibid.*, s.20.
s. 62A, order 86/1382.
s. 62B, order 86/1436.
ss. 78, 79, repealed in pt.: 1986, c.31, sch. 6.; c.44, sch. 9.

CAP.
1981—cont.

64. New Town Act 1981—*cont.*
sch. 10, order 86/502.
sch. 12, repealed in pt.: 1986, c.31, sch. 6.

65. Trustee Savings Bank Act 1981.
s. 1, 4, 32, see *Ross* v. *Lord Advocate* [1986] 1 W.L.R. 1077, H.L.
ss. 1, 32, see *Ross* v. *Lord Advocate,* 1986 S.L.T. 602.
s. 31, amended: 1986, c.45, sch. 14.
s. 53, order 86/841.
s. 54, amended: 1986, c.45, sch. 14.
sch. 5, order 86/453.

67. Acquisition of Land Act 1981.
s. 8, repealed in pt.: 1986, c.31, sch. 6; c.44, sch. 7.
s. 28, amended: *ibid.*
s. 29, amended: 1986, c.63, sch. 8.
s. 32, repealed in pt.: 1986, c.31, sch. 6.
sch. 4, repealed in pt.: S.L.R. 1986; c.31, sch. 6; c.63, sch. 12.

68. Broadcasting Act 1981.
s. 4, see *R.* v. *Horseferry Road Magistrates, ex p. Independent Broadcasting Authority* [1986] 3 W.L.R. 132, D.C.
s. 20, see *R.* v. *Independent Broadcasting Authority, ex p. Rank Organisation, The Times,* March 14, 1986, Mann J.
s. 32, order 86/629.
s. 32, amended: order 86/626; 1986, c.41, sch. 22; repealed in pt.: *ibid.*, schs. 22, 23.
s. 34, repealed in pt.: *ibid.*, sch. 23.
s. 35, amended: *ibid.*, sch. 22; repealed in pt.: *ibid.*, schs. 22, 23.
sch. 4, amended: *ibid.*, sch. 22.

69. Wildlife and Countryside Act 1981.
see *Walsall Metropolitan Borough Council and Robert M. Douglas Holdings* (Ref. T/APP/V4630/A/85/026623/P7) (1986) 1 P.A.D. 341.
s. 1, see *Kirkland* v. *Robinson, The Times,* December 4, 1986, D.C.
s. 32, amended: 1986, c.49, s.20.
s. 37, regs. 86/143.
s. 41, amended: 1986, c.49, s.20, sch. 3; repealed in pt.: *ibid.*, sch. 4.

1982

1. Civil Aviation (Amendment) Act 1982.
s. 1, repealed: 1986, c.31, sch. 6.

2. Social Security (Contributions) Act 1982.
sch. 1, repealed in pt.: 1986, c.48, sch. 5.

10. Industrial Training Act 1982.
ss. 5, 10, amended: 1986, c.15, s.1.

13. Fire Service College Board (Abolition) Act 1982.
repealed: S.L.R. 1986.

14. Reserve Forces Act 1982.
s. 3, order 86/2026.

16. Civil Aviation Act 1982.
s. 2, amended: 1986, c.31, s.72.
s. 7, regs. 86/1544.
s. 23, amended: 1986, c.31, sch. 4.

CAP.

1982—cont.

16. Civil Aviation Act 1982—*cont.*
ss. 27, 29, 32, repealed: *ibid.*, sch. 6.
s. 33, order 86/311.
ss. 33, 34 (in pt.), repealed: 1986, c.31, sch. 6.
s. 35, order 86/1348.
ss. 35 (in pt.), 37, 38 (in pt.), 40, 58, repealed: 1986, c.31, sch. 6.
ss. 60, 61, orders 86/599, 1304.
ss. 60, 61, repealed in pt.: 1986, c.31, sch. 6.
ss. 73, 74, regs. 86/403, 1202, 2120, 2153.
s. 74, see *R.* v. *Civil Aviation Authority, ex p. Emery Air Freight Corp., The Times,* November 10, 1986, C.A.
s. 75, regs. 86/1953.
s. 88, orders 86/312, 1347.
ss. 88, 99, repealed in pt.: 1986, c.31, sch. 6.
s. 93, order 86/2016.
s. 97, order 86/1892.
ss. 101, 102, orders 86/599, 1304.
s. 105, amended: order 86/948; repealed in pt.: 1986, c.31, sch. 6; c.44, sch. 9.
s. 108, order 86/1162.
s. 108, amended: 1986, c.31, sch. 4.
schs. 5, 13 (in pt.), 14 (in pt.), 15 (in pt.), repealed: *ibid.*, sch. 6.

23. Oil and Gas (Enterprise) Act 1982.
ss. 9–17, repealed: 1986, c.44, sch. 9.
s. 11, direction 86/980.
s. 21, orders 86/27–51, 89–93, 106–109, 117, 118, 130–134, 157, 163–166, 200–206, 215, 236, 353–363, 433, 434, 460–462, 546, 548–550, 552, 605, 606, 815, 816, 818–822, 824, 826–830, 865, 889, 915, 941–943, 1007, 1008, 1012, 1092, 1101, 1130–1132, 1193–1200, 1281–1284, 1392–1396, 1462–1466, 1577–1586, 1665–1667, 1741–1747, 1838–1845, 2050–2052, 2055–2059.
ss. 32 (in pt.), 33, 34, 36 (in pt.), sch. 1, repealed: 1986, c.44, sch. 9.
sch. 3, repealed in pt.: *ibid.*, c.48, sch. 5.

24. Social Security and Housing Benefits Act 1982.
see *R.* v. *Secretary of State for Health and Social Security, ex p. Sheffield* (1985) 18 H.L.R. 6, Forbes J.; *R.* v. *Housing Benefits Review Board of the London Borough of Ealing, ex p. Saville* (1986) 18 H.L.R. 349, Kennedy J; *R.* v. *Housing Benefit Review Board for Sedgemoor District Council, ex p. Weaden* (1986) 18 H.L.R. 355, Schiemann J.
s. 1, amended: 1986, c.50, s.68.
s. 2, regs. 86/477; amended: *ibid.*
s. 3, regs. 86/477.
s. 3, amended: 1986, c.50, sch. 10.
s. 7, order 86/67.
s. 7, amended: order 86/67; 1986, c.50, s.67; repealed in pt.: *ibid.*, sch. 11.
s. 8, repealed: *ibid.*

CAP.

1982—cont.

24. Social Security and Housing Benefit Act 1982—*cont.*
s. 9, regs. 86/318.
s. 9, amended: 1986, c.50, s.67; repealed in pt.: *ibid.*, sch. 11.
ss. 11–16, repealed: *ibid.*
ss. 17, 18, regs. 86/477.
ss. 19–21, repealed: 1986, c.50, sch. 11.
s. 23A, repealed in pt.: 1986, c.48, sch. 5.
s. 25, repealed: 1986, c.50, sch. 11.
s. 26, regs. 86/318, 477.
s. 28, regs. 86/84, 852, 1009, 1156.
Pt. II (ss. 28–36), repealed: 1986, c.50, sch. 11.
s. 32, orders 86/430, 2042.
s. 36, see *R.* v. *Secretary of State for Social Services, ex p. Association of Metropolitan Authorities* [1986] 1 W.L.R. 1, Webster J.
s. 36, orders 86/430, 2042.
ss. 38, 41, 42 (in pt.), 44 (in pt.), repealed: 1986, c.50, sch. 11.
s. 45, regs. 86/1009.
s. 45, amended: 1986, c.50, sch. 10; repealed in pt.: *ibid.*, sch. 11.
s. 47, regs. 86/318.
s. 47, schs. 2, 4, repealed in pt.: 1986, c.50, sch. 11.

25. Iron and Steel Act 1982.
sch. 4, amended: 1986, c.45, sch. 14.
sch. 6, repealed in pt.: S.L.R. 1986.

27. Civil Jurisdiction and Judgments Act 1982.
Commencement orders: 86/1781, 2044.
s. 9, order 86/2027.
s. 18, amended: 1986, c.32, s.39; c.45, sch. 14.
s. 40, repealed in pt. (S.): 1986, c.47, sch. 5.
s. 48, Acts of Sederunt 86/1941, 1946, 1947.
s. 53, orders 86/1781, 2044.
sch. 5, amended: 1986, c.39, sch. 2; c.45, sch. 14; c.50, sch. 10; c.60, s.188.
sch. 8, amended: 1986, c.39, sch. 2.

28. Taking of Hostages Act 1982.
s. 5, order 86/2015.

30. Local Government (Miscellaneous Provisions) Act 1982.
see *Lambeth London Borough Council* v. *Grewal* (1986) 82 Cr.App.R. 301, C.A.
s. 2, see *Sheptonhurst* v. *Newham London Borough Council* (1985) 984 L.G.R. 97, C.A.
s. 30, repealed in pt.: 1986, c.44, sch. 9.
s. 40, see *Sykes* v. *Holmes and Maw* [1985] Crim.L.R. 791, D.C.
sch. 3, see *Westminster City Council* v. *Croyalgrange* [1986] 1 W.L.R. 674, H.L.; *Sheptonhurst* v. *Newham London Borough Council* (1985) 84 L.G.R. 97, C.A.; *R.* v. *Peterborough City Council, ex p. Quietlynn, The Times,* July 28, 1986, C.A.

1982—cont.

30. Local Government (Miscellaneous Provisions) Act 1982—*cont.*
sch. 4, see *R.* v. *Bristol City Council, ex p. Pearce* (1985) 83 L.G.R. 711, Glidewell J.
sch. 6, repealed in pt.: 1986, c.63, sch. 12.

32. Local Government Finance Act 1982.
s. 8, amended: 1986, c.54, sch. 1; repealed in pt.: *ibid.*, schs. 1, 2.
ss. 15, 19, see *R.* v. *District Auditor for Leicester, ex p. Leicester City Council* (1985) 25 R.V.R. 191, Woolf J.
s. 17, see *Oliver* v. *Northampton Borough Council, The Times*, May 8, 1986, D.C.
ss. 19, 20, amended: order 86/2293.
ss. 19, 20, 22, see *Smith* v. *Skinner, Gladden* v. *McMahon* (1986) 26 R.V.R. 45, D.C.
s. 20, see *Hood* v. *McMahon, The Times*, August 1, 1986, C.A.
ss. 32, 35, regs. 86/1271.
sch. 2, amended: 1986, c.54, sch. 1; repealed in pt.: *ibid.*, schs. 1, 2

34. Forfeiture Act 1982.
ss. 1, 2, see *Patterson, Petr.* (O.H.), 1986 S.L.T. 121.
s. 4, amended: 1986, c.50, ss. 4, 76.
s. 5, amended: *ibid.*, s.76.

36. Aviation Security Act 1982.
s. 9, orders 86/2012, 2014.
s. 27, repealed in pt.: 1986, c.31, sch. 6.
s. 29, amended: *ibid.*, sch. 4; repealed in pt.: *ibid.*, sch. 6.
s. 30, repealed in pt.: *ibid.*
s. 38, amended: order 86/948; repealed in pt.: 1986, c.31, sch. 6.
s. 39, orders, 86/2012, 2014.

37. Merchant Shipping (Liner Conferences) Act 1982.
s. 9, Act of Sederunt 86/799.

38. Northern Ireland Act 1982.
s. 5, order 86/1036.

39. Finance Act 1982.
s. 28, amended: 1986, c.53, sch. 18.
s. 41, amended: 1986, c.41, s.23.
s. 70, amended: *ibid.*, sch. 16; repealed in pt.: *ibid.*
s. 147, repealed: 1986, c.44, sch. 9.
sch. 7, orders 86/386, 1440.
sch. 7, amended: 1986, c.53, sch. 18.
sch. 11, repealed in pt.: 1986, c.41, sch.16.
sch. 12, amended: *ibid.*, s.56.
sch. 18, amended: *ibid.*, sch. 21; repealed in pt.: *ibid.*

41. Stock Transfer Act 1982.
s. 1, repealed: 1986, c.44, sch. 9.

43. Local Government and Planning (Scotland) Act 1982.
ss. 14, 34, see *Caithness District Council* v. *Highland Regional Council*, 1986 S.L.T. 519.

44. Legal Aid Act 1982.
s. 1, regs. 86/445, 1559.

1982—cont.

44. Legal Aid Act 1982—*cont.*
s. 7, amended: 1986, c.50, sch. 10.
s. 9, see *R.* v. *Huntingdon Magistrates' Court, ex p. Yapp* [1986] Crim.L.R. 689, D.C.

45. Civic Government (Scotland) Act 1982.
s. 20, regs. 86/1238.
s. 46, see *Allan* v. *McGraw*, 1986 S.C.C.R. 257.
ss. 62, 63, amended: 1986, c.64, sch. 2; repealed in pt.: *ibid.*, sch. 3.
ss. 64, 65, amended: *ibid.*, sch. 2.
s. 66 amended: *ibid.*; repealed in pt.: *ibid.*, sch. 3.

46. Employment Act 1982.
s. 15, see *Express & Star* v. *NGA (1982)* [1986] I.C.R. 589, C.A.

48. Criminal Justice Act 1982.
s. 1, see *R.* v. *Bates (John)* (1985) 7 Cr.App.R.(S.) 105, C.A.; *R.* v. *Bradbourn* (1985) 7 Cr.App.R.(S.) 180, C.A.; *R.* v. *Grimes* (1985) 7 Cr.App.R.(S.) 137, C.A.; *R.* v. *Jeoffrey* (1985) 7 Cr.App.R.(S.) 135, C.A.
s. 7, see *R.* v. *Fairhurst, The Times*, August 2, 1986, C.A.
s. 9, see *Howley* v. *Oxford* (1985) 81 Cr.App.R. 246, D.C.
s. 21, see *R.* v. *Horrocks, The Times*, February 8, 1986, C.A.
ss. 44, 45, repealed: 1985, c.31, sch. 6.
s. 69, repealed in pt.: 1986, c.21, sch. 2.
s. 81, order 86/1884.
s. 81, repealed in pt.: 1985, c.31, sch. 6.
sch. 1, amended: 1986, c.32, s.24; c.64, sch. 2; repealed in pt.: *ibid.*, sch. 3.

49. Transport Act 1982.
Commencement order: 86/1326.
s. 29, orders 86/555(S.), 1327.
s. 29, amended: *ibid.*
s. 49, regs. 86/1330.
s. 70, amended: 1986, c.50, sch. 10.
s. 73, orders 86/1327, 1330.
s. 76, order 86/1326.

50. Insurance Companies Act 1982.
s. 7, amended: 1986, c.60, s.134.
s. 21A, added: *ibid.*, s.135.
s. 31A, added: *ibid.*, s.136.
s. 47A, amended: *ibid.*, sch. 13.
ss. 53–56, amended: 1986, c.45, sch. 14.
s. 59, rules 86/341, 1918, 2002.
s. 59, amended: 1986, c.45, sch. 14.
s. 71, amended: 1986, c.60, ss.135, 136.
s. 73, repealed: *ibid.*, sch. 17.
s. 78 amended: *ibid.*, s.137.
s. 79, repealed: *ibid.*, sch. 17.
s. 94A, regs. 86/446.
s. 96, amended: 1986, c.45, sch. 14.
s. 97, regs. 86/446.
sch. 5, repealed in pt.: 1986, c.53, sch. 19.

51. Mental Health (Amendment) Act 1982.
s. 70, repealed in pt.: S.L.R. 1986.

CAP.

1982—cont.

52. Industrial Development Act 1982.
s. 14, amended: 1986, c.63, sch. 11.
s. 14A, added: *ibid.*
s. 15, sch. 2, repealed in pt.: *ibid.*, sch. 12.
s. 15, sch. 2, repealed in pt. (S.): *ibid.*

53. Administration of Justice Act 1982.
Commencement order: 86/2259.
see *Food Corporation of India* v. *Marastro Cia. Naviera S.A.: the Trade Fortitude* [1985] 2 Lloyd's Rep. 579, Leggatt J.
s. 13, amended (S.): 1986, c.9, sch. 1.
s. 35A, see *Edmunds* v. *Lloyds Italico, The Times*, February 15, 1986, C.A.
s. 38, repealed in pt.: 1986, c.57, s.4.
s. 39, amended: *ibid.*, s.5.
s. 42, repealed in pt.: 1986, c.60, sch. 17.
s. 76, order 86/2259.

1983

2. Representation of the People Act 1983.
regs. 86/1091.
ss. 7, 10, 14–16, 18, regs. 86/1081, 1111(S.).
s. 36, regs. 86/1081, 1111(S.); rules 86/2215.
s. 53, regs. 86/104, 105, 139, 1081, 1111(S.).
s. 56, regs. 86/1081, 1111(S.).
s. 57, regs 86/1111(S.).
s. 60, see *R.* v. *Phillips (C. K.)* (1984) 6 Cr.App.R.(S.) 293, C.A.
s. 75, regs. 86/1081, 1111(S.).
s. 76A, order 86/383.
s. 89, regs. 86/1081, 1111(S.).
s. 197, order 86/383.
s. 201, regs. 86/104, 105, 139, 1081, 1111(S.).
s. 202, regs. 86/1111(S.)
sch. 1, regs. 86/1081, 1111(S.).
sch. 2, regs. 86/104, 105, 139, 1081, 1111(S.).
sch. 4, regs. 86/1081, 1111(S.).
sch. 8, repealed in pt.: S.L.R. 1986.

3. Agricultural Marketing Act 1983.
s. 1, amended: 1986, c.49, s.8.
s. 7, amended: *ibid.*; repealed in pt.: *ibid.*, sch. 4.
sch. 1, amended: *ibid.*, s.8; repealed in pt.: *ibid.*, s.8, sch. 4.

6. British Nationality (Falkland Islands) Act 1983.
s. 2, amended: order 86/948.

12. Divorce Jurisdiction, Court Fees and Legal Aid (Scotland) Act 1983.
sch. 1, repealed in pt.: 1986, c.9, sch. 2; S.L.R. 1986; 1986, c.47, sch. 5.

19. Matrimonial Homes Act 1983.
s. 1, see *Harris* v. *Harris* (1986) 1 F.L.R. 12, C.A.; *Summers* v. *Summers* (1986) 16 Fam. Law 56, C.A.

CAP.

1983—cont.

19. Matrimonial Homes Act 1983—*cont.*
s. 19, see *Seray-Wurie* v. *Seray-Wurie, The Times*, March 25, 1986, C.A.; *Essex County Council* v. *T., The Times*, March 15, 1986, C.A.
sch. 2, repealed in pt.: S.L.R. 1986.

20. Mental Health Act 1983.
s. 1, see *R.* v. *Mental Health Review Tribunal, ex p. Clatworthy* [1985] 3 All E.R. 699, Mann J.
s. 3, see *Waldron, Ex p.* [1985] 3 W.L.R. 1090, C.A.; *R.* v. *Hallstrom, ex p. W.; R.* v. *Gardner, ex p. L.* [1986] 2 W.L.R. 883, McCullough J.
ss. 17, 20, see *R.* v. *Hallstrom, ex p. W; R.* v. *Gardner, ex p. L.* [1986] 2 W.L.R. 883, McCullough J.
s. 29, see *B., Re*, November 29, 1985; Liverpool County Ct.
ss. 37, 47, 49, see *R.* v. *Castro* (1985) 81 Cr.App.R. 212, C.A.
s. 72, see *R.* v. *Mental Health Review Tribunal, ex p. Pickering* [1986] 1 All E.R. 99, Forbes J.; *Grant* v. *Mental Health Review Tribunal, The Times*, April 28, 1986, McNeil J.; *Secretary of State for the Home Department* v. *Mental Health Review Tribunal for Mersey Regional Health Authority* [1986] 1 W.L.R. 1170, Mann J.
s. 73, see *Secretary of State for the Home Department* v. *Mental Health Review Tribunal* [1986] 1 W.L.R. 1170, D.C.; *R.* v. *Oxford Regional Mental Health Review Tribunal, ex p. Secretary of State for the Home Department* [1986] 1 W.L.R. 1180; C.A.; *Grant* v. *Mental Health Review Tribunal, The Times*, April 28, 1986, McNeil J.
s. 94, amended: 1986, c.57, s.2.
ss. 106–108, rules 86/127.
s. 111 amended: 1986, c.57, s.2.
s. 139, see *Waldron, Ex p.* [1985] 3 W.L.R. 1090, C.A.
s. 145, see *Secretary of State for the Home Department* v. *Mental Health Review Tribunal for Mersey Regional Health Authority* [1986] 1 W.L.R. 1170, Mann J.
sch. 4, repealed in pt.: S.L.R. 1986.

21. Pilotage Act 1983.
Commencement order: 86/1051.
s. 3, order 86/402.
s. 9, order 86/568.
ss. 55, 58, order 86/1051.

25. Energy Act 1983.
s. 33, order 86/2018.

28. Finance Act 1983.
s. 26, amended: 1986, c.41, s.40.
sch. 5, amended: *ibid.*, s.40, sch. 9; c.45, sch. 14; repealed in pt.: 1986, c.41, schs, 9, 23.

(67)

CAP.

1983—cont.

29. **Miscellaneous Financial Provisions Act 1983.**
sch. 2, repealed in pt.: 1986, c.44, sch. 9.
30. **Diseases of Fish Act 1983.**
s. 9, amended: 1986, c.62, s.38.
34. **Mobile Homes Act 1983.**
s. 1, see *Balthasar* v. *Mullane* (1985) 17 H.L.R. 561; (1986) 84 L.G.R. 55, C.A.
36. **Social Security and Housing Benefits Act 1983.**
repealed: 1986, c.50, sch. 11.
37. **Importation of Milk Act 1983.**
s. 1, S.Rs. 1986 Nos. 21, 119.
41. **Health and Social Services and Social Security Adjudications Act 1983.**
s. 19, schs. 8, 9, repealed in pt.: 1986, c.50, sch. 11.
44. **National Audit Act 1983.**
sch. 4, repealed in pt.: 1986, c.31, sch. 6; c.44, sch. 9.
47. **National Heritage Act 1983.**
ss. 1–16, sch. 1, functions transferred: order 86/600.
schs. 4, 5, repealed in pt.: 1986, c.63, sch. 12.
49. **Finance (No. 2) Act 1983.**
s. 7, amended: 1986, c.56, sch. 3.
52. **Local Authorities (Expenditure Powers) Act 1983.**
s. 1, order 85/2038(S.).
53. **Car Tax Act 1983.**
s. 8, sch. 1, regs. 86/306.
54. **Medical Act 1983.**
s. 17, amended: order 86/23.
s. 32, order 86/149.
sch. 1, order 86/1390.
sch. 2, amended: order 86/23.
55. **Value Added Tax 1983.**
s. 3, orders 86/896, 1989.
s. 16, order 86/530.
s. 16, amended: 1986, c.41, s.12.
s. 17, orders 86/704, 716.
s. 19, orders 86/939, 1989.
s. 19, amended: 1986, c.41, s.13.
s. 20, orders 86/336, 532.
s. 22, regs. 86/335.
s. 40, amended: 1986, c.41, s.10.
s. 45, order 86/1989.
s. 48, orders 86/530, 704, 716.
sch. 1, order 86/631.
sch. 1, amended: order 86/631; 1986, c.41, s.10.
sch. 4, amended: *ibid.*, s.11.
sch. 5, amended: order 86/530.
sch. 6, amended: orders 86/704, 716.
sch. 7, see *E.M.I. Records* v. *Spillane* [1986] 1 W.L.R. 967, Browne-Wilkinson, V.-C.; *Grunwick Processing Laboratories* v. *C. & E. Comrs.* [1986] S.T.C. 441, Macpherson J.
sch. 7, regs. 86/71, 305.
sch. 8, rules 86/590.
56. **Oil Taxation Act 1983.**
s. 8, sch. 1, amended: 1986, c.41, sch. 110.
ss. 9, 12, orders 86/1644, 1645.

CAP.

1984

1. **Consolidated Fund Act 1984.**
repealed: 1986, c.42, sch. (C).
2. **Restrictive Trade Practices (Stock Exchange) Act 1984.**
repealed: 1986, c.60, sch. 17.
5. **Merchant Shipping Act 1984.**
sch. 1, amended: 1986, c.23, s.5.
8. **Prevention of Terrorism (Temporary Provisions) Act 1984.**
continued in force: order 86/417.
s. 17, order 86/417.
10. **Town and Country Planning Act 1984.**
s. 1, amended: 1986, c.63, sch. 7.
s. 1, amended (S.): *ibid.*
s. 5, see *Stafford Borough Council and Midland Counties Securities* (Ref. T/APP/Y3425/A/84/018365–8/P5) (1986) 1 P.A.D. 108.
11. **Education (Grants and Awards) Act 1984.**
s. 1, regs. 86/1031.
s. 2, amended: 1986, c.1, s.1.
12. **Telecommunications Act 1984.**
s. 9, order 86/1113.
s. 68, amended: 1986, c.45, sch. 14.
s. 82, see *Rudd* v. *Department of Trade and Industry, The Times*, April 16, 1986, D.C.
s. 104, order 86/1113.
sch. 2, repealed in pt.: 1986, c.44, sch. 9.
sch. 4, S.R. 1985 No. 366.
sch. 4, repealed in pt.: 1986, c.31, sch. 6.
sch. 5, order 86/1275.
13. **Road Traffic (Driving Instruction) Act 1984.**
Commencement order: 86/1336.
s. 5, order 86/1336.
19. **Trade Marks (Amendment) Act 1984.**
Commencement order: 86/1273.
s. 1, amended: 1986, c.39, s.2; repealed in pt.: *ibid.*, sch. 3.
s. 2, order 86/1273.
s. 2, amended: 1986, c.39, sch. 2; repealed in pt.: *ibid.*, sch. 3.
sch. 1, amended: *ibid.*, sch. 2; repealed in pt.: *ibid.*, sch. 3.
sch. 2, repealed in pt.: *ibid.*
22. **Public Health (Control of Disease) Act 1984.**
s. 14, repealed in pt.: 1986, c.31, sch. 6.
s. 46, repealed in pt.: 1986, c.50, sch. 11.
23. **Registered Homes Act 1984.**
ss. 5, 8, 16, regs. 86/457.
ss. 23, 27, 56, regs. 86/456.
24. **Dentists Act 1984.**
s. 45, regs. 86/887.
sch. 2, amended: order 86/23.
25. **Betting, Gaming and Lotteries (Amendment) Act 1984.**
Commencement order: 86/102.
s. 4, order 86/102.
26. **Inshore Fishing (Scotland) Act 1984.**
s. 1, order 86/59.
s. 2, order 86/60.

CAP.

1984—cont.

27. Road Traffic Regulation Act 1984.
Commencement order: 86/1147.
see *Rodgers* v. *Taylor, The Times*, October 28, 1986, D.C.
s. 6, see *Greater London Council* v. *Secretary of State for Transport* [1986] J.P.L. 513, C.A.
s. 43, repealed in pt.: 1986, c.31, sch. 6.
s. 44, order 86/225.
s. 45, amended and repealed in pt.: 1986, c.27, s.1.
s. 51, substituted: *ibid.*, s.2.
s. 64, regs. 86/1859.
ss. 73–75, amended: order 86/315.
s. 82, regs. 85/1888(S.).
s. 86, regs. 86/1175.
s. 95, order 86/1328.
ss. 99, 101, regs. 86/183.
s. 103, regs. 86/184.
s. 106, order 86/1177.
s. 115, amended: 1986, c.27, s.2.
s. 122, see *Greater London Council* v. *Secretary of State for Transport* [1986] J.P.L. 513, C.A.
s. 124, regs. 86/178–181, 259.
s. 129, repealed in pt.: 1986, c.63, sch. 12.
s. 129, repealed in pt. (S.): *ibid.*
s. 131, order 86/1224.
s. 134, regs. 85/1888(S.); 86/178–180.
s. 145, order 86/1147.
sch. 4, regs. 86/262.
sch. 6, amended: regs. 86/1175.
sch. 9, regs. 86/178–181, 259.
sch. 12, orders 86/56, 1329, 1875(S.).
sch. 13, repealed in pt.: 1986, c.31, sch. 6.

28. County Courts Act 1984.
s. 2, order 86/754.
s. 14, see *Stilwell* v. *Williamson, The Times*, September 1, 1986, C.A.
s. 14, repealed in pt.: S.L.R. 1986.
s. 38, see *Ainsbury* v. *Millington* [1986] 1 All E.R. 73, C.A.
s. 50, see *H.H. Property Co.* v. *Rahim, The Times*, November 8, 1986, C.A.
s. 75, see *Sharma* v. *Knight* [1986] 1 W.L.R. 757, C.A.
ss. 79, 92, repealed in pt.: S.L.R. 1986.
ss. 98, 102, 109, amended: 1985, c.45, sch. 14.
s. 118, repealed in pt.: S.L.R. 1986.
s. 141, repealed: *ibid.*
sch. 2, repealed in pt.: 1986, c.53, sch. 19.

30. Food Act 1984.
ss. 2, 3, 8, see *Barton* v. *Unigate Dairies, The Times*, October 27, 1986, D.C.
s. 4, regs. 85/2026; 86/720, 721, 987.
s. 7, regs. 85/2026; 86/987.
s. 13, regs. 86/720.
s. 30, regs. 86/722.
s. 33, regs. 86/721.
s. 38, regs. 86/723.
s. 68, order 86/429.
s. 74, regs. 86/722, 723.

CAP.

1984—cont.

30. Food Act 1984—*cont.*
s. 118, regs. 85/2026; 86/720–723, 987.
s. 119, regs. 85/2026.

31. Rating and Valuation (Amendment) (Scotland) Act 1984.
ss. 13 (in pt.), 21 (in pt.), sch. 3, repealed: S.L.R. 1986.

32. London Regional Transport Act 1984.
s. 13, order 86/156.
sch. 6, repealed in pt.: 1985, c.5, sch. 15.

33. Rates Act 1984.
s. 1, orders 86/212, 230, 265, 329.
s. 2, orders 86/265, 344.
s. 2, amended: order 86/344.
s. 4, see *R.* v. *Secretary of State for the Environment, ex p. Greenwich London Borough Council, The Times*, December 19, 1985, C.A.
s. 4, orders 86/212, 230, 265, 329.

35. Data Protection Act 1984.
ss. 9, 40, regs. 86/1899.

36. Mental Health (Scotland) Act 1984.
s. 9, order 86/374.

37. Child Abduction Act 1984.
s. 1, amended: 1986, c.55, s.65.
s. 6, amended (S.): 1986, c.9, sch. 1.

38. Cycle Tracks Act 1984.
s. 3, amended: 1986, c.5, sch. 14.

39. Video Recordings Act 1984.
Commencement orders: 86/1125, 1182(S.).
s. 23, orders 86/1125, 1182(S.).

40. Animal Health and Welfare Act 1984.
see *Malins* v. *Cole & Attard*, Knightsbridge Crown Court.
s. 10, regs. 85/1857(S.), 1858(S.).

41. Agricultural Holdings Act 1984.
repealed: 1986, c.5, sch. 15.

42. Matrimonial and Family Proceedings Act 1984.
Commencement orders: 86/635, 1049, 1226(S.).
ss. 5, 6, Pt. II (ss.3–8), see *Sandford* v. *Sandford* (1986) 16 Fam. Law 104, C.A.
s. 12, see *Chebarow* v. *Chebarow* [1986] 3 W.L.R. 95, Sheldon J.
s. 32, amended: 1986, c.55, sch. 11.
s. 47, orders 86/635, 1049, 1226(S.).
sch. 1, repealed in pt.: 1986, c.55, sch. 2.

43. Finance Act 1984.
s. 20, repealed in pt.: 1986, c.41, sch. 23.
sch. 8, orders 86/771; amended: *ibid.*
sch. 10, amended: 1986, c.41, ss. 22, 23.
sch. 13, repealed in pt.: *ibid.*, sch. 23.
sch. 19, amended: *ibid.*, s.50.

44. Appropriation Act 1984.
repealed: 1986, c.42, sch.(C).

46. Cable and Broadcasting Act 1984.
Commencement order: 86/537.
s. 2, order 86/900.
s. 27, repealed: 1986, c.64, schs. 2, 3.
s. 28, amended: *ibid.*, sch. 2.
s. 33, repealed in pt.: *ibid.*, schs. 2, 3.
s. 40, repealed in pt.: 1986, c.41, sch. 23.
s. 59, order 86/537.

1984—cont.

47. Repatriation of Prisoners Act 1984.
s. 9, orders 86/598, 2226.

48. Health and Social Security Act 1984.
Commencment order: 86/974.
s. 22, repealed: 1986, c.50, sch. 11.
s. 27, order 86/974.
s. 27, repealed in pt.: 1986, c.50, sch. 11.
s. 28, regs. 86/965, 975, 976.
schs. 4, 5, repealed in pt.: 1986, c.50, sch. 11.

49. Trade Union Act 1984.
s. 10, see *Monsanto* v. *Transport and General Workers Union, The Times*, July 16, 1986, C.A.
ss. 10, 11, see *Express & Star* v. *NGA (1982)* [1985] I.R.L.R. 455, Skinner J.

50. Housing Defects Act 1984.
s. 23, regs. 86/843(S.).

51. Inheritance Tax Act 1984.
Capital Transfer Tax Act renamed: 1986, c.41, s.100.
amended: *ibid.*
s. 3A, added: *ibid.*, sch. 19.
s. 7, amended: *ibid.*; repealed in pt.: *ibid.*, schs. 19, 23.
s. 8, order 86/528.
ss. 8, 9, 19, amended: 1986, c.41, sch. 19.
s. 26A, added: *ibid.*
ss. 30–32, 32A, 33, 35, 38, amended: *ibid.*
s. 39A, added: *ibid.*, s.105.
ss. 49, 55, 66–68, 78, 98, amended: *ibid.*, sch. 19.
s. 105, amended: *ibid.*, s.106.
ss. 113A, 113B, 124A, 124B, added: *ibid.*, sch. 19.
ss. 131, 142, amended: *ibid.*
ss. 148, 149, repealed: *ibid.*, sch. 23.
s. 155, amended: order 86/948.
s. 167, repealed in pt.: 1986, c.41, sch. 23.
ss. 199, 201, amended: *ibid.*, sch. 19.
s. 204, amended: *ibid.*; repealed in pt.: *ibid.*, schs. 19, 23.
s. 216, amended: *ibid.*, sch. 19.
s. 225, repealed in pt.: S.L.R. 1986.
ss. 226, 227, amended: 1986, c.41, sch. 19.
s. 230, functions transferred: order 86/600.
s. 233, order 86/1944.
s. 233, amended: 1986, c.41, sch. 19; order 86/1944.
s. 234, amended: 1986, c.41, s.107.
s. 236, amended: *ibid.*, sch. 19; repealed in pt.: *ibid.*, sch. 23.
ss. 237, 239, amended: *ibid.*, sch. 19.
sch. 1, substituted: *ibid.*
sch. 2, amended: *ibid.*; repealed in pt.: *ibid.*, schs. 19, 23.
schs. 4, 6, amended: *ibid.*, sch. 19.

53. Local Government (Interim Provisions) Act 1984.
s. 6, orders 86/466, 2202.
s. 7, see *R.* v. *District Auditor No. 3 Audit District of West Yorkshire Metropolitan County Council, ex p. West Yorkshire Metropolitan County Council* [1986] 26 R.V.R. 24, D.C.

1984—cont.

54. Roads (Scotland) Act 1984.
s. 17, regs. 85/2080.
s. 21, regs. 86/509.
s. 60, regs. 86/642.
s. 71, regs. 86/252.
s. 143, regs. 85/2080; 86/252, 509, 642; order 85/1953.
s. 152, regs. 86/252.
s. 157, order 85/1953.
sch. 9, repealed in pt.: 1986, c.44, sch. 9.

55. Building Act 1984.
ss. 4, 59, repealed: 1986, c.31, sch. 6.
ss. 77, 79, amended: 1986, c.63, sch. 9.
s. 80, amended: 1986, c.44, sch. 7; c.63, sch. 5.
s. 81, amended: 1986, c.63, sch. 5.
s. 126, repealed in pt.: 1986, c.44, sch. 9.
sch. 1, amended: order 86/452.

56. Foster Children (Scotland) Act 1984.
ss. 3, 4, 14, regs. 85/1798.

57. Co-operative Development Agency and Industrial Development Act 1984.
s. 7, order 86/128.

60. Police and Criminal Evidence Act 1984.
s. 9, sch. 1, see *R.* v. *Central Criminal Court, ex p. Adegbesan* [1986] Crim.L.R. 691; [1986] 3 All E.R. 113, D.C.; *Ex. p. Bristol Press & Picture Agency, The Times*, November 11, 1986, D.C.
s. 17, amended: 1986, c.64, sch. 2; repealed in pt.: *ibid.*, schs. 2, 3.
ss. 56, 58, 65, amended: 1986, c.32, s.32.
s. 113, order 86/307.
s. 116, amended: 1986, c.32, s.36.

61. Consolidated Fund (No. 2) Act 1984.
repealed: 1986, c.42, sch.(C).

62. Friendly Societies Act 1984.
s. 4, order 86/768.

1985

4. Milk (Cessation of Production) Act 1985.
s. 1, schemes 86/1612, 1614(S.).

6. Companies Act 1985.
see *Taylor* v. *McGirr, The Times*, April 11, 1986, D.C.
ss. 13, 44, amended: 1986, c.45, sch. 13.
Pt. III (ss.56–79), 81–83, 84 (in pt.), 85 (in pt.), 86, 87, repealed: 1986, c.60, sch. 17.
s. 97, amended: *ibid.*, sch. 16; repealed in pt.: *ibid.*, sch. 17.
s. 103, amended: 1986, c.45, sch. 13.
s. 125, see *Cumbrian Newspapers Group* v. *Cumberland & Westmorland Herald Newspaper & Printing Co.* [1986] 3 W.L.R. 26, Scott J.
s. 131, amended: 1986, c.45, sch. 13.
s. 137, see *Willaire Systems, Re, The Times*, July 17, 1986, C.A.
s. 140, amended: 1986, c.45, sch. 13.

1985—cont.

6. Companies Act 1985—cont.

s. 153, amended: 1986, c.45, sch. 13; c.60, s.196.

s. 156, amended: 1986, c.45, sch. 13.

s. 158, see *Cornhill Insurance* v. *Improvement Services* (1986) 1 W.L.R. 114, Harman J.

s. 163, amended: 1986, c.60, sch. 16.

s. 173, amended: 1986, c.45, sch. 13.

s. 185, amended: 1986, c.60, s.194.

s. 196, substituted: 1986, c.45, sch. 13.

s. 209, amended: 1986, c.60, s.197, sch. 16.

ss. 222, 225, amended: 1986, c.45, sch. 13.

s. 248, amended: regs. 86/1865.

s. 251, regs. 86/1865.

s. 265, amended: 1986, c.60, sch. 16.

s. 295, amended: 1986, c.53, sch. 18.

ss. 295–299, repealed: 1986, c.46, sch. 4.

s. 301, regs. 86/2067.

ss. 301, 302, repealed: 1986, c.46, sch. 4.

s. 302, amended: 1986, c.53, sch. 18.

s. 329, amended: 1986, c.60, sch. 16.

s. 380, amended: 1986, c.45, sch. 13.

ss. 396, 410, amended: 1986, c.39, sch. 2.

ss. 428–430, substituted: 1986, c.60, s.172, sch. 12.

s. 433, repealed in pt.: *ibid.*, sch. 17.

s. 437, amended: *ibid.*, sch. 13.

s. 440, amended: *ibid.*, s.198.

s. 441, amended: 1986, c.45, sch. 13.

s. 446, amended: *ibid.*, schs. 13, 16; repealed in pt.: *ibid.*, schs. 13, 17.

s. 447, see *Gomba Holdings UK* v. *Homan* [1986] 3 All E.R. 94, Hoffmann J.

s. 449, order 86/2046.

s. 449, amended: 1986, c.45, sch. 13; c.60, sch. 13; repealed in pt.: *ibid.*, sch. 17.

s. 451A, added: *ibid.*, sch. 13.

s. 459, see *Company, A, Re (No. 00477 of 1986), The Times*, April 8, 1986, Hoffman J.; *XYZ, Re, The Financial Times*, August 12, 1986, Hoffman J.; *Ward* v. *Coulson, Sanderson and Ward* [1986] P.C.C. 57, C.A.

s. 461, see *Company, A, Re (No. 005287 of 1985)* [1986] 1 W.L.R. 281, Hoffman J.

ss. 461, 462, amended: 1986, c.45, sch. 13.

s. 463, amended: *ibid.*; repealed in pt.: *ibid.*, sch. 12.

s. 464, amended: *ibid.*, sch. 13.

s. 467–473, repealed: *ibid.*, sch. 12.

s. 473, see *Inverness District Council* v. *Highlands Universal Fabrications* (O.H.), 1986 S.L.T. 556.

ss. 474–485, 486 (in pt.), 488–650, repealed: 1986, c.45, sch. 12.

s. 494, see *Potter Oils, Re, Financial Times*, November 22, 1985, Hoffman J.

s. 499, see *Gomba Holdings UK* v. *Homan* [1986] 3 All E.R. 94, Hoffmann J.

s. 512, order 86/1361.

1985—cont.

6. Companies Act 1985—cont.

s. 517, see *Ward* v. *Coulson, Sanderson and Ward* [1986] P.C.C. 57, C.A.

s. 518, see *Byblos Bank* v. *Al Khudhairy, Financial Times*, November 7, 1986, C.A.

s. 520, see *Company, A, Re*, May 20, 1986, H.H. Judge Cox; Exeter County Court; *Ward* v. *Coulson, Sanderson and Ward* [1986] P.C.C. 57, C.A.

s. 561, see *Rhodes (John T.), Re, The Times*, July 12, 1986, Hoffmann J.

s. 630, see *Augustus Barnett and Son, Re* [1986] P.C.C. 167, Hoffmann J.

s. 645, see *Palmer Marine Surveys, Re* [1986] 1 W.L.R. 573, Hoffmann J.

ss. 657, 658, amended: 1986, c.45, sch. 13.

ss. 659–674, repealed: *ibid.*, sch. 12.

s. 663, rules 86/341.

s. 693, repealed in pt.: 1986, c.60, sch. 17.

s. 709, repealed in pt.: 1986, c.45, sch. 12; c.60, sch. 17.

s. 710, repealed in pt.: 1986, c.45, sch. 12.

s. 711, amended: *ibid.*, sch. 13.

ss. 716, 717, amended: 1986, c.60, sch. 16.

s. 724, repealed: 1986, c.45, sch. 12.

s. 726, see *Speed Up Holdings* v. *Gouch* [1986] F.S.R. 330, Evans-Lombe Q.C.

s. 733, amended and repealed in pt.: 1986, c.45, sch. 13.

s. 735A, added: *ibid.*

s. 744, repealed in pt.: 1986, c.60, sch. 17.

sch. 3, repealed: *ibid.*

schs. 4, 9, amended: 1986, c.39, sch. 2; c.60, sch. 16.

sch. 12, repealed: 1986, c.46, sch. 4.

sch. 13, amended: 1986, c.60, sch. 16.

sch. 16, repealed: 1986, c.45, sch. 12.

sch. 22, amended: 1986, c.60, sch. 16; repealed in pt.: *ibid.*, sch. 17.

sch. 24, amended: *ibid.*, sch. 16; repealed in pt.: 1986, c.45, sch. 12: c.46, sch. 4; c.60, sch. 17.

8. Companies Securities (Insider Dealing) Act 1985.

s. 2, amended: 1986, c.60, s.173.

s. 3, amended: *ibid.*, s.174; repealed in pt.: *ibid.*, sch. 17.

s. 4, amended: *ibid.*, s.174.

s. 6, substituted: *ibid.*, s.175.

s. 13, amended: *ibid.*, ss.174, 176; repealed in pt.: *ibid.*, sch. 17.

s. 15, repealed: *ibid.*

s. 16, amended: *ibid.*, sch. 16.

9. Companies Consolidation (Consequential Provisions) Act 1985.

s. 7, repealed: 1986, c.60, sch. 17.

s. 31, see *Taylor* v. *McGirr* [1986] Crim.L.R. 544, D.C.

sch. 2, repealed in pt.: 1986, c.53, sch. 19; c.59, sch.; c.60, sch. 17.

13. Cinemas Act 1985.

s. 3, order 86/207, 320; amended: order 86/207.

CAP.
1985—cont.

15. Hong Kong Act 1985.
sch., orders 86/948, 1160, 1298.

17. Reserve Forces (Safeguard of Employment) Act 1985.
s. 22, order 86/2025.

20. Landlord and Tenant Act 1985,
s. 11, see *Davies* v. *Brenner*, July 31, 1986; H.H. Judge Tibber, Edmonton County Ct.

23. Prosecution of Offences Act 1985.
Commencement orders: 86/1029, 1334.
s. 1, see *Bray, Ex p., The Times*, October 7, 1986, D.C.
s. 14, regs. 86/405, 842, 1250, 1818.
ss. 19, 20, regs. 86/1335.
s. 31, orders 86/1029, 1334.

24. Rent (Amendment) Act 1985.
s. 1, see *Hewitt* v. *Lewis* [1986] 1 All E.R. 927.

27. Coal Industry Act 1985.
s. 3, order 86/631.

29. Enduring Powers of Attorney Act 1985.
Commencement order: 86/125.
s. 2, regs. 86/126.
s. 10, rules 86/127.
s. 14, order 86/125.

30. Ports (Finance) Act 1985.
s. 1, order 86/714; amended: *ibid.*

33. Rating (Revaluation Rebates) (Scotland) Act 1985.
s. 1, order 86/150.

35. Gaming (Bingo) Act 1985.
Commencement order: 86/832.
s. 3, regs. 86/834.
s. 5, order 86/832.
sch., order 86/833.

37. Family Law (Scotland) Act 1985.
Commencement order: 86/1237.
s. 27, amended: 1986, c.9, sch. 2.
s. 29, order 86/1237.

47. Further Education Act 1985.
s. 3, amended: order 86/452.

48. Food and Environment Protection Act 1985.
s. 1, orders 86/1027, 1059, 1121, 1179, 1185, 1232, 1247, 1294, 1331, 1344, 1360, 1384, 1410–1413, 1422, 1431, 1432, 1435, 1479, 1483, 1491, 1508, 1535, 1540, 1547, 1552, 1574, 1576, 1592, 1595, 1615, 1616, 1621, 1662, 1664, 1681, 1688, 1689, 1707, 1720, 1756, 1765, 1775, 1837, 1849, 1900, 1993.
s. 16, regs. 86/1510.
s. 24, orders 86/1059, 1247, 1294, 1331, 1344, 1360, 1411, 1413, 1422, 1431, 1432, 1435, 1479, 1483, 1491, 1508, 1535, 1540, 1547, 1552, 1574, 1576, 1592, 1595, 1615, 1616, 1621, 1662, 1664, 1681, 1688, 1689, 1707, 1720, 1756, 1765, 1775, 1837, 1849, 1900, 1993; regs. 86/1510.

50. Representation of the People Act 1985.
Commencement orders: 86/639, 1080.
regs. 86/1091.
ss. 2, 3, 6–9, 15, regs. 1081, 1111(S.)

CAP.
1985—cont.

50. Representation of the People Act 1985— *cont.*
s. 27, regs. 86/1111(S.).
s. 27, repealed in pt.: 1986, c.58, sch.
s. 29, orders 86/639, 1080.

51. Local Government Act 1985.
s. 3, repealed in pt.: 1986, c.63, sch. 12.
s. 10, order 86/413, 564.
s. 11, order 86/208.
s. 16, order 86/265.
ss. 31, 32, amended: 1986, c.10, s.10.
s. 40, order 86/425.
s. 40, amended: 1986, c.31, sch. 4.
s. 43, repealed in pt.: 1986, c.8, ss.1, 3, sch.
s. 44, order 86/148.
s. 45, order 86/413.
s. 46, order 86/226.
ss. 46, 47, functions transferred: order 86/600.
s. 47, order 86/148.
s. 48, see *R.* v. *London Boroughs Grants Committee, ex p. Greenwich London Borough Council, The Times*, May 6, 1986, D.C.
s. 52, orders 86/192, 297, 298, 399, 425, 426, 523, 573, 582.
s. 56, regs. 86/867.
s. 58, orders 86/436, 439.
s. 62, orders 86/148, 573.
s. 66, orders 86/96, 437, 471, 501, 553, 563, 1398.
s. 67, order 86/1774.
s. 68, orders 86/212, 265.
s. 69, repealed in pt.: 1986, c.54, sch. 2.
s. 77, orders 86/2063, 2093.
s. 80, repealed in pt.: 1986, c.54, sch. 2.
s. 89, orders 86/442.
s. 97, see *Westminster City Council, Re* [1986] 2 W.L.R. 807, H.L.
s. 98, orders 86/148, 452, 564.
s. 100, orders 86/148, 211, 256, 297, 298, 330, 413, 442, 564, 624, 2293.
s. 101, orders 86/1, 81, 148, 208, 227, 297, 298, 300, 330, 379, 399, 413, 425, 442, 452, 454, 564, 613, 615–618, 711, 1929, 2063, 2092, 2093, 2293.
s. 103, orders 86/208, 227, 613, 615–618, 711.
sch. 1, amended: 1986, c.63, schs. 10, 11; repealed in pt.: *ibid.*, sch. 11.
sch. 2, repealed in pt.: *ibid.*, sch. 12.
sch. 3, order 86/561.
sch. 4, see *Richmond Borough Council* v. *Secretary of State for Transport*, (1986) 136 New L.J. 941, Sir Neil Lawson.
sch. 4, orders 86/256, 278.
sch. 5, orders 86/154, 315, 316.
sch. 5, repealed in pt.: 1986, c.27, s.3.
sch. 13, amended: 1986, c.10, s.9; c.63, schs. 4, 5; repealed in pt.: *ibid.*, schs. 4, 12.

1985—cont.

51. Local Government Act 1985—*cont.*
sch. 14, amended: 1986, c.10, s.11; repealed in pt.: 1986, c.63, schs. 4, 12.
sch. 17, repealed in pt.: 1986, c.8, sch.

53. Social Security Act 1985.
s. 5, regs. 86/1718.
ss. 5, 9, amended: 1986, c.50, sch. 10.
ss. 15–17, 22, 27 (in pt.), repealed: *ibid.*, sch. 11.
s. 32, regs. 86/478.
s. 32, schs. 4, 5, repealed in pt.: 1986, c.50, sch. 11.

54. Finance Act 1985.
Commencement orders: 86/337, 365, 934, 968–970.
s. 2, repealed: 1986, c.41, sch. 23.
s. 12, order 86/969.
s. 16, amended: 1986, c.41, s.47.
s. 17, amended: *ibid.*, s.15.
s. 20, orders 86/906, 909, 970.
s. 27, order 86/934.
s. 30, order 86/365.
s. 32, order 86/337.
s. 49, repealed: 1986, c.41, sch. 23.
s. 56, amended: *ibid.*, s.57, sch. 13.
s. 57, amended and repealed in pt.: *ibid.*, s.57.
ss. 62, 67 (in pt.), repealed: *ibid.*, sch. 23.
s. 78, amended and repealed in pt.: *ibid.*, s.73; repealed (prosp.): *ibid.*, s.74, sch. 23.
s. 79, amended: *ibid.*, s.73; c.45, sch. 14; repealed in pt.: 1986, c.41, s.73; c.45, sch. 14; repealed (prosp.): 1986, c.41, s.74, sch. 23.
s. 80, repealed: *ibid.*
sch. 5, repealed in pt.: *ibid.*
sch. 19, regs. 86/387.
sch. 23, amended: 1986, c.41, sch. 17; repealed in pt.: *ibid.*, sch. 23.

56. Interception of Communications Act 1985.
Commencement order: 86/384.
s. 12, order 86/384.

57. Sporting Events (Control of Alcohol etc.) Act 1985.
ss. 1A, 2A, 5A–5D, added: 1986, c.64, sch. 1.
ss. 2, 3, 7, amended: *ibid.*
s. 8, amended: *ibid.*; repealed in pt.: *ibid.*, sch. 3.

58. Trustee Savings Bank Act 1985.
Commencement orders: 86/1219–1223.
s. 1, order 86/1222.
s. 4, orders 86/1220, 1223.
s. 6, order 86/100.
sch. 1, order 86/1219.
sch. 1, amended: 1986, c.53, sch. 19.
sch. 5, order 86/1221.

60. Child Abduction and Custody Act 1985.
Commencement order: 86/1048.
s. 2, order 86/1159.
s. 9, amended: 1986, c.55, sch. 1.

60. Child Abduction and Custody Act 1985—*cont.*
s. 10, S.Rs. 1986 Nos. 203, 218, 219; Acts of Sederunt 86/1955.
s. 20, amended: 1986, c.55, s.67, sch. 1.
s. 24, S.Rs. 1986 Nos. 203, 218, 219; Acts of Sederunt 86/1955, 1966.
s. 24A, added: 1986, c.55, s.67.
s. 27, amended: *ibid.*, s.67, sch. 1.
s. 29, order 86/1048.

61. Administration of Justice Act 1985.
Commencement orders: 86/364, 1503, 2260.
s. 66, repealed: 1986, c.53, sch. 19.
s. 69, orders 86/364, 1503, 2260.

62. Oil and Pipelines Act 1985.
s. 3, order 86/585.
s. 7, repealed in pt.: 1986, c.44, sch. 9.

65. Insolvency Act 1985.
Commencement orders: 86/6, 185, 463, 840, 1924.
s. 1, amended: 1986, c.53, sch. 18.
ss. 1–11, repealed: 1986, c.45, sch. 12.
s. 3, order 86/1764.
ss. 4, 5, regs. 86/951, 1995.
s. 10, regs. 86/951, 1764, 1995.
s. 12, amended: 1986, c.53, sch. 18.
ss. 12–14, repealed: 1986, c.46, sch. 4.
s. 15, repealed: 1986, c.45, sch. 12.
s. 16, repealed: 1986, c.46, sch. 4.
s. 17, repealed: 1986, c.45, sch. 12.
s. 18, repealed: 1986, c.46, sch. 4.
ss. 19, 20–107, repealed: 1986, c.45, sch. 12.
s. 97, amended: 1986, c.44, sch. 7.
s. 106, rules 86/304, 385, 611, 612, 619, 626(S.), 1916(S.).
s. 108, repealed in pt.: 1986, c.45, sch. 12; c.46, sch. 4.
ss. 109–214, repealed: 1986, c.45, sch. 12.
s. 200, amended: 1986, c.44, sch. 7.
ss. 216, 217 (in pt.), 221–234, repealed: 1986, c.45, sch. 12.
s. 226, rules 86/385.
s. 325, repealed in pt.: 1986, c.45, sch. 12.
s. 236, orders 86/6, 185, 463, 840, 1924.
s. 236, repealed in pt.: 1986, c.45, sch. 12.
sch. 1, rules 86/952.
sch. 1, repealed in pt.: 1986, c.45, sch. 12.
sch. 2, repealed: 1986, c.46, sch. 4; amended: 1986, c.53, sch. 18.
schs. 3–5, repealed: 1986, c.45, sch. 12.
sch. 4, repealed in pt.: 1986, c.50, schs. 10, 11.
sch. 5, rules 86/304.
sch. 6, repealed in pt.: 1986, c.45, sch. 12; c.46, sch. 4.
sch. 7, repealed: 1986, c.45, sch. 12.
sch. 8, repealed in pt.: 1986, c.5, sch. 15.
sch. 9, repealed in pt.: 1986, c.45, sch. 12; c.46, sch. 4.
sch. 10, repealed: 1986, c.45, sch. 12.

1985—cont.

66. Bankruptcy (Scotland) Act 1985.
Commencement orders: 85/1924; 86/1913.
s. 1, Acts of Sederunt 86/514, 517.
ss. 6–8, 11, order 85/1925.
s. 10, amended: 1986, c.60, sch. 16.
s. 14, Acts of Sederunt 86/514, 517.
ss. 15, 19, 22, 23, order 85/1925.
s. 25, order 85/1925; Act of Sederunt 86/517.
ss. 45, 48, 49, 51, 54, order 85/1925.
s. 62, Act of Sederunt 86/514.
s. 67, order 85/1925; regs. 86/1914.
s. 69, order 85/1925.
s. 70, amended: 1986, c.44, sch. 7.
s. 73, order 85/1925; regs. 86/1914.
s. 74, order 85/1925.
s. 78, orders 85/1924; 86/78, 1913.
sch. 2, Act of Sederunt 86/517.
sch. 3, regs. 86/1914.
sch. 3, repealed in pt.: 1986, c.50, schs. 10, 11.
sch. 4, order 85/1925.
sch. 5, order 85/1925; Acts of Sederunt 86/514, 517.
sch. 7, repealed in pt.: 1986, c.45, sch. 12.

67. Transport Act 1985.
Commencement orders: 86/80, 414, 1088, 1450, 1794, 1874.
s. 6, regs. 86/1671.
s. 7, regs. 86/1030.
s. 8, regs. 86/1671.
s. 9, regs. 86/1030.
s. 10, regs. 86/1779.
s. 12, regs. 86/566, 567, 1239(S.).
s. 13, orders 86/1386, 1387.
s. 17, regs. 86/1188.
s. 23, regs. 86/1245.
s. 27, regs. 86/1668.
s. 42, regs. 86/1691.
s. 60, orders 86/1287(S.), 1648–1653, 1672–1677, 1880(S.).
ss. 69, 70, orders 86/1702, 1703, 1780.
s. 76, order 86/1874(S.).
ss. 93, 94, 96, 97, 100, 134, regs. 86/77.
s. 140, orders 86/80, 414, 1088, 1450, 1794.
sch. 4, rules 86/1547.
sch. 6, regs. 86/1253.

68. Housing Act 1985.
s. 4, amended: order 86/1; 1986, c.63, sch. 5.
ss. 20, 21, amended: *ibid.*, sch. 5.
ss. 27, 27A, 27B, substituted: *ibid.*, s.10.
s. 27C, added: *ibid.*, s.11.
s. 30, repealed in pt.: *ibid.*, schs. 5, 12.
s. 36, amended: *ibid.*, sch. 5.
s. 46, repealed: *ibid.*, schs. 5, 12.
ss. 47, 48, amended: *ibid.*, sch. 5.
s. 57, amended: 1986, c.63, sch. 5.
s. 58, amended: *ibid.*, s.14.
ss. 60, 62, see *R.* v. *Gravesham Borough Council, ex p. Winchester* (1986) 18 H.L.R. 207, Simon Brown J.
s. 69, amended: 1986, c.63, s.14.

1985—cont.

68. Housing Act 1985—*cont.*
s. 80, amended: *ibid.*, sch. 5.
ss. 100, 101, amended: *ibid.*, sch. 3.
s. 106A, added: *ibid.*, s.6.
s. 109A, added: *ibid.*, sch. 5.
s. 115, amended: *ibid.*, sch. 4.
s. 117, amended: *ibid.*, sch. 5.
s. 125, amended: *ibid.*, s.4, sch. 5.
ss. 125A–125C, added: *ibid.*, s.4.
s. 127, amended: *ibid.*, s.4; repealed in pt.: *ibid.*, schs. 5, 12.
s. 129, amended: *ibid.*, s.2.
s. 130, amended: *ibid.*, sch. 5.
s. 131, order 86/2193.
ss. 137, 140, 142, 151, 152, amended: 1986, c.63, sch. 5.
s. 154, amended: 1986, c.26, s.2.
s. 156, amended: 1986, c.63, sch. 5.
s. 157, order 86/1695.
s. 158, amended: 1986, c.63, sch. 5.
s. 160, see *R.* v. *Rushmoor Borough Council, ex p. Barrett, The Times,* September 5, 1986, Reeve J.
ss. 171A–171H, added: 1986, c.63, s.8.
ss. 187, 188, 207, amended: *ibid.*, sch. 5.
s. 231, repealed: 1986, c.5, sch. 15.
s. 239, amended: 1986, c.63, s.21.
s. 240, amended and repealed in pt.: *ibid.*
s. 244, amended: *ibid.*, sch. 3.
s. 250, repealed in pt.: *ibid.*, s.21.
s. 251 amended: *ibid.*, sch. 5.
s. 255, amended: *ibid.*, sch. 3.
s. 256, amended: *ibid.*, sch. 5.
ss. 257, 258, amended: *ibid.*, sch. 21.
ss. 259A, 259B, added: *ibid.*
s. 322, amended: *ibid.*, sch. 5.
s. 352, see *Thrasyvoulou* v. *London Borough of Hackney* (1986) 18 H.L.R. 370, C.A.
ss. 425, amended: 1986, c.50, sch. 10.
s. 427A, added: 1986, c.63, sch. 5.
s. 429A, added: *ibid.*, s.16.
s. 434, amended: *ibid.*, sch. 5.
s. 442, amended: 1986, c.52, sch. 18.
s. 444, amended: 1986, c.63, sch. 5.
s. 445, order 86/1511.
s. 447, order 86/1489.
s. 447, amended: 1986, c.52, sch. 18.
s. 448, order 86/1490.
s. 450, substituted: 1986, c.53, sch. 18.
ss. 450A–450C, added: 1986, c.63, s.5.
ss. 452, 453, repealed in pt.: *ibid.*, s.5, sch. 12.
ss. 458, 459, amended: *ibid.*; repealed in pt.: 1986, c.53, sch. 19.
s. 460, amended and repealed in pt.: 1986, c.63, sch. 3.
ss. 462, 463, amended: *ibid.*
s. 464A, added: *ibid.*
s. 466, amended: *ibid.*
ss. 498A–489G, added: *ibid.*
ss. 499, 511, amended: *ibid.*
s. 513, amended and repealed in pt.: *ibid.*

1985—cont.

68. Housing Act 1985—*cont.*
ss. 514, 515, 518, 519, 526, 535, amended: *ibid.*
s. 543, order 86/1494.
s. 568, regs. 86/797.
s. 618, amended: 1986, c.63, sch. 5.
s. 621A, added: *ibid.*
s. 622, amended: 1986, c.53, sch. 18.
sch. 1, amended: 1986, c.5, sch. 14.
sch. 2, amended: 1986, c.63, s.9.
sch. 3, amended: *ibid.*, sch. 5.
sch. 3A, added: *ibid.*, s.6, sch. 1.
sch. 4, amended: *ibid.*, sch. 5; repealed in pt.: *ibid.*, schs. 5, 12.
sch. 5, amended: *ibid.*, sch. 1.
sch. 6, amended: *ibid.*, s.4, sch. 5; repealed in pt.: *ibid.*, schs. 5, 12.
sch. 9A, added: *ibid.*, s.8, sch. 2.
sch. 11, amended: *ibid.*, sch. 5.
sch. 14, amended: 1986, c.50, sch. 10.
sch. 18, amended: 1986, c.45, sch. 14.
schs. 22, 24, amended: 1986, c.63, sch. 5.

69. Housing Associations Act 1985.
s. 4, amended: 1986, c.63, s.19; c.65, s.13(S.).
s. 8, amended (S.): *ibid.*, sch. 2.
s. 10, amended: 1986, c.63, sch. 5.
s. 15, amended: 1986, c.65, sch. 2.
s. 15A, added (S.): *ibid.*, s.14.
ss. 40, 42, amended: *ibid.*, sch. 2.
ss. 44, 45, 52, amended (S.): *ibid.*, s.16.
s. 62, amended: 1986, c.63, sch. 5.
ss. 63–66, repealed: 1986, c.53, schs. 18, 19.
ss. 67, 68, amended: 1986, c.63, sch. 5.
s. 69A, added: *ibid.*
s. 72, repealed in pt.: 1986, c.53, schs. 18, 19.
s. 73, amended: 1986, c.63, sch. 5; repealed in pt.: 1986, c.53, schs. 18, 19.
s. 84, amended: *ibid.*, sch. 18.
s. 86, amended: *ibid.*; c.65, sch. 2.
s. 100, repealed (S.): *ibid.*, sch. 3.
s. 101, amended: 1986, c.53, sch. 18.
s. 106, amended (S.): 1986, c.65, s.13, sch. 2; repealed in pt.: *ibid.*, sch. 3.
s. 107, amended: *ibid.*, sch. 2; repealed in pt.: *ibid.*, sch. 3.
sch. 2, amended: 1986, c.63, sch. 5.

70. Landlord and Tenant Act 1985.
s. 14, amended: 1986, c.5, sch. 14.
s. 20A, added: 1986, c.63, sch. 5.
s. 21, amended: *ibid.*

71. Housing (Consequential Provisions) Act 1985.
sch. 2, amended: 1986, c.63, sch. 5; repealed in pt.: 1986, c.5, sch. 15; c.31, sch. 6; c.53, sch. 19; c.63, sch. 12.
sch. 3, amended: *ibid.*, sch. 5.

72. Weights and Measures Act 1985.
ss. 4, 5, orders 86/1684, 1685.
s. 11, regs. 86/1210, 1320, 1682, 1683, 2109.
s. 12, regs. 86/1210, 1320.

1985—cont.

72. Weights and Measures Act 1985—*cont.*
s. 15, regs. 86/1210, 1320, 1682, 1683, 2109.
ss. 47–49, 51, 54, 63, 65, 66, 68, regs. 86/2049.
s. 86, regs. 86/1210, 1260, 1320, 1682–1685, 2049, 2109.
s. 94, regs. 86/1210, 1320, 1682–1685, 2049, 2109.

73. Law Reform (Miscellaneous Provisions) (Scotland) Act 1985.
Commencement orders: 85/1908, 1945, 2055.
s. 15, amended: 1986, c.39, sch. 2.
s. 16, repealed: 1986, c.55, sch. 2.
s. 60, orders 85/1908, 1945, 2055.

1986

1. Education (Amendment) Act 1986.
Royal Assent, February 17, 1986.

2. Australia Act 1986.
Royal Assent, February 17, 1986.
Commencement order: 86/319.
s. 17, order 86/319.

3. Atomic Energy Authority Act 1986.
Royal Assent, February 19, 1986.

4. Consolidated Fund Act 1986.
Royal Assent, March 18, 1986.

5. Agricultural Holdings Act 1986.
Royal Assent, March 18, 1986.
Commencement order: 86/1596.
s. 12, see *Buckinghamshire County Council* v. *Gordon* (1986) E.G. 853, H.H. Judge Barr.
s. 24, order 86/1596.
sch. 6, order 86/1256.
sch. 14, repealed in pt.: 1986, c.63, sch. 12.

6. Prevention of Oil Pollution Act 1986.
Royal Assent, March 18, 1986.

7. Marriage (Wales) Act 1986.
Royal Assent, March 18, 1986.

8. Museum of London Act 1986.
Royal Assent, March 26, 1986.

9. Law Reform (Parent and Child) (Scotland) Act 1986.
Royal Assent, March 26, 1986.
schs. 1, 2, repealed in pt.: 1986, c.50, sch. 11.

10. Local Government Act 1986.
Royal Assent, March 26, 1986.

11. Gaming (Amendment) Act 1986.
Royal Assent, May 2, 1986.

12. Statute Law (Repeals) Act 1986.
Royal Assent, May 2, 1986.
sch. 2, repealed in pt.: 1986, c.56, sch. 4.

13. Highways (Amendment) Act 1986.
Royal Assent, May 2, 1986.

14. Animals (Scientific Procedures) Act 1986.
Royal Assent, May 20, 1986.
Commencement order: 86/2088.
s. 8, order 86/2089.
s. 12, rules 86/1911.

1986—cont.

14. Animals (Scientific Procedures) Act 1986
—*cont.*
s. 28, order 86/2089.
s. 30, order 86/2088.

15. Industrial Training Act 1986.
Royal Assent, May 20, 1986.

16. Marriage (Prohibited Degrees of Relationship) Act 1986.
Royal Assent, May 20, 1986.
Commencement order: 86/1343.
s. 6, order 86/1343.

17. Drainage Rates (Disabled Persons) Act 1986.
Royal Assent, June 26, 1986.

18. Corneal Tissue Act 1986.
Royal Assent, June 26, 1986.

19. British Shipbuilders (Borrowing Powers) Act 1986.
Royal Assent, June 26, 1986.

20. Horticultural Produce Act 1986.
Royal Assent, June 26, 1986.

21. Armed Forces Act 1986.
Royal Assent, June 26, 1986.
Commencement orders: 86/2071, 2124.
s. 17, orders 86/2071, 2124.

22. Civil Protection in Peacetime Act 1986.
Royal Assent, June 26, 1986.

23. Safety at Sea Act 1986.
Royal Assent, June 26, 1986.
Commencement order: 86/1759.
s. 15, order 86/1759.

24. Health Service Joint Consultative Committee (Access to Information) Act 1986.
Royal Assent, June 26, 1986.

25. Commonwealth Development Corporation Act 1986.
Royal Assent, June 26, 1986.

26. Land Registration Act 1986.
Royal Assent, June 26, 1986.
Commencement order: 86/2117.
s. 6, order 86/2117.

27. Road Traffic Regulation (Parking) Act 1986.
Royal Assent, July 8, 1986.

28. Children and Young Persons (Amendment) Act 1986.
Royal Assent, July 8, 1986.

29. Consumer Safety (Amendment) Act 1986.
Royal Assent, July 8, 1986.

30. Forestry Act 1986.
Royal Assent, July 8, 1986.

31. Airports Act 1986.
Royal Assent, July 8, 1986.
Commencement orders: 86/1228, 1487.
s. 2, orders 86/1228, 1229.
s. 10, repealed: 1986, c.60, sch. 17.
ss. 36, 38, order 86/1544.
s. 40, order 86/1502.
s. 41, regs. 86/1544.
s. 47, regs. 86/1543.
ss. 48, 51, regs. 86/1544.
s. 75, order 86/1801.

1986—cont.

31. Airports Act 1986—*cont.*
s. 79, order 86/1228.
s. 85, orders 86/1228, 1487.

32. Drug Trafficking Offences Act 1986.
Royal Assent, July 8, 1986.
Commencement orders: 86/1488, 1546, 2145.
s. 40, orders 86/1488, 1546, 2145.

33. Disabled Persons (Services, Consultation and Representation) Act 1986.
Royal Assent, July 8, 1986.
s. 15, repealed: 1986, c.66, s.5.

34. Protection of Children (Tobacco) Act 1986.
Royal Assent, July 8, 1986.

35. Protection of Military Remains Act 1986.
Royal Assent, July 8, 1986.

36. Incest and Related Offences (Scotland) Act 1986.
Royal Assent, July 18, 1986.
Commencement order: 86/1803.
s. 3, order 86/1803.

37. Latent Damage Act 1986.
Royal Assent, July 18, 1986.

38. Outer Space Act 1986.
Royal Assent, July 18, 1986.

39. Patents, Designs and Marks Act 1986.
Royal Assent, July 18, 1986.
Commencement order: 86/1274.
s. 4, order 86/1274.

40. Education Act 1986.
Royal Assent, July 18, 1986.

41. Finance Act 1986.
Royal Assent, July 25, 1986.
s. 92, orders 86/1710, 1833.
s. 92, amended: orders 86/1710, 1833.
s. 98, order 86/1711.
sch. 8, regs. 86/1948.

42. Appropriation Act 1986.
Royal Assent, July 25, 1986.

43. Crown Agents (Amendment) Act 1986.
Royal Assent, July 25, 1986.

44. Gas Act 1986.
Royal Assent, July 25, 1986.
Commencement orders: 86/1315, 1316, 1809.
s. 3, order 86/1316.
ss. 10, 47, regs. 86/1448.
s. 49, orders 86/1317, 1318.
s. 58, repealed: 1986, c.60, sch. 17.
ss. 62, 64, order 86/1810.
s. 68, orders 86/1315, 1809.
sch. 7, amended: 1986, c.63, sch. 7; repealed in pt.: 1986, c.45, sch. 12.
sch. 7, amended (S.): 1986, c.63, sch. 7.

45. Insolvency Act 1986.
Royal Assent, July 25, 1986.
ss. 53, 54, 62, 65–67, 70, 71, regs. 86/1917(S.).
ss. 184, 206, 273, 346, 354, 358, 360, 361, 364, amended: order 86/1996.
ss. 390, 392, 393, regs. 86/1995.

1986—cont.

45. Insolvency Act 1986—*cont.*
s. 411, rules 86/1915(S.), 1916(S.), 1918(S.), 1925, 2000, 2002; regs. 86/1994.
s. 412, regs. 86/1994.
s. 414, order 86/2030.
s. 415, order 86/2030.
ss. 416, 418, order 86/1996.
s. 419, regs. 86/1995.
s. 420, order 86/2142.
s. 421, order 86/1999.
s. 426, order 86/2123.
ss. 439, 441, order 86/2001.
sch. 6, order 86/1996.
sch. 8, regs. 86/1994.

46. Company Directors Disqualification Act 1986.
Royal Assent, July 25, 1986.
s. 8, amended: 1986, c.60, s.198.
s. 18, regs. 86/2067.
s. 21, order 86/2142.

47. Legal Aid (Scotland) Act 1986.
Royal Assent, July 25, 1986.
Commencement order: 86/1617.
ss. 8, 11, amended: 1986, c.50, sch. 10.
s. 46, order 86/1617.

48. Wages Act 1986.
Royal Assent, July 25, 1986.
Commencement order: 86/1998.
s. 7, amended: 1986, c.50, sch. 10.
s. 33, order 86/1998.

49. Agriculture Act 1986.
Royal Assent, July 25, 1986.
Commencement orders: 86/1419, 1484, 1485(S.), 1596, 2301.
s. 9, order 86/1419.
s. 24, orders 86/1484, 1485(S.), 1596, 2301.
sch. 1, order 86/1530.
sch. 2, order 86/1475.

50. Social Security Act 1986.
Royal Assent, July 25, 1986.
Commencement orders: 86/1609, 1719, 1958, 1959.
s. 39, regs. 86/1561.
ss. 46–48, 50, regs. 86/1960.
s. 51, regs. 86/1541, 1960.
s. 54, regs. 86/1960.
s. 83, order 86/1609; regs. 86/1960.
s. 84, regs. 86/1541, 1716, 1960.
s. 88, orders 86/1609, 1719, 1958, 1959.
s. 89, regs. 86/1541.
sch. 4, regs. 86/1960.

51. British Council and Commonwealth Institute Superannuation Act 1986.
Royal Assent, July 25, 1986.
Commencement order: 86/1860.
s. 3, order 86/1860.

52. Dockyard Services Act 1986.
Royal Assent, July 25, 1986.
s. 1, orders 86/2243, 2244.

1986—cont.

53. Building Societies Act 1986.
Royal Assent, July 25, 1986.
Commencement order: 86/1560.
s. 10, order 86/2099.
s. 15, order 86/1877.
s. 18, order 86/1715.
s. 23, order 86/2098.
s. 45, order 86/1878.
s. 101, amended: 1986, c.60, sch. 16.
s. 126, order 86/1560.
sch. 8, order 86/1763.

54. Rate Support Grants Act 1986.
Royal Assent, October 21, 1986.

55. Family Law Act 1986.
Royal Assent, November 7, 1986.

56. Parliamentary Constituencies Act 1986.
Royal Assent, November 7, 1986.

57. Public Trustee and Administration of Funds Act 1986.
Royal Assent, November 7, 1986.
Commencement order: 86/2261.
s. 6, order 86/2261.

58. European Communities (Amendment) Act 1986.
Royal Assent, November 7, 1986.

59. Sex Discrimination Act 1986.
Royal Assent, November 7, 1986.
Commencement order: 86/2313.
s. 10, order 86/2313.

60. Financial Services Act 1986.
Royal Assent, November 7, 1986.
Commencement orders: 86/1940, 2031, 2246.
s. 180, order 86/2046.
s. 195, repealed: 1986, c.60, sch. 17.
s. 211, orders 86/1940, 2031, 2246.

61. Education (No. 2) Act 1986.
Royal Assent, November 7, 1986.
Commencement order: 86/2203.
s. 66, order 86/2203.

62. Salmon Act 1986.
Royal Assent, November 7, 1986.

63. Housing and Planning Act 1986.
Royal Assent, November 7, 1986.
Commencement order: 86/2262.
s. 57, order 86/2262.

64. Public Order Act 1986.
Royal Assent, November 7, 1986.
Commencement order: 86/2041.
s. 41, order 86/2041.

65. Housing (Scotland) Act 1986.
Royal Assent, November 7, 1986.

66. National Health Service (Amendment) Act 1986.
Royal Assent, November 7, 1986.

67. Consolidated Fund (No. 2) Act 1986.
Royal Assent, December 18, 1986.

68. Advance Petroleum Revenue Tax Act 1986.
Royal Assent, December 18, 1986.

INDEX

This is the third part of the Current Law Statute Index 1986 and is up to date to December 31, 1986. References, e.g. 2/44 are to the Statutes of 1986, Chapter 2, section 44

Index

COMPANY LAW—*cont.*

extortionate credit transactions, **45**/244
foreign dividends: income tax, **41**/48
fraudulent trading, **45**/213, 215, **46**/4
insolvency,
building societies, **53**/26–29, schs. 6, 15
co-operation with office-holder, **45**/235
Crown, application, **45**/434, **46**/21
evidence, **45**/433
extortionate credit transactions, **45**/244
fees order, **45**/414, **46**/21
floating charges: avoidance, **45**/245
inquiry into dealings, **45**/236, 237
jurisdiction, **45**/117–119
co-operation between courts, **45**/426
Scotland, **45**/120, 121
liens on books etc. and, **45**/246
offences, **45**/432
punishments, **45**/430, sch.10
summary proceedings, **45**/431, **46**/21
office-holders: provisions as to, **45**/230–246
personal liability of directors, **45**/212, 217
preferences, **45**/239–241, sch. 11
prior transactions: adjustment, **45**/238–246
property, getting in, **45**/234
recognised banks, ets., **45**/422, **46**/21
re-use of company names, **45**/216
rules, **45**/411, schs. 8, 11, **46**/21
committee, **45**/413
security, **45**/247
Service, financial provisions, **45**/403–409
services: restrictive practices, **45**/428
transactions at undervalue, **45**/238, 240, 241
transitional provisions and savings, **45**/437,
sch. 11
unfit directors: disqualification, **46**/6–9,
sch. 1
utilities: supply, **45**/233
voluntary arrangements, **45**/1–7, 140
winding up, *see* winding up, *infra.*
insolvency practitioners, **45**/230, 388–398
regulations, as to, power to make, **45**/419
Insolvency Practitioners Tribunal,
45/396–398, sch. 7
insolvent partnerships, **45**/420, **46**/21
insurance companies. *See* INSURANCE.
investment business,
activities constituting, **60**/sch. 1
administration orders, **60**/74
auditors, **60**/107–111
authorised persons, **60**/7 *et seq.*, schs. 2, 3
designated agency, transfer of functions to,
60/114–118, schs. 7–9
excluded activities, **60**/sch. 1
exempted persons, **60**/36–46, schs. 4, 5
fees, **60**/112, 113
meaning, **60**/1, sch. 1
regulation, **60**/1 *et seq.*
restriction on carrying on, **60**/3–6
winding up orders, **60**/72, 73
managers, **45**/29, 31, 33–49, 72, sch. 11
members' voluntary winding up, **45**/90–95, 97,
107–116
oversea company, unregistered: winding up,
45/225
preferences, **45**/239–241

COMPANY LAW—*cont.*

receivers, **45**/28–49, 72, sch. 11
Scotland, **45**/50–72, schs. 2, 11
securities, **41**/59, 61, 64, 65, 113, schs. 17, 18,
60/sch. 1
insider dealing, **60**/173–178
official listing, **60**/142–157
unlisted: offers, **60**/158–171
stamp duty. *See* STAMP DUTY.
takeover offers, **60**/172, sch. 12
transactions at undervalue, **45**/238, 240, 241,
423–425
unregistered company,
meaning, **45**/220
winding up, **45**/220
winding up, **45**/73 *et seq.*
adjourned meetings: resolutions, **45**/194
affidavits, **45**/200
building societies, **53**/90, sch. 15
contributories, **45**/74–83, 139, 141, 142,
147–152, 154, 155, 157, 158, 161, 194,
195
court, by, **45**/73, 117 *et seq.*, 167, 168, 172,
174, sch. 11
general powers, **45**/147–160
creditors' voluntary, **45**/90, 96–116, 166
disclaimer, **45**/178–182, 186
dissolution after, **45**/201–205
evidence, **45**/191, 196, 197, 433
execution etc., effect of, **45**/183, 184
Financial Services Act 1986, under, **60**/72,
73, 198
floating charges, **45**/122
fraud, deceit etc., **45**/206–211, **46**/4
interest on debts, **45**/189
liquidation committee, **45**/101, 141
liquidators, **45**/85, 91–95, 100, 103–106,
108–115, 133, 136–140, 143–146, 163 *et
seq.*, 246, sch. 11
dissolution, **45**/201–205
powers and duties, **45**/165–170, sch. 4
provisional, **45**/131, 135–144, 230–246
release, **45**/173, 174
removal: vacation of office, **45**/171
malpractice, **45**/206 *et seq.*
investigation and prosecution, **45**/218,
219
penalties, **45**/212–217
members' voluntary, **45**/90–95, 97, 107–116
monetary limits under Act, **45**/416, 417
notice of, **45**/188
offences, **45**/432
punishments, **45**/430, sch. 10
summary proceedings, **45**/431
official receiver, **45**/132, 133, 136, 143, 202,
203, 205, 399–401, **46**/21
pending: information as to, **45**/192
preferential debts, **45**/175, 386, 387, sch. 6
public examination of officers, **45**/133
recognised banks, etc., **45**/422
rescission of contracts, **45**/186
Scotland. *See* SCOTLAND.
special manager: appointment, **45**/177
stamp duty exemptions, **45**/190
transitional provisions and savings, **45**/437,
sch. 11

[5]

Index

REVENUE AND FINANCE—*cont.*
investment business—*cont.*
restrictive practices: prevention, **60**/119–128
winding up orders, **60**/72, 73
local loans: limit, **41**/112
National Debt Commissioners: expenses, **57**/5
oil taxation, **41**/108–110, sch. 21
rate support grants, **54**/1–4
stamp duty. *See* STAMP DUTY.
supply, **42**/1, 2
value added tax. *See* VALUE ADDED TAX.
ROAD TRAFFIC,
airports, **31**/65, 66
vehicles excise duty, **41**/3, schs. 1, 2
Road Traffic Regulation (Parking) Act 1986 (c.27)

Safety at Sea Act 1986 (c.23)
Salmon Act 1986 (c.62)
SCOTLAND,
Building (Scotland) Act 1959, amendment, **65**/19, sch. 2
children,
actions for declarator, **9**/7
adoption, **9**/9
born out of wedlock, **9**/1, 5, sch. 1
domicile, **9**/9
legal equality, **9**/1
savings and supplementary provisions, **9**/9
companies,
administration, **45**/16
Insolvency Act 1986, application, **45**/440
receivers, **45**/50–72, sch. 2
winding up,
court, by, **45**/120, 121, 133, 135, 138, 157, 161, 162, 169, sch. 3
diligence, effect of, **45**/185
dissolution after, **45**/204
examination of persons, **45**/198
gratuitous alienations, **45**/242
leave to proceed: costs, **45**/199
liquidation committee, **45**/142
unclaimed dividends, **45**/193
unfair preferences, **45**/243
consumer safety, **29**/5, 7
corporal punishment in schools: abolition, **61**/48
custody orders,
jurisdiction, **55**/8–18
recognition, **55**/26
disabled persons: provisions as to, **33**/12–15
drug trafficking, **32**/40
enforcement etc. of confiscation orders, **32**/20–23
sequestration of defendant, **32**/16
housing, **65**/9–12
displaced persons: compensation, **65**/20
expenditure and grants, **65**/17, 18
homeless persons, **65**/21
lists, **65**/8, sch. 1
public sector tenants, right to buy, **63**/3, **65**/1–6, sch. 1
secure tenancies, **65**/1–12, 20, sch. 1
housing associations, **65**/8, 13–16

SCOTLAND—*cont.*
incest and related offences, **36**/1, 2, schs. 1, 2
legal aid, **47**/1 *et seq.*
advice and assistance, **47**/6–12
children, proceedings as to, **47**/29
civil, **47**/13–20, sch. 2
contempt of court, **47**/30
criminal, **47**/21–25
Crown, application, **47**/44
expenses, taxations, **47**/43
indemnity, rights of, **47**/39
information, **47**/34, 35
interpretation, **47**/6, 13, 41, 42
meaning, **47**/41
regulations, **47**/36, 37
rules of court, **47**/38
Scottish Legal Aid Board, **47**/1–3, sch. 1
Scottish Legal Aid Fund, **47**/4, 5
solicitors and counsel, **47**/31
solicitors: employment by Board, **47**/26–28
transitional provisions and savings, **47**/45, sch. 4
marriage, prohibited degrees, **16**/2, 6, sch. 2
milk quotas, **49**/14, 16, sch. 2
minors: tobacco products, sale to, **34**/2
opencast coal, **63**/sch. 8
Outer Space Act 1986, application, **38**/15
parentage,
blood sample, determination by, **9**/6
decrees of, **9**/sch. 1
presumptions as to, **9**/5
parental rights, **9**/1, 3
public airport company: capital expenses, **31**/23
salmon fisheries: administration, **62**/1–19, schs. 2–3
salmon, miscellaneous provisions, **62**/20–30
town and country planning,
appeals and applications, **63**/49, sch. 11
conservation areas, **63**/50, sch. 9
development orders, **63**/49, sch. 11
hazardous substances, **63**/35–38, sch. 7
local inquiries, **63**/53, sch. 11
local plans, **63**/53, sch. 11.
National Scenic Areas, **63**/53, sch. 11
offences: daily penalties, increase, **63**/53, sch. 11
planning permission: conditions, **63**/49, sch. 11
purchase notices, **63**/53, sch. 11
redevelopment etc.: grants, termination, [S] **63**/52
simplified planning zones, **63**/26, sch. 6
town schemes: repair grants, **63**/51
Use Classes Order, **63**/53, sch. 11
waste land, proper maintenance, **63**/53, sch. 11
tutor or curator, power to appoint, **9**/4
SEARCH, POWERS OF,
Public Order Act 1986, under, **64**/24
Sex Discrimination Act 1986 (c.59)
SHIPPING AND MARINE INSURANCE,
British Shipbuilders: borrowing powers, **19**/1, 2